Common Stock Valuation
Valuation of a Zero or Constant Growth Stock
Valuation of a Supernormal Growth Stock
Required Rate of Return Calculation and Common Stock Valuation in Sequence
Rate of Return (Dollar-Weighted)
Holding Period Return
Rate of Return, Given a PV and a FV
Rate of Return, Given PV and a Series of Ordinary Annuity Payments
Rate of Return, Given PV and a Series of Unequal Payments at End of Equal Time Periods
Portfolio Weighted Average Return and Average Beta
Rate of Return (Time-Weighted)
Financial Statement Analysis
Bond Valuation and Duration
Yields
Current Yield and Yield to Maturity
Taxable Equivalent Yield
Convertible Bond Calculations
Given Conversion Price
Given Conversion Ratio
Option Valuation
Calculate Option Value
Implied Variability of Underlying Stock
Portfolio Evaluation

Directions

To run the software, open the file "starthere.htm," located in the root of the CD, in either browser (Microsoft® Internet Explorer™ 4.0/5.0 or Netscape® Communicator 4.5/Navigator 4.08). After loading the Investment Analysis Calculator, a title (splash) screen will appear. Clicking on this screen brings up the main menu listing the calculation categories.

Suppose you want to access the Statistical Calculator to perform a linear regression. Click Statistical Calculator on the main menu, and the corresponding submenu appears. This screen contains a list of the functions available in the Statistical Calculator. Then click on Simple Linear Regression, and the screen containing the linear regression applet is displayed. Enter the number of entries in your data set in the field at the top, and then proceed to enter the data in the spreadsheet on the left. As soon as all the relevant data fields have been entered, the results are calculated and displayed in the output fields shaded in light green, on the right. The results are auto-calculated whenever data is modified in any input field.

To export data from a report, highlight the data and copy it as you would in a Word® document, and paste it into your Excel® or Word® document.

A Word of Caution

The primary purpose of the Investment Analysis Calculator is to save you time. While using the software, you must remember that you make the final decisions. The Investment Analysis Calculator provides answers to numerical problems, but you must evaluate the output to determine a logical course of action. The software is not a substitute for your ability to think; instead, it is a tool that helps you evaluate various problems encountered by investors.

Herbert B. Mayo

Investments

An Introduction

Seventh Edition

with Investment Analysis Calculator CD

Australia · Canada · Mexico · Singapore · Spain · United Kingdom · United States

Investments: An Introduction, 7e
Herbert B. Mayo

Editor-in-Chief:
Jack W. Calhoun

Vice President,Team Director:
Michael P. Roche

Executive Editor:
Michael R. Reynolds

Sr. Developmental Editor:
Jeff Gilbreath

Developmental Editor:
Amy Holmes

Sr. Marketing Manager:
Charlie Stutesman

Production Editor:
Daniel C. Plofchan

Media Technology Editor:
Vicky True

Media Developmental Editor:
John Barans

Media Production Editor:
Mark Sears

Manufacturing Coordinator:
Sandee Mileski

Compositor:
The Clarinda Company

Printer:
QuebecorWorld
Versailles, KY

Internal Design:
Casey Gilbertson

Cover Design/ Illustration:
Casey Gilbertson

Printed in the United States of America
1 2 3 4 5 05 04 03 02

For more information contact South-Western, 5191 Natorp Boulevard, Mason, Ohio 45040.
Or you can visit our Internet site at: http://www.swcollege.com

Library of Congress Cataloging-in-Publication Data
Mayo, Herbert B.
Investments : an introduction / Herbert B. Mayo.—7th ed.
p. cm.
"With investment analysis calculator CD."
Includes index.
ISBN 0-324-18008-X
1. Investments. 2. Investment Analysis. I. Title.
HG4521 .M37 2002
332.67'8--dc21
2002021809

Text ISBN: 0-324-18008-X
Package ISBN: 0-324-18007-1

for Sharon

Brief Contents

Contents

Part 1 | The Environment of Investing 1

Points of Interest

Preface

Many individuals find investments to be fascinating because they can actively participate in the decision-making process and see the results of their choices. Of course, not all investments will be profitable because you will not always make the correct investment decision. Over a period of years, however, you should earn a positive return on a diversified portfolio. In addition, there is a thrill from a major success, along with the agony associated with the stock that dramatically rose after you sold or did not buy. Both the big fish you catch and the big fish that get away can make wonderful stories.

Investing, of course, is not a game, but a serious subject that can have a major impact on your future well-being. Virtually everyone makes investments. Even if the individual does not select specific assets such as the stock of AT&T or federal government Series EE (Patriot) bonds, investments are still made through participation in pension plans and employee savings programs or through the purchase of whole life insurance or a home. Each of these investments has common characteristics such as the potential return and the risk you must bear. The future is uncertain, and you must determine how much risk you are willing to bear since a higher return is associated with accepting more risk.

You may find investing daunting because of specialized jargon or having to deal with sophisticated professionals. A primary aim of this textbook is to make investing less difficult by explaining the terms, by elucidating the possible alternatives, and by discussing many of the techniques used by professionals to value an asset and to construct a portfolio. While this textbook cannot show you a shortcut to financial wealth, it can reduce your chances of making uninformed investment decisions.

This textbook uses a substantial number of examples and illustrations employing data that are generally available to the investing public. This information is believed to be accurate; however, you should not assume that mention of a specific firm and its securities is a recommendation to buy or sell those securities. The examples have been chosen to illustrate specific points, not to pass judgment on individual investments.

Many textbooks on investments are written for students with considerable background in accounting, finance, and economics. Not every student, however, who takes an investment course has such background, and these students cannot cope with (or be expected to cope with) the material in advanced textbooks on investments. *Investments: An Introduction* is aimed at these students and covers the basics of investing ranging from descriptive material to the theory of portfolio construction and efficient markets. Some of the concepts (for example, portfolio theory) and some of the alternative investments (such as derivatives) are difficult to understand. There are no shortcuts to learning this material just as there are no shortcuts to wealth. The textbook does assume that the student has a desire to tackle a fascinating subject and to devote real energy to the material.

Changes from the Previous Edition

Both reviewers and users have made suggestions for improving *Investments: An Introduction.* This seventh edition of the text retains its five divisions and the order of its twenty-four chapters. In response to several comments, the tone in each chapter introduction has been lightened to increase student interest in the ensuing material.

Many of the chapters feature new problems, and some exercises from the previous edition have been clarified. All other changes in this edition revolve around coverage, content, selected details, and updating of the federal income tax laws.

One of the most important changes in the previous edition was the inclusion of Internet addresses as a source of information. These addresses included government agencies, advisory and data services, publicly held companies, and investment companies. For this edition, the number of Internet sites has been expanded. Addresses have been checked for accuracy, but addresses do change. Some disappear or merge into other sites, and an Internet word search for the name may locate the current address. Advisory services are usually fee based but may offer complimentary information. Some services are initially free, but after a "teaser" period, they charge for their information. Because I cannot know which services will continue to be complimentary, no attempt is made to differentiate sources on the basis of cost.

The changes in the individual chapters are as follows:

Chapter 2 (The Creation of Financial Assets) has more material on initial public offerings (IPOs) and new material on lock-ups.

Chapter 3 (Security Markets) has new material on the short-interest ratio, and the discussion of types of orders has been clarified.

Chapter 4 (Sources of Information) now includes material on financial analysts' recommendations as a source of information.

Chapter 6 (The Tax Environment) has new information on taxation. The new federal income and estate tax laws are being phased in over a number of years, so the exact provisions and tax rates will vary each year. Current information may be obtained through the IRS Web address: http://www.irs.gov.

Chapter 7 (Risk and Portfolio Management) has new material on semivariance and clarification of statistical tools such as the coefficient of variation and the calculation of beta.

Chapter 8 (Investment Companies) has new material on exchange-traded funds (ETFs). A new appendix is devoted to the taxation of mutual fund returns.

Chapter 9 (The Valuation of Common Stock) now includes material on the PEG ratio, and the discussion of the use of cash flow in stock valuation has been expanded.

Chapter 10 (The Return on Common Stock Investments) has additional material on the calculation of the Dow Jones Industrial Average and the impact of the exclusion of dividend income on returns. The coverage of the importance of time with regard to risk and compounding has been expanded.

Chapter 11 (Dividends: Past, Present, and Future) has a better illustration of the impact of repeated stock splits on the number of shares owned.

Chapter 13 (Security Selection: Analysis of Financial Statements) includes new material on generally accepted accounting principles, and the coverage of the DuPont method of financial analysis has been expanded. Hershey Foods financial statements have replaced Chesapeake Corporation financial statements as the comprehensive example of the application of ratio analysis. New material has been added to integrate the analysis of financial statements, security selection, and Internet sources.

Chapter 15 (The Bond Market) includes new material on "securitization" and the taxation of original issue discounts.

Chapter 16 (The Valuation of Fixed-Income Securities) contains expanded coverage of duration and the active management of bond portfolios. A new appendix illustrates bond valuation based on the structure of yields.

Chapter 17 (Government Securities) has new coverage of inflation-indexed federal government bonds.

Chapter 19 (An Introduction to Options) has been reorganized to reduce the coverage of warrants and to integrate the coverage of rights offerings into the chapter instead of in an appendix.

Chapter 20 (Option Valuation and Strategies) includes new material on the application of Black-Scholes valuation to employee stock options and the use of "collars" to lock in security gains. A brief discussion of the binomial option pricing model has been included in a new appendix.

Chapter 21 (Commodity and Financial Futures) has expanded coverage of swaps to include equity swaps.

Chapter 24 (Portfolio Planning and Management) has been completely rewritten and reorganized to tighten the discussion of portfolio planning. New material on exchange-traded funds as a tool of risk management has been added. A new section summarizes the various tools for risk management and refers the reader back to the chapters in which the tools are covered.

Pedagogical Features

This textbook has a variety of features designed to assist the student in the learning process. Each chapter starts with a set of **learning objectives.** These point out topics to look for as the chapter develops. **Terms to remember** are defined in the **marginal glossary** that appears as each term is introduced in the text. Chapters also include **questions** and, where appropriate, **problems.** The questions and problems are straightforward and designed primarily to review the material. Answers to selected problems are provided in Appendix B.

This edition retains the short **cases.** These are not cases in the general usage of the term, in which a situation is presented and the student is required to determine the appropriate questions and formulate an answer or strategy. The cases in this textbook are essentially problems that are cast in real-world situations. For example, a case may ask how much an individual would lose following one investment strategy instead of an alternative when either could be appropriate to meet a specific financial goal. Thus, the primary purpose of the cases is to help illustrate how the material may apply in the context of real investment decisions.

Time value of money problems permeate this text. While the use of interest tables is an excellent means to teach and illustrate time value problems, many students have financial calculators. Time value calculations using a financial calculator are placed in the margin to avoid breaking the flow of the text material.

Many instructors have their students construct a paper portfolio. An **Investment Project** is included which allows students to select stocks and track their performance during the semester. When I use this project, I encourage students to buy *The Wall Street Journal* as a source of information, since I want to encourage them to get in the habit of reading this paper. I realize, however, that many students will obtain information from the Internet. The project is not a trading game but is essentially a buy-and-hold strategy. Even with the buy-and-hold strategy, I have some reluctance to use this pedagogical tool. Since my personal financial goals have a longer time dimension than a semester, I want students to develop a longer time horizon for investing and to realize the importance of diversification and not to chase the latest investment fad.

There are also interesting points that may not fit neatly into a particular chapter. To include these, I have added boxed Points of Interest features to the chapters. These boxes may amplify the next material or present new material to supplement the coverage in the text. The tone of the Points of Interest features is often lighter than the text and is designed to increase reader interest in the chapter as a whole.

Supplementary Materials

A number of supplements are included in the Investments package and are available free of charge to instructors who adopt the textbook.

Instructor's Manual and Test Bank. The *Instructor's Manual* includes points to consider when answering the questions as well as complete solutions for the problems. In addition, suggestions are given for using the **Investment Project** feature in the classroom; teaching notes are provided for the cases; and instructions are provided for the *Investment Analysis Calculator* CD-ROM that accompanies the book. The *Test Bank* section of the manual includes approximately 1,000 true/false and multiple-choice questions. It is available on disk in Word format for simple word-processing purposes and also in a computerized version for Windows that has full test preparation capabilities. (ISBN 0-324-18011-X)

Investment Analysis Calculator CD-ROM. This dual-platform CD-ROM is designed to accompany the book and is free to adopters of the text. It includes numerous routines that may be used to help solve the end-of-chapter problems. The software is menu driven and is a useful tool for solving complex problems. Please note that it is not designed as a substitute for understanding the mechanics of problem analysis and solution. Thus, while the CD-ROM may help determine a stock's value, it cannot answer the question of whether or not the stock should be bought or sold; such a judgment must come from the user of the CD-ROM. (ISBN 0-324-18009-8)

PowerPoint™ slides are available on the Web site for use by instructors for enhancing their lectures. These slides bring out the most important points in the chapter. They also include important charts and graphs from the text, which will aid students in the comprehension of significant concepts.

Instructor's Resource CD-ROM. Get quick access to all instructor ancillaries from your desktop. This easy-to-use CD-ROM lets you review, edit, and copy exactly what you need in the format you want. The IRCD contains electronic versions of the Instructor's Manual, the Test Bank, the resource PowerPoint™ presentation, and the ExamView files. (ISBN 0-324-17761-5)

ExamView. This computerized testing software contains all of the questions in the printed Test Bank. ExamView is easy-to-use test creation software that is compatible with both Microsoft Windows and Macintosh. Instructors can add or edit questions, instructions, and answers and select questions by previewing them on the screen, selecting them randomly, or selecting them by number. Instructors can also create and administer quizzes online, whether over the Internet, a local-area network (LAN), or a wide-area network (WAN). (ISBN 0-324-18010-1)

Web site. The support Web site for *Investments: An Introduction*, Seventh Edition (http://mayo.swcollege.com) includes the following features:

- Instructor Resources
- Internet Applications
- Student Resources
- CaseNet
- Finance in the News
- Thomson Financial Network
- Digital Finance Case Library
- Investment Analysis Calculator
- Talk to Us
- About the Product

Possible Organizations of Investment Courses

The textbook has 24 chapters, but few instructors are able to complete the entire book in a semester course. Many of the chapters are self-contained units, so individual chapters may be omitted (or transposed) without loss of continuity. There are, however, exceptions. For example, the valuation of bonds uses the material on the time value of money. The valuation of common stock employs much of the material covered in the chapter on risk.

Part 1 covers investment fundamentals. It includes how securities come into existence and the role of financial intermediaries (Chapter 2); how securities are traded (Chapter 3); and risk, its measurement, and portfolio management (Chapter 7). These chapters are not easily omitted. Other chapters in Part 1 could be omitted if the students have covered the material in other courses (for example, the time value of money in Chapter 5 and taxation in Chapter 6).

The bread and butter of investing in financial assets is the analysis and selection of common stocks (Part 2) and fixed income securities (Part 3). Virtually all of this material should be covered in class with the possible exceptions of the material on technical analysis, high-yield securities, and convertibles.

The remaining parts of this text leave the individual instructor considerable choice. Since each instructor has personal preferences, any of the remaining eight chapters is easily omitted or included depending on the availability of time. My personal preference is to include the basic material on options (Chapter 19), which many students find both difficult and exciting, and the material on financial planning (Chapter 24), as the latter serves as a means to tie the course together.

Acknowledgements

A textbook requires the input and assistance of many individuals in addition to its author. Over the years, my publisher has provided thoughtful reviews from individuals who sincerely offered suggestions for improvement. Unfortunately, suggestions sometimes are contradictory. Since an author cannot please all of the reviewers at the same time, I trust that individuals whose advice was not (or could not be) taken will not be offended.

The following individuals provided valuable suggestions for improving the seventh edition: Joe Walker, University of Alabama–Birmingham; Lynn Leary Meyers, University of Utah; Perry Hubbs, University of South Florida and Arden Associates; James Felton, Central Michigan University; Barbara Childs, University of Texas–Austin, and Ron Meier, College for Financial Planning.

In addition, I received advice, help, and suggestions from several financial professionals. These included Frank Heiner, Scott & Stringfellow; Leo Kelly, Merrill Lynch Private Asset Management; Scott Boatwright; and Leon Konecny, Jr. All of these individuals and several who made anonymous suggestions contributed their time to this text. I appreciate their efforts.

I owe my greatest debt and offer my largest "thank you" to Ron Meier of the College for Financial Planning. Over the years, he has encouraged and supported my efforts to improve this book. He read portions of the manuscript and offered suggestions throughout the text. His help and suggestions have been invaluable.

At this point in the preface, it is traditional for the author to thank members of the editorial and production staff for their help in bringing the book to fruition. Over the years, I have been spoiled by the publisher's staff, who have worked on the various editions of Investments: An Introduction. The crew at South-Western/Thomson Learning that worked on this edition is no exception. I wish to thank Mike Reynolds, my editor; Charlie Stutesman, my marketing manager; Jeff Gilbreath and Amy Holmes, my developmental editors; Dan

Plofchan, my production editor; John Barans, my media developmental editor; and Mark Sears, my media production editor. I also wish to thank the staff at The Clarinda Company for providing the composition services. They deserve a special thank you for help, support, and efficiency with which the text proceeded through the production process.

I encourage readers to contact me with suggestions and comments. Please feel free to write me at 26 Back Brook Road, Ringoes, NJ 08551, or, if you prefer, please use my e-mail address, mayoher@tcnj.edu.

The Environment of Investing

PART 1

To enhance the learning process, this textbook has been divided into distinct sections. The first considers the environment in which investment decisions are made. This background can have an impact on which investments the individual chooses to include in his or her portfolio. Before constructing a portfolio, the individual should specify financial goals. Investing is a means to an end, such as financial security during retirement or the ability to make the down payment on a home or start a business. These financial goals should be specified because not all assets will serve to meet a particular financial goal.

Once these goals are established, the individual needs to know the mechanics of investing. These include the process by which securities are issued (Chapter 2) and subsequently bought and sold (Chapter 3). Investors also should be aware of at least some of many sources of information, such as data on specific firms and mutual funds, economic data, or general material on investing (Chapter 4). Since the development of the Internet, access to much of this information is a mere click away and readily available to any individual with a personal computer.

Understanding the financial background leads to several important general financial concepts. The first is the time value of money (Chapter 5). A dollar received today and a dollar received tomorrow do not have the same value. Linking the future and the present is the essence of the time value of money. The second is taxation (Chapter 6). Investment returns are subject to federal and state taxation, and different assets may receive different tax treatments. Taxation permeates investment decision making.

The next general concept is the construction of a diversified portfolio (Chapter 7). Because virtually all investments involve risk, the management of this risk through diversification may be the most important financial concept the investor must face. Failure to diversify subjects the individual to additional risk but may not generate additional return. The objective is to construct a diversified portfolio that maximizes the return for a given level of risk.

Investments are made in exceedingly competitive markets. Rapid dissemination of information and stiff competition among investors produce efficient markets. Efficient markets imply that the individual cannot expect to earn abnormally high returns over an extended period of time. Although an individual investment may do exceptionally well, such performance on a consistent basis is rare. Instead, the investor who constructs a well-diversified portfolio should earn a return that compensates for the risk taken.

The material in the subsequent parts of this text covers various investment alternatives and the variety of securities available for inclusion in a portfolio. The last chapter in Part 1, however, introduces investment companies, of which mutual funds are the most important (Chapter 8). The individual may choose not to analyze and acquire the different assets covered in the remainder of this text.

Instead, the investor may delegate that decision making to the portfolio managers of the investment companies. These portfolio managers, of course, use the same analytical techniques and acquire the same assets that comprise the body of the remainder of the text.

An Introduction to Investments

1

In 1986, Microsoft Corporation first offered its stock to the public. Within ten years, the stock's value had increased over 5,000 percent—a $10,000 investment was worth over $500,000. In the same year, Worlds of Wonder also offered its stock to the public. Ten years later, the company was defunct—a $10,000 investment was worth nothing. These are two examples of emerging firms that could do exceedingly well or fail. Would investing in large, well-established firms generate more consistent returns? The answer depends, of course, on which stocks were purchased and when. In 1972, the common stock of Xerox reached a high of $171.87 per share.[1] The price subsequently declined and did not exceed the old high until 1998. Obviously, limiting investments to large firms does not ensure a positive return. Over the years, some investments have generated extraordinary gains, while others have produced only mediocre returns, and still others have resulted in substantial losses.

Today the field of investments is even more dynamic than it was only a decade ago. World events occur rapidly—events that alter the values of specific assets. The individual has so many assets from which to choose, and the amount of information available to the investor is staggering and continually growing. The development of personal computers and the dissemination of information on the Internet have increased individuals' ability to track investments and to perform investment analysis. Furthermore, the inflation of the early 1980s, the recession of the early 1990s, the large decline in stock prices during 2000–2001, and the frequent changes in the tax laws have increased awareness of the importance of financial planning and wise investing.

Learning Objectives

After completing this chapter you should be able to:

1. Explain why individuals should specify investment goals.
2. Differentiate between liquidity and marketability.
3. Distinguish between primary and secondary markets.
4. Identify the sources of risk and the sources of return.
5. Understand why financial markets are considered efficient.

Portfolio Construction

Once an individual receives income, there are two choices: to spend it or to save it. If the individual chooses to save, an additional decision must be made: What is to be done with the savings? This is an extremely important question because in 1999, Americans' personal income was $7,789.6 billion and they saved $147.6 billion.[2] The saver must decide where to invest this command over goods and services that is currently not being used. This is an important decision because these

[1]Beginning on August 28, 2000, the New York Stock Exchange began a pilot program that traded stocks in decimal price increments rather than in the two-centuries-old practice of eighths and sixteenths of a dollar. Decimal pricing of all NYSE stocks was fully implemented on January 29, 2001.

[2]*Survey of Current Business* (June 2001): D-7.

portfolio
An accumulation of assets owned by the investor and designed to transfer purchasing power to the future.

assets are the means by which today's purchasing power is transferred to the future. In effect, the saver must decide on a **portfolio** of assets to own. A portfolio is a combination of assets designed to serve as a store of value. Poor management of these assets may destroy the portfolio's value, and the individual will not achieve his or her investment goals.

There are many assets (e.g., stocks, bonds, derivatives) that the investor may include in the portfolio. While this textbook will discuss many of them, the stress will be on long-term financial assets. While the saver may hold a portion of the portfolio in short-term assets, such as savings accounts, these assets do not seem to present the problem of valuation and choice that accompanies the decision to purchase a stock or a bond. Understanding the nature of long-term assets (i.e., how they are bought and sold, how they are valued, and how they may be used in portfolio construction) is the primary focus of this text.

Several factors affect the construction of a portfolio. These include the goals of the investor, the risks involved, the taxes that will be imposed on any gain, and a knowledge of the available opportunities and alternative investments. This text will cover the range of these alternative investments, their use in a portfolio, the risks associated with owning them, and their valuation.

The investor's goals should largely determine the construction and management of the portfolio. Investing must have a purpose, for without a goal a portfolio is like a boat without a rudder. Some objective must guide the composition of the portfolio.

There are many reasons for saving and accumulating assets. Individuals may postpone current consumption to accumulate funds to make the down payment on a house, finance a child's education, start a business, meet financial emergencies, finance retirement, leave a sizable estate, or even accumulate for the sake of accumulating. For any or all of these reasons, people acquire portfolios of assets rather than spend all their current income.

The motives for saving should dictate, or at least affect, the composition of the portfolio. Not all assets are appropriate to meet the investor's financial goals. For example, savings that are held to meet emergencies, such as an extended illness or unemployment, should not be invested in assets whose return and safety of principal are uncertain. Instead, emphasis should be placed on safety of principal and assets that may be readily converted into cash, such as savings accounts or shares in money market mutual funds. The emphasis should not be on growth and high returns. However, the funds should not sit idle, but should be invested in relatively safe assets that offer a modest return.

Other goals, such as financing retirement or a child's education, have a longer and more certain time horizon. The investor knows approximately when the funds will be needed and so can construct a portfolio with a long-term horizon. Bonds that mature when the funds will be needed or common stocks that offer the potential for growth would be more appropriate than savings accounts or certificates of deposit. The longer time period means the individual can acquire long-term assets that may offer a higher yield.

Most investors have several financial goals that must be met simultaneously. Thus, it is not surprising to learn that their portfolios contain a variety of assets. Of course, priorities and needs differ. The individual who is employed in a cyclical industry and may be laid off during a recession may place more stress on funds to cover unemployment than would the tenured professor. An individual with a poor medical history may seek to have more short-term investments than the person with good health. Medical coverage or disability insurance will also affect the individual's need for funds to cover a short-term emergency. If the investor has this coverage, more of the portfolio may be directed toward other financial goals. If the investor lacks such coverage, a greater proportion of the portfolio may have to be devoted to meeting this financial goal, and correspondingly fewer resources may be devoted to meeting alternative financial goals.

In addition to the individual's goals, his or her capacity or willingness to bear risk plays an important role in constructing the portfolio. Some individuals are more willing and able to bear (that is, assume) risk. These persons will tend to select assets on which the return involves greater risk to obtain the specified investment goals. For example, if the saver wants to build a retirement fund, he or she can choose from a variety of possible investments. However, not all investments are equal with regard to risk and potential return. Those investors who are more willing to accept risk may construct portfolios with assets involving greater risk that may earn higher returns. While low-risk investors may select securities issued by the more financially stable firms, investors who are less averse to taking risk may select stocks issued by younger, less-seasoned firms that may offer better opportunities for growth over a period of years.

Taxes may also affect the composition of an individual's portfolio. Income such as interest and realized capital gains are taxed. When a person dies, the federal government taxes the value of the estate, and several states levy a tax on an individual's inheritance. Such taxes and the desire to reduce them affect the composition of each investor's portfolio.

Portfolio decisions are obviously important. They set a general framework for the asset allocation of the portfolio among various types of investments. Individuals, however, rarely construct a portfolio all at once but acquire assets one at a time. The decision revolves around which specific asset to purchase: Which mutual fund? Which bond? or Which stock? Security analysis considers the merits of the individual asset. Portfolio management determines the impact that the specific asset has on the portfolio.

A large portion of this text is devoted to descriptions and analysis of individual securities, because it is impossible to know an asset's effect on the portfolio without first knowing its characteristics. Stocks and bonds differ with regard to risk, potential return, and valuation. Even within a type of asset such as bonds there can be considerable variation. For example, a corporate bond is different from a municipal bond, and a convertible bond differs from a straight bond that lacks the conversion feature. The investor needs to know and to understand these differences as well as the relative merits and risks associated with each of the assets. After understanding how individual assets are valued, the investor may then construct a portfolio that will aid in the realization of his or her financial goals.

Some Preliminary Definitions

I went to the doctor and he said, "You have a contusion." I asked, "What is a contusion?" and he said, "A bruise." My mind thought: "A bruise by another name is still a bruise" and immediately wanted to ask (but did not), "Why not call it a bruise?"

Every discipline or profession has its own terminology. The field of investments is no different. Some of the jargon is colorful (e.g., *bull* and *bear*); some is descriptive (e.g., *primary* and *secondary markets*); and some, like *contusion,* seems to confuse or muddy the waters (e.g., *purchasing power risk,* which is the risk associated with loss from inflation). In order to proceed, it is desirable to know some initial definitions concerning investments, and the best time to learn them and to start using them is now.

investment (in economics)
The purchase of plant, equipment, or inventory.

investment (in lay terms)
Acquisition of an asset such as a stock or a bond.

The term **investment** can have more than one meaning. In economics, it refers to the purchase of a physical asset, such as a firm's acquisition of a plant, equipment, or inventory or an individual's purchase of a new home. To the layperson the word denotes buying stocks or bonds (or maybe even a house), but it probably does not mean purchasing a plant, equipment, or inventory.

In either case, the firm or the individual wants a productive asset. The difference in definition rests upon the aggregate change in productive assets that results from the investment. When firms invest in plant and equipment, there is a net increase in productive assets. This increase generally does not occur when individuals purchase stocks and bonds. Instead, for every investment by the buyer there is an equal *dis*investment by the seller. These buyers and sellers are trading one asset for another: The seller trades the security for cash, and the buyer trades cash for the security. These transactions occur in secondhand markets, and for that reason securities markets are often referred to as **secondary markets**. Only when the securities are initially issued and sold in the **primary market** is there an investment in an economic sense. Then and only then does the firm receive the money that it, in turn, may use to purchase a plant, equipment, or inventory.

secondary market
A market for buying and selling previously issued securities.

primary market
The initial sale of securities.

In this text, the word *investment* is used in the layperson's sense. Purchase of an asset for the purpose of storing value (and, it is hoped, increasing that value over time) will be called an investment, even if in the aggregate there is only a transfer of ownership from a seller to a buyer. The purchases of stocks, bonds, options, commodity contracts, and even antiques, stamps, and real estate are all considered to be investments if the individual's intent is to transfer purchasing power to the future. If these assets are acting as stores of value, they are investments for that individual.

Assets have **value** because of the future benefits they offer. The process of determining what an asset is worth today is called **valuation**. An investor appraises the asset and assigns a current value to it based on the belief that the asset will generate cash flows (e.g., interest) or will appreciate in price. After computing this value, the individual compares it with the current market price to determine if the asset is currently overpriced or underpriced.

value
What something is worth; the present value of future benefits.

valuation
The process of determining the current worth of an asset.

In some cases this valuation is relatively easy. For example, the bonds of the federal government pay a fixed amount of interest each year and mature at a specified date. Thus, the future cash flows are known. However, the future cash flows of other assets are not so readily identified. For example, although the investor may anticipate future dividends, neither their payment nor their amount can be known with certainty. Forecasting future benefits may be very difficult, but they are still crucial to the process of valuation. Without forecasts and an evaluation of the asset, the investor cannot know if the asset should be purchased or sold.

Because the valuation of some assets is complicated, people may have different estimates of the future cash flows. It is therefore easy to understand why two individuals may have completely divergent views on the worth of a particular asset. One person may believe that an asset is overvalued and hence seek to sell it, while another may seek to buy it in the belief that it is undervalued. Valuation may be subjective, which leads to one person's buying while the other is selling. That does not mean that one person is necessarily irrational or incompetent. People's goals and perceptions (or estimates) of an asset's potential may change, affecting their valuation of the specific asset.

An investment is made because the investor anticipates a **return**. The total return on an investment is what the investor earns. This may be in the form of **income**, such as dividends and interest, or in the form of **capital gains**, or appreciation if the asset's price rises. Not all assets offer both income and capital appreciation. Some stocks pay no current dividends but may appreciate in value. Other assets, including savings accounts, do not appreciate in value, and the return is solely the interest income.

return
The sum of income plus capital gains earned on an investment in an asset.

income
The flow of money or its equivalent produced by an asset; dividends and interest.

capital gain
An increase in the value of a capital asset, such as a stock.

Return is frequently expressed in percentages, such as the **rate of return**, which is the annualized return that is earned by the investment relative to its cost. Before purchasing an asset, the investor anticipates that the return will be greater than that of other assets of similar risk. Without this anticipation, the purchase would not be made. The *realized* return may, of course, be quite different from the *anticipated* rate of return. That is the element of risk.

rate of return
The annual percentage return realized on an investment.

Risk is the uncertainty that the anticipated return will be achieved. As is discussed in the next section, there are many sources of risk. The investor must be

risk
The possibility of loss; the uncertainty of future returns.

willing to bear this risk to achieve the expected return. Even relatively safe investments involve some risk; there is no completely safe investment. For example, savings accounts that are insured still involve some element of risk of loss. If the rate of inflation exceeds the rate of interest that is earned on these insured accounts, the investor suffers a loss of purchasing power.

The term *risk* has a negative connotation, but uncertainty works both ways. For example, events may occur that cause the value of an asset to rise more than anticipated. Certainly the stockholders of Rubbermaid reaped returns that were larger than had been anticipated when it was announced the firm would merge with Newell. The price paid for the stock was considerably higher than the price the security commanded before the announcement of the merger.

speculation

An investment that offers a potentially large return but is also very risky; a reasonable probability that the investment will produce a loss.

A term that is frequently used in conjunction with risk is **speculation**. Many years ago virtually all investments were called "speculations." Today the word implies a high degree of risk. However, risk is not synonymous with speculation. Speculation has the connotation of gambling, in which the odds are against the player. Many securities are risky, but over a period of years the investor will reap a positive return. The odds are not really against the investor, and such investments are not speculations.

The term *speculation* is rarely used in this text, and when it is employed, the implication is that the investor runs a good chance of losing the funds invested in the speculative asset. Although a particular speculation may pay off handsomely, the investor should not expect that many such gambles will reap large returns. After the investor adjusts for the larger amount of risk that must be borne to own such speculative investments, the anticipated return may not justify the risk involved.

marketability

The ease with which an asset may be bought and sold.

liquidity

Moneyness; the ease with which assets can be converted into cash with little risk of loss of principal.

Besides involving risk and offering an expected return, stores of value have marketability or liquidity. These terms are sometimes used interchangeably, but they may also have different definitions. **Marketability** implies that the asset can be bought and sold. Many financial assets, such as the stock of AT&T, are readily marketable. In academic writings on investments, the term **liquidity** generally means the ease of converting an asset into cash *without risk of loss.* This definition clearly differentiates *marketability* from *liquidity,* since the stock of AT&T is marketable but not necessarily liquid. A savings account with a commercial bank is not marketable because the investor withdraws the funds (i.e., does not sell the account), but it is liquid, because a federally insured savings account has virtually no risk of loss of principal.

This distinction between marketability and liquidity need not apply to writings in the popular press on investments. In that context, liquidity generally refers to the ease of converting an asset into cash at the current price. If the individual is able to sell 300 shares of AT&T at the current price, the asset is considered to be liquid as well as marketable. Real estate, on the other hand, would be considered illiquid, since it may take months to sell and the sale may require that the asking price be lowered. The asset remains marketable but is certainly not liquid, because the investor knows neither how much will be obtained from the sale nor when the funds will be received.

This distinction between the academic and popular definitions of liquidity is subtle. If the individual purchases 100 shares of AT&T for $20, there is a risk of loss, because the future price is unknown. If the investor subsequently sells the stock for $15, this individual sustains a loss even though the shares were easily sold at the current market price. Such an asset would not be considered liquid in an academic sense, but the popular press would associate the easy sale with the stock's liquidity.

Because both definitions of liquidity are used, the student of investments needs to be aware of both meanings. The context in which the term is used generally indicates its definition. In this text, the academic definition is used because it implies something about the riskiness of the asset as well as the ability to convert the asset into cash. The term *liquid,* then, will be applied only to an asset that is readily convertible into cash without the investor sustaining a loss. *Marketability* will be used to refer to the ease of selling an asset, even if the sale results in the investor sustaining a loss.

All assets that serve as potential stores of value possess some combination of marketability, liquidity, and the potential to generate income and/or appreciate in price. These features, along with the risk associated with each asset, are considered when including the asset in the individual's portfolio. Because assets differ with regard to their features, it is important for the investor to know the characteristics of each asset. Much of the balance of this text considers each asset's features as well as the sources of its risk and return.

Sources of Risk

systematic risk
Associated with fluctuation in security prices; e.g., market risk.

As was mentioned previously, risk refers to the uncertainty that the actual return the investor realizes will differ from the expected return. As is illustrated in Exhibit 1.1, the sources of this variability in returns is often differentiated into two types of risk: systematic and unsystematic risk. **Systematic risk** refers to those factors that affect the returns on all comparable investments. For example, when the market as a whole rises, the prices of most individual securities also rise. There is a systematic relationship between the return on a specific asset and the return on all other assets in its class (i.e., all other comparable assets). Because this systematic relationship exists, diversifying the portfolio by acquiring other comparable assets does not reduce this source of risk; thus, systematic risk is often referred to as *nondiversifiable risk.* While constructing a diversified portfolio has little impact on systematic risk, you should not conclude that this nondiversifiable risk cannot be managed. One of the objectives of this text is to explain a variety of techniques that help manage the various sources of systematic risk. Chapter 24 has a section that consolidates these risk-management strategies.

unsystematic risk
The risk associated with individual events that affect a particular security.

Unsystematic risk, which is also referred to as *diversifiable risk,* depends on factors that are unique to the specific asset. For example, a firm's earnings may decline because of a strike. Other firms in the industry may not experience the same labor problem, and thus their earnings may not be hurt or may even rise as customers divert purchases from the firm whose operations are temporarily halted. In either case, the change in the firm's earnings is independent of factors that affect the industry, the market, or the economy in general. Because this source of risk applies only to the specific firm, it may be reduced through the construction of a diversified portfolio.

EXHIBIT 1.1

The Sources of Risk

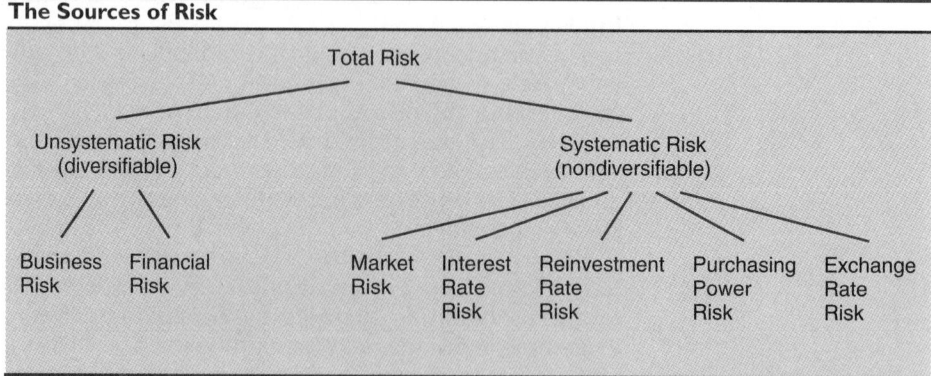

The total risk the investor bears therefore consists of unsystematic and systematic risk. The sources of unsystematic risk may be subdivided into two general classifications: business risk and financial risk. The sources of systematic risk may be subdivided into market risk, interest rate risk, reinvestment rate risk, purchasing power risk, and exchange rate risk.

business risk
The risk associated with the nature of a business.

Business risk is the risk associated with the nature of the enterprise itself. Not all businesses are equally risky. Drilling for new oil deposits is more risky than running a commercial bank. The chances of finding oil may be slim, and only one of many new wells may actually produce oil and earn a positive return. Commercial banks, however, can make loans that are secured by particular assets, such as residences or inventories. While these loans are not risk-free, they may be relatively safe because even if the debtor defaults, the creditor (the bank) can seize the security to meet its claims. Some businesses are by their very nature riskier than others, and, therefore, investing in them is inherently riskier.

All assets must be financed. Either creditors or owners or both provide the funds to start and to sustain the business. Firms use debt financing for two primary reasons. First, under current tax laws interest is a tax deductible expense while dividends paid to stockholders from earnings are not. Second, debt financing is a source of financial leverage that may increase the return on equity (i.e., the return to the owners). If the firm earns more on the borrowed funds than it must pay in interest, the return on equity is increased.

For many firms the use of debt financing is a major source of funds. Leveraged buyouts and corporate restructuring often involve the issuing of a substantial amount of debt and have led to the development of so-called *junk bonds.* Even conservatively managed firms use debt financing. Virtually every firm has some debt outstanding even if the debt is limited to accrued wages and accounts payable generated by the normal course of business.

financial risk
The risk associated with a firm's sources of financing.

This use of financial leverage is the source of **financial risk**. Borrowing funds to finance a business may increase risk, because creditors require that the borrower meet certain terms to obtain the funds. The most common of these requirements is the paying of interest and the repayment of principal. The creditor can (and usually does) demand additional terms, such as collateral or restrictions on dividend payments, that the borrower must meet. These restrictions mean that the firm that uses debt financing bears more risk because it must meet these obligations in addition to its other obligations. When sales and earnings are rising, these constraints may not be burdensome, but during periods of financial stress the failure of the firm to meet these terms may result in financial ruin and bankruptcy. A firm that does not use borrowed funds to acquire its assets does not have these additional responsibilities and does not have the element of financial risk.

market risk
Systematic risk; the risk associated with the tendency of a stock's price to fluctuate with the market.

Market risk refers to the tendency of security prices to move together. While it may be frustrating to invest in a firm that appears to have a minimum amount of business risk and financial risk and then to watch the price of its securities fall as the market as a whole declines, that is the nature of market risk. Security prices do fluctuate, and the investor must either accept the risk associated with those fluctuations or not participate in the market.

While market risk is generally applied to stocks, the concept also applies to other assets, such as stamps, art objects, and real estate. The prices of each of these assets fluctuate. If the value of houses were to rise in general, then the value of a particular house would also tend to increase. But the converse is also true because the prices of houses could decline, causing the value of a specific house to fall. Market risk cannot be avoided if the individual acquires assets whose prices may fluctuate.

interest rate risk
The uncertainty associated with changes in interest rates; the possibility of loss resulting from increases in interest rates.

Interest rate risk refers to the tendency of security prices, especially fixed-income securities, to move inversely with changes in the rate of interest. As is explained in detail in Chapter 16, the prices of bonds and preferred stock depend in part on the current rate of interest. Rising interest rates decrease the current price of fixed-income securities because current purchasers require a competitive yield. The investor who acquires these securities must face the uncertainty of fluctuating interest rates that, in turn, cause the price of these fixed-income securities to fluctuate.

reinvestment rate risk
The risk associated with reinvesting earnings on principal at a lower rate than was initially earned.

Reinvestment rate risk refers to the risk associated with reinvesting funds generated by an investment. If an individual receives interest or dividends, these funds could be spent on goods and services. For example, many individuals who live on a pension consume a substantial portion, and perhaps all, of the income generated by their assets. Other investors, however, reinvest their investment earnings in order to accumulate wealth.

Consider an individual who wants to accumulate a sum of money and purchases a $1,000 bond that pays $100 a year and matures after ten years. The anticipated annual return based on the annual interest and the amount invested is 10 percent ($100/$1,000). The investor wants to reinvest the annual interest, and the question then becomes what rate will be earned on these reinvested funds: Will the return be more or less than the 10 percent initially earned? The essence of reinvestment rate risk is the uncertainty that the investor will earn less than the anticipated return when payments are received and reinvested.

In addition to the previously mentioned risks, the investor must also bear the risk associated with inflation. Inflation is the loss of purchasing power through a general rise in prices. If prices of goods and services increase, the real purchasing power of the investor's assets and the income generated by them is reduced. Thus, **purchasing power risk** is the risk that inflation will erode the buying power of the investor's assets and income.[3]

purchasing power risk
The uncertainty that future inflation will erode the purchasing power of assets and income.

Investors will naturally seek to protect themselves from loss of purchasing power by constructing a portfolio of assets with an anticipated return that is higher than the anticipated rate of inflation. It is important to note the word *anticipated,* because it influences the selection of particular assets. If inflation is expected to be 4 percent, a savings account offering 6 percent will produce a gain and thereby "beat" inflation. However, if the inflation rate were to increase unexpectedly to 7 percent, the savings account would result in a loss of purchasing power. The real rate of return is negative. If the higher rate of inflation had been expected, the investor might not have chosen the savings account but might have purchased some other asset with a higher potential return.

exchange rate risk
The uncertainty associated with changes in the value of foreign currencies.

The last source of systematic risk is **exchange rate risk**, which is the uncertainty of the value of a currency that occurs when one currency is converted into another. This source of risk applies only if the investor acquires foreign assets denominated in a foreign currency. Avoiding such assets means the investor avoids this source of risk. However, because the individual may acquire shares in domestic firms with foreign operations or shares in mutual funds that make foreign investments, the individual still may indirectly bear exchange rate risk.

If the investor bears more risk, he or she may earn a higher return. This is the essential trade-off that all investors must face. Federally insured savings accounts offer lower yields but are less risky than bonds issued by AT&T, and AT&T bonds are less risky than the stock of a small, emerging firm whose securities are traded over the counter.

The investor may select riskier assets in anticipation of a higher return, but this higher return is not necessarily superior to a lower return. The investor must decide if the anticipated additional return is worth the additional risk. The aim, then, is for the investor to optimize the risk/return trade-off and to construct a portfolio that offers the highest expected return for the individual's willingness to bear risk.

By now it should be obvious that all investors bear risk. Even an investor who does nothing cannot avoid risk. By "doing nothing" and holding cash or placing

[3]The opposite of inflation is deflation, which is a general decline in prices. During a period of deflation, the real purchasing power of the investor's assets and income is increased (unless the value of the assets or the total amount of income is also declining).

the funds in a savings account, the investor is still making an investment and is bearing some element of risk. The very nature of transferring purchasing power from today to tomorrow requires accepting some risk, because the future is uncertain. Risk simply cannot be avoided, as any choice will involve at least one of the sources of risk: business risk, financial risk, market risk, interest rate risk, reinvestment rate risk, purchasing power risk, and exchange rate risk.

Efficient and Competitive Markets

Have you ever been fishing? (If not, substitute playing golf or some similar activity.) Did you catch any fish? Which fish did you talk about? The answer to that question is probably the "big one" or the "big one that got away." What is more important, of course, is the size of the average fish (or average golf score). If you go fishing several times, you will not catch a "big one" every time or even frequently. The average size of the fish you catch becomes the norm. And other individuals who fish in the same waters will have comparable results. Unless they have special skills or knowledge, most individuals' catch should be similar to and approach the average size of fish that is caught.

In many ways, the fishing analogy applies to investing in stock. Individuals tend to talk about the big return ("I bought X and it doubled within a week") or the lost opportunity ("I bought Plain and Fancy Doughnuts of America. It rose 80 percent within an hour and I did not sell"). But what matters is the return you earn after making many investments over an extended period of time. Unless you have special skills or knowledge, that return should tend to be comparable to the return earned by other investors in comparable investments.

Why is this so? The answer lies in the reality that investors participate in efficient and competitive financial markets. Economics teaches that markets with many participants (i.e., buyers and sellers) who may enter and exit freely will be competitive. That certainly describes financial markets. Investors may participate freely in the purchase and sale of stocks and bonds. Virtually anyone, from a child to a grandmother, may own a financial asset, even if it is just a savings account. Many firms, including banks, insurance companies, and mutual funds, compete for the funds of investors. The financial markets are among the most (and perhaps *the* most) competitive of all markets.

Financial markets tend to be very efficient. As is explained throughout this text, security prices depend on future cash flows, such as interest or dividend payments. If new information suggests that these flows will be altered, the market rapidly adjusts the asset's price. Thus, an efficient financial market implies that a security's current price embodies all the known information concerning the potential return and risk associated with the particular asset. If an asset, such as a stock, were undervalued and offered an excessive return, investors would seek to buy it, which would drive the price up and reduce the return that subsequent investors would earn. Conversely, if the asset were overvalued and offered an inferior return, investors would seek to sell it, which would drive down its price and increase the return to subsequent investors. The fact that there are sufficient investors who are informed means that a security's price will reflect the investment community's consensus regarding the asset's true value and also that the expected return will be consistent with the amount of risk the investor must bear to earn the return.

The concept of an efficient financial market has an important and sobering corollary. Efficient markets imply that investors (or at least the vast majority of investors) cannot expect on average to beat the market *consistently*. Of course, that does not mean an individual will never select an asset that does exceedingly well. Individuals can earn large returns on particular assets, as the stockholders of many firms know. Certainly the investor who bought Heller Financial stock on July 29, 2001, for $35.90 and sold it on July 30, 2001, for $52.99 made a large return on that investment.[4] The concept of efficient markets implies that this investor will not consistently select those individual securities that earn abnormally large returns.

If investors cannot expect to outperform the market consistently, they also should not consistently underperform the market. (That is, you would not always be the investor who sold Heller Financial just prior to the large increase in its price.) Of course, some securities may decline in price and inflict large losses on their owners, but efficient markets imply that the individual who constructs a well-diversified portfolio will not always select the stocks and bonds of firms that fail. If such individuals do exist, they will soon lose their resources and will no longer be able to participate in the financial markets.

Thus, efficient financial markets imply that investors should, over an extended period of time, earn neither excessively positive nor excessively negative returns. Instead, their returns should mirror the returns earned by the financial markets as a whole and the risk assumed by the investor. As is covered in Chapter 10, the Ibbotson studies (which are considered the benchmark for aggregate returns) indicate that the historical return on investments in stock in the country's largest firms has been approximately 11 percent annually. Smaller, but riskier, companies have generated higher returns. These historical returns are consistent with the risk–return trade-off, that higher returns require more risk. In an efficient market framework, it would be reasonable to assume that over an extended period of time the typical investor earns returns that are consistent with these historical returns.

Although security prices and returns are ultimately determined by the interactions of buyers and sellers (i.e., investors), there is little an individual can do to affect a security's price. Instead, the investor should select among alternatives to build a portfolio that is consistent with his or her financial goals and willingness to bear risk. That is, the investor allocates his or her resources to construct a well-diversified portfolio that over time meets the reasons for saving and postponing current spending.

Portfolio Assessment

Much of the popular press places emphasis on returns without considering risk. Mutual funds are often ranked on the basis of return. Statements such as "portfolio manager of growth fund X earned the highest return for the last three months" often appear in the popular financial press. The portfolio managers of the best-performing funds appear on *Wall $treet Week* or CNBC. Obviously, some fund manager had to earn the highest return for the last quarter. (Some student also earned the highest grade on my last test.)

While it can be useful to rank and compare returns, investments involve risk. You certainly will not read in *Money* or see on *Wall $treet Week* the portfolio manager of fund X who achieved the highest level of risk! But it could also be useful to rank and compare risk as well as returns. Throughout this text, risk and return are often related. You make an investment in order to earn an expected return and have to bear the risk associated with that investment. After the investment is sold (or redeemed), both the realized returns and the variability of those returns may be calculated. While particular sections of this text may discuss only risk or return, the fusion of the two cannot be far away.

You should start now to think of return in a risk context. How does this investment decision affect my risk exposure? Can I reduce risk without reducing my return? How may I compare returns on a risk-adjusted basis? Chapter 8 on invest-

[4]On July 30, 2001, GE announced that it would acquire Heller Financial, which explains the large, unexpected increase in the price of the stock.

ment companies presents several methods for ranking returns on a risk-adjusted basis. In both the professional and academic investment environments, these risk adjustments are important. As an informed investor, you too should want to compare returns and portfolio performance on a risk-adjusted basis.

The Internet

Although Chapter 4 discusses sources of information, Internet sources (Web addresses or URLs, for Uniform Resource Locator) begin in Chapter 1. These sources are spread throughout the book, and, in some cases, phone numbers and mailing addresses are also provided. (You should, of course, realize that Web addresses, phone numbers, and mailing addresses may change.) Information can be obtained through the Internet free of charge, but some vendors do charge a fee for the material. While many of the Web sites provided in the text are free, fee sites are included. Some of these fee sites have complementary information that you may find useful.

With the existence of the Internet, you face several important problems. First, too much information may be available, or contradictory information may be obtained from different sites. A defined topic, such as growth mutual funds, will generate more facts and data than you could possibly assimilate. The information problem is compounded because growth mutual funds are tied to other areas of investments, such as taxation or financial planning. Selecting a growth mutual fund (or any investment) may be tied to psychology, which can help explain why some investors prefer a particular fund or have a particular financial strategy.[5] Sorting through the information and putting it into a useful form takes time and computer expertise.

The second problem with information received through the Internet concerns its accuracy. You may not know the provider's motivation! If you access a company's or government agency's Web page, the information should be accurate. If you make a general search for information on a company, the data, analysis, and recommendations you find may be inaccurate or even purposefully misleading. In addition, misleading information can be sent directly to you through the Internet. *The Wall Street Journal* (August 17, 1998, p. C22) reported a story concerning individuals who had received an e-mail stock tip promoting a company called Maxnet Inc. The stock was selling for $3 but an unnamed analyst believed the stock could reach $50. After the bogus e-mail generated buying, the price of Maxnet Inc. stock quickly rose but just as quickly declined when the scam was discovered.

Buying stock based on such unsolicited recommendations is a recipe for disaster. Unscrupulous individuals can create stories designed to persuade people to buy a stock and inflate its price so the creators of the stories can unload the security. Such actions are not new. Touting a stock to unsuspecting investors has probably occurred since trading in stocks began. The Internet, however, creates the possibility of such fraud on a large scale. My broker has told me that he often receives stock recommendations through e-mail. While some of these recommendations may come from legitimate financial analysts, others appear to be scams.

There is probably little you (or anyone else) can do to stop the dissemination of inaccurate information through the Internet, but you do not have to act on it. If you limit your search to reliable sources, then the Internet (or any other source of data or advice) can help you make investment decisions. If you indiscriminately use the Internet (or any other source) to make investment decisions, then you too

[5]A developing area of finance, behavioral finance, would argue that you will select the information that justifies or supports your preconceived investment ideas. For an introduction to behavioral finance, consult Hersh Shefrin, *Beyond Greed and Fear: Understanding Behavioral Finance and the Psychology of Investing* (Boston, MA: Harvard Business School Press, 2000).

can become a victim of a scheme to drive up prices so those perpetrating the scam can sell securities at inflated prices.

The Author's Perspective and Investment Philosophy

Financial textbooks present material that is factual (e.g., the features of bonds), theoretical (e.g., the theory of portfolio construction and diversification), and the result of empirical studies. This text is no exception. Effort is made to avoid the author's bias or perspective. In reality, however, an author's viewpoint cannot be completely disregarded. It affects the space devoted to a topic and how the topic is covered.

The first tenet that affects my perspective is a belief that investment decisions are made in exceedingly competitive financial markets (the efficient markets referred to earlier). Information is disseminated so rapidly that few individual investors are able to take advantage of new information. This theme of efficient markets reappears throughout the book. You could conclude that the reality of efficient markets ends your chances of making good investments, but that is the wrong conclusion. The presence of efficient markets ensures that you can make investments on a level playing field. In other words, the return you earn does not have to be inferior to the returns generated by more seasoned or professional investors.

A second tenet that affects my perspective is my investment philosophy. I began the first edition of this text during the 1970s, so it is possible to infer how long I have been investing. Over the years I have developed my personal investment strategy that stresses patience and long-term wealth accumulation. Additional considerations are taxation and transaction costs. The philosophy and strategies of other individuals and portfolio managers may be the exact opposite. They may have a shorter time horizon and may be less concerned with current taxes or the costs of buying and selling securities.

Understanding yourself and specifying financial goals is important when developing an investment philosophy and making investment decisions. If your investments cause you to worry (frequently expressed as causing you to lose sleep), you need to look inside yourself to determine why. If I had to buy and sell securities frequently, I would have a conflict with my personality and long-term financial goals. As a graduate student, I would often buy and sell for small gains. I found such trading to be fun and stimulating, but I observed that stocks I sold always seemed to rise and those I did not sell always seemed to decline. In effect, I violated one of investing's cardinal rules: "Let your winners run but cut your losses." It was many years before I realized that a buy-and-sell strategy (a trading strategy) did not work for me. Part of the reason was my inability to sell the losers. (Behavioral finance might suggest that I had a problem with "letting go" or that I wanted to avoid the "pain of regret" in which I refused to face the reality that I had made a bad investment decision.) I also had failed to specify why I was investing. I was treating investment as a game and not a means to reach a financial goal.

Your background also affects your investment strategies. I grew up in a family of homebuilders. As would be expected, family members had a bias, which I continue to have, for companies related to real estate (e.g., the real estate investment trusts discussed in Chapter 23). Natural resources for building (e.g., trees for lumber), building materials (e.g., plumbing supplies), and appliances for homes were often the topic of discussion at dinner. Such companies as Georgia-Pacific (lumber) or Maytag (appliances) I remember from childhood. The same applies to such companies as the local gas and electric (Dominion Resources) or phone utility (AT&T before divestiture), because I grew up with their names.

In addition to efficient markets, financial goals, and your background, the time you have to devote to investing affects your decisions. I teach courses in finance, have contact with former students who work in the area, and know investment professionals. Daily news coverage, programs like *The Nightly Business Report* on public TV, 1-800 phone numbers, and materials I have retained, such as annual reports, mean I can obtain information even when I am away from my personal computer and the Internet! I think about some topic in finance and investments every day, holidays and vacations included.

Most individuals do not have such continuous contact with investments. Their jobs and family obligations preclude it. These individuals may not develop financial goals and investment strategies, but their need for financial planning does not disappear. When individuals lack time or believe they do not have expertise, they may use professional financial planners or other professionals, such as brokers, to facilitate the construction of a diversified portfolio. The growth in the popularity of mutual funds is partially explained by individuals who do not want to select specific securities and who turn over that process to portfolio managers. These investors, however, continue to need specific investment goals and strategies.

Your background, time available to devote to investments, and financial goals may produce an investment philosophy and strategy that are different from mine. The material in this text presents alternative investments and strategies, some of which I have not used (and would not use). I will, however, try to present all the material in an unbiased manner so that you may draw your own conclusions and develop your own financial goals, investment philosophy, and strategy.

Investments and Business Finance

Finance is one business discipline that may be studied from two perspectives. One is the perspective of the investor who puts up the funds that finance the business. The other is the perspective of the corporate manager who is responsible for using those funds profitably to earn a return for the investor. While it is often assumed that management takes actions designed to increase the value of the firm and generate a return for the investors, there can be conflict between these perspectives. Managers may pursue their own best interests and not take actions that are in the best interest of the firm's owners. For example, higher management salaries reduce earnings and the investors' return, in which case the two perspectives are in conflict.

As stated, this text is presented from the perspective of the individual investor, financial planner, and portfolio manager. While the text covers techniques, strategies, and concepts from an investment perspective, corporate managers also employ many of the same techniques, strategies, and concepts. These include:

- The issuing of stock to raise funds (Chapter 2)
- The measurement of risk (standard deviation and beta coefficients in Chapter 7)
- The determination of value using discounted cash flow models and price/earnings (P/E) ratios (Chapters 9 and 13)
- The calculation of returns on investments (the internal rate of return in Chapter 10)
- The distribution of earnings (Chapter 11)
- The impact of the aggregate economy on the individual company (Chapter 12)
- The use of financial ratios to analyze a firm (Chapter 13)
- The use and management of debt financing to obtain financial leverage (Chapter 13)

- The various debt instruments and their features (Chapter 15)
- The use of derivatives to manage risk (Chapter 19–21)
- The valuation of options (Chapter 20)

There are many texts that present much of the material in this text from the perspective of management.[6] A corporate finance course, therefore, often repeats material covered in an investment course. However, the perspective and emphasis are different. Corporate management does employ many of the concepts covered in investments and financial management courses. That usage has been verified by surveys of corporate executives.[7] If you believe that you have already learned some of the material in this text in other courses, do the appropriate problems as a means to check your understanding and knowledge, and move on to something new. Time is a precious resource. Use it wisely.

The Plan and Purpose of This Text

Because the individual participates in efficient financial markets and competes with informed investors, including professional securities analysts and portfolio managers, each investor needs fundamental information concerning investments. This text helps those individuals to increase their knowledge of the risks and returns from various investment alternatives. Perhaps because investing deals with individuals' money and the potential for large gains or losses, it seems more mysterious than it should. By introducing the various investments and the methods of their analysis, valuation, and acquisition, this text removes the mystery associated with investing.

The number of possible investment alternatives is virtually unlimited. Shares in thousands of corporations are actively traded, and if an investor does not want to select individual stocks, he or she still has over 8,000 mutual funds from which to choose. Corporations, the federal government, and state and local governments issue a variety of debt instruments that range in maturity from a few days to 30 or 40 years. More than 10,000 commercial banks and thrift institutions (e.g., savings banks) offer a variety of savings accounts and certificates of deposit. Real estate, futures, options, and collectibles further increase the available alternatives, and, as if there were insufficient domestic choices, the investor may purchase foreign securities. The problem is not one of availability but of choice. The investor cannot own every asset but must choose among the alternatives.

Frequently, investment alternatives are classified as short-term (one year) or long-term (greater than one year), variable-income or fixed-income, or defensive or aggressive (even speculative). Short-term assets, such as certificates of deposit and shares in money market mutual funds, are readily converted into cash and offer investors modest returns. Bonds and stocks have a longer time horizon and are referred to as long-term investments. Common stock is also referred to as a variable-income security because the dividends and capital gains may fluctuate from year to year. Bonds are illustrative of a fixed-income security. While the investor's return from such investments can vary, the flow of income generated by bonds and preferred stock is fixed, so these securities are referred to as fixed-income securities. Options, convertible bonds, and futures may be considered aggressive

[6]See, for instance, Eugene F. Brigham and Michael C. Ehrhardt, *Financial Management Theory and Practice,* 10th ed. (Cincinnati, OH: South-Western/Thomson Learning, 2002).

[7]For an extensive survey of management usage of concepts presented in this text and other financial concepts (e.g., cost of capital, option valuation applied to investments in plant and equipment), see John R. Graham and Campbell R. Harvey, "The Theory and Practice of Corporate Finance: Evidence from the Field," *Journal of Financial Economics* (Vol. 60, No. 1, 2001).

investments because they may offer high returns but require the investor to bear substantial risk. Other possible investments include nonfinancial assets (tangible or real assets) such as real estate, gold, and collectibles.

The subject of investments is sometimes viewed as complex, but the approach in this text is to isolate each type of asset. The sources of return, the risks, and the features that differentiate each are described. Techniques for analyzing and valuing the assets are explained. Most of the material is essential information for all investors, whether they have large or small portfolios.

The text is divided into several parts. The first lays the foundation on which security selection is based. This encompasses how securities come into existence (Chapter 2), the mechanics of buying and selling securities (Chapter 3), sources of information (Chapter 4), the process of compounding and discounting (Chapter 5), the tax environment (Chapter 6), and the analysis of risk and its measurement (Chapter 7). Because investment companies (e.g., mutual funds) are such a large component of the financial environment, Part I ends with a description of these funds (Chapter 8).

Part 2 is devoted to investments in common stock. Chapter 9 discusses the valuation of common stock. This is followed by measures of the market and historical returns (Chapter 10), dividends (Chapter 11), and the economic and industrial environment (Chapter 12). The last two chapters of Part 2 consider techniques used to analyze a specific stock: the analysis of financial statements (Chapter 13) and technical analysis (Chapter 14).

Part 3 covers fixed-income securities. Chapter 15 describes the features common to all debt instruments, and Chapter 16 discusses the pricing of bonds and the impact of changing interest rates. Next follow the various types of federal, state, and local government bonds (Chapter 17). The last chapter of Part 3 (Chapter 18) discusses convertible bonds and convertible preferred stock, which may be exchanged for the issuing firm's common stock.

Part 4 considers derivatives whose value is related to (derived from) another asset. Chapter 19 provides a general introduction to options (calls, puts, and warrants), and Chapter 20 expands this material to include option valuation and option strategies. Chapter 21 covers futures, which are perhaps the riskiest of all the investments covered in this text.

Part 5 considers the construction of a diversified portfolio. It begins by adding two classes of alternative investments: foreign securities (Chapter 22) and nonfinancial assets (Chapter 23). Chapter 24 is devoted to the construction and management of a well-diversified portfolio. Initially, the discussion is devoted to financial planning: financial goals, the investor's resources, and the management and evaluation of the portfolio. While the individual may acquire a variety of assets and construct a diversified portfolio, the easiest means for many investors is to acquire shares in an investment company. The text ends by comparing active management of one's portfolio through selection of individual securities to passive portfolio management through selection of shares in mutual funds.

Questions

1) What is the distinction between liquidity and marketability?
2) What is risk and what are the sources of risk that every investor must face?
3) A significant part of this text is devoted to valuation. What causes an asset to have value today?
4) What is the relationship between risk and expected return?
5) What is the implication of an efficient securities market for the return an investor will earn over a period of time?

THE FINANCIAL ADVISOR'S INVESTMENT CASE

Introduction to Chapter Cases

You are employed as a financial advisor. You could work for a bank specializing in trusts, an insurance company, or a brokerage firm. While financial planners do work for divisions within these financial institutions, there are also firms that specialize in the development of financial plans for individuals. These fee-only financial planners are compensated for the development of plans instead of solely on commissions based on the sale of financial products.

As a financial advisor, you work with a variety of individuals with a wide range of backgrounds and financial experience who seek advice and answers to their financial questions. Some questions may require simple numerical answers, while others may require judgments instead of factual responses. Your clients also want clear, straightforward explanations and guidance regarding possible alternative investments.

The chapters in this text present such problems or case studies faced by financial planners. By necessity, these cases must be brief, but they apply the material in the chapter (and sometimes more than one chapter) to a financial planning problem. When answering a specific question in a case, you should consider how the solution illustrates an important financial concept—such as the importance of contributing to a retirement account or constructing a diversified portfolio.

INVESTMENT PROJECT

Investment is one subject in which you, the student, can participate actively, at least on paper, in the content of the course. Constructing a paper portfolio is not the same as actually investing your own money. Nothing is at risk when following a paper portfolio; you cannot lose money. A paper portfolio, however, can illustrate several points developed in this text. This investment project asks you to collect weekly data on stock prices throughout the semester.

The project requires you to complete the following data sheet during the semester. How you complete the data sheet is at your discretion. The purpose of the project is to encourage you to develop the habit of following security prices and to see their relationship to the market as a whole. The purpose is not to simulate actual trading in securities. If you want to simulate trading securities, try an investment game. Examples include:

Greenline Collegiate Investment Challenge
http://www.ichallenge.net
The League of American Investors
http://www.investorsleague.com
Money Game
http://www.moneygame.com
SMG Worldwide
http://www.smg2000.com
Stock-Trak
http://www.stocktrak.com

THE DATA SHEET

	Week														
Stock	**1**	**2**	**3**	**4**	**5**	**6**	**7**	**8**	**9**	**10**	**11**	**12**	**13**	**14**	**15**
1 S&P 500															
2 CSK															
3 HSY															
4 IBM															
5 MSFT															
6															
7															
8															
9															

On the first row, record the value of the Standard & Poor's 500 stock index, which is an aggregate measure of the stock market. If the market rises during the semester, the value of the index will rise. Conversely, if the market declines, the value of the index will fall. On rows 2 through 5, record the prices of four stocks I have selected. On rows 6 through 9, record the prices of the stocks you have chosen. Unless your instructor specifies otherwise, you may use any method for picking your stocks. My choices are Chesapeake Corporation (CSK), Hershey Foods (HSY), International Business Machines (IBM), and Microsoft (MSFT). The capital letters that follow each firm's name are the ticker symbols used to identify each firm whose shares are traded on the New York and American stock exchanges or through the National Securities Dealers Automated Quotation System, which is referred to as the

Nasdaq stock market. If you follow specific securities for a period of time, you will remember them in terms of the symbols instead of the companies' names.

The data needed to complete this project are readily available in *The Wall Street Journal* or through the Internet.

Security prices are also available through the Internet. Possible Web sites for obtaining stock prices include:

http://www.msn.com
http://www.wrsn.com
http://www.wallstreetcity.com
http://www.bloomberg.com
http://www.quote.yahoo.com
http://www.finance.lycos.com

The layout for each site differs, but in each case, you enter the ticker symbol and hit enter (or search). If you do not know the ticker symbol, there are usually instructions for obtaining the symbol.

An alternative approach for obtaining price data is to set up a "watch account" or "watch list" through an Internet source such as those listed here. The list will provide you with the daily prices of the securities you are following. As the project begins, you should have nine entries: the S&P 500 stock index and the eight individual stock prices. You will be asked later to use the information, so record the price as of a given day (e.g., Friday closing price) throughout the semester. If you are using a watch list to obtain the prices, save your weekly printouts.

APPENDIX 1

Supply and Demand

Because students' backgrounds and experiences regarding a specific topic vary, this text includes two appendixes that review important material. This appendix considers the determination of price through the analysis of supply and demand. The appendix to Chapter 7 briefly addresses statistical topics, such as correlation and regression.

The phrase *supply and demand* is often encountered in economics and investments, especially regarding the determination of price. The demand for a specific product depends on several variables, such as (1) its price, (2) the prices of other goods—especially those used in conjunction with the product (*complementary goods*) or instead of the product (*substitute goods*), (3) consumers' income, and (4) consumers' tastes. The supply of a particular product depends on (1) its price, (2) the costs of production (such as labor), and (3) the level of technology.

Supply and demand analysis is applied to the relationship between the willingness of individuals to purchase (demand) the good, the willingness of producers to sell (supply) the good, and the resulting determination of the good's *equilibrium price*—when the quantity supplied equals the quantity demanded. The other factors are held constant in order to focus on the determination of the price that equates supply and demand.

In Figure 1A.1, the horizontal axis denotes quantity, while price is read on the vertical axis. The line *DD* represents the quantity that individuals demand of the

FIGURE 1A.1

The Determination of Price

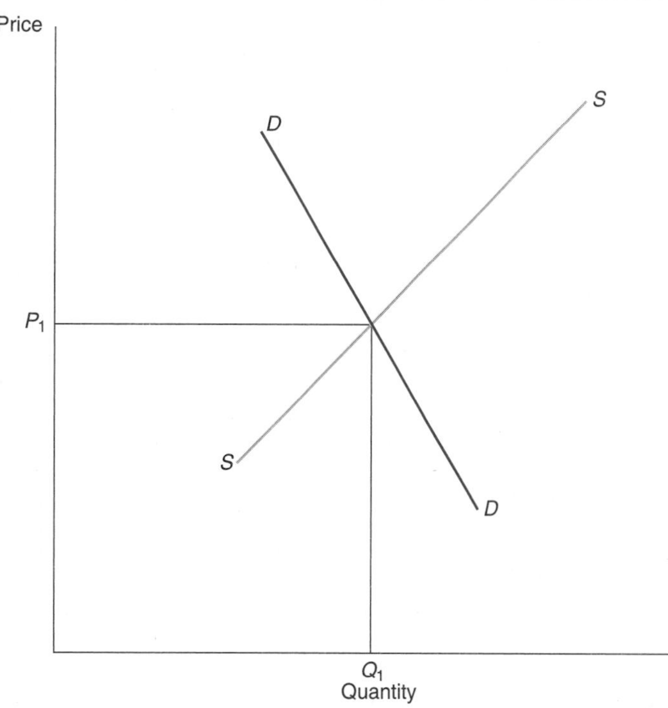

product at each price. As the price of the product increases, the quantity demanded declines, and as the price of the product decreases, the quantity demanded increases. Line *SS* represents the quantity the producers are willing to supply at each price. As the price of the product increases, the quantity supplied increases, and as the price falls, the quantity supplied decreases. Lines *DD* and *SS* intersect at price P_1 and quantity Q_1. At that price (and only at that price) the quantity demanded by consumers and the quantity supplied by producers are equal. Because demand and supply are equal, there is no reason for the price to change, and the market is at equilibrium.

If the price were higher than P_1, producers would seek to supply more of the good, but users would buy less of it (i.e., the quantity demanded would be lower), as shown in Figure 1A.2. At P_2, the quantity demanded is Q_2 and the quantity supplied is Q_3: The quantity supplied exceeds the quantity demanded. In order to sell the excess goods, producers lower prices, which increases the quantity demanded. The price decline continues until the equilibrium price (i.e., P_1) is restored, and the quantity demanded equals the quantity supplied.

If the price were lower than P_1, producers would supply less of the good, but users would seek to buy more of it (i.e., the quantity demanded would be higher). At P_2 in Figure 1A.3, the quantity demanded is Q_3 and the quantity supplied is Q_2. The quantity supplied is less than the quantity demanded; there is excess demand. In order to ration the good, the price rises, which increases the quantity supplied and decreases the quantity demanded. The price increase continues until the equilibrium price (P_1) is restored—demand equals supply.

In the previous analysis, the movement in the price of the good results from a disequilibrium in the market. If the quantity demanded does not equal the quantity supplied, the price changes, and an equilibrium price is established. No other

FIGURE 1A.2

Excess Supply: Quantity Supplied Exceeds Quantity Demanded

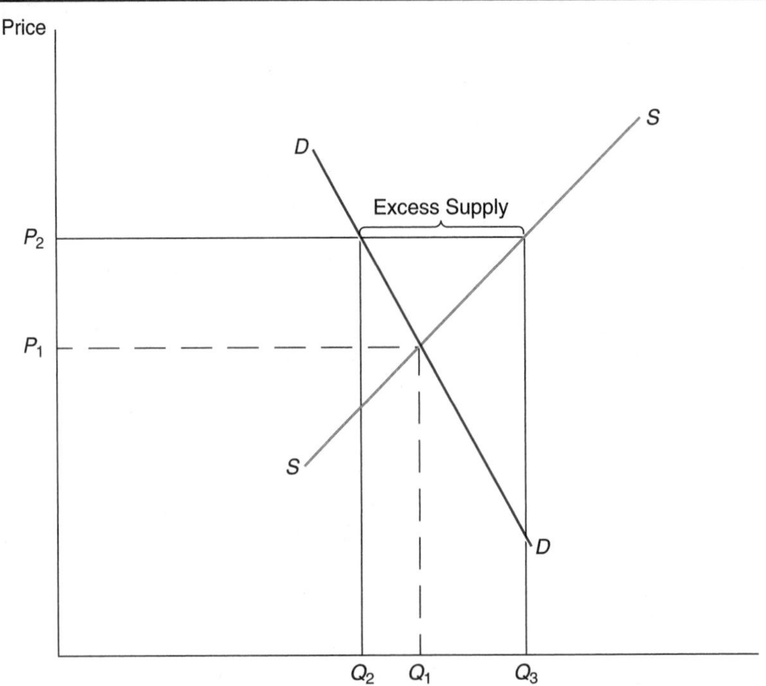

variables are considered (i.e., they are held constant and assumed not to change). If one of the other variables were to change, then it would affect the price of the good. For example, if incomes were to increase, the demand curve would shift to the right (i.e., D_1D_1 to D_2D_2 in Figure 1A.4 on p. 24). At the old price P_1, which previously equated the quantity demanded and the quantity supplied, the quantity demanded (Q_3) exceeds the quantity supplied (Q_1). The excess demand causes the price to rise. As the price increases, the quantity supplied is increased until a new equilibrium price and quantity are determined at P_2 and Q_2.

Changes in the other variables being held constant would produce similar results. A change in consumer tastes in favor of the good or an increase in the price of a substitute good would increase the demand for this good and shift the demand curve to the right. The analysis would be the same: The price of the good would rise, which induces an increase in the quantity supplied, and the market would move toward a new equilibrium level of price and quantity.

In the previous analysis, the change was generated by a change in income that caused the demand curve to shift. All other variables were held constant. Similar analyses may be applied to supply. If one of the variables affecting supply were to change, that too would affect the price of the good. For example, if costs of production were to decrease, the supply curve shifts to the right (i.e., S_1S_1 to S_2S_2 in Figure 1A.5 on p. 24). At the original equilibrium price P_1, the quantity supplied (Q_3) will exceed the quantity demanded (Q_1), forcing the price to decline. As the price decreases, the quantity demanded increases until a new equilibrium price and quantity are determined at P_2 and Q_2.

Changes in the other variables being held constant produce similar results. An improvement in technology or productivity would shift the supply curve to the right, indicating an increase in the supply of the good at each price. The results are

FIGURE 1A.3

Excess Demand: Quantity Demanded Exceeds Quantity Supplied

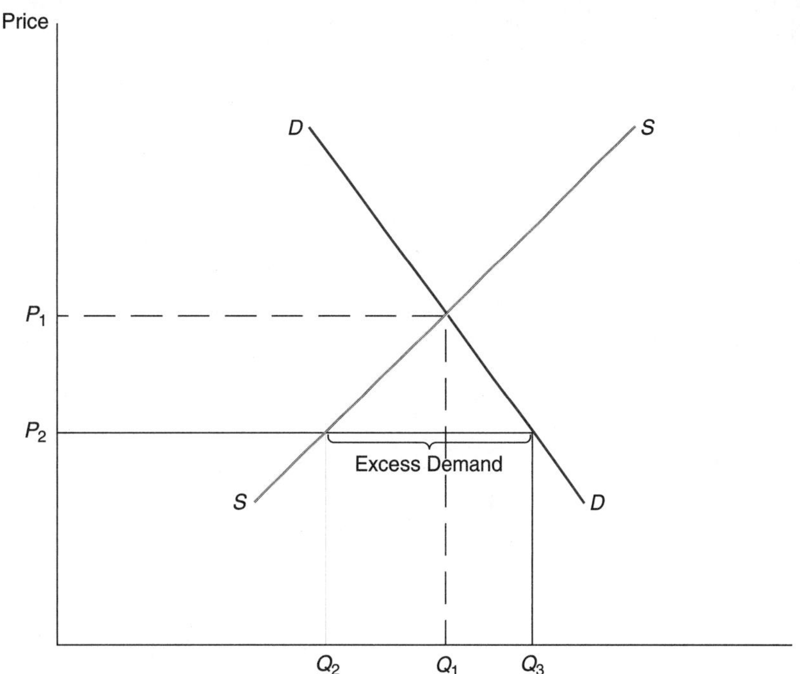

FIGURE 1A.4

An Increase (Shift) in Demand

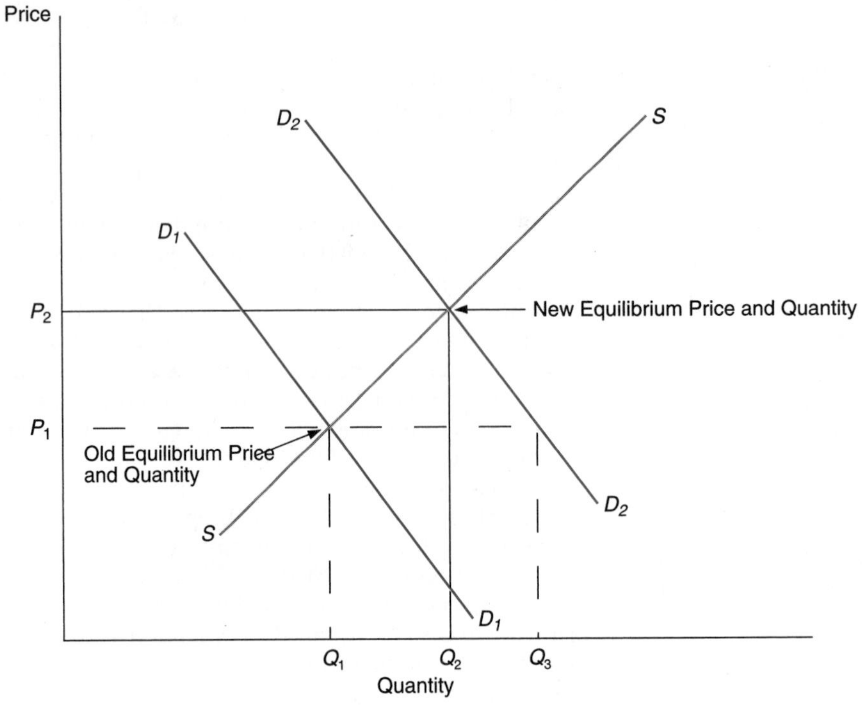

FIGURE 1A.5

An Increase (Shift) in Supply

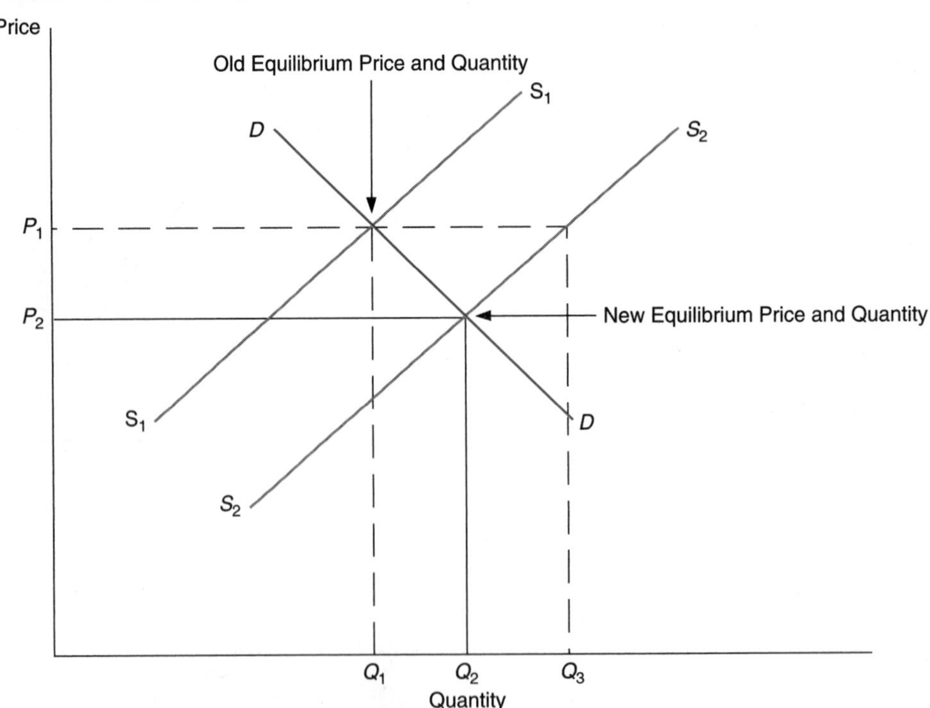

the same: The price of the good falls, causing an increase in the quantity demanded, and the market moves toward a new equilibrium level of price and quantity.

Notice the difference between Figures 1A.4 and 1A.5. In both illustrations, a variable previously held constant in Figures 1A.1–1A.3 changes, which shifts the demand or supply curves. In both cases, the shift initially causes disequilibrium in the market, which sets into motion forces that generate a change in the price of the good. The price change affects both the quantity supplied and the quantity demanded. These changes in price and quantity continue until a new equilibrium price is established, and the quantity demanded equals quantity supplied.

The preceding analysis considers the impact of altering one variable while holding other variables constant. In reality, however, several variables may change simultaneously. For this reason, the general "law" of supply and demand may not appear to hold. For example, during a period of inflation, the observed quantity demanded may not decline with an increase in price. The reason, of course, is that individuals' expectations of higher prices are simultaneously increasing the demand for the goods. If the increased demand exceeds the decline in the quantity demanded generated by the higher prices, the result will be higher prices and no reduction in the quantity purchased. Such a result does not invalidate supply and demand analysis; it merely illustrates how difficult it may be to isolate the impact of one variable while holding other variables constant.

For supply and demand analysis to apply, prices and quantities must be allowed to change. Price and quantity will not achieve equilibrium if they are not permitted to respond to the forces of supply and demand. For example, if the price is not allowed to rise in Figure 1A.3, the excess demand for the good cannot be erased. This excess demand will continue, but additional supply will not be forthcoming because the price has not risen. The existing supply will have to be rationed by some means other than price.

It should also be noted that the actual quantity bought always equals the quantity sold. For example, in Figure 1A.3, Q_2 represents the quantity bought and sold at price P_2 (the quantity supplied also must be the quantity purchased). The important point is that at price P_2 there is more quantity demanded than quantity supplied—the excess demand drives up the price. When it is reported that stock prices rose because buyers exceeded sellers (or demand exceeded supply), the wording is inaccurate: The stock prices rose because quantity demanded exceeded the supply and drove the prices higher. The actual number of shares bought (i.e., buyers) must equal the number of shares sold (i.e., sellers), even if the quantity demanded exceeds the quantity supplied.

Supply and demand analysis is frequently employed in economics and finance to explain price or quantity change or to examine the impact of a change in economic policy (e.g., imposing taxes on specific goods or reducing trade barriers). The analysis may be used in a macro (or aggregate) context or in a micro (or individual) context. To study an increase in the money supply by the Federal Reserve and its subsequent impact on interest rates illustrates a macro analysis; GM raising car prices and estimating its competitors' responses demonstrates a micro context.

CHAPTER

2 The Creation of Financial Assets

In July 2001, the Office of Thrift Supervision closed the Superior Bank of Chicago because it had lost nearly all of its $2.1 billion in assets. The bank became the responsibility of the FDIC, which provided $1.5 billion in credit to open a new banking institution to service the depositors. Because funds deposited in the bank were insured, depositors would not sustain losses up to the $100,000 legal limit. Of course, taxpayers would be providing the funds to the FDIC to cover the bailout.

Superior Bank, like other banks, made loans with the funds obtained from depositors. While its losses were the result of management's engaging in poor lending practices and inadequate employee supervision, the vast majority of banks profitably transfer funds from savers to borrowers through the lending process. All businesses need funds, and these funds come from creditors such as commercial banks that lend funds to the firm and from owners who have equity in the firm.

It is through this process of financing business that securities come into existence. Firms issue stocks and bonds, which are bought by the general public and by financial institutions, such as pension plans and commercial banks. Once issued, many of these securities may be traded in the secondary markets, such as the New York Stock Exchange. These secondary markets make securities more attractive to individuals because investors know there is a place to sell the securities should the need arise.

This chapter is concerned with the financing business needs, the role of financial intermediaries, and the advantages offered to individuals by short-term investments in various financial intermediaries. It begins with a general discussion of transferring funds from savers to business. This transfer occurs either directly, when firms issue new securities, or indirectly through financial intermediaries. The second section describes the process of issuing new securities and the role of the investment banker. The last sections of the chapter are devoted to the role of financial intermediaries. Increased competition and the deregulation of banking have led to a blurring of distinctions among the various intermediaries; however, all offer individuals modest yields and safe short-term investments. The chapter concludes with a discussion of money market mutual funds that directly compete for investors' funds with the traditional financial intermediaries (e.g., commercial banks).

Learning Objectives

After completing this chapter you should be able to:

1 Explain the roles of the investment banker and the financial intermediary.

2 Illustrate the flow of funds from savers to firms.

3 Identify the components necessary for the sale of securities to the general public.

4 Differentiate an underwriting from a best-efforts sale of securities.

5 Contrast the various financial instruments offered by commercial banks and other depository institutions.

6 Distinguish money market mutual funds from commercial banks and savings banks.

7 List several money market instruments.

The Transfer of Funds to Business

Securities and other financial assets facilitate the transfer of savings from those with funds to those who need funds. Savers may include individuals, firms, or governments. Savings represent a command of resources that are currently not being used. Thus a government that has collected tax receipts but has not spent the funds has, in effect, savings. So has a firm that has earned profits from the sale of goods but has not distributed the earnings. Until the earnings are distributed, the firm has savings.

Those in need of funds may include individuals, firms, and governments. For example, an individual may need funds to purchase a house, the local school board may need funds to build a school, or AT&T may require funds to purchase new equipment. The individual cannot obtain a mortgage to purchase a house, the school board cannot build the school, or AT&T cannot purchase the equipment if some individual, firm, or government does not put up the funds.

All financial assets (e.g., stocks, bonds, bank deposits, and government bonds) are created to facilitate this transfer. The creation of financial assets and the transfer of funds are crucial for the well-being of every economy. The individual could not obtain the resources to acquire the house, the local government could not build the school, and AT&T could not obtain the new equipment without the transfer of resources. And this transfer could not occur without the creation of financial assets.

All financial assets represent claims, and these claims may be divided into two types: debt obligations and equity obligations. Debt obligations, such as bonds or certificates of deposit with a commercial bank, are loans. The borrower pays interest for the use of the funds and agrees to repay the principal after some specified period of time. These debt obligations represent *legal obligations* on the part of the borrower that are enforceable in a court of law.

An equity claim represents ownership. Owners of common stock are the owners of the corporation that issued the stock. The individual who owns a home has equity in the home. Equity claims are paid after all debt obligations are met. This residual status means that owners reap the rewards when a business is successful but may sustain substantial losses when the operation is unsuccessful. This does not mean that lenders (creditors) may not sustain losses. It means that the owner has a riskier position than the creditor. Correspondingly, the owner may earn a greater return for bearing more risk.

While all financial assets represent a debt or an equity claim, the individual instruments have a variety of differing features. One of the purposes of this text is to explain this variety and to clarify the advantages and risks associated with each financial asset. Not all financial assets are clearly debt or equity instruments. Some have elements of both, such as the convertible bond, which is a debt instrument that may be converted into equity. Such bonds have to be analyzed from both perspectives: as a debt instrument and as an equity instrument.

The Direct and Indirect Transfer of Funds

financial intermediary
A financial institution, such as a commercial bank, that borrows from one group and lends to another.

There are basically two methods for transferring funds to businesses. One is the direct investment of funds into businesses by the general public. This occurs when firms issue new securities that are purchased by investors or when individuals invest in partnerships or sole proprietorships. The second method is the indirect transfer through a **financial intermediary**, which transfers funds to firms and other borrowers from individuals, or from firms that currently are not using the funds. The financial intermediary stands between the ultimate supplier and the ultimate user of the funds and facilitates the flow of money and credit between the suppliers and the users.

When a corporation issues a new security such as a bond and sells it to the general public, the following transaction occurs:

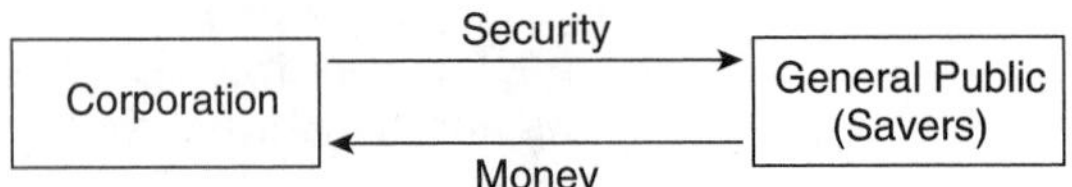

The saver purchases the security with money, thereby trading one asset for another. The firm acquires the funds by issuing the security; thus there is a direct transfer of money from the saver to the firm.

The indirect transfer is more complicated because an intermediary operates between the saver and the firm. The intermediary acquires funds from savers by issuing a claim on itself, such as a savings account at a commercial bank. The intermediary then lends the funds or buys new securities.

The flow of funds to the financial intermediary is illustrated by the following chart:

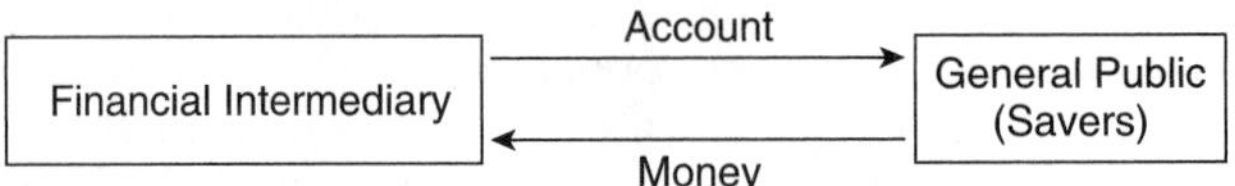

The saver trades one asset (the money) for another (the claim on the financial intermediary), and the financial intermediary acquires the funds by issuing a claim on itself.

The financial intermediary then lends the funds to an entity, such as a firm, government, or household, in need of the funds. That is, the financial intermediary buys a security such as a bond or makes a new loan, at which time the following transaction occurs:

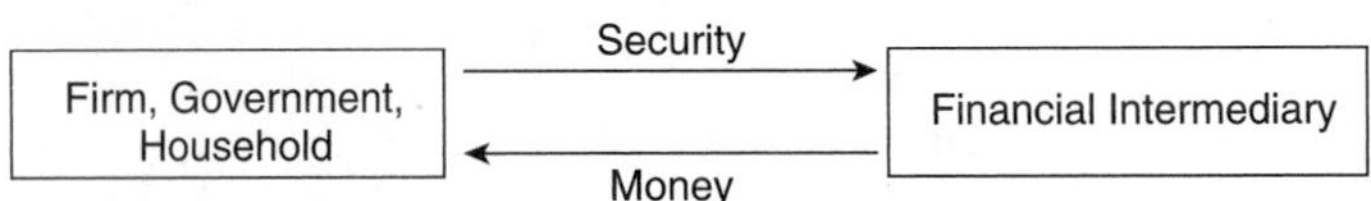

The financial intermediary gives up one asset, the money, to acquire another asset, the claim on the borrower. The borrower acquires the funds by promising to return them in the future and to pay interest while the loan is outstanding.

The preceding charts may be combined to illustrate the process of transferring funds from the ultimate lender (the saver) to the ultimate borrower.

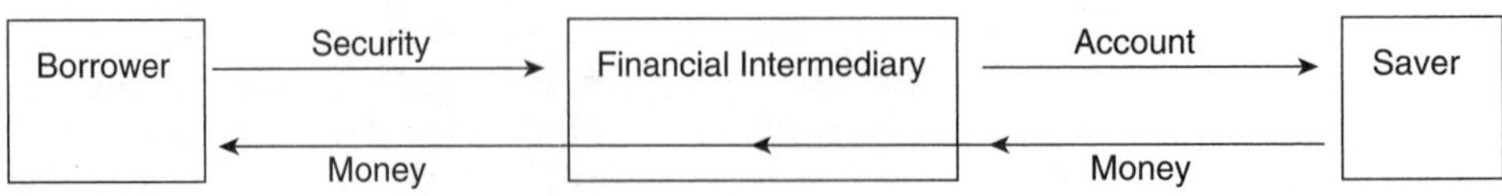

The saver's funds are transferred to the borrower through the financial intermediary. Through this process the borrower is able to acquire the funds because the financial intermediary was able to issue a *claim on itself* (i.e., the account) that the saver would accept.

private placement
The nonpublic sale of securities.

The direct sale of an entire issue of bonds or stock to an investor (or group of investors) or to a financial institution, such as a pension fund or a life insurance company, is called a **private placement**. The primary advantages of a private placement to the firm are the elimination of the cost of selling securities to the general public and the ready availability of large amounts of cash. In addition, the firm does not have to meet the disclosure requirements that are necessary to sell securities to the general public. This disclosure of information is for the protection of the investing public; it is presumed that the financial institution can protect itself by requiring information as a precondition for granting a loan. The disclosure requirements are both a cost to the firm when securities are issued to the public and a possible source of information to its competitors that the firm may wish to avoid divulging. An additional advantage of a private placement to both the firm and the financial institution is that the terms of securities may be tailored to meet both parties' needs.

A private placement has similar advantages for the firm that is investing the funds. A substantial amount of money may be invested at one time, and the maturity date can be set to meet the lender's needs. In addition, brokerage fees associated with purchasing securities are avoided. The financial intermediary can gain more control over the firm that receives the funds by building restrictive covenants into the agreement. These covenants may restrict the firm from issuing additional securities without the prior permission of the lender and may limit the firm's dividends, its merger activity, and the types of investments that it may make. All these restrictive covenants are designed to protect the lender from risk of loss and are part of any private sale of securities from a firm to a financial institution. Because each sale is separately negotiated, the individual terms vary with the bargaining powers of the parties and the economic conditions at the time of the agreement.

venture capitalist
Firm specializing in investing in the securities, especially stock, of small, emerging companies.

Private placements are especially important for small, emerging firms. The size of these firms or the risk associated with them often precludes their raising funds from traditional sources such as commercial banks. Firms that do make private placements of securities issued by emerging firms are called **venture capitalists**. Venture capital is a major source of finance for small firms or firms developing new technologies. The venture capitalists thus fill a void by acquiring securities issued by small firms with exceptional growth potential.

Of course, many small firms do not realize this potential, and venture capitalists often sustain large losses on their investments. Success, however, can generate a very large return. In a sense, it is a numbers game. If a venture capitalist invests in five projects and four fail, the one large gain can more than offset the investments in the four losers.

Once the emerging firm does grow, the securities purchased by the venture capitalist may be sold to the general public through a public offering. (The process of selling new securities to the general public is covered in the next section.) Many initial public offerings combine the sale of new securities to raise additional funds for the firm and a sale of securities by current shareholders. These current holdings often include the shares originally purchased by the venture capitalists, who are using the initial public sale as a means to realize the profits on their investments.[1]

[1]Not all investments made by venture capitalists are profitable. *The Wall Street Journal* (March 12, 2001) reported that Capital Research & Management invested $41 million just prior to the initial public offering of Loudcloud (LDCL) and lost $26 million in the first day of trading.

The Issuing and Selling of New Securities

investment banker

An underwriter, a firm that sells new issues of securities to the general public.

initial public offering (IPO)

The first sale of common stock to the general public.

Firms, in addition to acquiring funds through private placements, may issue new securities and sell them to the general public, usually through **investment bankers**. If this sale is the first sale of common stock to the general public, it is referred to as an **initial public offering (IPO)**. Firms sell securities when internally generated funds are insufficient to finance the desired level of investment spending and when the firm believes it to be advantageous to obtain outside funding from the general public instead of from a financial intermediary. Such outside funding may increase public interest in the firm and its securities and may also bypass some of the restrictive covenants that are required by financial institutions.

The following section addresses the sale of new securities to the general public through an investment banker. It covers the role played by the investment banker, the mechanics of selling new securities, and the potential volatility of the new-issue market. Although the discussion is limited to the sale of stock, it also applies to new issues of bonds sold to the general public.

The Role of Investment Bankers

A corporation can market its securities directly to the public. For example, Dominion Resources had a dividend reinvestment plan, in which cash dividends are used to purchase additional stock, and, at one time, had a stock purchase plan for customers in which they made cash contributions to buy stock with their electric bill payments. If a firm does directly sell shares to the general public, the formal offer to sell these securities must be made by a prospectus, and the securities must be registered with the Securities and Exchange Commission (SEC).[2] This process of registering the securities and their subsequent sale to the general public is discussed below.

Direct plans to sell securities to the general public involve expenses, so many firms employ investment bankers to market new securities. In effect, an investment banker serves as a middleman to channel money from investors to firms that need the capital. Although investment bankers are conduits through which the money flows, they are not financial intermediaries, since they do not create claims on themselves. With a financial intermediary, the investor has a claim on the intermediary. With an investment banker, however, the investor's claim is on the firm that issues the securities and not on the investment banker who facilitated the initial sale.

Investment banking is an important but often confusing financial practice, partly because of the misnomer. An *investment banker* is often not a banker and generally does not invest. Instead, the investment banker is usually a brokerage firm, such as Merrill Lynch or Legg Mason. Although these brokerage firms may own securities, they do not necessarily buy and hold the newly issued securities on their own account for investment purposes. (When an investment bank does commit its own funds and buys the securities as an investment, it is referred to as a *merchant bank* and its activity as *merchant banking*.)

Because brokerage firms have many customers, they are able to sell the securities without the costly search that the individual firm may have to undertake to sell its own securities. Thus, although the firm in need of financing must pay for the service, it is able to raise external capital at less expense through the investment banker than it could by selling the securities itself.

[2]Small issues of securities may be able to obtain an exemption from the federal and state registration laws. When the Hopewell Valley Community Bank directly sold stock to the general public in the geographic area served by the bank, its prospectus stated that the securities were being sold "in reliance upon exemptions from the registration requirements."

POINTS OF INTEREST

Green Shoes

When a firm and an investment banker agree to an underwriting, only the approximate number of shares and their approximate price can be established. Obviously, conditions can change, and underwriters need flexibility when selling the securities. If market conditions worsen, the underwriters may seek to sell a smaller issue at a lower price. If conditions improve, the issue may be increased. Firms often grant the underwriters an option to increase the size of the issue. This option is sometimes referred to as a *green shoe* after the first company that gave the option to its underwriters.

How the option works is simple. Suppose the initial agreement calls for the sale of 1,000,000 shares at approximately $10 a share. The issuing firm grants the underwriter an option to purchase up to 10 percent additional shares. If the issue is well received, the underwriter can sell up to an additional 100,000 shares. Of course, the underwriters do not have to sell any additional shares, nor do they have to sell all 100,000 shares if they do exercise the option. They may only accept, for example, an additional 45,600 shares if that number is needed to balance the market's initial demand for the stock.

The Mechanics of Underwriting

underwriting
The process by which securities are sold to the general public and in which the investment banker buys the securities from the issuing firm.

If a firm needs funds from an external source, it can approach an investment banker to discuss an underwriting. The term **underwriting** refers to the process of selling new securities. In an underwriting the firm that is selling the securities, and not the firm that is issuing the shares, bears the risk associated with the sale. The investment banker buys the securities with the intention of reselling them. If it fails to sell the securities, the investment banker must still pay the agreed-upon sum to the firm at the time of the offering (i.e., the sale) of the securities. Failure to sell the securities imposes significant losses on the underwriter, who must remit funds for securities that have not been sold.

The firm in need of financing and the investment banker discuss the amount of funds needed, the type of security to be issued, the price and any special features of the security, and the cost to the firm of issuing the securities. All these factors are negotiated by the firm seeking capital and the investment banker. If mutually acceptable terms are reached, the investment banker will be the intermediary through which the securities are sold by the firm to the general public.

originating house
An investment banker that makes an agreement with a firm to sell a new issue of securities and forms the syndicate to market them.

Because an underwriting starts with a particular brokerage firm that manages the underwriting, that firm is called the **originating house**. The originating house need not be a single firm if the negotiation involves several investment bankers. In this case, several firms can jointly underwrite and sell the securities to the general public.

syndicate
A selling group assembled to market an issue of securities.

The originating house does not usually sell all the securities by itself but instead forms a **syndicate** to market them. The syndicate is a group of brokerage houses that join together to underwrite a specific sale of securities. The members of the syndicate may bring in additional brokerage firms to help distribute the securities. The firm that manages the sale is frequently referred to as the *lead underwriter.* It is the lead underwriter that allocates the specific number of securities each member of the syndicate is responsible for selling.

The use of a syndicate has several advantages. First, the syndicate may have access to more potential buyers for the securities. Second, by using a syndicate the number of securities that each brokerage firm must sell is reduced. The increase in the number of potential customers and the decrease in the amount that each broker must sell increases the probability that the entire issue of securities will be sold. Thus, syndication makes possible both the sale of a large offering of securities and a reduction in the risk borne by each member.

In some cases, the firm seeking funds may not choose to negotiate the terms of the securities with an underwriter. Instead, the firm designs the issue and auctions the securities to the investment banker making the highest bid. In preparation for bidding, the investment banker will form a syndicate as well as determine the price it is willing to pay. The underwriter and its syndicate that wins the auction and purchases the securities marks up the price of the securities and sells them to the general public. Obviously, if the investment banker bids too high, it will be unable to sell the securities for a profit. Then the underwriter may sustain a loss when it lowers the securities' price in order to sell them.

Types of Agreements

best-efforts agreement
Agreement with an investment banker who does not guarantee the sale of a security but who agrees to make the best effort to sell it.

firm commitment
Agreement with an investment banker who guarantees a sale of securities by agreeing to purchase the entire issue at a specified price.

The agreement between the investment bankers and the firm may be one of two types. The investment bankers may make a **best-efforts agreement** in which they agree to make their best effort to sell the securities but do not guarantee that a specified amount of money will be raised. The risk of selling the securities rests with the firm issuing the securities. If the investment bankers are unable to find buyers, the firm does not receive the desired amount of money.

The alternative is a **firm commitment**, an underwriting in which the investment bankers purchase (i.e., underwrite) the entire issue of securities at a specified price and subsequently sell them to the general public. Most sales of new securities are made through firm commitments, and best-effort sales are generally limited to small security issues by less well known firms. In an underwriting, the investment bankers pay the expenses with the anticipation of recouping these costs through the sale. Because the underwriters have agreed to purchase the entire issue, they must pay the firm for all the securities even if the syndicate is unable to sell them. Thus, the risk of the sale rests with the underwriters.

It is for this reason that the pricing of the underwritten securities is crucial. If the initial offer price is too high, the syndicate will be unable to sell the securities. When this occurs, the investment bankers have two choices: (1) to maintain the offer price and hold the securities in inventory until they are sold or (2) to let the market find a lower price level that will induce investors to purchase the securities. Neither choice benefits the investment bankers. If the underwriters purchase the securities and hold them in inventory, they either must tie up their own funds, which could be earning a return elsewhere, or must borrow funds to pay for the securities. Like any other firm, the investment bankers pay interest on these borrowed funds. Thus, the decision to support the offer price of the securities requires the investment bankers to invest their own capital or, more likely, to borrow substantial amounts of capital. In either case, the profit margins on the underwriting are substantially decreased, and the investment bankers may even experience a loss on the underwriting.

Instead of supporting the price, the underwriters may choose to let the price of the securities fall. The inventory of unsold securities can then be sold, and the underwriters will not tie up capital or have to borrow money from their sources of credit. If the underwriters make this choice, they take losses when the securities are sold at less than cost. But they also cause the customers who bought the securities at the initial offer price to sustain a loss. The underwriters certainly do not want to inflict losses on these customers, because if they experience losses continually, the underwriters' market for future security issues will vanish. Therefore, the investment banks try not to overprice a new issue of securities, for overpricing will ultimately result in their suffering losses.

There is also an incentive to avoid underpricing new securities. If the issue is underpriced, all the securities will be readily sold and their price will rise because demand will have exceeded supply. The buyers of the securities will be satisfied, for the price of the securities will have increased as a result of the underpricing. The initial purchasers of the securities reap windfall profits, but these gains are really at the expense of the company whose securities were underpriced. If the underwriters had assigned a higher price to the securities, the company would have raised more capital. Underwriting is a very competitive business, and each security issue is negotiated individually; hence, if one investment banker consistently underprices securities, firms will choose competitors to underwrite their securities.

Although there are reasons for the underwriters to avoid either underpricing or overpricing, there appears to be a greater incentive to underprice the securities. Underpricing facilitates the sale and generates immediate profits for the initial buyers. One academic study did find that *initial* purchases earned higher returns as the buyers were given a price incentive to buy the new offering.[3] Subsequent buyers, however, did not fare as well, and any initial underpricing appears to disappear soon after the original offering. In addition, many initial public offerings subsequently underperform the market during the first years after the original sale.

Marketing Securities

preliminary prospectus (red herring)
Initial document detailing the financial condition of a firm that must be filed with the SEC to register a new issue of securities.

Securities and Exchange Commission (SEC)
Government agency that enforces the federal securities laws.

registration
Process of filing information with the SEC concerning a proposed sale of securities to the general public.

Once the terms of the sale have been agreed upon, the managing house may issue a **preliminary prospectus**. The preliminary prospectus is often referred to as a *red herring,* a term that connotes the document should be read with caution as it is not final and complete. (The phrase "red herring" is derived from British fugitives' rubbing herring across their trails to confuse pursuing bloodhounds.) The preliminary prospectus informs potential buyers that the securities are being registered with the **Securities and Exchange Commission (SEC)** and may subsequently be offered for sale. **Registration** refers to the disclosure of information concerning the firm, the securities being offered for sale, and the use of the proceeds from the sale.[4]

The cost of printing the red herring is borne by the issuing firm. This preliminary prospectus describes the company and the securities to be issued; it includes the firm's income statement and balance sheets, its current activities (such as a pending merger or labor negotiation), the regulatory bodies to which it is subject, and the nature of its competition. The preliminary prospectus is thus a detailed document concerning the company and is, unfortunately, usually tedious reading.

The preliminary prospectus does not include the price of the securities. That will be determined on the day that the securities are issued. If security prices decline or rise, the price of the new securities may be adjusted for the change in market conditions. In fact, if prices decline sufficiently, the firm has the option of postponing or even canceling the underwriting.

After the SEC accepts the registration statement, a final prospectus is published.[5] The SEC does not approve the issue as to its investment worth but rather sees that all information has been provided and the prospectus is complete in format and content. Except for changes that are required by the SEC, it is virtually identical to the preliminary prospectus. Information regarding the price of the security, the underwriting discount, and the proceeds to the company, along with

[3]See Roger G. Ibbotson, "Price Performance of Common Stock New Issues," *Journal of Financial Economics* (September 1975): 235–272. For additional literature on IPOs, consult Seth Anderson, *Initial Public Offerings* (Boston: Kluwer Academic Publishers, 1995) and Jay R. Ritter, "Initial Public Offerings," *Contemporary Financial Digest* (Spring 1998): 5–30.

A wealth of information on IPOs may be found at Hoover's IPO Central (http://www.ipocentral.com) and http://www.ipopros.com, a site codeveloped by R.R. Donnelley Financial and IPO Crossroads that includes a searchable database of current and historical IPOs.

[4]While there are exceptions, generally unregistered corporate securities may not be sold to the general public. The debt of governments (e.g., state and municipal bonds), however, is *not* registered with the SEC and may be sold to the general public. Information concerning the SEC may be obtained from htpp://www.sec.gov, the Securities and Exchange Commission's home page.

[5]Because corporate securities cannot be sold to the general public before the registration statement becomes effective, information concerning the proposed sale is accompanied by statements such as "orders to buy may not be accepted prior to the registration becoming effective" or "this information concerning the securities is not a solicitation to buy or sell."

any more recent financial data, is added. Exhibit 2.1 illustrates the title page of the final prospectus for an issue of 2,600,000 shares of Yahoo! Inc. The name of the managing underwriters is in large print at the bottom of the page. These managing underwriters formed the syndicate that sold the shares to the general public. In this example, 17 firms participated in the selling group.

The cost of the underwriting (also called *flotation costs* or *underwriting discount*) is the difference between the price of the securities to the public and the proceeds to the firm. In this example, the cost is \$0.91 per share, which is 7.5 percent of the proceeds received by the firm for each share. The total cost is \$2,366,000 for the sale of these shares. Underwriting fees tend to vary with the dollar value of the securities being underwritten and the type of securities being sold. Some of the expenses are fixed (e.g., preparation of the prospectus), so the unit cost for a large underwriting is smaller. Also, because it may be more difficult to sell speculative bonds than high-quality bonds, underwriting fees for speculative issues tend to be higher.

In addition to the fee, the underwriter may receive indirect compensation, which may be in the form of an option (called a "warrant") to buy additional securities.[6] Such indirect compensation may be as important as the monetary fee because it unites the underwriter and the firm. After the initial sale, the underwriter often becomes a market maker for the securities, which is particularly important to the investing public.[7] Without a secondary market in which to sell the security, investors would be less interested in buying the securities initially. By maintaining a market in the security, the brokerage firm eases the task of selling the securities originally.

Volatility of Initial Public Offerings

The new-issue market (especially for common stock) is extremely volatile. There have been times when the investing public seemed willing to purchase virtually any new security that was being sold on the market. There have also been periods during which new companies were simply unable to raise money, and large, well-known companies did so only under onerous terms.

The market for initial public offerings is volatile regarding not only the number of securities that are offered but also the price changes of new issues. It is not unusual for prices to rise dramatically. In April 1996, Yahoo!'s stock was initially offered at \$13 and closed at \$33 after reaching a high of \$43 during the first day of trading. Two years later the stock was trading in excess of \$180.

Few new issues perform as well as Yahoo!, and many that initially do well subsequently fall on hard times. Boston Chicken went public in 1993 at \$20 a share and rose to \$48.50 by the end of the first day of trading. However, in 1998, the company's rapid expansion overextended the firm's ability to sustain profitable operations. Boston Chicken declared bankruptcy, and the stock traded for less than \$1 a share.

The late 1990s saw a large increase in the number of IPOs, many of which were very speculative at best. Many companies, especially those related to technology in general and the Internet in particular raised large amounts of capital. Their stock prices rose dramatically and just as dramatically fell. Ask Jeeves went public in July 1999 at a price of \$14. It closed after the first day of trading at \$64.94 and reached almost \$200 in September. In July 2001, the stock was trading for about \$2. Another highflyer, Ariba, saw its stock decline from \$242 to \$4 in less than a year.

[6]This warrant is similar to the options discussed in Chapter 19 except there is no *public trading* in these warrants granted the underwriters.

[7]For a detailed discussion of making a market, see "Market Makers" in Chapter 3.

EXHIBIT 2.1

Title Page for the Prospectus of an Issue of Common Stock of Yahoo! Inc.

2,600,000 Shares

Yahoo! Inc.

Common Stock
(par value $0.001 per share)

All of the shares of Common Stock offered hereby are being offered by Yahoo! Inc. Prior to this offering, there has been no public market for the Common Stock of the Company. For factors considered in determining the initial public offering price, see "Underwriting".

In connection with this offering, the Underwriters have reserved approximately 200,000 shares of Common Stock for sale at the initial public offering price to persons associated with the Company.

See "Risk Factors" commencing on page 6 for certain considerations relevant to an investment in the Common Stock.

The Common Stock has been approved for quotation on the Nasdaq National Market under the symbol "YHOO".

THESE SECURITIES HAVE NOT BEEN APPROVED OR DISAPPROVED BY THE SECURITIES AND EXCHANGE COMMISSION OR ANY STATE SECURITIES COMMISSION NOR HAS THE SECURITIES AND EXCHANGE COMMISSION OR ANY STATE SECURITIES COMMISSION PASSED UPON THE ACCURACY OR ADEQUACY OF THIS PROSPECTUS. ANY REPRESENTATION TO THE CONTRARY IS A CRIMINAL OFFENSE.

	Initial Public Offering Price	Underwriting Discount(1)	Proceeds to Company(2)
Per Share	$13.00	$0.91	$12.09
Total(3)	$33,800,000	$2,366,000	$31,434,000

(1) The Company has agreed to indemnify the Underwriters against certain liabilities, including liabilities under the Securities Act of 1933. See "Underwriting".
(2) Before deducting estimated offering expenses of $700,000 payable by the Company.
(3) The Company has granted the Underwriters an option for 30 days to purchase up to an additional 390,000 shares at the initial public offering price per share, less the underwriting discount, solely to cover over-allotments. If such option is exercised in full, the total initial public offering price, underwriting discount and proceeds to the Company will be $38,870,000, $2,720,900 and $36,149,100, respectively. See "Underwriting".

The shares offered hereby are offered severally by the Underwriters, as specified herein, subject to receipt and acceptance by them and subject to their right to reject any order in whole or in part. It is expected that certificates for the shares will be ready for delivery in New York, New York, on or about April 17, 1996, against payment therefor in immediately available funds.

Goldman, Sachs & Co.

Donaldson, Lufkin & Jenrette
Securities Corporation

Montgomery Securities

The date of this Prospectus is April 12, 1996.

Source: Reproduced with permission of Yahoo! Inc. © 2000 by Yahoo! Inc. YAHOO! and the YAHOO! logo are trademarks of Yahoo! Inc.

While the late 1990s may be considered an aberration, they were not unique. In a sense, it was a repeat of the late 1960s when stocks of franchising and nursing home companies went public, rose dramatically, and subsequently declined. For example, Four Seasons Nursing Homes went public on May 10, 1968, at $11 a share. The stock rose to $102, but within two years the company was bankrupt and the stock sold for $0.16. In retrospect, a price of $102 seems absurd. The company had 3.4 million shares outstanding, so at a price of $102, the value of the company was $346.8 million ($102 × 3.4). The firm had revenues of only $19.3 million and earnings of less than $2 million, so it made no sense in terms of earnings capacity to value the firm in excess of $300 million.

The new-issue market in the late 1990s, however, was different in one very important respect. Ask Jeeves and Ariba didn't have earnings, and even at the collapsed price of $4 a share, the total market value of Ariba exceeded $1 billion. When the price of that stock reached $242, the total value of the company exceeded $60 billion! So if it made little sense to value Four Seasons Nursing Homes, which actually had earnings, at $300 million, it would make even less sense to value Ariba at $60 billion when it was operating at a loss. (This question of valuation is an essential question, perhaps the most important question, in finance. The process of valuation and techniques used to analyze a stock are covered in Chapters 9 and 13. Subsequent material also considers a growth strategy that might justify purchasing an Ariba versus a value strategy that would never consider such a stock.)

The lure of large gains is, of course, what attracts speculative investors. All firms were small at one time, and each one had to go public to have a market for its shares. Someone bought the shares of IBM, Microsoft, and Johnson & Johnson when these firms went public. The ability to spot the companies that promise the greatest growth for the future is rare. However, the new-issue market has offered and continues to offer the opportunity to invest in emerging firms, some of which may produce substantial returns for those investors or speculators who are willing to accept the risk. It is the possibility of such large rewards that makes the new-issue market so exciting. However, if the past is an indicator of the future, many small, emerging firms that go public will fail and will inflict significant losses on those investors who have accepted this risk by purchasing their securities.

Lock-ups

In addition to price volatility caused by speculative buying of an initial public offering, the possibility exists that insiders could use a new public issue of securities as a means to sell their stock. Such sales may also lead to price volatility, although in this case it would be price declines and not increases. (There is an additional ethical question concerning insiders profiting at the expense of the general investing public.) To understand the possible source of the price volatility, consider a privately held company that is considering going public. Before the initial public offering, managers and other employees are allowed to purchase the stock in a "nonpublic" or "private" transaction (e.g., $1 a share) or are granted options to buy the stock at a low price. Because there is no market in the stock, the price cannot be determined, so the sale price to insiders could be artificially low. (Such stock sales and the granting of options prior to the initial public offering are often viewed as "compensation" for those privileged employees.)

Private sales of securities are not illegal, but SEC guidelines indicate that stock acquired through a nonpublic transaction cannot be publicly sold unless it is held for at least one year. If the initial public offering were to occur after a year, the shares could be sold as part of the underwriting or immediately in the secondary market after the completion of the underwriting. For example, insiders who purchased the shares at $1 could sell the stock for a large profit, if the initial offering price to the general public were $10 a share. Such sales may destabilize the market and cause the price of the stock to fall.

To avoid this possible source of price volatility (and also the conflict of interest), the insiders may be forbidden by an agreement with the underwriter to sell their holdings for a period of time. Since the insiders are locked into the shares, the process is referred to as a *lock-up*. Obviously the lock-up cannot remain in effect indefinitely, and once it expires, the employees may sell their holdings.[8] This suggests there may be selling pressure on the stock once the lock-up period has expired.[9]

While lock-ups are not required by the SEC and are negotiated by the issuing firm and the underwriter, the full disclosure laws do require that issuing firms disclose potential sales by insiders. Because large sales may destabilize the market and cause the stock's price to fall, underwriters prefer long lock-ups. The period can range from 90 to 365 days, but 180 days is the most common. If there were no lock-up agreement, insiders could sell shares immediately provided they have met the SEC requirement to disclose the possible sale of previously restricted stock.

Shelf-Registrations

The preceding discussion was cast in terms of firms initially selling their stock to the general public (i.e., the "initial public offering" or "going public"). Firms that have previously issued securities and are currently public also raise funds by selling new securities. If the sales are to the general public, the same basic procedure applies. The new securities must be registered with and approved by the SEC before they may be sold to the public, and the firm often uses the services of an investment banker to facilitate the sale.

There are, however, differences between an initial public offering and the sale of additional securities by a publicly held firm. The first major difference concerns

POINTS OF INTEREST
SCOR

Small firms often have difficulty raising money (especially equity funds), but changes in selected state securities laws have eased the process of selling new stock to the general public. Companies seeking to raise up to $1,000,000 may complete a Small Company Offering Registration (SCOR) instead of the traditional prospectus. This disclosure statement uses a question-and-answer format and is less complicated than the traditional registration statement. A SCOR may be completed by a lawyer and/or an accountant who need not be an expert in public security offerings.

SCORs also permit the issuing firm to sell securities directly to individual investors and bypass the use of investment bankers. Stocks issued through the use of SCORs may be traded through brokerage firms who make a market in the securities. Because the dollar value of the offerings and the number of investors participating in these markets are small, these securities tend to be inactively traded. Increased use of SCORs, however, may expand trading in the securities. For information on additional means for small companies to raise funds, see Bruce G. Posner, "How to Finance Anything," *Inc.* (April 1992): 50–62.

[8]Once insiders have bought stock that they cannot sell, the possibility exists that the stock's price will decline after the underwriting. For strategies using derivatives to protect an insider from losses, see the discussions of protective puts and collars in Chapters 19 and 20. If such hedging strategies are in effect, they must be disclosed on SEC Form 144.

[9]One empirical analysis of lock-ups and their impact on stock values found that prices do decline prior to the release of restricted shares. This suggests that unrestricted investors are selling their shares prior to the release date. See Terrill R. Keasler, "Underwriter Lock-up Release and After-Market Performance," *The Financial Review* (May 2001): 1–20.

the price of the securities. Because a market already exists for the firm's stock, the problem of an appropriate price for the additional shares is virtually eliminated. This price will approximate the market price on the date of issue. Second, because the firm must periodically publish information (for instance, the annual report) and file documents with the SEC, there is less need for a detailed prospectus. Many publicly held firms construct a prospectus describing a proposed issue of new securities and file it with the SEC. This document is called a *shelf-registration.* After the shelf-registration has been accepted by the SEC, the firm may sell the securities whenever the need for funds arises. Such shelf-registrations offer the issuing firm considerable flexibility because the securities do not have to be issued but can be quickly sold if the firm deems that the conditions are optimal for the sale.

The Role of Financial Intermediaries

Although the securities of publicly held firms had to be sold to the public initially, these same firms acquire a substantial portion of their financing from financial intermediaries. This is particularly true of short-term funds that are borrowed from commercial banks or are obtained by issuing short-term debt obligations that are purchased by a variety of financial intermediaries. Of course, for the intermediaries to make these loans, they too must have funds. These funds are acquired from savers and other economic units who do not currently need them and who invest the money in obligations issued by the financial intermediary. In effect, the savers are ultimately supplying the funds to the firms (or to any economic unit) in need of the funds. However, this transfer of money occurs indirectly through the financial intermediary instead of directly.

In advanced economies, a variety of financial intermediaries have developed to facilitate the indirect transfer of savers' funds to borrowers. These intermediaries include commercial banks, savings and loan associations, mutual savings banks, credit unions, life insurance companies, pension plans, and money market mutual funds. Whenever these firms borrow from one group and lend to another, they are acting as financial intermediaries. However, it should be noted that if they purchase existing financial assets, such as stock traded on the New York Stock Exchange or existing mortgages, they are not acting as financial intermediaries. Instead, they are investing in assets traded in secondary markets, in which case funds flow from buyer to seller and not to the economic unit that initially issued the security.[10]

Historically, a clear differentiation existed among the various financial intermediaries. For example, the differences between commercial banks and "thrift institutions," such as savings banks and savings and loan associations (S&Ls), encompassed both the types of assets they acquired and the types of liabilities (accounts) they offered. Savings and loan associations were depository organizations that issued savings accounts and used the savers' funds to originate home mortgage loans. Such thrift institutions were clearly differentiated from commercial banks, which issued a variety of accounts, especially checking accounts, and made various loans, including personal loans (such as car loans) and short-term financing for businesses and governments.

Today, it is probably safe to assert that many savers and potential borrowers are no longer aware of differences among financial intermediaries. Commercial banks, savings and loan associations, savings banks, and credit unions offer similar services (e.g., checking accounts and savings accounts) and pay virtually the

[10]Secondary markets, such as the New York Stock Exchange, are discussed in the next chapter.

same rates of interest on deposits. In addition, the portfolio of assets acquired by each depository institution is more similar than in the past. For example, previously S&Ls made primarily mortgage loans, but now their portfolios have broadened to include a more varied mix of assets.

This blurring of the distinctions among the various financial intermediaries is the result of changes in the regulatory environment. Under the Depository Institutions Deregulation and Monetary Control Act of 1980, all depository institutions became subject to the regulation of the Federal Reserve. These regulations extended to the types of accounts these institutions may offer and the amount they must hold in reserve against deposits.[11] In return for this change in the regulatory environment, the depository institutions were permitted to offer more accounts to depositors, such as checking accounts, which previously could be offered only by commercial banks. The intermediaries were also permitted to broaden the services offered to depositors, such as brokerage services that link the accounts in the bank to brokerage accounts.[12] Deregulation also led to the end of controls on maximum interest rates. Now the depository institutions may pay whatever rate of interest on deposits they deem necessary to compete with other financial intermediaries, such as the money market mutual funds discussed later in this chapter.

Advantages Offered by Financial Intermediaries

Investors will not deposit funds with a financial intermediary unless some benefit is offered. The advantages provided by the intermediaries include convenience, interest income, and safety of principal. Checking accounts are a convenient means by which to make payments. Savings and checking accounts accommodate small deposits and small withdrawals. Other assets, such as stocks and bonds, may not be divisible into such small units or the commission costs associated with small units may make them impractical.

certificate of deposit (CD)
A time deposit with a specified maturity date.

Interest is paid on some checking accounts, savings accounts, and time deposits that are called **certificates of deposit** or **CDs**. Funds deposited in savings accounts and checking accounts may be withdrawn at will, making them among the most liquid assets available to investors. Certificates of deposit are time deposits that have a specified maturity date but that may be redeemed prior to maturity. Such early redemptions result in a penalty, such as the loss of interest for a quarter. The yields offered by these accounts depend on the term of the instrument. Exhibit 2.2 (p. 40) gives the term and yields provided by the savings accounts and certificates of deposit offered by a savings bank. Notice that as the term increases, the interest rate paid on the certificate also increases.

Exhibit 2.2 also illustrates that interest rates change over time. The yields on CDs offered in 1989 were considerably greater than those available to savers in 2001. For example, the yield on the two-year CD fell from 8.79 percent in 1989 to 4.10 percent in 2001. This decline in yields illustrates reinvestment rate risk. Individuals who owned certificates issued in 1989 that matured in 1992 were unable to reinvest the funds at old rates, because comparable certificates of deposit offered lower yields. If these investors wanted to earn higher rates, they would have had to invest elsewhere and probably bear additional risk in order to earn the higher returns that were previously available on investments in certificates of deposit.

negotiable certificate of deposit
A certificate of deposit in which the rate and the term are individually negotiated by the bank and the lender and which may be bought and sold.

If the investor has $100,000 or more to invest, depository institutions will sell **negotiable certificates of deposit** or **jumbo CDs** directly to the investor—in which case the yield and term of these certificates is agreed upon by the investor and the

[11]The importance of the reserve requirement and the other tools of monetary policy are discussed in Chapter 12.

[12]Brokerage firms have also encroached on the domain of the commercial banks through the creation of cash management accounts. Such accounts link checking accounts; credit, debit, and ATM cards; and money market yields.

EXHIBIT 2.2

Savings and Time Deposits Offered by a Savings Bank

Type of Deposit	Minimum Amount Required*	Term	Annual Rate of Interest 1989	1992	1995	1998	2001
Money market account	$1,000	None	7.15%	4.14%	2.55%	2.70%	2.20%
Savings account	100	None	5.25	4.14	2.65	2.50	2.50
Certificate of deposit	500	6 months	7.86	4.75	5.25	4.50	3.60
Certificate of deposit	500	1 year	8.33	4.95	5.50	5.00	3.80
Certificate of deposit	500	2 years	8.79	5.25	5.75	5.25	4.10
Certificate of deposit	500	3 years	9.11	5.40	5.95	5.75	4.40
Certificate of deposit	500	5 years	9.29	5.40	6.00	5.75	4.70

*Minimum deposit as of August 2001.

depository institution. Once issued, negotiable CDs may be bought and sold (hence the name "*negotiable* CD"). The ability to buy and sell jumbo CDs differentiates them from other CDs. Negotiable CDs can have maturities up to one year, and yields are comparable to those earned on other money market instruments, such as corporate commercial paper.

Eurodollar CD
Time deposit in a foreign bank and denominated in dollars.

Large American banks with foreign operations also issue **Eurodollar certificates of deposit (Eurodollar CDs)**. These CDs are similar to domestic negotiable CDs except they are issued either by the branches of domestic banks located abroad or by foreign banks. Eurodollar CDs are denominated in dollars (instead of a foreign currency) and are actively traded, especially in London, which is the center of the Eurodollar CD market. Because they are issued in a foreign country, these CDs are considered riskier than domestic CDs, so Eurodollar CDs offer higher yields to induce investors to purchase them.

The large amount required to purchase a negotiable CD (i.e., the $100,000 minimum investment, with $1 million being the usual unit of trading) precludes purchase by most investors. However, many investors do indirectly invest in negotiable certificates of deposit when they acquire shares in money market mutual funds, since these funds invest in negotiable certificates of deposit.

Perhaps one of the most appealing features of an account with a depository institution is its safety. Although there is the possibility of loss of purchasing power through the inflation rate exceeding the rate earned on the account, there is no risk of loss from default because the majority of these accounts are insured by the federal government. If an individual places $1,000 in a federally insured savings account, the $1,000 is safe. If the investor had invested $1,000 in a corporate bond, the market value of the bond could decline or the firm could default on the interest payment or principal repayment.

Federal Deposit Insurance Corporation (FDIC)
Federal government agency that supervises commercial banks and insures commercial bank deposits.

Federal government deposit insurance was one of the positive results of the Great Depression in the 1930s. The large losses sustained by commercial banks' depositors led to the establishment of the **Federal Deposit Insurance Corporation (FDIC)**. As of this writing, the FDIC insures depositors' accounts in commercial banks and savings banks up to $100,000. If a commercial bank were to fail, the FDIC would reimburse each depositor up to the $100,000 limit. As most individuals do not have more than $100,000 on deposit, these investors know that their principal is completely safe. However, the investor should note that the insurance is *not* automatic but must be purchased from the FDIC by the bank. A few banks have chosen not to purchase the insurance. Thus, if safety of principal is a major concern, it is best for the funds to be deposited only in an account insured by the federal government.

Money Market Mutual Funds and Money Market Instruments

money market mutual funds
Mutual funds that specialize in short-term securities.

money market instruments
Short-term securities, such as Treasury bills, negotiable certificates of deposit, or commercial paper.

As the name implies, **money market mutual funds** are investment companies that acquire **money market instruments**, which are short-term securities issued by banks, nonbank corporations, and governments. Money market mutual funds differ from regular mutual funds, which are discussed in Chapter 8, in that they specialize solely in short-term securities and provide investors with an alternative to savings and time deposits offered by banks. Money market mutual funds thus compete directly with commercial banks and other depository institutions for the deposits of savers, while regular mutual funds offer an alternative means to own stocks and bonds.

Until the deregulation of the banking system (the Monetary Control Act of 1980), money market mutual funds offered investors an asset that was unique. Under regulation, the maximum rate of interest that banks could pay was constrained. Thus, when interest rates paid by other short-term securities rose, the banks could not raise the rate they paid to be competitive with the money market mutual funds, which were not subject to the same regulations. The money funds gave individuals the opportunity to invest indirectly in short-term securities and earn the higher yields. As a result, deposits flowed out of the banks into the money funds. This rapid growth in their assets during the early 1980s is clearly seen in Figure 2.1 (p. 42), which charts the assets of these funds from 1980 through 2000.

With the deregulation of the banking system, banks could pay competitive rates, which temporarily slowed the rate of growth in the money funds' assets during 1982 through 1984. However, after a period of adjustment to the new regulatory environment, the assets of money market mutual funds resumed their growth, reaching almost $2 trillion by 2001.

The money funds invest in a variety of short-term securities that include the negotiable CDs just discussed. Other money market instruments include the short-term debt of the federal government (Treasury bills), commercial paper issued by corporations, repurchase agreements (commonly referred to as *repos*), bankers' acceptances, and tax anticipation notes. Of course, the individual investor may acquire these securities directly, but the large denominations of some short-term securities (e.g., the minimum denomination of negotiable CDs and commercial paper is $100,000) exclude most investors.

U.S. Treasury bill
Short-term debt of the federal government.

The safest short-term security is the **U.S. Treasury bill** (commonly referred to as a *T-bill*), which is issued by the federal government. Prior to the political confrontation over the federal budget in 1995, there was no question that the federal government would retire the principal and pay the interest on its obligations. (The pricing of and yields earned on T-bills are covered in Chapter 17.) The short term of the bills also implies that if interest rates were to rise, the increase would have minimum impact on the bills, and the quick maturity means that investors could reinvest the proceeds in the higher-yielding securities.

commercial paper
Unsecured, short-term promissory notes issued by the most creditworthy corporations.

Commercial paper is an unsecured *promissory note* (i.e., debt) issued by a corporation as an alternative to borrowing funds from commercial banks. Because the paper is unsecured, only firms with excellent credit ratings are able to sell it; hence, the risk of default is small, and the repayment of principal is virtually assured. Once again, the term is short, so there is little risk from an investment in commercial paper.

repurchase agreement (repo)
Sale of a short-term security in which the seller agrees to buy back the security at a specified price.

A **repurchase agreement** (or "repo") is a sale of a security in which the seller agrees to buy back (repurchase) the security at a specified price at a specified date.

FIGURE 2.1

Money Market Mutual Fund Assets, 1980-2000 (in billions)

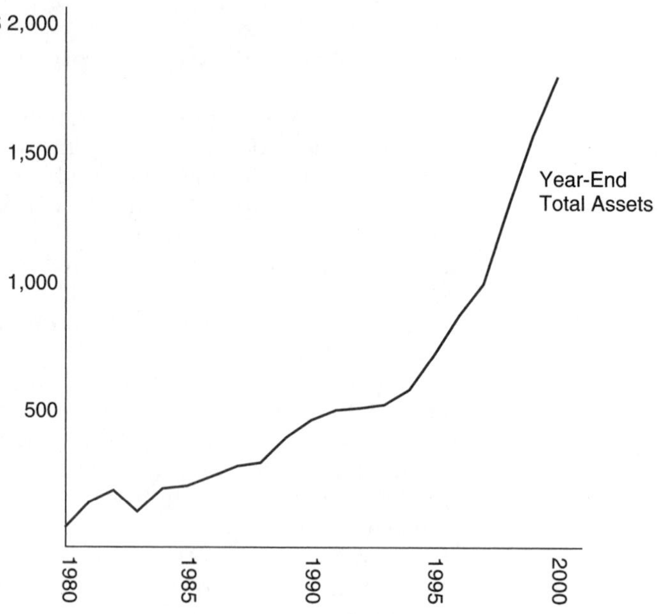

Source: Derived from the *Mutual Fund Fact Book*, published annually by the Investment Company Institute (http://www.ici.org).

Repos are usually executed using federal government securities, and the repurchase price is higher than the initial sale price. The difference between the sale price and the repurchase price is the source of the return to the holder of the security. By entering into the repurchase agreement, the investor (the buyer) knows exactly how much will be made on the investment and when the funds will be returned.

banker's acceptance
Short-term promissory note guaranteed by a bank.

Banker's acceptances are short-term promissory notes guaranteed by a bank. These acceptances arise through international trade. Suppose a firm ships goods abroad and receives a draft drawn on a specific bank that promises payment after two months. If the firm does not want to wait for payment, it can take the draft to a commercial bank for acceptance. Once the bank accepts the draft (and stamps it "accepted"), the draft may be sold. The buyer purchases the draft for a discount, which becomes the source of the return to the holder. Bankers' acceptances are considered to be good short-term investments because they are supported by two parties: the firm on which the draft is drawn and the bank that accepts the draft.

tax anticipation note
Short-term government security secured by expected tax revenues.

Tax anticipation notes are issued by states or municipalities to finance current operations before tax revenues are received. As the taxes are collected, the proceeds are used to retire the debt. Similar notes are issued in anticipation of revenues from future bond issues and other sources, such as revenue sharing from the federal government. These anticipation notes do not offer the safety of Treasury bills, but the interest is exempt from federal income taxation.[13] Commercial banks and securities dealers maintain secondary markets in them, so the notes may be liquidated should the noteholder need cash.

[13]The tax exemption of interest paid by state and local municipal debt is discussed in Chapter 6.

Money market mutual funds can invest in any of the money market instruments (negotiable certificates of deposit, Eurodollar CDs, Treasury bills, commercial paper, repurchase agreements, bankers' acceptances, and tax anticipation notes). Some of the funds, however, do specialize, such as the Schwab U.S. Treasury Money Fund, which invests solely in U.S. government securities or securities that are collateralized by obligations of the federal government. Other funds invest in a wider spectrum of short-term debt obligations. For example, as of June 30, 1998, the Schwab Money Fund had 0 percent of its assets in Treasury obligations, 12.4 percent in negotiable CDs, 78.7 percent in commercial paper, and the remaining percentage in various other short-term assets, such as repurchase agreements.

The investor may readily withdraw funds invested in a money market mutual fund. The individual who redeems the shares receives the amount invested plus any dividends that are credited daily to the account. Unless all investors sought to redeem their shares at the same time and thus forced the fund to liquidate its portfolio rapidly and perhaps at a loss, there is little risk that the individual investor would not receive the full value of the shares.

The yields earned on investments in money market funds closely mirror the yields on short-term securities. Since the Schwab U.S. Treasury Money Fund invests solely in government or government-backed securities, the yield it offers investors mirrors the return on these government securities. This relationship must occur because when the short-term debt held by the fund matures, the proceeds can be reinvested only at the going rate of interest paid by short-term government securities. Hence changes in short-term interest rates paid by these securities are quickly transferred to the individual money market mutual fund.

In addition to offering safety and money market yields, many money market funds provide a service that is similar to a checking account. The investor is permitted to write drafts against his or her shares. The drafts are technically not checks, but they do permit the transfer of funds from the money market mutual fund to whomever the draft is payable. While there may be a limit as to the minimum amount of the draft (e.g., $250), these instruments are an excellent means for increased money management. The investor can accumulate shares in the funds and, when disbursements become necessary, pay by the draft drawn on the fund. The funds invested in the money market fund continue to earn interest until the draft clears, at which time shares are redeemed to cover the amount of the draft. This service permits the investor to earn interest while waiting for the disbursement of funds. Money that may previously have been sitting in a non-interest-bearing checking account is now put to work for the investor.

Many brokerage firms have arrangements with money market funds that facilitate transfers of money between the two. Once a security is sold and the funds received by the broker on the settlement date, the broker transfers the funds to the money market fund. Later, when the investor buys a new security and must make payment, the funds are transferred back to the broker from the money market fund. All these transactions can occur without processing checks, as the money is transferred electronically from one account to another. This service permits the investor to earn interest on funds between investments even if the amount of time is only a few days. The amount of interest that the investor can earn by such transfers can be substantial. For example, at 4 percent, an investor earns about $11 per day on an investment of $100,000. Thus the transfer of $100,000 to a money market mutual fund for just one week will earn over $76.71 (i.e., $100,000 × 7/365 × 0.04).

Given the advantages offered by money market mutual funds, their initial popularity was not surprising. However, the growth in the assets of the money funds was nothing short of phenomenal. This is documented in Figure 2.1, which shows the huge increase in funds invested in money market mutual funds as the value of their assets rose from $76 billion in 1980 to $498 billion in 1990 to $1.845 trillion in 2000.

Summary

All firms must have a source of funds with which to acquire assets and retire outstanding liabilities as they come due. Besides retaining earnings, a firm may obtain these funds from savers who are not currently using all their income to buy goods and services. The transfer of these savings may occur directly when firms issue new securities, or indirectly through a financial intermediary.

When a firm issues new stocks or bonds, it usually employs the services of an investment banker to facilitate the sale of the securities by acting as a middleman between the firm and the savers. In many cases, investment bankers underwrite the issue of new securities, which means that they guarantee a specified amount of money to the issuing firm and then sell the securities to the public. Because the underwriters are obligated to remit the specified amount for the securities, they bear the risk of the sale.

Firms may also obtain funds by borrowing from financial intermediaries, who raise funds by creating liabilities on themselves (e.g., a savings account), then lend the funds to the ultimate users. Prior to the deregulation of the banking system, the various types of financial intermediaries were clearly distinguished from one another. However, now that regulation is centralized with the Federal Reserve and depository institutions may offer whatever interest rates they deem necessary to raise funds, the differences among the intermediaries are disappearing, as they tend to offer comparable yields and services.

One of the newest and most important financial intermediaries is the money market mutual fund, which offers savers a significant alternative to the traditional depository institution. These funds offer services similar to those of banks (e.g., checking privileges) and pay yields that are comparable to those available on money market instruments, such as negotiable certificates of deposit, commercial paper, Treasury bills, and repurchase agreements. Since the minimum denominations of these money market instruments are sufficiently large, such that most individuals are excluded from participating in the market for them, the money market mutual funds offer savers a means to indirectly acquire these securities.

Questions

1) In an underwriting, what role does each of the following play? (a) the investment banker, (b) the syndicate, (c) the red herring, (d) the SEC, and (e) the saver (investor).
2) Why is it important that in an underwriting the investment banker does not overvalue (that is, overprice) the securities? If the securities are overpriced, who suffers the loss?
3) What differentiates an underwriting from a best-efforts agreement? Who bears the risk in each of these agreements?
4) Why do investors buy new issues of securities? Besides the risk associated with fluctuations in the market as a whole and the loss of purchasing power through inflation, what is the source of risk associated with initial public offerings?
5) The text used Ask Jeeves (ASKJ) and Ariba (ARBA) as illustrations of stocks that soared after the IPO only to dramatically decline. Investor A bought 100 shares of ASKJ at its initial offering price of $14. Investor B bought 100 shares on the first day of trading at $65. Investor C bought 100 shares three months later at $190. What are those shares worth today? If investors A, B, and C sustained losses, who profited?
6) What is a financial intermediary? What role does it play? What differentiates a financial intermediary from an investment banker?

7) What features differentiate savings accounts, certificates of deposit, and negotiable certificates of deposit?
8) If a saver had $12,540 to invest for a short period of time, what alternatives would be available?
9) What assets do money market mutual funds acquire? Could an individual saver acquire these assets?
10) Why are money market mutual funds among the safest investments available to savers?

THE FINANCIAL ADVISOR'S INVESTMENT CASE

The Demise of a Savings Account

After completing a degree in education administration, Michael Nugent accepted a position with the New Jersey Department of Education. He has worked there for seven years and has experienced annual salary increments and steady promotions. His benefit package includes full medical and dental insurance, pension plan, and life insurance equal to twice his annual salary. A year after graduating from college he married his childhood sweetheart, Mary Monahan, who works as an administrative assistant for the state. Mike and Mary are relatively frugal people and have accumulated $100,000, which is held in a National Bank of New Jersey savings account and which earns a modest 3 percent annually. They also own a three-bedroom home with a 7.5 percent mortgage that has 20 years left before it is entirely paid off.

Although Mary has worked steadily, she is now pregnant with their first child. The Nugents are uncertain what changes this addition to the family will have on their economic situation. They doubt that Mary will be able to continue to work for a period of time, and Mike doubts that he will be able to add to their current savings account. He also thinks that this savings account may not be the best vehicle for their savings.

Mike decided that one possible course of action was to explore the various accounts and savings programs offered by the bank. National Bank of New Jersey is a moderate-sized regional bank that offers a variety of savings and checking accounts and a range of certificates of deposit. It also offers retirement plans, such as individual retirement accounts (IRAs), and has a working relationship with Strauss and Strauss Incorporated (S & S), a regional brokerage firm that will buy and sell securities for the bank's customers. Since the brokerage firm offers only minimal research services, it charges discount rates for transactions. Funds may be transferred directly from an account with the bank to S & S and vice versa. Mike asked a representative of the bank for suggestions and alternatives to the savings account. The representative made the following suggestions:

1) Close the savings account.
2) Purchase four $20,000 CDs, one of each of the following:

Maturity	Interest Rate
1 year	4%
2 years	4¼
3 years	4½
4 years	5%

3) Open a money market account with $20,000. The account currently pays 3 percent, but the rate varies weekly with changes in short-term interest rates. The individual may write checks against the account and deposit or withdraw funds without penalties. There are no service charges unless the amount in the account is less than $2,500.
4) Make a $10,000 gift to the child soon after birth and invest the funds in the highest-yielding CD offered by the bank.
5) Complete the paperwork to open a brokerage account with S & S, even if any purchase decisions will be deferred.

To help make this investment decision, Mike asked you the following questions:

1) How safe is each investment and is it insured against loss?
2) How liquid is each investment?
3) Why did the bank's representative suggest alternatives 4 and 5?
4) Will closing the savings account and executing the suggestions improve their (i.e., Mike and Mary's) portfolio?

Security Markets

3

On July 13, 2001, 7,660,600 shares of IBM traded on the New York Stock Exchange. In all, 1,106,566,490 shares of stock traded that day on the New York Stock Exchange. Not one penny of the proceeds of those sales went to the firms whose stocks were exchanged. Instead, all these transactions were among investors. Obviously, many individuals were altering their portfolios either through buying or selling these existing securities.

This buying and selling of securities has a certain mystique or fascination both for the novice and for the seasoned investor. Investors may be drawn to securities by the jargon used in the stock market or the excitement generated by trading securities. Perhaps the investor's fascination is the result of the fact that many dollars can be earned or lost through investments in stocks and bonds. For whatever reason, investors who are drawn to Wall Street must understand both how security markets work and the mechanics of buying and selling securities.

It is the purpose of this chapter to explain the machinations of the market and the mechanics of buying and selling securities. The first section discusses security dealers and the role of security exchanges. The bulk of the chapter describes how the individual buys securities. The role of the broker, the types of orders and accounts, the delivery of the securities, and the brokerage cost of buying and selling are explained. The chapter ends with a brief discussion of the regulation of the securities industry and the Securities Investor Protection Corporation (SIPC), which insures investors against losses incurred from the failure of a brokerage firm.

Learning Objectives

After completing this chapter you should be able to:

1. Explain the role of market makers and distinguish between security exchanges and over-the-counter markets.
2. List the services provided by brokers and brokerage firms.
3. Differentiate between the types of security orders and identify the costs of investing in securities.
4. Contrast cash and margin accounts.
5. Contrast long and short positions and explain the source of profit from each.
6. Define American depositary receipts (ADRs) and explain their advantages.
7. State the purpose of the Securities and Exchange Commission (SEC) and the Securities Investor Protection Corporation (SIPC) and the role of regulation in security markets.

Market Makers

rganized exchange
formal market for buying ıd selling securities or com- ıodities.

Securities are bought and sold every day by investors who never meet each other. The market impersonally transfers securities from individuals who are selling to those who are buying. This transfer may occur on an **organized exchange**, such as the New York Stock Exchange, or on an unorganized, informal market that is

over-the-counter (OTC) market
The informal secondary market for unlisted securities.

dealers
Market makers who buy and sell securities for their own accounts.

specialist
A market maker on the New York Stock Exchange who maintains an orderly market in the security.

round lot
The general unit of trading in a security, such as 100 shares.

odd lot
A unit of trading, such as 22 shares, that is smaller than the general unit of sale.

bid and ask
Prices at which a security dealer offers to buy and sell stock.

spread
The difference between the bid and the ask prices.

called the **over-the-counter (OTC) market**. In either case, professional security dealers make markets in securities and facilitate their transfer from sellers to buyers. The Securities and Exchange Act of 1934 defines a **dealer** as anyone who engages in the "business of buying and selling for his *own account.*" Buying and selling for your own account has the effect of making a market in the security, and dealers in over-the-counter securities are referred to as "market makers." Dealers for securities traded on the New York Stock Exchange (http://www.nyse.com) and the American Stock Exchange (http://www.amex.com) are referred to as **specialists**. These specialists offer to buy securities from any seller and to sell securities to any purchaser. In effect, specialists make a market in the stock.[1]

Transactions are made in either round lots or odd lots. A **round lot** is the basic unit for trading. For stock, it is usually 100 shares. Smaller transactions (for example, 37 shares), are called **odd lots**. The round lot does not have to be 100 shares for all stocks. For example, for very cheap stocks (sometimes called *cats and dogs*), a round lot may be 500 or 1,000 shares. For bonds, a round lot may be five $1,000 bonds (i.e., $5,000) or bonds totaling $10,000 or even $100,000 in face value. Odd lots are less profitable for brokerage firms and market makers because the paperwork and the time involved in executing a trade are the same for 10 shares or 100 shares, but the dollar volume of the trade is smaller for the odd lot. Thus, the price per share that the buyer is charged for an odd lot is usually higher than the price per share for a round lot. This additional fee may be hidden in a higher asking price for the security rather than being explicitly stated.

Both specialists and dealers quote prices on a **bid and ask** basis; they buy at one price and sell at the other. For example, a market maker may be willing to purchase a specific stock for $20 per share and sell it for $21. The security is then quoted "20–21," which are the bid and ask prices. Selected quotes are illustrated in Exhibit 3.1. As can be seen in the exhibit, the market makers in Sun Microsystems are willing to purchase (bid for) the stock at 14.66 and to sell (ask) the stock for 14.67.

The Spread

The difference between the bid and ask is the **spread** (i.e., the $0.01 difference between 14.66 and 14.67 for Sun Microsystems). Although the value of the security is the bid price, the investor pays the asking price. The spread, like brokerage commissions, is part of the cost of investing. These two costs should not be confused. The spread is one source of compensation for maintaining a market in the security. The broker's commission is compensation for executing the investor's purchase or sale order.

EXHIBIT 3.1

Selected Bid and Ask Quotes, the Spread, and Number of Shares Outstanding as of July 23, 2001

Company	Price: Bid Ask	Spread	Number of Shares Outstanding
UFP Technologies	$1.52–1.60	$0.08	1,950,000
Harmonic	11.65–11.69	0.04	58,100,000
Sun Microsystems	14.66–14.67	0.01	3,335,600,000

[1]As of December 31, 2000, 479 individuals operated as specialists. New York Stock Exchange, *2000 Annual Report,* available at http://www.nyse.com.

The spread may be large (at least as a percentage of the bid price). In Exhibit 3.1, for example, the spread is $0.08 for UFP Technologies, which is 5.3 percent of the bid price. The spread for Sun Microsystems is 0.07 percent of the bid. Because the spread is larger, the investor's effective cost of buying and selling the stock of UFP Technologies is greater than the cost of buying and selling the stock of Sun Microsystems.

The size of the differential between the bid and the ask is affected by various factors. If there are several market makers in a particular security, the spread tends to be smaller because of competition. The difference is also affected by the volume of transactions in the security and the number of shares that the firm has outstanding. If the volume of transactions or the number of outstanding securities is large, then the spread between the bid and the ask is small. Sun Microsystems has almost 3.3 billion shares outstanding, and millions of shares are traded daily. When the number of outstanding securities is small (i.e., it is a **thin issue**), the spread is usually larger. In the case of UFP Technologies in Exhibit 3.1, the firm has 1.9 million shares outstanding, and only a few hundred may be traded on a given day.

thin issue
An issue of securities with either a small number of securities in the hands of the general public or a small volume of transactions.

The spread is one source of profit for dealers as they turn over the securities in their portfolios. Market makers also earn income when they receive dividends and interest from the securities they own. Another source of profit is an increase in security prices, for the value of the dealers' portfolios rises. These profits are a necessary element of security markets because they induce the market makers to serve the crucial functions of buying and selling securities and of bearing the risk of loss from unforeseen price declines. These market makers guarantee to buy and sell at the prices they announce. Thus, an investor knows what the securities are worth at any given time and is assured that there is a place to sell current security holdings or to purchase additional securities. For this service, the market makers must be compensated, and this compensation is generated through the spread between the bid and ask prices, dividends and interest earned, and profits on the inventory of securities should their prices rise. (Of course, the market makers must bear any losses on securities that they hold when prices fall.)

Determination of Prices

Although the bid and ask prices are quoted by market makers, the security prices are set by the demand from all buyers and the supply from all sellers of securities. Market makers try to quote an **equilibrium price** that equates the supply with the demand. If market makers bid too low a price, too few shares will be offered to satisfy the demand. If they ask too high a price, too few shares will be purchased, which will result in a glut, or excess shares, in their portfolios.

equilibrium price
A price that equates supply and demand.

Could market makers set a security's equilibrium price? For large companies the answer is probably no. If the market makers tried to establish a price above the equilibrium price that is set by supply and demand, they would have to absorb all of the excess supply of securities that would be offered at the artificially higher price. Conversely, if the market makers attempted to establish a price below the equilibrium price, they would have to sell a sufficient number of securities to meet the excess demand that would exist at the artificially lower price. The buying of securities requires the delivery of the securities sold. Market makers do not have an infinite well of money with which to purchase the securities nor an unlimited supply of securities to deliver. They may increase or decrease their inventory, but they cannot support the price indefinitely by buying securities, nor can they prevent a price increase by selling them.

Although market makers cannot set the market price, they perform an extremely important role: They maintain an orderly market in securities so that buyers and sellers will have an established market in which to trade. To establish this orderly market, the market makers offer to buy and sell at the quoted bid and ask prices but guarantee only one round-lot transaction at these prices. If a market maker sets too low a price for a certain stock, a large quantity will be demanded by investors. The market maker is required to sell only one round lot at this price and then may increase the bid and ask prices. The increase in the price of the stock will (1) induce some holders of the stock to sell their shares and (2) induce some investors who wanted to purchase the stock to drop out of the market.

If the market maker sets too high a price for the stock, a large quantity of shares will be offered for sale, but these shares will remain unsold. If the market maker is unable to or does not want to absorb all these shares, the security dealer may purchase a round lot and then lower the bid and ask prices. The decline in the price of the stock will (1) induce some potential sellers to hold their stock and (2) induce some investors to enter the market by purchasing the shares, thereby reducing any of the market maker's surplus inventory.

Security Exchanges

listed security
A security that is traded on an organized exchange.

When a company first sells its securities to the public, the securities are often traded in the over-the-counter market. However, the firm may subsequently desire to have its securities **listed** on one of the major organized exchanges—the New York Stock Exchange (NYSE, or "the big board") or the American Stock Exchange (AMEX, or "the curb").[2] (Although the inclusion of the word *stock* in the names implies markets that deal solely in stock, bond issues and options are also traded on these exchanges.) The listing of a firm's securities on a major exchange has an element of prestige, for it indicates that the company has grown above local importance and has attained a specified level of size and profitability.[3]

In addition to these national exchanges, there are several regional stock exchanges, including the Philadelphia Exchange, the Boston Exchange, and the Pacific Exchange. These regional exchanges list companies of particular interest to their geographic areas. Some firms, like Plum Creek, are listed on several exchanges. This company has a national market for its stock but is also of particular interest to investors living on the West Coast, since it has large timber holdings there. Its securities are actively traded on both the New York and the Pacific stock exchanges.

The NYSE is the largest exchange and lists the securities of companies of national interest. The AMEX is smaller than the NYSE but, unlike the regional exchanges, lists smaller firms with national followings. Some of the firms listed on the NYSE were originally listed on the AMEX. After achieving larger earnings and size, these firms transferred their listings from the AMEX to the NYSE.

The listing requirements for both exchanges are presented in Exhibits 3.2 and 3.3. As may be seen in the exhibits, the criteria that must be fulfilled in order to be listed are similar for the two exchanges, but the required sums are larger for the NYSE. In addition to the conditions stated in the exhibits, listing requires the firm to conform to certain procedures, including publishing quarterly reports, soliciting proxies, and publicly announcing any developments that may affect the value of the securities.

Once the securities are accepted for trading on an exchange, the firm must continue to meet the listing requirements. The exchange may delist the securities if the firm is unable to continue to meet the criteria for listing. While delistings do

[2]For histories of the New York and American stock exchanges, consult Robert Sobel, *The Big Board: A History of the New York Stock Market* (New York: The Free Press, 1965) and Robert Sobel, *The Curbstone Brokers: The Origins of the American Stock Exchange* (New York: Macmillan, 1970). For a history of the evolution of the stock market, see B. Mark Smith, *Toward Rational Exuberance* (New York: Farar, Straus and Giroux, 2001).

[3]Many corporations (e.g., Microsoft and Intel) choose *not* to be listed.

EXHIBIT 3.2

Listing Requirements: New York Stock Exchange (U.S. Standards)

Minimum Quantitative Standards: Shares	
Round-lot holders	2,000 (U.S.)
or	
Total stockholders	2,200 (U.S.)
Together with:	
Average monthly trading volume (most recent six months)	100,000 shares
or	
Total shareholders	500
Together with:	
Average monthly trading volume	1,000,000 shares
Market value of public shares	$100,000,000
Public shares outstanding	1,100,000 shares
Minimum Quantitative Standards: Earnings	
Aggregate pretax earnings over the last three years of $6,500,000 achievable as:	
Pretax earnings (most recent year)	$2,500,000
Pretax earnings (each of two preceding years)	$2,000,000
or	
Pretax earnings in most recent year (all three years must be profitable)	$4,500,000
or	
Aggregate operating cash flow for three years (and all three years must be positive)	$25,000,000

Source: New York Stock Exchange, Inc. Web page (3/19/02): http://www.nyse.com/listed/domesticstandards.html. Reprinted with permission.

occur, over a period of years the number of listed securities has increased. Whereas 1,536 stocks were traded on the NYSE in 1973, the 2000 NYSE Annual Report showed that the number had grown to over 3,000 issues of 2,862 companies.

Reporting of Transactions

Daily transactions on the listed exchanges are reported by the financial press (e.g., *The Wall Street Journal*). Weekly summaries are also reported in several publications (e.g., *The New York Times* and *Barron's*). Although there is variation in this reporting, the format used in *The Wall Street Journal* appears as follows:

	52 WEEKS									
YTD %CHG	HI	LO	STOCK	(SYM)	DIV	YLD %	PE	VOL 100s	LAST	NET CHG
+4.1	99.38	45.83	BigGrn	**BGN**	2.16	4.2	30	20046	51.63	−1.75

The YTD %CHG represents the percentage change in the price of the stock during the current calendar year, so in this illustration the current price of the stock is 4.1 percent higher than the close at the end of the previous year. The HI and LO represent the high and low prices of the stock ($99.38 and $45.83, respectively) during the past 52 weeks. Notice that the percentage change in the price of the stock covers only the calendar year while the high and low prices cover the preceding 12 months.

EXHIBIT 3.3

Listing Requirements: American Stock Exchange

Quantitative Standards:	
Pretax income	$750,000
(latest fiscal year or two of three most recent years)	
Stock price	$3
Market value of public stock	$3,000,000
Stockholders' equity	$4,000,000
or	
Pretax income	—
Operating history	2 years
Stock price	$3
Market value of public stock	$15,000,000
Stockholders' equity	$4,000,000
Distribution of Stock Standards:*	
Alternative 1:	
Public float	500,000 shares
Public stockholders	800
Average daily volume	—
Alternative 2:	
Public float	1,000,000 shares
Public stockholders	400
Average daily volume	—
Alternative 3:	
Public float	500,000 shares
Public stockholders	400
Average daily volume	2,000 shares

*Alternative listing guidelines permit the listing of firms that are not operating profitably but have the financial resources to continue operations for an extended period of time.

Source: American Stock Exchange Web page (7/23/01): http://www.amex.com. Reprinted with permission.

Next is the name of the company (usually in abbreviated form) and the ticker symbol in bold print (BigGrn **BGN**). The DIV represents the firm's annual dividend paid during the preceding 12 months or the annual dividend rate based on four quarterly payments. The YLD % is the dividend divided by the price of the stock ($2.16 / $51.63 = 4.2 %). This dividend yield is a measure of the flow of income produced by an investment in BigGrn. (Dividends are discussed in detail in Chapter 11.)

PE is the ratio of the price of the stock to the company's per share earnings. This price/earnings (P/E) ratio is a measure of value and tells what the market is currently paying for $1 of the firm's earnings. P/E ratios permit comparisons of firms relative to their earnings and, as is explained in Chapter 13, is one analytical tool that is often used in the selection of stock.

The last entries concern trading during the day. Vol 100s is the volume of shares traded expressed in hundreds, so 20046 represents 2,004,600 shares. LAST represents the closing price of the stock ($51.63) and NET CHG is the change from the closing price on the previous day of trading. In this illustration the price of the stock declined $1.75 from the previous day of trading.

Many daily newspapers report trading in stocks listed on the New York Stock Exchange in this general form (or similar format). *The Wall Street Journal* provides this data and additional information that the investor may find useful. Exhibit 3.4 (p. 54) is an excerpt from the stock pages for trading on August 1, 2001.

The additional information includes significant changes in prices. If the price of the stock changed by more than 5 percent from the previous day, the entries are in boldface, (AK Steel). If the stock is a new issue within the past 52 weeks, the symbol *n* is given (Aetna). If the stock has been split during the last 12 months, that is indicated by the symbol *s* (AdvMicro). If the stock traded at a new 52-week high or low price, an arrow indicates the direction of this trade. If the stock is trading exclusive of the dividend, which means that the owners of the stock on the previous day are entitled to receive the dividend, that is indicated by the symbol *x* (Alcoa). The cloverleaf symbol indicates that complimentary annual or quarterly reports are available through *The Wall Street Journal* by calling a toll-free number.

Nasdaq
National Association of Securities Dealers Automatic Quotation system; quotation system for over-the-counter securities.

Securities of companies with shares issued to the general public that are not traded on an exchange are traded over-the-counter. The prices of many of these securities are also reported daily in the financial sections of newspapers. In *The Wall Street Journal* these entries are subdivided into the Nasdaq national-market issues and Nasdaq small-cap issues. **Nasdaq** is an acronym for National Association of Securities Dealers Automated Quotation system, which is the impressive system of communication for over-the-counter price quotations.[4] All major unlisted stocks are included in the Nasdaq stock market. A broker may thereby readily obtain the bid and ask prices for many stocks and bonds by simply entering the firm's code into the Nasdaq system.

The reporting of Nasdaq national-market issues is essentially the same as the reporting of listed securities. The information given includes the 52-week high and low prices, the firm's dividend, the volume of transactions, the closing price, and the net change from the previous day. Some papers also include the dividend yield and the P/E ratio.

In addition to the Nasdaq national-market issues, *The Wall Street Journal* and other papers that give thorough coverage of security prices report smaller, less actively traded Nasdaq stocks, called Nasdaq small-cap issues. This reporting is limited to the company, the dividend (if any), the volume of transactions, the closing price, and the net change in price from the previous day.

Composite Transactions

With the development of the Nasdaq stock market (http://www.nasdaq.com), the distinction between the various exchanges and the over-the-counter market is being erased. (The distinction between exchanges and over-the-counter markets was reduced by the merger of the AMEX and Nasdaq in November 1998.) Since New York Stock Exchange securities trade on other exchanges, the actual reporting of New York Stock Exchange listings includes all the trades and is reported as the NYSE-Composite transactions. The bulk of the transactions in listed securities, however, still occurs on the NYSE.

third market
Over-the-counter market for securities listed on an exchange.

In addition to the primary market (the initial sale of the security) and the secondary market (subsequent trading in the security), there is also the **third market**, which is over-the-counter trading in listed securities. While any trades in listed securities off the exchange may be referred to as the third market, the bulk of these trades are large transactions. Such large trades (i.e., 10,000 shares or more) are called *blocks*, and the market makers who organize and execute the trades are referred to as *block positioners*.

The participants in the third market are usually institutional investors, such as pension plans, mutual funds, or insurance companies, who want to buy or sell

[4]For reference books on the Nasdaq market system that provide information on trading procedures, acquire Leo M. Loll, Jr. and Julian G. Buckley, *The Over-the-Counter Securities Markets* (Englewood Cliffs, N.J.: Prentice-Hall, 1986) and National Association of Securities Dealers, *The NASDAQ Handbook*, rev. ed. (Chicago: Probus Publishing, 1992).

EXHIBIT 3.4

Reporting of Security Transactions

THE WALL STREET JOURNAL THURSDAY, AUGUST 2, 2001 **C3**

NEW YORK STOCK EXCHANGE COMPOSITE TRANSACTIONS

NOTICE TO READERS

Wall Street Journal stock tables reflect composite regular trading as of 4 p.m., and changes in closing prices from 4 p.m. the previous day. Trading after regular hours is summarized in the Late-Trading Snapshot that appears on this page.

Wednesday, August 1, 2001

Boldface—Price changed by more than 5 percent

s Stock split within last 52 weeks

n New issue within last 52 weeks

x Trading exclusive of dividend

▲ New 52-week high

YTD % CHG	52 WEEKS HI	52 WEEKS LO	STOCK (SYM)	DIV	YLD %	PE	VOL 100S	LAST	NET CHG
			-A-A-A-						
+ 31.2	17.10	9.75	AAR **AIR**	.34	2.1	24	623	16.57	+ 0.05
+ 21.6	38.20	23.94	ABM Indus **ABM**	.66	1.8	19	564	37.25	+ 0.70
− 21.8	26.50	16.81	ABN Am ADR **ABN**	.81e	4.6	...	1197	17.80	+ 0.01
− 18.5	43.94	31.59	♣ACE Ltd **ACE**	.60f	1.7	17	11718	34.60	− 0.31
+ 48.2	39.55	18.75	ACLN Ltd **ASW** s		...	10	1889	34.65	+ 1.38
− 29.8	72.81	33.60	♣AES Cp **AES**		...	34	20282	38.88	+ 0.58
− 28.2	110	55	AES Tr	3.38	5.5	...	176	61.74	− 0.26
− 17.6	37.47	23.38	AFLAC **AFL** s	.20	.7	24	9902	29.74	+ 0.16
− 13.7	13.13	7.90	AGCO Cp **AG**	.04	.4	70	2372	10.46	+ 0.15
+ 8.6	24.25	17.91	AGL Res **ATG**	1.08	4.5	13	1351	23.95	− 0.05
− 3.9	20	10.44	AgSvcAm **ASV**		...	12	12	13.22	− 0.20
▲+ 76.4	47.25	15	AIPC **PLB**		...	30	3160	47.30	+ 0.05
+ 60.1	**15**	**7.50**	**♣AK Steel AKS**	**.25**	**1.8**	**33**	**7912**	**14.01**	**+ 0.90**
− 2.5	26.06	22.50	♣AMB Prop **AMB**	1.58	6.3	17	1391	25.16	+ 0.16
+ 27.4	7.81	2.88	AMCOL **ACO**	.06f	1.0	38	150	6.05	− 0.01
− 5.2	25.31	20.13	♣AMLI Resdntl **AML**	1.88	8.0	9	318	23.40	− 0.05
− 7.5	43.94	27.63	AMR **AMR**	stk	...	dd	8573	36.23	+ 1.08
+ 6.8	25.05	21.38	AMR PINES	1.97	7.9	...	176	25.04	+ 0.14
+ 32.4	62.27	31.50	AOL Time **AOL**		...	dd	87710	46.08	+ 0.63
+ 23.1	5.31	2.63	APT Satelt **ATS**	.21e	5.9	...	83	3.54	+ 0.14
− 72.7	49.88	5	♣APW		...	...	1725	9.20	+ 0.20
+ 9.8	28.25	15.29	AT&T Wrls **AWE**		...	...	96713	19.01	+ 0.32
+ 56.5	24.76	12.41	AT&T **T** s	.15	.7	...	101208	20.30	+ 0.09
+ 3.6	26.35	23.88	AT&T 8 1/4 PNS	2.06	8.0	...	135	25.83	+ 0.08
+ 2.1	25.90	23.63	AT&T 8 1/8 PNS	2.03	8.0	...	282	25.53	+ 0.06
+ 35.6	31.75	15.13	♣AVX Cp **AVX**	.15	.7	8	6657	22.20	+ 0.20
− 18.4	39.88	24.58	AXA ADS **AXA** s	.50e	1.7	...	1968	29.31	+ 0.34
+ 39.9	25.79	14.63	AZZ **AZZ**	.16	.6	15	92	24.65	− 0.15
+ 116.0	4	0.44	AamesFnl **AAM**		...	dd	26	1.35	+ 0.04
+ 31.6	19.50	11.75	AaronRent **RNT**	.04	.2	14	274	18.51	+ 0.06
− 33.5	18.95	10.22	ABB ADS **ABB** n		...	...	188	11.19	+ 0.14
+ 8.9	25.09	20.63	AbbeyNtl **SUA**	1.75	7.2	...	181	24.43	+ 0.03
+ 8.6	25.25	21.75	AbbeyNtl 7 1/4% **SUD**	1.81	7.2	...	33	24.98	+ 0.05
+ 9.6	56.25	39.31	AbbottLab **ABT**	.84	1.6	48	38337	53.10	− 0.49
+ 83.4	**47.50**	**14.75**	**Abercrombie A ANF**		**...**	**23**	**26088**	**36.68**	**− 2.14**
− 17.5	11.44	7	Abitibi g **ABY**	.40g	...	...	1027	7.58	+ 0.03
+ 25.3	7.22	5.50	♣AcadiaRlty **AKR**	.48	6.8	10	140	7.05	+ 0.32
▲+ 2.2	15.29	14.50	Accenture **ACN** n		...	...	20764	15.50	+ 0.54
+ 8.4	6.94	3.70	♣AcceptIns **AIF**		...	dd	1138	5.69	− 0.11
+ 44.3	15.06	7.88	AckrlyGp **AK**	.02	.2	...	54	12.99	− 0.06
+ 20.6	27.19	10.94	Actuant A **ATU** s		...	dd	157	18.09	+ 0.59
− 19.8	20.40	10.89	Adecco **ADO** s		...	...	346	12.55	+ 0.08
+ 0.4	**44.56**	**15.40**	**Administaff ASF s**		**...**	**55**	**5082**	**27.30**	**+ 2.12**
+ 20.5	24.45	19.95	AFP Prov ADR **PVD**	1.38e	5.7	...	383	24.40	+ 0.40
+ 51.5	20.95	9.63	♣AdvMktg **MKT** s	.03	.2	16	496	17.55	+ 0.20
+ 36.8	38.25	13.56	♣AdvMicro **AMD** s		...	9	81139	18.90	+ 0.64
− 4.5	6.14	2.26	AdSemiEng ADS **ASX** sn	stk	...	...	129	2.50	+ 0.01
− 11.2	48	30.05	Advo **AD**		...	16	209	39.39	+ 0.34
− 31.9	43	25.92	♣AEGON **AEG**	.68e	2.4	20	1192	28.20	+ 0.42
+ 2.1	25.99	25.08	Aetna8.5% **AEF** n		...	...	670	25.80	+ 0.05
− 32.6	42.69	23.01	Aetna **AET** n		...	dd	15807	27.67	− 0.54
+ 36.5	86	43.13	AffilCmptr A **ACS**		...	34	6536	82.85	+ 0.01
▲+ 24.8	68.90	41.20	AffilMangr **AMG**		...	29	3529	68.51	+ 0.77
− 10.0	9.50	4.10	AgereSys A **AGRA** n		...	...	70238	5.42	− 0.11
− 42.0	**68**	**25**	**AgilentTch A**		**...**	**20**	**25077**	**31.75**	**+ 3.14**
+ 36.2	9.63	4.88	♣AgnicoEgl **AEM**	.02	.2	cc	852	8.17	− 0.12
+ 40.2	20.05	13.63	AgreeRlty **ADC**	1.84	9.5	11	72	19.28	− 0.22
− 29.2	14.75	8.50	Agrium **AGU**	.11	1.1	16	3329	10.35	...
− 7.0	33.49	26.31	Ahold **AHO**	.56e	1.9	...	482	30.24	+ 0.22
+ 88.4	7.65	3.06	AirNetSys **ANS**		...	16	438	7.30	− 0.10
− 0.1	49	30.50	AirProduct **APD**	.80f	2.0	15	14817	40.96	+ 0.13
+ 31.6	16.50	8.25	AirborneInc **ABF**	.16	1.2	dd	4851	12.83	+ 0.19
+ 82.0	12.85	5.19	Airgas **ARG**		...	29	2099	12.40	+ 0.47
− 14.9	13.13	8.16	Airlease **FLY**	1.52	15.1	13	33	10.05	+ 0.03
+ 11.4	15.63	12.50	AlamoGp **ALG**	.24	1.6	13	15	14.55	...
+ 8.1	35.25	19.50	AlaskaAir **ALK**		...	dd	1466	32.15	+ 0.51
+ 48.8	23	9.63	♣AlbanyInt **AIN**	j	...	15	768	20	+ 0.05
− 13.5	26.13	18.50	Albemarle **ALB**	.52	2.4	13	640	21.40	+ 0.64
− 18.3	50.90	34	♣AlbEngy g **AOG**	.60fg	...	...	1667	39.40	− 0.30
+ 0.4	44.70	27.38	AlbertoCl **ACV**	.33	.8	23	984	43	− 0.38
− 2.4	37.40	23.50	AlbertoCl A **ACVA**	.33	.9	20	677	35.58	− 0.34
+ 23.7	34.05	20.06	Albertsons **ABS**	.76	2.3	18	9964	32.77	+ 0.04
+ 7.8	48.75	28.19	♣Alcan **AL**	.60g	1.6	20	13785	36.86	− 0.65
− 67.2	**86.25**	**14.75**	**Alcatel ADS ALA**	**.43e**	**2.3**	**...**	**18943**	**18.32**	**+ 0.92**
+ 14.7	45.71	23.13	Alcoa **AA** x	.60	1.6	23	19215	38.41	− 0.67
− 3.4	82.31	58.38	Alexanders **ALX**		...	13	2	65.40	+ 0.21
▲+ 7.2	39.80	31.50	AlexRlEstEq **ARE**	1.84	4.6	25	404	39.85	+ 0.55
+ 7.2	216.06	167.59	Allghny **Y**	stk	...	4	76	216	+ 0.10
− 9.8	55.09	31.25	AllghnyEngy **AYE**	1.72	4.0	13	4958	43.48	+ 0.36
+ 20.6	22.63	12.50	AllghnyTch **ATI**	.80	4.2	26	1409	19.15	+ 0.09
− 26.4	24	10.80	AllenTele **ALN**		...	29	1132	13.21	− 0.65
− 22.5	101.13	59	♣Allergan **AGN**	.36	.5	52	15879	75	− 0.29
− 2.3	26.13	20.13	♣ALLETE **ALE**	1.07	4.4	13	2642	24.24	+ 0.55
+ 4.5	59.35	37.40	AllncCapMgt **AC**	3.01e	5.7	18	1741	52.88	+ 0.88
+ 7.1	17.40	12.50	AllianceData **ADS** n		...	...	192	15	...
+ 58.6	16.80	9	AllncFrstPdt **PFA**		...	13	44	15.36	− 0.14
− 1.1	13.30	13	Alliance **AIQ** n		...	...	6610	13	− 0.01
− 9.8	33.20	26.25	AlliantEngy **LNT**	2.00	7.0	6	1237	28.75	+ 0.18
+ 42.3	102	46.67	AlliantTech **ATK** s		...	20	3115	95	− 4.20
− 24.1	37.88	26.10	Allianz ADS **AZ** n	.14p	...	...	55	28.45	+ 0.30
+ 13.6	25.72	17.96	AlldCap **ALD**	2.04f	8.6	11	3602	23.71	+ 0.46
− 17.5	6.50	2.21	♣AlldHldg **AHI**		...	dd	18	2.27	+ 0.01
− 10.0	25.81	16.31	AlldIrishBk **AIB**	.46e	2.2	...	282	21.14	− 0.24
+ 32.7	19.90	7.50	AlliedWaste **AW**		...	cc	8440	19.32	+ 0.48
− 25.7	74.25	46.30	AllmericaFnl **AFC**	.25	.5	18	2698	53.85	+ 0.20
− 19.1	45.90	26.88	Allstate **ALL**	.76	2.2	14	42796	35.25	+ 0.29
+ 2.9	27.15	25	AllstFnn CorTS n				9	26.25	

LATE-TRADING SNAPSHOT 8/1/01

LATE-TRADING ACTIVITY (4 P.M.-6:35 P.M. Eastern Time)

	WEDNESDAY	TUESDAY	MONDAY	FRIDAY	THURSDAY
ISSUES TRADED	2,192	2,906	2,466	2,034	2,560
ADVANCES	428	512	400	470	467
DECLINES	348	439	340	481	548
UNCHANGED	1,416	1,955	1,726	1,083	1,545
ADVANCING VOLUME	30,030,200	30,730,200	16,568,800	17,658,200	26,312,000
DECLINING VOLUME	16,147,900	27,283,400	12,554,100	19,785,000	31,158,900
TOTAL VOLUME	71,398,910	85,713,200	50,939,800	52,320,900	78,676,100

LATE MOST ACTIVE ISSUES

ISSUE	EXCH	VOL(000)	LAST	NET CHG	% CHG
LucentTch	(N)	5,670.3	6.19	+ 0.06	+ 1.0
CiscoSys	(Nq)	1,534.9	20.26	− 0.04	− 0.2
SunMicrsys	(Nq)	1,375.7	17.46	+ 0.11	+ 0.6
NanophsTch	(Nq)	1,290.2	6.34	....	....
Intel	(Nq)	1,214.5	30.80	+ 0.05	+ 0.2
ATI Tch	(Nq)	1,168.9	10.66	− 0.08	− 0.7
WorldCom	(Nq)	1,151.8	14.66	− 0.04	− 0.3
OracleCp	(Nq)	1,072.3	18.39	+ 0.07	+ 0.4
Microsoft	(Nq)	963.6	66.64	+ 0.17	+ 0.3
StratosLght	(Nq)	954.3	7.46	....	....
PMC Sierra	(Nq)	923.9	36.68	+ 3.34	+ 10.0
Nextel	(Nq)	650.3	17.00	....	....
NASDAQ100	(A)	585.4	43.17	+ 0.07	+ 0.2
Danaher	(N)	521.4	55.25	− 1.05	− 1.9
ExpresScrpt	(Nq)	518.1	54.93	....	....
DellCptr	(Nq)	511.5	27.23	+ 0.05	+ 0.2
GenSemi	(N)	510.5	12.81	− 0.01	− 0.1
FrptMcCG B	(N)	491.4	11.00	....	....
Priceline	(Nq)	487.3	9.52	....	....
WbMthds	(Nq)	485.1	15.95	+ 0.35	+ 2.2
SapientCp	(Nq)	473.1	6.22	....	....
MellonFnl	(N)	450.0	38.20	− 0.11	− 0.3
ADC Tel	(Nq)	443.7	4.94	....	....
BroadVisn	(Nq)	440.2	3.65	....	....
QuakerOats	(N)	433.8	99.50	− 0.80	− 0.8
Comcast spA	(Nq)	431.4	38.65	+ 0.60	+ 1.6
ONI Sys	(Nq)	429.7	22.75	− 0.73	− 3.1
Corvis	(Nq)	420.6	3.94	− 0.01	− 0.3
i2 Tch	(Nq)	419.3	10.59	+ 0.10	+ 1.0
GlblCross	(N)	415.6	7.17	+ 0.17	+ 2.4

LATE PRICE PERCENTAGE GAINERS...

ISSUE	EXCH	VOL(000)	LAST	NET CHG	% CHG
DocuSci	(Nq)	2.0	3.28	+ 0.47	+ 16.7
Acterna	(Nq)	254.3	6.85	+ 0.82	+ 13.6
PMC Sierra	(Nq)	923.9	36.68	+ 3.34	+ 10.0
McLeodUSA A	(Nq)	337.7	3.09	+ 0.27	+ 9.6
ThrmaWave	(Nq)	7.4	15.55	+ 1.25	+ 8.7
AsiaGlbCrossA	(N)	29.5	5.50	+ 0.41	+ 8.1
DialgSemi ADS	(Nq)	7.0	3.23	+ 0.23	+ 7.7
TBC	(Nq)	57.5	11.73	+ 0.80	+ 7.3
Nutractl	(Nq)	11.8	4.60	+ 0.27	+ 6.2
CptrSci	(N)	144.3	35.50	+ 1.96	+ 5.8
eSpeed A	(Nq)	12.6	16.00	+ 0.87	+ 5.8
Medcath	(SC)	164.1	22.28	+ 1.08	+ 5.1
MRV Comm	(Nq)	23.0	7.28	+ 0.32	+ 4.6
BiolaseTch	(SC)	10.2	6.25	+ 0.25	+ 4.2
Recoton	(Nq)	25.7	19.50	+ 0.75	+ 4.0

AND LOSERS

ISSUE	EXCH	VOL(000)	LAST	NET CHG	% CHG
ASE Tst	(Nq)	76.3	11.25	− 1.17	− 9.4
Univision A	(N)	49.2	36.00	− 2.70	− 7.0
IntgtCircuit	(Nq)	47.3	20.15	− 1.45	− 6.7
AmylinPharm	(Nq)	2.8	7.50	− 0.44	− 5.5
LTX	(Nq)	18.0	22.75	− 1.24	− 5.2
Awarelnc	(Nq)	2.0	7.37	− 0.39	− 5.0
MicroLinear	(Nq)	41.7	3.61	− 0.17	− 4.5
NtlMercBcp	(SC)	2.4	7.75	− 0.35	− 4.3
CA McroDvc	(Nq)	4.0	8.30	− 0.35	− 4.0
Orbotech	(Nq)	77.6	26.02	− 0.98	− 3.6
BkUtdFnl A	(Nq)	9.0	14.00	− 0.52	− 3.6
MKS Instr	(Nq)	21.9	27.88	− 1.00	− 3.5
ONI Sys	(Nq)	429.7	22.75	− 0.73	− 3.1
Genesis	(Nq)	28.5	17.30	− 0.54	− 3.0
AdvPwrTch	(Nq)	10.0	14.00	− 0.39	− 2.7

The Late-Trading Snapshot reflects trading activity after regular trading hours in NYSE and Amex issues reported by electronic trading services, securities dealers and regional exchanges between 4 p.m. and 6:35 p.m. Eastern time, and in Nasdaq NMS issues between 4 p.m. and 6:30 p.m., with a minimum price of $3 and volume of 2,000. The primary market is indicated for each issue. N-NYSE A-Amex Nq-Nasdaq SC-Nasdaq SmallCap

WSJ.com **Journal Link:** For additional data from after-hours stock trading, see the online Journal at **WSJ.com/JournalLinks**

YTD % CHG	52 WEEKS HI	52 WEEKS LO	STOCK (SYM)	DIV	YLD %	PE	VOL 100S	LAST	NET CHG
− 3.6	50.63	42.45	AvalnBay **AVB**		...	19	2268	48.32	+ 0.47
+ 23.8	26	9.88	Avaya **AV** n		...	dd	6576	12.77	+ 0.24
− 8.0	87.50	66.63	Aventis ADS **AVE**	.44e	.6	...	1063	77.55	+ 0.55
− 11.8	14.50	9.35	Aventis ADS wt		...	...	30	12.35	+ 0.15
− 7.0	60.50	41.13	AveryDensn **AVY**	1.20	2.4	1	1752	51.05	− 0.21
+ 102.1	11.25	4.50	♣Aviall **AVL**		...	15	644	10.23	− 0.19
− 50.0	6.50	1.08	AviatnSales **AVS**		...	dd	63	1.25	− 0.01
− 16.1	30.44	15	Avista **AVA**	.48	2.8	5	1893	17.20	− 0.10
+ 14.7	32.56	17.19	Avnet **AVT** s	.30	1.2	8	5684	24.65	+ 0.76
− 4.7	49.75	35	AvonPdts **AVP**	.76	1.7	22	8923	45.62	− 0.77
+ 15.9	15.75	8.88	AztarCp **AZR**		...	13	1588	15	+ 0.08
			-B-B-B-						
− 8.0	47.31	33.25	BASF ADS **BF**	1.87e	4.6	...	534	40.90	+ 0.25
− 0.4	38.25	24.63	BB&T Cp **BBT**	1.04f	2.8	21	5403	37.15	+ 0.24
+ 3.8	17.60	14.06	BBV A Banco **BB**	.68e	4.4	...	6	15.38	− 0.22
− 34.9	**31.49**	**9.25**	**BcoFran ADR BFR**	**1.05e**	**7.7**	**...**	**738**	**13.68**	**− 0.77**
− 7.4	29.56	21	BCE Inc g **BCE**	1.20g	...	...	2657	26.80	+ 0.07
− 3.6	22.53	17.60	BG Gp ADS **BRG**	.52e	2.6	...	71	19.65	− 0.30
+ 1.3	12.04	9.13	BHPBilliton ADS **BHP** s	.53e	5.1	...	2938	10.33	+ 0.48
+ 43.9	57.24	28.88	BJs WhslClb **BJ**		...	30	3016	55.24	− 0.76
− 30.0	43.10	21.18	♣BJ Svc **BJS** s		...	15	31596	24.10	− 1.12
+ 56.2	34.80	16	BKF CapGp **BKF**		...	...	70	28.50	− 0.20
+ 0.5	7.50	4.19	BMC Ind **BMM**	.06	1.2	82	167	4.90	+ 0.10
+ 44.3	33	13	♣BMC Sftwr **BMC**		...	dd	11145	20.20	+ 0.20
− 5.8	33	23.25	BOC Gp **BOX**	1.16e	4.0	...	136	28.86	+ 1.16
+ 4.0	57.81	45.13	♣BP Plc ADS **BP**	1.38e	2.8	...	14256	49.77	+ 0.35
+ 18.9	17.41	10.50	BP Prudhoe **BPT**	3.11e	21.1	...	453	14.72	− 0.13

YTD % CHG	52 WEEKS HI	52 WEEKS LO	STOCK (SYM)	DIV	YLD %	PE	VOL 100S	LAST	NET CHG
− 4.6	33.69	26.20	BRE Prop **BRE**	1.86	6.2	39	552	30.23	− 0.13
+ 28.1	10.75	7.63	BRT RltyTr **BRT**	.22p	...	7	5	10.25	+ 0.10
+ 53.7	7.19	2.60	BWAY **BY**		...	dd	368	6.05	+ 0.25
+ 8.8	28.50	21.81	BacouUSA **BAU**		...	18	125	28.30	+ 0.05
− 20.5	8.60	6	Bairnco **BZ**	.20	3.3	9	28	6.06	+ 0.05
− 17.4	45.29	29.80	BakrHughs **BHI**	.46	1.3	57	35144	34.32	− 1.26
+ 3.2	25.15	18.38	♣BaldorElec **BEZ**	.52	2.4	21	216	21.80	− 0.23
+ 8.2	51.15	28.56	Ball Cp **BLL**	.60	1.2	dd	1491	49.84	+ 0.41
− 25.6	34.88	21.44	BallyTtlFit **BFT**		...	9	3165	25.20	− 0.20
− 15.2	16.63	11.41	BcoBilViz **BBV**	.35e	2.8	...	3324	12.45	+ 0.22
+ 22.6	17.55	11.38	BcoAEdw ADR **AED**	.06e	.4	...	71	16.55	...
+ 0.8	37.70	24.44	BcoLatin **BLX**	1.88	5.4	6	50	34.84	− 0.13
− 13.0	15.20	7	BcoRioP ADS **BRS**	1.33e	18.5	...	3	7.18	+ 0.08
+ 9.0	19.80	12	BcoSantdr CH **BSB**	.69e	4.2	...	1209	16.49	− 0.01
− 17.2	11.94	7.98	BcoSantdr **STD**	.25e	2.9	...	2244	8.75	+ 0.05
+ 8.1	24.40	17.25	BcoSanti ADR **SAN**	1.58e	7.5	...	13	21.15	− 0.50
− 27.5	4.31	1.35	Bancolom ADS **CIB**	.02e	1.1	...	1247	1.45	+ 0.10
+ 32.5	17	11.88	Bncpsouth **BXS**	.56	3.5	20	462	16.15	+ 0.05
+ 33.3	34.84	16.75	BancWest **BWE**	.76	2.2	18	2194	34.82	+ 0.03
− 26.3	46.75	25.70	Bandag **BDG**	1.22	4.1	14	124	29.90	− 0.11
− 23.3	38.69	20.90	Bandag A **BDGA**	1.22	4.7	10	15	25.70	+ 0.35
+ 3.0	26.70	23.50	BangorHyd **BGR**	.80	3.0	18	542	26.45	+ 0.02
+ 37.3	64.70	36.31	BankAm **BAC**	2.24	3.6	15	30122	63	− 0.62
− 0.3	42	24	BkIreland **IRE**	1.01e	2.6	...	54	39.12	+ 1.42
+ 0.1	29.15	20.19	♣BkMontreal g **BMO** sx	1.12g	...	...	396	26.37	+ 0.04
− 19.5	59.38	40.15	BankNY **BK**	.72	1.6	22	19797	44.40	− 0.46
+ 4.7	41.56	30.75	BkOne **ONE**	.84	2.2	31	36597	38.35	− 0.36
▲+ 184.0	10.29	3.38	BkAtlBcp A **BBX**	.12f	1.1	...	5766	10.65	+ 0.40

POINTS OF INTEREST

The P/E Ratio

One term often used by investors is the P/E ratio, which is the ratio of a stock's price to the firm's per-share earnings. By expressing each firm's stock price relative to its earnings, this ratio facilitates the comparison of firms. The P/E ratio indicates the amount that the market is willing to pay for each dollar of earnings. A P/E of 12 means that the stock is selling for 12 times the firm's earnings and that the market believes that $1 of earnings is currently worth $12. There is also the implication that if earnings increase by $1, the price of the stock will rise by $12.

Pharmaceutical Company	Per-Share Earnings for the Preceding 12 Months	Price of the Stock	P/E Ratio
Bristol-Myers Squibb	$2.06	$73.93	36
Bard (C.R.)	2.28	46.56	20
Forest Laboratories	1.28	132.87	96
GlaxoSmithKline	1.81	56.00	31
Johnson & Johnson	2.94	105.06	36
Merck	2.45	93.82	38
Mylan Labs	1.18	25.18	21
Pharmacia	0.91	61.0	67
Schering Plough	1.42	56.75	35

Source: Standard & Poor's *Stock Guide*, Year End 2000.

Firms in the same industry tend to have similar P/E ratios. This is illustrated in the accompanying exhibit, which gives the earnings, the price of the stock, and the P/E ratio for several pharmaceutical companies. The average P/E ratio for the group (i.e., 42) may be indicative of the appropriate P/E ratio for an individual firm's stock. If the company's ratio is higher than the industry's average (e.g., Pharmacia), the stock may be overpriced. Conversely, if the P/E ratio is lower than the industry's average (e.g., Mylan Labs), it may indicate that the stock is undervalued.

Unfortunately, security analysis and selection are not that simple. If a firm has an excellent record of earnings growth and the security market anticipates that this growth will continue, the P/E ratio tends to be higher than the industry's average. This higher growth has value. These earnings may achieve a higher price, in which case the stock sells for a higher P/E ratio. If a firm is considered to be riskier than is typical of firms in its industry, the P/E ratio tends to be lower. The earnings of a firm involving greater risk are worth less. Thus, the stock's price and the P/E ratio are lower than the industry's average.

While the P/E ratio is frequently used, it does not tell the investor much about the firm. Of course, it does permit easy comparison of firms, but it considers only the earnings and the price of the stock. It tells nothing of how the earnings were achieved or why the market may view one firm's earnings as inferior or superior to the earnings of another firm.

large amounts of stocks in listed securities, such as the stock of IBM, which trades on the NYSE. The institutional investor works through a large brokerage firm that completes the transaction. If the investor desires to buy a large position, the brokerage firm (or security dealer) seeks potential sellers. After the required seller (or sellers, for a sufficiently large block) is found, the securities are traded off the floor of the exchange.

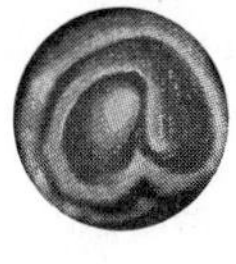

In the *fourth market,* the financial institutions do not use brokerage firms or security dealers but may trade securities through a computerized system, such as *Instinet* (http://www.instinet.com), which provides bid and ask price quotations and executes orders. This system is limited to those financial institutions that subscribe to the service. Transactions through Instinet are reported in the financial press through the composite transactions just like trades on the various exchanges.

Block trades, the third market, and the fourth market offer financial institutions two advantages: lower commissions and quicker executions. Competition among brokerage firms for this business has reduced the commission fees. In addition, the effort and time required to put together a block to purchase or to find buyers for a sale is reduced through the development of block trading and over-the-counter trading of listed securities. The effect of this trading and the change in the regulatory environment for financial institutions has led to a national market for the execution of security orders, since these orders need not go through an exchange in a particular geographical area.

The Mechanics of Investing in Securities

broker
An agent who handles buy and sell orders for an investor.

Individual investors usually purchase stocks and bonds through **brokers**, who buy and sell securities for their customers' accounts. (Some brokerage firms use different titles, such as "account executive" or "assistant vice president." These individuals perform the traditional functions of "brokers.") While a few companies (e.g., ExxonMobil) offer investors the option to purchase shares directly from the corporation, the majority of purchases are made through brokerage firms, such as Merrill Lynch or A.G. Edwards. Many brokerage firms also act as market makers and may be referred to as "broker-dealers" since different divisions within the firm perform both functions. The firm has individuals who buy and sell for the firm's account (i.e., are security dealers) and other individuals who buy and sell for customers' accounts (i.e., are brokers).

The broker services an individual's account and is the *investor's agent* who executes buy and sell orders. To be permitted to buy and sell securities, brokers must pass a proficiency examination administered by the National Association of Securities Dealers. Once the individual has passed the test, he or she is referred to as a **registered representative** and can buy and sell securities for customers' accounts.

registered representative
A person who buys and sells securities for customers; a broker.

Although registered representatives must pass this proficiency examination, the investor should not assume that the broker is an expert. There are many aspects of investing, and even an individual who spends a considerable portion of the working day servicing accounts cannot be an expert on all the aspects of investing. Thus, many recommendations are based on research that is done by analysts employed by the brokerage firm rather than by individual salespersons.

The investor should realize that brokers make their living through transactions (i.e., buying and selling for their customers' accounts). There are essentially two types of working relationships between the brokerage firm and the salesperson. In one case, the firm pays a basic salary, but the salesperson must bring in a specified amount in commissions, which go to the firm. After the minimum amount of sales has been met, the registered representative's salary is increased in proportion to the amount of additional commissions generated. In the second type of relationship, the salesperson's income is entirely related to the commissions generated. In either case, the investor should realize that the broker's livelihood depends on the sale of securities. Thus, the broker's advice on investing may be colored by the desire to secure commissions. However, the investor is ultimately responsible for the investment decisions. Although advice may be requested from the broker, and it is sometimes offered even though unsolicited, the investor must weigh the impact of a specific investment decision in terms of fulfilling his or her financial goals.

Selecting a brokerage firm can be a difficult task. Various firms offer different services; for example, some may specialize in bonds and others may deal solely in the securities of corporations located in a particular geographic region. The best source of information on stocks of local interest (e.g., local commercial banks) is often the regional brokerage firm. Other brokerage firms offer a full range of services, including estate planning and life insurance, as well as trading of stocks and bonds. Still other firms offer virtually no services other than executing orders at discount (i.e., lower) commissions. Each investor therefore needs to identify his or her personal investment goals and decide on the strategies to attain those goals in order to select the firm that is best suited to that individual's needs.

Choosing a registered representative is a more difficult task than selecting a brokerage firm. This individual will need to know specific information, including the investor's income, other assets and outstanding debt, and financial goals, in order to give the best service to the account. People are reluctant to discuss this information, so trust and confidence in the registered representative are probably the most important considerations in selecting a broker. Good rapport between the broker and the investor is particularly important if the relationship is going to be mutually successful.

The Long and Short Positions

long position
Owning assets for their income and possible price appreciation.

bullish
Expecting that prices will rise.

short position
Selling borrowed assets for possible price deterioration; being short in a security or a commodity.

bearish
Expecting that prices will decline.

market order
An order to buy or sell at the current market price or quote.

limit order
An order placed with a broker to buy or sell at a specified price.

day order
An order placed with a broker that is canceled at the end of the day if it is not executed.

good-till-canceled order
An order placed with a broker that remains in effect until it is executed by the broker or canceled by the investor.

stop order
A purchase or sell order designed to limit an investor's loss or to assure a profit on a position in a security.

Essentially, an investor has only two courses of action, which involve opposite positions. They are frequently referred to as the *bull* and *bear* positions and are symbolized by a statue, which is located outside the NYSE, of a bull and a bear locked in mortal combat.[5]

If an investor expects a security's price to rise, the security is purchased. The investor takes a **long position** in the security in anticipation of the price increase. The investor is **bullish** because he or she believes that the price will rise. The long position earns profits for the investor if the price rises after the security has been purchased. For example, if an investor buys 100 shares of AB&C for $55 (i.e., $5,500 plus brokerage fees) and the price rises to $60, the profit on the long position is $5 per share (i.e., $500 on 100 shares before commissions).

Opposite the long position is the **short position** (**bearish**), in which the investor anticipates that the security's price will fall. The investor sells the security and holds cash or places the funds in interest-bearing short-term securities, such as Treasury bills or a savings account. Some investors who are particularly bearish or who are willing to speculate on the decline in prices may even "sell short," which is a sale for future delivery. (The process of selling short is discussed later in this section.)

Types of Orders

After an investor decides to purchase a security, a buy order is placed with the broker. The investor may ask the broker to buy the security at the best price currently available, which is the asking price set by the market maker. Such a request is a **market order**. The investor is not assured of receiving the security at the currently quoted price, since that price may change by the time the order is executed. However, the order is generally executed at or very near the asking price.

The investor may enter a **limit order** and specify a price below the current asking price and wait until the price declines to the specified level. Such an order may be placed for one day (i.e., a **day order**), or the order may remain in effect indefinitely (i.e., a **good-till-canceled order**). Such an order remains on the books of the broker until it is either executed or canceled. If the price of the security does not decline to the specified level, the purchase is never made. While a good-till-canceled order may remain in effect indefinitely, brokerage firms generally have a time limit (e.g., one month or three months) that specifies when the order will be canceled if it has not been executed.

After purchasing the security an investor may place a **stop order** to sell, which may be at a higher or lower price.[6] Once the stock reaches that price, the stop order becomes a market order. An investor who desires to limit potential losses may place a stop-loss order, which specifies the price below the cost of the security at which the broker is authorized to sell. For example, if an investor buys a stock for $50 a share, a stop-loss order at $45 limits the loss to $5 a share, plus the commission fees for the purchase and the sale. If the price of the stock should fall to $45, the stop-loss order becomes a market order, and the stock is sold. (Since the order

[5]The derivations of "bull" and "bear" are lost in time. "Bearish" may originate from trading in pelts when bearskins were sold before the bears were caught. Bullbaiting and bearbaiting were also sports in the eighteenth century. See Steele Commager, "Watch Your Language," *Forbes* (October 27, 1980): 113–116.

[6]For a description of the 21 possible orders recognized by NYSE Rule 13, see Morris Mendelson and Junius W. Peake, "The ABCs of Trading on a National Market System," *Financial Analyst Journal* (September–October 1979): 39–40.

is now a market order, there is no assurance that the investor will get $45. If there is an influx of sell orders, the sale may occur at less than $45.) Such a sale protects the investor from riding the price of the stock down to $40 or lower. Of course, if the stock rebounds from $45 to $50, the investor has sold out at the bottom price.

The investor may also place a stop-sell order above the purchase price. For example, the investor who purchases a stock at $50 may place a sell order at $60. Should the price of the stock reach $60, the order becomes a market order, and the stock is sold. Such an order limits the potential profit, for if the stock's price continues to rise, the investor who has already sold the stock does not continue to gain. However, the investor has protected the profit that resulted as the price increased from $50 to $60. In many cases the investor watches the stock's price rise, decides not to sell, and then watches the price subsequently decline. Stop-sell orders are designed to reduce this possibility.

The placing of sell orders can be an important part of an investor's strategy. For example, in the previous case the investor who purchased a stock at $50 may place sell orders at $45 and $60. If the price of the stock subsequently rises, this investor may change these sell orders. For example, if the price rises to $56 per share, the investor may change the sell orders to $52 and $64. This will preserve the capital invested, for the price of the stock cannot fall below $52 without triggering the sell order, but the price can now rise above $60, which was the previous upper limit for the sell order. By continuously raising the prices for the sell orders as the stock's price rises, the investor can continue to profit from any price increase and at the same time protect the funds invested in the security against price declines.

Because both limit orders and stop orders specify a price, they are easy to confuse. The limit order specifies a price at which a stock is to be bought or sold. (The purchase could be made at a lower price, and the sale could occur at a higher price.) Limits orders are filled in order of receipt. A limit order to buy stock at $10 may not be executed if other investors have previously entered purchase orders at that price.[7]

A stop order also specifies a price. Once the price is reached, the order becomes a market order and is executed. Since the stop becomes a market order, the actual price at which it is executed may not necessarily be the specified price. For example, an investor buys a stock for $25 and enters a "stop-loss order" to sell at $20 to limit the possible loss on the stock. If the price declines to $20, the stop loss becomes a market order and stock is sold. As mentioned before, the investor may anticipate receiving $20, but there is no guarantee that the stock will be sold at that price. If, for example, the stock reported lower earnings and the price immediately dropped from $25 to $19, the stop-loss order would be executed at $19 instead of the specified $20.

If the investor were unwilling to accept a price less than $20, the individual could enter the sale order as a "stop-limit" order that combines a stop-loss with a limit order. However, the stock would not be sold if the price declined through the specified price before the limit order was executed. If, after the earnings announcement the price immediately dropped from $22 to $19, a stop-limit order at $20 would not be executed unless the stock subsequently rose to $20. With any limit order there is no assurance that the order will be executed. In other words, investors cannot have their cake and eat it too. Once the specified price is reached, a stop order guarantees an execution but not the price, whereas a limit order guarantees the price but not an execution.

confirmation statement
A statement received from a brokerage firm detailing the sale or purchase of a security and specifying a settlement date.

Once the purchase has been made, the broker sends the investor a **confirmation statement**, an example of which is shown in Exhibit 3.5. This confirmation statement gives the number of shares and name of the security purchased (100 shares

[7]Since individuals tend to think in terms of simple numbers such as $10 or $15, it may be a wise strategy to enter the buy order at $10.05, so that the order would be executed before all orders placed at $10. The same applies to sell orders. A limit to sell at $13 is executed once the stock price rises to $13 and prior sell orders are executed. A sell order at $12.90 stands before all sell orders at $13.

EXHIBIT 3.5

Confirmation Statement for the Purchase of 100 Shares of Clevepak Corporation

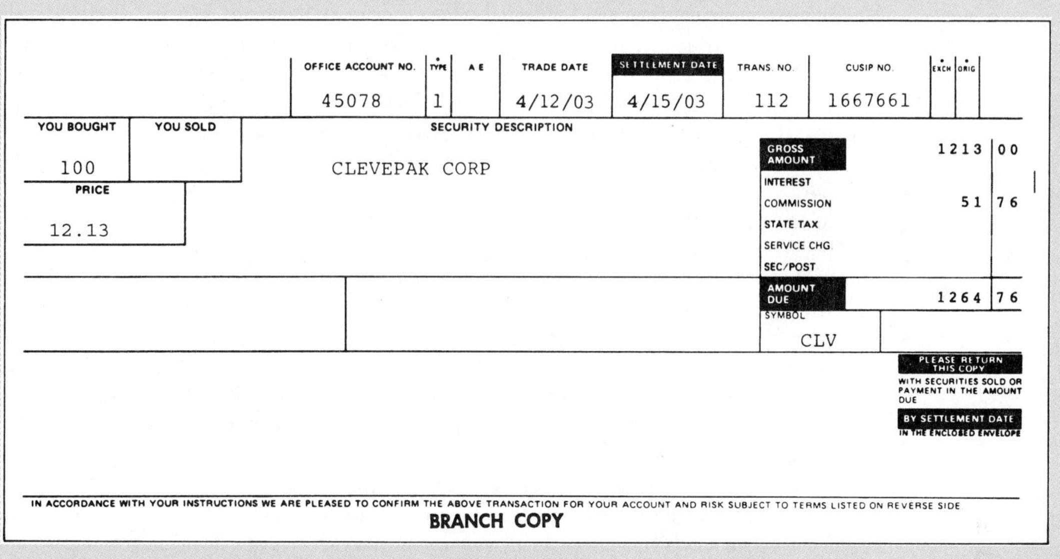

OFFICE ACCOUNT NO.	TYPE	A E	TRADE DATE	SETTLEMENT DATE	TRANS. NO.	CUSIP NO.	EXCH	ORIG
45078	1		4/12/03	4/15/03	112	1667661		

YOU BOUGHT	YOU SOLD	SECURITY DESCRIPTION
100		CLEVEPAK CORP

PRICE: 12.13

GROSS AMOUNT	1213	00
INTEREST		
COMMISSION	51	76
STATE TAX		
SERVICE CHG		
SEC/POST		
AMOUNT DUE	1264	76

SYMBOL: CLV

PLEASE RETURN THIS COPY WITH SECURITIES SOLD OR PAYMENT IN THE AMOUNT DUE BY SETTLEMENT DATE IN THE ENCLOSED ENVELOPE

IN ACCORDANCE WITH YOUR INSTRUCTIONS WE ARE PLEASED TO CONFIRM THE ABOVE TRANSACTION FOR YOUR ACCOUNT AND RISK SUBJECT TO TERMS LISTED ON REVERSE SIDE

BRANCH COPY

Source: Adapted from Scott & Stringfellow, Inc.

of Clevepak Corporation), the unit price ($12.13) and the total amount that is due ($1,264.76).[8] The amount that is due includes both the price of the securities and the transaction fees. The major transaction fee is the brokerage firm's commission, but there may also be state transfer fees and other miscellaneous fees. The investor has three business days after the trade date (the day the security is purchased—April 12, 200x) to pay the amount that is due. The settlement date (the day the payment is due—April 15, 200x) is three business days after the trade date, and this time difference is frequently referred to as $T + 3$.

Cash and Margin Accounts

margin
The amount that an investor must put down to buy securities on credit.

The investor must pay for the securities as they are purchased. This can be done either with cash or with a combination of cash and borrowed funds. The latter is called buying on **margin.** The investor then has either a cash account or a margin account. A cash account is what the name implies: The investor pays the entire cost of the securities (i.e., $1,264.76 in Exhibit 3.5) in cash.

When an investor uses margin—that is, purchases the security partially with cash and partially with credit supplied by the brokers—he or she makes an initial payment that is similar to a down payment on a house and borrows the remaining funds necessary to make the purchase. To open a margin account, the investor signs an agreement with the broker that gives the use of the securities and some control over the account to the broker. The securities serve as collateral for the loan. Should the amount of collateral on the account fall below a specified level, the broker can require that the investor put more assets in the account. This is called a *margin call,* and it may be satisfied by cash or additional securities. If the

[8]The CUSIP in the confirmation statement (1667661) refers to the Committee for Uniform Securities Identification Procedures, which assigns a unique number for each security issue.

investor fails to meet a margin call, the broker will sell some securities in the account to raise the cash needed to protect the loan.

margin requirement
The minimum percentage, established by the Federal Reserve, that the investor must put up in cash to buy securities.

The **margin requirement** is the minimum percentage of the total price that the investor must pay and is set by the Federal Reserve Board. Individual brokers, however, may require more margin. The minimum payment required of the investor is the value of the securities times the margin requirement. Thus, if the margin requirement is 60 percent and the price of 100 shares is $1,000, the investor must supply $600 in cash and borrow $400 from the broker, who in turn borrows the funds from a commercial bank. The investor pays interest to the broker on $400. The interest rate will depend on the rate that the broker must pay to the lending institution. The investor, of course, may avoid the interest charges by paying the entire $1,000 and not using borrowed funds.

Investors use margin to increase the potential return on the investment. When they expect the price of the security to rise, some investors pay for part of their purchases with borrowed funds. If the price rises from 10 to 14, the profit is $400. If the investor pays the entire $1,000, the percentage return is 40 percent. However, if the investor uses margin and pays for the stock with $600 in equity and $400 in borrowed funds, the investor's percentage return is increased (before the interest expense) to 67 percent. In this case, the use of margin is favorable because it increases the investor's return on the invested funds.

Of course, if *the price of the stock falls,* the reverse occurs—that is, *the percentage loss is greater.* If the price falls to $7, the investor loses $300 before commissions on the sale. The percentage loss is 30 percent. However, if the investor uses margin, the percentage loss is increased to 50 percent. Because the investor has borrowed money and thus reduced the amount of funds that he or she has committed to the investment, the percentage loss is greater. The use of margin magnifies not only the potential gain but also the potential loss. Because the potential loss is increased, buying securities on credit increases the element of risk that must be borne by the investor.

Maintenance Margin

The margin requirement establishes the minimum amount the investor must deposit (and the maximum amount the investor may borrow) when purchasing a security. If the price of the stock subsequently rises, the investor's position improves because the amount borrowed as a proportion of the total value of the stock declines. If, however, the value of the stock falls, the investor's position deteriorates and the amount owed becomes a larger proportion of the value of the stock.

maintenance margin
The minimum equity required for a margin position

In order to protect the broker from the investor's defaulting (not repaying the loan), a second margin requirement is established. This **maintenance margin** sets the minimum equity the investor must have in the position. If the stock's price declines sufficiently so that the investor violates the maintenance margin requirement, the investor receives a *margin call* and must advance additional funds or the broker will sell the stock and close the position.

Assume the maintenance margin requirement is 35 percent in the previous illustration. The initial margin requirement was 60 percent, so the investor paid $600 in cash (the investor's equity in the position) and borrowed $400 through the broker. If the investor's equity falls to below 35 percent, additional cash will be required. Suppose the price of the stock declines to $7, and the value of the stock is $700. Since $400 is owed, the investor's equity is $300, which is 42.9 percent of the value of the stock ($300/$700). Since 42.9 exceeds 35 percent, the investor is meeting the maintenance margin requirement. If, however, the price of the stock were $6, the investor's equity is $200—only 33.3 percent ($200/$600 = 33.3%) of the value of the stock. Since the maintenance margin requirement is 35 percent, the required margin is $210 (0.35 × $600). The investor will receive a margin call and be

POINTS OF INTEREST

Determining the Percentage Return on a Margin Purchase, Including Commissions, Interest Paid, and Dividends Received

The body of the text illustrated the potential magnification of the percentage return on a margin purchase versus a cash purchase. The example was an oversimplification because it excluded commissions, interest on any borrowed funds, and dividends received (if any). The following is a more complete illustration.

Assume the investor buys 100 shares of stock for \$10 a share and sells it for \$14. Also assume the margin requirement is 60 percent, the commission rate is 5 percent of the purchase or sale price, the interest rate is 10 percent, and the stock pays a dividend of \$1.00 a share. The following illustrates the two positions:

	Cash	Margin
Sale price	\$1,400	\$1,400
Commission	70	70
Proceeds of sale	1,330	1,330
Loan repayment	0	420
Cash received	1,330	910
Dividends received	\$100	\$100
Interest paid	0	42

Percentage earned on the cash purchase:

$$\frac{\$1{,}330 + \$100 - \$1{,}050}{\$1{,}050} = 36.2$$

Percentage earned on the margin purchase:

$$\frac{\$1{,}330 - \$1{,}050 + \$100 - \$42}{\$630} = 53.7\%$$

Notice that the profit on the purchase and sale (\$1,330 − \$1,050) and the dividend payment are the same in both cases. The difference in the percentage earned is the result of having to pay interest (\$42) and the fact that the investor only put up 60 percent of the funds (\$630) and borrowed \$420. It is the commitment of less than the full purchase price plus commissions and borrowing the balance that is the source of the magnification of the percentage return.

The percentage returns are also different from those in the simple illustration in the body of the text. When commissions, interest, and dividends are included, the return on the all-cash investment is 36.2 percent versus 30 percent in the simplified illustration. The return on the margin investment is 53.7 percent instead of 67 percent because the commissions and interest consume part of the return.

required to commit an additional \$10 to raise the equity to \$210 and meet the maintenance margin requirement.

The price of the stock (P) that triggers a margin call is determined by Equation 3.1, in which B is the amount borrowed per share and MM is the maintenance margin requirement. In this illustration, the price that produces a margin call is

$$P = B/(1 - MM) \tag{3.1}$$

$$P = \$4/(1 - 0.35) = \$6.15$$

At \$6.15 the investor's equity is \$215 (\$615 − \$400) which is 35 percent of the value of the stock (\$215/\$615 = 0.35 = 35%). As long as the price of the stock remains above \$6.15, the investor will not receive a margin call to commit additional cash to meet the maintenance margin requirement.

Delivery of Securities

Once the shares have been purchased and paid for, the investor must decide whether to leave the securities with the broker or to take delivery. (In the case of a margin account, the investor *must* leave the securities with the broker.) If the shares are left with the broker, they will be registered in the brokerage firm's name

street name
The registration of securities in a brokerage firm's name instead of in the buyer's name.

(i.e., in the **street name**). The brokerage firm then becomes custodian of the securities, is responsible for them, and sends a statement of the securities that are being held in the street name to the investor. The statement (usually monthly) also includes any transactions that have taken place and any dividends and interest that have been received. The investor may either leave the dividends and interest payments to accumulate or receive payment from the broker.

A simple example of the general form used for monthly statements is given in Exhibit 3.6.[9] The statement has three parts. The first gives summary data, such as the beginning and closing cash balances and interest and dividends received to date. The summary of dividend and interest income received so far during the year may help the investor plan for income tax purposes. The statement may also include the value of securities for which prices are available. If, for example, a stock is inactively traded (e.g., CCC Communications), price data may not be available.

The second part of the statement gives the activity during the month. In this case, 100 shares of Chesapeake Corp. were purchased and 58 shares of IBM were sold. The investor deposited 220 shares of Conquest Corporation in the account, and no securities were delivered. Dividends were received from two companies, and the NJ Housing Authority bond paid $150 in interest. Also during the month, the investor deposited $2,000 in the account but later withdrew $6,070.10.

The last part of the statement enumerates the various securities (i.e., positions) held in street name by the brokerage firm for the investor. This information may include the number of shares or principal amount of debt, the ticker symbol (if available), prices of the securities on the statement's closing day, and the value of each holding. In this case the investor owns stock in seven companies and $5,000 face amount of bonds.

The main advantage of leaving the securities with the brokerage firm is convenience, and the vast majority of investors (possibly in excess of 95 percent) have their securities registered in street name. The investor does not have to store the securities and can readily sell them, since they are in the brokerage firm's possession. The accrued interest and dividends may be viewed as a kind of forced savings program, for they may be immediately reinvested before the investor has an opportunity to spend the money elsewhere. The statements are a readily accessible source of information for tax purposes.

The requirement that securities be paid for within three days after purchase or delivered within three days after sale is often used by brokerage firms as an argument for registering securities in street name. Many brokerage firms require investors to have the securities or cash in their accounts before executing sales or purchases. As an additional deterrent, some brokerage firms charge for the delivery of securities.

Brokerage firms, however, cannot require the investor to leave the securities in the street name.[10] There are also important disadvantages to leaving the securities in the brokerage firm's name. If the brokerage firm fails or becomes insolvent, the investor may encounter difficulty in transferring the securities to his or her name and even greater difficulty in collecting any accrued dividends and interest.[11] In addition, because the securities are registered in the brokerage firm's name, interim financial statements, annual reports, and other announcements that are sent by the firm to its stockholders may be mailed to the brokerage firm and not to the investor.[12]

[9]Statements sent by brokerage firms may include considerably more information than is illustrated in Exhibit 3.6. This additional information may cover (1) the asset allocation of the various investments by type (e.g., stocks, fixed income, money market mutual funds), (2) year-to-date portfolio performance and major stock indices, (3) cost basis of the securities and unrealized gains, and (4) dividends to be received in the next period.

[10]There are exceptions, because some debt instruments (e.g., municipal bonds) are issued only as "book" entries. No certificates are created, so the "securities" must be registered in the street name.

[11]The Securities Investor Protection Corporation (SIPC) has reduced the investor's risk of loss from the failure of a brokerage firm. SIPC is discussed later in this chapter.

[12]Some corporations maintain lists of stockholders who registered their securities in the street name and mail statements directly to these investors.

EXHIBIT 3.6

Adapted Brokerage Firm Monthly Statement

Statement of Security Account

Account #876 55352
SS# or ID# 123 45 4321
Account Executive A. B. Broker, III

Statement Period	Financial Summary	
Beginning 06-29-XX	Opening Money Balance	$.00
Ending 07-30-XX	Closing Money Balance	$120.00
	Priced Portfolio Balance	$54,073.49

Year-to-Date	
Dividends	$1200.00
Interest	.00
Municipal Bond Interest	150.00

Activity for This Period

Date	Bought/ Received	Sold/ Delivered	Description	Price	Amount Charged	Amount Credited
07-01			GC&B	Div		160.00
07-01			NJ Housing Auth.	Int		150.00
07-03			Funds received			2000.00
07-04	100		Chesapeake Corp.	19	1950.00	
07-10		58	IBM	100		5710.10
07-13			Check balance		6070.10	
07-25	220		Conquest Corp.	Rec		
07-25			Harsco	Div		120.00

Positions

Long		Ticker Symbol	Price	Value
200	CCC Communications	NA°	NA°	NA
250	Chesapeake Corporation	CSK	20	5000.00
220	Conquest Corporation	CQX	2	440.00
300	GC&B	GCB	58.38	17514.00
400	Harsco	HSC	27.50	11000.00
259	Georgia Pacific	GP	49.11	12719.49
100	Oracle	ORCL	24	2400.00
5000	NJ Housing Auth. 6.00% 07-01-05	NA†	100	5000.00

°The symbols and prices of inactively traded OTC stocks may not be reported.
†Ticker symbols do not apply to municipal bonds.

This disadvantage, however, has diminished and perhaps ceased because the investor may access a firm's financial statements through the Internet.

trader
An investor who frequently buys and sells.

Whether the investor ultimately decides to leave the securities with the broker or to take delivery depends on the individual. If the investor frequently buys and sells securities (i.e., is a **trader**), the securities ought to be left with the broker to facilitate the transactions. If the investor is satisfied with the services of the broker and is convinced that the firm is financially secure, leaving the securities registered in the street name may be justified for reasons of convenience.

If the investor chooses to take delivery of the securities, that individual receives the stock certificates or bonds. Because the certificates may become negotiable, the investor may suffer a loss if they are stolen. Therefore, care should be taken to store them in a safe place (e.g., a lockbox or safe-deposit box in a bank). If the certificates are lost or destroyed, they can be replaced, but only at considerable expense in terms of money and effort.[13]

The Cost of Investing

commissions
Fees charged by brokers for executing orders.

Investing, like everything else, is not free. The individual must pay certain costs, the most obvious of which are **commission** fees. There may also be transfer fees, and while these last expenses tend to be trivial, they can add up as the dollar value or the number of trades increases.

Commission costs are not trivial, and for small investors they may constitute a substantial portion of the total amount spent on the investment. Commission rates are supposed to be set by supply and demand, but in reality only large investors (e.g., financial institutions such as insurance companies or mutual funds) are able to negotiate commissions with brokerage firms. These institutions do such a large dollar volume that they are able to negotiate lower rates. For these institutions, the commission rates (as a percentage of the dollar amount of the transaction) may be small.

Individuals, however, do not have this influence and generally have to accept the rate that is offered by the brokerage firm. Although the fee schedule may not be made public by the brokerage firm, the registered representative will generally tell (if asked) the investor what the fee will be before executing the transaction.

In general, commission rates are quoted in terms of round lots of 100 shares. Most firms also set a minimum commission fee (e.g., $50) that may cover all transactions involving $1,000 or less. Then, as the value of the 100 shares increases to greater than $1,000, the fee also increases. However, this commission fee as a percentage of the dollar value of the transaction will usually fall.

discount broker
A broker who charges lower commissions on security purchases and sales.

Some brokerage firms, known as **discount brokers**, offer lower commissions. (Full-service brokers may offer discounts, but the investor must ask for them. Receiving the requested discount will depend on such factors as the volume of trades generated by the investor.) Discount brokerage firms do not offer the range of services available through the full-service brokerage houses, but if the individual does not need these services, discount brokers may help to reduce the cost of investing by decreasing commissions.

Investors may further reduce commission costs by trading on-line. Firms that offer this service initially charged substantially lower commissions than were assessed by discount brokers. Even discount brokerage firms like Charles Schwab offered its customers discounts from its regular commissions if these investors used its electronic trading system. Obviously, individuals who feel comfortable using on-line trading and who do not need regular brokerage services may be able to obtain substantial reductions in the cost of buying and selling securities.

Even among the on-line brokers there are perceptible differences in commissions. Discount brokers like Schwab, which offers lower commissions for its customers who trade on-line, have even lower commissions for frequent traders. These commissions, however, exceed the rates charged by the deep-discount cyberbrokers such as Ameritrade (http://www.ameritrade.com), E*TRADE secu-

[13]For example, the financial statements of Dominion Resources direct stockholders who lost certificates to write the transfer agent for instructions on how to obtain replacements. Bond is required to protect the stockholder and the transfer agent should the lost certificates return to circulation. The cost of the bond is 2 percent of the current market value (not the investor's cost) of the stock plus a processing fee.

EXHIBIT 3.7

Effect of the Spread on the Cost of Investing

Purchase price	Brokerage commission	Total cost
$2,100.00	$61.80	$2,161.80
Sale price	Commission	Total received
$2,000.00	$61.00	$1,939.00
Net loss (total cost minus total received = net loss)		
$2,161.80 − $1,939.00 = $222.80		

rities (http://www.etrade.com), or Ameritrade Plus (http://www.ameritradeplus.com), which offer no-frills on-line service. These cheapest electronic brokers may not be the cheapest means to invest if the individual has to buy other services or sources of information. Some higher-priced on-line brokers provide access to research and other services that justify the higher costs. Comparison of costs and services may be found in such publications as *AAII Computerized Investing*. Presumably, such publications maintain currency in their comparisons of on-line brokerage firms, their costs, and services provided.

The Spread

Whereas commissions and other fees are explicit costs, there is also an important implicit cost of investing. This cost is the spread between the bid and the ask prices of the security. As was explained earlier in this chapter, the investor pays the ask price but receives only the bid price when the securities are sold. This spread should be viewed as a cost of investing. Thus, if an investor wants to buy 100 shares of a stock quoted 20–21, he or she will have to pay $2,100 plus commissions to buy stock that is currently worth (if it were to be sold) only $2,000. If the commission rate is 2.5 percent on purchases and sales, the cost of a round trip in the security (i.e., a purchase and a subsequent sale) is substantial. The total cost is illustrated in Exhibit 3.7. First, the investor pays $61.80 to buy the stock, for a total cost of $2,161.80 ($2,100 + $61.80). If the stock is then sold, the investor receives $1,939. Although the investor paid $2,161.80, only $1,939 is received if the stock is sold at the bid price. The total cost of this purchase and the subsequent sale exceeds $220. Thus, the bid price of the security must rise sufficiently to cover both the commission fees and the spread before the investor realizes any capital appreciation.

Another possible cost of investing is any impact on the price of the stock. If the portfolio manager of a mutual fund wants to buy (or sell) 50,000 shares of a stock, it is highly unlikely that this order can be filled without it affecting the stock's price. To fill the buy order, the market makers may have to raise the price to induce other investors to sell. This price effect may even apply to stocks that trade over a million shares daily. For stocks with only a modest number of shares outstanding, filling the order can certainly increase (or decrease in the case of a sale) the price. Any impact on the price of the security should be considered as a cost of investing.

To understand this potential cost, consider a market order to buy 600 shares of a small OTC stock with an asking price of $12. The total anticipated outlay is $7,200 (before commissions). The dealer, however, fills the order with 350 shares at $12 and 250 shares at $12.10 for a total outlay of $7,225. The $25 is an additional cost of buying the stock. The market was insufficiently deep to accept the market order without affecting the stock's price.

This illustration also points out the risk associated with a market order. Since the asking price was $12, the investor might assume that he or she can buy any number of shares, but that is not the case. To avoid the possibility of two transactions (and possibly two commission fees), the investor may ask the broker how many shares are being offered at the asking price. If the answer is 350 shares, there is no reason to expect that a market order for 600 shares will be filled at $12.

The investor could place an "all-or-nothing order" at the specified price, in which case he or she buys the entire 600 shares if they become available at the asking price. Once again, there is no assurance the order will be fulfilled. Thus, the investor may specify the complete order (i.e., price and all-or-nothing) and accept the risk that the order will not be filled. Or the investor may place a market order with the assurance that the order will be filled but accept the risk that the price may be affected by the size of the order.[14]

The Short Sale

short sale
The sale of borrowed securities in anticipation of a price decline; a contract for future delivery.

How does an investor make money in the security markets? The obvious answer is to buy at low prices and to sell at high prices. For most people this implies that the investor first buys the security and then sells it at some later date. Can the investor sell the security first and buy it back later at a lower price? The answer is yes, for a **short sale** reverses the order. The investor sells the security first with the intention of purchasing it in the future at a lower price.

Because the sale precedes the purchase, the investor does not own the securities that are being sold short. Selling something that a person does not own may sound illegal, but there are many examples of such short selling in normal business relationships. A magazine publisher who sells a subscription, a professional such as a lawyer, engineer, or teacher who signs a contract for future services, and a manufacturer who signs a contract for future delivery are all making short sales. When your school collected the semester's tuition, it established a short position; it contracted for the future delivery of educational services. If the cost of fulfilling the contract increases, the short seller loses. If the cost declines, the short seller profits. Selling securities short is essentially no different: It is a current sale with a contract for future delivery. If the securities are subsequently purchased at a lower price, the short seller will profit. However, if the cost of the securities rises in the future, the short seller will suffer a loss.

The mechanics of the short sale can be illustrated by a simple example employing the stock of XYZ, Inc. If the current price of the stock is $50 per share, the investor may buy 100 shares at $50 per share for a total cost of $5,000. Such a purchase represents taking a long position in the stock. If the price subsequently rises to $75 per share and the stock is sold, the investor will earn a profit of $2,500 ($7,500 − $5,000).

The short position reverses this procedure: The investor sells the stock first and buys it back at some time in the future. For example, an investor sells 100 shares of XYZ short at $50 ($5,000). Such a sale is made because the investor believes that the stock is *overpriced* and that the price of the stock will *fall*. In a short sale the investor does not own the 100 shares sold. The buyer of the shares, however, certainly expects delivery of the stock certificate. (Actually, the buyer does not know

[14]The author experienced this illustration when he placed an order for 600 shares of a small company traded OTC. Initially, 350 shares were purchased at $12 and 250 shares were purchased at $12.25. The broker allocated the commission costs over the two purchases so only one commission was charged. This experience taught me to ask the broker how many shares the dealer is offering to buy or sell at the bid and ask prices, and then decide whether to place a market order or an all-or-nothing order. This information may also be obtained through detailed quotes when using an on-line broker.

FIGURE 3.1

The Flow of Money and Certificates in a Short Sale

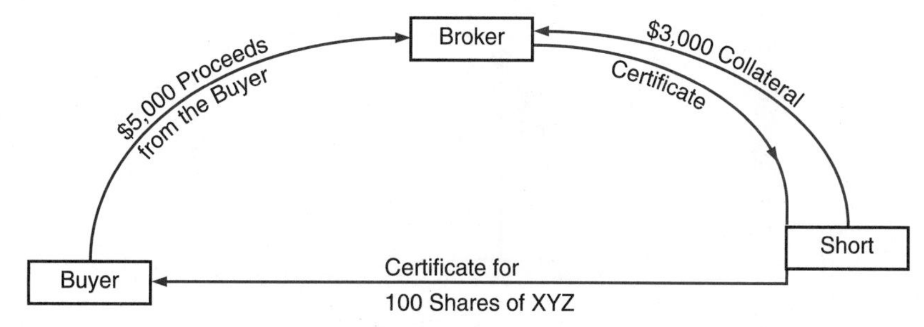

if the shares come from an investor who is selling short or an investor who is liquidating a position in the security.) The short seller has to *borrow* 100 shares to deliver to the buyer. The shares are usually borrowed from a broker, who in turn probably borrows them from clients who have left their securities with the broker. (Shares held in a margin account may be used by the broker, and one such possible use is to lend the shares to a short seller. However, shares left with the broker in a cash account cannot be lent to a short seller.)

covering the short sale
The purchase of securities to close a short position.

Although the investor has sold the securities, the proceeds of the sale are not delivered to the seller but are held by the broker. These proceeds will be subsequently used to repurchase the shares. (In the jargon of security markets such repurchases are referred to as **covering the short sale**.) In addition, the short seller must deposit with the broker an amount of money equal to the margin requirement for the purchase of the stock. Thus, if the margin requirement is 60 percent, the short seller in the illustration must deposit $3,000 ($5,000 × 0.6) with the broker. This money protects the broker (i.e., it is the short seller's collateral) and is returned to the short seller plus any profits or minus any losses when he or she buys the shares and returns them to the broker. This flow of certificates and money is illustrated in Figure 3.1. The broker receives the money from the short seller (the $3,000 collateral) and from the buyer of the stock (the $5,000 in proceeds from the sale). The investor who sells the stock short receives nothing, but the borrowed securities flow through this investor's account en route to the buyer. The buyer then receives the securities and remits the funds to pay for them.

If the price of a share declines to $40, the short seller can buy the stock for $4,000. This purchase is no different from any purchase made on an exchange or in the over-the-counter market. The stock is then returned to the broker, and the loan of the stock is repaid. The short seller will have made a profit of $1,000 because the shares were purchased for $4,000 and sold for $5,000. The investor's collateral is then returned by the broker plus the $1,000 profit. These events are illustrated in Figure 3.2. The 100 shares of XYZ stock are purchased for $4,000 by the short seller. When the certificate for the 100 shares is received, it is returned by the short seller to the broker (who, in turn, returns the shares to whomever they were borrowed from). The broker returns the investor's $3,000 that was put up for collateral. Since the investor uses only $4,000 of the $5,000 in proceeds from the short sale to purchase the stock, the broker sends the investor the remainder of the proceeds (the $1,000 profit).

If the price of the stock had risen to $60 per share and the short seller had purchased the shares and returned them to the broker, the short position would have

FIGURE 3.2

The Flow of Money and Certificates When Covering a Profitable Short Sale

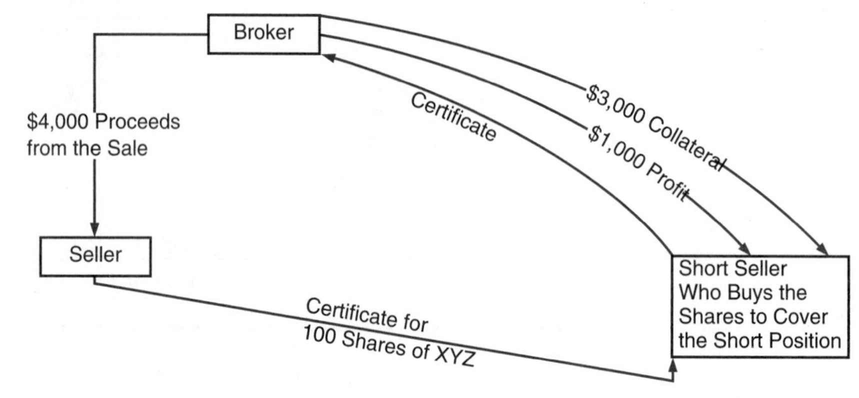

resulted in a $1,000 loss. The proceeds from the short sale would have been insufficient to purchase the shares. One thousand dollars of the collateral would have had to be used in addition to the proceeds to buy the stock and cover the short position. The broker would owe the short seller only what was left of the collateral ($2,000) after the transactions had been completed.

Although the previous transactions may sound complicated, they really are not. All that has occurred is that an investor has bought and sold a security. Instead of the investor's first purchasing the security and then selling it, the investor initially sold the security and subsequently purchased the shares to cover the short position. Because the sale occurred first, there is additional bookkeeping to account for the borrowed securities, but the transaction itself is not complicated.

Unfortunately, many individuals believe that short selling is gambling. They believe that if investors sell short and the price of the stock rises substantially, the losses could result in financial ruin. However, short sellers can protect themselves by placing stop-loss purchase orders to cover the short position if the stock's price rises to a particular level. Furthermore, if these investors fail to place stop-loss orders, the brokers will cover the position for them once their collateral has shrunk and can no longer support the short position. Thus, the amount that an investor can lose is limited to the collateral. Short selling really involves no greater risk than purchasing securities, for investors who buy securities can lose all their invested funds.

Actually, short selling is consistent with a rational approach to the selection of securities. If an investor analyzes a company and finds that its securities are overpriced, the investor will certainly not buy the securities, and any that are currently owned should be sold. In addition, if the individual has confidence in the analysis and believes that the price will decline, the investor may sell short. The short sale, then, is the logical strategy given the basic analysis. Securities that are overpriced should be considered for short sales, just as securities that the investor believes are undervalued are the logical choice for purchase.

Short selling is not limited to individual investors; market makers may also sell short. If there is an influx of orders to buy, the market makers may partially satisfy this demand by selling short. They will then repurchase the shares in the future to cover the short position after the influx of orders has subsided. Frequently, this transaction can be profitable. After the speculative increase in price that results from the increased demand, the price of the security may decline. When this occurs, the market makers profit because they sell short when the price rises but cover their positions after the price subsequently falls.

The Uptick Rule

There is one important constraint on an investor's ability to sell short: the *uptick* rule. An investor may buy stock and sell existing holdings at will, but the uptick rule is a major constraint on selling short, which is designed to stop price manipulation by short sellers.

Uptick refers to the direction of price change. If the price of a stock moves up from the previous trade, that is an uptick. If the price of the stock declines from the previous trade, that is a downtick. Short sales can be executed only when the previous change in the price of the stock was an uptick. Thus, if the price of the stock moves from $10 to $9.90, a short sale cannot be executed. If, however, the price moves back to $10 from $9.90, that is an uptick and a short sale may be made.[15]

The purpose of the uptick rule is to reduce the ability of investors and speculators to manipulate the market. Without this regulation, short sellers could borrow large quantities of stock that, when sold, would drive down the stock's price. By such manipulation, the short sellers could guarantee themselves profits. By instituting the uptick rule, the SEC has reduced the ability of short sellers to manipulate the market for their own benefit.

Short-Interest Ratio

The short selling of a stock requires that the shares must eventually be repurchased. Such repurchases imply future demand for the stock, which may increase its price. Of course, the argument could be expressed in reverse. Increased short selling suggests that those in the know are anticipating lower stock prices. For either reason, some investors track short sales as a means to forecast price changes.

Such tracking requires obtaining data on short sales. The number of shares that have been sold short is referred to as the *short interest.* Since companies have differing amounts of stock outstanding, the absolute number of shares sold short may be meaningless. Instead, the number of shares short is often divided by the number of shares outstanding and expressed as the *short-interest ratio.* An alternative ratio considers the number of shares sold short relative to the average daily trading. If this ratio exceeds 1.0, that means more than one day's volume has been sold short. A ratio of less than 1.0 suggests the opposite: The average daily volume exceeds the number of shares sold short.

The number of shares sold short and the short-interest ratio are readily available; they are published monthly in financial publications such as *The Wall Street Journal* or national newspapers such as *The New York Times.*[16] Depending on the investor's interpretation, an increase in the short-interest ratio suggests that short sellers will ultimately have to repurchase the shares or it suggests that investors are becoming more bearish and are selling the stock in anticipation of a price decline.

If an investor does sell short, there is always the possibility of being unable to repurchase the shares. Such a situation is referred to as a *short squeeze.* A short squeeze occurs when short sellers are unable to buy the stock to close their positions. This results in their bidding up the price as they frantically seek to buy the stock before its price rises further. Such a short squeeze is unlikely in a stock for

[15]An uptick refers to the last change in price. If a stock trades for $10 and then trades for $9.90, $9.90, $9.90, and $9.90, the last change was down. Until the stock rises (e.g., to $9.92), the last change was a downtick.

[16]Data on the short interest may also be located through Multex Investor (http://www.multexinvestor.com) under the heading "Performance Report" for a specific stock. The data include (1) the number of shares sold short, (2) shares sold short as a percentage of shares outstanding, and (3) the number of days necessary to cover existing short positions based on the average volume of daily transactions.

which there are many shares outstanding and that actively trades. If, however, the stock has only a few shares publicly traded, the possibility does exist that short sellers will be unable to buy shares, which pushes up the price as the short sellers panic and bid increasingly higher prices to close their positions. (The short squeeze essentially applies to commodity markets. If the long positions can control the supply of the commodity, that is, obtain a monopoly or a "corner on the market" for the commodity, they can demand virtually any price from the shorts, who must pay in order to cover their positions.)

Foreign Securities

Foreign companies, like U.S. companies, issue a variety of securities as a means to acquire funds. These securities subsequently trade on foreign exchanges or foreign over-the-counter markets. For example, there are stock exchanges in London, Paris, Tokyo, and other foreign financial centers. Unless Americans and other foreigners are forbidden to acquire these securities, Americans can buy and sell stocks through these exchanges in much the same way that they purchase domestic U.S. stocks and bonds. Thus, foreign securities may be purchased through the use of U.S. brokers who have access to trading on these exchanges. In many cases this access is obtained through a correspondent relationship with foreign security brokers.

Foreign securities may differ from U.S. securities. Consider terminology, for example. In Britain a "debenture" is a debt obligation secured by the firm's assets, while in the United States a debenture is an unsecured, general obligation of the company. Foreign dividends are usually paid semiannually or annually, and the amount is expressed as a percentage of par and not as an amount, as is done in the United States (e.g., 10% of $2 par instead of $0.20). The unit of trading may be greater than the 100-share round lot used in the United States. Foreign investors, such as Americans, may be limited to acquiring only nonvoting shares. This practice is common in developing nations in which only nationals may own voting stock and foreign investors own stock that lacks voting power. Such a practice keeps control within the country.

There are also differences in business practices. For example, Japanese firms use more debt financing (financial leverage) than is customary in the United States. It is not unusual for more than three-fourths of a Japanese firm's assets to be financed with debt. Accounting practices, such as the consolidation of subsidiaries' balance sheets or the depreciation of assets, differ from U.S. generally accepted accounting practices. Such differences make comparisons of foreign and U.S. accounting data exceedingly difficult.

By far, the easiest way to acquire foreign stocks is to purchase the shares of firms that are traded in the United States on an exchange or through the Nasdaq stock market. To be eligible for such trading, the foreign securities must be registered with the SEC. As of 1998, over 300 foreign stocks were traded on the NYSE and many more were traded on the AMEX and through Nasdaq. Exhibit 3.8 provides a sample of these securities and includes the company, the country of origin, its primary industry, and where the shares are traded. As may be seen in the exhibit, many foreign stocks, such as SONY and Royal Dutch Airlines, are traded on the New York Stock Exchange. Others, such as BAT Industries (British Tobacco), trade on the American Stock Exchange, and many others trade through Nasdaq.[17] The majority of the firms whose securities are actively traded in the United States are either Japanese or Canadian.

[17]Foreign stock exchanges may also list U.S. securities. The London Stock Exchange is the most liberal and actually encourages foreign listings.

EXHIBIT 3.8

Selected Foreign Securities Traded on the New York Stock Exchange, on the American Stock Exchange, and through Nasdaq

Firm	Country of Origin	Primary Industry	Where Traded in the United States
Alcan Aluminum	Canada	Aluminum	NYSE
BAT Industries	Great Britain	Tobacco products	AMEX
Campbell Resources	Canada	Gold mining	NYSE
Hitachi	Japan	Electronics	NYSE
Japan Airlines	Japan	Airline	Nasdaq
KLM Royal Dutch Airlines	Netherlands	Airline	NYSE
Kloof Gold Mines	South Africa	Gold mining	Nasdaq
Sony	Japan	Electronics	NYSE
TDK	Japan	Electronics	NYSE
Volkswagenwerk	Germany	Automobiles	Nasdaq

American Depositary Receipts (ADRs)
Receipts issued for foreign securities held by a trustee.

These domestic markets do not actually trade the foreign shares but trade receipts for the stock, called **American Depositary Receipts (ADRs)** or American Depositary Shares. These receipts are created by large financial institutions such as commercial banks. The ADRs are sold to the public and continue to trade in the United States.[18]

There are two types of ADRs. *Sponsored* ADRs are created when the firm wants the securities to trade in the United States. The firm employs a bank to perform the paperwork to create the ADRs and to act as transfer agent. In this case the costs are absorbed by the firm. All ADRs listed on the NYSE and AMEX are sponsored ADRs. *Unsponsored* ADRs are created when a brokerage firm believes there will be sufficient interest in a stock or bond to make a market in the security. The brokerage firm buys a block of securities and hires a commercial bank to create the ADRs and to act as transfer agent. However, fees for this service and for converting dividend payments from the foreign currency into U.S. dollars will be paid by the stockholders, not the issuing firm.

The creation of ADRs greatly facilitates trading in foreign securities. First, ADRs reduce the risk of fraud. If the investor purchased a foreign stock issued by a Japanese firm, the stock certificate would be written in Japanese. It is highly unlikely that the U.S. investor could read the language, and thus the investor could become prey to bogus certificates. ADRs erase that risk, since the certificates are in English and their authenticity is certified by the issuing agent. The investor is assured that the receipt is genuine even though it is an obligation of the issuing agent. The ADR represents only the underlying securities held by the agent and is not an obligation of the foreign firm that issued the stock.

Besides reducing the risk of fraud, ADRs are convenient. Securities do not have to be delivered through international mail, prices are quoted in dollars, and dividend payments are received in dollars. The ADR can represent any number of foreign shares. For example, one ADR of Telefonos de Mexico, which is traded on the NYSE, represents 20 regular Mexican shares.

If there are no ADRs issued for the stock the investor wants to purchase, then the actual foreign securities will have to be acquired. The individual instructs the

[18]Information concerning foreign securities (e.g., financials, earnings estimates, prices, and linkages to the company) may be found at http://www.adr.com, a Web site that is a joint project of J. P. Morgan and the Carson Group.

broker to purchase the foreign stock in the appropriate foreign market. As with any other security purchase, the shares or bonds are acquired through exchanges or over the counter from dealers who make a market in the security. The trading practices followed by foreign exchanges need not coincide with U.S. practices. For example, after a stock is purchased, a settlement date is established at which time payment is due. This settlement date may not coincide with the U.S. practice of payment due after three business days. However, such differences are more a matter of detail than substance and are diminishing with increased global investing. After the purchases are completed, the investor may choose to leave the securities registered with the broker or may take delivery.

The prices of a number of foreign stocks are given daily in the U.S. financial press. For example, *The Wall Street Journal* gives prices for selected securities traded on several foreign exchanges. The information is limited to prices—there is no reporting of volume of transactions, dividends, or P/E ratios. The number of foreign stock prices reported in the U.S. press is small compared to the population of foreign stocks. If the investor seeks to track the prices of many foreign stocks, that will require access to a foreign publication, such as the *Financial Times,* a British newspaper that is comparable to *The Wall Street Journal.*

Regulation

Like many industries, the securities industry is subject to a substantial degree of regulation both from the federal and from state governments. Since the majority of securities are traded across state lines, most regulation is at the federal level.

The purpose of these laws is to protect the investor by ensuring honest and fair practices. The laws require that the investor be provided with information upon which to base decisions. Hence, these acts are frequently referred to as the **full disclosure laws**, because publicly owned companies must inform the public of certain facts relating to their firms. The regulations also attempt to prevent fraud and the manipulation of stock prices. However, they do not try to protect investors from their own folly and greed. The purpose of legislation governing the securities industry is not to ensure that investors will profit from their investments; instead, the laws try to provide fair market practices while allowing investors to make their own mistakes.

full disclosure laws
The federal and state laws requiring publicly held firms to disclose financial and other information that may affect the value of their securities.

Although current federal regulation developed during the 1930s as a direct result of the debacle in the security markets during the early part of that decade, state regulations started in 1911 with the pioneering legislation in the state of Kansas. These state laws are frequently called *blue sky laws* because fraudulent securities were referred to as pieces of blue sky. Although there are differences among the state laws, they generally require that (1) security firms and brokers be licensed, (2) financial information concerning issues of new securities be filed with state regulatory bodies, (3) new securities meet specific standards before they are sold, and (4) regulatory bodies be established to enforce the laws.

The Federal Security Laws

The first modern federal legislation governing the securities industry was the Security Act of 1933, which primarily concerns the issuing of new securities. It requires that new securities be "registered" with the Securities and Exchange Commission (SEC). As discussed in Chapter 2, registration consists of supplying the SEC with information concerning the firm, the nature of its business and competition, and its financial position. This information is then summarized in the prospectus (refer to Exhibit 2.1), which makes the formal offer to sell the securities to the public.

EXHIBIT 3.9

Summary of the Objectives of the SEC

1. To ensure that individuals have sufficient information to make informed investment decisions.
2. To provide the public with information by the registration of corporate securities prior to their sale to the general public, and to require timely and regular disclosure of corporate information and financial statements.
3. To prevent manipulation of security prices by regulating trading in the securities markets; by requiring insiders to register the buying and selling of securities; and by regulating the activities of corporate officers and directors.
4. To regulate investment companies (e.g., mutual funds) and investment advisors.
5. To work in conjunction with the Federal Reserve to limit the use of credit to acquire securities.
6. To supervise the regulation of member firms, brokers, and security dealers by working with the National Association of Securities Dealers, which is the self-regulatory association of brokers and dealers.

Information concerning the SEC may be found in Samuel L. Hayes III, ed., *Wall Street and Regulation* (Boston: Harvard Business School Press, 1987) and K. Fred Skousen, *An Introduction to the SEC*, 5th ed. (Cincinnati: South-Western/Thomson Learning, 1990).

The most recent information concerning the SEC may be found at its Web site: http://www.sec.gov.

Once the SEC has determined that all material facts that may affect the value of the firm have been disclosed, the securities are released for sale. When the securities are sold, the buyer must be given a copy of the prospectus. If the investor incurs a loss on an investment in a new issue of securities, a suit may be filed to recover the loss if the prospectus or the registration statement that was filed with the SEC contained false or misleading information. Liability for this loss may rest on the firm, its executives and directors, the brokerage firm selling the securities, and any experts (e.g., accountants, appraisers) who were employed in preparing the documents. Owing to this legal accountability, those involved exercise caution and diligence in the preparation of the prospectus and the registration statement.

Although the Securities Act of 1933 applies only to new issues, the Securities Exchange Act of 1934 (and subsequent amendments) extends the regulation to existing securities. This act forbids market manipulation, deception and misrepresentation of facts, and fraudulent practices. The SEC was also created by this act to enforce the laws pertaining to the securities industry. A summary of the SEC's objectives is provided in Exhibit 3.9.

Under the Securities Exchange Act of 1934, publicly held companies are required to keep current the information on file with the SEC. This is achieved by having the firm file an annual report (called the *10-K report*) with the SEC. The 10-K report contains a substantial amount of factual information concerning the firm, and this information is usually sent in summary form to the stockholders in the company's annual report. (Companies must upon request and without charge send a copy of the 10-K report to stockholders. The 10-K report may also be obtained from EDGAR, which is described in the next chapter on sources of information.)

Firms are also required to release any information during the year that may materially affect the value of their securities. Information concerning new discoveries, lawsuits, or a merger must be disseminated to the general public. The SEC has the power to suspend trading in a company's securities for up to ten days if, in its opinion, the public interest and the protection of investors necessitate such a ban on trading. If a firm fails to keep investors informed, the SEC can suspend trading pending the release of the required information. Such a suspension is a drastic act and is seldom used, for most companies frequently issue news releases that inform the investing public of significant changes affecting the firm. Sometimes the company itself asks to have trading in its securities halted until a news release can be prepared and disseminated.

POINTS OF INTEREST

Illegal Use of Inside Information

The use of inside (privileged) information for personal gain is illegal. Management cannot buy a stock, make an announcement that causes the value of the stock to rise, and then sell the stock for a profit. If insiders do this, the corporation or its stockholders may sue, and if the defendants are found guilty, any profits must be returned to the corporation.

The law does not forbid insiders from buying and subsequently selling the stock. However, the Securities Exchange Act of 1934 requires that each officer, director, and major stockholder (i.e., any individual who owns more than 5 percent of the stock) of a publicly held corporation must file a report with the SEC disclosing the amount of stock held. These individuals must also file a monthly report if there are any changes in the holdings. This information is subsequently published by the SEC. If these insiders make a profit on a transaction that is completed (i.e., the stock is bought and sold) within six months, it is assumed the profit is the result of illegally using confidential corporate information.

Individuals who may be considered insiders are not limited to the corporation's officers and directors. An insider is any individual with "material information" not yet disclosed to the public. Material information implies information that could reasonably be expected to affect the value of the firm's securities. The individual need not necessarily be employed by the firm but could have access to inside information through business relationships, family ties, or being informed (tipped off) by insiders. Use of such privileged information even by nonemployees is also illegal. In one of the most famous cases concerning the illegal use of inside information, several officers and directors of Texas Gulf Sulfur became aware of new mineral discoveries. Their stock purchases, along with purchases made by individuals they had informed, were ruled illegal. Thus, an insider who may not directly profit through the use of inside information cannot pass that information to another party who profits from using that knowledge.

The disclosure laws do not require that the company tell everything about its operations. All firms have trade secrets that they do not want known by their competitors. The purpose of the full disclosure laws is not to restrict the corporation but (1) to inform the investors so that they can make intelligent decisions and (2) to prevent a firm's employees from using privileged information for personal gain.

It should be obvious that employees, ranging from president of the company to mailroom clerk, may have access to information before it reaches the general public. Such information (called *inside information*) may significantly enhance the employees' ability to make profits by buying or selling the company's securities before the announcement is made. Such profiteering from inside information is illegal. Officers and directors of the company must report their holdings and any changes in their holdings of the firm's securities to the SEC.[19] Thus, it is possible for the SEC to determine if transactions have been made prior to any public announcement that affected the value of the securities. If insiders do profit illegally from the use of such information, they may be prosecuted under criminal law and their gains may have to be surrendered to the firm.

Other Regulations

Although the Securities Act of 1933 and the Securities Exchange Act of 1934 are the backbone of regulations, subsequent laws have been passed. These include the Public Holding Company Act of 1935, which reorganized the utility industry by requiring better methods of financial accounting and more thorough reporting and by constraining the use of debt financing. The Investment Company Act of

[19]The use of reports of insider transactions to forecast stock prices is discussed in Chapter 9 in the section on the efficient market hypothesis.

1940 extended the regulations to include mutual funds and other investment companies. The most recent act of importance is the Securities Investor Protection Act of 1970, which is designed to protect investors from brokerage firm failures and bankruptcies. The act also created the Securities Investor Protection Corporation, which is discussed in the following section.

In addition to the laws affecting the issuing of securities and their subsequent trading, laws require disclosure by investment advisors (the Investment Advisers Act of 1940). Investment advisory services and individuals who "engage for compensation in the business of advising others about securities shall register" with the SEC.[20] This registration brings investment advisors within the regulation of the SEC. Under this law, investment advisors must disclose their backgrounds, business affiliations, and the compensation charged for their services. Failure to register with the SEC can lead to an injunction against supplying the service or to prosecution for violating securities laws.

Besides the state and federal securities laws, the industry itself regulates its members. The stock exchanges and the trade association, the National Association of Securities Dealers, have established codes of behavior for their members. These include relationships between brokers and customers, the auditing of members' accounts, and proficiency tests for brokers. While such rules may not have the force of law, they can have a significant impact on the quality and credibility of the industry and its representatives.

Securities Investor Protection Corporation

Most investors are aware that accounts in virtually all commercial banks are insured by the Federal Deposit Insurance Corporation (FDIC—http://www.fdic.gov). As of 2002, should an insured commercial bank fail, the FDIC reimburses the depositor for any losses up to $100,000. If a depositor has more than $100,000 on account at the time of the commercial bank's failure, the depositor becomes a general creditor for the additional funds.

This insurance has greatly increased the stability of the commercial banking system. Small depositors know that their funds are safe and therefore do not panic if a commercial bank fails (as one occasionally does). This stability simply did not exist before the formation of the FDIC. When panicky depositors tried to make withdrawals, some commercial banks could not meet the sudden requests for cash. Many had to close, which only increased the panic that had caused the initial withdrawals. Since the advent of the FDIC, however, such panic and withdrawals should not occur because the FDIC reimburses depositors (up to the limit) for any losses they sustain.

Securities Investor Protection Corporation (SIPC)
The agency that insures investors against failures by brokerage firms.

Like commercial banks, brokerage firms are also insured by an agency that was created by the federal government—the **Securities Investor Protection Corporation (SIPC)**. The SIPC (http://www.sipc.org) is managed by a seven-member board of directors. Five members are appointed by the President of the United States, and their appointments must be confirmed by the Senate. Two of the five represent the general public, and three represent the securities industry. The remaining two members are selected by the secretary of the treasury and the Federal Reserve board of governors.

The SIPC performs a role similar to that of the FDIC. Its objective is to preserve public confidence in the securities markets and industry. Although the SIPC does not protect investors from losses resulting from fluctuations in security prices, it does insure investors against losses arising from the failure of a brokerage firm.

[20]Securities and Exchange Commission, *The Work of the Securities and Exchange Commission* (Washington, D.C.: Government Printing Office, 1978), p. 17.

The insurance provided by the SIPC protects a customer's cash and securities up to $500,000.[21] If a brokerage firm fails, the SIPC reimburses the firm's customers up to this specified limit. If a customer's claims exceed the $500,000 limit, that customer becomes a general creditor for the remainder of the funds.

The cost of this insurance is paid for by the brokerage firms that are members of the SIPC. All brokers and dealers that are registered with the Securities and Exchange Commission (SEC) and all members of national security exchanges must be members of the SIPC. Most security dealers are thus covered by the SIPC insurance. Some firms have even chosen to supplement this coverage by purchasing additional insurance from private insurance firms.

Summary

This chapter has covered security markets and the mechanics of buying securities. Securities are traded on organized exchanges, such as the NYSE, or in the informal over-the-counter markets, including the Nasdaq stock market. Securities are primarily bought through brokers, who buy and sell for their customers' accounts. The brokers obtain the securities from dealers, who make markets in them. These dealers offer to buy and sell at specified prices (quotes), which are called the bid and the ask. Brokers and investors obtain these prices through a sophisticated electronic system that transmits the quotes from the various dealers.

After securities are purchased, the investor must pay for them with either cash or a combination of cash and borrowed funds. When the investor uses borrowed funds, that individual is buying on margin. Buying on margin increases both the potential percentage return and the potential risk of loss for the investor.

Investors may take delivery of their securities or leave them with the brokerage firm. Leaving securities registered in the street name offers the advantage of convenience because the brokerage firm becomes the custodian of the certificates. Since the advent of the SIPC and its insurance protection, there is little risk of loss to the investor from leaving securities with the brokerage firm.

Investors establish long or short positions. With a long position, the investor purchases stock in anticipation of its price rising. If the price of the stock rises, the individual may sell it for a profit. With a short position, the individual sells borrowed stock in anticipation of its price declining. If the price of the stock falls, the individual may repurchase it at the lower price and return it to the lender. The position generates a profit because the selling price exceeds the purchase price.

Both the long and short positions are the logical outcomes of security analysis. If the investor thinks a stock is underpriced, a long position (i.e., purchase of the stock) should be established. If the investor thinks a stock is overvalued, a short position would be sensible. If the investor is correct in either case, the position will generate a profit. Either position may, however, generate a loss if prices move against the investor's prediction.

Investors living in the United States may assume a global view and acquire stocks and bonds issued in foreign countries. These securities may be bought and sold through U.S. brokers in much the same way that investors acquire domestic securities. American depositary receipts (ADRs) representing foreign securities have been created to facilitate trading in foreign stocks. These ADRs are denominated in dollars, their prices are quoted in dollars, and their units of trading are consistent with those in the United States.

---

[21]Only $100,000 of the $500,000 insurance applies to cash balances on an account.

The federal laws governing the securities industry are enforced by the Securities and Exchange Commission (SEC). The purpose of these laws is to ensure that individual investors have access to information upon which to base investment decisions. Publicly owned firms must supply investors with financial statements and make timely disclosure of information that may affect the value of the firms' securities.

Investors' accounts with brokerage firms are insured by the Securities Investor Protection Corporation (SIPC). This insurance covers up to $500,000 worth of securities held by the broker for the investor. The intent of SIPC is to increase public confidence in the securities industry by reducing the risk of loss to investors from failure by brokerage firms.

Questions

1) What is the role of market makers, and how do they earn profits?
2) What is the difference between listed securities and securities traded through the Nasdaq stock market?
3) How is the market price of a security determined?
4) What is the difference between a market order, a good-till-canceled order, and a stop-loss order?
5) In addition to commission fees, are there any other costs of investing?
6) What are the advantages of leaving securities registered in the street name?
7) Why is it riskier to buy stocks on margin?
8) When should an investor sell short? How can an investor sell something that he or she does not own? How is the short position closed? What is the source of profit in a short position?
9) Why do U.S. investors purchase ADRs in preference to the actual securities? How do ADRs come into existence?
10) How is the SIPC similar to the FDIC?
11) Why are the laws governing the securities industry frequently referred to as "full disclosure laws"?
12) What are the roles of the SIPC and the SEC? Can trading in a security be suspended?

Problems

1) A stock sells for $10 per share. You purchase 100 shares for $10 a share (i.e., for $1,000), and after a year the price rises to $17.50. What will be the percentage return on your investment if you bought the stock on margin and the margin requirement was (a) 25 percent, (b) 50 percent, and (c) 75 percent? (Ignore commissions, dividends, and interest expense.)
2) Repeat Problem 1 to determine the percentage return on your investment but in this case suppose the price of the stock falls to $7.50 per share. What generalization can be inferred from your answers to Problems 1 and 2?
3) Investor A makes a cash purchase of 100 shares of AB&C common stock for $55 a share. Investor B also buys 100 shares of AB&C but uses margin. Each holds the stock for one year, during which dividends of $5 a share are distributed. Commissions are 2 percent of the value of a purchase or sale; the margin requirement is 60 percent, and the interest rate is 10 percent annually on borrowed funds. What is the percentage earned by each investor if he or she sells the stock after one year for (a) $40, (b) $55, (c) $60, and (d) $70? If the

margin requirement had been 40 percent, what would have been the annual percentage returns? What conclusion do these percentage returns imply?

4) An investor sells a stock short for $36 a share. A year later, the investor covers the position at $30 a share. If the margin requirement is 60 percent, what is the percentage return earned on the investment? Redo the calculations, assuming the price of the stock is $42 when the investor closes the position.

THE FINANCIAL ADVISOR'S INVESTMENT CASE

Investing an Inheritance

The Flynn brothers, Victor and Darin, could not be more different. Victor is assertive and enjoys taking risks, while Darin is reserved and is exceedingly risk averse. Both have jobs that pay well and provide fringe benefits, including medical insurance and pension plans. You are the executor for their grandfather's estate and know that each brother will soon inherit $85,000 from the estate. Neither has an immediate need for the cash, which could be invested to meet some long-term financial goal.

Once the funds have been received, you expect Victor to acquire some exceedingly risky investment (if he does not immediately squander the money). You would be surprised, however, if Darin chose to do anything other than place the funds in a low-yielding savings account. Neither alternative makes financial sense to you, so before the distribution of the funds you decide to offer financial suggestions that would reduce Victor's risk exposure and increase Darin's potential return.

Given the brothers' ages and financial condition, you believe that equity investments are appropriate. Such investments may satisfy Victor's propensity to take risks and increase Darin's potential return without excessively increasing his risk exposure (willingness to assume risk). Currently, the stock of Choice Juicy Fruit is selling for $60 and pays an annual dividend of $1.50 a share. The company's line of low-to-no-sugar juice offers considerable potential. The margin requirement set by the Federal Reserve is 60 percent, and brokerage firms are charging 7 percent on funds used to purchase stock on margin. While commissions vary among brokers, you decide that $70 for a 100-share purchase or sale is a reasonable amount to use for illustrative purposes. Currently, commercial banks are paying only 3 percent on savings accounts.

To give the presentation focus, you decide to answer the following questions:

1) What is the percent return earned by Darin if he acquires 100 shares, holds the stock for a year, and sells the stock for $80?
2) What is the percent return earned by Victor if he acquires 100 shares on margin, holds the stock for a year, and sells the stock for $80? What advantage does buying stock on margin offer Victor?
3) What would be the percent returns if the sale prices had been $50 or $100?
4) Must the two brothers leave the stock registered in street name? If not, what would be the advantage of leaving the stock with the broker? Does leaving the stock increase their risk exposure?
5) What would be the impact on the brothers' returns if the rate of interest charged by the broker increases to 10 percent?
6) If the maintenance margin requirement were 30 percent and the price of the stock declined to $50, what impact would that have on each brother's position? At what price of the stock would they receive a margin call?
7) Why would buying the stock be more advantageous to both brothers than the alternatives you anticipate them to select?

4 Sources of Information

Super investor Gordon Gekko in the movie *Wall Street* thrived on information. He would aggressively go to any length to obtain knowledge, facts, and data that would give him an edge. And it was this drive for information that led to his downfall, as he obtained and illegally used inside information.

All investors need information, but they do not have to commit illegal acts to obtain it. Today investors have a vast supply of readily available data and facts. An investor's problem is not obtaining information but determining what is useful and then interpreting it. This chapter will describe and illustrate a variety of these sources. The sources covered in this chapter are limited to information on financial assets, especially stocks. Other types of investments such as art or real estate require more specialized knowledge, and sources concerning those investments are not covered in this chapter.

Major sources of information include corporate publications, brokerage firms' research reports, and investment advisory services. Some of this information such as a company's annual report is complimentary and easily obtainable. Other information, such as the *Value Line Investment Survey,* may be purchased through subscription, but some of the subscription services may be available in a public or college library.

The Internet, of course, has made a huge amount of information concerning investments available with the click of a mouse. Internet sources (Web addresses) appear throughout this text in addition to those provided in this chapter. In many cases, same or similar information may be obtained through different sites. Some of it is free and some is available by subscription, and even subscription services tend to offer complimentary information. You should be able to obtain sufficient data and information from free or complimentary sources to determine if additional information obtained through subscription is worth the cost.

One word of warning: Web addresses were checked during the production process for this text, but addresses may change. Some sites fold, others merge, and some sites obtain new addresses or have several different Web addresses but only one is given in this text. Even addresses you would not expect to change may change. While there are often links between old and new addresses, you should not take for granted that such links exist.

Learning Objectives

After completing this chapter you should be able to:

1 Name four categories of financial information that are generally available to investors.

2 List several publications concerning investments that are available in many libraries.

3 Distinguish among the contents of an annual report, a brokerage firm's research report, and an investment advisory report.

4 Define inside information.

5 Identify several government publications concerning economic conditions.

Why Information?

Unless individuals follow a very simple investment strategy (e.g., investing all funds in savings accounts and certificates of deposit at the local bank) or a very naive strategy (e.g., randomly selecting securities and holding them indefinitely), they need to be informed. The regulatory environment (e.g., the SEC) encourages access to information, and corporations, advisory services, brokerage firms, and the popular press provide voluminous amounts of information, which is readily available.

Much of the analysis explained and illustrated in this text requires such readily available information. This is particularly true for the examination of financial statements, which are the foundation of the fundamental analysis discussed in detail in Chapter 13. The investor can measure such things as a firm's profitability, its sources of funds, the return it earns for its stockholders, and its capacity to meet debt obligations.

Many investors, of course, do not perform the analysis themselves. Instead, they may consult such publications as Standard & Poor's *The Outlook*, the *Value Line Investment Survey*, and brokerage firm reports on specific firms or industries. These publications report the results of fundamental analyses and apply them to recommendations for specific securities or investment strategies. The existence of these publications means that the individual investor does not have to redo what has already been done. However, the investor still needs to know where the results of an analysis may be obtained and how to understand and interpret the material.

Corporate Sources of Information

Publicly held firms are required by both federal and state laws, including the full-disclosure laws, to publish annual and quarterly reports. Furthermore, the SEC requires publicly held firms to publish news bulletins detailing any pertinent changes that may affect the value of their securities. These news releases will cover such items as announcements of major new products, merger activity, dividend payments, new financing or refinancing of existing debt, stock repurchases, and management changes.

Although publicly held corporations do send stockholders information, the Internet has become an important, perhaps even favored, means for these companies to communicate with stockholders and the general public. Publicly held American firms have Web pages that are readily accessed. Because the information that firms are required to disseminate is available through the Internet, many firms have stopped sending to stockholders material other than the annual report.

The easiest way to obtain information from the corporation may be to use the firm's Web address. For example, suppose you want information from Hershey Foods, which is used in Chapter 13 to illustrate the analysis of financial statements. Go to http://www.hersheys.com. Because Hershey Foods is a consumer products company, a substantial proportion of the available material concerns its products, but there is also a section on investor relations, which includes:

1 Investors' overview
2 Analyst coverage
3 Annual reports
4 Corporate governance
5 Dividend history
6 Earnings estimates

POINTS OF INTEREST

Reading an Annual Report

Although there is no correct way to read an annual report, the fact that the report includes both factual financial information and public relations material suggests that the prudent investor should read the annual report with caution. The tone of most annual reports, especially the message from management or the descriptions of the firm's products, markets, and potential for success and growth, is upbeat and positive. Even a year in which the firm experienced serious problems, such as declining sales and earnings, labor unrest, or internal strife, may be described with optimistic rhetoric.

With this in mind, the investor approaching an annual report should probably stress reading the numbers and how they were computed (i.e., the financial statements and the footnotes). Immediately after the financial statements, the firm must state the general accounting principles used in the construction of the financial statements. These principles, along with the subsequent footnotes, may offer a better clue to the firm's true financial condition than the blurbs describing sales, earnings, and dividends. Legal problems, nonrecurring sources of income, unfunded pension liabilities, lease obligations not on the balance sheet, current and deferred tax obligations, and the calculation of fully diluted earnings will be discussed (if applicable) in the various footnotes. Because any of these factors could affect the future value of the firm's securities, the prudent investor should take the time and effort to be aware of them.

7 Financial releases
8 Fundamentals
9 SEC filings
10 Stock purchase plans

The Annual Report

Perhaps the most important publication is the firm's annual report. This report covers a wide variety of topics and generally includes a corporate overview and descriptions of the firm's business, audited financial statements, management's discussions of the firm's operations and financial condition, and a letter from the corporation's president or chief executive officer or both.

Although the annual report includes a substantial amount of factual and financial information, it should be viewed as a public relations document. It is frequently printed on expensive paper and filled with colorful pictures of products and of smiling employees. There are exceptions. For example, Verizon's 2000 annual report contains no pictures, and is printed on recycled paper to demonstrate the company's concern for the environment. Prior to 1991, the company published the colorful, public relations type of annual report favored by most firms.

Firms use the annual report to explain, at least superficially, their achievements of the past year. These discussions are in general terms, but the firm's careful selection of words may allow the investor to read between the lines. Generally, the more substantive material is presented in the financial statements, particularly in the explanatory footnotes.

The typical annual report begins with a letter from the president of the company to the stockholders. The chair of the board of directors also frequently signs this letter. The letter reviews the highlights of the year and points out certain noteworthy events, such as a dividend increase or a merger. It may also forecast events in the immediate future, such as next year's sales growth and earnings.

POINTS OF INTEREST

The President's Letter

Every annual report includes a letter from the president or chair of the board. Generally, these are carefully worded documents that summarize the firm's achievements during the fiscal year. A discussion of the firm's prospects for the future may also be included. Does this forecast have useful information for investors? Does it "signal" how the firm's stock will perform in the near future?

These questions were addressed in a study that analyzed letters by corporate presidents or chairs of firms whose stocks subsequently performed very well or very poorly.* The letters of firms whose stocks subsequently did well tended to forecast gains and indicated confidence in the firm's potential. The letters of firms whose stock did poorly discussed the potential for losses and made references to forthcoming problems. Few of these letters forecasted gains.

The results of this research clearly suggest that the president's letter to stockholders offers more than public relations material. Instead, the investor may associate discussions of imminent losses, lack of confidence, or poor growth potential with poor future performance by the stock.

*See Dennis McConnell, John Haslem, and Virginia Gibson, "The President's Letter to Stockholders," *Financial Analysts Journal* (September–October 1986): 66–70.

After the letter to the stockholders, the annual report may describe the various components of the business. For example, it may illustrate with words and pictures the various products that the firm makes, the type of research and development in which the company is engaged, the particular application of the firm's goods and services in different industries, and the outlook for the firm's products in the various industries in which it operates.

After the descriptive material, there follows a set of financial statements. These statements include the balance sheet as of the end of the firm's fiscal year, its income statement for the fiscal year, and the statement of cash flows. A summary of financial information for the past several years may also be given. This summary permits the investor to view the firm's growth in sales, earnings, and dividends as well as the book value of the stock. Since the financial data have been audited, the investors may assume that the information is accurate and that the appropriate accounting principles have been applied consistently. Without this audit, year-by-year comparisons may be meaningless.

Quarterly Reports and SEC Filings

During the year, the firm publishes quarterly reports that summarize its performance during the preceding 3 months. These reports usually include a brief account of pertinent events as well as various financial statements. Although these statements are rarely as complete as the financial statements in the annual report, they do permit the investor to determine changes in the firm's earnings and sales for the quarter and often for the past 12 months. Such quarterly statements are not audited and may subsequently be restated.

10-K report
A required annual report filed with the SEC by publicly held firms.

Firms must file several documents with the Securities and Exchange Commission (SEC), which are available to investors.[1] The **10-K report** is the firm's annual report to the SEC. Because it gives a much more detailed statement of the firm's fundamental financial position than is provided in the stockholders' annual report, the 10-K is the basic source of data for the professional financial analyst. The contents of the 10-K include audited financial statements, breakdowns of sales

[1]For a complete list of forms required by the SEC, see K. Fred Skousen, *An Introduction to the SEC,* 4th ed. (Cincinnati: South-Western/Thomson Learning, 1987), 57–61.

and expenses by product lines, more detailed information about legal proceedings, management compensation including deferred compensation and incentive options, and environmental issues. Some of these items may involve considerable future costs and may take years to resolve, which could be detrimental to future earnings and the financial health of the company. Although the 10-K is not automatically sent to stockholders, a company must supply stockholders this document upon written request, and it is generally available through the company's Web site.

10-Q report
A required quarterly report filed with the SEC by publicly held firms.

8-K report
A document filed with the SEC that describes a change in a firm that may affect the value of its securities.

The **10-Q report** is the firm's quarterly report to the SEC. Like the 10-K, it is a detailed report of the firm's financial condition. The quarterly report the firm sends to its stockholders is basically a summary of the 10-Q. The **8-K report** must be filed with the SEC within 15 days after an event that may materially affect the value of the firm's securities. This document often details materials previously announced through a press release.

The firm also must file a prospectus when it sells securities to the general public. While the firm prepares a 10-K report annually, a prospectus is required only when the securities are initially sold to the general public. For an initial public offering a preliminary prospectus may be prepared. The final prospectus is published when the securities are sold, and the buyers receive a copy of it along with their confirmation statements. (See Exhibit 2.1 for the cover page of a prospectus for an issue of Yahoo! Inc. common stock that was sold to the general public.)

13-D report
Document filed with the SEC by an individual who acquires 5 percent of a publicly held firm's stock.

Individuals as well as firms may have to file forms with the SEC. Any stockholder who acquires 5 percent of a publicly held corporation's stock must submit a **13-D report**. This document requires crucial information, such as the intentions of the stockholder acquiring the large stake. Many takeover attempts start with the acquiring stockholder accumulating a substantial stake in the corporation. The required filing of the 13-D means that once the position reaches 5 percent of the outstanding shares, the buyer's intentions can no longer be hidden.

The SEC may be reached through its Web address: http://www.sec.gov. The SEC home page includes investor assistance and complaints, basic information concerning the SEC and its rule-making and enforcement powers, and specialized information for small business. The home page also provides entry to the EDGAR database.

Of all the information available from the SEC, perhaps the EDGAR database is the most important. EDGAR is an acronym for Electronic Data Gathering Analysis and Retrieval, which is the government's database of SEC filings by public companies and mutual funds. Data collection began in 1994 with a phase-in period. As of May 1996, all publicly held companies were required to file financial information electronically. From this site, an investor may obtain (download) a firm's 10-K or 10-Q.

If the investor wants only the data a firm files with the government, EDGAR should be sufficient. Although EDGAR is a major source of free data, the data may not be in a useful form. Several firms have processed this data into more useful forms and sell their services by subscription. These include Disclosure (http://www.disclosure.com) and EDGAR Online (http://www.edgar-online.com).

Inside Information

inside information
Privileged information concerning a firm.

In addition to the sources that have been previously discussed, there is the possibility of an investor's obtaining **inside information**. Inside information is not available to the general public, and it may be of great value in guiding investments in a particular firm. For example, news of a dividend cut or increment may affect a stock's price. Such knowledge before it is made public should increase the individual's ability to make profitable investment decisions. However, the use of such information for personal gain by employees of the firm, brokers or investment managers, or anyone else is illegal.

The reasons for insiders buying or selling their shares are varied. For example, an individual may be using the proceeds of a sale to retire personal debt or an executive may be exercising an option to buy the stock. Such transactions are legal and are done for reasonable, legitimate financial purposes. However, some financial analysts and investors believe that inside transactions offer a clue to management's perception of the future price performance of the stock. If many insiders sell their shares, this may be interpreted as a bearish sign, indicating that the market price of the stock will decline in the future. Conversely, a large number of purchases by insiders implies that management expects the price of the stock to rise. Such purchases by insiders are interpreted as being bullish. The reason for these interpretations is obvious: If managers believe that the firm's earnings are growing, they will buy the stock. Insiders' purchases and sales may mirror management's view of the company's potential. As is further explained in Chapter 9 on stock valuation and the efficient market hypothesis, information on insider transactions may be used by outside investors as an indicator of the direction of a stock's price.

Because officers, directors, and other insiders must file purchases and sales with the SEC, this information is public. (The value of this information may be asymmetric. While insiders will buy in anticipation of a price increase, a sale need not imply that the price of the stock will decline. Insiders may have other reasons for selling, such as a desire to lock in gains from stock options or to obtain funds for other purposes.) Once again, the investor is faced with the problem of putting the information collected by the SEC into useful form. Several Internet sources offer information concerning insider purchases and sales but charge for the service. Possible sources include Dow Jones (http://dowjones.com/corp/index.html), MarketEdge (http://www.marketedge.com), Standard & Poor's (http://www.stockinfo.standardpoor.com), and Wall Street City (http://www.wallstreetcity.com).

Brokerage Firms' Research Reports and Recommendations

One service that some brokers offer to their customers is research on specific securities; many brokerage firms have research staffs who analyze firms and their securities. The purpose of such research is to identify undervalued securities that have the potential for price appreciation. In some cases these findings are published by the brokerage firm and are readily available to its customers. The cost of such research is included in the commission fee.

Brokerage firms analysts' recommendations take the general form of "buy," "hold," or "sell." There are often gradients with the recommendations such as "strong buy" or "OK to buy" or "short-term hold/strong long-term buy." It is easy to accept these recommendations at face value. That is, "buy" means the stock should be acquired and "hold" means maintain current positions but do not add to them.

Unfortunately, analysts' recommendations should not necessarily be taken at face value. In most cases brokerage firm research reports tend to recommend purchases. Rarely do such recommendations recommend the outright sale of securities. There are two obvious reasons for the purchase recommendations. First, brokerage firms and brokers profit from commissions, and initial commissions are made through purchases of securities by investors. Second, brokerage firms make large fees through underwriting securities for firms and providing consulting services such as valuations and opinions in merger negotiations. If the firm's financial analysts are recommending the sale of the stock, that will not endear the firm to the company whose stock is being recommended for sale.

The firms certainly assert that their investment banking and brokerage operations are independent of each other and that their financial analysts are free to make judgments and recommendations based on their analysis. However, as was vividly demonstrated during the market declines of 2000 into 2001, many financial analysts continued to recommend purchases of stocks whose prices were dramatically declining and continuing to decline. This experience suggests that investors should be cautious when using analysts' recommendations when making investment decisions. Perhaps the individual should reinterpret recommendations such as "hold" to really mean "sell" or "avoid." At the very least the investor should use the research reports in conjunction with other sources of information.[2]

Business Publications Related to Investments

The investor may buy a variety of publications and services rendering information that is potentially useful in making investment decisions. This section will describe several of these sources of information. Emphasis is placed on general investment information, advisory services that recommend investments in specific firms, and services available to individual investors. Information on mutual funds is deferred to Chapter 8 and Chapter 24, which discuss mutual funds and portfolio management.

Newspapers and Magazines

The foremost financial newspaper is *The Wall Street Journal.* This daily newspaper publishes not only daily stock prices but also 12-month high and low prices, volume of transactions, option prices, quotes on Treasury securities, and prices of commodities and foreign currencies. In addition to financial news, *The Wall Street Journal* includes news bulletins that are issued by firms and editorial comments on national economic policy. Editorials tend to stress those policies that affect the investment community (e.g., the fiscal policy of the federal government, the monetary policy of the Federal Reserve Board, and proposed changes in the federal tax laws). *The Wall Street Journal Interactive Edition* at http://www.wsj.com provides links to related stories in the print edition.

In addition to *The Wall Street Journal,* Dow Jones publishes *Barron's,* a weekly newspaper that reports security transactions, various feature articles of interest to the financial community, and investment advisory reports. One particularly important piece of information is the *Barron's* confidence index, described in Chapter 14 on technical analysis. *Barron's* on-line (http://www.barrons.com) provides overviews of a company's performance and links to articles on the company.

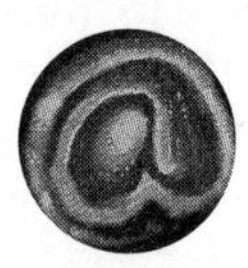

Media General, whose publicly held stock trades on the American Stock Exchange (MEG.A), also publishes a weekly paper, the *Media General Financial Weekly,* with emphasis on financial data. More important, however, is the vast amount of information available on-line through Media General Financial Services (http://www.mgfs.com). This database encompasses descriptions of the firm's securities and its financial statements, and price/earnings (P/E) ratios. Essentially the database provides all the types of analysis covered in this text. These include stock returns (Chapter 10), estimates of growth rates and earnings estimates (Chapter 11), an analysis of financial statements (Chapter 13), and technical indicators (Chapter 14). Much of the information is more detailed than individual investors generally need.

A variety of magazines also report financial news. These range from *Money,* which is a popular press magazine related primarily to personal finance and financial planning, to more sophisticated publications. General investors should be

[2]For a fascinating discussion of the conflict of interest between financial analysis and investment banking and other means by which financial analysts "sell the investor down the river," see Benjamin Mark Cole, *The Pied Pipers of Wall Street* (Princeton, NJ: Bloomberg Press, 2001).

particularly interested in *BusinessWeek* (http://www.businessweek.com), *Forbes* (http://www.forbes.com), and *Fortune* (http://www.fortune.com), all of which publish analytical articles concerning the general financial community and specific companies.

These publications also cover specific topics on investment decisions and security selection. For example, *Forbes* periodically devotes specific issues to the reporting of financial information that facilitates comparisons of firms. For instance, the *Annual Report on American Industry* ranks more than 1,000 firms with regard to sales and growth in earnings, stock price performance, and return on equity. The issue also classifies the firms by industry and reports such additional information as use of debt and profit margins for the individual firms and medians for the industry.

In addition to the *Annual Report on Industry, Forbes* also periodically presents other specialized information, such as an enumeration of the largest non-American firms and the annual performance of mutual funds. (*Barron's* also publishes quarterly the performance rating of mutual funds.) Perhaps one of the most awaited issues of *Forbes* is devoted to enumerating the 400 richest Americans. While that issue may not help the individual investor, it can illustrate the potential return for the successful management of investments and careers.

The academically and professionally oriented journals are more specialized, and their contents tend to be more difficult for the inexperienced or untrained investor to understand. *Financial Management* and the *Journal of Finance* are primarily designed for individuals doing research in financial topics, such as capital budgeting, cost of funds, or valuation theory. The *Harvard Business Review* is not limited to topics in finance but covers the gamut of business operations. The *Journal of Portfolio Management* and the *Financial Analysts Journal* are a cross between academic and professional publications, as they include articles by both practitioners and academicians. The *Financial Analysts Journal,* which is a professional magazine published six times a year by the Association for Investment Management and Research, is almost exclusively devoted to professional financial analysts.

The recent interest in financial planning has spawned publications devoted to the professional financial planner, such as *Financial Planning,* published by the International Association for Financial Planning, and the *Journal of Financial Planning,* published by the Institute of Certified Financial Planners. These publications

POINTS OF INTEREST

Background Readings

In addition to the material presented in this chapter, the reader may consult the following general source material:

Encyclopedia of Investments. 2d ed. Boston: Warren Gorham & Lamont, 1991. A standardized compilation of articles on over 50 possible investments. Each piece is individually written by an expert in that particular field. The length and format of each article are uniform, and each includes a glossary and bibliography. Each article covers practical considerations, such as how to buy and sell the asset, the primary factors that determine the asset's value, for whom the asset is suitable, and where professional advice may be obtained. Approximately half the book is devoted to nontraditional assets, such as folk art, gemstones, period furniture, and stamps. Since there is a dearth of conveniently compiled material on nontraditional investments, this encyclopedia is a convenient source of information for interested investors.

Levine, Sumner, and Caroline Levine. *Irwin Business and Investment Almanac.* 19th ed. Burr Ridge, IL: Irwin Professional Publishing, 1995.

Rosenberg, Jerry M. *Dictionary of Investing.* 2d ed. New York: John Wiley and Sons, 1992.

Stock Market Encyclopedia. New York: Standard & Poor's, published annually.

Woelfel, Charles J. *Encyclopedia of Banking and Finance.* 10th ed. Burr Ridge, IL: Irwin Professional Publishing, 1996. Includes definitions of terms, historical background, illustrations, laws and regulations, data, and a detailed bibliography concerning banking, finance, and investing.

have a more macro or aggregate emphasis than do journals designed for financial analysts and encompass such topics as tax shelters, retirement and estate planning, mutual funds, and portfolio management.

The individual who is interested in a particular area of investments may also read specialized trade journals. For example, those who are considering oil and gas investments may find the *Oil and Gas Journal* a good source of information concerning discoveries in new oil fields and the amounts of reserves that have been determined to exist in the fields. Such trade publications will help the investor keep abreast of events in a particular industry. (A source for trade publications is the *Guide to Industry Publications for Security Analysts,* published by the New York Society for Securities Analysts.)

One particularly important source of information for investors is the American Association of Individual Investors (AAII). This organization publishes a variety of useful material that includes the *AAII Journal, AAII Computerized Investing,* and the *Individual Investor's Guide to Low-Load Mutual Funds.* Because the purpose of the organization is educational, AAII accepts no advertising. Costs are covered through membership in the association (625 North Michigan Avenue, Chicago, IL 60611, or http://www.aaii.com).

The *AAII Journal* annually includes a guide to investment Web sites, which can be directly accessed from AAII's Web site. The Web addresses include stock exchanges, brokerage firms, advisory services, and government agencies. Brief descriptions of each site include services offered, functions performed, data available, types of securities covered, and documents provided. Whether the provider charges a fee or offers its services for free is also given.

Investment Advisory Services

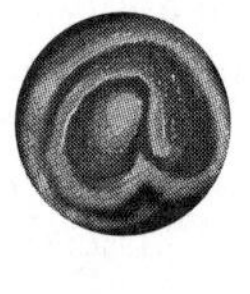

For the investor who wants additional information or advice, a variety of sources may be purchased, some of which are illustrated in this chapter. These sources include the corporate records that are published by Standard & Poor's (http://www.stockinfo.standardpoor.com) and by Mergent (http://www.mergent.com). In addition, Standard & Poor's publishes each month a *Stock Guide* and a *Bond Guide.* Exhibit 4.1 reproduces a page from the *Stock Guide.* As may be seen in the exhibit, which highlights the stock of Hershey Foods, a considerable amount of information is given, including not only the price but also financial data, such as dividends, earnings per share, and certain balance sheet items (current assets, current liabilities, long-term debt, and number of shares outstanding). Because this publication packs so much information into such a small space and is updated monthly, it is a widely used reference.

In addition to the *Stock Guide, Bond Guide,* and *Corporation Records,* Standard & Poor's publishes *The Outlook,* an investment advisory service that lists stocks appropriate for investors seeking income or growth. It also lists moderately speculative securities that may offer more potential for higher returns. Each issue describes several securities that the publisher believes are attractive investments. These lists and suggestions are continuously updated so that subscribers may alter their portfolios as conditions and suggestions change. It should be noted that material is generally descriptive and does not report how the conclusions were determined.

One important investor advisory service is the *Value Line Investment Survey* (http://www.valueline.com). Each week this publication includes new information on selected industries and specific firms within these industries and updates previously published information. During a three-month period, *Value Line* evaluates most of the important firms that trade their securities on the major exchanges or in the over-the-counter markets. In addition to evaluating individual firms, this service analyzes the industry and makes a recommendation for the price perfor-

EXHIBIT 4.1

Page from Standard & Poor's *Stock Guide*

92 **HAV-HEX** Standard & Poor's

¶ S&P 500 # MidCap 400 ◇ SmallCap 600 • Options

Index	Ticker	Name of Issue (Call Price of Pfd. Stocks)	Market	Com. Rank. & Pfd. Rating	Inst. Hold Cos	Inst. Hold Shs. (000)	Principal Business	Price Range 1971-99 High	1971-99 Low	2000 High	2000 Low	2001 High	2001 Low	May, 2001 May. Sales in 100s	Last Sale Or Bid High	Low	Last	%Div Yield	P-E Ratio	EPS 5 Yr Growth	% Annualized Total Return 12 Mo	36 Mo	60 Mo
		Haverty Furniture (Cont.)																					
1	HVT.A	Cl'A'	NY	A	5	493		18.50	2.67	13.18	9.31	14.90	10.00	180	14.6	3.40	13.40B	1.5	10	23	19.3	10.7	17.6
2	HA	✓Hawaiian Airlines	AS,Ph,P	NR	15	6345	Regional airline service	13.50	1.50	2.87	1.75	3.25	1.81	6343	3.24	2.80	3.08	...	d	Neg	23.2	5.5	−8.0
#3•[1]	HE	✓Hawaiian Elec Indus	NY,B,Ch,P,Ph	B+	167	8742	Hldg:electric/finl svc,Hawaii	44.62	7.06	37.93	27.68	37.95	33.56	29782	37.75	35.88	37.07	6.7	28	−14	12.5	6.2	8.9
4	HWK	✓Hawk Corp 'A'	NY	NR	27	4120	Aerospace friction pds	19.93	3.81	8.87	4.37	7.40	5.31	1667	6.79	5.37	6.75	...	13	...	−0.9	−28.2	...
5	HAZ	✓Hayes Lemmerz Intl	NY	NR	51	4238	Dsgn, mfr car & truck wheels	41.25	13.87	21.37	4.50	8.50	5.12	4727	8.50	7.00	8.25	...	d	NM	−42.9	−40.5	...
¶6•[2]	HCA	✓HCA-The Healthcare Company	NY,P	B	676	414758	Health care facilities/svcs	44.87	6.49	45.25	18.75	44.16	33.93	525221	41.08	35.60	40.34	0.2	22	52	49.8	...	...
#7•[3]	HCC	✓HCC Insurance Hldgs	NY,Ch,Ph	B+	190	42750	Prop & casualty insur,agency	32.75	3.20	27.18	10.93	29.65	20.50	60832	28.32	23.50	24.79	1.0	22	1	46.8	5.4	3.6
8	HED	✓Head N.V.	NY	NR	10	3036	Mfr,mkt sporting goods	....	....	10.00	4.25	5.99	3.81	4913	4.65	3.85	4.08	...	5	...	...	...	...
9	HEA	✓Headway Corporate Res	AS	NR	14	1019	Human resources services	12.75	1.50	5.75	1.06	2.40	1.10	904	1.85	1.20	1.34	...	3	NM	−56.3	−49.5	−23.5
10	HCP	Health Care Prop Inv	NY,B,Ch,P	NR	176	23945	Real estate investment trust	40.37	9.50	30.43	23.06	36.80	29.25	52444	35.92	34.05	34.12	9.0	17	−1	41.0	9.3	10.0
11•[1]	HCN	Health Care REIT	NY,Ch,P	NR	97	3703	Real estate investment trust	29.25	6.16	19.25	13.81	23.99	16.06	18215	23.20	21.50	22.74	10.3	13	−4	59.6	7.7	12.0
#12•[4]	HMA	✓Health Management Assoc	NY,Ph,P	B+	434	214434	Oper acute care hospitals	25.75	0.93	22.75	9.62	20.56	13.42	324123	18.40	15.75	17.76	...	22	15	50.3	−3.7	11.7
#13•[5]	HNT	✓Health Net'A'	NY	NR	274	109718	Manage HMO's western U.S.	37.12	5.87	26.93	7.62	26.18	17.42	147239	21.82	18.13	19.25	...	12	NM	60.4	−14.2	−8.3
14	HII	Healthcare Integrated Svcs	AS	C	..	...	Establish/oper MRI centers	87.50	3.75	11.87	0.37	2.00	0.62	815	2.00	0.87	2.00	...	d	−42	−44.8	−48.2	−38.4
15	HR	✓Healthcare Realty Tr	NY,Ph	NR	167	18375	Real estate investment trust	30.00	14.50	21.81	15.43	25.50	20.75	27204	25.50	23.80	24.92	9.2	14	4	62.9	6.0	11.4
16	HCRI	✓Healthcare Recoveries	NNM	NR	23	5317	Health insurance subrogation	26.00	2.56	5.18	2.56	4.99	2.37	4458	4.99	4.17	4.46	...	12	−7	27.4	−37.4	...
17	HCEN	✓HealthCentral.com	NNM	NR	15	1372	Dvlp stge:online hlth care sv	12.75	6.87	14.37	0.12	0.62	0.04	526705	0.40	0.12	0.31	...	..	...	−91.4	...	...
¶18•[6]	HRC	✓HEALTHSOUTH Corp	NY,Ch,Ph,P	B	472	286343	Medical rehabilitation svc	30.81	1.00	17.50	4.75	16.50	11.25	481081	14.04	11.31	12.70	...	16	3	99.2	−23.5	−6.2
19	HPP	Healthy Planet Prod	AS,Ch	C	2	62	Dsgn,mkt stationery/card prd	134.00	0.21	1.62	0.25	0.62	0.20	645	0.54	0.23	0.30	...	d	Neg	−56.4	−44.4	−46.7
20•[7]	HEAR	✓HearMe	NNM	NR	25	4277	Internet'live community'svcs	51.25	9.25	34.37	0.62	1.93	0.25	44432	0.83	0.35	0.56	...	d	...	−90.8	...	...
21•[8]	HTV	✓Hearst-Argyle Television 'A'	NY,Ph	NR	96	10289	Own/oper T.V. stations	41.25	19.93	29.25	17.06	24.75	18.42	15908	22.75	19.60	21.23	...	35	−13	12.1	−16.1	...
22	HTL	Heartland Partners L.P. 'A'[54]	AS	NR	4	399	Real estate development	23.25	6.25	23.75	18.12	19.00	16.50	86	17.35	16.75	16.90B	...	5	NM	−13.3	2.6	19.1
23	EAR	✓HEARx Ltd	AS,Ch	C	17	928	Oper hearing care centers	73.75	3.25	6.75	1.00	2.45	1.12	5845	2.05	1.20	1.63	...	d	40	−58.6	−52.3	−50.9
24	HL	✓Hecla Mining	NY,B,Ch,P,Ph	C	42	3479	Silver producer: lead,gold	35.83	1.43	2.00	0.50	1.70	0.50	106409	1.70	0.71	1.05	...	d	−25	−1.2	−40.6	−33.4
25	Pr B	Sr'B'cm Cv Pfd([56]51.40)	NY,Ch	D	6	497		59.12	22.18	28.12	6.00	12.00	5.93	1553	12.00	6.25	10.80	...	...	...	...	...	...
26	HCT	✓Hector Communications	AS	B	19	618	Oper tel cos,cable TV:WI,MN	17.25	2.75	15.75	10.00	11.93	9.60	604	11.93	10.10	11.75B	...	16	6	−7.8	2.6	10.1
27	HEI	✓HEICO Corp	NY,B,Ch,P,Ph	B+	53	2055	Mfr jet aircraft engine parts	31.59	0.06	20.25	11.13	20.50	13.01	6896	20.50	17.70	18.10	0.3	14	22	56.7	−12.1	25.5
28	HEI.A	Cl'A'	NY	B	52	4693		28.40	11.02	19.31	9.56	19.92	11.00	7584	19.92	16.70	17.58	0.3	13	22	64.3	−7.9	...
¶29•[9]	HNZ	✓Heinz (H.J.)	NY,B,Ch,Ph,P	A−	735	206531	Major mfr of processed foods	61.75	1.00	48.00	30.81	47.93	36.90	194881	43.60	38.61	43.31	3.6	15	12	13.8	−3.5	8.7
30	Pr	$1.70 3d cm Cv 1st Pfd(28.50)[57]	NY,B	NR	..	...	ketchup,soups,baby foods	805.00	25.50	616.00	481.00	....	....	....	....	....	584.75B	0.3	..	...	...	...	...
31•[1]	HELE	✓Helen of Troy Ltd	NNM	B+	37	9827	Hair care appliances	26.50	0.01	9.56	4.00	9.41	4.87	51425	9.41	6.16	9.13	...	15	1	39.1	−21.8	6.4
◇32•[10]	HELX	✓Helix Technology	NNM	B+	170	15649	Mfr of cryogenic equipment	49.50	0.09	80.18	19.31	32.90	20.37	55048	31.50	26.49	28.22	1.7	54	37	−15.6	19.2	12.3
33	OTE	✓Hellenic Telecommunic ADS[58]	NY	NR	65	26271	Telecommunication svc,Greece	16.50	9.50	15.87	6.81	8.25	6.37	15349	7.48	6.62	6.82	4.3	..	...	−41.9	...	...
34•[10]	HF	✓Heller Financial 'A'	NY	NR	187	42732	Provide financial svcs	31.93	15.50	32.62	16.50	39.30	28.75	90428	35.25	29.00	34.40	1.2	13	...	84.8	8.8	...
#35•[11]	HP	✓Helmerich & Payne	NY,B,Ch,Ph,P	B+	296	38817	Contract driller:o&g prod'n	45.56	1.16	44.81	19.75	58.73	38.06	124431	51.24	39.27	39.54	0.8	13	4	7.0	17.4	18.2
36•[4]	HEB	✓Hemispherx BioPharma	AS,Ph	NR	16	1407	Pharmaceutical R&D	13.18	1.62	19.00	4.43	5.81	3.01	14457	5.60	4.26	5.50	...	d	1	−5.4	11.8	...
37	WS	Wrrt(Pur 1 com at $4)	AS	...	3	140		9.00	0.50	15.00	0.87	2.25	0.60	3319	1.95	0.90	1.80	...	...	...	...	...	...
#38•[12]	JKHY	✓Henry(Jack) & Assoc	NNM	A	226	45387	Data process'g svcs to banks	14.12	0.06	33.12	12.06	31.37	18.56	103236	29.50	24.80	29.15	0.4	51	33	34.7	53.8	40.7
39•[5]	HERBA	✓Herbalife Intl'A'	NNM	B+	53	3269	Weight ctrl/hlth care prod	37.37	0.34	16.37	6.87	10.00	7.00	3334	8.75	7.30	8.30	7.2	6	−4	2.2	−27.7	−7.9
¶40•[9]	HPC	✓Hercules, Inc	NY,B,Ch,P,Ph	B+	282	68552	Spcl chemicals/food prod	66.25	4.08	28.00	11.37	20.00	11.30	130362	14.45	11.30	13.36	...	27	−25	−17.4	−30.4	−22.9
41	HPG	✓Heritage Propane Ptnrs L.P.	NY	NR	11	111	Propane retail marketer	25.50	16.75	23.87	16.50	31.00	21.62	5215	31.00	26.90	28.25	8.5	..	...	66.6	17.6	...
#42•[13]	MLHR	✓Herman Miller	NNM	B+	257	45808	Office furniture & systems	36.25	0.09	33.93	18.37	28.93	22.87	61566	28.61	25.93	26.96	0.6	15	32	0.4	−0.3	29.3
43	HT	Hersha Hospitality Trust	AS	NR	..	...	Real estate investment trust	6.37	4.81	6.12	4.00	6.06	4.80	868	6.00	5.34	5.94	12.1	18	...	22.3	...	...
¶44•[14]	HSY	✓Hershey Foods	NY,B,Ch,P,Ph	A	480	52385	Mfr chocolate,candy,pasta	76.37	0.70	66.43	37.75	70.15	55.12	128027	62.15	58.55	60.64	1.8	22	7	19.2	−2.5	12.7
¶45•[15]	HWP	✓Hewlett-Packard	NY,B,C,Ch,P,Ph	A+	1535	1021405	Mfr computer products	59.21	0.46	77.75	29.12	37.95	25.00	1709361	31.37	25.00	29.32	1.1	28	3	...	...	...
46•[8]	HXL	Hexcel Corp	NY,Ch,P	B−	100	13363	Honeycomb cores: plastics	43.00	1.90	15.43	4.75	12.40	8.76	27767	10.90	9.18	10.60	...	8	NM	36.8	−27.1	−6.7

Uniform Footnote Explanations-See Page 1. Other: [1]P:Cycle 2. [2]ASE,CBOE,P:Cycle 2. [3]Ph:Cycle 1. [4]ASE,CBOE:Cycle 2. [5]CBOE:Cycle 1. [6]ASE,CBOE,P,Ph:Cycle 3. [7]ASE,CBOE:Cycle 3. [8]P:Cycle 1. [9]ASE,CBOE,P:Cycle 3. [10]ASE:Cycle 1. [11]CBOE:Cycle 3. [12]ASE:Cycle 3. [13]CBOE:Cycle 2. [14]ASE:Cycle 2. [15]ASE,CBOE,P,Ph:Cycle 2. [51]Excl subsid pfd. [52]Approx. [53]To be determined. [54]Units. [55]Excl Cl'B' L.P.. [56]Thru 6-30-2000,scale to $50 in 2003. [57]0.50 vtg. [58]Ea ADS rep 0.50 ord,750 Drs. [59]If com exceeds $9 for 20 con trad days. [60]Incl 3.3M Sub Units. [61]Fiscal Dec'99 & prior. [62]8 Mo Aug'00. [63]Stk dstr of Agilent Technologies Inc.

Common and Convertible Preferred Stocks **HAV-HEX** 93

Index	Splits ◆ Cash Divs. Ea. Yr. Since	Dividends: Latest Payment Period $	Date	Ex. Div.	Total $ So Far 2001	Ind. Rate	Paid 2000	Financial Position Mil-$ Cash& Equiv.	Curr. Assets	Curr. Liab.	Balance Sheet Date	Capitalization Lg Trm Debt Mil-$	Shs. 000 Pfd.	Com.	Earnings $ Per Shr. Years End	1997	1998	1999	2000	2001	Last 12 Mos.	Interim Earnings Period	$ per Shr. 2000	2001	Index
1◆	1986	Q0.05	5-31-01	5-17	0.10	0.20	0.19¼	....	...	...		....	...	4756	Dc	±v0.57	v±0.72	v±1.19	Pv□1.31	....	1.31				1
2	....	None Since Public			...	Nil	....	85.2	142	215	3-31-01	13.4	...	33715	Dc	vd0.02	v0.19	v□d0.70	vPd0.48	....	d0.41	3 Mo Mar	v□d0.06	v0.01	2
3	1901	Q0.62	6-12-01	5-8	1.24	2.48	2.48	Total Assets $8469M			12-31-00	2538	[51]...	32991	Dc	v2.75	v2.64	v3.00	v1.40	....	1.33	3 Mo Mar	v0.90	v0.83	3
4	....	None Since Public			...	Nil	....	3.15	73.3	34.7	3-31-01	97.4	2	8553	Dc	pv0.74	v□1.51	v0.71	v0.66	....	0.51	3 Mo Mar	v0.25	v0.10	4
5◆	....	None Paid			...	Nil	....	....	533	644	1-31-01	1621	...	28455	Ja	v1.12	v□1.60	v2.06	vd1.41	....	d1.41				5
6	1993	0.02	9-1-01	7-30	0.06	0.08	0.08	188	4425	3089	3-31-01	6426	...	±537521	Dc	v□d0.38	v0.59	v±1.11	v±0.39	E1.82	0.46	3 Mo Mar	v±0.52	v±0.59	6
7	1996	Q0.06	4-9-01	3-29	0.12	0.24	0.21	Total Assets $2792M			3-31-01	57.5	...	★58776	Dc	v1.07	v1.48	v0.51	□v1.10	....	1.12	3 Mo Mar	v□0.26	v0.28	7
8	2001	[52]0.185	6-18-01	5-24	[52]0.185	[53]....	....	6.12	249	201	6-30-00	p70.2	...	★39821	Dc	...	...	pv2.23	Pv0.86	....	0.86				8
9	....	None Paid			...	Nil	....	1.02	58.6	25.1	3-31-01	75.7	1	11590	Dc	v0.28	v□0.47	v0.40	Pv0.41	....	0.42	3 Mo Mar	v0.13	v0.14	9
10	1985	Q0.77	5-18-01	5-1	1.53	3.08	2.94	Total Assets $2405M			9-30-00	1156	7400	★54562	Dc	v2.19	v2.54	v2.25	Pv2.13	....	2.07	3 Mo Mar	v0.45	v0.39	10
11	1971	Q0.58½	5-21-01	4-27	1.17	2.34	2.33½	Total Assets $1162.28M			9-30-00	438	6000	28693	Dc	v2.12	v2.24	v2.21	Pv1.91	....	1.80	3 Mo Mar	v0.52	v0.41	11
12◆	....	None Since Public			...	Nil	....	433	536	205	12-31-00	492	...	243587	Sp	v0.43	v0.54	v0.59	v0.68	E0.80	0.68	6 Mo Mar	v0.35	v0.35	12
13	....	None Since Public			...	Nil	....	1727	2323	1788	3-31-01	646	...	122980	Dc	±vd1.52	v±d1.35	v□1.21	v±1.33	E1.58	1.39	3 Mo Mar	v0.28	v0.34	13
14◆	....	None Paid			...	Nil	....	0.48	11.9	10.4	12-31-00	131	634	1362	Dc	vd1.30	v1.00	v1.25	vd17.69	....	d17.08	3 Mo Mar	vd0.50	v0.11	14
15	1993	Q0.575	6-7-01	5-11	1.14½	2.30	2.23	Total Assets $1589M			3-31-01	549	3000	40560	Dc	v1.68	v1.65	v1.99	v1.82	....	1.82	3 Mo Mar	v0.47	v0.47	15
16	....	None Since Public			...	Nil	....	0.72	30.1	19.5	9-30-00	14.5	...	10048	Dc	v0.37	v0.77	v0.46	Pv0.33	....	0.37	3 Mo Mar	v0.10	v0.14	16
17	....	None Since Public			...	Nil	....	3.37	18.9	16.8	3-31-01	1.11	480	50661	Dc	...	vpd0.10	vd4.96	vn/a	....	....	3 Mo Mar	vd1.10	vd0.16	17
18◆	....	None Since Public			...	Nil	....	183	1475	273	3-31-01	3227	...	389662	Dc	v0.91	v0.11	v0.18	v0.71	E0.81	0.73	3 Mo Mar	v0.17	v0.19	18
19	....	None Paid			...	Nil	....	0.17	2.62	1.58	9-30-00	0.09	31	3841	Dc	vd0.97	vd1.39	vd0.76	vPd0.47	....	d0.47				19
20	....	None Since Public			...	Nil	....	40.6	49.0	9.00	9-30-00	2.00	...	28914	Dc	...	vpd0.95	vd1.29	Pvd3.16	....	d2.83	3 Mo Mar	vd0.50	vd0.17	20
21	....	None Since Public			...	Nil	....	6.88	184	111	3-31-01	1444	22	±91763	Dc	vp0.96	v□1.08	±v□0.41	vΔ0.44	....	0.61	3 Mo Mar	v0.05	v0.22	21
22	....	0.75	1-7-98	12-29	...	Nil	....	Total Assets $53.2M			9-30-00	25.2	...	[55]2142	Dc	vd0.99	vd2.76	vNil	Pv2.76	....	3.77	3 Mo Mar	vNil	v1.01	22
23◆	....	None Since Public			...	Nil	....	5.24	12.3	9.99	12-29-00	0.18	6	11845	Dc	vd1.20	vd1.30	vd0.45	vd0.39	....	d0.57	3 Mo Mar	vd0.07	vd0.25	23
24	....	0.05	12-21-90	11-15	...	Nil	....	3.24	30.7	30.5	3-31-01	10.0	2300	66799	Dc	vd0.16	vd0.15	v□d0.75	v□d1.37	....	d1.13	3 Mo Mar	v□d0.13	v0.11	24
25	1993	0.87½	7-1-00	6-16	...	[53]...	2.62½	Cv into 3.2154 com, $15.55				....	2300	...	Dc	...	...	...	...	....	....	Arrears $2.625 to 4-1-01			25
26	....	None Paid			...	Nil	....	13.2	20.8	12.0	3-31-01	83.2	221	3481	Dc	v0.93	v1.15	v1.96	v0.86	....	0.75	3 Mo Mar	v0.30	v0.19	26
27◆	1976	0.02½	1-18-01	1-4	0.02½	0.05	0.045	5.94	76.2	25.1	1-31-01	27.0	...	±17555	Oc	v0.45	v0.62	v±0.85	v±1.32	....	1.32	6 Mo Apr	v±0.44	v±0.44	27
28◆	1998	S0.02½	1-18-01	1-4	0.02½	0.05	0.045	....	...	...		....	...	9003	Oc	±v0.45	v±0.62	±v0.85	v±1.32	....	1.32	6 Mo Apr	v±0.44	v±0.44	28
29	1911	Q0.39¼	4-10-01	3-22	0.78½	1.57	1.49½	208	3381	4668	1-31-01	1895	...	348676	Ap	v0.81	v2.15	v1.29	v2.47	E2.81	2.16	9 Mo Jan	v2.19	v1.88	29
30	1976	Q0.42½	4-1-01	3-22	0.85	1.70	1.70	Cv into 13.5 common				....	20	...	Ap	...	...	...	...	....	....				30
31◆	....	0.04	8-3-77	7-15	...	Nil	....	2.03	208	54.2	11-30-00	55.0	...	28051	Fb	v0.77	v0.96	v0.44	Pv0.60	....	0.60				31
32◆	1987	Q0.12	5-15-01	5-3	0.24	0.48	0.48	31.1	100	26.2	3-31-01	....	...	22537	Dc	v1.07	vd0.09	v0.70	v2.02	E0.52↓	1.89	3 Mo Mar	v0.35	v0.22	32
33	1999	0.291	9-5-00	6-27	...	0.29	0.291	183	1395	889	6-30-98	475	...	★504054	Dc	v0.68	...	...	...	....	....				33
34	1998	Q0.10	5-15-01	4-27	0.20	0.40	0.40	Total Assets $20001M			3-31-01	11595	7750	±96909	Dc	pv1.70	v1.91	v±2.74	v±2.69	E2.75	2.61	3 Mo Mar	v±0.70	v±0.62	34
35◆	1959	q0.07½	6-1-01	5-11	0.15	0.30	0.29	147	320	81.3	3-31-01	50.0	...	50609	Sp	v1.67	v2.00	v0.86	v1.64	E3.04	2.33	6 Mo Mar	v0.80	v1.49	35
36	....	None Since Public			...	Nil	....	6.14	6.72	1.24	3-31-01	....	...	29991	Dc	vd0.35	vd0.32	vd0.35	vd0.29	....	d0.30	3 Mo Mar	vd0.07	vd0.08	36
37	....	Terms&trad. basis should be checked in detail						Wrrts expire 11-2-2001				....	...	4620	Dc	...	...	...	...	....	....	Callable at 5¢[59]			37
38◆	1990	Q0.03	5-18-01	5-1	0.06	0.12	0.10	26.1	114	78.7	3-31-01	0.25	...	88466	Je	v0.20	v0.27	v0.38	v0.40	....	0.57	9 Mo Mar	v0.27	v0.44	38
39	1992	Q0.15	5-10-01	4-24	0.30	0.60	0.60	118	297	154	9-30-00	....	...	±28724	Dc	±v1.72	v±1.60	v±1.86	Pv±1.22	....	1.32	3 Mo Mar	v±0.19	v±0.29	39
40	1913	Div Postponed 11-14-00			...	Nil	0.62	161	1107	919	3-31-01	2412	...	108007	Dc	v□3.18	v0.10	v1.62	v0.91	E0.50	0.48	3 Mo Mar	v0.34	vd0.09	40
41	1996	Q0.60	4-16-01	3-29	1.18¾	2.40	2.263	15.5	141	127	2-28-01	408	...	[60]±12980	Au	0.64	v1.04	v[61]1.11	v[62]d0.66	....	....	6 Mo Feb	n/a	v3.45	41
42◆	1945	Q0.036	7-15-01	5-30	0.10⅞	0.15	0.145	74.3	432	454	3-03-01	67.9	...	75936	My	v0.77	v1.39	v1.67	v1.74	E1.81	1.93	9 Mo Feb	v1.24	v1.43	42
43	1999	0.18	4-27-01	3-26	0.36	0.72	0.72	Total Assets $96M			3-31-01	61.2	...	2275	Dc	...	n/a	pv0.50	Pv0.37	....	0.34	3 Mo Mar	v0.05	v0.02	43
44	1930	Q0.28	6-15-01	5-23	0.56	1.12	1.08	26.3	1120	573	3-31-01	878	...	±136646	Dc	v±2.23	±v2.34	v±3.26	v±2.42	E2.75	2.48	3 Mo Mar	v±0.51	v±0.57	44
45◆	1965	Q0.08	7-11-01	6-18	0.24	0.32	h[63]0.32	2852	22639	15225	1-31-01	3037	...	p1942829	Oc	v1.48	v1.39	v1.67	v1.80	E1.05	1.31	6 Mo Apr	v0.80	vΔ0.31	45
46	....	0.11	11-16-92	10-27	...	Nil	....	5.10	326	198	12-31-00	652	...	35100	Dc	v1.74	v1.24	vd0.64	v1.32	....	1.40	3 Mo Mar	v0.07	v0.15	46

◆Stock Splits & Divs By Line Reference Index [1]2-for-1,'99. [5]2-for-1,'97. [12]3-for-2,'97,'98. [14]1-for-10 REVERSE,'00. [18]2-for-1,'97. [23]1-for-10 REVERSE,'99. [27]10%,'97:3-for-2,'97:3-for-2 in Cl'A','98:10% Cl'A','00. [28]10%,'00. [31]2-for-1,'97. [32]2-for-1,'97. [35]2-for-1,'98. [38]3-for-2,'97:2-for-1,'00,'01. [42]2-for-1,'97,'98. [45]No adj for stk dstr,'00.

Source: Standard & Poor's *Stock Guide* (June 2001): 92–93. Reprinted with permission.

mance of specific stocks relative to the price movements of the market for the immediate future. These recommendations consist of scores ranging from 5 (the lowest performance) to 1 (the highest performance). A score of 1 does not necessarily mean that the stock will earn a positive return; rather, it indicates that *Value Line* believes the stock should outperform the market, which in declining markets may mean that the investor will still suffer losses but that the losses will be smaller.

A page from the *Value Line Investment Survey* is given in Exhibit 4.2. As may be seen from this exhibit, *Value Line* reports a considerable amount of information. Most of these data are factual, but there are some projections. In this example *Value Line* suggests that the stock of Hershey Foods will perform in tandem with the market (i.e., the timeliness rating is 3) in the near term.

Value Line asserts that the securities it recommends have outperformed the market.[3] It also maintains that the stocks ranked 1 and 2 by its analysis consistently achieve higher returns than those ranked 4 and 5. There is some outside empirical support for *Value Line*'s claims, for one study found that stocks ranked 1 by *Value Line* consistently outperformed (even after adjusting for risk) a strategy of randomly selected stocks.[4]

For individual investors, *Value Line*'s performance is somewhat misleading because to achieve the same results, they would have to duplicate the recommendations. *Value Line* assigns a ranking of 1 to 100 stocks. Thus, if only $1,000 is invested in each, a total outlay of $100,000 would be required. Even if the investor could make the purchases as soon as the recommendations were made (which may be impossible), the commission costs on so many small purchases would reduce the return. Generally, investors must select among the recommendations, so the results could be very different from the return earned by all of *Value Line*'s recommendations. Some of the individual securities will outperform the market but others will not, and there is no reason to assume the investor will always select the winners. (There is, of course, no reason to assume the investor will always select the losers.)

Value Line also manages several funds that permit the investor to obtain a diversified portfolio based on its analysts' recommendations. However, the investor should realize that while the ranking system for picking stocks has done well, the mutual funds managed by Value Line have not performed as well. For example, the Value Line growth fund earned −15.3 percent in 1997 when the average return for growth funds was 3.3 percent. (The five-year return for the Value Line growth fund was 13.9 percent, while the average return for growth funds was 16.1 percent. See *The Individual Investor's Guide to Low-Load Mutual Funds,* 20th ed. [Chicago: American Association of Individual Investors, 2001].)

Specialized Investment Advisory Services

In addition to the information published by publicly held firms, Standard & Poor's, and Mergent, and advisory services such as Value Line, there is a host of specialized investment advice that the investor may purchase. Because these publishers and authors earn their living by selling these services, the purchaser should be

[3]See, for instance, "The Value Line Ranking System," *The Value Line Investment Survey Selection & Opinion* (January 18, 1985): 960. How the system is constructed is discussed in Zvi Bodie, Alex Kane, and Alan J. Marcus, *Essentials of Investments* (Boston, MA: Irwin McGraw-Hill, 1998), 427–428.

[4]Fisher Black, "Yes, Virginia, There Is Hope: Tests of the *Value Line* Ranking System," paper presented at the Center for Research in Security Prices, Graduate School of Business, University of Chicago, May 1971; and Thomas E. Copeland and David Mayers, "The *Value Line* Enigma (1965–1978): A Case Study of Performance Issues," *Journal of Financial Economics* (November 1982): 289–321. However, there have been periods when the *Value Line* recommendations did poorly. For example, during the first eight months of 1992, the *Value Line* selections declined over 11 percent while the S&P 500 stock index rose 1 percent. See John Dorfman, "*Value Line*'s Top Picks Flopped in 1st Half," *The Wall Street Journal* (September 14, 1992): C1–2.

EXHIBIT 4.2

Page from *Value Line Investment Survey*

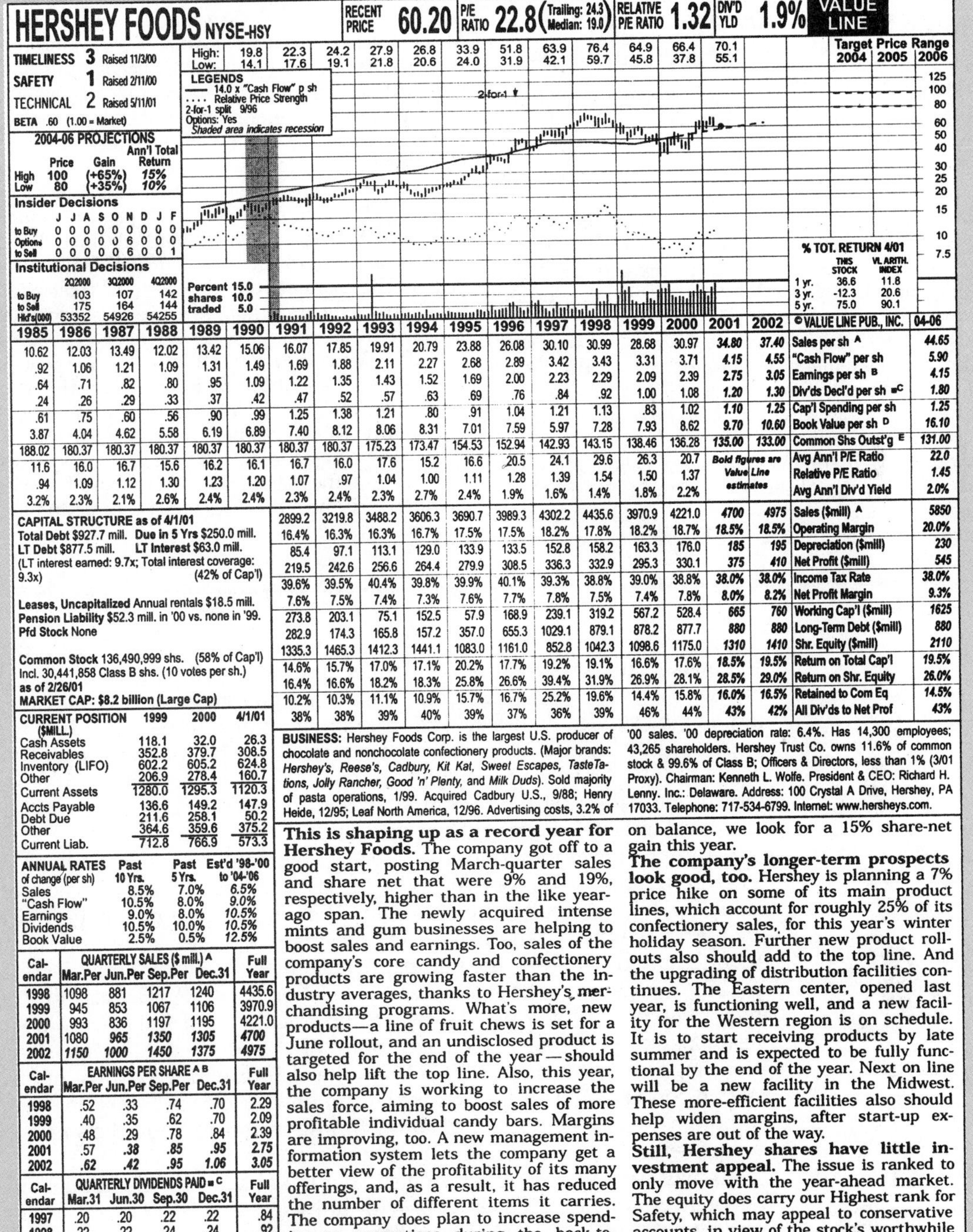

HERSHEY FOODS NYSE-HSY | RECENT PRICE 60.20 | P/E RATIO 22.8 (Trailing: 24.3, Median: 19.0) | RELATIVE P/E RATIO 1.32 | DIV'D YLD 1.9% | VALUE LINE

TIMELINESS 3 Raised 11/3/00
SAFETY 1 Raised 2/11/00
TECHNICAL 2 Raised 5/11/01
BETA .60 (1.00 = Market)

	1991	1992	1993	1994	1995	1996	1997	1998	1999	2000	2001
High:	19.8	22.3	24.2	27.9	26.8	33.9	51.8	63.9	76.4	64.9	66.4
Low:	14.1	17.6	19.1	21.8	20.6	24.0	31.9	42.1	59.7	45.8	37.8

High: 19.8, 22.3, 24.2, 27.9, 26.8, 33.9, 51.8, 63.9, 76.4, 64.9, 66.4, 70.1
Low: 14.1, 17.6, 19.1, 21.8, 20.6, 24.0, 31.9, 42.1, 59.7, 45.8, 37.8, 55.1

LEGENDS
— 14.0 x "Cash Flow" p sh
.... Relative Price Strength
2-for-1 split 9/96
Options: Yes
Shaded area indicates recession

2-for-1

Target Price Range 2004 | 2005 | 2006

125, 100, 80, 60, 50, 40, 30, 25, 20, 15, 10, 7.5

2004-06 PROJECTIONS

	Price	Gain	Ann'l Total Return
High	100	(+65%)	*15%*
Low	80	(+35%)	*10%*

Insider Decisions

	J	J	A	S	O	N	D	J	F
to Buy	0	0	0	0	0	0	0	0	0
Options	0	0	0	0	0	6	0	0	0
to Sell	0	0	0	0	0	6	0	0	1

Institutional Decisions

	2Q2000	3Q2000	4Q2000
to Buy	103	107	142
to Sell	175	164	144
Hld's(000)	53352	54926	54255

Percent shares traded 15.0, 10.0, 5.0

% TOT. RETURN 4/01

	THIS STOCK	VL ARITH. INDEX
1 yr.	36.6	11.8
3 yr.	-12.3	20.6
5 yr.	75.0	90.1

1985	1986	1987	1988	1989	1990	1991	1992	1993	1994	1995	1996	1997	1998	1999	2000	2001	2002	© VALUE LINE PUB., INC.	04-06
10.62	12.03	13.49	12.02	13.42	15.06	16.07	17.85	19.91	20.79	23.88	26.08	30.10	30.99	28.68	30.97	*34.80*	*37.40*	Sales per sh A	*44.65*
.92	1.06	1.21	1.09	1.31	1.49	1.69	1.88	2.11	2.27	2.68	2.89	3.42	3.43	3.31	3.71	*4.15*	*4.55*	"Cash Flow" per sh	*5.90*
.64	.71	.82	.80	.95	1.09	1.22	1.35	1.43	1.52	1.69	2.00	2.23	2.29	2.09	2.39	*2.75*	*3.05*	Earnings per sh B	*4.15*
.24	.26	.29	.33	.37	.42	.47	.52	.57	.63	.69	.76	.84	.92	1.00	1.08	*1.20*	*1.30*	Div'ds Decl'd per sh ■C	*1.80*
.61	.75	.60	.56	.90	.99	1.25	1.38	1.21	.80	.91	1.04	1.21	1.13	.83	1.02	*1.10*	*1.25*	Cap'l Spending per sh	*1.25*
3.87	4.04	4.62	5.58	6.19	6.89	7.40	8.12	8.06	8.31	7.01	7.59	5.97	7.28	7.93	8.62	*9.70*	*10.60*	Book Value per sh D	*16.10*
188.02	180.37	180.37	180.37	180.37	180.37	180.37	180.37	175.23	173.47	154.53	152.94	142.93	143.15	138.46	136.28	*135.00*	*133.00*	Common Shs Outst'g E	*131.00*
11.6	16.0	16.7	15.6	16.2	16.1	16.7	16.0	17.6	15.2	16.6	20.5	24.1	29.6	26.3	20.7	*Bold figures are*		Avg Ann'l P/E Ratio	*22.0*
.94	1.09	1.12	1.30	1.23	1.20	1.07	.97	1.04	1.00	1.11	1.28	1.39	1.54	1.50	1.37	*Value Line*		Relative P/E Ratio	*1.45*
3.2%	2.3%	2.1%	2.6%	2.4%	2.4%	2.3%	2.4%	2.3%	2.7%	2.4%	1.9%	1.6%	1.4%	1.8%	2.2%	*estimates*		Avg Ann'l Div'd Yield	*2.0%*
						2899.2	3219.8	3488.2	3606.3	3690.7	3989.3	4302.2	4435.6	3970.9	4221.0	*4700*	*4975*	Sales ($mill) A	*5850*
						16.4%	16.3%	16.3%	16.7%	17.5%	17.5%	18.2%	17.8%	18.2%	18.7%	*18.5%*	*18.5%*	Operating Margin	*20.0%*
						85.4	97.1	113.1	129.0	133.9	133.5	152.8	158.2	163.3	176.0	*185*	*195*	Depreciation ($mill)	*230*
						219.5	242.6	256.6	264.4	279.9	308.5	336.3	332.9	295.3	330.1	*375*	*410*	Net Profit ($mill)	*545*
						39.6%	39.5%	40.4%	39.8%	39.9%	40.1%	39.3%	38.8%	39.0%	38.8%	*38.0%*	*38.0%*	Income Tax Rate	*38.0%*
						7.6%	7.5%	7.4%	7.3%	7.6%	7.7%	7.8%	7.5%	7.4%	7.8%	*8.0%*	*8.2%*	Net Profit Margin	*9.3%*
						273.8	203.1	75.1	152.5	57.9	168.9	239.1	319.2	567.2	528.4	*665*	*760*	Working Cap'l ($mill)	*1625*
						282.9	174.3	165.8	157.2	357.0	655.3	1029.1	879.1	878.2	877.7	*880*	*880*	Long-Term Debt ($mill)	*880*
						1335.3	1465.3	1412.3	1441.1	1083.0	1161.0	852.8	1042.3	1098.6	1175.0	*1310*	*1410*	Shr. Equity ($mill)	*2110*
						14.6%	15.7%	17.0%	17.1%	20.2%	17.7%	19.2%	19.1%	16.6%	17.6%	*18.5%*	*19.5%*	Return on Total Cap'l	*19.5%*
						16.4%	16.6%	18.2%	18.3%	25.8%	26.6%	39.4%	31.9%	26.9%	28.1%	*28.5%*	*29.0%*	Return on Shr. Equity	*26.0%*
						10.2%	10.3%	11.1%	10.9%	15.7%	16.7%	25.2%	19.6%	14.4%	15.8%	*16.0%*	*16.5%*	Retained to Com Eq	*14.5%*
						38%	38%	39%	40%	39%	37%	36%	39%	46%	44%	*43%*	*42%*	All Div'ds to Net Prof	*43%*

CAPITAL STRUCTURE as of 4/1/01
Total Debt $927.7 mill. **Due in 5 Yrs** $250.0 mill.
LT Debt $877.5 mill. **LT Interest** $63.0 mill.
(LT interest earned: 9.7x; Total interest coverage: 9.3x) (42% of Cap'l)

Leases, Uncapitalized Annual rentals $18.5 mill.
Pension Liability $52.3 mill. in '00 vs. none in '99.
Pfd Stock None

Common Stock 136,490,999 shs. (58% of Cap'l)
Incl. 30,441,858 Class B shs. (10 votes per sh.)
as of 2/26/01
MARKET CAP: $8.2 billion (Large Cap)

CURRENT POSITION ($MILL.)	1999	2000	4/1/01
Cash Assets	118.1	32.0	26.3
Receivables	352.8	379.7	308.5
Inventory (LIFO)	602.2	605.2	624.8
Other	206.9	278.4	160.7
Current Assets	1280.0	1295.3	1120.3
Accts Payable	136.6	149.2	147.9
Debt Due	211.6	258.1	50.2
Other	364.6	359.6	375.2
Current Liab.	712.8	766.9	573.3

ANNUAL RATES of change (per sh)	Past 10 Yrs.	Past 5 Yrs.	Est'd '98-'00 to '04-'06
Sales	8.5%	7.0%	*6.5%*
"Cash Flow"	10.5%	8.0%	*9.0%*
Earnings	9.0%	8.0%	*10.5%*
Dividends	10.5%	10.0%	*10.5%*
Book Value	2.5%	0.5%	*12.5%*

Calendar	QUARTERLY SALES ($ mill.) A Mar.Per	Jun.Per	Sep.Per	Dec.31	Full Year
1998	1098	881	1217	1240	4435.6
1999	945	853	1067	1106	3970.9
2000	993	836	1197	1195	4221.0
2001	1080	*965*	*1350*	*1305*	*4700*
2002	*1150*	*1000*	*1450*	*1375*	*4975*

Calendar	EARNINGS PER SHARE A B Mar.Per	Jun.Per	Sep.Per	Dec.31	Full Year
1998	.52	.33	.74	.70	2.29
1999	.40	.35	.62	.70	2.09
2000	.48	.29	.78	.84	2.39
2001	.57	*.38*	*.85*	*.95*	*2.75*
2002	*.62*	*.42*	*.95*	*1.06*	*3.05*

Calendar	QUARTERLY DIVIDENDS PAID ■ C Mar.31	Jun.30	Sep.30	Dec.31	Full Year
1997	.20	.20	.22	.22	.84
1998	.22	.22	.24	.24	.92
1999	.24	.24	.26	.26	1.00
2000	.26	.26	.28	.28	1.08
2001	.28				

BUSINESS: Hershey Foods Corp. is the largest U.S. producer of chocolate and nonchocolate confectionery products. (Major brands: *Hershey's, Reese's, Cadbury, Kit Kat, Sweet Escapes, TasteTations, Jolly Rancher, Good 'n' Plenty,* and *Milk Duds*). Sold majority of pasta operations, 1/99. Acquired Cadbury U.S., 9/88; Henry Heide, 12/95; Leaf North America, 12/96. Advertising costs, 3.2% of '00 sales. '00 depreciation rate: 6.4%. Has 14,300 employees; 43,265 shareholders. Hershey Trust Co. owns 11.6% of common stock & 99.6% of Class B; Officers & Directors, less than 1% (3/01 Proxy). Chairman: Kenneth L. Wolfe. President & CEO: Richard H. Lenny. Inc.: Delaware. Address: 100 Crystal A Drive, Hershey, PA 17033. Telephone: 717-534-6799. Internet: www.hersheys.com.

This is shaping up as a record year for Hershey Foods. The company got off to a good start, posting March-quarter sales and share net that were 9% and 19%, respectively, higher than in the like year-ago span. The newly acquired intense mints and gum businesses are helping to boost sales and earnings. Too, sales of the company's core candy and confectionery products are growing faster than the industry averages, thanks to Hershey's merchandising programs. What's more, new products—a line of fruit chews is set for a June rollout, and an undisclosed product is targeted for the end of the year—should also help lift the top line. Also, this year, the company is working to increase the sales force, aiming to boost sales of more profitable individual candy bars. Margins are improving, too. A new management information system lets the company get a better view of the profitability of its many offerings, and, as a result, it has reduced the number of different items it carries. The company does plan to increase spending on promotions during the back-to-school and Halloween seasons, which will put downward pressure on margins. Still, on balance, we look for a 15% share-net gain this year.

The company's longer-term prospects look good, too. Hershey is planning a 7% price hike on some of its main product lines, which account for roughly 25% of its confectionery sales, for this year's winter holiday season. Further new product rollouts also should add to the top line. And the upgrading of distribution facilities continues. The Eastern center, opened last year, is functioning well, and a new facility for the Western region is on schedule. It is to start receiving products by late summer and is expected to be fully functional by the end of the year. Next on line will be a new facility in the Midwest. These more-efficient facilities also should help widen margins, after start-up expenses are out of the way.

Still, Hershey shares have little investment appeal. The issue is ranked to only move with the year-ahead market. The equity does carry our Highest rank for Safety, which may appeal to conservative accounts, in view of the stock's worthwhile total-return potential.

George A. Niemond *May 11, 2001*

(A) Year ends Dec. 31; qtrs. end first Sunday of April, July, Oct. (B) Primary egs. until '96. Dil. after. Excl. gain (loss) from discont. oper.: '85, (3¢); '88, 5¢. Excl. net nonrecur.: '88, 15¢; '90, 6¢; '93, d18¢; '94, d23¢; '96, d12¢; '98, 5¢; '99, $1.17, '00, 3¢. Quarters may not add to total due to change in shs. out. Next egs. rpt. due late July. (C) Next div'd mtg. about Aug. 1. Next ex date abt. Aug. 25. Approx. div'd pmt. dates: 15th of Mar., June, Sept., Dec. ■ Div'd reinv. plan avail. (D) Incl. intang. In '00: $474.4 mill., $3.48/sh. (E) In mill., adj. for stock split.

Company's Financial Strength	A+
Stock's Price Stability	95
Price Growth Persistence	70
Earnings Predictability	85

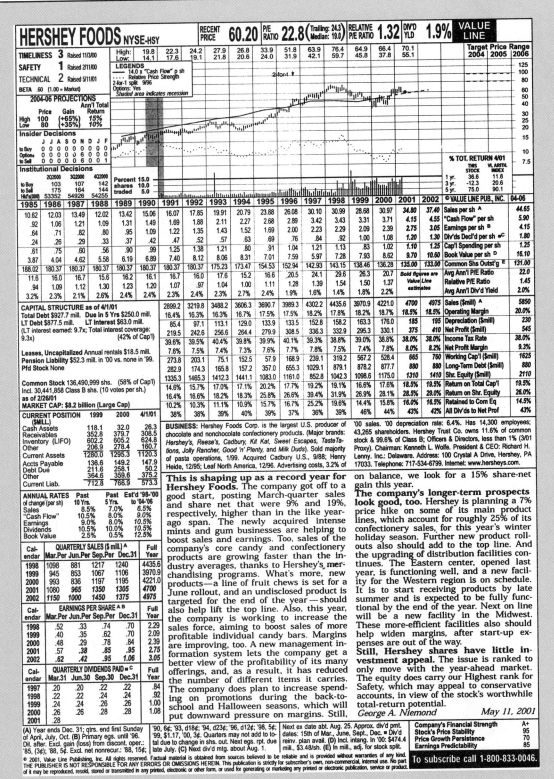

Source: *Value Line Investment Survey* (May 11, 2001). Reprinted with permission.

POINTS OF INTEREST

Standard & Poor's *Corporation Records* and Mergent's Manuals

Two of the most important sources of factual information concerning firms and their securities are the *Corporation Records* published by Standard & Poor's and the various manuals published by Mergent. S&P's *Corporation Records* contains descriptions of companies listed on the major exchanges and many over-the-counter stocks. (Firms that are included must pay a fee for the service. As of 2001, Mergent charged from $2,200 to $6,900 depending on the extent of the coverage.) These corporate records are updated quarterly and include the most recent fiscal year's financial statements. For larger firms, S&P's *Corporation Records* includes descriptions of the firm's various securities, its earnings, dividends, and the annual range of security prices for the previous decade.

Previously, Mergent manuals were called Moody's manuals and were published by Financial Information Services (FIS). That named has been changed to Mergent FIS and the manuals now bear the Mergent name.

Mergent's manuals compile information similar to S&P's *Corporation Records,* but Mergent publishes this material in specialized volumes. The titles include: *Mergent Industrial Manual, Mergent Bank and Finance Manual, Mergent Public Utility Manual, Mergent Municipal & Government Manual, Mergent Transportation Manual, Mergent International Manual,* and *Mergent OTC Industrial Manual.* In addition to these annually published manuals, Mergent also publishes *News Reports,* which continually updates the material in the manuals.

Like S&P's *Corporation Records,* Mergent manuals require that the firm or government pay an annual fee for inclusion. Material in these manuals includes descriptions of the firm, its securities, and recent financial statements. The manuals are an excellent reference for descriptions of the important features of a firm's securities, especially its bonds.

S&P's *Corporation Records* and the Mergent manuals include essentially the same information. However, occasionally a firm is listed in one and not the other. This is particularly true for small firms whose securities are traded over-the-counter. Corporations whose securities are traded on the major exchanges generally choose to be included in both S&P's *Corporation Records* and Mergent's manuals.

somewhat cautious when acting on any specific recommendations. Previous recommendations that proved successful do not guarantee future success.[5] Furthermore, if the service makes several recommendations, some, according to the laws of probability, should be correct. The service's true performance may be reflected in the number of successes relative to the number of recommendations or in the returns earned on all the recommendations relative to a measure of the market, such as Standard & Poor's 500 stock index.

Before the development of the Internet, you could obtain investment newsletters through the postal service. Today, these newsletters have Web addresses, and many are delivered solely electronically. The number of sites is large and growing, and because anyone can develop an investment strategy and sell it through subscription on the Internet, the number of such newsletters will only increase.

One means to access several newsletters is INVESTools (http://www.investools.com), which provides portfolio tracking and linkages to about 30 investor newsletters that encompass many of the fundamental and technical approaches covered in this textbook. The site also provides a source of basic information concerning a firm or a mutual fund and a means to obtain stock quotes. Although the newsletters are obtained through subscriptions, the site permits you to register and receive complimentary information.

As may be expected, INVESTools is not the only Web site that has links to investment newsletters. Other sites with links include The Market Line Letter at Wall Street City (http://www.wallstreetcity.com), Investors Newsletter Digest (http://www.investorsnews.com), NETworth (http:/www.networth.galt.com).

[5]The SEC and state regulatory agencies forbid advisory services from providing single illustrations or examples of previously successful recommendations. All recommendations ever made must be presented.

POINTS OF INTEREST

Learning While You Drive: Investment Cassettes

If you can learn French or listen to a novel on your way to work, why can't you learn about investments? The answer: You can! The American Association of Individual Investors (http://www.aaii.com) has developed an "Audio Cassette Collection," so you can pop in a cassette when you are on the road. The tapes are 1½ to 3 hours in duration and each is accompanied by a workbook. The subjects include such varied investment topics as retirement and financial planning, understanding financial statements, investment fundamentals, small stock investing, stock valuation models, municipal bonds, mutual funds, and real estate investment trusts. Similar material is also available on videotape. These materials may be ordered directly from the association: 625 North Michigan Avenue, Chicago, IL 60611.

This list is representative and not exhaustive of means of accessing sites of investment newsletters.

One source for comparing the performance of various investment advisory services is the *Hulbert Financial Digest,* a monthly publication that objectively rates the performance of over 150 services and includes profiles of better performers. The editor, Mark Hulbert, also writes columns on performance for *Forbes* and is the author of the *Hulbert Financial Digest Almanac,* a guide to investment newsletters.

Socially Responsible Investing

Socially responsible investing refers to buying securities in firms that produce socially desirable goods and services or pursue socially desirable policies. Of course, what is considered socially desirable is determined by each individual. For one investor, manufacturers of military and defense products or electric utilities with nuclear facilities may be examples of firms that do not produce socially desirable products. The securities of these firms would be excluded from consideration for possible investments. Another investor, however, may believe that a strong defense is socially responsible or that nuclear power is less polluting than oil and coal-fired generators and would include the securities of defense contractors and nuclear utilities as possible investments.

Socially responsible investing may be applied not only to products but to other facets of business enterprise. Does the firm have a good record for promoting women and minorities? Does the firm perform research on live animals? Does the firm sponsor socially desirable programs, such as research on cancer or AIDS? These are but a few of the possible social considerations individual investors may apply when selecting firms for possible investment.

If socially responsible investing appeals to an individual, he or she must determine which firms meet whatever social goals or criteria that are deemed important. In one sense, this process is another illustration of selecting among alternatives using a screening process, except the social criteria are added to (or substituted for) financial criteria to identify acceptable investments. Initial results suggest results are comparable to returns generated by the major stock indices, which suggests that the investor is not hurt (or helped) by making socially conscientious investments.

If the investor does not want to select individual socially conscientious firms, a possible alternative is to invest in a socially conscientious mutual fund with a portfolio that is consistent with the investor's social criteria. The *2000 AAII Guide to Low-Load Funds* lists nine socially conscientious mutual funds. The Social Investment Forum is a nonprofit organization that promotes the practice of socially

responsible investing. Its Web site (http://www.socialinvest.org) explains the concept, has recent information concerning social investing, and provides a link to Co-op America (http://www.coopamerica.org), which lists mutual funds that are members of the Social Investment Forum.[6] Whether these funds meet the individual's social goals, however, is up to the investor to determine.

Other Sources of Information

The U.S. government publishes a considerable amount of material that may be useful to investors. These publications include the *Survey of Current Business,* which presents business statistics, and the *Business Conditions Digest,* which provides information on business indicators. The *Economic Report of the President* and the *Annual Report of the Council of Economic Advisors* are published annually; they cover business conditions and provide economic forecasts. For statistics on interest rates, the money supply, national income, and unemployment rates, the investor may consult the *Federal Reserve Bulletin,* which is published monthly by the board of governors of the Federal Reserve. (For Web addresses, see the accompanying Points of Interest.)

The investor may also join an investment club. Such clubs pool the members' funds and invest them in securities.[7] Most clubs invest only moderate sums. For

POINTS OF INTEREST

Finding Government Publications on the Web

The federal government and its agencies publish a substantial amount of material, some of which may interest the individual investor. This material includes historical data, forecasts, and regulations, such as the tax laws. Although the information is available in print form, the investor may find it easier to access the documents directly through the Internet.

The following is a list of Web addresses that should facilitate obtaining government material:

Federal Government

Economic Report of the President:
http://www.access.gpo.gov/eop/
Bureau of Labor Statistics:
http://stats.bls.gov
Bureau of Economic Analysis:
http://www.bea.doc.gov
U.S. Budget Information:
http://www.access.gpo.gov/omb/omb003.html
Federal Deposit Insurance Corporation:
http://www.fdic.gov
Internal Revenue Service:
http://www.irs.ustreas.gov/prod
U.S. Treasury:
http://www.ustreas.gov

Federal Reserve

Federal Reserve Board of Governors:
http://www.federalreserve.gov
Federal Reserve Bank of New York:
http://www.ny.frb.org

From this list, you may obtain the *Economic Report of the President,* information on interest rates (from the Federal Reserve or the Federal Reserve Bank of New York), employment statistics and consumer prices (Bureau of Labor Statistics), foreign exchange rates (Federal Reserve), and copies of tax laws and tax forms (IRS). There is also a Government Information Locator (http://www.gils.net/index.html) to facilitate locating specific information and data published by the federal government.

[6] Other possible Web sites include the Coalition for Environmentally Responsible Economies (http://www.ceres.org), the Investor Responsibility Research Center (http://www.irrc.org), and SocialFunds.com (http://www.socialfunds.com).

[7] For a description of the procedures of establishing an investment club, consult the *Investors Manual* published by the National Association of Investors Corporation, Box 220, Royal Oak, MI 48068. The Web address is http://www.better-investing.org.

example, members pay $10 per month in dues, which are then invested in the club's name. Although such sums of money are trivial, the potential knowledge and experience that can be gained through membership in such clubs are not. Because members must agree on the club's investment goals, strategies, and choice of investments, the individual may learn a considerable amount concerning investments as the club formulates and executes policy. These clubs may have an additional advantage in that they may be able to obtain professional help at a fraction of the cost. For example, a broker may be willing to talk with members of the club and execute orders for them. The broker may provide this service for the potential commissions not only from the club but also from individual members of the club who may become clients. Unfortunately, the club may be dominated by one or a few outspoken individuals, and the club's goals may not coincide with the individual's goals or financial needs. Because of these factors, the individual should not rely solely on investment clubs to make personal investment decisions.[8]

The individual should also consider taking courses in investments. Many adult education programs offer noncredit courses in areas of investments. These may range from basic financial planning or investment fundamentals to more specialized topics such as financing college education, value investing, investments for women, or using options. Such courses are usually taught by financial professionals. Unless they are thinly disguised sales presentations, they can be a useful source of investment information.

Last, there are an almost unlimited number of Web sites that provide information for investors. Many Web addresses have already been provided in the body of this chapter, but the following is a list of several additional sites the investor may find useful:

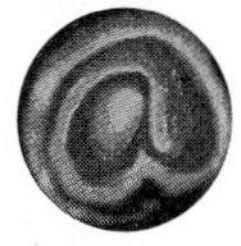

BigCharts (http://www.bigcharts.com) permits the investor to chart and compare stocks, mutual funds, and stock indices

DirectAdvice (http://www.directadvice.com) is a source primarily devoted to financial planning services.

FinanCenter (http://www.financenter.com) provides financial calculators and facilitates comparing borrowing alternatives.

Financial Engines (http://www.financialengines.com) and Morningstar ClearFuture (a subdivision of Morningstar, http://www.morningstar.com) specialize in retirement planning.

Gómez.com (http://www.gomez.com) compares on-line brokers.

Motley Fool (http://www.fool.com) provides basic financial information and advice in a somewhat irreverent way that removes some of the excessive seriousness associated with investment information.

Thomson Investors Network (http://www.thomsoninvest.net) provides stock data, charts, tools of financial analysis, a firm's earnings history, and industry comparisons.

Validea (http://www.validea.com) tracks analysts' recommendations.

As the preceding has illustrated, there is no shortage of readily available information. The problem for the investor is separating "the wheat from the chaff" and

[8]While an investment club may be a means to learn about investments and to socialize, it is not necessarily a means to earn higher returns. One study [Brad M. Barber and Terrance Odean, "Too Many Cooks Spoil the Profits: Investment Club Performance," *Financial Analysts Journal* (January–February 2000): 17–25] found that on average investment clubs earned lower returns than the market as measured by the S&P 500 stock index. The explanation for the lower returns revolves around the tendency of club members to trade excessively, which generates higher commissions and requires having to cover the spread. (See the section on the cost of investing in Chapter 3.)

processing it into a useful form from which to draw conclusions.[9] Even if the investor relies solely on the advice of others, such as brokers or investment services, that individual must still select from the alternatives that are suggested. For example, each week the *Value Line Investment Survey* recommends 100 stocks that should, in its opinion, outperform the market. No investor is going to buy all of them. If an investor follows the advice of the publication and purchases several of its recommended stocks, he or she must still choose from the various recommended investment alternatives. Hence, the final investment decision rests with the individual investor, who earns the returns and bears the risk.

Summary

This chapter has described some of the extensive literature that is available to investors. These publications range from the annual and quarterly reports of publicly held firms to specialized investment advisory services. Some of this information is readily available and may be obtained with little effort and at little cost. Other sources require that the investor pay a substantial sum for the material. Many brokerage firms carry some of the publications that have been described, and the investor may often find them at a local library.

Although none of the publications can consistently predict the future (and the investor should be skeptical of any publication claiming that the subscriber can make a fortune), investors do need to be well informed. Reading financial literature from diverse sources is an excellent means of keeping abreast of events in the financial markets. The investor should be aware of the many sources of potentially useful financial information.

There is no shortage of information on financial markets and investing. Instead, the problems for the investor are processing this information and putting it into a usable form for making financial decisions. Ultimately, it is the individual who reaps the returns earned by the investment and bears the risk of loss.

Questions

1) Describe the contents of an annual report.
2) What is a 10-K report? What is a prospectus?
3) Name several sources of information on investments that are available to individuals. In general, is there a shortage of available information?
4) Why may investment advisory research reports and financial analysts' recommendations be self-serving?
5) The act of finding information is one of the best means to learn about the literature that is available to the investor. Locate the following and skim through each to become familiar with its contents: *The Wall Street Journal* and *Barron's; Value Line Investment Survey, The Outlook,* or some other advisory service publication; *Forbes, Fortune,* or *Business Week;* and *Mergent Industrial Manual* or Standard & Poor's *Corporation Records.*

[9]This problem of separating useful information from irrelevant, misleading, or even incorrect information is exacerbated if the individual visits "chat rooms" on the Internet. Because you cannot determine the motivation of the person providing the material, it may be best for the serious investor to completely avoid this source of "information."

The Time Value of Money

5

For 40 years, you diligently put $2,000 in your retirement account at the local bank. The bank pays you 4 percent interest. If, however, you had placed that money in a mutual fund that earned twice as much (8 percent), you would have accumulated $391,062 more in the mutual fund. The account at the bank will be worth $190,051, but the mutual fund will be worth $581,113. Ben Franklin said: "Money makes money. And the money that money makes makes more money." Mr. Franklin, however, did not point out the importance of the rate at which money makes more money.

The time value of money is one of the most crucial concepts in finance. An investment decision is made today. You buy stock in IBM now, but the sale and the return on the investment will be in the future. You believe you need $50,000 to make the down payment on a house. You want to know how much you must save each year. Or if you are able to save $4,000 annually, how long will it take to accumulate the $50,000? You save $50,000 and buy a $200,000 home; now you have a $150,000 mortgage. What will be your periodic payments required by the loan? There has to be a way to express these future amounts in the present. The process of expressing the future in the present and of expressing the present in the future is the essence of the time value of money.

This chapter covers four concepts: (1) the future value of $1, (2) the present value of $1, (3) the future sum of an annuity, and (4) the present value of an annuity. Several examples apply these concepts to investments. The chapter closes with an introduction to security valuation, using the time value of money.

You may use financial calculators or computer programs such as the software accompanying this text to solve these problems. However, every problem may not readily fit into a preprogrammed calculator or computer template. Computer programs may facilitate the calculations, but only if you can properly set up the problem. Even then the specific question being asked may not be answered. You may have to work with the numbers or interpret them.

The purpose of understanding the time value of money is to facilitate understanding investments and to perform problems that pertain to valuation of assets and financial planning. If you already know the topic, you may proceed to the next chapter. If you do not understand the time value of money, careful attention to this chapter is critical because knowledge of the topic and the ability to work problems are essential for comprehending important concepts in investments.

Learning Objectives

After completing this chapter you should be able to:

1 Explain why a dollar received tomorrow is not equal in value to a dollar received today.

2 Differentiate between compounding and discounting.

3 Distinguish among the future value of $1, the future value of an annuity, the present value of $1, and the present value of an annuity.

4 Solve problems concerning the time value of money.

The Future Value of $1

If $100 is deposited in a savings account that pays 5 percent annually, how much money will be in the account at the end of the year? The answer is easy to determine: $100 plus $5 interest, for a total of $105. This answer is derived by multiplying $100 by 5 percent, which gives the interest earned during the year, and then by adding this interest to the initial principal. That is,

Initial principal + (Interest rate × Initial principal) = Principal after one year.

This calculation is expressed in algebraic form in Equation 5.1, in which P represents the principal and i is the rate of interest. This equation employs subscripts to represent time. The subscript 0 indicates the present, and 1 means the end of the first year. (The second year, third year, and so on to any number of years will be represented by 2, 3, . . . n, respectively. This use of subscripts occurs throughout this text.)

(5.1)
$$P_0 + iP_0 = P_1.$$

If P_0 is the initial principal ($100) and i is the interest rate (5%), the principal after one year (P_1) will be

$$\$100 + 0.05(\$100) = \$105.$$

How much will be in the account after two years? This answer is obtained in the same manner by adding the interest earned during the second year to the principal at the beginning of the second year—that is, $105 plus 0.05 times $105 equals $110.25, which may be expressed in algebraic terms:

(5.2)
$$P_1 + iP_1 = P_2.$$

compounding
The process by which interest is paid on interest that has been previously earned.

After two years the initial deposit of $100 will have grown to $110.25; the savings account will have earned $10.25 in interest. This total interest is composed of $10 representing interest on the initial principal and $0.25 representing interest that has accrued during the second year on the $5 in interest earned during the first year. This earning of interest on interest is called **compounding**. Money that is deposited in savings accounts is frequently referred to as being compounded, for interest is earned on both the principal and the previously earned interest.

The words *interest* and *compounded* are frequently used together. For example, banks may advertise that interest is compounded daily for savings accounts, or the cost of a loan may be expressed as 12 percent compounded annually. In the previous example, interest was earned only once during the year; thus it is an example of interest that is compounded annually. In many cases, interest is not compounded annually but quarterly, semiannually, or even daily. The more frequently it is compounded (i.e., the more frequently the interest is added to the principal), the more rapidly the interest is put to work to earn even more interest.

How much will be in the account at the end of three years? This answer can be determined by the same general formula that was previously used. The amount in the account at the end of the second year ($110.25) is added to the interest that is earned during the third year (5% × $110.25); that is,

$$\$110.25 + \$5.5125 = \$115.76,$$

or the formula may be expressed algebraically as

(5.3)
$$P_2 + iP_2 = P_3.$$

By continuing with this method, it is possible to determine the amount that will be in the account at the end of 20 or more years, but doing so is obviously a lot of work. Fortunately, there are easier ways to ascertain how much will be in the account after any given number of years. The first is to use an interest table called the future value of $1 table.

The first table in Appendix A gives the interest factors for the future value of $1. The interest rates at which $1 is compounded periodically are read horizontally at the top of the table. The number of periods (e.g., years) is read vertically along the left-hand margin. To determine the amount to which $100 will grow in three years at 5 percent interest, find the interest factor (1.158) and multiply it by $100. That calculation yields $115.80, which is the answer that was derived previously by working out the equations (except for rounding). To ascertain the amount to which $100 will grow after 25 years at 5 percent interest compounded annually, multiply $100 by the interest factor, 3.386, to obtain the answer $338.60. Thus, if $100 were placed in a savings account that paid 5 percent interest annually, there would be $338.60 in the account after 25 years.

Interest tables for the future value of $1 are based on a general formulation of the simple equations used previously. To determine the amount in the savings account at the end of Year 1, the following equation was used:

(5.1) $$P_0 + iP_0 = P_1,$$

which may be written as

$$P_0(1 + i) = P_1.$$

To calculate the amount after two years, the following equation was used:

(5.2) $$P_1 + iP_1 = P_2,$$

which may be written as

$$P_1(1 + i) = P_2.$$

Since P_1 equals $P_0(1 + i)$, the amount in the account at the end of Year 2 may be expressed as

$$P_0(1 + i)(1 + i) = P_2.$$

This equation uses the term $1 + i$ twice, for P_0 is being multiplied by $1 + i$ twice. Thus, it is possible to write Equation 5.2 as

$$P_0(1 + i)^2 = P_2.$$

The amount to which $1 will grow may always be expressed in terms of the initial dollar (i.e., P_0). The general formula for finding the amount to which $1 will grow in n number of years, if it is compounded annually, is

(5.4) $$P_0(1 + i)^n = P_n.$$

Thus, the general formula for finding the future value of $1 for any number of years consists of (1) the initial dollar (P_0), (2) the interest $(1 + i)$ and (3) the number of years (n). Taken together, $(1 + i)^n$, the interest rate and time, are referred to as the *interest factor.* This interest factor for selected interest rates and time periods is given in the interest tables in Appendix A.

FIGURE 5.1

Future Value of $1.00

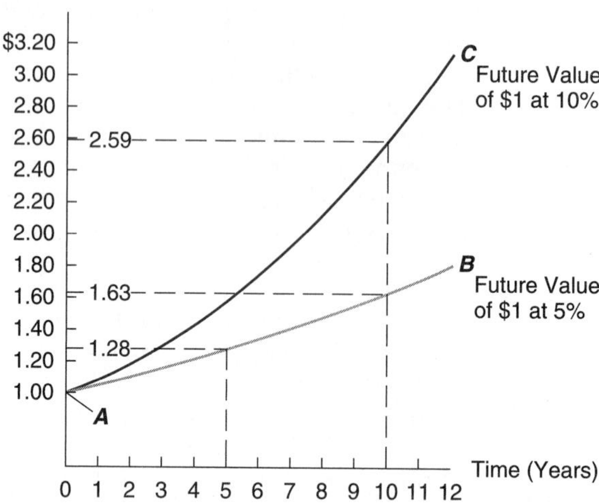

As may be seen in the first table in Appendix A, the value of $1 grows with increases in the length of time and in the rate of interest. These relationships are illustrated in Figure 5.1. If $1 is compounded at 5 percent interest (*AB* in the figure), it will grow to $1.28 after five years and to $1.63 after ten years. However, if $1 is compounded at 10 percent interest (*AC* on the graph), it will grow to $2.59 in ten years. These cases illustrate the basic nature of compounding: The longer the funds continue to grow and the higher the interest rate, the higher will be the ultimate value.

It also should be noted that doubling the interest rate more than doubles the amount of interest that is earned over a number of years. In the example just given, the interest rate doubled from 5 percent to 10 percent; however, the amount of interest that will have accumulated in ten years rises from $0.63 at 5 percent to $1.59 at 10 percent. This is the result of the fact that compounding involves a geometric progression. The interest $(1 + i)$ has been raised to some power (n).

Future value problems may also be easily solved with the use of a financial calculator designed for business applications. These calculators have been programmed to solve time value problems. (Some financial calculators also have other business applications, such as determining depreciation expense and statistical analysis. Many employers expect new hires to be able to use financial calculators, so an inability to use them may put you at a disadvantage.)

Although there are differences among models, financial calculators generally have five special function keys:

N   I or **%   PV   PMT   FV**

These keys represent the time period (N), the interest rate (I or %), the amount in the present (PV for *present value*), the periodic payment (PMT for *annuity*, which will be discussed later in this chapter), and the amount in the future (FV for *future value*).

To illustrate how easy financial calculators are to use, consider the preceding illustration of the future value of $1 in which $100 grew to $338.60 after 25 years when the annual interest rate was 5 percent. Using a financial calculator, enter the present amount (PV = − 100), the interest rate (I = 5), and time (N = 25). Since there are no annual payments, be certain that PMT is set equal to zero (PMT = 0). Then instruct the calculator to determine the future value (FV = ?). The calculator should arrive at a future value of $338.64, which is almost the same amount derived using the interest table for the future value of $1. (The difference is the result of the interest tables being rounded to three places.)

You may wonder why the present value was entered as a negative number. Financial calculators consider payments as either cash inflows or cash outflows. Cash inflows are entered as positive numbers, and cash outflows are entered as negative numbers. In the example, the initial amount is an outflow because the individual invests the $100. The resulting future amount is a cash inflow since the investor receives the terminal amount. That is, the investor gives up the $100 (the outflow) and after 25 years receives the $338.64 (the inflow).

Problems involving time value permeate this text and are illustrated with the use of interest tables and with financial calculators. Illustrations using interest tables clarify the basic concept, while the illustrations that employ the financial calculator indicate the ease with which the answer may be derived. The financial calculator illustrations use the following general form:

PV = ?
FV = ?
PMT = ?
N = ?
I = ?

followed by the answer. When applied to the preceding illustration, the form is

PV = $−100
FV = ?
PMT = 0
N = 25
I = 5

FV = $338.64

The final answer is separated from the data that is entered. Except for the first illustrations in this chapter, each example is placed in the margin so that it does not break the flow of the written material.

The Present Value of $1

present value
The current worth of an amount to be received in the future.

discounting
The process of determining present value.

In the preceding section, $1 grew, or compounded, over time. This section considers the reverse. How much is $1 that will be received in the future worth today? For example, how much will a $1,000 payment 20 years hence be worth today if the funds earn 10 percent annually? This question incorporates the time value of money, but instead of asking how much $1 will be worth at some future date, it asks how much that future $1 is worth today. This is a question of **present value**. The process by which this question is answered is called **discounting**. Discounting determines the worth of funds that are to be received in the future in terms of their present value.

In the earlier section, the future value of $1 was calculated by Equation 5.4:

$$P_0(1 + i)^n = P_n. \tag{5.4}$$

Discounting reverses this equation. The present value (P_0) is determined by dividing the future value (P_n) by the interest factor $(1 + i)^n$. This is expressed in Equation 5.5:

(5.5)

$$P_0 = \frac{P_n}{(1 + i)^n}.$$

The future is discounted by the appropriate interest factor to determine the present value. For example, if the interest rate is 10 percent, the present value of $100 to be received five years from today is

$$\begin{aligned} P_0 &= \frac{\$100}{(1 + 0.1)^5} \\ &= \frac{\$100}{1.611} \\ &= \$62.07. \end{aligned}$$

As with the future value of $1, interest tables and financial calculators ease the calculation of present values. The second table in Appendix A gives the interest factors for the present value of $1 for selected interest rates and time periods. The interest rates are read horizontally at the top, and time is read vertically along the left-hand side. To determine the present value of $1 that will be received in five years if the current interest rate is 10 percent, multiply $1 by the interest factor, which is found in the table under the vertical column for 10 percent and in the horizontal column for five years. The present value of $100 is

$$\$100 \times 0.621 = \$62.10.$$

Thus, $100 that will be received after five years is currently worth only $62.10 if the interest rate is 10 percent. This is the same answer that was determined with Equation 5.5 (except for rounding).

To solve this problem using a financial calculator, enter the future amount (FV = 100), the interest rate (I = 10), and the number of years (N = 5). Set the payments equal to zero (PMT = 0), and instruct the calculator to compute the present value (PV = ?). The calculator should determine the present value to be −62.09; once again the answer is virtually the same as that derived from the interest tables. Notice that the calculator expresses the present value as a negative number. If you receive a $100 cash inflow after ten years, that will require a current outflow of $62.09 if the rate of interest is 10 percent.

As may be seen in Equation 5.5, the present value of $1 depends on (1) the length of time before it will be received and (2) the interest rate. The farther into the future the dollar will be received and the higher the interest rate, the lower the present value of the dollar. This is illustrated by Figure 5.2, which gives the relationship between the present value of $1 and the length of time at various interest rates. Lines *AB* and *AC* give the present value of $1 at 4 percent and 7 percent, respectively. As may be seen in this graph, $1 to be received after 20 years is worth considerably less than $1 to be received after five years when both are discounted at the same percentage rate. At 4 percent (line *AB*) the current value of $1 to be received after 20 years is only $0.456, whereas $1 to be received after five years is worth $0.822. Also, the higher the interest rate (i.e., discount factor), the lower the present value of $1. For example, the present value of $1 to be received after five years is $0.822 at 4 percent, but it is only $0.713 at 7 percent.

FIGURE 5.2

Present Value of $1 to Be Received in the Future

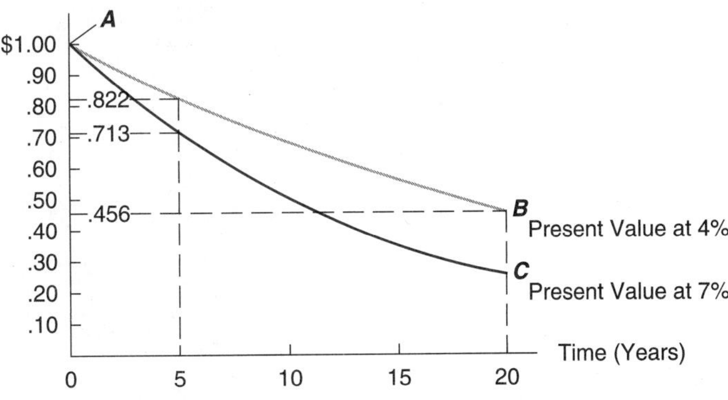

The Future Sum of an Annuity

annuity
A series of equal annual payments.

future sum of an annuity
Compound value of a series of equal annual payments.

annuity due
A series of equal annual payments with the payments made at the beginning of the year.

ordinary annuity
A series of equal annual payments in which the payments are made at the end of each year.

How much will be in a savings account after three years if $100 is deposited annually and the account pays 5 percent interest? This is similar to the future value of $1 except that the payment is not received as one lump sum but as a series. If the payments are equal, the series is called an **annuity**. The question is an illustration of the **future sum of an annuity**.

To determine how much will be in the account we must consider not only the interest rate earned but also whether deposits are made at the beginning of the year or the end of the year. If each payment is made at the beginning of the year, the series is called an **annuity due**. If the payments are made at the end of the year, the series is an **ordinary annuity**. What is the future sum of an annuity if $100 is deposited in an account for three years starting right now? What is the future sum of an annuity if $100 is placed in an account for three years starting at the end of the first year? The first question concerns an annuity due, while the second question illustrates an ordinary annuity.

The flow of payments for these two types of annuities is illustrated in Exhibit 5.1 (p. 104). In both cases, the $100 is deposited for three years in a savings account that pays 5 percent interest. The top half of the figure shows the annuity due, while the bottom half illustrates the ordinary annuity. In both cases, three years elapse from the present to when the final amount is determined and three payments are made. The difference in the timing of the payment results in a difference in the interest earned. Because in an annuity due the payments are made at the beginning of each year, the annuity due earns more interest ($31.01 versus $15.25) and thus has the higher terminal value ($331.01 versus $315.25). As will be illustrated later in the chapter, the greater the interest rate and the longer the time period, the greater will be this difference in terminal values.

The procedures for determining the future sum of an annuity due (FSAD) and the future sum of an ordinary annuity (FSOA) are stated formally in Equations 5.6 and 5.7, respectively. In each equation, *PMT* represents the equal, periodic payment, *i* represents the rate of interest, and *n* represents the number of years that elapse from the present until the end of the time period. For the annuity due, the equation is

$$\text{FSAD} = PMT(1 + i)^1 + PMT(1 + i)^2 + \cdots + PMT(1 + i)^n. \quad (5.6)$$

EXHIBIT 5.1

The Flow of Payments for the Future Value of an Annuity Due and an Ordinary Annuity

	Annuity Due				
	1/1/×0	1/1/×1	1/1/×2	1/1/×3	Sum
	$100.00	5.00	5.25	5.51	$115.76
		100.00	5.00	5.25	110.25
			100.00	5.00	105.00
Amount in the account	$100.00	205.00	315.25	331.01	$331.01
	Ordinary Annuity				
	1/1/×0	1/1/×1	1/1/×2	1/1/×3	Sum
	—	$100.00	5.00	5.25	$110.25
			100.00	5.00	105.00
				100.00	100.00
Amount in the account	—	$100.00	205.00	315.25	$315.25

When this equation is applied to the previous example in which $i = 0.05$, $n = 3$, and the annual payment $PMT = \$100$, the accumulated sum is

$$\begin{aligned}\text{FSAD} &= \$100(1 + 0.05)^1 + 100(1 + 0.05)^2 + 100(1 + 0.05)^3\\ &= \$105 + 110.25 + 115.76\\ &= \$331.01.\end{aligned}$$

For the ordinary annuity the equation is

$$\text{FSOA} = PMT(1 + i)^0 + PMT(1 + i)^1 + \cdots + PMT(1 + i)^{n-1}. \quad (5.7)$$

When this equation is applied to the preceding example, the accumulated sum is

$$\begin{aligned}\text{FSOA} &= \$100(1 + 0.05)^0 + 100(1 + 0.05)^1 + 100(1 + 0.05)^{3-1}\\ &= \$100 + 105 + 110.25\\ &= \$315.25.\end{aligned}$$

Although it is possible to derive the sum of an annuity in this manner, it is very cumbersome. Fortunately, interest tables and financial calculators facilitate these calculations.[1] In the third table in Appendix A we find the interest factors for the future sum of an ordinary annuity for selected time periods and selected interest rates. (Interest tables are usually presented only for ordinary annuities. How these tables may be used for annuities due is discussed later.) The number of periods is read vertically at the left, and the interest rates are read horizontally at the top. To ascertain the future sum of the ordinary annuity in the previous example, this table is used as follows. The FSOA at 5 percent interest for three years (three annual $100 payments with interest being earned for two years) is $100 times the interest factor found in Table 3 of Appendix A for three periods at 5 percent. This interest factor is 3.153; therefore, the future value of this ordinary annuity is $100

[1]The equations for the interest factors for the future value of an ordinary annuity and for the present value of an ordinary annuity are provided in the section on electronic calculators. See Equations 5.12 and 5.13, respectively.

FIGURE 5.3

Future Sum of an Ordinary Annuity of $1

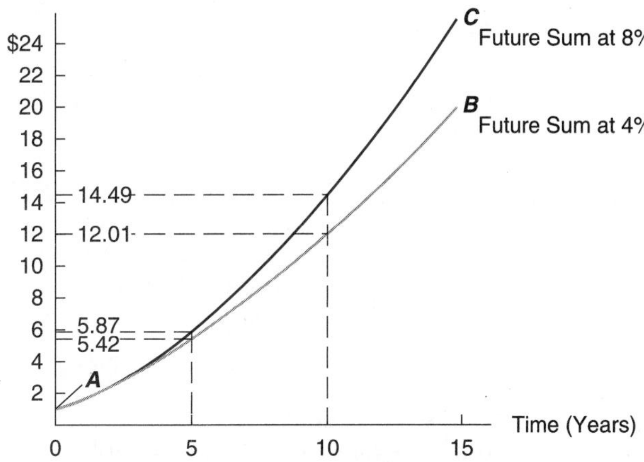

times 3.153, which equals $315.30. This is the same answer that was derived by determining the future value of each $100 deposit and totaling them. (The slight difference in the two answers is the result of rounding.)

To use the financial calculator to solve for the ordinary annuity, enter the number of years (N = 3) the rate of interest (I = 5), and the amount of each payment (PMT = −100). Because there is no single initial payment, enter zero for the present value (PV = 0), and instruct the calculator to solve for the future value (FV = ?). When this data is entered, the calculator determines that the future value is $315.25. (The calculator requires you to express the $100 payment as a negative number because it is assuming you are making a cash outflow of $100 each period and receiving a $315.25 cash inflow at the end of the three years.)

The value of an ordinary annuity of $1 compounded annually depends on the number of payments (i.e., the number of periods over which deposits are made) and the interest rate. The longer the time period and the higher the interest rate, the greater will be the sum that will have accumulated in the future. This is illustrated by Figure 5.3. Lines *AB* and *AC* show the value of the $1 annuity at 4 percent and 8 percent, respectively. After five years the value of the annuity will grow to $5.87 at 8 percent but to only $5.42 at 4 percent. If these annuities are continued for another five years, they will be worth $14.49 and $12.01, respectively. Thus, both the rate at which the annuity compounds and the length of time affect the annuity's value.

While Table 3 in Appendix A is constructed for an ordinary annuity, it may be converted into a table for an annuity due by multiplying the interest factor given in the table by $(1 + i)$. For example, in the illustration of the $100 deposited annually in the savings account for three years, the interest factor for the ordinary annuity was 3.153. This interest factor may be converted for an annuity due at 5 percent for three years by multiplying 3.153 by 1 + 0.05. That is,

$$3.153(1 + 0.05) = 3.3107.$$

When this interest factor is applied to the example of $100 deposited in the bank at 5 percent for three years with the deposits starting immediately, the resulting terminal value is

$$\$100(3.3107) = \$331.07.$$

This is the same answer as derived by making each calculation individually and summing them. (Once again the small difference in the two answers is the result of rounding.)

To use a financial calculator to solve for the future value of an annuity due, use the key that informs the calculator that the payments are to be made at the beginning rather than the end of each time period. Enter the amount of the payment (PMT = −100), the rate of interest (I = 5), and the number of years (N = 3). Set the present value equal to zero (PV = 0) and instruct the calculator to solve for the future value.

The difference between the terminal value of the two kinds of annuity payments can be quite substantial as the number of years increases or the interest rate rises. Consider a retirement account in which the saver places $2,000 annually for 20 years. If the deposits are made at the end of the year (an ordinary annuity) and the rate of interest is 7 percent, the terminal amount will be

$$\$2{,}000(40.995) = \$81{,}990.$$

However, if the deposits had been made at the beginning of each year (an annuity due), the terminal amount would be

$$\$2{,}000(40.995)(1 + 0.07) = \$87{,}729.30.$$

The difference is $5,739.30! Almost $6,000 in additional interest is earned if the deposits are made at the beginning, not at the end, of each year.

The difference between the ordinary annuity and the annuity due becomes even more dramatic if the interest rate rises. Suppose the account offered 12 percent instead of 7 percent. If the deposits are made at the end of each year, the terminal value is

$$\$2{,}000(72.052) = \$144{,}104.$$

If the payments are at the beginning of the year, the terminal value will be

$$\$2{,}000(72.052)(1 + 0.12) = \$161{,}396.48.$$

The difference is now $17,292.48.

The Present Value of an Annuity

present value of an annuity
The present worth of a series of equal payments.

In investment analysis, the investor is often not concerned with the future value but with the **present value of an annuity**. The investor who receives periodic payments often wishes to know the current (i.e., present) value. As with the future sum of an annuity, this value depends on whether the payments are made at the beginning of each year (an annuity due) or at the end of each period (an ordinary annuity).

The present value of an annuity is simply the sum of the present value of each individual cash flow. Each cash inflow is discounted back to the present at the appropriate discount factor and the amounts summed. Suppose you expect to receive $100 at the end of each year for three years and want to know how much this series of payments is worth if you can earn 8 percent in an alternative investment. To answer the question, you discount each payment at 8 percent:

Payment	Year	Interest Factor	Present Value
$100	1	0.926	$92.60
100	2	0.857	85.70
100	3	0.794	79.40
			$257.70

The process determines the present value to be \$257.70. That is, if you invest \$257.70 now and earn 8 percent annually, you can withdraw \$100 at the end of each year for the next three years.

This process is expressed in more general terms by Equation 5.8. The present value (PV) of the annual payments (PMT) is then found by discounting these payments at the appropriate interest rate (i) for n time periods.

(5.8)
$$\begin{aligned} \text{PV} &= \frac{PMT}{(1+i)^1} + \cdots + \frac{PMT}{(1+i)^n} \\ &= \sum_{t=1}^{n} \frac{PMT}{(1+i)^t}. \end{aligned}$$

When the values from the previous example are inserted into the equation, it reads

$$\begin{aligned} \text{PV} &= \frac{\$100}{(1+0.08)} + \frac{\$100}{(1+0.08)^2} + \frac{\$100}{(1+0.08)^3} \\ &= \frac{\$100}{1.080} + \frac{\$100}{1.166} + \frac{\$100}{1.260} \\ &= \$257.70 \end{aligned}$$

Since the payments are equal and made annually, this example is an annuity, and the present value is simply the product of the payment and the interest factor. Interest tables have been developed for the interest factors for the present value of an annuity (see the fourth table in Appendix A). Selected interest rates are read horizontally along the top, and the number of periods is read vertically at the left. To determine the present value of an annuity of \$100 that is to be received for three years when interest rates are 8 percent, find the interest factor for three years at 8 percent (2.577) and then multiply \$100 by this interest factor. The present value of this annuity is \$257.70, which is the same value that was derived by obtaining each of the individual present values and summing them. The price that one would be willing to pay at the present time in exchange for three future annual payments of \$100 when the rate of return on alternative investments is 8 percent is \$257.70.

To use the financial calculator to solve for the present value of the ordinary annuity, enter the number of years (N = 3), the rate of interest (I = 8), and the amount of each payment (PMT = 100). Since there is no single future payment, enter zero for the future value (FV = 0), and instruct the calculator to solve for the present value (PV = ?). When this data is entered, the calculator determines that the present value is −257.71. (Once again the calculator expresses the \$257.71 as a negative number because it is assuming you make an initial cash outflow of \$257.71 and receive a \$100 cash inflow each period. If you enter the \$100 payment as a negative number, the present value will be a positive number. The calculator will then assume you initially received a \$257.71 cash inflow through a loan and are making a \$100 cash repayment or outflow each period.)

As with the present value of \$1, the present value of an annuity is related to the interest rate and the length of time over which the annuity payments are made. The lower the interest rate and the longer the duration of the annuity, the greater the present value of the annuity. Figure 5.4 illustrates these relationships. As may be seen by comparing lines *AB* and *AC*, the lower the interest rate, the higher the present dollar value. For example, if payments are to be made over five years, the present value of an annuity of \$1 is \$4.45 at 4 percent but only \$3.99 at 8 percent. The longer the duration of the annuity, the higher the present value; hence, the

FIGURE 5.4

Present Value of an Ordinary Annuity of $1

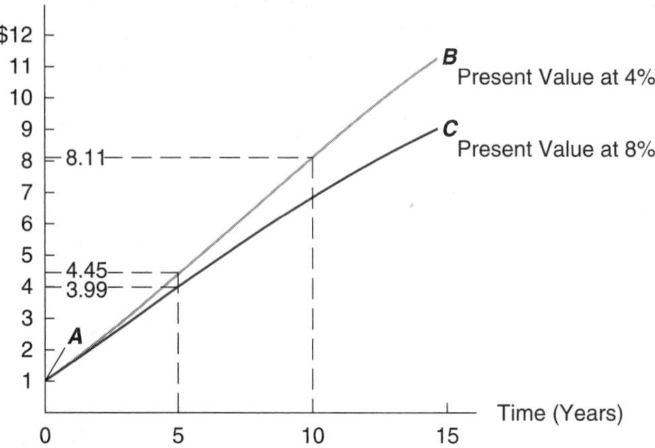

present value of an annuity of $1 at 4 percent is $4.45 for five years, whereas it is $8.11 for ten years.

Many payments to be received in investments occur at the end of a time period and not at the beginning and thus are illustrative of ordinary annuities. For example, the annual interest payment made by a bond occurs after the bond is held for a while, and distributions from earnings (e.g., dividends from stock or disbursements from a real estate tax shelter) are made after, not at the beginning of, a period of time. There are, however, payments that may occur at the beginning of the time period, such as the annual distribution from a retirement plan; these would be illustrative of annuities due.

The difference in the flow of payments and the determination of the present values of an ordinary annuity and an annuity due are illustrated in Exhibit 5.2. In

EXHIBIT 5.2

Flow of Payments and Determination of the Present Value of an Ordinary Annuity and an Annuity Due at 10 Percent for Three Years

Ordinary Annuity

1/1/x0	1/1/x1	1/1/x2	1/1/x3
$1,818 ←	(0.909) 2,000		
1,652 ←		(0.826) 2,000	
1,505 ←			(0.751) 2,000
$4,972			

Annuity Due

1/1/x0	1/1/x1	1/1/x2	1/1/x3
$2,000			
1,818 ←	(0.909) 2,000		
1,652 ←		(0.826) 2,000	
$5,470			

each case, the annuity is for $2,000 a year for three years and the interest rate is 10 percent. In the top half of the exhibit, the payments are made at the end of the year (an ordinary annuity), while in the bottom half of the exhibit, the payments are made at the beginning of the year (an annuity due). As may be seen by the totals, the present value of the annuity due is higher ($5,470 versus $4,972). This is because the payments are received sooner and, hence, are more valuable. As may also be seen in the illustration, because the first payment of the annuity due is made immediately, its present value is the actual amount received. Because the first payment of the ordinary annuity is made at the end of the first year, that amount is discounted, and, hence, its present value is less than the actual amount received.

The interest tables for the present value of an annuity presented in this text (and in other finance and investment texts) apply to ordinary annuities. These interest factors may be converted into annuity due factors by multiplying them by $(1 + i)$. Thus the interest factor for the present value of an ordinary annuity for $1 at 10 percent for three years (2.487) may be converted into the interest factor for an annuity due of $1 at 10 percent for three years as follows:

$$2.487(1 + i) = 2.487(1 + 0.1) = 2.736.$$

When this interest factor is used to determine the present value of an annuity due of $2,000 for three years at 10 percent, the present value is

$$\$2,000(2.736) = \$5,472.$$

The present value of an ordinary annuity of $2,000 at 10 percent for three years is

$$\$2,000(2.487) = \$4,974.$$

These are essentially the same answers given in Exhibit 5.2; the small differences result from rounding.

To use a financial calculator to solve for the present value of the annuity due, use the key that informs the calculator that the payments are to be received at the beginning rather than the end of each time period. Enter the amount of the payment to be received (PMT = 2,000), the rate of interest (I = 10), and the number of years (N = 3). Set the future value equal to 0 (FV = 0), and instruct the calculator to solve for the present value.

Illustrations of Compounding and Discounting

The previous sections have explained the various computations involving time value, and this section will illustrate them in a series of problems that the investor may encounter. These illustrations are similar to examples that are used throughout the text. Understanding these examples will make comprehending the rest of the text material much easier, because the emphasis can then be placed on the analysis of the value of specific assets instead of on the mechanics of the valuation.

Calculator Solution

Function Key	*Data Input*
PV =	−10
FV =	?
PMT =	0
N =	10
I =	9
Function Key	*Answer*
FV =	23.67

1 An investor buys a stock for $10 per share and expects the value of the stock to grow annually at 9 percent for ten years, at which time the individual plans to sell it. What is the anticipated sale price? This is an example of the future value of $1 growing at 9 percent for ten years. The future value is

$$\begin{aligned} P_n &= P_0(1 + i)^n, \\ P_{10} &= \$10(1 + 0.09)^{10} \\ &= \$10(2.367) = \$23.67, \end{aligned}$$

in which 2.367 is the interest factor for the future sum of $1 at 9 percent for ten years. The investor anticipates selling the stock for $23.67.

2 An investor sells a stock for $23.67 that was purchased ten years ago. A return of 9 percent was earned. What was the original cost of the investment? This is an example of the present value of $1 discounted back at 9 percent for ten years. The initial value is

Calculator Solution

Function Key	Data Input
PV =	?
FV =	23.67
PMT =	0
N =	10
I =	9
Function Key	**Answer**
PV =	−10

$$P_0 = \frac{P_n}{(1 + i)^n}$$
$$= \frac{\$23.67}{(1 + 0.09)^{10}}$$
$$= \$23.67(0.4224) = \$10,$$

in which 0.4224 is the interest factor for the present value of $1 discounted at 9 percent for ten years. The investment cost $10 when it was purchased ten years ago.

The student should know that Questions 1 and 2 are two views of the same investment. In Question 1 the $10 investment grew to $23.67. In Question 2 the value at the time the stock was sold was brought back to the value of the initial investment. Another variation of this question would be as follows. If an investor bought stock for $10, held it for ten years, and then sold it for $23.67, what was the return on the investment? In this case the values of the stock at the time it was bought and sold are known, but the rate of growth (the rate of return) is unknown. The answer can be found by using *either* the future value of $1 table or the present value of $1 table.

If the future value table is used, the question is at what rate (x) will $10 grow in ten years to equal $23.67. The answer is

Calculator Solution

Function Key	Data Input
PV =	−10
FV =	23.67
PMT =	0
N =	10
I =	?
Function Key	**Answer**
I =	9%

$$P_0(1 + x)^n = P_n,$$
$$\$10(1 + x)^{10} = \$23.67,$$
$$(1 + x)^{10} = 2.367.$$

The interest factor is 2.367, which, according to the future value of $1 table for ten years, makes the growth rate 9 percent. This interest factor is located under the vertical column for 9 percent and in the horizontal column for ten years.

If the present value table is used, the question asks what discount factor (x) at ten years will bring $23.67 back to $10. The answer is

$$P_0 = \frac{P_n}{(1 + x)^n},$$
$$\$10 = \frac{\$23.67}{(1 + x)^{10}},$$
$$0.4224 = \frac{1}{(1 + x)^{10}}.$$

The interest factor is 0.4224, which may be found in the present value of $1 table for ten years in the 9 percent column (i.e., the growth rate is 9 percent). Thus, this problem may be solved by the proper application of either the future value or present value tables.

3 An employer starts a pension plan for a 45-year-old employee. The plan requires the employer to invest $1,000 at the end of each year. If that

investment earns 8 percent annually, how much will be accumulated by retirement at age 65?

This is an example of the future value of an ordinary annuity. The payment is \$1,000 annually and grows at 8 percent for 20 years. The fund will be

Calculator Solution

Function Key	Data Input
PV =	0
FV =	?
PMT =	−1000
N =	20
I =	8
Function Key	**Answer**
FV =	45,761.96

$$\begin{aligned} FV &= PMT(1+i)^0 + \cdots + PMT(1+i)^{n-1} \\ &= \$1{,}000(1+0.08)^0 + \cdots + \$1{,}000(1+0.08)^{19} \\ &= \$1{,}000(45.762) = \$45{,}762. \end{aligned}$$

(45.762 is the interest factor for the future sum of an ordinary annuity of \$1 compounded annually at 8 percent for 20 years.)

4 The same employer decides to place a lump sum in an investment that earns 8 percent and to draw on the funds to make the annual payments of \$1,000. After 20 years all the funds in the account will be depleted. How much must be deposited initially in the account?

This is an example of the present value of an ordinary annuity. The annuity is \$1,000 per year at 8 percent for 20 years. Thus, the present value (i.e., the amount of the initial investment) is

Calculator Solution

Function Key	Data Input
PV =	?
FV =	0
PMT =	1000
N =	20
I =	8
Function Key	**Answer**
PV =	−9815.15

$$\begin{aligned} PV &= \sum_{t=1}^{n} \frac{PMT}{(1+i)} + \cdots + \frac{PMT}{(1+i)^n} \\ &= \frac{\$1{,}000}{1+0.08} + \cdots + \frac{\$1{,}000}{(1+0.08)^{20}} \\ &= \$1{,}000(9.818) = \$9{,}818, \end{aligned}$$

in which 9.818 is the interest factor for the present value of an ordinary annuity of \$1 at 8 percent for 20 years. Thus, the employer need invest only \$9,818 in an account now that earns 8 percent to meet the \$1,000 annual pension payment for the next 20 years.

Notice the difference between the answers in the equations in Examples 3 and 4. In the equation in Example 3, a set of payments earns interest, and thus the future value is larger than just the sum of the 20 payments of \$1,000. In the equation in Example 4, a future set of payments is valued in present terms. Since future payments are worth less today, the current value is less than the sum of the 20 payments of \$1,000.

Also notice that if the employer sets aside \$9,818 today and earns 8 percent annually for 20 years, the terminal value is \$45,761.28, which is essentially the same amount derived in the third illustration. From the employer's viewpoint, the \$9,818 may be used to cover a required \$1,000 annual payment or used to accumulate a required \$45,762 future value. Essentially, either approach achieves the required terminal value.

5 An investment pays \$50 per year for ten years, after which \$1,000 is returned to the investor. If the investor can earn 9 percent, how much should this investment cost? This question really contains two questions: What is the present value of an ordinary annuity of \$50 at 9 percent for ten years, and what is the present value of \$1,000 after ten years at 9 percent? The answer is

Calculator Solution

Function Key	Data Input
PV =	?
FV =	1000
PMT =	50
N =	10
I =	9
Function Key	**Answer**
PV =	−743.29

$$\begin{aligned} PV &= \sum_{t=1}^{n} \frac{PMT_1}{(1+i)^1} + \cdots + \frac{PMT_n}{(1+i)^n} + \frac{FV_n}{(1+i)^n} \\ &= \frac{\$50}{(1+0.09)} + \cdots + \frac{\$50}{(1+0.09)^{10}} + \frac{\$1{,}000}{(1+0.09)^{10}} \\ &= \$50(6.418) + \$1{,}000(0.422) = \$742.90. \end{aligned}$$

(6.418 and 0.422 are the interest factors for the present value of an ordinary annuity of $1 and the present value of $1, respectively, both at 9 percent for ten years.)

This example illustrates that an investment may involve both a series of payments (an annuity component) and a lump-sum payment. This particular investment is similar to a bond, the valuation of which is discussed in Chapter 16. Other examples of valuation and the computation of rates of return are given in Chapters 9 and 10, which consider investments in common stock.

Calculator Solution

Function Key		Data Input
PV	=	−5.40
FV	=	?
PMT	=	0
N	=	10
I	=	5
Function Key		*Answer*
FV	=	8.80

6 A corporation's dividend has grown annually at the rate of 5 percent. If this rate is maintained and the current dividend is $5.40, what will the dividend be after ten years? This is a simple future value of $1 problem. The dividend will grow to

$$\begin{aligned} P_n &= P_0(1 + i)^n \\ &= \$5.40(1 + 0.05)^{10} \\ &= \$5.40(1.629) = \$8.80. \end{aligned}$$

(1.629 is the interest factor for the future value of $1 at 5 percent for ten years.) Although such a growth rate in future dividends may not be achieved, this problem illustrates how modest annual increments can result in a substantial increase in an investor's dividend income over a number of years. (In the calculator solution, if you enter the 5.40 as a positive number, the answer is a negative 8.80. Either is acceptable as long as you interpret the answer correctly.)

The previous examples illustrate the use of interest tables and the financial calculator. These problems can also be done without the tables or a financial calculator if you have access to an electronic calculator with a y^x key and/or logs. Also, computer programs, such as the Investment Analysis programs that accompany this text, may be used as substitutes for interest tables or financial calculators to solve the problems. (The use of nonfinancial calculators to determine interest factors that are not in the tables is discussed later in this chapter.)

Nonannual Compounding

semiannual compounding
The payment of interest twice a year.

You should have noticed that in the previous examples compounding occurred only once a year. Since compounding can and often does occur more frequently—for example, **semiannually**—the equations that were presented earlier must be adjusted. This section extends the discussion of the compound value of $1 to include compounding for time periods other than a year.

Converting annual compounding to other time periods necessitates two adjustments. First, a year is divided into the same number of time periods that the funds are being compounded. For semiannual compounding a year consists of two time periods, whereas for quarterly compounding the year comprises four time periods.

After adjusting for the number of time periods, the individual adjusts the interest rate to find the rate per time period. This is done by dividing the stated interest rate by the number of time periods. If the interest rate is 8 percent compounded semiannually, then 8 percent is divided by 2, giving an interest rate of 4 percent earned in *each* time period. If the annual rate of interest is 8 percent compounded quarterly, the interest rate is 2 percent (8% ÷ 4) in each of the four time periods.

POINTS OF INTEREST

The Rule of 72

Do you want a shortcut method that answers the question, "How long will it take to double my money if I earn a specified percent?" The rule of 72 does just that! Divide 72 by the rate earned, and the answer is an approximation of how long it takes for the initial amount to double. For example, if the rate is 6 percent, funds double in 72/6 = 12 years. At 10 percent, funds double in 7.2 years.

How accurate is this shortcut? As may be seen from this table, the rule of 72 gives a rather accurate approximation of the time necessary to double one's funds at a specific rate of growth.

Rate (%)	Years for Funds to Double Using the Rule of 72	Actual Years for Funds to Double
5	14.4	14.2
7	10.3	10.2
10	7.2	7.3
12	6.0	6.1
16	4.5	4.7
20	3.6	3.8

These adjustments may be expressed in more formal terms by modifying Equation 5.4 as follows:

$$P_0\left(1+\frac{i}{c}\right)^{n\times c}=P_n. \tag{5.9}$$

The only new symbol is *c*, which represents the frequency of compounding. The interest rate *(i)* is divided by the frequency of compounding *(c)* to determine the interest rate in each period. The number of years *(n)* is multiplied by the frequency of compounding to determine the number of time periods.

The application of this equation may be illustrated in a simple example. An individual invests $100 in an asset that pays 8 percent compounded quarterly. What will the future value of this asset be after five years—that is, $100 will grow to what amount after five years if it is compounded quarterly at 8 percent? Algebraically, this is

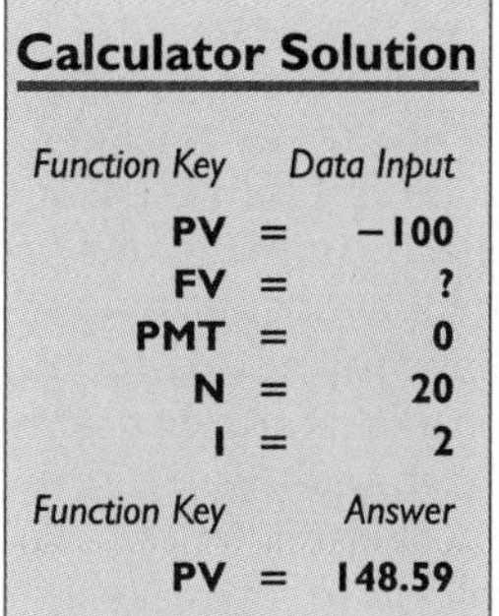

Calculator Solution

Function Key	Data Input
PV =	−100
FV =	?
PMT =	0
N =	20
I =	2
Function Key	**Answer**
PV =	148.59

$$\begin{aligned} P_n &= P_0\left(1+\frac{i}{c}\right)^{n\times c}\\ &= \$100\left(1+\frac{0.08}{4}\right)^{5\times 4}\\ &= \$100(1+0.02)^{20}. \end{aligned}$$

In this formulation the investor is earning 2 percent for 20 time periods. To solve this equation, the interest factor for the future value of $1 at 2 percent for 20 years (1.486) is multiplied by $100. Thus, the future value is

$$P_5 = \$100(1.486) = \$148.60.$$

The difference between compounding annually and compounding more frequently can be seen by comparing this problem with one in which the values are identical except that the interest is compounded annually. The question is, then, to what amount will $100 grow after five years at 8 percent compounded annually? The answer is

Calculator Solution

Function Key	Data Input
PV =	−100
FV =	?
PMT =	0
N =	5
I =	8
Function Key	Answer
FV =	146.93

$$\begin{aligned} P_5 &= \$100(1 + 0.08)^5 \\ &= \$100(1.469) \\ &= \$146.90. \end{aligned}$$

This sum, $146.90, is less than the amount that was earned when the funds were compounded quarterly, which suggests the general conclusion that the more frequently interest is compounded, the greater will be the future amount.

The discussion throughout this text is generally limited to annual compounding. There is, however, one important exception: the valuation of bonds. Bonds pay interest semiannually, and this affects their value. Therefore, semiannual compounding is incorporated in the bond valuation model that is presented in Chapter 16.

Present Value and Security Valuation

The valuation of assets is a major theme of this text. Investors and financial analysts must be able to analyze securities to determine their current value. This process requires forecasting future cash inflows and discounting them back to the present. The present value of an investment, then, is related to future benefits, in the form of either future income or capital appreciation. For example, stocks are purchased for their *future* dividends and potential capital gains but *not* for their previous dividends and price performance. Bonds are purchased for *future* income. Real estate is bought for the *future* use of the property and for the potential price appreciation. The concept of discounting future cash inflows back to the present applies to all investments: It is the future and not the past that matters. The past is relevant only to the extent that it may be used to predict the future.

Some types of analysis (including the technical approach to selecting investments that is discussed in Chapter 14) use the past in the belief that it forecasts the future. Technical analysts employ such information as the past price movements of a stock to determine the most profitable times to buy and sell a security. However, most of the analytical methods that are discussed in this text use some form of discounting future cash flows to value an asset. Prices are the present value of anticipated future cash inflows, such as dividends.

Subsequent chapters will discuss a variety of assets and the means for analyzing and valuing them. For debt, the current price is related to the series of interest payments and the repayment of the principal, both of which are discounted at the current market interest rate. The current price of a stock is related to the firm's future earnings and dividends and the individual's alternative investment opportunities. Cash flows are discounted back to the present at the appropriate discount factor. For these reasons it is important that the reader start in this introductory chapter to view current prices as the present value of future cash inflows. The various features of the different investments, including stocks and bonds, will be discussed, and their prices will be analyzed in terms of present value. If the reader does not understand the material on the time value of money presented in this chapter, the analytical sections of subsequent chapters may be incomprehensible.

Electronic Calculators

Once you have mastered the concepts of future value and present value and understand how the amounts are determined, the tedium associated with the actual calculations is reduced through the use of financial calculators programmed to solve time value problems. Even if your calculator is not preprogrammed to perform these types of problems, you may still be able to derive the interest factors for the future value of $1 and the present value of $1. This derivation requires that the calculator have the exponent key (y^x).[2]

The equation for the interest factor for the future value of $1 (FVIF) is

(5.10) $$\text{FVIF} = (1 + i)^n.$$

To find the interest factor for 6 percent for three years [i.e., $(1 + 0.06)^3$], first enter 1 plus the interest rate: 1.06. The display should read 1.06. Next, raise this amount to the third power, which is achieved by striking the y^x key and the number 3. Press "equal," and the display should read 1.191, which is the interest factor that may be found in the first table of Appendix A under the column for 6 percent and three years.

The equation for the interest factor of the present value of $1 (PVIF) is

(5.11) $$\text{PVIF} = \frac{1}{(1 + i)^n}.$$

The interest factor for the present value is the reciprocal of the interest factor for the future value of $1. To derive the interest factor for the present value of $1 at 6 percent for three years, do the preceding steps used to determine the future value of $1 and then take the reciprocal. If the calculator has the $1/x$ key, press this key, and the reciprocal is automatically determined. If the calculator lacks this key, the reciprocal is found by dividing 1 by the number just derived. In the illustration, the reciprocal for 1.191 is 0.8396 (1/1.191), which is the interest factor for the present value of $1 at 6 percent for three years. You may verify this number by looking under the column for the present value of $1 at 6 percent for three years in the second table in Appendix A, which gives the interest factor as 0.840. The difference is, of course, the result of rounding.

This discussion indicates that the interest factors for the future value of $1 and the present value of $1 may be derived using a nonfinancial electronic calculator. The interest factors for the future value of an annuity and the present value of an annuity may also be derived using a nonfinancial calculator with an exponent key.

The equation for the interest factor for the future sum of an annuity (FVAIF) is

(5.12) $$\text{FVAIF} = \frac{(1 + i)^n - 1}{i}.$$

Thus, if the interest rate is 5 percent and the number of years is four, then the interest factor is

$$\text{FVAIF} = \frac{(1 + 0.05)^4 - 1}{0.05} = \frac{1.2155 - 1}{0.05} = 4.310,$$

which is the same number found in the table for the future value of an annuity for four years at 5 percent.

[2]For example, scientific calculators are obviously not designed to solve business problems, but they do have an exponent key.

The equation for the interest factor for the present value of an annuity (PVAIF) is

(5.13)
$$\text{PVAIF} = \frac{1 - \dfrac{1}{(1+i)^n}}{i}.$$

If the interest rate is 6 percent and the number of years is three, then the interest factor is

$$\text{PVAIF} = \frac{1 - \dfrac{1}{(1+0.06)^3}}{0.06} = \frac{1 - 0.8396}{0.06} = 2.673,$$

which is the interest factor found in the table for the present value of an annuity at 6 percent for three years.

In addition to facilitating the calculation of interest factors, the electronic calculator also offers a major advantage over the use of interest tables. Interest tables are limited to exact rates (e.g., 5 percent) and whole years (e.g., six years). Unless the individual interpolates between the given interest factors, the tables cannot provide the interest factor for 6.7 percent for five years and three months. However, this interest factor can be determined by using the electronic calculator. The interest factor for the future value of $1 at 6.7 percent for five years and three months may be found as follows:

Calculator Solution

Function Key	Data Input
PV =	−100
FV =	?
PMT =	5
N =	5.25
I =	6.7
Function Key	*Answer*
FV =	140.56

1. Enter 1.067.
2. Raise 1.067 by 5.25 (i.e., $y^x = 1.067^{5.25}$).
3. Press "equal" to derive the interest factor: 1.4056.

Thus, if $100 is invested at 6.7 percent, compounded annually for five years and three months, the future value is $140.56.

While financial calculators may ease the burden of the arithmetic, they cannot set up the problems to be solved. You must still determine if the problem concerns future value or present value and whether the problem deals with a lump sum or an annuity. Failure to set up the problem correctly will only lead to incorrect results, so it is imperative that the student be able to determine what is being used and which of the various cases applies to the particular problem.

Summary

Money has time value. A dollar to be received in the future is worth less than a dollar received today. People will forgo current consumption only if future growth in their funds is possible. Invested funds earn interest, and the interest in turn earns more interest—a process called compounding. The longer funds compound and the higher the rate at which they compound, the greater will be the final amount in the future.

Discounting, the opposite of compounding, determines the present value of funds to be received in the future. The present value of a future sum depends on how far into the future the funds are to be received and on the discount rate. The farther into the future or the higher the discount factor, the lower will be the present value of the sum.

Compounding and discounting may apply to a single payment (lump sum) or to a series of payments. If the payments are equal, the series is called an annuity.

When the payments start at the beginning of each time period, the series is called an annuity due; when the payments are made at the end of each time period, the series is called an ordinary annuity.

Although an investment is made in the present, returns are earned in the future. These returns (e.g., the future flows of interest and dividends) must be discounted by the appropriate discount factor to determine the investment's present value. It is this process of discounting by which an investment's value is determined. As is developed throughout this text, valuation of assets is a crucial step in the selection of assets to acquire and hold in an investor's portfolio.

Questions

1) What is the difference between a lump-sum payment and an annuity? What is the difference between an ordinary annuity and an annuity due? Are all series of payments annuities?
2) What is the difference between compounding (the determination of future value) and discounting (the determination of present value)?
3) For a given interest rate, what happens to the following as time increases?
   a) future value of $1
   b) future value of an annuity
   c) present value of $1
   d) present value of an annuity
4) For a given time period, what happens to the following as the interest rate increases?
   a) future value of $1
   b) future value of an annuity
   c) present value of $1
   d) present value of an annuity
5) What does the phrase "discounting the future at a high rate" imply?
6) As is explained in subsequent chapters, increases in interest rates cause the value of assets to decline. Why would you expect this relationship?

Problems

1) A saver places $1,000 in a certificate of deposit that matures after 20 years and that each year pays 4 percent interest, which is compounded annually until the certificate matures.
   a) How much interest will the saver earn if the interest is left to accumulate?
   b) How much interest will the saver earn if the interest is withdrawn each year?
   c) Why are the answers to (a) and (b) different?
2) An investor bought a stock ten years ago for $20 and sold it today for $35. What is the annual rate of growth (rate of return) on the investment?
3) At the end of each year a self-employed person deposits $1,500 in a retirement account that earns 10 percent annually.
   a) How much will be in the account when the individual retires at the age of 65 if the savings program starts when the person is age 45?
   b) How much additional money will be in the account if the saver defers retirement until age 70 and continues the annual contributions?
   c) How much additional money will be in the account if the saver discontinues the contributions but does not retire until the age of 70?

4) A saver wants $100,000 after ten years and believes that it is possible to earn an annual rate of 8 percent on invested funds.
   a) What amount must be invested each year to accumulate $100,000 if (1) the payments are made at the beginning of each year or (2) if they are made at the end of each year?
   b) How much must be invested annually if the expected yield is only 5 percent?
5) An investment offers $10,000 per year for 20 years. If an investor can earn 8 percent annually on other investments, what is the current value of this investment? If its current price is $120,000, should the investor buy it?
6) Graduating seniors may earn $35,000 each year. If the annual rate of inflation is 4 percent, what must these graduates earn after 20 years to maintain their current purchasing power? If the rate of inflation rises to 8 percent, will they be maintaining their standard of living if they earn $150,000 after 20 years?
7) A person who is retiring at the age of 65 and who has $200,000 wants to leave an estate of at least $30,000. How much can the individual draw annually on the $200,000 (starting at the end of the year) if the funds earn 8 percent and the person's life expectancy is 85 years?
8) A 40-year-old individual establishes a retirement account that is expected to earn 7 percent annually. Contributions will be $2,000 annually at the beginning of each year. Initially, the saver expects to start drawing on the account at age 60.
   a) How much will be in the account when the saver is age 60?
   b) If this investor found a riskier investment that offered 10 percent, how much in additional funds would be earned?
   c) The investor selects the 10 percent investment and retires at the age of 60. How much can be drawn from the account at the beginning of each year if life expectancy is 85 and the funds continue to earn 10 percent?
9) You are offered $900 five years from now or $150 at the end of each year for the next five years. If you can earn 6 percent on your funds, which offer will you accept? If you can earn 14 percent on your funds, which offer will you accept? Why are your answers different?
10) The following questions illustrate nonannual compounding.
   a) One hundred dollars is placed in an account that pays 12 percent. How much will be in the account after one year if interest is compounded annually, semiannually, or monthly?
   b) One hundred dollars is to be received after one year. What is the present value of this amount if you can earn 12 percent compounded annually, semiannually, or monthly?
11) At the end of each year, Tom invests $2,000 in a retirement account. Joan also invests $2,000 in a retirement account but makes her deposits at the beginning of each year. They both earn 9 percent on their funds. How much will each have in his or her account at the end of 20 years?
12) You purchase a $100,000 life insurance policy for a single payment of $35,000. If you want to earn 9 percent on invested funds, how soon must you die for the policy to have been the superior alternative? If you die within ten years, what is the return on the investment in life insurance? (Morbid questions, but you might want to view life insurance as an investment alternative. As one financial analyst told the author: "Always look at the numbers; analyze life insurance as an investment.")
13) You are offered an annuity of $12,000 a year for 15 years. The annuity payments start after five years have elapsed. If the annuity costs $75,000, is the annuity a good purchase if you can earn 9 percent on invested funds?

14) You purchase a $1,000 asset for $800. It pays $60 a year for seven years at which time you receive the $1,000 principal. Prove that the annual return on this investment is not 9 percent.

15) You invest $1,000 a year for ten years at 10 percent and then invest $2,000 a year for an additional ten years at 10 percent. How much will you have accumulated at the end of the 20 years?

16) You are promised $10,000 a year for six years after which you will receive $5,000 a year for six years. If you can earn 8 percent annually, what is the present value of this stream of payments?

17) A township expects its population of 5,000 to grow annually at the rate of 5 percent. The township currently spends $300 per inhabitant, but, as the result of inflation and wage increments, expects the per-capita expenditure to grow annually by 7 percent. How much will the township's budget be after 10, 15, and 20 years?

18) A financial manager with $1,000 to invest is faced with two competing alternatives, both of which cost $1,000. Alternative A will annually pay $275 for five years while Alternative B pays $300 a year for two years and $250 for three years. If the manager wants to earn at least 10 percent, which investment should be selected?

19) Suppose you purchase a home for $150,000. After making a down payment of $50,000, you borrow the balance through a mortgage loan at 8 percent for 20 years. What is the annual payment required by the mortgage? If you could get a loan for 25 years but had to pay 9 percent annually, what is the difference in the annual payment?

20) You have an elderly aunt, Aunt Kitty, who has just sold her house for $165,000 and entered a retirement community that charges $30,000 annually. If she can earn 6 percent on her funds, how long will the funds from the sale of the house cover the cost of the retirement community?

21) A widower currently has $107,500 yielding 8 percent annually. Can he withdraw $18,234 a year for the next 10 years? If he cannot, what return must he earn in order to withdraw $18,234 annually?

22) You want $100,000 after eight years in order to start a business. Currently you have $26,000, which may be invested to earn 7 percent annually. How much additional money must you set aside each year if these funds also earn 7 percent in order to meet your goal of $100,000 at the end of eight years? By how much would your answer differ if you invested the additional funds at the beginning of each year instead of at the end of each year?

23) You have accumulated $325,000 in a retirement account and continue to earn 8 percent on invested funds.

- **a)** What amount may you withdraw annually starting today based on a life expectancy of 20 years? How much will be in the account at the end of the first year?
- **b)** Suppose you only take out 1/20 of the funds today and the remainder continues to earn 8 percent. How much will be in the account at the end of the first year? Compare your answer to (a). Why are they different?

24) Your first child is now a 1-year-old. It currently costs a total of $60,000 to attend a public college for four years. If these costs rise 5 percent annually, how much must you invest each year to cover the expenses after 18 years if you are able to earn 10 percent annually?

25) Which is the better choice when purchasing a $20,000 car:

- **a)** a four-year loan at 4 percent,
- **b)** an immediate rebate of $2,000 and a four-year loan at 10 percent?

Supplemental Problems

All the preceding problems can be solved using the interest tables supplied in the appendix. To test your ability to construct your own interest factors or to use the computer programs available with this text, solve the following problems.

1) You place $1,300 in a savings account that pays 5.3 percent annually. How much will you have in the account at the end of six years and three months?

2) You invest $1,000 annually for seven years and earn 7.65 percent annually. How much interest will you have accumulated at the end of the seventh year?

3) An investment promises to pay you $10,000 each year for ten years. If you want to earn 8.42 percent on your investments, what is the maximum price you should pay for this asset?

4) You bought a stock for $10 a share and sold it for $25.60 after 5½ years. What was your annual return (rate of growth) on the investment?

5) You can earn 7.2 percent annually; how much must you invest annually to accumulate $50,000 after five years?

THE FINANCIAL ADVISOR'S INVESTMENT CASE

Funding a Pension Plan

Erin O'Reilly was recently employed by the human resources department of a moderate-sized engineering firm. Management is considering the adoption of a defined-benefit pension plan in which the firm will pay 75 percent of an individual's last annual salary if the employee has worked for the firm for 25 years. The amount of the pension is to be reduced by 3 percent for every year less than 25, so that an individual who has been employed for 15 years will receive a pension of 45 percent of the last year's salary [75 percent − (10 × 3%)]. Pension payments will start at age 65, provided the individual has retired. There is no provision for early retirement. Continuing to work after age 65 may increase the individual's pension if the person has worked for less than 25 years or if the salary were to increase.

One of the first tasks given O'Reilly is to estimate the amount that the firm must set aside today to fund pensions. While management plans to hire actuaries to make the final determination, the managers believe the exercise may highlight some problems that they will want to be able to discuss with the actuaries. O'Reilly was instructed to select two representative employees and estimate their annual pensions and the annual contributions necessary to fund the pensions.

O'Reilly decided to select Arnold Berg and Vanessa Barber. Berg is 58 years old, has been with the firm for 27 years, and is earning $34,000. Ms. Barber is 47, has been with the firm for 3 years, and earns $42,000 annually. O'Reilly believes that Berg will be with the firm until he retires; he is a competent worker whose salary will not increase by more than 4 percent annually, and it is anticipated he will retire at age 65. Barber is a more valuable employee, and O'Reilly expects Barber's salary to rise at least 7 percent annually in order to retain her until retirement at age 65.

To determine the amount that must be invested annually to fund each pension, O'Reilly needs (in addition to an estimate of the amount of the pension) an estimate of how long the pension will be distributed (i.e., life expectancy) and how much the invested funds will earn. Since the firm must pay an interest rate of 8 percent to borrow money, she decides that the invested funds should be able to earn at least that amount.

While O'Reilly believes she is able to perform the assignment, she has come to you for assistance to help answer the following questions.

1) If each individual retires at age 65, how much will his or her estimated pension be?

2) Life expectancy for both employees is 15 years at age 65. If the firm buys an annuity from an insurance company to fund each pension and the insurance company asserts it is able to earn 9 percent on the funds invested in the annuity, what is the cost or the amount required to purchase the annuity contracts?

3) If the firm can earn 8 percent on the money it must invest annually to fund the pension, how much will the firm have to invest annually to have the funds necessary to purchase the annuities?

4) What would be the impact of each of the following on the amount that the firm must invest annually to fund the pension?

- **a)** Life expectancy is increased to 20 years.
- **b)** The rate of interest on the annuity contract with the insurance company is reduced to 7 percent.
- **c)** Barber retires at age 62 instead of 65.

6 The Tax Environment

Oliver Wendell Holmes, Jr. said that "taxes are what we pay for civilized society." If you judge by the variety and amount of taxes, we live in a very civilized society. Income from all sources is taxed. Sales taxes are levied on consumer purchases. Excise taxes are levied on imported goods and selected domestic goods, such as beer, wine, and gasoline. Property taxes are levied on real estate. Tolls are levied when you use some highways, bridges, and tunnels.

While there are many types of taxes, only two affect investment decision making: income taxes, which alter the return earned on an investment, and wealth taxes, which affect the value of an estate. Estate taxation is, of course, levied only once, but income taxation recurs throughout the investor's life. For this reason, considerable time and effort are devoted to reducing taxes and sheltering income from taxation.

This chapter briefly covers the main sources of taxation and offers several illustrations of tax shelters. Tax laws and regulations change virtually every year. This is unfortunate because it means that investment decisions made under one set of laws may be taxed under a different set of laws. Changes in tax laws will also mean that some of the specific information in this chapter (e.g., tax rates) may become outdated. However, the basic tax principles tend to remain the same.

Learning Objectives

After completing this chapter you should be able to:

1. Identify the taxes that affect investment decision making.
2. Define progressive, proportionate, and regressive taxes.
3. Illustrate how capital losses are used to offset capital gains and ordinary income.
4. Explain how pension plans, IRAs, Keogh accounts, and 401(k) accounts are tax shelters.
5. Explain the tax advantages associated with municipal bonds, annuities, and life insurance.
6. Differentiate between estate and inheritance taxes.
7. Explain the impact of accelerated depreciation on taxes owed.

Tax Bases

Since one of the main purposes of taxes is to raise revenues, a tax base must be large in order to produce any sizable amount of revenue. In general, there are three bases that can be taxed: one's income, one's wealth, and one's consumption (i.e., spending). In the United States all three are used as tax bases at various levels of government. The federal government and many states tax income. Several states and virtually all local governments tax wealth (e.g., property taxes). The federal government also may tax an individual's wealth when that person dies (i.e., estate taxes). Many state governments tax spending (i.e., sales taxes), and the federal government taxes specific spending when it levies import duties, taxes telephone usage, and levies excise taxes on gasoline.

All three major sources of taxation may affect investment decisions. For many individuals, the tax that has the most impact on investments is the federal income tax, which is levied on investment income (i.e., interest and dividends) and on capital gains. Hence, the material on taxes appearing throughout this text emphasizes the federal income tax. However, taxes on wealth, such as the federal estate tax or property taxes on real estate, can be very important considerations for individual investors in specific circumstances. The least important general tax from an investment viewpoint is the sales tax (i.e., taxes on consumption). The purchase of securities or the acquisition of a savings account or shares in a mutual fund are not subject to sales tax. There are, however, a few investments, such as the purchase of gold or collectibles such as antiques, that are subject to sales tax in some localities. These taxes, of course, reduce the potential return from the investments and may reduce their attractiveness in comparison to financial assets that are exempt from sales taxes.

Income Taxation

Personal and corporate income is subject to taxation. These taxes are levied both by the federal government and by many state governments. Some states also permit the taxation of income by their municipalities. For example, the income of New York City residents is subject to federal, state, and city taxes.

In general, income taxes apply to all sources of income. Thus, dividend and interest income is subject to this taxation. However, the tax is not applied evenly to the returns from all investments. For example, dividend income is taxed by the federal government, while interest on municipal bonds is not.

progressive tax
A tax whose rate increases as the tax base increases.

regressive tax
A tax whose rate declines as the tax base increases.

proportionate tax
A tax whose rate remains constant as the tax base changes.

Income taxes levied by the federal government and by many state governments are progressive. A tax is **progressive** if the tax rate increases as the tax base (income) rises. If the tax rate declines as the base increases, the tax is **regressive**. If the tax rate remains constant, the tax is **proportionate**.

The differences in progressive, regressive, and proportionate taxes are illustrated in Exhibit 6.1. The first column gives an individual's income. The second and third columns illustrate a progressive tax (the tax rate increases with the increases in income). The fourth and fifth columns illustrate a regressive tax (the tax rate declines as income rises). The last two columns illustrate a proportionate tax (the rate remains constant as income changes). As shown, the absolute amount of tax paid increases in each case. However, the effect of the higher tax rates on the total amount of tax is considerable as income rises from $10,000 to $50,000. With

EXHIBIT 6.1

Differences in Taxes Paid Under Hypothetical Progressive, Regressive, and Proportionate Rates

	Progressive		Regressive		Proportionate	
Income	Tax Rate	Total Tax Paid	Tax Rate	Total Tax Paid	Tax Rate	Total Tax Paid
$10,000	10%	$1,000	10%	$ 1,000	20%	$ 2,000
20,000	15	3,000	9	1,800	20	4,000
30,000	20	6,000	8	2,400	20	6,000
40,000	25	10,000	7	2,800	20	8,000
50,000	30	15,000	6	3,000	20	10,000

the regressive tax structure, the tax rises from $1,000 to $3,000. With the progressive tax, the amount paid in taxes rises to $15,000.

Many people believe that taxes should be progressive, so that individuals with higher incomes bear a larger portion of the cost of government. Regressive taxes are criticized on this basis. Regressive taxes place a greater share of the cost of government on those individuals with the least ability to afford the burden. The argument for progressive taxes is based on ethical or normative beliefs. It is a moral judgment that some taxpayers should pay a proportionately higher amount of tax.

The federal personal income tax is progressive because as the individual's income rises, the tax rate increases. For example, as of January 1, 2001, the federal income tax rates for a married couple filing a joint return were:

Taxable Income	Marginal Tax Rate
0–45,200	15%
45,201–109,250	28
109,251–166,450	31
166,451–297,300	36
above 297,300	39.6

Given this tax schedule, an individual with taxable income of $25,000 owes income taxes of $3,750 (0.15 × $25,000). If taxable income is $60,000, the taxes owed are $10,924 ($45,200 × 0.15 + 14,800 × 0.28). This tax is 18.21 percent ($10,924/$60,000) of the couple's taxable income.

marginal tax rate
The tax rate paid on an additional last dollar of taxable income; an individual's tax bracket.

The right-hand column (i.e., the tax rate on additional income) is often referred to as the **marginal tax rate**. As may be seen from the schedule, the tax rate increases as income increases, which indicates that the federal income tax structure is progressive. The tax brackets (e.g., $109,251–166,450) change every year, because the brackets are adjusted for inflation (i.e., there is a *cost-of-living adjustment*, or COLA). As prices increase, the tax brackets are raised so that individuals are not taxed at a higher marginal tax rate solely as the result of higher prices.

During 2001, a new income tax law was passed that changed the income tax rates. A new 10 percent bracket was created for taxable income of $0 to $12,000, and the remaining marginal tax rates will be decreased over time. For 2002–2003, the 28 percent bracket becomes 27 percent, and the 31 percent, 36 percent, and 39.6 percent brackets become 30 percent, 35 percent, and 38.6 percent, respectively. If it is assumed that the tax laws will not be changed again, in 2006 there will be five brackets: 10 percent, 25 percent, 28 percent, 33 percent, and 35 percent. The income subject to each rate will change annually as the brackets are adjusted for inflation.

Tax Shelters

tax shelter
An asset or investment that defers, reduces, or avoids taxation.

Even though the 2001 tax legislation reduced marginal tax rates, individuals are still concerned with sheltering income from taxation. A **tax shelter**, as the name implies, is anything that avoids, reduces, or defers taxes; it is a shelter or protection against taxes. An investor does not have to be wealthy to enjoy these benefits, and many investors of modest means use tax shelters. Unfortunately, the term *tax shelter* may evoke a variety of emotions and misunderstandings. In the minds of some people, tax shelter connotes all those taxes that other people are not paying. For some investors, the possibility of sheltering income from taxation may be sufficient to make irrational (and costly) investments. Still others may not realize the tax shelters that they themselves enjoy.

POINTS OF INTEREST

Keeping Abreast of the Tax Laws

It is both difficult and time-consuming to stay current on the tax laws, which partially explains why tax services, such as H&R Block, can be profitable. The individual should realize that changes in the tax laws quickly render as outdated much of the material previously published on federal income taxes.

The American Association of Individual Investors (http://www.aaii.com) publishes a personal guide for tax and financial planning, *Personal Tax and Financial Planning Guide.* This annual publication covers charitable contributions, the alternative minimum tax, deferral of earned income, and other crucial tax topics from the individual investor's perspective.

Investors who do not use accountants to prepare their tax papers often do use the services of tax consultants. For the current federal tax laws, the investor may consult:

West Federal Taxation: Individual Income Taxes. Cincinnati: South-Western/Thomson Learning.

This book is published annually and continues to set the standard for reference in introductory tax. With its thorough, accessible coverage, no other text helps users better master the ever changing Individual Tax Code.

Lasser Institute. *J. K. Lasser's Your Income Tax.* New York: Simon & Schuster.

This annual publication is designed to help an individual file federal income tax forms; thus, it has current information on many of the tax laws pertaining to investments. It is also considerably easier to read than the *Federal Tax Course;* the latter, however, is both more comprehensive and more thorough. The Lasser Institute also publishes a guide to retirement planning that is updated annually.

Lasser, J. K. *All You Should Know About IRA, Keogh, and Other Retirement Plans.* New York: Prentice-Hall.

In addition to its annual *U.S. Master Tax Guide,* CCH Incorporated (http://tax.cch.com) offers specialized tax publications that cover such topics as tax preparation, state tax guides, estate and gift taxes, retirement benefits, charitable gifts, IRA fundamentals, and record retention requirements.

The investor may also obtain tax information on the Web. Using the Web may be the best single means to maintain currency in the tax laws. The IRS's address is http://irs.ustreas/gov. This site provides tax forms, educational materials, and links to other sites. Tax information may also be obtained from accounting firms (see, for instance, Deloitte & Touche: http://www.tdonline.com), the American Institute of CPAs (http://www.aicpa.org), and tax services such as H&R Block (http://www.hrblock.com). Other possible sources for current tax information include TurboTax Online through the Quicken Financial Network (http://www.quicken.com/taxes) and 1040.com (http://www.1040.com).

tax-exempt bond
A bond whose interest is excluded from federal income taxation.

An example of a tax shelter that avoids taxation is the municipal bond. These bonds are generally referred to as **tax-exempt bonds**, because the interest earned on most state and municipal debt is exempt from federal income taxation. (Correspondingly, interest on federal debt is exempt from state and local income taxation.) The interest is also exempt from state and local income taxes if the owner is a resident of the state of issue. Thus, for a resident of New York City, the interest on a New York state bond is exempt from federal income taxes, New York state income taxes, and New York City income taxes. This can be a significant tax shelter as one's income and marginal tax bracket rise. An individual living in New York City who has a combined federal, state, and local marginal tax rate equaling 40 percent will find that the after-tax yields on a 5.4 percent New York state bond equals the yield on a 9.0 percent corporate bond. (The equivalence of taxable and nontaxable yields is explained in Chapter 17.)

An example of a tax shelter that reduces taxes is the deductibility of interest on mortgages and property taxes. A home is, in part, an investment, and the deductibility of these expenses associated with home ownership reduces the individual's federal income taxes. In addition to being a major tax shelter, this makes home ownership less expensive and more attractive.

An example of a tax shelter that defers taxes is the tax-deferred retirement account. While the individual does not avoid paying the tax, the payment is postponed until some time in the future. In effect, the individual has the free use of the funds until the tax must be paid, which in this case will be during retirement. For a 30-year-old worker, this will be in the distant future.

Capital Gains and Losses

capital gain
The increase in the value of an asset such as a stock or a bond.

capital loss
A decrease in the value of an asset such as a stock or a bond.

Many investments are purchased and subsequently sold. If the sale results in a profit, that profit is considered a **capital gain**; if the sale results in a loss, that is a **capital loss**. If the gain or loss is realized within a year, it is a short-term capital gain or loss. If the sale occurs after a year from the date of purchase, it is a long-term gain or loss.

Short-term capital gains are taxed at the individual's marginal tax rate. Thus, if an investor buys a stock for $10,000 and sells it for $13,000 after nine months, the $3,000 short-term capital gain is taxed as any other source of taxable income. If the stock had been held for fifteen months, the $3,000 long-term capital gain is taxed at either 10 or 20 percent, depending on the individual's marginal tax rate. Taxpayers in the 15 percent bracket pay 10 percent and all others pay 20 percent.[1] Thus, for individuals in the 31 percent marginal tax bracket, long-term capital gains are taxed at 20 percent. An individual in the 31 percent tax bracket would pay $930 of a $3,000 short-term capital gain, while a $3,000 long-term capital gain generates $600 in taxes, a reduction of $330.

The investor may use capital losses to offset capital gains. If the investor bought a second stock for $15,000 and sold it for $12,000, the $3,000 loss would offset the $3,000 capital gain. This offsetting of capital gains by capital losses applies to both short- and long-term gains. However, there is a specified order in which losses offset gains.

Initially short-term losses are used to offset short-term gains, and long-term losses are used to offset long-term gains. If there is a net short-term loss (i.e., short-term losses exceed short-term gains), it is used to offset long-term gains. For example, if an investor has realized net short-term losses of $3,000, that short-term loss may be used to offset up to $3,000 in long-term capital gains. If net short-term losses are less than long-term gains, the resulting net capital gain is taxed as long-term.

If there is a net long-term loss (i.e., long-term losses exceed long-term gains), the loss is used to offset short-term gains. For example, $3,000 in net long-term capital losses is used to offset up to $3,000 in short-term capital gains. If net long-term losses are less than short-term gains, the resulting net capital gain is taxed as short-term.

If the investor has a net short- or long-term capital loss after subtracting short- or long-term capital gains, that net capital loss is used to offset income from other sources, such as dividends or interest. However, only $3,000 in capital losses may be used in a given year to offset income from other sources. If the individual has a larger loss (e.g., $5,000), only $3,000 may be used in the current year. The remainder ($2,000) is carried forward to offset capital gains or income received in future years. Under this system of carry-forward, a current capital loss of $10,000 offsets only $3,000 in current income and the remaining $7,000 is carried forward to offset capital gains and income in subsequent years. If the investor has no capital gains in the second year, only $3,000 of the remaining loss offsets income in the second year and the balance ($4,000) is carried forward to the third year. In the case of a large capital loss, this $3,000 limitation may be an incentive for the investor to take gains in the current year rather than carry forward the loss.

paper profits
Price appreciation that has not been realized.

Even if capital gains are taxed at the same rate as ordinary income, they are still illustrative of a tax shelter. The taxes on capital gains may be deferred indefinitely, because investment profits are taxed only after they have been realized. Many profits on security positions are only **paper profits**, because some investors do not

[1]Recent changes in long-term capital gains taxation include a provision that assets purchased after December 31, 2000, and held for more than five years will be taxed at 8 or 18 percent, instead of 10 or 20 percent. In addition, long-term capital gains on the sale of an individual's personal residence will not be subject to tax unless the gain exceeds $500,000 on a joint return ($250,000 for single taxpayers).

sell the securities and realize the gains. The tax laws encourage such retention of securities by taxing the gains only when they are realized.

If the holder gives the securities to someone as a gift (for example, if a grandparent gives securities whose value has risen to a grandchild), the cost basis is transferred to the recipient, and the capital gains taxes continue to be deferred. If the recipient sells the securities and realizes the gain, then capital gains taxes will have to be paid by the owner of the securities (i.e., the recipient of the gift).

Capital gains taxes can be avoided entirely if the individual holds the securities until he or she dies. The value of securities is taxed as part of the deceased's estate. The securities are then transferred through the deceased's will to other individuals, such as children or grandchildren, and the cost basis becomes the security's value as of the date of death. For example, suppose an individual owns shares of IBM that were purchased in the 1960s. The current value of the shares is probably many times their cost. If the investor were to sell these shares, he or she would incur a large capital gain. However, if the shares are held until the investor dies, their new cost basis becomes the current value of the shares, and the capital gains tax on the appreciation is avoided.[2]

The Wash Sale

Suppose an investor had purchased Merck for $70 a share and it is currently selling for $50. The investor has a paper loss. Can the investor sell a stock for the loss and immediately repurchase it? The answer is yes, but the investor cannot take a tax loss on the sale. The sale of a stock for a loss and an immediate repurchase is a "wash sale," and the loss is not allowed for tax purposes. While the federal tax code does not prohibit the investor from repurchasing the stock, the laws disallow the loss if the taxpayer buys the stock within 30 days prior to or 30 days after the date of the sale.

What other options are available? First, the investor could sell the stock and repurchase it after the 30 days have lapsed. Of course, the stock's price could rise during the 30 days, in which case the individual forgoes the potential gain. Second, the investor could buy an additional 100 shares of Merck, hold the 200 shares for the required 30 days, and then sell the initial 100 shares. The risk associated with this strategy is a continued price decline, in which case the investor would sustain a loss on both the original shares *and* the second purchase. Third, the investor could buy a stock in a similar company (e.g., sell Merck and purchase Johnson & Johnson). This strategy's risk is that Merck and Johnson & Johnson may not be perfect substitutes for each other; Merck stock could rise while Johnson & Johnson stock declines.

The wash sale rule applies not only to sales of stock but also to other financial assets, such as bonds and shares in mutual funds. The basic principle is that the individual cannot purchase "substantially identical" securities within the 30 days before or after the sale. Selling Merck and immediately repurchasing it is obviously a trade in substantially identical securities. Selling Merck and immediately repurchasing Johnson & Johnson is obviously *not* a substantially identical security trade. However, selling AT&T 6 percent bonds due in 2020 and repurchasing AT&T 5.8 percent bonds due in 2019 is ambiguous. The bonds are so similar that they may be considered "substantially identical." If the 5.8 percent bonds had been issued by Verizon, or were even issued by AT&T but due in 2005, then the securities are not substantially identical.

[2]Under the 2001 tax law, the estate tax is being phased out and repealed in 2010. Because Congress can change the tax laws, whether the complete abolition of the estate tax will occur is conjecture. If the estate tax is abolished, the ability to step up a security's cost basis and avoid capital gains taxes will also disappear.

An investor in mutual funds may encounter a problem if the dividend distributions are reinvested. If an investor sells part of his or her holdings for a loss on December 10 and the mutual fund pays a dividend that is reinvested (used to purchase additional shares) on December 20, 30 days have not lapsed. This is a wash sale and the tax loss will be disallowed. This scenario will be avoided if individuals accumulate but do not sell the shares. For individuals, such as retirees, who reinvest dividend payments while systematically withdrawing cash from the mutual fund, the possibility exists that the wash sale rule will disallow the tax benefits of selling the shares for a loss.

Tax-Deferred Pension Plans

One tax shelter that may also ease the burden of retirement is the pension plan. Many firms contribute to these plans for their employees. The funds are invested in income-earning assets, such as stocks and bonds. In some cases, the individual employee is required to make payments in addition to the employer's contributions. The amount of the employer's contribution is usually related to the employee's earnings. These contributions are not included in taxable income, so the worker does not have to pay taxes on the employer's payments to the pension plan. Instead, the funds are taxed when the worker retires and starts to use the money that has accumulated through the plan.

Deductible IRAs

One criticism of employer-sponsored pension plans was that they were not available to all workers. However, Congress passed legislation that enables all employees as well as the self-employed to establish their own pension plans; thus, the tax shelter that was previously provided only through employer-sponsored pension plans is now available to all workers. An employee who is not covered by a pension plan may set up an **individual retirement account (IRA)**. In 1981 Congress passed additional legislation that extended IRAs to all employees, even if they were already participating in an employer-sponsored pension plan.

IRA
A retirement plan (individual retirement account) that is available to workers.

As of January 2002, an individual worker may open an account with a financial institution, such as a commercial bank, savings and loan association (S&L), brokerage firm, or mutual fund company, and may deposit up to $3,000 per year. (The annual contribution rises to $4,666 in 2005.) The funds must be earned, which means that any employee who earns $3,000 or more may place as much as $3,000 in an IRA account. However, if the individual's source of income is dividends or interest, these funds cannot be placed in an IRA.

The amount invested in the IRA is deducted from the individual's taxable income. Income earned by the funds in the account is also not taxed. All taxes are deferred until the funds are withdrawn from the IRA, and then they are taxed as ordinary income. If the individual prematurely withdraws the funds (before age 59½), the money is taxed as ordinary income and a penalty tax is added.

IRA accounts soon became one of the most popular tax shelters, but Congress placed important restrictions on the deductibility of the IRA contribution. For workers *covered by a pension plan,* full deductibility is applicable only for couples filing a joint return with adjusted gross income (in 2002) of *less than* $54,000. (For single workers covered by a pension plan the limit is $34,000.) Note that adjusted gross income is used and not earned income. If an individual earns a modest salary but has significant amounts of interest or dividend income, this additional income counts when determining the deductibility of IRA contributions. Once the cutoff level of income is reached, the deductibility of the contribution is reduced, so that it is completely phased out once the couple reaches adjusted gross income of $64,000 ($44,000 for individuals).

It is important to emphasize that the complete loss of deductibility of the IRA contribution applies only to workers filing a joint return who earn more than $64,000 ($44,000 filing a single return). For the majority of workers, the deductibility of the IRA contribution still applies. And the deductibility still applies to any individual, no matter what the level of income, who is not covered by an employer-sponsored pension plan.

Even if the individual loses the deductibility of the IRA contributions, there is still reason to establish an IRA because the income earned by the funds invested in the account is tax-deferred. If a worker places $3,000 in the account for 20 years, it would earn a substantial return that would not have been taxed. For example, if $3,000 were placed in an IRA each year for 20 years and it earns 8 percent annually, the amount in the account would grow to $137,286. Only $60,000 of the total represents the annual contributions. The remaining $77,256 is earnings that have not been taxed—but will be taxed when the funds are withdrawn from the account.

Initially, the deductible IRA required the individual to be working in order to set up the account. For married couples, this meant that both had to be working for both to take advantage of a tax-deductible IRA. Under current tax laws, both spouses may have a tax-deductible IRA provided that at least one of them has earned income equal to the retirement contributions. This means that in 2002, a married couple with one wage earner could invest $6,000 in two IRA accounts with $3,000 being contributed to each spouse's account.

Even if the couple is unable to save enough to fund the entire $6,000, it is still desirable to invest as much as their budget permits. Then the question arises: In whose account, the husband's or the wife's, should the funds be placed? From a tax perspective, the answer is whoever is younger, which is probably the wife. If the couple can save only $1,700, the funds should be invested in the wife's account if she is younger because the potential tax shelter is greater. Since withdrawals do not have to start until the individual is 70½, the funds may remain in the account for a longer period of time, continuing to compound tax-deferred. In addition, the wife may have a greater need for the funds during her old age since the probability is higher that she will be the surviving spouse. Of course, once the funds are in the wife's name, she is the owner and controls the account.

POINTS OF INTEREST

When to Start an IRA

While an individual worker's ability to establish an IRA is constrained by the availability of funds, the earlier the account is started, the better. Since many young workers often have other priorities for which they are saving (e.g., a down payment on a house) and are not contemplating retirement, they may delay opening an IRA. This is unfortunate, because the final amount in the account is greatly enhanced if the deposits are made at an early age.

This difference in the terminal value is illustrated by the following examples. An individual deposits $1,000 in an IRA starting at age 25 and continues the contribution for 40 years (i.e., until age 65). If the funds earn 8 percent annually, the acount grows to $259,050. If the same individual started the account at age 45 and contributed $2,000 annually until age 65, the account would have $91,524. Even though total contributions in both cases are $40,000, the final amounts are considerably different. When the funds are deposited earlier, they earn more interest, which produces the larger terminal value. Thus it is to the individual's benefit to start IRA contributions as soon as possible, even if the amount of the contributions is modest.

POINTS OF INTEREST

The Use of Personal Computers to Complete Your 1040

For many investors, record keeping, tax planning, and the completion of tax forms required for filing with the IRS can be complicated, time-consuming, and expensive. However, by using a personal computer and a tax preparation package, the investor may significantly reduce the amount of work necessary for the completion of the required tax forms. There are many tax packages to choose among, including *Turbo Tax* from Intuit and J. K. Lasser's *Your Income Tax*. The following is a list of factors the investor should consider when acquiring such a program.

1) The investor needs to identify the use of the program. There are many tax packages available, offering a wide range of features. Modest tax packages will complete the most frequently used tax schedules (e.g., form 1040 and schedules A, B, C, D, and E). If, however, the investor needs to complete other schedules, a more elaborate (and more expensive) program may be necessary.
2) The investor must be certain the program is compatible with the computer to be used, as many programs can be used only with specfic hardware. The investor may want to examine the tax packages before buying the personal computer.
3) Because tax laws change frequently, the investor should consider the adaptability of the program to changes in the tax laws. Otherwise, he or she may have to purchase new programs to handle alterations in the tax laws.
4) Computer programs designed to complete tax papers are "cookbooks." They can only do what the investor tells them to perform. Their primary advantages are the reduction in mathematical errors and the simplification of both tax planning and the completion of the tax forms. For example, the investor may enter into the program charitable deductions, interest expenses, or business deductions throughout the year. Such running entries will simplify year-end tax planning. However, the investor must still know what to enter. The tax preparation package is not a substitute for knowledge of the tax laws.

Keogh Accounts

Keogh account (HR-10 plan)
A retirement plan that is available to self-employed individuals.

Self-employed persons may establish a pension plan called a **Keogh account** or **HR-10 plan**. The account is named after the congressman who sponsored the enabling legislation. A Keogh is similar to an IRA or a company-sponsored pension plan. The individual places funds in the account and deducts the amount from taxable income. The maximum annual contribution is the lesser of 25 percent of income or $35,000. (Future limits will be adjusted for inflation.) The funds placed in the account earn a return that (like the initial contributions) will not be taxed until the funds are withdrawn. As in the case of the IRA, there is a penalty for premature withdrawals before age 59½ and withdrawals must start after reaching the age of 70½.

The determination of the amount an individual may contribute to a Keogh account is somewhat confusing. The individual may contribute up to 25 percent of net earned income, but the calculation of net earned income subtracts the pension contribution as a business expense. The effect is that the individual can contribute 20 percent of income before the contribution. Consider a self-employed individual who earns $100,000 before the pension contribution. If that individual contributes $20,000 (i.e., 20 percent of $100,000), he or she has contributed 25 percent of income after deducting the pension contribution:

Net income after contribution: $100,000 − $20,000 = $80,000.

Contribution as percent of net earned income: $20,000/$80,000 = 25%.

It is probably easier to determine one's maximum possible contribution by taking 20 percent of income before the contribution than by determining 25 percent of net earned income.[3]

A self-employed person may open an IRA in addition to a Keogh account. The contribution to the IRA, however, may not be deductible from taxable income if the individual's income exceeds the limits discussed above. If the self-employed person has funds to finance only one account, it is probably more advantageous to have the Keogh account since the amount that may be contributed (and sheltered from current income taxes) is larger.

If a self-employed person does open a Keogh plan, it must also apply to other people employed by this individual. There are some exceptions, such as new and young employees; however, if a self-employed individual establishes a Keogh account for himself or herself, other regular employees cannot be excluded. By establishing the account, the self-employed individual takes on fiduciary responsibilities for the management of Keogh accounts for his or her employees. This individual can avoid these responsibilities by establishing a Simplified Employee Pension (SEP) plan. SEPs were designed by Congress to encourage small employers to establish pension plans for their employees while avoiding the complexities of the pension laws.

401(k) Plans

Many employers also offer supplementary retirement accounts (SRAs), which are often referred to as *401(k) plans.* These programs permit individuals to contribute a portion of their earned income, up to a specified limit, to a savings plan. The contribution is deducted from the individual's earnings before determining taxable income; thus, a 401(k) plan is similar in its effect on the employee's federal income taxes to IRAs and Keogh accounts. The funds may be invested in one of several plans offered by the company. These often include a stock fund, a bond fund, and a money market fund. The individual has the choice as to the distribution of the contributions among the plans and may be allowed to shift the funds at periodic intervals. (The allocation of funds among the various choices is covered in Chapter 24 on portfolio management.)

403(b) Plans

Nonprofit organizations, such as hospitals, religious organizations, foundations, and public and private schools, sometimes offer similar salary reduction plans, referred to as *403(b) plans.* They work essentially in the same way as 401(k) plans for employees of for-profit organizations. In both cases, the employee's income is reduced by the contribution so that federal income tax is deferred until the funds are withdrawn from the account. The contributions are invested, and the tax on the earnings is also deferred until the funds are withdrawn.

SEPs

In addition to regular pension plans, 401(k)s, and 403(b)s, pension plans include the *Simplified Employee Plan (SEP).* As mentioned previously, pension plans and

---

[3]The formula for determining the maximum contribution is

$$\frac{\text{Income} \times 0.25}{1 + 0.25}.$$

If the individual's income is $100,000, the maximum contribution is

$$\frac{\$100{,}000 \times 0.25}{1 + 0.25} = \frac{\$25{,}000}{1.25} = \$20{,}000.$$

EXHIBIT 6.2

Potential Savings with a Tax-Sheltered Retirement Account

	Case A	Case B
Present		
Taxable income	$50,000.00	$50,000.00
Contribution	0	2,000.00
Net taxable income	50,000.00	48,000.00
Taxes	14,000.00	13,440.00
Disposable income	36,000.00	34,560.00
Contribution to savings	2,000.00	0
Net disposable income	34,000.00	34,560.00
Tax savings	0	560.00
Year 1		
Amount invested	$2,000.00	$2,000.00
Interest earned	200.00	200.00
Taxes on interest	56.00	0
Net interest earned	144.00	200.00
Year 2		
Amount in account	$2,144.00	$2,200.00
Interest earned	214.40	220.00
Taxes on interest	60.03	0
Net interest earned	154.37	220.00
Year 3		
Amount in account	$2,298.37	$2,420.00
	.	.
	.	.
	.	.
Year 20		
Amount in account	$8,033.89	$13,455.00
Tax savings	0	5,421.00

the laws governing them are complex and may be costly for an employer to administer. For this reason, many small employers do not set up pension plans. To overcome this criticism of pension laws, Congress enacted legislation that enables small firms to set up simplified plans (i.e., SEPs). In a SEP plan, employers make IRA contributions on behalf of employees and thus avoid the administrative costs associated with developing their own pension plans. The limitations on contributions to regular IRA accounts do not apply to SEP plans. In addition to employee contributions, the tax law permits employers to use salary reductions to make contributions to their SEP, so the SEP-IRA can also serve as a 401(k) plan.

Savings from Tax-Deferred Pension Plans

An example of the savings that are possible with these tax shelters is presented in Exhibit 6.2. For illustrative purposes, it is assumed that the individual earns $50,000. The individual's personal income tax rate on all taxable income is assumed to be 28 percent, so for each dollar of income, the individual must pay

$0.28 in taxes.[4] The example illustrates two cases. In case A, the individual pays the income tax and then saves $2,000, which is placed in a taxable investment (e.g., a corporate bond) that pays 10 percent annually. The interest income earned by the account is, of course, taxable. In case B, the individual places $2,000 in a tax-sheltered retirement account, which also pays 10 percent annually. However, the tax on this interest is deferred until the individual retires and withdraws the money.

In case A the saver starts with the $50,000 and pays the income tax ($14,000), which leaves a disposable income of $36,000. Of this, $2,000 is invested, leaving $34,000. In case B the saver initially contributes $2,000 to an IRA, which reduces taxable income by $2,000 to $48,000. Taxes of $13,440 are then paid, which leaves a spendable income of $34,560. By placing $2,000 in the IRA account and reducing taxable income, the saver reduces taxes by $560.

The initial tax saving, however, is only the first part of the potential savings. The $2,000 in case A now earns $200 in interest, but $56 of that is lost in taxes. Hence, the saver nets only $144 in interest. The 10 percent interest rate generates a return after taxes of only 7.2 percent. The $2,000 in the IRA earns $200 but none of that interest is currently subject to tax.

After the first year (i.e., the beginning of the second year), there is $2,144 in the account in case A, but in case B, in which the saver placed funds in the retirement account, the amount in the account is $2,200. The amounts in the accounts in case A and in case B grow to $2,298.37 and $2,420, respectively, at the beginning of the third year. After 20 years the initial $2,000 placed in the account in case A will have grown to $8,033.89 after taxes have been paid, but the proceeds in the tax-deferred account will have grown to $13,455. The tax savings over 20 years will amount to $5,421.[5]

This example assumes that the saver makes only one payment of $2,000. However, savings plans usually imply that the investor periodically places funds in the account. If the investor were to place at the beginning of each year $2,000 in the taxable investment or the tax-sheltered retirement account every year for 20 years, the tax savings would be even greater. In that case, the tax-sheltered account would have $126,005 but the taxable alternative would have $89,838 after taxes. The difference then would be $36,167. This difference is the result of the tax savings on the interest alone and does not include the $560 tax savings generated each year by depositing the $2,000 in the account. In 20 years, $11,200 ($560 each year × 20) would be saved in taxes, for a total tax savings of more than $47,300.

These tax savings would be greater if the investor were to place a larger sum each year in the retirement plan account or if income tax rates were higher. For the self-employed professional with a substantial amount of taxable income, retirement plans such as the Keogh account offer one of the best means available to shelter income from current taxation. However, the individual will still have to pay tax on this income when the funds are withdrawn from the plan, while the tax has already been paid on the funds in the taxable alternative.

Nondeductible IRAs—The Roth IRA

In 1997, enabling legislation created the Roth IRA, named after its sponsor, Senator Roth from Delaware. Like the deductible IRA, the Roth IRA is designed to encourage saving for retirement and is an illustration of a tax shelter. However, unlike the traditional IRA in which the contributions are deducted up front, the Roth IRA's advantage occurs when the funds are withdrawn. While the contributions

[4]This example uses the 28 percent tax rate in effect on January 2001. This rate will decline over time so that by 2006, the 28 percent rate will be 25 percent. Other tax brackets will also be reduced, as the 31 percent tax bracket will become 28 percent in 2006.

[5]This example assumes that the tax on interest in case A is deducted from the interest and is not paid from other disposable income. Therefore, case A uses an after-tax return of 7.2 percent while case B uses a 10 percent return.

are not tax deductible, the withdrawals are not subject to income tax. As was explained earlier, withdrawals from a deductible IRA are subject to income taxation.

Like the deductible IRA, the Roth IRA is subject to limitations concerning the amount of the contribution. For 2002–2004 the limitation is $3,000 annually for an individual's account. Contributions may be made as long as adjusted gross income is less than $150,000 ($95,000 if single). For adjusted gross income in excess of these levels, the contributions are phased out. Complete phaseout occurs at adjusted gross incomes of $160,000 and $110,000, respectively. (These phaseout income limitations are more generous than the limitations for deductible IRAs and may encourage the individual to select the Roth IRA in preference to the deductible IRA.)

The individual can have both types of IRAs but cannot contribute $3,000 to both. Thus, the investor could invest $1,500 in each account (for a total of $3,000), but that strategy avoids the important question: Which is better, the deductible or the nondeductible IRA?

The Deductible Versus the Nondeductible IRA

Although it may appear that the nondeductible IRA is preferred because all the return on the investments is exempt from taxation, that is not necessarily the correct choice. Instead, the choice depends on the investor's current income tax bracket and anticipated tax bracket in the future when the funds are withdrawn. In general, if the tax bracket is higher when the contributions are made, the deductible IRA should be preferred. The converse would be true if the investor expects to be in a higher tax bracket when the funds are withdrawn. Then the nondeductible IRA should be preferred. If the tax brackets are the same, it may not matter which IRA the individual chooses. (There are other differences between the deductible and the nondeductible plans, such as mandatory withdrawal from a deductible IRA starting at age 70½. The nondeductible IRA does not have mandatory withdrawals. Such differences may favor one plan over the other independently of the individual's tax bracket.)

To verify this, consider the following three cases in which an investor has $40,000 in adjusted gross income and can earn 8 percent annually on invested funds for 20 years. In the first case, the investor is in the 25 percent income tax bracket and expects to be in that bracket when the funds are withdrawn. (For simplicity, assume that the 25 percent tax rate applies to all taxable income instead of part of the income being taxed at a lower rate and some being taxed at the marginal rate as currently required by the federal income tax code.) With the deductible IRA, disposable income after the IRA contribution and taxes is as follows:

Adjusted gross income	$40,000
Deductible IRA contribution	2,000
Taxable income	38,000
Income taxes	9,500
Disposable income	$28,500

If this individual chooses the nondeductible IRA, the following analysis applies:

Adjusted gross income	$40,000
Deductible IRA contribution	0
Income taxes	10,000
Nondeductible IRA contribution	1,500
Disposable income	$28,500

Notice that in both cases disposable income is the same, so the situations are comparable.

Calculator Solution

Function Key	Data Input
(a) PV =	0
FV =	?
PMT =	−2,000
N =	20
I =	8
Function Key	*Answer*
FV =	91,524
(b) PV =	0
FV =	?
PMT =	−1,500
N =	20
I =	8
Function Key	*Answer*
FV =	68,643
(c) PV =	−91,524
FV =	0
PMT =	?
N =	20
I =	8
Function Key	*Answer*
PMT =	9,322
(d) PV =	−68,643
FV =	0
PMT =	?
N =	20
I =	8
Function Key	*Answer*
PMT =	6,991

The $2,000 annual contribution in the deductible IRA grows to $91,524[(a)] over 20 years at 8 percent, while the $1,500 in the nondeductible IRA grows to $68,643.[(b)] If the funds are withdrawn over 20 years and continue to earn 8 percent annually, the deductible IRA will generate $9,322[(c)] a year. Taxes then are paid on the entire distribution, so the investor gets to keep $6,991 [$9,322 − 0.25($9,322)]. The nondeductible IRA yields $6,991,[(d)] which the investor may keep; there is no further tax liability. Notice that the net amount received after taxes is the same independently of which IRA the individual selected.

To prefer one IRA over the other requires differences in the assumed tax rates for the amounts invested. Consider the effect of assuming a 25 percent tax rate when the funds are invested but a 20 percent tax rate when the funds are withdrawn. With the deductible IRA, disposable income after the IRA contribution and taxes is as follows:

Adjusted gross income	$40,000
Deductible IRA contribution	2,000
Taxable income	38,000
Income taxes	9,500
Disposable income	$28,500

If this individual chooses the nondeductible IRA, the following analysis applies:

Adjusted gross income	$40,000
Deductible IRA contribution	0
Income taxes	10,000
Nondeductible IRA contribution	1,500
Disposable income	$28,500

Since the initial 25 percent income tax rate is unaltered, the analysis is the same as above. The difference occurs when the funds are withdrawn.

Once again, the $2,000 annual contribution in the deductible IRA grows to $91,524[(a)] and the $1,500 annual contribution to the nondeductible IRA grows to $68,643.[(b)] When the funds are withdrawn, the deductible IRA generates $9,322[(c)] a year, and the investor nets after taxes $7,457.60 [$9,322 − 0.2($9,322)]. The nondeductible IRA yields only $6,991,[(d)] so the deductible IRA is the better choice because there is more tax saving up front.

The opposite occurs if the tax rates are assumed to be 20 percent when the funds are contributed to the retirement account but 25 percent when they are withdrawn. In that case the IRA contribution and taxes are as follows:

Adjusted gross income	$40,000
Deductible IRA contribution	2,000
Taxable income	38,000
Income taxes	7,600
Disposable income	$30,400

If this individual chooses the nondeductible IRA, the following analysis applies:

Adjusted gross income	$40,000
Deductible IRA contribution	0
Taxable income	8,000
Nondeductible IRA contribution	1,600
Disposable income	$30,400

Calculator Solution

Function Key	Data Input
(e) PV =	0
FV =	?
PMT =	−1,600
N =	20
I =	8
Function Key	*Answer*
FV =	73,219
(f) PV =	73,219
FV =	0
PMT =	?
N =	20
I =	8
Function Key	*Answer*
FV =	7,458

The initial income tax rate is now 20 percent, so the results are altered. Since disposable income is increased for the deductible IRA, the contribution to the nondeductible IRA is increased to maintain comparability.

Once again, the $2,000 annual contribution in the deductible IRA grows to $91,524[(a)] but the $1,600 in the nondeductible IRA grows to $73,219.[(e)] When the funds are withdrawn, the deductible IRA generates $9,322[(c)] a year, and the investor retains $6,992 [$9,322 – 0.25($9,322)]. The nondeductible IRA yields $7,458,[(f)] so the nondeductible IRA is the better choice because the tax saving is greater when the funds are withdrawn (i.e., the tax rate is higher during the withdrawal period than during the accumulation period).

The first case illustrates that if disposable income is maintained under each IRA and the tax rates are the same during the accumulation and withdrawal periods, there is no difference between the deductible and the nondeductible IRAs. The subsequent cases showed that if the tax rate is higher during the accumulation stage, the deductible IRA is better and that if the tax rate is higher during the withdrawal stage, the nondeductible IRA is better.

The last case considers when the tax rates are the same (25 percent during the accumulation and the withdrawal periods) and the annual contribution is the same ($2,000) for either IRA. To compare equal contributions, the investor must reduce disposable income to cover the taxes paid on the income contributed to the nondeductible IRA.

For the deductible IRA, the analysis is as follows:

Adjusted gross income	$40,000
Deductible IRA contribution	2,000
Taxable income	38,000
Income taxes	9,500
Disposable income	$28,500

For the nondeductible IRA, the analysis is:

Adjusted gross income	$40,000
Deductible IRA contribution	0
Income taxes	10,000
Nondeductible IRA contribution	2,000
Disposable income	$28,000

The difference in disposable income is $500, which is the tax on the income invested in the nondeductible IRA.

The question now is what does the investor who chose the deductible IRA do with the $500? If the money is spent, then there is no question that the nondeductible IRA will produce the higher flow of income during the withdrawal period. The withdrawals will be the same in both cases, but the deductible IRA payments will be subject to income tax while the nondeductible payments will be tax-exempt. If the individual invests the $500, there is an array of possibilities, but unless it is assumed the return exceeds the return on the nondeductible IRA, the analysis will favor the Roth IRA. The following analysis considers two possibilities: (1) the $500 is invested in a tax-exempt security and (2) the $500 is invested in a non-dividend-paying stock, so that any profits will be taxed as long-term capital gains.

Calculator Solution

Function Key	Data Input
(g) PV =	0
FV =	?
PMT =	−500
N =	20
I =	6
Function Key	*Answer*
FV =	18,393

If the individual annually invests $500 for 20 years in a tax-exempt fund and the fund earns 6 percent, the total grows to $18,393.[(g)] (In the 25 percent tax bracket, 6 percent after taxes is equivalent to 8 percent before taxes. See the discussion of tax-equivalence in the section on municipal bonds in Chapter 17.) If the funds continue to earn 6 percent for 20 years, the saver may withdraw $1,604[h] annually. This $1,604 plus the $6,992 after-tax withdrawal from the deductible IRA generates total cash flow of $8,596, which is inferior to the $9,322 generated by the nondeductible IRA.

If the saver annually invests the $500 in non-dividend-paying growth stocks that grow at 8 percent, the total is $22,881,[i] of which $10,000 is the amount invested and $12,881 is the appreciation that is subject to long-term capital gains taxation. If the long-term capital gains tax rate is 20 percent, the investor nets $10,305 after tax for a total of $20,305. At 8 percent, $20,305 generates $2,068[j] before tax for the next 20 years. Thus, $2,068 plus $6,992 after taxes from the deductible IRA totals $9,060. This amount is also inferior to the $9,322 annual withdrawal from the nondeductible IRA.

In both scenarios, the nondeductible IRA is the better choice. Why is this so? The answer lies in the fact that the extra $500 generates a return that will not be taxed when withdrawn from the nondeductible IRA. However, the $500 investment outside of the IRA will have tax implications, which must be considered when selecting between the two strategies. In the first case, the nontaxable 6 percent return can never exceed the 8 percent return earned in the nondeductible IRA. In the second case, the 8 percent growth is the same as that earned in the Roth IRA but is subject to long-term capital gains taxation. In both cases, the after-tax return is insufficient to cover the tax break from the nondeductible IRA. Unless a higher return is assumed for the additional $500 investment, the nondeductible IRA is always the superior choice, because the return will be insufficient to offset the tax advantage. (Of course, assuming a higher return can justify any strategy.)

In summary, if the individual can forgo current spending (that is, make the $2,000 contribution *and cover the taxes on that income*), the nondeductible IRA will be the better choice. If, however, the individual can only save the $2,000 and not cover the tax, there is no substantive difference between the two IRAs. The cash withdrawals will be the same as long as the tax rates are the same. The choice between the deductible and the nondeductible then depends on the expected income tax rate when the funds are withdrawn. If the expected income tax rate exceeds the current rate, the individual should choose the nondeductible IRA.[6] If the expected income tax rate is less than the current rate, the saver should select the deductible IRA.[7]

Calculator Solution

	Function Key	Data Input
(h)	PV =	−18,393
	FV =	0
	PMT =	?
	N =	20
	I =	6
	Function Key	Answer
	PMT =	1,604
(i)	PV =	0
	FV =	?
	PMT =	−500
	N =	20
	I =	8
	Function Key	Answer
	FV =	22,881
(j)	PV =	−20,305
	FV =	0
	PMT =	?
	N =	20
	I =	8
	Function Key	Answer
	PMT =	2,068

Tax-Deferred Annuities

tax-deferred annuity
A contract sold by an insurance company in which the company guarantees a series of payments and whose earnings are not taxed until they are distributed.

In addition to tax-deferred pension plans, an individual may acquire a **tax-deferred annuity**, which is a contract for a series of payments in the future whose earnings are not subject to current income taxation. Tax-deferred annuities are sold by life insurance companies, and they work like life insurance in reverse. Instead of periodically paying for the insurance, the individual who owns the annuity receives regular payments from the insurance company.[8] A tax-deferred annuity has two components: a period in which funds accumulate and a period in which payments are made by the insurance company to the owner of the annuity.

[6]Differences in the income limitations on contributions and when funds must be withdrawn also favor the nondeductible Roth IRA over the deductible IRA.

[7]The Roth IRA offers interesting possibilities for students who are currently earning modest amounts and who are in low tax brackets. For example, if a 17-year-old high school student earns $1,000, that income will not be subject to federal income tax. If the $1,000 were invested in a Roth IRA that earned 8 percent and the funds were left to compound until age 67 (50 years), the account would be worth $46,902. This amount could then be withdrawn and not be subject to income tax. This illustration assumes, of course, the student is willing to part with the $1,000 and that Congress does not change the tax laws.

[8]For descriptions of various types of annuities, see Robert S. Rubinstein, "Life Insurance Investments—Annuities," in *The Encyclopedia of Investments*, ed. M. E. Blume and J. P. Friedman (Boston: Warren, Gorham & Lamont, 1982), 355–382.

The investor buys the annuity by making a payment to the insurance company (e.g., a lump-sum distribution from a pension plan may be used to buy an annuity). The insurance company then invests the funds and contractually agrees to a repayment schedule, which can start immediately or at some other time specified in the contract. While the funds are left with the insurance company, they earn a return for the annuity's owner. The individual's personal income tax obligation on these funds is deferred until the earnings are actually paid out by the insurance company.

Since the tax on the earnings is deferred, it is possible that the amount of tax actually paid will be less than would have been the case if the earnings were taxed as accumulated. Many individuals use these annuities to accumulate funds for retirement. If after reaching retirement their income has fallen, their tax bracket may be reduced. In this case, the withdrawals from the annuity will be taxed at a lower rate. Of course, it is possible that if the individual has saved sufficiently through pension plans, IRA accounts, Keogh accounts, and personal savings, the tax bracket could be higher instead of lower when funds are withdrawn from any of the tax-sheltered accounts (including the tax-deferred annuity). But even if a higher tax rate were to occur in the future, the individual still has had the advantage of tax-free accumulation during the period when the tax obligation was deferred.

Life Insurance as a Tax Shelter

The primary focus of this text is on investing in stocks and bonds, but an individual's portfolio may include life insurance. Such insurance offers both financial protection from premature death and a means to accumulate wealth. The death protection offered by the insurance policy is the amount or **face value** of the policy. It is this face value that is paid to the named beneficiary at the insured's death.

face value
An insurance policy's death benefit.

Life insurance may be classified into two types: policies with a savings program and policies without savings. Life insurance with a savings component accumulates funds, which are referred to as the policy's **cash value**. The owner of the policy may cancel it and receive the cash value. As long as the policy is in force, the cash value continues to grow as the invested funds earn interest.

cash value
The amount that would be received if a life insurance policy were canceled.

Life insurance policies that lack the savings feature are called **term insurance**. The individual purchases insurance for a specified period of time (i.e., the term). The cost of the policy covers only the financial protection in the event of death. There is no savings component and no investment. Term life insurance is essentially no different from property or casualty insurance. In each case the buyer acquires protection against some peril for the term of the policy.

term insurance
Life insurance with coverage for a specified time and excluding a savings plan.

Because term insurance lacks a savings component, it is cheaper, but more costly insurance policies with savings programs offer important advantages. If the individual has difficulty saving, the periodic insurance payment (i.e., the policy's premium) is a means to force saving. Perhaps the most important advantage of this type of insurance is the tax shelter associated with the savings component.

Returns earned on many investments such as interest on a certificate of deposit or dividends earned on a common stock are taxed in the year earned. Even if the individual leaves the funds in the bank to earn interest or participates in a dividend reinvestment program that accumulates additional shares, that individual is subject to income tax on the funds as if they were received. Reinvesting funds does not result in tax deferral.

The taxation of the return earned on funds invested in the savings component of life insurance policies is perceptibly different from the taxation of interest earned on savings accounts or dividends from stock. The funds earned on the policy's cash value are subject to tax only when they are received. Current interest earned on the cash value is sheltered from current income taxation. Furthermore, if the insured should die before the policy is cashed in, the interest is *never* subject to federal income tax.

Under federal income tax laws, taxation of the policy's cash value occurs only if the policyholder cashes in the policy and removes the funds. In this case, the individual is subject to federal income taxation but only if the amount received exceeds the total premiums paid. For example, if the insured had made policy payments over the years of $2,000, cashed in the policy, and received $1,500, there would be no federal income tax. The amount received is less than the cost of the policy. If, however, the insured had made payments of $2,000 and received $3,200, then the individual would be subject to federal income taxes on the amount that exceeds the payments (i.e., $1,200 in this illustration).

This tax treatment of the receipts from an insurance policy is not truly taxation of earned interest. No attempt is made to differentiate what part of the cost of the policy covers the death benefit and what part is the savings component. The individual is able to recover the entire amount spent to maintain the policy before there are any tax implications. Only after the cash value has grown sufficiently that the amount the contributions have earned exceeds the total premiums does the policyholder become subject to federal income taxation.

While there is considerable variety in the types of policies that offer a savings component, most are purchased through periodic payments. These premium payments may be made annually, quarterly, or even monthly, and as long as the payments are made, the policy remains in force.

Insurance companies, however, also offer a single-payment (i.e., single-premium) policy in which the individual makes only one payment. If an individual were to receive a large payment (e.g., a distribution from a pension plan or an inheritance), the individual could use those funds to purchase a single-premium life insurance policy. The policy offers the same general features associated with traditional life insurance. It protects the insured's beneficiaries against the financial impact of premature death, and the cash value of the policy generates a tax-deferred return with a guaranteed minimum return.

Single-premium life insurance policies offer a major cost advantage over traditional policies. In the typical life insurance policy, a large percentage of the initial payments is used to cover the commissions associated with selling the policy. Only a modest amount is actually invested to increase the policy's cash value. With a single-premium policy, sales commissions and other fees are paid from the earnings generated by the policy's cash value. Virtually all the initial payment of the policy is invested and immediately contributes to increasing the policy's cash value.[9]

Employee Stock Option Plans as a Tax Shelter

One tax shelter available to some corporate employees is the employee stock option plan, which permits individuals to buy their employer's stock at a specified price within a specified time period.[10] These stock option plans are considered a tax shelter because they defer tax obligations until the employees realize gains from exercising their options. Taxes will be owed only after the employee sells the stock acquired through the stock option for a profit.

There are two types of corporate stock option plans: the *stock purchase plan* and *incentive stock options*. The stock purchase plan permits employees to buy their corporate employer's stock at a price that is generally set at a modest discount (up to

[9]For descriptions of the various types of life and casualty insurance, see George E. Rejda, *Principles of Risk Management and Insurance*, 6th ed. (New York: HarperCollins, 1997).

[10]Stock options that are traded in secondary markets such as the Chicago Board Options Exchange are covered in Chapter 19.

15 percent). If the company has a stock purchase plan, it must be offered to virtually all employees. Only new hires, part-time employees, highly compensated personnel, and employees owning more than 5 percent of the stock are excluded.

For tax purposes, employees receive no taxable income when they receive or when they exercise the option granted under a stock purchase plan. If the shares are held for at least a year after the option is exercised *and* for at least two years after the option was granted, any profits on the sale of the stock are considered to be long-term capital gains. Thus, if an employee is granted the option and exercises it after five months, that individual must hold the stock for another nineteen months (for a total of two years after the option is granted) for any profit on the sale to be treated as a long-term capital gain. If the stock is held for a shorter time period, the profit is treated as ordinary income for the year in which the gain is realized.

Unlike stock purchase options, incentive stock options are granted to selected employees. These plans, which require stockholder approval, specify the number of shares that may be purchased and the employees (or class of employees) eligible to receive the options. The price at which the option may be exercised must be equal to or exceed the market price of the stock when the option is granted. This option must be exercisable within ten years and may not be transferred by the recipient (except through an estate). For options granted after 1986, the value of the stock that may be purchased through the option cannot exceed $100,000 per employee.

The recipient of the incentive stock option experiences no taxable income when the option is granted or exercised. If the employee exercises the option and holds the stock for one year and for two years after the option was granted, any profit on exercising the option and subsequent sale of the stock is a long-term capital gain. If the time requirements are not met, the profit is considered ordinary income for the year in which the gain is realized.[11]

The distinction between treating incentive stock option profits as ordinary income or as capital gains is obviously important if the tax rate on long-term capital gains differs from the rate on ordinary income. Currently, the long-term capital gains tax rates are 10 percent for individuals in the 15 percent income tax bracket and 20 percent for all other brackets. The difference in the rates can produce substantial tax savings. For an individual in the 36 percent tax bracket, the difference between long-term capital gains taxes and ordinary income taxes is $16,000 per $100,000 of long-term capital gains.

Even if the rates on ordinary income and long-term capital gains were the same, the distinction between the two is still important. If an employee realizes a long-term capital gain through exercising the option and selling the stock, that gain may be offset by losses realized on the sale of other capital assets. (Correspondingly, if the stockholder realizes a loss through the employee stock option plan, that loss may be used against capital gains from other transactions.) There is no limitation on the dollar amount of this offset. An individual who previously made a poor investment and has, for example, a $36,000 capital loss can use that loss to offset long-term capital gains realized by exercising the incentive stock option and selling the stock. By such judicious timing of realizing gains and losses, the employee may be able to erase capital gains generated through exercising the incentive stock option and selling the stock.

If the gains from the incentive stock options are considered ordinary income, the taxpayer's ability to use capital losses from other sources to offset the gains from the incentive stock options is severely limited. As explained earlier in this chapter, only $3,000 ($1,500 for married individuals filing separately) of ordinary

[11]Waiting for time to pass to convert a short-term paper profit into long-term capital gain can, of course, mean that the gain could evaporate if the price of the stock were to fall. One strategy to lock in the gain and maintain the position until sufficient time has passed is a "collar." See Chapter 20 for an explanation of how a collar is used to maintain a position after exercising an option without running the risk of loss from a decline in the price of the underlying stock.

income may be offset by capital losses in a given year. The ability to use capital losses to offset capital gains from incentive stock option plans requires that the latter be treated as capital gains and not as ordinary income. Thus, the classification of profits from employee stock option plans as capital gains instead of ordinary income can have a positive tax implication even if the tax rate on capital gains and ordinary income are equal.

Taxation of Wealth

There are also taxes on wealth in the form of estate, gift, and property taxes. Two types of taxes are exacted when a person dies: estate taxes and inheritance taxes. Estate taxes are imposed on the corpus or body of the deceased's estate. That includes the value of investments, such as stocks and bonds, as well as the value of personal effects, such as automobiles and other personal property. The inheritance tax is levied on the share of an estate received by another individual. Like the estate tax, it is imposed on the value of personal effects as well as on financial assets.

estate tax
A tax on the value of a deceased individual's assets.

Estate taxes are primarily the domain of the federal government, while both estate and inheritance taxes are levied by state governments. Like the personal income tax, estate and inheritance taxes are usually progressive. Selected rates as of 2001 from the federal estate tax are given in Exhibit 6.3.[12] As may be seen from this exhibit, the marginal tax rates increase with the value of the estate up to 55 percent on estates in excess of $3,000,000.

EXHIBIT 6.3

Selected Federal Estate Tax Rates as of January 2001

Taxable Value of the Estate	Tax On the Base*	Tax Plus Percentage†	Tax On Excess Over
0–10,000	$ 0	18%	$ 0
10,000–20,000	1,800	20	10,000
20,000–40,000	3,800	22	20,000
.	.	.	.
.	.	.	.
.	.	.	.
100,000–150,000	23,800	30	100,000
150,000–250,000	38,800	32	150,000
250,000–500,000	70,800	34	250,000
500,000–750,000	155,800	37	500,000
.	.	.	.
.	.	.	.
.	.	.	.
2,500,000–3,000,000	1,025,800	53	2,500,000
above 3,000,000	1,290,000	55	3,000,000

*This is the tax paid on the minimum amount shown in the left-hand column under the heading "Taxable Value of the Estate."

†The percentage applies to any amount in excess of the minimum and up to the maximum amount shown under the heading "Taxable Value of the Estate."

[12]These rates also apply to gifts.

Estate tax laws are extremely complex, and an investor who is planning the distribution of an estate should consult a lawyer or financial planner. However, the basic components of these taxes are as follows. First, a married individual may leave the entire estate to a spouse without the spouse's paying any tax. Thus, a married individual with a net worth of $10,000,000 may leave the entire estate to a spouse and avoid estate taxes. (This is really only a deferment of the tax liability, because this wealth is added to the wealth of the surviving spouse and is subject to estate tax when the spouse dies.) Second, the estate receives a tax credit, which reduces the amount of taxes owed. In 2001, the tax credit was $211,300, so all estates worth $675,000 or less did not pay tax.

Beginning in 2002, the estate tax is being phased out. During this transition period, the maximum estate tax rate and the exemption from estate taxes are as follows:

Year	Maximum Rate	Exemption
2002	50%	$1 million
2003	49	$1 million
2004	48	$1.5 million
2005	47	$1.5 million
2006	46	$2 million
2007	45	$2 million
2008	45	$2 million
2009	45	$3.5 million
2010	Tax repealed	

Based on these schedules beginning in 2002, all estates less than $1 million will be exempt. For a married couple with $1 million in each spouse's name, the effect is an exemption of the joint estate of $2 million. And the total possible exemption for a married couple rises to $7 million in 2009.

inheritance tax
A tax on what an individual receives from an estate.

Inheritance taxes are levied by state governments on the distribution of the estates of individuals living in the state. Even though the recipient of the inheritance may live in another state, that individual's inheritance is subject to tax by the state in which the deceased resided.

As with state income taxes, there are substantial differences in state inheritance taxes. There are also differences in the tax rates for recipients of an inheritance, depending on their relation to the deceased. The deceased's immediate family pays lower rates. Maximum rates apply to nonrelatives who receive a share of the estate.

property tax
A tax levied against the value of real or financial assets.

In addition to estate and inheritance taxes, the investor must also be concerned with **property taxes**. These are primarily levied by counties, municipalities, and townships. Since there are thousands of such local governments, there is great diversity in property taxes.

Personal property taxes may be levied on tangible or intangible personal property. Tangible property is physical property, such as a house or an automobile. Intangible personal property includes nonphysical assets and financial assets, such as stocks and bonds. Many localities tax only tangible property, with particular emphasis on real estate. However, some states permit the taxation of intangible personal property. In such states the individual's portfolio of stocks and bonds may be subject to property taxation. For example, a portfolio of stocks and bonds worth over $100,000 is taxed in Florida at the rate of $2 per $1,000 of value. A $2,000,000 portfolio pays $4,000 in intangible personal property tax. (Florida also has local property taxes on real estate but does not have a personal income tax. The Florida legislature recently voted to phase out the intangible property tax.) Because there is considerable variation in this type of taxation, the investor would be wise to learn the specific tax laws that apply in his or her own state.

Corporate Taxation

Like individuals, firms are subject to taxation by the various levels of government. Income, capital gains, and property may all be subject to taxation. Although any of these taxes may affect the individual firm, this brief discussion is limited to the federal corporate income tax.

As of January 2002, the federal corporate tax structure for income earned in 2001 was the following:

Taxable Corporate Income	Marginal Tax Rate
$0–50,000	15%
$50,001–75,000	25
$75,001–100,000	34
$100,001–335,000	39
$335,001–10,000,000	34
$10,000,001–15,000,000	35
$15,000,001–18,300,000	38
over $18,300,000	35

The 39 percent bracket recaptures the benefits of the 15 and 25 percent brackets. The 38 percent tax bracket recaptures the benefits of the 34 percent bracket. Once corporate income exceeds $18,300,000, all corporate income is taxed at 35 percent.

Under this tax structure, the maximum rate applies to virtually all corporations of any significant size. Certainly for publicly held firms, the investor might as well view the amount of taxes owed as being about one-third of the firm's taxable income. Although it is difficult to isolate who ultimately bears the cost of the corporate income tax, it is at least partially borne by investors, since the tax reduces either cash dividends and/or the firm's capacity to reinvest its earnings and grow.

straight-line depreciation
The allocation of the cost of plant and equipment by equal annual amounts over a period of time.

accelerated depreciation
The allocation of the cost of plant and equipment in unequal annual amounts such that most of the cost is recovered in the early years of an asset's life.

investment tax credit
A direct reduction in taxes owed resulting from investment in plant or equipment.

Like individual investors, corporate managements seek to reduce or at least to defer tax payments by taking advantage of certain deductions and making selected investments. For example, the cost of long-term assets, such as plant and equipment, is allocated (i.e., deducted from income) over a period of time; that is, the asset is depreciated. Under **straight-line depreciation**, the amount of the deduction is the same each year, but under **accelerated depreciation** this expense is increased during the early years of the asset's life. The effect of accelerated depreciation is to increase expenses in the early years of the asset's life, which decreases current income and current taxes. The tax is deferred until after the period of accelerated depreciation has elapsed.

Previously, another means to alter the amount of taxes owed was the **investment tax credit**, which, as the name implies, is a credit to be applied against taxes for making certain investments. In an effort to stimulate spending on plant and equipment, the federal government permitted corporations to reduce their taxes if they made certain investments in plant and equipment. By channeling a firm's funds into these investments, management was able to reduce the amount of income tax that the firm had to pay.

Any proposal to change corporate income tax rates or reinstate the investment tax credit could have a major implication for investors if the tax credit applies to firms in industries that require a substantial investment in plant and equipment. The future profitability of these firms may be increased whereas firms that provide services, such as retail operations, may experience reduced profitability. The investment tax credit offers service firms few tax benefits, but higher tax rates should decrease their future net income.

Another way corporate financial managers can reduce income taxes is through investments in the stock of other corporations. Only 30 percent of any dividends received are subject to corporate income tax, and the remaining 70 percent are excluded from federal income taxation.[13] If the stock's value rises and is subsequently sold for a profit, this profit is considered a capital gain and is taxed as any other source of income. However, as with individuals, corporate capital gains taxes are paid only after the profits are realized. Management may defer this tax indefinitely by not realizing the gains. Thus, the exclusion of 70 percent of dividend income and the tax deferral of capital gains help explain why some firms own stock in other firms instead of operating assets, such as plant and equipment.[14]

Accelerated depreciation and investments in other corporations' stocks are two means available to corporate management to reduce the firm's income taxes. The potential impact of taxes influences management's decision making (just as it affects an individual investor's choice of assets). From the viewpoint of the individual investor, corporate income tax laws make analyzing and comparing companies more difficult. However, if a firm pays less than one-third of its earnings in taxes, that may be a clue to the investor to examine the firm more closely. Although management may be able to reduce taxes temporarily, this may also imply that current earnings are overstated and that taxes may be higher in the future.

Summary

Tax laws have a significant impact on the environment of investing. These laws are issued by all levels of government, but the most important laws affecting investment decisions have been passed by the federal government.

The federal government taxes income from investments, capital gains, and the individual's estate. Federal income tax rates are progressive, which means that as the tax base increases, the tax rate increases. This taxation—especially the progressivity of tax rates—induces individuals to find ways to reduce their tax liabilities. Investments that reduce, defer, or avoid taxes are called tax shelters. Important tax shelters include tax-exempt bonds and pension plans. The interest on tax-exempt bonds completely avoids federal income taxes, while pension plans (including IRAs, Keogh accounts, and 401(k) plans) defer taxes until the funds are withdrawn from the plans.

In addition to tax-deferred pension plans, the investor has the option to establish a nondeductible IRA plan in which the withdrawals are not subject to federal income taxation. The choice between the tax-deductible and the nondeductible IRA depends on (1) the ability of the saver to pay the tax on the current contribution and (2) the assumption made concerning the individual's expected income tax rate when withdrawals will be made compared to the current income tax rate.

Capital gains occur when an investor buys an asset such as stock and subsequently sells it for a profit. Gains that are realized within a year are short-term and are taxed as ordinary income. Gains that are realized after one year are long-term

[13]If corporation A owns 20 to 80 percent of corporation B, only 20 percent of dividends are taxable. If A owns over 80 percent of B, the books of the two firms are consolidated, and there are no federal income taxes if one pays dividends to the other.

[14]For additional discussion of the corporate dividend exclusion, see the section on preferred stock in Chapter 16.

and receive favorable tax treatment, as they are taxed at a maximum rate of 20 percent. A capital loss occurs when the asset is sold for a loss. Such losses are used to offset capital gains. If the investor has capital losses that exceed capital gains, the losses may be used to offset up to $3,000 annually in income from other sources.

Estate taxes are levied on the value of a decedent's estate, and some states also levy taxes on an individual's share of an estate (i.e., the inheritance). State and local governments also tax an individual's property, which may include the investor's financial assets.

Corporations also pay federal and state income taxes. The tax reform law enacted in 1986 reduced both corporate income tax rates and the ability of corporations to avoid paying income taxes. However, accelerated depreciation and the 70 percent exclusion of dividends earned on investments in the stock of other companies permit corporations to reduce or defer the current amount of taxes they must pay.

Questions

1) What is a progressive tax? Why is the federal estate tax illustrative of a progressive tax?
2) Does a tax shelter necessarily imply that the investor avoids paying taxes?
3) What is a capital gain? When are capital gains taxes levied? May capital losses be used to offset capital gains and income from other sources?
4) Which of the following illustrate a tax shelter?
   a) Dividend income
   b) Interest earned on a savings account
   c) A stock purchased for $10 that is currently worth $25
   d) Interest earned on a municipal bond
   e) Interest earned on the cash value of an insurance policy
5) What are Keogh, 401(k), and IRA plans? What are their primary advantages to investors?
6) What is the difference between an estate tax and an inheritance tax?
7) What differentiates a deductible IRA from a Roth (nondeductible) IRA? What conditions favor the nondeductible IRA?
8) What differentiates term insurance from other types of life insurance? Why is term insurance not an example of a tax shelter?
9) What is depreciation? How does it reduce a firm's taxes? Should a firm use accelerated depreciation instead of straight-line depreciation?
10) How can a corporation shelter income by purchasing stock in another company?

11) Go to the IRS Web site (http://www.irs.ustreas.gov) and locate the federal income tax rates for the current year.

Problems

1) a) An individual in the 28 percent federal income tax bracket and 20 percent long-term capital gains tax bracket bought and sold the following securities during the year:

	Cost Basis of Stock	Proceeds of Sale
ABC	$24,500	$28,600
DEF	35,400	31,000
GHI	31,000	36,000

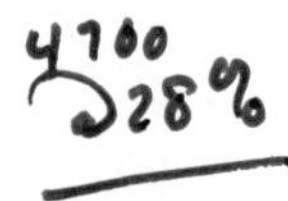

What are the taxes owed on the short-term capital gains?

b) An individual in the 35 percent federal income tax bracket and 20 percent long-term capital gains tax bracket bought and sold the following securities during the year:

	Cost Basis of Stock	Proceeds of Sale
ABC	$34,600	$28,600
DEF	29,400	31,000
GHI	21,500	19,000

What are the taxes owed or saved as a result of these sales?

2) An investor is in the 31 percent tax bracket and pays long-term capital gains taxes of 20 percent. What are the taxes owed (or saved in the cases of losses) in the current tax year for each of the following situations?
   a) Net short-term capital gains of $3,000; net long-term capital gains of $4,000
   b) Net short-term capital gains of $3,000; net long-term capital losses of $4,000
   c) Net short-term capital losses of $3,000; net long-term capital gains of $4,000
   d) Net short-term capital gains of $3,000; net long-term capital losses of $2,000
   e) Net short-term capital losses of $4,000; net long-term capital gains of $3,000
   f) Net short-term capital losses of $1,000; net long-term capital losses of $1,500
   g) Net short-term capital losses of $3,000; net long-term capital losses of $2,000

3) You are in the 30 percent income tax bracket and pay long-term capital gains taxes of 20 percent. What are the taxes owed or saved in the current year for each of the following sets of transactions?
   a) You buy 100 shares of ZYX for $10 and after seven months sell it on December 31, 200X, for $23. You buy 100 shares of WER for $10 and after fifteen months sell it on December 31, 200X, for $7. You buy 100 shares of DFG for $10 and after nine months, on December 31, 200X, it is selling for $15.
   b) You buy 100 shares of ZYX for $60 and after seven months sell it on December 31, 200Y, for $37. You buy 100 shares of WER for $60 and after fifteen months sell it on December 31, 200Y, for $67. You buy 100 shares of DFG for $60 and after nine months sell it on December 31, 200Y, for $76.
   c) On January 2, 200X, you buy 100 shares of ZYX for $40 and sell it for $31 after twenty-two months. On January 2, 200X, you buy 100 shares of WER for $40 and sell it for $27 after fifteen months. On January 2, 200X, you buy 100 shares of DFG for $40 and sell it for $16 after eighteen months.
   d) On January 2, 200X, you buy 100 shares of ZYX for $60. On October 2, 200X, you sell 100 shares of ZYX for $40. On October 10, 200X, you purchase 100 shares of ZYX for $25.

4) You are in the 25 percent income tax bracket. What are the taxes owed or saved if you
   a) Contribute $2,000 to a 401(k) plan
   b) Contribute $2,000 to a Roth IRA
   c) Withdraw $2,000 from a traditional IRA
   d) Withdraw $2,000 from a Keogh account

5) Your traditional IRA account has stock of GFH, which cost $2,000 20 years ago when you were 50 years old. You have been very fortunate, and the stock is now worth $23,000. You are in the 35 percent income tax bracket and pay 20 percent on capital gains.
   a) What was the annual rate of growth in the value of the stock?
   b) What are the taxes owed if you withdraw the funds?
6) You are 60 years old. Currently, you have $10,000 invested in an IRA and have just received a lump-sum distribution of $50,000 from a pension plan, which you roll over into an IRA. You continue to make $2,000 annual payments to the regular IRA and expect to earn 9 percent on these funds until you start withdrawing the money at age 70 (i.e., after ten years). The IRA rollover will earn 9 percent for the same duration.
   a) How much will you have when you start to make withdrawals at age 70?
   b) If your funds continue to earn 9 percent annually and you withdraw $17,000 annually, how long will it take to exhaust your funds?
   c) If your funds continue to earn 9 percent annually and your life expectancy is 18 years, what is the maximum you may withdraw each year?
7) Bob places $1,000 a year in his IRA for ten years and then invests $2,000 a year for the next ten years. Mary places $2,000 a year in her IRA for ten years and then invests $1,000 a year for the next ten years. They both have invested $30,000. If they earn 8 percent annually, how much more will Mary have earned than Bob at the end of 20 years?
8) Bob and Barbara are 55 and 50 years old. Bob annually contributes $1,500 to Barbara's IRA. They plan to make contributions until Bob retires at age 65 and then to leave the funds in as long as possible (i.e., age 70 to ease calculations).

   Mike and Mary are 55 and 50 years old. Mike annually contributes $2,000 to Mike's IRA. They plan to make contributions until Mike retires at age 65 and then leave the funds in as long as possible (i.e., age 70 to ease calculations). Both Barbara's and Mike's IRAs yield 10 percent annually.

   The combined life expectancy of both couples is to age 85 of the wife. What will be each couple's annual withdrawal from the IRA based on life expectancy? (This problem is designed to illustrate an important point in financial planning for retirement. What is the point?)
9) A corporation owns 10,000 shares of MNO Corp. The stock pays a dividend of $2.35 a share. If the corporation that owns the stock is in the 34 percent federal income tax bracket, how much tax does it owe on the dividend income?
10) A corporation in the 34 percent federal income tax bracket collects the following investment income:

Dividends on preferred stock owned	$12,000
Interest on municipal bonds	10,000
Interest on corporate bonds	7,000
Dividends on common stock owned	8,500
Interest on federal government bonds	5,000

How much federal income tax does this firm owe on its investment income?

THE FINANCIAL ADVISOR'S INVESTMENT CASE
Retirement Planning and Federal Income Taxation

Your financial planning practice services several sophisticated individuals who have accumulated a substantial amount of assets but who are naive concerning potential strategies to reduce taxes. To increase their awareness, one client suggested that you offer a complimentary seminar to explain fundamental means for reducing taxes. Your immediate reaction was that each individual's tax situation differs, so the seminar would be of little benefit. On further reflection, however, you thought a focused presentation could be beneficial, especially if you limit the discussion to one topic, retirement planning, and cover other tax strategies such as capital gains or estate planning only to the extent that they affect retirement planning.

To illustrate the differences in retirement planning, you selected two very different case studies. Mary Ewing is a single parent with one teenage son. She has a well-paying, secure job that offers a 401(k) plan, life insurance, and other benefits. While Ms. Ewing has sufficient resources to finance her son's college education, he works in a local CPA office that provides him with sufficient spending money, including the cost of insurance for his car.

Jason Montagno has two young children and his wife has returned to graduate school to complete an advanced degree. He is self-employed in an industry with large cyclical swings in economic activity. Although Montagno did not sustain any losses during the prior recession, he has previously experienced losses that have affected his willingness to assume risk. During the good years, he has accumulated a sizable amount of liquid assets that he believes may be needed during any future periods of economic downturn.

You decide that both individuals offer sufficient differences to cover many facets of tax planning for retirement. To ease your presentation, you assume that both are in the 25 percent marginal tax bracket and that retirement will not occur for at least 20 years. Although you would like to illustrate how much each individual could accumulate, you believe that discussion should be deferred until some other time in order to concentrate on the tax implications of possible retirement strategies. To help generate discussion, you decide to start your presentation by answering the following specific questions that you distributed prior to the seminar:

1) Can Mary set up an IRA and deduct the contribution from her income that is subject to federal income taxation? Does the same apply to Jason? Could Mary's or Jason's children have IRA accounts?
2) Can Mary or Jason set up a Keogh account and deduct the contribution from income that is subject to federal income taxation? Could their children establish Keogh accounts?
3) Is there any reason why Mary or Jason should prefer a 401(k) or Keogh retirement account to an IRA?
4) Is the income generated by Mary's 401(k) account subject to current federal income taxation? If Jason created a retirement account, would the income be subject to current federal income taxation?
5) If either Mary or Jason were to withdraw funds from their retirement accounts, would they pay federal income taxes and penalties?
6) If Mary or Jason purchased stock outside of a retirement account, should the purchases emphasize

income or capital gains? Would purchasing stock outside a retirement account be a desirable strategy?

7) Would the purchase of an annuity offer tax benefits that are similar to a retirement account?

8) Would the funds in Mary's or Jason's retirement accounts be subject to federal estate taxation?

9) What general strategies would you suggest to an individual seeking to accumulate funds for retirement?

7 Risk and Portfolio Management

In August 2001, the Power Ball jackpot reached $280 million. People drove for miles and stood in long lines to buy a ticket. The odds of their winning were approximately 80 million to 1. The odds were obviously not on any individual's side. Perhaps they should have listened to George Patton, who in *War As I Knew It*, wrote, "Take calculated risks; that is quite different from being rash." All investments involve risk because the future is uncertain, but the possible returns on investments are perceptibly more certain than the returns on a state-sponsored lottery.

This chapter is an introduction to the sources and measurements of risk and how these measurements are used in portfolio theory. Risk may be measured by a standard deviation, which measures the dispersion (or variability) around a central tendency, such as an average return. Risk also may be measured by a beta coefficient, which is an index of the volatility of a security's return relative to the return on the market. Much of this chapter is devoted to an exposition of these measures of risk and the reduction of risk through the construction of diversified portfolios.

The chapter ends with a discussion of portfolio theory and explanations of security returns. Portfolio theory is built around the investor seeking to construct an efficient portfolio that offers the highest return for a given level of risk or the least amount of risk for a given level of return. Of all the possible efficient portfolios, the individual investor selects the portfolio that offers the highest level of satisfaction or utility.

Models of security returns are built around the specification of what variables affect an asset's return. In the capital asset pricing model, a security's return primarily depends on interest rates (such as the rate of safe Treasury securities), movements in security prices in general, and how the individual stock responds to changes in the market. In arbitrage pricing theory, security returns are related to more variables, which may include unexpected changes in inflation or industrial production.

Learning Objectives

After completing this chapter you should be able to:

1. Identify the sources of risk.
2. Identify the relationship between securities that is necessary to achieve diversification.
3. Contrast the sources of return and differentiate between expected and realized returns.
4. Explain how standard deviations and beta coefficients measure risk. Interpret the difference between beta coefficients of 1.5, 1.0, and 0.5.
5. Contrast efficient and inefficient portfolios and identify which portfolio the individual will select.
6. Compare the explanation of a stock's return according to the capital asset pricing model and arbitrage pricing theory.

Return

Investments are made to earn a return. To earn the return, the investor must accept the possibility of loss. Portfolio theory is concerned with risk and return. Its purpose is to determine the combination of risk and return that allows the investor to achieve the highest return for a given level of risk. To do this, means for measuring risk and return must be devised. Initially, this chapter considers various usages for the term *return*, followed by an extensive discussion of the measurement of risk. Risk and return are then combined in the discussion of portfolio theory.

expected return
The sum of the anticipated dividend yield and capital gains.

The word *return* is often modified by an adjective, including the *expected return*, the *required return*, and the *realized return*. The **expected return** is the anticipated flow of income and/or price appreciation. An investment may offer a return from either of two sources. The first source is the flow of income that may be generated by the investment. A savings account generates interest income. The second source of return is capital appreciation. If an investor buys stock and its price subsequently increases, the investor receives a capital gain. All investments offer the investor potential income and/or capital appreciation. Some investments, like the savings account, offer only income, whereas other investments, such as an investment in land, may offer only capital appreciation. In fact, some investments may require that expenditures (e.g., property tax on the land) be made by the investor.

This expected return is summarized in Equation 7.1:

$$E(r) = \frac{E(D)}{P} + E(g). \tag{7.1}$$

The symbols are

$E(r)$ the expected return (as a percentage)
$E(D)$ the expected dividend (or interest in the case of a debt instrument)
P the price of the asset
$E(g)$ the expected growth in the value of the asset (i.e., the capital gain).

If an investor buys a stock for \$10 and expects to earn a dividend of \$0.60 and sell the stock for \$12 so there is a capital gain of 20 percent, the expected return is

$$E(r) = \frac{\$0.60}{\$10} + 0.2 = 0.26 = 26\%.$$

The investor expects to earn a return of 26 percent during the time period.[1]

required return
The return necessary to induce the investor to purchase an asset.

It is important to realize that this return is anticipated. The yield that is achieved on the investment is not known until after the investment is sold and converted to cash. It is important to differentiate between the *expected return*, the *required return*, and the *realized return*. The expected return is the incentive for accepting risk, and it must be compared with the investor's **required return**, which is the return necessary to induce the investor to bear the risk associated with a particular investment. The required return includes (1) what the investor may earn on alternative investments, such as the risk-free return available on Treasury bills,

[1]Since the time period has not been specified, this return should not be confused with an *annual* rate of return. In Chapter 10, returns that do not specify the time period are referred to as *holding period returns*. The calculation of *annual rates of return* is also addressed in Chapter 10.

and (2) a premium for bearing risk that includes compensation for the expected rate of inflation and for fluctuations in security prices. Since the required return includes a measure of risk, the discussion of the required return must be postponed until the measurement of risk is covered.

realized return
The sum of income and capital gains earned on an investment.

The **realized return** is the return actually earned on an investment and is essentially the sum of the flow of income generated by the asset and the capital gain. The realized return may, and often does, differ from the expected and required returns.[2]

The realized return is summarized by Equation 7.2:

$$r = \frac{D}{P} + g. \quad (7.2)$$

This is essentially the same as the equation for expected return with the expected value sign, *E*, removed. If an investor buys a stock for $10 and collects $0.60 in dividends, and the stock appreciates by 20 percent, the realized return is

$$r = \frac{\$0.60}{\$10} + 0.2 = 0.26 = 26\%.$$

Expected Return Expressed as a Probability

Probability theory measures or indicates the likelihood of something occurring. If you are certain that something will happen, the probability is 100 percent. (Remember the old joke about death and taxes.) The sum of all the probabilities of the possible outcomes is 100 percent. The expected value (the anticipated outcome) is the sum of each outcome multiplied by the probability of occurrence. For example, an investor is considering purchasing a stock. The possible returns and the investor's estimate of their occurring are as follows:

Return	Probability
3%	10%
10	45
12	40
20	5

The sum of all the probabilities is 100 percent, and the returns encompass all the possible outcomes. The expected value or, in this illustration, the expected return [$E(r)$] is the probability of the outcome times each individual price. That expected value is

$$\begin{aligned} E(r) &= (0.10).03 + (0.45).10 + (0.40).12 + (0.05).20 \\ &= 0.003 + 0.045 + 0.048 + 0.01 = 0.106 = 10.6\%. \end{aligned}$$

Each of the expected returns is weighted by the probability of occurrence. The results are then added to determine the expected return, 10.6%.

While it is possible that the return on the stock could be as low as 3 percent or as high as 20 percent, their weights are relatively small. They contribute only modestly to the expected return. The return of 10 percent carries more weight (45 percent) in the determination of the expected return. Notice, however, that the expected return is not 10 percent, nor is it any of the four possible outcomes. The expected return is a weighted average in which each outcome is weighted by the probability of the outcome occurring.

[2]The calculation of annual rates of return that *have been realized* is covered in Chapter 10.

The investor may also use this information to construct cumulative probabilities. Cumulative probability distributions answer questions such as, What is the probability that the return will be least 10 percent, or What is the probability that the investor will not earn 12 percent? The answer to the former question is 90 percent (45% + 40% + 5%) percent, because that percentage includes all the probabilities that the return will be 10 percent or greater. The answer to the second question is 55 percent, because it includes all the probabilities that the stock's return will be less than 12 percent.

Probability lends itself to studying different situations. By changing the individual probabilities, the outcome (the expected value) is altered. For example, the probabilities in the preceding example could be changed, which would affect the weighted average (i.e., the expected return). If the individual returns remain the same but their probability of occurring are changed as follows:

Return	Probability
3%	20%
10	35
12	40
20	5

the expected return $[E(r)]$ becomes

$$E(r) = (0.20).03 + (0.35).10 + (0.40).12 + (0.05).20$$
$$= 0.006 + 0.035 + 0.048 + 0.01 = 0.099 = 9.9\%$$

A greater weight is now assigned to the lowest return, which has the effect of reducing the expected return from 10.6 percent to 9.9 percent.

In addition to changing the probabilities and determining the impact of the expected return, it is also possible to change the individual returns to determine how sensitive the expected return is to an individual observation. (This type of analysis cannot be applied to the probabilities. Changing one probability requires changing another since the sum of the probabilities must equal 100 percent.) Suppose the third return (the third observation) were to change by 1 percent from 12 percent to 13 percent. The impact on the expected return is

$$E(r) = (0.20).03 + (0.35).10 + (0.40).13 + (0.05).20$$
$$= 0.006 + 0.035 + 0.052 + 0.01 = 0.103 = 10.3\%$$

If the fourth observation were changed by 1 percent from 20 percent to 21 percent, the expected return would be

$$E(r) = (0.20).03 + (0.35).10 + (0.40).12 + (0.05).21$$
$$= 0.006 + 0.035 + 0.048 + 0.0105 = 0.0995 = 9.95\%$$

The expected return is more sensitive to the change in the first case when the individual return rose from 12 to 13 percent. In the second illustration, the expected return is not sensitive to the change.

This type of sensitivity analysis can play an important role in portfolio management. It helps answer questions such as, If stock A's return declines, what impact will the decline have on the portfolio's return? How sensitive is the portfolio return to a specific stock's return? If, for example, a large proportion of an individual's portfolio had been invested in Enron when it imploded during 2001, the impact was significant. The portfolio return was sensitive to the Enron bankruptcy. If, however, Enron constituted a small proportion of an individual's portfolio, the impact would have been minor. The portfolio return would not have been sensitive to the return of an individual stock. (An investor might want to answer the following series of questions: What is the worst case scenario? What is the probability that the worst case will occur? What is the impact if the worst case does occur?)

A Monte Carlo simulation takes this process to an extreme. Named after combining mathematics with gambling casinos, a Monte Carlo approach ties together simulations and probability distributions. A computer randomly selects a value for each variable and computes the expected value and the dispersion around that expected value. (That variability or dispersion around the expected value is measured by the standard deviation, which is discussed later in this chapter.) This process of selecting values for each variable and determining the expected value is repeated numerous times. The results are then combined into one final expected value and measure of dispersion around that value.

Sources of Risk

Risk is concerned with the uncertainty that the realized return will not equal the expected return. As was explained in the initial chapter, there are several sources of risk. These are frequently classified as diversifiable (or unsystematic) risk or nondiversifiable (or systematic) risk. Diversifiable risk refers to the risk associated with the specific asset and is reduced through the construction of a diversified portfolio. Nondiversifiable risk refers to the risk associated with (1) fluctuating security prices in general, (2) fluctuating interest rates, (3) reinvestment rates, (4) the loss of purchasing power through inflation, and (5) loss from changes in the value of exchange rates. These sources of risk are not affected by the construction of a diversified portfolio.

Nondiversifiable Risk

Asset returns tend to move together. If security prices rise in general, the price of a specific security tends to rise with the market. Conversely, if the market were to decline, the value of an individual security would also tend to fall. Thus there is a systematic relationship between the price of a specific asset, such as a common stock, and the market as a whole. As long as investors buy securities, they cannot avoid bearing this source of systematic risk.

Asset values are also affected by changes in interest rates. As is explained in Chapter 16, rising interest rates depress the prices of fixed-income securities, such as long-term bonds and preferred stock. Conversely, if interest rates fall, the value of these assets rises. A systematic negative (i.e., inverse) relationship exists between the prices of fixed-income securities and changes in interest rates. As long as investors acquire fixed-income securities, they must bear the risk associated with fluctuations in interest rates.

Common stock prices are also affected by changes in interest rates. Just as there is a negative relationship between interest rates and the prices of fixed-income securities, the same relationship exists between common stock and interest rates. First, future cash flows from common stocks are being discounted at higher rates, so their present values are lower. In addition, higher rates make fixed-income securities more attractive, so investors substitute bonds and other fixed-income investments for common stock. The movement from stock to higher-paying debt instruments tends to depress stock prices. The converse is true when interest rates fall. The rotation from lower-yielding fixed-income securities to equities should lead to higher stock prices.

Investors receive payments, such as dividends or interest, that may be reinvested. When yields change (e.g., when interest rates rise or decline), the amount received on these reinvested funds also changes. This, then, is the source of reinvestment risk. In the early 1980s, when interest rates were relatively high, investors benefited when their funds were reinvested. However, in the 1990s, when yields were the lowest in 20 years, many investors' incomes declined as they earned less on reinvested funds. This was particularly true for savers such as retirees with low-risk investments such as certificates of deposit. When higher yielding CDs came due, investors had to accept lower interest yields when they renewed the certificates.

Investors must also endure the loss of purchasing power through inflation. It is obvious that rising prices of goods and services erode the purchasing power of both investors' income and assets. Like fluctuating security prices or changes in interest rates, there is nothing the individual can do to stop inflation; therefore, the goal should be to earn a return that exceeds the rate of inflation. If the investor cannot earn such a return, he or she may benefit more from spending the funds and consuming goods now.

The last source of systematic risk is the risk associated with changes in the value of currencies. If investors acquire foreign investments, the proceeds of the sale of the foreign asset must be converted from the foreign currency into the domestic currency before they may be spent. (The funds, of course, may be spent in the foreign country without the conversion.) Since the values of currencies change, the value of the foreign investments will rise or decline with changes in the value of the currencies. If the value of the foreign currency rises, the value of the foreign investment increases and the domestic investor gains. The converse occurs when the price of the foreign currency declines.[3]

Individuals can avoid exchange-rate risk by not acquiring foreign assets and, of course, miss the opportunities such investments may offer. However, investors may still bear some of this risk because many firms are affected by changes in the value of foreign currencies. Many U.S. firms invest abroad. For example, over two-thirds of the Coca-Cola Company's revenues are generated abroad. Even if a company does not invest abroad, it may compete with foreign firms in domestic markets. Hence investors who do not own foreign assets are affected, albeit indirectly, by changes in the value of foreign currencies relative to their own.

Besides the sources of nondiversifiable systematic risk, the investor also faces the unsystematic risk associated with each asset. Since the investor buys specific assets, for example, the common stock of IBM or bonds issued by the township of Princeton, that individual must bear the risk associated with each specific investment.

For firms, the sources of unsystematic risk are the business and financial risks associated with the operation. Business risk refers to the nature of the firm's operations, and financial risk refers to how the firm finances its assets (i.e., whether the firm uses a substantial or modest amount of debt financing). For example, the business risk associated with United or Delta Airlines is affected by such factors as the cost of fuel, the legal and regulatory environment, the capacity of planes, and seasonal changes in demand. Financial risk for airlines depends on how the airline finances its planes and other assets—that is, whether the assets were acquired by issuing bonds, preferred stock, or common stock; by leasing; or by borrowing from other sources.

The investor may be unable to anticipate all the events that will affect a certain firm, such as a strike or natural disaster, but these events may affect the value of the firm's securities in positive or negative ways. In either case, the possibility of these events occurring increases the risk associated with investing in a specific asset.

[3]The individual may also have to endure political risks if investments are made in unstable countries with unstable governments.

POINTS OF INTEREST
Other Terms Used to Describe Sources of Risk

The body of the text dichotomized the sources of risk into unsystematic/diversifiable risk, which may be reduced through the construction of well-diversified portfolios, and systematic/nondiversifiable risk, which cannot be reduced through diversification. These two general classes of risk were then subdivided into the sources of risk illustrated in Exhibit 1.1. Other terms or words are also used to describe sources of risk. Whether these are different sources or subsets for (or synonymous with) the sources in Exhibit 1.1 is probably open to debate. But if an investor's goal is risk management, such semantic discussions are probably immaterial.

Default risk refers to the probability that borrowers (e.g., a firm or government) will not meet their debt obligations. Such risk is firm-specific and may be considered as part of financial risk, the impact of which is reduced through the construction of a well-diversified portfolio. *Country risk* refers to the risk associated with investing in a specific country. Such risk is obvious for an investment in a country whose government may subsequently nationalize the assets—as occurred when Castro seized power in Cuba. Country risk may also apply to investments in emerging nations, whose economies and political environments are not stable. Since country risk applies to specific nations, its impact may be reduced through diversification or avoided entirely by not investing in countries with unstable, volatile economies and governments.

Event risk refers to the possibility of loss from a specific event. This source of risk may be firm-specific. For example, AH Robin's Dalkon Shield bankrupted the company but the impact on an individual's diversified portfolio was probably negligible. Specific events, however, can affect the market as a whole. The oil embargo of the 1970s caused a dramatic shift in the price of oil, which, in turn, had an impact on inflation and the level of economic activity. Stock prices and interest rates were also negatively affected. Whether the investor wants to consider as the source of risk the specific "event" or the expected increases in inflation and higher interest rates is probably immaterial. The ultimate effect was a general reduction in stock prices and lower bond prices, the impact of which could not have been reduced through the construction of a well-diversified portfolio.

Total (Portfolio) Risk

portfolio risk
The total risk associated with owning a portfolio; the sum of systematic and unsystematic risk.

diversification
The process of accumulating different securities to reduce the risk of loss.

The combination of systematic and unsystematic risk is defined as the total risk (or **portfolio risk**) that the investor bears. Unsystematic risk may be significantly reduced through **diversification**, which occurs when the investor purchases the securities of firms in different industries. Buying the stock of five telephone companies is not considered diversification, because the events that affect one company tend to affect the others. A diversified portfolio may consist of stocks and bonds issued by a telephone company, an electric utility, an insurance firm, a commercial bank, an oil refinery, a retail business, and a manufacturing firm. This is a diversified mixture of industries and types of assets. The impact of particular events on the earnings and growth of one firm need not apply to all the firms; therefore, the risk of loss in owning the portfolio is reduced.

How diversification reduces risk is illustrated in Figure 7.1, which shows the price performance of three stocks and their composite. Stock A's price initially falls, then rises, and starts to fall again. Stock B's price ultimately rises but tends to fluctuate. Stock C's price fluctuates the least of the three but ends up with only a modest gain. Purchasing stock B and holding it would have produced a substantial profit, while A would have generated a moderate loss.

The last quadrant illustrates what happens if the investor buys an equal dollar amount of each stock (i.e., buys a diversified portfolio).[4] First, the value of the portfolio as a whole may rise even though the value of an individual security may not. Second, and most important, the fluctuation in the value of the portfolio is

[4]Later in this chapter, the statistical condition that must be met to achieve diversification is discussed and illustrated using returns from investments in the common stocks of Mobil and Public Service Enterprise Group.

FIGURE 7.1

Prices of Three Stocks

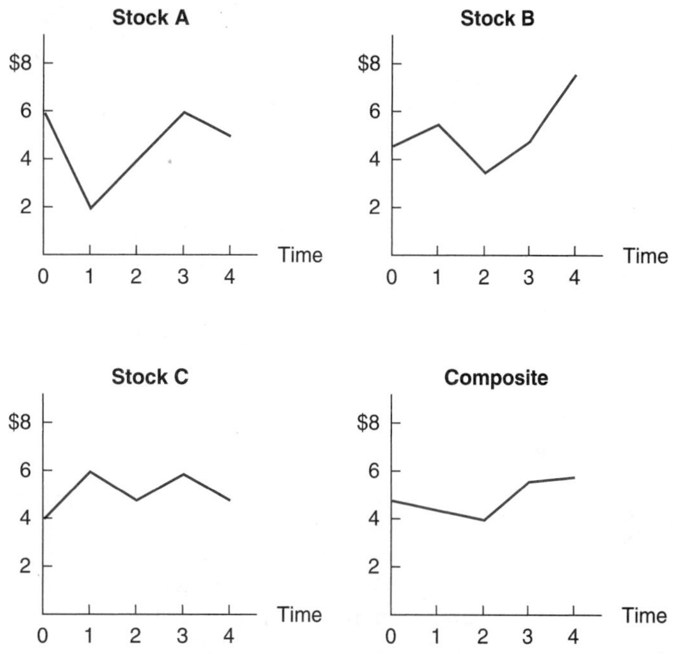

less than the fluctuations in individual security prices. By diversifying the portfolio, the investor is able to reduce the risk of loss. Of course, the investor also gives up the possibility of a large gain (as was achieved by stock B).

In effect, a diversified portfolio reduces the element of unsystematic risk. The risk associated with each individual investment is reduced by accumulating a diversified portfolio of assets. Even if one company fails (or does extremely well), the impact on the portfolio as a whole is reduced through diversification. Distributing investments among different industries, however, does not eliminate market risk and the other types of systematic risk. The value of a group of securities will tend to follow the market values in general. The price movements of securities will be mirrored by the diversified portfolio; hence, the investor cannot eliminate this source of systematic risk.

How many securities are necessary to achieve a diversified portfolio that reduces and almost eliminates unsystematic risk? The answer may be "surprisingly few." Several studies have found that risk has been significantly reduced in portfolios consisting of from 10 to 15 securities.[5]

This reduction in unsystematic risk is illustrated in Figure 7.2 (p. 158). The vertical axis measures units of risk, and the horizontal axis gives the number of securities. Since systematic risk is independent of the number of securities in the portfolio, this element of risk is illustrated by a line, *AB*, that runs parallel to the

[5]For further discussion, see the following: John Evans and Stephen Archer, "Diversification and the Reduction of Dispersion: An Empirical Analysis," *Journal of Finance* (December 1968): 761–767; Bruce D. Fielitz, "Indirect versus Direct Diversification," *Financial Management* (winter 1974): 54–62; William Sharpe, "Risk, Market Sensitivity and Diversification," *Financial Analysts Journal* (January–February 1972): 74–79, and Meir Statman, "How Many Stocks Make a Diversified Portfolio?" *Journal of Financial and Quantitative Analysis* (September 1987): 353–364. However, George Frankfurter suggests that even well-diversified portfolios have a substantial amount of nonsystematic risk. See his "Efficient Portfolios and Nonsystematic Risk," *The Financial Review* (fall 1981): 1–11.

FIGURE 7.2

Portfolio Risk: The Sum of Systematic and Unsystematic Risk

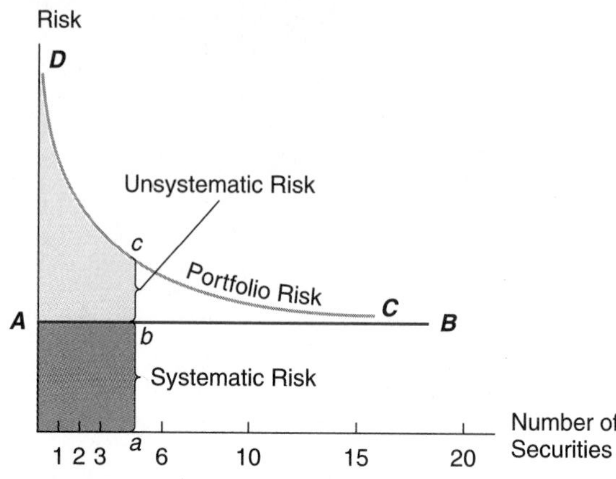

horizontal axis. Regardless of the number of securities that an individual owns, the amount of nondiversifiable risk remains the same.[6]

Portfolio risk (i.e., the sum of systematic and unsystematic risk) is indicated by line *CD*. The difference between line *AB* and line *CD* is the unsystematic risk associated with the specific securities in the portfolio. The amount of unsystematic risk depends on the number of securities held. As this number increases, unsystematic risk diminishes; this reduction in risk is illustrated in Figure 7.2 where line *CD* approaches line *AB*. For portfolios consisting of ten or more securities, the risk involved is primarily systematic.

Such diversified portfolios, as mentioned previously, do not consist of ten public utilities but of a cross section of U.S. businesses. Investing $20,000 in ten stocks (i.e., $2,000 for each) may achieve a reasonably well-diversified portfolio. Although such a portfolio costs more in commissions than two $10,000 purchases, the small investor achieves a diversified mixture of securities, which should reduce the risk of loss associated with investment in a specific security.[7] Unfortunately, the investor must still bear the systematic risk associated with movements in the markets, the risk of loss in purchasing power that results from inflation, and the other sources of nondiversifiable risk.

The Measurement of Risk

Portfolio theory determines the combination of risk and return that allows the investor to achieve the highest return for a given level of risk. The previous section addressed the expected and realized return; the measurement of risk is the focus of the next sections of this text.

Risk is concerned with the uncertainty regarding whether the realized return will equal the expected return. The measurement of risk places emphasis either on the extent to which the return varies from the average return or on the volatility of

[6]The sources of systematic risk may be managed through techniques that are covered throughout this text. For example, the investor bears less market risk by constructing a portfolio that is less responsive to changes in security prices. (See the discussion of beta coefficients later in this chapter.) Interest rate and reinvestment rate risk may be managed using "duration" or constructing a laddered bond portfolio (covered in Chapter 16). Exchange-rate risk may be reduced through the use of derivatives. (See the discussions of options, futures, and swaps in Chapters 19–21.)

[7]As is discussed in the next chapter, diversification is one advantage offered by mutual funds.

the return relative to the return on the market. The variability of returns is measured by a statistical concept called the *standard deviation*, while volatility is measured by what has been termed a *beta coefficient*. (In terms of Figure 7.2, the standard deviation measures the total risk—that is, the distance *ac*. The beta measures systematic risk—distance *ab*. As may be seen in the figure, total risk approaches systematic risk as the portfolio becomes more diversified, so that in a well-diversified portfolio, the two measures of risk are essentially equal.) This section considers the standard deviation as a measure of risk. Beta coefficients are covered later in the chapter.

A measurement of risk is implied when individuals refer to the annual range in an asset's price. One may encounter such statements as "The stock is trading near its low for the year," or "245 stocks reached new highs while only 41 fell to new lows." Some individuals plan their investment strategy as if a stock trades within a price range. If the stock is near the low for the year, it may be a good time to purchase. Correspondingly, if it is trading near the high for the year, it may be a good time to sell. The range in the stock's price, then, can be used as a guide to strategy, because the price tends to gravitate to a mean between these two extremes. In other words, there is a *central tendency* for the price of the stock. The range in a stock's price then becomes a measure of risk. Stocks with wider ranges are "riskier" because their prices tend to deviate farther from the average (mean) price.

One problem with using the range as a measure of risk is that two securities with different prices can have the same range. For example, a stock whose price ranges from $10 to $30 has the same range as a stock whose price varies from $50 to $70. The range is $20 in both cases, but an increase from $10 to $30 is a 200 percent increment, whereas the increase from $50 to $70 is only a 40 percent increase. The price of the latter stock appears to be more stable; hence, less risk is associated with this security, even though both stocks involve equal risk according to the range.

Dispersion Around an Investment's Return

dispersion
Deviation from the average.

The problem inherent in using only two observations (e.g., a stock's high and low prices) to determine risk may be avoided by analyzing **dispersion** around an average value, such as an investment's average return. This technique considers all possible outcomes. If there is not much difference among the individual returns (i.e., they are close together), then the dispersion is small. If most of the returns are near the extremes and differ considerably from the average return, then the dispersion is large. The larger this dispersion, the greater the risk associated with a particular stock.

This concept is perhaps best illustrated by a simple example. An investment in either of two stocks yields an average return of 15 percent, but stocks could have the following returns:

Stock A	Stock B
13½%	11%
14	11½
14¼	12
14½	12½
15	15
15½	17½
15¾	18
16	18½
16½	19

Although the average return is the same for both stocks, there is an obvious difference in the individual returns. Stock A's returns are close to the average value,

FIGURE 7.3

Distribution of the Returns of Two Stocks

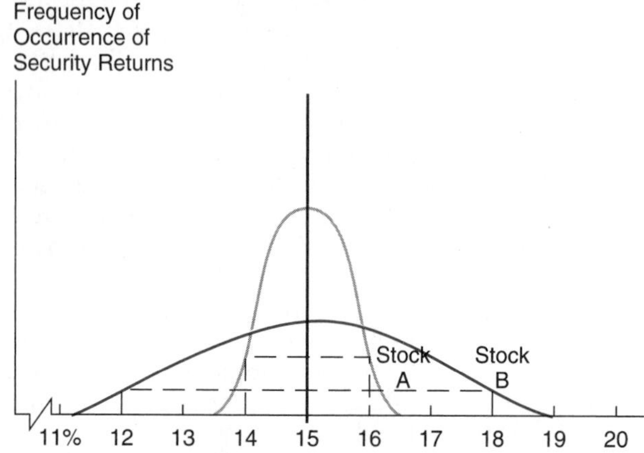

whereas stock B's returns are closer to the high and low values. The returns of stock A cluster around the average return. Because there is less variability in returns, it is the less risky of the two securities.

These differences in risk are illustrated in Figure 7.3, which plots returns on the horizontal axis and the frequency of their occurrence on the vertical axis. (This is basically the same information that was previously given for stocks A and B, except that more observations would be necessary to construct such a graph. While only nine observations are used in the illustration, the figure is drawn as if there were a large number of observations.) Most of stock A's returns are close to the average return, so the frequency distribution is higher and narrower. The frequency distribution for stock B's return is lower and wider, which indicates a greater dispersion in that stock's returns.

The large dispersion around the average return implies that the stock involves greater risk because the investor can be less certain of the stock's return. The larger the dispersion, the greater is the chance of a large loss from the investment, and, correspondingly, the greater is the chance of a large gain. However, this potential for increased gain is concomitant with bearing more risk. Stock A involves less risk; it has the smaller dispersion. But it also has less potential for a large gain. A reduction in risk also means a reduction in possible return on the investment.

Standard Deviation as a Measure of Risk: One Asset

This dispersion around the mean value (i.e., the average return) is measured by the standard deviation.[8] Since the standard deviation measures the tendency for the individual returns to cluster around the average return and is a measure of the variability of the return, it may be used as a measure of risk. The larger the dispersion, the greater the standard deviation and the larger the risk associated with the particular security.

The standard deviation of the returns for stock A is 1.01. The actual calculation of the standard deviation is illustrated in the appendix to this chapter. Plus or minus one standard deviation has been shown to encompass approximately 68 percent of

[8]The variance, which is the square of the standard deviation, is also used to measure risk. See the discussion of the variance and semivariance in the appendix to this chapter.

FIGURE 7.4

Distribution of the Returns of Two Stocks (Including Standard Deviations)

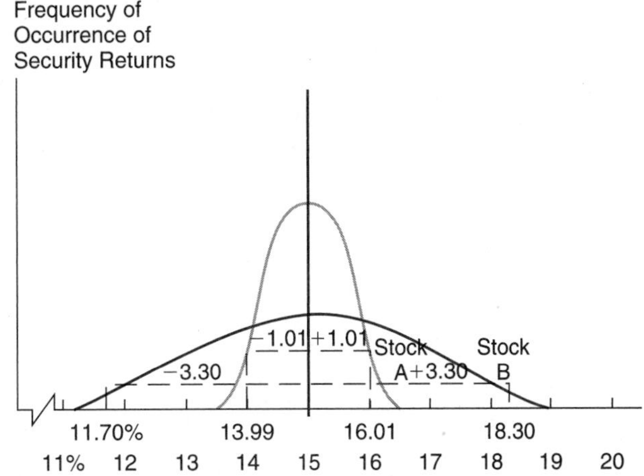

all observations (in this case, 68 percent of all the returns). Since the standard deviation for A is 1.01, then approximately 68 percent of the returns fall between 13.99 and 16.01 percent. These returns are simply the average return (15 percent) plus 1.01 and minus 1.01 (i.e., plus or minus the standard deviation).

For stock B the standard deviation is 3.30, so approximately 68 percent of the returns fall between 11.7 and 18.3 percent. Stock B's returns have a wider dispersion from the average return, and this fact is indicated by the greater standard deviation.

These differences in the standard deviations are illustrated in Figure 7.4, which reproduces Figure 7.3 but adds the standard deviations. The average return for both stocks is 15 percent, but the standard deviation is greater for stock B than for stock A (i.e., 3.30 for B versus 1.01 for A). By computing the standard deviation, the analyst quantifies risk. This will help in the selection of individual securities, since the investor will prefer those assets with the least risk for a given expected return.

If this were an illustration of selecting between two securities, the individual would select investment A because it has the lower standard deviation for a given return. If this were an illustration comparing the historical or actual returns between two investments, the individual would conclude that investment A had outperformed investment B since the returns were the same but B's return had been more variable.

Such comparisons are easy when the returns are the same, because the analysis is limited to comparing the standard deviations. The comparisons are also easy when the standard deviations are the same, because then the analysis is limited to comparing the returns. Such simple comparisons are rare, since investment returns and standard deviations often differ. Investment A may offer a return of 10 percent with a standard deviation of 4 percent, while investment B offers a return of 14 percent with a standard deviation of 6 percent. Since neither the returns nor the standard deviations are the same, they may not be compared. Investment A offers the lower return and less risk; therefore, it cannot be concluded that it is the superior investment.

This inability to compare may be overcome by computing the *coefficient of variation*, which divides the standard deviation by the return. This process, which is illustrated in the appendix to this chapter, expresses risk relative to return. Higher coefficients of variation imply more risk, because a higher numerical value means more variability per unit of return.

The Return and Standard Deviation of a Portfolio

Although the preceding discussion was limited to the return on an individual security and the dispersion around that return, the concepts can be applied to an entire portfolio. A portfolio also has an average return and a dispersion around that return. The investor is concerned not only with the return and the risk associated with each investment but also with the return and risk associated with the portfolio as a whole. This aggregate is, of course, the result of the individual investments and of each one's weight in the portfolio (i.e., the value of each asset, expressed in percentages, in proportion to the total value of the portfolio).

Consider a portfolio consisting of the following three stocks:

Stock	Return
1	8.3%
2	10.6
3	12.3

If 25 percent of the total value of the portfolio is invested in stocks 1 and 2 and 50 percent is invested in stock 3, the return is more heavily weighted in favor of stock 3. The return is a weighted average of each return times its proportion in the portfolio.

Return	×	Weight (Percentage Value of Stock in Proportion to Total Value of Portfolio)	=	Weighted Average
8.3%	×	0.25	=	2.075%
10.6	×	0.25	=	2.650
12.3	×	0.50	=	6.150

The return is the sum of these weighted averages.

2.075%
2.650
6.150
10.875%

The previous example is generalized in Equation 7.3, which states that the return on a portfolio r_p is a weighted average of the returns of the individual assets $[(r_1)\ldots(r_n)]$, each weighted by its proportion in the portfolio $(w_1 \ldots w_n)$:

$$r_p = w_1(r_1) + w_2(r_2) + \cdots + w_n(r_n). \tag{7.3}$$

Thus, if a portfolio has 20 securities, each plays a role in the determination of the portfolio's return. The extent of that role depends on the weight that each asset has in the portfolio. Obviously those securities that compose the largest part of the individual's portfolio have the largest impact on the portfolio's return.[9]

Unfortunately, an aggregate measure of the portfolio's risk (i.e., the portfolio's standard deviation) is more difficult to construct than the weighted average of the

[9]The same general equation may be applied to expected returns, in which case the expected return on a portfolio, $E(r_p)$, is a weighted average of the expected returns of the individual assets $[(E(r_1)\ldots E(r_n)]$, each weighted by its proportion in the portfolio $(w_1 \ldots w_n)$:

$$E(r_p) = w_1E(r_1) + w_2E(r_2) + \cdots + w_nE(r_n).$$

FIGURE 7.5

Stock Returns, Individually and Combined

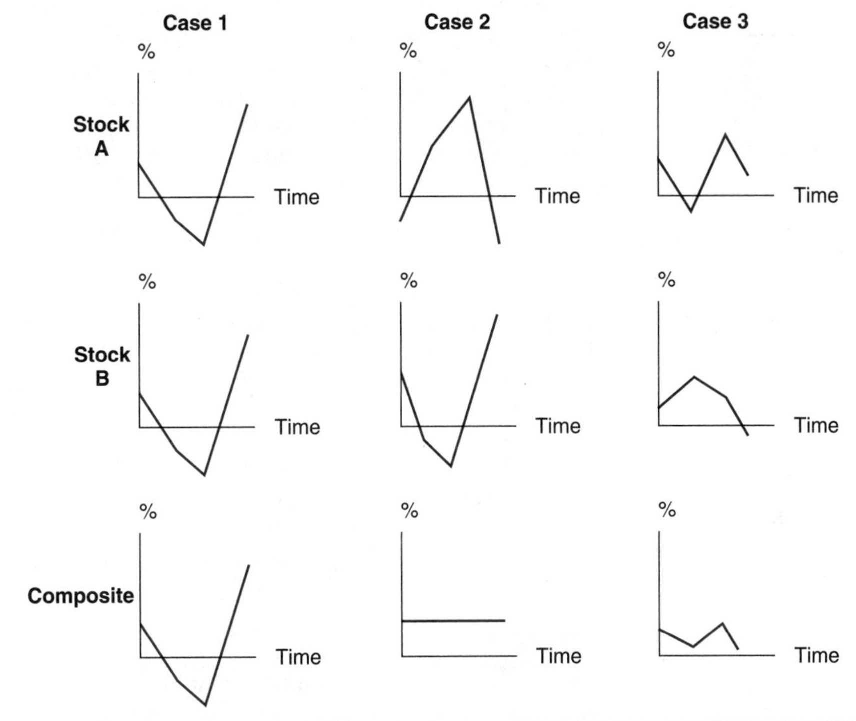

returns. This is because security prices are not independent of each other. However, while security prices do move together, there can be considerable difference in these price movements. For example, prices of stocks of firms in home building may be more sensitive to recession than stock prices of utilities, whose prices may decline only moderately. These relationships among the assets in the portfolio must be considered in the construction of a measure of risk associated with the entire portfolio. These inner relationships among stocks are called *covariation.* Covariation considers not only the variability of the individual asset but also its relationship with the other assets in the portfolio.

Since the determination of a portfolio's standard deviation becomes very complicated for a portfolio of many assets, the following illustrations will be limited to portfolios of only two assets. Three cases are illustrated in Figure 7.5. In the first case, the two assets' returns move exactly together; in the second, the two assets' returns move exactly opposite; and in the third, the returns are independent of each other. While these examples are simple, they do illustrate how a portfolio's standard deviation is determined and the effect of the relationships among the assets in the portfolio on the risk associated with the portfolio as a whole.

The standard deviation of the returns on a portfolio (S_d) with two assets is given in Equation 7.4:

(7.4)
$$S_d = \sqrt{w_a^2 S_a^2 + w_b^2 S_b^2 + 2w_a w_b \text{ cov}_{ab}}$$

Although this looks formidable, it says that the standard deviation of the portfolio's return is the square root of the sum of (1) the squared standard deviation of the return of the first asset (S_a) times its squared weight in the portfolio (w_a) plus

(2) the squared standard deviation of the return on the second asset (S_b) times its squared weight (w_b) in the portfolio plus (3) two times the weight of the first asset times the weight of the second asset times the covariance of the two assets.[10]

The calculation of covariation (like the calculation of the standard deviation) is illustrated in the appendix to this chapter. As is also explained in the appendix, the correlation coefficient combines the standard deviations of the two variables and the covariance, so the covariance is computed before the correlation coefficient. However, it is often convenient to express the covariance of returns on assets a and b (cov_{ab}) in terms of the correlation coefficient:

$$\textbf{cov}_{ab} = S_a \times S_b \times \textbf{(correlation coefficient of } a \textbf{ and } b\textbf{)}.$$

Although the calculation of the correlation coefficient is illustrated in the appendix to this chapter, for this discussion it is necessary to know only that the numerical values of the correlation coefficient range from +1.0 for perfect positive correlation to −1.0 for perfect negative correlation.

To illustrate the determination of the portfolio's standard deviation, consider the returns earned by securities A and B and the returns' standard deviations in the following three cases in which the portfolio is divided equally between the two securities. The three cases are also shown in Figure 7.5, which plots the returns on the assets and on the portfolio composed of equal amounts invested in each (i.e., 50 percent of the portfolio in each asset).

CASE I

Perfect Positive Correlation (Correlation Coefficient = 1.0)

Year	Return on Security A	Return on Security B	Return on Portfolio
1	10%	10%	10%
2	−12	−12	−12
3	−25	−25	−25
4	37	37	37
Average return	2.5%	2.5%	2.5%
Standard deviation of security returns	27.16	27.16	?

[10]While Equation 7.4 expresses the standard deviation of a portfolio consisting of two assets, most portfolios consist of more than two assets. The standard deviations of portfolios consisting of more assets are computed in the same manner, but the calculation is considerably more complex. For a three-security portfolio, the calculation requires portfolio weights for securities a, b, and c, and the covariance of ab, ac, and bc. For a six-security portfolio, the calculation requires each security's weight and the covariance of ab, ac, ad, ae, af, bc, bd, be, bf, cd, ce, cf, de, df, and ef for a total of 15 covariances. The number of required covariances is

$$\frac{(n^2 - n)}{2},$$

in which n is the number of securities in the portfolios. For a six-security portfolio that is

$$\frac{(6^2 - 6)}{2} = 15.$$

For a portfolio with 100 securities, the required number of covariances is

$$\frac{(100^2 - 100)}{2} = 4{,}950.$$

While such calculations can be performed by computers, a two-security portfolio is sufficient to illustrate the computation of the portfolio standard deviation and its implication for diversification.

In this case, the securities move exactly together (i.e., their correlation coefficient is 1.0). The standard deviation of the portfolio is computed as follows:

$$\begin{aligned}
S_d &= \sqrt{w_a^2 S_a^2 + w_b^2 S_b^2 + 2w_a w_b \, \textbf{cov}_{ab}} \\
&= \sqrt{w_a^2 S_a^2 + w_b^2 S_b^2 + 2w_a w_b \, S_a S_b \, \textbf{Correlation Coefficient}_{ab}} \\
&= \sqrt{0.5^2(27.16)^2 + 0.5^2(27.16)^2 + 2(0.5)(0.5)(27.16)(27.16)(1)} \\
&= 27.16.
\end{aligned}$$

CASE 2

Perfect Negative Correlation (Correlation Coefficient = −1.0)

Year	Return on Security A	Return on Security B	Return on Portfolio
1	−15%	25%	5%
2	12	−2	5
3	25	−15	5
4	−37	47	5
Average return	−3.75%	13.75%	5%
Standard deviation of security returns	27.73	27.73	?

In this case the returns move exactly opposite (i.e., the correlation coefficient is −1.0), and the standard deviation of the portfolio is

$$\begin{aligned}
S_d &= \sqrt{w_a^2 S_a^2 + w_b^2 S_b^2 + 2w_a w_b \, \textbf{cov}_{ab}} \\
&= \sqrt{0.5^2(27.73)^2 + 0.5^2(27.73)^2 + 2(0.5)(0.5)(27.73)(27.73)(-1)} \\
&= 0.
\end{aligned}$$

CASE 3

Partial Negative Correlation (Correlation Coefficient = −0.524)

Year	Return on Security A	Return on Security B	Return on Portfolio
1	10%	2%	6%
2	−8	12	2
3	14	6	10
4	4	−2	1
Average return	5%	4.5%	4.75%
Standard deviation of security returns	9.59	15.97%	?

In this last case the returns do not move together. In the first and third years they both generated positive returns, but in the other two years one generated a loss while the other produced a positive return. In this illustration the correlation coefficient between the returns equals −0.524. Thus, the standard deviation of the portfolio is

$$S_d = \sqrt{w_a^2S_a^2 + w_b^2S_b^2 + 2w_aw_b \text{ cov}_{ab}}$$
$$= \sqrt{0.5^2(9.59)^2 + 0.5^2(5.97)^2 + 2(0.5)(0.5)(9.59)(5.97)(-0.524)}$$
$$= 4.11.$$

Notice how, in the first case, the standard deviation of the portfolio is the same as the standard deviation of the two assets. Combining these assets in the portfolio has no impact on the risk associated with the portfolio. In Case 2, the portfolio's risk is reduced to zero (i.e., the portfolio's standard deviation is zero). This indicates that combining these assets whose returns fluctuate exactly in opposite directions has the effect on the portfolio of completely erasing risk. The fluctuations associated with one asset are exactly offset by the fluctuations in the other asset, so there is no variability in the portfolio's return.

Notice that in the second case the elimination of risk does not eliminate the positive return. Of course, if one asset yielded a return of +10 percent while the other asset yielded −10 percent, the net return is 0 percent. That is, however, a special case. If in one period the return on one asset is +15 percent while the other is −5 percent, the net is 5 percent.[11] If, in the next period, the first asset yielded −1 percent while the other yielded 11 percent, the net is still 5 percent. The swing in the first asset's return is −16 percent (+15 to −1), while the swing in the second asset's return is +16 percent (−5 to +11). The movements are exactly opposite, so the correlation coefficient would be −1.0, but the return on a portfolio *equally* invested in the two securities would be +5 percent for both periods.

In the third case, which is the most realistic of the three illustrations, the standard deviation of the portfolio is less than the standard deviations of the individual assets. The risk associated with the portfolio as a whole is less than the risk associated with either of the individual assets. Even though the assets' returns do fluctuate, the fluctuations partially offset each other, so that by combining these assets in the portfolio, the investor reduces exposure to risk with almost no reduction in the return.

Diversification and the reduction in unsystematic risk require that assets' returns not be highly positively correlated. When there is a high positive correlation (as in Case 1), there is no risk reduction. When the returns are perfectly negatively correlated (as in Case 2), risk is erased (i.e., there is no variability in the combined returns). If one asset's return falls, the decline is exactly offset by the increase in the return earned by the other asset. The effect is to achieve a risk-free return. In the third case, there is neither a perfect positive nor a perfect negative correlation. However, there is risk reduction, because the returns are poorly correlated. The lower the positive correlation and the greater the negative correlation among the returns, the greater will be the risk reduction achieved by combining the various assets in the portfolio.

While the above illustration is extended, it points out a major consideration in the selection of assets to be included in a portfolio. The individual asset's expected return and risk are important, but the asset's impact on the portfolio as a whole is also important. The asset's return and the variability of that return should be considered in a portfolio context. It is quite possible that the inclusion of a volatile asset will reduce the risk exposure of the portfolio as a whole if the return is negatively correlated with the returns offered by the other assets in the portfolio.

[11]Remember: The return is a weighted average of the individual returns, so in this illustration the return is (0.5) (0.15) + (0.5) (−0.05) = 0.05 = 5%.

Failure to consider the relationships among the assets in the portfolio could prove to be counterproductive if including the asset reduces the portfolio's potential return without reducing the variability of the portfolio's return (i.e., without reducing the element of risk).[12]

Risk Reduction through Diversification: An Illustration

The previous discussion has been abstract, but the concept of diversification through securities whose returns are not positively correlated may be illustrated by considering the returns earned on two specific stocks, Public Service Enterprise Group and Mobil Corporation. Public Service Enterprise Group is primarily an electric and gas utility whose stock price fell with higher interest rates and inflation. Prior to its merger with Exxon, Mobil was a resource company whose stock price rose during inflation in response to higher oil prices but fell during the 1980s as oil prices weakened and inflation receded.

The annual returns (dividends plus price change) on investments in these two stocks are given in Figure 7.6 for the period 1971 through 1991. As may be seen in the graph, there were several periods when the returns on the two stocks moved

FIGURE 7.6

Annual Returns for Mobil and PSEG: Individually and Combined

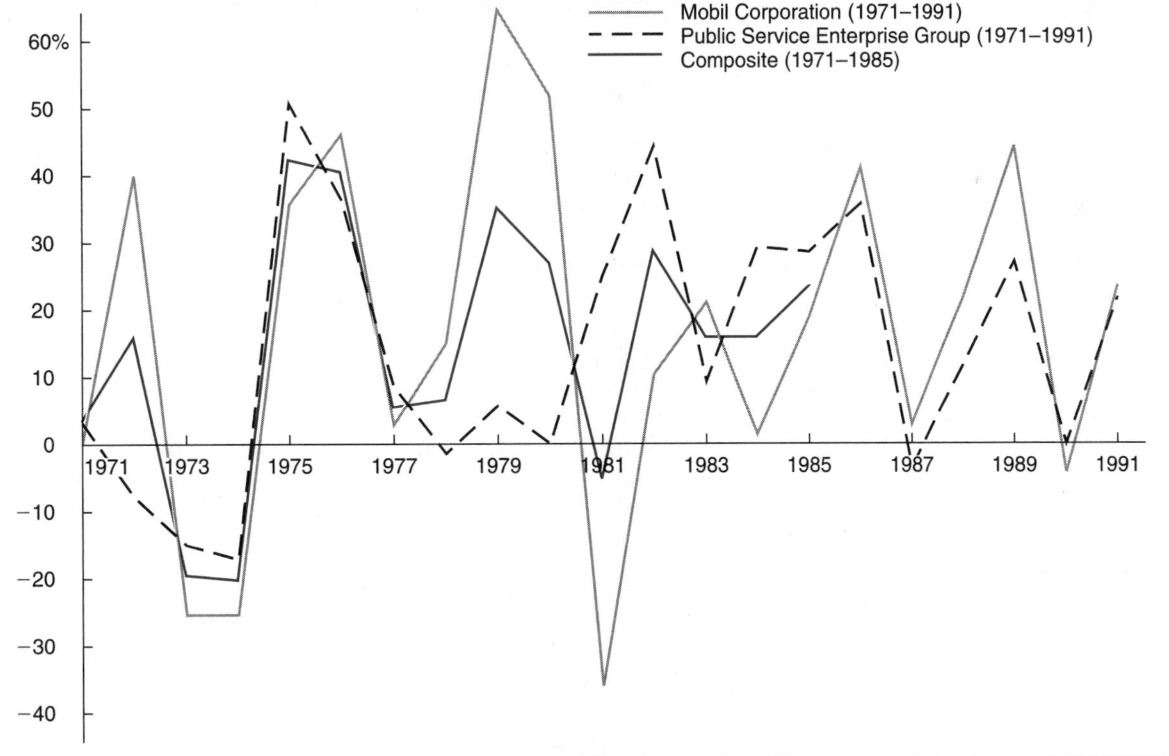

[12]The correlation between assets is an essential topic in portfolio management and appears frequently in this text, especially when considering diversification through the use of fixed-income securities, real estate, collectibles, or foreign securities.

FIGURE 7.7

Scatter Diagram of Returns for Mobil and PSEG

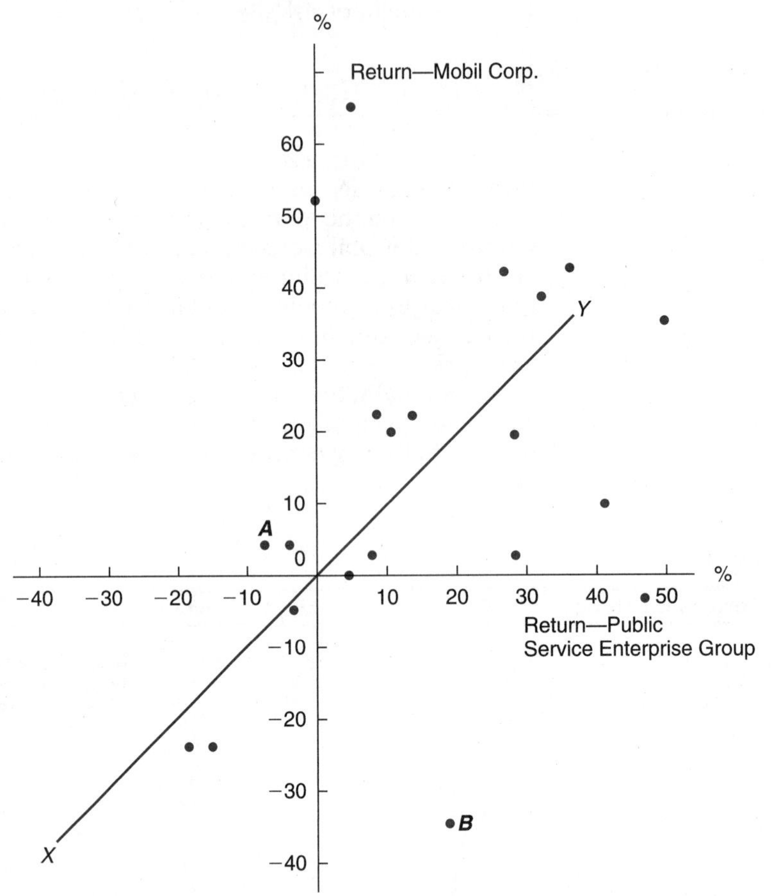

in opposite directions. For example, during 1971 and 1978, an investment in Public Service Enterprise Group generated a loss while an investment in Mobil produced profits. However, the converse occurred during 1981 as the trend in Public Service Enterprise Group's stock price started to improve. From 1980 to 1985 the price of Public Service Enterprise Group doubled, but the price of Mobil's stock declined so that most of the return earned on Mobil's stock during the mid-1980s was its dividend.

Figure 7.7 presents a scatter diagram of the returns on these two stocks for 1971–1991. The horizontal axis presents the average annual return on Public Service Enterprise Group, while the vertical axis presents the average annual return on Mobil Corporation. As may be seen in the graph, the individual points lie throughout the plane representing the returns. For example, point A represents a positive return on Mobil but a negative return on Public Service Enterprise Group, and point B represents a positive return on Public Service Enterprise Group but a negative return on Mobil.

Combining these securities in a portfolio reduces the individual's risk exposure, as is also shown in Figures 7.6 and 7.7. The line representing the composite return in Figure 7.6 runs between the lines representing the returns on the individual securities. Over the entire time period, the average annual returns on Mobil and Public Service Enterprise Group were 16.6 and 13.0 percent, respectively. The average annual return on the composite was 14.8 percent. The risk reduction (i.e., the reduction in the dispersion of the returns) can be seen by comparing the standard deviations of the returns. For the individual stocks, the standard deviations were 26.5 percent and 19.4 percent, respectively, for Mobil and Public Service Enterprise Group. However, the standard deviation for the composite return was 18.9, so the dispersion of the returns associated with the portfolio is less than the dispersion of the returns on either stock by itself.[13]

In this illustration the correlation coefficient between the two returns is 0.34. This lack of correlation is visible in Figure 7.7. If there were a high positive correlation between the two returns, the points would lie close to the line *XY*. Instead, the points are scattered throughout the figure. Thus, there is little correlation between the two returns, which is why combining the two securities reduces the individual's risk exposure.

It should be noted that combining these two stocks achieved diversification in the past because their returns were not highly correlated. Such diversification, however, may not be achieved in the future if the returns become highly positively correlated. This higher correlation appears to have occurred since 1985. The annual returns plotted in Figure 7.6 appear to have moved together from 1985 through 1991. This movement suggests that investing in these two stocks had little impact on diversification after 1985. This inference is confirmed because the correlation coefficient for years 1971 through 1985 is 0.231, but 0.884 for years 1986 through 1991.[14]

Although diversification is a prime goal because it reduces the investor's risk exposure without necessarily reducing the portfolio's return, the investor is faced with the problem of identifying those assets whose returns will not be positively correlated in the future. Unfortunately, the returns on many financial assets are positively correlated. In addition, as illustrated in Figure 7.6, returns that are negatively correlated under one set of economic conditions may not be negatively correlated in a different economic environment.

If investors include a broad spectrum of assets in their portfolios, a substantial level of diversification and risk reduction should be achieved. A portfolio that includes stocks, bonds, money market mutual funds, real estate, tangible assets, and foreign securities should be well diversified. The sample of correlation coefficients in Exhibit 7.1 (p. 170) tends to confirm this general conclusion. The numerical values of the correlation coefficients relating the returns from investing in U.S. stocks to the returns from alternative investments are low (i.e., near 0), which suggests the possibility of diversification does exist. This potential for diversification is one of the strongest arguments for including foreign investments, real estate, and collectibles in an individual's portfolio.

Portfolio Theory

Harry Markowitz is credited with being the first individual to use the preceding material to develop a theory of portfolio construction employing returns and risk

[13]The calculation is $\sqrt{(0.5)^2\,(26.5)^2 + (0.5)^2\,(19.4)^2 + 2(0.5)\,(0.5)\,(26.5)\,(19.4)\,(0.34)} = 18.9$

[14]The correlation remained high after 1991 and was 0.732 for 1985–1999, which suggests that using these two stocks to create a portfolio had little impact on the variability of the portfolio's return during that period.

EXHIBIT 7.1

Selected Correlation Coefficients for Returns from Various Alternative Investments

	Correlation Coefficient	Time Period
U.S. common stocks and Treasury bills	−0.03	1926–1997[1]
U.S. common stocks and long-term government bonds	0.19	1926–1997[1]
U.S. common stocks and Japanese stocks	0.28	1970–1990[2]
U.S. common stocks and Mexican stocks	0.25	1989–1995[3]
U.S. common stocks and U.S. real estate	0.02	1979–1996[4]

[1]*Stocks, Bonds, Bills, and Inflation, 1998 Yearbook* (Chicago, Ill.: Ibbotson Associates, 1998), 118.
[2]Roger Ibbotson and Gary Brinson, *Global Investing* (New York: McGraw-Hill, 1993), 146.
[3]Michael Keppler and Martin Lechner, *Emerging Markets* (Chicago: Irwin Professional Publishing, 1997), 96.
[4]Michael Paladino and Herbert Mayo, "Investments in REITS Do Not Help Diversify Stock Portfolios: An Update," *Real Estate Review* (winter 1998), 39.

as measured by a portfolio's standard deviation.[15] This contribution was a major advance in finance and led to the development of the capital asset pricing model (CAPM) and subsequently to the arbitrage pricing model, generally referred to as *arbitrage pricing theory* (APT). Both the CAPM and the APT seek to explain portfolio and security returns as a response to change in identifiable variables.

The Markowitz Model

The Markowitz model is premised on a risk-averse individual constructing a diversified portfolio that maximizes the individual's satisfaction (generally referred to as *utility* by economists) by maximizing portfolio returns for a given level of risk. This process is depicted in Figures 7.8 through 7.10, which illustrate the optimal combinations of risk and return available to investors, the desire of investors to maximize their utility, and the determination of the optimal portfolio that integrates utility maximization within the constraint of the available portfolios.

Figure 7.8 illustrates the determination of the optimal portfolios available to investors. The vertical axis measures portfolio expected returns expressed as a percentage. The horizontal axis measures the risk associated with the portfolio, using the portfolio's standard deviation (σ_p). In Figure 7.8, the shaded area represents all the possible portfolios composed of various combinations of risky securities. This area is generally referred to as the *attainable* or *feasible* set of portfolios. Some of these portfolios are **inefficient** because they offer an inferior return for a given amount of risk. For example, portfolio *A* is inefficient since portfolio *B* offers a higher return for the same amount of risk.

inefficient portfolio
A portfolio whose return is not maximized given the level of risk.

efficient portfolio
The portfolio that offers the highest expected return for a given amount of risk.

All portfolios that offer the highest return for a given amount of risk are referred to as **efficient**. The line that connects all these portfolios (*XY* in Figure 7.8) defines the *efficient frontier* and is referred to as the *efficient set* of portfolios. Any portfolio that offers the highest return for a given amount of risk must lie on the efficient frontier. Any portfolio that offers a lower return is inefficient and lies below the efficient frontier in the shaded area. Since inefficient portfolios will not be selected, the efficient frontier establishes the best set of portfolios available to investors.

[15]Harry M. Markowitz, "Portfolio Selection," *The Journal of Finance* (March 1952); and Harry M. Markowitz, *Portfolio Selection: Efficient Diversification of Investments* (New York: Wiley, 1959).

FIGURE 7.8

The Efficient Frontier

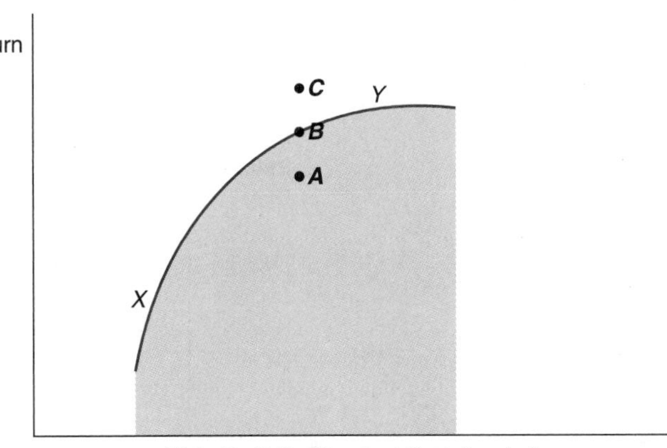

A portfolio such as C that lies above the efficient frontier offers a superior yield for the amount of risk. Investors would prefer that portfolio to portfolio *B* on the efficient frontier because C offers a higher return for the same level of risk. Unfortunately, combination C of risk and return does not exist. It is not a feasible solution. No combination of risk and expected return that lies above the efficient frontier is attainable.

While the efficient frontier gives all the best attainable combinations of risk and return, it does not tell *which* of the possible combinations an investor will select. That selection depends on the individual's willingness to bear risk. The combining of the efficient frontier and the willingness to bear risk determines the investor's optimal portfolio. Figure 7.8 gives only the efficient frontier; it says nothing about the investor's willingness to bear risk.

This willingness to bear risk may be shown by the use of indifference curves, which are often used in economic theory to indicate levels of an individual's utility (i.e., consumer satisfaction) and the impact of trading one good for another. While satisfaction cannot be measured, the analysis permits the *ranking of levels of satisfaction*. A higher level of satisfaction may be reached by obtaining more of one good without losing some of an alternative good. For example, a consumer will prefer a combination of five apples and five oranges to a combination of five apples and four oranges, because the individual has more apples but has not lost any oranges.

While five apples and five oranges is preferred to five apples and four oranges, it cannot be concluded that the individual will prefer six apples and four oranges to five apples and five oranges. To obtain the sixth apple, the consumer gave up one orange. If the consumer prefers the additional apple to the lost orange, then a higher level of satisfaction is achieved. If the consumer does not prefer the additional apple, then the level of satisfaction is reduced. It is also possible that the additional satisfaction gained by the additional apple exactly offsets the satisfaction lost, so the individual is indifferent between five apples and five oranges and six apples and four oranges. Notice that instead of measuring satisfaction, the analysis seeks to determine *levels* of satisfaction—that is, which combination of goods is preferred.

When applied to portfolio theory, the economic theory of consumer behavior develops the trade-off between risk and return (instead of the trade-off between two goods such as apples and oranges). This trade-off between risk and return is

FIGURE 7.9

Indifference Map

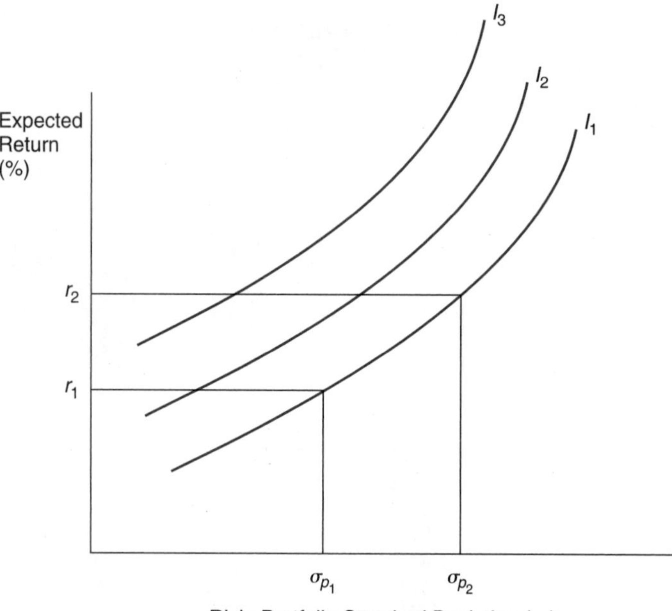

also shown by indifference curves. A set of these indifference curves is illustrated in Figure 7.9. Each indifference curve represents a level of satisfaction, with higher curves indicating higher levels of satisfaction. Movements along a given curve indicate the same level of satisfaction (the individual is indifferent). For example, on indifference curve I_1, the investor would be willing to accept a modest return, such as r_1 and bear a modest amount of risk (σ_{p_1}). The same investor would also be willing to bear more risk for a higher return (e.g., r_2 and σ_{p_2}). The additional return is sufficient to induce bearing the additional risk so the investor is *indifferent between the two alternatives*. Thus, all the points on the same indifference curve represent the same level of satisfaction.

The indifference curves in Figure 7.9 are for a risk-averse investor; hence, additional risk requires more return. However, notice that these curves are concave from above; their slope increases as risk increases. This indicates that investors require ever-increasing amounts of additional return for equal increments of risk to maintain the same level of satisfaction.

Investors would like to earn a higher return without having to bear additional risk. A higher return without additional risk increases total satisfaction. Higher levels of satisfaction are indicated by indifference curves I_2 and I_3, which lie above indifference curve I_1. Once again the investor is *indifferent between any combination of risk and return* on I_2. All combinations of risk and return on indifference curve I_2 are preferred to all combinations on indifference curve I_1. Correspondingly, all points on indifference curve I_3 are preferred to all points on I_2. Since there is an indefinite number of levels of satisfaction, an indefinite number of indifference curves could be constructed for an individual. Each would represent a different level of satisfaction, and the higher the curve, the higher the level of satisfaction. (One of the advantages offered by this type of analysis is that indifference curves

FIGURE 7.10

Determination of the Optimal Portfolio

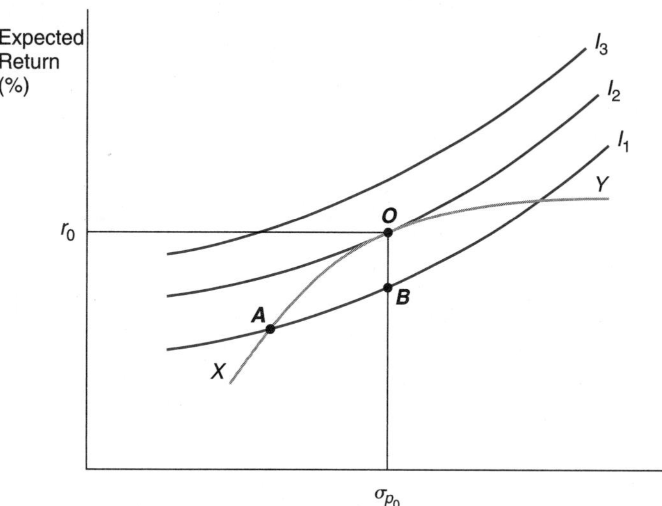

themselves do not measure satisfaction; they only indicate rankings—that is, I_2 is preferred to I_1.)

The investor seeks to reach the highest level of satisfaction but is, of course, constrained by what is available. The best combinations of risk and return available are given by the efficient frontier. Superimposing the indifference curves on the efficient frontier defines the investor's optimal portfolio. This is shown in Figure 7.10, which combines Figures 7.8 and 7.9. The optimal combination of risk and return represented by point *O* is the investor's optimal combination of risk and return.

If the investor selects any other portfolio with a different combination of risk and return on the efficient frontier (e.g., *A*), that portfolio would not be the individual's best choice. While portfolio *A* is an efficient combination of risk and return, it is not the optimal choice, as may be seen using the following logic. Portfolio *B* is equal to portfolio *A* (i.e., the investor is indifferent between *A* and *B*), but *B* is not efficient and is inferior to portfolio *O*, since *O* offers a higher level of return for the same amount of risk. Portfolio *O* must be preferred to *B*, and because *A* and *B* are equal, *O* must also be preferred to *A*. By similar reasoning, only one portfolio offers the highest level of satisfaction *and* lies on the efficient frontier. That unique combination of risk and return is represented by portfolio *O*, which occurs at the *tangency* of the efficient frontier and indifference curve I_2.

If an indifference curve cuts through the efficient frontier (e.g., I_1), it is attainable but inferior, and it can always be shown that the investor can reach a higher level of satisfaction by altering the portfolio. If an indifference curve lies above the efficient frontier (e.g., I_3), such a level of satisfaction is not obtainable. The investor would like to reach that level of satisfaction, but no combination of assets offers such a high expected return for that amount of risk.

Different investors may have varying indifference curves. If the investor is very risk-averse, the curves tend to be steep, indicating a large amount of additional return is necessary to induce this individual to bear additional risk and maintain the

FIGURE 7.11

Different Optimal Portfolios for Different Investors

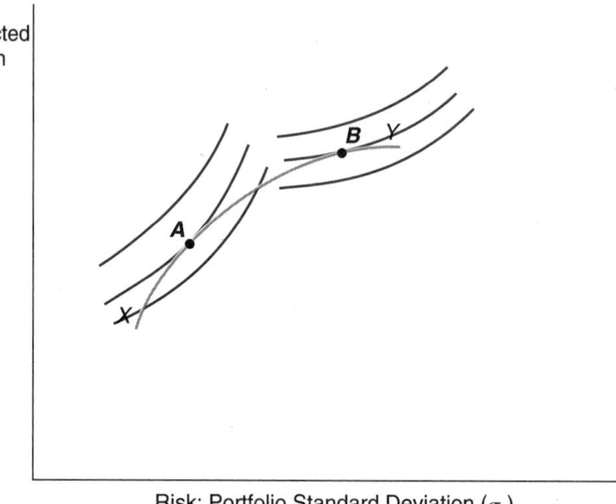

same level of satisfaction. If the curves are relatively flat, the individual is less risk-averse. Only a modest amount of additional return is necessary to induce this individual to bear additional risk and still maintain the same level of satisfaction. However, both investors are still averse to bearing risk. The difference is the degree of risk aversion.

This difference in attitude toward risk is illustrated in Figure 7.11, which has two sets of indifference curves imposed on the efficient frontier. One investor is more risk-averse and selects the combination of risk and return represented by point *A*, while the other investor is more willing to bear risk and selects the combination of risk and return represented by point *B*. Both investors, however, select a combination of risk and return that lies on the efficient frontier. Each selects that particular combination determined by the tangency of their highest obtainable indifference curve and the efficient frontier.

The Capital Asset Pricing Model

Although indifference curves cannot be observed or estimated, combining them with the efficient frontier produced a major step forward for portfolio theory. For the first time, the Markowitz model explained diversified portfolio construction in the utility-maximization framework generally used by economists. This model subsequently led to the development of the capital asset pricing model (CAPM) by William F. Sharpe, John Lintner, and Jan Mossin.[16] The CAPM is among the most important *theoretical concepts* in finance; it advances the relationship between risk and return in an efficient market context, adds the possibility of earning a risk-free return, and is easier to implement than the Markowitz model. The CAPM

[16]For the seminal work on CAPM, see William Sharpe, "Capital Asset Prices: A Theory of Market Equilibrium," *The Journal of Finance* (September 1964): 425–442; John Lintner, "The Valuation of Risk Assets and the Selection of Risk Investments in Stock Portfolios and Capital Budgets," *Review of Economics and Statistics* (February 1965): 13–37; and Jan Mossin, "Equilibrium in a Capital Asset Market," *Econometrica* (October 1966): 768–783. The contributions of Markowitz and Sharpe to the analysis of risk and the development of portfolio theory are so important that they, along with Merton Miller, were awarded the Nobel Prize in economics in 1990.

FIGURE 7.12

Capital Market Line

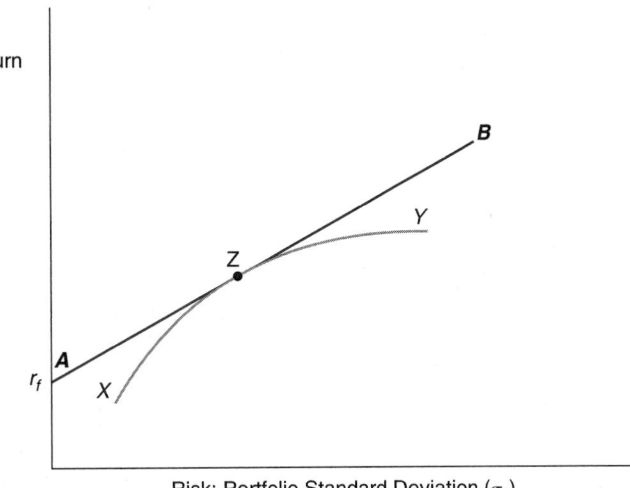

is an outgrowth of the Markowitz model and extends the concept of optimal diversified portfolios to the market in general and to the valuation of individual securities. That is, the concept is applied in both a *macro* context that specifies the relationship between risk and the return on a portfolio and a *micro* context that specifies the relationship between risk and the return on a specific asset.

The macro aspect of the CAPM is the development of the *capital market line.* Figure 7.12 begins with all the possible efficient portfolios of risky securities and adds line *AB,* which begins at r_f on the *Y*-axis and is tangent to the efficient frontier. *AB* is the capital market line specified by the capital asset pricing model. Each point on the line represents a combination of the risk-free security and a portfolio encompassing risky securities. If investors bear no risk and invest their entire portfolios in risk-free assets, they should earn a return equal to r_f. As investors substitute risky securities for the risk-free assets, both risk and return increase (i.e., there is movement along the capital market line). Point *Z,* the point of tangency, represents a portfolio consisting solely of risky securities. To the right of *Z,* an investor is using margin to increase return further, but the use of margin continues to increase risk. In effect, the capital market line *AZB* becomes the efficient frontier. Combinations of risk and return on this line represent the best attainable portfolios, and these combinations range from portfolios with no risk earning only the risk-free return to portfolios in which securities are bought on margin.

The equation for the capital market line is based on the equation for a straight line:

$$Y = a + bX$$

in which *Y* becomes the return on the portfolio (r_p); *a,* the intercept, becomes the risk-free rate (r_f), *X* becomes the risk premium; and *b* is the slope of the line. The equation for the capital market line is

(7.5)
$$r_p = r_f + \left(\frac{r_m - r_f}{\sigma_m}\right)\sigma_p.$$

FIGURE 7.13

Different Portfolios for Different Investors

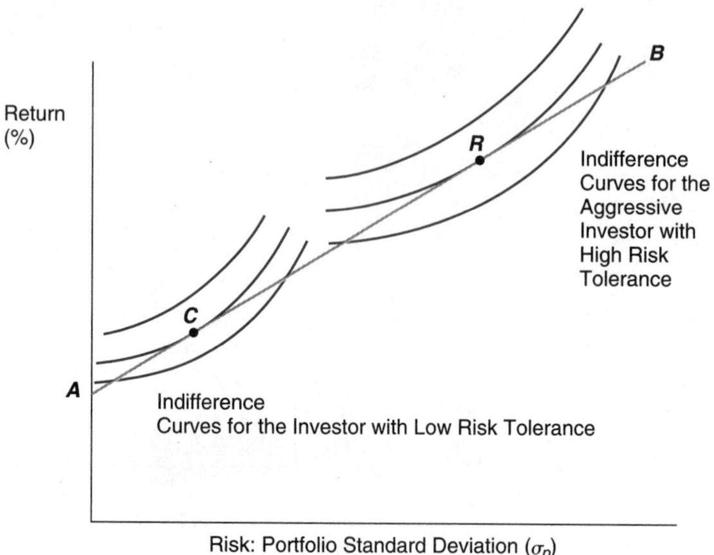

This equation states that the return on a portfolio (r_p) is the sum of the return earned on a risk-free asset (risk-free return = r_f) such as a Treasury bill and a risk premium that depends on (1) the extent to which the return on the market exceeds the risk-free return (i.e., $r_m - r_f$) and (2) the dispersion of the portfolio (σ_p) relative to the dispersion of the market (σ_m). If the dispersion of the portfolio is equal to the dispersion of the market, these two considerations cancel; the return on such a portfolio depends solely on the risk-free rate and the risk premium associated with investing in securities. If, however, the dispersion of the portfolio is greater than the dispersion of the market, the return will have to exceed the return associated with the market. The risk premium is larger. Thus, the capital market line indicates that to earn larger returns, the investor is required to take greater risks.

The capital market line by itself does not determine which portfolio the individual will acquire. The actual portfolio the individual selects depends on the capital market line and the individual's willingness to bear risk, as indicated by indifference curves. Figure 7.13 represents the combination of risk and return selected by both an investor with low risk tolerance and an investor with high risk tolerance. The investor with low risk tolerance is represented by the steeper indifference curves and is very averse to bearing risk and selects a portfolio represented by point C, in which a large proportion of the portfolio consists of the risk-free asset. The more aggressive investor (i.e., the flatter indifference curves) selects a portfolio, represented by *R*, in which part of the securities are purchased on margin and the portfolio is leveraged.

The Capital Asset Pricing Model and Beta Coefficients

The second component of the capital asset pricing model is the specification of the relationship between risk and return for the *individual* asset. At the micro level this relationship is referred to as the *security market line* (SML). Although this relationship is very similar to the capital market line, the difference is important. In the capital market line, risk is measured by the portfolio's standard deviation. In the security market line, the individual asset's risk is measured by a *beta coefficient*. Understanding the security market line requires understanding beta coefficients. Thus, it is necessary to explain this measure of risk before discussing its use in the capital asset pricing model.

Beta Coefficients

beta coefficient
An index of risk; a measure of the systematic risk associated with a particular stock.

When an individual constructs a well-diversified portfolio, the unsystematic sources of risk are diversified away. That leaves the systematic sources of risk as the relevant risks. A **beta coefficient** is a measure of systematic risk; it is an index of the volatility of the individual asset relative to the volatility of the market. The beta coefficient for a specific security (β_i) is defined as follows:

(7.6)
$$\beta_i = \frac{\textbf{Standard deviation of the return on stock } i}{\textbf{Standard deviation of the return on the market}} \times \textbf{Correlation coefficient between the return on the stock and the return on the market}$$

Thus, beta depends on (1) the variability of the individual stock's return, (2) the variability of the market return (both measured by their respective standard deviations), and (3) the correlation between the return on the security and the return on the market. (The computation of beta is illustrated in the section on regression analysis in the appendix to this chapter.)

The ratio of the standard deviations measures how variable the stock is relative to the variability of the market. The more variable a stock's return (i.e., the larger the standard deviation of the stock's return) relative to the variability of the market's return, the greater the risk associated with the individual stock. The correlation coefficient indicates whether this greater variability is important.

The impact of different numerical values for the standard deviation of the stock's return and for the correlation coefficient on the beta coefficient is illustrated in Exhibit 7.2 (p. 179). The exhibit has two parts. In the first, the stock return moves exactly with the market, so the correlation coefficient between the return on the stock and the return on the market is 1.0. Since the correlation coefficient is equal to 1.0, there is a strong, positive relationship between the return on the market and the return on the stock. Whether the stock has more or less market risk depends on the variability of the stock's return relative to the variability of the market return. When the stock's return is less variable than the market return (e.g., when the standard deviation is 2 percent), the beta is 0.2. The stock is less volatile than the market, and the stock has only a small amount of market risk. When the standard deviation is 18 percent, the beta is 1.8. The stock is more volatile than the market and has a large amount of market risk.

In the second part of Exhibit 7.2, the standard deviations of the stock and the market are equal, but the value of the correlation coefficient varies. When the returns on the stock and the market move in exactly opposite directions, the correlation coefficient is −1.0 and the beta is −1.0. While the variability of the stock and the market are the same, the volatility of the stock and the market returns are exactly opposite. Conversely, if the correlation coefficient is +1.0, the beta is +1.0. The variability of the stock and market returns are identical, and the volatility of the stock is the same as the market. If there is no relationship between returns on the stock and the market (i.e., the correlation coefficient is 0.0), the beta equals 0.0. The return on the stock does not respond to changes in the market;

POINTS OF INTEREST

A Practical Capital Market Line

The prior discussion indicates that one facet of the capital asset pricing model is a theory explaining the determination of an individual's optimal portfolio as a combination of a riskless asset and a portfolio of risky securities in which the capital market line specifies the relationship between a portfolio's risk and return. The slope of the line indicates the additional return associated with each additional unit of risk. Illustrations such as Figure 7.14 are sometimes used to indicate how individual classes of assets may fall on the capital market line and how the substitution of one class of assets increases the investor's return and risk exposure.

Although the discussion of each type of security in Figure 7.14 is deferred until its appropriate place in the text, the illustration suggests that there are specific assets, such as short-term U.S. Treasury bills or federally insured savings accounts, that generate a modest return without risk. As you move farther to the right, returns increase as the investor acquires riskier assets. Risk-free assets are followed by money market securities with marginally higher yields. These are succeeded by bonds with intermediate term maturities of one to ten years. Bonds with longer terms to maturity tend to offer higher returns but expose the investor to greater risk. Stocks of large corporations and small firms offer even more return but require the individual to bear even greater risk. At the extreme right of the figure, such assets as options, foreign investments, real estate, collectibles, and futures contracts produce the highest returns but carry the greatest amount of risk.

While Figure 7.14 indicates that some assets offer higher returns for additional risk-taking, the capital asset pricing model suggests that investors combine these various assets in efficient diversified portfolios. If an investor's particular portfolio does not lie on the efficient frontier, that individual alters the combination of assets to obtain an efficient portfolio. Then the investor determines if that efficient portfolio offers the highest level of satisfaction. If it does not, the investor further alters the portfolio until both conditions are met, so that the portfolio is efficient while achieving the highest level of satisfaction.

This process is no different than individuals' allocating their income among various goods and services so that the highest level of consumer satisfaction is achieved with the given amount of income. The amount of income constrains the consumer just as the efficient frontier constrains the investor. Given these constraints, individuals still behave in such a way as to maximize their consumer satisfaction. In portfolio theory, that maximization is indicated by the tangency of the efficient frontier and the individual investor's indifference curves.

FIGURE 7.14

A Pragmatic Capital Market Line

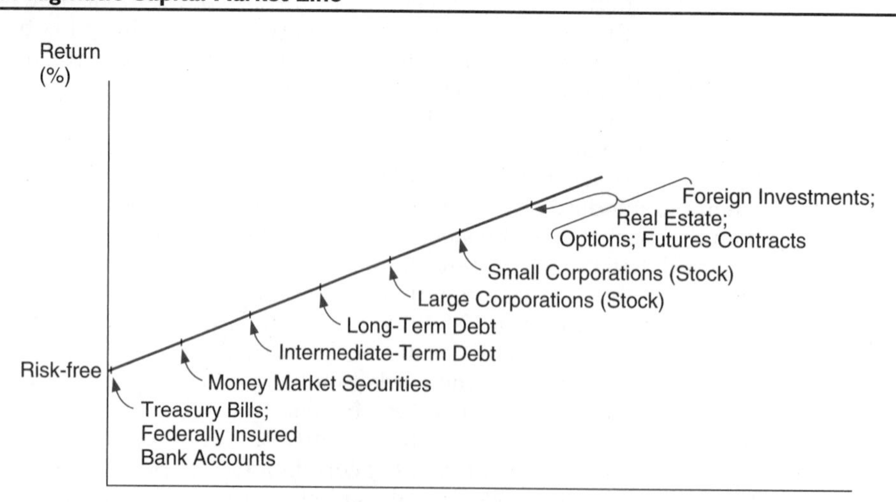

EXHIBIT 7.2

Various Values of Beta Coefficients

Part 1	
Standard deviation of the market	10%
Correlation coefficient of the returns on the stock and on the market	1.0
Standard Deviation of the Stock	**Beta**
2%	(2/10)(1) = 0.2
6	(6/10)(1) = 0.6
10	(10/10)(1) = 1.0
14	(14/10)(1) = 1.4
18	(18/10)(1) = 1.8

Part 2	
Standard deviation of the market	10%
Standard deviation of the stock	10%
Correlation Coefficient	**Beta**
−1.0	(10/10)(−1.0) = −1.0
−0.5	(10/10)(−0.5) = −0.5
0.0	(10/10)(0.0) = 0.0
0.5	(10/10)(0.5) = 0.5
1.0	(10/10)(1.0) = 1.0

there is no market risk. The stock's return can vary, but this variability must be explained by other sources of risk.

As long as there is a strong relationship between the return on the stock and the return on the market (i.e, the correlation coefficient is not a small number), the beta coefficient has meaning. Since the numerical values of the correlation coefficients can range from −1.0 to +1.0, they are often squared to obtain the *coefficient of determination*, or (R^2). As is explained in the statistical appendix to this chapter, the coefficient of determination gives the proportion of the variation in one variable explained by the variation in the other variable. Beta coefficients with low coefficients of determination suggest that the beta is of little use in explaining the movements in the stock, because some factor other than the market is causing the variation in the stock's return.

If a stock has a beta of 1.0, the implication is that the stock's return moves exactly with an index of the market. A 10 percent return in the market could be expected to produce a 10 percent return on the specific stock. Correspondingly, a 10 percent decline in the market would result in a 10 percent decline in the return on the stock. A beta coefficient of less than 1 implies that the return on the stock would tend to fluctuate less than the market as a whole. A coefficient of 0.7 indicates that the stock's return would rise by only 7 percent as a result of a 10 percent increase in the market but would fall by only 7 percent when the market declined by 10 percent. A coefficient of 1.2 means that the return on the stock could be expected to be 12 percent if the market return was 10 percent, but the return on the stock would decline by 12 percent when the market declined by 10 percent.

The greater the beta coefficient, the more systematic market risk associated with the individual stock. High beta coefficients may indicate higher profits during rising markets, but they also indicate greater losses during declining markets. Stocks with high beta coefficients are referred to as *aggressive*. The converse is true for stocks with

FIGURE 7.15

Stock with a Beta Coefficient of Greater Than 1.0

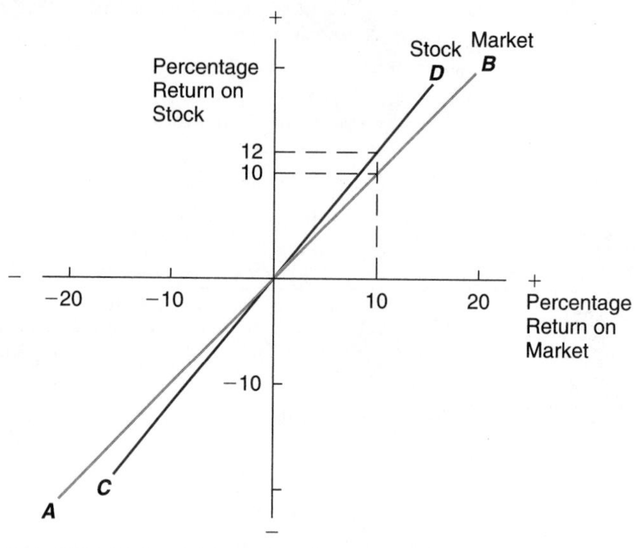

FIGURE 7.16

Stock with a Beta Coefficient of Less Than 1.0

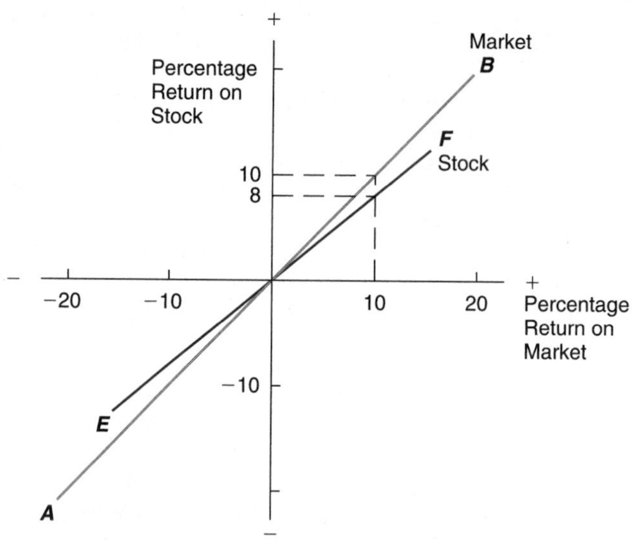

low beta coefficients, which should earn lower returns than the market during periods of rising stock prices but earn higher (or less negative) returns than the market during periods of declining prices. Such stocks are referred to as *defensive*.

This relationship between the return on a specific security and the market index as a whole is illustrated in Figures 7.15 and 7.16. In each graph the horizontal axis represents the percentage return on the market index and the vertical axis represents the percentage return on the individual stock. The line *AB*, which represents the market, is the same in both graphs. It is a positive-sloped line that runs through the point of origin and is equidistant from both axes (i.e., it makes a 45-degree angle with each axis).

Figure 7.15 illustrates a stock with a beta coefficient of greater than 1. Line *CD* represents a stock whose return rose and declined more than the market. In this case the beta coefficient is 1.2, so when the return on the market index is 10 percent, this stock's return is 12 percent.

Figure 7.16 illustrates a stock with a beta coefficient of less than 1. Line *EF* represents a stock whose return rose (and declined) more slowly than that of the market. In this case the beta coefficient is 0.8, so when the market's return is 10 percent, this stock's return is 8 percent.

Beta coefficients do vary among firms. This is illustrated in Exhibit 7.3, which presents the beta coefficients for selected firms as computed by *Value Line*. As may be seen in the table, some firms (e.g., ExxonMobil) have relatively low beta coefficients, while the coefficients for other firms (e.g., GE) are higher. Investors who are willing to bear more risk may be attracted to these stocks with higher beta coefficients. Investors who are less inclined to bear risk may prefer the stocks with low beta coefficients. Although these investors forgo some potential return during rising market prices, they should suffer milder losses during periods of declining stock prices.

Computing beta coefficients for a significant number of securities over a reasonably long period is a time-consuming, tedious job. (How betas are estimated is illustrated in the appendix to this chapter.) Fortunately, the investor may obtain beta coefficients from several sources. (Standard deviations of portfolio returns are not available.) For example, the *Value Line Investment Survey* supplies beta coefficients for all securities covered by the service. Betas are also available through Standard & Poor's ComStock, which, like *Value Line*, is a subscription service (http://www.spcomstock.com). The investor, however, should be warned that betas from different sources may vary for the same stock![17] (See the accompanying Points of Interest box: Will the Real Beta Please Stand Up?)

To be useful, beta coefficients must be reliable predictors of future stock price behavior. For example, a low-risk investor who desires stocks that will be stable will probably purchase stocks with low beta coefficients. An investor selecting a stock with a beta coefficient of 0.6 will certainly be upset if the market prices decline by 10 percent and this stock's price falls by 15 percent, since a beta coefficient of 0.6 indicates that the stock should decline by only 6 percent when the market declines by 10 percent.

Beta coefficients are constructed with historical price data. Although such data may be accumulated and tabulated for many years, this does not mean that coefficients based on historical data will be accurate predictors of future movements in stock prices. Beta coefficients can and do change over time. Empirical studies have shown that beta coefficients for individual securities may be unstable (e.g., the decrease in Boeing's beta or increase in AT&T's beta in Exhibit 7.3).[18] Therefore, the investor should not rely solely on these coefficients for selecting a particular security. However, beta coefficients do give the investor some indication of the market risk associated with specific stocks and thus can play an important role in the selection of a security.

[17]For a discussion of differences in betas, see Frank K. Reilly and David J. Wright, "A Comparison of Published Betas," *Journal of Portfolio Management* (spring 1988): 64–69.

[18]See, for instance, Robert A. Levy, "Stationarity of Beta Coefficients," *Financial Analysts Journal* (November/December 1971): 55–62. In general, the evidence suggests that the numerical value of beta coefficients moves toward 1.0 (i.e., riskier securities become less volatile and vice versa). See Marshall E. Blume, "Portfolio Theory: A Step Toward Its Practical Application," *Journal of Business* (April 1970): 152–173; and Marshall Blume, "Beta and Their Regression Tendencies," *Journal of Finance* (June 1975): 785–796.

EXHIBIT 7.3

Selected Beta Coefficients as Computed by *Value Line*

	Beta Coefficient					
Company	**1978**	**1986**	**1992**	**1995**	**1998**	**2001**
AT&T	0.65	0.90	0.85	0.85	NMF	1.00
ExxonMobil	0.90	0.80	0.75	0.60	0.85	0.80
Philip Morris, Inc.	0.90	0.95	1.05	1.20	1.00	0.70
Johnson & Johnson	0.95	0.95	1.05	1.10	1.10	0.85
IBM	0.95	1.05	0.95	1.00	1.15	1.00
GE	1.00	1.05	1.10	1.10	1.25	1.25
CBS, Inc./Viacom*	1.00	1.05	1.00	1.05	0.90	1.20
E. I. Du Pont	1.05	1.20	1.10	1.00	1.10	1.00
Kmart	1.05	1.15	1.20	1.25	0.80	1.05
McDonald's	1.05	1.10	0.95	1.05	0.90	0.85
Alcoa	1.15	1.15	1.25	1.05	0.95	0.90
Boeing	1.25	1.20	1.05	1.00	0.95	0.95

NMF = No meaningful figure; result of spin-offs of Lucent Technologies and NCR.
*Viacom acquired CBS in 2000.
Source: *http://www.valueline.com.*

Unlike the beta coefficient for individual securities, the beta coefficient for a diversified portfolio is fairly stable over time. Changes in the different beta coefficients tend to average out; while one stock's beta coefficient is increasing, the beta coefficient of another stock is declining. A portfolio's historical beta coefficients, then, can be used as a tool to forecast its future beta coefficient, and this projection should be more accurate than forecasts of an individual security's beta coefficient. For example, in both 1978 and 1998 the average beta coefficient of the portfolio illustrated in Exhibit 7.3 is approximately 1.[19] If an equal dollar amount were invested in each security, the value of the portfolio should follow the market value fairly closely, even though individual beta coefficients are greater or less than 1. This tendency of the portfolio to mirror the performance of the market should occur even though selected securities may achieve a return that is superior (or inferior) to that of the market as a whole.

Beta and the Security Market Line

Beta's primary use in finance has been its incorporation into the capital asset pricing model as the key variable that explains individual security returns. The relationship between risk, as measured by beta, and an asset's return is specified in the security market line (SML). The security market line stipulates the return on a stock (r_s) as

(7.7) $$r_s = r_f + (r_m - r_f)\beta.$$

The return on a stock depends on the risk-free rate of interest (r_f) and a risk premium composed of the extent to which the return on the market (r_m) exceeds the

[19]The average for the 12 stocks in Exhibit 7.3 was 0.992 in 1978, 1.031 in 1986, 1.025 in 1992, 1.021 in 1995, 0.995 in 1998, and 0.963 in 2001. This consistency suggests that the beta for a portfolio consisting of these stocks would have changed only marginally over the years even though the individual betas may have changed.

POINTS OF INTEREST

Will the Real Beta Please Stand Up?

Exhibit 7.3 provided the beta coefficient for several stocks as computed by the Value Line Investment Survey. The following table reproduces those beta coefficients and adds the beta coefficients estimated by Market Guide and available through Multex-Investor (http://www.multexinvestor.com). Although the Value Line betas may be obtained through subscribing to its service (http://www.valueline.com), the Market Guide betas are complimentary.

Company	*Value Line* Beta	Market Guide Beta
Alcoa	0.90	1.07
AT&T	1.00	0.99
Boeing	0.95	0.56
E. I. Du Pont	1.00	0.71
ExxonMobil	0.80	0.41
GE	1.25	1.17
IBM	1.00	1.26
Johnson & Johnson	0.85	0.60
Kmart	1.05	0.92
McDonald's	0.85	0.69
Philip Morris	0.70	0.25
Viacom	1.20	NA

Immediately it is apparent that the estimated beta coefficients differ, and the differences are not consistent in one direction. While most of the Market Guide betas are lower, some are higher.

Why are there differences, and do the differences matter? The answer to the first question is easier. Beta coefficients are calculated using regression analysis that estimates the slope of a line that relates an independent variable (the market) to a dependent variable (the stock). Differences in the slope (the beta) may arise because the estimates use a different measure of the market (e.g., the *Value Line* stock index and not the Standard & Poor's 500 stock index). Another possible source of the difference is the time period covered. For example, one estimate may use weekly returns over five years while another uses weekly returns over three years. Betas will also differ if the calculation considers only price changes in the stock and the market instead of total returns, which include price changes and dividends received.

Whether the differences are important may depend on the usage of the betas. If the purpose is to determine which stocks have more systematic risk (i.e., to determine the relative amount of systematic risk), variations in the betas may not be a problem. Even if the estimates differ, it is unlikely that one estimate will be 2.1 (indicating a large amount of market risk) while another estimate is 0.9, indicating less volatility than the market. Beta coefficients, however, are also used in the valuation of stock (see Chapter 9) and in measuring performance of mutual funds (see Chapter 8). Since lower beta coefficients indicate less risk, that argues for a higher valuation, in which case the investor would be willing to pay more for the stock. Unfortunately, there is no answer as to which estimate is "correct." While an individual could accept one beta as the basis for stock valuation, an alternative strategy would be to use more than one beta and develop a range of stock values before making a final investment decision.

risk-free rate and the individual stock's beta coefficient.[20] This relationship (i.e., the security market line) is shown in Figure 7.17 (p. 184).

The similarity of the capital market line and the security market line are immediately apparent if Figure 7.17 is compared to Figure 7.12. The *Y*-axis is the same, and the relationship between risk and return is represented as a straight line (i.e., $Y = a + bX$). The difference between the two figures is the measure of risk on the X-axis. The capital market line uses the portfolio's standard deviation, while the security market line uses the individual security's beta coefficient.

The difference between the two concepts, however, is more than the distinction between the two measures of risk. Both the capital market line (Equation 7.5) and the security market line (Equation 7.7) are part of the capital asset pricing model,

[20]The return on Standard & Poor's 500 stock index is often used as a proxy for the return on the market. Another alternative measure is the return estimated by Ibbotson Associates and reported in the *Stocks, Bonds, Bills, and Inflation (SBBI) Annual Yearbook*. Both the S&P 500 stock index and the Ibbotson data are discussed in Chapter 10.

Although these measures of the returns on the market may be appropriate for investments in many securities and diversified portfolios, they may be inappropriate for particular investments—such as the returns on the mutual fund specializing in gold stocks. The return on an index of gold or precious metal stocks may be a more relevant measure of the market return in such cases.

FIGURE 7.17

Security Market Line

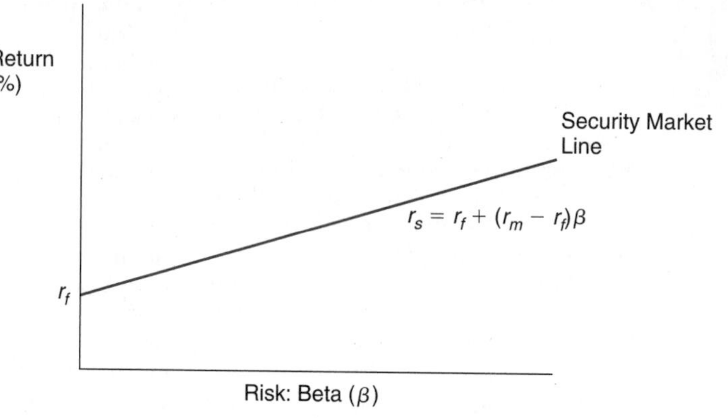

which seeks to explain security returns. The capital market line, or the macro component, suggests that the return on a well-diversified portfolio depends on the yield of a risk-free security and the portfolio's response to an aggregate measure of risk—the portfolio's standard deviation. The security market line, or the micro component, suggests that the return on an individual asset depends on the risk-free rate and the security's response to changes in the market, with that response being measured by an index of the security's market risk—the beta coefficient.

In addition to being a theory of the determination of security returns, the capital asset pricing model plays an important role in the valuation of securities and the analysis of portfolio performance. For example, in Chapter 9, the security market line component of the CAPM is used to determine the required return for an investment in common stock. This return is then used in the dividend-growth model to determine the value of a common stock. The model is also used in portfolio evaluation in Chapters 8 and 24, in which a realized return is compared to the required return specified by using the capital asset pricing model. Thus, the CAPM not only is an integral part of the theory of portfolio construction and the determination of security returns but also establishes a criterion for assessing portfolio performance.

Portfolio Betas

The security market line relates a particular stock's beta to the security's return. However, beta coefficients may also be computed for an entire portfolio and related to the portfolio's return. If a portfolio is well diversified, its beta is an appropriate index of the portfolio's risk, since diversification virtually eliminates the portfolio's unsystematic risk. The portfolio beta is a weighted average of each security in the portfolio and its beta. Thus, if a portfolio has the following stocks and their betas,

Stock	Amount Invested	Percent of Portfolio	Beta
A	$100	10%	0.9
B	200	20	1.2
C	300	30	1.6
D	400	40	1.7

the portfolio's beta is

$$(0.1)(0.9) + (0.2)(1.2) + (0.3)(1.6) + (0.4)(1.7) = 1.49.$$

This portfolio's beta is greater than 1.0, which indicates that the portfolio is more volatile than the market. Of course, the portfolio beta would have been different if the weights were different. If the portfolio had been more heavily weighted in stock A instead of stock D, for example, the numerical value of the beta would have been lower.

In addition to betas for individual stocks, betas may be computed for portfolios or mutual funds. For example, Morningstar provides beta coefficients for the mutual funds in its database, and the American Association of Individual Investors supplies betas for the funds covered by its *Guide to Low-Load Mutual Funds*. The interpretation of these betas is essentially the same as that for common stock. A numerical value of beta that is greater than 1.0 suggests an aggressive mutual fund whose return is more volatile than the market. A numerical value less than 1.0 suggests the opposite: that the fund has less market risk. (Morningstar also provides the coefficient of determination, [R^2], which is one measure of the quality of the estimated beta. A small R^2 would suggest that nonmarket factors are the primary contributors to the variability of the fund's return. See the appendix to this chapter for a discussion of the correlation coefficient and the coefficient of determination.)

In addition to indicating market risk, portfolio betas can play an important role in the evaluation of performance, since betas are a means to standardize each fund's return relative to its market risk. The discussion of assessing portfolio performance is deferred until the material on portfolio assessment in Chapter 8 on investment companies.

Arbitrage Pricing Theory

The previous material discussed beta coefficients and their use in the capital asset pricing model. While the CAPM is a major component in financial theory, it has been criticized as being too limited. The model reduces the explanation of a stock's return to two variables: (1) the market return and (2) the volatility of the stock in response to movements in the market (i.e., the beta). Of course in a well-diversified portfolio, systematic risk is *the* important source of risk. However, unsystematic risk may be important in the determination of an individual stock's return, if the stock's price is responsive to changes in some other variable. For example, an increase in the rate of inflation or a decrease in the rate of interest could have an important impact on an individual stock's return. Thus, other factors could play an important role in the explanation of security returns.

arbitrage
Simultaneous purchase and sale to take advantage of price differences in different markets.

Arbitrage pricing theory (APT), initially developed by Stephen A. Ross, seeks to add additional variables to the explanation of security returns.[21] It is a multivariable model in which security returns are dependent on several variables in addition to the volatility of the market. APT derives its name from the economic premise that prices cannot differ in two markets. **Arbitrage** is the act of buying a good or security and simultaneously selling it in another market at a higher price. (Individuals who participate in these transactions are called "arbitrageurs.")[22] If

[21]See Stephen A. Ross, "The Arbitrage Theory of Capital Asset Pricing," *Journal of Economic Theory* (December 1976): 341–360; and "Return, Risk, and Arbitrage," in I. Friend and J. L. Bicksler, eds., *Risk and Return in Finance* (Cambridge, MA: Ballinger, 1977), Section 9. A more advanced discussion of portfolio theory and arbitrage pricing theory may be found in advanced textbooks on investments, such as Robert C. Radcliffe, *Investments: Concepts, Analysis, Strategy*, 5th ed. (Glenview, IL: Scott, Foresman/Little Brown Higher Education, 1997).

[22]Arbitrage is discussed further in the chapters on options and futures.

IBM stock were selling for $50 in New York and $60 in San Francisco, an opportunity for a riskless profit exists. Arbitrageurs would buy the stock in New York and simultaneously sell it in San Francisco, thus earning the $10 profit without bearing any risk. Of course, the act of buying in New York will drive up the stock's price and the act of selling in San Francisco will drive down the price until the prices in the two markets are equal and the opportunity for arbitrage is erased.

Arbitrage also implies that portfolios with the same risk generate the same returns. If portfolio A has the same risk as portfolio B, the two are substitutes for each other. Just as the stock of IBM must trade for the same price in New York and San Francisco, the returns on portfolios A and B must be the same or an opportunity for arbitrage would exist. Once again, the role of arbitrage is to erase differentials. Differences in returns then must be related to differences in how the portfolios respond to the changes in the sources of risk that the investor faces. These sources of risk may be a major determinant of the return the investor earns.

In arbitrage, the security's price movement and return are *not* explained by a relationship between risk and return. The CAPM is built on an assumption concerning investors' willingness to bear risk (i.e., investors must expect to earn a higher return to be induced to bear more risk). While this assumption may be reasonable, APT explains movements in security prices without making an assumption concerning risk preferences. Security returns are the result of arbitrage as investors seek to take advantage of perceived differences in prices of risk exposure.

Arbitrage pricing theory states that the return on a security (r_s) depends on the expected return (r_e) and on a set of factors ($F_1 \ldots F_n$). For example, if the number of factors were four, the general model would be

(7.8) $$r_s = r_e + b_1F_1 + b_2F_2 + b_3F_3 + b_4F_4 + e$$

The individual parameters (i.e., the estimated coefficients $b_1 \ldots b_4$) measure the responsiveness or sensitivity of the return on the stock (or portfolio) to changes in the respective factors. The e represents an error term. If the model captures the important factors, the errors tend to cancel out (i.e., a positive error is canceled by a negative error), and the numerical value of the error term should be zero ($e = 0$). If there is a consistent error, the error term will not be equal to zero and the model is misspecified—that is, at least one important factor has been excluded.

The factors that could affect the return on a stock (or a portfolio) are numerous. Empirical work on APT generally classifies these variables into *sector* influences and *systematic* influences. An example of a sector variable is a firm's industry. What affects a bank stock may not affect a retailer or an airline. A systematic influence may be interest rates or the level of economic activity. For example, high dividend-paying stocks may more readily respond to changes in interest rates, while cyclical stocks may more readily respond to changes in the level of economic activity.

While there could be a large number of possible variables, empirical results suggest that only a few seem to have a lasting or continuous impact on security returns. For example, a change in inflation may have an important impact on security returns. However, it is unanticipated (rather than anticipated) inflation that has the impact. In competitive financial markets, expected inflation is already incorporated into a security's price. If inflation is expected to rise from 4 percent to 8 percent, security prices would have been previously adjusted downward and yields would be higher. It is the unexpected change that arbitrage pricing theory is seeking to build into the return. The expected return plus the responsiveness to the unexpected change in inflation (and to other factors) determine the realized return.

Unexpected events will always occur, so realized returns usually deviate from expected returns. What the investor does not know is which unexpected events will occur and how the individual stock will respond to the change. In addition, not all securities or portfolios will respond in the same direction or by the same amount. Two portfolios may respond differently to a change in a particular factor; hence, the returns on two (or more) portfolios may also differ.

Consider the following three-variable multifactor model:

$$r_s = 0.12 + b_1F_1 + b_2F_2 + b_3F_3 + e$$

in which the return on a stock will be 12 percent (the expected return) plus the impact of three risk factors. However, the estimated parameters for two stocks differ. Suppose the estimated equations for stocks A and B are

$$r_{sA} = 0.12 + 0.02F_1 - 0.01F_2 + 0.01F_3$$

and

$$r_{sB} = 0.12 + 0.05F_1 + 0.01F_2 + 0.02F_3.$$

The error terms wash out (i.e., $e = 0$), and the equations for the returns on the two stocks differ. The stocks have different responsiveness to changes in the risk factors, so the returns on each stock must differ. For example, the estimated coefficients for the second factor have different signs (minus versus plus), indicating this factor has an opposite impact on the returns of the two stocks.

Suppose the numerical values of the factors are 0, 1, and 2, respectively. The returns on the stocks will be

$$r_{sA} = 0.12 + 0.02(0) - 0.01(1) + 0.01(2) = 0.13 = 13\%$$

and

$$r_{sB} = 0.12 + 0.05(0) + 0.01(1) + 0.02(2) = 0.17 = 17\%$$

Since the numerical value of factor 1 is 0 during the time period, the expected value for this factor and the actual value were the same (i.e., $F_1 = 0$), so this factor had no impact on the returns. The actual values of factors 2 and 3 differed from the expected values; thus, these two variables affected each security's return. Factor 2 had a negative impact on stock A and a positive impact on stock B, while factor 3 had a positive influence on both stocks, with a slightly larger effect (0.02 versus 0.01) on stock B.

While there may be many possible factors, research suggests that four are preeminent. These are (1) unexpected inflation, (2) unexpected changes in the level of industrial production, (3) unanticipated shifts in risk premiums, and (4) unanticipated changes in the structure of yields (measured by the slope of the curve illustrating term structure of interest rates).[23]

Again, since expected changes are already incorporated into the expected return, APT stresses the importance of unanticipated change. If the actual values and expected values are equal, the factor washes out. If factor 1 in the preceding model is the difference between the actual rate of inflation and the expected rate of inflation, the equation would be

[23]The term structure of interest rates is discussed in Chapter 15 in the section on yields and in the appendix.

$$r_s = 0.12 + b_1 \text{ (actual rate of inflation} - \text{expected rate of inflation)} + b_2F_2 + b_3F_3.$$

If the actual rate of inflation is 4 percent and the expected rate of inflation is also 4 percent, this factor has no impact on the stock's return, that is, $b_1(0.04 - 0.04) = 0$.

The factors will have an impact on the stock's return only when the actual values differ from the expected values. If the actual rate of inflation is 7 percent (an increase from the expected 4 percent), this risk factor becomes relevant and has an impact on the stock's return. The amount of impact and its direction depend on the estimated parameter (i.e., the estimated coefficient and its sign). An increase in the rate of inflation could cause the returns on some stocks (e.g., utilities) to fall and cause the returns to rise on others (e.g., resource companies).

How each stock and each portfolio responds to the differences between the realized and the expected variables is crucial to the returns earned. Even though two stocks have the same beta coefficients and have responded in a similar fashion to a change in the market, they may respond differently to changes in other factors. For this reason, a portfolio stressing fixed-income securities may experience a larger response to a change in inflation than a portfolio stressing economic growth. This difference in responsiveness may play a crucial role in security selection or portfolio management. It suggests that buying low beta stocks may not be a defensive strategy if the securities are responsive to another variable that is subject to change.

Unfortunately, one of the largest problems facing the investor or portfolio manager who seeks to apply APT is the measurement of unanticipated changes in the factors. If one of the factors changes (e.g., an unanticipated increase in the rate of inflation) and the financial portfolio manager seeks to analyze how the market (or particular stock) responds to the change, that individual cannot separate the movement in the price caused by changes in expected inflation and the movement caused by unanticipated inflation. The movement in the market or the stock's price would encompass both. This is, of course, a major hurdle in the implementation of the model.

APT is currently in the process of being further developed and may someday supplant the capital asset pricing model as the primary model relating risk and return. Intuitively, APT is appealing because it is less limiting than the capital asset pricing model. The CAPM is based on an assumption concerning risk preferences and explains returns solely in terms of movements in the market. In the CAPM, the impact of asset-specific variables is erased through the construction of a diversified portfolio, so the volatility of the stock relative to the volatility of the market is the prime variable that explains an asset's risk and return. APT, however, suggests that differences in returns are driven by an arbitrage process and that two securities or portfolios with the same risk must generate the same return. APT permits the inclusion of more explanatory variables. The inclusion of these other factors, especially economic variables, such as unexpected changes in industrial production, make APT an appealing alternative explanation of an asset's return. Additional econometric research obviously is necessary to make the model more usable by individuals and portfolio managers, but it is reasonable to anticipate that further research will occur and that arbitrage pricing theory will remain at the forefront of security valuation and portfolio management.

Summary

Because the future is uncertain, all investments involve risk. The return the investor anticipates through income and/or capital appreciation may differ considerably from the realized return. This deviation of the realized return from the expected return is the risk associated with investing.

Risk emanates from several sources, which include fluctuations in market prices, fluctuations in interest rates, changes in reinvestment rates, fluctuations in exchange rates, and loss of purchasing power through inflation. These sources of risk are often referred to as *systematic risk* because the returns on assets tend to move together (i.e., there is a systematic relationship between security returns and market returns). Systematic risk is also referred to as *nondiversifiable risk* because it is not reduced by the construction of a diversified portfolio.

Diversification does, however, reduce *unsystematic risk*, which applies to the specific firm and encompasses the nature of the firm's operation and its financing. Because unsystematic risk applies only to the individual asset, there is no systematic relationship between the source of risk and the market as a whole. A portfolio composed of 10 to 15 unrelated assets—for example, stocks in companies in different industries or different types of assets, such as common stock, bonds, mutual funds, and real estate—virtually eradicates the impact of unsystematic risk on the portfolio as a whole.

Risk may be measured by the standard deviation, which measures the dispersion around a central tendency, such as an asset's or a portfolio's average return. If the individual returns differ considerably from the average returns, the dispersion is larger (i.e., the standard deviation is larger) and the risk associated with the asset is increased.

An alternative measure of risk, the beta coefficient, measures the responsiveness or variability of an asset's return relative to the return on the market as a whole. If the beta coefficient exceeds 1, the stock's return is more volatile than the return on the market; but if the beta is less than 1, the return on the stock is less volatile. Since the beta coefficient relates the return on the stock to the market's return, it is an index of the systematic risk associated with the stock.

Portfolio theory is built around risk and return. Portfolios that offer the highest return for a given amount of risk are *efficient*; portfolios that do not offer the highest return for a given level of risk are *inefficient*. A major component of portfolio theory is the capital asset pricing model (CAPM), which has a macro (aggregate) and a micro component. In the macro component, the capital market line gives the return on each efficient portfolio associated with each level of risk, which is measured by the portfolio's standard deviation. The individual investor selects the efficient portfolio that generates the highest level of satisfaction or utility.

In the micro component of the capital asset pricing model, beta coefficients are used to explain an individual security's return. Riskier securities with higher beta coefficients should have greater returns to justify bearing the additional risk. The security market line gives the return on a specific asset associated with each level of risk as measured by the asset's beta coefficient.

The use of beta as the primary explanatory variable of security returns has been criticized as too limiting. An alternative explanation of security returns is arbitrage pricing theory (APT), which is a multivariable model. In this model, such variables as unexpected inflation or unexpected changes in industrial production may affect security returns in addition to the security's response to changes in the market.

Questions

1) What is the difference between nondiversifiable (systematic) risk and diversifiable (unsystematic) risk?
2) What is a diversified portfolio? What type of risk is reduced through diversification? How many securities are necessary to achieve this reduction in risk? What characteristics must these securities possess?
3) What are the sources of return on an investment? What are the differences among the expected return, the required return, and the realized return?

4) If the expected returns of two stocks are the same but the standard deviations of the returns differ, which security is to be preferred?
5) If an investor desires diversification, should he or she seek investments that have a high positive correlation?
6) Indifference curves used in portfolio theory relate risk and return. How is the portfolio's risk measured? If one investor's indifference curves are steeper than another investor's, what does that indicate about their respective willingness to bear risk?
7) What is a beta coefficient? What do beta coefficients of 0.5, 1.0, and 1.5 mean?
8) If the correlation coefficient for a stock and the market equals 0, what is the market risk associated with the stock?
9) How are the capital market line and the security market line different? What does each represent?
10) How does arbitrage pricing theory advance our understanding of security returns?

11) Locate and compare the current Market Guide betas (http://www.marketguide.com or http://www.multexinvestor.com) with the beta coefficients for the stocks in the Points of Interest box. Have the individual betas changed? Has the average beta coefficient for the 12 stocks increased?

Problems

1) You are considering three stocks with the following expected dividend yields and capital gains:

	Dividend Yield	Capital Gain
A	14%	0%
B	8	6
C	0	14

a) What is the expected return on each stock?
b) How may transactions costs and capital gains taxes affect your choices among the three securities?

2) A portfolio consists of assets with the following expected returns:

	Expected Return	Weight in Portfolio
Real estate	16%	20%
Low-quality bonds	15	10
AT&T stock	12	30
Savings account	5	40

a) What is the expected return on the portfolio?
b) What will be the expected return if the individual reduces the holdings of the AT&T stock to 15 percent and puts the funds into real estate investments?

3) You are given the following information concerning two stocks:

	A	B
Expected return	10%	14%
Standard deviation of the expected return	3.0	5.0
Correlation coefficient of the returns	−.1	

a) What is the expected return on a portfolio consisting of 40 percent in stock A and 60 percent in stock B?
b) What is the standard deviation of this portfolio?
c) Discuss the risk and return associated with investing (a) all your funds in stock A, (b) all your funds in stock B, and (c) 40 percent in A and 60 percent in B. (This answer *must* use the numerical information in your answers derived above.)

4) You are given the following information:

Expected return on stock A	12%
Expected return on stock B	20%
Standard deviation of returns:	
stock A	1.0
stock B	6.0
Correlation coefficient of the returns on stocks A and B	+.2

a) What are the expected returns and standard deviations of a portfolio consisting of:
   1) 100 percent in stock A?
   2) 100 percent in stock B?
   3) 50 percent in each stock?
   4) 25 percent in stock A and 75 percent in stock B?
   5) 75 percent in stock A and 25 percent in stock B?
b) Compare the above returns and the risk associated with each portfolio.
c) Redo the calculations assuming that the correlation coefficient of the returns on the two stocks is −0.6. What is the impact of this difference in the correlation coefficient?

5) What is the beta of a portfolio consisting of one share of each of the following stocks given their respective prices and beta coefficients?

Stock	Price	Beta
A	$10	1.4
B	24	0.8
C	41	1.3
D	19	1.8

How would the portfolio beta differ if (a) the investor purchased 200 shares of stocks B and C for every 100 shares of A and D and (b) equal dollar amounts were invested in each stock?

6) What is the return on a stock according to the security market line if the risk-free rate is 6 percent, the return on the market is 10 percent, and the stock's beta is 1.5? If the beta had been 2.0, what would be the return? Is this higher return consistent with the portfolio theory explained in this chapter? Why?

7) You are considering purchasing two stocks with the following possible returns and probabilities of occurrence:

Investment A	Return	Probability of Occurrence
	−10%	20%
	5	40
	15	30
	25	10

Investment B	Return	Probability of Occurrence
	−5	20%
	5	40
	7	30
	39	10

Compare the expected returns and risk (as measured by the standard deviations) of each investment. Which investment offers the higher expected return? Which investment is riskier? Compare their relative risks by computing the coefficient of variation. For explanations and illustrations of the required calculations, see the appendix to this chapter.

8) Using the material on the standard deviation and the coefficient of variation presented in the appendix to this chapter, rank the following investments with regard to risk.

a)

Investment Returns	
Stock A	**Stock B**
2.50%	7.50%
2.75	8.25
3.00	9.00
3.25	9.75
3.50	10.50

b)

Investment Returns	
Stock A	**Stock B**
1.70%	7.40%
1.85	7.70
2.00	8.00
2.15	8.30
2.30	8.60

9) This problem illustrates how beta coefficients are estimated and uses material covered in the appendix to this chapter. It may be answered using any program that performs linear regression analysis, (e.g., Excel) or the beta calculation in the Investment Analysis package that accompanies this text. The following information is given:

		Return on	
Period	**Market**	**Stock X**	**Stock Y**
1	10%	−2%	13%
2	26	13	41
3	−2	3	3
4	−14	−7	−7
5	7	9	9
6	14	5	19
7	−5	2	−8
8	19	13	13
9	8	−3	17
10	−5	8	−14

a) Using regression analysis, compute the estimated equations relating the return on stock X to the return on the market and the return on stock Y to the return on the market. According to the equations, what is each stock's beta coefficient? What does each beta coefficient imply about the systematic risk associated with each stock?
b) What is the difference between the return on each stock given by the estimated equation for period 10 and the actual return? What may account for any differences in the estimated return and the actual return? (To answer this question, use the estimated equation, and compare the results with the actual results.)
c) What is the R^2 for each equation? Interpret the R^2. What does the R^2 imply about the other sources of risk as they apply to stocks X and Y?

THE FINANCIAL ADVISOR'S INVESTMENT CASE

Inferior Investment Alternatives

Although investing requires the individual to bear risk, the risk can be controlled through the construction of diversified portfolios and by excluding any portfolio that offers an inferior return for a given amount of risk. While this concept seems obvious, one of your clients, Marcy LaRossa, is considering purchasing a stock that you believe will offer an inferior return for the risk she will bear. To convince her that the acquisition is not desirable, you want to demonstrate the trade-off between risk and return.

While it is impractical to show the trade-off for all possible combinations, you believe that illustrating several combinations of risk and return and applying the same analysis to the specific investment should be persuasive in discouraging the purchase. Currently, U.S. Treasury bills offer 7 percent. Three possible stocks and their betas are as follows:

Security	Expected Return	Beta
Stock A	9%	0.6
Stock B	11	1.3
Stock C	14	1.5

1) What will be the expected return and beta for each of the following portfolios?
   - **a)** Portfolios 1 through 4: All of the funds are invested solely in each asset (the corresponding three stocks and the Treasury bill).
   - **b)** Portfolio 5: One-quarter of the funds are invested in each alternative.
   - **c)** Portfolio 6: One-half of the funds are invested in stock A and one-half in stock C.
   - **d)** Portfolio 7: One-third of the funds are invested in each stock.

2) Are any of the portfolios inefficient?

3) Is there any combination of the Treasury bill and stock C that is superior to portfolio 6 (i.e., half the funds in stock A and half in stock C)?

4) Since your client's suggested stock has an anticipated return of 12 percent and a beta of 1.4, does that information argue for or against the purchase of the stock?

5) Why is it important to consider purchasing an asset as part of a portfolio and not as an independent act?

INVESTMENT PROJECT

This chapter explains how beta coefficients are used as an index of systematic risk. Find the beta coefficient for the eight stocks that you are following and record the information on the data sheet. Beta coefficients are published in the *Value Line Investment Survey*. If *Value Line* is not available, you may be able to locate betas using the Internet. Possible sources include Yahoo (http://biz.yahoo.com), Wall Street Research Net (http://www.wsrn.com), and MultexInvestor (http://www.multexinvestor.com). Since the location of the beta coefficients varies with each source, you may have to search to find the beta. A good starting point may be "company profile," "company snapshot," or "company statistics."

What is the average beta for the portfolio of eight stocks? To determine this average for a portfolio in which you invest an equal dollar amount in each stock, the portfolio beta is the simple average of the eight individual betas. That is

	Stock	Beta
1	CSK	
2	HSY	
3	IBM	
4	MSFT	
5		
6		
7		
8		
Average beta		Sum/8 =

For a portfolio in which you purchase the same number of shares (and the dollar amount invested in each stock differs), determine the weight of each stock in the portfolio and use that weight to construct a weighted average beta for the portfolio. That is,

		Cost of 100 Shares	Weight in Portfolio	Beta	Weighted Beta
1	CSK				
2	HSY				
3	IBM				
4	MSFT				
5					
6					
7					
8					

(The total cost of the portfolio is the sum of the amount invested in each stock. Each stock's weight is its cost/total cost. The weighted beta is the beta times the weight for each stock. The weighted average portfolio beta is the sum of the individual weighted betas.)

Remember, the beta for the market is 1.0, so if the portfolio beta is less than 1.0, the portfolio has less systematic risk than the market. Of course, if the beta exceeds 1.0, the portfolio should tend to be more volatile than the market as a whole.

APPENDIX 7

Statistical Tools

The old saying that "statistics never lie, but liars use statistics" certainly may apply to investments. Mathematical computations and statistics often play an important role in financial and security analysis and in portfolio construction. You do not have to be a statistician or a security analyst to have a fundamental knowledge of the statistics provided by such investment services as Value Line or Morningstar. Understanding these basic statistical concepts should increase your comprehension of investment analysis.

This appendix briefly explains and illustrates with financial examples common mathematical computations and statistical concepts that appear in the body of the text. These include the computation of averages, measures of variability (such as the standard deviation), regression analysis, and the reliability of the estimates.

Averages

Averages, which are measures of central tendency, are often used in investments. For example, an industry average price/earnings ratio was illustrated in Chapter 3 in a Points of Interest box. Averages are also used in the construction of indexes. For example, the Standard & Poor's 500 stock index is a weighted average of stock prices with 1943, the *base* year, as the starting point.

Arithmetic Average

While the *average* (or *mean*) may appear to be an easy concept, there is more than one method for computing averages. First, there is the simple or arithmetic average in which all the observations are treated equally. The arithmetic average is the sum of all the individual numbers divided by the number of observations. Consider the following three stocks and their prices:

Stock	Price
A	\$10
B	\$17
C	\$42

The arithmetic mean or average price is

$$\frac{\$10 + 17 + 42}{3} = \$23.$$

Notice that the average price (\$23) exceeds the value of two of the stocks. The \$23 does not imply that the average is biased. If the investor owns one share of each stock, the simple average does reflect the value of a share.

If the investor owns five shares of A, two shares of B, and one share of C, then the \$23 average price does not accurately measure the value of a share in the portfolio. In this case a *weighted average*, which considers not only the price of each stock but also its weight in the portfolio, is more appropriate. The weighted average price of a share is

$$\frac{5(\$10) + 2(\$17) + 1(\$42)}{\text{Total number of shares}} = \frac{\$126}{8} = \$15.75.$$

The weighted average price is closer to $10 because stock A constitutes a larger portion of the total portfolio.

Weighted averages are often used to determine expected returns. Suppose you anticipate that a stock will earn 5 percent during a recession, 9 percent during periods of modest economic growth, and 16 percent during a period of rapid economic expansion. What is the expected return on the stock? The answer partially depends on the probability of each event occurring. If you expect the probability of recession to be 20 percent, the probability of modest growth to be 65 percent, and the probability of rapid growth to be 15 percent, the expected return $E(r)$ is

$$E(r) = (0.20)(5) + (0.65)(9) + (0.15)(16) = 9.25\%.$$

(Expected values are often denoted by E; notice also that the sum of the weights—i.e., probabilities—must equal 1 and, unlike the previous illustrations of the computation of averages, no division was performed.) If the probabilities had been different (e.g., 40 percent, 45 percent, and 15 percent), the expected return would have been different:

$$E(r) = (0.40)(5) + (0.45)(9) + (0.15)(16) = 8.45\%.$$

The greater weight toward recession has decreased the expected return.

You should realize that the actual return will deviate from the expected return because only one of the three scenarios will occur. The investor will earn 5, 9, or 16 percent even though the weighted averages are 9.25 or 8.45 percent.

Geometric Average

An alternative method for calculating averages is the *geometric average*. Instead of adding the individual numbers and dividing by the number of entries, a geometric average multiplies the individual numbers and then takes the nth root, with n equal to the number of individual entries. For example, if the prices of three stocks are $10, $17, and $42, the geometric average is

$$\sqrt[3]{(\$10)(\$17)(\$42)} = \$19.26.$$

Although the calculation of the nth root appears to be formidable, it is easy if your calculator has a y^x key.[1] First, take the reciprocal of the exponent expressed as a decimal (i.e., convert the 3 into 1/3: .33333). Second, express the equation using the decimal:

$$\textbf{Geometric average price} = (\$10)(\$17)(\$42)^{.3333}.$$

Third, use the y^x key to perform the calculation, so

$$\sqrt[3]{(\$10)(\$17)(\$42)} = (\$10)(\$17)(\$42)^{.3333} = \$19.26.$$

This value is different than the average price determined by using the arithmetic mean. Both averages are mathematically correct, and there are cases when one may be preferred to the other. Actually, all three types of averages are used in the construction of aggregate measures of the stock market. The Dow-Jones industrial average is an arithmetic average, the Standard & Poor's 500 stock index is

[1]The square root is a special case that determines the second root. Many calculators have a special key to square a number (x^2) and to take the square root, $\sqrt{x}$.

a value-weighted average, and the *Value Line* stock index is constructed using a geometric average.

There is one case in investments, the computation of average returns, in which the difference between the calculations of the arithmetic and geometric averages is crucial. Consider the following stock prices and the percentage change in each.

Year	Price of Stock	Percentage Change
1	$20	—
2	34	70.0%
3	25	−26.5
4	30	20.0

The percentage changes indicate what the investor earned each year and may be used to compute a return. (Returns are generally expressed as a percentage, while profits or capital gains are expressed in dollars.) The average return for the three years is 21.17 percent:

$$\frac{(70.0 - 26.5 + 20.00)}{3}.$$

You would think that if an investor earned 21.17 percent each year, the total gain would be

$$\$20 \times 3 \times .2117 = \$12.70$$

and the $20 would now be worth $32.70 instead of $30. Something is obviously wrong, and the error would be even larger if the calculation had used compounding:

$$\$20(1 + 0.2117)^3 = \$35.58.$$

The error is the result of averaging plus and minus percentage changes. A price movement from $20 to $25 is a 25 percent gain. A price change from $25 to $20 is a 20 percent decline. Averaging the two percentage changes produces an average of 2.5 percent, but a change from $20 to $25 to $20 indicates no change and no return. In both cases the stock moves $5, but the percentage changes differ because the base or starting price differs—thus biasing the return upward.

This problem is avoided if a geometric average return is computed. The computation is as follows:

$$\sqrt[3]{(1 + 0.70)(1 + [-0.265])(1 + 0.2)} = \sqrt[3]{1.4994} = 1.1446.$$

The geometric average return is

$$1.1446 - 1 = 14.46\%.$$

Notice that the calculation is not

$$\sqrt[3]{(70)(-26.5)(2)} = \sqrt[3]{-3710},$$

which fails to consider the decimal (i.e., 70 percent does not equal 70) and produces a negative number. The correct calculation requires adding the percentage, expressed as a decimal, to 1. Positive percentage changes generate numbers greater than 1. Negative percentage changes result in numbers less than 1, but all numbers must be positive. After the appropriate root is determined, the 1 is subtracted to obtain the geometric average return, which in the illustration is an annual return of 14.46 percent.

Does the 14.46 percent seem reasonable? The answer is yes. Suppose a \$20 investment earned 14.46 percent each year; the gain would be

$$\$20 \times 3 \times 0.1446 = \$8.676$$

and the \$20 would now be worth \$28.676. Something still remains wrong, but once compounding is considered, the correct return is verified:

$$\$20(1 + 0.1446)^3 = \$29.99 \approx \$30.$$

Since the use of the geometric average has generated the true return, its use is crucial to investments. (The calculation reappears in Chapter 10, which covers the rates of return earned on various alternative investments.)

The Standard Deviation

While averages are often used in investment analysis, they indicate nothing about the variability of the individual observations. Do the observations cluster around the average or is there considerable variation in the individual numbers? Consider two stocks presented in the body of the text that earned the following annual returns:

	Return	
Year	Stock A	Stock B
1	13.5%	11.0%
2	14.0	11.5
3	14.25	12.0
4	14.5	12.5
5	15.0	15.0
6	15.5	17.5
7	15.75	18.0
8	16.0	18.5
9	16.5	19.0

The arithmetic average return is 15 percent (135/9) in both cases, but B's returns are obviously more diverse than A's. In B the individual observations cluster around the extreme values, so there is more variation in the annual returns.

This dispersion or variability around the mean is measured by the *standard deviation*. The equation for the computation of the standard deviation (σ) is

(7A.1)
$$\sigma = \sqrt{\frac{\Sigma(r_n - \bar{r})^2}{n - 1}}$$

This equation states that the standard deviation is the square root of the sum of the squared differences between the individual observation (r_n) and the average ($\bar{r}$), divided by the number of observations (n) minus 1.[2] The steps necessary to calculate the standard deviation follow:

[2]The subscript n represents the total observations from 1 through n. The line over the r indicates that the number is the average of all the observations. The $n - 1$ represents the *degrees of freedom*, because there can be only $n - 1$ independent observations. Consider the following analogy. If you know (1) the average of a series of 10 numbers and (2) 9 of the 10 numbers, the remaining number can be determined. It cannot be independent, so there are only $10 - 1$ (i.e., $n - 1$) independent numbers.

When computing the standard deviation from sample data, $n - 1$ is generally used in the denominator. However, the difference between n and $n - 1$ is very small for large numbers of observations. For large samples, n and $n - 1$ are virtually the same, and n may be used instead of $n - 1$. When all observations are known (i.e., when

1 For the range of possible returns, subtract the average return from the individual observations.
2 Square this difference.
3 Add these squared differences.
4 Divide this sum by the number of observations less 1.
5 Take the square root.

For stock A, the standard deviation is determined as follows:

Individual Return	Average Return	Difference	Difference Squared
13.50%	15%	−1.5	2.2500
14	15	−1	1.0000
14.25	15	−0.75	0.5625
14.50	15	−0.5	0.25
15	15	0	0
15.50	15	0.5	0.25
15.75	15	0.75	0.5625
16	15	1	1.000
16.50	15	1.5	2.2500
	The sum of the squared differences: 8.1250		

The sum of the squared differences divided by the number of observations less 1:

$$\frac{8.1250}{8} = 1.0156.$$

The square root:

$$\sqrt{1.0156} = \pm 1.01$$

Thus, the standard deviation is 1.01. (A square root is a positive [+] or negative [−] number. For example, the square root of 9 is +3 *and* −3 since (3)(3) = 9 and (−3)(−3) = 9. However, in the calculation of the standard deviation, only positive numbers are used—that is, the sum of the squared differences—so the square root must be a positive number.)

The investor must then interpret this result. Plus and minus 1 standard deviation has been shown to encompass approximately 68 percent of all observations (in this case, 68 percent of the returns). The standard deviation for stock A is 1.01, which means that approximately two-thirds of the returns fall between 13.99 and 16.01 percent. These returns are simply the average return (15 percent) plus 1.01 and minus 1.01 percent (i.e., plus and minus the standard deviation).

The standard deviation for B is 3.30, which means that approximately 68 percent of the returns fall between 11.7 percent and 18.3 percent. Stock B's returns

computing the standard deviation of a population), n is also used. See, for instance, a text of statistics, such as David R. Anderson, Dennis J. Sweeney, and Thomas A. Williams, *Statistics for Business and Economics*, 8th ed. (Cincinnati, OH: South-Western/Thomson Learning, 2002).

Average rates of return (and their standard deviations) are illustrations of samples, because not every possible period is included. Even computations of annual rates of return are samples because the annual returns may be computed for January 1, 20X0 through January 1, 20X1 but exclude rates computed using January 2, 20X0 through January 2, 20X1; January 3, 20X0 through January 3, 20X3; etc. The presumption is that if enough periods are included in the computation, the results are representative of all possible outcomes (representative of the population). The large sample would also mean that the difference between n and $n - 1$ is small and should not affect the estimate of the variability around the mean.

have a wider dispersion from the average return, and this fact is indicated by the greater standard deviation.

While the standard deviation measures the dispersion around the mean, it is an absolute number. In the previous illustration, the average return was 15 percent for both A and B, so the larger standard deviation for B indicates more variability. If the average returns for A and B differed, a comparison of their standard deviations may not indicate that B's returns are more diverse.

The standard deviation may also be computed for expected values and their probabilities. The body of this chapter illustrated the computation of an expected return. In that illustration, the returns and their probabilities were as follows:

Return	Probability
3%	10%
10	45
12	40
20	5

The expected value (return) was

$$E(r) = (0.10).03 + (0.45).10 + (0.40).12 + (0.05).20$$
$$= 0.003 + 0.045 + 0.048 + 0.01 = 0.106 = 10.6\%$$

To calculate the dispersion (the standard deviation) around the expected value, use the following process:

Individual Return	Expected Return	Difference	Difference Squared and Weighted by the Probability
3%	10.6%	−7.6	(57.76)(0.10) = 5.776
10	10.6	−.6	(0.36)(0.45) = 0.162
12	10.6	1.4	(1.96)(0.40) = 0.784
20	10.6	9.4	(88.36)(0.05) = 4.418
			11.14

Subtract the expected value from the individual observation. Square the difference and weight the squared difference by the probability of occurrence. The sum of the weighted squared differences is the variance (11.14). The standard deviation is the square root of the variance ($\sqrt{11.14} = 3.338$). The standard deviation is simply a weighted average of the differences from the expected value.

Although the standard deviation measures the dispersion around the mean (or expected mean), it is an absolute number. In the first illustration of the calculation of the standard deviation, the average return was 15 percent for both A and B, so the larger standard deviation for B indicates more variability.

Suppose that over a period of years, firm A had average earnings of $100 with a standard deviation of $10, while firm B's average earnings were $100,000 with a standard deviation of $100. Since $10 is less than $100, it would appear that firm A's earnings were less variable. Such a conclusion, however, does not make sense, since B's average earnings are so much larger than A's average earnings.

The *coefficient of variation* (CV) is used to adjust for such differences in scale. The coefficient of variation is a relative measure of dispersion and is defined as the ratio of the standard deviation divided by the mean. That is,

(7A.2)
$$CV = \frac{\text{The standard deviation}}{\text{The average}}.$$

The coefficients of variation for firms A and B are

$$CV_A = \frac{\$10}{\$100} = 0.1 \quad \text{and} \quad CV_B = \frac{\$100}{\$100{,}000} = 0.001.$$

From this perspective, B's earnings are less variable than A's, even though B's standard deviation is larger. (The Sharpe index discussed in Chapter 8 for evaluating portfolio performance is, in effect, a coefficient of variation since it is the ratio of the return divided by the standard deviation.)

In some cases, the *variance* is used instead of the standard deviation as a measure of risk. (It is not unusual for the risk/return model to be referred to as the "mean–variance" model.) The variance is the square of the standard deviation (i.e., the variance is the sum of the squared differences). As with the standard deviation, variances can be used to rank the amount of risk, but the variance is harder to interpret. While a mean of 25 percent with a standard deviation of 10 percent suggests that approximately two-thirds of the returns fall between 15 and 35 percent, the variance has no such useful interpretation.

The standard deviation does have a weakness in that it considers both positive and negative performance. Investors are probably not disappointed if the return is higher than the average. It is the negative return that concerns them, but the standard deviation does not differentiate between upside and downside variability. The computation of the standard deviation squares both the returns that exceed the average (the positive differences) and the returns that are less than the average (i.e., the negative differences).

Semivariance

Risk is often measured by the dispersion around a central value such as an investment's average return or the investment's required or target returns. As was illustrated in the previous section, dispersion may be measured by the variance or the standard deviation, which is the square root of the variance. The standard deviation is easier to interpret since approximately two-thirds of all observations lie within 1 standard deviation of the mean. If a mutual fund's average return is 12 percent with a standard deviation of 3, then approximately two-thirds of the time, the fund's return lies between 9 and 15 percent.

The variance and the standard deviation do not differentiate between variability that exceeds the average, which presumably investors want, and variability that is less than the average, which investors do not want. Investors are primarily concerned with downside risk, the possibility of loss and not the possibility of a large gain. When variance is used as a measure of risk, it may be advantageous to analyze only the extent to which the return is less than the average or target (i.e., to consider downside variability).

An alternative to the variance is the *semivariance*, which considers only the returns that fall below the average or target.[3] Since the semivariance isolates only

[3]Semivariance is primarily used by professional portfolio managers. See, for instance, David Spaulding, *Measuring Investment Performance* (New York: McGraw-Hill, 1997) and Frank J. Fabozzi, *Investment Management*, 2nd ed. (Upper Saddle River, NJ: Prentice Hall, 1999.)

the returns below the average, it is a measure of downside risk. Consider the two following investments and their returns for each time period:

Period	Investment A	Investment B
1	−7%	0%
2	−5	−2
3	6	−7
4	8	11
5	13	13

The average returns, variances, and standard deviations are the same (3.0 percent, 74.5, and 8.6, respectively). In terms of return and risk, the two investments are the same. Investment A, however, has larger losses, which are offset by the larger gains, so the two investment returns are the same.

The semivariance uses the same method of computation as the variance but only includes the observations below the average. The affect of considering only the observations that are less than the average may be seen by computing the sum of the squared differences for both investments but limiting the calculation to only those observations that are below the average return. For investment A that calculation is

Investment A

Average Return	Individual Return	Difference	Difference Squared
3%	−7	−10	100
3	−5	−8	64
The sum of the squared differences:			164

For investment B the calculation is

Investment B

Average Return	Individual Return	Difference	Difference Squared
3%	0	0	0
3	−2	−5	25
3	−7	−10	100
The sum of the squared differences:			125

The sum of the squared differences is larger for investment A, which suggests that A is the riskier investment.

Covariation and Correlation

Sometimes it is desirable to know not only how a return varies relative to its average return but also its variability to other returns. This variability is measured by the *covariance* or *correlation coefficient*. To illustrate the calculation of covariance and the correlation coefficient, consider the following annual returns for two mutual funds.

Year	Return Fund A	Fund B
1	10%	17%
2	14	3
3	8	16
4	8	21
5	10	3
Average return	10%	12%

The arithmetic average return is 10 percent for A and 12 percent for B. (The standard deviations of the returns are 2.449 and 8.426, respectively.)

Both funds have positive returns, and the higher return for B is associated with more variability—that is, a higher standard deviation. There is also variability between the returns in a given year. For example, A did well in year 5 when B earned a small return, but B did very well in year 4 when A earned a modest return. Covariance and correlation measure the variability of the returns on funds A and B relative to each other and indicate if the returns move together or inversely.

The covariance is found by considering simultaneously how the individual returns of A differ from its average and how the individual returns of B differ from its average. The differences are multiplied together, summed, and the sum is divided by the number of observations minus 1 $(n - 1)$. For the previous returns, the calculation of the covariance is as follows:

Average Return on A	Individual Return on A	Difference	Average Return on B	Individual Return on B	Difference	Product of the Difference
10%	10	0	12%	17	−5	0
10	14	−4	12	3	9	−36
10	8	2	12	16	−4	−8
10	8	2	12	21	−9	−18
10	10	0	12	3	9	0
					The sum of the product of the differences:	−62

To determine the covariance (cov_{AB}), the sum of the product of the differences is divided by the number of observations minus 1:

$$\text{cov}_{AB} = \frac{-62}{5 - 1} = -15.5.$$

Notice that unlike the computation for the standard deviation, the differences are not squared, so the final answer can have a negative number. The negative number indicates that the variables move in opposite directions, and a positive number indicates they move in the same direction. Large numerical values indicate a strong relationship between the variables, while small numbers indicate a weak relationship between the variables.

Since the covariance is an absolute number, it is often converted into the *correlation coefficient*, which measures the strength of the relationship and is easier to interpret than the covariance. The correlation coefficient (R_{AB}) is defined as

(7A.3)
$$R_{AB} = \frac{\text{Covariance of AB}}{\text{(Standard deviation of A)(Standard deviation of B)}}$$

(By algebraic manipulation, the covariance is

$$\text{cov}_{ab} = S_a \times S_b \times \text{(correlation coeficient of a and b)}$$

and is frequently used in this form in this text).

The numerical value of the correlation coefficient ranges from +1 to −1. If two variables move exactly together (i.e., if there is a perfect positive correlation between the two variables), the numerical value of the correlation coefficient is 1. If the two variables move exactly opposite of each other (i.e., if there is a perfect negative correlation between the two variables), the numerical value of the correlation coefficient is −1. All other possible values lie between the two extremes. Low numerical values, such as −0.12 or 0.19, indicate little relationship between the two variables. In this example, the correlation coefficient of AB is

$$R_{AB} = \frac{-15.5}{(2.499(8.426)} = -0.7511.$$

A correlation coefficient of −0.7511 indicates a reasonably strong negative relationship between the two variables.

The correlation coefficient is often converted into the coefficient of determination, which is the correlation coefficient squared and is often referred to as R^2. The coefficient of determination gives the proportion of the variation in one variable explained by the other variable. In the preceding illustration, the coefficient of determination is 0.5641 ((−0.7511)(−0.7511)), which indicates that 56.41 percent of the variation in fund A's return is explained by the variation in fund B's return. (Correspondingly, 56.41 percent of the variation in B's return is explained by A's return. No causality is claimed by the coefficient of determination. It is the job of the analyst to determine if one of the variables is dependent on the other.) Obviously, some other variable(s) must explain the remaining 43.59 percent of the variation.

Since the R^2 gives the proportion of the variation in one variable explained by the other, it is an important statistic in investments. For example, Morningstar reports the volatility of a mutual fund's return relative to the return on the market. This volatility is measured by an index referred to in the chapter as a *beta coefficient*. The beta has little meaning if the relationship between the fund's return and the market return is weak. The strength of the relationship is indicated by the R^2. If the $R^2 = 0.13$, the beta has little meaning, since the variation in the return is caused by something other than the movement in the market (i.e., the stock has little market risk). If the $R^2 = 0.94$, it is reasonable to conclude that the variability of the return is primarily the result of the variability of the market, (i.e., the stock's primary source of risk is movements in the market).

Regression Analysis[4]

Although the correlation coefficient and the coefficient of determination provide information concerning the closeness of the relationship between two variables, they cannot be used for forecasting. Regression analysis, on the other hand, estimates an equation between two variables that may be used in forecasting. Regression analysis is also used to estimate the beta coefficient referred to in the previous paragraph. As was explained in the body of this chapter, betas are very important in investments as an index of the systematic, nondiversifiable risk.

Correlation coefficients do not imply any causality. The correlation coefficient relating X to Y is the same as the correlation coefficient for Y to X. Regression does

[4]For a more detailed explanation of regression analysis, consult a specialized statistics textbook such as William Mendenhall and Terry Sincich, *A Second Course in Statistics: Regression Analysis*, 5th ed. (Upper Saddle River, New Jersey: Prentice Hall, 1996).

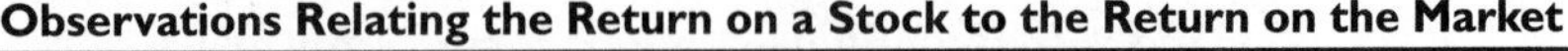

FIGURE 7A.1

Observations Relating the Return on a Stock to the Return on the Market

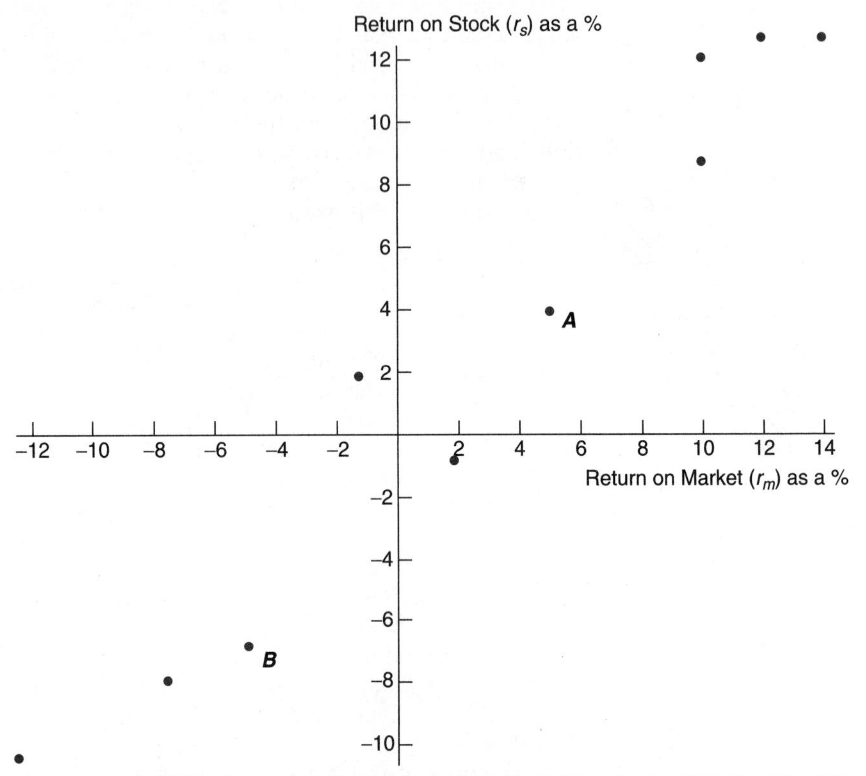

have an implication of a causal relationship, because variables are specified as *independent* and *dependent*. Consider the following data relating the independent variable, the return on the market (r_m), and the dependent variable, the return on a stock (r_s).

Return on the Market (r_m)	Return on a Stock (r_s)
14%	13%
12	13
10	12
10	9
5	4
2	−1
−1	2
−5	−7
−7	−8
−12	−10

Each pair of observations represents the return on the market and the return on the stock for a period of time, such as a week or a year. The data are plotted in Figure 7A.1, with each point representing one set of observations. For example, point

A represents a 4 percent return on the stock in response to a 5 percent increase in the market. Point B represents a −7.0 percent return on the stock and a −5.0 percent return on the market.

The individual points like A and B tell very little about the relationship between the return on the market and the return on the stock, but all the observations, taken as a whole, may. In this illustration, the points suggest a strong positive relationship between the return on the market and the return on the stock, but inferences from visual inspection may be inaccurate.

The problem of accuracy is reduced by regression analysis, in which the individual observations are summarized by a linear equation relating the return on the market—the independent variable—and the return on the stock—the dependent variable. (In this illustration there is only one independent variable. Multiple regression, however, incorporates more than one independent variable.) The general form of the equation is

(7A.4)
$$r_s = a + br_m + e$$

in which r_s and r_m are the return on the stock and the return on the market, respectively, a is the Y-intercept, b is the slope of the line, and e is an error term. (The analysis assumes that the error term is equal to 0, since errors should be both positive and negative and tend to cancel out. If the errors do not cancel out, the equation is misspecified.)

Although the actual computations of the intercept and slope are performed by a computer, a manual demonstration of the process is presented in Exhibit 7A.1, from which the following equation is derived:

$$r_s = -0.000597 + 0.9856\ r_m.$$

EXHIBIT 7A.1

Manual Calculation of a Simple Linear Regression Equation

$X(r_m)$	$Y(r_s)$	X^2	Y^2	XY
0.14	0.13	0.0196	0.0169	0.0182
0.12	0.13	0.0144	0.0169	0.0156
0.10	0.12	0.0100	0.0144	0.0120
0.10	0.09	0.0100	0.0081	0.0090
0.05	0.04	0.0025	0.0016	0.0020
0.02	−0.01	0.0004	0.0001	−0.0002
−0.01	0.02	0.0001	0.0004	−0.0002
−0.05	−0.07	0.0025	0.0049	0.0035
−0.07	−0.08	0.0049	0.0064	0.0056
−0.12	−0.10	0.0144	0.0100	0.0120
$\Sigma X = 0.28$	$\Sigma Y = 0.27$	$\Sigma X^2 = 0.0788$	$\Sigma Y^2 = 0.0797$	$\Sigma XY = 0.0775$

n = the number of observations (10)

$$b = \frac{n\,\Sigma XY - (\Sigma X)(\Sigma Y)}{n\,\Sigma X^2 - (\Sigma X)^2}$$

$$= \frac{(10)(0.0775) - (0.28)(0.27)}{(10)(0.0788) - (0.28)(0.28)}$$

$$= \frac{0.7750 - 0.0756}{0.7880 - 0.0784} = 0.9856$$

The a is computed as follows:

$$a = \frac{\Sigma Y}{n} - b\frac{\Sigma X}{n}$$

$$= \frac{0.27}{10} - (0.9856)\frac{0.28}{10} = -0.000597$$

The estimated equation is $r_s = -0.000597 + 0.9856\ r_m$.

FIGURE 7A.2

Regression Line Relating the Return on a Stock to the Return on the Market

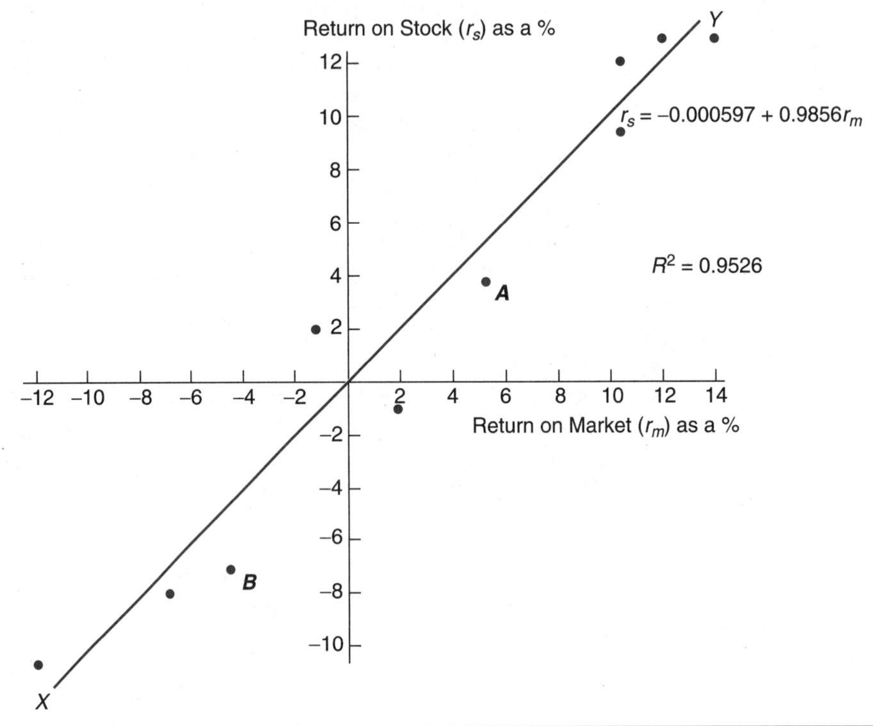

The Y-intercept is -0.000597 and the slope of the line is $+0.9856$. In the body of this chapter, this slope is referred to as the stock's beta coefficient. This equation is given as line XY in Figure 7A.2, which reproduces Figure 7A.1 but adds the regression line. As may be seen from the graph, line XY runs through the individual points. Some of the observations are above the line, while others fall below it. Some of the individual points are close to the line, while others appear farther away. The closer the points are to the line, the stronger is the relationship between the two variables.

Since the individual observations lie close to the estimated regression line, that suggests a high correlation between the two variables. In this illustration, the actual correlation coefficient is 0.976, which indicates a very strong relationship between the return on the stock and the return on the market. The coefficient of determination, the R^2, is 0.9526, which indicates that over 95 percent of the return on the stock is explained by the return on the market.

A small R^2 (e.g., $R^2 = 0.25$) would suggest that other factors affected the stock's return. The stock would have more unsystematic, diversifiable risk, and the beta coefficient may be a poor predictor of the stock's future performance. That, however, need not imply that the beta is useless. The portfolio beta, which is an aggregate of the individual betas, may be a good predictor of the return the investor can expect from movements in the market. Factors that adversely affect the return on one security may be offset by factors that enhance the return earned on other securities in the portfolio. In effect, the errors cancel.

Manually calculating the regression equation, the correlation coefficient, and the coefficient of determination is tedious and time-consuming. Fortunately, spreadsheet software applications, such as Excel and Lotus, include a simple linear regression program. Some electronic calculators also perform regression, although the number of observations is limited. The Investment Analysis software package that accompanies this text also includes a simple linear regression program.

8 Investment Companies

Because many investors find managing their own portfolios to be difficult or time-consuming or both, they purchase shares in investment companies. The managements of these companies then invest the funds primarily in a diversified portfolio of stocks and bonds. Because the individual owns shares in the investment company, he or she owns a claim on the diversified portfolio. By purchasing these shares, the saver can achieve the advantage of diversification even if he or she can invest only a modest amount. These advantages have resulted in investment companies becoming a popular vehicle for many individuals, and they play a significant role in security markets.

There are two general types of investment companies: *closed-end* and *open-end.* The open-end investment company is commonly referred to as a "mutual fund" and is by far the more popular. This chapter discusses both types of investment companies, the mechanics of buying and selling their shares, the costs associated with these investments, and the potential sources of profit. Also included in the discussion are the various specialized investment companies, such as stock index funds or high-yield bond funds, that offer investors a broad spectrum of alternatives to the direct purchase of stocks and bonds through brokers.

The chapter ends with means to compare investment companies' performance. Although the absolute return is important, the risk assumed to earn that return is also important. The measures of performance assessment encompass both risk and return. As was discussed in the previous chapter, risk may be measured by a portfolio's standard deviation of the return or the beta coefficient; and the relationship between risk and return are specified in the capital market line and the security market line. This material is used to construct indexes of performance on the basis of risk and return.

This chapter introduces investment companies but does not explicitly cover factors to consider when selecting among the thousands of mutual funds and closed-end investment companies. The allocation of funds among various investment alternatives, the selection of mutual funds, and mutual fund performance relative to the market as a whole will be covered after all the investment alternatives have been discussed—that is, in Chapter 24 on portfolio planning and management.

Learning Objectives

After completing this chapter you should be able to:

1 Differentiate between closed-end and open-end investment companies.
2 Define *net asset value.*
3 Identify the costs of investing in mutual funds and closed-end investment companies.
4 List the advantages offered by investment companies.
5 Distinguish among the types of mutual funds.
6 Identify hidden capital gains and losses.
7 Differentiate between a unit trust and an actively managed portfolio.
8 Distinguish between loading fees, exit fees, and 12b-1 "plans."
9 Compare performance on the basis of risk and return.

Investment Companies: Origins and Terminology

closed-end investment company
An investment company with a fixed number of shares that are bought and sold in the secondary security markets.

open-end investment company
A mutual fund; an investment company from which investors buy shares and to which they resell them.

mutual fund
An open-end investment company.

Investment companies are not a recent development but were established in Britain during the 1860s. Initially, these investment companies were referred to as *trusts* because the securities were held in trust for the firm's stockholders. These firms issued a specified number of shares and used the funds that were obtained through the sale of the stock to acquire shares of other firms. Today, the descendants of these companies are referred to as **closed-end investment companies** because the number of shares is fixed (i.e., closed to new investors).

Whereas the first trusts offered a specific number of shares, the most common type of investment company today does not. Instead, the number of shares varies as investors buy more shares from the trust or sell them back to the trust. This **open-end investment company** is commonly called a **mutual fund**. Such funds started in 1924 when Massachusetts Investor Trust offered new shares and redeemed (i.e., bought) existing shares on demand by stockholders.

The rationale for investment companies is simple and appealing. The firms receive the funds from many investors, pool them, and purchase securities. The individual investors receive (1) the advantage of professional management of their money, (2) the benefit of ownership in a diversified portfolio, (3) the potential savings in commissions, as the investment company buys and sells in large blocks, and (4) custodial services (e.g., the collecting and disbursing of funds).[1]

The advantages and service help to explain why both the number of mutual funds and the dollar value of their shares have grown dramatically during the last 25 years. According to data available through the Investment Company Institute (http://www.ici.org), the total number of funds in 1970 was 361. At the end of 1990, the number had risen to 2,362, and by the beginning of 2001, the number of mutual funds exceeded 8,100. (As of 2000, fewer than 3,000 companies were traded on the NYSE. The number of funds more than doubled the number of common stocks traded on the NYSE!) Of the 8,184 funds, 4,394 were equity funds and 2,222 bond funds. Money market funds accounted for 1,013 funds, and the balance consisted of hybrid funds. Although 8,184 may seem like a large number of equity and bond funds, there are over 27,000 funds worldwide.

Just as the number of funds has grown, so have their total assets. Excluding money market mutual funds' assets, total mutual fund assets grew from $17.9 billion in 1970 to $570.8 billion in 1990 (an annual compound growth rate of 14.85 percent). The growth then exploded from total assets of $570.8 in 1990 to $5,121.4 billion in 2000 (an annual compound growth rate of 24.5 percent).

Although total assets grew partially in response to higher stock prices, annual net sales (gross sales minus redemptions, which are shares sold back to the fund) also grew rapidly during the 1990s. This growth is illustrated in Figure 8.1 (p. 212), which presents annual net sales from 1970 through 2000. Prior to 1983, annual net sales never exceeded $10 billion. In 2000, net sales exceeded $252 billion, and that large amount was down from the over $300 billion net sales during each of the preceding two years. During the 1970s there were even periods (e.g., 1972–1973) when redemptions exceeded sales, so net sales were negative. These redemptions plus the general decline in the market produced a 23 percent *decrease* in mutual funds' total assets in 1974. However, the bull market of the 1990s plus increased net sales generated unprecedented growth in mutual funds' total assets.[2]

Investment companies receive special tax treatment. Their earnings (i.e., dividends and interest income) and realized capital gains are exempt from taxation.

[1]The services provided by investment companies are enumerated in George Benigno, "At Your Service," *Mutual Funds* (April 1995): 51–54.

[2]The value of closed-end investment companies also grew, but the total value of their assets is less than one-tenth of the value of mutual funds' assets.

FIGURE 8.1

Mutual Funds Net Sales 1970–2000 (in billions)

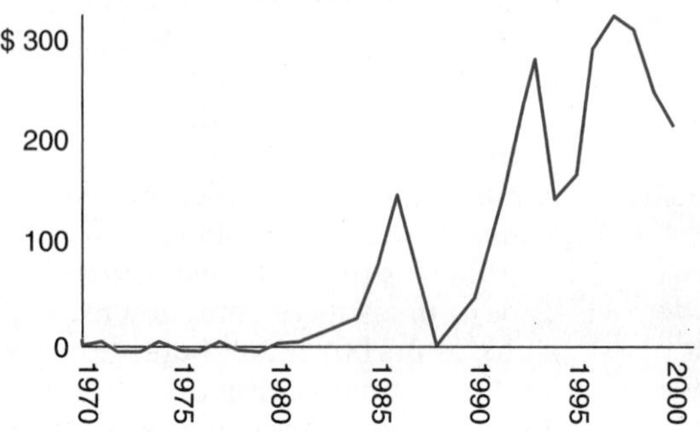

Source: *Mutual Fund Fact Book*, published annually by the Investment Company Institute (http://www.ici.org).

Instead, these profits are taxed through their stockholders' tax returns. Dividends, interest income, and realized capital gains (whether they are distributed or not) of the investment companies must be reported by their shareholders, who pay the appropriate income taxes.

For this reason, income that is received by investment companies and capital gains that are realized are usually distributed. The companies, however, offer their stockholders the option of having the fund retain and reinvest these distributions. While such reinvestments do not erase the stockholders' tax liabilities, they are an easy, convenient means to accumulate shares. The advantages offered by the dividend reinvestment plans of individual firms that will be discussed in Chapter 11 also apply to the dividend reinvestment plans offered by investment companies. Certainly the most important of these advantages is the element of *forced savings.* Because the stockholder does not receive the money, there is no temptation to spend it. Rather, the funds are immediately channeled back into additional income-earning assets.

net asset value
The asset value of a share in an investment company; total assets minus total liabilities divided by the number of shares outstanding.

One term frequently encountered in a discussion of an investment company is its **net asset value**. The asset value of an investment company is the total value of its stocks, bonds, cash, and other assets minus any liabilities (e.g., accrued fees).[3] The net asset value of any share of stock in the investment company is the total asset value of the fund divided by the number of shares outstanding. Thus, net asset value may be obtained as follows:

Value of stock owned	$1,000,000
Value of debt owned	+1,500,000
Value of total assets	$2,500,000
Liabilities	−100,000
Net worth	$2,400,000
Number of shares outstanding	1,000,000
Net asset value per share	$2.40

[3]Some closed- and open-end investment companies use debt financing to leverage the returns for their stockholders. For example, the High Yield Income Fund (a closed-end investment company) reported in its August 31, 2000, *Annual Report* that the fund has a $21,000,000 loan outstanding. This loan was 23 percent of the fund's total assets. The Kaufman Fund (an open-end mutual fund) stated in its May 1, 1998, prospectus that it may borrow funds subject to the provision that the value of assets minus the liabilities is at least 300 percent of the amount borrowed. Although the amount that these investment companies may borrow is modest relative to their assets, such use of margin increases the potential return or loss and increases their stockholders' risk exposure.

The net asset value is extremely important for the valuation of an investment company, for it gives the value of the shares should the company be liquidated. Changes in the net asset value, then, alter the value of the investment company's shares. Thus, if the value of the fund's assets appreciates, the net asset value will increase, which may also cause the price of the investment company's stock to increase.

Closed-End Investment Companies

Based on the number of mutual funds and their total assets, open-end investment companies are more important than closed-end investment companies. This discussion, however, begins with closed-end investment companies. These companies developed before mutual funds, and they have characteristics that are similar to the stocks and bonds traded in the security markets. (Such trading was discussed in Chapter 3).

As was mentioned in the previous section, a closed-end investment company has a set capital structure that may be composed of all stock or a combination of stock and debt. The number of shares and the dollar amount of debts that the company may issue are specified. In an open-end investment company (i.e., a mutual fund), the number of shares outstanding varies as investors purchase and redeem them. Because the closed-end investment company has a specified number of shares, an individual who wants to invest in a particular company must purchase existing shares from current stockholders. Conversely, any investor who owns shares and wishes to liquidate the position must sell the shares. Thus, the shares in closed-end investment companies are bought and sold, just as the stock of IBM is traded. Shares of these companies are traded on the New York Stock Exchange (e.g., Adams Express), on the American Stock Exchange (e.g., First Australia Fund), and in the over-the-counter markets (e.g., Z Seven Fund).

Discounts and Premiums

The market value of these shares is related to the potential return. The market price of stock in a closed-end company, however, need not be the net asset value per share; it may be above or below this value, depending on the demand and the supply of stock in the secondary market. If the market price is below the net asset value of the shares, the shares are selling for a **discount**. If the market price is above the net asset value, the shares are selling for a **premium**.

discount (from net asset value)
The extent to which the price of a closed-end investment company's stock sells below its net asset value.

premium (over net asset value)
The extent to which the price of a closed-end investment company's stock exceeds the share's net asset value.

These differences between the investment company's net asset value per share and the stock price are illustrated in Exhibit 8.1 (p. 214), which gives the price, the net asset value, and the discount or the premium for several closed-end investment companies. Four of the shares sold for a discount (i.e., below their net asset values) and one sold for a premium. The cause of this discount is not really known, but it is believed to be the result of taxation. The potential impact of capital gains taxation on the price of the shares is illustrated in the following example.

A closed-end investment company initially sells stock for $10 per share and uses the proceeds to buy the stock of other companies. If transaction costs are ignored, the net asset value of a share is $10, and the shares may trade in the secondary market for $10. The value of the firm's portfolio subsequently rises to $16 (i.e., the net asset value is $16). The firm has a potential capital gain of $6 per share. If it is realized and these profits are distributed, the net asset value will return to $10 and each stockholder will receive $6 in capital gains, for which he or she will pay the appropriate capital gains tax.

Suppose, however, that the capital gains are not realized (i.e., the net asset value remains at $16). What will the market price of the stock be? This is difficult to determine, but it will probably be below $16. Why? Suppose an investor bought

POINTS OF INTEREST

Initial Public Offerings of Closed-End Investment Companies

As was explained in Chapter 2, the shares of companies are originally sold to the public through investment bankers in an initial public offering (or IPO). The shares of closed-end investment companies are originated through the same process. These shares are initially sold to the public for a *premium* over their net asset value. If the price to the public is $15 and the investment banking fee is $0.85, then the net asset value is reduced from $15.00 to $14.15. In effect, the shares are sold for a premium of 6 percent over their net asset value.

While some initial public offerings do well in the secondary markets, many do not. The prices of these closed-end investment company shares decline until the premium disappears, and the shares may even sell for a discount. The SEC has reported that the shares of bond and stock closed-end investment funds declined 6 and 23 percent, respectively, within the first four months of trading.* These results suggest that it is not prudent to purchase initial offerings of closed-end investment companies. While no satisfactory explanation has been given as to why individuals pay the initial premium, the usual explanation involves the persuasive power of the brokers who sell the securities for the investment bankers.

*See Kathleen Weiss, "The Post-Offering Price Performance of Closed-End Funds," *Financial Management* (autumn 1989): 57–67; and "Closed-End Fund Offerings: Popular but Perilous," *Mutual Funds* (June 1995): 112–115.

EXHIBIT 8.1

Net Asset Values and Market Prices of Selected Closed-End Investment Companies as of July 13, 2001

Company	Price	Net Asset Value	(Discount) or Premium as a Percentage of Net Asset Value
Adams Express	17.52	19.53	(10.3) %
General American Investors	36.30	37.56	(3.4)
Salomon Brothers Fund	14.03	14.79	(5.1)
Tri-Continental	21.54	24.33	(11.5)
Zweig Total Return	9.80	8.59	14.1

Source: *The Wall Street Journal*, July 16, 2001, C16.

a share for $16 and the firm then realized and distributed the $6 capital gain. After the distribution of the $6, the investor would be responsible for any capital gains tax, but the net asset value of the share would decrease to $10.

Obviously this is not advantageous to the buyer. Individuals may be willing to purchase the shares only at a discount that reduces the potential impact of realized capital gains and the subsequent capital gains taxes. Suppose the share had cost $14 (i.e., it sold for a discount of $2 from the net asset value) and the fund realized and distributed the gain. The buyer who paid $14 now owns a share with a net asset value of $10 and receives a capital gain of $6. Although this investor will have to pay the appropriate capital gains tax, the impact is reduced because the investor paid only $14 to purchase the share whose total value is $16 (the $10 net asset value plus the $6 capital gain).

Although many closed-end investment companies sell for a discount, some do sell for a premium. In Exhibit 8.1, Zweig Total Return sold for $9.80 in July 2001, when its net asset value was $8.59, a premium of 14.1 percent above the net asset value. Often, closed-end investment companies that sell for a premium have a specialized portfolio that appeals to some investors. For example, the Spain Fund and the Turkish Fund commanded premiums of 10.2 and 21.4 percent, respectively. These funds invest primarily in countries that place restrictions on foreign investments. If individuals want to acquire shares in firms in these countries (perhaps for potential growth or for diversification purposes), the closed-end investment company is the only viable means to make the investments. The effect may be to bid up the price of the shares so that the closed-end investment company sells for a premium over its net asset value.

Since the shares may sell for a discount or a premium relative to their net asset value, it is possible for the market price of a closed-end investment company to fluctuate more or less than the net asset value. For example, during 1996, the net asset value of Salomon Brothers Fund rose from \$15.43 to \$17.26 (an 11.9 percent increase), but the stock increased 19.6 percent (\$13.375 to \$16.00) as the discount fell from 13.3 to 7.3 percent. Since the market price can change relative to the net asset value, an investor is subject to an additional source of risk. The value of the investment may decline not only because the net asset value may decrease but also because the shares may sell for a larger discount from their net asset value.

Some investors view the market price relative to the net asset value as a guide to buying and selling the shares of a closed-end investment company. If the shares are selling for a sufficient discount, they are considered for purchase. If the shares are selling for a small discount or at a premium, they are sold. Of course, determining the premium that will justify the sale or the discount that will justify the purchase is not simple (and may even be arbitrary).

Sources of Return from Investing in Closed-End Investment Companies

Profits are the difference between costs and revenues. Investing in closed-end investment companies involves several costs. First, since the shares are purchased in the secondary markets, there is the brokerage commission for the purchase and for any subsequent sale. Second, the investment company charges a fee to manage the portfolio. This fee is subtracted from any income that the firm's assets earn. These management fees generally range from 0.5 to 2 percent of the net asset value. Third, when the investment company purchases or sells securities, it also has to pay brokerage fees, which are passed on to the investor.

The purchase of shares in closed-end investment companies thus involves three costs that the investor must bear. Some alternative investments, such as savings accounts in commercial banks, do not involve these costs. Although commission fees are incurred when stock is purchased through a broker, the other expenses associated with a closed-end investment company are avoided.

Investors in closed-end investment companies earn returns in a variety of ways. First, if the investment company collects dividends and interest on its portfolio, this income is distributed to the stockholders in the form of dividends. Second, if the value of the firm's assets increases, the company may sell the assets and realize the gains. These profits are then distributed as capital gains to the stockholders. Such distributions usually occur in a single payment near the end of the calendar year and, for most individuals, the tax year. Third, the net asset value of the portfolio may increase, which will cause the market price of the company's stock to rise. In this case, the investor may sell the shares in the secondary market and realize a capital gain. Fourth, the market price of the shares may rise relative to the net asset value (i.e., the premium may increase or the discount may decrease); the investor may then earn a profit through the sale of the shares.

These sources of return are illustrated in Exhibit 8.2 (p. 216), which presents the distributions and price changes over seven years for Salomon Brothers Fund from

EXHIBIT 8.2

Annual Returns on an Investment in Salomon Brothers Fund, a Closed-End Investment Company

Distributions and Price Changes	2000	1999	1998	1997	1996	1995	1994	1993
Per-share income distributions	0.14	0.18	0.27	$0.27	0.33	0.35	0.33	0.34
Per-share capital gains distributions	2.41	3.63	3.19	$2.63	2.09	1.49	1.39	1.51
Year-end net asset value	16.27	19.24	18.76	$18.51	17.26	15.43	12.88	14.88
Year-end market price	16.25	20.375	18.19	$17.625	16.00	13.375	10.50	12.75
Annual return based on prior year's market price								
a. Dividend yield	0.7	1.0	1.5	1.7%	2.5	3.3	2.6	—
b. Capital gains yield	11.8	20.2	18.1	16.4%	15.6	14.2	10.9	—
c. Change in price	−20.2	12.0	3.2	10.2%	19.6	27.4	−17.6	—
Total return	−7.7	33.2	22.8	28.3%	37.7	44.9	−4.1	—

Source: Salomon Brothers Fund (SBF) annual reports.

December 31, 1993, through December 31, 2000. As may be seen in the exhibit, the investment company distributed cash dividends of $0.27 and capital gains of $2.63 in 1997. The net asset value rose from $17.26 to $18.51, and the price of the stock likewise rose (from $16 to $17.625). An investor who bought the shares on December 31, 1996, earned a total annual return of 28.3 percent (before commissions) on the investment.[4]

The potential for loss is also illustrated in Exhibit 8.2. If the investor bought the shares on December 31, 1999, he or she suffered a loss during 2000. While the fund distributed $0.14 in income and $2.41 in capital gains, the net asset value and the price of the stock declined sufficiently to more than offset the income and capital gains distributions.

Unit Trusts

unit trust
A passive investment company with a fixed portfolio of assets that are self-liquidating.

A variation on the closed-end investment company is the fixed-unit investment trust, commonly referred to as a **unit trust** or unit investment trust (UIT). These trusts, which are formed by brokerage firms and sold to investors in units of $1,000, hold a fixed portfolio of securities. The portfolio is designed to meet a specified investment objective, such as the generation of interest income, in which case the portfolio would include federal government or corporate bonds, municipal bonds, or mortgage loans. An example of such a trust is Merrill Lynch's Government Securities Income Fund, which invests solely in U.S. Treasury securities and other obligations backed by the full faith and credit of the federal government.

A unit trust is a passive investment, as its assets are not traded but are frozen. No new securities are purchased, and securities originally purchased are rarely sold. The trust collects income (e.g., interest on its portfolio) and, eventually, the repayment of principal. The trust is self-liquidating because as the funds are received, they are not reinvested but are distributed to stockholders. Such trusts are primarily attractive to such investors as retirees who seek a steady, periodic flow of payments. If the investor needs the funds earlier, the shares may be sold back to the trust at their current net asset value, which may be lower than the initial cost.

[4]The calculation of the annual return is

$$\frac{\$17.625 + \$0.27 + \$2.63 - \$16}{\$16} = 28.3\%.$$

Unit trusts are primarily of interest to investors whose financial goals are matched by the objectives of the trust. Such individuals acquire shares in a diversified portfolio of assets that are sold in affordable units. Unlike other investment companies, the fixed portfolio means that operating expenses, which would reduce the current flow of income to the owners of the trust, are minimal.

As with any investment, however, unit trusts do have disadvantages. The investor pays an initial up-front fee of 3 to 5 percent when the trust is formed, and even though there are no management fees, the trustees do have custodial and bookkeeping expenses that are paid from the earnings of the trust. Although the trust may acquire high-quality securities, there is no certainty that the bonds will not default. There is the risk that the realized return may be less than anticipated.

The concept of a unit trust has been extended to a broader spectrum of securities. For example, Merrill Lynch developed a trust consisting solely of emerging growth stocks. After a specified period of time, the stocks will be sold and the funds distributed to unit holders. Once again, the trust is a passive investment that holds a portfolio for a specified time period and is liquidated. Such a trust may appeal to an investor seeking capital appreciation through a diversified portfolio but who needs the funds at a specific time in the future (e.g., at retirement). Because the liquidation date is specified, that individual knows when the funds will be received.

Although the investor knows when the funds will be received, he or she does not know the amount. The prices of the stocks held by the trust could rise or fall. If the value of the stocks were to rise, the investor would earn a profit. However, if the prices of the securities were to decline, the trust's management cannot wait beyond the liquidation date for the stocks to recoup their lost value.

Mutual Funds

Although open-end investment companies (*mutual funds*) are similar to closed-end investment companies, there are important differences. The first concerns their capital structure. Shares in mutual funds are not traded in the secondary markets. Instead, an investor purchases shares directly from the fund at the net asset value plus any applicable sales charge. After receiving the money, the mutual fund issues new shares and purchases assets with these newly acquired funds. If an investor owns shares in the fund and wants to liquidate the position, the shares are sold back to the company at the net asset value minus any applicable sales charge. The shares are redeemed, and the fund pays the investor from its cash holdings. If the fund lacks sufficient cash, it will sell some of the securities it owns to obtain the money to redeem the shares. The fund cannot suspend this redemption feature except in an emergency, and then it may be done only with the permission of the Securities and Exchange Commission.

The second difference between closed-end and open-end investment companies is the source of the return to the investor. As with closed-end investment companies, individuals may profit from investments in mutual funds from several sources. Any income that is earned from the fund's assets in excess of expenses is distributed as dividends. If the fund's assets appreciate in value and the fund realizes these profits, the gains are distributed as capital gains. If the net asset value of the shares appreciates, the investor may redeem them at the appreciated price. Thus, in general, the open-end mutual fund offers investors the same means of earning profits as the closed-end investment company does, with one exception. In the case of closed-end investment companies, the price of the stock may rise relative to the net asset value of the shares. The possibility of a decreased discount or an increased premium is a potential source of profit that is available only through closed-end investment companies. It does not exist for mutual funds because their shares never sell at a discount. (They actually sell for a premium if a sales charge is added to the net asset value.) Hence, changes in the discount or premium are a source of profit or loss to investors in closed-end but not in open-end investment companies.

A third important difference between open-end and closed-end investment companies pertains to the cost of investing. Mutual funds continuously offer to sell new shares, and these shares may be sold at their net asset value plus a sales fee, which is commonly called a *loading charge* (also called a *load fee* or simply *load*). This cost and others, such as the 12b-1 fee covered later in this chapter, are disclosed in the fund's prospectus. When the investor liquidates the position, the shares are redeemed at their net asset value. For most funds no additional fees are charged for the sale.

no-load mutual fund
A mutual fund that does not charge a commission for buying or selling its shares.

load fund
A mutual fund that charges a commission to purchase or sell its shares.

The loading fee may range from zero for **no-load mutual funds** to between 3 and 6 percent for **load funds**. If the individual makes a substantial investment, the loading fee is usually reduced. For example, the American Balanced Fund (ABALX, or http://www.americanfunds.com) offers the following schedule of fees:

Investment	Fee
$0–50,000	5.75%
over 50,000	4.5
over 100,000	3.5
over 250,000	2.5

The investor should be warned that mutual funds state the loading charge as a percentage of the *offer* price. For example, if the net asset value is $20 and the loading charge is 5.75 percent, then the offer price is $20/(1 − 0.0575) = $21.22. Since the loading fee is based on the offer price, then you pay a fee of $1.22, which is 5.75 percent of the offer price (0.0575 × $21.22 = $1.22). The effect of the fee being a percentage of the offer price and not a percentage of the net asset value is to increase the effective percentage charged. If American Balanced Fund's loading charge is 5.75 percent, the effective loading charge based on the net asset value is 5.75%/(1 − 0.575) = 5.75/0.9425 = 6.1%, which is higher than the stated 5.75 percent loading charge. (The effective rate may also be determined by dividing the load fee by the net asset value. In this example, that is $1.22/$20 = 6.1%.)

In addition to loading charges, investors in mutual funds have to pay a variety of other expenses. Each mutual fund is required to disclose in its prospectus these various costs, which are generally referred to as "fees and expenses." The costs associated with researching specific assets, brokerage fees charged when the fund buys and sells securities, and compensation to management are all costs that the investor must bear. These expenses are the cost of owning the shares and are in addition to any sales fees (loading charges) the investor pays when the shares are purchased. The costs of owning the shares are generally expressed as a percentage of the fund's assets. A total expense ratio of 1.6 percent tells the investor that the fund's expenses are $1.60 for every $100 of assets. It should be obvious that the fund must earn at least $1.60 for each $100 in assets just to cover these costs, so if a fund earns 11.2 percent on its assets, the investor nets 9.6 percent.

The fees and expenses for three no-load mutual funds (Legg Mason High Yield Portfolio, Legg Mason Total Return Trust, and Schwab International Index Fund) are illustrated in Exhibit 8.3. The first three rows list the fees related to purchasing the shares. Because all three funds are no-load funds, there are no sales costs, but the Schwab International Fund does have a fee for early withdrawals. Such exit fees are designed to discourage frequent redemptions by investors seeking short-term gains. If the investor holds the shares for six months, the charge does not apply.

EXHIBIT 8.3

Cost Disclosures for Selected No-Load Mutual Funds

	Legg Mason High Yield Portfolio	Legg Mason Total Return Trust	Schwab International Index Fund
Sales load	None	None	None
Early withdrawal fees	None	None	0.75%
Exchange fees	None	None	None
Management fees	0.65%	0.75%	0.45
Operating expenses	0.44	0.19	0.50
12b-1 fees	0.50	1.00	None
Total expenses	1.59	1.91	0.95

Sources: Each fund's prospectus.

The management fee compensates the investment advisor for the general management of the fund's affairs. This fee generally runs from 0.5 to 1.0 percent of the fund's assets. Operating expenses cover record keeping, transaction costs, directors' fees, and legal and auditing expenses. The sum of these expenses tends to range from 0.3 to 0.7 percent of the fund's assets; including management and other expenses, the range increases to 0.8 to 1.7 percent of the fund's assets.

While management and other expenses are necessary fees, 12b-1 fees are nonessential costs. As is discussed later in this chapter, these are special charges for marketing and distribution services and may include commissions to brokers who sell the shares. The Schwab fund does not have a 12b-1 fee, but the two Legg Mason funds do. In contrast to the Legg Mason full-service brokerage firm, Schwab's brokers do not work on commission. The 12b-1 fee then compensates the Legg Mason brokers for selling the shares and covers any other expenses associated with advertising and marketing the fund. (The 12b-1 fee is discussed in the section on returns.)

The Portfolios of Mutual Funds

The portfolios of investment companies may be diversified or specialized, but most may be classified into various types, such as income, growth, special situations, and balanced. Income funds stress assets that produce income; they buy stocks and bonds that pay generous dividends or interest income. The Value Line Income Fund is an example of a fund whose objective is income. Virtually all of its assets are income stocks, such as those of utilities, which distribute a large proportion of their earnings and periodically increase the dividend as their earnings grow.

Growth funds stress appreciation in the value of the assets, and little emphasis is given to current income. The portfolio of the Value Line Fund is an example of a growth fund. The majority of the assets are the common stocks of companies with potential for growth. These growth stocks include the shares of very well known firms as well as those of smaller firms that may offer superior growth potential.

Even within the class of growth funds there can be many differences. Some stress riskier securities in order to achieve larger returns and faster appreciation in their investors' funds. For example, Janus Venture seeks capital appreciation by investing in smaller companies. Other growth funds, however, are more conservative. The

POINTS OF INTEREST

Services Offered by Mutual Funds

Custodial services, such as monthly statements and the reinvestment of dividends and capital gains distributions, are obvious services offered by mutual funds. These funds, however, offer the investor other services, designed to encourage the investor to acquire shares in that particular fund or family of funds. Some of these services include check writing and credit cards to access money market funds. While subject to a minimum amount, the money market fund may pay a rate of interest higher than that available through an interest-bearing checking account with a commercial bank. A fund may offer an automatic investment or an automatic withdrawal plan in which money is transferred from or to the investor's checking account.

Other possible services include direct deposit of payroll checks, access to automated teller machines, telephone or on-line exchange of shares from one fund to another within a family of funds, telephone redemption of shares, statements sent to a third party (such as an accountant or financial planner), trading through a personal computer, cross reinvestment (in which the distributions from one fund are used to purchase shares in another fund), and faxed transactions.

Not all funds offer all services, and changes in technology and customer demand will affect which services continue to be offered. The investor, however, should realize that the costs of the services are hidden in the fund's expenses and thus reduce the return the fund earns. Individuals who do not need or want these services are, in effect, subsidizing those who do use them.

Fidelity Fund is a growth fund emphasizing larger companies that still are considered to offer capital appreciation but whose earnings are more stable and reliable.

Special situation investment companies specialize in more speculative securities that, given the "special situation," may yield large returns but require the investor to bear more risk. The portfolio of Value Line Special Situations Fund illustrates this element of risk. The stocks in this portfolio tend to be in small companies or companies that have fallen on bad times but whose course may be changing. Investments in special situation securities can be very rewarding, but some do not fulfill their potential return.

Balanced funds own a mixture of securities that sample the attributes of the assets of other mutual funds. A balanced fund, such as the Fidelity Balanced Fund, owns a variety of stocks, some of which offer potential growth while others are primarily income producers. A balanced portfolio may also include short-term debt (such as U.S. Treasury bills), long-term debt, and preferred stock. Such a portfolio seeks a balance of income from dividends and interest and capital appreciation.

Mutual funds may also be classified according to *investment style*. Investment style refers to a portfolio manager's investment philosophy or investment strategy. Possible styles include the size of firms acquired by the fund or the approach (growth or value) used to select the firms.

Firm size refers to *large cap, mid-cap,* or *small cap*. The word "cap" is short for *capitalization,* which refers to the market value of the company. The market value is the number of shares outstanding times the market price. Large cap stocks are the largest companies, with market value exceeding $5 billion. A small cap stock is a much smaller firm, perhaps with a total value of less than $1 billion. Mid-cap is, of course, between the two extremes. Actually the difference among a small cap, a mid-cap, and a large cap stock is arbitrary. A small cap stock could be less than $1 billion, less than $500 million, or less than $300 million total market value, depending on whose value is being used. (Some classifications divide stocks into large cap and small cap and exclude mid-cap, and there are classifications that include micro- or mini-cap for even smaller firms.)

POINTS OF INTEREST

The Internet and Information Concerning Mutual Funds

As you might expect, the Internet can be a major source of information concerning mutual funds. Presumably, all mutual funds post information on the Internet and have Web addresses. While shares are usually purchased directly from the fund through brokers or direct withdrawals from a bank account, most funds will also execute transactions on-line. (Don't, however, conclude that on-line purchases of a load fund let you avoid paying the sales charge. You still pay the load fee but instead of the payment going to a salesperson, it is kept by the fund.)

Besides the funds themselves, possible on-line sources of information include

American Association of Individual Investors:
http://www.aaii.com

Bloomberg L.P.:
http://www.bloomberg.com

ICI Mutual Fund Connection:
http://www.ici.org

Morningstar:
http://www.morningstar.net

Mutual Fund Investor's Center:
http://www.mfea.com

Mutual Funds Magazine Online:
http://www.mfmag.com

Quicken Financial Network:
http://www.quicken.com

Value Line Investment Research and Asset Management:
http://www.valueline.com

Yahoo! Finance:
http://quote.yahoo.com

These sources offer basic information such as net assets, performance measures, and comparisons. Several offer links to other sites. For example, *Mutual Fund* magazine's site (http://www.mfmag.com) provides links to a mutual fund's site and to other fund services such as Morningstar.

Two companies that use paper or produce paper products illustrate this difference in size. Chesapeake Corporation (CSK), a manufacturer of specialty displays, has 15.1 million shares outstanding; at a price of $23, the total value of the stock is $347.3 million and would be classified as a small cap stock. Georgia Pacific (GP), a manufacturer of disposable paper products and building supplies, has 224.7 million shares outstanding. At a price of $34, the total value is $7.4 billion and would be classified as a large cap stock. It is obvious that CSK is small compared to GP and would not be an acceptable investment for a large cap portfolio even if the portfolio manager believed that the stock was undervalued.

An alternative strategy to capitalization-based investing is *style investing* based on *growth* or *value.* A growth fund portfolio manager identifies firms offering exceptional growth by employing techniques that analyze an industry's growth potential and the firm's position within the industry. A value manager acquires stock that is undervalued or "cheap." A value approach stresses fundamental analysis and is based on investment tools such as P/E ratios and comparisons of financial statements. (Contrarian investors may be considered value investors since they are identifying strong stocks that are currently out of favor with the investment community.) Many technology stocks illustrate the difference between the growth and value approaches. During 1998, Amazon.com appealed to many growth portfolio managers because the company was the first to market books via the Internet and had large growth potential. From a value perspective, the firm had no earnings and was selling substantially above its value based on its accounting statements. Such a stock appealed to few value investors.

A fund can have more than one style, such as "small cap–value," which suggests that the portfolio manager acquires shares in small companies that appear to be undervalued. A "small cap–growth" fund would stress small companies offering potential growth but not necessarily operating at a profit.

While various investment styles may seem complementary, a portfolio manager's style can be important, especially when evaluating performance. Presumably, a style portfolio manager offers the investor two things: (1) the style and (2) the investment skill. If a portfolio manager's style stresses small cap growth, that fund's performance should not be compared to the performance of large cap funds. Only through a consistent comparison of funds with similar strategies or styles can the portfolio manager's investment skill be isolated.

The Portfolios of Specialized Mutual Funds

Investment trusts initially sought to pool the funds of many savers to create a diversified portfolio of assets. Such diversification spread the risk of investing and reduced the risk of loss to the individual investor. While a particular investment company had a specified goal, such as growth or income, the portfolio was still sufficiently diversified so that the element of firm-specific, unsystematic risk was reduced.

Today, however, a variety of funds have developed that have moved away from this concept of diversification and the reduction of risk. Instead of offering investors a cross section of American business, many funds have been created to offer investors specialized investments. For example, an investment company may be limited to investments in the securities of a particular sector of the economy (e.g., Fidelity Select Multimedia) or a particular industry, such as gold (e.g., INVESCO Gold). There are also funds that specialize in a particular type of security, such as bonds (e.g., American General Bond Fund).

While these funds have a specialization in a sector, industry, or security, they are usually diversified within their area of concentration. For example, a high-yield bond fund may acquire poor-quality bonds, but the fund would own a variety of these bonds issued by different firms in different industries. Thus, the portfolio is diversified even though the fund is specialized. For example, in 2000, the Corporate High Yield Fund reported in its *2000 Annual Report* that it held bonds issued by over 100 companies in almost 40 different industries. While its portfolio would certainly react to changes in interest rates and to changes in the market for high-yield securities, the impact of one specific bond on the portfolio as a whole would be marginal.

There are, however, a few funds that are not well diversified and have a portfolio focused on a few securities. The FPA Paramount Fund, the Sequoia Fund, and the Yacktman Fund each have fewer than 20 stocks in their portfolios. If the fund's management selects well, the fund can achieve high returns. The converse, however, is also true. By focusing on only a few investments, the ability of diversification to reduce the variability of returns is diminished; a focused fund's return may be exceptionally high during one period and exceptionally low during another.[5]

In addition to funds with specialized portfolios, there are also other investment companies that offer individuals real alternatives to the traditional, diversified stock mutual fund. The money market fund (discussed in Chapter 2) provides a means to invest in money market securities. Funds that acquire foreign securities permit the individual to have foreign investments without having to acquire foreign stocks. (The discussion of these funds is deferred to Chapter 22 on international investments.) Other examples of specialized funds that help investors manage risk or participate in other markets include the index fund, the exchange-traded fund, and the municipal bond fund.

[5]The success achieved by Warren Buffett is partially the result of his using a focused approach. The stock portfolio of Berkshire Hathaway consists of fewer than ten stocks and is heavily weighted with Coca-Cola. The composition of the Buffett portfolio is chronicled in Robert G. Hagstrom, *The Warren Buffett Portfolio: Mastering the Power of the Focus Investment Strategy* (New York: John Wiley & Sons, Inc., 1999).

index fund
A mutual fund whose portfolio seeks to duplicate an index of stock prices.

An **index fund** duplicates a particular measure (index) of the market. The fund's purpose is almost diametrically opposed to the traditional purpose of a mutual fund. Instead of identifying specific securities for purchase, the managements of these funds seek to duplicate the composition of an index of the market. The Vanguard Index Trust–500 Portfolio is based on the Standard & Poor's 500 stock index. Other funds seek to duplicate different indexes. The Vanguard Index Trust–Extended Market Portfolio seeks to duplicate the Wilshire 4500 stock index, which is even more broadly based than the S&P 500 stock index. Some index funds are less broadly based, such as the Rushmore Over-the-Counter Index Plus. This index, based on the Nasdaq 100 stock index, is limited to the 100 largest over-the-counter stocks. (The composition of stock indices is covered in Chapter 10.)

exchange-traded fund
A mutual fund whose shares are traded in the secondary markets.

An **exchange-traded fund (ETF)** is a mutual fund whose shares are bought and sold on an exchange such as the New York Stock Exchange. Unlike the traditional mutual fund, whose shares are bought from the fund and redeemed through the fund, the shares of an ETF may be traded in the secondary markets just like the shares of IBM. This ability to trade funds gives the investor flexibility. When an investor buys or redeems a mutual fund's shares, the investor may not execute the transactions at specified prices. Instead, the shares are bought (or sold) at the end of the day when the fund's net asset value is determined. If an investor wanted to liquidate a position during the day in response to a declining market, such a sale could not occur.[6] Instead, the investor would receive the net asset value at the end of the trading day, and the prices of the underlying stocks and the fund's net asset value could be lower.

Exchange-traded funds overcome this possible disadvantage associated with mutual funds. The investor may buy and sell at will. The individual may also establish limit orders that specify prices at which to buy and sell shares, enter stop-loss orders, and buy the shares using margin. The investor may even sell the shares short. (Mutual fund shares cannot be purchased on margin and cannot be sold short because there is no market for the shares.)

Currently, exchange-traded funds are variations on index funds. Like all index funds, they are a means to take a position in the market without having to select specific securities. While investors may buy and sells ETFs in an attempt to time changes in the market, they are essentially tools for portfolio and risk management. For this reason, ETFs will be discussed in more detail in Chapter 24 on portfolio management.

Another recently introduced specialized mutual fund is the investment company whose portfolio is devoted to tax-exempt bonds. Until 1976, open-end mutual funds were legally barred from this market. However, with the passage of enabling legislation, mutual funds were permitted to own tax-exempt bonds, and several funds were immediately started to specialize in these securities. These funds offer investors, especially those with modest funds to invest, an opportunity to earn tax-free income while maintaining a diversified portfolio. Municipal bonds are sold in units of $5,000, and minimum purchases may require $10,000 or more. Thus, a sizable sum is required for an individual to obtain a diversified portfolio. Ten bonds of ten different state and local governments could cost $100,000, making the advantages of tax-free income and a well-diversified portfolio virtually impossible for many investors. Investment companies that specialize in tax-exempt bonds offer a means to overcome this problem, since the funds are sold in smaller denominations and their portfolios are diversified.

[6] This inability of investors to time their purchases and sales of mutual fund shares is not necessarily a disadvantage from the fund's perspective. If the fund had a large influx of sell orders during the day, the management might be forced to sell large blocks of stock into a declining market.

POINTS OF INTEREST

Family Funds and Supermarkets

One major trend in financial services is to offer investors a wide variety of products from the same financial institution. Along with their traditional services and products, many commercial banks offer brokerage services, mutual funds, pension plans, trust departments, life insurance, and a single encompassing financial statement that summarizes the investor's positions. Brokerage firms have also created similar packages of products, some of which (e.g., Merrill Lynch) they have developed themselves. In other cases (e.g., Charles Schwab), the brokerage firm teams with mutual fund sponsors to offer investors a laundry list of financial products.

One means to obtain information concerning a mutual fund is to contact its sponsor, especially if the fund is a member of a family. The following lists the Web addresses of several sponsors. From the sponsor's address you may access information concerning individual funds. All the following sponsors offer funds that are covered in *The Individual Investor's Guide to Low-Load Mutual Funds.* This publication excludes funds with selling expenses in excess of 3 percent and provides a snapshot of each fund's performance and risk. (Inclusion in the following list does not imply superior performance nor does exclusion imply the opposite.)

American Century
http://www.americancentury.com
Columbia Funds
http://www.columbiafunds.com
Dreyfus
http://www.dreyfus.com
Fidelity Investments
http://www.fidelity.com
Founders
http://www.founders.com
Gabelli Asset Management Inc.
http://www.gabelli.com
Galaxy Funds
http://www.galaxyfunds.com
Janus
http://www.janus.com
Midas Funds
http://www.midasfunds.com
The Montgomery Funds
http://www.montgomeryfunds.com
Neuberger Berman
http://www.nbfunds.com
RS Investments
http://www.rsim.com
Scudder Investments
http://www.scudder.com
Strong
http://www.strong-funds.com
T. Rowe Price
http://www.troweprice.com
The Vanguard Group
http://www.vanguard.com

Most mutual funds are created by investment management companies that administer money for institutional investors (e.g., pension plans, foundations, and endowments) and individuals. These money management firms include commercial banks, insurance companies, or investment counsel firms (e.g., Fidelity Investments). After a mutual fund is created, it has its own portfolio managers who select the assets included in the fund's portfolio. The originating investment management company then becomes an investment advisor to the fund.

Many investment management firms offer a wide spectrum of mutual funds, often referred to as a "family of funds." (See the accompanying Points of Interest box.) Each fund has a separate financial goal and hence a different portfolio designed to achieve the fund's objective. For example, Fidelity Investments offers investors the opportunity to choose among over 125 different mutual funds covering a wide spectrum of alternatives. An investor seeking income may acquire shares in an equity income fund, a government bond fund, or a corporate bond fund. These varied investments give the individual a diversified portfolio of income-earning assets.

In addition to offering a variety of funds from which to choose, a family of funds generally permits the individual to shift investments from one fund to another within the family without paying fees. An individual currently invested in a growth fund may shift to an income fund upon retiring. Such a shift can be achieved by redeeming the shares in the growth fund and buying shares in the income fund. While the redemption is a taxable event (unless the shares are in a tax-deferred account), the switch may be made without the investor paying commissions (i.e., load charges) on the transactions.

The Returns Earned on Investments in Mutual Funds

As was previously explained, the securities of investment companies offer individuals several advantages. First, the investor receives the advantages of a diversified portfolio, which reduces risk. Some investors may lack the resources to construct a diversified portfolio, and the purchase of shares in an investment company permits these investors to own a portion of a diversified portfolio. Second, the portfolio is professionally managed and under continuous supervision. Many investors may not have the time, desire, or expertise to manage their own portfolios and, except in the case of large portfolios, may lack the funds to obtain professional management. By purchasing shares in an investment company, individuals buy the services of professional management, which may increase the investor's return. Third, the administrative detail and custodial aspects of the portfolio are performed by the management of the company.

However, there are also disadvantages to using investment companies. Their services are not unique but may be obtained elsewhere. For example, the trust department of a commercial bank offers professional management and custodial services, and leaving the securities with the broker and registering them in the broker's name relieves the investor of storing the securities and keeping some of the records. In addition, the investor may acquire a diversified portfolio with only a modest amount of capital. Diversification does not require 100 different stocks. If the investor has $20,000, a reasonably diversified portfolio may be produced by investing in the stock of eight to ten companies in different industries. One does not have to purchase shares in an investment company to obtain the advantage of diversification.

Investment companies do offer the advantage of professional management, but this management cannot guarantee to outperform the market. A particular fund may do well in any given year, but it may do poorly in subsequent years. Several studies have been undertaken to determine if professional management results in superior performance for mutual funds.

The first study, conducted for the SEC, covered the period from 1952 through 1958.[7] This study found that the performance of mutual funds was not significantly different from that of an unmanaged portfolio of similar assets. About half the funds outperformed Standard & Poor's indices, but the other half underperformed these aggregate measures of the market. In addition, there was no evidence of superior performance by a particular fund over a number of years. These initial results were confirmed by later studies.[8] When loading charges are included in the analysis, the return earned by investors tends to be less than that which would be achieved through a random selection of securities.

More recent studies generated somewhat different conclusions. Even if funds in the aggregate do not outperform the market, some individual funds—or "hot

[7]See Irwin Friend et al., *A Study of Mutual Funds* (Washington, DC: U.S. Government Printing Office, 1962).

[8]See, for instance, William F. Sharpe, "Mutual Fund Performance," *Journal of Business*, special supplement, 39 (January 1966): 119–138; Michael C. Jensen, "The Performance of Mutual Funds in the Period 1945–64," *Journal of Finance* 23 (May 1968): 389–416; Patricia Dunn and Rolf D. Theisen, "How Consistently Do Active Managers Win?" *Journal of Portfolio Management* 9 (summer 1983): 47–50; and Frank J. Fabozzi, Jack C. Francis, and Cheng F. Lee, "Generalized Functional Form for Mutual Fund Performance," *Journal of Financial and Quantitative Analysis* 15 (December 1980): 1107–1120.

FIGURE 8.2

Annual Percentage Returns, 1985–2000

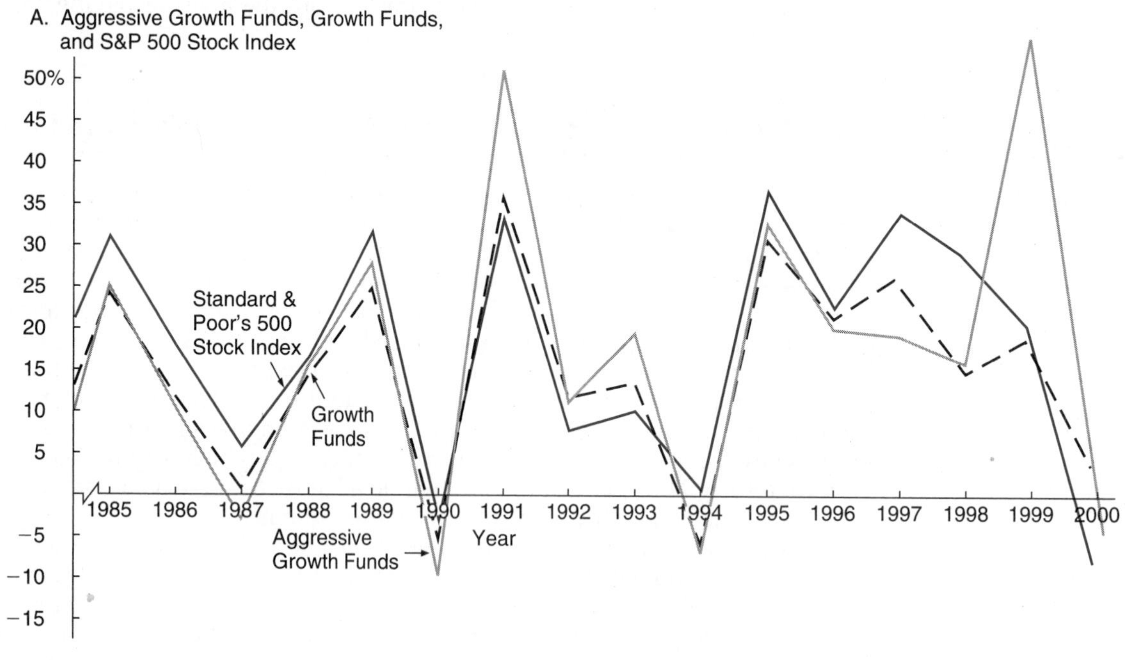

hands"—may earn higher returns and continue to perform well.[9] If this is true, an obvious strategy would be to acquire shares in the best-performing mutual funds in one period in the expectation that their performance will repeat in the next period. However, additional studies have indicated that while persistence may be documented during the 1970s, such a pattern of performance did not continue.[10] Investment strategies designed to take advantage of the alleged consistency of returns failed to earn higher returns. Once again, the general conclusion appears to be that investments in mutual funds do not offer superior returns.

These results are mirrored in the graphs presented in Figure 8.2, which plots annual returns for 1985 through 2000 earned by various types of no-load mutual funds and the Standard & Poor's 500 stock index. (As is discussed in Chapter 10, the S&P 500 stock index is composed of the largest firms traded on the exchanges or through Nasdaq.) The returns include change in net asset value and all distributions. Part A gives the annual returns of funds classified as aggressive growth and growth. The primary emphasis of these funds is appreciation of capital and not generation of current income. Aggressive growth funds may take a considerable amount of risk, such as buying and selling options, to obtain their specified investment goal.

[9]See, for instance, William N. Goetzmann and Roger Ibbotson, "Do Winners Repeat? Patterns in Mutual Fund Behavior," Yale University Working Paper, 1991; Mark Grinblatt and Sheridan Titman, "The Persistence of Mutual Fund Performance," *Journal of Finance* (December 1992): 1977–1984; and Darryll Hendricks, Jayendu Patel, and Richard Zeckhauser, "Hot Hand in Mutual Funds: Short-Run Persistence of Relative Performance," *Journal of Finance* (March 1993), 93–130.

[10]See Burton G. Malkiel, "Return from Investing in Equity Mutual Funds 1971–1991," Center for Economic Policy Studies Working Paper No. 15, December 1993; and Thomas M. Krueger and Richard E. Callaway, "The Persistence of Three-Year Mutual Fund Performance," *Journal of Financial Planning* (July 1995): 136–141.

FIGURE 8.2 CONTINUED

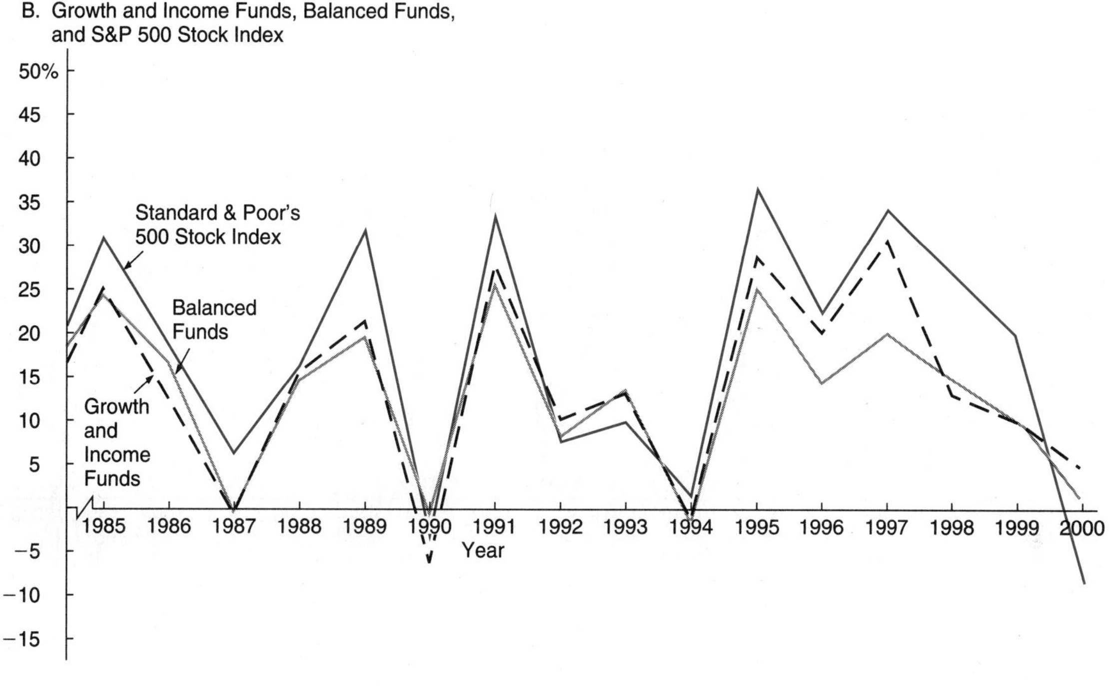

Part B presents the aggregate annual returns for no-load funds stressing growth and income and funds with balanced portfolios. These funds have portfolios with less market risk than the portfolios of those funds seeking capital appreciation. Such funds tend to perform better than more aggressive funds during declining markets (such as in 1990).

Part C compares the annual returns on international funds whose portfolios are invested solely in foreign securities to the returns on the S&P 500. As is explained in Chapter 22 on international investments, fluctuations in the value of currencies affect the yields on foreign investments. If the value of the dollar declines relative to other currencies, these moneys are worth more when they are converted into dollars. During the 1980s, the dollar declined relative to foreign currencies, which may help explain the international funds' exceptional performance in the mid-1980s. However, when the dollar declined dramatically against the yen and the German mark during 1994, the international funds generated a loss while the S&P 500 achieved a small positive return.

Exhibit 8.4 (p. 228) provides annualized, five-year returns and their standard deviations for the five classes of funds (as reported by the American Association of Individual Investors) in Figure 8.2. All five groups earned returns that were less than the Standard & Poor's 500 stock index. In addition, the variability of the index return (i.e., its standard deviation) was less than the variability of the returns for the growth, aggressive growth, and international funds. Perhaps what is most surprising is that the aggressive growth funds earned inferior returns to the growth funds and were riskier. During the time period, additional risk does not appear to have been rewarded.

Individuals, however, do not earn the return achieved by an aggregation of funds. Individuals choose specific funds, whose performance could have been

FIGURE 8.2 CONTINUED

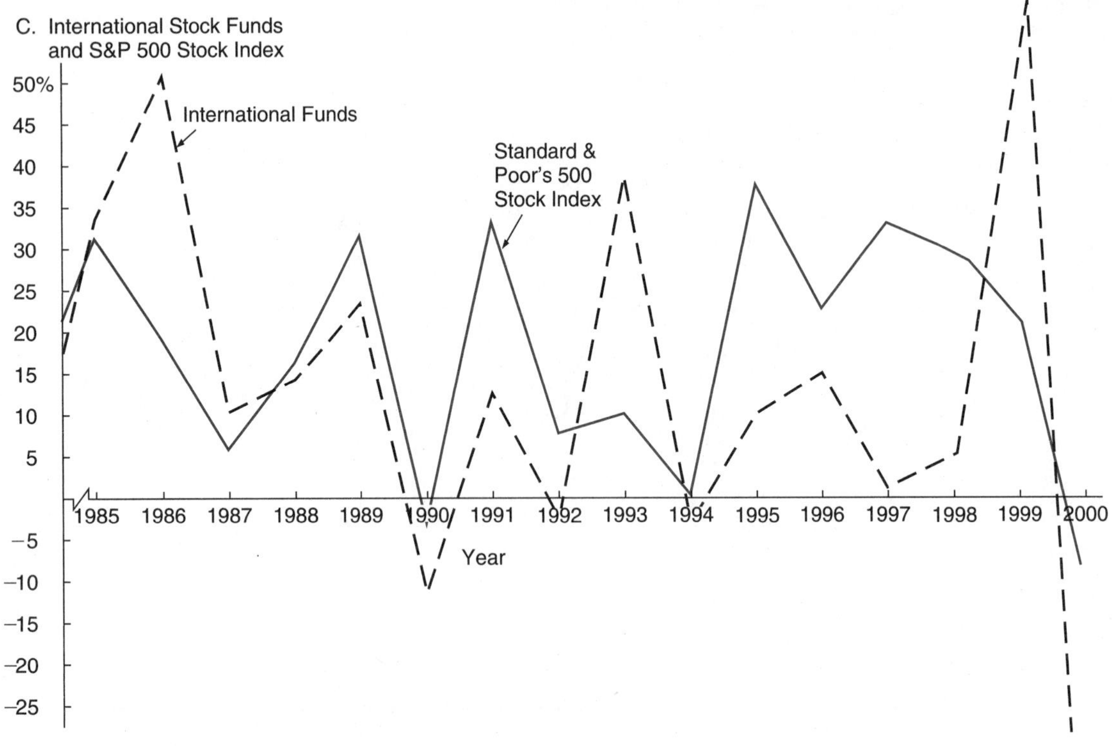

Source: *The Individual Investor's Guide to No-Load Mutual Funds,* 8th, 14th, 17th, and 20th eds. (Chicago: American Association of Individual Investors, 1989, 1995, 1998, and 2001).

EXHIBIT 8.4

Returns on Various Types of Low-Load and No-Load Mutual Funds (1996–2000)

Fund Classification	Return	Standard Deviation of Return
Growth	16.1%	19.5%
Growth and income	14.3	17.4
Aggressive growth	14.6	32.5
Balanced	11.4	11.0
International	8.3	22.7
Standard & Poor's 500 stock index	18.3	17.7

Source: *The Individual Investor's Guide to Low-Load Mutual Funds,* 20th ed. (Chicago: American Association of Individual Investors, 2001), p. 30.

better or worse than the average returns presented in Figure 8.2. This is illustrated in Figure 8.3, which presents the annual returns for the Liberty Acorn/Z Fund and the USAA Mutual Growth Fund. As may be seen in the figure, the Acorn Fund did better over the time period than the USAA Growth Fund. If the investor had selected the Liberty Acorn/Z Fund in 1990 and held it through 2000, his or her

FIGURE 8.3

Annual Percentage Returns 1985–2000, Liberty Acorn/Z Fund and USAA Mutual Growth Fund

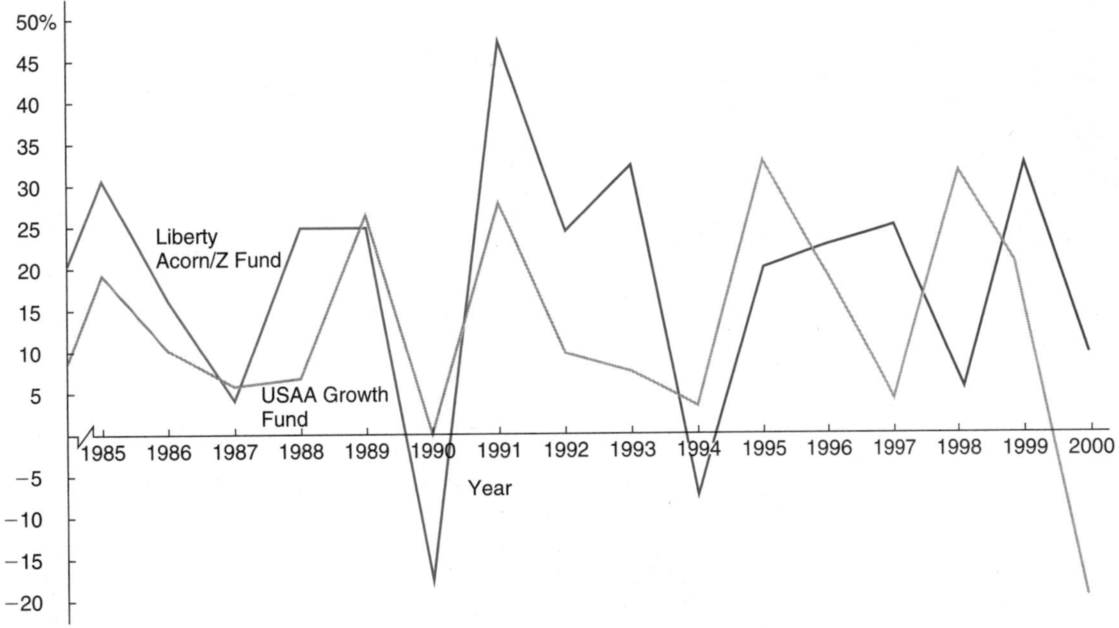

Source: *The Individual Investor's Guide to No-Load Mutual Funds*, 8th, 14th, 17th, and 20th eds. (Chicago: American Association of Individual Investors, 1989, 1995, 1998, and 2001).

investment would have yielded a higher return than an investment in the USAA Mutual Growth Fund during the same time period.

Fund performance may also vary during rising and falling markets. A fund that has historically done well during a rising market may be an inferior performer during declining markets. The period used in Figure 8.3 was a time of positive returns, and the *Individual Investor's Guide to Low-Load Mutual Funds* ranks both Acorn and USAA Mutual Growth Fund as less than average performers during rising markets but ranks USAA Mutual Growth Fund as above average during declining markets.[11] If the investor could forecast which type of market was going to occur, that individual could switch between the two funds.

Such successful market timing should increase returns earned by individuals or professional investment managers. However, empirical evidence suggests that few managers are able to achieve superior timing.[12] These findings are consistent with the prior studies of investment performance by mutual funds. In the aggregate, the returns earned by mutual funds over a period of years do not exceed the return earned by the market as a whole.

[11]*The Individual Investor's Guide to Low-Load Mutual Funds* is published annually by the American Association of Individual Investors, but this publication is limited to no-load and low-load funds. *Forbes,* in its annual issue devoted to mutual funds, ranks both load and no-load funds with regard to their performance in up and down markets. Another means to compare fund performance in rising and declining markets is to ask this question: If $10,000 were invested in the fund, how much would the investor have after five years or ten years, assuming all dividends and capital gains distributions are reinvested? *Barron's* publishes the answer to that question in its periodic reviews of mutual fund performance.

[12]Roy D. Hendriksson, "Market Timing and Mutual Fund Performance: An Empirical Investigation," *Journal of Business* 57 (January 1984): 73–96; and Stanley J. Kon, "The Market-Timing Performance of Mutual Fund Managers," *Journal of Business* 56 (July 1983): 323–347.

POINTS OF INTEREST

The Regulation of Mutual Funds

Mutual funds operate under the Investment Company Act of 1940, which is administered by the Securities and Exchange Commission. The general purpose of this regulation is the same as that which applies to the securities market: the disclosure of information so the individual investor can make an informed decision. Mutual funds must register their shares with the SEC and provide prospective shareholders with a prospectus. The prospectus specifies the fund's investment objectives, the composition of its portfolio, fees and expenses that the investor pays, the composition of the fund's board of directors, and insider transactions.

Regulation does not specify maximum fees nor does it apply to the execution of the fund's objective or its performance. It is assumed that excessive fees or poor performance will lead to the demise of the fund, just as the poor management of a firm will lead to its failure. Regulation cannot ensure that investors will earn profits, nor does it protect them from their own folly or greed.

These results are easy to misinterpret. They do not imply that the managements of mutual funds are incompetent. The findings give support for the efficient market hypothesis discussed in Chapter 9. In an efficient market, only competent managers would be able to match the market over a period of years. The incompetent would be forced out by their inferior results.

What these findings imply is that mutual funds and other investment companies may offer investors a means to match the performance of the market and still obtain the advantages of diversification and custodial services. For many individuals, these are sufficient reasons to invest in the shares of investment companies instead of directly in stocks and bonds. These investors do not have to concern themselves with the selection of individual securities.

Impact of Income Taxes and Fees on the Investor's Return

The previous section considered returns earned by groups of mutual funds. These were aggregations, so the investor need not have earned the same returns. Even if the discussion had covered the return earned by every specific fund, the fund's return and the investor's need not be the same. This statement should be obvious since the investor would have to make the investment on the same starting or base day and reinvest all distributions. Even if the individual invested on the same day and reinvested all distributions, the statement would still apply since mutual funds' reported returns are before taxes and load charges.

Taxation

Mutual fund earnings and capital gains are not taxed at the fund level. Instead, the fund's distributions are taxed as income or capital gains through the shareholders' tax returns. (See the appendix to this chapter on the determination of taxes owed.) The mutual fund could not know its stockholders' tax brackets, which would differ among the various taxpayers, and reports return on a before-tax basis rather than an after-tax basis. The investors, however, need to be aware that the return reported by the fund is a before-tax return and is not comparable to the after-tax return the investor realizes.

Consider a case in which a fund has a net asset value of $10 when an individual in the 28 percent tax bracket acquires 100 shares. The fund earns $1 a share, which

POINTS OF INTEREST

Retaining Your Mutual Fund Statements

While the IRS requires that you retain your 1040 for only three years, you must retain information concerning the cost of your investments until it is needed to complete your tax forms. If, for example, you purchased a stock for $1,000 in 1965, you should retain the purchase confirmation because the cost basis of the stock is necessary to complete your 1040 when the stock is sold. (The confirmation statement will also verify the cost in case of an audit.) This retention principle applies to mutual fund statements, especially if you are reinvesting distributions.

Distributions are taxed even though they may be reinvested. If you do not retain these statements indicating the purchases, you will not have the cost basis to complete the required tax forms. You may even forget that the shares were purchased with after-tax funds and pay tax on the entire proceeds of the sale. Failure to retain mutual fund statements only increases the probability that you will be unaware of the cost basis of your shares.

If you take distributions in cash and do not reinvest them, the need to retain statements to determine the cost basis is eliminated. You may find this less burdensome, especially when receiving monthly distributions from a fixed-income fund and making periodic share purchases by check. And, of course, if the shares are held in your tax-deferred retirement account and distributions are reinvested, there are no tax implications until you withdraw the funds—at which time the entire distribution is taxed, and the cost basis of the shares is irrelevant.

it distributes. The individual receiving the $100 has two choices: (1) reinvest the funds and (2) use the money elsewhere. In either case, the $28 in income taxes must be paid. If the individual wants to maintain the investment and reinvests in the fund (i.e., reinvests the $100), he or she must finance the $28 tax payment from another source. In effect, the investor commits more funds to maintain the investment since the funds used to pay the taxes must come at the expense of something.[13]

In the previous illustration, the distribution was income. If the fund's net asset value increased by $1 per share through the appreciation of its portfolio, the fund could realize and distribute the capital gain. Once again, the investor is faced with having to pay the tax on the distribution. The distribution of the capital gain has the same implication for taxes as the distribution of income except the tax rate will be lower if the distribution is a long-term capital gain. The investor must finance the tax payment, and the before-tax return reported by the fund will exceed the after-tax return realized by the investor. (The ability of a fund's management to reduce the tax obligations of its shareholders is referred to as the fund's "tax efficiency." As is discussed in Chapter 24 on portfolio management, tax efficiency may be a reason to prefer one fund to another fund.)

Fees

The fund's fees also affect the return earned by the investor. Management fees, commissions to brokers for executing the fund's trades, and 12b-1 fees (discussed below) are paid from the fund's income before determining the fund's earnings available to shareholders. These expenses are across all shares and are already accounted for in the return reported by the fund. Presumably, lower expenses contribute to a higher return, and differences in expenses among the funds may be a reason for selecting a particular fund.

[13]This problem, of course, applies to all investments subject to income taxation. However, the general existence of the problem does not erase the fact that it reduces the comparability of the individual's realized after-tax return and the before-tax return reported by the mutual fund. See "Sure, I Made Money. . . . But What's Left after Taxes?" *Mutual Funds* (March 1995): 21–22, which discusses a fund's after-tax return as a percentage of its pretax return.

Front-end load fees are paid when the shares are purchased, and exit fees are paid when the shares are redeemed. These fees apply only to those individuals who are buying and redeeming shares and do not apply to other shareholders who are neither buying nor redeeming shares. These fees, however, affect the investor's realized return and increase the difficulty of comparing the performance reported by the fund and the return actually realized by the investor.

Consider a front-loaded mutual fund that charges 6.0 percent. If the net asset value of the fund is $10, the investor must remit $0.64 to purchase a share.[14] The mutual fund earns $1 during the year, so the net asset value grows to $11. The fund's management reports a return of 10 percent, but the individual investor has certainly not earned 10 percent. Instead, the actual amount invested ($10.64) has grown to $11, an increase of less than 3 percent. Over a period of years, the loading fee significantly reduces the return. For example, if the fund were to earn 12 percent compounded annually for seven years, its net asset value would grow from $10 to $22.11.[(a)] However, the investor's return would be only 11 percent as the actual amount invested ($10.64) rises to $22.11.[(b)]

Calculator Solution

(a)

Function Key	Data Input
PV =	−10
FV =	?
PMT =	0
N =	7
I =	12
Function Key	Answer
FV =	22.11

(b)

Function Key	Data Input
PV =	−10.64
FV =	22.11
PMT =	0
N =	7
I =	?
Function Key	Answer
I =	11.01

(c)

Function Key	Data Input
PV =	−10
FV =	22.44
PMT =	0
N =	7
I =	?
Function Key	Answer
I =	11.51

(d)

Function Key	Data Input
PV =	−10.64
FV =	21.44
PMT =	0
N =	7
I =	?
Function Key	Answer
I =	10.53

The return is further decreased if the fund has a deferred exit fee (or nuisance fee) that applies if shares are redeemed within a specified time period. For example, the Dean Witter Natural Resources Fund has a redemption fee even though it is considered to be a no-load fund. The fee starts at 5 percent and declines to 1 percent if the shares are held six years. Several funds have both a loading fee and a redemption fee. Such fees may be designed to reduce switching investments and cover the costs to the funds of handling withdrawals. Such deferred fees reduce the return and make comparisons of the fund's stated return and the individual's realized return more difficult.

This problem of comparisons created by fees is considerably lessened for a no-load mutual fund if (1) the management fees of the no-load fund are no higher than the management fees of the load fund and (2) the no-load fund does not have an exit fee. Some no-load funds assess a sales charge when the investor redeems the shares (i.e., a load fee in reverse). Since the fund lacks a traditional front-end load fee, it may refer to itself as a no-load fund.

The impact of a back-end load fee can be considerable even though the charge may be expressed as a modest 2 or 3 percent. Consider the preceding illustration in which the net asset value grew from $10 to $22.11 in seven years for a 12 percent annual increase. If the fund assesses a 3 percent back-end fee, the investor receives $21.44 ($22.11 − [0.03][$22.11]), so the realized return is reduced from 12 percent annually to 11.5 percent.[(c)]

If the fund has both a front-end and back-end load, the investor's return is reduced even further. To continue the preceding example, the individual spends $10.64 to acquire a share with a net asset value of $10. The net asset value then compounds at 12 percent for seven years to $22.11, and the fund assesses a 3 percent back-end load. The investor receives $21.44, so that individual has in effect invested $10.64 to receive $21.44 over seven years. This is a return of 10.5 percent annually, which is almost two percentage points below the 12 percent that the fund can report as the growth in the net asset value.[(d)]

Actually, the impact on the terminal value of an investment in the fund is the same for a back-end and a front-end loading fee as long as the percentages are the same. For example, fund A charges a 3 percent front-end load fee, while fund B charges a 3 percent exit fee. The initial net asset value of each is $10, which grows

[14]This cost of the share is determined as follows:

$\$10/(1 - 0.06) = \$10/0.94 = \$0.64.$

The loading fee is $0.64, which is 6.0 percent of the amount invested ($10.64 × 0.06 = $0.64). As was discussed earlier in this chapter, loading fees are figured on the amount invested and not on the net asset value.

Calculator Solution

(e)

Function Key	Data Input
PV =	−10
FV =	?
PMT =	0
N =	12
I =	12

Function Key	Answer
FV =	38.96

(f)

Function Key	Data Input
PV =	−10.31
FV =	38.96
PMT =	0
N =	12
I =	?

Function Key	Answer
I =	11.72

(g)

Function Key	Data Input
PV =	−10.00
FV =	37.79
PMT =	0
N =	12
I =	?

Function Key	Answer
I =	11.72

(h)

Function Key	Data Input
PV =	−50,000
FV =	?
PMT =	0
N =	20
I =	12

Function Key	Answer
FV =	482,315

(i)

Function Key	Data Input
PV =	−47,000
FV =	?
PMT =	0
N =	20
I =	12

Function Key	Answer
FV =	453,376

12b-1 fees
Fees that a mutual fund may charge to cover marketing and advertising expenses.

annually at 12 percent for 12 years. The investor spends $10.31 ($10/[1 − 0.03]) to acquire a share of fund A and $10 to acquire a share of fund B. The terminal value of both funds is

$10(3.8960) = $38.96.[(e)]

The investor in fund B, however, only receives $37.79 ($38.96 − [0.03][$38.96]). The return on each investment, however, is 11.72 percent: $10.31 grows to $38.96 at 11.72 percent[(f)], and $10.00 grows to $37.79 at 11.72 percent.[(g)] In both cases the return is the same.

The impact of these differences in loading fees is substantial when the rate differences are compounded over many years. Consider a $50,000 investment in a fund that is left to compound at 12 percent for 20 years. The $50,000 grows to $482,315.[(h)] However, if the fund had charged an initial load fee of 6.0 percent, the investor would have only $47,000 ($47,000/[1 − 0.06] = $50,000) actually invested by the fund. At 12 percent compounded annually for 20 years, the terminal value would be $453,376.[(i)] This is $28,939 less than would be earned with the no-load fund.

Suppose the investor had purchased shares in a no-load fund with an exit fee of 3 percent. In this case, the investor receives $467,846 ($482,315 − $14,469). If the investor had purchased a load mutual fund with a 6.0 percent front load and a 3 percent back-end load, this individual would have netted only $439,775, or $42,540 less than the no-load fund with no exit fee. Obviously, the loading fees can have a considerable impact on the net return the investor ultimately earns, even though the net asset value increased by the same percentage in each case!

While individuals who sell load funds may disagree, the preceding illustrations suggest that the investor should not view the load as a one-time fee whose impact is reduced over time as it is spread over an ever-increasing investment. Instead, the opposite is true. The longer the investor holds the shares, the greater the absolute differential will be between the terminal values of the load and no-load funds. The funds not lost to the load fee are being compounded over a longer period of time; thus, the terminal value of the no-load fund becomes even larger.

While this discussion suggests that investors should purchase no-load mutual funds in preference to those with load fees, the investor still needs to be aware of an expense some no-load funds charge that may prove over a period of time to be more costly than the loading fees. The purpose of the loading fee is to compensate those individuals who sell the fund's shares. No-load funds do not have a salesforce and thus do not have this expense. They may, however, use other marketing devices, such as advertising, that must be paid for.

Some load and no-load funds have adopted an SEC rule that permits management to use the fund's assets to pay for these marketing expenses. These are referred to as **12b-1 fees**, which are often called a *12b-1 plan* by the industry. 12b-1 fees are named after the SEC rule that enables funds to assess the fee which, in effect, is an ongoing charge that shareholders pay. The fee covers a variety of costs, such as advertising, distribution of fund literature, and even sales commissions to brokers. Unlike a front-load fee, which is charged when the shares are purchased, this 12b-1 fee can be a continuous annual expense. Thus, over a number of years, investors in funds assessing this charge may pay more than they would have paid in loading fees.

Over a period of years, 12b-1 fees can significantly reduce the return the investor earns, because the fee is paid not only in good years but also in years when the fund experiences losses and a decline in its net asset value. The investor needs to be aware of 12b-1 fees when selecting a mutual fund, since the growth in the fund's net asset value will be reduced by the fee. Suppose one fund charges a fee that averages 1.0 percent of total assets and another fund does not assess the fee. Both funds earn 12 percent on assets before the fees, so after the fee is paid the returns are 12 percent for the fund without the fee but 11 percent for the fund with the 12b-1 fee. Obviously, the stockholder's return is reduced, and over time the impact of this reduction can be surprisingly large. Consider an initial investment of $1,000. After 20 years the $1,000 at 12 percent grows to $9,646 in the fund without the fee but only grows to $8,062 in the fund with the fee. The difference ($1,584) is, of course, the result of the 12b-1 fee. Thus, unless the fees lead to higher investment returns, they must reduce the return earned by the investor.[15]

Performance Evaluation: Risk Adjustment for Comparing Returns

There are two essential concerns when assessing investment performance: return *and* risk. Even if the investor determines the returns that various funds have earned, these returns may not be comparable, because comparing absolute returns omits one of the crucial elements in investing: risk. Unfortunately, many investors and the popular press appear to stress return and omit risk.

It should be obvious that returns from funds with different objectives are not comparable. Returns on money market mutual funds are obviously not comparable to returns on small cap growth funds. Even returns on funds with the same objective, such as capital appreciation, may not be comparable if they are not equally risky. From the investor's perspective, a return of 15 percent achieved by a low-risk portfolio is preferred to 15 percent earned on a high-risk portfolio. If the investor compares absolute returns, he or she is implicitly assuming that both funds are equally risky. To compare returns, the investor needs to *standardize for differences in risk.* After making this adjustment, then the individual can better determine if the fund's management outperformed other funds or the market.

The phrases "outperformed the market" or "beat the market" are often used regarding performance. (They were used in the previous section on returns.) Unfortunately, the phrases can be misleading. In the popular press, the phrases are essentially comparing the portfolio manager's return to the market return. This implies the goal of the fund is to earn a return that exceeds the market return. In addition, two considerations are omitted: (1) What is the appropriate market or benchmark and (2) risk. In the academic and (usually) the professional literature, the phrases mean a *risk-adjusted* return in excess of the market return. If the portfolio manager's risk-adjusted return exceeds the market return, then the fund outperformed the market (i.e., beat the market).

Three techniques for the measurement of performance that incorporate both risk and return have been developed. These measures, which are often referred to as *composite performance measures,* are (1) the Jensen index, (2) the Treynor index, and (3) the Sharpe index, each named after the individual who first used the technique to measure performance. All three measures address the questions of the index of the aggressive market and the adjustment of the return for risk associated with the portfolio. Thus, all three composite measures provide risk-adjusted measures of performance. They encompass both elements of investment performance: the return and the risk taken to earn that return.

The benchmark frequently used to measure the market is the S&P 500 stock index, since it is a comprehensive, value-weighted index. Because many portfolios,

[15]See *The Individual Investor's Guide to Low-Load Mutual Funds,* 20th ed. (Chicago: American Association of Individual Investors, 2001), for a discussion of the impact of 12b-1 and other fees.

especially mutual funds, trust accounts, and pension plans, are comprised of the securities represented in the S&P 500 index, this index is considered to be an appropriate proxy for the market. However, if the portfolios include bonds, real estate, and numerous types of money market securities, the S&P 500 stock index may be an inappropriate benchmark for evaluating portfolio performance. (Possible solutions to this problem are addressed later, in Chapter 24 on portfolio management.)

The differences among the three composite performance measures rest primarily with the adjustment for risk and the construction of the measure of evaluation. The measurement of risk is particularly important because a lower return is not necessarily indicative of inferior performance. Obviously, the return on a money market mutual fund should be less than the return earned by a growth fund during a period of rising security prices. The more relevant question is this: Was the growth fund manager's performance sufficient to justify the additional risk?

All three composite measures are an outgrowth of the capital asset pricing model (CAPM), presented in Chapter 7. That model specified that the return on an investment (r) depends on (1) the return the individual earns on a risk-free asset, such as a U.S. Treasury bill, and (2) a risk premium. This risk-adjusted return was expressed as

$$r = r_f + (r_m - r_f)\beta$$

in which r_f represents the risk-free rate and r_m is the return on the market. The risk premium depends on the extent to which the market return exceeds the risk-free rate (i.e., $r_m - r_f$) adjusted by the systematic risk associated with the asset (i.e., its beta coefficient). This relationship is shown in Figure 8.4, which replicates Figure 7.17, the security market line. The Y-axis represents the return, and the X-axis represents the risk as measured by beta. Line AB gives all the combinations of return at each level of risk. If the investor bears no risk, the return on the Y-axis represents the risk-free rate, and higher returns are associated with bearing increased risk.

The Jensen Performance Index

Although the CAPM is used to determine the return that is required to make an investment, it may also be used to evaluate realized performance for a well-diversified portfolio: that is, given the realized return and the risk, did the investment earn a sufficient return? The Jensen performance index determines by

FIGURE 8.4

CAPM Risk-Adjusted Returns

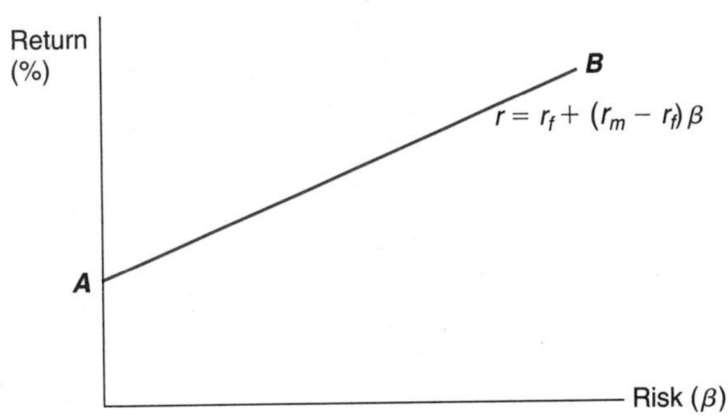

how much the realized return differs from the return required by the CAPM.[16] The realized return (r_p) on a portfolio (or on a specific investment if applied to the return on an individual asset) is

$$r_p = r_f + (r_m - r_f)\beta + e. \tag{8.1}$$

Equation 8.1 is basically the same as the CAPM equation except that (1) the *realized* return is substituted for the return and (2) a random error term (e) has been added.[17] In this form, the model is used to evaluate performance and not to determine the required return necessary to make an investment.[18]

If the risk-free return is subtracted from both sides, the equation becomes

$$r_p - r_f = (r_m - r_f)\beta + e. \tag{8.2}$$

In this form, Equation 8.2 indicates that the actual risk premium earned on the portfolio equals the market risk premium times the beta plus the error term. Since the errors are assumed to be random, the value of e should be zero.

Figure 8.5 reproduces Figure 8.4 and adds line CD, which represents Equation 8.1. The two lines, AB and CD, are parallel, and since the risk-free rate has been subtracted from both sides of Equation 8.1 to derive Equation 8.2, line CD has no positive intercept on the Y-axis. Equation 8.2 indicates that after subtracting the risk-free rate, higher returns are related solely to the additional risk premium as-

FIGURE 8.5

Jensen Performance Index—Risk-Adjusted Returns Including and Excluding the Risk-Free Rate

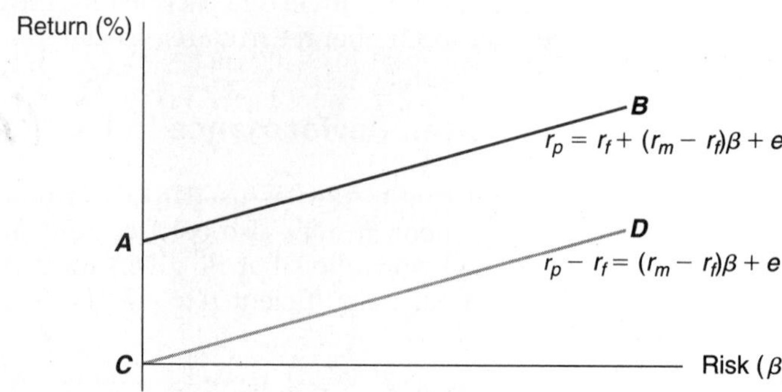

[16]Jensen's seminal work on portfolio evaluation may be found in Michael C. Jensen, "The Performance of Mutual Funds in the Period 1945–1964," *Journal of Finance* (May 1968): 389–416.

[17]Two methods for computing returns, dollar-weighted and time-weighted rates of return, are discussed in Chapter 10. The dollar-weighted return (the internal rate of return) determines the rate that equates all an investment's cash inflows with its cash outlays. The time-weighted return computes the return for each period and averages these holding period returns. The computation may be an arithmetic or a geometric average, with the latter being preferred because it considers compounding.

While dollar-weighted or time-weighted rates of return may be used for comparisons, the investor needs to apply the computation consistently. If, for instance, an individual computes time-weighted rates of return as required by the Association for Investment Management and Research, then any comparisions must be made with rates computed using the same method. If the investor or portfolio manager compares his or her performance with rates derived from another source, such as the returns earned by mutual funds reported in Morningstar, that individual needs to be certain that all returns were calculated using the same method of computation.

[18]Application of the Jensen model may require an adjustment in the risk-free rate. Usually, a short-term security, such as a U.S. Treasury bill, is the appropriate proxy for this rate. However, if the time period being covered by the evaluation is greater than a year, it is inappropriate to use a short-term rate, and a different risk-free rate is required for each time interval during the evaluation period. If, for example, the evaluation of the performance of two portfolio managers is being done on an annual basis over five years, a different one-year risk-free rate would have to be used for each of the five years during the evaluation period.

sociated with the portfolio. Actual performance, however, may differ from the return implied by Equation 8.2. The possibility that the realized return may differ from the expected return is indicated by

(8.3)
$$r_p - r_f = a + (r_m - r_f)\beta,$$

in which a (often referred to as *alpha*) represents the extent to which the realized return differs from the required return or the return that would be anticipated for a given amount of risk.

After algebraic manipulation, Equation 8.3 is often presented in the following form:

(8.4)
$$a = r_p - [r_f + (r_m - r_f)\beta],$$

Jensen performance index
A measure of performance that compares the realized return with the return that should have been earned for the amount of risk borne by the investor.

which is referred to as the **Jensen performance index**. Because alpha is the difference between the realized return and the risk-adjusted return that should have been earned, the numerical value of a indicates superior or inferior performance.

If the portfolio manager consistently does better than the capital asset model projects, the alpha takes on a positive value. If the performance is consistently inferior, the alpha takes on a negative value. For example, if portfolio manager X achieved a return of 15.0 percent with a beta of 1.1 when the market return was 14.6 percent and the risk-free rate was 7 percent, the alpha is

$$a = 0.15 - [0.07 + (0.146 - 0.07)1.1] = -0.0036,$$

which indicates inferior performance. If portfolio manager Y achieved a 13.5 percent return with a beta of 0.8, the alpha is

$$a = 0.135 - [0.07 + (0.146 - 0.07)0.8] = 0.0042,$$

which indicates superior performance. Even though portfolio manager Y had the lower realized return, the performance is superior on a risk-adjusted basis.

The Jensen performance index permits the comparison of portfolio managers' performance relative to one another or to the market. The numerical values of alpha permit the ranking of performance, with the higher scores indicating the best performance. The sign of the alpha indicates whether the portfolio manager outperformed the market after adjusting for risk. A positive alpha indicates superior performance relative to the market, and a negative alpha indicates inferior performance. Thus, in the previous example, portfolio manager Y's performance was superior not only to portfolio manager X's performance but also to the market. In other words, portfolio manager Y outperformed the market on a risk-adjusted basis.

The Jensen performance index measures risk premiums in terms of beta, so the index assumes that the portfolio is well diversified. Since a well-diversified portfolio's total risk is primarily its systematic risk, beta is the appropriate index of that risk. Thus, the Jensen performance index would be an appropriate measure for large cap growth mutual funds whose portfolios are well diversified. If the portfolio were not sufficiently diversified, portfolio risk would include both unsystematic and systematic risk, and the standard deviation of the portfolio's returns would be a more appropriate measure of risk. Thus, the Jensen performance index is not an appropriate measure of performance for specialized sector funds, such as Fidelity Select Regional Banks, or aggressive small cap growth funds that specialize in a class of stocks, such as Fidelity Emerging Growth.

The Treynor Performance Index

Treynor index
A risk-adjusted measure of performance that standardizes the return in excess of the risk-free rate by the portfolio's systematic risk.

The Treynor and Sharpe indexes are alternative measures of portfolio evaluation. The **Treynor index** (T_i) for a given time period is

$$T_i = \frac{r_p - r_f}{\beta}, \tag{8.5}$$

in which r_p is the realized return on the portfolio and r_f is the risk-free rate.[19] The extent to which the realized return exceeds the risk-free rate (i.e., the risk premium that is realized) is divided by the portfolio beta (i.e., the measure of systematic risk). Thus, if portfolio manager X achieved a return of 15 percent when the risk-free rate was 7 percent and the portfolio's beta was 1.1, the Treynor index is

$$T_X = \frac{0.15 - 0.07}{1.1} = 0.0727.$$

If portfolio manager Y achieved a return of 13.5 percent with a beta of 0.8, the Treynor index is

$$T_Y = \frac{0.135 - 0.07}{0.8} = 0.08125.$$

This indicates that portfolio manager Y outperformed portfolio manager X on a risk-adjusted basis, which is the same conclusion regarding the relative performance of the two portfolio managers derived by the Jensen index of performance. However, it *cannot* be concluded from the Treynor index that either portfolio manager outperformed or underperformed the market, because there is no source for comparison. The Treynor performance index must be computed for the market to determine whether the portfolio manager outperformed the market. If, during the time period, the market return was 14.6 percent, then the Treynor index for the market is

$$T_M = \frac{0.146 - 0.07}{1.0} = 0.076.$$

(Notice that the numerical value of the beta for the market is 1.0.) Since the Treynor index for the market is 0.076, portfolio manager X underperformed while portfolio manager Y outperformed the market on a risk-adjusted basis.

This conclusion is illustrated in Figure 8.6. Line *AB* represents the returns (r_p) that would be anticipated using the capital asset pricing model for a given risk-free rate, a given return on the market, and different levels of beta. The *Y*-intercept measures the risk-free return, which in the preceding illustration is 7.0 percent. The return on the market is 14.6 percent, and the *X*-axis gives different levels of beta. Thus, the equation for line *AB* is

$$r_p = r_f + (r_m - r_f)\beta = 0.07 + (0.146 - 0.07)\beta.$$

If the portfolio manager outperforms the market on a risk-adjusted basis, the realized combination of risk and return will lie above line *AB*. Conversely, if the performance is inferior to the market, the realized combination of risk and return will lie below line *AB*.

[19]Jack L. Treynor, "How to Rate Management Investment Funds," *Harvard Business Review* (January/February 1966): 63–74.

FIGURE 8.6

Realized Returns Compared to the Market Return

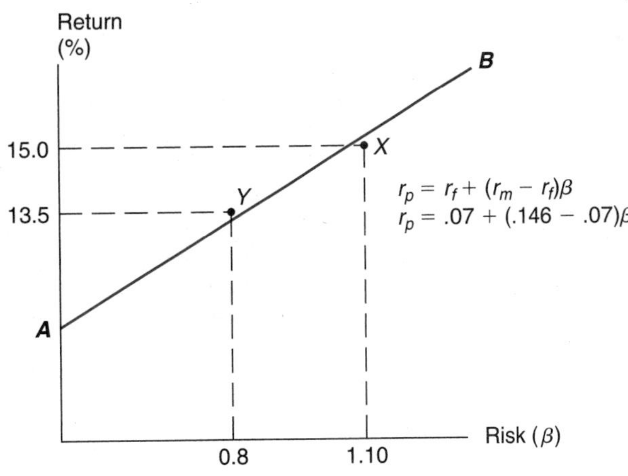

The beta of portfolio X is 1.1, so the anticipated return is

$$r_x = 0.07 + (0.146 - 0.07)1.1 = 15.36\%.$$

The *realized return* is 15.0 percent, which is less than the expected return of 15.36 percent, and the portfolio underperformed the market after adjusting for risk. This realized return is represented by point *X* in Figure 8.6, and the point does lie below line *AB*.

The beta of portfolio Y is 0.8, so the anticipated return is

$$r_y = 0.07 + (0.146 - 0.07)0.8 = 13.08\%.$$

The realized return is 13.5 percent, which exceeds the expected return of 13.08 percent; thus, the portfolio outperformed the market after adjusting for risk. The realized return is represented by point *Y* in Figure 8.6, and the point does lie above line *AB*.

The Jensen and Treynor performance measures are very similar. They include the same information: the return on the portfolio, the risk-free and the market returns earned during the time period, and the portfolio's beta. The Treynor measure computes a relative value, the return in excess of the risk-free rate divided by the measure of risk. While the Treynor index may be used to determine whether a portfolio's performance was superior or inferior to the market on a risk-adjusted basis, the numerical value of the index may be difficult to interpret. For example, in the preceding illustration, the Treynor indices for portfolios X and Y were 0.0727 and 0.08125, respectively. When these values were compared to the Treynor index for the market (0.076), the comparisons indicated inferior and superior results, but the results do not indicate by how much each portfolio under- or outperformed the market.

The Jensen measure computes an absolute value, the alpha, which may be easier to interpret and does indicate the degree to which the portfolio over- or underperformed the market. In the example, the alphas of portfolios X and Y were

−0.0036 and 0.0042, respectively. Portfolio X performed 0.36 percent less than the market, while portfolio Y performed 0.42 percent better than the market.[20]

DOES NOT ASSUME PORTFOLIO IS DIVERSIFIED

The Sharpe Performance Index

The third measure of performance, the **Sharpe performance index** (S_i), is

$$S_i = \frac{r_p - r_f}{\sigma_p}. \tag{8.6}$$

Sharpe performance index
A risk-adjusted measure of performance that standardizes the return in excess of the risk-free rate by the standard deviation of the portfolio's return.

The only new symbol in the index is σ_p, which represents the standard deviation of the portfolio.[21] If the previous examples are continued and portfolio manager X's returns had a standard deviation of 30 percent (0.3), while portfolio manager Y's returns had a standard deviation of 25 percent, their respective indices are

$$S_X = \frac{0.15 - 0.07}{0.3} = 0.267$$

and

$$S_Y = \frac{0.135 - 0.07}{0.25} = 0.260.$$

Because portfolio manager X has the higher score, the performance is superior to that of portfolio manager Y. The additional return (i.e., 15 versus 13.5) more than compensates for the additional risk (i.e., the higher standard deviation).

The Sharpe ranking of X over Y is opposite to the ranking determined using the Treynor and Jensen indices of performance. In those measurements, portfolio manager Y had the higher score, which indicated better performance. The reason for the difference in the rankings is the measure of risk. The Sharpe performance index uses the standard deviation of the returns as the measure of risk. Since the index uses the standard deviation, it does not assume the portfolio is well diversified. In effect, the index standardizes the return in excess of the risk-free rate by the *variability* of the return. The Treynor index uses the portfolio's beta and does assume the portfolio is well diversified. In effect, it standardizes the return in excess of the risk-free rate by the *volatility* of the return.

It is important to realize that variability and volatility do not mean the same thing. (At least in an academic usage; words may be interchanged in the popular press.) Variability compares one period's return with the portfolio's average return. That is, how much did the return vary from period to period? A variable return implies that over time there will be large differences in the annual returns. Volatility compares the return relative to something else. That is, how volatile was the stock's return compared to the market return? A volatile return implies that the return on the portfolio fluctuates more than some base (i.e., the return on the portfolio is more volatile than the return on the market). A portfolio could have a

[20]The Jensen measure offers an additional advantage. By using regression analysis it may be possible to determine if the alpha is statistically significant. For example, portfolio Y's alpha was 0.42 percent—but that difference could be the result of chance. If the alpha is statistically significant, then the difference is not the result of chance and confirms that the portfolio manager outperformed the market on a risk-adjusted basis.

[21]William F. Sharpe, "Mutual Fund Performance," *Journal of Business* (January 1966): 1119–1138.

low beta; its return relative to the market would not be volatile (i.e., the return on the market would fluctuate more). However, from year to year there could be a large variation in the portfolio's return, so the returns are variable even though the portfolio is less volatile than the market.

Because the measures of risk used in the Sharpe and Treynor indices differ, it is possible for the two indices to rank performance differently. Suppose the average return on a utility fund is 8 percent with a standard deviation of 9 percent. This indicates that during 68 percent of the time, the return ranges from −1 to 17 percent. Returns ranging from −1 to 17 percent may indicate large variability in the return for that type of fund and indicate considerable risk unique to that fund (i.e., a large amount of diversifiable risk). The fund, however, may have a beta of only 0.6, indicating that its returns are less volatile than the market returns. The fund has only a modest amount of nondiversifiable, systematic risk. The large standard deviation may generate an inferior risk-adjusted performance using the Sharpe index because the fund has excessive diversifiable risk. The low beta may generate a superior risk-adjusted return when the Treynor index is used because that index considers only the fund's nondiversifiable risk.

As with the Treynor index, the Sharpe measure of performance does not indicate whether the portfolio manager outperformed the market. No statement can be made concerning performance relative to the market unless the Sharpe performance index also is computed for the market. If the standard deviation of the market return is 20 percent (0.2), the Sharpe index for the market is

$$S_M = \frac{0.146 - 0.07}{0.2} = 0.38.$$

Since this value exceeds the numerical values computed for portfolio managers X and Y (i.e., 0.267 and 0.26), the inference is that both *underperformed* the market on a risk-adjusted basis.

Preference for one performance measure may depend on the portfolios being evaluated and whether the evaluation should be based on total risk or diversifiable risk. If the specific portfolio constitutes all of an individual's assets, total risk is the appropriate measure. This argues for the Sharpe performance index because it uses the standard deviation of the returns, which measures total risk. If, for instance, an individual had most of his or her funds invested in a growth equity fund in a 401 (k) plan, then the Sharpe index would indicate how that plan performed based on the total risk borne by the individual.

If the portfolio manager being evaluated constitutes only one of many portfolios the individual holds, then the Treynor or Jensen indexes may be preferred. If the individual has acquired the shares of several diverse funds, then that individual has achieved diversification—each fund does not represent the investor's total risk. Instead, the investor is concerned with the nondiversifiable risk associated with each fund, in which case beta is the appropriate measure of risk. In effect, the investor is evaluating the ability of the portfolio manager to generate a return for the systematic risk the investor bears. (The individual could then determine the aggregate return and standard deviation of all the various funds to evaluate the fund selection process.)

To some extent, the performance index chosen by the individual may depend on which is readily available. If, for example, Morningstar provides the alphas and the Sharpe index for each fund, individuals cannot use the Treynor index unless they are willing to compute it for themselves. However, since the Sharpe index is computed using the standard deviation of each fund's return and the alphas are computed using each fund's beta, both measures of risk are covered, and it is probably unnecessary to compute the Treynor index.

The Benchmark Problem

The Jensen, Treynor, and Sharpe indexes of performance use an index such as the S&P 500 stock index to measure the market. However, the index may not be an appropriate measure of the market. Certainly a stock index would be an inappropriate benchmark for a mutual fund with a portfolio devoted to long-term government bonds. A stock index may even be inappropriate for a portfolio devoted to stock if that portfolio is not similar in composition to the composition of the benchmark (e.g., the portfolio consists of foreign instead of domestic stocks).

This problem is referred to as the *benchmark problem,* and it permeates all attempts to evaluate portfolio performance. The essence of the problem is that performance of many portfolios should not be compared to a limited aggregate measure of the U.S. stock market. One possible solution is to use different measures of the market or to create specific measures that are more appropriate. That discussion, however, will be deferred to after the coverage of different indexes of the market (Chapter 10) and the various securities that may be included in a portfolio. The coverage of these specific assets comprises the bulk of the remainder of this textbook. After coverage of the various securities and the indexes is completed, portfolio assessment and the benchmark problem will return in Chapter 24 on portfolio management.

In addition to the benchmark problem, a problem has been pointed out concerning the Treynor or Jensen performance indexes. Richard Roll has suggested in a series of articles that computing beta coefficients using aggregate indexes as proxies for the market may produce biased betas.[22] This bias is potentially a major problem, because estimated betas are used in the capital asset pricing model for the valuation of individual securities and as part of the process for evaluating portfolio performance that employs the capital asset pricing model (i.e., the Treynor and the Jensen measures of performance).

Summary

Instead of directly investing in securities, individuals may buy shares in investment companies. These firms, in turn, invest the funds in various assets, such as stocks and bonds.

There are two types of investment companies. A closed-end investment company has a specified number of shares that are bought and sold in the same manner as the stock of firms such as AT&T. An open-end investment company (i.e., a mutual fund) has a variable number of shares sold directly to investors. Investors who desire to liquidate their holdings sell them back to the company.

Investment companies offer several advantages, including professional management, diversification, and custodial services. Dividends and the interest earned on the firm's assets are distributed to stockholders. In addition, if the value of the company's assets rises, the stockholders profit as capital gains are realized and distributed.

Mutual funds may be classified by the types of assets they own. Some stress income-producing assets, such as bonds, preferred stock, and common stock of firms that distribute a large proportion of their income. Other mutual funds stress

[22]The seminal works on the benchmark problem include four articles by Richard Roll: "A Critique of the Asset Pricing Theory's Test," *Journal of Financial Economics* (March 1977): 129–176; "Ambiguity When Performance is Measured by the Securities Market Line," *Journal of Finance* (September 1978): 1051–1069; "Performance Evaluation and Benchmark Errors I," *Journal of Portfolio Management* (summer 1980): 5–12 and "Performance Evaluation and Benchmark Errors II," *Journal of Portfolio Management* (winter 1981): 17–22. See also Robert Ferguson, "The Trouble with Performance Measurement," *Journal of Portfolio Management* (spring 1986): 4–9.

growth in their net asset values through investments in firms with the potential to grow and generate capital gains. There are also investment companies that specialize in special situations, particular sectors of the economy, and tax-exempt securities. There are even mutual funds that seek to duplicate an index of the stock market.

Although investment companies are professionally managed, the returns that mutual funds have earned over a period of years have not consistently outperformed the market.

Performance may be judged using the Jensen index by comparing the realized return with the risk-adjusted return that should have been earned. If the realized return exceeds this risk-adjusted return, then there was truly an excess return, and the investor beat the market during that time period. Alternative approaches for portfolio evaluation standardize the realized return by a measure of risk, such as the portfolio's standard deviation (the Sharpe index) or its beta (the Treynor index). The resulting index of performance may be compared with similar standardized indices of performance by mutual funds or the market to determine if the particular portfolio did exceptionally well during the time period.

If the portfolio's performance was exceptional, the investor should realize that repeating such superior returns will be difficult. Efficient financial markets imply that the investor cannot expect to outperform the market consistently, but they do not imply that such performance is impossible.

Questions

1) What is the difference between a closed-end and an open-end investment company?
2) Are mutual funds subject to federal income taxation?
3) What is a loading charge? Do all investment companies charge this fee?
4) What is a specialized mutual fund? How is it different from a special situation fund? What differentiates large and small cap funds?
5) Should an investor expect a mutual fund to outperform the market? If not, why should the investor buy the shares?
6) What are the differences among loading fees, exit (or nuisance) fees, and 12b-1 fees? Why is it reasonable to assume that closed-end investment companies do not have these expenses?
7) Why may the annual growth in a fund's net asset value not be comparable to the return earned by an individual investor?
8) How may beta coefficients be used to standardize returns for risk to permit comparisons of mutual fund performance?
9) If a portfolio manager earned 15 percent when the market rose by 12 percent, does this prove that the manager outperformed the market?
10) How may realized returns be adjusted for risk so that investment performance may be judged on a risk-adjusted basis?

Problems

1) What is the net asset value of an investment company with $10,000,000 in assets, $790,000 in current liabilities, and 1,200,000 shares outstanding?
2) If a mutual fund's net asset value is $23.40 and the fund sells its shares for $25, what is the load fee as a percentage of the net asset value (i.e., the amount actually invested in the shares)?

3) If an investor buys shares in a no-load mutual fund for $31.40 and the shares appreciate to $44.60 in a year, what would be the percentage return on the investment? If the fund charges an exit fee of 1 percent, what would be the return on the investment?

4) An investor buys shares in a mutual fund for $20 per share. At the end of the year the fund distributes a dividend of $0.58, and after the distribution the net asset value of a share is $23.41. What would be the investor's percentage return on the investment?

5) You are given the following information concerning several mutual funds:

Fund	Return in Excess of the Treasury Bill Rate	Beta
A	12.4%	1.14
B	13.2	1.22
C	11.4	0.90
D	9.8	0.76
E	12.6	0.95

During the time period the Standard & Poor's stock index exceeded the Treasury bill rate by 10.5 percent (i.e., $r_m - r_f = 10.5\%$).

a) Rank the performance of each fund without adjusting for risk and adjusting for risk using the Treynor index. Which, if any, outperformed the market? (Remember, the beta of the market is 1.0.)

b) The analysis in part (a) assumes each fund is sufficiently diversified so that the appropriate measure of risk is the beta coefficient. Suppose, however, this assumption does not hold and the standard deviation of each fund's return was as follows:

Fund	Standard Deviation of Return
A	0.045 (= 4.5%)
B	0.031
C	0.010
D	0.014
E	0.035

Thus, fund A earned a return of 12.4 percent, but approximately 68 percent of the time this return has ranged from 7.9 percent to 16.9 percent. The standard deviation of the market return is 0.01 (i.e., 1 percent), so 68 percent of the time, the return on the market has ranged from 9.5 to 11.5 percent. Rank the funds using this alternative measure of risk. Which, if any, outperformed the market on a risk-adjusted basis?

THE FINANCIAL ADVISOR'S INVESTMENT CASE

Retirement Plans and Investment Choices

Ken Morsovich's 22-year-old daughter Bozena has just accepted a job with Doctor Medical Systems (DMS), a firm specializing in computer services for doctors. DMS offers employees a 401(k) plan to which employees may contribute 5 percent of their salary. DMS will match $0.50 for every dollar contributed. Bozena's starting salary is $32,000, so she could contribute up to $1,600 and DMS would contribute an additional $800. If she did decide to contribute to the plan, she has the following choices of funds, all managed by Superior Investments. She may select any combination of the funds and change the selection quarterly.

- **a)** U.S. Value Fund—a fund invested solely in stocks of U.S. firms that management believes to be undervalued
- **b)** Research & Technology Fund—a fund specializing in stocks of companies or firms primarily emphasizing computer services and programming
- **c)** Global Equities—a fund invested solely in stocks of firms with international operations, such as Sony
- **d)** Government Bond Fund—a fund devoted to debt issued or guaranteed by the federal government
- **e)** High-Yield Debt—a fund devoted to bonds with non-investment grade ratings
- **f)** Money Fund—a fund investing solely in short-term money market instruments

The historic returns of each fund, the standard deviation of the returns, the fund's beta (computed relative to the S&P 500 stock index), and the R^2 of beta are as follows:

	Return	Standard Deviation of Return	Beta	R^2
a. USVF	13%	20%	0.7	0.3
b. RTF	12	10	1.1	0.9
c. GE	15	40	1.5	0.6
d. GBF	7	8	0.3	0.2
e. HYD	10	12	0.4	0.3
f. MF	4	1	0.0	0.0

Ken's employer offers a defined benefit pension plan in which his retirement income depends on the average of his salary for the last five years in which he works. Since the employer guarantees and funds the plan, Ken does not understand Bozena's choices. He believes that she should participate but does not know the advantages and risks associated with each choice. Since Ken is your cousin, he has asked you to answer the following questions to convince Bozena to participate in the 401(k) plan and to help her choose among the six alternative funds.

1) If Bozena participates and the 401(k) earns 10 percent annually, how much will she have accumulated in 45 years (to age 67) even if her salary does not change?
2) If she does not participate and annually saves $1,600 on her own, how much will she have accumulated if she earns 10 percent and is in the 20 percent federal income tax bracket?
3) If she retires at age 67, given the amounts in 1 and 2, how much can Bozena withdraw and spend

each year for 20 years from each alternative? Assume she continues to earn 10 percent (before tax) and remains in the 20 percent federal income tax bracket.

4) If her salary grows, what impact will the increase have on the 401(k) plan? To illustrate the effect on her accumulated funds, assume a $5,000 increment every five years so that she is earning $72,000 in years 35–40 (ages 63–67).

5) What are the risks and potential returns associated with each of the six alternative funds?

6) Who bears the risk associated with Bozena's retirement income?

7) Why does Ken not have to make these investment decisions? What are the risks associated with his retirement plan?

8) At this point in Bozena's life, which alternative(s) do you suggest she select?

APPENDIX 8

The Taxation of Mutual Fund Distributions

Income and capital gains from investments in mutual funds are subject to federal income taxation just like income and capital gains from any other investments. Distributions from the funds are specified as income or capital gains on the 1099 forms sent to the individual so the investor knows the proper classification of the distributions for tax purposes.

Sales of fund shares, however, are trickier. The general rule is first purchased–first sold. For example, if an investor buys 100 shares in January and 100 shares in February and sells 100 shares in December, the shares purchased in January are considered to have been sold. Over time, security prices have risen, so the use of first-in–first-sold will probably result in the shares with the lowest cost basis being sold first. Selling the shares with the lower cost basis results in the investor owing more capital gains taxes.

If the investor only makes a few purchases, the record keeping required for tax purposes is modest. But, if additional shares are acquired through the reinvestment of distributions, accurate record keeping can be a substantial chore. Consider the following series of purchases.

Date	Shares Acquired	How Acquired	Average Price	Cost Basis
1/2/X0	100	Initial purchase	$20	$2,000
12/30/X0	4	$100 distribution	25	100
6/6/X1	50	Second purchase	72	3,600
12/30/X1	6	$360 distribution	60	360
1/31/X2	40	Third purchase	155	6,200

The investor has acquired 200 shares with a total cost basis of $12,260, which includes the purchases and the distributions. Notice that the cost basis of the shares acquired through the reinvestment of a distribution is the amount of the distribution. Each distribution was taxed in the year in which it was received even though the funds were reinvested. If the investor does not add in the amount of the distributions ($460) to the cost basis, he or she may believe that the total cost of the shares is $11,800. If all the shares are sold and the investor uses only $11,800 as the cost basis, any capital gain will be overstated and hence the taxes owed will be higher.

The investor now sells 40 shares. Under first-purchased–first-sold, 40 of the initial 100 shares were sold, so the cost basis of the 40 sold shares is $800 ($20 × 40). If the last 40 shares had been sold, the cost basis would have been $6,200. Any capital gains would have been smaller (or capital loss would have been larger). To have the higher cost basis apply, the investor writes the fund or broker and instructs that the shares purchased on 1/31/X2 be sold. Such documentation is necessary if the investor wants the 1/31/X2 shares sold for tax purposes in preference to the shares acquired on 1/2/X0.

Now consider what happens if the investor sells 150 shares. Under first-bought–first-sold, the 100 shares purchased 1/2/X0, the 4 shares purchased on 12/30/X0 with the $100 distribution, and 46 of the 50 shares acquired on 6/6/X1 are sold. The cost basis is $5,412 [$2,000 + 100 + (46/50)$3,600]. If the investor makes frequent purchases (e.g., a monthly purchase plan) and has distributions reinvested, the record keeping can become substantial.[1]

An alternative technique lets the investor determine the average cost of all the shares and use that for the cost basis. In the preceding illustration, the average cost of a share is $61.30 ($12,260/200). If 40 shares are sold, the cost basis is $2,452, and if 150 shares are sold, the cost basis is $9,195. Averaging *ends* the investor's ability to select which shares to sell. If, for instance, the investor wanted to sell the 40 shares that were purchased last and at the highest cost, such a strategy is precluded once the investor has started averaging the cost basis.

[1]One means of keeping track of a portfolio's cost basis is to use an Internet service. Possible sites include:

http://www.quicken.com
http://www.moneycentral.msn.com
http://www.morningstar.com
http://www.cnbc.com
http://www.clearstation.com
http://www.gainskeeper.com

While each site's services differ, they do facilitate tracking a portfolio. Investors can keep track of holdings bought at different times and different prices, and in some cases the services will print out reports of long- and short-term capital gains that can be attached to the investor's tax return.

Investing in Common Stock

PART 2

For many individuals the word *investing* is synonymous with buying and selling common stock. Although alternatives are certainly available, common stocks are a primary instrument of investing, perhaps because of the considerable exposure individuals have to them. Newspapers report stock transactions, market averages are quoted on the nightly news, and brokerage firms advertise the attractiveness of such investments.

Unlike bonds, which pay a fixed amount of interest, common stocks may pay a dividend and offer the potential to grow. As the economy prospers and corporate earnings rise, the dividends and the value of common stocks may also increase. For this reason, common stocks are a good investment for individuals who have less need for current income but desire capital appreciation.

This section discusses investing in common stocks. Various techniques are used to analyze a firm and its financial statements with the purpose of identifying the stocks that have the greatest potential or are the most undervalued. This section also considers how measures of the market are constructed and the returns that investors in the aggregate have earned over a period of years.

CHAPTER

9 The Valuation of Common Stock

You are considering purchasing IBM's stock and want information to facilitate your decision. From a source such as Quicken or Yahoo! Finance, you type in the IBM ticker symbol, which leads you to price quotes and various links such as company profile, analyst ratings, and financials. Financials sounds dull and you believe that you already know IBM's profile. You click on analyst ratings and find 20 ratings ranging from "strong buy" to "strong sell." You also find earnings estimates for the next year which range from $4.84 to $5.55. You click on an additional link for evaluation. The evaluation tells you the stock's price is in a "buy zone" and the buy zone ranges from $66 to $111. If you do buy the stock at its current price of $104, the stock could decline 40 percent and still be in the buy zone.

You are facing one of the most elusive and perplexing questions facing every investor. What is the stock worth? What is its current value? Without some estimate of the current value, the decision to buy will be based on hunches, intuition, or tips. What do you do? A financial psychologist (or cynic) might suggest that you latch on to the specific information that confirms a preconceived desire to buy IBM. But in any event, you must have some notion as to the value of the stock in order to justify the purchase of IBM.

Conceptually, the valuation of a stock is the same as the valuation of a bond or any asset. In each case, future cash flows are discounted back to their present value. For debt instruments this process is relatively easy because debt instruments pay a fixed amount of interest and mature at a specified date. Common stock, however, does not pay a fixed dividend, nor does it mature. These two facts considerably increase the difficulty of valuing common stock.

Initially in this chapter the features of common stock are described. Then follows a simple model for the valuation of common stock. Next a means for adjusting this model for risk is suggested. This dividend-growth model is then related to P/E ratios and other techniques for selecting stocks.

The chapter ends with a discussion of the efficient market hypothesis and the empirical evidence that supports the hypothesis. This hypothesis asserts that financial markets are so efficient that security prices properly measure what a stock is worth and that the investor cannot expect to consistently outperform the market on a risk-adjusted basis. While empirical evidence generally supports the efficient market hypothesis, there are some anomalies that suggest some investors may be able to earn a return in excess of the return they should earn relative to the market as a whole.

Learning Objectives

After completing this chapter you should be able to:

1 Identify the components of an investor's required rate of return.

2 Distinguish between required and expected returns.

3 Examine the determinants of a stock's price.

4 Calculate the value of a stock using a simple present value model.

5 Explain how to use P/E ratios, price-to-sales ratios, price-to-book ratios, and PEG ratios to select stocks.

6 Differentiate the three forms of the efficient market hypothesis.

7 Describe several anomalies that are inconsistent with the efficient market hypothesis.

The Corporate Form of Business and the Rights of Stockholders

stock
A security representing ownership in a corporation.

certificate of incorporation
A document creating a corporation.

charter
A document specifying the relationship between a firm and the state in which it is incorporated.

bylaws
A document specifying the relationship between a corporation and its stockholders.

voting rights
The rights of stockholders to vote their shares.

director
A person who is elected by stockholders to determine the goals and policies of the firm.

A corporation is an artificial legal economic unit established by a state. **Stock**, both common and preferred, represents ownership, or equity, in a corporation. Under state laws, the firm is issued a **certificate of incorporation** that indicates the name of the corporation, the location of its principal office, its purpose, and the number of shares of stock that are authorized (i.e., the number of shares that the firm may issue). In addition to a certificate of incorporation, the firm receives a **charter** that specifies the relationship between the corporation and the state. At the initial meeting of stockholders, **bylaws** are established that set the rules by which the firm is governed, including such issues as the **voting rights** of the stockholders.

Firms may issue both preferred and common stock. As the name implies, preferred stock holds a superior position to common stock. For example, preferred stock receives dividend payments before common stock and, in the case of liquidation, preferred stockholders are compensated before common stockholders. While preferred stock is legally equity and hence represents ownership, its features are more similar to the characteristics of debt than of common stock. For this reason, the discussion of preferred stock is deferred to Chapter 16, which covers the valuation of fixed-income securities.

In the eyes of the law, a corporation is a legal entity that is separate from its owners. It may enter into contracts and is legally responsible for its obligations. Creditors may sue the corporation for payment if it defaults on its obligations, but the creditors cannot sue the stockholders. Therefore, an investor knows that if he or she purchases stock in a publicly held corporation such as General Motors, the maximum that can be lost is the amount of the investment.[1] Occasionally, a large corporation (e.g., Columbia Gas, Macy's, or Texaco) does go bankrupt, but owing to limited liability, its stockholders cannot be sued by its creditors.[2]

Because stock represents ownership in a corporation, investors who purchase shares obtain all the rights of ownership. These rights include the option to vote the shares.[3] The stockholders elect a board of **directors** that selects the firm's management. Management is then responsible to the board of directors, which in turn is responsible to the firm's stockholders. If the stockholders do not think that the board is doing a competent job, they may elect another board to represent them.

For publicly held corporations, such democracy rarely works. Stockholders are usually widely dispersed, while the firm's management and board of directors generally form a cohesive unit. Rarely does the individual investor's vote mean much.[4] However, there is always the possibility that if the firm does poorly, another firm may offer to buy the outstanding stock held by the public. Once such

[1]Stockholders in privately held corporations who pledge their personal assets to secure loans do not have limited liability. If the corporation defaults, the creditors may seize the assets that the stockholders have pledged. In this event, the liability of the shareholders is not limited to their investment in the firm.

[2]Bankrupt large corporations rarely cease to exist but are reorganized or bought out by viable companies. Both Columbia Gas and Texaco used the bankruptcy filing as a strategic maneuver to increase their bargaining power in legal actions. Macy's bankruptcy resulted from its inability to meet current obligations as they came due. Macy's was subsequently purchased by Federated Department Stores.

[3]For convenience, stockholders may vote over the Internet. Go to http://www.proxyvote.com and follow the instructions.

[4]Exceptions do occur. In 1994, Kmart stockholders defeated a proposal to create separate classes of stock representing minority positions in four specialty units. One of the biggest occurred when Penn Central stockholders voted down a merger with Colt Industries. Management supported the merger but lost the vote: 10,245,440 shares against versus 10,104,220 shares in favor. For evidence of the impact of proxy fights on stockholder returns, see Lisa F. Borstadt and Thomas J. Swirlein, "The Efficient Monitoring Role of Proxy Contests: An Empirical Analysis of Post-Contest Control Changes and Firm Performance," *Financial Management* (autumn 1992): 22–34.

purchases are made, the stock's new owners may remove the board of directors and establish new management. To some extent this encourages a corporation's board of directors and management to pursue the goal of increasing the value of the firm's stock.

cumulative voting
A voting scheme that encourages minority representation by permitting each stockholder to cast all of his or her votes for one candidate for the firm's board of directors.

A stockholder generally has one vote for each share owned, but there are two ways to distribute this vote. With the traditional method of voting, each share gives the stockholder the right to vote for one individual for *each* seat on the board of directors. Under this system, if a majority group voted as a block, a minority group could never elect a representative. The alternative system, **cumulative voting**, gives minority stockholders a means to obtain representation on the firm's board. While cumulative voting is voluntary in most states, it is mandatory in several, including California, Illinois, and Michigan.

How cumulative voting works is best explained by a brief example. Suppose a firm has a board of directors composed of five members. With traditional voting, a stockholder with 100 shares may vote 100 votes for a candidate for each seat. The total 500 votes are split among the seats. Under cumulative voting, the individual may cast the entire 500 votes for a candidate for one seat. Of course, then the stockholder cannot vote for anyone running for the remaining four seats.

A minority group of stockholders can use the cumulative method of voting to elect a representative to the firm's board of directors. By banding together and casting all their votes for a specific candidate, the minority may be able to win a seat. Although this technique cannot be used to win a majority, it does offer the opportunity for representation that is not possible through the traditional method of distributing votes (i.e., one vote for each elected position). As would be expected, management rarely supports the cumulative voting system.

Since stockholders are owners, they are entitled to the firm's earnings. These earnings may be distributed in the form of cash dividends, or they may be retained by the corporation. If they are retained, the individual's investment in the firm is increased (i.e., the stockholder's equity increases). However, for every class of stock, the individual investor's relative position is not altered. Some owners of common stock cannot receive cash dividends, whereas others have their earnings reinvested. The distribution or retention of earnings applies equally to all stockholders.[5]

Although limited liability is one of the advantages of investing in publicly held corporations, stock ownership does involve risk. As long as the firm prospers, it may be able to pay dividends and grow. However, if earnings fluctuate, dividends and growth may also fluctuate. It is the owners—the stockholders—who bear the business risk associated with these fluctuations. If the firm should default on its debt, it can be taken to court by its creditors to enforce its obligations. If the firm should fail or become bankrupt, the stockholders have the last claim on its assets. Only after all the creditors have been paid will the stockholders receive any funds. In many cases of bankruptcy, this amounts to nothing. Even if the corporation survives bankruptcy proceedings, the amount received by the stockholders is uncertain.

preemptive rights
The right of current stockholders to maintain their proportionate ownership in the firm.

rights offering
Sale of new securities to stockholders.

Preemptive Rights

Some stockholders have **preemptive rights**, which is their prerogative to maintain their proportionate ownership in the firm. If the firm wants to sell additional shares to the general public, these new shares must be offered initially to the existing stockholders in a sale called a **rights offering**. If the stockholders wish to maintain their proportionate ownership in the firm, they can exercise their rights by purchasing the new shares. However, if they do not want to take advantage of

[5]Some corporations have different classes of stock. For example, Food Lion, Inc., has two classes of common stock, both of which are publicly traded. The class A stock does not have voting power while the class B does. However, if management chooses to pay dividends to the class B stock, it must pay a larger dividend to the class A stock.

this offering, they may sell their privilege to whoever wants to purchase the new shares.

Preemptive rights may be illustrated by a simple example. If a firm has 1,000 shares outstanding and an individual has 100 shares, that individual owns 10 percent of the firm's stock. If the firm wants to sell 400 new shares and the stockholders have preemptive rights, these new shares must be offered to the existing stockholders before they are sold to the general public. The individual who owns 100 shares would have the right to purchase 40, or 10 percent, of the new shares. If the purchase is made, then that stockholder's relative position is maintained, for the stockholder owns 10 percent of the firm both before and after the sale of the new stock.

Although preemptive rights are required in some states for incorporation, their importance has diminished and the number of rights offerings has declined.[6] Some firms have changed their bylaws in order to eliminate preemptive rights. For example, AT&T asked its stockholders to relinquish these rights. The rationale for this request was that issuing new shares through rights offerings was more expensive than selling the shares to the general public through an underwriting. Investors who desired to maintain their relative position could still purchase the new shares, and all stockholders would benefit through the cost savings and the flexibility given to the firm's management. Most stockholders accepted management's request and voted to relinquish their preemptive rights. Now AT&T does not have to offer any new shares to its current stockholders before it offers them publicly.

Investors' Expected Return

total return
The sum of divixdend yield and capital gains.

Investors purchase stock with the anticipation of a **total return** consisting of a dividend yield and a capital gain. The dividend yield is the flow of dividend income paid by the stock. The capital gain is the increase in the value of the stock that is related to the growth in earnings. If the firm is able to achieve growth in earnings, then dividends can be increased, and over time the shares should grow in value.

The expected return on an investment, which was discussed in Chapter 7 and expressed algebraically in Equation 7.1, is reproduced here:

(7.1)

$$E(r) = \frac{E(D)}{P} + E(g)$$

The expected return, $E(r)$, is the sum of the dividend yield, which is the expected dividend $E(D)$ divided by the price of the stock (P) plus the expected growth rate $E(g)$. If a firm's \$1 annual dividend is expected to grow at 7 percent and the price of the stock is \$25, the anticipated return on an investment in the stock is

$$E(r) = \frac{\$1}{\$25} + 0.07 = 0.11 = 11\%.$$

For an investment to be attractive, the expected return must be equal to or exceed the investor's required return. (Specification of the required return will be discussed later in this chapter.) If an individual requires an 11 percent return on investments in common stock of comparable risk, then this stock meets the investor's requirement. If, however, the investor's required rate of return is in excess of 11 percent, the anticipated yield on this stock is inferior, and the investor will

[6]Rights offerings and their valuation are discussed in Chapter 19, which covers options. The majority of NYSE and AMEX firms with rights offerings are foreign, not domestic, corporations.

POINTS OF INTEREST
Real Returns

As used in this text, the word *returns* implies nominal returns; no adjustment is made for the rate of inflation. If such an adjustment were made, the resulting returns would be expressed in *real* terms. Real returns measure the increase in purchasing power earned by the investor. If the nominal return was 15 percent when the rate of inflation was 10 percent, the investor is worse off than the investor who earns a nominal return of 10 percent during a period when prices increase by only 3 percent. In the latter case, the investor earns a higher real return.

The real return (i.e., the inflation-adjusted return) that the investor earns may be determined by the following equation:

$$\left(\frac{1 + \text{nominal return}}{1 + \text{rate of inflation}} - 1\right) \times 100\%$$

Thus, if the rate of nominal return is 15 percent when the rate of inflation is 10 percent, the real return is

$$\left(\frac{1 + 0.15}{1 + 0.10} - 1\right) \times 100\% = 4.545\%.$$

This rate is less than the real return when the nominal return is 10 percent and the rate of inflation is 3 percent. Under that circumstance the real return is

$$\left(\frac{1 + 0.10}{1 + 0.03} - 1\right) \times 100\% = 6.796\%.$$

There is no doubt that inflation has eroded the purchasing power of the dollar. Figure 10.7, in the next chapter, illustrates the real loss investors experienced after adjusting for inflation during the 1970s. However, during the 1980s, investors in common stock experienced a positive real return. Research on returns and inflation indicates that, over an extended period, the return on common stocks has exceeded the rate of inflation by about 6 percent.* This suggests that individuals who invested for the long haul earned a real return on their positions in common stock.

*See *Stocks, Bonds, Bills, and Inflation Yearbook* (Chicago, IL: Ibbotson Associates, published annually). The Web address is http://www.ibbotson.com.

not purchase the shares. Conversely, if the required rate of return on comparable investments in common stock is 10 percent, this particular stock is an excellent purchase because the anticipated return exceeds the required rate of return.

In a world of no commission fees and in which the tax on dividends is the same as on capital gains, investors would be indifferent to the composition of their return. An investor seeking an 11 percent return should be willing to accept a dividend yield of zero if the capital gain is 11 percent. Conversely, a capital growth rate of zero should be acceptable if the dividend yield is 11 percent. Of course, any combination of growth rate and dividend yield with an 11 percent return should be acceptable.

However, because of commissions and taxes, the investor may be concerned with the composition of the return. To realize the growth in the value of the shares, the investor must sell the security and pay commissions. This cost suggests a preference for dividend yield. In addition, capital gains occur in the future and may be less certain than the flow of current dividends. The uncertainty of future capital gains versus the likelihood of current dividends also favors dividends over capital appreciation.

Differences in the capital gains tax rate and the income tax on dividend income may have the opposite effect. If the long-term capital gains tax rate is lower than the income tax rate, investors may prefer to own stocks that pay minimal or even no dividends. Instead of collecting dividends and paying the tax, they hold the shares until they need the funds, then sell the stock (paying the commissions) and realize the capital gains. As of 2001, the difference between the highest income tax rate and the long-term capital gains tax rate was almost 20 percent (39.1 percent on income versus 20 percent on long-term capital gains), which strongly argues for preferring growth over dividend income.

Because each investor's situation and financial goals are different, it is not surprising that the preference for dividends or capital gains differs for various investors. Retired people may prefer a dividend yield for the income it provides. Investors with other sources of income may prefer growth and capital gains, since the capital gains tax is deferred until the shares are sold. Because an individual's financial needs and goals change, it is not surprising to find investors making changes in their portfolios. It is the role of security markets to bring these buyers and sellers together.

Valuation as the Present Value of Dividends and the Growth of Dividends

Value investing primarily focuses on what an asset is worth—its intrinsic value. As with the valuation of any asset, the valuation of stock involves bringing future cash inflows (e.g., dividends) back to the present at the appropriate discount factor.[7] For the individual investor, that discount factor is the required return, which is the return the investor demands to justify purchasing the stock. This return includes what the investor may earn on a risk-free security (e.g., a Treasury bill) plus a premium for bearing the risk associated with investments in common stock.

The process of valuation and security selection is similar to comparing expected and required returns, except the emphasis is placed on determining what the investor believes the security is worth. Future cash inflows are discounted back to the present at the required rate of return. The resulting valuation is then compared with the stock's current price to determine if the stock is under- or overvalued. Thus, valuation compares dollar amounts. That is, the dollar value of the stock is compared with its price. Returns compare percentages. That is, the expected percentage return is compared to the required return. In either case, the decision will be the same. If the valuation exceeds the price, the expected return will exceed the required return.

The process of valuation and security selection is readily illustrated by the simple case in which the stock pays a fixed dividend of $1 that is not expected to change. That is, the anticipated flow of dividend payments is

Year	1	2	3	4	...
Dividend	$1	$1	$1	$1	...

The current value of this indefinite flow of payments (i.e., the dividend) depends on the discount rate (i.e., the investor's required rate of return). If this rate is 12 percent, the stock's value (V) is

[7]For a basic explanation of the dividend-growth model and other techniques used to value securities, see: John Bajkowski, "From Theory to Reality: Applying the Valuation Models," *AAII Journal* (January 1993): 34–38; and John Markese, "A Fundamental Guide to Common Stock Valuation," *AAII Journal* (January 1993): 30–33.

Valuation is a major topic covered in depth in more advanced texts. See, for instance: Zvi Bodie, Alex Kane, and Alan J. Marcus, *Investments,* 4th ed. (Boston: Irwin McGraw-Hill, 1999); and William F. Sharpe, Gordon J. Alexander, and Jeffrey V. Bailey, *Investments,* 6th ed. (Upper Saddle River, NJ: Prentice-Hall, 1999).

Corporate professionals and investment managers may prefer the following trade publications to an advanced textbook. The following cover analysis of cash flow, differences between valuation and accounting practices, and value-based management: Tom Copeland, Time Koller, and Jack Murrin, *Valuation: Measuring and Managing the Value of Companies,* 2d ed. (New York: John Wiley & Sons, 1994); Aswath Damodaran, *The Dark Side of Valuation* (Upper Saddle River, NJ: Prentice-Hall, 2001).

For an opposing view (i.e., the excessive use of financial theory and its inapplicability to financial investment decisions), consult: Louis Lowenstein, *Sense and Nonsense in Corporate Finance* (Reading, MA: Addison-Wesley, 1991).

$$V = \frac{\$1}{(1 + 0.12)} + \frac{1}{(1 + 0.12)^2} + \frac{1}{(1 + 0.12)^3} + \frac{1}{(1 + 0.12)^4} + \cdots$$

$$V = \$8.33.$$

This process is expressed in the following equation in which the new variables are the dividend (D) and the required rate of return (k):

(9.1) $$V = \frac{D}{(1 + k)^1} + \frac{D}{(1 + k)^2} + \cdots + \frac{D}{(1 + k)^\infty}$$

which simplifies to

(9.2) $$V = \frac{D}{k}.$$

Thus, if a stock pays a dividend of \$1 and the investor's required rate of return is 12 percent, then the valuation is

$$\frac{\$1}{0.12} = \$8.33.$$

Any price greater than \$8.33 will result in a yield that is less than 12 percent. Therefore, for this investor to achieve the required rate of return of 12 percent, the price of the stock must not exceed \$8.33.

There is, however, no reason to anticipate that common stock dividends will be fixed indefinitely into the future. Common stocks offer the potential for growth, both in value and in dividends. For example, if the investor expects the \$1 dividend to grow annually at 6 percent, the anticipated flow of dividend payments is

Year	1	2	3	4	...
Dividend	\$1	\$1.06	\$1.124	\$1.191	...

The current value of this indefinite flow of growing payments (i.e., the growing dividend) also depends on the discount rate (i.e., the investor's required rate of return). If this rate is 12 percent, the stock's value is

$$V = \frac{\$1}{(1 + 0.12)} + \frac{1.06}{(1 + 0.12)^2} + \frac{1.124}{(1 + 0.12)^3} + \frac{1.191}{(1 + 0.12)^4} + \cdots$$

$$V = \$17.67.$$

dividend-growth valuation model
A valuation model that deals with dividends and their growth properly discounted back to the present.

Equation 9.2 may be modified for the growth in dividends. This is expressed in Equations 9.3 and 9.4. The only new variable is the rate of growth in the dividend (g), and it is assumed that this growth rate is fixed and will continue indefinitely into the future. Given this assumption, the **dividend-growth valuation model** is

(9.3) $$V = \frac{D(1 + g)^1}{(1 + k)^1} + \frac{D(1 + g)^2}{(1 + k)^2} + \frac{D(1 + g)^3}{(1 + k)^3} + \cdots + \frac{D(1 + g)^\infty}{(1 + k)^\infty}$$

which simplifies to

(9.4) $$V = \frac{D_0(1 + g)}{k - g}.$$

The stock's intrinsic value is thus related to (1) the current dividend, (2) the growth in earnings and dividends, and (3) the required rate of return.[8] Notice the current dividend is D_0, with the subscript 0 representing the present. The application of this dividend-growth model may be illustrated by a simple example. If the investor's required rate of return is 12 percent and the stock is currently paying a $1 per share dividend growing at 6 percent annually, the stock's value is

$$V = \frac{\$1(1 + 0.06)}{0.12 - 0.06} = \$17.67.$$

Any price greater than $17.67 will result in a total return of less than 12 percent. Conversely, a price of less than $17.67 will produce an expected return in excess of 12 percent. For example, if the price is $20, according to Equation 7.1 the expected return is

$$E(r) = \frac{\$1(1 + 0.06)}{\$20} + 0.06$$
$$= 11.3\%.$$

Because this return is less than the 12 percent required by the investor, this investor would not buy the stock and would sell it if he or she owned it.[9]

If the price is $15, the expected return is

$$E(r) = \frac{\$1(1 + 0.06)}{\$15} + 0.06$$
$$= 13.1\%.$$

This return is greater than the 12 percent required by the investor. Since the security offers a superior return, it is undervalued. This investor then would try to buy the security.

Only at a price of $17.67 does the stock offer a return of 12 percent. At that price it equals the return available on alternative investments of the same risk. The investment will yield 12 percent because the dividend yield during the year is 6 percent and the earnings and dividends are growing annually at the rate of 6 percent. These relationships are illustrated in Figure 9.1 (p. 258), which shows the growth in dividends and prices of the stock that will produce a constant yield of 12 percent. After 12 years, the dividend will have grown to $2.02 and the price of the stock will be $35.55. The total return on this investment will still be 12 percent. During that year, the dividend will grow to $2.14, giving a 6 percent dividend yield, and the price will continue to appreciate annually at the 6 percent growth rate in earnings and dividends.

If the growth rate had been different (and the other variables remained constant), the valuation would have differed. The following illustration presents the value of the stock for various growth rates:

Growth Rate	Value of the Stock
0%	$ 8.83
3%	$ 11.78
9%	$ 35.33
11%	$106.00
12%	undefined (denominator = 0)

[8]For a derivation of the equation, see Eugene F. Brigham and Louis G. Gapenski, *Intermediate Financial Management*, 5th ed. (Fort Worth, TX: The Dryden Press, 1996), 126.

[9]Notice the expected dividend is $1.06, which is the $1 current dividend plus the anticipated $0.06 (6 percent) increment in the dividend.

FIGURE 9.1

Earnings, Dividends, and Price of Stock over Time Yielding 12 Percent Annually

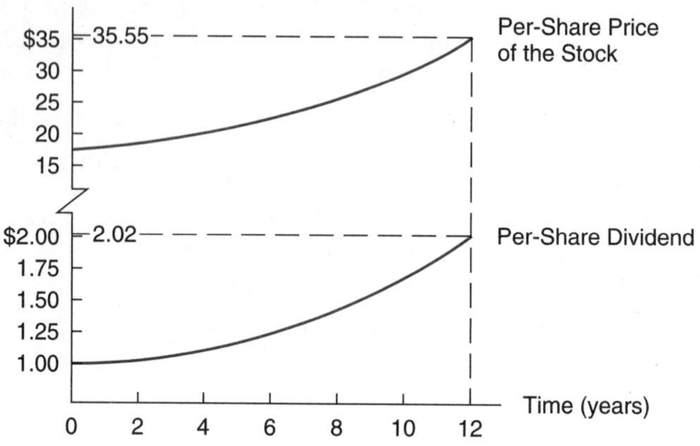

FIGURE 9.2

Earnings Growth Averaging 6 Percent Annually

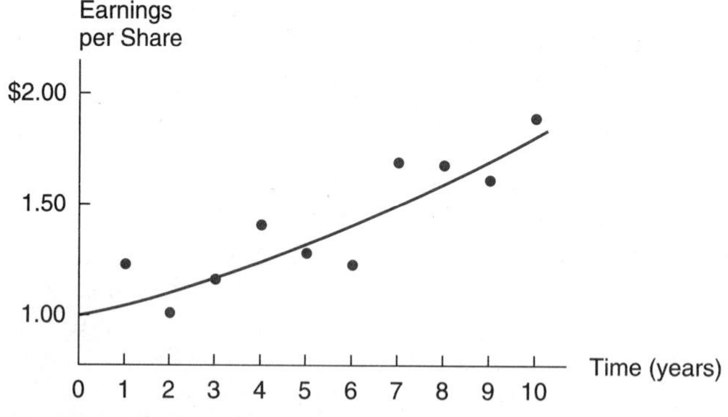

As the growth rate increases, so does the valuation, until the value becomes undefined (an exceedingly large number) when the growth rate equals the required return. This positive relationship indicates that when a stock offers more potential for capital gains, its valuation increases (if the dividend and the required return are *not affected* by the growth).

The dividend-growth valuation model assumes that the required return exceeds the rate of growth (i.e., $k > g$). While this may appear to be a restrictive assumption, it is logical. The purpose of the dividend-growth model is to determine what the stock is worth and then to compare this value to the actual price in order to determine whether the stock should be purchased. If a stock offers 14 percent when the investor requires 12 percent, the valuation is immaterial. It does not matter what the stock costs. Whether the price is $1 or $100,000 is irrelevant because the individual anticipates earning 14 percent on the amount invested when only 12 percent is required. Valuation can be material only if the growth rate (i.e., the potential capital gain) is less than the required return.

In the preceding illustration, the firm's earnings and dividends grew at a steady 6 percent rate. Figure 9.2 illustrates a case in which the firm's earnings grow annually at an average of 6 percent, but the year-to-year changes stray considerably from 6 percent. These fluctuations are not in themselves necessarily reason for concern. The firm does exist within the economic environment, which fluctuates over time. Exogenous factors, such as a strike or an energy curtailment, may also affect earnings during a particular year. If these factors continue to plague the firm, they will obviously play an important role in the valuation of the shares. However, the emphasis in valuation is on the flow of dividends and the growth in earnings over a period of years. This longer time dimension smoothes out temporary fluctuations in earnings and dividends.[10]

Although the previous model assumes that the firm's earnings will grow indefinitely and that the dividend policy will be maintained, such need not be the case. The dividend-growth model may be modified to encompass a period of increasing or declining growth or one of stable dividends. Many possible variations in growth patterns can be built into the model. Although these variations change the equation and make it appear far more complex, the fundamentals of valuation remain unaltered. Valuation is still the process of discounting future dividends and growth in earnings and dividends back to the present at the appropriate discount rate.

To illustrate such a variation, consider the following pattern of expected earnings and dividends.

Year	Earnings	Yearly Dividends	Percentage Change in Dividends from Previous Year
1	$1.00	$0.40	. . .
2	1.60	0.64	60.0%
3	1.94	0.77	20.3
4	2.20	0.87	13.0
5	2.29	0.905	4.0
6	2.38	0.941	4.0
7	2.48	0.979	4.0

After the initial period of rapid growth, the firm matures and is expected to grow annually at the rate of 4 percent. Each year the firm pays dividends, which contribute to its current value. However, the simple model summarized in Equation 9.4 cannot be used, because the earnings and dividends are not growing at a constant rate. Equation 9.3 can be used, and when these values, along with a required rate of return of 12 percent, are inserted into the equation, the stock's value is

$$\begin{aligned} V &= \frac{\$0.40}{(1+0.12)^1} + \frac{\$0.64}{(1+0.12)^2} + \frac{\$0.77}{(1+0.12)^3} + \frac{\$0.87}{(1+0.12)^4} \\ &\quad + \frac{\$0.905}{(1+0.12)^5} + \frac{\$0.941}{(1+0.12)^6} + \frac{\$0.979}{(1+0.12)^7} + \cdots \\ &= \$9.16. \end{aligned}$$

This answer is derived by dividing the flow of dividends into two periods: a period of super growth (years 1 through 4) and a period of normal growth (from year 5 on). The present value of the dividends in the first four years is

$$\begin{aligned} V_{1-4} &= \frac{\$0.40}{(1+0.12)^1} + \frac{\$0.64}{(1+0.12)^2} + \frac{\$0.77}{(1+0.12)^3} + \frac{\$0.87}{(1+0.12)^4} \\ &= \$0.36 + \$0.51 + \$0.55 + \$0.55 \\ &= \$1.97. \end{aligned}$$

[10]Methods for estimating growth rates are discussed after the material on dividends in Chapter 11.

The dividend-growth model is applied to the dividends from year 5 on, so the value of the dividends during normal growth is

$$V_{5-\infty} = \frac{\$0.87(1 + 0.04)}{0.12 - 0.04} = \$11.31.$$

This $11.31 is the value at the end of year 4, so it must be discounted back to the present to determine the current value of this stream of dividend payments. That is,

$$\frac{\$11.31}{(1 + 0.12)^4} = \$11.31(0.636) = \$7.19.$$

The value of the stock, then, is the sum of the two parts.[11]

$$\begin{aligned} V &= V_{1-4} + V_{5-\infty} \\ &= \$1.97 + 7.19 = \$9.16. \end{aligned}$$

As this example illustrates, modifications can be made in this valuation model to account for the different periods of growth and dividends. Adjustments can also be made for differences in risk. The student should realize that the model does not by itself adjust for different degrees of risk. If a security analyst applies the model to several firms to determine which stocks are underpriced, there is the implication that investing in all the firms involves equal risk. If the analyst uses the same required rate of return for each firm, then no risk adjustment has been made. The element of risk is assumed to be the same for each company.

The Investor's Required Return and Stock Valuation

One means to adjust for risk is to incorporate into the valuation model the beta coefficients presented earlier in Chapter 7. In that chapter, beta coefficients, which are an index of the market risk associated with the security, were used as part of the capital asset pricing model to explain returns. In this context, beta coefficients and the capital asset pricing model are used to specify the risk-adjusted required return on an investment.

The required return has two components: the risk-free rate (r_f) that the investor can earn on a risk-free security such as a U.S. Treasury bill, and a risk premium. The risk premium is also composed of two components: (1) the additional return that investing in securities offers above the risk-free rate, and (2) the volatility of

[11]This valuation procedure may be summarized by the following general equation:

$$V = V_s + V_n.$$

V_s is the present value of the dividends during the period of super growth; that is,

$$V_s = \sum_{t=1}^{n} \frac{D_0(1 + g_s)^t}{(1 + k)^t}.$$

V_n is the present value of the dividends during the period of normal growth; that is,

$$V_n = \left[\frac{D_n(1 + g)}{k - g}\right]\left(\frac{1}{(1 + k)^n}\right).$$

The value of the stock is the sum of the individual present values; that is,

$$V = \sum_{t=1}^{n} \frac{D_0(1 + g_s)^1}{(1 + k)^t} + \left[\frac{D_n(1 + g)}{k - g}\right]\left(\frac{1}{(1 + k)^n}\right).$$

the particular security relative to the market as a whole (i.e., the beta). The additional return is the extent to which the return on the market (r_m) exceeds the risk-free rate ($r_m - r_f$). Thus, the required return (k) is

(9.5) $$k = r_f + (r_m - r_f)\beta.$$

Equation 9.5 is the same general equation as the security market line in Chapter 7, which was used to explain a stock's return. In that context, the capital asset pricing model states that the realized return depends on the risk-free rate, the risk premium associated with investing in stock, and the market risk associated with the particular stock. In this context, the same variables are used to determine the return the investor requires to make the investment. The investor seeks a return that covers the yield on a risk-free asset, the risk premium associated with investing in stock, and the market risk associated with the specific stock. The difference between the two uses concerns time. In one case, the variables are being used to determine if a specific stock should currently be purchased; in the other, they are explaining what affected the realized return from an investment made in the past.

The following examples illustrate how the equation for the required return is used. The risk-free rate is 9 percent and it is anticipated that the market will rise by 12 percent. Stock A is relatively risky and has a beta coefficient of 1.80, while stock B is relatively safe and has a beta of 0.83. What return is necessary to justify purchasing either stock? Certainly it would not be correct to require a return of 12 percent for either, since that is the expected return on the market. Since stock A is riskier than the market, the required return for A should exceed 12 percent. However, the required return for B should be less than 12 percent because it is less risky than the market as a whole.

Given this information concerning the risk-free rate and the anticipated return on the market, the required rates of return for stocks A and B are

$$k_A = 9\% + (12\% - 9\%)1.80 = 9\% + 5.4\% = 14.4\%$$

and

$$k_B = 9\% + (12\% - 9\%)0.83 = 9\% + 2.5\% = 11.5\%.$$

Thus the required rates of return for stocks A and B are 14.4 percent and 11.5 percent, respectively. These required returns are different from each other and from the expected return on the market, because the analysis now explicitly takes into consideration risk (i.e., the volatility of the individual stock relative to the market). Stock A's required rate of return is greater than the expected return on the market (14.4 percent versus 12 percent) because stock A is more volatile than the market. Stock B's required rate of return is less than the return expected for the market (11.5 percent versus 12 percent) because stock B is less volatile than the market as a whole.

The relationship between the required rate of return and risk expressed in Equation 9.5 is illustrated in Figure 9.3 (p. 262). The horizontal axis represents risk as measured by the beta coefficient, and the vertical axis measures the required rate of return. Line *AB* represents the required rates of return associated with each level of risk. Line *AB* uses the information given in the preceding example: The Y-intercept is the risk-free return (9 percent), and the slope of the line is the difference between the market return and the risk-free return (12 percent minus 9 percent). If the beta coefficient were 1.80, the figure indicates that the required return would be 14.4 percent; if the beta coefficient were 0.83, the required return would be 11.5 percent.

The security market line will change if the variables that are used to construct it change. For example, if the expected return on the market were to increase from 12

FIGURE 9.3

Relationship between Risk and Required Rate of Return

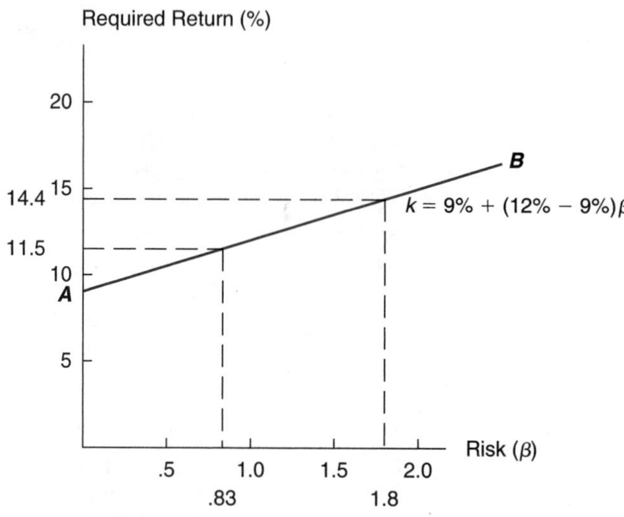

FIGURE 9.4

Relationship between Risk and Required Rate of Return

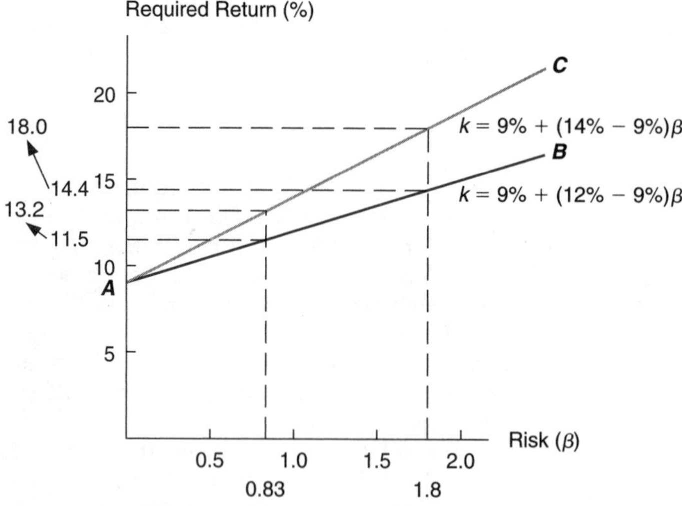

percent to 14 percent and there was no simultaneous change in the risk-free rate, then *AB* would pivot to *AC* in Figure 9.4. At each beta the required return is increased. For example, the required return for a stock with a beta of 1.80 now rises from 14.4 percent to 18 percent, and the required return for a stock with a beta of 0.83 increases from 11.5 percent to 13.2 percent.

How this risk-adjusted discount rate may be applied to the valuation of a specific stock is illustrated by the following example. Suppose a firm's current dividend of $2.20 would grow at 5 percent, U.S. Treasury bills of six-month duration offer a risk-free return of 6.5 percent, and an investor anticipates that the market would rise annually at a compound rate of 12.5 percent (i.e., about 6 percentage points more than the risk-free rate).[12] What would be the maximum price this investor should pay for the stock?

The first step in answering the question is to determine the risk-adjusted required return. If the firm's beta is 0.75, the required return is

$$\begin{aligned} k &= r_f + (r_m - r_f)\beta \\ &= 0.065 + (0.125 - 0.065)0.75 \\ &= 0.11. \end{aligned}$$

Next, this risk-adjusted required return is used in the dividend-growth model presented earlier:

$$\begin{aligned} V &= \frac{D_0(1 + g)}{k - g} \\ &= \frac{\$2.20(1 + 0.05)}{0.11 - 0.05} = \frac{\$2.31}{0.06} \\ &= \$38.50. \end{aligned}$$

At a price of $38.50 (and only at $38.50), the expected and required returns are equated. If the market price is below $38.50, the stock would be considered undervalued and a good purchase. Correspondingly, if the price exceeds $38.50, the stock should not be purchased but should be sold short.

Alternative Valuation Techniques

The dividend-growth model is theoretically sound: It discounts future cash flows back to the present at the required return, and the required return incorporates differences in market risk. Making the model operational, however, is difficult. A problem immediately arises if the stock does not pay a dividend, and many firms do not pay dividends. Without a dividend payment, the numerator is $0.00, which makes the value equal to $0.00.

While this problem is obvious, there are additional problems associated with each of the variables in the model. One problem is the choice of the beta coefficient. As was discussed in Chapter 7, there can be differences in estimated betas for the same stock, which raises a question as to which beta to use. The same question applies to the risk-free rate. Although a short-term rate on federal government securities may be used, investments in stock often have a longer time horizon. The question becomes which to use, a short-term or long-term rate? (A corollary question is this: Is it appropriate to use a short-term rate for valuing a long-term investment?) Even if the analyst does use a short-term rate, there is still the question of which short-term rate: a three-month, a six-month, or any other risk-free short-term rate?

[12]Ibbotson found that over a period of years stocks have yielded a return of approximately 6 to 7 percent in excess of the return on U.S. Treasury bills. Thus, if bills are yielding 6.5 percent, an expected return on the market of 12.5 percent is reasonable. See *Stocks, Bonds, Bills and Inflation Yearbook* (Chicago, IL: Ibbotson Associates, published annually).

POINTS OF INTEREST
Inflation and the Investor's Required Return

Although inflation is not explicitly part of the equation for the required rate of return, it is implicitly included. Anticipation of inflation will increase the rate on Treasury bills and the required return on the market. Higher rates of inflation will increase the T-bill rate as (1) the Federal Reserve takes steps to reduce inflation and (2) individuals seek to protect themselves by investing only if yields are sufficiently high to compensate them for the anticipated inflation.

A higher T-bill rate will result in an increase in the required return on the market. Investors certainly will not buy risky securities in general if their return declines relative to the T-bill rate. Increases in the T-bill rate must lead to corresponding increases in the required return on the market. The net effect will be to increase the required rate of return on an investment in common stock. For example, suppose the expected rate of inflation rises by 2 percent from 4 to 6 percent, which, in turn, causes the T-bill rate to rise from 6 to 8 percent and the required return on the market to increase from 12 to 14 percent. If a stock has a beta of 1.2, the required return rises from

$$k = 0.06 + (0.12 - 0.06)1.2 = 13.2\%$$

to

$$k = 0.08 + (0.14 - 0.08)1.2 = 15.2\%.$$

Similar problems exist with the return on the market and the future growth rate. One possible solution is to use historical data. Historical stock returns are discussed in the next chapter, and the computation of growth rates using past dividend payments is covered in Chapter 11. Historical returns may depend on the period selected, and the growth rate may depend on the method used for the calculation. In addition, using historical data assumes that the past is applicable to the future. The analyst is once again forced to make hard choices and simplify.

The problems with making the dividend-growth model applicable, however, are not a sufficient basis for discarding it or any other valuation model. Valuation models are built on discounting future cash flows. The analyst is forced to identify real economic forces (e.g., earnings and growth rates) and the returns on alternative investments (e.g., the risk-free rate and the return on the market). Without such analysis, the investor may have to rely on hunches, intuition, and just plain guessing to select assets. Such an approach has no conceptual or theoretical basis.

P/E Ratios

Value investing is concerned with the components of the dividend-growth model even if the analyst does not apply the actual model. The financial analyst or portfolio manager may employ alternative approaches to identify stocks for possible purchase. One of these approaches is the use of the ratio of the stock's price to earnings per share, or the P/E ratio.

The P/E ratio was introduced in Chapter 3 in the section on the reporting of security transactions by the financial press. That discussion suggested that firms in the same industry tend to have similar price/earnings ratios. In addition, as is discussed below, there is the suggestion that a firm's stock tends to trade within a range of price/earnings ratios.

The process by which price/earnings ratios may be used to value a stock is summarized by the following simple equation:

$$P = (m)(EPS), \tag{9.6}$$

which states that the value of the stock is the product of the earnings per share (*EPS*) and some multiple. This multiple is the appropriate price/earnings ratio. Once the earnings and the appropriate multiple are known, the value of the stock is easily determined. For example, if the financial analyst determines that the appropriate P/E ratio is 10 and the firm will earn $4.50 per share, the value of the stock is

$$(10)(\$4.50) = \$45.$$

The implication is that if the stock is currently selling for $35, it is undervalued and should be purchased. If it is selling for $55, it is overvalued and should be sold.

An alternative method using P/E ratios is to divide the current price by forecasted earnings to express the P/E ratio in terms of future earnings. For example, suppose the price of the stock is $36 when the estimated earnings are $4.50. The P/E using the estimated earnings is $36/$4.50 = 8.0. If the appropriate P/E is 10, a P/E of 8 suggests that the stock is undervalued and that the price of the stock will rise over time as the forecasted earnings are realized. The difference between these two approaches is the starting point. In the first case, the earnings and the appropriate P/E ratio are used to determine a value, which is compared to the current price. In the second case, the current price is divided by the estimated earnings to determine a P/E ratio, which is compared to the appropriate P/E ratio. In either case, the crux of the analysis is (1) the appropriate P/E ratio and (2) earnings.

The use of a P/E approach to valuation and security selection is often found in the financial press (if not the academic press). For example, the Argus Research Corporation Portfolio Selector recommended purchase of Genuine Parts Co. by stating that the "shares trade at 12.7 times our EPS projection of $2.90." A similar statement was made concerning Three Five Systems: "The shares appear undervalued at 13 times our earnings estimate of $2.25." Such material is typical of brokerage firms' purchase recommendations for common stocks.[13]

The previous discussion considered a unique P/E ratio, but stocks may be treated as if they trade within a range of P/E ratios. Consider the P/E ratios over a ten-year period for Bristol-Myers Squibb in Exhibit 9.1. On the average, the P/E ratio has ranged from a high of 27.8 to a low of 18.8. Unless there has been a

EXHIBIT 9.1

Price/Earnings Ratio for Bristol-Myers Squibb

Year	High	Low
2000	32	18
1999	38	28
1998	43	28
1997	30	16
1996	20	14
1995	17	11
1994	21	17
1993	23	18
1992	33	22
1991	21	16
Average	27.8	18.8

[13]Similar techniques are used in other areas to value an asset. For example, a house may sell for $100 per square foot, or a horse may sell for 30 times stud fees. Thus, a 2,560-square-foot house would have a valuation of $256,000, and a yearling whose stud fee had been $10,000 would be worth $300,000. Whether such valuations are excessive are, of course, up to the potential buyer to determine.

change in the composition of the firm, the investor will not expect a stock that has traded within a range of 27.8 to 18.8 to start selling for a P/E ratio of 40. Instead a P/E ratio of 40 would indicate that the stock is overpriced (such as in 1998 in Exhibit 9.1), while a P/E ratio of 10 would indicate the opposite.

Weakness in the Use of P/E Ratios

The first major weakness concerning the use of P/E ratios is the appropriate ratio. The preceding illustration employs a P/E ratio of 10, but no explanation is given to explain why 10 is appropriate. In the Bristol-Myers Squibb illustration, the point is made that the ratio ranged on the average between 27.8 and 18.8 but does not explain why either of these numbers would be the appropriate P/E ratio or why the ratio should stay within the range.

One possible solution is to use the industry average P/E ratio. This is a common solution to the problem of determining an appropriate ratio, but it does implicitly assume that a particular firm is comparable to the firms used to determine the average P/E ratio. Although many firms in an industry are similar, each is unique in some way. For example, is Phillips comparable to ExxonMobil? Both are large, integrated oil companies, but Phillips' oil reserves are primarily in Alaska while ExxonMobil's reserves are more diverse. Such differences in resources, markets served, or internal structure do raise the question of comparability. Financial analysts who use industry average P/E ratios may not address this question but view the average P/E ratio as a pragmatic solution to the problem of determining an appropriate P/E ratio for use in security valuation.

The second problem with the use of P/E ratios concerns earnings. There are essentially two problems: (1) the definition of earnings and (2) estimating future earnings. While companies report total and per-share earnings, these "bottom-line" numbers may include extraordinary items that are nonrecurring. Should the earnings be adjusted for these isolated events? For example, Chesapeake Corporation reported EPS of $12.29 in 1991, but these earnings included a $10.03 gain from the sale of its paper and forest products divisions. Without the nonrecurring gain, EPS would have been $2.26.

Obviously, the P/E ratio will be affected by the choice of earnings. Higher earnings will lower the P/E ratio and perhaps suggest that the stock is undervalued, especially if the industry average P/E ratio is higher. If the gain is excluded and EPS are lower, the P/E ratio will be higher. The higher P/E ratio may indicate that the stock is not undervalued. The converse applies to extraordinary charges to income. Chesapeake reported in 2000 a per-share loss of $4.26, which included a charge of $4.87. Without the nonrecurring loss, EPS would have been $0.71. The decline in EPS causes the P/E ratio to be higher (or in this example, undefined), so the stock may appear to be overvalued.

One possible solution is to adjust EPS for extraordinary items and use that figure to calculate the P/E. This is a reasonable approach if the items are unique, nonrecurring events. A firm, however, may have extraordinary items on a recurring basis. In one year, bad investments may be written off. In the next year, management may sell a subsidiary for a loss. In the third year, a loss of foreign exchange transactions may decrease earnings. Recurring extraordinary losses may imply poor management, so the use of the actual, *unadjusted* earnings may be appropriate. (One possible means to standardize recurring gains and losses may be to average the earnings over a period of years. Such an approach would acknowledge the extraordinary items but reduce the impact of a large extraordinary gain or loss in a particular year.)

Even if the investor resolves the problem of the definition of earnings, forecasting future earnings is daunting. As is illustrated in Chapter 13, the investor may compute many ratios based on data found in a firm's financial statements. By combining an analysis of the firm's financial statements, its position in its industry, and the direction of the economy, the financial analyst may be able to forecast earnings. It is doubtful, however, that the individual investor has the time or inclination to make such estimates.

If the individual obtains projected earnings from other sources, such earnings remain only forecasts. (See the Points of Interest box in Chapter 13 on the buy-side and the sell-side of the street for earnings forecasts.) Firms often report earnings that are perceptibly different from the forecasts of Wall Street's security analysts. Stock prices can move dramatically when actual earnings differ from the forecasts. For example, in June 2001, Juniper Networks announced that it would miss analysts' earnings projections. The price of the stock declined from $46.63 to $38.02, a decline of 18.5 percent. Such a large price change reflects the tendency of many investors, including professional portfolio managers, to react—perhaps overreact—to good or bad news.

Similarities Between the Use of P/E Ratios and the Dividend-Growth Valuation Model

Even though P/E ratios have serious weaknesses from the perspective of common-stock valuation, they are useful for comparing firms with different earnings and stock prices. Current earnings and the price of the stock are combined in a P/E ratio, and this standardization facilitates comparisons. If a firm's P/E ratio differs from the industry average, the investor may want to ask why and analyze the firm further before making an investment decision.

The previous discussion suggested how P/E ratios may be used to compare firms and help select individual stocks. The approach appears to be different from the dividend-growth model presented earlier in this chapter. They are, however, essentially similar. The dividend-growth model was

$$V = \frac{D_0(1 + g)}{k - g}$$

The firm's current dividend (D_0) is related to its current earnings (E_0) and the proportion of the earnings that are distributed (d). That is, the dividend is the product of the earnings and the proportion distributed:

$$D_0 = dE_0.$$

When this is substituted back into the dividend-growth model, the model becomes

$$V = \frac{dE_0(1 + g)}{k - g}$$

If both sides of the equation are divided by earnings (E_0), the stock's valuation is expressed as a P/E ratio:

$$\frac{V}{E_0} = \frac{d(1 + g)}{k - g}$$

From this perspective, a P/E ratio depends on the same fundamental financial variables as the dividend-growth model: the dividend (which depends on earnings), the firm's ability to grow, and the required return.

The use of P/E ratios instead of the dividend-growth model offers one major advantage and one major disadvantage. As previously stated, the advantage is that P/E ratios may be applied to common stocks that are not currently paying cash dividends. The dividend-growth model assumes that the firm will eventually pay cash dividends and that it is these future dividends that give the stock current value. The major weakness of the use of P/E ratios is that these ratios do not tell the analyst if the security is under- or overvalued. The ratio may indicate whether the firm's stock is selling near its historic high or low P/E ratio and then the investor draws an inference from this information. The dividend-growth model establishes a value based on the investor's required rate of return, the firm's dividends, and the future growth in those dividends. This valuation is then compared to the actual price to answer the question of whether the stock is under- or overvalued.

Price/Book Value

An alternative to P/E ratios for the selection of stocks is the ratio of the price of the stock to the per-share book value. (Book value is the sum of stock, additional paid-in capital, and retained earnings on a firm's balance sheet.) Essentially the application is the same as with the P/E ratio. The security analyst compares the price of the stock with its per-share book value. A low ratio suggests that the stock is undervalued while high ratios suggest the opposite. Determining what constitutes a "low" or a "high" value is left to the discretion of the analyst, but the ratio (like all ratios) does facilitate comparisons of firms.

P/E ratios and the ratio of market to book are convenient means to compare stocks and are important to the value approach for security selection. Value investing emphasizes stocks that are anticipated to grow more slowly than average but may be selling for low prices (i.e., are undervalued). These stocks often have low P/E and market-to-book ratios, and the firms often operate in basic or low-tech industries. The essence of this approach is that the market has overlooked these stocks. A value strategy is obviously opposite to a growth strategy, which emphasizes the selection of stocks with greater-than-average growth potential.

Price/Sales (P/S) Ratio

A third valuation ratio is the ratio of the stock price to per-share sales (P/S). This ratio offers one particular advantage over the P/E ratio. If a firm has no earnings, the P/E ratio has no meaning, and the ratio breaks down as a tool for valuation and comparisons. The P/S ratio, however, can be computed even if the firm is operating at a loss, thus permitting comparisons of all firms, including those that are not profitable.

Even if the firm has earnings and thus has a positive P/E ratio, the price/sales ratio remains a useful analytical tool. Earnings are ultimately related to sales. A low P/S ratio indicates a low valuation; the stock market is not placing a large value on the firm's sales. Even if the firm is operating at a loss, a low P/S ratio may indicate an undervalued investment. A small increase in profitability may translate these sales into a large increase in the stock's price. When the firm returns to profitability, the market may respond to the earnings, and both the P/E and P/S ratios increase. Thus, a current low price/sales ratio may suggest that there is considerable potential for the stock's price to increase. Such potential would not exist if the stock were selling for a high price/sales ratio.

How the price/sales ratios is used is illustrated in Exhibit 9.2, which gives the price/sales, price/book, and price/earnings ratios for four firms classified in the paper and paper products industry. The exhibit also includes Georgia Pacific, which manufactures paper products and building supplies. All these ratios are readily available through the Internet. See, for instance, http://www.morningstar.com, http://biz.yahoo.com, or http://www.quicken.com. Exhibit 9.2 uses Wall

EXHIBIT 9.2

Price/Sales, Price/Book, and Price/Earnings Ratios

Selected Firms in the Paper and Paper Products Industry			
	Price/Sales	**Price/Book**	**Price/Earnings**
Chesapeake Corporation	0.47	0.89	29.4
Westvaco Corporation	0.78	1.23	11.3
Weyerhaeuser Company	0.70	1.63	13.6
Willamette Industries	1.10	2.16	15.0
Paper Products and Building Products			
Georgia Pacific	0.32	1.26	16.0

Source: Wall Street Research Net (http://www.wsrn.com), August 11, 2001.

Street Research Net (http://www.wsrn.com), which reports data from Media General Financial Services. (Wall Street Research Net and Media General provide an excellent set of definitions of the data. For example, click on "AboutQuick-Source Data" in the section on Fundamental Data and Ratios in Wall Street Research Net's Financials.)

As may be seen in the exhibit, Chesapeake has the lowest P/S and P/B ratios of the paper and paper products firms. The low ratios would suggest that Chesapeake is the most undervalued of the four firms. Unfortunately, it also has the highest P/E ratio, which would suggest the exact opposite conclusion. Based solely on the P/S ratio, Georgia Pacific is the best buy.

While the ratio of price/sales is used as a tool for security selection, the weaknesses that apply to P/E ratios (and to price/book ratios) also apply to price/sales. Essentially, there is no appropriate or correct ratio to use for the valuation of a stock. While some financial analysts believe that a low P/E ratio is indicative of financial weakness, other security analysts draw the opposite conclusion. The same applies to price/sales ratios. Some financial analysts isolate firms with low ratios and then suggest that these firms are undervalued. Other analysts, however, would argue the opposite. Low price/sales ratios are characteristic of firms that are performing poorly and not worth a higher price. The low ratio then does not indicate undervaluation but is a mirror of financial weakness.

PEG Ratio

PEG ratio
The price/earnings ratio divided by the growth rate of earnings.

Another alternative valuation technique that came into prominence during the late 1990s is the **PEG ratio**. This ratio is

$$\frac{\textbf{Price/earnings ratio}}{\textbf{Earnings growth rate}}.$$

If the stock's P/E ratio is 20 and the per-share earnings growth rate is 10 percent, the value of the ratio is

$$\frac{20}{10} = 2.$$

The PEG ratio standardizes P/E ratios for growth. It gives a relative measure of value and facilitates comparing firms with different growth rates.

If the growth rate exceeds the P/E ratio, the numerical value is less than 1.0 and suggests that the stock is undervalued. If the P/E ratio exceeds the growth rate, the PEG ratio is greater than 1.0. The higher the numerical value, the higher the valuation and the less attractive is the stock. A PEG of 1.0 to 2.0 may suggest the stock is reasonably valued, and a ratio greater than 2.0 may suggest the stock is overvalued. (What numerical value determines under- and overvaluation depends on the financial analyst or investor.)

As with the price/earnings, price/sales, and price/equity ratios, the PEG ratio can have significant problems. Certainly all the questions concerning the use of price/earnings ratios apply to the PEG ratio, since the P/E ratio is the numerator in the PEG ratio. Should earnings include nonrecurring items or be adjusted for nonrecurring items? Should the analyst use historical earnings? Should an estimated or expected P/E ratio be used?

Consistency requires that the P/E ratio and the earnings growth rate have common definitions. If the forecasted growth rate is based on current earnings that exclude nonrecurring items, that argues for using a P/E based on recurring current earnings. Price/earnings ratios based on expected earnings, however, should not be used in the calculation of the PEG ratio, because both the numerator and denominator would be based on the same growth rate.[14]

Because the PEG ratio standardizes for growth, it offers one major advantage over P/E ratios. The PEG ratio facilitates comparisons of firms in different industries that are experiencing different rates of growth. Rapidly growing companies may now be compared to companies experiencing a lower rate of growth. This comparison is illustrated in Exhibit 9.3, which gives the PEG and P/E ratios for several firms. Several of the firms (e.g., Capital One Financial and Honeywell) have high P/E ratios and may be considered overvalued based solely on that ratio. However, these same firms are expected to grow more rapidly, so when the P/E ratio is standardized for growth, these stocks appear less overvalued. Other firms such as EMC have relatively high PEG and P/E ratios, which would suggest they are overvalued. And at the other extreme, Phillips Petroleum has a low P/E and a low PEG, which suggests the stock is undervalued. Of course, the investor may want to ask why both ratios are so low for Phillips. The low PEG and the low

EXHIBIT 9.3

Selected PEG Ratios as of August 2001

Firm	PEG Ratio	P/E Ratio
Capital One Financial	0.9	25.8
Cisco	5.1	N/E
Coca-Cola	2.2	33.1
Dominion Resources	1.4	21.8
EMC	2.7	30.7
ExxonMobil	2.3	15.8
Hershey Foods	2.3	23.3
Honeywell	1.2	47.7
Phillips Petroleum	0.8	6.4

Source: Quicken (http://www.quicken.com), August 10, 2001.

[14]Some analysts obviously do use P/E ratios based on expected earnings when computing PEG ratios. In Exhibit 9.3 Quicken reported a 5.1 PEG for Cisco even though the service also reported N/E (no earnings) for Cisco's P/E ratio. This presentation would suggest that the PEG ratio for Cisco must be based on projected and not historical earnings.

P/E ratios may be a good starting point but are probably not sufficient to conclude the stock is a good purchase.

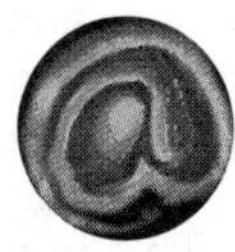

The investor could calculate PEG ratios, but it may be more practical to obtain them from an existing source. Possible sources include Morningstar (http://www.morningstar.com) or Quicken (http://www.quicken.com). As in the case of beta coefficients, a problem exists concerning which source to use, since PEG ratios may differ from different sources.[15] For example, the PEG ratio for Hershey Foods located at Quicken was 2.3 but was 1.7 from INVESTools (http://www.investools.com). Certainly if an investor wants to compare firms, only one source should be used to maintain consistency.

Cash Flow

An alternative to using earnings in security valuation is cash flow and the ability of the firm to generate cash. (The statement of cash flows, which emphasizes the change in a firm's cash position, is covered in Chapter 13, which discusses the analysis of financial statements.) For young, growing firms, the ability to generate cash may be initially as important as earnings since generating cash implies the firm is able to grow without requiring external financing. After the initial period of operating at a loss but producing positive cash flow, the firm may grow into a prosperous, profitable operation.

The valuation process using cash flow is essentially the same as is used with P/E ratios, except cash flow is substituted for earnings and emphasis is placed on the growth in cash flow rather than the growth of earnings. For example, in its August issue of *Private Client Monthly* a Scott & Stringfellow analyst recommended purchasing XTO stock. Besides the company's successful exploration for and production of natural gas, the analyst pointed out that XTO was trading "below 5× 2002 discretionary cash flow." In this illustration, 5 times cash flow was being used instead of 5 times earnings to justify purchasing the stock.

The estimation of future cash flow and the determination of the appropriate multiplier are, of course, at the discretion of the investor or analyst. For firms with substantial investments in plant or natural resources, noncash depreciation (and depletion expense) helps recapture the cost of these investments and contribute to the firm's cash flow. The same applies to real estate investments, and funds from operations are often used instead of earnings when valuing properties and real estate investment trusts.[16] Such valuations are the essence of value investing practiced by individuals such as Warren Buffett. Whether a value approach is superior to a growth approach will be addressed in the next section on efficient markets and possible anomalies to the efficient market hypothesis.

The Efficient Market Hypothesis

Perhaps it is conceit that makes some individuals think they can use the dividend-growth model or P/E ratios or price-to-book ratios or any other technique to beat the market. The important consideration, however, is not beating the market but outperforming the market on a risk-adjusted basis. Notice the use of the phrase *risk-adjusted basis.* This distinction between the phrases "beating the market" and "beating the market on a risk-adjusted basis" is important. The popular press often compares returns to the return on the market and announces that X outperformed (or underperformed) the market.

[15]Differences in beta coefficients were illustrated in Chapter 7 in the Points of Interest: Will the Real Beta Please Stand Up?

[16]See also the discussion of depreciation in Chapter 6 under corporate taxation and the discussion of real estate investment trusts (REITs) in Chapter 23.

Of course, if a particular portfolio manager pursues a risky strategy, that individual should "beat" the market. Conversely, an individual who manages a conservative, low-risk portfolio should not beat the market. Failure to consider risk is, in effect, omitting one of the most important considerations in investing. Thus, to beat the market, the portfolio manager or individual investor must do better than the return that would be expected given the amount of risk. This implies that the investor could earn a lower return than the market but still outperform the market after adjusting for risk.

efficient market hypothesis (EMH)
A theory that security prices correctly measure the firm's future earnings and dividends and that investors should not consistently outperform the market on a risk-adjusted basis.

The **efficient market hypothesis (EMH)** suggests that investors cannot expect to outperform the market consistently on a risk-adjusted basis. Notice that the hypothesis does not say an individual will not outperform the market, since obviously some investors may do exceptionally well for a period of time. Being an occasional winner is not what is important, however, since most investors have a longer time horizon. The efficient market hypothesis suggests that investors will not outperform the market on a risk-adjusted basis over an extended period of time.

The efficient market hypothesis is based on several assumptions, including (1) the fact that there are a large number of competing participants in the securities markets, (2) information is readily available and virtually costless to obtain, and (3) transaction costs are small. The first two conditions seem obvious. That there are a large number of participants cannot be denied. Brokerage firms, insurance companies, investment and asset management firms, and many individuals spend countless hours analyzing financial statements seeking to determine the value of a company. The amount of information available on investments is nothing short of staggering, and the cost of obtaining much of the information used in security analysis is often trivial.

The third condition may not hold for individual investors, who must pay commissions to brokerage firms for executing orders. The condition does apply to financial institutions, such as trust departments and mutual funds. These institutions pay only a few cents per share and this insignificant cost does not affect their investment decisions. Today, as a result of electronic trading, even the individual investor may now be able to buy and sell stock at a cost that is comparable to financial institutions. However, investors who continue to use traditional full-service brokers pay substantial commissions to trade stocks, and these commissions do affect the investment's return.

Because security markets are highly competitive, information is readily available, and transactions may be executed with minimal transaction costs, the efficient market hypothesis argues that security prices adjust rapidly to new information and must reflect all known information concerning the firm. Since security prices fully incorporate known information and prices change rapidly, day-to-day price changes will follow in a *random walk* over time. A random walk essentially means that price changes are unpredictable and patterns formed are accidental. If prices do follow a random walk, trading rules are useless, and various techniques, such as charting, moving averages, or odd-lot purchases relative to sales, cannot lead to superior security selection. (These techniques are discussed in Chapter 14.)

The conventional choice of the term *random walk* to describe the pattern of changes in security prices is perhaps unfortunate for two reasons. First, it is reasonable to expect that over a period of time, stock prices will rise. Unless the return is entirely the result of dividends, stock prices must rise to generate a positive return. In addition, stock prices will tend to rise over time as firms and the economy grow.

Second, the phrase *random walk* is often misinterpreted as meaning that security prices are randomly determined, an interpretation that is completely backwards. It is *changes* in security prices that are random. Security prices themselves are rationally and efficiently determined by such fundamental considerations as earnings, interest rates, dividend policy, and the economic environment. Changes in

FIGURE 9.5

Adjustments in Expected Returns When Securities Are Under- or Overvalued

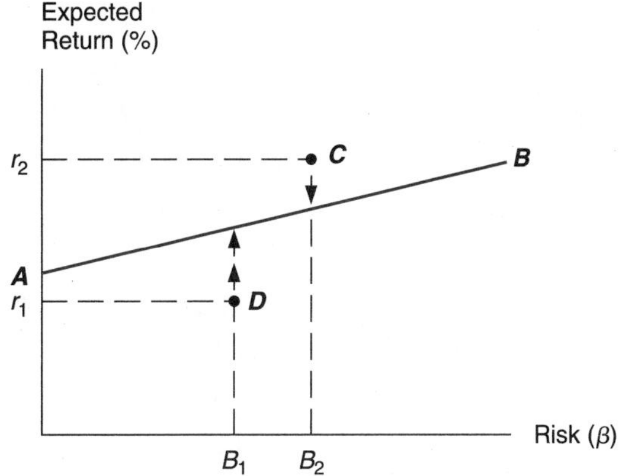

these variables are quickly reflected in a security's price. All known information is embodied in the current price, and only new information will alter that price. New information has to be unpredictable; if it were predictable, the information would be known and stock prices would have already adjusted for that information. Hence, new information *must be random,* and security prices should change randomly in response to that information. If changes in security prices were not random and could be predicted, then some investors could consistently outperform the market (i.e., earn a return in excess of the expected return given the amount of risk) and security markets would not be efficient.

Because security prices incorporate all known information concerning a firm, the current price of a stock must properly value the firm's future growth and dividends. Today's price, then, is a true measure of the security's worth. Security analysis that is designed to determine if the stock is over- or underpriced is futile, because the stock is neither. If prices were not true measures of the firm's worth, an opportunity to earn excess returns would exist. Investors who recognized these opportunities (e.g., that a particular stock is undervalued) and took advantage of the mispricing (e.g., bought the undervalued stock) would consistently outperform the market on a risk-adjusted basis.

This process by which security prices would adjust may be illustrated by using the figure relating risk and return presented earlier in the chapter. Figure 9.5 reproduces this relationship between risk and return. Suppose stock C offered an expected return of r_2 for bearing B_2 of risk. What would the investor do? The obvious answer is rush to purchase the stock, because it offers an exceptional return for the given amount of risk. If several investors had a similar perception of this risk/return relationship, they also would seek to purchase the stock, which would certainly increase its price and reduce the expected return. This price increase and reduction in expected return stops when point C in Figure 9.5 moves back to line *AB,* which represents all the optimal combinations of risk and expected returns that are available. Thus, the security that was initially undervalued becomes fairly priced and no longer offers an exceptional return.

The converse case (i.e., overvaluation) is illustrated by stock D in Figure 9.5, which offers an inferior expected return for the given amount of risk. In this case, investors perceive the stock as being overvalued and will seek to sell it. This increased desire to sell will depress the stock's price and thus increase the expected return. The decline in the stock's price will cease only after the expected return has

FIGURE 9.6

Daily Closing Prices of AMR (American Airlines)

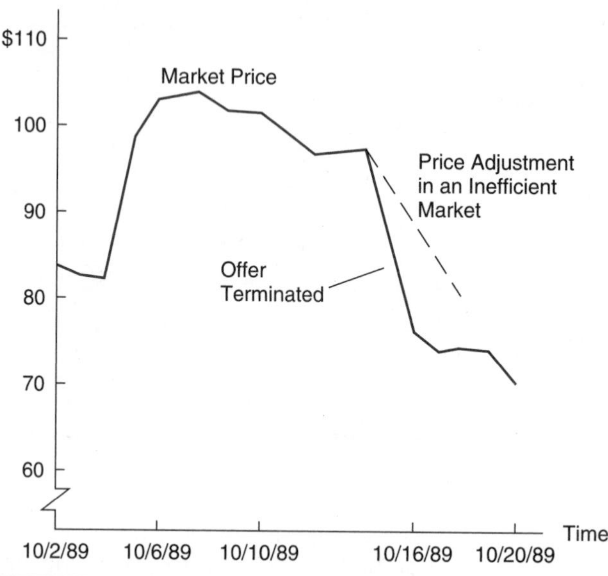

risen sufficiently to move point D in Figure 9.5 back to the line representing the optimal risk/return relationship. The efficient market hypothesis thus asserts that the price of any under- or overvalued stock is unstable and will change. The security's equilibrium price (when there is no incentive to change) is a true valuation of what the investment community believes the asset is worth.

The Speed of Price Adjustments

For security markets to be efficient, security prices must adjust rapidly. The efficient market hypothesis asserts that the market prices adjust extremely rapidly as new information is disseminated. In the modern world of advanced communication, information is rapidly dispersed in the investment community. The market then adjusts security prices in accordance with the impact of the news on the firm's future earnings and dividends. By the time that the individual investor has learned the information, security prices probably will have already changed. Thus, the investor will not be able to profit from acting on the information.

This adjustment process is illustrated in Figure 9.6, which plots the price of AMR (American Airlines) stock. In early October 1989, AMR received a buyout offer at $120, and the stock rose quickly and dramatically. However, the offer was terminated on October 16, and the price of the stock fell 22⅛ points from $98⅝ to $76½. Such price behavior is exactly what the efficient market hypothesis suggests: The market adjusts very rapidly to new information. By the time the announcement was reported in the financial press on October 17, it was too late for the individual investor to react, as the price change had already occurred. Today, with announcements being rapidly disseminated via the Internet, it is unlikely that many, if any, individuals could receive and act on the information before the price changes. Once the announcement has been made, security dealers will immediately alter the bid and ask prices to adjust for the new information.

If the market were not so efficient and prices did not adjust rapidly, some investors would be able to adjust their holdings and take advantage of differences in investors' knowledge. Consider the broken line in Figure 9.6. If some investors knew that the agreement had been terminated but others did not, the former could sell their holdings to those who were not informed. The price then may fall over a period of time as the knowledgeable sellers accepted progressively lower prices in order to unload their stock. Of course, if a sufficient number of investors had learned quickly of the termination, the price decline would be rapid as these investors adjusted their valuations of the stock in accordance with the new information. That is exactly what happened, because a sufficient number of investors were rapidly informed and the efficient market quickly adjusted the stock's price.

If an investor were able to anticipate the termination of the merger before it was announced, that individual could avoid the price decline. Obviously, some investors did sell their shares just before the announcement, but it is also evident that some individuals bought those shares. Certainly one reason for learning the material and performing the various types of analysis throughout this text is to increase one's ability to anticipate events before they occur. However, the investor should realize that considerable evidence supports the efficient market hypothesis and strongly suggests few investors will, over a period of time, outperform the market consistently.

Forms of the Efficient Market Hypothesis

The previous discussion of the efficient market hypothesis suggested that financial markets are efficient. The competition among investors, the rapid dissemination of information, and the swiftness with which security prices adjust to this information produce efficient financial markets in which an individual cannot expect to consistently outperform the market. Instead, the investor can expect to earn a return that is consistent with the amount of risk he or she bears.

While the investor may know that financial markets are efficient, he or she may not know *how* efficient. The degree of efficiency is important, because it determines the value the individual investor places on various types of analysis to select securities. If financial markets are inefficient, then many techniques may aid the investor in selecting securities, and these techniques will lead to superior results. However, as markets become more efficient and various tools of analysis become well known, their usefulness for security selection is reduced, since they will no longer produce superior results (i.e., beat the market on a risk-adjusted basis).

The investor may believe that the financial markets are weakly efficient, semistrongly efficient, or strongly efficient. The *weak form* of the efficient market hypothesis suggests that the fundamental analysis discussed in Chapter 13 may produce superior investment results but that the technical analysis discussed in Chapter 14 will not. Thus, studying past price behavior and other technical indicators of the market will not produce superior investment results. For example, if a stock's price rises, the next change cannot be forecasted by studying previous price behavior. According to the weak form of the efficient market hypothesis, technical indicators do not produce returns on securities that are in excess of the return consistent with the amount of risk borne by the investor.

The *semistrong* form of the efficient market hypothesis asserts that the current price of a stock reflects all the public's information concerning the company. This knowledge includes both the firm's past history and the information learned through studying a firm's financial statements, its industry, and the general economic environment. Analysis of this material cannot be expected to produce superior investment results. Notice that the hypothesis does not state that the analysis cannot produce superior results. It just asserts that superior results should not be expected. However, there is the implication that even if the analysis of information produces superior results in some cases, it will not produce superior results over many investment decisions.

This conclusion should not be surprising to anyone who thinks about the investment process. Many investors and analysts study the same information. Their thought processes and training are similar, and they are in competition with one another. Certainly, if one perceives a fundamental change in a particular firm, this information will be readily transferred to other investors, and the price of the security will change. The competition among the potential buyers and the potential sellers will result in the security's price reflecting the firm's intrinsic worth.

As may be expected, the investment community is not particularly elated with this conclusion. It implies that the fundamental analysis considered in Chapter 13 will not produce superior investment results. Thus, neither technical nor fundamental analysis will generate consistently superior investment performance. Of course, if the individual analyst is able to perceive fundamental changes before other analysts do, that individual can outperform the market as a whole. However, few, if any, individuals should be able to consistently perceive such changes. Thus, there is little reason to expect investors to achieve *consistently* superior investment results.

There is, however, one major exception to this general conclusion of the semistrong form of the efficient market hypothesis. If the investor has access to *inside information,* that individual may consistently achieve superior results. In effect, this individual has information that is not known by the general investing public. Such privileged information as dividend cuts or increments, new discoveries, or potential takeovers may have a significant impact on the value of the firm and its securities. If the investor has advance knowledge of such events and has the time to act, he or she should be able to achieve superior investment returns.

Of course, most investors do not have access to inside information or at least do not have access to information concerning a number of firms. An individual may have access to privileged information concerning a firm for which he or she works. But as was previously pointed out, the use of such information for personal gain is *illegal.* To achieve continuous superior results, the individual would have to have a continuous supply of correct inside information and to use it illegally. Probably few, if any, investors have this continuous supply, which may explain why both fundamentalists and technical analysts watch sales and purchases by insiders as a means to glean a clue as to the true future potential of the firm as seen by its management.

The *strong form* of the efficient market hypothesis asserts that the current price of a stock reflects all known (i.e., public) information and all privileged or inside information concerning the firm. Thus, even access to inside information cannot be expected to result in superior investment performance. Once again, this does not mean that an individual who acts on inside information cannot achieve superior results. It means that these results cannot be expected and that success in one case will tend to be offset by failure in other cases, so over time the investor will not achieve superior results.

This conclusion rests on a very important assumption: Inside information cannot be kept inside! Too many people know about the activities of a firm. This information is discerned by a sufficient number of investors, and the prices of the firm's securities adjust for the informational content of this inside knowledge. Notice that the conclusion that the price of the stock still reflects its intrinsic value does not require that all investors know this additional information. All that is necessary is for a sufficient number to know. Furthermore, the knowledge need not be acquired illegally. It is virtually impossible to keep some information secret, and there is a continual flow of rumors concerning a firm's activities. Denial by the firm is not sufficient to stop this spread of rumors, and when some are later confirmed, it only increases the credibility of future rumors as a possible means to gain inside information.

Although considerable empirical work has been designed to verify the forms of the efficient market hypothesis, these tests generally support only the weak and semistrong forms. The use of privileged information may result in superior investment performance, but the use of publicly known information cannot be expected to produce superior investments. Thus, neither technical nor fundamental analysis may be of help to the individual investor, because the current price of a stock fully incorporates this information.

Empirical Evidence for the Efficient Market Hypothesis: The Anomalies

While it is generally believed that security markets are efficient, the question as to how efficient markets are remains to be answered. This raises a second question: If the financial markets are not completely efficient, what are the exceptions? The question of degree has led to three forms of the efficient market hypothesis referred to as the *weak form,* the *semistrong form,* and the *strong form.* The second question has led to the identification of exceptions to market efficiency, referred to as *anomalies.* A market anomaly is a situation or strategy that cannot be explained away but would not be expected to happen if the efficient market hypothesis were true. For example, if buying shares in companies that announced a dividend increase led to excess returns, such a strategy would imply that security markets are not completely efficient. (How such a test may be constructed is explained in the appendix to this chapter).

Empirical testing of various types of technical indicators supports the weak form of the efficient market hypothesis, and the techniques explained in Chapter 14, generally referred to as *technical analysis,* do not lead to superior investment results. The evidence suggests that successive price changes are random and that the correlation between stock prices from one period to the next period is virtually nil. Thus, past price behavior provides little useful information for predicting future stock prices.[17]

Further support that security returns are not related is found in the returns estimated by Ibbotson Associates for 1926–1999.[18] The results found the serial correlation between returns for common stocks and for small stocks to be virtually nil (0.01 and 0.08, respectively). The lack of serial correlation in the returns supports the weak form of the efficient market hypothesis since the returns in one period are not

---

[17]For a summary of this empirical work, see James H. Lorie et al., *The Stock Market: Theories and Evidence,* 2d ed. (Homewood, IL: Richard D. Irwin, 1985).

[18]*Stocks, Bonds, Bills, and Inflation, 2000 Yearbook* (Chicago, IL: Ibbotson Associates, 2000), 119. In the statistical appendix to Chapter 7, the correlation coefficient measured the extent to which two series are correlated. For example, if returns on assets A and B were

Period	A	B
1	15%	12%
2	10	10
3	6	4
4	−4	−9
5	−8	−6

there is obvious positive correlation between the two series. Serial correlation measures the correlation between the data for one of the variables. For example, the individual returns for A appear to be serially correlated since the return for each subsequent period is smaller than the return in the previous period. This serial correlation suggests that the return in one period forecasts the return in the next period.

related to the returns in the previous or subsequent time periods. Hence the returns in one period cannot be used to predict the returns in the next period. However, there is some empirical evidence that suggests inefficiencies do exist, and more recent results suggest that simple trading rules could improve returns.[19] Whether the inefficiencies are sufficient to permit investors to develop trading strategies that cover their costs and generate excess returns has not been determined.

At the other extreme, the strong form of the efficient market hypothesis asserts that even access to inside information will not lead to excess returns. Initial empirical evidence does not support the strong form and suggests that insiders may be able to trade profitably in their own stocks.[20] More recent evidence confirms these initial results that insider trading anticipates changes in stock prices. Insider purchases rise before an increase in the stock's price and insider sales precede decreases in the stock's price.[21] Such evidence suggests that financial markets are not completely efficient.

Noninsiders may track purchases and sales by insiders because the latter must register their trading activity with the SEC, which publishes monthly an *Official Summary of Security Transactions and Holdings.* (See also the Web sites provided in Chapter 4.) Unfortunately, knowledge of this inefficiency and tracing insider activity does not guarantee that the investor will earn superior investment results. One study found that a strategy of buying after insider purchases and selling after insider sales failed to produce a return that was large enough to overcome the commissions associated with the trading strategy.[22] While this result supports the strong form of the efficient market hypothesis, it may not be applicable today. Currently, investors may buy and sell stocks on-line with minimal commissions (e.g., $10 a trade). These commission rates suggest the investor may be able to take advantage of information concerning insider trading.

In a recent study, H. Nejat Seyhun provided a comprehensive analysis of insider trading.[23] Seyhun compared insider trading to other valuation techniques (e.g., price/earnings and price/book ratios). Insiders tend to buy stocks with low P/E and low price/book ratios. He also compared insider trading by chief executives to trading by corporate officers, directors, and large shareholders to determine which trades have the better forecasting power. As would be expected, insider trading by chief executives had better forecasting ability because these insiders have the best overall view of the firm's prospects. Seyhun extended the analysis to encompass the size of the firm and the size of the trades and found that insider trading in the shares of small cap stocks tends to have more predictive power than trading in large cap stocks. The same relationship applied to the size of the trade; large trades had more predictive power than small trades. Insider purchases also give better signals than insider sales.

By far the most research and the most interest lie with the semistrong form of the efficient market hypothesis. Studies of strategies that use publicly available information, such as the data found in a firm's financial statements, have generally

---

[19]See Andrew W. Lo and A. Craig MacKinley, "Stock Market Prices Do Not Follow Random Walks: Evidence from a Simple Specification Test," NBER Working Paper No. 2168 (February 1987); Donald B. Keim and Robert F. Stambaugh, "Predicting Returns in the Stock and Bond Markets," *Journal of Financial Economics* (December 1986); and Willim Brock, Josef Lakonishok, and Blake LeBaron, "Simple Technical Trading Rules and the Stochastic Properties of Stock Returns," *Journal of Finance* (December 1992): 1731–1764.

[20]See Joseph E. Finnerty, "Insiders and Market Efficiency," *Journal of Finance* (September 1976): 1141–1148, and the references given in this article.

[21]See, for instance, Dan Givoly and Dan Palmon, "Insider Trading and the Exploitation of Inside Information: Some Empirical Evidence," *Journal of Business* (January 1985): 69–87; R. Richardson Pettit and P. C. Venkatesh, "Insider Trading and Long-Run Return Performance," *Financial Management* (summer 1995): 88–103; and Stephen H. Penman, "Insider Trading and Dissemination of Firms' Forecast Information," *Journal of Business* (October 1982): 479–503.

[22]H. Nejat Seyhun, "Insiders' Profits, Costs of Trading, and Market Efficiency," *Journal of Financial Economics* (1986): 189–212.

[23]H. Nejat Seyhun, *Investment Intelligence From Insider Trading* (Cambridge, MA: The MIT Press, 1998).

concluded that this information does not produce superior results. Prices change very rapidly once information becomes public, and thus the security's price embodies all known information. If an investor could anticipate the new information and act before the information became public, that individual might be able to outperform the market, but once the information becomes public, it rarely can be used to generate superior investment results.

While the evidence generally supports the semistrong form of the efficient market hypothesis, there are exceptions. Two of the most important anomalies are the *P/E effect* and the *small-firm effect*. The *P/E effect* suggests that portfolios consisting of stocks with low price/earnings ratios have a higher average return than portfolios with higher P/E ratios. The *small-firm effect* (or *small cap* for small capitalization) suggests that returns diminish as the size of the firm rises. Size is generally measured by the market value of its stock. If all common stocks on the New York Stock Exchange are divided into five groups, the smallest quintile (the smallest 20 percent of the total firms) has tended to earn a return that exceeds the return on investments in the stocks that comprise the largest quintile, even after adjusting for risk.

Subsequent studies have found that the small-firm effect occurs primarily in January, especially the first five trading days. This anomaly is referred to as the *January effect*. However, there is no negative mirror-image December effect (i.e., small stocks do not consistently underperform the market in December) that would be consistent with December selling and January buying. The January effect is often explained by the fact that investors buy stocks in January after selling for tax reasons in December. And there is some evidence that within a size class those stocks whose prices declined the most in the preceding year tend to rebound the most during January.

The *neglected-firm effect* suggests that small firms that are neglected by large financial institutions (e.g., mutual funds, insurance companies, trust departments, and pension plans) tend to generate higher returns than those firms covered by financial institutions. By dividing firms into the categories of highly researched stocks, moderately researched stocks, and neglected stocks (based on the number of institutions holding the stock), researchers have found that the last group outperformed the more well-researched firms. This anomaly is probably another variation of the small-firm effect, and both the neglected-firm effect and the small-firm effect suggest that the market gets less efficient as firms get smaller. Because large financial institutions may exclude these firms from consideration, their lack of participation reduces the market's efficiency.

Besides the January effect, there is also a *day-of-the-week effect*. Presumably, there is no reason to anticipate that day-to-day returns should differ except over the weekend, when the return should exceed the return earned from one weekday to the next. However, research has suggested that the weekend does not generate a higher return but a *lower* return. If this anomaly is true, it implies that investors anticipating the purchase of stock should not buy on Friday but wait until Monday. Investors anticipating the sale of stock should reverse the procedure. If this anomaly does exist, it should be erased by investors selling short on Friday and covering their positions on Monday (i.e., an act of arbitrage should erase the anomaly). The existence of the anomaly is generally resolved by asserting that the excess return is too small to cover transaction costs.

The *Value Line Investment Survey* (see Exhibit 4.2) weekly ranks all the stocks that it covers into five groups, ranging from those most likely to outperform the market during the next 12 months (stocks ranked "1") to those most likely to underperform the market during the next 12 months (stocks ranked "5"). Several studies have found that using the Value Line ranking system (i.e., selecting stocks ranked "1") generates an excess return, hence the *Value Line effect*. Once again, the smaller firms tended to generate the largest excess return. While the amount of this excess return differed among the various studies, its existence is inconsistent with the efficient market hypothesis. However, it may be exceedingly difficult for the individual investor to take advantage of the anomaly since the Value Line rankings change weekly, which will require substantial transaction costs as the investor frequently adjusts his or her portfolio.

The *overreaction effect* is the tendency of security prices to overreact to new information and is also inconsistent with efficient markets. There are many illustrations in this text of security prices experiencing large changes in response to new information. For example, in October 1998, Guilford Mills announced that it had discovered accounting irregularities that overstated earnings. The stock immediately dropped 18 percent. Is such a decline an overreaction or a correct valuation based on the new information? An overreaction implies the price will correct, and the investor could exploit the overreaction to earn higher returns. Evidence does support this anomaly that the market does overreact, but the overreaction appears to be asymmetric.[24] Investors overreact to bad news but not to good news. This would suggest that Guilford Mill's stock would rebound (at least in the short term).

There also appears to be evidence that security prices may drift in a particular direction over a period of time (a *drift* anomaly), especially after a surprise announcement of some magnitude.[25] Bad news is interpreted by the market to be prolonged and stocks continue to decline even if the firm's fundamentals subsequently change. The converse would also be true: The market assumes good news will continue indefinitely. The former situation creates a buying opportunity, while the latter creates a selling opportunity. Presumably, in efficient markets, the change would occur immediately, since the new price embodies the new information. To continue the Guilford Mills example, this inefficiency implies the initial price decline will continue, which suggests that selling the stock short would lead to superior returns.[26] (The overreaction and the drift anomalies appear to be at odds, but that interpretation need not be correct. The subsequent rebound may occur soon following the initial price change after which the price drift resumes.)

book-to-price ratio
The accounting value of a stock divided by the market price of the stock.

The **book-to-price ratio** considers the ratio of a stock's book value on the firm's balance sheet to the market value of the stock.[27] Stocks with high book-to-market-value ratios are sometimes referred to as *value stocks* to differentiate them from stocks with low ratios of book value to market value, which may be referred to as *growth stocks.* According to this anomaly, the prices of growth stocks are bid up by investors anticipating higher growth in earnings. The higher price reduces the ratio of book value to the stock's market value. As the ratio of book value of equity to market value decreases, the stock becomes more risky because there is increased variability of returns. These riskier stocks should generate higher returns.

In research published in 1992, Fama and French considered the relationship between stock returns and the ratio of book value to the market value for the period 1962–1990.[28] Fama and French's results indicated that firms with low ratios of book value to market value (i.e., the growth stocks) generated lower returns. The immediate implication is that investors who use the ratio of book to market to select securities (i.e., individuals who invest in value stocks) will earn a higher return without bearing additional risk. Such a result is inconsistent with the efficient

---

[24]See, for instance, Werner DeBondt and Richard Thaler, "Does the Market Overreact?" *Journal of Finance* (July 1985): 793–805; and Keith C. Brown and W. V. Harlow, "Market Overreaction: Magnitude and Intensity," *Journal of Portfolio Management* (winter 1988): 6–13.

[25]See, for instance, George Foster, Chris Olsen, and Terry Shevlin, "Earnings Releases and the Behavior of Security Returns," *The Accounting Review* (October 1984).

[26]Guilford Mills' stock did continue to drift downwards and closed at $1.62 on December 31, 2000. The stock's price was in the midteens when the initial announcement concerning accounting irregularities was made.

[27]This ratio is the reciprocal of the ratio of market value to book value. While both ratios essentially say the same thing from different perspectives, each appears in the financial literature. Price-to-book primarily appears in the professional literature and the popular press. Book-to-price appears in the academic research pertaining to investments.

[28]Eugene F. Fama and Kenneth R. French, "The Cross-Section of Expected Returns," *The Journal of Finance* (June 1992): 427–465. The French–Fama study also reported that returns were not related to the beta used in the capital asset pricing model. Low beta stocks generated higher returns, which is inconsistent with the capital asset pricing model.

market hypothesis, which asserts that higher returns are only available if the investor bears more risk.[29]

The Fama and French study is also important for its implications concerning a value strategy versus a growth strategy. The results certainly support a value strategy since they suggest that this approach leads to higher returns. The results also indicate that a growth strategy generates lower returns. Companies classified as growth stocks often have low book-to-price ratios, and these are precisely the stocks that the Fama and French results show produce lower returns and higher risks. The obvious implication is that a growth strategy is inferior. However, research done by Richard Bernstein of Merrill Lynch Capital Markets suggests there may be periods when one strategy generates superior results followed by a period when the opposing strategy produces higher returns.[30]

While evidence does support the efficient market hypothesis, the preceding discussion indicates that there appear to be exceptions. Perhaps the observed exceptions are the result of flaws in the research methodology. Furthermore, any evidence supporting a particular inefficiency cannot be used to support other possible inefficiencies; it applies only to the specific anomaly under study.

Before any investor rushes out to take advantage of these alleged inefficiencies, that individual should remember several sobering considerations. First, the empirical results are only consistent with inefficiencies; they do not prove their existence. Second, for the investor to take advantage of the inefficiency, it must be ongoing. Once an inefficiency is discovered and investors seek to take advantage of it, the inefficiency may disappear. Third, transaction costs are important, and the investor must pay the transaction costs associated with the strategy. If a substantial amount of trading is required, any excess return may be consumed by transaction costs. Fourth, the investor still must select individual issues. Even if small firms outperform the market in the first week of January, the individual investor cannot purchase all of them. There is no assurance that the selected stocks will be those that outperform the market in that particular year. Fifth, for an anomaly to be useful for an active investment strategy, its signals must be transferable to the individual investor. Just because the *Value Line* rankings produce excess returns in an empirical study does not mean that the individual investor may be able to receive the information rapidly enough to act on it. The anomaly may exist for those investors with the first access to the information, but not to all investors who receive the recommendations.

Implications of the Efficient Market Hypothesis

Ultimately, investors must decide for themselves the market's degree of efficiency and whether the anomalies are grounds for particular strategies. Any investor who has a proclivity toward active investment management may see the anomalies as an opportunity. Those investors who prefer more passive investment management may see them as nothing more than interesting curiosities.[31]

---

[29]Further support for these results may be found in Josef Lakonishok, "Contrarian Investment, Extrapolation, and Risk," *The Journal of Finance* (December 1994): 1541–1578. This study found that value strategies (investments in firms whose stock price is low relative to earnings and other fundamentals, such as the book value of the equity) did better than growth strategies. For a basic discussion of the value approach, see Robert A. Haugen, *The New Finance: The Case Against Efficient Markets,* 2d ed. (Old Tappan, NJ: Prentice-Hall, 1999).

[30]Richard Bernstein, *Style Investing* (New York: John Wiley & Sons, 1995); and Richard Bernstein, "Growth & Value," *Merrill Lynch Quantitative Viewpoint* (June 4, 1991).

[31]For an excellent perspective on market efficiency, see Simon M. Keane, "The Efficient Market Hypothesis on Trial," *Financial Analysts Journal* (March/April 1986): 58–63. Keane suggests that the burden of proof of market inefficiency must fall on those individuals advocating an active strategy designed to take advantage of market inefficiencies. Even if inefficiencies were perceived by highly skilled financial specialists, that is insufficient evidence that the market is inefficient for the vast number of participants. For ordinary investors to benefit, any inefficiencies used by the financial specialist must be transmittable to the nonspecialist. Without evidence of such transferability of a market inefficiency, only passive strategies are defensible given the cost to execute an active strategy.

POINTS OF INTEREST

The Money Masters

The efficient market hypothesis suggests that few, if any, investors will outperform the market for an extended period of time. Nine individuals who seem to have achieved that feat are highlighted in a fascinating book, *The Money Masters,* by John Train (Harper and Row, 1980). In this book, Train explores the ideas and strategies of these nine portfolio managers who achieved extraordinary records of capital appreciation for a period of at least ten years.*

The strategies and characteristics of these nine individuals have common threads. They sought undervalued securities and tended to avoid stocks that were currently popular. They avoided new ventures, well-known firms (the so-called *blue chips*), and gimmicks, such as options. They made realistic appraisals and favored stocks that tended to sell below book value. Each of these investors was patient and willing to wait until the prices of his stocks rose to reflect the securities' true value.

These nine men (there were no women) tended to be loners. While they were obviously very well informed concerning Wall Street, they were geographically dispersed and not necessarily located in New York City. While their success could be interpreted to refute the efficient market hypothesis, the opposite inference is more correct. The paucity of individuals who have achieved such success is strong support for the hypothesis that few individuals will achieve superior returns over an extended period of time.

*In 1987, John Train published *The New Money Masters* (Harper and Row), which added the next generation of portfolio managers (e.g., Peter Lynch) to Train's initial list. He repeated the process in 2000 when he published *Money Masters of Our Time* (HarperBusiness).

Whether the investor tends to follow a more passive strategy or one that is designed to take advantage of an anomaly, the individual needs to understand the efficient market hypothesis. First, an efficient market implies that investors and financial analysts are using known information to value correctly what a security is worth. The individual may not be able to use public information to achieve superior investment results because the investment community is already using and acting on that information. If the investment community did not use this information and properly apply it to security valuation, the individual could achieve superior investment results. It is the very fact that investors as a whole are competent and are trying to beat each other that helps to produce efficient financial markets.

Second, while security markets are efficient, such efficiency may not apply to other markets. For example, the investor may not buy and sell nonfinancial assets in an efficient market. This means that the current prices of these assets need not reflect their intrinsic value—that is, the price may not reflect the asset's potential flow of future income or price appreciation. If the markets for assets other than financial assets are dispersed and all transactions are, in effect, over-the-counter, the dissemination of information and prices is limited. This tends to reduce the efficiency of markets and to result in prices that can be too high or too low. While such a situation may offer excellent opportunities for the astute and the knowledgeable, it can also spell disaster for the novice.[32]

The third and perhaps most important implication of the efficient market hypothesis applies to an individual's portfolio. The efficient market hypothesis seems to suggest that the individual investor could randomly select a diversified portfolio of securities and earn a return consistent with the market as a whole. Furthermore, once the portfolio has been selected, there is no need to change it. The strategy, then, is to buy and hold. Such a policy offers the additional advantage of minimizing commissions.

[32]One reason often given for investing in foreign markets is that they are less efficient than U.S. markets. However, even if these markets are less efficient, it does not necessarily follow that U.S. investors are able to take advantage of the inefficiencies.

The problem with this naive policy is that it fails to consider the reasons an investor saves and acquires securities and other assets. The goals behind the portfolio are disregarded, and different goals require different portfolio construction strategies. Furthermore, goals and conditions change, which in turn requires changes in an individual's portfolio. Altering the portfolio for the sake of change will result in additional commissions and not produce superior investment returns. However, when the investor's goals or financial situation change, the portfolio should be altered in a way that is consistent with the new goals and conditions.

The importance to the individual investor of the efficient market hypothesis is not the implication that investment decision making is useless. Instead, it brings to the foreground the environment in which the investor must make decisions. The hypothesis should make the investor realize that investments in securities may not produce superior returns. Rather, the investor should earn a return over a period of time that is consistent with the return earned by the market as a whole and the amount of risk borne by the investor. This means that individual investors should devote more time and effort to the specifications of their investment goals and the selection of securities to meet those goals than to the analysis of individual securities. Since such analysis cannot be expected to produce superior returns, it takes resources and time away from the important questions of why we save and invest.

Summary

A corporation is an economic unit created (i.e., chartered) by a state. Ownership in the corporation is represented by stock, which may be readily transferred from one individual to another. In addition, investors in publicly held corporations have limited liability.

Investors in common stock anticipate a return in the form of cash dividends and/or capital appreciation. Capital gains taxation laws favor price appreciation over cash dividends: Cash dividends are taxed as received, while capital gains receive favorable tax treatment. Such gains are taxed only when realized (i.e., when the stock is sold).

A simple model of stock valuation suggests that this value depends on the firm's earnings, its dividend policy, and investors' required rate of return. According to the model, future dividends should be discounted back to the present to determine a stock's value. The discount factor used depends on returns available on alternative investments and the risk associated with the particular stock. An alternative to the dividend-growth model is the use of P/E ratios and forecasted earnings to determine if the stock should be purchased. Both the dividend-growth model and the use of P/E ratios place emphasis on future earnings and dividends.

Risk is incorporated into the valuation of stock through the application of the capital asset pricing model. In the CAPM, the risk adjustment uses a firm's beta coefficient, which is an index of the stock's market risk. These beta coefficients alter the investor's required return so that individual stocks with higher numerical betas have greater required returns.

Financial assets are bought and sold in competitive financial markets. This competition as well as the rapid dissemination of information among investors and the rapid changes in security prices results in efficient security markets. The efficient market hypothesis suggests that the individual investor cannot expect to outperform the market on a risk-adjusted basis over an extended period of time. Instead, the investor should earn a return that is consistent with the market return and the amount of risk the individual bears.

Empirical work tends to support the efficient market hypothesis, at least the weak and semistrong forms. These studies give evidence that investors cannot use public information to earn a return in excess of what could be expected given the return on the market and the risk the investor bears. There are, however, several anomalies, such as the January effect, the small-firm effect, or the analysis of P/E ratios, that are inconsistent with the efficient market hypothesis. These anomalies suggest that the investor may be able to earn excess returns and that financial markets may have pockets of inefficiency.

Summary of Equations

Valuation of common stock (constant dividend):

$$V = \frac{D}{k} \tag{9.2}$$

Valuation of common stock (constant rate of growth):

$$V = \frac{D_0(1 + g)}{k - g} \tag{9.4}$$

Required return:

$$k = r_f + (r_m - r_f)\beta \tag{9.5}$$

Valuation using a multiple (e.g., a P/E ratio):

$$P = (m)(EPS) \tag{9.6}$$

Questions

1) What does it mean for investors in the shares of IBM to have limited liability?
2) What role does each of the following play for the investor?
   a) Preemptive rights
   b) Cumulative voting
   c) Board of directors
3) What is the difference between the expected return and the required return? When should the two returns be equal?
4) What is the difference between the value of a stock and its price? When should they be equal?
5) What variables affect the value of a stock according to the dividend-growth model? What role do earnings play in this model?
6) How do interest rates and risk affect a stock's price in the capital asset pricing model?
7) Does the efficient market hypothesis suggest that an investor cannot outperform the market? What effect do the dissemination of information and the speed with which security prices change have on the efficient market hypothesis?
8) What are the three forms of the efficient market hypothesis?
9) While security markets are generally believed to be efficient, there appear to be some exceptions. For these exceptions (i.e., the anomalies) to be important for the individual investor, what must apply?
10) If investors had to limit themselves to one anomaly, which exception to the efficient market hypothesis seems to offer the most hope?
11) Compare the following information (as of January 1999) concerning several stocks with current information obtained from an Internet source.

	P/E	P/S	Price/Book
Amazon.com	NC	36.2	94.2
Yahoo!	NC	150.0	53.4
Barnes & Noble	54.5	1.0	5.5
Disney	61.5	2.7	3.2
Sprint	29.0	2.3	3.1

NC = not computed because firm was operating at a loss.

What has happened to the valuations of each stock since January 1999?

Problems

1) Given the following data, what should the price of the stock be?

Required return	10%
Present dividend	$1
Growth rate	5%

   a) If the growth rate increases to 6 percent and the dividend remains $1, what should the stock's price be?
   b) If the required return declines to 9 percent and the dividend remains $1, what should the price of the stock be? If the stock is selling for $20, what does that imply?

2) An investor requires a return of 12 percent. A stock sells for $25, it pays a dividend of $1, and the dividends compound annually at 7 percent. Will this investor find the stock attractive? What is the maximum amount that this investor should pay for the stock?

3) A firm's stock earns $2 per share, and the firm distributes 40 percent of its earnings as cash dividends. Its dividends grow annually at 7 percent.
   a) What is the stock's price if the required return is 10 percent?
   b) The firm borrows funds and, as a result, its per-share earnings and dividends increase by 20 percent. What happens to the stock's price if the growth rate and the required return are unaffected? What will the stock's price be if after using financial leverage and increasing the dividend to $1, the required return rises to 12 percent? What may cause this required return to rise?

4) The annual risk-free rate of return is 9 percent and the investor believes that the market will rise annually at 15 percent. If a stock has a beta coefficient of 1.5 and its current dividend is $1, what should be the value of the stock if its earnings and dividends are growing annually at 6 percent?

5) You are considering two stocks. Both pay a dividend of $1, but the beta coefficient of A is 1.5 while the beta coefficient of B is 0.7. Your required return is

$$k = 8\% + (15\% - 8\%)\beta$$

   a) What is the required return for each stock?
   b) If A is selling for $10 a share, is it a good buy if you expect earnings and dividends to grow at 5 percent?
   c) The earnings and dividends of B are expected to grow annually at 10 percent. Would you buy the stock for $30?
   d) If the earnings and dividends of A were expected to grow annually at 10 percent, would it be a good buy at $30?

6) You are offered two stocks. The beta of A is 1.4 while the beta of B is 0.8. The growth rates of earnings and dividends are 10 percent and 5 percent, respectively. The dividend yields are 5 percent and 7 percent, respectively.
   a) Since A offers higher potential growth, should it be purchased?
   b) Since B offers a higher dividend yield, should it be purchased?
   c) If the risk-free rate of return were 7 percent and the return on the market is expected to be 14 percent, which of these stocks should be bought?

7) Your broker suggests that the stock of QED is a good purchase at $25. You do an analysis of the firm, determining that the $1.40 dividend and earnings should continue to grow indefinitely at 8 percent annually. The firm's beta coefficient is 1.34, and the yield on Treasury bills is 7.4 percent. If you expect the market to earn a return of 12 percent, should you follow your broker's suggestion?

8) The required return on an investment is 12 percent. You estimate that firm X's dividends will grow as follows:

Year	Dividend
1	$1.20
2	2.00
3	3.00
4	4.50

For the subsequent years you expect the dividend to grow but at the more modest rate of 7 percent annually. What is the maximum price that you should pay for this stock?

9) Management has recently announced that expected dividends for the next three years will be as follows:

Year	Dividend
1	$2.50
2	3.25
3	4.00

For the subsequent years, management expects the dividend to grow at 5 percent annually. If the risk-free rate is 4.3 percent, the return on the market is 10.3 percent, and the firm's beta is 1.4, what is the maximum price that you should pay for this stock?

10) Management has recently announced that expected dividends for the next three years will be as follows:

Year	Dividend
1	$3.00
2	2.25
3	1.50

The firm's assets will then be liquidated and the proceeds invested in the preferred stock of other firms so that the company will be able to pay an annual dividend of $1.25 indefinitely. If your required return on investments in common stock is 10 percent, what is the maximum you should pay for this stock?

THE FINANCIAL ADVISOR'S INVESTMENT CASE

Determining the Value of a Business

Erik Satie has just inherited his father's company. Prior to his death, Mr. Satie was the sole stockholder, and he left the entire company to his only son. Although Erik has worked for the firm for many years as a commercial artist, he does not feel qualified to manage the operation. He has considered selling the firm while it is still a viable operation and before his father's absence causes the value of the firm to deteriorate. Erik realizes that selling the firm will result in his losing control, but his father granted him a long-term contract that guarantees employment or a generous severance package. Furthermore, if Erik were to sell for cash, he should receive a substantial amount of money, so his financial position would be secure.

Even though Erik would like to sell out, he has enough business sense to realize that he does not know how to place an asking price (a value) on the firm. The IRS had established a value on his father's stock of $100 a share, and since he owned 100,000 shares, the value of the company for estate tax purposes was $10,000,000. Erik thought that was a reasonable amount but decided to consult with Sophie Ryer, a CPA who completed the estate tax return.

Ryer suggested that the firm could be valued using a discounted cash flow method in which the current and future dividends are discounted back to the present to determine the value of the firm. She explained to Erik that this technique, the dividend-growth model, is an important theoretical model used for the valuation of companies. In addition, she suggested that the price/earnings ratio of similar firms may be used as a guide to the value of the firm. Erik asked Ryer to prepare a valuation of the stock based on P/E ratios and the dividend-growth model. While Erik realized that he could get only one price, he requested a range of values from an optimistic price to a minimum, rock-bottom value.

To aid in the valuation process, Ryer assembled the following information. The firm earned $8.50 a share and distributed 60 percent in cash dividends during its last fiscal year. This payout ratio had been maintained for several years, with 40 percent of the earnings being retained to finance future growth. The per-share earnings for the past five years were as follows:

Year	Per-Share Earnings
1998	$6.70
1999	7.40
2000	7.85
2001	8.20
2002	8.50

Publicly held firms in the industry have an average P/E ratio of 12, with the highest being 17 and the lowest 9. The betas of these firms tend to be less than 1.0, with 0.85 being typical. While the firm is not publicly held, it is similar in structure to other firms in the industry. It is, however, perceptibly smaller than the publicly held firms. The Treasury bill rate is currently 5.2 percent, and most financial analysts anticipate that the market as a whole will average a return of 6 to 6.5 percent greater than the Treasury bill rate.

Satie has come to you to help devise a financial plan after the company is sold. Such a plan would encompass the construction of a well-diversified portfolio with sufficient resources to meet temporary needs for cash. You do not want to accept blindly the IRS estate value of $10,000,000. Obviously, if the firm could be sold for more, that would be beneficial to your client. In addition, you want an indication of the value Ryer may place on the firm, so you resolve to answer the following questions.

1) Based on the background information, what are the highest and lowest values of the stock based on P/E ratios?
2) What has been the firm's earnings growth rate (i.e., the rate of growth from $6.70 to $8.50) for the prior five years?
3) What is the highest and lowest value of the stock based on the dividend-growth model?
4) What assumptions must be made to determine these values using these two techniques?
5) Explain the impact each of the following would have on the valuation of the stock:
   a) The anticipated return on the market rises.
   b) The rate of growth declines.
   c) The average P/E were 15 instead of 12.
6) What is the tax implication if the stock is sold for more than the $100 used to value the stock for the estate?

Testing the Efficient Market Hypothesis: The Event Study

One method employed to test the efficient market hypothesis is to study how a stock responds to the change in a variable, such as an unexpected increase in earnings or a decrease in the dividend. This technique is called an *event study*. If the market anticipated the event, the price should have already adjusted (i.e., the information is fully discounted), and the announcement of the event should have no impact. If the market did not anticipate the event, the price should immediately adjust for the new information so that few, if any, individuals are able to profit by acting on the announcement of the event. If the market is not completely efficient, prior to the announcement the price should move in the direction implied by the event but not fully discount the event.

These three scenarios are illustrated in Figure 9A.1 (p. 290). Panel a illustrates the case in which the information is fully discounted and the price has already adjusted before the event, which occurs at t_l. Even though some individuals may acquire the stock before the announcement, the time lapse between the price increase (from *A* to *B* in panel a) is sufficient that the time value of money consumes any possible excess return. For example, if individuals buy a stock in anticipation of a $1 dividend increment and bid up the stock's price, any excess return implied by the dividend increment is consumed by the cost of carrying the security until the announcement is made. This pattern is consistent with market efficiency.

Panel b illustrates the case in which there is no price change prior to the event, at which time the price quickly adjusts for the new information. Since the price change (i.e., the vertical distance *AB* in panel b) is rapid and by an amount equal to the valuation of the event, there is no opportunity for an excess gain once the information is public. This price pattern also is consistent with efficient markets.

Panel c illustrates the case in which the market is not efficient; some price change (i.e., the movement from *A* to *B* in panel c) occurs prior to the event, but either the amount of the increment or its timing is insufficient to discount fully the impact of the announcement. Thus, investors who buy the stock prior to the announcement earn an excess return. If this pattern exists for several events (e.g., for all dividend increments), then the individual investor who perceives the pattern may earn consistent excess returns. For such inefficiency to exist, it is not necessary that every, or even many, investors perceive the pattern. If some investors, be they skilled or have some particular knowledge of the event, are able to outperform the market consistently, the market is not completely efficient.

Testing for the patterns illustrated in Figure 9A.1 would appear to be easy, but two important observations need to be made. First, at any moment in time many factors (e.g., a movement in the market, a change in interest rates, a change in expected inflation, or a political event) may be affecting a stock's price, so the impact of one event must be isolated to determine if it has an impact on the stock's price and hence on the return. Second, returns must be adjusted for risk. One individual may acquire a very risky portfolio and achieve a higher return than the market. Another individual may acquire a portfolio consisting of certificates of deposit and achieve a lower return. The different returns earned by these individuals are not sufficient evidence that the former outperformed the market while the latter underperformed the market. A higher (or lower) return may be the result of a different amount of risk. Thus, returns must be adjusted for risk. To demonstrate market inefficiency, the individual must consistently achieve a higher (or lower) return on a *risk-adjusted basis*. Thus, it is possible for a return to be less than the market return but still be considered superior after adjusting for risk, in which case the return indicates an inefficient market.

FIGURE 9A.1

Stock Price Changes in Response to an Event

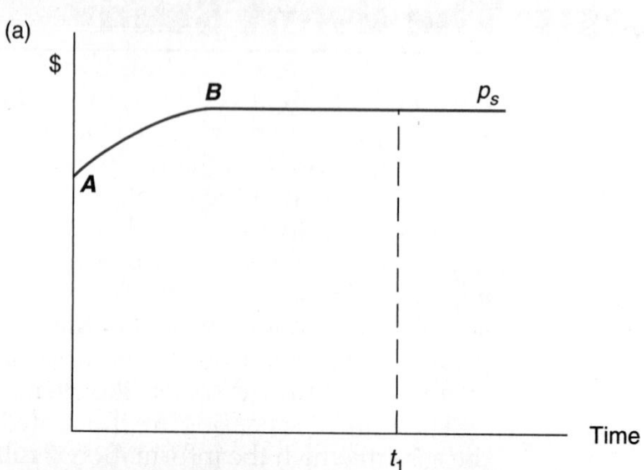

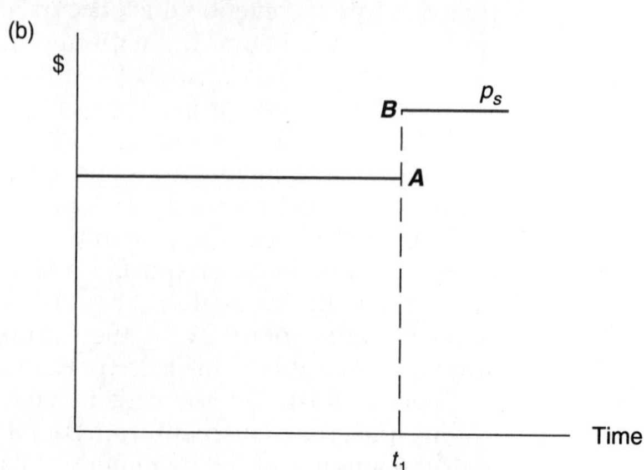

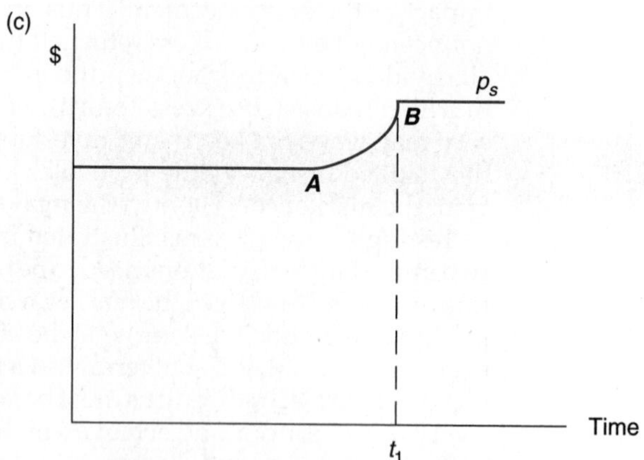

Testing of the efficient market hypothesis using event studies assumes that the stock's return (r_s) is a function of the return the security would earn in response to the return on the market ($a + br_m$) and the impact of a firm-specific event represented by the e in the following equation:

$$r_s = a + br_m + e.$$

The a measures the return the stock would earn if the market return equals zero. The r_m measures the market return during the period, while the b gives the response of the individual stock's return to the market return (i.e., it is the stock's beta). The e, or error term, picks up the impact of a firm-specific event, such as a reduction in the dividend.

Rearranging the equation to solve for e gives an estimate of the firm-specific component of the return:

$$e = r_s - (a + br_m).$$

This equation states that if the return associated with changes in the market (i.e., $a + br_m$) is subtracted from the actual return (i.e., r_s), the residual is the firm-specific component of the return. The impact of this residual, of course, plays an important role in the rationale for the diversification of a portfolio. Because diversification erases the impact of firm-specific events, the value of e approaches zero as the number of securities increases, and the impact of firm-specific events is eliminated.

In an event study, however, the e is used to test for the impact of a firm-specific event, such as a dividend cut. The value of e will not equal zero if the event has an impact on the stock's return. If, for example, a dividend cut has a negative impact on a stock's return, e will be negative after subtracting the return generated by the movements in the market. It is possible that e could be positive if the market approves of the dividend cut and causes the stock's return to exceed the return associated with movements in the market as a whole. If the firm-specific event has no impact, the value of e is zero, and the stock's return is completely explained by the movement in the market.

Even though an investor can earn an excess return or sustain an excess loss in a single event, that is not sufficient evidence to verify an inefficiency. To overcome this, researchers measure superior performance by computing the "cumulative excess return" the investor earns. If the individual consistently outperforms the market, these excess returns will grow over time. The three possible patterns (i.e., consistently superior excess returns, consistently inferior returns, and no excess returns) are illustrated in Figure 9A.2 (p. 292). The efficient market hypothesis suggests that the pattern of cumulative excess returns should look like panel c, in which returns fluctuate around zero. If the investor consistently outperforms the market, the cumulative excess returns will rise (i.e., panel a). Conversely, if the performance is consistently inferior, the cumulative excess returns will be negative and falling (i.e., panel b).

How cumulative excess returns may be used to test for an inefficiency can be illustrated by employing one of the so-called "technical" indicators, such as the 200-day moving average. (Technical analysis is covered in Chapter 14.) The 200-day moving average suggests buying or selling a stock when the price of the stock goes through the 200-day moving average. For example, if the moving average has been declining, the daily price of the stock will have been less than the moving average. If the price of the stock rises sufficiently so that it is equal to the moving average and then moves above the average, the movement is interpreted to be a buy signal. Conversely, if the moving average has been rising, the daily price of the stock will have been greater than the moving average. If the price of the stock declines sufficiently to equal the moving average and subsequently moves below the average, that is interpreted as a sell signal.

FIGURE 9A.2
Cumulative Returns

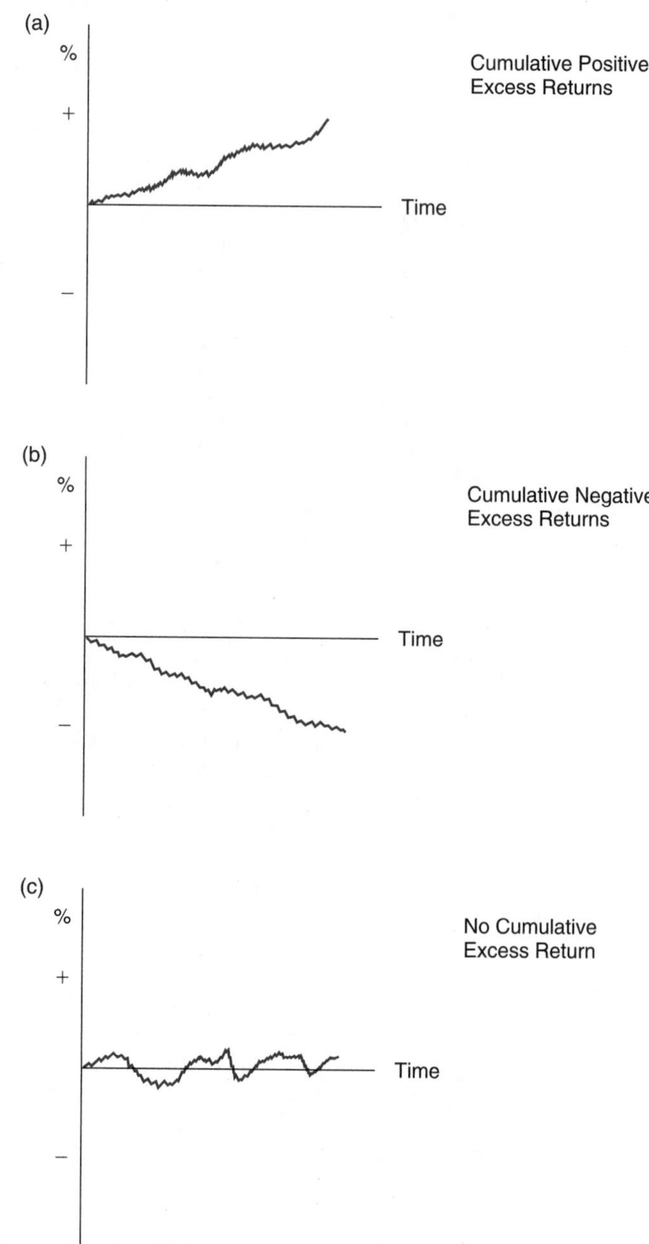

Such buy and sell signals beg to be tested. The stock returns generated by strategies such as this should be compared to the returns generated by the market during each time period. That is, the residuals (i.e., the excess returns) are isolated and summed. If the strategy outperformed the market, then the cumulative excess return would rise over time. Such a pattern would indicate superior performance and suggest the market is not efficient, at least with regard to the particular buy-sell strategy being tested.

The Return on Common Stock Investments

10

From 1996 through 1999, the Standard & Poor's 500 stock index rose 26.435 percent annually. Is it reasonable to expect that stock prices will continue to increase annually at 26.435 percent? At that rate, $1,000 will grow to $108,980 in 20 years. If you could invest $1,000 each year, you would have $408,473 after 20 years.

That's not going to happen. What return is it reasonable to assume will occur? What return has the market achieved over an extended period of time, such as 20 years? As will be covered later in this chapter, the large companies that comprise the S&P 500 index have averaged about 11 percent annually. Even at that rate, $1,000 grows to $8,062 in 20 years and $1,000 invested every year grows to $64,203. Of course, you won't get to keep the entire amount because you will have to pay taxes on the gains. However, even if combined state and federal taxes consume 30 percent of the total, you still walk away with $5,643 and $44,942, respectively.

Historical market returns are important because they give you perspective and are useful when forecasting future returns. The discounted cash flow valuation model presented in the previous chapter had three components: the annual dividend, the growth rate, and the required return. The required return depended on the risk-free rate on Treasury securities, the firm's beta, and the return on the market. Dividends and growth rates will be developed in the next chapter. Treasury bills were discussed in Chapter 2 in the section on money market securities. Beta was considered in Chapter 7 on the measurement of risk. This chapter considers the return on the market.

The measurement of performance and the historical returns earned by investments in stocks are the primary focus of this chapter. The first section discusses the construction of aggregate measures of the stock market. These include the Dow Jones averages, Standard & Poor's 500 stock index, the New York Stock Exchange index, the Wilshire 5000 Total Market stock index, and the specialized indexes that have recently been developed.

The second section is devoted to the historical returns earned on investments in securities. It includes an explanation of the methods employed to compute rates of return, the various methods used to show the returns, and academic studies of the returns actually earned by investments in common stock. The chapter concludes with a discussion of buying stock systematically to smooth out price fluctuations and reduce the average cost of a position in a stock.

Learning Objectives

After completing this chapter you should be able to:

1. Differentiate between a simple price-weighted average, a value-weighted average, an equal-weighted average, and a geometric average.
2. Contrast the Dow Jones averages with other aggregate measures of the stock market.
3. Explain the differences among the holding period return, an average rate of return, and the true annual rate of return.
4. Compute the rate of return on an investment.
5. Compare the results of various studies concerning the rates of return earned on investments in common stock.

6 Compare the risks and returns associated with alternative investments based on the Ibbotson Associates studies of returns.

7 Identify the advantages associated with dollar cost averaging and averaging down.

Measures of Stock Performance: Averages and Indexes

Constructing an aggregate measure of stock prices may appear to be easy, but there are several possible problems. The first concerns the choice of which securities to include and how many. Although the number to include certainly was a problem before the advent of computers, it is not a major concern today when a measure may include any number of securities (e.g., all stocks listed on the NYSE). However, the question of which specific companies remains. Unless all are included, choices must be made among the possible securities to include in the aggregate measure of the market.

A second important problem concerns the weight that should be given to each security. For example, consider two stocks. Company A has 1 million shares outstanding and the stock sells for \$10. Company B has 10 million shares outstanding, and its stock sells for \$20. The total market value (or capitalization) of A is \$10 million while the total market value of B is \$200 million. How should these two securities be weighted? There are several choices: to treat each stock's price equally, to adjust for B's larger number of shares, or to use an equal dollar amount invested in each stock.

A Price-Weighted Arithmetic Average

The first choice is the arithmetic average of both stocks whereby the two prices are treated equally and the average price is

$$\frac{(\$10 + \$20)}{2} = \$15.$$

If the prices of the stocks rise to \$18 and \$22, respectively, the new average price is

$$\frac{(\$18 + \$22)}{2} = \$20.$$

In both calculations, the simple average gives equal weight to each stock and does not recognize the difference in the number of shares outstanding.

A Value-Weighted Average

An alternative means used to measure stock performance is to construct an average that allows for differences in the number of shares each company has outstanding. If the preceding numbers are used, the total value of A and B is

	Price × Number of shares =	Total value
	\$10 × 1,000,000 =	\$ 10,000,000
+	\$20 × 10,000,000 =	200,000,000
		\$210,000,000.

The average price of a share of stock is

$$\text{Average price} = \text{Total value of all shares} \div \text{Total number of shares}$$

$$\text{Average price} = \frac{\$210{,}000{,}000}{(10{,}000{,}000 + 1{,}000{,}000)} = \$19.09.$$

If the prices of the stocks rise to $18 and $22, respectively, the new total value of all shares is

$$\begin{array}{lr} \$18 \times 1{,}000{,}000 = & \$\ 18{,}000{,}000 \\ + & \\ \$22 \times 10{,}000{,}000 = & 220{,}000{,}000 \\ \hline & \$238{,}000{,}000. \end{array}$$

The average value of a share of stock becomes

$$\text{Average price} = \frac{\$238{,}000{,}000}{(10{,}000{,}000 + 1{,}000{,}000)} = \$21.64.$$

The value-weighted average gives more weight to companies with more shares outstanding.

An Equal-Weighted Average

An alternative to the price-weighted and the value-weighted averages is the equal-weighted average price, which assumes an equal dollar invested in each stock. If, in the preceding illustration, $100 is invested in each stock, the investor would acquire 10 shares of stock A and 5 shares of stock B. The total cost of the 15 shares is $200, so the average price of a share is

$$\frac{\$200}{15} = \$13.33.$$

If the prices of the stocks rise to $18 and $22, respectively, the value of the shares is

$$\$180 + \$110 = \$290.$$

The new average value of a share is

$$\frac{\$290}{15} = \$19.33.$$

A Geometric Average

A fourth alternative means to calculate an aggregate measure of security prices is to construct a geometric average. Instead of adding the prices of the various stocks and dividing by the number of entries, a geometric average multiplies the various prices and then takes the *n*th root with *n* equal to the number of stocks. For example, if the prices of two stocks are $10 and $20, the geometric average is

$$\text{Average price} = \sqrt[2]{(\$10)(\$20)} = \$14.14.$$

If the prices of the stocks rise to $18 and $22, the new geometric average price is

$$\textbf{Average price} = \sqrt[2]{(\$18)(\$22)} = \$19.90.$$

As this discussion indicates, there are several ways to view an aggregate market price. Each of these methods produces a different average price, and when the stock prices are changed, the changes in the averages differ. In the illustration, the simple average rose from $15 to $20 for a 33.3 percent increase, but the value-weighted average price rose from $19.09 to $21.64, which is only a 13.34 percent increase. The equal-weighted average rose from $13.33 to $19.33, a 45 percent increase, while the geometric average price rose from $14.14 to $19.90, a 40.74 percent increase.

As is discussed later in this chapter, annual returns are often computed using geometric averages. Compounding, which the arithmetic average does not consider, is exceedingly important in investments. As was explained in Chapter 5, the $1 + i$ component of the interest factor is raised to the nth power (i.e., $[1 + i]^n$). The n represents the number of periods and captures compounding. If the purpose is to compare the order of returns, the investment with the higher arithmetic average will also be the higher compound return. The order of the returns is not changed. If the purpose is to determine the true annualized return, then compounding must be considered—which requires computing the geometric average and not the arithmetic average.

Different Movements in Price Averages

The previous discussion illustrated how different types of stock price averages may be computed, resulting in different percentage changes in the averages. Even though the percentage changes vary, it would seem reasonable to assume that the average prices change in the same direction. However, that need not be the case; consider three stocks with the following prices and number of shares outstanding:

Stock	A	B	C
Number of shares outstanding	1,000	10,000	3,000
Price as of 1/1/0X	$10	$15	$25
Price as of 1/1/0Y	18	13	25

The price-weighted averages for the two years are

$$\frac{(\$10 + \$15 + \$25)}{3} = \$16.67$$

$$\frac{(\$18 + \$13 + \$25)}{3} = \$18.66.$$

The value-weighted averages are

$$\frac{(\$10 \times 1{,}000) + (\$15 \times 10{,}000) + (\$25 \times 3{,}000)}{14{,}000} = 16.78$$

$$\frac{(\$18 \times 1{,}000) + (\$13 \times 10{,}000) + (\$25 \times 3{,}000)}{14{,}000} = \$15.93.$$

These examples show that the average value of a share of stock differs in each case, and the price change can move in opposite directions.[1] The value of a share of stock rose from $16.67 to $18.66 according to the simple average, but when the value-weighted average was used, the price of a share decreased from $16.78 to $15.93.

The previous discussion covered the calculation of average price. Average price is generally converted into an index whose advantage is ease of comparison over time. In the example of price-weighted average, the initial price was $16.67. This amount could be used as the base year to which all subsequent years are compared. In the second year, the average price rose to $18.66. The new average price is expressed relative to the average in the initial year, which is called the base year:

$$\frac{\$18.66}{\$16.67} = 1.1193.$$

The result, 1.1193, means that the current price is 0.1193 (1.1193 − 1), or 11.9 percent greater than the prior year's price. If the price rises to $19.56 in the next year, then the increase relative to the base year is

$$\frac{\$19.56}{\$16.67} = 1.1734.$$

Thus, the price in the second year is 17.34 percent higher than in the initial year.

The Dow Jones Averages

Dow Jones Industrial Average
An average of the stock prices of 30 large firms.

One of the first measures of stock prices was the average developed by Charles Dow.[2] Initially, the average consisted of the stock from only 11 companies, but it was later expanded to include more firms. Today, this average is called the **Dow Jones Industrial Average**, and it is probably the best known and most widely quoted average of stock prices.

The Dow Jones Industrial Average is a simple price-weighted average. Initially, it was computed by summing the price of the stocks of 30 companies and then dividing by 30. Over time, the divisor has been changed so that substitutions of one firm for another or a stock split has no impact on the average. If the computation were simply the sum of the current prices of 30 divided by 30, the substitution of one stock for another or a stock split would affect the average.

To see the possible impact of substituting one stock for another, consider an average that is computed using three stocks (A, B, and C) whose prices are $12, $35, and $67, respectively. The average price is $38. For some reason, the composition of

---

[1]The geometric averages are

$$\sqrt[3]{(\$10 \times \$15 \times \$25)} = \$15.54$$

and

$$\sqrt[3]{(\$18 \times \$13 \times \$25)} = \$18.02.$$

Geometric averages may be computed using any electronic calculator with a y^x key. Take the reciprocal of the exponent and express it as a decimal (i.e., convert the 3 into ⅓, expressed as .3333). The average price for the first stock is ($10) ($15) $(\$25)^{.3333}$; use the y^x key to perform the calculation. Thus, the geometric average price of a share of this stock is

$$\sqrt[3]{(\$10 \times \$15 \times \$25)} = (\$10)(\$15)(\$25)^{.3333} = \$15.54.$$

[2]In 1882 Edward Jones joined Charles Dow to form a partnership that grew into Dow, Jones and Company. Information on the Dow Jones averages may be found at http://www.djindexes.com.

the average is changed. Stock B is dropped and replaced by stock D, whose price is \$80. The average price is now \$53 [(\$12 + 35 + 80/30]. The substitution of D for B has caused the average to increase even though there has been no change in stock prices. To avoid this problem, the divisor is changed from 3 to the number that does not change the average. To find the divisor, set up the following equation:

$$(\$12 + 67 + 80)/X = \$38.$$

Solving for X gives a divisor of 4.1842. When the prices of stocks A, C, and D are summed and divided by 4.1842, the average price is

$$(\$12 + 67 + 80)/4.1842 = \$38,$$

so the average price has not been altered by the substitution of stock D for B.

A similar situation occurs when one of the stocks is split. (Stock splits and their impact on the price of a share is covered in Chapter 11.) Suppose stock D is split 2 for 1 so its price becomes \$40 instead of \$80 (two new shares at \$40 = one old share at \$80). The investor's wealth has not changed; the individual continues to hold stock worth a total of \$159 (\$12 + 67 + 40 + 40). The price average, however, becomes (\$12 + 67 + 40)/4.1842 = \$28.44 instead of \$38. According to the average, the stock is worth less. The average has been affected by something other than a price movement—in this case, the stock split. Once again, this problem is solved by changing the divisor so that the average price remains \$38. To find the divisor, set up the following equation:

$$(\$12 + 67 + 40)/X = \$38.$$

Solving for X gives a divisor of 3.1316. When the individual prices of stocks A, C, and D are summed and divided by 3.1316, the average price is

$$(\$12 + 67 + 40)/3.1316 = \$38,$$

so the average price has not been altered by the stock split.

While the Dow Jones Industrial Average (and the Utility Average, the Transportation Average, and the Composite Average) are adjusted for stock splits, stock dividends in excess of 10 percent, and the substitution of one firm for another, no adjustment is made for the distribution of cash dividends. Hence, the average declines when stocks like ExxonMobil go ex-div (pay a dividend) and their prices decline. (The reason for a stock's price to decline when the firm pays a dividend is explained in Chapter 11.)

The failure to include dividend payments means that the annual percentage change in the Dow Jones Industrial Average understates the true return. This failure to include the dividend can have an amazing impact when compounding is considered. Suppose the average rises 8 percent annually when dividends are excluded but the return is 10 percent when dividends are included and reinvested. (The dividend yield on the Dow Jones Industrial Average was 1.66% as of January 2001.) Over 20 years, \$1,000 grows to \$4,661 at 8 percent but to \$6,728 at 10 percent. If the time period is extended to 50 years, these values become \$46,902 and \$117,391, respectively.[3]

[3]One study found that from its inception through December 31, 1998, the Dow Jones Industrial Average grew from 40.94 to 9,181.43, for a 5.42 percent annual growth rate. However, if dividends had been reinvested, the Dow Jones would have been 652,230.87, for an annual growth rate of 9.89 percent. See Roger G. Clarke and Meir Statman, "The DJIA Crossed 652,230," *The Journal of Portfolio Management* (winter 2000): 89–93.

This understatement of the true annual return is, of course, true for all stock indexes that do not add back the dividend payment. The bias is greater for those indexes that cover the largest companies, since they tend to pay dividends. Although some small cap stocks do distribute dividends, they tend to pay out a smaller proportion of their earnings, and the dividend constitutes a small, perhaps even trivial, part of the total return.

The Dow Jones Industrial Average for the period from 1950 through 2000 is presented in Figure 10.1 (p. 300), which plots the high and low values of the average for each year. During the 1960s and 1970s, the Dow Jones Industrial Average (and the stock market) was erratic and certainly did not experience the steady growth achieved during the 1950s. In 1970 and in 1974 the Dow Jones Industrial Average even fell below the highs achieved during 1959. The period from 1985 through 1998, however, showed a different pattern, as stock prices soared and the Dow Jones Industrial Average reached new highs, in spite of suffering a major setback in 1987.

The period 1996–1999 was another period of major growth for stock markets, during which the Dow Jones Industrial Average rose from 5,117 at year-end 1995 to 11,497 at year-end 1999. However, this large growth came to a crashing end in 2000, when the average declined to 10,787 for a 6.18 percent decrease.

In addition to the industrial average, Dow Jones computes an average for transportation stocks, utility stocks, and a composite of all the stocks included in the three separate averages. All three averages are composed of a relatively small number of companies. Thirty stocks are included in the industrial average, 20 stocks compose the transportation average, and 15 stocks make up the utilities average. The firms included are among the largest (in terms of sales and total assets) and best known in the nation. (The current composition of the Dow Jones averages is reported daily in *The Wall Street Journal.*) However, many prominent firms (e.g., Johnson & Johnson) are excluded from these averages.

This small number of firms is one source of criticism of the Dow Jones averages. It is argued that the small sample is not indicative of the market as a whole. For this reason, other measures of stock prices that have broader bases, such as the NYSE index or Standard & Poor's 500 stock index, may be better indicators of the general market's performance.

Graphical Illustrations

While a picture may be worth 1,000 words, pictures can be misleading. So, before proceeding to the discussion of other indexes of stock prices, it is desirable to consider the composition of graphs (i.e., the pictures) used to illustrate indexes of stock prices. The choice of the scale affects the graph. This choice can influence the reader's perception of the index and, hence, the performance of the stock market.

This impact may be illustrated by the following monthly range of stock prices and percentage increases:

Month	Price of Stock	Percentage Change in Monthly Highs
January	$ 5–10	—
February	10–15	50
March	15–20	33
April	20–25	25

Even though the monthly price increases are equal ($5), the percentage increments decline. The investor who bought the stock at $10 and sold it for $15 made $5 and earned a return of 50 percent. The investor who bought it at $20 and sold for $25 also made $5, but the return was only 25 percent.

FIGURE 10.1

Annual Price Range of the Dow Jones Industrial Average, 1950–2000

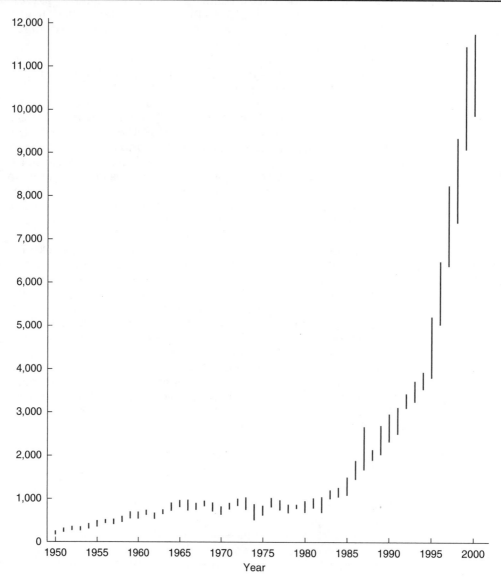

Source: First issue of *The Wall Street Journal* for each year.

These monthly prices may be plotted on graph paper that uses absolute dollar units for the vertical axis. This is done on the left-hand side of Figure 10.2. Such a graph gives the appearance that equal price movements yield equal percentage changes. However, this is not so, as the preceding illustration demonstrates.

To avoid this problem, a different scale can be used, as illustrated in the right-hand side of Figure 10.2. Here, equal units on the vertical axis represent percentage change. Thus, a price movement from \$10 to \$15 appears to be greater than one from \$20 to \$25, because in percentage terms it *is* greater.

FIGURE 10.2

The Use of Different Scales to Illustrate Stock Price Movements

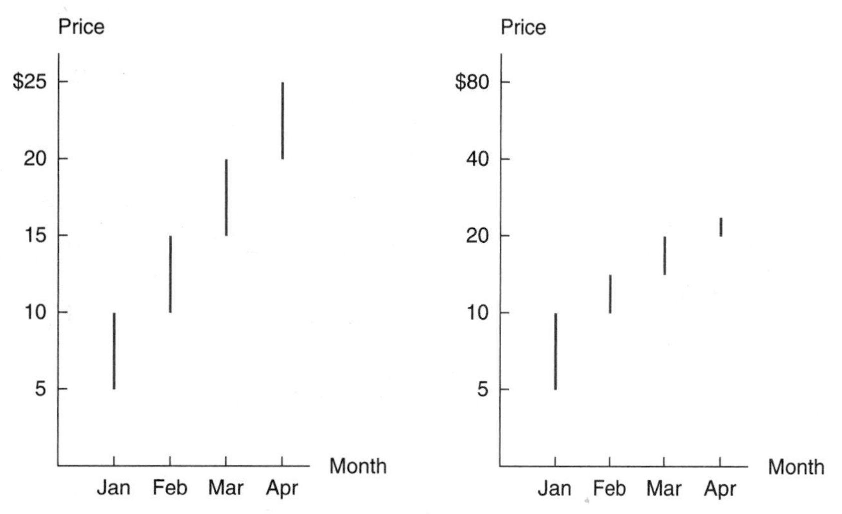

The impact of using the percentage scale may be seen by comparing Figures 10.1 and 10.3. Both present the annual price range of the Dow Jones Industrial Average, but Figure 10.1 uses an absolute scale while Figure 10.3 (p. 302) expresses prices in relative terms. The general shape is the same in both cases, but the large absolute increase in the Dow Jones Industrial Average during the late 1990s is considerably less impressive in Figure 10.3. Because absolute price changes are reduced to relative price changes, graphs like Figure 10.3 are better indicators of security price movements and the returns investors earn. Several of the figures in this text that indicate movements in stock prices are constructed to show relative price changes rather than absolute prices. (Such figures are common in the financial press. For example, the figure in Exhibit 4.2 that illustrates the *Value Line Investment Survey* uses percentage changes on the vertical axis, not absolute price changes.)

Other Major Indexes of Stock Prices

Standard & Poor's 500 stock index
A value-weighted index of 500 stocks.

Unlike the Dow Jones Industrial Average, the **Standard & Poor's 500 stock index** (commonly referred to as the S&P 500) is a value-weighted index. The index was 10 in the base year, 1943. Thus, if the index is currently 100, the value of these stocks is ten times their value in 1943. Standard & Poor's also computes an index of 400 industrial stocks and indexes of 20 transportation, 40 utility, and 40 financial companies.

Although the number of stocks in the S&P 500 remains constant, the composition of the index changes over time. Mergers and acquisitions are a major cause of a change in the index as one firm is acquired and is replaced by another stock. A financially weak firm whose stock has experienced a major decline in value may be dropped in favor of a company in better financial condition. The impact on the price of a stock that is added to the index is usually positive. Any price increase, however, is the result not of the company receiving more favorable recognition, but of buying by the index funds, which must now include the stock in their portfolios.

NYSE composite index
New York Stock Exchange index; an index of prices of all the stocks listed on the New York Stock Exchange.

The **New York Stock Exchange composite index** includes all common stocks listed on the NYSE. Like the Standard & Poor's indexes, the NYSE index is value-

FIGURE 10.3

Annual Price Range of the Dow Jones Industrial Average, 1950–2001

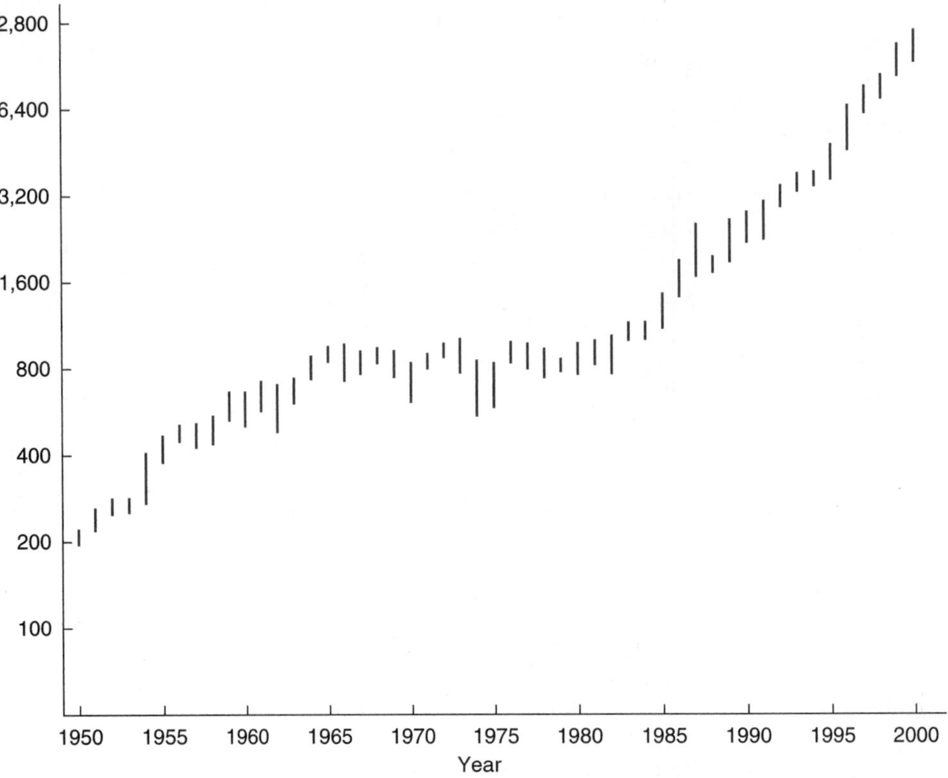

Source: First issue of *The Wall Street Journal* for each year.

weighted, with a base of 50 as of December 31, 1965. Value Line computes an index of more than 1,700 stocks that includes stocks traded on the New York Stock Exchange, on the American Stock Exchange, and on Nasdaq. Unlike the Dow Jones Industrial Average, which is a simple arithmetic average, and the S&P 500, which is a value-weighted average, the Value Line index is a geometric average that gives equal weight to each stock included in the average.

The Wilshire 5000 stock index is the broadest-based aggregate measure of stock prices. It is constructed using all stocks traded on the New York and American stock exchanges plus the actively traded over-the-counter stocks (i.e., virtually every publicly traded U.S. company). Other stock indexes include the American Stock Exchange index, which is a value-weighted index that encompasses all the common stocks on that exchange. The National Association of Security Dealers Automatic Quotation System (Nasdaq) index of over-the-counter stocks covers more than 3,000 issues. The National Association of Securities Dealers also publishes nonindustrial OTC indexes for banking and insurance. A summary of major aggregate measures of the U.S. stock market (including their coverage and means of computation) is given in Exhibit 10.1.

Initially, market indexes covered some concept of the market as a whole. Now, however, a variety of indexes have been developed, many of which are devoted to

EXHIBIT 10.1

The Coverage and Computation of Selected Aggregate Measures of U.S. Stock Markets*

Market Measure	Coverage	Computation
Dow Jones Industrial Average	30 large firms	Price-weighted arithmetic average
Standard & Poor's 500 stock index	500 actively traded stocks (400 industrial, 20 transportation, 40 utility, and 40 financial firms)	Value-weighted
Standard & Poor's 400 stock index	400 industrial companies	Value-weighted
Standard & Poor's 100 stock index	100 large cap stocks	Value-weighted
Standard & Poor's MidCap index	400 medium-sized firms with median market values (stock price times number of shares outstanding) of approximately $2 billion	Value-weighted
NYSE composite index	All stocks listed on the NYSE	Value-weighted
AMEX composite index	All stocks listed on the AMEX	Value-weighted
Value Line average	Approximately 1,700 stocks covered by the *Value Line Investment Survey*	Equally-weighted geometric average
National Association of Securities Dealers (Nasdaq) composite index	3,000 over-the-counter stocks	Value-weighted
Wilshire 5000 index	Approximately 7,000 NYSE, AMEX, and Nasdaq stocks	Value-weighted

*Information on these and other indexes is available through the Nasdaq–AMEX index descriptions at http://www.amex.com/reference/indexdescriptions.stm.

a subsection of the market, such as all stocks that meet a certain condition or belong to a particular subgroup. Examples of these indexes include the Nasdaq Industrials, Nasdaq Banks, Nasdaq Computer, and Nasdaq Telecommunications indexes.[4] Additional indexes and their components include:

Russell 1000	the largest 1,000 firms
Russell 2000	next-largest 2,000 firms
Russell 3000	combines the firms in the Russell 1000 and Russell 2000
Standard & Poor's 400 MidCap	index of moderate-sized firms
Standard & Poor's 600 SmallCap	index of relatively small firms
Standard & Poor's 1500 Index	combines all the stocks in the S&P 500, S&P 400 MidCap, and the S&P 600 SmallCap indexes

[4]Many of these indexes are reported daily in *The Wall Street Journal* or are available through other sources, especially the Internet. For example, over 90 indexes are reported at http://www.timely.com. (There are stock indexes of foreign stock markets such as the Japanese Nikkei 225 stock average, the London Financial Times Stock Exchange 100, and the Toronto Stock Exchange 300 composite index. Foreign indexes are discussed in Chapter 22 on international investments.)

The S&P 500 and the NYSE composite are primarily measures of large cap stocks. The Nasdaq index is limited to securities traded through Nasdaq, and the Wilshire 5000 is a very broad-based measure of stocks. The Russell 1000 is also a measure of the largest companies, but the Russell 2000 encompasses the next-largest companies. Because it excludes the largest companies and very small companies, this aggregate measure of one segment of the market has increasingly become the benchmark measure for the performance of small stocks.

As may be seen in Exhibit 10.1 and the preceding list, a large variety of indexes exists. While it may seem unnecessary to have so many indexes (and obviously the individual cannot follow all of them), each index can serve an important purpose. In Chapter 8 on mutual funds, it was observed that assessing a portfolio manager's performance requires a benchmark for comparison. While a large cap growth fund may be compared to the S&P 500 stock index, such a comparison would not be valid for the manager of a fund that specialized in energy stocks or small cap stocks. This question of comparability, of course, applies to any specialized investment portfolio and has led to the creation of specialized indexes. If assessment is going to be based on market comparisons, then appropriate measures of the relevant market's performance are necessary.

In addition to indexes of stock prices, there are also aggregate measures of the bond market. These averages may be expressed in terms of yields, such as the yields used to construct Figures 15.3, 16.4, and 17.1, or in terms of prices. One illustration of a bond price index is the Dow Jones composite corporate bond average, which consists of ten public utility and ten industrial bonds. The average is expressed as a percentage of the debt face amount. If the composite of the 20 bonds is 103.49, the average price of a bond is $1,034.90.

Actually, several hundred different bond indexes exist in addition to the Dow Jones 20 corporate bond average. Other bond indexes include the Lehman Brothers Aggregate index, the Merrill Lynch Domestic Master bond index, and the Salomon Brothers Corporate Bond index. These three indexes are similar. Each includes bonds with more than one year to maturity. Individual bonds are weighted by their market value, and selected bonds (e.g., high-yield, convertible, and variable rate bonds) are excluded from each index.

Price Fluctuations

Fluctuations in stock prices are illustrated in Figure 10.4, which plots the Dow Jones Industrial Average, the Standard & Poor's 500 stock index, and the NYSE composite index for 1980 through 2000. (The Dow Jones values have been divided by 10 to put them on a common basis with the two indexes.) All three aggregate measures show the large increase in stock prices that occurred during the time period. Over the 21 years, the Dow Jones increased at an annual rate of 12.63 percent, while the S&P 500 and the NYSE composite increased at annual rates of 12.12 and 11.46 percent, respectively. (Those slight differences in rates illustrate the importance of compounding over an extended period of time. Over 21 years, $100 grows to $1,104.96 at 12.63 percent, but only $976.11 at 11.46 percent.)

As would be expected, all three aggregate measures of the stock market move together, but the amount of movement does vary. For example, from January 1986 to January 1989, the Dow Jones rose by 39 percent, but the NYSE rose only 31 percent. Generally, the correlation among the various aggregate measures is very high.[5] There is, however, some difference in the variability of these aggregate mea-

[5]Merrill Lych Quantitative Analysis Group has estimated the correlation coefficient relating the S&P 500 and the Dow Jones Industrial Average to be 0.95. The correlation coefficient between the S&P 500 and the NYSE composite index was 1.0. The correlation coefficients of the monthly returns for the data used in Figure 10.4 were 0.99. For additional correlation coefficients, see Frank J. Fabozzi, *Investment Management* (Englewood Cliffs, NJ: Prentice-Hall, 1995), 49.

FIGURE 10.4

Aggregate Measures of Stock Prices, 1980–2000

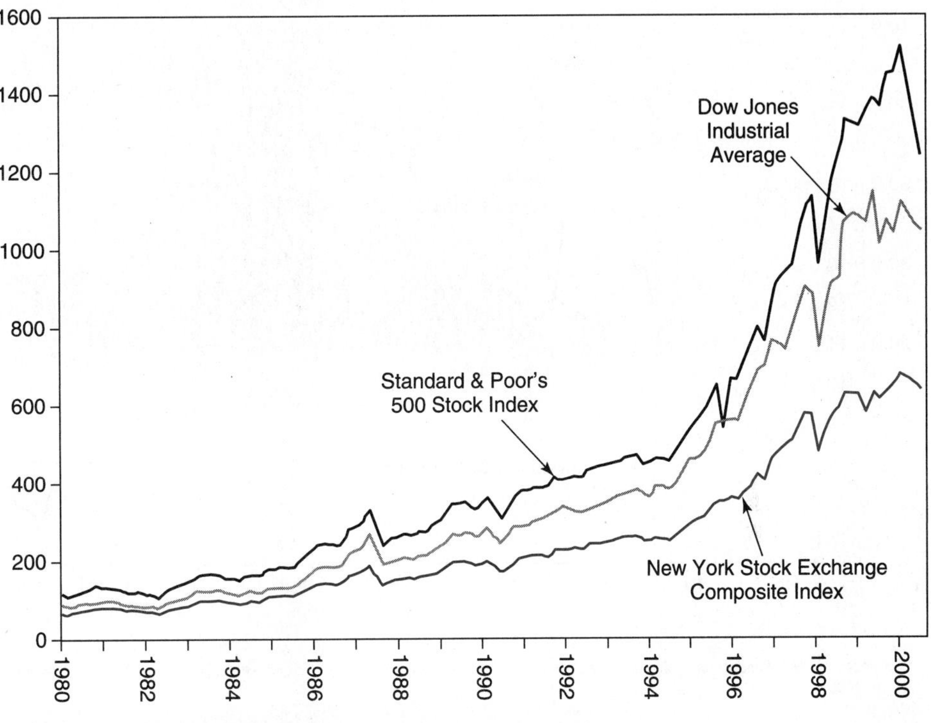

Source: *Federal Reserve Bulletin,* various issues.

sures. The standard deviations of the monthly returns based on the data used to construct Figure 10.4 were 6.12 percent for the Dow Jones Industrial Average and 6.48 percent for the S&P 500. The standard deviation for NYSE composite index was lower (5.88 percent).

Figure 10.4 also shows that security prices can and do fall. One particularly severe decline occurred in late 1987. However, in a matter of months, stock prices were back to approximately the levels at the beginning of 1987, and by 1990, stock prices had climbed back to and exceeded the highs reached prior to the debacle experienced during October 1987. A similar large decline was experienced during 2000 (especially in over-the-counter stocks, some of which are included in the S&P 500).

Figure 10.5 (p. 306) illustrates fluctuations in bond prices and compares the Dow Jones 20-bond composite average and the yield on Moody's Aaa-rated bonds from 1978 through 2000. The figure vividly illustrates an inverse relationship between bond prices and yields. For example, the bond average fell from 85.4 to 55.4 between January 1979 and September 1981, when interest rates on the Aaa-rated bonds rose from 9.3 percent to over 15 percent. However, from May 1984 through year-end 1993, the price of bonds rose as interest rates fell. (This negative relationship between interest rates and bond prices is explained in detail in Chapter 16 on the valuation of fixed-income securities.)

Figure 10.5 shows the relationship between bond prices and yields; Fig. 10.6 (p. 307) shows the relationship between bond prices and stock prices. Although changes in interest rates do affect changes in stock prices, over time bond prices

FIGURE 10.5

Dow Jones Bond Average and Yields on Mergent's (Moody's) Aaa-Rated Bonds, 1978–2000

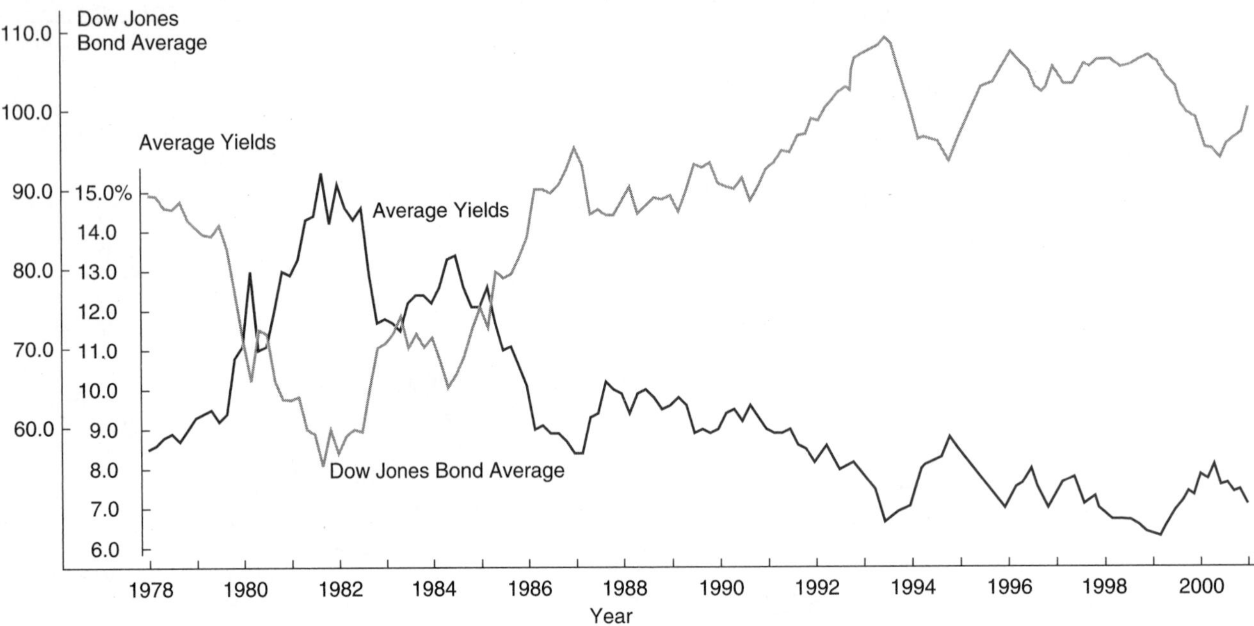

Source: *Moody's Bond Record,* various issues, 1978–1999; *Mergent's Bond Record,* various issues, 2000; *The Wall Street Journal Index* (Ann Arbor, MI: UMI Company), 1978–2000.

and stock prices are independent of each other. For the period illustrated in Figure 10.6 (January 1, 1993, through January 1, 2001), the Dow Jones Industrial Average rose from 3,310 to 10,887, while the bond average started at 1,050 and ended at 1,003. Over time, stock prices rose while bond prices fluctuated around their principal value of $1,000 per bond. However, you should not conclude that investors in bonds earned no or negative returns. Instead of experiencing the capital appreciation generated by stocks, these investors collected the interest payments. (For returns earned by stock and bond investors, see the section on investment returns later in this chapter.)

Security Prices and Investors' Purchasing Power

Another means to measure security price performance is to compare one of the measures of the market with a general price index. This gives an indication of the losses inflicted on the investing public by inflation. If the general price index rises more rapidly than the index of security prices, the implication is that stockholders suffer a loss of purchasing power. This loss occurs even if stock prices rise if the increase is at a slower rate than consumer prices.[6]

The loss of purchasing power is illustrated in Figure 10.7 (pp. 308–309), which is divided into three panels. The first plots the Dow Jones Industrial Average from

[6]Because stock indexes exclude dividends, the actual loss in purchasing power is overstated.

FIGURE 10.6

Dow Jones Industrial Average and Dow Jones Bond Average, 1993–2000

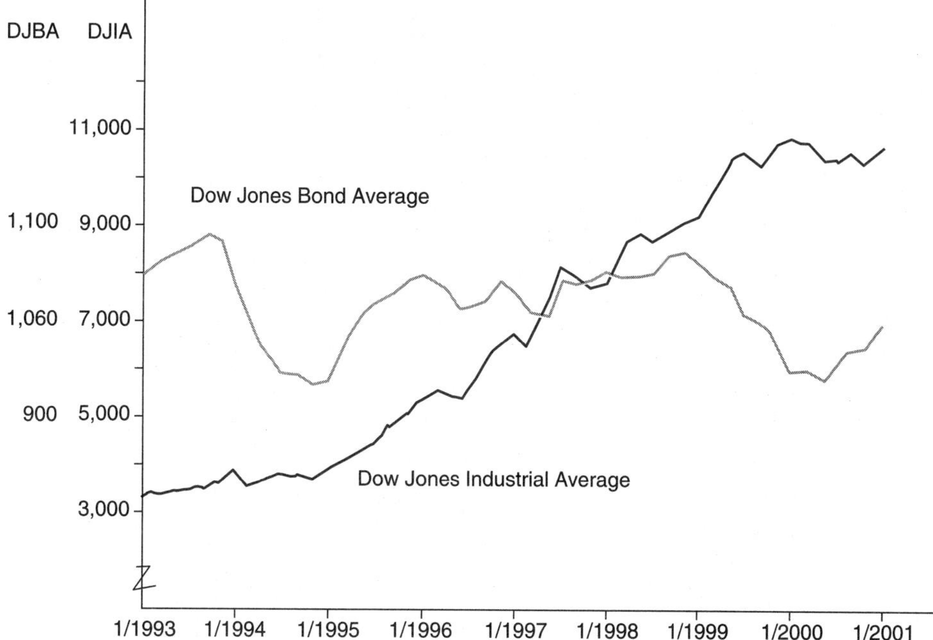

Source: *The Wall Street Journal Index*, published annually. Ann Arbor, MI: UMI Company, various issues.

1970 through 2000 and the Dow Jones deflated average (i.e., expressed relative to the Consumer Price Index). As may be seen in this panel, stock prices did not grow during the 1970s, but a different pattern emerged during the 1980s. The figure also shows the purchasing power of stocks declined from 1970 to 1981 and then started to rise. However, at the end of 1991, the purchasing power of the Dow Jones was approximately the same as at the beginning of the period, because from 1970 through 1991, the Consumer Price Index rose annually at 6.1 percent while the Dow rose at 6.5 percent. Of course, investors who purchased these stocks earned a higher return through the receipt of dividends, but the purchasing power of the value of the stocks was virtually unchanged at the end of 20 years.

The second panel presents the annual percentage change in the Dow and the Consumer Price Index. While the CPI fluctuates from year to year, the amount of fluctuation is perceptibly smaller than for stock prices. Furthermore, the CPI never declines (i.e., all the annual changes are positive), while stocks can, and do, suffer years of large, negative change.

The third panel presents the real change in annual stock prices. In some years, stock prices rose more than the rate of inflation (e.g., 1995–1999), so that investors experienced a positive real return. There were years in which stock prices fell while consumer prices continued to rise (e.g., 1984 and 2000), and there were years in which stock prices increased, but not at the level that consumer prices increased. For example, during 1979 and 1980, stock prices rose but inflation exceeded the stocks' price increase, so that investors experienced negative real returns even though they earned positive returns on the securities.

FIGURE 10.7

Purchasing Power of Dow Jones Industrial Average, 1970–2000

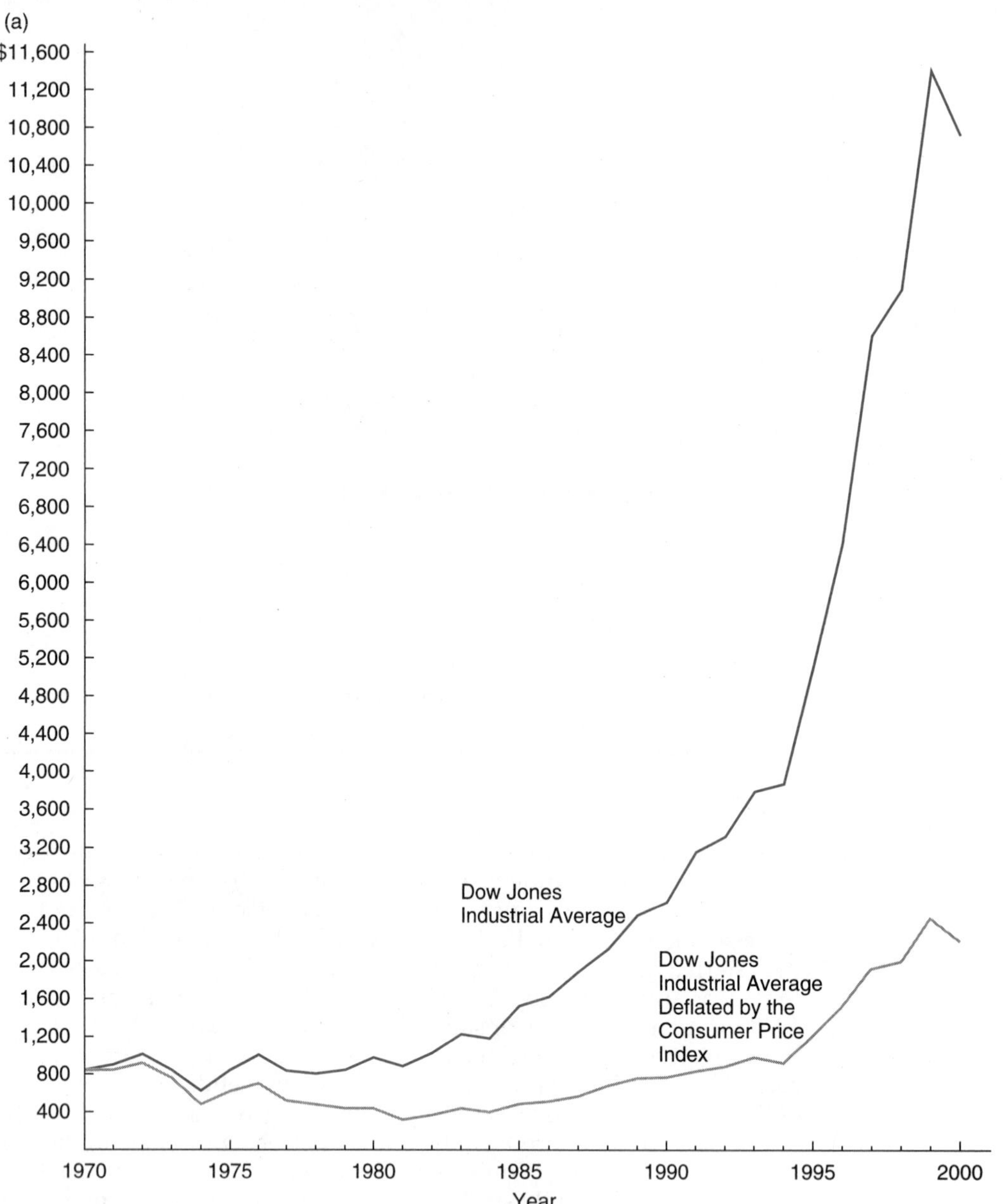

Source: *Federal Reserve Bulletin,* various issues.

FIGURE 10.7, CONTINUED

Purchasing Power of Dow Jones Industrial Average, 1970–2000

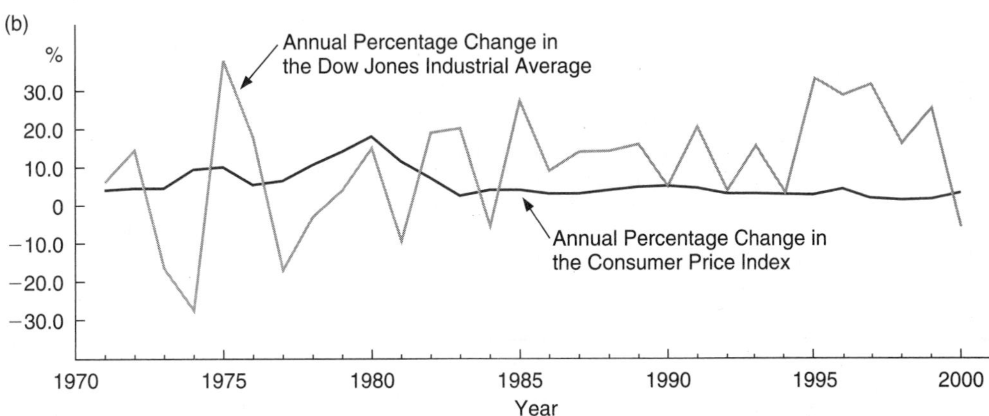

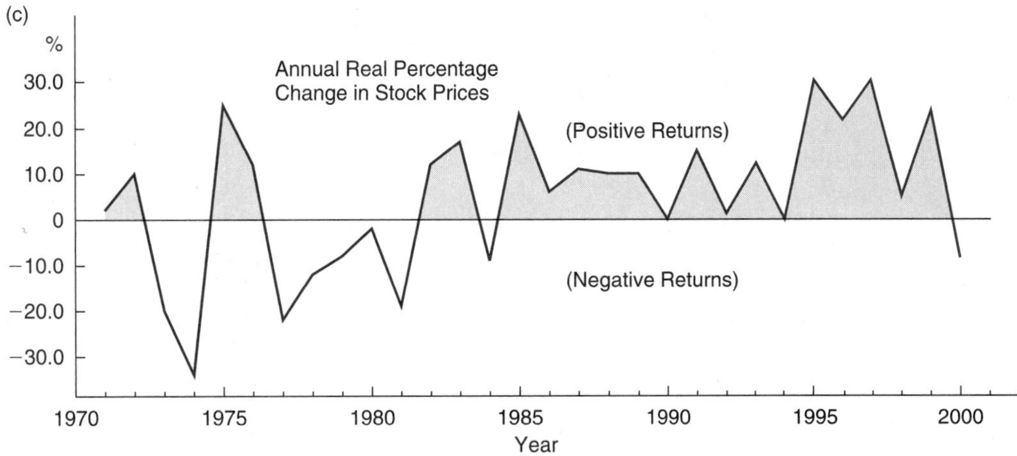

Source: *Federal Reserve Bulletin*, various issues.

Figure 10.7 also suggests that inflation is detrimental to stock prices. Once inflation started to diminish in the early 1980s, common stock prices began to rise. Although inflation did not cease in the 1980s, the rate was perceptibly smaller and stock prices rose dramatically after 1984, reaching new highs virtually every year.

Rates of Return on Investments in Common Stock

holding period return (HPR)
Total return (income plus price appreciation during a specified time period) divided by the cost of the investment.

What returns have been earned on investments in securities? To answer this question, the investor should consider the purchase price of the security, the sale price, the flow of income (such as dividends or interest), and how long the investor owned the asset. The easiest (and perhaps the most misleading) return is the **holding period return (HPR)**. It is derived by dividing the profit (or loss) plus any income by the price paid for the asset. That is,

POINTS OF INTEREST
Overstating the Rate of Appreciation in the Value of a House

Holding period returns are frequently used when discussing real estate investments, and, because of the long time periods involved, they can be very misleading. Their simplest form would include such a statement as, "I bought my house in 1970 for $35,000 and sold it for $175,000 in 2000." The large price increase ($140,000) generates a holding period return of 400 percent ($140,000/$35,000). However, the true annualized rate of return is 8.38 percent. The purchase price of $35,000, deposited in an investment that paid 8.38 percent, compounded annually during the same time period, would have grown into $175,000. While this illustration does not consider (1) the use of the house, (2) any expenses associated with upkeep, and (3) any tax advantages associated with home ownership, it does illustrate how misleading holding period returns can be. In the context of this illustration, the house's price appreciation is not particularly impressive.

$$\text{HPR} = \frac{P_1 + D - P_0}{P_0}, \tag{10.1}$$

in which P_1 is the sale price, D is the income, and P_0 is the purchase price. If an investor buys a stock for $40, collects dividends of $2, and sells the stock for $50, the holding period return is

$$\text{HPR} = \frac{\$50 + \$2 - \$40}{\$40} = 30\%.$$

The holding period return has a major weakness because it fails to consider how long it took to earn the return. This problem is immediately apparent if the information in the previous example had been a stock that cost $40, paid annual dividends of $1, and was sold at the end of the *second* year for $50. Given this information, what is the return? While the holding period return remains the same, 30 percent is obviously higher than the true annual return. If the time period is greater than a year, the holding period return overstates the true annual return. (Conversely, for a period that is less than a year, the holding period return understates the true annual return.)

Because the holding period return is easy to compute, it is frequently used, producing misleading results. Consider the following example. An investor buys a stock for $10 per share and sells it after ten years for $20. What is the holding period return on the investment? This simple question can produce several misleading answers. The individual may respond by answering, "I doubled my money!" or "I made 100 percent!" That certainly sounds impressive, but it completely disregards the *length of time* needed to double the individual's money. The investor may compute the arithmetic average and assert that he or she made 10 percent annually (100% ÷ 10 years). This figure is less impressive than the claim that the return is 100 percent, but it is also misleading because it fails to consider compounding. Some of the return earned during the first year in turn earned a return in subsequent years, which was not taken into consideration when the investor averaged the return over the ten years.

rate of return
The discount rate that equates the cost of an investment with the cash flows generated by the investment.

The correct way to determine what **rate of return** was earned is to phrase the question as follows: "At what rate does $10 grow to $20 after ten years?" The student should recognize this as another example of the time value of money. The equation used to answer this question is

$$P_0(1 + r)^n = P_n,$$

in which P_0 is the cost of the security, r is the rate of return per period, n is the number of periods (e.g., years), and P_n is the price at which the security is sold. When the proper values are substituted, the equation becomes

$$\$10(1 + r)^{10} = \$20,$$

which asks at what rate $10 will grow for ten years to become $20. To answer this question, the interest factor must be determined:

$$(1 + r)^{10} = \$20 \div \$10 = 2.$$

Thus, 2 is the interest factor for the future value of $1 for ten years. Locating this factor in the compound value of a dollar table (Appendix A), reveals the value of r to be approximately 7 percent.

The use of the table for the compound value of $1 leads only to an approximate answer. If the investor desires a more accurate answer, the appropriate root must be found. That is,

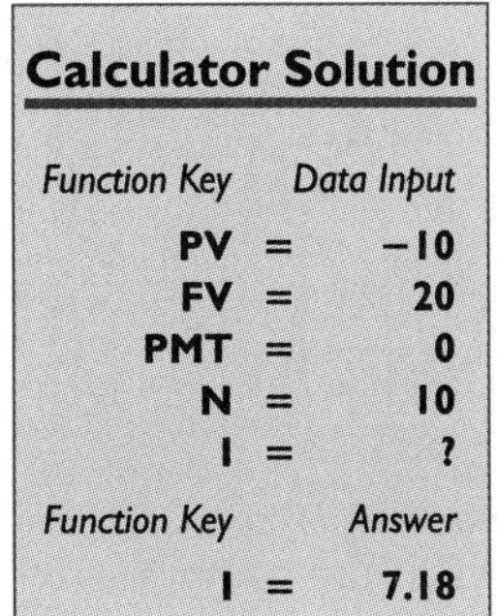

Calculator Solution

Function Key	Data Input
PV =	−10
FV =	20
PMT =	0
N =	10
I =	?
Function Key	**Answer**
I =	7.18

$$\$10(1 + r)^{10} = \$20.00,$$
$$(1 + r)^{10} = 2,$$
$$r = \sqrt[10]{2} - 1 = 1.0718 - 1 = 7.18\%,$$

so the annual rate of return is 7.18 percent. The correct rate of return on the investment (excluding any dividend income) is considerably less impressive than "I doubled my money!" or "I averaged 10 percent each year."

An individual who does not have access to interest tables or a financial calculator, or who does not want to go through the procedure of taking the nth root, may be tempted to determine the percentage return for each year. For example, if the price of the stock were to rise from $20 to $22, the annual return would be 10 percent ($2 ÷ $20). If the stock were to fall in price from $20 to $15, the annual rate of return would be −25 percent (−$5 ÷ $20).

There is nothing wrong with this technique until the investor averages the resulting annual percentage changes. Like the average of the ten-year holding period return, this procedure can be misleading. Consider the following example. An investor buys a stock for $20. At the end of the year it is selling for $25, but the investor holds the stock for a second year and then sells it at cost (i.e., $20). What is the rate of return? Obviously, the investor earned nothing and the rate of return should indicate this fact.

If, however, the investor computes the annual rate of return each year, and then averages these annual rates, the investment will have a positive rate of return. In the first year, the stock's price rose from $20 to $25, indicating a 25 percent gain ($5 ÷ $20). During the second year, the stock declined from $25 to $20, for a 20 percent loss (−$5 ÷ $25). What is the average rate of return? The answer is

$$25\% - 20\% = 5\%$$
$$\frac{5\%}{2} = 2.5\%.$$

Owing to the magic of numbers, the investor has earned a 2.5 percent average return, even though the investment produced neither a gain nor a loss. This example illustrates how the averaging of positive and negative percentage changes can provide misleading results.

The correct method to determine the annual rate of return is to use a geometric average. In the first year, the stock rose from $20 to $25 (or $25 ÷ $20 = 1.25). In the second year, the stock declined from \$25 to \$20 (or \$20 ÷ \$25 = 0.8). The geometric average is

$$\sqrt[2]{(1.25)(0.80)} = 1.00,$$

so the average return is 1.00 − 1.00 = 0.0%.[7]

Geometric averages are often used to obtain rates of return over a period of years. Suppose the annual rates of return are as follows:

Year	Rate of Return
1	25%
2	3
3	−18
4	−10
5	15

The geometric average return is

$$\sqrt[5]{(1.25)(1.03)(0.82)(0.90)(1.15)} - 1 = 0.0179 = 1.79\%.$$

This annual return is lower than the arithmetic return of 3 percent that would be obtained by adding each of the returns and dividing by 5. As in the previous example, the averaging of positive and negative annual returns (i.e., the computation of an arithmetic average) overstates the true return.

The inclusion of income makes the calculation of a rate of return more difficult. Consider the example that started this section in which the investor bought a stock for \$40, collected \$2 in dividends for two years, and then sold the stock for \$50. What is the rate of return? The holding period return is overstated because it fails to consider the time value of money. If the investor computes the rate of growth and only considers the original cost and the terminal value, the rate of return is understated because the dividend payments are excluded.

internal rate of return
Percentage return that equates the present value of an investment's cash inflows with its cost.

These problems are avoided by computing an investment's **internal rate of return**, an approach that determines the rate that equates the present value of all an investment's future cash inflows with the present cost of the investment. An example of an internal rate of return is the yield to maturity on a bond (discussed in Chapter 16). Since the yield to maturity equates the present value of the cash inflows (the interest and principal repayment) with the present cost of the investment, it is the true, annualized rate of return.

The general equation for the internal rate of return (r) for a stock is

$$P_0 = \frac{D_1}{(1+r)} + \cdots + \frac{D_n}{(1+r)^n} + \frac{P_n}{(1+r)^n}, \qquad (10.2)$$

in which D is the annual dividend received in n years, and P_n is the price received for the stock in the nth year.[8]

[7]See the appendix to Chapter 7 for the computation of geometric averages using percentages.

[8]The same equation will be used to determine the yield to maturity in Chapter 16. The yield to maturity is, in effect, the internal rate of return on an investment in a bond that is purchased today and redeemed at maturity.

If the internal rate of return were computed for the previous illustration of a stock that cost \$40, paid an annual dividend of \$1, and was sold at the end of the second year for \$50, the equation to be solved is

$$\$40 = \frac{\$1}{(1 + r)} + \frac{\$1}{(1 + r)^2} + \frac{\$50}{(1 + r)^2}.$$

Notice that there are three cash inflows: the dividend received each year and the sale price. The internal rate of return equates *all* cash inflows to the investor with the cost of the investment. These cash inflows include periodic payments as well as the sale price. (The calculation for the holding period return combined the dividend plus the capital gain on the investment and treated them as occurring at the end as a single cash inflow.)

Solving this equation is very tedious, especially if there is a large number of years. Select a rate (e.g., 12 percent) and substitute it into the equation. If the results equate both sides of the equation, the internal rate of return has been determined. If the sides are not equal, select another rate and repeat the process. For example, if 12 percent is selected, then

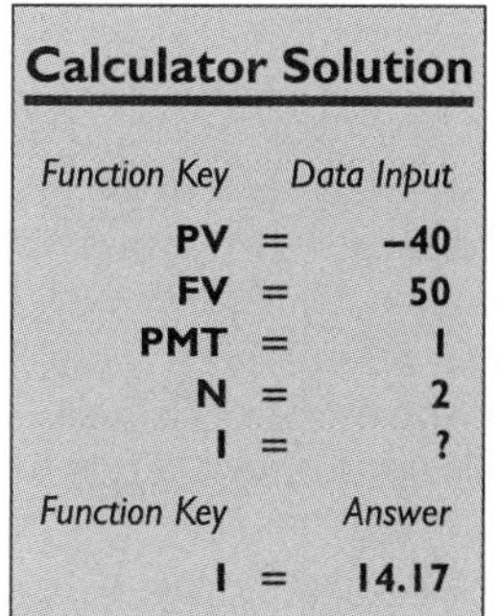

Calculator Solution

Function Key	*Data Input*
PV =	−40
FV =	50
PMT =	1
N =	2
I =	?
Function Key	*Answer*
I =	14.17

\$40 = \$1 × (interest factor for the present value of an annuity at 12 percent for two years) + \$50 × (interest factor for the present value of \$1 at 12 percent for two years)
= \$1(1.690) + \$50(0.797) = \$41.54.

Since the two sides are not equal, 12 percent is not the internal rate of return. Since \$41.54 exceeds \$40, the rate is too small, so a greater rate would be selected and the process repeated.

This tedious process is made considerably easier with the use of a financial calculator or the software that accompanies this text. When the data are entered into the calculator, the internal rate of return on the investment, 14.17 percent, is readily determined. This 14.17 percent is the true, annualized rate of return on the investment. (The use of a financial calculator facilitates the computation of the internal rate of return, but calculators do have weaknesses. In this illustration, the yearly payments are equal and are entered into the calculator as an annuity. If the yearly payments were unequal, each payment would have to be individually entered. Because calculators limit the number of individual entries, they may not be used to determine the internal rate of return for problems with large numbers of cash inflows.)

The internal rate of return has two potential problems. The first concerns the reinvestment of cash inflows received by the investor. The internal rate of return assumes that cash inflows are *reinvested at the investment's internal rate.* In the preceding illustration that means the \$1 received in the first year is reinvested at 14.17 percent. If the dividend payment is reinvested at a lower rate or not reinvested (e.g., it is spent), the true return on the investment will be less than the rate determined by the equation. Conversely, if the investor earns more than 14.17 percent when the \$1 is reinvested, the true return on the investment will exceed the internal rate of return determined by the equation.

The second problem occurs when the investor makes more than one purchase of the security. While the problem is not insurmountable, it makes the calculation more difficult. Suppose the investor buys one share for \$40 at the beginning of the first year, buys a second share for \$42 at the end of the first year, and sells both shares at the end of the second year for \$50 each. The firm pays an annual dividend of \$1, so \$1 is collected at the end of year 1 and \$2 at the end of year 2. What is the rate of return on the investment?

To answer this question using the internal rate of return, the investor must equate the present value of the cash inflows and the cash outflows. The cash flows are as follows:

Time	Year 0	End of Year 1	End of Year 2
Cash outflow	$40	$42	—
Cash inflow	—	$ 1	$2 + $100

There are two cash outflows (the purchases of $40 and $42) that occur in the present (year 0) and at the end of year 1. There are two cash inflows, the $1 dividend received at the end of year 1 and the $2 dividend at the end of year 2 plus the receipts from the sale of the shares ($100) at the end of year 2. The equation for the internal rate of return is

$$\$40 + \frac{42}{(1 + r)} = \frac{\$1}{(1 + r)} + \frac{2 + 100}{(1 + r)^2}$$

and the internal rate of return is 16.46 percent.

In this example, the investor owns one share during the first year and two shares during the second year. The return in the second year has more impact on the overall return than the rate earned during the first year when the investor owned only one share. Since the number of shares and hence the amount invested differ each year, this approach to determining rates of return is sometimes referred to as a **dollar-weighted rate of return.**

dollar-weighted rate of return
The rate that equates the present value of cash inflows and cash outflows; the internal rate of return.

time-weighted rate of return
Average of individual holding period returns.

An alternative to the dollar-weighted or internal rate of return is the **time-weighted return**, which ignores the amount of funds invested during each time period. This technique computes the return for each period and averages the results. In effect, it computes the holding period return for each period and averages them. In the illustration, the initial price was $40; the investor collected $1 in dividends and had stock worth $42 at the end of the year. The return for the first year was

$$(\$42 + 1 - 40) \div 40 = 7.5\%.$$

During the second year, a share rose from $42 to $50 and paid a $1 dividend. The return was

$$(\$50 + 1 - 42) \div 42 = 21.43\%.$$

The simple average return is

$$(7.5\% + 21.43) \div 2 = 14.47\%,$$

and the geometric average return is

$$\sqrt{(1.075)(1.2143)} - 1 = \sqrt{1.3054} - 1 = 1.1425 - 1 = 14.25\%.$$

As discussed earlier, the geometric average is the true compound rate, while the simple average tends to overstate the true annual rate of return.

In this illustration, the dollar-weighted return (i.e., the internal rate of return) is higher than the time-weighted return. This is the result of the stock performing better in the second year when the investor owned more shares. The results would

POINTS OF INTEREST

When a 75 Percent Return Produces a Loss

You invest $100 in a mutual fund that earns 25 percent annually for three years. Unfortunately, it loses 75 percent during the fourth year but then comes back and earns 25 percent for the next three years. That's a total return of 75 percent. Because seven years were required to earn the 75 percent, the average return is 10.7 percent. This percentage is comparable to the annual return determined by the historical studies of returns earned on common stocks.

Unfortunately, the implication that the fund's performance is comparable to the market return is incorrect. The calculation (6) (25) − 75 does give 75, but that is not the rate of return. What actually happened to the investment is as follows:

Year	Value of Investment
0	$100.00
1	125.00
2	156.25
3	195.31
4	48.83
5	61.04
6	76.29
7	95.37

You lost money; the true rate of return is negative!

This example points out two things. First, adding percentage changes is misleading. This problem is avoided by the following calculation:

$$(1.25)(1.25)(1.25)(0.25)(1.25)(1.25)(1.25) = 0.9537.$$

On an annualized basis, the rate of return is

$$\$100\ (1 + r)^7 = \$95.37$$

$$r = 0.9537^{0.14286} - 1 = -0.7\%.$$

Second, one bad year can wipe out the gains of several good years. The 5 percent loss in the fourth year requires a 300 percent increase to offset it. If your stock declines from $195.31 to $48.83 (a 75 percent decrease), the stock must rise by 400 percent to go from $48.83 to $195.31, which is a 300 percent increase.

You may not experience such a large decline in the value of your stock. If, however, such a decline occurs when you need to sell the securities, the large loss will obviously have an impact on your wealth. The possibility of a worst-case scenario (i.e., a large loss when funds are needed) should be a consideration if you are anticipating selling the securities for a specific purpose. If, for example, your aim is to finance your daughter's college education, taking profits early may be desirable to avoid the possibility of a large loss occurring when the tuition bill comes due!

have been reversed if the stock had performed better the first year than during the second year (i.e., 21.4 percent in year 1 and 7.5 percent in year 2). In that case, the larger amount invested would have earned the smaller return, so the dollar-weighted return would have been less than the time-weighted return.

Which of the two methods, the dollar-weighted return or the time-weighted return, is preferred? There is no absolute right answer. Because the investor is concerned with the return earned on *all* the dollars invested, the dollar-weighted return would appear to be superior. However, there is an argument for the use of a time-weighted return to evaluate the performance of a portfolio manager. For example, a firm may make periodic contributions to its employee pension plan. Because the timing and amount of the cash inflows are beyond the pension plan manager's control, the use of a dollar-weighted return is inappropriate. Thus, money managers often use a time-weighted return instead of a dollar-weighted return to evaluate portfolio performance.[9]

[9]The Association for Investment Management and Research (AIMR) *requires* its members to calculate time-weighted returns at least quarterly using a geometric average. The purpose of the calculation is to inform clients of the portfolio manager's performance. The portfolio managers must also present measures of risk, such as the standard deviations of the returns. See AIMR, *Performance Presentation Standards* (Charlottesville, VA: Association for Investment Management and Research, 1993).

Studies of Investment Returns

Several studies have been conducted by academicians on the returns earned by investments in common stocks; hence, these reports should not contain any bias. Unfortunately, research done by brokerage firms, investment advisory services, or the trust departments of commercial banks may involve a conflict of interest. Although the results may seem valid, one may still be hesitant to accept them as honest appraisals of the returns earned by investors.

Calculator Solution

Function Key	Data Input
PV =	−1000
FV =	?
PMT =	0
N =	20
I =	9.3
Function Key	*Answer*
FV =	5,921

An early study on the rates of return earned by investments in common stocks was done by Fisher and Lorie. They studied the annual rates of return from investments in all common stocks listed on the NYSE from 1926 through 1965 and found that the annual rate of return was 9.3 percent.[10] (The student should remember that an annual return of 9.3 percent means $1,000 will grow to $5,921 in 20 years.) The rates of return were even higher during the 1950s and early 1960s when the country and the stock market experienced prosperity and rapid growth. During this time the annual rates of return averaged as high as 15 percent.

Studies of the stock market by Holmes and by Brigham and Pappas corroborated the results of Fisher and Lorie.[11] Holmes's study covered the period between 1871 and 1971. The annual rate of return earned for the 100-year period was 7.8 percent. For the years that overlapped with Fisher and Lorie's study, the rate of return was 9.7 percent. This small difference (9.7 versus 9.3 percent) could be attributed to commission costs: Fisher and Lorie included a commission cost for stock purchases, while Holmes's study did not. Hence, one would expect Fisher and Lorie's rates of return to be less.

Brigham and Pappas's study covered the period from 1946 to 1965. They concluded that the annual rate of return was about 15 percent. Although this figure is considerably higher than the overall returns in the Fisher and Lorie and Holmes studies, it is similar to their returns for the comparable time period.

Ibbotson and Sinquefield initially extended the results of previous studies to 1981.[12] Their study was more comprehensive than the previous studies in that it considered not only stocks but also corporate bonds, federal government bonds and bills, and the rate of inflation. Since 1981 the results have been updated annually, and this work is generally considered to be the most definitive study of rates of return on alternative investments.[13] A summary of the results is presented in Exhibit 10.2. As may be seen in the exhibit, the annual rate of return for common stocks as measured by the Standard & Poor's 500 common stock index was 11.3 percent. If only smaller stocks are considered, the annual rate of return rises to 12.6 percent. Ibbotson Associates defines small stocks as the lowest one-fifth of New York Stock Exchange firms in total value (i.e., price times number of shares outstanding).

Exhibit 10.2 includes the annual rates of return earned by long-term corporate debt, federal government bonds, and Treasury bills. In addition, the exhibit includes the standard deviation of each rate of return, which indicates the associated risk. As would be expected, the risk is largest for the small stocks. While their annual return was 12.6 percent, the standard deviation was 33.6 percent, which means that in 68 percent of the years the annual return ranged from 46.2 percent to −21.0 percent. This is a very large range in returns when compared to that of Treasury bills, which had a standard deviation of 3.2 percent. Obviously, if the investor

[10] Lawrence Fisher and James H. Lorie, "Rates of Return on Investments in Common Stock: The Year-by-Year Record, 1926–1965," *Journal of Business* 40 (July 1968): 1–26.

[11] See John Russell Holmes, "100 Years of Common Stock Investing," *Financial Analysts Journal* 30 (November/December 1974): 38–45; and Eugene F. Brigham and James L. Pappas, "Rates of Return on Common Stock," *Journal of Business* 42 (July 1969): 302–316.

[12] Roger Ibbotson and Rex Sinquefield, *Stock, Bonds, Bills, and Inflation: The Past and the Future* (Charlottesville, VA: Financial Analysts Research Foundation, 1982).

[13] The annual updates are published by Ibbotson Associates in *The Stocks, Bonds, Bills, and Inflation (SBBI) Yearbook*. Information concerning SBBI is available at http://www.ibbotson.com.

EXHIBIT 10.2

Annual Rates of Return, 1926–1999, Estimated by Ibbotson Associates

Security	Annual Rate of Return	Standard Deviation of Return
Large company common stocks	11.3%	20.1%
Small company stocks	12.6	33.6
Long-term corporate bonds	5.6	8.7
Long-term government bonds	5.1	9.3
Treasury bills	3.8	3.2
Rate of Inflation	3.1	4.5

Source: *Stocks, Bonds, Bills, and Inflation, 2000 Yearbook* (Chicago, IL: Ibbotson Associates, 2000). (Data in the *SBBI Yearbook* updated annually.)

EXHIBIT 10.3

Average, Highest, and Lowest Returns: 1945–1995, 1980–1995, and 1988–1999

		1945–1995	1980–1995	1988–1999
Large company stocks	average return	12.4%	15.8%	19.1%
	highest return	52.6 (1954)	37.4 (1995)	37.4 (1995)
	lowest return	−26.5 (1974)	−4.9 (1981)	−3.2 (1990)
Small company stocks	average return	14.7	15.6	15.3
	highest return	83.6 (1967)	44.6 (1991)	44.6 (1991)
	lowest return	−30.9 (1973)	−21.6 (1990)	−21.6 (1990)
Rate of Inflation	average	4.3	4.4	3.2
	highest	18.2 (1945)	12.4 (1980)	6.1 (1990)
	lowest	0.4 (1955)	1.1 (1986)	1.7 (1997)

Source: *Stocks, Bonds, Bills, and Inflations, 2000 Yearbook* (Chicago, IL: Ibbotson Associates, 2000).

limited the portfolio to riskier securities and was forced to sell the stocks, the investor could sustain a large loss if the sale occurred during a declining market. Conversely, over a period of years, the riskier stocks produced a higher return.

Exhibit 10.2 gives the annual rate of inflation, and it is interesting to note that the rate earned on Treasury bills slightly exceeded the rate of inflation. This suggests that the investor who is concerned with maintaining purchasing power can meet this goal (at least before federal income taxes are considered) by acquiring Treasury bills. The exhibit also suggests that over time, the yield on stocks tends to be approximately 7 percent above the rate on Treasury bills. This information may be important when trying to establish a return necessary to justify purchasing equities. For example, a current yield on Treasury bills of 4.5 percent suggests that a return of 11.5 percent may be necessary to justify purchasing a corporation's common stock (before adjusting for the risk associated with the specific company).

Because the results in Exhibit 10.2 may have been affected by the returns earned during the depression of the 1930s, Exhibit 10.3 presents the returns for more recent time periods: 1945–1995, 1980–1995, and 1988–1999. For all three periods, the returns on stocks exceeded the returns presented in Exhibit 10.2. Exhibit 10.3 also indicates considerable range in the returns. During 1954, the return on large stocks exceeded 50 percent, while the losses in 1974 exceeded 25 percent. The returns on small stocks experienced an even greater range, from a high of 83.6 percent in 1967

EXHIBIT 10.4

Highest and Lowest Returns for Different Time Horizons (since 1994)

	Common Stocks	Small Company Stocks
One-year		
Lowest return	−26.5% (1974)	−30.9% (1973)
Highest return	52.6% (1954)	83.6% (1967)
Five-year time horizon:		
Lowest return	−2.4% (1970–1974)	−12.6% (1970–1974)
Highest return	28.6% (1995–1999)	39.8% (1975–1979)
Ten-year time horizon:		
Lowest return	1.4% (1965–1974)	3.2% (1965–1974)
Highest return	20.1% (1949–1958)	30.4% (1975–1984)
Twenty-year time horizon:		
Lowest return	6.5% (1959–1978)	8.2% (1955–1974)
Highest return	17.9% (1980–1999)	20.3% (1975–1994)

Source: *Stocks, Bonds, Bills and Inflation, 2000 Yearbook* (Chicago, IL: Ibbotson Associates, 2000), various pages.

to a loss of 30.9 percent in 1973. Even during the most recent time period, 1988–1999, the returns on stocks ranged from 37.4 percent to −3.2 percent, and the range in the returns on small stocks was even larger (44.6 percent to −21.6 percent). Perhaps the most unexpected result revealed in Exhibit 10.3 is the performance of small stocks compared to large stocks. During 1980–1995 and 1988–1999, the smaller stocks earned a lower return, indicating that the additional risk associated with investments in smaller companies did not generate corresponding higher returns.

Exhibits 10.2 and 10.3 indicate that investments in common stock have generated positive returns, but the standard deviations in Exhibit 10.2 and the lowest returns in Exhibit 10.3 confirm that investment in stocks can produce losses over short periods of time. While the −26.5 percent return in 1974 was the worst case for the large companies and −30.9 percent in 1973 the worst for the small companies, these two years were not unique. Common stocks generated negative returns during 11 of the 55 years from 1945 through 1999.

This pattern of returns changes when longer time periods are considered. Exhibit 10.4 presents the high–low returns for time periods varying from one year to twenty years. As the number of years increases, the range of the return diminishes *and* the worst-case scenario improves. Over all ten-year time periods, investments in stock *did not produce a loss.* The worst case for common stocks and small stocks occurred from 1965 through 1974 when they earned annualized returns of 1.4 percent and 3.2 percent, respectively.

For twenty-year time periods, the range of returns continued to decline and the minimum returns increased. The worst period for stocks (1959 through 1978) generated annual returns of 6.53 percent, and for the small stocks the lowest return was 8.21 percent earned during 1955 through 1974. In addition, for every ten-year period since 1974, common stock annual returns have exceeded 10 percent. These results suggest that if individuals take a long perspective, they should earn positive returns on investments in common stocks. If they do sustain losses during a particular period, perseverance and patience should be rewarded and the losses erased.

The investor may ask whether securities traded in a particular market, such as the Nasdaq stock market, generate higher returns than the stocks traded on the

New York Stock Exchange. Such a conclusion may be drawn from Figure 10.8 (p. 320), which plots the Nasdasq stock index and the S&P 500. Even though the S&P 500 includes some Nasdaq stocks, it is primarily a measure of large capitalization NYSE stocks. Figure 10.8 has three parts. Part (a) covers the entire 21-year time period, January 1980 through to January 2001. As may be seen in the figure, the two aggregate measures are almost coincident for the first 15 years. Parts (b) and (c) break down the 21 years into two subperiods. The first 15 years, 1980 through 1994, are presented in (b), and the last 6 years, 1995–2000, are presented in (c). While there is divergence in (b), the movements are similar. The S&P 500 grew annually at 9.7 percent; the Nasdaq grew annually at 10.9 percent. The period from 1995 through 2000, however, was different. During 1999, the Nasdaq stock market rose dramatically and then retreated just as dramatically during 2000 and 2001, as the prices of technology stocks declined.

Over the entire period, the S&P grew annually at 12.1 percent and Nasdaq grew at 13.4 percent. Nasdaq stocks did generate higher returns than the securities listed on the NYSE. However, these over-the-counter stocks were more volatile, which indicates more risk. Presumably, in efficient financial markets, if an investment involves greater risk, it should earn a higher return.

The Reinvestment Assumption

Before jumping to conclusions as to what an investor in the stock market will earn, the student should realize that studies of investment return are aggregates. The investor's portfolio may not mirror the market return. In addition, historical returns may not be indicators of future returns. Studies of historical returns make a crucial assumption that investors may not be able to fulfill. The studies compute internal rates of return that assume that dividend and interest income are reinvested at the internal rate. For most individuals, that assumption does not apply. While it obviously does not apply if the individual spends the payments, the assumption still would not apply if the income were reinvested. Because income taxes would have to be paid on the dividend and interest income, the funds available would be reduced. If all the funds were reinvested, the investor would have to pay the tax from other sources. In either case, the comparability of the historical returns with the return the investor earns is diminished. (This is, of course, the same problem covered in Chapter 8. In that discussion, the fund's return was stated before tax while the individual had to pay the income tax on the distributions, so the realized returns were after tax.)

At best, historical returns may be taken as starting points in the valuation of stock. They may be used in the capital asset pricing model to help determine the required return, which in turn is used as the discount factor in the dividend-growth model. Thus, historical returns are important to the determination of whether a stock is overvalued or undervalued.

Time Diversification

Historical returns can also lead to an incorrect conclusion concerning risk. As the time period increases, the variability of returns appears to decrease, implying a decrease in risk. This misperception is sometimes referred to as "time diversification," and it suggests that as the investor's time horizon is increased, risk is reduced. This conclusion concerning risk reduction is counterintuitive. A longer time horizon should imply greater uncertainty and greater risk. Certainly the next six months are more certain than the next twelve months, and the next year is more certain than ten years into the future. This uncertainty should increase as the time horizon increases.

FIGURE 10.8

S&P 500 Stock Index and Nasdaq Stock Index, 1980–2000

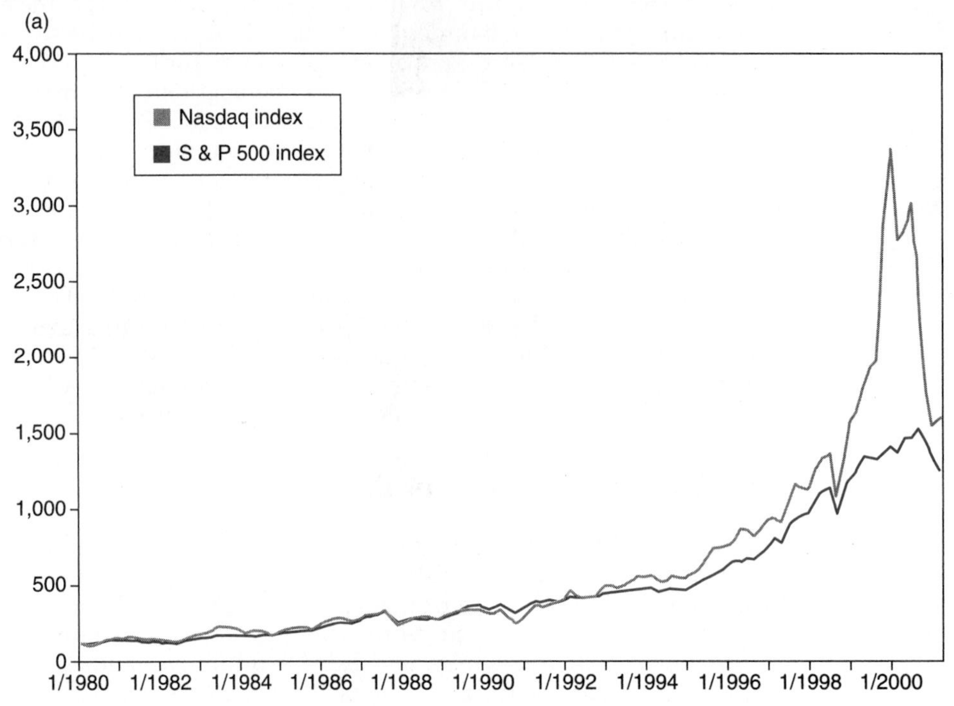

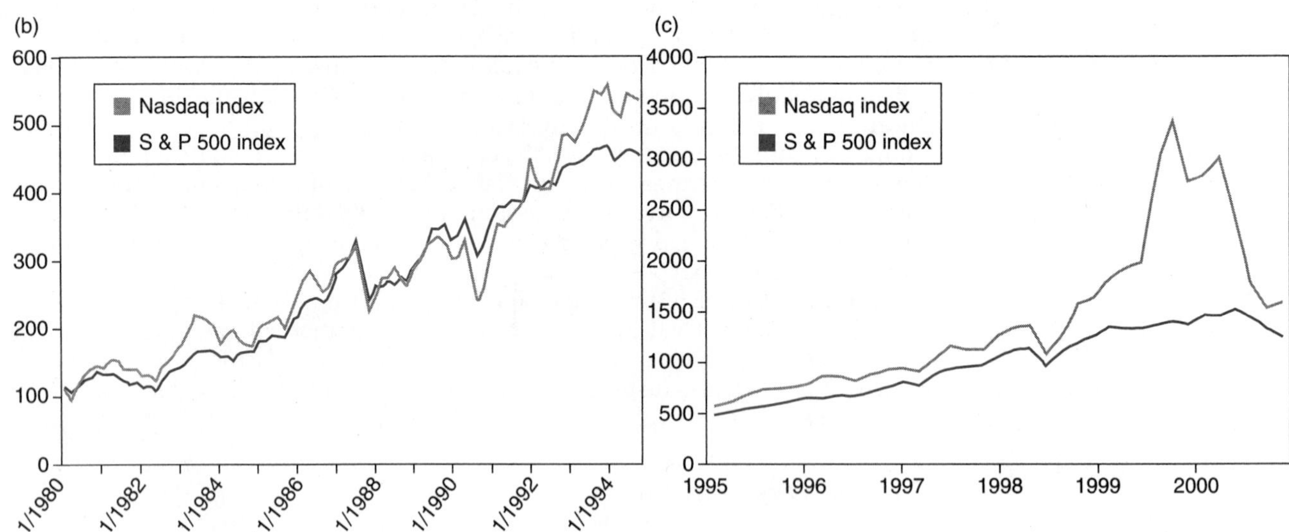

Source: Data from Commodity Systems, Inc. (CSI) available through Yahoo! at http://finance.yahoo.com under the section "Historical Prices."

Actually, the concept of time diversification is the result of the mathematical calculation of the standard deviation. Consider the following prices of a stock and the annualized returns:

	One-Year Returns	Two-Year Returns	Four-Year Returns	Five-Year Returns
$100	—			
120	20.0%	—		
130	8.3	14.0%	—	
160	23.1	15.5	—	
140	−12.5	3.8	8.8%	—
170	21.4	3.1	9.1	11.2%
Geometric average return	11.2%	9.0%	9.0%	11.2%
Standard deviation of the return	14.9	6.6	0.2	0.0

In this illustration, the standard deviation of the returns declines as the number of years increases. In fact, there is no variability in the return for the five-year time period. The standard deviation is 0.0, indicating no variability and no risk. This lack of variability is, of course, the result of only one observation, the five-year return.

The conclusion that there is no risk is false. Certainly the individual making the investment now does not know the value of the portfolio at the end of the time period. Risk is the uncertainty of the future value, when the asset is sold. This future price cannot be known with certainty, and the future price should become less certain as the time period increases. The standard deviation does measure the variability of returns and is an important tool for comparing performance (as in the Sharpe Index for ranking risk-adjusted performance of portfolio managers, presented in Chapter 8). Its use, however, to justify a longer investment time horizon on the basis of risk reduction is a misuse of an important mathematical tool.

The importance of time rests not with risk reduction, but with the realization that time works in the investor's favor. Most individuals have limited resources; the accumulation of wealth through investments requires the passage of time. The Ibbotson studies suggest that over time equity investors earn the highest returns when compared to other financial assets. Compounding has its greatest impact the longer the time period. These considerations obviously argue for the investor to adopt a long time horizon.

While long time horizons are important, any investor who had to liquidate in late October 1987 or during the last half of 2000 into 2001 learned that investments still involve risk even if the assets were accumulated over an extended period of time. "Time diversification" and its implication that increased time reduces risk is unfortunate, since risk management and diversification are among the most important concepts in investments. The construction of a diversified portfolio reduces the risk associated with specific securities. Once the investor has constructed a well-diversified portfolio, the risk exposure essentially depends on movements in the market and the portfolio's response to those movements. That risk is not reduced if the investor has a long time horizon.

Reducing the Impact of Price Fluctuations: Averaging

One strategy for accumulating shares and reducing the impact of security price fluctuations is to "average" the position. By buying shares at different times, the investor accumulates the shares at different prices. Such a policy may be achieved through the dividend reinvestment plans offered by mutual funds and many

EXHIBIT 10.5

Average Position When $2,000 in EMEC Stock is Purchased Each Quarter

Date	Price of Stock	Number of Shares Purchased	Cumulative Number of Shares Owned	Average Cost of Share
1/1/X0	$25	80	80	$25.00
4/1/X0	28	71	151	26.50
7/1/X0	33	60	211	28.44
10/1/X0	27	74	285	28.07
1/1/X1	21	95	380	26.32
4/1/X1	18	111	491	24.44
7/1/X1	20	100	591	23.69
10/1/X1	25	80	671	23.85

companies. An alternative is for the investor to systematically purchase shares of stock through a broker. There are two basic methods for achieving this averaging: the periodic purchase of shares and the purchase of additional shares if the stock's price falls.

Periodic Purchases

Under the periodic purchase plan, the investor buys additional shares of a stock at regular intervals. For example, the investor may elect to buy $2,000 worth of a stock every quarter or every month. This purchase is made at the appropriate interval, no matter what the price of the stock is. Since the dollar amount is the same, this technique is referred to as **dollar cost averaging**.

dollar cost averaging
The purchase of securities at different intervals to reduce the impact of price fluctuations.

The effect of such a program is illustrated in Exhibit 10.5, which shows the number of shares of EMEC stock purchased at various prices when $2,000 is invested each quarter. The first column gives the dates of purchase, and the second column presents the various prices of the stock; the third and fourth columns list the number of shares purchased and the total number of shares held in the position. The last column presents the average price of the stock held in the position. The student should notice that when the price of the stock declines, $2,000 buys more shares. For example, at $33 per share, $2,000 buys only 60 shares, but at $18 per share the investor receives 111 shares. Because more shares are acquired when the price of the stock falls, this has the effect of pulling down the average cost of a share. In this example, after two years the average cost of the stock had fallen to $23.85 and the investor had accumulated 671 shares. If the price of the stock subsequently rises, the investor will earn more profits on the lower-priced shares and thus will increase the return on the entire position.[14]

Averaging Down

Some investors find it difficult to purchase stock periodically, especially if the price of the stock has increased. Instead, they prefer to purchase additional shares

[14]For arguments *against* using dollar cost averaging, see John R. Knight and Lewis Mandell, "Nobody Gains from Dollar Cost Averaging: Analytical, Numerical and Empirical Results," *Financial Services Review* 2, no. 1 (1992/1993): 51–61, and Steven Thorley, "The Fallacy of Dollar Cost Averaging," *Financial Practice and Education* (fall/winter 1994): 138–143.

EXHIBIT 10.6

Averaging Down Strategies

Price of the Stock	Number of Shares Purchased ($1,000 Each Purchase)	Cost of 100 Shares
$30	33	$ 3,000
25	40	2,500
20	50	2,000
15	66	1,500
10	100	1,000
	289 shares	$10,000
	(for a cost of $5,000 and an average cost of $17.30 per share)	(500 shares, for a cost of $10,000 and an average cost of $20 per share)

of the stock only if the price declines. Such investors are following a policy of averaging down. Averaging down is a means by which the investor reduces the cost basis of an investment in a particular security by buying more shares as the price declines so that the average cost of the entire position in the security is reduced. This may be particularly rewarding if the price subsequently rises, because the investor has accumulated shares at decreased prices and earns a gain when the price increases. The investor may dollar cost average, which means that the same dollar amount is spent on shares each time a purchase is made. Or the investor may average down by purchasing the same number of shares (i.e., **share averaging**) every time a purchase is made.

share averaging
A system for the accumulation of shares in which the investor periodically buys the same number of shares.

Exhibit 10.6 illustrates these averaging down strategies. The price of the stock is given in column 1. Column 2 uses the dollar cost averaging method; the investor purchases $1,000 worth of stock every time the price declines by $5. As is readily seen in column 2, the number of shares in each successive purchase is larger. The last entries in the column give the total amount that the investor has spent ($5,000), the total number of shares that have been purchased (289), and the average cost of the shares ($17.30). The average cost of the total position has declined perceptibly below the $30 price of the initial commitment. However, if the price of the stock were to increase to $30, the entire position would be worth $8,670. The investor would have made a profit of $3,670 and earned a gain of 73 percent on the entire position.

Column 3 in Exhibit 10.6 illustrates the share averaging method, which means that the same number of shares are bought every time the investor makes a purchase. When the price declines by $5, the investor buys 100 shares. If the price of the stock were to fall to $10, the investor would have accumulated 500 shares under share averaging, for a total cost of $10,000. If the price of the stock were to return to $30, the entire position would be worth $15,000, and the investor's profit would be $5,000, for a gain of 50 percent.

There is a greater reduction in the average cost of the entire position with dollar cost averaging than with share averaging. When the investor dollar cost averages, the amount spent is held constant and the number of shares purchased varies. When the investor share averages, the number of shares purchased is held constant and the dollar amount varies. Because the investor purchases a fixed number of shares with share averaging regardless of how low the price falls, the average cost of a share in the position is not reduced to the extent that it is with dollar cost averaging.

The preceding discussion and examples explain the essentials of averaging. The investor may choose any number of variations on this basic concept. For example, the investor may choose to average down on declines of any dollar amount in the price of the stock or may select any dollar amount to invest for periodic purchases or for averaging down. The effect is the same—that is, to reduce the average cost basis of the position in that particular security.

Averaging down obviously requires that the investor have the funds to acquire the additional shares once the price has declined. In addition, dollar cost averaging will involve purchasing odd lots (33 shares, for example) or combinations of odd and even lots (such as 133 shares, composed of one round lot of 100 shares and one odd lot of 33 shares). Such purchases may not be cost-efficient when considering commissions. Dividend reinvestment plans that permit additional contributions may alleviate the problem of commission costs, but the purchases then cannot be made at a particular desired price.[15] Instead, the investor must accept the price on the day the funds are invested.

The investor who follows a policy of dollar cost averaging should not assume that such a strategy will lead to a positive return. The stock's price may continue to decline, or many years may pass before the price of the security rises to its previous level. The individual should view the funds spent on the initial investment as a fixed or sunk cost that should not influence the decision to buy additional shares. This type of reasoning is difficult to put into practice. Many individuals will not readily admit that they have made a poor investment. Unfortunately, they then follow a program of averaging down in the belief that it will vindicate their initial investment decision.

The investor should not automatically follow a policy of averaging down. Before additional purchases are made, the stock should be reanalyzed. If the potential of the company has deteriorated (which may be why the price of the stock has fallen), the investor would be wiser to discontinue the policy of averaging down, to sell the stock, and to take a tax loss. If the stock lacks potential, it makes no sense to throw good money (the money used to buy the additional shares) after bad (the money previously invested in the stock). Some questions that the investor should ask are "Does the firm still have potential?" or "Is there a substantive reason for maintaining the current position in the stock?" If the answer is yes, then averaging down and periodic purchases are two means of accumulating shares while reducing their average cost basis. Such strategies reduce the impact of security price fluctuations, but it cannot be assumed the strategies produce superior returns, since excess returns are inconsistent with the efficient market hypothesis. Averaging strategies do, however, offer a means to save and systematically accumulate securities.

Summary

Security prices fluctuate daily. Many averages and indices have been developed that track these price movements. Aggregate measures of the market include the Dow Jones averages, Standard & Poor's stock indexes, the NYSE index, the Russell stock indexes, and the Value Line stock index. There are even measures of segments of the market (e.g., large cap stocks) or sectors (e.g., tech stocks).

The composition and method of calculation of each measure differ. The composition ranges from the Dow Jones Industrial Average of 30 companies to the Russell 5000, which encompasses over 7,000 companies. The method of calculation is based on averages, which include price-weighted averages (e.g., the Dow Jones industrials), value-weighted averages (e.g., the S&P 500), and geometric averages (e.g., the Value Line index).

[15]Corporate dividend reinvestment plans are discussed in Chapter 11.

An index may be used to compute stock returns. Just as there are several ways to calculate an average, there are several ways to compute a return. The holding period return is the percent change in the price of the investment over the entire time period. The holding period return may also include any income generated by the investment. Since the holding period return does not consider time, it does not include the impact of compounding and often overstates the true, compounded return. Dollar-weighted returns and time-weighted returns do include the impact of time. The dollar-weighted return (or internal rate of return) equates the present value of an investment's cash inflows with the investment's cash outflows. The time-weighted return is a geometric average of each period's return.

Studies of common stock returns found that investors have earned a return in excess of 10 percent annually. The returns earned during the 1970s, however, were lower, and the real return was even smaller after adjusting for inflation. During the late 1980s and 1990s, returns once again achieved or exceeded their historical averages.

Averaging is one strategy designed to reduce the impact of price fluctuations. An investor may either make periodic purchases (dollar cost averaging) or buy additional shares after the price has declined (averaging down). Such strategies may reduce the average cost of the position in the stock and result in larger gains if the price of the stock subsequently rises.

Questions

1) What is a value-weighted average? Why does such an average place more emphasis on such firms as General Motors or ExxonMobil than on other companies?
2) How does the Dow Jones Industrial Average differ from Standard & Poor's 500 stock index, the NYSE composite index, and the Value Line index?
3) What has happened to the real return (i.e., the return adjusted for price-level changes) earned by investors in common stock?
4) Why may averaging percentage changes produce an inaccurate measure of the true rate of return?
5) Historically, what rates of return have investors earned on investments in common stocks?
6) What is the advantage of using a relative rather than an absolute scale to construct graphs of security prices?
7) What is dollar cost averaging? What is averaging down? Why may averaging down result in poor investment decisions?
8) The 1998 year-end values of several measures of the market were as follows:

Dow Jones Industrial Average	9,181
S&P 500 stock index	1,229
Nasdaq stock index	2,193

What were the percentage changes for these measures of the stock market in subsequent years?

9) You purchase $1,000 of IBM stock on the 15th of each month starting in 1999. Excluding commissions, how many shares have you accummulated? What is the average cost of a share? What is the position currently worth? Is this an illustration of averaging down or dollar cost averaging? (One possible source of historical security price data is http://chart.yahoo.com/d?s=. Fill in the stock symbol after the =.)

Problems

1) What is the holding period return and the annual rate of return on a stock that cost $32 and was sold for $99 after ten years?
2) An investor buys a stock for $35 and sells it for $56.38 after five years.
   a) What is the holding period return?
   b) What is the true annual rate of return?
3) A stock costs $80 and pays a $4 dividend each year for three years.
   a) If an investor buys the stock for $80 and expects to sell it for $100 after three years, what is the anticipated rate of return?
   b) What would be the rate of return if the purchase price were $60?
   c) What would be the rate of return if the dividend were $1 annually and the purchase price were $80 and the sale price were $100?
4) You purchase a stock for $100 that pays an annual dividend of $5.50. At the beginning of the second year, you purchase an additional share for $130. At the end of the second year, you sell both shares for $140. Determine the dollar-weighted return and the time-weighted compounded (i.e., geometric) return on this investment. Repeat the process but assume that the second share was purchased for $110 instead of $130. Why do the rates of return differ?
5) You purchase a stock for $40 and sell it for $50 after holding it for five years. During this period you collected an annual dividend of $2. Did you earn more than 12 percent on your investment? What was the annual dollar-weighted rate of return?
6) You purchase a mutual fund for $35 a share. The fund makes the following distributions:

Year	Distribution
1	$1.00
2	3.15
3	2.09
4	1.71

   At the end of the fourth year, you redeem the shares for $41. What was the dollar-weighted rate of return on your investment?
7) You invest $100 in a mutual fund that grows 10 percent annually for four years. Then the fund experiences an exceptionally bad year and declines by 60 percent. After the bad year, the fund resumes its 10 percent annual return for the next four years.
   a) What is the average percentage change for the nine years?
   b) If you liquidate the fund after nine years, how much do you receive?
   c) What is the annualized return on this investment using a dollar-weighted calculation and using a time-weighted calculation?
8) You sold a stock short for $50 and maintained the position for two years during which the stock paid an annual dividend of $2. At the end of two years, you closed the position when the stock was selling for $35. The margin requirement for short sales was 100 percent. Excluding the impact of any interest charge on borrowed funds and commissions on purchases and sales, what was the annual rate of return on this investment?
9) You read that stock A is trading for $50 and is down 50 percent for the year. Stock B is also trading for $50 but has risen 100 percent for the year. If the

investor had purchased one share of each stock at the beginning of the year, what can you conclude has happened to the value of the portfolio?

10) You believe that QED stock may be a good investment and decide to buy 100 shares at $40. You subsequently buy an additional $4,000 worth of the stock every time the stock's price declines by an additional $5. If the stock's price declines to $28 and rebounds to $44, at which time you sell your holdings, what is your profit? (Assume that no fractional shares may be purchased.)

11) Given the following information concerning four stocks,

	Price	Number of Shares
Stock A	$10	100,000
Stock B	17	50,000
Stock C	13	150,000
Stock D	20	200,000

a) Construct a simple price-weighted average, a value-weighted average, and a geometric average.

b) What is the percentage increase in each average if the stocks' prices become:

1) A: $10, B: $17, C: $13, D: $40

2) A: $10, B: $34, C: $13, D: $20?

c) Why were the percentage changes different in (1) and (2)?

12) You are given the following information concerning four stocks:

Stock	A	B	C	D
Shares outstanding	1,000	300	2,000	400
Price 20X0	$50	30	20	60
20X1	50	30	40	60
20X2	50	60	20	60

a) Using 20X0 as the base year, construct three aggregate measures of the market that simulate the Dow Jones Industrial Average, the S&P 500 stock index, and the Value Line stock index (i.e., a simple average, a value-weighted average, and a geometric average).

b) What is the percentage change in each aggregate market measure from 20X0 to 20X1, and 20X0 to 20X2? Why are the results different even though only one stock's price changed and in each case the price that changed doubled?

c) If you were managing funds and wanted a source to compare your results, which market measure would you prefer to use in 20X2?

13) Determine the Dow Jones Industrial Average as of your date of birth and as of your most recent birthday. What was the annualized rate of growth, on the average, between the two dates? Since this rate of growth does not include dividend income, it understates your rate of return. Assume that you collected dividends of 2 percent annually and compare your total return with the data for stock returns in Exhibits 10.2 and 10.3. (Information on the Dow Jones averages may be found at http://www.djindexes.com.)

THE FINANCIAL ADVISOR'S INVESTMENT CASE

The Calculation of Returns

As a portfolio manager, you are required to provide clients with a measure of your performance, a comparison with the market, and a measure of risk. Initially, your portfolio was worth $10 a share. During the last five years, the ending values of the portfolio, the cash distributions, and the annual return on the market were as follows:

Year	Ending Value of Your Portfolio	Cash Distributed	Market Return
1	$10.50	$0.30	12%
2	12.00	1.00	17
3	11.25	0.50	2
4	12.50	1.00	−3
5	14.00	1.25	14

1) Over the entire five years, what was the time-weighted compound annual rate of return and the comparable rate of return on the market?
2) Was your return more or less volatile than the market? Did your investors bear more or less systematic risk than the market?
3) Were your returns more or less variable than the market returns?
4) Do your answers to questions 2 and 3 indicate that your portfolio was more or less risky than the market?
5) Over the entire five years, what was the dollar-weighted compound annual rate of return?
6) If an individual bought 100 shares (i.e., $1,000) at the beginning of year 1, how much did the investor have in the account at the end of year 5 assuming that all cash distributions were reinvested in your fund at the year-end values? Based on these beginning and ending values, what was the annual rate of return?
7) Why do the rates calculated in questions 1, 5, and 6 differ?
8) If an individual invested $1,000 at the beginning of each year, how much did the investor have in the account at the end of year 5 if cash distributions were also reinvested? (Assume that the year-end values are the beginning values of the subsequent year.) Using this strategy, the dollar-weighted internal rate of return is almost 20 percent. (Using the CD program yields 19.9 percent.) Why is the annual rate so much higher than those in which the investor made only the initial investment? Which of these rates best indicates your performance even when the individual invests $1,000 each year?

CHAPTER

Dividends: Past, Present, and Future 11

As of August 27, 2001, Cornerstone Realty Income (TCR) paid a dividend of $1.12. At a price of $11.27, that was a dividend yield of 9.9 percent. Berkshire Hathaway (BRK.A) paid no dividend but commanded a price of $69,800 a share. Dominion Resources (D) paid $2.58, an amount that had not changed in over five years, but Coca-Cola (KO) raised its dividend for the 39th consecutive year. Obviously, there can be great diversity in firms' dividend policies.

This chapter is concerned with dividends and dividend policy. Although this is among the briefer chapters in the text, you should not conclude the topic is unimportant even though investor interest appears to have waned. The large percentage increases in the stock market during the late 1990s resulted in (1) low dividend yields by historical standards and (2) investor interest primarily in capital gains instead of dividend income. The reduction in the long-term capital gains tax rate also encourages investing for growth instead of dividends since the latter are income. At the federal level, income tax rates rise to 39.1 percent.

Dividends, however, are important. Dividend payments come at the expense of retaining earnings, which could be used to retire debt or finance additional investment in plant and equipment. Even though dividend payments reduce retained earnings, management may use continued dividend payments or dividend increments to signal that the firm is prospering and should continue to do well. Also, for investors who want a flow of income, cash dividends are one possible source.

This chapter covers the various forms of dividend payments, ranging from regular quarterly cash dividends to irregular dividend payments, and stock dividends, stock splits, and the retention of earnings. Emphasis is placed on the impact of dividend payments on the price of a stock. The chapter also includes a discussion of estimating a firm's future dividend growth because that growth rate is a crucial component of the dividend-growth model discussed in Chapter 9.

Learning Objectives

After completing this chapter you should be able to:

1. List the important dates for dividend payments.
2. Explain why changes in dividends generally follow changes in earnings.
3. Determine the impact of stock dividends and stock splits on the earning capacity of the firm.
4. Explain the effect of stock splits and stock dividends on the price of a stock and on the stockholder's wealth.
5. Identify the advantages of dividend reinvestment plans.
6. Analyze the tax implications of dividend reinvestment plans, stock repurchases, and liquidations.
7. Estimate the growth rate in a firm's cash dividend.

Cash Dividends

dividend
A payment to stockholders that is usually in cash but may be in stock or property.

regular dividends
Steady dividend payments that are distributed at regular intervals.

extra dividend
A sum paid in addition to the firm's regular dividend.

irregular dividends
Dividend payments that either do not occur in regular intervals or vary in amount.

A **dividend** is a distribution from earnings. Many companies pay cash dividends and have a dividend policy that is known to the investment community. Even if the policy is not explicitly stated by management, the continuation of such practices as paying a quarterly cash dividend implies a specific policy.

Most American companies that distribute cash dividends pay a **regular dividend** on a quarterly basis. A few companies make monthly distributions (e.g., Winn-Dixie Stores), and some make the distribution semiannually or annually. In the case of semiannual and annual payments, the dollar amount is small. Instead of paying $0.025 per share quarterly, the company pays $0.10 per share annually.

Although most companies with cash dividend policies pay regular quarterly dividends, there are other types of dividend policies. Some companies pay quarterly dividends plus an additional or **extra dividend**. In 2001, ExxonMobil paid its regular quarterly dividend but also distributed an extra dividend because the company had an exceptional year. Such a policy is appropriate for a firm in a cyclical industry because earnings fluctuate over time and the firm may be hard-pressed to maintain a higher level of regular quarterly dividends. By having a set cash payment that is supplemented with extras in good years, the firm is able not only to maintain a fixed payment that is relatively assured but also to supplement the cash dividend when the extra is warranted by the earnings.

Occasionally a firm distributes property as a supplement to or instead of cash dividends. For example, Freeport-McMoran distributed shares in two of its subsidiaries, Freeport-McMoran Energy Partners, Ltd. and Freeport-McMoran Copper and Gold Company. These property distributions supplemented the firm's usual quarterly cash dividend. Distributing property (i.e., stock in the subsidiaries) permits the stockholders to benefit directly from the market value of the subsidiaries, both of which became publicly traded, and from any of the subsidiaries' cash dividends.[1]

Other firms pay cash dividends that are **irregular**: There is no set dividend payment. For example, real estate investment trusts (frequently referred to as REITs and discussed in Chapter 23) are required by law to distribute their earnings to maintain their favorable tax status. These trusts are, in effect, closed-end investment companies and pay no corporate income tax; instead, their earnings are distributed and the stockholders pay the tax. To ensure this favorable tax treatment, REITs must distribute at least 90 percent of their earnings. Since the earnings of such trusts fluctuate, the cash dividends also fluctuate. The special tax laws pertaining to REITs cause them to have irregular dividend payments.

Since management seeks to maximize the wealth of the stockholders, the dividend decision should depend on who has the better use for the funds, the stockholders or the firm. If management can earn a higher return on the funds, then retaining and reinvesting the earnings is the logical choice. Management, however, probably does not know the stockholders' alternative uses for the funds and thus pursues a policy that it believes is in the stockholders' best interest. Stockholders who do not like the dividend policy may sell their shares. If sellers exceed buyers, the price will fall, and management will be made aware of the investors' attitude toward the dividend policy.

Some managements view dividends as a residual. Their rationale is simple and pragmatic. They do not know with certainty the stockholders' preference and the firm has investment opportunities that may be financed through the retention of earnings. After all attractive investments have been made, any residual is left for

[1]Freeport-McMoran Copper and Gold subsequently paid cash dividends to its preferred stockholders based on the price of gold.

POINTS OF INTEREST
The Longevity of Cash Dividends

The dividend-growth model presented in Chapter 9 assumes that firms pay cash dividends indefinitely. Do firms in fact continue to pay cash dividends year after year? For many corporations the answer is "yes!" Several have paid a cash dividend every year for more than 100 years.

Many of these firms are banks because banking was one of the first important industries to develop. The Bank of New York started paying dividends in the eighteenth century (1785).

America's industrial giants developed after the banks, and while their dividend longevity records may not be as impressive as those of the banks, the accompanying list illustrates the extended period over which some industrial firms have maintained cash dividends.

Do dividend payments ever end? Unfortunately, the answer is also yes. The financial difficulty Unisys experienced in 1990 caused the firm to cease paying cash dividends. Previously the firm had paid a cash dividend every year since 1895.

Firm	Year Annual Cash Dividends Began
Cincinnati Gas and Electric (CINergy)	1853
Stanley Works	1877
AT&T	1881
Exxon	1882
Carter Wallace	1883
Consolidated Edison	1885
Eli Lilly	1885
UGI	1885
Procter & Gamble	1891
Westvaco Corp	1892
Coca-Cola	1893
Colgate-Palmolive	1895
General Mills	1898
General Electric	1899
PPG Industries	1899

distribution to stockholders. Such a policy places emphasis on growth and, if the firm does have excellent investment alternatives, may lead to higher stock prices over a period of time.

payout ratio
The ratio of dividends to earnings.

retention ratio
The ratio of earnings not distributed to earnings.

Management may also view dividend policy as the distribution of a certain proportion of the firm's earnings. This policy may be expressed in terms of a **payout ratio**, which is the proportion of the earnings that the firm distributes. Conversely, the **retention ratio** is the proportion of the earnings that are not paid out and are retained. For example, Hershey Foods earned $2.42 in 2000 and paid cash dividends of $1.08. The payout ratio is 44.6 percent ($1.08/$2.42), and the retention ratio is $1.08/$2.42 = 55.4 percent. (The retention ratio is also equal to 1 − payout ratio, which is 1 − 0.466 = 55.4 percent for Hershey Foods.)

For some firms, the payout ratio has remained relatively stable over time. Such consistency suggests that management views the dividend policy in terms of distributing a certain proportion of the firm's earnings to stockholders. The obvious implication is that higher earnings will lead to higher dividends as management seeks to maintain the payout ratio.[2]

Management, however, rarely increases the cash dividend immediately when earnings increase because it wants to be certain that the higher level of earnings will be maintained. The managements of many publicly held corporations are especially reluctant to reduce the dividend because the decrease may be interpreted as a sign of financial weakness. In addition, a decrease in earnings may not imply that the firm's capacity to pay the dividend has diminished. For example, an increase in noncash expenses, such as depreciation, reduces earnings but not cash, and the same applies to a write-down of the book value of an asset. In both cases,

[2]SCANA's management stated in the company's *2001 First Quarter Interim Report* that the "goal is to increase the common stock dividend at a rate that reflects the growth in our principal businesses, while maintaining a payout ratio of 50–55 percent of earnings."

FIGURE 11.1

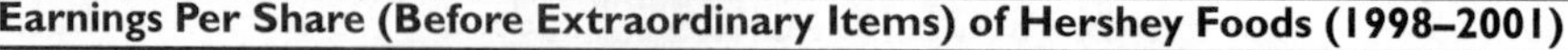

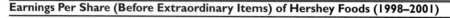

Earnings Per Share (Before Extraordinary Items) of Hershey Foods (1998–2001)

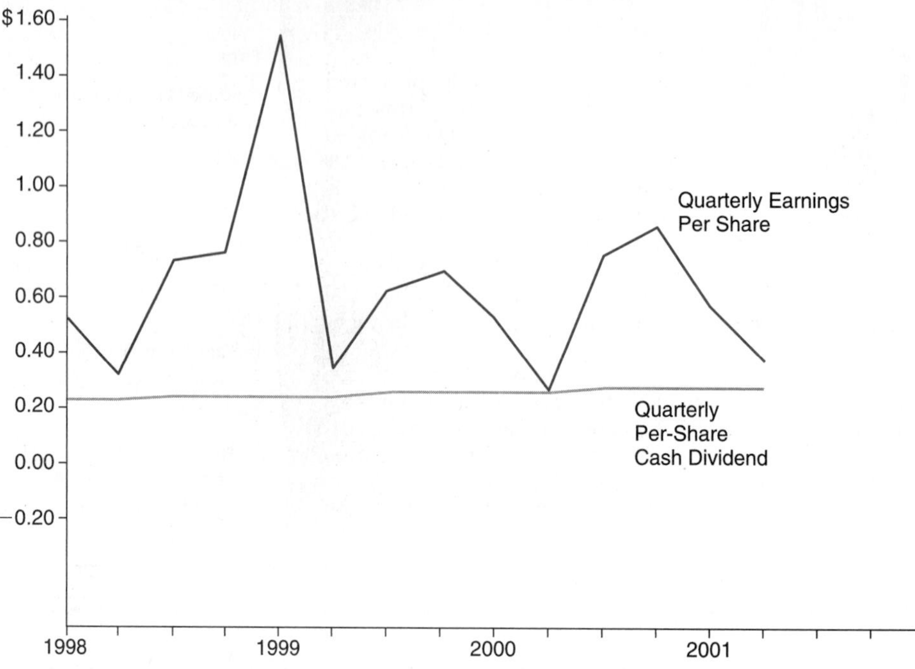

Source: *Hershey Foods Annual Report*, various issues.

the firm's capacity to pay the dividend is not affected, because the expense does not affect cash. Management then maintains the dividend payment to signal that the firm's financial condition has not deteriorated.[3]

This pattern is illustrated in Figure 11.1, which presents the quarterly per-share earnings (after extraordinary gains) and the cash dividend for Hershey Foods for 1998 through 2001. As may be seen in the figure, earnings fluctuate more than the cash dividend. During the first quarter of 1999, Hershey experienced a large one-time gain from the sale of its pasta business. The large increase in earnings did not result in a dividend increment. The decline in earnings during the first two quarters of 2000 also did not result in a dividend decrease. Instead, the quarterly cash dividend has been periodically increased each year from $0.22 in 1998 to $0.3025 as of August 2001.

While U.S. firms tend to follow a policy of quarterly dividend distributions, firms in other countries do not. Instead, they may make two payments. The first payment may be called a preliminary dividend and the second (made at the end of the firm's fiscal year) may be called a final dividend. For example, British Telecommunications paid $1.5819 per share in February 1997 and then distributed $2.4348 in September.

[3]A survey of corporate managers suggests that management (1) is concerned with dividend continuity, (2) believes dividends help maintain or increase stock prices, and (3) believes dividend payments indicate the future prospects of the firm. These results are reported in H. Kent Baker, Gail E. Farrelly, and Richard B. Edelman, "A Survey of Management Views on Dividend Policy," *Financial Management* (autumn 1985): 78–84.

Even if the cash payments from foreign firms were to occur at regular intervals, the dollar amount tends to vary. This variation is the result of fluctuation in the dollar value of each currency. While the discussion of fluctuations in exchange rates is deferred to Chapter 22, it should be obvious that if the value of the dollar falls relative to the euro, for example, any dividends that are distributed in euros translate into more dollars when the euros are converted. The converse is also true. If the dollar value of the euro should fall, the dividend buys fewer dollars when the currency is converted. Americans who want predictable flows of dividends are usually advised to purchase American stocks and avoid foreign securities.

The Distribution of Dividends

date of record
The day on which an investor must own shares in order to receive the dividend payment.

ex-dividend
Stock that trades exclusive of any dividend payment.

ex-dividend date
The day on which a stock trades exclusive of any dividends.

The process by which dividends are distributed occurs over time. First, the firm's directors meet. When they declare a dividend, two important dates are established. The first date determines who is to receive the dividend. On the **date of record**, the ownership books of the corporation are closed, and everyone who owns stock in the company at the end of that day receives the dividend.

If the stock is purchased after the date of record, the purchaser does not receive the dividend. The stock is traded **ex-dividend**, for the price of the stock does not include the dividend payment. This **ex-dividend date** is two trading days prior to the date of record, because the settlement date for a stock purchase is three working days after the transaction.

This process is illustrated by the following time line:

Declaration date (January 2)	Ex div date (January 30)	Date of record (February 1)	Distribution date (March 1)

On January 2, the board of directors declares a dividend to be paid March 1 to all stockholders of record February 1. To receive the dividend, the individual must own the stock at the close of trading on February 1. To own the stock on February 1, the stock must have been purchased on or before January 29. If the stock is bought January 29, settlement will occur after three days on February 1 (assuming three workdays), so the investor owns the stock on February 1. If the investor buys the stock on January 30, that individual does not own the stock on February 1 (the seller owns the stock) and cannot be the owner of record on February 1. On January 30, the stock trades exclusive of the dividend (ex-dividend or "ex-div"), and the buyer does not receive the dividend.

In the financial press, transactions in the stock on the ex-dividend date are indicated by an x. The following entry, taken from *The Wall Street Journal,* indicates the stock of Reynolds and Reynolds traded exclusive of the dividend.

	DIV	%	PE	100s	LAST	NET CHG
Reyn&Reyn REY x	.44	2.0	17	1453	22.50	+0.31

The $0.11 (i.e., $0.44 ÷ 4) quarterly dividend will be paid to whomever bought the stock on the previous day and will not be paid to investors who purchased the stock on the ex-dividend date.

The investor should realize that buying or selling stock on the ex-dividend date may not result in a windfall gain or a substantial loss. If a stock that pays a $1.00 dividend is worth $100 on the day before it goes ex-dividend, it cannot be worth $100 on the ex-dividend date. If it were worth $100 on both days, investors would purchase the stock for $100 the day before the ex-dividend date, sell it for $100 on the ex-dividend date, and collect the $1 dividend. If investors could do this, the price would exceed $100 on the day preceding the ex-dividend date and would be less than $100 on the ex-dividend date. In effect, this price pattern does occur because this stock would sell for $100 and then be worth $100 minus $1 on the ex-dividend date.[4]

This price change is illustrated in the previous example from *The Wall Street Journal.* There was an increase in the price of Reynolds and Reynolds stock for the ex-dividend date. This indicates that the closing price on the previous day was $22.30 and not $22.19 (22.50 − 0.31), as might be expected. Since the current buyers will not receive the dividend, the net change in the price of the stock is reduced for the dividend. The net change is figured from the adjusted price (i.e., $22.30 minus the $0.11 dividend). If the stock had closed at 23.00, the net change would have been +0.81, and if it had closed at 22.00, the net change would have been −0.19.

distribution date
The date on which a dividend is paid to stockholders.

The second important date established when a dividend is declared is the day on which the dividend is paid, or the **distribution date**. The distribution date may be several weeks after the date of record, as the company must determine who the owners were as of the date of record and process the dividend checks. The company may not perform this task itself; instead, it may use the services of its commercial bank, for which the bank charges a fee. The day that the dividend is received by the stockholder is thus likely to be many weeks after the board of directors announces the dividend payment. For example, the distribution date for a Black & Decker dividend that was declared on July 17 was September 25, which was almost two weeks after the date of record, September 14.

Many firms try to maintain consistency in their dividend payment dates. Textron makes payments on the first business days of January, April, July, and October. Public Service Enterprise Group pays its dividends on the last days of March, June, September, and December. Such consistency in payments is beneficial to investors and the firm, as both can plan for this receipt and disbursement.

Stock Dividends

stock dividend
A dividend paid in stock.

recapitalization
An alteration in a firm's sources of finance, such as the substitution of long-term debt for equity.

Some firms make a practice of paying stock dividends in addition to or in lieu of cash dividends. **Stock dividends** are a form of **recapitalization** and do *not* affect the assets or liabilities of the firm. Since the assets and their management produce income for the firm, a stock dividend does not by itself increase the potential earning power of the company. Some investors, however, may believe that stock dividends will enhance the earning capacity of the firm and consequently the value of the stock. They mistakenly believe that the stock dividend increases the firm's assets.

The following balance sheet demonstrates the transactions that occur when a firm issues a stock dividend:

Assets		Liabilities and Equity	
Total assets	$10,000,000	Total liabilities	$2,500,000
		Equity: $2 par common stock (2,000,000 shares authorized; 1,000,000 outstanding)	2,000,000
		Additional paid-in capital	500,000
		Retained earnings	5,000,000

[4]Since dividend payments are not necessarily the same amount as price changes (e.g., a dividend of $0.095 is not equal to $0.09 or $0.10), the opportunity for abnormal returns may exist. See David A. Dubofsky, "A Market Microstructure Explanation of Ex-Day Abnormal Returns," *Financial Management* (winter 1992): 32–43. Some empirical work also suggests that the prices of stocks with high dividend yields tend to fall *more* than the amount of the dividend. See John D. Finnerty, "The Behavior of Electric Utility Common Stock Prices Near the Ex-Dividend Date," *Financial Management* (winter 1981): 59–69.

Since a stock dividend is only a recapitalization, the assets and the liabilities are not affected by the declaration and payment of the stock dividend. However, the entries in the equity section of the balance sheet are affected. The stock dividend transfers amounts from retained earnings to common stock and additional paid-in capital. The amount transferred depends on (1) the number of new shares issued through the stock dividend and (2) the market price of the stock.

If the company in the preceding example issued a 10 percent stock dividend when the price of the common stock was $20 per share, 100,000 shares would be issued with a market value of $2,000,000. This amount is subtracted from retained earnings and transferred to common stock and additional paid-in capital. The amount transferred to common stock will be 100,000 times the par value of the stock ($2 × 100,000 = $200,000). The remaining amount ($1,800,000) is transferred to additional paid-in capital. The balance sheet then becomes:

Assets		Liabilities and Equity	
Total assets	$10,000,000	Total liabilities	$2,500,000
		Equity: $2 par common stock (2,000,000 shares authorized; 1,100,000 outstanding)	2,200,000
		Additional paid-in capital	2,300,000
		Retained earnings	3,000,000

The student should note that no funds (i.e., money) have been transferred. While there has been an increase in the number of shares outstanding, there has been no increase in cash and no increase in assets that may be used to earn profits. All that has happened is a recapitalization: The equity entries have been altered.

The major misconception concerning the stock dividend is that it increases the ability of the firm to grow. If the stock dividend is a substitute for a cash dividend, then this belief may be partially true, because the firm still has the asset cash that would have been paid to stockholders if a cash dividend had been declared. However, the firm will still have the cash even if it does not pay the stock dividend because a firm may retain its earnings. Hence, the decision to pay the stock dividend does not increase the amount of cash; it is the decision *not to pay* the cash dividend that conserves the money. When a stock dividend is paid in lieu of cash, it may even be interpreted as a screen: The stock dividend is hiding the firm's reluctance to pay cash dividends.

Although the stock dividend does not increase the wealth of the stockholder, it does increase the number of shares owned. In the previous example, a stockholder who owned 100 shares before the stock dividend had $2,000 worth of stock. After the stock dividend is distributed, this stockholder owns 110 shares that are also worth $2,000, for the price of the stock falls from $20 to $18.18. The price of the stock declines because there are 10 percent more shares outstanding, but there has been no increase in the firm's assets and earning power. The old shares have been diluted, and hence the price of the stock must decline to indicate this **dilution**.[5]

dilution
A reduction in earnings per share due to the issuing of new securities.

If the price of the stock did not fall to adjust for the stock dividend, all companies could make their stockholders wealthier by declaring stock dividends. However, because the stock dividend does not increase the assets or earning power of the firm, investors are not willing to pay the former price for a larger number of shares; hence, the market price must fall to adjust for the dilution of the old shares.

[5]A stock dividend must reduce the price of the stock because the firm does not receive funds and earnings per share must decline. However, when new shares are issued, dilution may not occur. Presumably, management will use the funds for profitable investments or to retire debt, so earnings per share may not decline. One study, however, found that management is concerned with the dilution of existing stockholders' positions and this concern affects their decision to issue *new* stock to raise funds. See John Graham and Campbell Harvey, "The Theory and Practice of Corporate Finance: Evidence from the Field," *Journal of Financial Economics* 60 (May/June 2001): 187–243.

POINTS OF INTEREST
Cisco Systems' Frequent Stock Splits

The impact of the stock split on the number of shares owned may be illustrated by the extreme example of Cisco Systems, which went public in March 1990 and closed the first day at $24.25. Since then, the stock has been frequently split. The splits and the resulting number of shares are as follows:

Date of Split	Split	Number of Shares
3/91	2 for 1	200
3/92	2 for 1	400
3/93	2 for 1	800
3/94	2 for 1	1,600
2/96	2 for 1	3,200
12/97	3 for 2	4,800
9/98	3 for 2	7,200
6/99	2 for 1	14,400
3/00	2 for 1	28,800

As of March 2001, Cisco Systems was trading for $23. If 100 shares were initially purchased at the close of trading on the first day for $2,425, their value in March 2001 was $662,400. That is an annualized return of 66.53 percent (PV = −2,425; FV = 662,400; PMT = 0, and N = 10. I = 66.53). Of course, this performance is exceptional, but it is probably not related to Cisco Systems' stock splits but to its growth in revenues and earnings. During that period, revenues grew annually at 52 percent, and earnings per share rose from $0.01 to $0.53.

There are some significant disadvantages associated with stock dividends. The primary disadvantage is the expense. The costs associated with these dividends include the expense of issuing new certificates, payments for any fractional shares, any taxes or listing fees on the new shares, and the revision of the firm's record of stockholders. These costs are indirectly borne by the stockholders. There are also costs that fall directly on the stockholders, including increased transfer fees and commissions (if the new securities are sold), additional odd-lot differentials, and the cost of storage.

Perhaps the primary advantage of the stock dividend is that it brings to the current stockholders' attention the fact that the firm is retaining its cash in order to grow. The stockholders may subsequently be rewarded through the firm's retention of assets and its increased earning capacity. By retaining its assets, the firm may be able to earn more than the stockholders could if the funds were distributed. This should increase the price of the stock in the future. However, this same result may be achieved without the expenses associated with the stock dividend.

The Stock Split

stock split
Recapitalization that affects the number of shares outstanding, their par value, the earnings per share, and the price of the stock.

After the price of a stock has risen substantially, management may decide to split the stock. The rationale for the **stock split** is that it lowers the price of the stock and makes it more accessible to investors. For example, when Finova split its stock 2 for 1, management stated in the *Annual Report* that "the split would help broaden our investor base." The management of MindSpring went even further in a 1999 press release announcing a 2-for-1 split: "This action will help widen the distribution and enhance the marketability of MindSpring's common stock, and bring the price per share . . . into a range which should generate increased interest from current and new shareholders." Implicit in this reasoning are the beliefs that investors prefer lower-priced shares and that reducing the price of the stock benefits the current stockholders by widening the market for their stock.

Like the stock dividend, the stock split is a recapitalization. It does not affect the assets or liabilities of the firm, nor does it increase its earning power. The wealth of the stockholder is increased only if investors prefer lower-priced stocks, which will increase the demand for this stock.

The balance sheet used previously for illustrating the stock dividend may also be used to illustrate a 2-for-1 stock split. In a 2-for-1 stock split, one old share becomes two new shares, and the par value of the old stock is halved. There are no changes in the additional paid-in capital or retained earnings. The new balance sheet becomes:

Assets		Liabilities and Equity	
Total assets	$10,000,000	Total liabilities	$2,500,000
		Equity: $1 par common stock (2,000,000 shares authorized; 2,000,000 outstanding)	2,000,000
		Additional paid-in capital	500,000
		Retained earnings	5,000,000

There are now twice as many shares outstanding, and each new share is worth half as much as one old share. If the stock had sold for $80 before the split, each share becomes worth $40. The stockholder with 100 old shares worth $8,000 now owns 200 shares worth $8,000 (i.e., $40 × 200).

An easy way to find the price of the stock after the split is to multiply the stock's price before the split by the reciprocal of the terms of the split. For example, if a stock is selling for $54 per share and is split 3 for 2, then the price of the stock after the split will be $54 × ⅔ = $36. Such price adjustments must occur because the old shares are diluted and the earning capacity of the firm is not increased.

Stock splits may use any combination of terms. Exhibit 11.1 illustrates the terms of several stock splits in 2001. Although 2-for-1 splits are the most common, there can be unusual terms, such as the 5-for-4 split of Chittenden Corporation in 2001. There is no obvious explanation for such terms except that management wanted to reduce the stock's price to a particular level and selected the terms that would achieve the desired price.

EXHIBIT 11.1

Selected Stock Splits Distributed in 2001

Company	Terms
NEC Corp.	5 for 1
Constellation Brands	2 for 1
H&R Block	2 for 1
Loews Corp.	2 for 1
National Fuel Gas	2 for 1
ExxonMobil	2 for 1
Biomet	3 for 2
REX Stores	3 for 2
Chittenden Corp.	5 for 4
Meritage	1 for 3

POINTS OF INTEREST

ExxonMobil's Shareholder Investment Program

In 1991, ExxonMobil replaced its dividend reinvestment plan with a *shareholder investment program.* Participants in the old dividend reinvestment plan were automatically transferred to the new plan. What makes the new program unique is that it is open to all investors, including those who do not own Exxon stock. These individuals may enroll in the plan and make their initial purchase of ExxonMobil through the program, thereby entirely avoiding using a brokerage firm.

The ExxonMobil investment program requires an initial investment of $250, but subsequent purchases may be made for as little as $50 up to $8,000 per month. Payments may be made as frequently as weekly. While ExxonMobil pays all the costs associated with the purchases, there is a fee for sales. The investor may choose to receive all or a portion of ExxonMobil's regular quarterly dividend payment. Receipt of dividends does not terminate participation in the program, and investors may still make periodic purchases of the stock even though they choose to receive their quarterly dividend payments.

Occasionally there is a reverse split, such as the Meritage 1-for-3 split. A reverse split reduces the number of shares and raises the price of the stock. The purpose of such a split is to add respectability to the stock (i.e., to raise the price above the level of the "cats and dogs"). Since some investors will not buy low-priced stock and since commissions on such purchases are often higher (at least for full-service brokers), it may be in the best interest of all stockholders to raise the stock's price through a reverse split.

Stock splits, like stock dividends, do not increase the assets or earning capacity of the firm. The split does decrease the price of the stock and thereby may increase its marketability. Thus, the split stock may be more widely distributed, which increases investor interest in the company. This wider distribution may increase the wealth of the current stockholders over time.

Academic studies, however, are inconclusive as to whether stock splits or stock dividends increase the value of stock.[6] These studies generally show that other factors, such as increased earnings, increased cash dividends, or a rise in the general market, result in higher prices for individual stocks. In fact, stock splits generally occur *after* the price of the stock has risen. Instead of being a harbinger of good news, they mirror an increase in the firm's earnings and growth.

From the investor's point of view, there is little difference between a stock split and a stock dividend. In both cases the stockholders receive additional shares, but their proportionate ownership in the firm is unaltered. In addition, the price of the stock adjusts for the dilution of per-share earnings caused by the new shares.

Accountants, however, do differentiate between stock splits and stock dividends. Stock dividends are generally less than 20 to 25 percent. A stock dividend of 50 percent would be treated as a 3-for-2 stock split. Only the par value and the number of shares that the firm has outstanding would be affected. There would be no change in the firm's retained earnings. A stock split of 11 for 10 would be treated as a 10 percent stock dividend. In this case, retained earnings would be reduced, and the amount would be transferred to the other accounts (i.e., common stock and paid-in capital accounts). Total equity, however, would not be affected.

[6]See, for instance, Michael T. Maloney and J. Harold Mulherin, "The Effect of Splitting on the Ex: A Microstructure Reconciliation," *Financial Management* (winter 1992): 44–59. This article has over 50 references on the impact of stock splits. Evidence that stock splits may increase investors' wealth is provided in David L. Ikenberry, Graeme Rankine, and Earl K. Stice, "What Do Stock Splits Really Signal," *Journal of Financial and Quantitative Analysis* (September 1996): 357–375. For an extensive review of the literature on stock splits *and* stock dividends, refer to H. Kent Baker, Aaron L. Philips, and Gary E. Powell, "The Stock Distribution Puzzle: A Synthesis of the Literature on Stock Splits and Stock Dividends," *Financial Practice and Education* (spring/summer 1995): 24–37.

Dividend Reinvestment Plans

dividend reinvestment plan (DRIP)
A plan that permits stockholders to have cash dividends reinvested in stock instead of received in cash.

Many corporations that pay cash dividends also have **dividend reinvestment plans (DRIPs)** in which the cash dividends are used to purchase additional shares of stock. Dividend reinvestment programs started in the 1960s, but the expansion of the programs occurred in the early 1970s, so that currently more than 2,000 companies offer some version of the dividend reinvestment plan.[7]

Types of Dividend Reinvestment Plans

There are two general types of dividend reinvestment programs. In most plans a bank acts on behalf of the corporation and its stockholders. The bank collects the cash dividends for the stockholders and in some plans offers the stockholders the option of making additional cash contributions. The bank pools all the funds and purchases the stock on the open market (i.e., in the secondary market). Since the bank is able to purchase a larger block of shares, it receives a reduction in the per-share commission cost of the purchase. This reduced brokerage fee applies to all the shares purchased by the bank. Thus, all investors, ranging from the smallest to the largest, receive this advantage. The bank does charge a fee for its service, but this fee is usually modest, does not offset the savings in brokerage fees, and in some cases is paid for by the firm.[8]

In the second type of reinvestment plan, the company issues new shares of stock for the cash dividend, and the money is directly rechanneled to the company. The investor may also have the option of making additional cash contributions. This type of plan offers the investor an additional advantage in that the brokerage fees are completely circumvented. The entire amount of the cash dividend is used to purchase shares, with the cost of issuing the new shares being paid by the company.

Some brokerage firms also offer dividend reinvestment plans. For example, Charles Schwab will reinvest dividends for stock registered in street name. Referred to as the *StockBuilder Plan,* Schwab purchases the shares for the investor and charges a small fee for the service. Schwab benefits by any profits on the spread between the bid and ask prices on securities bought and sold and by inducing individuals to invest through Schwab instead of competing brokerage firms.

Advantages of Dividend Reinvestment Plans

Dividend reinvestment plans offer advantages to both firms and investors. For stockholders, the advantages include the purchase of shares at a substantial reduction in commissions. Even reinvestment plans in which the fees are paid by the stockholder offer this savings. Both types of plans are particularly attractive to the small investor, for few brokerage firms are willing to buy $100 worth of stock, and substantial commissions are charged on such small transactions.

[7]Mergent's annual *Dividend Record* lists the firms traded on the NYSE and AMEX that offer dividend reinvestment plans. The American Association of Individual Investors annually publishes similar information and includes phone numbers, minimum-maximum optional cash purchases, fees, and discounts (if available). There is even an investment advisory service, the DRIP Investor (http://www.dripinvestor.com), which provides timely information on the plans. Information concerning dividend reinvestment plans is readily available on the Internet from DRIP Central (http://www.dripcentral.com) and Netstock Direct (http://www.netstockdirect.com). Netstock Direct not only provides detailed plan summaries but its software also allows companies to publish their plans. Links to the firms provide investors with immediate access to each firm's dividend reinvestment or direct purchase stock plan.

[8]Some firms have eliminated dividend reinvestment plans to avoid the costs. For example, Asset Investors Corporation announced in 1998 that it discontinued "its dividend reinvestment plan in order to eliminate the plan's administrative costs." Other firms now levy purchase fees, maintenance fees, or fees for selling the shares. Information concerning these expenses is available through the DRIP Investor.

Perhaps the most important advantage to investors is the fact that the plans are automatic. The investor does not receive the dividends, for the proceeds are automatically reinvested. For any investor who lacks the discipline to save, such forced saving may be a means to systematically accumulate shares. For the firm, the primary advantages are the goodwill that is achieved by providing another service for its stockholders. The plans that involve the issue of new shares also raise new equity capital. This automatic flow of new equity reduces the need for the sale of shares through underwriters.

The Internal Revenue Service considers dividends that are reinvested to be no different from cash dividends that are received. Such dividends are subject to federal income taxation. The exclusion from federal income taxation of dividend income that is reinvested has been considered as one possible change in the tax code, but there is little chance of passage since Congress has been closing, rather than opening, loopholes.

Repurchases of Stock and Liquidations

stock repurchase
The buying of stock by the issuing corporation.

liquidation
The process of converting assets into cash; dissolving a corporation.

A firm with excess cash may choose to repurchase some of its outstanding shares of stock or to liquidate the corporation. This section briefly covers **stock repurchases** and **liquidations**. A repurchase is in effect a partial liquidation, as it decreases the number of shares outstanding. This reduction should increase the earnings per share because the earnings are spread over fewer shares.

While the repurchase of shares is a partial liquidation, it may also be viewed as an alternative to the payment of cash dividends. Instead of distributing the money as cash dividends, the firm offers to purchase shares from stockholders. If the stockholders believe that the firm's potential is sufficient to warrant the retention of the shares, they do not have to sell them. If the shares are sold back to the company, any resulting profits will be taxed as capital gains.

There are several reasons why management may choose to repurchase stock. Management may need to use the shares for another purpose, such as exercising stock options that have been granted to employees.[9] Management may want to alter the capital structure of the firm and use less equity financing relative to debt financing. The total equity of the firm is reduced by the repurchase, so that the return on the firm's equity may be increased. Since repurchases reduce the number of outstanding shares, the firm's earnings per share should be increased. These increases in the return on equity and the earnings per share could lead to a higher stock price.

Management may also repurchase shares to reduce the chance of an unwanted takeover attempt. If a firm has a large amount of cash, it may become the prey of another firm: The firm executing the takeover borrows the required cash from another source (such as a group of banks), acquires the firm, and then uses the cash obtained through the takeover to retire the loan. If management believes the firm has generated excess cash and may become a takeover candidate, then repurchasing the shares can serve two purposes: (1) It increases earnings per share and possibly increases the stock's price, and (2) it decreases the probability of an unsolicited attempted takeover. (The repurchase will also increase management's proportionate ownership and strengthen its control over the firm, assuming that management does not participate in the repurchase.)

[9]Repurchased shares are usually held in the firm's "treasury" for future use. See, for instance, the stockholders' equity section of Hershey Foods Corporation's balance sheet in Exhibit 13.1. While the cost of the repurchased shares reduces the firm's equity, the shares are not retired but held by the company. If the shares were retired and management subsequently wanted to issue the stock to employees or the general public, the shares would have to be reregistered with the SEC in order for them to be publicly traded.

One of the most spectacular repurchases occurred when Teledyne bought 8.7 million shares at $200 for a total outlay of $1.74 billion. Teledyne initially offered to repurchase 5 million shares. At that time the stock was selling for $156, so the offer represented a 28 percent premium over the current price. The large premium induced more than 5 million shares to be tendered. While Teledyne could have prorated its purchases, it chose to accept all the shares. The repurchase reduced the number of shares outstanding from 20 million to 11.3 million and raised per-share earnings by more than $7. After the repurchase the price of the stock did not decline back to $156 but continued to grow and sold for more than $240 a share within a few weeks. Such behavior by investors suggests that the repurchase served the best interests of the remaining stockholders.

Occasionally a firm is liquidated. The final distribution of the firm's assets is called a *liquidating dividend.* This is a bit misleading, because the distribution is not really a dividend. It is treated for tax purposes as a distribution of capital and is taxed at the appropriate capital gains tax rate. Thus, liquidating dividends are treated in the same manner as realized sales for federal income tax purposes.

A simple example illustrates how such a dividend works. A firm decides to liquidate and sells all its assets for cash. The stockholders then receive the cash. If the sales raise $25 in cash per share, a stockholder surrenders the stock certificate and receives $25 in cash. The capital gain is then determined by subtracting the stockholder's cost basis of the share from the $25. If the stockholder paid $10 for the share, the capital gain would be $15. The stockholder then pays the appropriate capital gains tax. If the cost basis were $40, the investor would suffer a capital loss of $15, which may be used for tax purposes to offset other capital gains or income. In either case, this is no different than if the stockholder had sold the shares. However, in a sale the stockholder does have the option to refuse to sell and thus may postpone any capital gains tax. In a liquidation the stockholder must realize the gain or loss. Once the firm has adopted a plan of liquidation, it must execute the plan or face penalties. When a firm liquidates, the stockholder cannot postpone the capital gains tax.

In the preceding example, the liquidating dividend was cash. However, the dividend need not be cash but may be property. For example, a real estate holding company could distribute the property it owns. Or a company that has accumulated stock in other companies could distribute the stock instead of selling it. Such distributions may be desirable if the stockholders want the particular assets being distributed. However, if the stockholders want or need cash (perhaps to pay the capital gains tax), then the burden of liquidating the assets is passed on to them.

An example of a firm that did liquidate is Tishman Realty. The stockholders adopted a plan of liquidation; the firm then sold most of its assets to Equitable Life Assurance for $200 million. The company paid an initial $11 per share liquidating dividend. After additional cash distributions were made, a partnership was established to hold the remaining assets, which consisted primarily of mortgages on properties sold. These partnership shares were then distributed to stockholders to complete the liquidation.

Estimating Dividend Growth Rates

To make the dividend-growth model operational, the analyst needs numerical values for three variables: (1) the current dividend (D_0) (2) the required rate of return (k), and (3) the growth rate of future dividends (g). The current dividend is known. The required return, which was discussed in the previous chapter, needs estimates of the risk-free rate and the risk premium applicable to the specific stock. The third variable, the growth rate, requires an estimate of future dividends. It may be the most difficult variable to calculate, and a small change in this estimate can have a large impact on the stock's valuation.

Growth as the Product of the Return on Equity and the Retention Ratio

Retained earnings may be used to acquire additional assets. If these assets generate income, they will permit future growth in the firm's cash dividends. This points out that current dividends and internally financed growth are mutually exclusive. If the firm retains earnings, it cannot pay dividends, and if the firm distributes earnings, this source of funds cannot be used to finance expansion of plant and equipment. Of course, the firm could expand by issuing new stock, but then the old stock may be diluted.[10] By not issuing new shares and by retaining earnings, all the potential for growth accrues to the existing stockholders.

The impact of different retention ratios may be seen by considering the following balance sheets.

Assets		Liabilities and Equity	
Assets	$20	Liabilities	$10
		Equity	10
	$20		$20

return on equity
The ratio of earnings to equity.

During the year, the firm earns $2 after deducting all operating and finance expenses. The **return on equity**, the ratio of earnings divided by equity, is $2/$10 = 20 percent. If the firm retains all its earnings (retention ratio = 1.0 and the payout ratio = 0), the new balance sheet becomes:

Assets		Liabilities and Equity	
Assets	$22	Liabilities	$10
		Equity	12
	$22		$22

Suppose, however, the firm had distributed $0.72 and retained only $1.28 (i.e., the retention ratio is 64 percent and the payout ratio is 36 percent). The new balance sheet becomes:

Assets		Liabilities and Equity	
Assets	$21.28	Liabilities	$10.00
		Equity	11.28
	$21.28		$21.28

The firm's assets and equity have not risen as much because the firm has retained less of its earnings. The future growth in earnings is now less, because management has made a smaller investment in assets.

This relationship between growth (g), the return on equity (ROE), and the retention ratio (RR) is summarized in Equation 11.1:

$$g = \text{ROE} \times \text{RR}. \tag{11.1}$$

In the first illustration, the growth rate is

$$g = 0.2 \times 1 = 20\%,$$

[10]See footnote 5.

while in the second illustration, the growth rate is

$$g = 0.2 \times 0.64 = 12.8\%.$$

Unless the return on the equity can be increased, future earnings (and hence future dividends) can only grow at 12.8 percent.

If the firm were able to increase the return on equity, the dividend could be increased without a corresponding decrease in the growth rate. For example, if the return on equity had been 31.25 percent, the firm could distribute 36 percent of its earnings and retain 64 percent and still achieve a 20 percent growth rate (i.e., $0.3125 \times 0.64 = 20\%$). If, however, the return on equity is not increased and management increases the dividend, the higher payment must imply lower retention of earnings. If the firm distributes $1.20, the retention ratio falls to 40 percent, and the rate of growth is reduced to 8 percent ($0.2 \times 0.4 = 8\%$).

What impact will the increased dividend at the expense of growth have on the price of the stock? The answer is indeterminate. Examine the arrows placed in the dividend-growth model from Chapter 9:

$$V = \frac{D_0\uparrow(1 + g\downarrow)}{k - g\downarrow}.$$

The increase in the dividend (i.e., a higher numerator) argues for a higher stock price, but the lower growth rate, which increases the denominator and decreases the numerator, argues for a lower stock price. The converse also applies. A lower dividend decreases the numerator and suggests a lower price while a higher growth rate means a smaller denominator and an increased numerator, which increases the valuation. Thus, a dividend increment at the expense of the retention of earnings could result in the price of the stock rising or falling.

Alternative Means to Estimate Growth Rates

An alternative means to estimate growth is to analyze past growth and use this information to project future growth. Suppose per-share dividends and their annual percentage change for the firm were as follows:

Year	Dividend	Percentage Change from Previous Year
1992	$0.33	—
1993	0.36	9.1%
1994	0.38	5.3
1995	0.39	2.6
1996	0.42	7.7
1997	0.43	2.4
1998	0.46	7.0
1999	0.52	11.5
2000	0.68	30.8
2001	0.72	5.9
2002	0.72	0.0

The base year is 1992, so the dividend rises from $0.33 to $0.72 over the ten-year period. The annual percentage change, which is given in the third column, varies from year to year. During 2000, the dividend rose over 30 percent, but in the last year the dividend was not increased. The arithmetic average of the ten percentage changes is 8.2 percent.

The arithmetic average of percentage changes can bias the growth rate. (See the discussion of averages in Appendix 7 on statistical tools.) If the calculation includes both positive and negative percentage changes, the growth rate is overstated. An alternative method is to compute a geometric average, which avoids the potential bias. If the geometric average of the ten percentage changes is computed, the growth rate is 7.9 percent.

Calculator Solution

Function Key	Data Input
PV =	−0.33
FV =	0.72
PMT =	0
N =	10
I =	?
Function Key	**Answer**
I =	8.11

A fourth method for computing the historical growth rate uses the future value equation from Chapter 5. The question to be solved is: What is the annual rate of growth if the dividend grew from \$0.33 during 1992 to \$0.72 during 2002 (i.e., ten completed years)? That is,

$$\$0.33(1 + g)^{10} = \$0.72$$
$$(1 + g)^{10} = 0.72/0.33 = 2.182.$$

The interest factor for the future value of \$1 for ten years is 2.182, which, according to Appendix A for the future value of \$1, yields an annual growth rate of about 8 percent. The exact rate is

$$g = \sqrt[10]{2.182} - 1 = 1.081 - 1 = 8.1\%.$$

The weakness of this approach is that the calculation uses only two observations, the first and last years. A fifth way to use the data estimates an equation that summarizes the observations relating dividends and time. Such an equation yields an estimate of the annual growth rate in the dividend. This technique, least-squares regression analysis, was explained in the appendix to Chapter 7. How regression may be used to estimate the growth rate is illustrated in the appendix to this chapter. Using this technique yields an annual growth rate of 8.6 percent.

An Application

Which growth rate should the individual use to value the stock? Currently there are five estimates: 12.8 percent using the return on equity and the retention ratio for the last year, 8.6 percent using regression analysis, 8.2 percent (the arithmetic average percentage change in the dividend), 8.1 percent (the rate using the terminal values of the dividend), and 7.9 percent (the geometric average percentage change). The answer requires judgment on the part of the analyst because the valuation will differ depending on the choice. Obviously, the lower rate, the more conservative choice, may be appropriate if the analyst anticipates that the pace of economic activity will decline. However, if the analyst believes that the firm's financial condition is improving, the use of a lower growth rate will argue against acquiring the stock. (Chapter 13 will consider the analysis of financial statements to help determine if the firm's performance is improving or deteriorating and thus help answer the question of which growth rate to use.)

Since 12.8 percent and 7.9 percent are the highest and lowest estimated growth rates, the analyst may decide to disregard these two extremes. The remaining estimates (8.6, 8.2, and 8.1) seem reasonable for extended periods of time. Since the 8.2 percent is an arithmetic average, the analyst may prefer the 8.1 percent because it was determined using a geometric function and thus includes compounding. The geometric average of 7.9 percent also lends support to the selection of 8.1 percent.

Next the analyst must determine the required rate of return. As was explained in Chapter 9, the required rate depends on the risk-free rate, the return on the market, and the firm's beta coefficient. The yield on six-month Treasury bills is readily available; assume for this discussion it is 5 percent.[11] If the Ibbotson–Sinquefield study is used, then the return on the market should be approximately 12 percent (i.e., a return on the market that is 5 to 7 percent greater than the Treasury bill rate). If the beta, found in a source such as the *Value Line Investment Survey,* is 0.9, the required rate of return is

$$\begin{aligned} k &= r_f + (r_m - r_f)\beta \\ &= 0.05 + (0.12 - 0.05)0.9 \\ &= 11.3\%. \end{aligned}$$

Since the required rate of return has been determined and the annual dividend is $0.72, the valuation model may be applied. In this illustration the value of the stock is

$$\begin{aligned} V &= \frac{D_0(1 + g)}{k - g} \\ &= \frac{\$0.72(1 + 0.081)}{0.113 - 0.081} \\ &= \$24.32. \end{aligned}$$

If the stock is selling for $24, the stock is reasonably priced (i.e., neither undervalued nor overvalued). If the stock is selling for $20, it is undervalued. At $30, it is overvalued.

If the valuation model generates a large divergence between the valuation and the market price (e.g., $40 when the price is $24), the investor should reconsider the estimates used in the model. A large divergence would indicate that the stock is either well undervalued or overvalued. Such mispricings should be rare because, as discussed in several places in this text, security markets are competitive and efficient. If a security were undervalued, investors would seek to buy it, which would drive up the price. If a security were overvalued, investors would seek to sell it, which would drive down the price. Thus, if the dividend-growth model indicates a large divergence between the estimated value and the current market price, it would be advisable for the analyst to determine if the data used in the model are inaccurate.

For example, if the analyst believes that the firm can sustain an 8.6 percent rate of growth, the valuation model yields:

$$\begin{aligned} V &= \frac{\$0.72(1 + 0.086)}{0.113 - 0.086} \\ &= \$28.96. \end{aligned}$$

This valuation indicates that the firm's stock at $24 is undervalued and should be purchased. The question then becomes: Can 8.6 percent be sustained? At 8.1 percent, the valuation is $24.32, which is close to the price of $24. It appears that the market consensus of a sustainable growth rate is around 8.1 percent, for at 8.1 percent the valuation is about $24.

[11]There may be a logical inconsistency in the use of the capital asset pricing model and the dividend-growth model. The dividend-growth model assumes an indefinite life for the stock (i.e., it is perpetual). No investor has indefinite life, so the stock will be held for a finite period of time. If that expected holding period can be determined, the analyst may use the yield on a Treasury bond with the same term to maturity to match the expected holding period of the stock and the bond.

There is, however, an argument against the use of the yield on the long-term bond. While such a bond does not have a default risk, there are still risks associated with unexpected inflation, fluctuations in interest rates, and the reinvestment of interest received. Only short-term Treasury bills are virtually risk-free, so if the expected holding period is not known, the use of the short-term Treasury bill rate is a reasonable proxy for the risk-free rate.

By now it should be obvious that stock valuation is more an art than a science. However, the use of equations such as the dividend-growth model may give valuation an appearance of being more exact than in reality it can be. The model determines a unique value but that number obviously depends on the data used. Instead of determining a unique value, an analyst may employ data derived under varying assumptions and derive a range of values for a given stock. This may lead to investment advice that reads something like "We believe that the stock is fairly priced at $23 to $25 and would buy the stock on any weakness that drives the price below $20." Prices do fluctuate and may briefly create buy or sell opportunities that may offer the individual the chance of opening or liquidating positions.

Earnings Estimates, Growth Rates, and the Internet

Earnings estimates for the next quarter and next year and historical growth rates are generally available through the Internet. While such information is readily available through subscription services, it may also be found as part of complimentary sources. The American Association of Individual Investors' *Computerized Investing* periodically surveys services that provide fundamental stock information, which includes earnings estimates and growth rates.

In Chapter 13, Hershey Foods Corporation's financial statements are used to illustrate the analysis of financial statements. Suppose an investor wants estimates of future earnings or growth rates as part of the financial analysis or to use in the dividend-growth model. According to the AAII September/October 2000 issue of *Computerized Investing,* possible sources of this information include:

Morningstar (http://www.morningstar.com)
Quicken (http://www.quicken.com)
SmartMoney (http://www.smartmoney.com)
Wall Street City (http://www.wallstreetcity.com)
Wall Street Research Net (http://www.wsrn.com)
Yahoo! (http://quote.yahoo.com)

These sources, however, may provide different information. Possible differences are illustrated in Exhibit 11.2, which gives estimated per-share earnings and estimated growth rates for Hershey Foods. The information from each site may

EXHIBIT 11.2

Growth Rates and Analysts' Estimates for Earnings per Share for Hershey Foods as of August 2001

	EPS Estimates	Growth Rates
MultexInvestor (http://www.multexinvestor.com)	$2.74	7.41%
Source: Market Guide	Year ending 2001	5 year
Quicken (http://www.quicken.com)	$2.74	9.30%
Source: Zacks for EPS estimate; Media General for growth rate	Year ending 2001	5 year
Wall Street Research Net (http://www.wsrn.com)	$3.04	14.79%
Source: Media General Financial Services	Year ending 2002	1 year
Zacks (http://www.zacks.com)	$2.74	9.35%
Source: Average of analysts' estimates	Year ending 2001	5 year

differ because each site may use a different source for the data it reports. Zacks Investment Research is often the primary source of earnings estimates. Zacks' estimates are, in turn, an average of analysts' estimates. (In addition to the sites in Exhibit 11.2, Morningstar and MSN (http://www.moneycentral.msn.com) also provide estimates by Zacks Investment Research.)

While the differences in Exhibit 11.2 for EPS are small, there are substantial differences in the growth rates. Such variation would produce substantial differences in the valuation of a stock, especially if varying rates are used in a discounted cash flow model such as the dividend-growth model. An investor needs to use some common sense when applying growth rates. A rate such as the one-year estimate of 14.79 percent in Exhibit 11.2 cannot be maintained indefinitely. Even a rate such as 9.35 percent is large when extrapolated many years into the future. If the available data suggest that a company's prospects are too good to be true and the information does not make reasonable sense, don't use it.

Summary

After a firm has earned profits, it may either retain them or distribute them in the form of cash dividends. Many publicly held corporations follow a stated dividend policy and distribute quarterly cash dividends. A few firms supplement this dividend with extra dividends if earnings warrant the additional distribution. Some firms pay irregular dividends that vary in amount from quarter to quarter.

Dividends are related to the firm's capacity to pay them. As earnings rise, dividends also tend to increase, but there is usually a lag between higher earnings and increased dividends. Most managements are reluctant to cut dividends and thus do not raise the dividend until they believe that the higher level of earnings can be sustained.

In addition to cash dividends, some firms distribute stock dividends. These dividends and stock splits do not increase the earning capacity of the firm. Instead, they are recapitalizations that alter the number of shares the firm has outstanding. Since stock dividends and stock splits do not alter the firm's earning capacity, they do not increase the wealth of the stockholders. The price of the stock adjusts for the change in the number of shares that results from stock dividends and stock splits.

The retention or distribution of earnings should be a question of who can put the funds to better use—the firm or its stockholders. If a firm retains earnings, it should grow and the value of the shares should increase. When this occurs, the stockholders may be able to sell their shares for a profit.

Many firms offer their stockholders the option of having their dividends reinvested in the firm's stock. This is achieved either through the firm's issuing new shares or purchasing existing shares. Dividend reinvestment plans offer the stockholders the advantages of forced savings and a reduction in brokerage fees.

Instead of paying cash dividends, a firm may offer to repurchase some of its existing shares. Such repurchases reduce the number of shares outstanding and may enhance the growth in the firm's per-share earnings because there will be fewer shares outstanding. Any profits earned on such repurchases are taxed as capital gains, as are liquidating dividends that occur when a corporation is disbanded and its assets are distributed to the stockholders.

Estimating the growth rate of a firm's future dividends is necessary for the application of the dividend-growth model. One possible estimation of the dividend-growth rate is the product of the firm's return on equity and its retention ratio. Other possible estimates are based on the annual changes in the firm's dividend or the use of regression analysis to estimate the growth rate based on the past dividends over a period of years.

Questions

1) Why may a firm distribute dividends even though earnings decline?
2) Why may a dividend increment lag after an increase in earnings?
3) Define *ex-dividend date, date of record,* and *distribution date.*
4) Explain the differences between the following dividend policies: (a) regular quarterly dividends; (b) regular quarterly dividends plus extras; and (c) irregular dividends.
5) How are stock dividends and stock splits similar?
6) What are the advantages to stockholders of dividend reinvestment plans?
7) What tax advantages apply to stock repurchases that do not apply to cash dividend distributions?
8) Why should dividend policy be a question of whether the firm or its stockholders can put the funds to better use?
9) Using one of the sources provided in the section on earnings estimates, growth rates, and the Internet, what are the estimates for Hershey Foods' (HSY) earnings in 2003 or 2004? Did HSY's 2001 and 2002 earnings match the estimates given in Exhibit 11.2?

10) As of July 2001, Quicken (http://www.quicken.com) had a site that provided the intrinsic value of a stock based on discounted cash flow. While the site has default values for growth rates and required returns (called the "discount rate"), the user may substitute other values. Type in the ticker symbol for Hershey Foods (HSY) and find its intrinsic value under Evaluator. Recalculate this value using the growth rates determined in Question 9. Repeat this process by recalculating the intrinsic value using a required return based on the current Treasury bill rate plus a risk premium.

Problems

1) A firm has the following items on its balance sheet:

Cash	$ 20,000,000
Inventory	134,000,000
Notes payable to bank	31,500,000
Common stock ($10 par; 1,000,000 shares outstanding)	10,000,000
Retained earnings	98,500,000

Describe how each of these accounts would appear after:

a) A cash dividend of $1 per share
b) A 10 percent stock dividend (fair market value of stock is $13 per share)
c) A 3-for-1 stock split
d) A 1-for-2 reverse stock split

2) A company whose stock is selling for $60 has the following balance sheet:

Assets	$30,000,000	Liabilities	$14,000,000
		Preferred stock	1,000,000
		Common stock ($12 par; 100,000 shares outstanding)	1,200,000
		Paid-in capital	1,800,000
		Retained earnings	12,000,000

   a) Construct a new balance sheet showing the effects of a 3-for-1 stock split. What is the new price of the stock?
   b) Construct a new balance sheet showing the effects of a 10 percent stock dividend. What will be the approximate new price of the stock?

3) An investor who buys 100 shares for $40 a share of a stock that pays a per-share dividend of $2 annually signs up for the dividend reinvestment plan. If neither the price of the stock nor the dividend is changed, how many shares will the investor have at the end of ten years?

4) A firm's dividend payments have been as follows:

Year	Dividend
1992	$1.00
1993	1.05
1994	1.12
1995	1.30
1996	1.30
1997	1.45
1998	1.50
1999	1.62
2000	1.70
2001	1.88
2002	2.00

Ten years have elapsed since the dividend rose from $1 at the *end* of 1992 to $2 at the *end* of 2002. You want to determine the annual rate of growth in the dividend.

   a) What was the average percentage change in the dividend?
   b) What was the rate of growth based on beginning and ending dividends?
   c) What was the rate of growth using the regression analysis illustrated in the appendix to this chapter?
   d) Does each technique give you the same rate of growth?

5) H.J. Heinz's annual dividends were as follows:

1990	$0.540
1991	0.620
1992	0.700
1993	0.780
1994	0.860
1995	0.940
1996	1.035
1997	1.135
1998	1.235
1999	1.344
2000	1.447

Use these payments to determine the historical growth rate of the dividend. Calculate growth rates based on (1) the average percentage change, (2) beginning and terminal values, and (3) regression analysis (illustrated in the appendix to this chapter). Find the current yield on the six-month Treasury bill and Heinz's beta and most recent annual dividend. You may assume that the return on the market is 5 to 7 percent higher than the Treasury bill rate. Develop a range of stock valuations based on this information. If your valuation differs from the current market price of the stock, what are some possible explanations for the divergence?

6) Go to a Web source that announces stock splits and determine a stock that will be split 2 for 1 in the near future. Possible sources are Equity Analytics, Ltd. (http://www.e-analytics.com), the 2 for 1 stock split newsletter (http://www.2-for-1.com), and Yahoo!'s Splits Calendar (http://biz.yahoo.com), which is located under Financial Calendars in the Research Center. What will be the new price of the stock after the split? What effect will the split have on the firm's total earnings, earnings per share, assets, and total equity?

THE FINANCIAL ADVISOR'S INVESTMENT CASE

Strategies to Increase Equity

Christina Holmes is preparing for a meeting of the board of directors of Chesapeake Bay Corporation, a developer of moderate-priced homes and vacation homes in the Chesapeake Bay area. The combination of the location near major metropolitan areas with the recreational facilities associated with the Chesapeake Bay has made the firm one of the most successful homebuilders in the nation. During the last five years, the firm's cash dividend has risen from $2.10 to $3.74, and the price of its stock has risen from $36 to $75. Since the firm has 1,200,000 shares outstanding, the market value of the stock is $90,000,000. Given the volatile nature of its industry, the increases in the price of the stock and in the dividend were substantial achievements.

Management, however, is considering entering into nonbuilding areas in an effort to diversify the firm. These new investments will require more financing. Although additional debt financing is a possibility, management believes that it is unwise to issue only new debt and not increase the firm's equity base. New equity could be obtained by issuing additional stock or reducing the dividend and thus retaining a larger proportion of the firm's earnings. Two major points had previously been raised against these strategies: Issuing additional shares may dilute the existing stockholders' position, and reducing the dividend could cause the value of the stock to decline.

Even though it is possible that no change will be made and that the firm will continue its present course, the board believes that a thorough discussion of all possibilities is desirable. Holmes has been instructed to develop alternatives to the two strategies for the next meeting of the board in two weeks.

The short period for preparation means that a thorough analysis may be impossible, especially of the possible impact of a dividend cut on the value of the stock, but Holmes presumes that some additional alternatives do exist. One of her assistants suggested that the firm institute a dividend reinvestment plan, in which additional shares would be sold to stockholders to raise additional equity capital. Her other assistant suggested that the company substitute a 5 percent stock dividend for the cash dividend. Before making either (or both) suggestions to the board, Holmes decided to seek your help in answering several questions:

1) Would implementing the suggestions dilute the existing stockholders' position?
2) How much new equity would be raised by each action?
3) What may happen to the price of the stock?
4) What are the costs associated with each strategy?
5) Would a stock split combined with either strategy help raise additional equity financing?
6) Would an increase in the cash dividend coupled with the dividend reinvestment plan help raise additional equity financing?
7) Is there any reason to prefer or exclude any one of the four strategies (that is, issuing new shares, reducing the dividend, instituting a dividend reinvestment plan, or substituting a stock dividend for the cash dividend)?

APPENDIX 11

Use of Regression Analysis to Estimate Growth Rates

In the appendix to Chapter 7, regression analysis was used to estimate beta coefficients. In this appendix, it is used to estimate growth rates. The equation to be estimated is

$$D_0(1 + g)^n = D_n.$$

This equation states that the initial dividend (D_0) will grow at some rate (g) for some time period (n) into the future dividend (D_n). This equation may be expressed in the following general form:

$$(a)(b)^x = Y,$$

in which $Y = D_n$, $a = D_0$, $b = (1 + g)$, and $x = n$.

The equation is exponential, which is difficult to estimate, but it may be restated in log-linear form as:

$$\log Y = \log a + (\log b)X.$$

In this form, the least-squares method of regression may be used to estimate a and b. This procedure using dividends (Y) and time (X) is as follows:

Year (X)	Dividend (Y)	Log Y	X^2	X(log Y)
1	0.33	−0.48184	1	−0.48148
2	0.36	−0.44369	4	−0.88739
3	0.38	−0.42021	9	−1.26064
4	0.39	−0.40893	16	−1.63574
5	0.42	−0.37675	25	−1.88375
6	0.43	−0.36653	36	−2.19918
7	0.46	−0.33724	49	−2.36069
8	0.52	−0.28399	64	−2.27197
9	0.68	−0.16749	81	−1.50741
10	0.72	−0.14266	100	−1.42667
11	0.72	−0.14266	121	−1.56934
66	5.41	−3.57168	506	−17.4843

$$\log b = \frac{(n)\Sigma X(\log Y) - (\Sigma \log Y)(\Sigma X)}{(n)\Sigma X^2 - (\Sigma X)^2}$$

$$= \frac{(11)(-17.4843) - (-3.57168)(66)}{(11)(506) - (66)^2}$$

$$= \frac{43.40352}{1210} = 0.035870.$$

$$\log a = \frac{\Sigma \log Y}{n} - \frac{(\log b)\Sigma X}{n}$$

$$= \frac{-3.57168}{11} - (0.035870)(66/11)$$

$$= -0.5399.$$

FIGURE 11A.1

Dividends and Estimated Regression Line

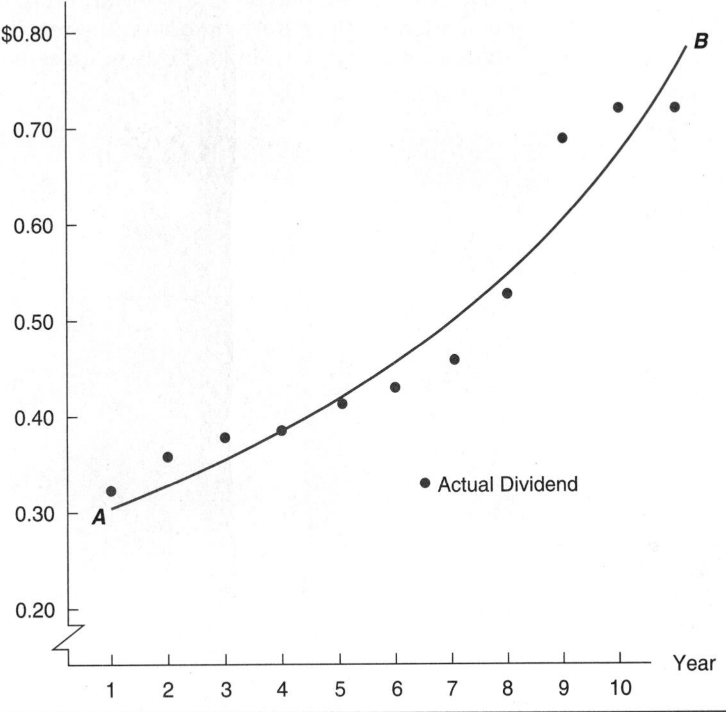

The estimated equation is

$$\log Y = -0.5399 + 0.03587X.$$

The estimated equation is not in the desired form

$$(a)(b)^x = Y$$

to obtain

$$D_0(1 + g)^n = D_n.$$

The estimated equation is in logs and must be converted out of logs.

Since $10^{-0.5399} = 0.2885$ and $10^{0.03587} = 1.0861$, the equation in the desired form is

$$(0.2885)(1.0861) = D_n.$$

Since $1.0861 = (1 + g)$, g must equal 0.0861 (i.e., $g - 1 = 0.0861$), so the growth rate is 8.61 percent.

Figure 11A.1 plots the dividends over time as well as the estimated equation (line *AB*). Although the observations lie both above and below the estimated line, they tend to follow closely the contour of the line, which suggests that the equation gives a good estimate of the historical rate of growth in the dividend. This conclusion is supported by the coefficent of determination (R^2), which is equal to 0.93—suggesting that 93 percent of the variation in the dividend is explained.

This example illustrates the mechanics of determining the regression equation. The same results may be obtained by using a regression program, such as the one in the Investment Analysis software that accompanies this text. Enter the year (1, 2, etc.) as the independent variable and the dividend *in logarithmic form* as the dependent variable. After you obtain the results, convert the equation back to exponential form to determine the rate of growth.

The Macroeconomic Environment for Investment Decisions

12

Many events affect investment decisions. Some events cause security markets to react; others do not. On April 18, 2001, the Federal Reserve unexpectedly lowered interest rates and the Dow Jones Industrial Average rose 372 points. Subsequently, on May 15 and July 26, the Federal Reserve again lowered interest rates, and the stock market yawned. Within a few months of the inauguration of President George W. Bush, the federal income tax code was, again, altered. During the first quarter of 2001, the rate of economic growth continued to decline, but the economy did continue to expand, although at a slower rate. In the second quarter, the country entered a recession and ended its record expansion of no recession for ten years.

Do these events matter from the investor's perspective? The answer is ambiguous. The positive response to the April 18th decline in interest rates certainly affected investors owning securities. But the May 15th decline had no immediate impact. The changes in the tax code will result in investors paying lower income tax rates, but the impact will be marginal at best. The lower rate of economic growth certainly did affect some industries, especially technology companies, and firms within those industries were adversely affected. Many employees were let go; some firms folded, and those that survived saw their stock prices decline.

This chapter considers the aggregate economic environment in which investment decisions are made. This macroeconomic framework is a precursor to the fundamental analysis of a firm's financial condition that follows in the next chapter. Emphasis is placed on the Federal Reserve's monetary and the federal government's fiscal policy, especially the impact on interest rates. Since the risk-free rate is part of the required return in the capital asset pricing model, anything that affects the rate of interest should affect security prices. The chapter also considers the impact on specific industries since firms operate within an industry. The chapter ends with a discussion of the expected economic environment and investment strategies.

The material in this chapter and the subsequent chapter form the backbone of fundamental analysis. The student should realize that two chapters cannot cover these important topics in depth; entire books have been written on each topic alone. This text can only include the basic methods and tools used in fundamental analysis and the valuation of common stock. The student should also remember the concept of efficient financial markets and that analysis of the economic environment and a firm's financial statements will not by themselves lead to superior investment decisions.

Learning Objectives

After completing this chapter you should be able to:

1. Define gross domestic product and specify its components.
2. Specify the factors that affect a specific rate of interest.
3. Describe the tools of monetary policy and the mechanics of open market operations.
4. Contrast the measures of the money supply.

5 Explain how monetary and fiscal policy and a federal government deficit or surplus may affect security prices.

6 Differentiate cyclical from stable industries and identify factors that affect the performance of an industry.

The Logical Progression of Fundamental Analysis

Fundamental analysis has a logical progression from the general to the specific. First, the analyst considers the economic environment, which may give some indication of the future direction of security prices. For example, rising inflation and interest rates argue that security prices should tend to fall. Second, the analyst considers the industry, since industries react differently to changes in the economic environment. The demand for durable items, such as cars, major appliances, and housing, tends to respond to changes in the level of economic activity, while the demand for other products, such as necessities (e.g., food) and some consumer goods, tends to be less responsive to changes in economic activity.

After considering the economy and the industry, the analyst considers the individual firm, since what applies to the economy or the industry may not apply to a specific firm. Some firms do poorly even when the general economy prospers. From 1989 through 1994, US Airways Group operated at a loss even when many airlines generated record profits. The converse is also true, since some firms do well and grow during periods of economic stagnation. These stocks may be good purchases even if it appears that the market as a whole will decline.

It may be difficult to justify purchasing stock when it appears that the economy or an industry is doing poorly. Some analysts, however, believe that this is the best time to purchase stock. If many investors are seeking to liquidate positions, security prices may be driven down, so that the buyer may be purchasing the stock at an undervalued price. These analysts are referred to as **contrarians**. Being a contrarian and going against the general sentiment is not easy.[1] Just think how difficult it would have been to have the courage to buy stock when the Dow Jones Industrial Average fell over 500 points on August 30, 1998.

contrarians
Investors who go against the consensus concerning investment strategy.

Most financial analysts and investors who use fundamental analysis are not contrarians. Instead, they follow the general logic of fundamental analysis of considering the economy, the industry, and the firm's performance and position within its industry. They use the analysis to help identify what they believe to be the general direction of the market and undervalued securities.

The Economic Environment

All investment decisions are made within the economic environment. This environment varies as the economy goes through stages of prosperity. These stages are often referred to as the **business cycle**. The name is perhaps a poor choice, since the word *cycle* suggests a regularly repeated sequence of events, such as the seasons of the year. The economy does not follow a regularly repeated sequence of events. Instead, the term *business cycle* refers to a pattern of changing economic output and growth: an initial period of rapid growth followed by a period of slow growth or even stagnation after which the economy contracts.

business cycle
An economic pattern of expansion and contraction.

[1]A similar type of approach is also one of the tools of technical analysis explained in Chapter 14. In technical analysis a contrarian emphasizes doing the opposite of what investment advisory services are recommending.

FIGURE 12.1

Phases of the Business Cycle

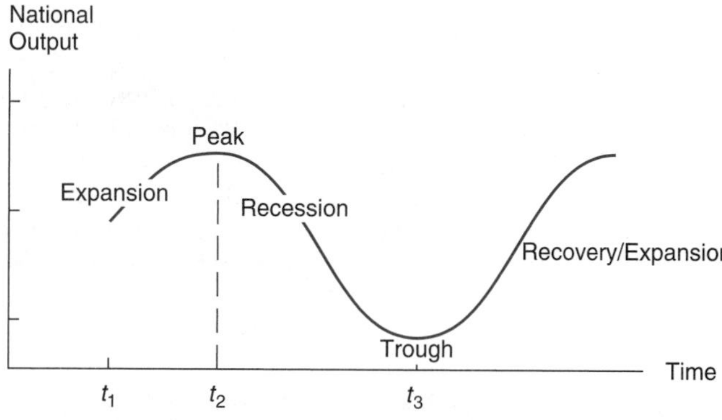

While each business cycle differs, there are common characteristics that are illustrated in Figure 12.1. Starting from a point of neutrality (t_1), the economy expands, reaching a peak at t_2. The economy then declines, reaching a trough at t_3 and subsequently starts to rebound to repeat the pattern. The peak may be accompanied by an increased rate of inflation as the economy gets "overheated." Since in the aggregate, prices of goods and services generally do not fall, there is no "deflation" (i.e., a period of *falling* prices, which is the opposite of inflation). Instead, the levels of employment and output tend to decline. Such a period of economic contraction is called a **recession**.

recession
A period of rising unemployment and declining national output.

One of the major advances within the social sciences is the increased understanding of events that affect the phases of the business cycle and of the causes of economic growth. This understanding has led to the development of tools, such as monetary and fiscal policy, that can alleviate the swings in economic activity. Unfortunately for policymakers, outside events also affect the level of economic activity. The capacity of policymakers to control the economy is constrained by these ever-changing social and political events.

In addition, circumstances that affect the economy during one period may not exist or may have less impact during subsequent periods. The oil embargo and its sudden and swift change in the price of crude oil severely affected the economy during the 1970s. Since the oil embargo, oil prices have been more stable, and fluctuations in the supply and price of oil ceased to be a disruptive force.

During the 1930s, the failures of many commercial banks had an enormous impact on the economy and contributed to the Great Depression. During the late 1980s, the failure of many savings and loan associations and commercial banks created a financial crisis but had little impact on the aggregate economy. Actions by the federal government to guarantee deposits stopped any run on the savings and loans. Of course, there was a large cost to taxpayers to finance the bailout of the banks, but that burden was spread over the population. This cost did not have the same impact on the aggregate economy as the 1930s liquidity crisis created when individual investors raced to withdraw funds from commercial banks.

Even the large plunge in the stock market during October 1987 appears in retrospect to have been a nonevent. At that time there were predictions that the large decline in stock prices was a harbinger of another depression. Such a depression did not occur. Instead, the economy continued to prosper, and the stock market reached new historic highs. Of course, some investors did sustain major losses during October 1987, but other individuals who purchased stocks after the decline probably earned profits. Such transfers among investors, however, do not have the same impact on the country that is associated with a decline in the general level of economic activity.

Each of these events was important. The dramatic increase in the price of oil, the collapse in a segment of the banking system, and the severe decline in stock prices did inflict losses on individual investors. It is possible that none of these events will be repeated; the next economic crisis may be perceptibly different from the preceding one. The economy is simply too complex to be characterized as a series of regularly repeated cycles of equal length and magnitude. Even if such repetition were possible, individuals would soon recognize the pattern and adjust accordingly. Such adjustments, of course, would ensure that the future will not be a replay of the past.

Measures of Economic Activity

gross domestic product (GDP)
Total value of all final goods and services newly produced within a country by domestic factors of production.

Economic activity is measured by aggregate indicators such as the level of production and national output. Perhaps the most commonly quoted measure is **gross domestic product (GDP)**, which is the total dollar value of all *final* goods and services newly produced within the country's boundaries with *domestic* factors of production. Cars made in the United States by Toyota are included in GDP, while IBM computers produced in Europe are not. Gross domestic product has replaced gross national product (GNP) as the primary measure of a nation's aggregate national output. (GNP is the total value of all final goods and services newly produced by an economy and includes income generated abroad—that is, income earned abroad by U.S. firms is added and income earned in the United States by foreign firms is subtracted.) The change from GNP to GDP emphasizes the country's output of goods and services within its geographical boundaries. Alternative measures of economic activity stress prices and employment. Emphasis is often placed on unemployment, especially the rate of unemployment, which measures output lost.

POINTS OF INTEREST
Means to Obtain Economic Data

Economic data emanates from numerous sources that include the federal government, the Federal Reserve, the National Bureau of Economic Research, the stock exchanges, and the SEC. Many of these sources may be accessed via the Internet, and their Web addresses appear throughout this text.

For federal government information, the Government Printing Office (GPO) has an index of government documents and data at http://www.access.gpo.gov.

One possible way to obtain Web addresses is through directories with links. These directories often have search engines that provide a means to obtain Web addresses for specific sites. One possibility is the Liberty Fund, whose Web page (www.libertyfund.org) provides links to government agencies such as the Bureau of Economic Analysis, the Bureau of Labor Statistics, the Federal Reserve, and the Census Bureau (source of economic indicators). The site also provides links to economic periodicals and university sources as well as international links to the World Bank, the International Monetary Fund (IMF), and the European Union.

If you want to broaden your knowledge of what is available through the Internet and how to access it, you may wish to obtain Ned L. Fielden's *Internet Research Theory and Practice,* 2nd ed. (Jefferson, NC: McFarland & Company, 2001). This book includes explanations of Internet tools such as search engines, techniques for information retrieval, and definitions or explanations of various abbreviations (e.g., HTTP, ISP, PDF, SMTP) that appear when using the World Wide Web or Internet documents.

GDP may be computed by adding the expenditures of the sectors of an economy or by adding all sources of income. From the individual investor's perspective, the former is more useful since corporate earnings are related to expenditures by the various sectors of the economy. These expenditures are personal consumption (C), gross private domestic investment (I), government spending (G), and net exports (E). The sum, GDP, is often indicated by the following equation:

$$\text{GDP} = C + I + G + E \tag{12.1}$$

Equation 12.1 points out the importance to economic activity of personal spending and investment in plant, equipment, and inventory by firms, government spending, and the exporting of goods. Government taxation, of course, reduces the ability of individuals and firms to spend, but the tax revenues are spent—they contribute to the nation's GDP. Correspondingly, the importing of goods increases the GDP of other nations, while foreign spending here increases gross domestic product. (In a sense the Mercantilists of the fifteenth through the seventeeth centuries had it right: Export goods and receive gold. Perhaps they placed the emphasis incorrectly on the accumulation of wealth and national power. They should have said, "Export goods and increase the domestic economy by increasing output and employment.")

Since the GDP is the sum of spending by each sector, if one sector of the economy were to decline, then GDP would also decline if another sector did not increase. For example, political pressure to reduce federal government spending puts pressure on business to expand jobs and invest in plant and equipment. Without such expansion in the business sector to offset the decline in government spending, consumer income and spending may not rise and the economy may stagnate.

Equation 12.1 also points out the importance of fiscal and monetary policies on the nation's economy. Excluding the direct impact of government spending, the thrust of a specific policy is its effect on the firms' and consumers' ability to, or incentive to, spend. For example, lower interest rates encourage additional spending by firms on plant, equipment, and inventory and by individuals on durable goods such as cars and homes. Higher interest rates have the opposite effect. These changes in business and consumer spending have an immediate impact on the aggregate level of output; that is, they affect the level of GDP.

Over time, the nation's output grows, but the rate of growth varies. The level of employment also rises as the economy grows, but the rate of employment (and unemployment) varies from year to year. From 1964 to 1990, the economy experienced four periods of recession as determined by the National Bureau of Economic Research (NBER): December 1969–November 1970, November 1973–March 1975, January 1980–July 1980, and July 1981–November 1982. The length of the recessions varied from a few months in 1980 to almost a year and a half from 1981 to 1982. The periods of economic growth also varied from the short period of growth in late 1980 to mid-1981, to the long period of growth that started at the end of 1982 and lasted to July 1990. That recession ended in March 1991, and as of January 2001, the subsequent period of economic expansion was continuing.

This variability in the length of the periods of recession and expansion and the variation in the rate of growth verifies that there is no readily identifiable, repeating business cycle. If the economy did go through identifiable patterns, they would be readily recognized by policymakers, who would adjust their strategies in an effort to stop (or at least reduce) the impact of economic stagnation or inflation. Even though the economy does not follow precise patterns, growth in the macro economy is closely watched by investors and financial analysts, since changes in the level of economic activity often bring responses from the federal government or the Federal Reserve in the form of economic policy.

Policy that emanates from the nation's capital may affect security markets by altering corporate earnings and the rate of interest. Investors and financial analysts follow various indicators of economic activity to forecast the direction of the economy, to anticipate changes in national economic policy, and to help formulate possible investment strategies. Individuals, who invest on the basis of relationships between security prices and economic activity, need to know the direction of economic change before it occurs. Hence the emphasis is placed on *leading* indicators of economic activity. The National Bureau of Economic Research tabulates a series of economic indicators. Eleven are leading indicators, four are coincident indicators, and seven are lagging indicators. The data is reported individually for each series, and the NBER groups these indicators into three composite indices.

The Conference Board also publishes composite economic indicators. As with the NBER indicators, some are leading while others are coincident and lagging indicators. The ten leading indicators are:

1. Average weekly hours of manufacturing production workers
2. Average weekly initial claims for unemployment insurance
3. Manufacturers' new orders (consumer goods and materials)
4. Time for deliveries
5. Manufacturers' new orders of nondefense capital goods
6. Building permits, new private housing units
7. Stock prices (S&P 500 stock index)
8. Money supply (M-2)
9. Interest rate spread (difference between ten-year Treasury bond yields and short-term rates)
10. Index of consumer expectations

Information concerning these indicators may be found at the Conference Board's home page, http://www.tcb.org. The index of leading indicators and the periods of the four previous recessions and economic expansion are illustrated in Figure 12.2. As may be seen in the figure, the index turns down prior to the decline in economic activity. However, there are two important caveats to consider. First, the time lapse between the initial decline in the index and the subsequent start of the recession differs. The 1973 recession started nine months after the decrease in the index, but the index declined for over a year and a half before the 1990 recession. Second, the index may give false signals. The index decreased in both 1984 and 1987 without a similar decline in the economy.

Measures of Consumer Confidence

One leading economic indicator that receives special attention is a measure of consumer sentiment or confidence. Consumer confidence affects spending, which has an impact on corporate profits and levels of employment. Two such measures include the Consumer Confidence Index (CCI) and the Consumer Sentiment Index (CSI). The CCI is published monthly by the Consumer Research Center of the Conference Board (http://www.conference-board.org) in the *Consumer Confidence Survey* and in the *Statistical Bulletin;* the CSI is published monthly by the Survey Research Center of the University of Michigan and is available by subscription. The CSI is used by the Department of Commerce as one of its leading indicators. Both the CCI and the CSI provide indicators of consumer attitudes by focusing on (1) consumer perceptions of business conditions, (2) consumer perceptions of their financial condition, and (3) consumer willingness to purchase durables, such as

FIGURE 12.2

Index of Leading Indicators, 1972–1994

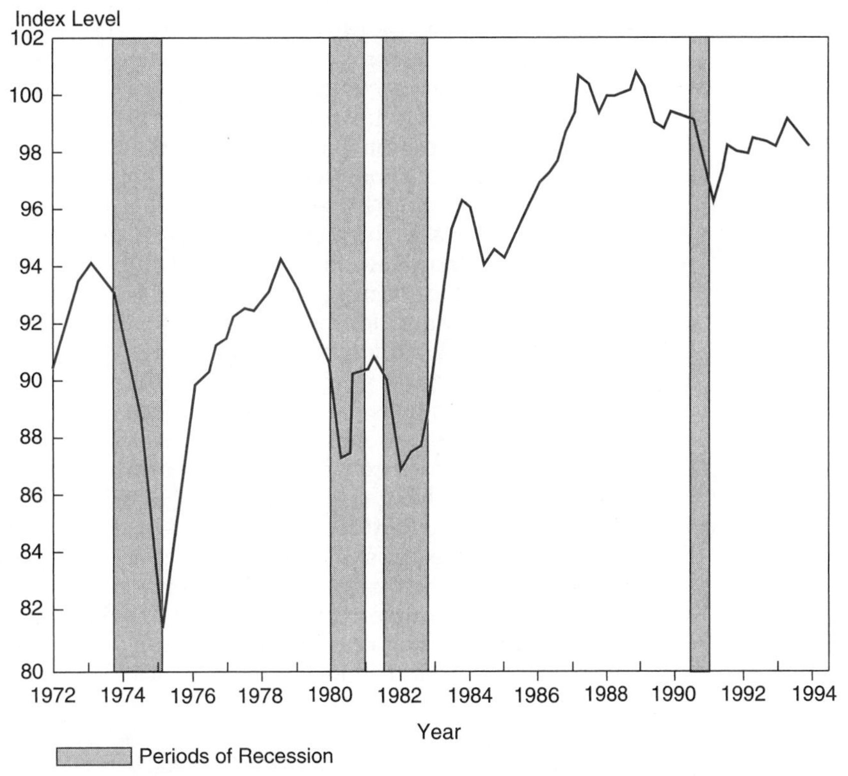

automobiles, homes, and other large dollar-cost items. An increase in confidence forecasts that consumers will increase spending, which leads to economic growth.

The absolute level of either index does not measure consumer optimism or pessimism. However, the level may be compared to previous economic periods, and changes in the indexes suggest changes in consumer optimism or pessimism. A decline in consumer confidence forecasts a reduction in the level of economic activity. Individuals who are worried about losing their jobs or who anticipate a decline in income will demand fewer goods and services and will not borrow to finance durable purchases. An increase in the indexes has, of course, the opposite implication. To some extent, a reduction in consumer confidence and a resulting decline in the demand for goods and services may be a self-fulfilling prophecy. If consumers do cut back and purchase fewer goods and services, firms will have to contract, laying off workers and cutting payrolls.

From an investor's perspective, the change in the economy resulting from a change in consumer confidence could lead to a shift in the individual's portfolio. A reduction in confidence that leads to economic contraction argues for movement out of growth companies into defensive stocks such as utilities or large firms (IBM or Merck) and debt instruments. The reduction in the level of economic activity should hurt firms' earnings and reduce their capacity to pay dividends or reinvest funds. However, the lower level of economic activity may induce the Federal Reserve to pursue a stimulatory monetary policy. At least initially, an easy-money policy will reduce interest rates, as the Federal Reserve puts money into the economy. Investors with long-term debt instruments in their portfolios should experience capital gains as bond prices rise in response to lower interest rates.

While investors may follow leading indicators to help formulate investment strategies, the usefulness of the index of leading indicators for trading in stocks is limited, because stock prices are one of the leading indicators.[2] By the time the index of indicators has given a signal, stock prices have (probably) already changed. It is still possible, however, that one of the specific leading indicators leads the stock market. For example, if changes in the stock market precede changes in economic activity by four months and changes in the money supply precede the change in economic activity by seven months, then changes in the money supply might predict changes in the stock market three months before the event. Unfortunately, there is variation in the individual components of the leading indicators. While a specific indicator may lead one recession by three months, it may lead another recession by nine months. One indicator by itself is not an accurate forecaster. (If it were, there would be no need for an *index* of leading indicators.)

In addition, it is virtually impossible to tell when an indicator has changed. Peaks and valleys (i.e., changes in the indicators) are generally determined after the fact. It is impossible to tell when a recession has started (or ended) until the change has occurred, and the same principle would apply to a specific indicator's forecasting changes in stock prices.

This inability to forecast changes in stock prices is consistent with the efficient market hypothesis. If one variable or an index of several variables could be used to forecast the direction of stock prices, individuals using the technique would consistently outperform the market. Such performance is unlikely using publicly known information, so the inability to use economic data to forecast stock prices is further support for the semistrong form of the efficient market hypothesis.

The Consumer Price Index

In addition to aggregate measures of economic activity and leading indicators, measures of inflation can have an important impact on investor behavior. Inflation is a general rise in prices and was previously discussed as an important source of risk. While prices are expressed in units of a currency (e.g., dollars), inflation is generally measured by an index. Two commonly used indexes are the Consumer Price Index (CPI) and the Producer Price Index (PPI). The CPI is calculated by the Bureau of Labor Statistics and measures the cost of a basket of goods and services over time. The PPI is calculated by the U.S. Department of Labor and measures the wholesale cost of goods over a period of time. Since goods are manufactured prior to their sale to consumers, changes in the Producer Price Index often forecast changes in the Consumer Price Index.[3]

While aggregate prices are measured by an index, the rate of inflation is measured by changes in the index. If the CPI rises from 100 to 105.6 during the year, the annual rate of inflation is 5.6 percent. Over time, there has been considerable variation in the rate of inflation. During 1930, the inflation rate was −6.0 percent

[2]Evidence from previous business cycles suggests that stock prices lead business activity, which implies that stock purchases should precede economic expansion and that sales should occur while the economy is still expanding (i.e., before recession starts). See Douglas Pearce, "Stock Prices and the Economy," *Economic Review,* Federal Reserve Bank of Kansas City (November 1983): 7–22; and Robert Shiller, "Theories of Aggregate Stock Price Movements," *The Journal of Portfolio Management* (winter 1984): 28–37.

[3]Information concerning federal government statistics such as the Consumer Price Index may be found through the Bureau of Labor Statistics home site: http://stats.bls.gov. Information concerning the various price indexes may be found at http://stats/bls.gov/cpi. Data for the Consumer Price Index from 1913 through the present may be found at ftp://ftp.bls.gov/pub/special.requests/cpi/cpiai.txt.

(i.e., prices in the aggregate fell). During 1980, the rate was 12.4 percent. Exhibit 10.2 reported that the annual rate of inflation for 1926 through 2000 was 3.1 percent, with a standard deviation of 4.5. This result indicates that for 68 percent of the years, the rate of inflation ranged from a low of −1.4 percent to a high of 7.6 percent. For the 1962–2000 period, there were no years in which consumer prices fell.

The impact of inflation on individuals varies with their consumption of goods and services. Since inflation is a general rise in prices and the Consumer Price Index measures the price of a basket of goods and services, the impact on individuals depends on the extent to which they consume the particular goods whose prices are inflating. For example, higher housing costs do not affect individuals equally. Homeowners seeking to sell may benefit from the higher prices at the expense of those seeking to acquire housing. Prices also do not rise evenly over geographic areas. Heating costs may rise more in the north than in the south, and correspondingly the cost of air-conditioning may rise more in the south than the north. These differences and other problems—such as how the index is calculated and the inability to adjust the index for technological change in the goods consumed—have led some analysts to argue that the CPI overstates the true rate of inflation. (The Bureau of Labor surveys buying patterns about every ten years and reconstructs the basket of goods and services consumed by the average household.)

During deflation, which is a general decline in prices, the real purchasing power of assets and income rises as the prices of goods and services decline. Since World War II, inflation has been a common occurrence, but deflation has not occurred since the depression of the 1930s. While prices of specific goods and services may decline in response to lower demand or to lower costs of production, prices in general tend to be "sticky"—they do not decline. This stickiness is apparent in the labor market, in which an aggregate reduction in the demand for labor does not result in lower wages. Instead, workers are laid off and individuals looking for jobs are unable to find them, so the level of unemployment rises.

While the effects of inflation vary among individuals, its impact on interest rates is the same for all individuals, firms, or governments who borrow or who lend funds. An increase in the rate of inflation will increase interest rates as investors seek a higher return to maintain the purchasing power of their funds. In addition, the Federal Reserve will pursue a tight-money policy designed to curb inflation. Such a policy drives up interest rates on short-term federal government securities. This increase in short-term rates permeates all interest rates, so that the policy is felt by all borrowers.

Inflation can also be deleterious to the stock market. Although higher prices of goods and services sold could lead to increased earnings, firms have to purchase inputs, so inflation increases the cost of production. Replacing aging plant and equipment becomes more costly, and inventory, labor, and financing costs rise in response to inflation. Although there have been periods when stock prices did rise when inflation heated up (e.g., between 1979 and 1980, the rate of inflation exceeded 10 percent annually and stock prices rose), empirical evidence generally supports the theory that high inflation decreases stock prices.[4] For example, during 1946 and from 1974 to 1975, the rate of inflation exceeded 10 percent annually and stock prices fell. The 1990s also support a negative relationship between stock prices and inflation: Stock prices consistently rose while the rate of inflation remained stable at a relatively modest 3 percent—perceptibly lower than during the late 1970s and early 1980s, when the annual inflation rate rose to over 13 percent.

[4]See, for instance, Charles R. Nelson, "Inflation and Rates of Return on Common Stock," *Journal of Finance* (May 1976): 471–483; and E. Fama and G. Schwert, "Asset Returns and Inflation," *Journal of Financial Economics* (November 1977): 115–146.

Discounted cash flow models of valuation, such as the dividend-growth model presented in Chapter 9, also suggest that inflation should tend to depress stock prices. Cash flows may not grow as rapidly as consumer prices during periods of rapid inflation, and the required return rises as investors seek to earn higher returns to compensate for the loss of purchasing power. When both of these factors are applied to cash flows, they indicate that inflation will lower stock prices.

The Federal Reserve

Federal Reserve
The central bank of the United States.

In addition to forecasts of aggregate economic activity, investors are concerned with the monetary policy of the **Federal Reserve** (the "Fed"). The Federal Reserve is the country's central bank.[5] Although in many countries the treasury and the central bank are one and the same, in the United States they are independent of each other. Such independence is an example of the checks and balances of the U.S. political system. However, both the U.S. Treasury and the Federal Reserve share the same general goals of full employment, stable prices, and economic growth.

The Federal Reserve pursues these economic goals through its impact on the supply of money and the cost of credit. Monetary policy refers to changes in the supply of money and credit. When the Federal Reserve wants to increase the supply of money and credit to help expand the level of income and employment, it follows an *easy* monetary policy. When it desires to contract the supply of money and credit to help fight inflation, it pursues a *tight* monetary policy.

Determination of Interest Rates[6]

The impact of the Federal Reserve's monetary policy is felt through its effect on the rate of interest—that is, the impact on the cost of borrowing funds. The rate of interest is determined by the demand for and supply of loanable funds, which is illustrated in Figure 12.3. As interest rates decline, the quantity demanded of loanable funds increases. Lower rates increase the profitability of investments in assets such as plant, equipment, and inventory; reduce the cost of carrying a home mortgage; and increase the quantity demanded of borrowed funds. As interest rates rise, the quantity supplied of loanable funds increases. Higher returns encourage individuals to spend less and save more, which increases the quantity supplied of loanable funds. The equilibrium rate of interest equates the quantity of funds demanded and the quantity of funds supplied.

Figure 12.3 indicates only one rate of interest, but there is actually a spectrum of rates. The actual rate an individual borrower pays (and the investor earns) depends on several variables, such as the term of the loan or the riskiness of the borrower. A specific interest rate may be expressed as a simple equation:

$$i = i_r + p_i + p_d + p_l + p_t. \tag{12.2}$$

[5]For a concise introduction to the structure and role of the Federal Reserve, obtain Board of Governors, *The Federal Reserve System: Purposes and Functions,* 8th ed. (Washington, DC: Government Printing Office, 1994). Publications of the Federal Reserve include the *Federal Reserve Bulletin*. This monthly publication reports financial data, including interest rates, employment, gross domestic product, and the money supply. Materials published by the Federal Reserve may be found at its Web address: http://www.federalreserve.gov.

[6]The types and features of bonds and the impact of fluctuations in interest rates on bond prices is covered in Part 3 of this text. This section discusses interest rates in general terms in order to understand how the Federal Reserve's monetary policy is transmitted to the aggregate economy.

FIGURE 12.3

Determination of the Interest Rate

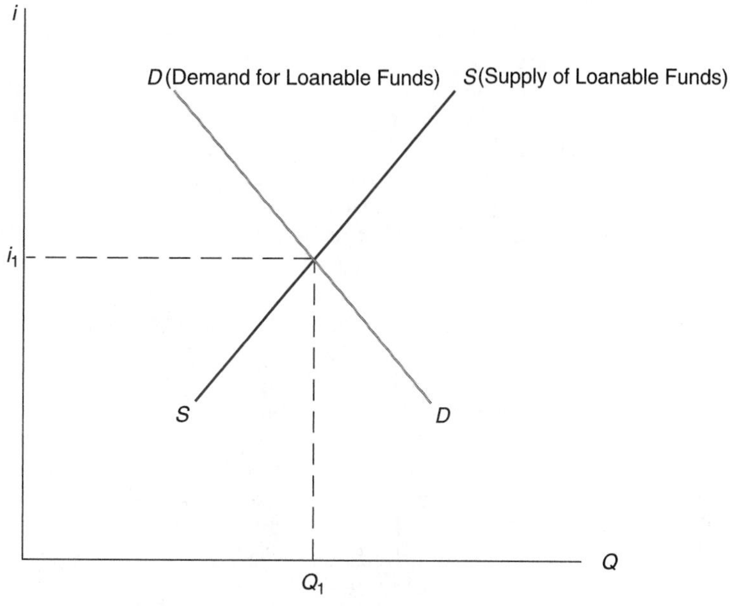

The current nominal interest rate (i) is the sum of the real risk-free rate (i_r) plus a series of premiums: the premium for expected inflation (p_i), the premium for default risk (P_d), the premium for liquidity (P_l), and the premium for the term to maturity (P_t). Thus, the observed current rate of interest is the result of the interplay of several complex variables, each of which is simultaneously affecting the rate.

The *real risk-free rate* is the return investors could earn without bearing any risk in a noninflationary environment. While no exact measure of the real risk-free rate exists, analysts generally believe it ranges from 2 to 4 percent. The real risk-free rate varies with the general level of economic activity, rising during periods of economic expansion and contracting during periods of economic stagnation. During a period of rapid economic growth, the real risk-free rate may rise to 4 percent, but the actual observed interest rate will be higher as a result of the other contributing factors.

The *inflation premium* depends on expectations of future inflation. A greater anticipated rate argues for a higher rate of interest. Since inflation may vary from year to year, the expectation also varies. If the expected inflationary rate is 4 percent for one year and 6 percent for the second year, the premiums will differ. In this case, the one-year rate of interest would be less than the two-year rate (assuming all other factors are held constant). The investor would have to earn only 4 percent for a one-year loan to cover the expected rate of inflation but would require a higher interest rate on a two-year loan to be compensated for the higher anticipated rate of inflation in the second year. This relationship would be reversed if the expected rate of inflation were 6 percent for the next year and 4 percent for the second year. In that case, the rate on a two-year debt instrument could be lower than the rate on a one-year security. (The inflation premium on the one-year security would have to be 6 percent to compensate for that year's rate of inflation, while the premium on the two-year security could be 5 percent annually to compensate the investor for the expected 10 percent inflation over the two-year time period.)

The *default premium* depends on investors' expectations or the probability that the lender will not pay the interest and retire the principal. The higher the probability of default, the greater will be the interest required to induce investors to purchase the securities. Rating systems give some indication of default risk, and the difference in yields and prices between bonds with different ratings is illustrated in Figure 16.4 in Chapter 16.

The *liquidity/marketability premium* is related to the ease with which the asset may be converted into cash near its original cost. Although there is an active secondary market in debt securities, there are differences in the depth of these markets. The bonds of a well-known company such as AT&T may be readily sold, but the secondary market for the bonds of a small company may be inactive. The size of an issue of bonds also affects its marketability. A large $500 million bond issue will have an active secondary market, and the spread between the bid and ask prices will be small (e.g., $10 to $20 per $1,000). A small issue, however, may not have an active secondary market, and the spread between the bid and ask prices is large. The bond may be quoted 97–100 or even 95–100, which is a bid price of $950 and an asking price of $1,000 per $1,000 face amount of debt. (Large spreads especially apply in the market for small issues of municipal bonds.) If investors realize that a bond purchased for $1,000 can only be sold for $950, these individuals will demand a higher interest rate to compensate for the loss that would occur if the bonds had to be sold.

The *term premium* is associated with the time (or term to maturity) when the bond will be redeemed. Investors prefer short-term to long-term bonds. As is explained in Chapter 16, when interest rates rise, bond prices fall, and the amount of the price decline is greater the longer the term of the bond. To compensate for the possibility of higher interest rates inflicting capital losses on bondholders, investors seek a higher interest rate as the term of the bond increases.

As this discussion indicates, the interest rate is affected by many factors. The actual observed current nominal rate of interest is the result of the simultaneous interplay of all these factors. Thus, anomalies in bond yields are possible. For example, the interest rate on a poor-quality bond that matures in one year may be less than the rate on a high-quality bond that matures in ten years, if the premium for the longer term exceeds the default premium. Another possible explanation for the difference in the yields could be that the poor-quality bond is actively traded, while the higher-quality bond is a small issue with an inactive secondary market. Or investors could anticipate a larger increase in the rate of inflation over the ten-year term of the higher-quality bond—an anticipation that would have little impact on the rate paid by a bond that matures within a year.

The Impact of the Federal Reserve on Interest Rates

The determination of interest rates is complicated by the role of the Federal Reserve. The Federal Reserve seeks to affect the level of economic activity by changing interest rates. Through its impact on the cost of credit, the Federal Reserve seeks to control inflation or to stimulate employment and economic growth. The Federal Reserve affects interest rates through its power to change the money supply by using the tools of monetary policy: the reserve requirements of banks, the discount rate, and open market operations.

The Federal Reserve influences the money supply and interest rates through the lending capacity of the fractional reserve banking system. Depository institutions (commercial banks and savings institutions, such as savings and loan associations) must hold reserves against their deposit liabilities. The amount of these reserves is determined by the Federal Reserve. Any transaction that affects banks' reserves affects their capacity to lend.

reserve requirement
The percentage of cash that banks must hold against their deposit liabilities.

When a cash deposit is made in a bank, the cash becomes part of the bank's reserves. These reserves are divided into *required reserves* and *excess reserves.* This division depends on the **reserve requirement**, which is the percentage set by the Federal Reserve that depository institutions must hold against deposit liabilities. (Deposit liabilities are primarily checking and savings accounts, but the Federal reserve may set reserve requirements against other accounts, such as time deposits.) If the reserve requirement is 10 percent and $100 cash is deposited, $10 must be held against the deposit (the required reserve) and $90 is available for lending (the excess reserves). Only a fraction of the new cash (10 percent) must be held against the deposit liability.

When the commercial banking system lends the excess reserves, the supply of money and credit is expanded. When the money created by the new loan returns to the banking system, the process of determining new required and excess reserves is repeated. Depository institutions with new excess reserves are able to create additional loans, and when these loans are made, the money supply is again increased. The maximum possible expansion in the money supply is $900, which is the new excess reserves divided by the reserve requirement (i.e., $90/0.10 = $900).[7] The converse occurs when deposits and reserves leave the banking system. As the fractional reserve banking system leads to expansion when new reserves are created, it will also contract when reserves are decreased.

Any transaction that affects the banking system's reserves or any change in the reserve requirement alters the system's ability to expand the supply of money. By lowering the reserve requirement, the Federal Reserve instantly creates new excess reserves (and new lending capacity). According to the previous illustration, if the reserve requirement were lowered from 10 percent to 5 percent, $95 instead of $90 of the $100 deposit would be considered excess reserves, so each bank could lend more and create more credit. These additional loans will be magnified as the new money works its way through the fractional reserve banking system. Thus, by lowering the reserve requirement, the Federal Reserve increases the capacity of banks to lend, and when they do lend, they effect an increase in the supply of credit and money within the economic system.

discount rate
The rate of interest that the Federal Reserve charges banks for borrowing reserves.

The **discount rate** is the interest rate the Federal Reserve charges depository institutions for borrowing reserves. When banks borrow from the Federal Reserve, they receive excess reserves. When these reserves are loaned, they expand the supply of money and credit. Depository institutions may also borrow from the Federal Reserve when they determine that they have insufficient reserves to meet their reserve requirements. In that case, borrowing the required reserves would not expand the supply of money and credit, because the expansion had already

[7]The actual amount of the expansion depends on what happens to the new funds generated by the loans. If the money does not return to the banking system (i.e., people retain cash), the money supply does not expand. However, since the vast majority of transactions use checks instead of cash, it is reasonable to assume that the funds created by the new loans will be returned to the banking system, permitting the system to expand further.

Another drain on the banking system occurs when the money is used to purchase foreign goods and services. The money leaves the country and lodges in foreign banks, which increases the foreign banks' capacity to lend but reduces the American lending capacity. Fortunately for the U.S. economy, the dollar is an international currency. U.S. payments for foreign goods result in increased deposits in foreign banks, but unless the dollars are converted into the local currency, these banks maintain deposits in U.S. banks. Foreign banks then can make loans denominated in dollars; since U.S. bank deposits are maintained, the American banking system does not contract.

The process of loan creation through the fractional reserve banking system is explained in money and banking texts. See, for instance, Frederic S. Miskin, *The Economics of Money, Banking, and Financial Markets,* 5th ed. (Reading, MA: Addison-Wesley, 1998).

occurred at the time the loans were made. By borrowing the necessary reserves, banks will not have to liquidate assets in order to obtain the funds to meet their reserve requirements. Such liquidations would cause the system to contract, so in this case, borrowing the reserves from the Federal Reserve maintains the supply of money and credit.

While changes in the reserve requirement and the discount rate can affect the supply of money and credit, they are infrequently used. Since 1963, the reserve requirement for checking accounts has been changed only eight times. During 1994, the Fed increased the discount rate from 3 percent to 5.25 percent over a period of 13 months to slow down the economy and help maintain the economic expansion. After a decrease to 5 percent in January 1996, the rate was not changed again until October 1998, when it was lowered to 4.75 percent.

During 2000 and 2001, the Federal Reserve used the discount rate more aggressively. Starting with a rate increase in November 1999, the Federal Reserve continued to increase the discount rate from 4.75 percent to 6 percent in June 1999. The increases were designed to dampen the economy, which was growing at a rate that was believed to be unsustainable and would lead to inflationary pressure. Then in January 2001, the Federal Reserve reversed the process and decreased the rate from 6 percent on January 1 to 1.25 percent on December 11. These unprecedented decreases were designed to rejuvenate an economy whose rate of growth had declined from 5.3 percent during the first half of 2000. By the second quarter of 2001, economic growth turned negative, and the economy entered its first recession in ten years.

While the Federal Reserve does change the discount rate, such changes may be more symbolic than substantive. There are other, more effective (and subtler) means to alter the supply of money and credit. Instead of relying on the discount rate and the reserve requirement, the Federal Reserve uses the **federal funds rate** (or *Fed funds rate*) and open market operations. While the term *federal funds rate* includes the word *federal,* the rate should not be confused with the discount rate. The federal funds rate is the interest charged by banks when they lend reserves to each other. Banks with excess reserves can put those funds to work by lending them to other banks in the federal funds market. Thus, the bank converts a sterile asset into an income-earning asset, and the bank in need of reserves acquires them without having to borrow from the Federal Reserve.

federal funds rate
The rate of interest a bank charges another for borrowing reserves.

Unlike the discount rate, the federal funds rate is not set by the Federal Reserve. Instead, it is established by the interaction of the demand and supply of funds available in the federal funds market. The Federal Reserve, however, can affect the supply of funds and thereby affect the federal funds rate. During the 1990s and early 2000s, the Federal Reserve preferred to set a target federal funds rate and changed that target as a tool of monetary policy instead of changing the discount rate.

The target federal funds rate is achieved through the most important tool of monetary policy, open market operations. **Open market operations** is the buying and selling of securities (primarily U.S. Treasury bills) by the Federal Reserve. The Federal Reserve may buy or sell these securities in any quantity at any time. When the Federal Reserve seeks to follow an expansionary policy, it purchases Treasury bills. When the Federal Reserve pays for the securities, the funds are deposited into commercial banks, which puts reserves into the banking system. Because only a percentage of the reserves will be required against the deposit liabilities, the remainder become excess reserves. When these newly created excess reserves are loaned by the banking system, the supply of money and credit is increased.

open market operations
The buying or selling of Treasury securities by the Federal Reserve.

A tight (contractionary) monetary policy is designed to drain reserves from the banking system. The Federal Reserve sells securities, which are then purchased by the general public or banks. When the securities are paid for, funds flow from deposits to the Federal Reserve. The effect is to reduce the reserves of depository institutions. Because only a small percentage of the lost reserves are required, the major-

FIGURE 12.4

Increase in the Supply of Loanable Funds

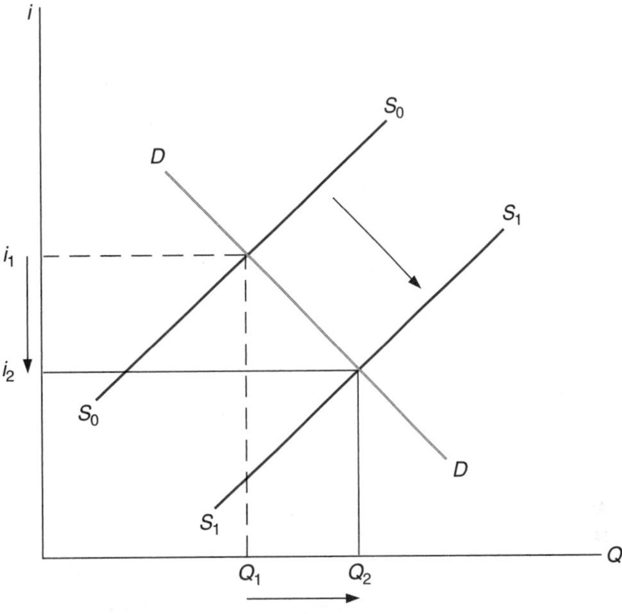

ity become lost excess reserves. The reduction in excess reserves then decreases the banks' capacity to lend and thus contracts the supply of money and credit.

Open market operations have a direct and immediate impact on interest rates. When the Federal Reserve purchases Treasury bills, demand is increased. This drives up prices (and simultaneously drives down yields) in order to induce investors to sell the securities. The opposite occurs when the Federal Reserve sells Treasury bills. In that case, the Fed increases the supply, which reduces their price (and simultaneously increases their yields) and induces investors to purchase the securities. Thus, by altering the demand for and supply of U.S. Treasury bills, the Federal Reserve affects their prices and their yields.

This impact on interest rates may be seen by the use of supply and demand curves from Figure 12.3. In Figure 12.4 an expansionary monetary policy increases the supply of loanable funds (S_0S_0 shifts to S_1S_1). At the old rate (i_1), excess quantity leads to lower interest rates. The opposite effect occurs if the Federal Reserve follows a tight monetary policy and drains funds out of the banking system. The decrease in supply (S_0S_0 to S_1S_1 in Figure 12.5 on p. 370) drives up the rate of interest.

The change in yields on Treasury bills is transferred to all other yields. As was explained earlier, interest rates are the result of the interaction of several factors, one of which is the risk-free rate of interest. Since U.S. Treasury bills are the safest of all securities, their yield is generally used as the risk-free rate. Any change in the Treasury bill rate (i.e., in the risk-free rate) must have an impact on interest rates in general. If the rate on Treasury bills rises, the rate on other short-term securities must also rise. In addition, short-term rates tend to be less than long-term rates, so the increase in short-term rates will be transferred to long-term rates. Of course, the amount of change in each rate varies, since the other factors that affect interest rates will simultaneously affect the rate on each security. Still, the general

FIGURE 12.5

Decrease in the Supply of Loanable Funds

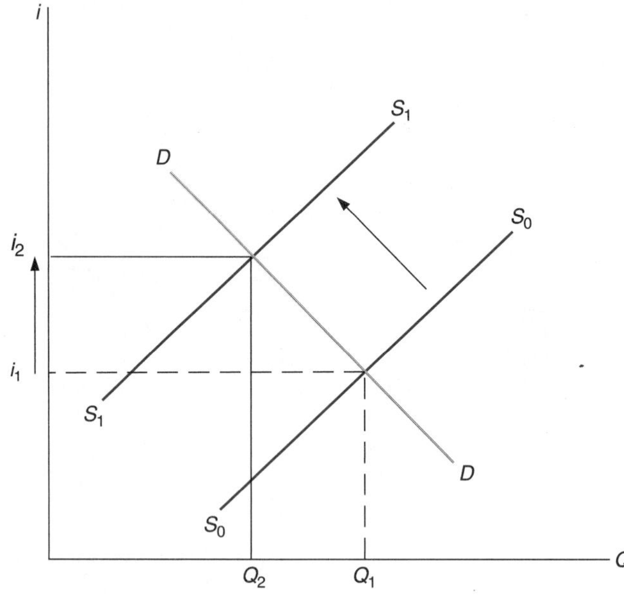

conclusion remains that all rates should rise in response to the Treasury bill rate increase.

The opposite impact occurs when the Federal Reserve puts reserves into the banking system. The initial impact will be to drive down the risk-free rate, which in turn will cause interest rates in general to decline. The extent to which rates fall and which specific rates decline then depends on the other factors. For example, if investors/lenders anticipate that easy money may lead to inflation, the expectation of increased inflation may cause long-term rates to remain stable or even rise even though current short-term rates have fallen.

The actual impact of any change in the supply of money and loanable funds is difficult to isolate, because the Federal Reserve uses monetary policy to pursue more than one economic goal. Over time, the Federal Reserve must increase the money supply to facilitate economic growth. If the money supply grows too slowly, it will put pressure on interest rates and there will be insufficient funds to sustain the growth. Conversely, the Federal Reserve does not want to increase the money supply too rapidly, because excess monetary expansion will lead to inflationary pressure.

The Impact of Monetary Policy on Stock Prices

The previous discussion suggested that the Federal Reserve's monetary policy affects interest rates through its impact on the reserves of the banking system. Monetary policy also has an impact on stock prices. This may be the direct result of the changes in interest rates or the indirect result of the monetary policy's effect on a firm's earning capacity.

The potential impact may be seen by referring to the dividend-growth model presented in Chapter 9. That model is

POINTS OF INTEREST
Fed Watching

Because changes in interest rates can have a major impact on security prices, it is not surprising that investors watch the Fed with the hope of determining the next change in monetary policy. This watching primarily revolves around meetings of the Federal Open Market Committee and the statements of the chairman of the Board of Governors of the Federal Reserve.

The Federal Open Market Committee is individually the most powerful component of the Fed because it has control over open market operations. The committee consists of 12 members, 7 of whom are the members of the Board of Governors of the Federal Reserve. The remaining 5 members are the presidents of the 12 Federal Reserve district banks. Membership on the Open Market Committee rotates among 11 of the district bank presidents. The president of the New York district bank is a permanent member.

The most important individual member of the Fed is the chairman of the Board of Governors. During the 1990s, Alan Greenspan served as chairman. An economist who served as head of the Council of Economic Advisors to President Ford, Chairman Greenspan is an economic conservative who has tended to follow a moderately expansionary monetary policy with a primary emphasis on stabilizing prices. However, the goal of stable prices does not mean that the Fed will not take action to stimulate economic growth. During the 1990 recession, the Federal Reserve put reserves into the banking system and lowered the discount rate to stimulate economic expansion. During the late 1990s, the Fed again lowered interest rates to maintain economic growth as the Asian economies declined and the fear arose that the Asian economic problems would cause the U.S. economy to falter and enter into a recession.

As chairman of the Board of Governors, Alan Greenspan is the chief spokesman for the Fed. His frequent testimony to Congress is eagerly anticipated for clues to future Fed actions. The market does react to his statements, which are often interpreted negatively. The fact that a major goal of the Fed is price stability suggests the Fed will raise rates at the first whiff of increased prices. For example, in December 1996, Chairman Greenspan remarked that recent increases in stock prices exhibited "irrational exuberance." The next day, the Dow Jones Industrial Average declined 145 points. Greenspan's remarks may also cause stock prices to rise. In September 1998, after a one-day drop in excess of 500 points, Chairman Greenspan hinted that interest rates might be reduced. The Dow Jones Industrial Average rose more than 380 points the next day. These illustrations indicate that Chairman Greenspan's remarks can have an impact on the market, but the impact may be short-lived. The market rose over 1,000 points within six months after the "irrational exuberance" statement and lost more than 380 points within a week after the hint of lower interest rates. Thus, it should be evident that Chairman Greenspan's remarks should not be the sole or even primary basis for investment decisions.

$$V = \frac{D_0(1 + g)}{k - g},$$

in which V is the value of the stock, D_0 is the dividend that is currently being paid, k is the investor's required rate of return, and g is the growth rate in the firm's dividend. Any factors that affect the model's variables then must have an impact on the valuation of the stock.

When the Federal Reserve tightens credit and drains money out of the system, interest rates rise. Higher interest rates increase the required return (k) and suggest that the value of the stock should decline. In addition, higher interest rates may reduce the firm's earnings, hurting its ability to grow and pay dividends. Either the g or the D_0 (or both) are reduced, so the value of the stock declines. In terms of the constant dividend-growth valuation model, tight money reduces the numerator and increases the denominator, which puts downward pressure on the value of the stock.

A loosening of credit has the opposite impact. Lower interest rates may increase a stock's price by increasing earnings, which leads to higher dividends or increased growth, and by reducing the required return. This suggests that if the investor anticipates lower interest rates, he or she should buy stocks and reduce holdings of short-term assets, such as shares of money market mutual funds or certificates of deposit.

Determining the Direction of Monetary Policy

To take advantage of changes in interest rates, the investor needs to know the direction that the Federal Reserve is following. It should come as no surprise then that Fed watching is a major activity among security analysts and portfolio managers. Major changes in monetary policy occur after the Federal Reserve's Board of Governors' monthly meetings. Such changes are signaled by changes in the federal funds rate or the discount rate. During the remainder of the month, analysts track changes in the nation's money supply and bank reserves in an effort to determine current monetary policy.

Unfortunately, monetary statistics, which are released weekly, may not clearly indicate the Federal Reserve's monetary policy. While the Fed's purpose is to control the money supply to stimulate economic growth and to maintain stable prices and full employment, there is disagreement as to the composition of the money supply. The simplest definition of the supply of money (commonly referred to as **M-1**) is the sum of currency, coins, and checking accounts (including interest-bearing checking accounts) in the hands of the public. A broader definition (**M-2**) adds savings accounts to this definition. Thus, if individuals shift funds from savings accounts to checking accounts, the money supply is increased under the narrow definition (M-1) but is unaffected under the broader definition (M-2).

M-1
Sum of demand deposits, coins, and currency.

M-2
Sum of demand deposits, coins, currency, and savings accounts at banks.

The growth rate in the money supply will depend on the definition used by the analyst. Figure 12.6 plots M-1 and M-2 for 1986 through 2000. Over the entire period, both M-1 and M-2 rose, but there were periods in which the rates of growth differed. For example, during 1988 and 1989, M-2 grew by 4 percent while M-1 was virtually unchanged. An opposite pattern occurred during 1991. There were even periods (such as early 1988) when M-1 declined while M-2 rose, and M-1 was virtually unchanged from 1994 through 2001.

While M-1 and M-2 may present conflicting signals, there is still consensus that the Federal Reserve systematically expands the money supply over time to maintain economic growth. (Over the 15-year period in Figure 12.6, M-1 and M-2 grew annually at 3.85 percent and 4.75 percent, respectively.) From the individual investor's perspective, the growth in the money supply is related to economic growth and economic growth is related to stock prices. If the money supply rises too slowly, economic growth will be constrained, which should reduce stock prices. If the money supply rises too rapidly, inflation will result, which is associated with higher rates of interest and lower stock prices. The goal is to determine what rate of growth in the money supply will over time sustain economic growth without creating stagnation or inflation.[8]

While the monetary policy of the Federal Reserve can have an important impact on bond and stock investments, developing a successful investment strategy based on monetary policy is exceedingly difficult, if not impossible. In addition, the stock market is a leading indicator of economic activity. The market anticipates change in monetary policy and does not react to the policy change unless the change is unanticipated. Hence, to use changes in monetary policy as a guide for an investment strategy, it is necessary to differentiate between expected changes—the effects of which are already embodied in stocks' prices—and unanticipated changes, which can have an impact on stock prices. This means that the investor must correctly anticipate and act before the unexpected change. In efficient financial markets, the investor must have superior insight or luck to use changes in monetary policy to consistently generate superior stock market profits.

[8]Some economists, especially Milton Friedman, argue that monetary policy is destabilizing. Because excessive monetary growth leads to inflation, controlling the expansion of the money supply is crucial to stable prices. However, the money supply must grow to facilitate economic growth. Limiting the power of the Federal Reserve to create reserves and requiring that it expand the money supply at a fixed rate should, according to this monetarist group of economists, lead to stable prices without constraining economic growth.

FIGURE 12.6

Money Supply (M-1 and M-2), 1986–2000 (in billions of dollars)

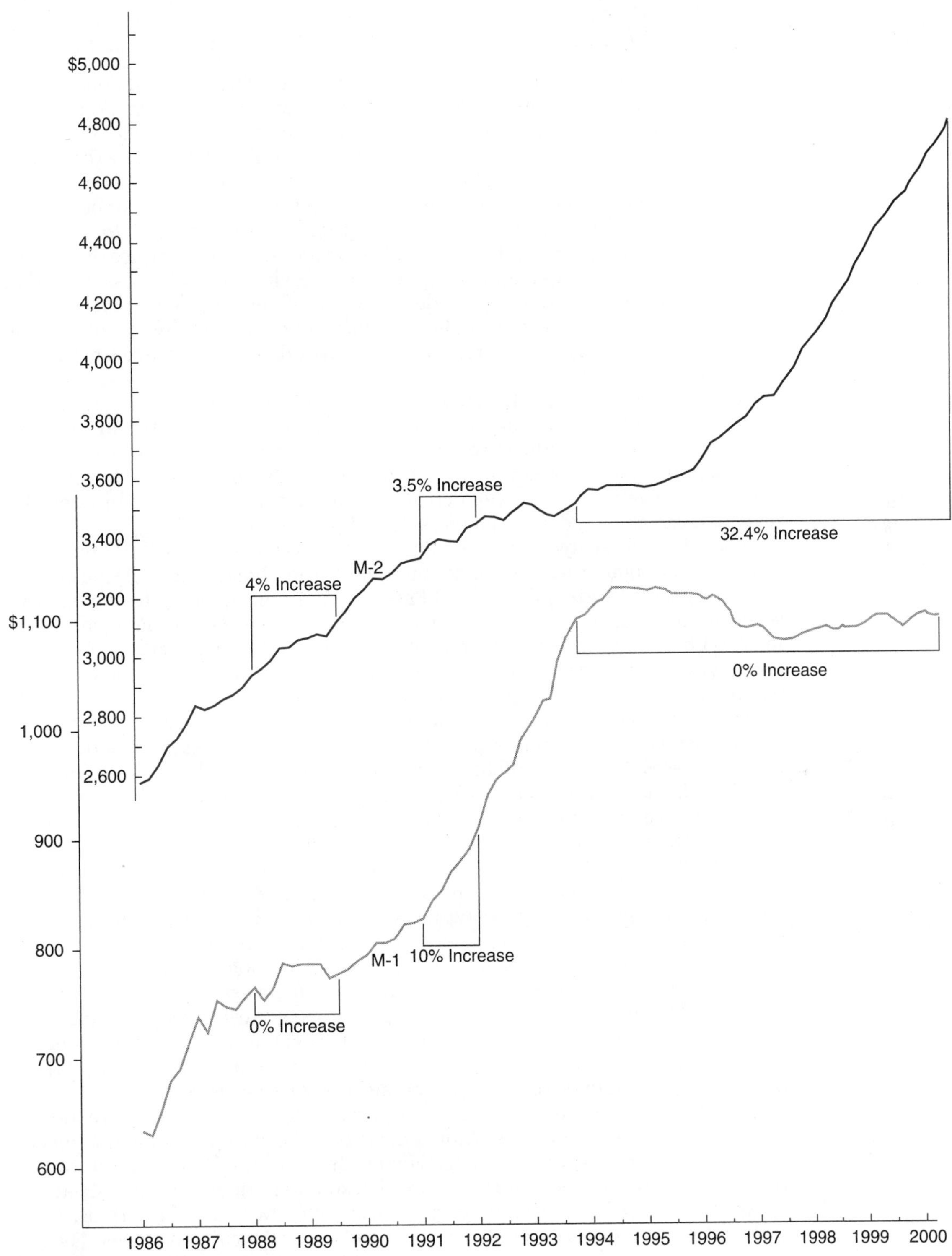

Source: *Federal Reserve Bulletin*, various issues.

Fiscal Policy

fiscal policy
Taxation, expenditures, and debt management of the federal government.

In addition to the monetary policy of the Federal Reserve, the fiscal policy of the federal government can have an important impact on the security markets. **Fiscal policy** is taxation, expenditures, and debt management by the federal government.[9] Like monetary policy, fiscal policy may be used to pursue the economic goals of price stability, full employment, and economic growth.

Obviously, taxation can have an impact on security prices. Corporate income taxes reduce corporate earnings and hence reduce firms' capacity to pay dividends and to retain earnings for growth. Personal income taxes reduce disposable income. This reduces demand for goods and services as well as savings that would be invested in some asset. Federal taxes also affect the demand for specific securities, such as tax-exempt bonds. Thus the tax policies may affect not only the level of security prices but also relative prices, as certain types of assets receive favorable tax treatment.

deficit spending
Government expenditures exceeding government revenues.

The potential impact of the federal government's fiscal policy is not limited to taxation. Expenditures can also affect security prices. This should be obvious with regard to the specific products bought by the government. Such purchases may increase a particular firm's earnings and help enhance its stock's price. However, expenditures in general, especially **deficit spending**, in which expenditures exceed revenues, can affect the financial markets and security prices.

When the federal government's expenditures exceed revenues, the federal government may obtain funds to finance this deficit from three sources: (1) the general public, (2) banks, and (3) the Federal Reserve. When the federal government sells securities to the general public to finance the deficit, these securities compete directly with all other securities for the funds of savers. This increased supply of federal government securities will tend to decrease security prices and increase their yields.

A similar conclusion applies to sales of Treasury securities to banks. If the banks lend money to the federal government, they cannot lend these funds to individuals and businesses. The effect will be to raise the cost of loans as the banks ration their supply of loanable funds. Higher borrowing costs should tend to reduce security prices for several reasons. First, higher costs should reduce corporate earnings, which will have an impact on dividends and growth rates. Second, higher borrowing costs should reduce the attractiveness of buying securities on credit (i.e., margin) and thus reduce the demand for securities. Third, the higher costs of borrowing will encourage banks to raise the rates they pay depositors. Since all short-term rates are highly correlated, increases in one rate will be transferred to other rates. Once again, the higher interest rates in general produce lower security prices.

If the Federal Reserve were to finance the federal government's deficit, the impact would be the same as if the Fed had purchased securities through open market operations. In either case, the money supply would be expanded. In effect, when the Fed buys the securities issued to finance the federal government's deficit, the Fed is monetizing the debt because new money is created.

surplus
Receipts exceeding disbursements.

The opposite of deficit spending is a **surplus**, in which government revenues exceed government expenditures. Prior to the late 1990s, the federal government had not had a budgetary surplus since the Nixon administration. Once receipts did exceed disbursements, the issue arose as to what should be done with the surplus.

As expected, politicians had different ideas as to how to use the surplus. These included reducing taxes and increasing spending on specific programs. The for-

[9]See the Council of Economic Advisors, *Economic Report of the President.* This annual publication reports the fiscal policy (i.e., taxation and expenditures) of the federal government and is available at http://www.access.gpo.gov/eop.

mer would decrease government revenues while the latter would increase disbursements, either of which would consume the surplus. Other suggestions included reducing part of the outstanding federal debt and supporting Social Security. Reducing the debt would, of course, restore the funds to the general public or commercial banks when these investors sold their securities back to the federal government.

Supporting Social Security would also return the funds to the private sector. Social Security payments go into trust funds that hold federal government debt. An influx of funds into these accounts would be invested in government securities. Since the federal government is running a surplus, it is reasonable to assume it is not issuing new bonds in excess of what is required to roll over existing debt. Thus, the surplus money contributed to the Social Security trust funds would not be used to buy new bonds but to purchase existing debt held by the general public and the banking system. Money taken from the general public when the surplus was created would be returned when the securities were purchased.

As was explained earlier, securities issued to finance the deficit compete with other securities, and an increase in federal government bonds should depress prices and raise interest rates. The surplus has the opposite effect. As the trust funds acquire government debt, the bonds' prices should rise while yields decline. In either case, a deficit or a surplus, the security markets are not immune to the fiscal policy of the federal government. Financing a government deficit or investing any surplus should have an impact on security prices and interest rates.

Industry Analysis

Industries go through a cycle that is analogous to the life cycle experienced by individuals. Initially, technology generates a product that spawns an industry. For example, the development of small chips led to the personal computer industry. In other cases, change in one area causes the rebirth of another. Film studios had many movies that were occasionally shown in rereleases or on late-night TV, but the development of home video cameras, videocassettes, and videotape players generated a new market for an old product: the rental and sale of movies on cassettes and subsequently DVDs for home use.

Initially, many firms enter a rapidly expanding industry, but as the number of participants increases, the markets become saturated. The rate of growth declines, producing a phase of consolidation. Some firms fail and cease operations while others merge with stronger firms. The benefits to the surviving firms include a larger market share and increased capacity to survive. A mature industry will tend to have a few remaining participants that share a stable market. Such markets may continue to grow, but the rate of growth is modest.

This life-cycle pattern of growth is illustrated in Figure 12.7 (p. 376), which shows the initial rapid growth in sales (t_0 to t_1), followed by the reduction in the rate of growth (t_1 to t_2), and the inevitable period of maturity (t_2 to t_3). In some cases, the industry may even start to decline as total sales diminish (t_3 and on). In a declining industry the competition can be especially fierce as the participants fight for the declining market.

The time necessary for this life cycle can be long or very short, depending on the rate of technological change, the amount of funds necessary to start operations, and the legal barriers to entry and competition, such as patents. Ease of entry will rapidly saturate the market. Today it may be difficult to realize that McDonald's and Burger King were once two of many rapidly growing fast-food enterprises serving primarily hamburgers. For each of these firms to have survived, Americans would have had to eat hamburgers for breakfast, lunch, and dinner. Only a handful of the initial entrants survived, and today the market is dominated by a few large firms.

FIGURE 12.7

Life Cycle of an Industry

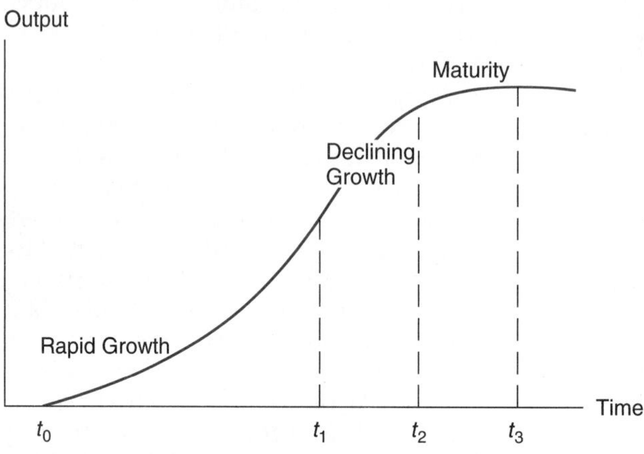

In some cases, saturated domestic markets have encouraged firms to expand abroad. Deteriorating domestic cigarette sales have driven R. J. Reynolds and Phillip Morris to expand foreign markets in an effort to maintain sales and profitability. According to the 2000 annual report, over 60 percent of Coca-Cola's revenues are generated by foreign sales.

If management has insight and perceives the decline in its industry, it may alter the firm's core businesses by diversifying into other areas still offering potential growth. For example, increased use of cars and planes led to a decline in the demand for long-distance bus travel. Greyhound, the former leader in city-to-city bus travel, sold its bus operations.[10] While the company continued to manufacture buses for sale to urban and inner-city transit systems, it no longer operated a bus system. In addition, Greyhound's management diversified into consumer products (e.g., Dial soaps and Purex laundry products) and services (e.g., Dobbs, which provides catering to airlines) and then changed the firm's name to Dial Corp. to acknowledge the firm's new configuration.[11]

cyclical industry
An industry whose sales and profits are sensitive to changes in the level of economic activity.

In addition to going through a cycle of growth and decay, industries respond to the level of economic activity. Some industries tend to be very cyclical and move with the economy. Examples of **cyclical industries** include automobiles and construction. Since consumers can defer such high-priced items from one year to the next, sales in these industries tend to be exaggerated by economic fluctuations. Car sales and housing starts vary from year to year, and, as would be expected, earnings of firms in these industries also tend to fluctuate.

These fluctuations in the revenues and earnings of a cyclical firm are illustrated by Lennar, which builds moderately priced homes in Florida, Texas, and Arizona, and, as noted, whose sales and earnings tend to be cyclical. This was evident during the late 1980s when both revenues and earnings rose rapidly, mirroring economic growth. Sales went from $154 million in 1984 to almost $400 million in 1989, and earnings per share rose from $0.22 to $0.93 during the same period. The

[10]The buyers of the bus operations took the new firm public in 1991, so Greyhound was reborn as a publicly held long-distance bus company.

[11]Dial subsequently sold the operations that manufactured buses and, in 1997, split into two companies—Dial, the manufacturer of consumer products, and Viad, a provider of services, such as contracting for trade shows, food services, and money order processing.

weaker economy in the early 1990s had a major impact on Lennar's revenues, and earnings per share fell to $0.45.

The second half of the 1990s was a period of rapid economic expansion. As may be expected, Lennar's revenues and earnings grew rapidly. From 1995 to 2000, revenues more than quadrupled, and earnings per share rose from $1.95 in 1995 to $3.64 in 2000. The combination of an expanding economy and influx of people into the areas served by Lennar produced financial prosperity for the firm.

While some industries are cyclical, others are not. Many firms operate in industries that are stable and experience growth even when the economy is in recession. For example, food processors, selected retailers, and producers of staples operate in industries that are not prone to recession. People have to eat and these purchases cannot be deferred. A company like Campbell Soups experienced revenue growth during the 1990 recession. Even a company such as Hershey Foods may experience growth during recession because consumers may defer spending on big-ticket items (e.g., new cars) but continue to treat themselves to candy.

The fact that some firms are in cyclical industries while others are in more stable industries does not imply that investors should purchase securities in the latter group to the exclusion of those in the former. Security markets tend to smooth out the fluctuations in earnings so the firm's value is related to its performance over time. As the valuation models presented in Chapter 9 indicated, cash flows, such as dividend income, and the growth in the firm's earnings over many years (all properly discounted back to the present) ultimately determine the value of the shares. The fact that a firm is in a cyclical industry does not by itself imply that the firm's securities are inferior investments. It indicates that returns from such investments may be more variable (i.e., riskier).

Perhaps the ideal investment is in a firm in a growing industry. Demand for the firm's output can be anticipated to increase, and even if more companies enter the market, the expansion of the market itself will permit the firm to maintain its profits in the face of increased competition. Identifying such industries is not easy. Airlines were considered a growth industry but fell on hard times, and mergers consolidated the industry. Technology-oriented industries, such as those that produce copiers and computers, have provided excellent examples of past growth. Even industries that were once considered mature (e.g., semiconductors) may regain their former growth.

While many previous growth industries were based on technological change, future growth need not necessarily be built on technology. Consumer tastes change, and, as incomes increase, consumers may buy different types of products. More income may be spent on services, travel, or fine-quality consumer durable goods, such as crystal instead of glass. Companies in these industries may become the next generation of growth firms. The best investments, then, should prove to be in the securities of firms that are able either to capitalize on technological change or to expand and take advantage of shifts in demand.

In addition to studying the type of industry, the financial analyst considers such factors as government regulations, labor conditions, and the financing requirements of the industry. While all industries are subject to regulation, some are more heavily regulated than others. For example, utilities such as electric and gas are subject to a large amount of regulation concerning the price firms may charge and the returns they may earn for their stockholders.[12] This regulatory climate

[12]Electric and gas utilities are currently undergoing deregulation, but the process of deregulating differs among the states. Some states are requiring that utilities separate transmission and distribution from the generation of electricity. Other states permit utilities to own both generation and distribution, but the firms must open their transmission lines to other suppliers. And some states have not started the deregulation process. The California experience illustrates one possible impact on consumers and electric companies. Deregulation has led to brownouts and the bankruptcy of Pacific Gas and Electric, when the utility had to pay more under deregulation for power but was precluded by regulation from passing on the higher costs to consumers.

EXHIBIT 12.1

Ratio of Revenues to Total Assets of Selected Firms (revenues and assets in billions)

Firm	Industry	Revenues	Assets	Sales to Total Assets
Public Service Enterprise Group	Gas and electric utility	$6.8	$20.8	0.33
Phillips Petroleum	Oil refining	20.8	20.5	1.01
Dial	Consumer products	1.6	1.4	1.14
The Limited	Retail clothing	10.1	4.1	2.61
Owens & Minor	Medical supplies distributors	3.5	0.9	3.9

Source: 2000 annual reports.

varies from state to state. If a utility operates in a state whose utility commission tends to be more stringent, that utility will often experience lower returns on assets and equity. This tends to result in lower dividends and a lower stock price.

Labor conditions also affect the analysis of an industry. The presence of labor unions or the industry's need for skilled labor can affect earnings. Unions such as those organized in airlines (e.g., the pilots' union) or mining (e.g., the United Mine Workers) can affect earnings through strikes and expensive contracts. The need for specialized labor such as engineers can also have an impact on earnings as firms pay generous salaries in an effort to bid away skilled workers from other firms. An analysis of previous labor negotiations or the supply of available skilled labor can give the financial analyst insight into the risk associated with the industry as a whole.

Financing requirements also can have an impact on firms' earnings. Industries that are growing or use a large amount of plant and equipment need more funds than more stable and less capital-intensive industries. For example, firms with oil operations need a substantial amount of plant and equipment, since drilling for oil requires investments in rigs, completed wells require transportation systems, and oil refining requires investment in plant and equipment. Differences in the amount of assets used to generate sales are illustrated in Exhibit 12.1, which presents the ratio of revenues to total assets for several firms with sales in excess of $1 billion. The table ranks the firms from the lowest to highest sales to total assets and lists each firm's industry. As may be expected, an electric and gas utility, such as Public Service Enterprise, must have substantial investment in plant and equipment to generate revenues. For every $1 in revenues, the firm had over $3 in assets. The need for substantial investments also applies to an oil refiner (Phillips). A retailer (The Limited) or a distributor (Owens & Minor) may not need large investments in plant and equipment to generate sales. Owens & Minor generates over $3 for every $1 invested in assets.[13]

The more assets needed to generate sales, the larger is the potential impact on earnings. All assets necessitate a source of funds. Debt financing requires future cash outflows (principal repayments and interest expense). Additional equity financing spreads earnings over more shares, which may decrease earnings per share. Thus, this need for funds to finance investments in plant and equipment

[13] The Limited's ratio of sales to total assets is probably overstated since The Limited rents (leases) space in malls for its retail stores. These leases do not appear on the balance sheet (i.e., they are not "capitalized"), but the use of the space is comparable to the use of any asset. The financial analyst may wish to recompute the firm's total assets to include the leases; failure to include the leased space as an asset understates The Limited's use of assets (i.e., the ratio of sales to total assets is overstated).

can affect the valuation of a firm's stock because the financing may reduce total earnings or earnings per share.

The Anticipated Economic Environment and Investment Strategies

Investing would certainly be easier if there were an identifiable relationship between a specific asset's return and the general economy. Then changes in the economy would lead to predictable changes in the asset's price and its return. In some cases, such relationships do exist. Real estate values tend to increase with higher prices in general since rents may also increase, and bond prices are responsive to changes in interest rates.

However, for many assets, especially common stocks, the linkage between an asset's price (i.e., the return it offers) and the general economy is complex. An expanding economy may increase the demand for a firm's product, which leads to higher earnings. The higher earnings may permit increased dividends or growth, since the firm has more funds to reinvest. If other factors are held constant, the expanding economy should lead to higher stock prices. Unfortunately, those factors cannot be relied on to remain constant. The expanding economy may result in higher wages and salaries, higher interest rates, increased competition, the deterioration of the value of the dollar in regard to other currencies, higher taxes, and rising prices. All these factors may have an adverse effect on the firm. The other factors offset the positive impact of the higher earnings and may even cause the increase in earnings never to materialize.

The relationship between the economy and investment selection is made more difficult when one realizes that security prices are a harbinger of economic activity and not a mirror. Changes in security prices tend to precede changes in economic activity. If an investor waits until the economy has changed before executing a particular strategy based on that economy, the action is often too late. Security prices may have already incorporated the economic change.

While this discussion suggests that it is not simple to link the economy to investing and security selection, there still are strategies the individual investor may follow. For example, changes in interest rates, changes in the rate of inflation or deflation, increased unemployment and recession, and continued economic growth may each suggest a particular strategy that is more desirable and should be followed.

Changes in Interest Rates

Those securities whose return primarily consists of a fixed flow of income, such as long-term bonds and preferred stock, are sensitive to changes in interest rates. In addition, the common stocks of financial institutions (e.g., commercial banks) and firms in cyclical industries (e.g., building supplies) are considered sensitive to interest rate changes.

Most long-term bonds pay a fixed dollar amount of interest each year. As yields rise elsewhere, this fixed flow of income is no longer competitive. Thus, anticipation of higher interest rates certainly implies that the investor should move out of long-term, fixed-income securities. Conversely, anticipation of lower interest rates implies that such securities should be acquired. Purchases of long-term bonds lock in the fixed flow of interest income, and the prices of these bonds will rise when interest rates fall.

The common stock of some firms is also sensitive to changing interest rates. For example, the prices of public utility stocks, especially those of electric power companies, fluctuate with changes in interest rates. Many of these companies distribute a large proportion of their earnings. Since much of the return the investor can anticipate is the flow of dividend income, the common stocks of public utilities are similar to long-term bonds. Unless the dividends increase to offset rising interest rates, the prices of public utility stocks will decline (the stocks' prices move inversely with changes in interest rates).

The common stocks of financial institutions are also sensitive to changes in interest rates because higher interest rates increase banks' cost of funds. Since their primary sources of funds are the various types of deposit accounts they offer, higher interest rates require banks to make higher interest payments to depositors. This reduces profitability. Thus the anticipation of higher interest rates suggests that investors shift funds from the common stocks of financial institutions into other investments.

Cyclical firms that produce such goods as houses, automobiles, and other consumer durables require a large expenditure by the consumer. The purchase of a new car or durable good may be deferred. The ability of consumers to postpone purchases of durables suggests that the demand for these products will fluctuate with changes in interest rates. Periods of high interest rates reduce demand, which, in turn, leads to lower sales and lower profits for firms in cyclical industries.

As this discussion implies, the anticipation of higher interest rates suggests that investors avoid (1) fixed-income investments, (2) firms (such as utilities or banks) whose cost of funds is sensitive to changes in interest rates and who are unable to pass on the increased cost, and (3) firms in cyclical industries whose product demand is affected by changes in interest rates. Of course, the opposite would hold for expectations of declining interest rates.

While the anticipation of higher interest rates implies that the individual should avoid many assets, that does not answer the question of which assets should be acquired. If the investor anticipates higher interest rates (and correspondingly lower security prices), he or she should acquire more liquid investments and debt instruments with short maturities, such as Treasury bills or shares of money market mutual funds. The yields on these assets will tend to increase with any increase in interest rates, and the principal is relatively safe. These short-term debt instruments frequently mature, providing an opportunity to reinvest the funds at the then current rates. Thus, if interest rates continue to increase, the investor is in the position to take advantage of the higher rates.

If the investor anticipates that interest rates will fall, he or she purchases interest-sensitive securities, such as long-term bonds. If the investor wants to follow a more aggressive strategy, that individual may purchase bonds with long terms to maturity or with poorer-quality ratings, since such bonds' prices will tend to rise more during periods of declining interest rates.

Inflation

The anticipation of inflation (i.e., expectation of higher prices of goods and services) also implies an expectation of higher interest rates for several reasons. In an attempt to slow inflation, the Federal Reserve tightens credit to reduce the supply of money and credit. In addition, creditors, aware that inflation reduces the purchasing power of the funds they lend, will protect this purchasing power by demanding a higher return for the use of their funds. These actions increase interest rates, so investors should avoid interest-sensitive securities and long-term debt instruments that pay fixed amounts of interest and should acquire short-term instruments (e.g., U.S. Treasury bills) whose yields will increase with the rate of inflation.

POINTS OF INTEREST

Deflation and the Asian Flu

Deflation in the U.S. and European economies has been virtually unheard of since the depression of the 1930s. However, the possibility of deflation in Asian economies became an issue during the late 1990s, when many Asian countries experienced major recessions. These economic downturns (sometimes referred to as the *Asian flu*) certainly hurt the earnings of U. S. and other foreign firms with operations in Asian countries. However, an additional question arose: Would deflation in Asian economies be transferred to Western economies? Would the Asian flu decrease demand for Western goods and services (reduce exports) and cause these economies to stop growing and begin to stagnate?

Price data reported by the International Monetary Fund (IMF), however, suggest that even if the Asian economies were in recession, they did not experience deflation. The International Monetary Fund (http://www.imf.org) is the standard source of statistics on international financial data such as exchange rates, prices, production, and government finance. While some commodity prices did decline, consumer price indexes reported by the IMF indicate that deflation did not occur.* This is illustrated in the following table of Asian price indexes. The table also includes the IMF's U.S. price index for comparison; 1995 is the base year with a value of 100.

Year	1995	1996	1997	1998	1999
Country					
Korea	100	104.9	109.6	117.8	121.5
Japan	100	100.1	101.8	102.5	102.2
Malaysia	100	103.5	106.2	111.8	114.9
Thailand	100	105.8	111.8	120.8	121.1
U.S.	100	102.9	105.3	107.0	109.3

Source: International Monetary Fund, *International Financial Statistics*, July 2001.

As may be seen in the table, each price index rose from 1995 through July 1999. The rate of inflation was the least in Japan, and during 1999 Japanese prices were virtually unchanged. While the Japanese economy stagnated, the data indicate that it had not entered into a period of deflation. As for the other Asian countries, the rate of inflation may have decreased, but in the aggregate prices did not fall.

Recession, of course, does reduce aggregate demand, including the demand for imports. Deflation is not required for Asian flu to spread to Western economies. So it is not surprising to learn that Western nations took steps to stimulate their economies. For example, to help reduce the possible impact that the Asian recessions could have on the U.S. economy, the Federal Reserve periodically lowered interest rates (the discount rate and the targeted federal funds rate) during 1998.

*The relationship between declining commodity prices and falling stock prices is discussed in John J. Murphy, *Technical Analysis of the Financial Markets* (New York: New York Institute of Finance, 1999). See, in particular, the discussion in Chapter 17 on falling commodity prices and their impact on commodity exporters.

However, the anticipation of inflation requires more than a passive strategy of holding short-term liquid assets. The investor should also acquire those assets that will benefit from the inflationary environment. The prices of real estate and other physical assets tend to increase during a period of inflation. Thus, the investor may seek to move out of financial assets into tangible assets.

The common stocks of selected firms may also do well in an inflationary environment. Companies that own substantial amounts of physical resources (e.g., oil, metals, land) tend to prosper during inflation, as their assets' value increases with the general rise in prices. The true value of these assets is usually hidden from investors, as firms carry the assets on their balance sheets at cost rather than at current market value. However, the prices of the common stocks of firms with such "hidden assets" may rise as the replacement cost of these assets increases. In general, any firm with a rich asset base, such as metals or real estate, may experience rapid growth in earnings that is directly attributable to the inflationary environment.

The expectation of an inflationary environment thus suggests that the investor should stress liquid assets, tangible assets, and the common stocks of firms whose asset base will be enhanced by increased asset values. Correspondingly, the investor should not acquire fixed-income instruments, long-term debt obligations, and the common stocks of firms lacking assets whose prices will rise with inflation. In a sense, the strategy is more defensive than offensive, as it is built around retaining and protecting the investor's current purchasing power and the real (deflated) value of assets held.

Deflation

Deflation, the opposite of inflation, is a period of declining prices. Deflation should not be confused with "disinflation," which is a decline in the rate of inflation. Prices are still rising but at a slower rate. During a deflationary period, the prices of tangible assets, such as real estate and precious metals, will fall.

The safest strategy is to acquire short-term liquid assets. Since deflation increases the purchasing power of money, the investor will want to hold interest-bearing liquid assets. However, deflation should also be accompanied by declining interest rates and rising bond prices. A deflationary environment should make long-term debt obligations good investments.

If the individual does acquire long-term bonds, he or she should purchase only bonds of excellent quality. Deflation may be accompanied by many bankruptcies as firms become unable to meet their financial obligations. The safest strategy for investors, then, may be to acquire only the bonds issued by the federal government and firms with strong financial statements. The investor should limit purchases to quality fixed-income securities because the bonds' value is related to the ability of the debtor firms to service the debt. If these firms are able to maintain timely interest and principal payments, the value of the bonds will appreciate as falling interest rates accompany the deflation.

Recession and Economic Stagnation

Periods of recession and economic stagnation will require different strategies. Recession is a period of rising unemployment (which may or may not be accompanied by deflation). During a recession, the Federal Reserve will expand the supply of money and credit. This expansion will at least initially decrease interest rates until the stimulus increases the level of economic activity.

The federal government may adopt an expansionary fiscal policy. Lower taxes and increased government expenditures increase aggregate demand for goods and services. This increased demand is designed to stimulate economic activity, which, in turn, should reduce the level of unemployment.

To take advantage of the economic stimulus, the investor moves out of short-term money market instruments into financial assets, especially the common stocks of firms that will benefit from the expansionary monetary and fiscal policy. Firms that produce consumer goods or durables such as automobiles and housing may profit from the expansion in the economy. Retailing firms and firms that produce leisure goods or provide services may prosper as the economy moves from the period of economic stagnation and recession toward expansion and economic growth. Increased business activity should also generate increased investment in plant and equipment. Manufacturers of capital goods, machine tools, and other inputs necessary for the production of consumer goods and services will experience increased demand, which may result in increased profits.

The investor, however, should realize that not all firms will perform well during a period of induced expansion. Expansionary monetary and fiscal policy does not imply that all firms will prosper. In addition, some forms of stimulatory policy are not general in their effect. The investment tax credit and more generous accelerated depreciation allowances, which have been used to stimulate economic expansion, favor firms that make substantial investments in plant and equipment. Firms that provide services may not require as much of an investment in long-term physical assets to generate sales. Thus these firms will not be helped as much as the firms that are able to take advantage of changes in the tax codes.

Economic Growth

A period of sustained economic growth (e.g., the 1990s) differs from a period of expansion generated through the use of stimulatory monetary and fiscal policy. As occurred during the later 1990s, monetary policy was often designed to thwart a return of inflation. During the same period, fiscal policy did not stimulate consumer demand for goods and services, as the federal government deficit shrank and moved toward a surplus. During such a period, the investor cannot rely on lower interest rates or expansionary fiscal policy to boost security prices.

Possible investments for such a period of economic growth may include common stock of firms with good financial positions and records of sustained earnings growth. An aggressive investor may emphasize firms with growth in revenues, industries with rapid technological change, and emerging industries. Such investments may supplant traditional growth companies, especially as current earnings and dividends become less important. However, during the late 1990s, some investors may have taken such a strategy to an extreme only to experience stock prices of firms emphasizing technology and emerging industries tumbling. A more defensive investor during the same period may have emphasized more traditional areas of growth and even added intermediate- and long-term bonds to generate current income, since dividend yields declined as stock prices rose.

The ability to move between strategies and to alter the portfolio's allocation of assets is obviously important as the perception of the economic environment changes or as the individual's financial objectives change. Although the investor could completely alter the portfolio by selling all positions designed for one scenario and buying securities consistent with an alternative scenario, such complete shifts may be expensive in terms of fees and in terms of taxes owed. Fortunately, there are other possibilities for rebalancing a portfolio, such as the exchange-traded fund. The discussion of these securities, however, will be deferred until Chapter 24, which covers portfolio management and asset allocation.

While portfolio management and asset selection can be designed to meet the investor's expectations of higher or lower interest rates, inflation or deflation, recession or economic growth, such portfolio construction requires active decision making. If the investor does not want to devote the time and effort to active portfolio management, that individual may buy the shares of investment companies. As was discussed in Chapter 8, each mutual fund identifies the strategies and goals (e.g., growth or income) that it follows. The investor then selects the funds whose strategies and goals are consistent with his or her own. For example, if the investor anticipates inflation and wants a position in gold, he or she may purchase shares in a gold fund. Anticipation of lower interest rates suggests purchasing shares in a bond fund.

Since more than one fund pursues a particular strategy, the individual must choose among the various funds. The investor is only relieved of the decision as to which individual securities to acquire.

Summary

Fundamental financial analysis selects stocks by identifying the strongest firms within an industry. The analysis starts by considering the direction of the aggregate economy, since security prices respond to economic activity. During periods of prosperity, stock prices tend to rise. Conversely, stock prices will fall when investors anticipate recession and sluggish economic growth.

The aggregate economy is affected by many factors, but the monetary policy of the Federal Reserve and the fiscal policy of the federal government are particularly important. Both the Fed and the federal government pursue the general economic goals of full employment, stable prices, and economic growth. The Federal Reserve affects economic activity through its impact on the supply of money and credit. The federal government affects the economy through taxation and expenditures. Both monetary and fiscal policy can alter security prices through their impact on interest rates and their impact on firms' earnings (and hence on dividends and growth rates).

Factors that affect an industry also have an impact on the individual firm. Government regulations, labor unions, skilled labor requirements, technological changes, and cyclical demand for an industry's output can and do alter the earnings of a firm. The financial analyst thus considers those characteristics of an industry that play an important role in determining the capacity of the individual firm to succeed and grow within its industry.

Investment strategies are affected by the economic environment. During a period of rising interest rates, the investor should seek liquid, short-term investments and avoid long-term, fixed-income securities. Expectations of increasing inflation also call for avoiding long-term financial investments, as well as for acquiring those tangible assets whose value will increase with the rate of inflation, such as real estate and precious metals. Expectation of deflation suggests that these assets should be avoided.

During a period of recession, the investor should acquire assets such as the common stocks of firms that will benefit from expansionary monetary and fiscal policy. While in a period of sustained economic growth, the individual may prefer long-term investments in firms whose position is sufficiently strong to sustain and finance growth.

None of these economic scenarios has one simple strategy. There are so many possible investments, ranging from low risk to high risk, that may be appropriate for a particular investment strategy. Also, some alternatives may not be appropriate for a particular investor whose willingness to bear risk differs from the risk exposure generated by the particular asset. However, these same assets may be combined in ways that will suit another investor's strategy and willingness to bear risk.

Active management of a portfolio based on moves in the economy requires portfolio shifts before the economy changes. The individual must anticipate when interest rates will rise or fall in order to take advantage of the price changes in fixed-income securities. The investor must anticipate inflation in order to purchase real assets before the inflation occurs. To take advantage of sustained economic growth, the investor must anticipate when that growth will occur and which firms it will benefit. Once economic change has occurred, it will be too late, as security prices will have already changed.

It is not sufficient to base portfolio decisions on today's economy. It is the future economic environment that is crucial, which helps explain why portfolio decisions based on the anticipated economy are among the most difficult decisions facing the individual investor.

Questions

1) What are the phases of a business cycle? Have the periods of expansion and contraction changed since the Great Depression?
2) What factors, besides the expected rate of inflation, may affect the rate of interest a borrower pays?
3) What is the Federal Reserve? What are its economic goals? How may the Fed pursue its economic goals? How may the tools of monetary policy affect security prices?
4) What are M-1 and M-2? How may the Federal Reserve alter M-1 or M-2?
5) What are the differences between monetary policy and fiscal policy?
6) What is a cyclical industry? Is it undesirable to invest in firms in cyclical industries? Why may leading economic indicators be important to the analysis of a cyclical firm?
7) Classify the following firms as cyclical, growth, or stable (based on the nature of their respective industries).
   a) Bristol-Myers Squibb (pharmaceuticals)
   b) Microsoft
   c) Dominion Resources
   d) Alcoa
   e) U.S. Homes
8) If an investor expects interest rates and prices to decline, what types of financial assets should be acquired? What are the linkages between higher interest rates and stock prices?
9) Should economic stimulus by the Federal Reserve generate higher or lower earnings? Why may an expansionary monetary policy encourage investments in long-term financial assets?
10) Which is more important from an investment perspective: current earnings or anticipated earnings?
11) Using the Internet addresses in footnote 3, determine the CPI as of the end of the last four years.

12) What were the revenues and earnings per share of Lennar Corporation (LEN) for the years after 2000? Information concerning the firm may be found through its home page (http://www.lennar.com) or through the SEC's EDGAR (http://www.sec.gov or http://www.edgar-online.com).

THE FINANCIAL ADVISOR'S INVESTMENT CASE

The Unionville Teachers' Investment Club

You have been invited to speak to the newly formed Unionville Teachers' Investment Club. Initially, each member contributed $500, and these funds were placed in an interest-bearing money market account pending the first investment decision. The club members decided to invite a stockbroker to discuss individual stocks and you to cover the macroeconomy. The members have little knowledge of the Federal Reserve's monetary policy and the federal government's fiscal policy except what they hear nightly on local and national news broadcasts.

While a sophisticated discussion of macroeconomics would be inappropriate, you believe that discussing possible linkages between stock prices and economic policy might help the members understand factors that affect stock prices. Since stock prices are related to earnings, dividends, and required returns, you decide to cover linkages between monetary and fiscal policy, and those three factors. To organize your talk, you decide to answer the following questions:

1) What is monetary policy and how does the Federal Reserve execute changes in monetary policy?
2) What is fiscal policy and how is it different from monetary policy?
3) How do monetary and fiscal policy affect a firm's earnings?
4) Why may this impact on earnings affect a firm's dividends and its ability to expand?
5) Why will a change in interest rates affect investors' willingness to own stock? Does the anticipation of higher interest rates argue for investing in stock?
6) Are all firms equally affected by changes in economic policy?
7) Why are expected changes in economic policy as important as the actual changes?

Security Selection: Analysis of Financial Statements

13

Even though financial markets are efficient, and the majority of investors, including professional portfolio managers, do not and will not outperform the market on a consistent basis, individuals do buy and sell securities. On a typical day, over a billion shares trade. It is not unusual for over a million shares to trade in an individual stock daily. On June 8, 2001, over 50 million shares of Cisco Systems traded on the Nasdaq.

Obviously, some one thought the shares were undervalued while other thought they were overvalued. How did they come to these conclusions? One method is to analyze a firm's financial statements. Such analysis is employed in "value investing," which focuses on the financial condition of the firm. "Growth investing," which focuses on changes in revenues or earnings, also uses selected financial data.

This chapter is devoted to ratios used to analyze a firm's financial statements. The analysis may cover a period of time to determine trends such as growth in earnings. An alternative approach compares one firm with similar firms or with industry averages to determine the firm's position within its industry.

While there are many ratios that the financial analyst may compute, they all may be classified into one of five groups. Liquidity ratios seek to determine if a firm can meet its financial obligations as they come due. Activity ratios tell how rapidly assets flow through the firm; profitability ratios measure performance. Leverage ratios measure the extent to which a firm uses debt financing, and coverage ratios measure the firm's ability to make ("cover") a specific payment.

Each ratio is defined, explained, and illustrated. This is followed by a discussion of which ratios are the most appropriate for bondholders and which are the most important from the stockholders' perspective. The third section applies ratio analysis to a firm's financial statements to determine the firm's financial condition. This analysis is the backbone of value investing and fundamental to the dividend-growth model presented in Chapter 9, which determined if a stock is under- or overvalued.

Because investments in plant and equipment, the repayment of debt, and the distribution of dividends require cash outflows, the chapter ends with a discussion of the firm's ability to generate cash. The firm's sources and uses of funds are enumerated in the statement of cash flows. Unfortunately, many investors overlook this financial statement. By enumerating where the firm obtained its sources of funds and how these funds were used, the statement of cash flows may provide the best indication of the firm's changing financial position.

Learning Objectives

After completing this chapter you should be able to:

1 Differentiate between (a) the current ratio and the quick ratio; (b) accounts receivable turnover and the average collection period; (c) gross profit margin, operating profit margin, and net profit margin; and (d) the return on assets and the return on equity.

2 Identify which ratios are of primary interest to creditors and stockholders.

3 Apply ratios to analyze the financial statements of a firm.

4 Compare a firm's ratios with those of other firms in its industry.
5 Illustrate how price/earnings (P/E), price/book (P/B), price/sales (P/S), and the PEG ratios are used to help value and select stocks.
6 Analyze the sources and uses of a firm's cash.
7 Explain why cash and earnings are not synonymous and how a firm could operate at a loss and generate cash.

Ratio Analysis

Ratios, which are probably the most frequently used tool to analyze a company, are popular because they are readily understood and can be computed with ease. In addition, the information used in ratio analysis is easy to obtain, for many ratios employ data available in a firm's annual and quarterly reports. Ratios are used not only by investors and financial analysts but also by a firm's management and its creditors. Management may use ratio analysis to plan, to control, and to identify weaknesses within the firm. Creditors use the analysis to establish the ability of the borrower to pay interest and retire debt. Stockholders are primarily concerned with performance and employ ratio analysis to measure profitability.[1]

Although a variety of people use ratio analysis, they should select those ratios that are best suited to their specific purposes. As is illustrated later in this chapter, a creditor is concerned primarily with the firm's ability to pay interest and repay principal and is less concerned with the rate at which the firm's equipment is used. While the rate at which fixed assets turn over may affect the ability of the company to pay the interest and principal, the typical creditor is more concerned with the firm's capacity to generate cash.

The investor may find that a specific industry requires additional ratios or more sophisticated versions of a particular ratio. For example, the ratios used to analyze public utilities are different from those used to analyze railroads. Although both are highly regulated and have similarities, such as large investments in plant and equipment, the natures of the industries are different, including factors such as the labor requirements, competition, and the demand for each service. Emphasis, then, is placed on different factors, such as miles traveled per ton of freight for railroads versus the peak load requirements relative to the average demand for electricity for an electric utility.

time-series analysis
An analysis of a firm over a period of time.

cross-sectional analysis
An analysis of several firms in the same industry at a point in time.

Ratios may be computed and interpreted from two perspectives. They may be compiled for a number of years to perceive trends, which is called **time-series analysis**, or they may be compared at a given time for several firms within the same industry, known as **cross-sectional analysis**. Time-series and cross-sectional analyses may be used together, as the analyst will compare the firm to its industry over a period of years.

One ratio by itself means little, but several ratios together may give a clear picture of a firm's strengths and weaknesses. Rarely will all the ratios indicate the same general tendency. However, when they are taken as a group, the ratios often give the investigator an indication of the direction in which the firm is moving and its financial position in comparison to other firms in its industry.

[1]Benjamin Graham is considered to be the father of modern financial analysis that employs ratio analysis of financial statements. His text is a classic and employs many of the ratios described in this chapter. See Benjamin Graham, David L. Dodd, Sidney Cottle, and Charles Tatham, *Security Analysis: Principles and Techniques*, 5th ed. (New York: McGraw-Hill, 1988). See especially part 4, "The Valuation of Common Stock," for the conservative financial approach to the analysis of common stock. Several books that are a cross between traditional text and publications for the sophisticated investor or financial analyst are also available. These include Leopold A. Bernstein, *Financial Statement Analysis Theory, Applications & Interpretation*, 6th ed. (New York: McGraw-Hill, 1998); Charles H. Gibson, *Financial Statement Analysis*, 7th ed. (Cincinnati, OH: South-Western Publishing Co., 1997); and Edward Renshaw, *The Practical Forecasters' Almanac* (Homewood, IL: Business-One Irwin, 1992).

EXHIBIT 13.1

Hershey Foods Corporation Consolidated Balance Sheet

December 31, (in millions)	1999	1998
ASSETS		
Current assets		
Cash and cash equivalents	$ 118.0	$ 39.0
Accounts receivable	353.8	451.3
Inventories	602.2	493.2
Deferred income taxes	80.3	58.5
Other	125.6	91.9
Total current assets	1,279.9	1,133.9
Property, plant, and equipment	1,510.5	1,648.1
Other assets	556.3	622.1
Total assets	$3,346.7	$3,404.1
LIABILITIES AND STOCKHOLDERS' EQUITY		
Current liabilities		
Accounts payable	$ 136.6	$ 156.9
Accrued liabilities	292.5	294.4
Short-term loans	209.2	345.9
Other	74.5	17.6
Total current liabilities	712.8	814.8
Long-term debt	878.2	879.1
Other long-term liabilities	331.0	346.8
Deferred income taxes	326.0	321.1
Total liabilities	2,248.0	2,361.8
Stockholders' equity		
Common stock shares outstanding 149.5 in 1999; 149.5 in 1998	149.5	149.5
Additional paid-in capital	30.4	30.4
Retained earnings	2,513.3	2,189.7
Treasury stock repurchased at cost	(1,552.7)	(1,267.4)
Other adjustments	(32.0)	(59.9)
Total stockholders' equity	1,098.7	1,042.3
Total liabilities and stockholders' equity	$3,346.7	$3,404.1

Source: Adapted from Hershey Foods Corporation *Proxy Statement* and *1999 Annual Report to Stockholders.*

The subsequent sections of this chapter cover a variety of ratios. The illustrations of these ratios employ data taken from the balance sheet and income statements of Hershey Foods Corporation (HSY—the NYSE trading symbol). Hershey's balance sheet and income statement for 1999 and 1998 are given in Exhibits 13.1 and 13.2 (p. 390). The 1999 data are used to illustrate the ratios, and both years plus several additional years' data are employed later in the chapter to illustrate the use of ratios in time-series analysis.

Before proceeding, the reader needs to be forewarned that several ratios have more than one definition. The definition used by one analyst may differ from that

EXHIBIT 13.2

Hershey Foods Corporation Statement of Income

For the years ended December 31, (in millions except per-share data)	1999	1998
Net Sales	$3,970.9	$4,435.6
Costs and expenses		
Cost of goods sold	2,354.7	2,625.1
Selling, marketing, and administrative	1,057.8	1,167.8
Gain on sale of business	243.7	—
Earnings before interest and taxes	802.1	642.7
Interest expense	74.3	85.7
Provision for income taxes	267.5	216.1
Net income	$ 460.2	$ 340.9
Net income per share	$ 3.29	$ 2.38
Net income per share—diluted	$ 3.26	$ 2.34
Cash dividends per share	$ 1.00	$ 0.96

Source: Adapted from Hershey Foods Corporation *Proxy Statement* and *1999 Annual Report to Stockholders.*

used by others. These differences can arise from averaging the data in two financial statements. (See, for instance, the two approaches to inventory turnover discussed below.) Another source of differences can be what is included or excluded. (See, for instance, the various definitions of the debt ratios.) As is illustrated later in this chapter, you cannot assume that the analysis obtained from one source is comparable to that provided by an alternative source. This problem may be particularly acute with analyses of financial statements that may be found on the Internet. Of course, you can avoid this problem by performing the analysis yourself!

Liquidity Ratios

Liquidity is the ease with which assets may be quickly converted into cash without the firm's incurring a loss. If a firm has a high degree of liquidity, it will be able to meet its debt obligations as they become due. Therefore, liquidity ratios are a useful tool for the firm's creditors, who are concerned with being paid. Liquidity ratios are so called because they indicate the degree of liquidity or "moneyness" of the company's assets.

The Current Ratio

current ratio
Current assets divided by current liabilities; a measure of liquidity.

The **current ratio** is the ratio of current assets to current liabilities.

$$\text{Current ratio} = \frac{\text{Current assets}}{\text{Current liabilities}}.$$

It indicates the extent to which the current liabilities, which must be paid within a year, are "covered" by current assets. For HSY, the current ratio as of December 31, 1999, was

POINTS OF INTEREST

Generally Accepted Accounting Principles (GAAP)

Accounting statements provide financial information concerning an enterprise. Although the emphasis in this text is the statements' applications to firms, financial statements may be constructed for governments (e.g., the local municipality), nonprofit organizations (such as the Metropolitan Opera), or individuals. In all cases, these statements show the financial condition of the entity and its assets and how they were financed. This information can then be used to aid financial decision making.

To be useful in decision making, financial statements must be reliable, understandable, and comparable. Reliability requires the statements to be objective and unbiased. The data included on the statements should be verifiable by independent experts. This does not mean that two accountants working with the same information will construct identical financial statements. Individual opinions and judgments may lead to different financial statements. An example that involves the accountant's judgment is the allowance for doubtful accounts receivable. Two accountants may establish differing amounts that will affect the firm's financial statements. However, it should not be concluded that two accountants will construct widely different statements. While the financial statements may differ, the amount of differentiation should be modest.

Accountants' second goal is that financial statements be understandable. The statement should be presented in an orderly manner and be readable by informed laypersons as well as professionals. Investors and other individuals who use financial statements need not know all the principles used to construct a financial statement. However, an intelligent individual should be able to read a firm's profitability, its assets and liabilities, and its cash flow.

Comparability requires that one set of financial statements can be compared to the same financial statements constructed over different accounting periods. The principles used to construct one year's statements should be used for subsequent years. If the principles being applied are changed, the previous years' statements should be restated. If the firm's operations change, the financial statements should also reflect these changes. If, for example, the firm discontinues part of its operations, its sales, expenses, and profits for previous years should be restated. If this adjustment is not made, the users of the financial statements will be unable to compare the firm's financial condition and performance over a period of time for its continuing operations.

To increase the objectivity of financial statements, a general framework for accounting and financial reports has been established by the Financial Accounting Standards Board (FASB). Accounting principles that are "generally accepted" also receive the support of the American Institute of Certified Public Accountants and the Securities and Exchange Commission (SEC). Although these bodies establish the principles under which financial statements are constructed, it should not be concluded that the principles are static. Their conceptual framework changes over time with changes in the business environment and the needs of the statements' users. For example, increases in foreign investments and fluctuations in the value of foreign currencies have generated a need for better methods of accounting for these foreign investments. This problem, plus others such as inflation, pension liabilities, and stock options, have resulted in changes in accounting principles as the profession seeks to improve the informational content of financial statements.

$$\frac{\$1{,}279.9}{\$712.8} = 1.80,$$

which indicates that for every $1 that the firm had to pay within the year, there was $1.80 in the form of either cash or an asset that was to be converted into cash within the year.

For most industries, it is desirable to have more current assets than current liabilities. It is sometimes asserted that a firm should have at least $2 in current assets for every $1 in current liabilities, or a current ratio of at least 2:1. If the current ratio is 2:1, then the firm's current assets could deteriorate in value by 50 percent and the firm would still be able to meet its short-term liabilities.

Although such rules of thumb are convenient, they need not apply to all industries. For example, electric utilities usually have current liabilities that exceed their current assets (i.e., a current ratio of less than 1:1). Does this worry short-term creditors? No, because the short-term assets are primarily accounts receivable from electricity users and are of high quality. Should a customer fail to pay an electricity bill, the company threatens to cut off service, and this threat is usually sufficient to induce payment. The higher the quality of the current assets (i.e., the greater the probability that these assets can be converted to cash at their stated value), the less vital it is for the current ratio to exceed 1:1. The reason, then, for selecting a rule of thumb such as a current ratio of at least 2:1 is for the protection of the creditors, who are aware that not all current assets will, in fact, be converted into cash.

Both creditors and investors want to know if the firm has sufficient liquid assets to meet its bills. Obviously, a low current ratio is undesirable because it indicates financial weakness, but a high current ratio may also be undesirable. A high current ratio may imply that the firm is not using its funds to best advantage. For example, the company may have issued long-term debt and used it to finance an excessive amount of inventory or accounts receivable. The high current ratio may also indicate that the firm is not taking advantage of available short-term financing or is mismanaging its current assets, which reduces its profitability. A high or low numerical value for the current ratio may be a signal to creditors and stockholders that the management of short-term assets and liabilities should be revised.

The Quick Ratio

quick ratio (acid test)
Current assets excluding inventory divided by current liabilities; a measure of liquidity.

The current ratio gives an indication of the company's ability to meet its current liabilities as they become due, but it has a major weakness. It is an aggregate measure of liquidity that does not differentiate between the degrees of liquidity of the various types of current assets, which may be in the form of cash, accounts receivable, or inventory. Cash is a liquid asset, but it may take many months before inventory is sold and turned into cash. This failure of the current ratio to distinguish between the degrees of liquidity has led to the development of the quick ratio, which omits inventory from the calculation. The **quick ratio** or *acid test* (both names are used) is determined as follows:

$$\textbf{Acid test ratio} = \frac{\textbf{Current assets} - \textbf{Inventory}}{\textbf{Current liabilities}}.$$

For HSY, the acid test ratio is

$$\frac{\$1{,}279.9 - \$602.2}{\$712.8} = 0.95,$$

which is lower than the current ratio of 1.80. The difference lies, of course, in the inventory that the company is carrying, which is excluded from the acid test.[2]

A low quick ratio implies that the firm may have difficulty meeting its current liabilities as they become due if it must rely on converting inventory into cash. However, a low quick ratio does not indicate that the firm will fail to pay its bills. The ability to meet liabilities is influenced by such factors as (1) the rate at which cash flows into the firm, (2) the time at which bills become due, (3) the relationship

[2]The quick ratio may also be defined as

$$\frac{\text{Cash} + \text{Cash equivalents} + \text{Accounts receivable}}{\text{Current liabilities}}.$$

It might appear the two definitions are the same, but they are not if the firm has current assets other than cash, cash equivalents, accounts receivable, and inventory. This second definition excludes other current assets such as prepaid expenses, while the definition in the text does not. If this second definition is used for Hershey, the quick ratio is (\$118.0 + \$353.8)/\$712.8 = 0.66, which is lower and suggests the firm is less liquid.

between the company and its creditors and their willingness to roll over debt, and (4) the firm's ability to raise additional capital. The acid test merely indicates how well the current liabilities are covered by cash and by highly liquid assets that may be converted into cash relatively quickly. Because this ratio takes into account that not all current assets are equally liquid, it is a more precise measure of liquidity than is the current ratio.

The Components of Current Assets

Another approach to analyzing liquidity is to rank current assets with regard to their degree of liquidity and to determine the proportion of each asset in relation to total current assets. The most liquid current asset is cash, followed by marketable securities (i.e., cash equivalents), such as Treasury bills or certificates of deposit, accounts receivable, and finally inventory. For HSY, the proportion of each asset to total current assets is

Current Assets	Proportion of Total Current Assets
Cash and cash equivalents	9.2%
Accounts receivable	27.6
Inventory	47.0
Other current assets	16.2
	100.0%

Since this technique ranks current assets from the most liquid to the least liquid, it gives an indication of the degree of liquidity of the firm's current assets. If a large proportion of total current assets is inventory, the company is not very liquid. HSY appears to be reasonably liquid, as almost 37 percent of its current assets are composed of cash, cash equivalents, and accounts receivable.[3]

This method of separating total current assets into their components and then ranking them according to their degree of liquidity gives management, creditors, and investors a better measure of the firm's ability to meet its current liabilities than does the current ratio. When used with the quick ratio, these two measures supplement the current ratio and should be used to analyze the liquidity of any firm that carries a significant amount of inventory in its operations.

Activity Ratios

Activity ratios indicate at what rate the firm is turning its inventory and accounts receivable into cash. The more rapidly the firm turns over its inventory and receivables, the more quickly it acquires cash. High turnover indicates that the firm is rapidly receiving cash and is in a better position to pay its liabilities as they become due. Such high turnover, however, need not imply that the firm is maximizing profits. For example, high inventory turnover may indicate that the firm is selling items for too low a price in order to induce quicker sales. A high receivables turnover may be an indication that the firm is offering large discounts for rapid payment, which could result in lower profits.

[3]The management may pay off current obligations prior to the end of the fiscal year. Such reductions in current liabilities improve the balance sheet, but they also reduce the firm's cash. If HSY follows this strategy, its year-end cash would constitute a minimal proportion of its current assets.

Inventory Turnover

inventory turnover
The speed with which inventory is sold.

Inventory turnover is defined as annual sales divided by average inventory. That is,

$$\textbf{Inventory turnover} = \frac{\textbf{Sales}}{\textbf{Average inventory}}.$$

This ratio uses average inventory throughout the year. Such an average reduces the impact of fluctuations in the level of inventory. If only year-end inventory were used and it was abnormally high at the end of the fiscal year, the turnover would appear to be slower. Conversely, if inventory was lower than normal at the year's end, the turnover would appear faster than in fact it was. Averaging the inventory reduces the impact of these fluctuations. Management may use any number of observations (e.g., monthly or weekly) to determine the average inventory. The information available to investors, however, may be limited to the level of inventory given in the firm's annual reports.

For HSY, the level of inventory was \$602.2 in 1999 and \$493.2 in 1998. The average for the two years was

$$\frac{\$602.2 + \$493.2}{2} = \$547.7.$$

Thus, for HSY, inventory turnover was

$$\frac{\textbf{Sales}}{\textbf{Average inventory}} = \frac{\$3,970.9}{\$547.7} = 7.25.$$

This indicates that annual sales are about 7 times the level of inventory. Inventory thus turns over 7.25 times a year, or about once every 7 weeks.

Inventory turnover may also be defined as the cost of goods sold divided by the inventory. That is,

$$\textbf{Inventory turnover} = \frac{\textbf{Cost of goods sold}}{\textbf{Average inventory}}.$$

If this definition is used, HSY's inventory turnover is

$$\frac{\$2,354.7}{\$547.7} = 4.3.$$

This definition places more emphasis on recouping the cost of the goods. However, creditors may prefer to use sales, since sales produce the funds to service the debt. Dun and Bradstreet uses sales in its industry averages, and any creditors who use Dun and Bradstreet data as a source of comparison must remember to use sales instead of cost of goods sold to be consistent.

Average Collection Period

average collection period (days sales outstanding)
The number of days required to collect accounts receivable.

The **average collection period**, which is also referred to as *days sales outstanding,* measures how long it takes a firm to collect its accounts receivable. The faster the company collects its receivables, the more rapidly it receives cash and hence can pay its obligations, such as its interest expense. The average collection period (ACP) is determined as follows:

$$\text{ACP} = \frac{\text{Receivables}}{\text{Sales per day}}.$$

Sales per day are total sales divided by 360 (or 365) days. For HSY the average collection period is

$$\frac{\$353.8}{\$3{,}970.9 \div 360} = 32.1.$$

This indicates that the firm takes 32 days to convert its receivables into money.

receivables turnover
The speed with which a firm collects its accounts receivable.

Receivables turnover, which is another way of viewing the average collection period, may be defined as annual credit sales divided by receivables.[4] By this definition,

$$\text{Receivables turnover} = \frac{\text{Annual credit sales}}{\text{Accounts receivable}}.$$

An alternative definition of receivables turnover substitutes annual sales for annual credit sales. That is,

$$\text{Receivables turnover} = \frac{\text{Annual sales}}{\text{Accounts receivable}}.$$

Either definition is acceptable as long as it is applied consistently. Although management has access to the information used in both formulas, investors may be limited to the data provided by the firm. If annual credit sales are not reported by the firm, the investor will have no choice but to use annual sales.

Since the HSY income statement does not give annual credit sales, the first definition cannot be used; hence, for HSY,

$$\text{Receivables turnover} = \frac{\$3{,}970.9}{\$353.8} = 11.2.$$

This indicates that annual sales are 11.2 times the amount of receivables. The larger the ratio, the more rapidly the firm turns its credit sales into cash. A turnover of 11.2 times per year indicates that receivables are paid off on the average of every 1.07 months. This is the same information that was derived by computing the average collection period, since 32 days is approximately 1.07 months.

All of the previously mentioned turnover ratios need to be interpreted with much caution. These ratios are static, for they use information derived at a given time (i.e., the year-end figures on the balance sheet). The ratios, however, are dealing with dynamic events; they are concerned with the length of time it takes for an event to occur. Because of this problem with time, these turnover ratios, which are based on year-end figures, may be misleading if the firm has (1) seasonal sales, (2) sporadic sales during the fiscal year, or (3) any growth in inventory and sales during the fiscal year. Creditors and bondholders need to be aware of these potential problems since they can lead to incorrect conclusions concerning the firm's capacity to service its debt.

Fixed Asset Turnover

Inventory and accounts receivable turnover stress the speed with which current assets flow up the balance sheet. Rapid inventory turnover means inventory is

[4] Some analysts may prefer to average the accounts receivable in the same way that inventory was averaged for the inventory turnover ratio.

quickly sold and converted into either cash or an account receivable. The average collection period tells how long it takes the firm to collect the account (i.e., how long it takes to receive cash from a credit sale).

Turnover ratios may also be constructed for long-term assets. Such a ratio is the **fixed asset turnover.**

fixed asset turnover
Ratio of sales to fixed assets; tells how many fixed assets are needed to generate sales.

$$\textbf{Fixed asset turnover} = \frac{\textbf{Annual sales}}{\textbf{Fixed assets}}.$$

Fixed assets are the firm's plant and equipment, and this ratio indicates the amount of plant and equipment that were used to generate the firm's sales. For HSY, the fixed asset turnover was

$$\textbf{Fixed asset turnover} = \frac{\$3{,}970.9}{\$1{,}510.5} = 2.63.$$

This indicates that HSY generated \$2.63 in sales for every \$1 invested in plant and equipment (i.e., fixed assets).

Many firms (such as utilities) must have substantial investment in plant and equipment to produce the output they sell. Other firms, especially those providing services, need only modest amounts of fixed assets. The more rapidly fixed assets turn over, the smaller the amount of plant and equipment the firm is employing. While the ratio is obviously sensitive to the firm's industry, it does help measure the efficiency with which management is using its long-term assets.

Profitability Ratios

The amount that a firm earns is particularly important to investors. Earnings accrue to stockholders and either are distributed to them as dividends or are retained. Retained earnings represent an additional investment in the corporation by stockholders. Obviously, a firm's performance is a crucial element in fundamental analysis.

Profitability ratios are measures of performance that indicate the amount the firm is earning relative to some base, such as sales, assets, or equity. The **gross profit margin** is

gross profit margin
Percentage earned on sales after deducting the cost of goods sold.

$$\textbf{Gross profit margin} = \frac{\textbf{Revenues} - \textbf{Cost of goods sold}}{\textbf{Sales}}.$$

For HSY, the gross profit margin for 1999 was

$$\textbf{Gross profit margin} = \frac{\$3{,}970.9 - 2{,}354.7}{\$3{,}970.9} = 40.7\%,$$

which indicates the firm earned almost \$0.41 on every dollar of sales before considering administrative expenses, depreciation, and financing costs.

The **operating profit margin** is operating income divided by sales.

operating profit margin
Percentage earned on sales before adjusting for nonrecurring items, interest, and taxes.

$$\textbf{Operating profit margin} = \frac{\textbf{Operating earnings}}{\textbf{Sales}}.$$

Operating income is often defined as earnings before interest and taxes, and in most cases that is sufficient unless the firm has extraordinary or nonrecurring items included in earnings before interest and taxes. While management will report these items as a separate entry, they may be reported as part of income before interest and taxes, in which case these earnings are not indicative of operating income.

For HSY, 1999 earnings before interest and taxes ($802.1 million) includes a large gain from the sale of a business ($243.7 million). In this case, using earnings before interest and taxes as a measure of operating income will be misleading. The analyst would use "income from operations" ($802.1 − $243.7 = $558.4 million) for the calculation of the operating profit margin:

$$\textbf{Operating profit margin} = \frac{\$558.4}{\$3{,}970.9} = 14.1\%.$$

(If the analyst had used earnings before interest and taxes, the ratio would have been $802.1/$3,970.9 = 20.2%, which is perceptibly higher than 14.1%.)

net profit margin
The ratio of earnings after interest and taxes to sales.

The **net profit margin** is the ratio of profits after taxes to sales. That is,

$$\textbf{Net profit margin} = \frac{\textbf{Earnings after taxes}}{\textbf{Sales}}.$$

For HSY, the net profit margin was

$$\textbf{Net profit margin} = \frac{\$460.2}{\$3{,}970.9} = 11.6\%.$$

The net profit margin indicates that HSY earned $0.116 on every $1 of sales. If the gain on the sale of the business had been excluded, the net profit margin would have been lower. Whether the analyst or investor should include or exclude the profit from the sale in the calculation of the net profit margin is a judgment call. The gain does generate earnings for stockholders, but such gains are unlikely to recur, in which case the analyst may subtract the nonrecurring gain prior to the calculation of the net profit margin.

POINTS OF INTEREST

When Is an Increase in Earnings a Loss?

Financial analysis may be more concerned with a firm's operating income than with the bottom line, or net income. Analysts will determine how that net income was achieved. Sometimes a firm's income from operations may have declined or the firm may have even operated at a loss, but as the result of other sources of income, such as interest, capital gains, or tax benefits, the firm is able to report an increase in net income.

Consider the following abridged income statements derived from McDermott International, Inc. Although sales rose, the firm operated at a loss but was able to report an increase in net income and earnings per share because of interest income, capital gains, and tax benefits. Many of these income-producing items are nonrecurring. For example, the firm may report the benefit of tax credits in the year in which they occur, but such tax savings will not necessarily occur every year. Thus the financial analyst may place more emphasis on the operating loss than on the net income as an indicator of the firm's earning capacity.

Years Ended March 31,	X1	X0
Revenues (in millions)	$3,257	$3,223
Costs of operations	2,879	2,892
Gross profit	378	331
Depreciation	158	149
Selling and administrative expenses	308	301
Operating income	**(88)**	**(109)**
Other income (interest, capital gains)	88	53
Tax benefits (e.g., investment tax credits)	71	90
Extraordinary items and minority dividends (net)	(12)	(3)
Net income	**$ 59**	**$ 31**
Earnings per share	$ 1.60	$ 0.83

Source: McDermott International *Annual Report*, various issues.

While the computation of all three profit margin ratios may seem unnecessary, they tell the analyst different things about profitability. The gross profit margin is sensitive only to changes in the cost of goods sold. The operating profit margin is affected by all operating expenses. Changes in advertising or depreciation affect the operating but not the gross profit margin. By computing both ratios, the financial analyst can determine whether changes in the cost of goods sold or changes in other operating expenses are affecting operating income.[5]

The net profit margin adds the impact of financing expenses and taxes on profitability. A change in income tax rates affects net profits but not operating profits. This impact may be important for stockholders who are concerned with the bottom line (net income) but not for bondholders whose interest is paid before income tax. Bondholders may be concerned with expenses that affect operating income but not those that affect net income.

return on assets
The ratio of earnings to total assets.

Other profitability ratios measure the **return on assets** and the return on equity. The return on assets is net earnings divided by assets. That is,

$$\textbf{Return on assets} = \frac{\textbf{Earnings after taxes}}{\textbf{Total assets}}.$$

For HSY, the return on assets was

$$\frac{\$460.2}{\$3{,}346.7} = 13.8\%.$$

Thus, HSY earned $0.138 on every $1 of assets. This ratio measures the return on the firm's resources (i.e., its assets). It is an all-encompassing measure of performance that indicates the total that management is able to achieve on all the firm's assets. This return on assets takes into account the profit margin and the rate at which the assets are turned over (e.g., the rate at which the firm sells its inventory and collects its accounts receivable) as well as taxes and extraordinary items.

Although return on assets gives an aggregate measure of the firm's performance, it does not tell how well management is performing for the stockholders. This performance is indicated by the return on equity, which was discussed in Chapter 11. The return on equity uses earnings after taxes, which are the earnings available to the firm's stockholders. For HSY, the return on equity is

$$\textbf{Return on equity} = \frac{\textbf{Earnings after taxes}}{\textbf{Equity}} = \frac{\$460.2}{\$1{,}098.7} = 41.9\%.$$

Equity is the sum of stock, additional paid-in capital (if any), and retained earnings (if any). The return on equity measures the amount that the firm is earning on the stockholders' investment.[6]

[5]Some financial analysts also determine profit margins using earnings before interest, taxes, and depreciation and amortization (EBITDA). As was explained in the section on corporate taxation in Chapter 6, depreciation is the allocation of the cost of a tangible asset (i.e., plant and equipment) over a period of time. Amortization is the allocation of an intangible asset such as goodwill over a period of time. Both depreciation and amortization are noncash expenses. As is explained later in this chapter in the section on the statement of cash flows, noncash expenses are added back to earnings to determine the cash generated by operations.

By using EBITDA instead of operating income (EBIT), the financial analyst is subtracting only cash expenses (e.g., cost of goods sold) from revenue. If two firms have identical EBIT but one has larger depreciation expenses, its cash expenses are lower. Lower cash expenses means that EBITDA is larger; the firm has lower cash outflows. By using earnings before interest, taxes, and depreciation and amortization expenses (EBITDA) as well as operating earnings (EBIT) and net earnings, the financial analyst is better able to determine the firm's ability to generate cash. Such cash then may be used to retire debt, distributed to stockholders, or invested in potentially profitable assets.

[6]A return on equity of 41.9% is exceptionally high. In this example, the return on equity includes the profitable sale of a business, which may artificially increase the percentage. For this reason, it is often desirable to remove extraordinary items such as a sale of part of the business before computing the return on equity. Another possibility is to compute the ratio over a period of time to establish a more accurate indication of the continuing return that management is able to earn for stockholders.

Many stockholders may be concerned not with the return on the firm's *total* equity but with the return earned on the equity attributable to the common stock. To determine this return on common stock, adjustments must be made for any preferred stock the firm has outstanding. First, the dividends that are paid to preferred stockholders must be subtracted from earnings to obtain earnings available to common stockholders. Second, the contribution of the preferred stock to the firm's equity must be subtracted to obtain the investment in the firm by the common stockholders. Thus, the return to common stockholders is

$$\text{Return on common equity} = \frac{\text{Earnings after taxes} - \text{Preferred stock dividends}}{\text{Equity} - \text{Preferred stock}}.$$

Of course, if the firm has no preferred stock, the return on equity and the return on the common equity are identical.

For HSY, the return on common equity for 1999 was

$$\text{Return on common equity} = \frac{\$460.2 - 0}{\$1{,}098.7 - 0} = 41.9\%.$$

The ratio indicates that HSY earned a return of \$0.419 for every \$1 invested by common stockholders. Thus, while HSY achieved only 13.8 percent on its total assets, it was able to earn 41.9 percent on the stockholders' investment.

Leverage or Capitalization Ratios

financial leverage
The use of borrowed funds to acquire an asset.

debt ratio
The ratio of debt to total assets; a measure of the use of debt financing.

How can a firm magnify the return on its stockholders' investment? One method is the use of **financial leverage**. As is explained in the appendix to this chapter, by successfully using debt financing, management can increase the return to the owners, the common stockholders. The use of financial leverage may be measured by capitalization ratios, which indicate the extent to which the firm finances its assets by debt. These ratios are also referred to as **debt ratios**.

Because debt financing can have such impact on the firm, each of these ratios is extremely valuable in analyzing the financial position of the firm. The most commonly used capitalization ratios are (1) the debt-to-equity ratio and (2) the debt-to-total assets ratio. These ratios are

$$\frac{\text{Debt}}{\text{Equity}} \text{ and } \frac{\text{Debt}}{\text{Total assets}}.$$

For HSY, the values for these ratios for 1999 were as follows:

$$\frac{\text{Debt}}{\text{Equity}} = \frac{\$2{,}248.0}{\$1{,}098.7} = 2.05.$$

$$\frac{\text{Debt}}{\text{Total assets}} = \frac{\$2{,}248.0}{\$3{,}346.7} = 67.2\%.$$

For HSY, the debt-to-equity ratio indicates that there was \$2.05 in debt for every \$1 of stock. The ratio of debt to total assets indicates that debt was used to finance 67.2 percent of the firm's assets.

Since these ratios measure the same thing (i.e., the use of debt financing), the student may wonder which is preferred. Actually, either is acceptable. The debt-to-equity ratio expresses debt in terms of equity, while the debt-to-total assets ratio gives the proportion of the firm's total assets that are financed by debt. Financial analysts or investors should choose the one they feel most comfortable working with.

POINTS OF INTEREST
The Numerical Difference Between the Return on Assets and the Return on Equity

As is developed in the appendix to this chapter, the return on equity may be increased by the use of debt financing. As the firm employs more debt financing and less equity financing, earnings are spread over a smaller equity base, which increases the return on equity. Thus it is possible for a firm to have a small return on its total assets but have a large return on its equity.

The conclusion may be illustrated by a profitable commercial bank. In its *2000 Annual Report,* Bank of America (BAC) reported that it earned $7.8 billion on total assets of $642.2 billion. While the return on assets (ROA) was only 1.2 percent, its return on equity (ROE) was 16.6 percent (i.e., more than 13 times the ROA). How could the small return on assets produce such a large return on equity? The answer lies in the company's successful use of financial leverage. Of the $642.2 billion in assets, $594.7 billion (92.6 percent) were financed with debt. Equity financed only $47.5 billion (7.4 percent). Obviously, BAC (and all other commercial banks) use a substantial amount of debt. By successfully using financial leverage, management is able to magnify a small return on assets into a large return on equity. A large difference between the return on assets and the return on equity indicates management's successful use of financial leverage.

When a firm uses a small amount of financial leverage, the numerical differences between the return on assets and the return on equity is small. (They would be equal if the firm used no debt.) In 2000, VF Corporation, the manufacturer of Wrangler and Lee jeans, had a return on assets of 6.0 percent and a return on equity of 11.9 percent (i.e., less than twice the ROA). The difference between VF's return on assets and return on equity was smaller than the difference between BAC's return on assets and equity. The smaller difference is the result of VF Corporation financing 49.7 percent of its assets with debt compared with BAC's 92.6 percent debt financing.

Whether a firm uses a large amount of financial leverage depends on the nature of the business and management's willingness to bear financial risk. Some firms inherently have a high degree of financial leverage. Commercial banks borrow from one group, the depositors, in order to make loans; the nature of the business results in a large amount of financial leverage (deposit liabilities). Manufacturing blue jeans and other clothing may be financed with debt or equity. VF Corporation's management has to answer the question of how much financial risk is appropriate for the firm and its stockholders. Management must determine the extent to which it desires to magnify the return on equity through the use of debt financing.

These capitalization ratios are aggregate measures. They both use *total* debt and hence do not differentiate between short-term and long-term debt. The debt-to-equity ratio uses total equity and therefore does not differentiate between the financing provided by preferred and common stock. The debt-to-total assets ratio uses total assets and hence does not differentiate between current and long-term assets.

Some definitions of debt ratio use only long-term debt (i.e., long-term debt/total assets). The argument is that short-term debt has to be quickly retired and is not part of the firm's permanent capital structure. There are three possible arguments against this reasoning. First, a firm may always have some current liabilities (e.g., trade accounts payable), and such liabilities are part of its permanent capital structure. Second, during periods of higher interest rates, management may issue short-term debt as a temporary source of funds prior to refinancing once interest rates have declined. Third, there are periods when short-term debt may be used prior to issuing long-term debt. For example, when a plant is being constructed, it may be financed with short-term debt prior to more permanent financing once the plant is completed and put into operation. In this text, the term *debt ratio* will always include both short- and long-term debt.

There is also the question of whether to include the deferred taxes as part of the debt structure and hence include them in the calculation of the debt ratio. Since deferred taxes finance 9.7 percent of HSY's assets ($326.0/$3,346.7), there is a strong argument for including them as part of the firm's debt obligations. The argument for exclusion of deferred taxes is that they may be deferred indefinitely. Inclusion ultimately depends on when the financial analyst believes the taxes will be paid. Changes in tax laws or in the firm's operations can accelerate or retard paying these deferred obligations. An acceleration, of course, argues for their inclusion in the calculation.

In spite of the variety of definitions of the debt ratio, all the ratios measure the extent to which assets are financed by creditors. The smaller the proportion of total assets financed by creditors, the larger the decline in the value of assets that may occur without threatening the creditors' position. Capitalization ratios thus give an indication of risk. Firms that have a small amount of equity capital are considered to involve greater risk because there is less cushion to protect creditors if the value of the assets deteriorates. For example, the ratio of debt to total assets for HSY was 61.2 percent. This indicates that the value of the assets may decline by 38.8 percent (100% − 61.2%) before only enough assets remain to pay off the debt. If the debt ratio had been 80 percent, a decline of only 20 percent in the value of the assets would endanger the creditors' position.

Capitalization ratios indicate risk as much to investors as they do to creditors, because firms with a high degree of financial leverage are riskier investments. If the value of the assets declines or if the firm experiences declining sales and losses, the equity deteriorates more quickly for firms that use financial leverage than for those that do not use debt financing. Hence, the debt ratios are an important measure of risk for both investors and creditors.

That capitalization ratios differ among firms is illustrated in Exhibit 13.3, which presents the debt ratios for five industrial and manufacturing firms. This exhibit is arranged in descending order from the firm that uses the greatest amount of debt financing (GenCorp) to the firm that uses the least (VF Corporation).

Financing not only varies from industry to industry but within an industry. Exhibit 13.4 (p. 402) presents the debt ratios for three telephone and telecommunications corporations. As in Exhibit 13.3, the proportion of a firm's total assets financed with debt varies, but there is less variation within the industry group than among the selected industrial firms.[7]

Financial theory suggests that there is an optimal combination of debt and equity financing that maximizes the value of a firm. The optimal use of financial leverage benefits common stockholders by increasing the per-share earnings of the company and by permitting faster growth and larger dividends. If, however, the firm uses too much financial leverage or is **undercapitalized**, creditors will require a higher interest rate to compensate them for the increased risk. Investors will invest their funds in a corporation with a large amount of financial leverage

undercapitalized
Having insufficient equity financing.

EXHIBIT 13.3

Ratio of Total Debt to Total Assets for Selected Firms as of December 2000

Firm	Debt Ratio
GenCorp	85.3%
Georgia-Pacific	81.4
Hershey Foods	61.2
Coca-Cola Company	55.3
VF Corp. (Vanity Fair)	49.7

Source: 2000 annual reports.

[7]The debt ratios calculated for Exhibits 13.3 and 13.4 use total debt. The ratios may be considerably different if only long-term debt is used. The Coca-Cola Company debt ratio declines to only 10.5 percent if current liabilities are excluded from the calculation.

EXHIBIT 13.4

Ratio of Total Debt to Total Assets for Three Telephone/Telecommunications Firms as of December 2000

Firm	Debt Ratio
Verizon	79.0
SBC Communications	69.1
Sprint	67.2

Source: 2000 annual reports.

only if the anticipated return is higher. Thus, the debt ratio, which measures the extent to which a firm uses financial leverage, is one of the most important ratios that managers, creditors, and stockholders may calculate.

DuPont Method of Financial Analysis

While each ratio gives an indication of one facet of a firm's operation, they may be combined to show the impact of interrelations of a firm's operations on its earning power. This is achieved by the use of the DuPont system of financial analysis, which combines profitability, asset management, and leverage to determine the return on the firm's equity. Essentially, the DuPont system determines the return on equity by multiplying three things: (1) the net profit margin, (2) total asset turnover, and (3) an equity multiplier that indicates the firm's use of financial leverage.

The product of the net profit margin and total asset turnover determines the return on assets. That is,

$$\textbf{Return on assets} = \frac{\textbf{Net earnings}}{\textbf{Sales}} \times \frac{\textbf{Sales}}{\textbf{Assets}} = \frac{\textbf{Net earnings}}{\textbf{Assets}}.$$

The product of the return on assets and the ratio of assets to equity (the equity multiplier) determines the return on equity. That is,

$$\textbf{Return on equity} = \frac{\textbf{Net earnings}}{\textbf{Assets}} \times \frac{\textbf{Assets}}{\textbf{Equity}}.$$

Thus, the DuPont system of financial analysis is

$$\textbf{Return on equity} = \frac{\textbf{Net earnings}}{\textbf{Sales}} \times \frac{\textbf{Sales}}{\textbf{Assets}} \times \frac{\textbf{Assets}}{\textbf{Equity}} = \frac{\textbf{Net earnings}}{\textbf{Equity}}.$$

All the ratios used in the DuPont system were previously defined except the equity multiplier, which is the ratio of total assets to equity (the reciprocal of the ratio of equity to total assets). Because the ratio of equity to total assets indicates the proportion of assets financed by equity, it is a measure of financial leverage. The smaller the percentage of assets financed by equity (i.e., the larger the proportion financed by debt), the larger will be that ratio of assets to equity. Thus, for a given return on assets, the greater will be the return on equity.

The DuPont system is illustrated in Exhibit 13.5, which presents the general layout of the system and applies it to the financial statements of Hershey Foods

EXHIBIT 13.5

The DuPont System of Financial Analysis

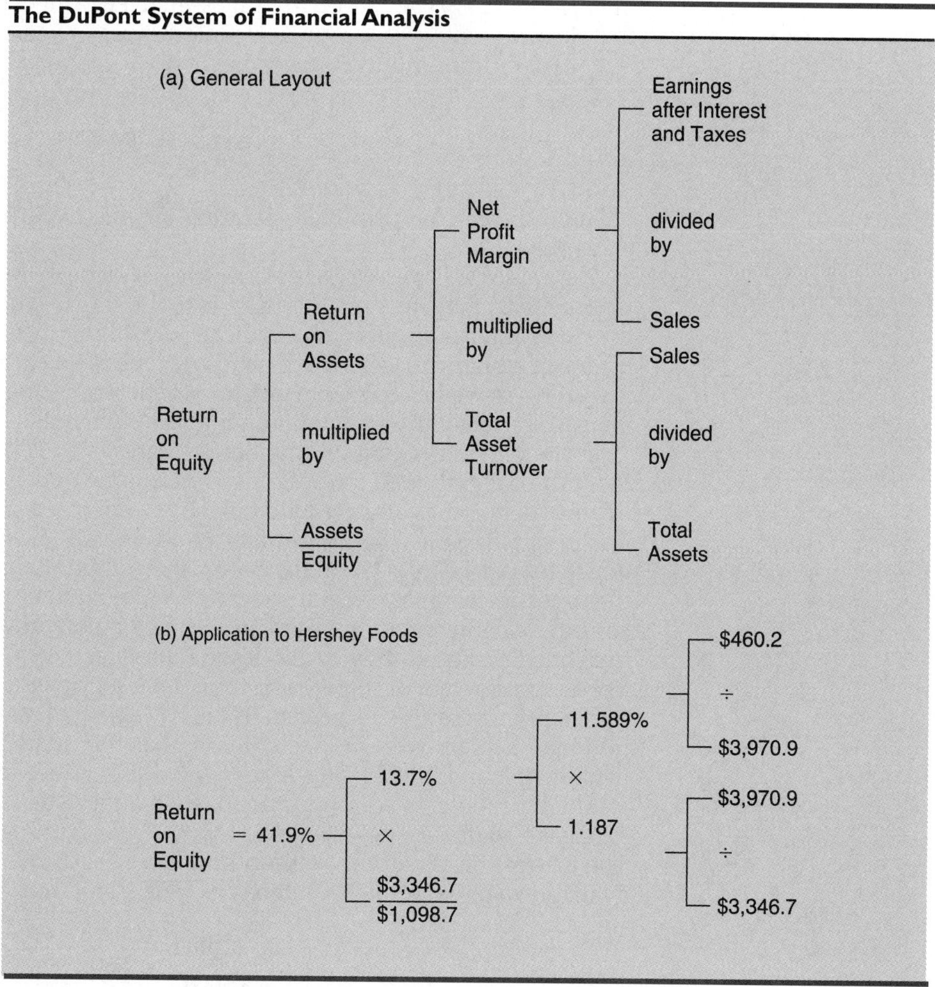

Corporation. While the end product of the system (i.e., the return on equity) is no different from the simple ratio of earnings to equity, the layout of the analysis facilitates locating internal sources of a firm's problems.

Coverage Ratios

times-interest-earned
Ratio of earnings before interest and taxes divided by interest expense; a coverage ratio that measures the safety of debt.

While leverage ratios measure the firm's use of debt, coverage ratios specifically measure its ability to service its debt. These ratios indicate to creditors and management how much the firm is earning from operations relative to what is owed. The coverage for interest payments is called **times-interest-earned**. Times-interest-earned is the ratio of earnings that are available to pay the interest (i.e., operating income) divided by the amount of interest. That is,

$$\textbf{Times-interest-earned} = \frac{\textbf{Earnings before interest and taxes}}{\textbf{Annual interest expense}}.$$

A ratio of 2 indicates that the firm has $2 after meeting other expenses to pay $1 of interest charges. The larger the times-interest-earned ratio, the more likely it is that the firm will be able to meet its interest payments.

For HSY, times-interest-earned is

$$\frac{\$802.1}{\$74.3} = 10.80,$$

which indicates the firm has operating income of $10.80 for every $1 of interest expense.

The ability to cover the interest expense is important, for failure to meet interest payments as they become due may throw the firm into bankruptcy. A decline in the times-interest-earned ratio indicates declining income relative to debt, or stable income but increased use of debt. It serves as an early warning to creditors and investors, as well as to management, of a deteriorating financial position and the increased probability of default on interest payments.

In the previous equation, the times-interest-earned ratio is an aggregate value that lumps together all interest payments. Some debt issues may be subordinated to other debt issues and are paid only after senior debt issues are redeemed. Thus, it is possible to pay the senior debt issues in full and to have no funds left with which to pay the interest on the subordinate debt. When this subordination exists, the times-interest-earned statistic may be altered to acknowledge it. For example, consider a company with $2,000 in earnings before interest and taxes and $10,000 in debt consisting of two issues. Issue A has a principal amount of $8,000 and carries an interest rate of 10 percent. Issue B has a principal amount of $2,000 and carries an interest rate of 14 percent. Issue B is subordinate to issue A. The subordination may explain why the second issue has the higher interest rate, for creditors usually demand higher rates in return for debt issues involving greater risk.

The times-interest-earned ratio for each debt issue is computed as follows. The firm has two debt issues (A and B) and $2,000 in earnings before interest and taxes. The interest on issue A is $800 and on issue B is $280. For issue A there is $2,000 available to pay the $800 in interest expense, and thus the coverage ratio is

$$\frac{\$2{,}000}{\$800} = 2.50.$$

For issue B there is $2,000 to cover the interest on A and B. Thus, for issue B the coverage ratio is

$$\frac{\$2{,}000}{\$800 + \$280} = 1.85.$$

It would be misleading to suggest that the coverage for issue B is the amount available after issue A was paid. In such a case that would indicate a coverage of

$$\frac{\$1{,}200}{\$280} = 4.29,$$

which is incorrect. Issue B would then have the higher coverage ratio and would appear to be safer than the senior debt. The proper way to adjust for subordination is to add the interest charges to the denominator and *not* to subtract the interest paid to the senior debt issue from the numerator. For successive issues of subordinated debt, the interest payments would be added to the denominator. Since the total amount of earnings available before taxes to pay the interest is spread out over ever-increasing interest payments, the coverage ratio declines and hence gives the true indication of the actual coverage of the subordinated debt.

Ratio Analysis for Specific Investors

An investor may not need to compute many ratios; a few selected ratios will probably provide sufficient information concerning the financial condition of the firm. The ratios that should be selected depend on the investor's need, which varies with the type of investment. Creditors, such as commercial banks or bondholders, are concerned with the firm's capacity to service its debt (i.e., pay the interest and retire the principal) as well as the extent to which the firm is financially leveraged. Stockholders, however, are more concerned with performance (i.e., earnings, dividends, growth, and valuation). While creditors and stockholders are both concerned with the financial condition of the firm, their emphases differ. Hence, they may compute different ratios to determine the firm's financial position as it applies to their specific investments.

Ratio Analysis for Creditors

Creditors are concerned with the firm's use of debt and its capacity to pay interest and retire its debt obligations as they come due. Debt financing may increase the return the firm is able to earn for its stockholders but also adds to the financial obligations of the firm, thus increasing the firm's financial risk. Creditors would prefer that the firm use less debt financing, since equity financing increases the safety of the firm's existing debt obligations.

The extent to which a firm uses debt financing is measured by the debt-to-total assets ratio or debt-to-equity ratio. The greater the proportion of the firm's assets financed with debt, the larger both ratios will be. Creditors may compute these ratios to ascertain the extent to which the firm uses debt financing and thereby may perceive the financial risk associated with the firm's sources of financing.

While creditors are concerned with the firm's sources of financing, they are even more concerned with the firm's liquidity position and its ability to generate cash to service the debt. The capacity of the firm to pay current interest obligations is measured by liquidity ratios (e.g., the current ratio and the quick ratio), selected activity ratios (e.g., inventory turnover and the average collection period), and the coverage ratio, times-interest-earned.

The liquidity ratios indicate the extent to which a firm has current assets relative to current liabilities. Since interest owed during the year is a current liability, the more current assets the firm has relative to current liabilities, the greater is the probability that the interest payment will be made. A high current ratio or high quick ratio implies interest will be paid when due.

The current and quick ratios do not indicate the firm's capacity to generate cash. They only indicate current assets relative to current liabilities. For most firms, a large percentage of the current assets will be inventory and accounts receivable. Because these assets must be converted into cash before interest can be paid, creditors may wish to analyze inventory turnover and the average collection period. These ratios indicate how rapidly inventory and accounts receivable flow up the balance sheet. The more rapidly inventory turns over, the more quickly the firm generates sales. These sales will be either for cash or on credit. The more rapidly the firm collects its accounts receivable, the more rapidly it is receiving cash. Rapid turnover of both inventory and accounts receivable is desirable from a creditor's perspective because it indicates that the firm is generating the funds with which it can make interest payments.

Lenders should also compute the coverage ratio, times-interest-earned, to determine if the firm is generating sufficient operating income to pay its interest obligations. Individually, this is one of the most important ratios, because it measures the extent to which operating income (i.e., earnings before interest and taxes) covers interest expense. Because lenders are paid after operating expenses are met but before income taxes, they must be concerned with the operating income generated by the firm. Ultimately, interest payments must be generated by operations. If the firm's operations cannot generate sufficient income to meet its interest expense, the lenders' position is tenuous.

Creditors are not concerned with net earnings, which are earnings after interest and taxes. It is the stockholders who are concerned with the net income that remains after interest and taxes are paid. This net income is the source of cash dividends and retained earnings, which will finance the firm's future growth and generate capital gains for the stockholders.

Any ratio by itself probably does not tell very much. A firm could be generating profitable sales but still not have cash. If a firm sells \$100 worth of inventory for \$120, that is a profitable sale. If the sale is for credit, the firm acquires an account receivable and not cash. Obviously, the firm is operating profitably, but until the account receivable is collected, the creditors cannot be paid. It is by combining several ratios (e.g., leverage, liquidity, and the turnover of short-term assets) that creditors perceive the safety of their current interest payments. The more rapidly the firm turns over inventory and accounts receivable, the more liquid its current position, and the higher the coverage of interest owed, the more certain should be the interest payment. (The firm's ability to generate cash is also indicated by the statement of changes in financial position, which is discussed later.)

In addition to interest payments, bondholders and other creditors are concerned with the repayment of their principal, which comes from the capacity of the firm to generate sufficient cash flow. This capacity may not be indicated by the firm's balance sheet or income statement. A firm could be operating at a profit but not be generating cash, and a firm could be reporting an accounting loss but still be generating cash.

Since the income statement does not tell if the firm is generating cash, lenders should study the firm's consolidated statement of cash flows. This statement enumerates the firm's sources and uses of funds and adjusts earnings that the firm reports but for which the firm did not receive cash. The consolidated statement of cash flows also adds back to earnings those expenses that did not involve an outlay of cash (e.g., depreciation). A firm with large depreciation expenses could be operating with little profit or even at a loss and still have the funds to retire its bonds as they mature.

The capacity of the firm to meet both the interest and principal repayment may be indicated by the following expanded coverage ratio, which includes interest, principal repayment, operating income, and depreciation expense:

$$\frac{\textbf{Earnings before interest and taxes} + \textbf{Depreciation}}{\left(\textbf{Interest expense} + \dfrac{\textbf{Principal repayment}}{(1 - \textbf{Firm's income tax rate})}\right)}.$$

For HSY, this ratio is

$$\frac{\$460.3 + 163.3}{\left(\$74.3 + \dfrac{0.4}{1 - 0.323}\right)} = 8.3.$$

The current portion of long-term debt due within the year is \$0.4, and 0.323 (32.3 percent) is the firm's average federal and state income tax rate in 1999. The ratio

POINTS OF INTEREST

The Buy Side and the Sell Side of the Street

As is explained in Chapter 3, investors buy stock at the asking price and sell at the bid. The purchases and sales are executed by brokers and are made through security dealers. Are these participants the "buy side" and "sell side" of Wall Street? If a financial analyst works the "buy side" or the "sell side" of Wall Street, does that mean he or she is buying or selling stocks and bonds?

The answer is no. A *financial* analyst (or *security* analyst or *investment* analyst—all three names are used) is an individual who analyzes financial statements, interviews corporate management, and uses other sources of information to construct earnings estimates and buy or sell recommendations for individual securities. These analysts are not brokers and are not security dealers, and they are not buying and selling for their own accounts. They are (very well) paid employees who work for money management firms and brokerage houses.

A buy-side analyst works for a nonbrokerage firm that manages mutual funds, pension plans, or trust services for corporate clients or individual investors. The buy-side analyst provides recommendations, which are given to the firm's portfolio managers, who buy and sell securities. Since these analysts are developing recommendations for possible purchases by their employers, they work the "buy side" of the Street.

A sell-side analyst does the same type of work but is employed by a brokerage firm. The sell-side analyst's recommendations are provided to the brokers who, in turn, give the recommendations to investors. The purpose of a sell-side analyst's reports is to generate security sales, hence the name "sell side."

Since buy-side analysts' reports are solely for their employers' use, the recommendations may remain private. Sell-side analysts' reports, however, become public, and this creates a potential conflict of interest or at least a potential bias in the analysis. There are several possible reasons for this bias. First, analysts may issue favorable reports to maintain good relationships with corporate management, since executives are one source of an analyst's information. Second, the corporation may employ an underwriter to issue new securities. Analysts do not want to lose this future business for their brokerage firms. Third, analysts' reports are designed to encourage security transactions, especially purchases, by the brokerage firm's customers. Any of these reasons could cause an analyst to issue a favorable report concerning a firm and its securities. Since more favorable reports are issued than negative reports, one could easily draw that conclusion.

Certainly, the individual investor should not blindly accept a security analyst's recommendations. There is, however, some evidence that financial analysts are able to forecast stock returns. (See, for instance, Kenneth Stanley, Wilbur G. Lewellen, and Gary C. Schlarbaum, "Further Evidence on the Value of Professional Investment Research," *Journal of Financial Research* [spring 1981]: 1–9.) Evidence also exists that suggests there is little difference among the forecasts of different analysts. (See Edwin Elton, Martin Gruber, and Seth Grossman, "Discrete Expectational Data and Portfolio Performance," *Journal of Finance* [July 1986]: 699–714.)

If an investor wants to follow analysts' estimates, there are several sources on the Internet. Possibilities include the general information sources such as CNBC on MSN Money, Quicken, or Yahoo!, which may provide summaries of analysts' estimates. If this complimentary information is insufficient, the premium fee-based sources are Zacks Investment Research (http://www.zacks.com) and First Call (http://www.firstcall.com). In addition to offering a subscription service that provides comprehensive estimates, these services may also permit the investor to buy reports devoted to specific companies.

indicates that HSY generates sufficient cash flow to cover not only its interest payments but also the principal repayments.[8]

Depreciation expense is added to earnings before interest and taxes (EBIT) in the numerator to determine cash flow from operations. (Other applicable noncash expenses, such as depletion and amortization, should also be added to EBIT.) The principal repayment is added to interest expense in the denominator. Because principal repayment is not a tax-deductible expense, the amount of the payment must be expressed before tax. This adjustment is achieved by dividing the principal repayment by 1 minus the firm's tax rate. As with times-interest-earned, the

[8]The numbers were taken from the statement of cash flows in Exhibit 13.8, p. 418. The tax rate is taxes divided by net income plus taxes.

larger the ratio, the safer should be the creditor's position, because the greater is the firm's capacity to pay the interest and repay the principal.

Ratio Analysis for Stockholders

Stockholders, like creditors, are investors, but stockholders earn their return not through interest payments but through dividends and growth in the value of the shares. Thus stockholders are primarily concerned with performance (i.e., the capacity of the firm to generate earnings). Performance is measured by such ratios as the profit margin on sales, return on assets, and return on equity. Stockholders are also concerned with the source of the return on their individual investments (i.e., dividends and capital gains). Measures of the distribution of earnings, growth in earnings and dividends, and the market's valuation of the stock are also important to the individual stockholder. Thus, in addition to profitability ratios, stockholders are concerned with the payout ratio, measures of growth, and the P/E ratio.

Sales are the firm's source of revenues and profits. Unless the firm earns its revenues from an investment portfolio, the ability to generate profitable sales is ultimately the source of the return earned by the firm for its stockholders. The ability to generate profitable sales is indicated by profitability ratios, especially the net profit margin (i.e., net earnings to sales). Firms with a high net profit margin or whose net profit margins exceed their industry's averages may be attractive investments.

The return on assets (earnings divided by total assets) indicates what the firm has earned on its resources. The ratio does not indicate what the firm earned on the stockholders' funds. Thus, for stockholders the return on equity (earnings divided by equity) is exceedingly important, because it indicates what management has earned on the stockholders' investment in the firm. A high return on equity indicates that the management has achieved high earnings for the stockholders relative to the funds they have invested in the firm.

A high return on equity is by itself not necessarily desirable. If the firm employs a substantial amount of debt financing (i.e., earning more on the assets acquired through the use of debt financing than must be paid in interest) to acquire assets, this may magnify the return on equity. However, if the firm were to operate at a loss, the use of financial leverage would magnify the loss to the stockholders. Thus stockholders, like bondholders, are concerned with the extent to which the firm uses debt financing. The debt ratios indicate the use of debt financing and hence measure the financial risk associated with the firm.

If a firm has both a high return on equity and a high debt ratio, the return on equity may be the result of successfully using financial leverage to magnify the return on the stockholders' funds. If the firm has a high return on equity but a low debt ratio, that indicates the firm has profitable operations and is not using debt financing as a major source of the return to its stockholders. The latter situation is less risky, as the profits are the result of operating decisions and not financing decisions. Small changes in sales or expenses should not have a large impact on earnings.

Since earnings are either distributed or retained, stockholders are concerned with the payout ratio, which was discussed in Chapter 11. For HSY, the per-share payout ratio in 1999 was

$$\textbf{Payout ratio} = \frac{\textbf{Dividends}}{\textbf{Earnings}} = \frac{\$1.00}{\$3.29} = 30.3\%.$$

POINTS OF INTEREST

Netscape and Locating Information on Hershey Foods Corporation

Netscape has a relatively easy process for obtaining general information concerning investing or on a particular company, such as Hershey Foods Corporation. Start at Netscape (http//www.netscape.com) and click on "Personal Finance." The section on Personal Finance has links to many investing and financial topics such as mortgage loans and insurance as well as links to a specific firm. It is a useful means to obtain general financial information.

If you are on the Personal Finance page and want information on a specific firm, enter the ticker symbol such as HSY for Hershey Foods. This takes you to the "Quote" page for current price information on the stock. (You can avoid going through the Personal Finance section by entering the ticker symbol on the home page.) From the Quote page, you have several choices for additional information concerning HSY. "News" provides current headlines, if any are available. "Charts" shows price movements in the stock for the prior 12 months. "Profile" gives basic financial information such as earnings, market capitalization, the existence of a dividend reinvestment plan, and ratios such as price/earnings, price/sales, and price/book. "Financials" gives HSY's income statement and balance sheet and some additional ratios such as debt/equity and return on equity. "Analysis" and "Insiders" provide earnings estimates and insider transactions and purchases and sales by mutual funds. "SEC Filings" gives a chronicle listing of the firm's filings (e.g., 10-K forms) with the SEC.

Although this process is a means to obtain information and data concerning a company, you will have to process it into a useful form. It only provides information on one firm and you will have to repeat the process if you wish to compare firms. If you have access to a database, then you should be able to compare firms more readily, but databases are generally available only through subscription. At least the process described is a means to obtain a considerable amount of complimentary information and data on specific stocks.

This indicates that management distributed about 30 percent of the firm's earnings. The distribution of earnings is a prerogative of the board of directors. Some managements prefer to retain earnings to finance future growth.

If an investor is primarily concerned with the flow of dividend income, a high payout ratio is desirable. Stockholders who seek growth and capital gains will prefer a lower payout ratio, which indicates that a larger proportion of earnings are being retained to finance future operations. The Coca-Cola Company in its 2000 *Annual Report* stated that the payout ratio was 45 percent (excluding the impact of extraordinary items) but the board of directors had voted to gradually reduce the ratio to 30 percent to "free up additional cash for reinvestment in our high-return beverage business." Even investors who seek income may not desire a payout ratio of 100 percent, since even modest growth in the dividends will require some retention of earnings.

The capacity of the firm to grow by internally generated funds depends on its return on equity and the distribution of its earnings. For example, consider a firm with \$100 in equity that earns \$10. The return on equity is 10 percent (\$10/\$100). If the firm distributes \$10, the equity cannot internally grow. If the \$10 are retained, the equity grows from \$100 to \$110, a 10 percent increase. If 40 percent of the earnings are distributed ($0.4 \times \$10 = \$4$), only \$6 are retained and the equity grows by 6 percent, from \$100 to \$106. The firm cannot increase its equity more than 6 percent and maintain the dividend unless it increases its profitability (i.e., increases the return on equity). Thus, the larger the return on equity and the smaller the payout ratio, the greater will be the firm's internal growth.

Stockholders who seek capital gains should be particularly interested in the payout ratio. The value of the shares will not appreciate over time unless earnings and dividends grow. The product of 1 minus the payout ratio and the return on equity provides the investor with a measure of internal growth (i.e., $[1 - 0.4][0.1] = 0.06 = 6\%$ rate of growth in equity). The payout ratio combined with the return on equity indicates the capacity of the firm to grow internally without (1) using additional debt financing, which may increase financial risk, or (2) selling additional shares, which may dilute the existing stockholders' equity and earnings.

The Need for Comparisons: The Problems with Interpretation

Although creditors and stockholders may emphasize different ratios that analyze a firm's financial statements, both should realize that one ratio by itself can be misleading. The usefulness of ratio analysis is the general picture derived from the ratios. Individual ratios may be contradictory, but the total analysis should provide any investor with an indication of the financial position of the firm.

Just as an individual ratio may be meaningless, so may be a set of ratios for a given firm if there is no benchmark with which to compare them. Thus the investor should either (1) compare individual ratios for a firm over a period of time to establish norms for the firm or (2) compare the individual firm's ratios to an industry average. Industry comparisons, however, are not easy to interpret. Many firms have a variety of product lines and may not be readily classified into a particular industry. In addition, industry averages may be dated. Material on industry averages published in the current year must be based on financial statements that are at least one year old. There may be inconsistencies comparing this year's financial statements with previous years' industry averages. Such comparisons will have meaning only if the industry averages are stable over time.

The problem of defining the industry may be illustrated by considering the industry comparisons available through MultexInvestor (http://www.multexinvestor.com). MultexInvestor provides Market Guide data and places Hershey Foods in the food processing industry, which encompasses beverages, crops, fish and livestock, tobacco, and even personal household products. Firms used for the comparison include Heinz, IBP (Iowa Beef), and Kellogg. While Hershey may be classified in the food processing industry, it specializes in candies. (Its primary competitors are Mars and Cadbury Schweppes.) Should Hershey be considered comparable to Heinz, IPB, or Kellogg? Are its ratios comparable to industry averages that include firms with perceptibly different products? Whether the answers are yes and Hershey should be compared to industry averages that include firms with different products is left to the individual using the data.

Problems concerning the use of ratio analysis are not limited to the availability and comparability of industry averages. Differences in accounting pratices may also alter a firm's finanacial statements and thus affect ratio analysis. For example, the use of LIFO (last in, first out) for inventory valuation instead of FIFO (first in, first out) can have an impact on the inventory carried on the balance sheet and on the cost of goods sold. During a period of inflation, many firms will choose to use LIFO instead of FIFO. This choice results in selling the last (and presumably most costly) inventory first. The firm's cost of goods sold is higher, which reduces the firm's earnings and taxes. The cost of the remaining inventory is lower, because the more costly inventory was sold first. Any ratio that uses inventory or earnings will be affected by the choice of LIFO instead of FIFO. If a financial analysis is comparing two firms, one of which uses LIFO and the other FIFO, the analysis will be biased. The firm using LIFO will appear to be less profitable. However, since its level of inventory is lower, it will have higher inventory turnover. In actuality, there may be little substantive difference between the two firms.

Other accounting choices may also alter the results of ratio analysis. The choice of leasing instead of buying, larger allowances for doubtful accounts, or the accounting for pension liabilities may have an impact on a firm's financial statements. Although the accounting profession standardizes the construction of financial statements, differences among firms can and do exist, which may raise questions concerning the use of ratio analysis to compare firms.

Even a trend analysis of a firm's financial statements may be suspect. The problems mentioned before also apply to a ratio analysis of one firm over time if it has made accounting changes from one accounting period to the next. Such changes will be noted in the financial statements, but they do raise questions concerning the comparability of ratios computed over a number of years.[9]

Although there can be weaknesses in the use of ratios to analyze a firm's financial statements, the technique is still an excellent starting point to analyze a firm's financial position. The limitations of the data do not necessarily negate the technique. Instead, the analyst needs to be aware of the weaknesses so that appropriate adjustments can be made in either the construction of the ratios or the interpretation of the results.

Financial Ratios and Stock Valuation

Many ratios have been presented throughout this chapter. In this section, several are used to analyze the financial position of Hershey Foods. The ratios provide background evidence for the valuation models explained and illustrated in Chapters 9 and 11.

Exhibit 13.6 (p. 412) reports a ratio analysis for Hershey Foods for the years 1995 through 1999. Figure 13.1 (p. 413) presents the same material in graph form for the ratios. As might be expected, there can be variation in the ratios from year to year. Some ratios are stable (e.g., the gross profit margin), while others fluctuate (e.g., the return on equity). When a ratio deviates from the average for the firm or if the firm's ratios deviate from an average used for comparisons (e.g., an industry average), the investor should ask why. As was stated earlier, Hershey Foods sold its pasta business for a profit and that produced a large increase in earnings for 1999. All the ratios that use earnings (e.g., the return on equity) may be overstated because the sale of the pasta operations is an extraordinary item that occurs only once. It is a *nonrecurring item.*

Even if there are no nonrecurring items, ratio analysis by itself cannot tell you whether to buy or sell a stock. First, ratios are constructed with historical data, and past performance may not be indicative of future performance. Second, even if past performance is repeated, the investor still needs a measure of what the stock is worth in order to determine if the current price is excessive. That, of course, is the purpose of discounted cash flow models and comparative ratios such as price/earnings (P/E), price/sales (P/S), and price/book (P/B).

Alternative Strategies For Selecting Common Stocks

Besides the valuation model, other techniques may be used to identify possible stocks for purchase. These include the ratio of price to book value, low P/E stocks, small capitalization stocks, and screening techniques. These methods are not necessarily a substitute for analysis of financial statements and valuation models, but they are helpful when used in conjunction with them.

[9]If possible, the financial analyst should put ratios on a common footing so that current operations are comparable to prior years' operations. For example, Hershey sold its pasta operations in 1999. The sale implies that all prior financial statements, which include the pasta operations, should be adjusted and the financial ratios recalculated.

EXHIBIT 13.6

Ratio Analysis of Hershey Foods, 1995–1999

	1999	1998	1997	1996	1995	Five-Year Average
Liquidity Ratios						
Current ratio	1.80	1.39	1.30	1.20	1.07	1.35
Quick ratio	0.95	0.78	0.70	0.63	0.61	0.73
Activity Ratios						
Average collection period (days)	32.1	36.6	30.1	26.6	31.8	31.4
Inventory turnover	7.3	8.9	8.5	8.4	9.3	8.5
Fixed asset turnover	4.3	2.6	2.7	2.5	2.6	2.9
Profitability (Performance) Ratios						
Gross profit margin	40.7%	40.8	42.2	42.3	42.3	41.7%
Operating profit margin	14.1%	14.5	14.7	14.1	13.8	14.2%
Net profit margin	11.6%	7.7	7.8	6.8	7.8	8.3%
Return on assets	13.8%	10.0	10.2	8.5	9.9	10.5%
Return on equity	41.9%	32.7	33.4	27.5	22.2	31.5%
Leverage and Coverage Ratios						
Debt ratio (debt/total assets)	61.2%	69.3	74.0	63.5	61.7	65.9%
Times-interest-earned	10.8	7.5	8.3	11.7	11.8	10.0
Other Ratios						
Payout ratio	30.3%	39.3	37.7	43.4	40.8	38.3%

Source: Data derived from Hershey Foods *Annual Report to Stockholders*, various issues.

Market Price Less Than Book Value

The ratio of market price to book value suggests that the investor should limit purchases to those stocks selling for less than their book value.[10] During 1990 and 1991, the stocks of savings and loan associations sold for less than their book value. For example, the book value of Columbia Savings & Loan exceeded $28, but the stock sold for less than $10. By implication, the stock would be an attractive investment. By the same reasoning, as of January 1, 2001, Hershey Foods' book value was $7.86 and the stock was selling for $64.37, so the stock would not be a good purchase.

The simplicity of this technique is very appealing, but it does not follow that just because a stock is selling below book value, it is a good investment. Unfortunately, the ratio does not answer the question "Why is the stock selling below book value?" The answer could be declining earnings or inflated assets. Many savings and loan institutions had problem loans on which no interest was being paid. In effect, their book value was overstated. The general negative cloud that hung over the entire savings and loan industry caused the stock prices of virtually all savings and loan institutions to fall. Of course, the problem facing the investor is to determine which firms are truly undervalued and which are in the greatest financial difficulty. The ratio of price to book cannot answer that question, but it can be a good starting point for analyzing securities.

[10] An investor may determine the book value per share by dividing the equity available to common stock by the number of shares outstanding. The equity available to common stock is the sum of the common stock, paid-in capital (if any), and retained earnings. These values are found on the firm's balance sheet.

FIGURE 13.1

Ratio Analysis of Hershey Foods, 1995–1999

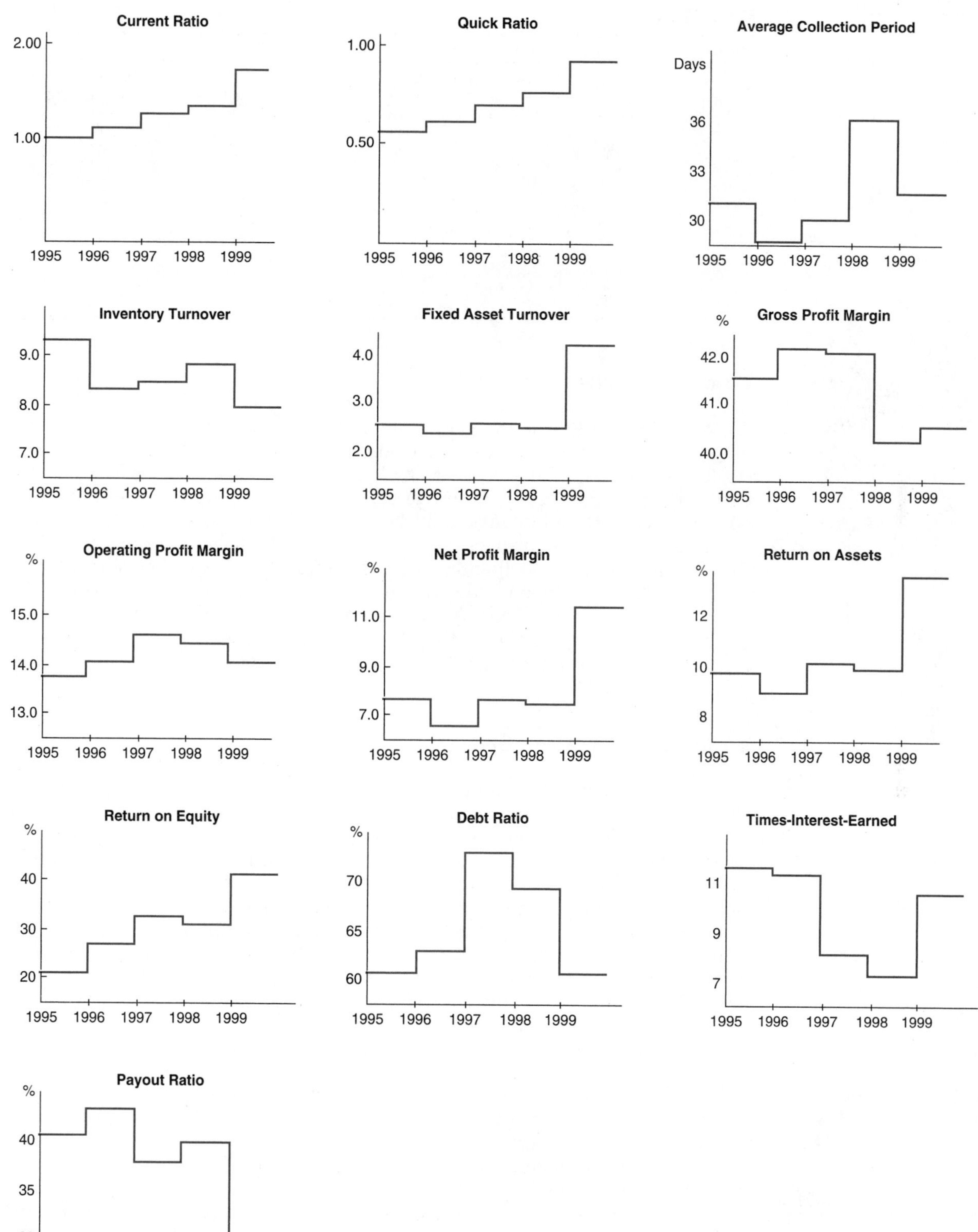

Source: Hershey Foods *Annual Report to Stockholders,* various issues.

EXHIBIT 13.7

Market Capitalization of Selected Stocks

Firm	Number of Shares Outstanding*	Price (1/01/01)	Market Value of Stock
R. G. Barry	9,372	$ 2.37	$ 22,211,640
Chesapeake Corporation	15,111	20.56	310,682,160
Apple Computer	335,882	14.87	4,994,565,340
Georgia-Pacific	224,723	31.02	6,999,379,760
AT&T	3,750,479	17.25	64,695,762,750

*Number of shares in thousands derived from *Standard & Poor's Stock Guide*, Year End 2001.

Low P/E Stocks

As was discussed in Chapter 9, P/E ratios are often used to compare and value firms and to help select securities for purchase. The strategy of buying low P/E stocks is similar to purchasing stocks with low market-to-book ratios. The investor limits purchases to stocks with low price/earnings multiples or those companies whose current P/E ratios are near the low end of their historic range. Once again, the technique does not answer the question "Why is the stock selling for a low P/E?" If investors believe that the firm's financial condition will decline, the low P/E ratio may be justified and certainly does not argue for the purchase of the stock. However, it should be reiterated that returns from investments in low P/E stocks is one of the anomalies to the efficient market hypothesis. Such an anomaly suggests that following a low P/E strategy for stock selection may lead to superior investment results.

Small Capitalization Stocks

Instead of analyzing the ratio of a firm's stock price to its book value or its per-share earnings, the individual may prefer to invest in firms that are small or that are not well followed by professional financial analysts. This group of stocks is referred to as small capitalization (*small cap*) stocks, which means that the total market value of the company's equity is modest (e.g., $500 million to $1 billion). The total market value of the equity is the number of shares outstanding times the stock's price. Exhibit 13.7 presents the capitalization (i.e., number of shares outstanding, price per share, and total market value) for selected stocks. The exhibit is constructed so the smallest cap stocks are listed first. Obviously, AT&T is a large firm whose stock, in the aggregate, is worth much more than the stock of Chesapeake Corporation, which in turn has a market capitalization considerably larger than that of R. G. Barry, manufacturer of Dearfoam slippers.

Small capitalization stocks may lack a following on Wall Street. Analysts often work for large financial institutions, such as life insurance companies or brokerage firms. These financial institutions tend to avoid investing in or recommending the stocks of small companies, so their analysts do not cover them. This lack of coverage by financial analysts suggests that small companies may offer the individual an investment opportunity. It should be pointed out that a strategy of investing in small capitalization stocks is based on the belief that the market for large companies is very efficient but the market for small companies is less efficient. It may be possible to identify a specific small company that is currently undervalued and hence is a good investment.

Analysis of Financial Statements, Security Selection, and the Internet

If investors do not want to calculate the ratios used in an analysis of a firm's financial statement, they may find the ratios at various sites. For example, Media General Financial Services (http://www.mgfs.com) provides ratios calculated on the basis of the last quarter, the previous fiscal year, and the preceding 12 months. Earnings estimates, price and volume of shares traded, and returns may also be obtained, but access to this information does cost.

Most of the basic ratios covered in this chapter may be found on the Internet at no cost. Three possible sources are MultexInvestor, which provides data by Market Guide (http://www.multexinvestor.com), Wall Street Research Net (WSRN), which provides data from Media General (http://www.wsrn.com), and INVESTools (http://www.investools.com). (Money Central MSN and Quicken also provide data from Media General; Reuters [http://www.reuters.com] reports Market Guide data.) These sources, however, do not necessarily present the same ratios, and the values may differ for the same ratios. These two points are illustrated by the following table, which provides selected financial ratios for Hershey Foods.

Ratios	MultexInvestor	WSRN	INVESTools
Current ratio	1.65	—	1.95
Profit margin	8.12%	7.9%	9.7%
Return on assets	10.43%	9.7%	18.9%
Return on equity	30.93%	28.5%	27.8%
Debt/Equity	0.75	0.75	0.75
Total debt/Equity	0.99	—	—
Price/Book	6.79	7.47	6.56
Price/Earnings	23.21	26.60	23.79
Price/Sales	1.88	2.08	—

Immediately it is apparent that not all the ratios are available and that the values differ. (In the case of the debt/equity ratios, MultexInvestor-Market Guide gives two ratios. One version uses long-term debt only while the other uses total debt.) Such differences could be the result of the time periods used (e.g., the last 12 months, referred to as "trailing twelve months"—TTM, versus the firm's last fiscal year). Different data may be used in the calculation. For example, one source may use earnings that have not been adjusted for extraordinary items, whereas another source may use adjusted earnings. Varying definitions of a particular ratio may also explain the differences.

These differences pose a problem for the investor who wants to make comparisons. One obvious solution is for the individual to compute the ratios, in which case the definitions and time periods can be applied consistently. A more pragmatic solution may be to use one source exclusively. The choice could depend on which source provides the desired data. For example, MultexInvestor provides the company's ratios and ratios for the industry, the sector, and the S&P 500.

Once the investor has determined the appropriate source for the data, ratios can be used to screen companies to isolate firms that meet specific criteria. For example, the investor can specify a return on equity of at least 20 percent, a dividend yield of 2.5 percent, and a price/earnings ratio of less than 15.0. The computer then screens the database to identify all firms that meet these specified criteria. If the number is large, the criteria may be made more stringent or additional criteria may be added to the screening process.

Screening techniques provide an excellent illustration of an Internet application, but the investor must subscribe to the service to have access to the database. In some cases, the individual will also have to obtain software to run the program. The costs for basic searches are relatively modest (e.g., less than $100 a year), but if the investor wants access to a larger database or to search on more variables, the cost will be higher. (Some services offer complimentary searches on a few variables.) Possible sources of screening services include:

American Association of Individual Investors (http://www.aaii.org)
INVESTools (http://www.investools.com)
Standard & Poor's (http://www.stockinfo.standardpoor.com)
Wall Street City (http://www.wallstreetcity.com)
Worth (http://www.worth.com)
Zachs Investment Research (http://www.zacks.com)

Perhaps the best initial strategy is to determine which variables the investor believes are crucial and then determine which services offer the appropriate data. The investor can then use the search screens and subsequently determine if the results warrant the cost and the effort to apply the screens.

The investor should realize that a data search does not answer the fundamental question: Is the stock under- or overvalued?[11] The search only isolates stocks that meet the specified criteria. If the investor seeks to identify all stocks with a dividend yield of 2.5 percent and a return on equity of 20 percent, the resulting list will be based on the current dividend. There is no assurance that the dividend will be maintained. The return on equity will be based on the firm's income statement and balance sheet, which are historical. The next year's earnings could be lower, so the desired return on equity is not maintained. While screening limits the number of stocks to those that meet the criteria, these filter techniques are at best starting points in the analysis of stocks for possible inclusion in a portfolio.

Analysis of Cash Flow

The bulk of this chapter has been devoted to the analysis of a firm's income statement and balance sheet with emphasis placed on profitability and net earnings available to the common stockholder. However, increased interest has developed among financial analysts in a firm's operating income and cash flow. Net income may be affected by numerous factors that have little meaning from the perspective of a firm's operations. For example, the use of straight-line depreciation instead of accelerated depreciation will increase earnings (and taxes) but does not affect the firm's operations. Other items, such as the sale of an appreciated asset, an increase in reserves to cover losses on accounts receivable, or changes in inventory valuation, can have an impact on the firm's net income, but these events need not affect current or future operations.

The previous examples suggest that earnings could be affected without affecting operations. Because these examples may be nonrecurring (e.g., the sale of an asset occurs only once), net income from different accounting periods may not be

[11]Quicken (http://www.quicken.com) does provide a system that determines a stock's intrinsic value. The technique uses a discounted cash flow model, which assumes a particular growth rate in earnings and an appropriate discount rate. In August 2001, Hershey Foods' intrinsic value was determined to be $42. Since the stock was selling for $58, the intrinsic value suggested that the stock was overvalued.

comparable. In addition, the firm could have recurring earnings and still not be generating cash. For example, if Firm A owns stock of Firm B, this investment can affect earnings but not operations. Firm A may report as part of its earnings the earnings of Firm B (i.e., Firm A picks up its proportional share of Firm B's earnings), but that does not necessarily mean that Firm A receives cash. If Firm B retains the earnings, Firm A obviously does not receive any cash for the earnings it is reporting. For a firm like Berkshire Hathaway, which has substantial equity investments in other firms, a large proportion of its earnings are independent of its own operations and do not represent the receipt of cash.

Because net earnings may be affected by nonrecurring items or need not represent cash, some financial analysts place more emphasis on cash flow. The argument is that the cash flow generated by a firm's operations is a better indication of its profitability and value. Instead of isolating income, these analysts determine the capacity of the firm to generate cash and use this information for their valuation of the firm.

Statement of Cash Flows

statement of cash flows
An accounting statement that enumerates a firm's cash inflows and cash outflows.

The increased emphasis on the generation of cash has led to the creation of the **statement of cash flows**. This statement determines changes in the firm's holding of cash and cash equivalents (i.e., short-term liquid assets, such as Treasury bills). The emphasis is not on income or the firm's assets and liabilities but on the inflows and outflows of cash from the firm's operations, investments, and financing decisions.

The statement of cash flows for Hershey Foods Corporation is presented in Exhibit 13.8 (p. 418). The statement is divided into three sections: (1) operating activities, (2) investment activities, and (3) financing activities. Each section enumerates the inflow and outflow of cash. The cash inflows are:

1. A decrease in an asset,
2. An increase in a liability, and
3. An increase in equity.

The cash outflows are:

1. An increase in an asset,
2. A decrease in a liability, and
3. A decrease in equity.

The statement of cash flows starts with a firm's earnings and works through various entries to determine the change in the firm's cash and cash equivalents. As is illustrated in Exhibit 13.8, Hershey Foods starts with earnings of $460.3 million. Since earnings are not synonymous with cash, adjustments must be made to put earnings on a cash basis. The first adjustment is to add back all noncash expenses and deduct noncash revenues. The most important of these adjustments is usually depreciation, the noncash expense that allocates the cost of plant and equipment over a period of time. Other noncash expenses may include depletion of raw materials and amortization of intangible assets such as goodwill. In this illustration, Hershey has depreciation expense of $163.2 million, which is added to the firm's earnings.

Next, deferred taxes are added to earnings plus noncash expenses. Earnings are determined after subtracting taxes owed for the time period but not necessarily paid. A firm may be able to defer paying some taxes until the future, so these deferred taxes do not result in an outflow of cash during the current accounting period. Although taxes actually paid are a cash outflow, deferred taxes recognized

EXHIBIT 13.8

Hershey Foods Corporation Consolidated Statement of Cash Flows

For the years ended December 31, (in millions)	1999	1998	1997
Operating activities			
Net income	$460.3	$340.9	$336.3
Adjustments to reconcile net income to net cash (used in) provided by operating activities:			
Depreciation and amortization	163.2	158.2	152.8
Deferred income taxes	(8.3)	82.2	16.9
(Gains) losses on sales of business net of tax	(165.0)	—	—
Changes in operating assets and liabilities, net of acquisitions and dispositions:			
Accounts receivable	77.9	(90.5)	(68.5)
Inventories	(136.5)	12.3	(33.5)
Other assets and liabilities	(55.2)	(124.1)	85.1
Accounts payable and accrued expenses	(8.7)	10.0	13.0
Net cash (used in) provided by operating activities	327.7	389.7	506.0
Investing activities			
Purchases of property, plant, and equipment	(115.4)	(161.3)	(172.9)
Proceeds from sale of businesses	450.0	—	—
Other	(11.9)	(33.6)	(7.7)
Net cash provided by (used in) investing activities	322.7	(194.9)	(180.7)
Financing activities			
Net borrowings (payments) on credit lines	(136.7)	(36.5)	(217.0)
Payments on long-term debt	(.4)	(25.2)	(15.6)
Proceeds from long-term debt	1.7	—	550.0
Proceeds from issuances of common stock	18.9	19.4	14.4
Purchases of outstanding common stock	(318.0)	(16.2)	(507.7)
Dividends paid	(136.7)	(129.0)	(121.5)
Other	—	(22.5)	(35.0)
Net cash (used in) provided by financing activities	(571.3)	(210.0)	(332.5)
Increase (decrease) in cash and cash equivalents	79.1	(15.2)	(7.2)
Cash and cash equivalents at beginning of year	39.0	54.2	61.4
Cash and cash equivalents at end of year	$118.1	$ 39.0	$ 54.2

Source: Adapted from Hershey Foods *1999 Annual Report to Stockholders.*

during the time period are not a cash outflow and are added back to earnings to determine the cash generated by operations. Hershey's statement of cash flows indicates that deferred taxes declined by $8.3 million. When part of the firm's operations were sold, the deferred taxes associated with those operations could no longer be deferred and hence *had to be paid.* Paying these income taxes is, of course, a cash outflow, so the entry is in parentheses.

Gains from the sale of plant and equipment are also subtracted. Since these gains are included in the sale of the plant and equipment that is part of the firm's investment activities, failure to subtract the gain would double count the profit as generating cash from the sale and from the earnings generated by the sale. For Hershey, the gain on the sale of business is $165.0 million. This amount is part of the proceeds from the sale of plant and equipment enumerated later in the statement and is subtracted from net income.

The next set of entries refers to changes in the firm's current assets and liabilities resulting from operations. Some of these changes generate cash while others consume it. If accounts receivable increase, that means during the accounting period the firm experienced a net increase in credit sales. These credit sales do not generate cash until the receivables are collected, so an increase in accounts receivable is a cash outflow.

An increase in inventory, like an increase in accounts receivable, is an outflow of cash. If the firm ends the period with more inventory than when it began, it has experienced a cash outflow. Hershey's inventory rose by $136.5 million, so this amount is subtracted to determine cash generated by operations. Once again, the cash outflow is indicated by the parentheses. If inventory had declined, that would indicate the firm sold more inventory than it acquired. This change would be an inflow of cash, and the amount would not be in parentheses.

These effects on cash by changes in accounts receivable and inventory also apply to other current assets. An increase in a current asset, other than cash or cash equivalents, is a cash outflow, while a decrease is a cash inflow. For example, if the firm prepays an insurance policy or makes a lease or rent payment at the beginning of the month, these payments are cash outflows. However, they are also increases in the asset prepaid expense; thus, the increase in the asset represents a cash outflow.

In addition to changes in current assets, normal day-to-day operations will alter the firm's current liabilities. Wages will accrue and other trade accounts may rise. An increase in the firm's payables is a cash inflow, because the cash has not yet been paid. A decrease in payables results when the accounts are paid, thus becoming a cash outflow. Hershey experienced a decrease of $8.7 million in accounts payable and other accrued expenses.

The sum of all the adjustments to income and the changes in operating current assets and current liabilities is the net cash provided by operating activities. Hershey experienced a net cash inflow from operations of $327.7 million during 1999. This operating cash flow is perceptibly different from the firm's reported income of $460.3 million.

After the adjustments to income and the changes in current assets and current liabilities from operations, the statement of cash flows considers cash generated by investment activities. The acquisition of plant and equipment requires a cash outflow, whereas the sale of plant and equipment generates cash (an inflow). Expanding firms often need additional investments in plant and equipment, which consumes cash. A stagnating firm with excess capacity may sell plant and equipment, which generates cash. Hershey purchased plant and equipment ($115.4 million), which is a cash outflow and is presented in parentheses. The firm also sold a business (a cash inflow of $450.0 million). The remaining entry, a cash outflow of $11.9 million, primarily is the result of long-term software purchases. The net effect of its investment decisions was a cash inflow of $322.7 million.

The third part of the statement of cash flows covers the firm's financing decisions. Financing activities can be for either the long- or the short-term. Issuing new debt produces a cash inflow, so an increase in short-term liabilities (such as a bank loan) or long-term liabilities (such as a bond) is a source of cash. (Notice that a change in the current liability "net borrowings on credit lines" is treated in the section on financing activities and is not included with the changes in other current liabilities under operating activities.) A reduction in bank loans or outstanding bonds requires a cash outflow. Issuing new stock (an increase in equity) generates a cash inflow, while redeeming stock or paying cash dividends are cash outflows.

The cash inflows and outflows from Hershey Foods Corporation's financing decisions consisted primarily of $136.7 million to retire current borrowings, $318.0

million to repurchase outstanding stock, and $136.7 million to pay cash dividends. There were some small cash inflows from issuing debt and stock, but the net effect of the firm's financing decisions was a cash outflow of $571.3 million.

The last line in the statement of cash flows indicates the firm's cash position at the end of the accounting period. If the sum of the cash inflows from operations, investments, and financing is positive, the firm experienced a cash inflow. If the sum is negative, the result is a cash outflow. For Hershey, the sum was a cash inflow of $79.1 million, which increased the firm's cash and cash equivalents from $39.0 million to $118.1 million.

What does the statement of cash flows add to the financial analyst's knowledge? By placing emphasis on cash, the statement permits the individual to see where the firm generated cash and how these funds were used. Hershey experienced a major increase in cash from the sale of part of its business. These funds were used to reduce outstanding short-term debt, and to repurchase some of its outstanding stock. These cash outflows, however, did not consume all the cash inflow, so the firm's cash holdings increased.

Problems with the Definition of *Cash Flow*

The statement of cash flows highlights the firm's ability to generate cash, but the term *cash flow* may be misleading because its varying meanings may depend on the context in which the term is used. Sometimes cash flow refers to the firm's cash cycle: the selling of inventory, the collection of accounts receivable, and the paying of current liabilities. In this context, cash flow is concerned with the speed with which cash flows through the firm. The emphasis is placed on selling inventory, speeding up the collection of accounts receivable, and retarding the payment of current liabilities. By collecting cash faster and holding it longer, management may increase the firm's profitability.

In other contexts, cash flow is variously defined as (1) earnings plus depreciation (and any other noncash expense), (2) net earnings plus noncash expenses minus principal repayments and preferred stock dividends, (3) net earnings plus

POINTS OF INTEREST
Valuation Techniques and Unique Values

The goal of valuation is to determine a unique value that can be compared to the stock's price. Unfortunately, the various techniques can lead to different values, and instead of determining a unique price, the analysis may generate a range of values. Both of these points are illustrated in the valuation provided to the management of Life Technologies by the investment banking firm Goldman Sachs. Life Technologies requested the valuation after Dexter Corporation offered to purchase the company for $37 a share. The board of Life Technologies employed Goldman Sachs as a financial advisor to determine if the $37 offer was reasonable and fair to Life Technologies' stockholders.

Goldman Sachs used several of the techniques developed in this text to determine the value of Life Technologies stock, including discounted cash flows and a comparable analysis of selected companies. The discounted cash flow models brought back to the present estimates of future cash flows. The comparability analysis compared the firm with similar firms using price/earnings ratios, forecasted earnings, and estimates of growth. Using these techniques, Goldman Sachs determined values ranging from $7.74 to $64.85. (See Life Technologies Schedule 14D-9 filed with the SEC, November 16, 1998.)

The implication of this illustration is obvious. The techniques used to value stock often produce different amounts, and in the final analysis the values are often expressed in terms of a range and not a unique number (although the range is usually smaller than in this illustration). Valuation is not an exact science. If it were, investment decisions would be obvious, and incorrectly priced stocks could not exist.

noncash expenses minus principal repayments and required maintenance capital expenditures, or (4) *pre*tax earnings plus noncash expenses minus principal payments and maintenance capital expenditures. Although these definitions differ, they share similarities. In each, cash flow considers earnings and noncash expenses. In the last three, an effort is being made to determine cash that is not encumbered by the need to retire debt or to restore plant and equipment. For this reason, principal repayments, preferred dividend payments, and cash required to maintain plant and equipment are subtracted to determine discretionary or net free cash flow.[12] Possible uses for this free cash flow include (1) the payment of dividends, (2) additional investments in plant and equipment, (3) acquisitions of other firms, (4) debt retirement, or (5) share repurchases.

Application of Cash Flow to Valuation

The previous discussion points out the increased emphasis on cash flow and the problems of isolating its definition. Once the investor or financial analyst has decided upon a definition and has calculated the estimated cash flow, the next step is to use this information for stock valuation. One method for using cash flow as a valuation tool is to multiply the cash flow per share by the appropriate multiple. This is essentially the same type of technique as employing P/E ratios. In that technique, the analyst multiplies the firm's per-share earnings by the appropriate multiple to determine the firm's value. The same method may be used with the firm's cash flow: The cash flow is multiplied by the appropriate multiple to determine the value of the stock. Of course, determining the appropriate multiple, like determining the appropriate P/E ratio, is one of the major problems facing the financial analyst or individual investor.

As was explained in Chapter 9, cash flow may also be used as a substitute for earnings and dividends in the dividend-growth model. Future estimated cash flows are discounted back to the present in much the same way that future dividends are discounted back to the present. The use of cash flow instead of dividends or earnings is particularly prevalent in the valuation of real estate operations since depreciation is a large proportion of expenses but does not represent an outflow of cash. The real estate analyst substitutes cash flow for earnings to determine the value of the firm.

Whether the financial analyst uses earnings and dividends, cash flows, or P/E ratios, the fundamental principle remains the same. In each case, the analyst is using a type of discounted cash flow technique to determine the value of the stock. In each case, an amount is being discounted back to the present. While there is no unique technique for valuation of a stock since future earnings, dividends, and cash flows are unknown, the importance of expressing the future in terms of the present is crucial to valuation and is the backbone of fundamental value investing.

Fundamental Analysis in an Efficient Market Environment

This chapter has been devoted to the analysis of the financial statements of an individual firm. The interpretation of the results helps identify under- and overvalued securities. However, the individual must not lose sight of the fact that investment decisions are made in efficient financial markets. Fundamental analysis may improve an individual's understanding and perception of the firm's financial condition, but it does not necessarily produce superior investment decisions.

[12]Unfortunately, information on maintenance may not be available to the individual investor. Financial institutions, however, may negotiate for this information as a precondition for granting a loan. The individual may obtain per-share estimates of a firm's cash flow through the *Value Line Investment Survey*.

While it is not necessary to repeat the material on the efficient market hypothesis presented in Chapter 9, it is desirable to remind the reader that there is a considerable body of empirical evidence supporting the hypothesis. There is, however, also evidence that is inconsistent with efficient markets, and these anomalies suggest there may be pockets of inefficiency. Several of the anomalies are built upon fundamental analysis. The small firm effect, low P/E ratios, the Value Line ranking system, and unexpected changes in earnings are illustrations of possible anomalies that use fundamental analysis.[13] In addition, the Fama–French findings discussed in Chapter 9 suggest that higher returns are not related to risk as measured by beta. Instead (1) the size of the firm as measured by the market value of the firm's equity and (2) the ratio of book value of equity to the market value of equity (the reciprocal of the ratio of market to book value discussed in this chapter) better explain returns. These inconsistencies with efficient markets and the capital asset pricing model give encouragement to investors and financial analysts to pursue "value" investing that employs fundamental analysis.

Of course, without fundamental analysis of accounting statements, financial markets would be less efficient. By performing the analysis and seeking to apply the results to the selection of securities, the investor contributes to the efficiency of the market. But the competition among investors helps ensure that a security's price is a fair representation of what the consensus believes the security is worth.

Investors should not bemoan the implications of efficient markets. If the individual does not reach for speculative returns (and hence does not take excess risks or become vulnerable to investment scams), efficient markets imply that an individual has the opportunity to earn a return consistent with the amount of risk the investor bears. Over a period of time, efficient security markets should reward the patient individual willing to accept the risk associated with investing in stocks and bonds. Participation in financial markets is open to all investors. Any individual may acquire financial assets either directly through the purchase of securities or indirectly through the purchase of shares in investment companies or through participation in pension plans and investment vehicles offered by other financial institutions. Over a period of years, these investors should earn returns that are consistent with the risk they bear and the returns earned by the efficient markets.

Summary

Ratio analysis is frequently used to analyze a firm's financial position. These ratios are easy to compute and employ data that are readily available on a firm's financial statements. The ratios include those designed to measure liquidity, activity, profitability, and capitalization (leverage).

While an investor may compute many ratios, it may be more efficient to select those ratios pertinent to the analysis. Creditors and investors in bonds are primarily concerned with determining the firm's capacity to meet its debt obligations as they come due, while investors who purchase stock may stress profitability and growth.

Ratios facilitate comparisons. A firm's current financial condition may be compared with previous years, and trends in the financial position may be identified. In addition, the firm may be compared with other firms within its industry. Some ratios have different definitions, so the analyst must be sure when comparing his

[13]It has been suggested that the anomaly associated with the Value Line ranking system (see footnotes 2 and 3 in Chapter 4) can be explained by unexpected changes in firms' earnings. Investing in firms whose earnings differ from analysts' projected earnings may lead to superior returns. Since an unanticipated change in earnings may lead to changes in the Value Line rankings, it is the earnings surprise and not the ranking system that is the anomaly. See John Affleck-Graves and Richard Mendenhall, "The Relationship between the Value Line Enigma and Post-Earnings Announcement Drift," *Journal of Financial Economics* (February 1992): 75–96.

or her analysis with industry averages from other sources that the same ratio definitions are employed.

Ratio analysis may be used in conjunction with the dividend-growth model to help identify under- or overvalued stocks. Other selection methods also use financial information to help in the process of security selection. These techniques include (1) the analysis of the ratio of price to book value and price to earnings, (2) the total market value of the firm's stock, and (3) various screening techniques designed to identify superior stocks for possible investments.

Emphasis may also be placed on the determination of the firm's ability to generate cash. The statement of cash flows enumerates the firm's cash inflows and outflows. Increases in liabilities and equity and decreases in assets are cash inflows, while decreases in liabilities and equity and increases in assets are cash outflows. By specifying cash inflows and outflows, the statement determines if the firm's cash position has improved or deteriorated. This cash flow may then be used as a basis for determining the value of the firm.

While many investment techniques may be used to help identify individual securities for purchase, such investments are made in efficient financial markets. This suggests that the individual cannot expect to outperform the market consistently on a risk-adjusted basis. Thus, fundamental analysis is important for efficient markets to exist, but it does not follow that the use of fundamental analysis by the individual will lead to superior investment decisions.

Questions

1) What is the difference between the current ratio and the quick ratio?
2) If accounts receivable increase, what effect will this have on the average collection period?
3) What is the difference between liquidity ratios and activity ratios?
4) What is times-interest-earned and what does it add to the analyst's knowledge of the firm? Would this ratio be of interest to a creditor?
5) What are the differences between the gross, operating, and net profit margins?
6) What does the debt ratio measure? Do all firms within an industry use the same proportion of debt financing? Why may the return on equity exceed the return on a firm's total assets?
7) Should you buy a stock with a high
   a) Current ratio?
   b) Return on equity?
   c) Payout ratio?
   d) Debt ratio?
8) What does the statement of cash flows add to the analyst's knowledge of the firm?

9) Use an Internet source such as Quicken (http://www.quicken.com) or Wall Street Research Net (http://www.wsrn.com) to obtain financial ratios indicating the use of debt and profitability for the following pharmaceutical firms: Bristol-Myers Squibb, Merck, Pfizer, and Schering-Plough. Rank the firms on the basis of (a) use of debt financing, (b) profitability, and (c) valuation based on P/E and price/sales ratios.

Problems

1) Using the income statement and balance sheet presented here, compute the following ratios. Compare your results with the industry averages. What strengths and weaknesses are apparent?

Ratio	Industry Average
Current ratio	2:1
Acid test (quick ratio)	1:1
Inventory turnover	
a. Annual sales	4.0 ×
b. Cost of goods sold	2.3 ×
Receivables turnover	
a. Annual credit sales	5.0 ×
b. Annual sales	6.0 ×
c. Average collection period	2.5 months
Operating profit margin	26%
Net profit margin	19%
Return on assets	10%
Return on equity	15%
Debt ratio	
a. Debt/equity	33%
b. Debt/total assets	25%
Times-interest-earned	7.1 ×

Income Statement for XYZ
for the period ending December 31, 20xx

Sales	$100,000
Cost of goods sold	60,000
Gross profit	40,000
Selling and administrative expense	15,000
Operating profit	25,000
Interest expense	5,000
Earnings before taxes	20,000
Taxes	3,200
Earnings available to stockholders	$ 16,800
Number of shares outstanding	10,000
Earnings per share	$1.68

(To compute the inventory turnover, assume that the prior year's inventory was $40,000.)

Firm XYZ
Balance Sheet as of December 31, 20xx
Assets

Current assets		
Cash and marketable securities		$ 10,000
Accounts receivable	$ 32,000	
Less allowance for doubtful accounts	2,000	30,000
Inventory		
Finished goods	30,000	
Work in progress	5,000	
Raw materials	7,000	42,000
Total current assets		$ 82,000

Firm XYZ
Balance Sheet as of December 31, 20xx
Assets *continued*

Investments		$ 10,000
Long-term assets		
Plant and equipment	100,000	
Less accumulated depreciation	30,000	70,000
Land		10,000
Total long-term assets		$ 80,000
Total assets		$172,000

Liabilities & Stockholders' Equity

Current liabilities	
Accounts payable	$ 10,000
Accrued wages	11,000
Bank notes	15,000
Accrued interest payable	4,000
Accrued taxes	1,000
Total current liabilities	$ 41,000
Long-term debt	$ 15,000
Total liabilities	$ 56,000
Stockholders' equity	
Common stock ($1 par value; 20,000 shares authorized; 10,000 shares outstanding)	$ 10,000
Additional paid-in capital	20,000
Retained earnings	86,000
Total stockholders' equity	$116,000
Total liabilities and equity	$172,000

2) You have taken the following information from a firm's financial statements. As an investor in the firm's debt instruments, you are concerned with its liquidity position and its use of financial leverage. What conclusions can you draw from this information?

	2002	2001	2000
Sales	$1,700,000	$1,500,000	$1,000,000
Cash	18,000	7,000	5,000
Accounts receivable	152,000	130,000	125,000
Inventory	200,000	190,000	200,000
Current liabilities	225,000	210,000	175,000
Operating income	170,000	145,000	90,000
Interest expense	27,000	23,000	20,000
Taxes	53,000	45,000	25,000
Net income	90,000	77,000	45,000
Debt	260,000	250,000	200,000
Equity	330,000	300,000	200,000

3) What is the debt/equity ratio and the debt ratio for a firm with total debt of $700,000 and equity of $300,000?
4) A firm with sales of $500,000 has average inventory of $200,000. The industry average for inventory turnover is four times a year. What would be the reduction in inventory if this firm were to achieve a turnover comparable to the industry average?
5) Company A has three debt issues of $3,000 each. The interest rate on issue A is 4 percent, on B the rate is 6 percent, and on C the rate is 8 percent. Issue B is subordinate to A, and issue C is subordinate to both A and B. The firm's operating income (EBIT) is $500. Compute the times-interest-earned ratio for issue C. What does the answer imply? Does the answer mean that the interest will not be paid?
6) If a firm has sales of $42,791,000 a year, and the average collection period for the industry is 40 days, what should this firm's accounts receivable be if the firm is comparable to the industry?
7) Two firms have sales of $1 million each. Other financial information is as follows:

	Firm A	Firm B
EBIT	$150,000	$150,000
Interest expense	20,000	75,000
Income tax	50,000	30,000
Equity	300,000	100,000

What are the operating profit margins and the net profit margins for these two firms? What is their return on equity? Why are they different? If total assets are the same for each firm, what can you conclude about their respective uses of debt financing?

8) In this chapter, ratio analysis was applied to the financial statements of HSY. Update Exhibit 13.6 for the years after 1999. The 2000 fiscal financial statements are provided here. For years after 2000, consult Hershey Foods' annual reports available at http://www.hersheys.com.

Hershey Foods Corporation Consolidated Balance Sheet as of December 31, 2000 (in millions)

ASSETS		**LIABILITIES AND STOCKHOLDERS' EQUITY**	
Current assets		**Current liabilities**	
Cash and cash equivalents	$ 32.0	Accounts payable	$ 149.2
Accounts receivable	379.7	Accrued liabilities	358.1
Inventories	605.2	Short-term loans	257.6
Deferred income taxes	76.1	Other	2.0
Other	202.3	Total current liabilities	766.9
Total current assets	1,295.3	**Long-term debt**	877.7
Property, plant, and equipment	1,585.4	**Other long-term liabilities**	327.7
		Deferred income taxes	300.5
Other assets	566.9	**Total liabilities**	2,272.7
Total assets	$3,447.6	**Stockholders' equity**	
		Common stock shares outstanding 149.5 in 2000	149.5
		Additional paid-in capital	13.1
		Retained earnings	2,702.9
		Treasury stock repurchased at cost	(1,645.0)
		Other adjustments	(45.5)
		Total stockholders' equity	$1,175.0
		Total liabilities and stockholders' equity	$3,447.7

Source: Adapted from Hershey Foods Corporation *Proxy Statement* and *2000 Annual Report to Stockholders.*

Hershey Foods Corporation Statement of Income for the year ended December 31, 2000 (in millions except per share data)

Net Sales	$4,221.0
Costs and expenses	
Cost of goods sold	2,295.1
Selling, marketing, and administrative	1,303.4
Gain on sale of business	—
Earnings before interest and taxes	622.5
Interest expense	76.0
Provision for income taxes	212.1
Net income	$ 334.4
Net income per share	$ 2.42
Cash dividends per share	$ 1.08

Source: Adapted from Hershey Foods Corporation *Proxy Statement* and *2000 Annual Report to Stockholders.*

THE FINANCIAL ADVISOR'S INVESTMENT CASE
Blue Jeans and Stock Selection

Bryan Szafranski often observed that the clothes worn by his daughters and their friends were made of denim. No matter what the style, blue jeans and other clothes made of denim were popular. While certain styles would remain popular for only brief periods, the use of denim continued year after year. Szafranski reasoned that the manufacturers of denim may be potentially attractive investments, as there appeared to him to be little fluctuation in the demand for denim.

Szafranski discovered that the primary manufacturer of denim was Dentex, a textile mill in North Carolina. Dentex specializes in denim and produces only a modest amount of other types of cloth. Its sales of denim account for one-third of the total denim market, both domestic and abroad. Dentex's balance sheets and income statements for the last two years are presented in Exhibit 1. Dentex's per-share earnings and dividends are given in Exhibit 2 (p. 430). With the exception of the most recent year, 2001, and 1998, per-share earnings have steadily increased, and dividends have risen every year for the last ten years. This pattern of earnings and dividend growth impressed Szafranski, who tended to think of textiles as a dull industry with little growth potential.

Szafranski realized that for the firm to be a good investment, it should have strong fundamentals and be financially sound. So he decided to use ratios to analyze the firm's financial statements. From other sources, he found the industry averages given in Exhibit 3 (p. 430).

Currently Dentex's stock sells for $50. Szafranski could invest in U.S. Treasury bills that yield 3.5 percent, but he believes that the stock market may offer a return over a period of years of 9.5 percent. Should he buy the stock of Dentex? To help Szafranski with his decision, answer the following questions:

1) What conclusion(s) are indicated by the ratio analysis?
2) What is the firm's current payout ratio compared to its historical payout ratio?
3) What are the annual growth rates in the earnings per share and the dividend?
4) Is there any reason to believe that the firm has changed its dividend policy?
5) Risk is affected by many factors. How may each of the following affect the firm-specific (unsystematic) risk associated with Dentex?
   a) The firm's geographical location
   b) Its product line
   c) Its use of debt financing
   d) Foreign competition
6) Does Dentex's P/E ratio suggest the firm is undervalued?
7) Why is the growth rate in the dividend not sustainable?
8) If a dividend growth rate of 4 percent can be sustained, is the stock a good purchase if the required return is 9.5 percent?
9) If the beta coefficient were 0.8 and the sustainable growth is assumed to be 4 percent, should the stock be purchased if the risk-free rate is 3.5 percent and the anticipated return on the market is 9.5 percent?

EXHIBIT 1

Financial Statements of Dentex

Consolidated Statement of Income (for the years ending)

	2001	2000
Sales (in thousands)	$668,000	$730,000
Cost of goods sold	531,000	571,000
Selling and administrative expense	54,000	52,000
Depreciation	24,000	22,000
Interest expense (net)	3,000	3,000
	612,000	648,000
Income before taxes	56,000	82,000
Income taxes	24,000	35,000
Net income	$ 32,000	$ 47,000
Earnings per share	$5.87	$8.82
Dividends per share	2.20	2.00

Consolidated Balance Sheet (as of December 31)

	2001	2000
Assets (in thousands)		
Current assets		
Cash and short-term investments	$ 23,000	$ 5,000
Accounts receivable	80,000	114,000
Inventory	120,000	118,000
Total current assets	223,000	237,000
Property, plant, and equipment		
Land	3,000	3,000
Buildings and equipment	177,000	156,000
Other	20,000	17,000
	200,000	176,000
Total assets	$423,000	$413,000

	2001	2000
Liabilities (in thousands)		
Current liabilities		
Long-term debt due within a year	$ 6,000	$ 4,000
Accounts payable	22,000	22,000
Accrued expenses	30,000	35,000
Income taxes owed	3,000	10,000
Total current liabilities	61,000	71,000
Long-term debt	20,000	22,000
Stockholders' equity		
Common stock	57,000	57,000
Paid-in capital	5,000	5,000
Retained earnings	280,000	258,000
Total stockholders' equity	342,000	320,000
Total liabilities and stockholders' equity	$423,000	$413,000

EXHIBIT 2

Earnings per Share and Dividends of Dentex

	Earnings per share	Dividends
2001	$5.87	$2.20
2000	8.82	2.00
1999	7.49	1.80
1998	6.21	1.60
1997	6.75	1.35
1996	4.90	0.95
1995	3.97	0.75
1994	2.51	0.70
1993	1.58	0.55
1992	1.33	0.51
1991	1.00	0.50

EXHIBIT 3

Industry Averages for Selected Ratios

Current ratio	3.2:1
Quick ratio	1.6:1
Average collection period	55 days
Inventory turnover (sales/average inventory)	3.7 a year
Fixed asset turnover	4.5 a year
Debt ratio (debt/total assets)	33%
Times-interest-earned	10 ×
Net profit margin	3.3%
Return on assets	4.5%
Return on equity	7.0%

APPENDIX 13

Financial Leverage and the Return on Equity

Financial leverage is the use of another person's money in return for a fixed payment. If a firm borrows funds, it issues debt and must make a fixed interest payment for the use of the money. A company may also obtain financial leverage by paying a fixed dividend on stock. This type of stock is given preference or prior claim on the earnings of the company (i.e., it is preferred stock). Since preferred stock has a fixed dividend, it is similar to debt and is a source of financial leverage.

A firm agrees to make fixed interest and dividend payments because it *anticipates* being able to earn more with the borrowed funds than it has to pay in interest to its creditors. This will increase the return on the common stockholders' investment. The creditors are willing to lend the money in return for the fixed payments because they receive a relatively assured flow of income from the loans but do not bear the risk of owning and operating the business. If the creditors had the skills and desired to do so, they would enter the business themselves. There are, however, many people who lack either the skills or the desire to enter a particular business and who are satisfied to let a corporation use their money for the promised fixed return. They are, of course, aware that the firm anticipates earning more with their money than it has agreed to pay.

Management wants to increase the value of the firm's stock. Since the use of financial leverage may increase the return on the common stockholders' equity, management may decide to use financial leverage. Its use, however, may also increase the level of risk. Thus, management must try to determine the optimal amount of financial leverage, for the use of insufficient leverage will decrease the stockholders' return on equity but the use of excessive leverage will subject the stockholders to excessive risk.

How Financial Leverage Increases the Rate of Return on Equity

How financial leverage works may be shown by a simple illustration. Firm A needs $100 in capital to operate and may acquire the money from the stockholders (owners) of the firm. Alternatively, it may acquire part of the money from stockholders and part from creditors. If management acquires the total amount from the owners, the firm uses no debt financing (financial leverage) and would have the following simple balance sheet:

Assets	Liabilities and Equity
Cash $100	Debt $0
	Equity $100

Once in business, the firm generates the following simplified income statement:

Sales	$100
Expenses	−80
Operating profit	$ 20
Taxes (40%)	−8
Net profit	$ 12

What is the return that the firm has earned on the owners' investment? The answer is 12 percent, for the investors contributed $100 and the firm earned $12 after taxes. The firm may pay the $12 to the investors in cash dividends or may retain the money to help finance future growth. Either way, however, the stockholders' rate of return on their investment is 12 percent.

By using financial leverage, management may be able to increase the owners' rate of return on their investment. What happens to their rate of return if management is able to borrow part of the capital needed to operate the firm? The answer to this question depends on (1) the proportion of total capital that is borrowed and (2) the interest rate that must be paid to the creditors. If management is able to borrow 50 percent ($50) of the firm's capital needs at an interest cost of 10 percent, the balance sheet becomes

Assets	Liabilities and Equity
Cash $100	Debt $50
	Equity $50

Since the firm borrowed $50, it is now obligated to pay interest. Thus, the firm has a new expense that must be paid before any earnings are available for the common stockholders. The simple income statement becomes

Sales	$100
Expenses	− 80
Operating profit	$ 20
Interest expense	−5
Taxable income	$ 15
Taxes	−6
Net Profit	$ 9

The use of debt causes the total net profit to decline from $12 to $9 but the owners' return on equity increases from 12 percent to 18 percent. Since the owners invested only $50 and earned $9 on that amount, they made 18 percent on their investment, whereas without the use of leverage they earned only 12 percent on their $100 investment.

There are two sources of this additional return. First, the firm borrowed money and agreed to pay a fixed return of 10 percent. The firm, however, was able to earn more than 10 percent with the money, and this additional earning accrued to the owners of the firm. Second, the entire burden of the interest cost was not borne by the firm. The federal tax laws permit the deduction of interest as an expense before taxable income is determined, and thus this interest expense is shared with the government. The greater the corporate income tax rate, the greater is the portion of interest expense borne by the government. In this case, 40 percent, or $2 of the $5 interest expense, was borne by the federal government in lost tax revenues. If the corporate income tax rate were 60 percent, the government would lose $3 in taxes by permitting the deduction of the interest expense.

As was seen in the preceding example, a firm's management may increase the owners' return on equity through the use of debt financing—that is, the use of financial leverage. By increasing the proportion of the firm's assets that are financed by debt (by increasing the debt ratio), management is able to increase the return on the owners' equity. Exhibit 13A.1 shows various combinations of debt and equity financing, along with the resultant earnings for the firm and the return on the investors' equity. The exhibit is constructed on the assumption that the interest rate is 10 percent regardless of the proportion of the firm's assets financed by debt.

EXHIBIT 13A.1

Relationship Between Debt Financing and the Return on Equity

Proportion of assets financed by debt (%)	0	20	50	70	90
Amount of debt outstanding ($)	0.00	20.00	50.00	70.00	90.00
Equity ($)	100.00	80.00	50.00	30.00	10.00
Sales ($)	100.00	100.00	100.00	100.00	100.00
Expenses ($)	−80.00	−80.00	−80.00	−80.00	−80.00
Operating profit ($)	20.00	20.00	20.00	20.00	20.00
Interest expense ($) (10% interest rate)	0.00	2.00	5.00	7.00	9.00
Taxable income ($)	20.00	18.00	15.00	13.00	11.00
Income tax ($) (40% tax rate)	−8.00	−7.20	−6.00	−5.20	−4.40
Net profit ($)	12.00	10.80	9.00	7.80	6.60
Return on equity (%)	12.00	13.50	18.00	26.00	66.00

As may be seen from Exhibit 13A.1, as the proportion of debt financing rises, the return on the owners' equity not only rises but does so at an increasing rate. This indicates dramatically how the use of financial leverage may significantly increase the return on a firm's equity.

Besides the possible increase in the return on stockholders' funds, the use of financial leverage may also increase earnings per share. Although total earnings declined in the preceding example when the firm borrowed funds, earnings per share would probably rise. This is because the firm is using less equity financing and therefore would have to issue fewer shares. The smaller earnings would be spread over a smaller number of shares, which may cause earnings per share to increase. However, as is subsequently explained, the increased per-share earnings may not necessarily lead to higher stock prices.

Financial Leverage and Risk

Since the use of financial leverage increases the owners' return on equity, why not use ever-increasing amounts of debt financing? The answer is that as the proportion of debt financing rises, the element of risk increases. This amplification of risk increases (1) the potential for fluctuations in the owners' returns and (2) the interest rate that the creditors charge for the use of their money.

How the use of financial leverage increases the potential risk to the owners is illustrated by employing the simple example presented in the previous section. What happens to the return on the equity if sales decline by 10 percent, from $100 to $90, but expenses remain the same? The income statements for two firms with and without financial leverage become:

	Firm without Leverage (0% Debt)	Firm with Leverage (50% Debt)
Sales	$90	$90
Expenses	−80	−80
Operating profit	$10	$10
Interest	−0	−5
Taxable income	$10	$ 5
Taxes	−4	−2
Net profit	$ 6	$ 3

The 10 percent decline in sales produces a substantial decline in the earnings and return on the owners' investment in both cases. For the firm without debt financing, the return on equity declines to 6 percent ($6 ÷ $100); for the firm with financial leverage, the return plummets from the 18 percent in the previous example to 6 percent. The decline is greater when financial leverage is used than when it is not.

The return decreased more for the firm with financial leverage because of the interest payment. When the firm borrowed the capital, it agreed to make a *fixed* interest payment. This fixed interest payment was the source of the increase in the owners' return on equity in the second example when sales were $100, and it is the cause of the larger decline in the owners' return on equity when the firm's sales declined from $100 to $90. If the firm had used leverage to a greater extent (i.e., if it had borrowed more), the decline in the return on the owners' investment would have been even greater. As the proportion of a firm's assets financed by fixed obligations increases, the potential fluctuation in the stockholders' return on equity also increases. Small changes in revenue or costs will produce greater fluctuations in the earnings of a firm with a considerable amount of financial leverage.

Firms that use large amounts of financial leverage are viewed by investors (both creditors and stockholders) as being risky. Creditors may refuse to lend to a firm that uses debt financing extensively, or they may do so only at higher interest rates or under more stringent loan conditions. Equity investors will also require a higher return to justify bearing the risk. As is explained in the next section, this increase in the required return may result in a decline in the value of the stock.

Financial Leverage and Valuation

Since financial leverage may increase earnings per share and the return on equity, investors may be willing to pay more for the stock. For example, for a particular required return on an investment, an increase in earnings from $1 to $1.20 per share should increase the value of the stock. If the investor desires a set return and the firm earns more, the investor should be willing to pay more for the stock.

This concept can be illustrated by the use of the following equation. The risk-free rate is 7.0 percent, and the investor expects the market to rise by 13.0 percent. If the beta coefficient is 0.83, the required rate of return is 12.0 percent (i.e., $k = 0.07 + [0.13 - 0.07]0.83 = 0.12$). If the firm earns $1 before using financial leverage, distributes $0.60, and retains the remaining $0.40 so that it can grow, the value of the stock using the dividend-growth model is

$$V = \frac{\$0.60(1 + 0.05)}{0.12 - 0.05}$$
$$= \$9$$

when the required return is 12 percent and the firm is able to grow annually at the rate of 5 percent.

If the firm now successfully uses financial leverage to increase earnings per share, it can increase its dividend *without* reducing its ability to grow, or it can increase its growth rate without decreasing its cash dividend. If the firm's per-share earnings rise to $1.20 and the additional $0.20 is distributed as cash dividends (i.e., cash dividends rise to $0.80), the value of the stock is

$$V = \frac{\$0.80(1 + 0.05)}{0.12 - 0.05}$$
$$= \$12.$$

Thus, the successful use of financial leverage results in an increase in the value of the stock.

The use of financial leverage, however, may increase the element of risk because per-share earnings and the return to stockholders become more variable. Therefore, to induce investors to bear this additional risk, the return must be larger. Suppose the beta coefficient rises to 1.17 because earnings are more volatile. The required return rises to 14 percent (i.e., $k = 0.07 + [0.13 - 0.07]1.17 = 0.14$). The required return, then, has increased as a result of the additional risk, which is attributable to the use of an increased amount of financial leverage.

The potential impact of this increase in the required rate of return may be illustrated by the preceding example. The cash dividends have increased to $0.80 as a result of the use of financial leverage but the required rate of return has increased from 12 percent to 14 percent. The value of the stock becomes

$$P = \frac{\$0.80(1 + 0.05)}{0.14 - 0.05}$$
$$= \$9.33.$$

Although the value of the stock does rise (from $9 to $9.33), the amount of the increase is small. The increase in the required return that occurred when the firm used more financial leverage almost completely offset the increase in value from the higher per-share earnings and higher cash dividends.

The use of financial leverage may not result in an increase in the value of stock. Although more financial leverage may result in higher per-share earnings, it may also cause investors' required return to rise. This increase in the required return will certainly offset part, if not all, of the effect of the increase in per-share earnings. It is even possible that the value of the stock will decline if the required return increases sufficiently.

Management, then, must be concerned with the extent to which the firm uses debt financing. One goal of management is to increase the value of the shares, but the extensive use of financial leverage may have the opposite effect and cause the value of the firm's stock to decline. Therefore, management must determine that combination of debt and equity financing that offers the benefits of financial leverage without unduly increasing the element of risk. Such a capital structure of debt and equity should help to maximize the value of the firm's stock.[1]

Differences in the Amount of Financial Leverage Used by Firms

Although virtually every firm uses financial leverage, there are differences in the extent to which it is used. For some firms, the nature of the business enterprise necessitates the extensive use of financial leverage, and this influences the behavior of the firms in the industry. For example, commercial banks use a large amount of financial leverage because most of their assets are financed by their deposit liabilities (e.g., checking accounts). Slight changes in the revenues of a commercial bank may produce greater fluctuations in the earnings. Bankers are well aware of this effect of financial leverage and are usually not willing to take inordinate risks. The nature of a bank's operations and the high use of financial leverage require bankers to be conservative.

Other firms need large amounts of fixed equipment to operate and may use leverage extensively if this equipment is financed through the issuance of debt.

[1]For a discussion of a firm's optimal capital structure, see Eugene Brigham, Louis C. Gapenski, and Michael C. Ehrhardt, *Financial Management: Theory and Practice,* 9th ed. (Fort Worth, TX: The Dryden Press, 1999).

EXHIBIT 13A.2

Earnings per Share (EPS) and the Use of Debt Financing by UAL (United Airlines)

Year	EPS	Debt as a Proportion of Total Assets
1999	$9.97	70.8%
1998	6.38	77.9
1997	9.04	81.9
1996	5.96	90.8
1995	5.47	NMF
1994	0.19	NMF
1993	(0.66)	90.6
1992	(4.33)	94.2
1991	(3.58)	83.8
1990	1.08	78.9
1989	3.97	78.3
1988	9.47	78.7
1987	1.44	60.7

EPS before extraordinary items.
NMF = No meaningful number; debt exceeded total assets.
Source: *Handbook of Common Stock,* Winter 2000–2001 edition (New York: Mergent FIS, Inc., 2001).

The airlines are an excellent example of an industry that has a large investment in equipment frequently financed by debt. This, in part, explains the large fluctuations in the earnings of airline companies. Exhibit 13A.2 presents the earnings per share (EPS) for UAL (United Airlines) and the proportion of its assets financed by debt. The information in this exhibit indicates that there have been large and sudden fluctuations in the earnings per share. These fluctuations are the result of changes in the demand for and in the cost to provide the service, and they are magnified by the use of debt financing. For example, United Airlines finances over three-quarters of its assets with debt and has experienced severe fluctuations in earnings that have ranged from profits of $1.08 per share in 1990 to a loss of $3.58 just one year later, followed by earnings of over $9 a share in 1997.

Technical Analysis

14 CHAPTER

In Bizet's *Carmen,* three gypsies use cards to foretell their future. One foresees a young lover who sweeps her off her feet to experience never-ending love. Another foresees a rich, old gentleman who marries her. She will have diamonds and gold and soon become a widow. Carmen foresees death.

Wouldn't investing be easier if we could read the cards and foresee the future? Or if we could find a trading rule that told us when to buy or sell? Then the investor would not have to perform the analysis described in the previous chapters. The technical approach to security selection purports to do just that. By analyzing how the market (or a specific stock) has performed in the past, the investor may forecast how the market (or a specific stock) will perform in the future. The study of historical data concerning prices or the volume of transactions is substituted for analysis of financial statements and forecasts of future dividends and the growth in earnings.

Technical analysis is a very broad topic because there are so many varieties of this type of analysis. This chapter covers several popular technical approaches to the market and security selection. These include the Dow Theory, odd-lot purchases and sales, point-and-figure charts, and moving averages. Since these techniques accumulate and summarize data in a variety of charts and graphs, investors who use these techniques are often referred to as *chartists.*

The discussion in this chapter is primarily descriptive. After presenting several technical approaches, the chapter ends with a consideration of the empirical studies that seek to verify the techniques. The results of these studies strongly suggest that *technical analysis does not lead to superior investment results.* However, this lack of empirical support has not stopped the use of technical analysis, and some of its jargon is commonly used by both professional and lay investors.

Learning Objectives

After completing this chapter you should be able to:

1. State the purpose of technical analysis.
2. Differentiate between the various technical approaches to security selection.
3. Construct X-O charts, bar graphs, and candlesticks.
4. Calculate a moving average.
5. Construct a portfolio based on the Dogs of the Dow.
6. Explain why the technical approach has little support from many investors.

The Purpose of the Technical Approach

The two previous chapters considered the economy and the analysis of financial statements. The investor or portfolio manager studied (1) the firm's financial condition as indicated in the firm's financial statements, (2) the position of the firm in its industry, and (3) the direction of the economy. Such systematic study of the firm's financial condition and potential is the backbone of security analysis and value investing. The techniques are the *fundamental* tools of financial analysis, hence its name. Ultimately, the purpose of such analysis is to help identify undervalued assets for possible inclusion in the individual's portfolio.

A different type of analysis uses charts and graphs of price movements, the volume of security transactions, or sales and purchases by selected investors. This approach, especially some of the charts, can appear to be technical, hence the name *technical analysis.* The name does not imply that fundamental analysis is simple. The analysis of financial statements can be complex; however, in the jargon of investments, technical analysis implies a particular approach to security selection that is completely different from the systematic study of a firm's financial statements, its position within its industry, and the aggregate economy. In technical analysis the emphasis is placed on determining when to buy or sell. Such buy or sell signals may be independent of the firm's financial condition. Thus, technical analysis may recommend selling a financially strong firm if there are indicators that security prices will decline.

The Variety of Technical Analysis

technical analysis
An analysis of past volume and/or price behavior to identify which assets to purchase or sell and the best time to purchase or sell them.

Technical analysis attempts to predict future stock prices by analyzing past stock prices. In effect, it asserts that tomorrow's stock price is influenced by today's price. That is a very appealing assertion, because it eliminates the need to perform fundamental analysis. No longer does the investor have to be concerned with ratios, estimating growth, and appropriate discount rates. Instead, he or she keeps a record of specific market factors, such as who is buying and selling the stock, and of specific information on individual stocks, such as the closing price and the volume of transactions. This information is then summarized in a variety of charts and graphs, which in turn tell the investor when to buy and sell the securities.

There are many different technical approaches to the selection of securities. Only a few will be discussed in this chapter. These are classified into two groups. The first techniques are designed to indicate the general direction of the market. Since security prices move together, the direction of the market is the important, perhaps overriding, factor in the decision to buy and sell securities. This first group of techniques includes the Dow Theory (which is perhaps the oldest of all the technical approaches to the market), Barron's confidence index, and odd-lot purchases versus odd-lot sales.

The second group of technical approaches discussed in this chapter is designed not only to discern the direction of the market but also to decide when to buy or sell specific securities. These include point-and-figure charts, bar graphs, and moving averages of stock prices. The information necessary to perform this analysis is also readily available in the financial press. Thus, the investor may either perform the analysis or pay advisory services to do so.

Before reading further, the student should be forewarned that the presentations of the various approaches make their application appear to be easy. Also, the examples have been constructed to illustrate the techniques. In actual practice the buy and sell signal indicated by technical analysis may be less obvious than the illustrations in the text (and in the sales material of vendors). A technical indicator is constructed with data as they become available. Often, you can look back and see that a pattern has developed (e.g., a sell signal), and if the investor had sold, the correct decision would have been made. Hindsight, however, is 20/20. Seeing the pattern after the fact is not the same as perceiving the pattern as it is unfolding. Of course, you must perceive the indicator as it develops to act on it.

The student should also realize that the efficient market hypothesis suggests that using technical analysis will not lead to superior investment decisions. As was explained in Chapter 9, most empirical results support this hypothesis. In addition, technical analysis may require frequent buying and selling, which generates commissions for the broker. The little evidence that does support technical analysis suggests that any superior results are marginal at best and do not cover the commission costs.[1] An obvious implication of these studies is that a strategy of buy and hold produces investment results that are equal to or better than those from trading securities using technical analysis.

Even though empirical results do not favor the use of technical analysis, some investors and portfolio managers continue to use this type of analysis. This usage has the potential to affect security prices. For example, breaking a trend line may suggest a buying (or selling) opportunity. Heavy buying (or selling) could occur even though the firm's fundamentals have not changed. By knowing technical trading rules, an investor may avoid buying when the technicians are buying and perhaps artificially raising the stock's price.

Even if investors and portfolio managers do not employ technical analysis as the sole criterion for investment decisions, they may apply the analysis to confirm decisions based on fundamental analysis. One possible explanation for the continued use is the accuracy of the empirical tests. These tests must specify a confidence level, such as 95 percent. Consider a technical approach that generates a return of 12.2 percent when the average return is 12 percent. Can the investor assert with a 95 percent level of confidence that the 0.2 percent difference is the result of the approach's ability to outperform or is the difference the result of chance?[2] Even if the returns had been 15 percent versus 12 percent and the probability of the difference being statistically significant were higher, the 3 percent difference could still be the result of chance.

Empirical tests often use 95 percent as the level of confidence, with 90 percent being the lowest acceptable level. If it cannot be shown with at least a 90 percent level of confidence that the results are attributable to the technical indicator, the empirical test concludes that the difference is the result of chance. Supporters of technical analysis may argue that 95 percent or even the less rigorous 90 percent are too high a level of confidence. If a technique works only 70 percent of the time, it still generates a higher return. If this return is 0.2 percent greater than the average return, then over a period of years the difference will generate a higher terminal value (i.e., in 20 years, $100,000 grows to $999,671 at 12.2 percent but only $964,629 at 12 percent). Even if the additional return is the result of chance, it is doubtful the investor would say, "I don't want the additional $35,000. It was not earned but was the result of luck!"

The debate concerning the efficacy of technical analysis will continue, and the Internet will increase access to technical analysis by the individual investor. Data are readily available that permit the investor to track stocks and apply technical analysis. (See the Points of Interest "Technical Analysis and the Internet" on page 440.) Even if the individual does not use the analysis, its jargon permeates the popular, if not the academic, press on investments. Thus, the student of investments needs to be aware of technical analysis even if he or she never uses it as part of an investment strategy.

Market Indicators

Dow Theory
A technical approach based on the Dow Jones averages.

The **Dow Theory** is one of the oldest technical methods for analyzing security prices. It is an aggregate measure of security prices and hence does not predict the

[1]Summaries of the empirical evidence that generally refute technical analysis are given in James H. Lorie and Mary T. Hamilton, *The Stock Market: Theories and Evidence,* 2d ed. (Homewood, IL: Richard D. Irwin, 1985); and Burton G. Malkiel, *A Random Walk Down Wall Street,* 6th ed. (New York: W. W. Norton & Co., 2000). The large body of evidence that does not support the use of technical analysis has caused many instructors to slight and even omit technical analysis. One text that does present a sympathetic coverage of technical analysis is Jerome B. Cohen, Edward D. Zinbarg, and Arthur Zeikel, *Investment Analysis and Portfolio Management,* 5th ed. (Homewood, IL: Richard D. Irwin, 1987), Chapter 8.

[2]An analogy with batting averages may help clarify the point. A player with a batting average of .256 has a .298 season. Since baseball is a game of streaks, is the higher average the result of improved skills or chance (i.e., a lucky streak during the season)? The answer is obviously important since management may pay for improved skills but trade the player if the improved average is the result of chance.

POINTS OF INTEREST

Technical Analysis and the Internet

Data for generating a technical indicator or the actual calculation of the indicator may be found through the Internet. Often the investor must subscribe to a service to obtain the analysis. Some technical tools, such as the moving averages discussed later in this chapter, are readily available at no cost. Subscription services may offer teasers, which permit the investor to sample an indicator before deciding to subscribe.

Possible sources of technical indicators or information on technical analysis include:

Ask Research:
http://www.askresearch.com
Dorsey Wright & Associates:
http://www.dorseywright.com
Equity Analytics, Ltd.:
http://www.e-analytics.com
Silicon Investor:
http://www.siliconinvestor.com
Wall Street City:
http://www.wallstreetcity.com

direction of change in individual stock prices. What it purports to show is the direction that the market will take. Thus, it is a method that identifies the top of a bull market and the bottom of a bear market.

The Dow Theory developed from the work of Charles Dow, who founded Dow Jones and Company and was the first editor of *The Wall Street Journal.*[3] Dow identified three movements in security prices: primary, secondary, and tertiary. Primary price movements are related to the security's intrinsic value. Such values depend on the earning capacity of the firm and the distribution of dividends. Secondary price movements, or "swings," are governed by current events that temporarily affect value and by the manipulation of stock prices. These price swings may persist for several weeks and even months. Tertiary price movements are daily price fluctuations to which Dow attributed no significance.

Although Charles Dow believed in fundamental analysis, the Dow Theory has evolved into a primarily technical approach to the stock market. It asserts that stock prices demonstrate patterns over four to five years and that these patterns are mirrored by indexes of stock prices. The Dow Theory employs two of the Dow Jones averages, the industrial average and the transportation average. The utility average is generally ignored.

The Dow Theory is built on the assertion that measures of stock prices tend to move together. If the Dow Jones Industrial Average is rising, then the transportation average should also be rising. Such simultaneous price movements suggest a strong bull market. Conversely, a decline in both the industrial and transportation averages suggests a strong bear market. However, if the averages are moving in opposite directions, the market is uncertain as to the direction of future stock prices.

If one of the averages starts to decline after a period of rising stock prices, the two are at odds. For example, the industrial average may be rising while the transportation average is falling. This suggests that the industrials may not continue to rise but may soon start to fall. Hence, the smart investor will use this signal to sell securities and convert to cash.

The converse occurs when, after a period of falling security prices, one of the averages starts to rise while the other continues to fall. According to the Dow Theory, this divergence suggests that the bear market is over and that security prices

[3]George W. Bishop, Jr., *Charles H. Dow and the Dow Theory* (New York: Appleton-Century-Crofts, 1960), 225–228.

in general will soon start to rise. The investor will then purchase securities in anticipation of the price increase.

There are several problems with the Dow Theory. The first is that it is not a theory but an interpretation of known data. It does not explain why the two averages should be able to forecast future stock prices. In addition, there may be a considerable lag between actual turning points and those indicated by the forecast. It may be months before the two averages confirm each other, during which time individual stocks may show substantial price changes.

Barron's Confidence Index

Barron's confidence index
An index designed to identify investors' confidence in the level and direction of security prices.

Barron's confidence index is based on the belief that the differential between the returns on quality bonds and bonds of lesser quality will forecast future price movements. During periods of optimism, investors will be more willing to bear risk and thus will move from investments in higher-quality debt to more speculative but higher-yielding, lower-quality debt. This selling of higher-quality debt will depress its price and raise its yield. Simultaneously, the purchase of poor-quality debt should drive up its price and lower the yield. Thus, the difference between the two yields will diminish.

The opposite occurs when sentiment turns bearish. The investors and especially those who "know" what the market will do in the future will sell poor-quality debt and purchase higher-quality debt. This will have the effect of increasing the spread between the yields, as the price of poor-quality debt falls relative to that of the higher-quality debt.

Barron's confidence index is constructed by using Barron's index of yields on higher- and lower-quality bonds. When the yield differential is small (i.e., when the yields on high-quality debt approach those that can be earned on poor-quality debt), the ratio rises. This is interpreted as showing investor confidence. Such confidence means that security prices will tend to rise. Conversely, when the index declines, that is an indication that security prices will fall.

Like the other technical approaches, Barron's confidence index may indicate a tendency; however, it does not give conclusive signals. Since the signals of the Barron's confidence index are often ambiguous or there is a considerable time lag between the signal and the change forecasted, the index can be of only modest use for investors. Like many technical indicators, it may point to the direction that security prices will follow, but it is not a totally reliable predictor of future stock prices.

Purchase and Sale of Odd Lots

odd-lot theory
A technical approach to the stock market that purports to predict security prices on the basis of odd-lot sales and purchases.

Another technical indicator of the market is the **odd-lot theory**, which concerns the purchase and sale of securities by small investors. These investors buy in small quantities (i.e., odd lots, or less than 100 shares). The volume of such odd-lot purchases and sales is reported in the financial press along with other financial data. The ratio of these odd-lot purchases to odd-lot sales is taken by some technicians as an indicator of the direction of future prices.

The rationale behind the use of the ratio of odd-lot purchases to sales is the assertion that small investors are frequently wrong, especially just before a change in the direction of the market. Such investors will get caught up in the enthusiasm of a bull market and expand their purchases just as the market is reaching the top. The converse occurs at the market bottom. During declining markets, small investors become depressed about the market. After experiencing losses, they sell out as the market reaches its bottom. Such sales are frequently referred to as the passing of securities from "weak" hands to "strong" hands. The weak hands are, of course, the small investors who are misjudging the market, and the strong hands are the large investors who are more informed and capable of making correct investment decisions.

Generally, the ratio of odd-lot purchases to odd-lot sales ranges from 1.4 to 0.6.[4] If the ratio approaches 1.25 to 1.30, that means the small investors are increasing their purchases relative to sales, which is a very bearish signal. According to the odd-lot theory, such purchases forecast a decline in stock prices. If the ratio approaches 0.6, odd-lot sales exceed purchases, indicating that the small investor is bearish. Such bearishness on the part of the small investor is then taken as a bullish sign by believers in the odd-lot theory.

Like the Dow Theory and Barron's confidence index, the odd-lot theory illustrates a tendency, but there is also little concrete evidence of its ability to forecast accurately when the market will change. It assumes that purchasers of odd lots make inferior investment decisions, but you should remember that many large investors are also sellers at the market bottom and buyers at the market top. It has even been suggested that the real "odd-lotters" are the institutional investors and that individual investors may profit by doing the opposite of professional money managers.[5]

Investment Advisory Opinions

While the odd-lot theory suggests that the small investor is often wrong, the advisory opinion theory suggests that financial advisors are often wrong. This approach is often referred to as a *contrarian* view, since it takes the opposite side of most financial advisors. The theory suggests that when most financial advisory services become bearish and forecast declining security prices, that is the time to purchase securities. When the majority become bullish and forecast rising security prices, the wise investor liquidates (i.e., sells securities). This technical indicator seems perverse, as it suggests that those most likely to know are unable to forecast the direction of security prices accurately.

Advances/Declines

The advance–decline cumulative series is an indicator based on the cumulative net difference between the number of stocks that rose in price relative to the number that declined. Consider the following summaries of daily trading on the New York Stock Exchange:

Day	1	2	3	4
Issues advancing	1,200	820	480	210
Issues declining	400	760	950	1,190
Issues unchanged	200	220	370	400
Net advances (declines)	800	60	(470)	(980)
Cumulative net advances (declines)	800	860	390	(590)

During the first day, 800 more stocks rose than declined. While this pattern continued during the second day, the number of stocks rising was less than during the previous day, so the cumulative total registered only a small increment. During

[4] See Jerome B. Cohen, Edward D. Zinbarg, and Arthur Zeikel, *Investment Analysis and Portfolio Management*, 5th ed. (Homewood, IL: Irwin, 1987), 270–272.

[5] See Mark Hulbert, "The New Odd-lotters," *Forbes*, December 23, 1991, 183.

the third day, the market weakened, and the prices of more stocks fell than rose. However, the cumulative total remained positive. During the fourth day, the number of stocks that declined rose farther, so that the cumulative total now became negative.

According to technical analysis, the cumulative total of net advances gives an indication of the general direction of the market. If the market is rising, the net cumulative total will be positive and expanding; however, when the market changes direction, the cumulative total will start to diminish and will become negative as prices continue to decline. Of course, the converse applies at market bottoms. When the market declines, the net advances fall (i.e., the negative cumulative total increases). Once the bottom in the market has been reached and security prices start to rise, the number of advances will start to exceed the number of declines, which will cause the net advances to increase. Changes in the direction of advances/declines becomes a barometer of the trend in the market. (This technique is similar to moving averages, which are discussed later in this chapter and which are used to measure both the direction of prices in individual stocks and in the market as a whole.)

Specific Stock Indicators

The preceding section discussed several technical approaches to the market as a whole. This section considers several techniques that may be applied to either the market or individual securities. When applied to the market, their purpose is to identify the general trend. When applied to individual securities, these techniques attempt to inform the investor when to buy, when to sell, or when to maintain current positions in a specific security.

Point-and-Figure Charts (X-O Charts)

Most technical analysis has an underlying basis (or perhaps rationalization) in economics. In effect, these analytical techniques seek to measure supply and demand. Because an increase in demand will lead to higher prices and an increase in supply will lead to lower prices, an analysis that captures shifts in supply and demand will be able to forecast future price movements. **Point-and-figure charts**, also called **X-O charts**, identify changes in supply and demand by charting changes in security prices.

point-and-figure chart (X-O chart)
A chart composed of Xs and Os that is used in technical analysis to summarize price movements.

If a stock's price rises, that movement is caused by demand exceeding supply. If a stock's price falls, then supply exceeds demand. If a stock's price is stable and trades within a narrow range, the supply of the stock coming onto the market just offsets the current demand. However, when the stock's price breaks this stable pattern of price movements, there has been a fundamental shift in demand and/or supply. Thus, a movement upward suggests a change in demand relative to supply, while a movement downward suggests the opposite.

Point-and-figure charts identify these fundamental changes through the construction of graphs employing Xs and Os. Such an X-O chart is constructed by placing an X on the chart when the price of the stock rises by some amount, such as $1 or $2, and an O on the chart when it declines by that amount. Such a chart requires tracking the stock on a daily basis, and if the price has changed by the specified amount, an entry is made on the chart.

This procedure is best explained by an illustration. Suppose the price of a stock had the following day-to-day price changes and the investor wanted to construct an X-O chart for price movements of $2. The procedure is illustrated in Figure 14.1 (p. 444).

Daily Closing Prices for January

Date	Prices				
1/1–1/5	$50.13	$51.38	$51.75	$52.50	$54.13
1/8–1/12	53.50	53.13	52.50	51.87	51.13
1/15–1/19	49.50	49.75	47.13	48.75	47.88
1/22–1/26	49.75	46.88	46.12	45.88	44.87

Figure 14.1 is divided into four quadrants, which illustrate the four steps necessary to create the chart.

The first quadrant (A) sets up the axes—time on the horizontal axis and dollars on the vertical axis. Time is measured in variable units since a movement along the X-axis could occur after a week, a month, or a year. The dollar unit depends on the prices of the stock. For lower-priced stocks, the units may be $1, but for higher-priced stocks the units may be larger, such as $2 or $3. Since a movement from $40 to $42 is the same percentage increase as a price movement from $20 to $21, the use of the large increments for higher-priced stocks does not reduce the quality of the X-O chart. In addition, the use of larger units reduces the number of entries necessary to create the chart. Since the price of the stock in question is in the $50 range, a $2 interval is selected, and the vertical axis shows the increments in $2 units.

The second quadrant (B) plots the price of the stock on the first day of observation. Since the price of the stock is rising, the chartist enters an X at $50 on the chart. Additional Xs are entered only after the price of the stock rises by $2 (e.g.,

FIGURE 14.1

The Construction of an X-O Chart

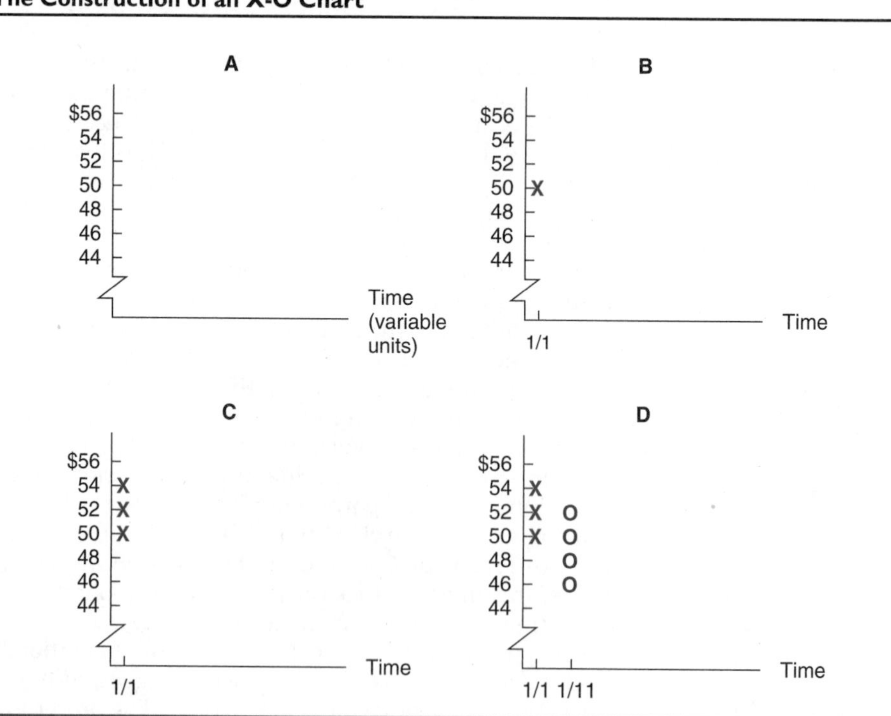

$50 to $52). All small movements in price both up and down are ignored, and only after the price has risen by $2 is a second X entered on the chart. Thus, although the price of the stock rose during the first three days, no entry is made. The effect of such omissions is both to reduce the work required to construct the chart and to minimize the effect of small daily price fluctuations.

The third quadrant (C) plots the price increases that occurred on days 4 and 5. The price closed above $52 on day 4, so an X is placed on the chart. The same applies to day 5, when the stock closed above $54.

The fourth quadrant (D) illustrates the decline in the stock's price. After reaching a high of $54.50, the price of the stock starts to fall. The chartist now uses only Os instead of Xs to indicate the declining price. Once again, the price must fall by $2 before an entry is made (i.e., the stock must sell for $52 or less, since $54 was the highest X entry). The date on which Os began to be recorded on the chart is noted on the horizontal axis. Once the price reaches $52, an O is placed on the chart. This occurs on January 11. The analyst will continue to place Os on the chart until the present downward trend is reversed and the price of the stock rises by the necessary $2. Then the analyst will start a new column and enter an X to indicate an increase in the stock's price.

In this case, the price of the stock continues to decline. Each time the stock breaks the two-point barrier, another O is placed on the chart. If the price continues to decline, the column will fill up with Os. If the stock's price stabilizes, no entries will be made until a two-point movement occurs.

After a period of stable prices, a deviation signals the direction of future price changes. Such signals are illustrated in Figure 14.2. On the left-hand side (A), after a period of trading between $52 and $58, the price of the stock rises to a new high of $60. This suggests that a new upward price trend is being established, which is a buy signal. On the right-hand side (B), the opposite case is illustrated. The price declines below $52, which suggests that a new downward price trend is being established. If the investor owns the stock, the shares should be sold.

FIGURE 14.2

Buy and Sell Signals

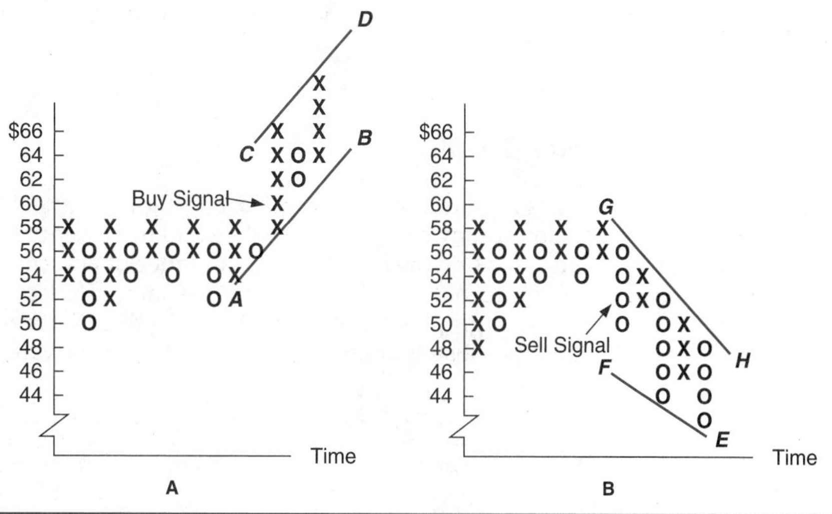

In both cases illustrated in Figure 14.2, the purchases and sales appear to be made at the wrong time. In the case of the purchase, it is made after the stock has already increased in price. Conversely, the sale is made after the stock has declined in price. Thus, purchases are not made at the lows, and sales are not made at the highs. Instead, the purchases appear to be made when the stock is reaching new highs, and the sales are made when the stock is reaching new lows. The rationale for this behavior rests primarily on the belief that the charts indicate new trends. Despite the fact that the investor missed the high prices for the sale and the low prices for the purchase, if the price change that is being forecasted proves accurate, then the investor will have made the correct investment decision even though the purchases and sales were not made at the exact turning points.

Besides indicating the buy or sell signals when trends are being established, these charts suggest possible trading strategies during the trends, which are also illustrated in Figure 14.2. While the left-hand side shows a price that is obviously rising, the price is still fluctuating. The right-hand side illustrates a downward trend, but the price is also fluctuating. During the upward trend, each high is higher than the preceding high price, and each low is higher than the preceding low price. Obviously, if an investor buys this stock and holds it, the return will be positive over this period. However, the return may be increased by judiciously buying at each low, selling at each high, and repeating the process when the cycle within the trend is repeated.

In order to isolate these opportunities, a set of lines has been drawn in Figure 14.2 connecting the high and the low prices that the stock is achieving. These lines are believed to have special significance because they indicate when to make the buy and sell decisions. The bottom lines (*AB* and *EF*), which connect the lowest prices, suggest a price level that generates "support" for the stock. Technical analysis asserts that when the price of the stock approaches a support line, the number of purchases will increase, which will stop further price declines. Hence, the approach of a stock's price toward a support line suggests that a buying opportunity is developing. Should the price reach the line and then start to climb, the investor should buy the stock.

The opposite occurs at the top lines (*CD* and *GH*), which represents "resistance." Since the price of the stock has risen to that level, more investors will want to sell their stock, which will thwart further price advances. Accordingly, the investor should sell the stock when the price reaches a line of resistance. After the stock has been sold, the investor then waits for the price to decline to the level of price support.

Bar Graphs

bar graph
A graph indicating the high, low, and closing prices of a security.

Bar graphs are similar to point-and-figure charts. Like the X-O charts, they require a day-to-day compilation of data and use essentially the same information. Preference for one over the other is a matter of choice, and, though the investor could construct both, such work would seem redundant.

A bar graph is constructed by using three price observations—the high, the low, and the closing price for the day. If the prices were

Price	Monday	Tuesday	Wednesday	Thursday	Friday
High	$10	$9.50	$9.88	$10.50	$12
Low	9	9	9.25	9.88	10.13
Close	9	9.37	9.87	10	11.50

the bar graphs for each day would be

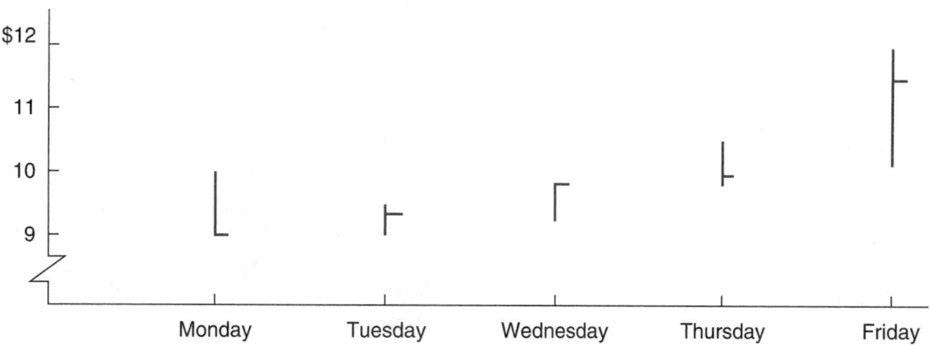

The vertical lines represent the range of the stock's price (i.e., the high and the low prices), and the horizontal lines represent the closing price.

As with the X-O chart, the bar graph is supposed to indicate future price movements in the stock by the pattern that emerges. There are several possible patterns. For example, one brief paperback book on charting identifies at least ten patterns, each with a descriptive name, such as head and shoulder, rounded tops, and descending triangles.[6] Space limits this discussion to only one pattern: the head and shoulder. The student who is interested in the variety of patterns should consult a book that explains the different patterns and how they are used to predict future stock prices.

head-and-shoulder pattern
A tool of technical analysis; a pattern of security prices that resembles a head and shoulders.

A **head-and-shoulder pattern** does just what its name implies: The graph forms a pattern that resembles a head and shoulders. Such a pattern is illustrated in Figure 14.3. Initially, the price of the stock rises. Then it levels off before rising to a

FIGURE 14.3

Head-and-Shoulder Pattern

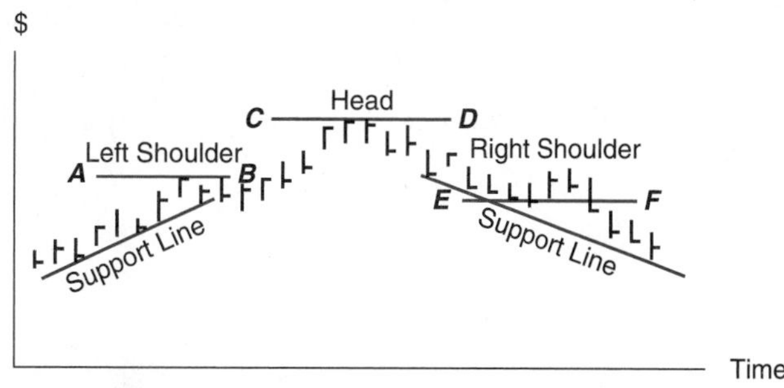

[6]Descriptions of various patterns may be found in Clifford Pistolese, *Using Technical Analysis,* rev. ed. (Chicago: Probus, 1994). This paperback includes self-teaching exercises designed to test the reader's ability to spot patterns in stock prices. Other books that explain and illustrate various methods of technical analysis include Steven B. Achelis, *Technical Analysis from A to Z* (Chicago: Probus, 1995); Jake Bernstein, *The Compleat Day Trader: Trading Systems, Strategies, Timing Indicators, and Analytical Methods* (New York: McGraw-Hill Book Company, 1995); Tushar Chande and Stanley Kroll, *The New Technical Trader: Boost Your Profit by Plugging Into the Latest Indicators* (New York: John Wiley & Sons, 1994); Richard Hexton, *Technical Analysis in the Options Market: The Effective Use of Computerized Trading Systems* (New York: John Wiley & Sons, 1995); John J. Murphy, *Technical Analysis of the Financial Markets* (New York: New York Institute of Finance, 1999); Rick Bensignor, ed., *New Thinking in Technical Analysis* (Princeton, NJ; Bloomberg Press, 2000); and Robert D. Edwards and John Magee, *Technical Analysis of Stock Trends,* 8th ed. (Boca Raton, FL: CRC Press, 2001).

new high, after which the price declines, levels off, and then starts to fall. To illustrate the head-and-shoulder pattern, several lines have been imposed on the graph. These lines are similar to the lines of resistance and support found on the X-O charts. Line *AB* shows the left shoulder and also represents a line of resistance. However, once it is penetrated, the price of the stock rises to a new high, where it meets new resistance (line *CD*).

When the stock is unable to penetrate this new resistance, the price starts to decline and forms the head. However, after this initial decline in price the stock reaches a new level of support, which forms the right shoulder (line *EF*). When the price falls below line *EF*, the head-and-shoulder pattern is completed. This is interpreted to mean that the stock's price will continue to fall and is taken as a very bearish sign by followers of this type of analysis.

While the head-and-shoulder pattern in Figure 14.3 indicates that the price of the stock will subsequently fall, the same pattern upside down implies the exact opposite. In this case, penetration of the right shoulder indicates that the price of the stock will rise and is taken as a very bullish sign by those who use bar graphs.

Candlesticks

Sometimes the bar graphs are drawn as "candlesticks." Candlestick graphs require four prices: the open, the close, the high, and the low. A thin line (the "shadow") connects the high and low prices. The body of the candlestick connects the opening and closing prices. If the open price exceeds the closing price, indicating that the price fell, the body of the candlestick is filled in (i.e., is black). If the open price is less than the closing price (the price rose), the body is left open (i.e., is white). For example, suppose a stock had the following prices during the week:

	Monday	Tuesday	Wednesday	Thursday	Friday
High	$10.00	$9.50	$10.00	$10.00	$10.00
Open	9.50	9.50	9.50	9.25	9.50
Close	9.25	9.25	9.75	9.50	9.50
Low	9.00	9.00	9.50	9.00	9.00

the candlestick graphs for each day would be

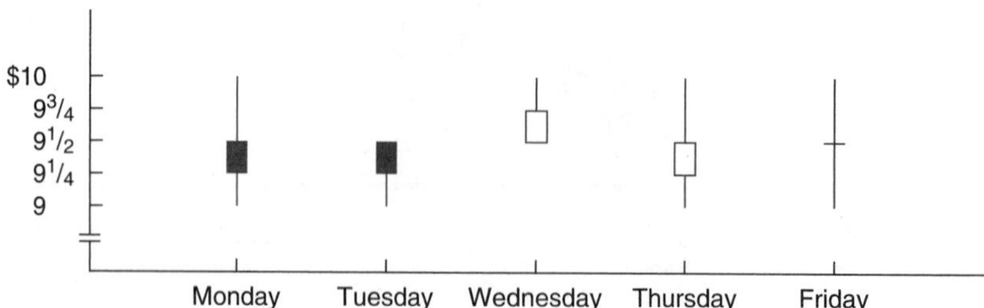

As perhaps would be expected, dark candlesticks (especially long sticks) are bearish indicators, while light candlesticks are bullish. Candlesticks may also be used to construct head-and-shoulder patterns and other configurations that technical analysts use to forecast the direction of stock prices.

Moving Averages

moving average
An average in which the most recent observation is added and the most distant observation is deleted before the average is computed.

A **moving average** is an average computed over time. For example, suppose the closing monthly values for the Dow Jones Industrial Average were as follows:

January	9,287	April	9,258	July	9,347	October	9,374
February	9,284	May	9,315	August	9,334	November	9,472
March	9,267	June	9,335	September	9,328	December	9,547

A six-month moving average of the Dow Jones industrials would be computed as follows. The average for the first six months is computed first.

$$\frac{9{,}287 + 9{,}284 + 9{,}267 + 9{,}258 + 9{,}315 + 9{,}335}{6} = \frac{55{,}746}{6} = 9{,}291.$$

Then the average is computed again, but the entry for July (9,347) is added in and the entry for January (9,287) is deleted:

$$\frac{9{,}284 + 9{,}267 + 9{,}258 + 9{,}315 + 9{,}335 + 9{,}347}{6} = \frac{55{,}806}{6} = 9{,}301.$$

The average is thus 9,301, which is greater than the average for the preceding six months (9,291).

To obtain the next entry, the average is computed again, with August being added and February being dropped. The average in this case becomes 9,309. By continuing this method of adding the most recent entry and dropping the oldest entry, the averages move through time.

Figure 14.4 (p. 450) presents both the Dow Jones Industrial Average for 1984 through 1994 and the six-month moving average. (The monthly data for continuing the figure are provided in Question 11.) As may be seen from the figure, the moving average follows the Dow Jones industrials. However, when the Dow Jones industrials are declining, the moving average is greater than the industrial average. The converse is true when the Dow Jones Industrial Average is rising: The moving average is less than the industrial average. At several points the two lines cross. For example, the Dow Jones Industrial Average crossed the six-month moving average in early 1988. Technicians place emphasis on such a crossover, for they believe that it is indicative of a change in the direction of the market. (It may also indicate a change in a specific security's price when the moving average is computed for a particular stock.) In this illustration, there appears to be some validity to the claim of the predictive power of the moving average, as the market rose after the buy signals and fell after the sell signals.

The average that is most frequently used is a 200-day moving average. (Other possibilities are 30-day, 60-day, weekly close, etc.) Thus, for a specific stock, the investor must keep a daily tabulation of 200 stock prices and recompute the average daily! Such calculations are obviously tedious if the investor does them.[7] A 200-day average may be approximated by using weekly prices for 35 to 40 weeks. There is little evidence that using moving averages of different durations produces results inferior (or superior) to the 200-day moving average.[8]

[7]Moving averages are one investment tool that is readily found on the Internet. Possible sources include http://home.microsoft.com, http://www.quicken.com, and http://quote.yahoo.com. From the home page, enter the stock's ticker symbol. Moving averages are then usually found under "charts" or "graphs." While the specific moving averages may vary, each source generally provides 50-, 100-, and 200-day moving averages of the stock's price. The user may also be able to customize the time period covered.

[8]Moving averages may be combined with other technical indicators. See, for instance, Kenneth Tower, "Applying Moving Averages to Point and Figure Charts," in Rick Bensignor, ed., *New Thinking in Technical Analysis* (Princeton, NJ: Bloomberg Press, 2000).

FIGURE 14.4

Dow Jones Industrial Average and a Six-Month Moving Average

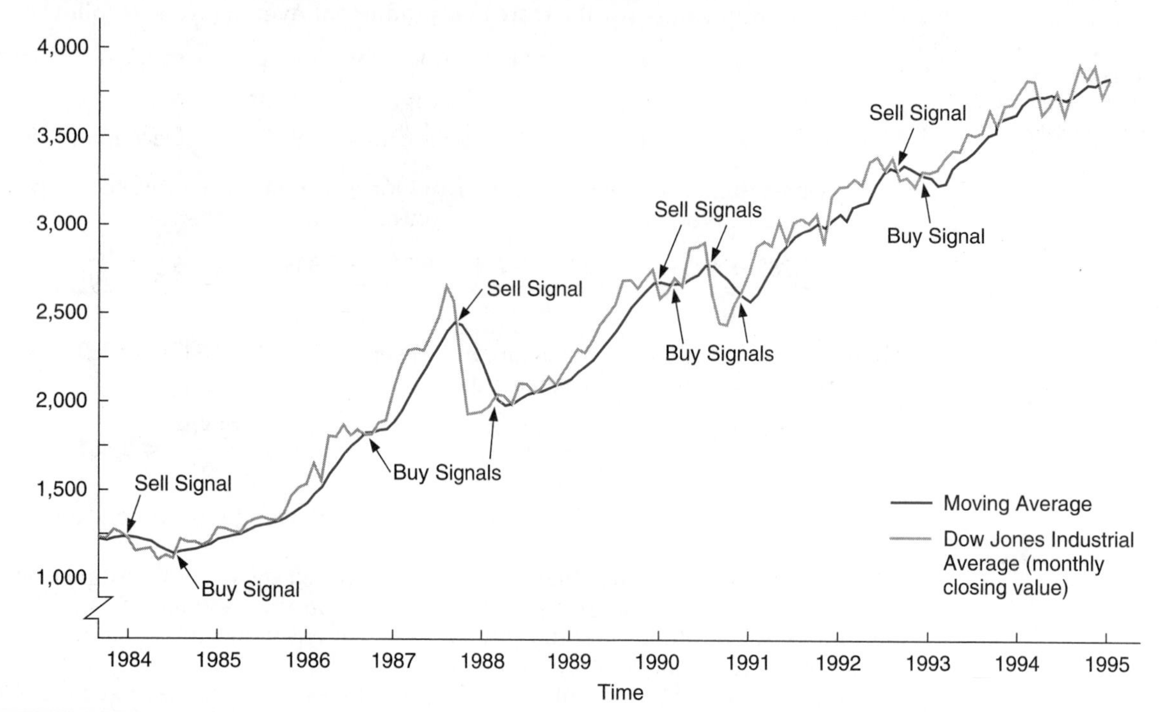

Volume

The preceding techniques emphasized price movements as measured by point-and-figure charts, bar graphs, and moving averages. Technical analysts also place emphasis on the volume of transactions and deviations from the normal volume of trading in a specific stock. A large deviation from normal volume is interpreted to mean a change in the demand for or supply of the stock.

Since a price change can occur on small volume or on large volume, the price change itself says nothing concerning the breadth of the change in demand or supply. A price increase on small volume is not as bullish as one accompanied by heavy trading. Conversely, a price decline on small volume is not as bearish as a decline accompanied by a large increase in the number of shares traded. When a price decline occurs on small volume, that indicates that only a modest increase in the supply of the stock was offered for sale relative to the demand. However, if the price decline were to occur on a large increase in volume, that would indicate many investors were seeking to sell the stock, which would be considered bearish.

Short Sales by Specialists

As was explained in Chapter 3, specialists make a market in securities listed on the organized exchanges (i.e., they offer to buy and sell securities for their own accounts). In order to make a market, specialists must be abreast of the events affecting securities. They continually adjust their portfolios in response to the flow of securities to and from the market. It is through this process that they make the market in the individual securities. If they misjudge demand and supply and subsequent price changes, they could suffer large losses.

If specialists believe that the supply of stock will increase and drive down a stock's price, they take short positions in the stock in anticipation of the price decline. Total short sales and specialists' short sales must be reported to the SEC and the NYSE. Generally, about half of all short sales are made by the specialists. If, however, the specialists' proportion of total short sales rises to above 65 percent, technical analysts believe this is a bearish indicator. The high ratio of specialists' short sales indicates that those who may be best able to perceive changes in supply and demand are anticipating price declines. If the ratio of specialists' short sales to total short sales falls to 40 percent, technical analysts interpret that as a bullish sign, indicative of rising future stock prices.[9]

The Verification of Technical Analysis

At first glance, technical analysis seems so very appealing. One needs only to obtain a set of charts and then follow the signals given by the analysis. Such simple rules for investing literally beg for verification to ascertain if they are, in fact, good predictors.

Several studies have sought to test the validity of technical analysis. The use of computers has eased calculations and made it possible to test several variations of the technical approach. For example, the investigator may have the computer calculate various moving averages (e.g., 200-day, 100-day, or 50-day averages) to determine if one is the best predictor.

The majority of this research has failed to verify the various technical approaches to investing.[10] This conclusion is the basis for the weak form of the efficient market hypothesis discussed in Chapter 9. The large body of empirical evidence has convinced many investors to believe that the technical approach does not lead to superior investment performance and that the investor would do just as well to buy a randomly selected portfolio and hold it. When commissions are included, the return from following the technical approach may be even less than that earned on a randomly selected portfolio. These conclusions have resulted in a general rejection of technical analysis by many academically trained teachers of finance.

Although technical analysis has found little support in the financial academic community, this may be changing since the publication of studies by respected researchers in investments that supported technical analysis.[11] These studies suggested that a simple set of trading rules using moving averages and support and resistance levels did have forecasting power for changes in the Dow Jones Industrial Average. The results also suggested that traders could improve returns over a

[9]See Cohen et al., *Investment Analysis and Portfolio Management,* 272–273.

[10]For example, see Michael C. Jensen and George A. Bennington, "Random Walks and Technical Theories: Some Additional Evidence," *Journal of Finance* 25 (May 1970): 469–482; Eugene Fama, "The Behavior of Stock Market Prices," *Journal of Business* 37 (January 1965): 34–105; F. E. James, Jr., "Monthly Moving Averages—An Effective Investment Tool?" *Journal of Financial and Quantitative Analysis* (September 1968): 315–326; and J. C. Van Horne and G. G. C. Parker, "The Random Walk Theory: An Empirical Test," *Financial Analysts Journal* (November/December 1967): 87–92. Empirical support for technical analysis may be found in Robert A. Levy, "Random Walks: Reality or Myth," *Financial Analysts Journal* (November/December 1967): 69–77.

[11]William Brock, Josef Lakonishok, and Blake LeBaron, "Simple Technical Trading Rules and the Stochastic Properties of Stock Returns," *Journal of Finance* 47 (December 1992): 1731–1764; and Andrew Lo, Harry Mamaysky, and Jiang Wang, "Foundation of Technical Analysis," *Journal of Finance* 55 (August 2000): 1705–1765.

POINTS OF INTEREST
The Market Technicians Association

The Market Technicians Association is an organization for individuals whose "professional efforts are spent practicing financial technical analysis that is either made available to the investing public or becomes a primary input into an active portfolio management process and for whom technical analysis is the basis of the decision making process." Affiliate memberships are open to individuals who are interested in technical analysis but do not meet the above requirements. The association publishes the *Market Technicians Association Journal* to "promote the investigation and analysis of price and volume activities of the world's financial markets." Information concerning the association and its journal may be obtained by writing the association at 71 Broadway, 2nd Floor, New York, NY 10006 or at http://www.mta-usa.org.

buy-and-hold strategy. Unfortunately, the improvement in returns requires frequent trading, which involves transaction costs. Another study found that when transaction costs are factored into the analysis, returns are not improved over buy-and-hold.[12] This result is, of course, consistent with efficient markets. (With the advent of electronic trading and its minimal transaction costs, it may become possible to use trading rules, pay the commissions, and beat a buy-and-hold strategy. Stay tuned.)

One major reason why technical approaches cannot lead to superior investment results is the speed with which security prices change. Information is readily disseminated among the investors, and prices adjust accordingly.[13] Thus, if an investor were to develop an approach that outperformed the market, it would only be a matter of time before the technique would be learned by others. The method would no longer achieve the initial results as additional investors applied it. A system that works (if one can be found) can succeed only if it is not known by many investors. Thus, it is naive for an investor to believe that he or she can use a known technical approach to beat the market. A new and unknown system is needed. However, when one realizes that many investors are looking for and testing various approaches, it is hard to believe that the individual investor will find a technical approach that can beat the market.

Although the technical approach may lack verification, it is still used by some portfolio managers as a supplement to fundamental analysis to help the timing of purchases and sales.[14] One frequently sees advertisements in the financial press or on the Internet for advisory services that employ various technical approaches. Perhaps the investor should ask why the service is being sold and not being applied exclusively by those who know the "secret." Certainly, if one knows how to beat the market, one should be able to earn a substantial return on investments and should not need to sell the secret for monetary gain.

[12]Hendrick Bessembinder and Kolok Chan, "Market Efficiency and the Returns to Technical Analysis," *Financial Management* (summer 1998): 5–17.

[13]One study found that the technical approach may be a lagging and not a leading indicator of stock prices. In an efficient market, prices may react before the technical indicator gives a signal of the change. Thus, by the time the signal is observed, prices have already responded, and there is no opportunity for the investor to take advantage of the signal. See Ben Branch and Thomas Schneeweis, "Market Movements and Technical Market Indicators," *The Mid-Atlantic Journal of Business* (summer 1986): 31–41.

[14]For an integration of fundamental and technical analysis, see Lawrence Stein, *The Fundamental Stock Market Technician* (Chicago: Probus, 1986); and Steven P. Rich and William Reichenstein, "Market Timing for the Individual Investor: Using the Predictability of Long-Horizon Stock Returns to Enhance Portfolio Performance," *Financial Services Review* (1993/1994): 29–43.

The Dogs of the Dow

One investment strategy that recently has come into prominence is the Dogs of the Dow.[15] (Weak stocks or low-priced stocks are sometimes referred to as "dogs.") This simple strategy is neither a technical approach nor a fundamental approach to the selection of securities. Since it requires no analysis of past stock prices, volume of trading, or any other method of technical analysis, it is not readily classifiable as a technical approach. The Dogs of the Dow, however, also avoids the fundamental analysis of financial statements, the valuation of cash flows, and the estimation of future growth rates. Since the Dow dog strategy is mechanical, it is more comparable to technical approaches than to valuation methods for selecting stocks and is included in this chapter.

The Dogs of the Dow strategy requires the investor to rank all 30 stocks in the Dow Jones Industrial Average from highest to lowest based on their dividend yields (dividend divided by the price of the stock). The investor then buys an equal dollar amount of the ten stocks with the highest dividend yields. (An alternative strategy is to buy the five lowest-priced "small dogs" of the ten highest-yielding dividend stocks.) After one year, the process is repeated. The Dow stocks are once again ranked, and, if a stock continues to be among the ten highest dividend yields, it is retained. If the stock is no longer among the ten, it is sold and replaced by a new Dow dog that is one of the ten stocks with the highest dividend yields.

This strategy has obvious appeal. First, since it is rebalanced only once a year, commission costs are modest. Second, by waiting one additional day so the portfolio adjustments occur after a year, all capital gains are long-term. (The dividend payments are, of course, taxed as income.) Third, by buying the Dow stocks with the highest dividend yields, this yield may offer some downside protection from further price declines. Fourth, buying the Dow dogs is acquiring the stocks in the Dow that are currently out of favor and is consistent with a contrarian strategy.

Does the system work? There is evidence that the Dow dividend strategy produces higher returns than the Dow itself.[16] The evidence, however, also shows that the standard deviations of the returns on the Dow dogs exceeded the standard deviations of the returns on the Dow Jones Industrial Average and the S&P 500 stock index. (A Dow dog portfolio is less diversified, so the expectation would be for greater variability in the returns.) This result is, of course, consistent with efficient markets: More risk-taking generates higher returns. The empirical results also suggest that over long periods, such as a decade, a strategy of buying and holding all the Dow stocks was a better alternative after considering risk, taxes, and transaction costs.

If an investor wants to execute the strategy, there are essentially two choices: (1) buy and hold the ten stocks or (2) purchase shares in a unit trust with a Dow dog portfolio. Several brokerage firms, such as Merrill Lynch, have developed unit trusts with portfolios that follow the strategy. These trusts may be especially appropriate for individuals with modest amounts to invest. Unit trusts were developed because mutual funds cannot exactly follow the Dow dog strategy. An SEC rule limits the amount of a fund's portfolio that can be invested in one stock to 5

---

[15]The Dow dividend strategy was popularized in Michael O'Higgins, *Beating the Dow* (New York: Harper Perennial, 1992). Information concerning the Dow dogs, such as which stocks would currently comprise a Dow dog portfolio, may be found at http://www.dogsofthedow.com.

[16]Evidence that the strategy generates larger returns but the returns are more variable may be found in George Wunder and Herbert Mayo, "Study Supports Efficient Market Hypothesis," *Journal of Financial Planning* (July 1995): 128–135; and Grant McQueen, Kay Shields, and Steven R. Thorley, "Does the Dow-10 Investment Strategy Beat the Dow Statistically and Economically?" *Financial Analysts Journal* (July–August 1997): 66–72.

percent, and the strategy requires 10 percent of the portfolio in each dog. Hennessy Balanced Fund invests 50 percent of its portfolio in the Dow dogs and the remaining 50 percent in U.S. Treasury bills, and Dogs of the Market Fund puts 50 percent in dogs and 50 percent in high-yielding stocks from the S&P 500. These variations are, of course, not pure Dow dog strategies but do offer investors an alternative means to invest in these particular stocks.

Summary

Technical analysis seeks to identify superior investments by examining the past behavior of the market and of individual securities. Technical analysts, or "chartists," stress the past as a means to predict the future. This approach is diametrically opposed to the fundamental approach, which stresses future earnings and dividends, (i.e., cash flows) appropriately discounted back to the present.

Several technical approaches (the Dow Theory, Barron's confidence index, and odd-lot purchases versus odd-lot sales) attempt to identify changes in the direction of the market. Because individual security prices move together, the determination of a change in the direction of the market should identify the future movement of individual security prices.

Other technical approaches (X-O charts, bar graphs, and moving averages) may be applied to individual securities. By constructing various charts and graphs, the technical analyst determines when specific securities should be bought or sold.

A strategy involving the use of Dow Jones Industrial Average stocks selects the ten Dow stocks with the highest yields. These stocks are held for exactly one year, at which time the portfolio is rebalanced to continue holding the Dow stocks with the highest dividend yields.

Whether technical approaches to market timing and security selection lead to superior results (i.e., higher risk-adjusted returns) is an empirical question. With some exceptions little support has been found to verify technical analysis. The results of these studies suggest that the investor may achieve similar results by purchasing and holding a well-diversified portfolio of securities.

Questions

1) What is the purpose of technical analysis?
2) Why are those who use technical analysis sometimes referred to as *chartists*?
3) What changes represent a sell signal in the Dow Theory, Barron's confidence index, and the odd-lot theory?
4) What is a moving average? What is the significance when a stock's price equals a moving average of that price?
5) Why may technical analysis produce self-fulfilling predictions?
6) What is the problem with time lags in technical analysis?
7) Why does technical analysis receive little support from academically oriented students of investments?
8) Which technical approach may be the best?
9) Which Dow Jones Industrial Average stocks would be considered "dogs"?
10) Locate graphs of moving averages for International Business Machines (IBM) and Cisco. Based on the moving averages, should you be long or short in each of these stocks? (Possible sources for moving averages include http://www.askresearch.com, http://www.siliconinvestor.com, and http://www.wsrn.com. Sites that provide price quotes such as http://www.

msn.com or http://quote.yahoo.com will also have links to "charts" that show a stock's moving average.)

11) Continue Figure 14.4 using the following data. You may need the 1994 data, which are provided, to continue the analysis of the buy and sell signals.

Year–month	DJIA	Six-Month Moving Average	Year–month	DJIA	Six-Month Moving Average
94–1	3834	3693	7	8223	7283
2	3832	3723	8	7622	7407
3	3636	3737	9	7945	7634
4	3682	3737	10	7442	7706
5	3758	3749	11	7823	7788
6	3625	3728	12	7908	7827
7	3765	3716	98–1	7907	7775
8	3918	3731	2	8546	7929
9	3843	3765	3	8800	8071
10	3908	3803	4	9063	8341
11	3739	3800	5	8900	8521
12	3834	3835	6	8952	8695
95–1	3843	3848	7	8883	8857
2	4011	3863	8	7539	8690
3	4158	3916	9	7843	8530
4	4329	3986	10	8592	8452
5	4465	4107	11	9117	8488
6	4606	4235	12	9181	8526
7	4727	4383	99–1	9359	8605
8	4616	4484	2	9307	8900
9	4817	4593	3	9786	9224
10	4801	4672	4	10789	9590
11	5119	4781	5	10560	9830
12	5117	4866	6	10971	10129
96–1	5409	4980	7	10655	10345
2	5531	5132	8	10829	10598
3	5645	5270	9	10337	10690
4	5580	5400	10	10730	10680
5	5643	5488	11	10878	10733
6	5655	5577	12	11497	10821
7	5529	5597	00–1	10941	10869
8	5616	5611	2	10128	10752
9	5882	5651	3	10922	10849
10	6029	5726	4	10734	10850
11	6522	5872	5	10522	10791
12	6448	6004	6	10448	10616
97–1	6813	6218	7	10522	10546
2	6878	6429	8	11215	10727
3	6583	6546	9	10651	10682
4	7009	6709	10	10971	10722
5	7330	6844	11	10414	10704
6	7673	7048	12	10646	10737

Source: Dow Jones (http://www.djindexes.com).

THE FINANCIAL ADVISOR'S INVESTMENT CASE

Moving Averages

Denise Chung has a background in math and has recently read about the use of moving averages to forecast the direction of a stock's price. Ms. Chung is skeptical, so she has selected a stock to study the potential return from the strategy. Through a database, she obtained the following monthly closing prices of the stock. She then computed a six-month moving average and the difference between the stock's price and the moving average. From this data, she wants to compare the profit or loss from various investment strategies.

1) If Chung limits transactions to buying and subsequently selling on the various signals, when does Chung make her first purchase? (For simplicity, assume all transactions are in units of 100 shares and there are no commissions.)
2) If she follows this strategy for the entire time period through January 2000, how many transactions does she make and what is her gain or loss?
3) If she follows a strategy of purchasing on buy signals and selling on subsequent sell signals with a strategy of shorting on sell signals and covering on buy signals, what is her gain and loss as of January 2000?
4) If Chung buys 100 shares of stock in January 1995 and holds them for the entire period, what is her gain or loss as of January 2000?
5) If Chung follows a share-averaging strategy of buying 100 shares every January and July, what is her gain or loss as of January 2000?
6) If Chung follows a strategy of dollar cost averaging and buying $10,000 worth of the stock every January and July, what is her profit or loss as of January 2000?
7) What are the merits and risks associated with the preceding strategies?

Date	Stock Price	Six-Month Moving Average	Difference
Jan-95	99.75		
Feb-95	98.38		
Mar-95	104.88		
Apr-95	105.88		
May-95	110.50		
Jun-95	119.50	106.48	13.02
Jul-95	118.00	109.52	8.48
Aug-95	108.13	111.15	−3.02
Sep-95	105.50	111.25	−5.75
Oct-95	108.25	111.65	−3.40
Nov-95	108.38	111.29	−2.91
Dec-95	112.50	110.13	2.37
Jan-96	112.13	109.15	2.98
Feb-96	126.88	112.27	14.61
Mar-96	131.00	116.52	14.48
Apr-96	112.63	117.25	−4.62
May-96	103.63	116.46	−12.83
Jun-96	102.00	114.71	−12.71
Jul-96	98.63	112.46	−13.83
Aug-96	100.25	108.02	−7.77
Sep-96	99.38	102.75	−3.37
Oct-96	98.25	100.36	−2.11
Nov-96	98.38	99.48	−1.10
Dec-96	89.00	97.32	−8.32
Jan-97	90.38	95.94	−5.56
Feb-97	89.25	94.11	−4.86
Mar-97	86.38	91.94	−5.56
Apr-97	81.75	89.19	−7.44
May-97	90.63	87.90	2.73
Jun-97	90.38	88.13	2.25
Jul-97	96.88	89.21	7.67
Aug-97	87.13	88.86	−1.73
Sep-97	86.00	88.80	−2.80
Oct-97	78.20	88.20	−10.00
Nov-97	76.25	85.81	−9.56
Dec-97	77.00	83.58	−6.58
Jan-98	80.38	80.83	−0.45
Feb-98	82.00	79.97	2.03

Date	Stock Price	Six-Month Moving Average	Difference	Date	Stock Price	Six-Month Moving Average	Difference
Mar-98	85.25	79.85	5.40	Mar-99	111.00	106.44	4.56
Apr-98	82.63	80.59	2.05	Apr-99	107.00	106.77	0.23
May-98	98.63	84.32	14.32	May-99	111.38	107.19	4.19
Jun-98	94.00	87.15	6.85	Jun-99	111.25	108.63	2.62
Jul-98	95.75	89.71	6.04	Jul-99	111.38	109.75	1.63
Aug-98	93.88	91.69	2.19	Aug-99	111.38	110.57	0.81
Sep-98	99.88	94.13	5.75	Sep-99	111.38	110.63	0.75
Oct-98	105.00	97.86	7.14	Oct-99	103.50	110.05	−6.55
Nov-98	108.88	99.57	9.32	Nov-99	105.66	109.09	−3.43
Dec-98	102.63	101.00	1.63	Dec-99	107.12	108.40	−1.28
Jan-99	104.63	102.48	2.15	Jan-00	108.00	107.84	0.16
Feb-99	106.50	104.59	1.91				

Investing in Fixed-Income Securities

PART 3

Part 3 considers investments in securities that pay a fixed annual income. The annual interest or dividend payments are the same each year. Since such investments consist primarily of long-term bonds issued by corporations and governments, most of Part 3 is devoted to these bonds. These securities produce a constant flow of income and for many years were considered to be good investments for conservative individuals. However, the wide fluctuations in bond prices and interest rates during the early 1980s and the expansion of the market for junk bonds during the late 1980s have increased the risk associated with investing in bonds. While bonds still offer a flow of interest income and the safety associated with the legal obligation to repay the principal, many individual bond issues can no longer be considered safe investments that are appropriate for conservative investors seeking income and the preservation of capital.

15 The Bond Market

In *The Merchant of Venice,* Antonio secured his debt with Shylock with a "pound of flesh." And you thought your credit card interest rate was bad! Perhaps that is why Polonious advised Hamlet "neither a borrower nor a lender be." The terms of a loan can be onerous, but corporations and governments do borrow, often under burdensome terms, to finance investments in plant, equipment, or inventory or for the construction of roads and schools. Internally generated funds are often insufficient to finance such investments on a pay-as-you-go basis. Bonds, which mature at the end of a term longer than one year, permit firms and governments to acquire assets now and pay for them over a period of years. This long-term debt is then retired for corporations by the cash flow that is generated by plant and equipment and for governments by the fees or tax revenues that are collected.

This chapter is concerned with bonds and covers (1) the characteristics common to all these debt instruments, (2) the risks associated with investing in debt, (3) the mechanics of purchasing bonds, and (4) the retirement of debt. Chapter 16 covers the valuation of fixed-income securities. Like stock, bonds may be purchased initially either by financial institutions in a private placement or by individuals through a public offering. Once the securities have been issued, secondary markets develop. These debt instruments may be bought and sold on the organized security exchanges or in the over-the-counter markets. These securities are generally very marketable, since there is an active secondary market in many corporate and government bonds.

Learning Objectives

After completing this chapter you should be able to:

1. Describe the features common to all bonds.
2. Explain the purpose of the indenture and the role of the trustee.
3. Identify the sources of risk to the bondholder.
4. Describe the procedure for buying a bond and the paying or receiving of accrued interest.
5. Differentiate among the types of corporate bonds.
6. Differentiate the variety of high-yield bonds, their sources of risk, and realized returns.
7. Distinguish among the ways bonds are retired.

General Features of Bonds

Interest and Maturity

bond
A long-term liability with a specified amount of interest and specified maturity date.

principal
The amount owed; the face value of a debt.

All **bonds** (i.e., long-term debt instruments) have similar characteristics. They represent the indebtedness (liability) of their issuers in return for a specified sum, which is called the **principal**. Virtually all debt has a **maturity date,** which is the particular date by which it must be paid off. When debt is issued, the length of time to maturity is set, and it may range from one day to 20 or 30 years or more. If

maturity date
The time at which a debt issue becomes due and the principal must be repaid.

interest
Payment for the use of money.

coupon rate
The special interest rate or amount of interest paid by a bond.

current yield
Annual income divided by the current price of the security.

yield to maturity
The yield earned on a bond from the time it is acquired until the maturity date.

yield curve
The relationship between time to maturity and yields for debt in a given risk class.

the maturity date falls within a year of the date of issuance, the debt is referred to as short-term debt. Long-term debt matures more than a year after it has been issued. (Debt that matures in from 1 to 10 years is sometimes referred to as *intermediate debt.*) The owners of debt instruments receive a flow of payments, which is called **interest**, in return for the use of their money. Interest should not be confused with other forms of income, such as the cash dividends that are paid by common and preferred stock. Dividends are distributions from earnings, whereas interest is an expense of borrowing.

When a debt instrument such as a bond is issued, the rate of interest to be paid by the borrower is established. This rate is frequently referred to as the bond's **coupon rate** (e.g., the 7½ percent for the AT&T bond in Exhibit 15.2). The amount of interest is usually fixed over the lifetime of the bond. (There are exceptions; for example, see the section on variable interest rate bonds later in this chapter.) The return earned by the investor, however, need not be equal to the specified rate of interest because bond prices change. They may be purchased at a discount (a price below the face amount or principal) or at a premium (a price above the face amount of the bond). The return actually earned, then, depends on the interest received, the purchase price, and what the investor receives upon selling or redeeming the bond.

The potential return offered by a bond is referred to as the *yield.* Yield is frequently expressed in two ways: the **current yield** and the **yield to maturity**. Current yield refers only to the annual flow of interest or income. The yield to maturity refers to the yield that the investor will earn if the debt instrument is held from the moment of purchase until it is redeemed at par (face value) by the issuer. The difference between the current yield and the yield to maturity is discussed at length in the section on the pricing of bonds in Chapter 16.

There is a relationship between yield and the length of time to maturity for debt instruments of the same level of risk. Generally, the longer the time to maturity, the higher the rate of interest. This relationship is illustrated in Figure 15.1 (p. 462), which plots the yield on various U.S. government securities as of May 2001. This figure, which is frequently referred to as a **yield curve**, shows that the bonds with the longest time to maturity have the highest interest rates. For example, short-term securities (three months to maturity) had yields of 3.72 percent; one-year bonds paid yields of 5.04 percent, and bonds that matured after 30 years paid in excess of 6.17 percent.

One would expect such a relationship because the longer the time to maturity, the longer the investor will tie up his or her funds. To induce investors to lend their money for lengthier periods, it is usually necessary to pay them more interest. Also, there is more risk involved in purchasing a bond with a longer period to maturity, since the future financial condition of the issuer is more difficult to estimate for the longer term. This means that investors will ordinarily require additional compensation to bear the risk associated with long-term debt.

Although such a relationship between time and yield does usually exist, there have been periods when the opposite has occurred (i.e., when short-term interest rates exceeded long-term interest rates). This happened from 1978 to 1979, and again in 1981, when short-term interest rates were higher than long-term rates. The yields on Treasury securities (securities issued by the Treasury Department) in June 1981 are illustrated in Figure 15.2 (p. 462). In this case the yield curve has a negative slope, which indicates that as the length of time to maturity increased, the interest rates declined. Thus, securities maturing in less than a year had a yield of greater than 14 percent, while the long-term debt that matured after ten years yielded 13 percent.

Such a yield curve can be explained by inflation, which exceeded 10 percent in 1981 to 1982. The Board of Governors of the Federal Reserve was pursuing a tight monetary policy in order to fight inflation. It sold short-term government securities (i.e., Treasury bills) in an effort to reduce the capacity of commercial banks to

FIGURE 15.1

Positively Sloped Yield Curve

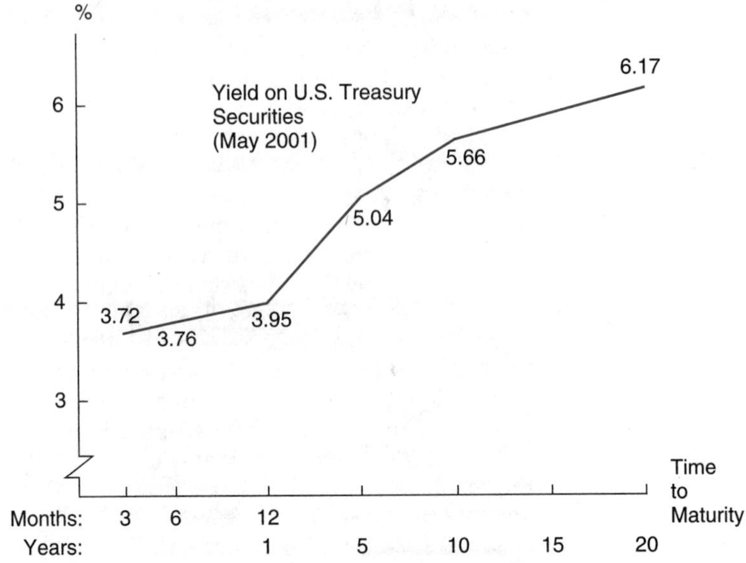

Source: Data derived from *The Wall Street Journal.*

FIGURE 15.2

Yield Curves (Yields on Federal Government Securities)

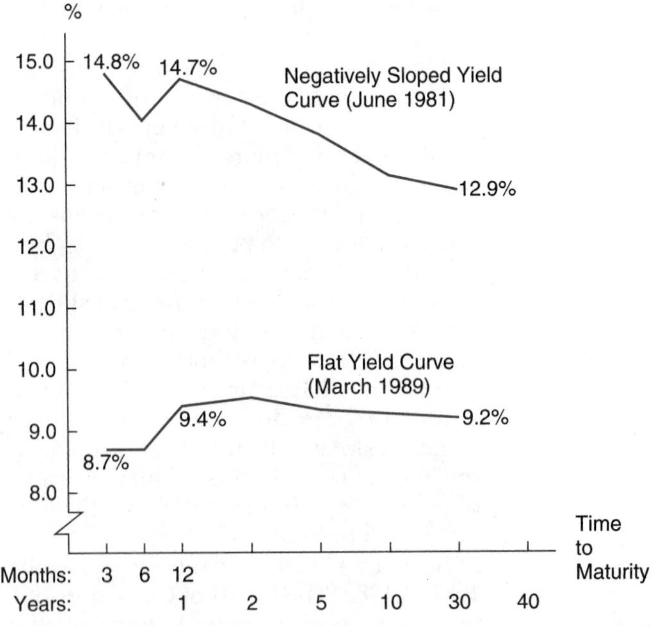

Source: Data derived from *The Wall Street Journal.*

FIGURE 15.3

Yields on Treasury Bills and Treasury Bonds (1980–April 2001)

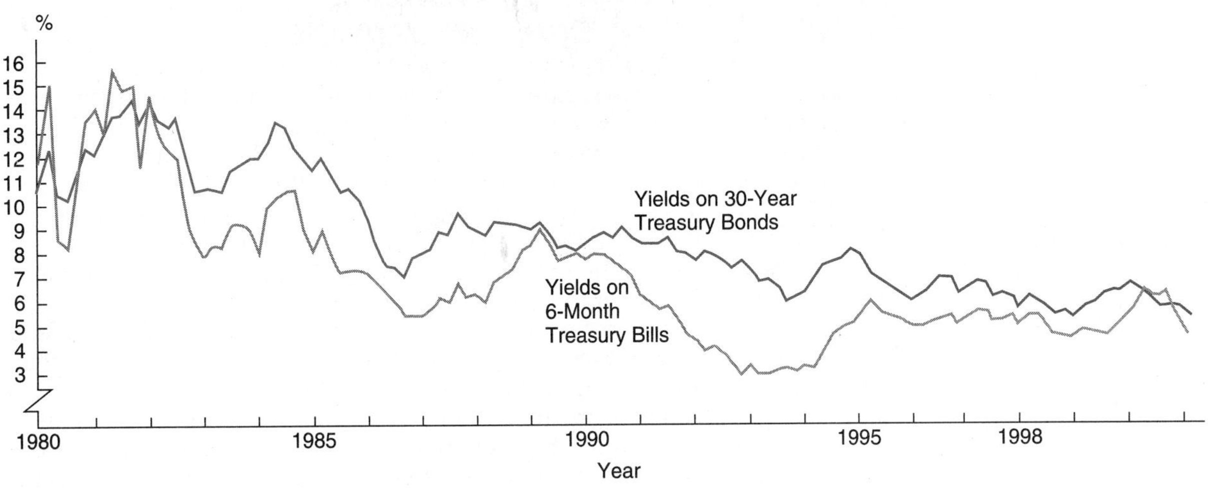

Source: *Federal Reserve Bulletin,* various issues.

lend. These sales depressed the prices of all fixed-income securities, which resulted in higher yields. (As is explained in detail in Chapter 16, yields on debt instruments rise as their prices fall.) The yields on short-term securities rose more than those on long-term securities, and this, coupled with other events in the money and capital markets, resulted in the negative-sloped yield curve. When the rate of inflation abated during the mid-1980s, the yield curve returned to the positive slope that it maintains during most periods.

There have also been periods when the yield curve was relatively flat. This is also illustrated in Figure 15.2 by the yield curve for March 1989. The yield on short-term debt with three to six months to maturity was approximately 8.7 percent, and the rate for 30-year bonds was 9.2 percent. While the long-term rate did exceed the short-term rate, the small difference produced a gently rising, or flat, yield curve.

Figures 15.1 and 15.2 also illustrate that interest rates do change. (The student should remember that the interest rate is the current rate paid for the use of credit. This should not be confused with the coupon rate, which is fixed when the debt instrument is issued.) Although all interest rates fluctuate, short-term rates are more volatile than long-term interest rates. This is illustrated in Figure 15.3, which plots the yields on a six-month Treasury bill and on a 30-year Treasury bond. As may be seen from the figure, the fluctuation in yields for the short-term bill is greater than that for the long-term bond. For example, the yield on a six-month Treasury bill decreased from 7.0 percent per year in late 1990 to below 4.0 percent in early 1992, while the yield on a 30-year Treasury bond declined from 8.5 to 7.9 percent during the same period. This figure illustrates not only the greater fluctuation in short-term yields but also how quickly changes can occur. For example, the annual short-term rate rose from 10.1 to 15 percent in only *three* months in early 1980 in response to changes in the demand for the supply of short-term credit.[1]

[1]In the fall of 2001, the U.S. Treasury announced it would no longer issue the 30-year bond. For more material on the structure of yields and how an investor may use yield curves, see the appendixes to this chapter and Chapter 17.

The Indenture

indenture
The document that specifies the terms of a bond issue.

Each debt agreement has terms that the debtor must meet. These are stated in a legal document called the **indenture**.[2] These terms include the coupon rate, the date of maturity, and any other conditions required of the debtor. One of the more frequent of these requirements is the pledging of collateral, which is property that the borrower must offer to secure the loan. For example, the collateral for a mortgage loan is the building. Any other assets owned by the borrower, such as securities or inventory, may also be pledged to secure a loan. If the borrower defaults on the debt, the creditor may seize the collateral and sell it to recoup the principal. **Default** occurs when the borrower fails to meet not only the payment of interest but *any* of the terms of the indenture. The other conditions of the indenture are just as important as meeting the interest payments on time, and often they may be more difficult for the debtor to satisfy.

default
The failure of a debtor to meet any term of a debt's indenture.

Examples of common loan restrictions include (1) limits on paying dividends, (2) limits on issuing additional debt, and (3) restrictions on merging or significantly changing the nature of the business without the prior consent of the creditors. In addition, loan agreements usually specify that if the firm defaults on any other outstanding debt issues, this debt issue is also in default, in which case the creditors may seek immediate repayment. Default on one issue, then, usually puts all outstanding debt in default.

These examples do not exhaust all the possible conditions of a given loan. Since each loan is separately negotiated, there is ample opportunity for differences among loan agreements. During periods of scarce credit, the terms of a loan agreement will be stricter, whereas during periods of lower interest rates and more readily available credit, the restrictions will tend to be more lenient. The important point, however, is that if any part of the loan agreement is violated, the creditor may declare that the debt is in default and may seek a court order to enforce the terms of the indenture.

The Role of the Trustee

Many debt instruments are purchased by individual investors who may be unaware of all the terms of the indenture. Even if individual investors are aware of the terms, they may be too geographically dispersed to take concerted action in case of default. To protect their interests, a **trustee** is appointed for each publicly held bond issue. It is the trustee's job to see that the terms of the indenture are upheld and to take remedial action if the company defaults on the terms of the loan. For performing these services, the trustee receives compensation from the issuer of the debt.

trustee
An appointee, usually a commercial bank, responsible for upholding the terms of a bond's indenture.

Trustees are usually commercial banks that serve both the debtor and the bondholders. They act as transfer agents for the bonds when ownership is changed through sales in the secondary markets. The signature of a trustee on the bond is a guarantee of the authenticity of the bond. These banks receive from the debtor the funds to pay the interest, and this money is then distributed to the individual bondholders. It is also the job of the trustee to inform the bondholders if the firm is no longer meeting the terms of the indenture. In case of default, the trustee may take the debtor to court to enforce the terms of the contract. If there is a subsequent reorganization or liquidation of the company, the trustee continues to act on behalf of the individual bondholders to protect their principal.

[2] For publicly held corporate bond issues, the indenture is filed with the Securities and Exchange Commission.

Forms of Debt

registered bond
A bond whose ownership is registered with the commercial bank that distributes interest payments and principal repayments.

bearer bond
A bond with coupons attached or a bond whose possession denotes ownership.

coupon bond
A bond with coupons attached that are removed and presented for payment of interest when due.

Debt instruments are issued in one of two forms: (1) **registered bonds** or (2) **bearer bonds** to which coupons are attached (therefore, they are also called **coupon bonds**). Registered bonds are similar to stock certificates; the bonds are registered in the owner's name. Delivery of the bonds is made to the registered owner, who also receives the interest payments from the trustee bank. When the bond is sold, it is registered in the name of the new owner by the transfer agent.

While many bonds may be registered in the name of the owner, most registered bonds are issued in *book form*. No actual bonds are printed; instead, a computer record of owners is maintained by the issuer or the issuer's agent, such as a bank. If a bond is sold only in book form, the investor cannot take delivery, and the bond must be registered in the street name of the investor's brokerage firm or whoever is holding the bond for the investor. Such a system is obviously more efficient than physically issuing the bond.

Bearer bonds are entirely different. Ownership is evidenced by mere possession of the bond and is transferred simply by passing the debt instrument from the seller to the buyer; no new certificates are issued. Thus, securities in this form are extremely easy to transfer. However, if they are lost, they are like currency. Therefore, the possibility of theft is a real concern that requires the owner to be extremely cautious when handling these bonds.

Since the debtor does not know the names of the owners of bearer securities, coupons for interest payments are attached to the bond. The owner must detach the coupon and send it to the paying agent (the trustee) to collect the interest. In the past, most bonds were of this type. Investors who relied on fixed-interest income for their livelihood were frequently called "coupon clippers."

Under current law, all newly issued corporate and municipal bonds have to be registered in the owner's name or whomever holds the bond for the owner (e.g., a brokerage firm). Previously issued coupon bonds still exist; however, the supply of coupon bonds is diminishing. It is only a matter of time before all corporate and municipal bonds will be in registered form.

Risk

An important characteristic of all debt is risk: risk that the interest will not be paid (i.e., risk of default); risk that the principal will not be repaid; risk that the price of the debt instrument may decline; risk that inflation will continue, thereby reducing the purchasing power of the interest payments and of the principal when it is repaid; risk that the bond will be retired (i.e., called) prior to maturity, thereby denying the investor the interest payments for the term of the bond; and risk that interest rates will fall, resulting in lower interest income when the proceeds are reinvested. These risks vary with different types of debt. For example, there is no risk of default on the interest payments and principal repayments of the debt of the federal government. The reason for this absolute safety is that the federal government has the power to tax and to create money. The government can always issue the money that is necessary to pay the interest and repay the principal.[3]

The procedure is more subtle than just printing new money. The federal government issues new debt and sells it to the Federal Reserve Board. With the proceeds of these sales, the federal government retires the old debt. The money supply increases because newly created money is used to pay for the debt. The effect

[3]The decline in the value of the dollar in foreign countries may reduce the attractiveness of federal obligations. Fluctuations in the value of the dollar, then, do impose risk for foreigners who invest in these securities.

EXHIBIT 15.1

Bond Ratings

Moody's Bond Ratings*

Aaa	Bonds of highest quality	B	Bonds that lack characteristics of a desirable investment
Aa	Bonds of high quality	Caa	Bonds in poor standing that may be defaulted
A	Bonds whose security of principal and interest is considered adequate but may be impaired in the future	Ca	Speculative bonds that are often in default
		C	Bonds with poor prospects of any investment value (lowest rating)
Baa	Bonds of medium grade that are neither highly protected nor poorly secured		
Ba	Bonds of speculative quality whose future cannot be considered well assured		

For ratings Aa through B, 1 indicates the high, 2 indicates the middle, and 3 indicates the low end of the rating class.

Standard & Poor's Bond Ratings†

AAA	Bonds of highest quality	BB	Bonds of lower-medium grade with few desirable investment characteristics
AA	High-quality debt obligations		
A	Bonds that have a strong capacity to pay interest and principal but may be susceptible to adverse effects	B through CCC	Primarily speculative bonds with great uncertainties and major risk if exposed to adverse conditions
BBB	Bonds that have an adequate capacity to pay interest and principal but are more vulnerable to adverse economic conditions or changing circumstances		
		C	Income bonds on which no interest is being paid
		D	Bonds in default

Plus (+) and minus (−) are used to show relative strength and weakness within a rating category.

***Source:** Adapted from *Mergent's Bond Record,* January 2001.
†**Source:** Adapted from *Standard & Poor's Bond Guide,* January 2001.

of selling debt to the Federal Reserve Board and then using the proceeds to retire existing debt (or to finance a current deficit) is no different from printing and spending new money. The money supply expands in either case. Thus, the federal government can always pay its interest expense and retire its debt when it becomes due.

Even though the federal government can refund its debt and hence is free of the risk of default, the prices of the federal government's bonds can and do fluctuate. In addition, the purchasing power of the dollar may decline as a result of inflation, and, therefore, the purchasing power of funds invested in debt also may decline. Thus, investing in federal government securities is not free of risk, since the investor may suffer losses from price fluctuations of the debt or from inflation.

credit rating systems
Classification schemes designed to indicate the risk associated with a particular security.

The debt of firms, individuals, and state and local governments involves even greater risk, for all these debtors may default on their obligations. To aid buyers of debt instruments, several companies have developed **credit rating systems**. The most important of these services are Moody, Dun and Bradstreet, and Standard & Poor's. Although these firms do not rate all debt instruments, they do rate the degree of risk of a significant number.

Exhibit 15.1 gives the risk classifications presented by Moody and Standard & Poor's. The rating systems are quite similar, for each classification of debt involving little risk (high-quality debt) receives a rating of triple A, while debt involving greater risk (poorer-quality debt) receives progressively lower ratings. Bonds rated triple B or better are considered investment grade, while bonds with lower ratings are often referred to as *junk bonds* or *high-yield securities.* The growth in this poor-quality debt was one of the phenomena within the financial markets during

EXHIBIT 15.2

Ratings for Selected Bonds (as of January 1, 2001)

Firm	Coupon Rate of Interest	Year of Maturity	Moody's Rating	Standard & Poor's Rating
AT&T	7½%	2006	A2	A
Consumers Energy	7⅜	2023	Baa3	BBB+
Dow Chemical	9	2021	A1	A
Paramount Communications*	8¼	2022	A3	BBB+
Mobil**	8⅝	2021	Aaa	AAA
Xerox	7.20	2016	A3	BBB−

*Merged with Viacom.
**Merged with Exxon to form ExxonMobil.
Sources: *Mergent's Bond Record*, January 2001, and *Standard & Poor's Bond Guide*, Year end 2000.

the 1980s. (The variety of features found in junk bonds is covered later in this chapter.)

Even within a given rating, both Moody and Standard & Poor's fine-shade their rankings. Moody adds the numbers 1 through 3 to indicate degrees of quality within a ranking, with 1 representing the highest rank and 3 the lowest. Thus a bond rated A1 has a higher rating than a bond rated A3. Standard & Poor's uses + and − to indicate shades of quality. Thus a bond rated A+ has a higher rating than an A bond, which, in turn, has a better rating than an A− bond.

Since the rating services analyze similar data, their ratings of specific debt issues should be reasonably consistent. This consistency is illustrated in Exhibit 15.2, which gives the ratings for several different bond issues. Generally, both Moody and Standard & Poor's assigned comparable ratings, such as the A2 and A to the AT&T bond. When the ratings are different, the discrepancies are small. Moody ranked the Consumers Energy bond Baa3, which is lower than the Standard & Poor's BBB+ rating. (BBB− would be the comparable rating.)

These ratings play an important role in the marketing of debt obligations. Since the possibility of default may be substantial for poor-quality debt, some financial institutions and investors will not purchase debt with a low credit rating. Many financial institutions, especially commercial banks, are prohibited by law from purchasing bonds with a rating below Baa. Thus, if the rating of a bond issued by a firm or a municipality is low or declines from the original rating, the issuer may have difficulty selling its debt. Corporations and municipal governments try to maintain good credit ratings, because high ratings reduce the cost of borrowing and increase the marketability of the debt.

While the majority of corporate and municipal bonds are rated, there are exceptions. If a firm or municipality believes it will be able to market the securities without a rating, it may choose not to incur the costs necessary to have the securities rated. Unrated securities tend to be small issues and, because they lack the approval implied by a rating, probably should be viewed as possessing considerable risk.

Besides the risk of default, creditors are also subject to the risk of price fluctuations. Once debt has been issued, the market price of the debt will rise or fall depending on market conditions. If interest rates rise, the price of existing debt must fall so that its fixed interest payments relative to its price become competitive with the higher rates. In the event that interest rates decline, the opposite is true. The higher fixed-interest payments of the bond make the debt more attractive than comparable newly issued bonds, and buyers will be willing to pay more for the debt issue. Why these fluctuations in the price of debt instruments occur is explained in more detail in Chapter 16, which discusses the valuation of debt instruments.

There is, however, one feature of debt that partially compensates for the risk of price fluctuations. The holder knows that the debt ultimately matures: The principal must be repaid. If the price of the bond decreases and the debt instrument sells for a discount (i.e., less than the face value), the value of the debt must appreciate as it approaches maturity, because on the day of maturity, the full amount of the principal must be repaid.

Since interest rates fluctuate, bondholders may also bear reinvestment rate risk. Of course, this risk does not apply if the investor is spending payments as they are received, but that is often not the case. Instead, the payments are reinvested, and lower interest rates imply the individual will earn less and accumulate a lower terminal value. The converse would also apply if interest rates were higher. The reinvested payments would earn more and the investor would accumulate a larger terminal value.

Bondholders and creditors also endure the risk associated with inflation, which reduces the purchasing power of money. During periods of inflation the debtor repays the loan in money that purchases less. Creditors must receive a rate of interest that is at least equal to the rate of inflation to maintain their purchasing power. If lenders anticipate inflation, they will demand a higher rate of interest to help protect their purchasing power. For example, if the rate of inflation is 3 percent, the creditors may demand 6 percent, which nets them 2.9 percent in real terms. (See the Points of Interest feature "Real Returns" in Chapter 9 for the calculation.) Although inflation still causes the real value of the capital to decline, the higher interest rate partially offsets the effects of inflation.

If creditors do not anticipate inflation, the rate of interest may be insufficient to compensate for the loss in purchasing power. Inflation, then, hurts the creditors and helps the debtors, who are repaying the loans with money that purchases less.

The supposed inability of creditors to anticipate inflation has led to a belief that during inflation it is better to be a debtor. However, creditors invariably make an effort to protect their position by demanding higher interest rates. There is a transfer of purchasing power from creditors to debtors only if the creditors do not fully anticipate the inflation and do not demand sufficiently high interest rates. A transfer of purchasing power from debtors to creditors will occur in the opposite situation. If inflation is anticipated but does not occur, many debtors may pay artificially high interest rates, which transfers purchasing power from them to their creditors.[4] Hence, the transfer of purchasing power can go either way if one group inaccurately anticipates the future rate of inflation.

If the investor acquires bonds denominated in a foreign currency, there is the additional risk that the value of the currency will decline relative to the dollar. Payments received in yen, euros, or pounds have to be converted into dollars before they may be spent in the United States, so fluctuations in the value of the currency affect the number of dollars the investor will receive. Of course, the value of the foreign currency could rise, which means the investor receives more dollars, but the value could also fall.

All the sources of risk to bondholders (default, fluctuations in bond prices from fluctuations in interest rates, reinvestment rate risk, loss of purchasing power from inflation, and foreign exchange rate risk) are essentially the same as the sources of risk to investors in stock. While a diversified bond portfolio reduces the

[4]Debtors may seek to protect themselves from the anticipated inflation *not* occurring by having the bond be callable. The call feature is discussed later in this chapter.

risk identified with a specific asset (i.e., the risk of default), the risks associated with bond investments in general are not reduced by diversification. Even diversified bond investors must still bear the risks of fluctuations in interest and reinvestment rates, loss of purchasing power from inflation, and declining exchange rates.

The Mechanics of Purchasing Bonds

Bonds may be purchased in much the same way as stocks. The investor can buy them through a brokerage firm, and some bonds (e.g., federal government securities) can be purchased through commercial banks. The various purchase orders that may be used to buy stock (e.g., the market order or the limit order with a specified price) also apply to the purchase of bonds. Bonds may be bought with cash or through the use of margin.

The bonds of many companies are listed on the New York and American stock exchanges. In addition, there is a large volume of trading in bonds in the over-the-counter markets. Like listed stocks, transactions in bonds are reported by the financial press. The following entry for an AT&T bond is typical of the form used by *The Wall Street Journal,* and other papers use a similar, if not identical, presentation to report bond prices:

Bonds	Current Yield	Volume	Close	Net Change
ATT 8⅛ 22	7.9	20	103	+½

The entry is for a $1,000 bond (though bonds generally trade in units greater than $1,000). Bond prices are reported as a percent of face value, so 103 means 103% of $1,000, or $1,030.00. The bond has a coupon rate of 8⅛ percent and matures in the year 2022, which is reported as 8⅛ 22. The current yield is the annual interest payment divided by the price ($81.25 ÷ $1,030.00 = 7.9%). The number of bonds traded was 20, which means that, according to face value, $20,000 worth of these bonds changed ownership.

confirmation statement
Statement received from a brokerage firm that specifies a purchase or sale of a security.

After the debt has been purchased, the broker sends a **confirmation statement**. Exhibit 15.3 (p. 470) presents simplified confirmation statements for the purchase and subsequent sale of $10,000 in face value worth of Tesoro Petroleum bonds. In addition to a description of the securities, the confirmation statements include the price, the commission, accrued interest, and net amount due.

accrued interest
Interest that has been earned but not received.

Bonds earn interest every day, but the firm distributes the interest payments only twice a year. Thus, when a bond is purchased, the buyer owes the previous owner **accrued interest** for the days that the owner held the bond. In the case of the first transaction, the purchase was made after the last interest payment, so the accrued interest amounted to $54.00. This interest is added to the purchase price that the buyer must pay. When the bond is sold, the seller receives the accrued interest. The second transaction occurred soon after the interest payment, and in this case the accrued interest was only $12.00, which was added to the proceeds of the sale.[5]

The profit or loss from the investment cannot be figured as the difference between the proceeds of the sale and the amount that is due after the purchase (i.e., $8,667.00 minus $7,899.00). Instead, an adjustment must be made for the accrued

[5]Interest on bonds accrues daily. At 5.25 percent, the interest on $10,000 is $525, or approximately $1.44 a day. If the purchase of the bond occurs 37 days after the payment date, the accrued interest owed is $53.28. If the sale occurs 8 days after the interest payment, the accrued interest received is $12.52. Accrued interest amounts in Exhibit 15.3 are rounded to facilitate the calculation of gains (or losses) in Exhibit 15.4.

EXHIBIT 15.3

Simplified Confirmation Statements for the Purchase and Sale of a Bond

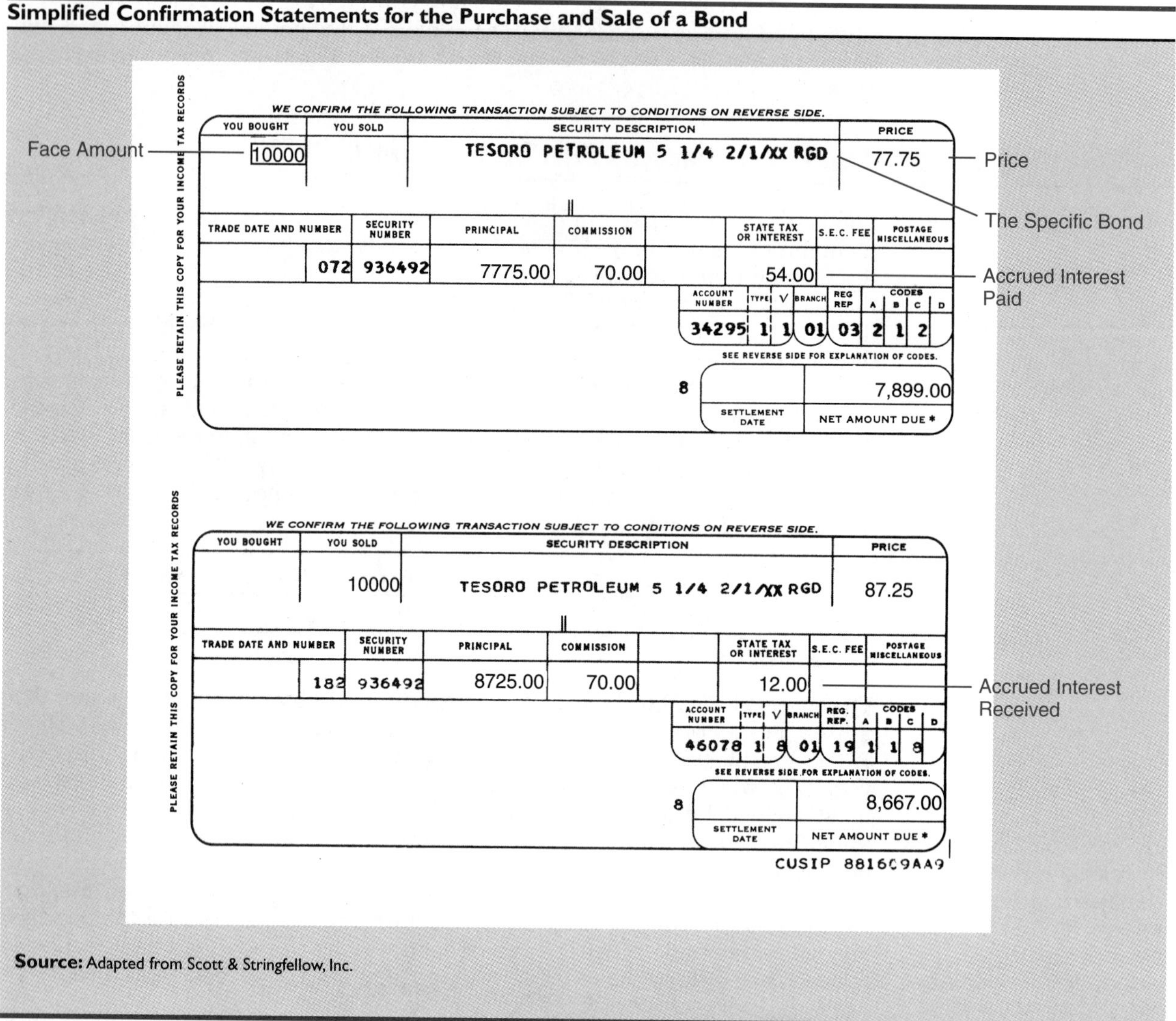

PLEASE RETAIN THIS COPY FOR YOUR INCOME TAX RECORDS

WE CONFIRM THE FOLLOWING TRANSACTION SUBJECT TO CONDITIONS ON REVERSE SIDE.

YOU BOUGHT	YOU SOLD	SECURITY DESCRIPTION	PRICE
10000		TESORO PETROLEUM 5 1/4 2/1/XX RGD	77.75

TRADE DATE AND NUMBER	SECURITY NUMBER	PRINCIPAL	COMMISSION		STATE TAX OR INTEREST	S.E.C. FEE	POSTAGE MISCELLANEOUS
072	936492	7775.00	70.00		54.00		

ACCOUNT NUMBER	TYPE	V	BRANCH	REG REP	A	B	C	D
34295	1	1	01	03	2	1	2	

SEE REVERSE SIDE FOR EXPLANATION OF CODES.

8

SETTLEMENT DATE	NET AMOUNT DUE *
	7,899.00

PLEASE RETAIN THIS COPY FOR YOUR INCOME TAX RECORDS

WE CONFIRM THE FOLLOWING TRANSACTION SUBJECT TO CONDITIONS ON REVERSE SIDE.

YOU BOUGHT	YOU SOLD	SECURITY DESCRIPTION	PRICE
	10000	TESORO PETROLEUM 5 1/4 2/1/XX RGD	87.25

TRADE DATE AND NUMBER	SECURITY NUMBER	PRINCIPAL	COMMISSION		STATE TAX OR INTEREST	S.E.C. FEE	POSTAGE MISCELLANEOUS
182	936492	8725.00	70.00		12.00		

ACCOUNT NUMBER	TYPE	V	BRANCH	REG. REP.	A	B	C	D
46078	1	8	01	19	1	1	8	

SEE REVERSE SIDE FOR EXPLANATION OF CODES.

8

SETTLEMENT DATE	NET AMOUNT DUE *
	8,667.00

CUSIP 88169AA9

Source: Adapted from Scott & Stringfellow, Inc.

interest. This procedure is illustrated in Exhibit 15.4. First, the accrued interest must be subtracted from the amount due to obtain the cost of the bond. Thus, $7,899.00 minus $54.00 is the cost ($7,845.00) of this purchase. Second, the accrued interest must also be subtracted from the proceeds of the sale. Thus, $8,667.00 minus $12.00 yields the revenues from the sale. To determine the profit or loss, the cost basis is subtracted from the sale value. In this particular instance, that is $8,655.00 (the sale value) minus $7,845.00 (the cost basis), which represents a gain of $810.00.

flat
A description of a bond that trades without accrued interest.

A few bonds do trade without accrued interest. These bonds are currently in default and are not paying interest. Such bonds are said to trade flat, and an *F* is placed next to them in the transactions reported by the financial press. These bonds are of little interest except to speculators. The risk in buying them is substantial, but some do resume interest payments that can result in substantial returns.

EXHIBIT 15.4

Determination of Profit or Loss on the Sale of a Bond

Cost basis of the bond:	
Amount due	$7,899.00
Less accrued interest	−54.00
	$7,845.00
Revenue from the sale:	
Proceeds of the sale	$8,667.00
Less accrued interest	−12.00
	$8,655.00
Profit (or loss) on the investment:	
Return from the sale of the bond	$8,655.00
Cost basis of the bond	7,845.00
Profit (or loss) on the investment	$810.00

Variety of Corporate Bonds

Corporations issue many types of bonds: mortgage bonds, equipment trust certificates, debenture bonds and subordinated debentures, income bonds, convertible bonds, variable interest rate bonds, and zero coupon bonds. These corporate debt instruments are either secured or unsecured. If a debt instrument is secured, the debtor pledges a specific asset as collateral. In case of default, the creditor may seize this collateral (through a court proceeding). Bonds that are not collateralized by specific assets are unsecured. If the debtor were to default, there would be no specific assets the creditors could seize to satisfy their claims on the borrower. Such unsecured debt instruments are supported by the general capacity of the firm to service its debt (i.e., pay the interest and repay the principal). Thus, the capacity of the borrower to generate operating income (i.e., earnings before interest and taxes) is crucial to the safety of unsecured debt obligations.

Mortgage Bonds

mortgage bond
A bond that is secured by property, especially real estate.

Mortgage bonds are issued to purchase specific fixed assets, which are then pledged to secure the debt. This type of bond is frequently issued by utility companies. The proceeds that are raised by selling the debt are used to build power plants, and these plants secure the debt. As the plants generate revenues, the firm earns the cash flow that is necessary to service (pay interest on) and retire the debt. If the firm defaults on the interest or principal repayment, the creditors may take title to the pledged property. They may then choose to hold the asset and earn income from it (to operate the fixed asset) or to sell it. These options should give investors cause for thought: How many creditors could operate a power plant? If the investors choose to sell it, who would buy it?

These two questions illustrate an important point concerning investing in corporate debt. Although property that is pledged to secure the debt may decrease the lender's risk of loss, the creditor is not interested in taking possession of and operating the property. Lenders earn income through interest payments and not through the operation of the fixed assets. Such creditors are rarely qualified to operate the assets should they take possession of them. If they are forced to seize and sell the assets, they may find few buyers and may have to sell at distress prices. Despite the fact that pledging assets to secure debt increases the safety of the principal, the lenders prefer the prompt payment of interest and principal.

Equipment Trust Certificates

equipment trust certificate
A serial bond secured by specific equipment.

Not all collateral has questionable resale potential. Unlike the mortgage bonds that are issued by utility companies, **equipment trust certificates** are secured by assets with substantial resale value. These certificates are issued to finance specific equipment, which is pledged as collateral. Equipment trust certificates are primarily issued by railroads and airlines to finance rolling stock (railroad cars) and airplanes. As the equipment is used to generate cash flow, the certificates are retired. The collateral supporting these certificates is generally considered to be of excellent quality, for, unlike some fixed assets (e.g., the aforementioned utility plants), this equipment may be readily *moved* and sold to other railroads and airlines in the event that the firm defaults on the certificates.

Investors, however, should realize that while equipment may be more readily sold than power plants, these investors could still suffer losses. For example, when Eastern, Pan Am, and several small airlines went bankrupt, they dumped a large number of aircraft on the market, so prices for used aircraft declined. This, of course, meant that even the secured creditors did not receive their principal from the proceeds of the sales of the planes.

Other Asset-Backed Securities and Securitization

While equipment trust certificates are secured by equipment such as railroad cars and mortgages are secured by real estate, other assets may also be used as collateral for a debt issue. For example, a firm may issue and sell debt securities backed by its accounts receivable. (The firm may also sell outright the receivables to a financial institution or factor, who, in turn, issues debt instruments secured by the assets.) As the accounts are collected, the funds are used to retire the securities and pay the interest. The advantage to the issuing firm is simple. It obtains the funds immediately and does not have to wait for the collection of the receivables. The advantage to the investors, especially large pension plans, is that they receive an interest-paying security that is relatively safe since it is secured by the underlying assets.

securitization
The process of converting an illiquid asset into a marketable security.

The process of converting illiquid assets such as accounts receivable into liquid assets is called **securitization**. Textron, a manufacturer of Bell helicopters, Cessna aircraft, automotive products, and fastening systems, sells a variety of products, which generates accounts receivable. In its 2000 annual report, Textron reported that it securitized over $1 billion in assets, including $763 million in aviation receivables and $275 million in equipment loans. The proceeds of the sales were then used to retire commercial paper previously issued by Textron.

Debentures

debenture
An unsecured bond.

Debentures are unsecured promissory notes that are supported by the general creditworthiness of the firm. This type of debt involves more risk than bonds that are supported by collateral. In the case of default or bankruptcy, the unsecured debt is redeemed only after all secured debt has been paid off. Some debentures are subordinated, and these involve even more risk, for they are redeemed after the other general debt of the firm has been redeemed. Even unsecured debt has a superior position to the subordinated debenture. These bonds are among the riskiest debt instruments issued by firms and usually have higher interest rates or other attractive features, such as convertibility into the stock of the company, to compensate the lenders for assuming the increased risk.

Financial institutions, such as commercial banks or insurance companies, prefer a firm to sell debentures to the general public. Since the debentures are general obligations of the company, they do not tie up its specific assets. Then, if the firm needs additional funds from a commercial bank, it can use specific assets as collateral, in which case the bank will be more willing to lend the funds. If the assets had been previously pledged, the firm would lack this flexibility in financing.

Although the use of debentures may not decrease the ability of the firm to issue additional debt, default on the debentures usually means that all senior debt is in default as well. A common indenture clause states that if any of the firm's debt is in default, all debt issues are also in default, and in this case the creditors may declare that all outstanding debt is due. For this reason, a firm should not overextend itself through excessive amounts of unsecured debt.

Income Bonds

income bond
A bond whose interest is paid only if it is earned by the firm.

Income bonds are the riskiest bonds issued by corporations. Interest is paid only if the firm earns it. If the company is unable to cover its other expenses, it is not legally obligated to pay the interest on these bonds. Owing to the great risk associated with them, income bonds are rarely issued by corporations. One notable exception is an issue of Disney bonds that could pay as much as 13.5 percent annually if a package of 20 Disney movies grosses over $800 million. If, however, the gross is less, the bonds could yield as little as 3 percent.

Although income bonds are rarely issued by firms, a similar type of security is often issued by state and municipal governments. These are *revenue bonds,* which are used to finance a particular capital improvement that is expected to generate revenues (e.g., a toll road or a municipal hospital). If the revenues are insufficient, the interest is not paid.

There is, however, one significant difference between income bonds and revenue bonds. Failure to pay interest does not result in default for an income bond, but it does mean that a revenue bond is in default. Most projects financed by revenue bonds have generated sufficient funds to service the debt, but there have been notable exceptions. Perhaps the most famous default was the multibillion-dollar default by the Washington Public Power Supply System. As of 2001, the defaulted bonds were virtually worthless.

Convertible Bonds

convertible bond
A bond that may be exchanged for (i.e., converted into) common stock.

Convertible bonds are a hybrid-type security. Technically they are debt: The bonds pay interest, which is a fixed obligation of the firm, and have a maturity date. But these bonds have a special feature: The investor has the option to convert the bond into a specified number of shares of common stock. For example, the Nextel Communications 5¼ percent of the year 2010 bond may be converted into 13.44 shares of Nextel common stock. The market price of convertible bonds depends on both the value of the stock and the interest that the bonds pay. If the price of the common stock rises, then the value of the bond must rise. The investor thus has the opportunity for capital gain should the price of the common stock rise. If, however, the price of the common stock does not appreciate, the investor still owns a debt obligation of the company and therefore has the security of an investment in a debt instrument.

Convertible bonds have been popular with some investors, and thus firms have issued these bonds as a means to raise funds. However, since convertible bonds are a hybrid-type security, they are difficult to analyze. For this reason, a detailed discussion is deferred until Chapter 18, which follows the discussion of nonconvertible debt and precedes the discussion of options.

Variable Interest Rate Bonds

variable interest rate bond
A long-term bond with a coupon rate that varies with changes in short-term rates.

Generally, the interest that a bond pays is fixed at the date of issuance; however, some corporations issue **variable interest rate bonds.** Citicorp was the first major American firm to offer bonds with variable interest rates to the general public. Two features of the Citicorp bond were unique at the time it was issued: (1) a variable interest rate that was tied to the interest rate on Treasury bills and (2) the right of the holder to redeem the bond at its face value.

The interest rate to be paid by the Citicorp bond was set at 1 percent above the average Treasury bill rate during a specified period. This variability of the interest rate means that if short-term interest rates rise, the interest rate paid by the bond must increase. The bond's owner participates in any increase in short-term interest rates. Of course, if the short-term interest rates decline, the bond earns a lower rate of interest.

The second unique feature of the Citicorp bond was that two years after it was issued, the holder had the option to redeem the bond for its face value or principal. This option recurred every six months. If the owner needed the money more quickly, the bond could have been sold in the secondary market, for it was traded on the New York Stock Exchange. An important implication of the variable coupon is that the market price of the bond fluctuates less than the price of a fixed coupon bond. As is explained in the next chapter, the price of a fixed coupon bond fluctuates inversely with interest rates. Such price changes will not occur with a variable rate bond because the interest paid fluctuates with interest rates in general. Hence these bonds avoid one of the major sources of risk associated with investing in bonds: higher interest rates driving down the bond's market value.

Zero Coupon and Discount Bonds

zero coupon bond
A bond on which interest accrues and is paid at maturity, and is initially sold at a discount.

In 1981 a new type of bond was sold to the general public. These bonds pay no interest and are sold at large discounts. The pathbreaking issue was the J.C. Penney **zero coupon bond.** This bond was initially sold for a discount ($330) but paid $1,000 at maturity in 1989. The investor's funds grew from $330 to $1,000 after eight years. The annual rate of growth (i.e., the yield on the bond) was 14.86 percent.[6]

Calculator Solution

Function Key	Data Input
PV =	−330
N =	8
PMT =	0
FV =	1000
I =	?
Function Key	**Answer**
I =	14.86

[6]The yield on a zero coupon is calculated using the time value formula (Equation 5.4):

$$P_0(1 + i)^n = P_n,$$

which is solved for i. In this example,

$$\$330(1 + i)^8 = \$1{,}000$$
$$(1 + i)^8 = \$1{,}000/\$330 = 3.030$$
$$i = \sqrt[8]{3.030} - 1$$
$$i = 0.1486 = 14.86\%.$$

The 14.86 percent was derived by the use of a financial calculator. If the student does not have access to a calculator with a y^x key or a financial calculator, then the future value table can be used, which will derive an answer of approximately 15 percent.

POINTS OF INTEREST

Original-Issue Discounts and Taxation

As mentioned in the body of the text, interest that accrues to a zero coupon and an original-issue discount bond is taxed as income even though it is not received until the bond's maturity. Consider the following four-year, $1,000 zero coupon bond. If the comparable rate is 10 percent, the price of the bond is $683.01. (FV = 1000, N = 4, I = 10, PMT = 0, PV = 683.01 when interest is compounded annually.) After one year (when the bond has three years to maturity), the price will be $751.31 if interest rates do not change. The appreciation from $683.01 to $751.31 ($68.30) is the accrual of interest, and that $68.30 is subject to federal income tax even though the investor has not received any payment. At the end of the second, third, and fourth years, the bond's values are $826.45, $909.09, and $1,000. The accrued interest amounts are $75.13, $82.64, and $90.91. These interest amounts accrue annually and are based on the bond's paying 10 percent annually.

The accrued interest increases each year as the previous year's interest is added to the amount owed. The $68.30 in accrued interest earned the first year is added to $683.01, which is the amount owed at the end of the first year ($751.31). The $751.31 earns $75.13, which is added to $751.31 to determine the amount owed at the end of the second year when the bond has two years to maturity. The process is repeated until the bond is redeemed at maturity for $1,000.

All of these bond prices and accrued interest were determined using the 10 percent the bond was to pay when it was issued. Interest rates do change. For example, if the current rate is 9 percent at the end of the first year (when the bond has three years to maturity), the price will be $772.18 instead of $751.31. If the investor sells the bond, there is a gain of $89.17 ($772.18 − $683.01). This gain, however, is not a capital gain since $68.31 is the appreciation associated with the accrual of interest. The capital gain is $20.86. The $68.31 is taxed as income and the $20.86 is taxed at the appropriate capital gains tax rate. If instead of declining from 10 to 9 percent, the interest rate rose from 10 percent to 12 percent, the price of the bond with three years to maturity is $711.78. If the investor sells the bond, the gain is only $28.77. The accrued interest, however, remains $68.31. The difference is −$39.54 ($28.77 − $68.31), which is a capital loss. The accrued interest continues to be taxed as income, but the loss has to be used to offset other capital gains before it may be applied against ordinary income such as accrued interest. (The use of capital gains to offset ordinary income was discussed in Chapter 6.)

After the initial success of this issue, other firms, including IBM Credit Corporation (the financing arm of IBM) and ITT Financial, issued similar bonds. In each case the firm pays no periodic interest. The bond sells for a large discount, and the investor's return accrues from the appreciation of the bond's value as it approaches maturity.

Because the return on an investment in a zero coupon bond depends solely on the firm's capacity to retire the debt, the quality of the firm is exceedingly important. Zero coupon bonds issued by such firms as Sears or IBM Credit Corporation are of excellent quality and should be retired at maturity. In these cases the investor will earn the expected return that accrues when the bond approaches maturity. If, however, the investor purchases low-quality zero coupon bonds, these bonds may never be redeemed. If the firm were to go bankrupt, the investor may receive nothing. Thus, it is possible for the individual who buys zero coupon bonds to lose the entire investment and never receive a single interest payment.

There is, however, a tax feature that reduces the attractiveness of zero coupon bonds. The IRS taxes the accrued interest as if it were received. Thus the investor must pay federal income tax on the earned interest even though the investor receives the funds only when the bond matures. Thus zero coupon bonds are of little interest to investors except as part of pension plans. Zero coupon bonds may be included in an individual's retirement account because the tax on the accrued interest in the account is deferred until the funds are withdrawn. So the primary reason for acquiring a zero coupon bond is to use it in conjunction with a tax-deferred retirement plan.

Eurobonds

Many U.S. firms also issue bonds in foreign countries to raise funds for foreign investments (e.g., plant and equipment).[7] These bonds fall into two basic types, depending on the currency in which they are denominated. U.S. firms can sell bonds denominated in the local currency (e.g., British pounds or European euros). For example, ExxonMobil reported in its 2000 10-k report that $650 million of its $7.28 billion of long-term debt (8.9 percent) was denominated in foreign currencies. The firm can also sell abroad bonds denominated in U.S. dollars called **Eurobonds**. This term applies even though the bonds may be issued in, say, Asia instead of Europe.

Eurobond
A bond denominated in U.S. dollars but issued abroad.

When a firm issues a Eurobond, the U.S. firm promises to make payments in dollars. This means that the U.S. investor does not have to convert the payments from the local currency (e.g., British pounds) into dollars. As is explained in Chapters 7 and 22, fluctuation in the value of one currency relative to another is a major source of risk that every individual who acquires foreign securities must bear. By acquiring Eurobonds, the U.S. investor avoids this currency risk. However, foreign investors do bear this risk. They have to convert the dollars into their currency, so the yields on Eurobonds tend to be higher than on comparable domestic securities. The higher yield is a major reason why investors find Eurobonds attractive.

High-Yield Securities

high-yield securities
Non-investment-grade securities offering a high return.

High-yield securities (sometimes referred to as *junk bonds*) are not a particular type of bond but refer to any debt of low quality (i.e., bonds rated below triple B). These bonds have the same general features associated with investment-grade debt. In addition to the interest payment (the coupon) and the maturity date, junk bonds often have call features and sinking funds. While junk bonds are usually debentures and may be subordinated to the firm's other debt obligations, some do have collateral (i.e., they are mortgage bonds). As is subsequently discussed, some high-yield securities have variations on the basic features associated with all bonds.

The poor quality of junk bonds requires that they offer high yields, at least relative to investment-grade debt. Generally, triple B or better is considered investment grade, and many financial institutions, such as trust departments of commercial banks, are only allowed to purchase investment-grade bonds. Anything with a lower credit rating is not an acceptable risk.

Junk bonds (and high-yield preferred stock) are often issued to finance takeovers and mergers or to finance start-up firms with little credit history. The bonds are purchased by financial institutions and individuals who are accustomed to investing in poor-quality debt and who are willing and able to accept the larger risk in order to earn the higher yields. These investors may treat the bonds as if they are equity instruments that will generate their potential return if the firm generates cash flow and survives. In many cases, the additional return may be 3 or 4 percentage points greater than the yield on investment-grade debt.

fallen angel
Investment-grade security whose quality has deteriorated.

High-yield securities may be divided into two classes. First are the bonds that were initially investment grade but whose credit ratings were lowered as the issuing firms developed financial problems. This type of high-yield bond is often referred to as a **fallen angel**. When RJR Nabisco was purchased and taken private, the surviving firm issued substantial new debt that resulted in the downgrading of

[7]Bonds are also issued in the United States by foreign firms and these are sometimes referred to as "Yankee" bonds. Other colorful names are also applied to foreign bonds issued in other domestic markets: the "Bulldog" market for foreign bonds issued in the United Kingdom and the "Samurai" market for foreign bonds issued in Japan.

POINTS OF INTEREST
Mezzanine Financing

While there are secondary markets for high-yield securities, junk bonds tend to lack liquidity. The spreads between the bid and ask prices are often large, and there may be little or no market for small issues. This lack of liquidity for small issues has led to "mezzanine financing." In a theater, the mezzanine is between the orchestra seats and the balcony seats. That analogy describes mezzanine financing, which tends to be a modest-sized debt issue ranging from $50 million to $200 million.

Modest-sized issues are often too small to attract buyers of high-yield securities (e.g., pension plans or mutual funds specializing in low-quality debt) but too large for most commercial banks. To place such issues, investment bankers have formed specialized groups to arrange offerings of mezzanine debt. The securities are privately placed with one or more buyers who intend to hold the securities until maturity. Since there will be no secondary market for the securities, the yields tend to be higher, which compensates the buyers for the lack of liquidity.

outstanding RJR Nabisco bonds. The prices of what were previously high-quality debt declined dramatically, and the issues became high-yield securities. Of course, the high yields were to be earned by new buyers and not by the original investors who suffered losses when the prices of the previously issued bonds declined.

Some fallen angels ultimately go bankrupt. Manville, Public Service of New Hampshire, and Texaco all went bankrupt and defaulted on their debts. However, bonds in default continue to trade, and there is always the possibility that the firm will recover and the price of the bonds will rise. This did occur in the case of Texaco. One of the attractions of the high-yield security market is the possibility that the financial condition of the issuing firm will improve. A higher credit rating should be beneficial to the holders of the firm's debt, because the bonds' prices should increase as the firm's financial condition improves.

The second class of high-yield securities is composed of bonds and preferred stock issued by firms with less than investment-grade credit ratings. The maturities of these securities can range from short-term (i.e., high-yield commercial paper) to long-term (i.e., bonds and preferred stock).

Pay-in-Kind (PIK) Securities

pay-in-kind (PIK) securities
Bonds or preferred stock whose interest or dividends are paid in additional debt or shares.

Pay-in-kind securities are bonds and preferred stock whose interest and dividends may be paid in additional debt or shares. The option to pay in paper instead of cash rests with the firm. In some cases, the option is granted only for the initial years, with payment in subsequent years to be made in cash. Since the investor may not receive dividends or interest in cash, PIK bonds and PIK preferred stock are among the riskiest of high-yield securities, so the stated yields are high even by high-yield security standards.

Paying the interest or dividend with additional securities has a positive long-term implication. The firm's current liquidity position is not hurt by the distribution of additional securities. Of course, issuing additional debt means the firm will have to pay more interest and to retire more debt at maturity, but that is some time in the future when the firm's capacity to service the debt may be better.

Although PIK securities may appeal to any investor seeking an extremely risky but high-yield security, they have major tax disadvantages. The payments, be they in cash or *in additional securities,* are subject to personal income taxation to the recipient. Securities received by holders of PIK preferred stocks and bonds must pay federal income tax as if the payments had been received in cash. In addition, Congress changed the tax laws so that interest paid in additional debt instead of cash is *not deductible* for corporate income tax purposes. While firms are not excluded from issuing PIK bonds, the tax deduction for interest paid in additional debt no longer exists. These changes in the tax laws suggest that few, if any, new PIK bonds will be issued and that they will cease to exist as bonds currently outstanding are retired.

Split Coupon Bonds

split coupon bond
Bond with a zero or low initial coupon followed by a period with a high coupon.

A **split coupon bond** combines the features of zero coupon and high coupon bonds. During the first three to five years, the bond pays initially no (or a small amount of) interest. The interest accrues like a zero coupon bond. After this initial period, the bond pays a high coupon. For example, Dr Pepper issued a split coupon bond that pays no interest for the first four years and then must pay a coupon of 11.5 percent for the next six years, until the bond matures.

These bonds, which are also referred to as *deferred interest bonds,* initially sell at a discounted price that is calculated using the coupon rate in effect when the bond starts to pay cash. For the Dr Pepper bond, the flow of payments per $1,000 bond is

Interest:	
Years 1–4	$0
Years 5–10	$115
Principal repayment at end of year 10:	$1,000

The advantage to the firm issuing split coupon bonds is that debt service is eliminated during the initial period. As with PIK securities, split coupon bonds conserve cash, but the accrual of interest is tax deductible to the issuing firm. Split coupon bonds are often issued in leveraged buyouts and other recapitalizations that result in the firm issuing substantial amounts of debt. (The RJR Nabisco buyout resulted in the surviving firm issuing both PIK and split coupon bonds.)

Split coupon bonds tend to be very costly to the firm issuing them. The high yield to investors means a high cost of funds to the issuers. There is an incentive for the firm to retire the securities as soon as possible. Thus most split coupon bonds have call features that permit the firm to retire the securities before their maturity. For example, Safeway Stores called half of its issue of junior subordinated debentures only 11 months after the bonds were originally issued.

Reset Securities and Increasing Rate Bonds

reset bond
Bond whose coupon is periodically reset.

Although the coupons are fixed when most high-yield securities are issued, there are exceptions. With a **reset bond**, the coupon is adjusted at periodic intervals, such as six months or every year. The coupon is usually tagged to a specified rate, such as the six-month Treasury bill rate plus 5 percent, and there is often a minimum and a maximum coupon. For example, American Shared Hospital Service issued a reset note whose coupon can range from 14 to 16.5 percent.

Since the coupon is permitted to change, price fluctuations associated with changes in interest rates are reduced. The minimum coupon, however, means that if interest rates fall on comparably risky securities, the price of the bond will rise since the coupon becomes fixed at the lower bound. And the same applies when interest rates rise. If the coupon reaches the upper limit, further increases in comparable yields will decrease the bond's price. However, within the specified range the changing coupon should stabilize the price of the bond. Of course, if the firm's financial condition changes, the price of the bond will change independently of changes in interest rates.

increasing rate bond
Bond whose coupon rises over time.

An **increasing rate bond** is a debt security whose coupon increases over time. For example, RJR Holdings issued $5 billion of increasing rate notes. One issue had an initial coupon of 14.5625 percent, but future coupons will be the higher of 13.4375 percent or 4 percent higher than the three-month London Interbank Offer (LIBOR) rate. Subsequent coupons increase by 0.5 percent quarterly for two years and 0.25 percent quarterly for years three and four. Unless yields decline dramatically so that 13.4375 percent becomes the coupon, the yield on this bond will rise over time. Obviously, increasing rate securities are an expensive means for any firm to raise funds, so the investor can anticipate that the issuer will seek to retire the debt as rapidly as possible, which is precisely what occurred as RJR Holdings refinanced after interest rates fell and its financial position improved.

Extendible Securities

extendible security
Bond whose maturity date may be extended into the future.

In the previous discussion, the high-yield securities had differing coupons but fixed maturity dates. PIK securities permit interest and dividends to be paid in additional securities. Split coupon bonds have periods during which interest accrues but is not paid. Reset and increasing rate notes and bonds have coupons that vary. Each of the types of high-yield securities has a fixed maturity date. However, a firm may issue an **extendible security** in which the term to maturity may be lengthened by the issuer. For example, Mattel issued a bond with an initial maturity date in 1990, but the company could extend the bond for one-, two-, or three-year periods with a final maturity in 1999. Thus the investor who acquired this bond did not know if the bond would be outstanding for one year or six years or longer. Only the final maturity in 1999 was known.

The ability to extend the maturity date is, of course, beneficial to the issuer. If the firm does not have the capacity to retire the debt at the initial maturity date, the date may be extended. This buys time for the firm to find the funds or to refinance the debt. Failure to retire the debt at the final maturity, of course, throws the bond into default.

Returns Earned by Investors in High-Yield Securities

The coupons on high-yield securities are promised or anticipated yields. In some cases the promised return will be realized if the firm makes timely payments and

---

POINTS OF INTEREST

The Internet and Sources of Information on Bonds

Descriptive information concerning bonds may be found at Smart Money's bond page (http://www.smartmoney.com). Since many of the ratios used to analyze a stock are also used to analyze a bond, the Internet sources provided in Chapter 13 for the analysis of stock may also be used to obtain information to analyze debt securities. There are, however, sites such as Bondsonline (http://www.bonds-online.com) that provide specialized information on bonds. In addition to educational material, Bondsonline can be especially useful since it has links to credit rating agencies, the Bureau of the Public Debt (http://www.publicdebt.treas.gov), and the EDGAR database (http://www.sec.gov) or Edgar Online (http://www.edgaronline.com), and the credit agencies such as Moody's Investors Services (http://www.moodys.com).

U. S. Treasury and some corporate bond prices are provided daily in the financial press (e.g., *The Wall Street Journal*). While stock prices are continuously reported through the Internet, finding bond prices is much more difficult. One possible source is the Bond Market Association (http://www.investinginbonds.com).

retires the securities on schedule. However, security markets and firms are dynamic entities. Change is always occurring, so the returns actually earned by investors will probably differ from the promised yields. The actual returns could be higher, especially if interest rates decline or the firm's financial condition improves. In either case, the price of the high-yield security should rise, so that the investor earns a higher return.

While earning higher returns is possible, the greater concern is usually that something will go wrong and that the investor will earn a lower return. Firms that issue high-yield securities are obviously not financially strong and some will not survive. If the investor is unfortunate enough to select those firms, he or she could lose a substantial amount of money—perhaps all the funds invested. Avoiding such an outcome is obviously desirable and is the purpose of analyzing the issuer's financial condition and determining the quality of its debt.

Analysis of investment-grade debt revolves around the firm's current and future capacity to service the debt. This analysis may start with such ratios as the debt ratio or times-interest-earned. However, for high-yield securities the emphasis is generally placed on cash flow (operating income plus noncash expenses such as depreciation) instead of total debt and earnings before interest and taxes. Many firms that issued high-yield securities used the funds to invest in plant and equipment. While they may currently be operating at a loss, noncash depreciation expense may generate sufficient cash flow to service the debt.[8]

Spreads in Yields and Realized Returns Prior to 1990

The spread between the yields to maturity on high-yield and investment-grade securities can be substantial. From 1982 to 1988, high-yield securities offered returns that exceeded the yields on Treasury securities by 3.2 to 5.0 percent.[9] A spread of 5 percent means if the yield to maturity on Treasury bonds is 7 percent, the yield to maturity on high-yield bonds is 12 percent.

The yield to maturity and the return actually earned are not necessarily the same. Studies of returns *actually earned* on portfolios of high-yield securities indicate that the returns exceeded the returns on investment-grade bonds. One study found the annual return on the high-yield securities from 1977 through 1986 was 11.04 percent, while investment grade bonds and federal government bonds earned 9.40 and 9.36 percent, respectively. Only common stock outperformed the high-yield bonds.[10] An alternative study for the period 1978 through 1986 found that high-yield securities returned 12.8 percent compared to 11.1 percent on long-term government securities, a spread of 1.7 percent.[11]

A spread of 1.7 percent seems small, especially since the average spread between the yields to maturity for high-yield securities and Treasury bonds often exceeds 5 percent. It must be remembered that yields to maturity are returns investors expect when the bonds are purchased and not necessarily the realized re-

[8]Models have been developed using accounting data to predict corporate bankruptcy. While these models are beyond the scope of this text, any individual who is considering investing in high-yield securities may readily apply the models to analyze specific firms. These models' track records in red-flagging possible defaults have been excellent. See E. Altman and S. Nammacher, *Investing in Junk Bonds: Inside the High Yield Debt Market* (New York: Lipper Analytical Services, Inc., 1986); and E. Altman, *Corporate Financial Distress: A Complete Guide to Predicting, Avoiding and Dealing with Bankruptcy* (New York: John Wiley & Sons, 1992).

[9]See Drexel Burnham Lambert's *1989 High Yield Market Report—Financing America's Future,* 112.

[10]Edward I. Altman, "The Anatomy of the High-Yield Bond Market," *Financial Analysts Journal* (July/August 1987): 12–25.

[11]Marshall E. Blume and Donald B. Keim, "Lower-Grade Bonds: Their Risks and Returns," *Financial Analysts Journal* (July/August 1987): 26–33.

turns. The returns just reported are realized returns. The 12.8 percent return included the impact of the defaults that occurred in the high-yield market. If the investor could be more selective and avoid defaults, the spread between the realized return on high-yield securities and alternative debt instruments would improve.

These studies also indicated that the prices of high-yield securities were *less* volatile. During periods of changing interest rates, their prices did not fluctuate as much as the prices of investment-grade corporate and federal government bonds. This result seems inconsistent with the concept of a risky, high-yield security. However, as discussed in the next chapter, the prices of bonds with higher coupons tend to fluctuate less than those of bonds with lower coupons. High-yield securities have higher coupons than investment-grade bonds, so their prices are less sensitive to fluctuations in interest rates. It is the firm-specific risk (i.e., the unsystematic risk) and not the market or interest rate risk that is the source of risk with which the investor in high-yield securities must contend.

The material in Chapter 7 suggested that unsystematic risk would be reduced through the construction of diversified portfolios. A portfolio of as few as 10 to 12 stocks could erase a substantial amount of the unsystematic risk. The same concept holds for investments in high-yield securities. A diversified portfolio of these securities will reduce firm-specific risk. However, adequate diversification may require 25 to 30 different issues, which is more than twice the number of issues required to diversify a stock portfolio.[12] Since high-yield securities are issued in minimum units of $5,000 and $10,000, diversification may require an investment in excess of $100,000.

Junk Bonds in the 1990s

Prior to 1989, high-yield securities did generate returns that compensated for the additional risk, but in 1989 the market for junk bonds began to falter. The recession combined with the large amount of debt financing put unbearable strain on the issuers of junk bonds. Some firms were late in making interest payments, and several prominent issues defaulted (for example, Resorts International, Macy's, and Integrated Resources). Campeau put up its prestigious department store, Bloomingdales, for sale in order to raise cash to service its debt. The sale did not go through, and Campeau went bankrupt. Other companies, such as Southland, owner of 7-Eleven stores, Orion Pictures, owner of the Oscar-winning movie *The Silence of the Lambs,* and retailer Carter Hawley Hale, defaulted and declared bankruptcy.

The large number of defaults tainted even the high-yield bonds that continued to pay interest, so that the prices of virtually all junk bonds fell. This produced a buying opportunity for the investor able to determine which of the firms would survive. Just as all the firms that issued high-yield securities could not survive, not every firm whose bonds were selling at significant discounts would fail. During 1991 and 1992, many firms that had previously issued debt now issued equity. Firms that had been taken private in leveraged buyouts were taken public through the issue of stock (e.g., Joy Technologies, Safeway, and Owens-Illinois). The prices of their bonds rose as dramatically as they had fallen, and many bonds that had sold for large discounts were redeemed at par after these firms issued new stock and once again became publicly held firms.[13]

Not all investors in high-yield securities fared so well, however. Many of the firms that did default were reorganized and the bondholders were forced to realize

[12]See Drexel Burnham Lambert's *1989 High Yield Market Report—Financing America's Future,* 51.

[13]While junk bonds generated negative returns in 1990, the returns in 1991 exceeded 30 percent. See Edward I. Altman, "Revisiting the High-Yield Bond Market," *Financial Management* (summer 1992): 79–80.

large losses. The holders of Southland's debt had to accept bonds with a lower face value and smaller interest payments as part of a court-sanctioned reorganization. The majority of holders of Harcourt Brace Jovanovich bonds accepted about $0.50 on the dollar as part of the HBJ merger agreement with General Cinema. The bondholders of the Trump Taj Mahal accepted equity in the casino and lower interest payments as part of Taj Mahal's reorganization. Why would the bondholders agree to these terms? In short, high-yield bonds are usually unsecured and subordinated to the firm's other debt obligations. Failure to accept the terms of the reorganization would probably result in the bondholders' losing their entire investment. Under the reorganization, there is always the possibility the firm will survive and that the bondholders will recoup some, if not all, of their investment.

The latter part of the 1990s was a period of relative quiet for the high-yield bond market. Although there were individual defaults and bankruptcies (e.g., Boston Chicken), in the aggregate yields were positive. According to the *Individual Investor's Guide to Low-Load Mutual Funds,* the average annual returns for high-yield mutual funds for 1996–1997 were 15.7 and 14.6 percent. (Returns declined to 1.9, 5.6, and −6.9 for 1998–2000 and Standard and Poor's reported that defaults reached historic highs in 2001.) As would be expected, these yields exceeded the returns on government and corporate bond funds but were less than the returns on equity funds.

Retiring Debt

Debt issues must ultimately be retired, and this retirement must occur on or before the maturity date of the debt. When the bond is issued, a method for periodic retirement is usually specified, for very few debt issues are retired in one lump payment at the maturity date. Instead, part of the issue is systematically retired each year. This systematic retirement may be achieved by issuing the bond in a series or by having a sinking fund.

Serial Bonds

serial bond
A bond issue in which specified bonds mature each year.

In an issue of **serial bonds,** some bonds mature each year. This type of bond is usually issued by corporations to finance specific equipment, such as railroad cars, which is pledged as collateral. As the equipment depreciates, the cash flow that is generated by profits and depreciation expense is used to retire the bonds in a series as they mature.

The advertisement presented in Exhibit 15.5 for equipment trust certificates issued by Union Pacific Railroad Company is an example of a serial bond. These equipment trust certificates were issued in 1985 and were designed so that one-fifteenth of the bonds matured each year. Thus, the firm retired $2,337,000 of the certificates annually as each series within the issue matured. At the end of 2001, the entire issue of certificates had been retired.

Few corporations, however, issue serial bonds. They are primarily issued by state and local governments to finance capital improvements, such as new school buildings, or by ad hoc government bodies, such as the Port Authority of New York, to finance new facilities or other capital improvements. The bonds are then retired over a period of years by tax receipts or by revenues generated by the investment (e.g., toll roads).

Sinking Funds

sinking fund
A series of periodic payments to retire a bond issue.

Sinking funds are generally employed to ease the retirement of long-term corporate debt. A **sinking fund** is a periodic payment to retire part of the debt issue.

EXHIBIT 15.5

Example of a Serial Bond Issue (Equipment Trust Certificate)

This announcement is under no circumstances to be construed as an offer to sell or as a soliciatation of an offer to buy any of these securities. The offering is made only by the Offering Circular Supplement and the Offering Circular to which it relates.

NEW ISSUE July 17, 1985

$35,055,000

Union Pacific Railroad Company

Equipment Trust No. 1 of 1985

Serial Equipment Trust Certificates
(Non-callable)

Price 100%
(Plus accrued dividends, if any, from the date of original issuance.)

MATURITIES AND DIVIDEND RATES.

(To mature in 15 equal annual installments of $2,337,000, commencing July 15, 1987.)

1987	6.500%	1992	7.500%	1997	7.800%
1988	7.000	1993	7.600	1998	7.800
1989	7.125	1994	7.700	1999	7.875
1990	7.300	1995	7.700	2000	7.875
1991	7.375	1996	7.750	2001	7.875

These Certificates are offered subject to prior sale, when, as and if issued and received by us, subject to approval of the Interstate Commerce Commission.

Merrill Lynch Capital Markets

Thomson McKinnon Securities Inc.

Source: Reprinted with permission of the Union Pacific Railroad Company.

One type of sinking fund requires the firm to make payments to a trustee, who invests the money to earn interest. The periodic payments plus the accumulated interest retire the debt when it matures.

Another type of sinking fund requires the firm to set aside a stated sum of money and to randomly select the bonds that are to be retired. The selected bonds are called and redeemed, and the holder surrenders the bond because it ceases to earn interest once it has been called. This type of sinking fund is illustrated in Exhibit 15.6 by an advertisement taken from *The Wall Street Journal.* The specific bonds being retired were selected by a lottery. Once they are chosen, these bonds are called. The owners must surrender the bonds to obtain their principal. If the bonds are not presented for redemption, they are still outstanding and are obligations of the company, but the debtor's obligation is limited to refunding the principal, since interest payments ceased at the call date.

Since each debt issue is different, there can be wide variations in sinking funds. A strong sinking fund retires a substantial proportion of the debt before the date of maturity. For example, if a bond issue is for $10 million and it matures in ten years, a strong sinking fund may require the firm to retire $1 million, or 10 percent, of the issue each year. Thus, at maturity only $1 million is still outstanding. With a weak sinking fund, a substantial proportion of the debt is retired at maturity. For example, a sinking fund for a debt issue of $10 million that matures in ten years may require annual payments of $1 million commencing after five years. In this example, only $5 million is retired before maturity. The debtor must then make a lump sum payment to retire the remaining $5 million. Such a large final payment is called a **balloon payment.**

balloon payment
The large final payment necessary to retire a debt issue.

Different sinking funds are illustrated in Exhibit 15.7 (p. 486), which presents the sinking fund requirements for two GT&E bonds. (GT&E subsequently merged with Bell Atlantic to form Verizon.) One of the sinking funds is quite strong. The 9⅛ percent bond has a sinking fund that retires 95 percent of the issue prior to maturity. However, there is no sinking fund for the 7.9 percent bond that matures in 2027. Unless GT&E calls the bond and retires it prior to maturity, the entire issue may be outstanding until it matures in 2027.

The strength of a sinking fund affects the element of risk. A strong sinking fund requirement means that a substantial amount of the debt issue is retired during its lifetime, which makes the entire debt issue safer. The sinking fund feature of a debt issue, then, is an important factor in determining the amount of risk associated with investing in a particular debt instrument.

Repurchasing Debt

discount
The sale of anything below its stated value.

If bond prices decline and the debt is selling at a **discount**, the firm may try to retire the debt by purchasing it on the open market.[14] The purchases may be made from time to time, in which case the sellers of the bonds need not know that the company is purchasing and retiring the debt. The company may also offer to purchase a specified amount of the debt at a certain price within a particular period. Bondholders may then tender their bonds at the offer price; however, they are not required to sell their bonds and may continue to hold the debt.[15] The firm must then continue to meet the terms of the debt's indenture.

The advantage of repurchasing debt that is selling at a discount is the savings to the firm. If a firm issued $10 million in face value of debt and the bonds are currently selling for $0.60 on the $1, the firm may reduce its debt by $1,000 with a cash outlay of only $600, resulting in a $400 savings for each $1,000 bond that is purchased. This savings is translated into income, because a reduction in debt at a discount is an extraordinary item that is treated in accounting as income. For example, General Cinema reported a gain of $419.6 million from the purchase of Harcourt Brace Jovanovich's debt at a discount as part of the acquisition of the

[14]Some indentures, however, forbid open market repurchases.

[15]If more bonds are tendered than the company offered to buy, the firm prorates the amount of money that it had allocated for the purchase among the number of bonds being offered.

EXHIBIT 15.6

Example of a Sinking Fund Retiring Debt

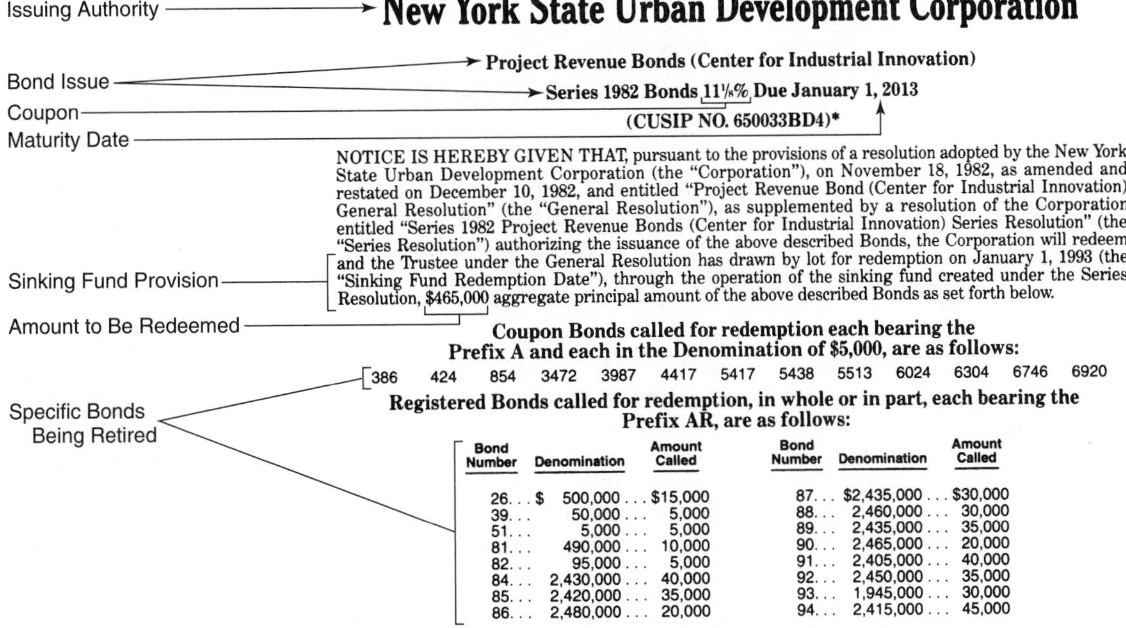

NOTICE OF REDEMPTION
To the Holders of

New York State Urban Development Corporation

Project Revenue Bonds (Center for Industrial Innovation)
Series 1982 Bonds 11 1/8% Due January 1, 2013
(CUSIP NO. 650033BD4)*

NOTICE IS HEREBY GIVEN THAT, pursuant to the provisions of a resolution adopted by the New York State Urban Development Corporation (the "Corporation"), on November 18, 1982, as amended and restated on December 10, 1982, and entitled "Project Revenue Bond (Center for Industrial Innovation) General Resolution" (the "General Resolution"), as supplemented by a resolution of the Corporation entitled "Series 1982 Project Revenue Bonds (Center for Industrial Innovation) Series Resolution" (the "Series Resolution") authorizing the issuance of the above described Bonds, the Corporation will redeem and the Trustee under the General Resolution has drawn by lot for redemption on January 1, 1993 (the "Sinking Fund Redemption Date"), through the operation of the sinking fund created under the Series Resolution, $465,000 aggregate principal amount of the above described Bonds as set forth below.

Coupon Bonds called for redemption each bearing the Prefix A and each in the Denomination of $5,000, are as follows:

386 424 854 3472 3987 4417 5417 5438 5513 6024 6304 6746 6920

Registered Bonds called for redemption, in whole or in part, each bearing the Prefix AR, are as follows:

Bond Number	Denomination	Amount Called	Bond Number	Denomination	Amount Called
26...	$ 500,000...	$15,000	87...	$2,435,000...	$30,000
39...	50,000...	5,000	88...	2,460,000...	30,000
51...	5,000...	5,000	89...	2,435,000...	35,000
81...	490,000...	10,000	90...	2,465,000...	20,000
82...	95,000...	5,000	91...	2,405,000...	40,000
84...	2,430,000...	40,000	92...	2,450,000...	35,000
85...	2,420,000...	35,000	93...	1,945,000...	30,000
86...	2,480,000...	20,000	94...	2,415,000...	45,000

On the Sinking Fund Redemption Date, there shall become due and payable on each of the above mentioned Bonds to be redeemed, the sinking fund redemption price, namely 100% of the principal amount thereof. Interest accrued on such Bonds to said Sinking Fund Redemption Date will be paid in the usual manner. From and after the Sinking Fund Redemption Date, interest on the Bonds described above shall cease to accrue.

IN ADDITION THE CORPORATION HAS ELECTED TO REDEEM ON JANUARY 1, 1993 (THE "REDEMPTION DATE") ALL REMAINING OUTSTANDING BONDS NOT HERETOFORE CALLED FOR SINKING FUND REDEMPTION AT A REDEMPTION PRICE EQUAL TO 103% OF THE PRINCIPAL AMOUNT THEREOF. INTEREST ACCRUED ON SUCH BONDS TO THE REDEMPTION DATE WILL BE PAID IN THE USUAL MANNER. FROM AND AFTER THE REDEMPTION DATE, INTEREST ON THE BONDS SHALL CEASE TO ACCRUE.

The Bonds specified herein to be redeemed shall be redeemed on or after both the Sinking Fund Redemption Date and the Redemption Date upon presentation and surrender thereof, together, in the case of coupon Bonds, with all appurtenant coupons attached, if any, maturing after January 1, 1993, to Bankers Trust Company, as Trustee and Paying Agent, in person or by registered mail (postage prepaid) at the following addresses:

IN PERSON:

Bankers Trust Company
Corporate Trust and Agency Group
First Floor
123 Washington Street
New York, New York

BY MAIL:

Bankers Trust Company
Corporate Trust and Agency Group
P.O. Box 2579
Church Street Station
New York, NY 10008
Attn: Bond Redemption

If any of the Bonds designated for redemption are in registered form, they should be accompanied by duly executed instruments of assignment in blank if payment is to be made to other than the registered holder thereof.

Coupons maturing January 1, 1993 appertaining to the coupon Bonds designated for redemption should be detached and presented for payment in the usual manner. Interest due January 1, 1993 on registered Bonds designated for redemption will be paid to the registered holders of such registered Bonds in the usual manner.

NEW YORK STATE URBAN DEVELOPMENT CORPORATION
By: BANKERS TRUST COMPANY, *as Trustee*

Source: Empire State Development Corporation.

EXHIBIT 15.7

Selected Examples of Sinking Funds for GT&E Bonds

GT&E (A Telephone Subsidiary of Verizon) Bonds		Sinking Fund Feature
9⅛%	2016	$12,500,000 face amount retired each year (sinking fund to start in 1997) to retire 95% of the issue prior to maturity.
7.9%	2027	No sinking fund.

publisher. The low interest rates of the late 1990s and early 2000s caused bond prices to rise. (See the next chapter for the explanation of changes in interest rates and their impact on bond prices.) The increase in bond prices meant the opportunity to repurchase bonds at a discount had disappeared.

On the surface, a firm's retiring debt at a discount may appear desirable. However, using money to repurchase debt is an investment decision, just like buying plant and equipment. If the company repurchases debt, it cannot use the funds for other purposes. Management must decide which is the better use of the money: purchasing other income-earning assets or retiring the debt and saving the interest payments. Unlike a sinking fund requirement (which management must meet), purchasing and retiring debt at a discount is a voluntary act. The lower the price of the debt, the greater the potential benefit from the purchase, but management must still determine if it is the best use of the firm's scarce resource, cash.

Call Feature

call feature
The right of an issuer to retire a debt issue prior to maturity.

Some bonds may have a **call feature** that allows for redemption prior to maturity. In most cases after the bond has been outstanding for a period of time (e.g., five years), the issuer has the right to call and retire the bond. The bond is called for redemption as of a specific date. After that date, interest ceases to accrue, which forces the creditor to relinquish the debt instrument.

Such premature retiring of debt through a call feature tends to occur after a period of high interest rates. If a bond has been issued during such a period and interest rates subsequently decline, it may be advantageous for the company to issue new bonds at the lower interest rate. The proceeds can then be used to retire the older bonds with the higher coupon rates. Such **refunding** reduces the firm's interest expense.

refunding
The act of issuing new debt and using the proceeds to retire existing debt.

call penalty
A premium paid for exercising a call feature.

Of course, premature retirement of debt hurts the bondholders who lose the higher-yield bonds. To protect these creditors, a call feature usually has a **call penalty**, such as the payment of one year's interest. If the initial issue had a 9 percent interest rate, the company would have to pay $1,090 to retire $1,000 worth of debt. This call penalty usually declines over the lifetime of the debt. Exhibit 15.8 illustrates the call penalty associated with the AT&T 8⅛ of 2020. In 2003 the penalty is $39.71 per $1,000, but it declines to nothing in 2015. Such a call penalty does protect bondholders, and the debtor has the right to call the bond and to refinance debt if interest rates fall sufficiently to justify paying the call penalty.[16]

Several such refinancings occurred during the 1990s when interest rates fell to lows that had not been seen in 20 years. In particular, utility companies that had issued debt when interest rates were higher sold new bonds with lower yields,

[16]How the call feature may affect the price of a bond is discussed in Chapter 16.

EXHIBIT 15.8

Schedule for the Call Penalty of the AT&T $8\frac{1}{8}$ Debenture Maturing in 2020

Year	Percentage of Face Value	Amount Required to Retire $1,000 of Debt	Amount of Call Penalty
2003	103.971	$1,039.71	$39.71
2004	103.640	$1,036.40	$36.40
2005	103.309	$1,033.09	$33.09
2006	102.978	$1,029.78	$29.78
2007	102.647	$1,026.47	$26.47
⋮	⋮	⋮	⋮
2010	101.655	$1,016.55	$16.55
⋮	⋮	⋮	⋮
2015	100.000	$1,000.00	0.00

called the old debt, and paid the call penalty. In 1998, Bell Atlantic retired $125 million of bonds with 7.5 percent coupons. The company paid 101.5 per bond (i.e., $1,015 per $1,000) for a penalty of $15 per bond. Nonutility companies also retired debt whose coupons exceeded the current rate of interest. Texas Instruments retired $200 million of its 12.7 percent bonds that were due in 2005. It paid $1,047 to retire $1,000 in face value of debt (i.e., a premium of $47 per bond). These refinancings sufficiently reduced the companies' interest expense to justify paying the call premium.

Summary

This chapter discussed the general features of long-term debt. The terms of a debt issue include the coupon rate of interest and the maturity date. A trustee is appointed for each bond issue to protect the rights of the individual investors. The risks associated with investing in debt are attributable to price fluctuations and inflation as well as to the possibility of default on interest and principal repayment. To help investors, several firms have developed rating services that classify debt issues according to risk.

The mechanics of purchasing debt are very similar to those of buying stocks. However, while stocks are purchased through brokerage firms, some debt instruments (e.g., federal government securities) may be purchased through banks.

Debt may be retired in several ways. Some bonds are issued in a series, with a specified amount of debt maturing each year. Other debt issues have sinking funds that retire part of the bond issue prior to maturity. For some debt issues, the firm has the right to call the bonds prior to maturity. The debtor can also offer to buy the debt back from investors before it matures. Since creditors are as concerned with the return of their principal as they are with the payment of interest, the ability of the firm or government to retire its liabilities is one of the foremost factors in determining the risks associated with investing in debt.

Questions

1) What is the difference between (a) bearer bonds and registered bonds? (b) The indenture and the trustee? (c) The coupon rate and the current rate of interest?

2) What is the relationship between the yield earned on bonds and the length of time to maturity? Does this relationship always hold?
3) Even though bonds are debt obligations, investing in them involves risk. What are the sources of risk? What service is available to aid the buyers of debt instruments in selecting a particular bond?
4) How may bonds be purchased?
5) What is the difference between a serial issue of bonds and term bonds with a specific maturity date and a sinking fund?
6) A call penalty protects whom from what? Why may firms choose to retire debt early after a period of high interest rates?
7) What advantages and disadvantages do bonds offer to investors?
8) What secures mortgage bonds and equipment trust certificates?
9) Why are many debentures and income bonds considered to be risky investments?
10) Figure 15.1 gives a yield curve as of May 2001. What is the current yield curve? Have interest rates on federal government securities risen or fallen since May 2001? (Treasury yields are given in *The Wall Street Journal;* they may also be found at http://www.bloomberg.com under U.S. Markets or at http://www.publicdebt.treas.gov.)

THE FINANCIAL ADVISOR'S INVESTMENT CASE

Corporate Bonds as a Viable Investment Vehicle

An investment club has recently asked you to give a presentation on investing in corporate bonds. Club members have previously invested solely in corporate stocks, but several members have expressed an interest in diversifying the portfolio through investing in bonds. Although you do not often give presentations, you believe that this one exception may introduce your financial planning services to potential clients.

Since you don't know the background of the club members or what they expect in the presentation, you suggested that they send you several questions as a means to start the general discussion. You received the following questions:

1) What are the primary differences between investments in corporate stock versus corporate bonds?
2) Since bonds pay interest, does that imply the individual's risk exposure is less for investing in bonds rather than stock?
3) What are the mechanics of purchasing bonds? May the investor leave the bonds with his or her broker?
4) Since a bond has a maturity date, does that imply the investor holds the bond to maturity?
5) Can the investor expect to earn higher returns on a firm's bonds than on its stock?
6) Are high-yield securities an acceptable investment for an investment club or its members?

The questions obviously cover many facets to consider when investing in bonds. You believe that the presentation will be improved if you also illustrate bond investments as part of a tax-deferred retirement account or a means to achieve diversification, so you pose these additional questions:

7) From a tax perspective, which should an investor acquire for a retirement account: a firm's stock or its bonds?
8) If an individual owns stock and acquires bonds issued by the same company, does the purchase diversify the investor's portfolio?
9) How does an individual construct a diversified bond portfolio? How can an investor use bonds to help diversify the total portfolio?

APPENDIX 15

The Term Structure of Interest Rates

The relationship between the rate of interest and the length of time to maturity is often referred to as the *term structure of interest rates.* During most periods of history, the longer the term to maturity, the higher the rate of interest (for example, see the yields offered by the savings and loan association in Exhibit 2.2 and the yields in Figure 15.1). One possible explanation for this relationship is that investors have a preference for liquidity. To induce these individuals to commit their funds for a longer term, the interest rate has to be higher to compensate them for the loss of liquidity.

This explanation is very plausible, but there have been periods when short-term interest rates have been higher than long-term rates. This has led to the development of an alternative explanation of the structure of yields based on investor expectations concerning future interest rates. This expectations theory suggests that the long-term rate is an average of the current short-term rate and the expected future short-term rate.

Consider an investor faced with the two following investment alternatives:

One-year bond	6%
Two-year bond	8%

If the investor purchases the two-year bond, the yield is locked in for two years. However, if the one-year bond is purchased, the investor will have to reinvest the proceeds when the bond matures. He or she will seek to earn the same return on either alternative: (1) the one-year bond in combination with a second one-year bond or (2) the two-year bond. Thus, the choice between the two alternatives depends on what the expected future rate on the one-year bond will be.

For the yields on the two alternatives to produce the same return over two years, the funds reinvested when the one-year bond matures must earn 10 percent during the second year. The average yield is 8 percent in both cases. The yield on the two-year bond equals the yield on the combination of the 6 percent and 10 percent one-year bonds.

However, suppose the investor anticipates that the one-year rate in the future will be 12 percent. If the current one-year bond is purchased, the individual can reinvest the funds when it matures and earn 12 percent for one year. The average return over the two years is 9 percent and beats the 8 percent annual yield on the two-year bond. Obviously, the two one-year securities will be preferred. However, if the investor anticipates that the future one-year rate will be 9 percent, the average yield over the two years is 7.5 percent annually, which is inferior to the 8 percent earned annually on the two-year bond.

Although an individual may move between the one- and two-year bonds, this is not true in the aggregate. Investors as a whole cannot alter their portfolios by selling one security and purchasing another. Such attempts to alter portfolios change the securities' prices and yields. If all investors expected the future one-year rate to be 12 percent, they would seek to sell the two-year bond. The effect would be to drive up its yield. One possible set of one-year and two-year yields that could emerge is:

One-year bond	8%
Two-year bond	10%

In this case, the average yield on the two one-year bonds is 10 percent (8 percent for one year and 12 percent for the other year). The average yield on the two-year bond is 10 percent. Since the average yield on either investment alternative is the same (for a given risk class), an expectation of higher future interest rates requires a positively sloped yield curve. If investors anticipate that the one-year rate next year will be 12 percent and that two-year bonds are paying 10 percent, the one-year rate today *must be 8 percent.* At 8 percent the average yield on the two alternatives is 10 percent for both. If the current rate on the one-year bond is 8 percent, the term structure is positive. The one-year bond is paying 8 percent and the two-year bond is paying 12 percent, which is a positive relationship between yields and time to maturity.

If, however, investors expect the future one-year rate to be 7 percent while the two-year bond pays 10 percent annually, the current one-year rate must be 13 percent. Only if the current rate is 13 percent will a combination of it and the expected future one-year rate of 7 percent equal the average annual yield offered by the two-year bond. If the current one-year rate is 13 percent, then the current term structure of yields is negative. The one-year bond offers 13 percent and the two-year bond offers 10 percent, which is a negative relationship between yields and time to maturity. Thus, the expectation of lower rates in the future requires a negatively sloped yield curve in the present.

In addition to the liquidity preference and expectations theories of the term structure of yields, a third alternative explanation has been suggested. It is referred to as the *segmentation theory,* and it suggests that yields depend on the demand for and supply of credit in various segments of the financial markets. For example, suppose funds were to flow from savings and loan associations and other savings institutions to money market mutual funds. Since the S&Ls make mortgage loans but money market mutual funds make only short-term loans and no mortgage loans, there has been a change in the supply of credit in the two markets. The supply of mortgage money has decreased, and the rate charged on these loans should rise. Simultaneously, the supply of short-term credit has increased, which should tend to reduce short-term interest rates. The structure of yields thus depends on the supply and demand for credit from the various segments of the economy. A flow from one segment to another alters the supply of this credit, causing yields (i.e., the term structure of interest rates) to change. A flow of funds from financial institutions that grant short-term loans to those making long-term loans will then result in a negatively sloped yield curve.

There is no consensus as to which of the three theories is correct. Each has appealing elements, but there is insufficient empirical evidence to suggest that the structure of yields is solely explained by only one of the three theories. It is probably safe to assume that all three play some role in the determination of the term structure of interest rates.[1]

[1]The illustration of the expectation theory in this appendix is limited to two years. However, it may be generalized into more time periods so that the current structure of yields reflects expected short-term rates in three, four, five, or more years. See David S. Kidwell, Richard L. Peterson, and David W. Blackwell, *Financial Institutions, Markets, and Money,* 7th ed. (Fort Worth, TX: The Dryden Press, 2000), 134–143.

CHAPTER

16 The Valuation of Fixed-Income Securities

In January 2001, *The Wall Street Journal* reported that a $1,000 federal government bond was selling for $1,260. Another was selling for $1,300. A $1,000 bond issued by Time-Warner was selling for $1,120. Why would anyone pay these high prices for a $1,000 bond? These investors will only receive $1,000 when the bonds mature. They could have bought a different $1,000 federal government bond for $1,000. And an alternative Time Warner bond was also available, and it cost only $995.

As was learned in the previous chapter, corporations issue a variety of debt instruments that are sold to the general public. There exists a very active secondary market for these bonds. Since the bonds trade daily, what establishes their prices? Why do some bonds trade for $1,300 while others trade for much less? Which bonds' prices tend to be more volatile? These are some of the essential questions concerning investing in fixed-income securities, especially bonds.

Although a variety of debt instruments exists, each with its specific name and characteristics, for the purpose of this chapter the term *bond* will be used to represent all types of debt instruments. As will be explained in detail, bonds are priced so their yields are the same. What is important is how much you earn and not how much you pay. The price of any bond (for a given risk class) is primarily related to (1) the interest paid by the bond, (2) the interest rate that investors may earn on comparable, competitive bonds, and (3) the maturity date. Bond pricing is followed by a discussion of the various uses of the word yield, including the current yield, the yield to maturity, and the yield to call.

After the coverage of pricing and yields, the chapter continues with a discussion of yields and risk, duration, and the management of fixed-income portfolios. The chapter ends with the consideration of preferred stock. Since preferred stock pays a fixed dividend, which is analogous to the fixed-interest coupon paid by a bond, the discussion of preferred stock has been deferred until the coverage of bonds and their valuation has been completed. This material includes a brief description of preferred stock and its valuation, the differences between bonds and preferred stock, and an analysis of the ability of the firm to meet preferred stock's fixed dividend payment.

Learning Objectives

After completing this chapter you should be able to:

1. Determine the price of a bond.
2. Isolate the factors that affect a bond's price.
3. Explain the relationship between changes in interest rates and bond prices.
4. Differentiate among current yield, yield to maturity, and yield to call.
5. Illustrate how discounted bonds may be used to help finance an individual's retirement.
6. Explain how the reinvestment of earned interest affects the investor's realized return.
7. Illustrate the relationship between a bond's duration and its price volatility.

8 Differentiate active and passive strategies for the management of bond portfolios.

9 Compare and contrast bonds and preferred stock.

Perpetual Bonds

perpetual bond
A debt instrument with no maturity date.

A **perpetual bond** is a bond that never matures. The issuer never has to retire the principal; it has only to meet the interest payments and the other terms of the indenture. Although such a bond may sound absurd, there are some in existence. For example, the British government issued perpetual bonds called *consols* to refinance the debt that was issued to support the Napoleonic Wars. These bonds will never mature, but they do pay interest, and there is an active secondary market in them.

How much can a perpetual bond be worth? The answer is the present value of the bond's cash flow, which depends on the interest paid by the bond and the return the investor can earn elsewhere. For example, a perpetual bond pays the following stream of interest income annually:

Year 1	Year 2	...	Year 20	...	Year 100	...	Year 1000	...
$80	$80		$80		$80		$80	

How much are these interest payments worth? The question really is, what is the present value of each one of these $80 payments? To answer the question, the investor must know the rate of interest that may be earned on alternative investments. If the investor can earn 10 percent elsewhere, the present value or price (P) of the perpetual stream of $80 payments is

$$\begin{aligned} P &= \frac{\$80}{(1+0.10)^1} + \frac{\$80}{(1+0.10)^2} + \cdots + \frac{\$80}{(1+0.10)^{20}} \\ &\quad + \cdots + \frac{\$80}{(1+0.10)^{100}} + \cdots + \frac{\$80}{(1+0.10)^{1000}} \\ &= \$80(0.909) + \$80(0.826) + \cdots + \$80(0.149) \\ &\quad + \cdots + \$80(0.000) + \cdots + \$80(0.000) \\ &= 72.72 + \$66.08 + \cdots + \$11.92 + \cdots + 0 \\ &= \$800. \end{aligned}$$

i↑ BP↓
i↓ BP↑

As may be seen in this example, the $80 interest payments received in the near future contribute most to the present value of the bond. Dollars received in the distant future have little value today. The sum of all of these present values is $800, which means that if alternative investments yield 10 percent, an investor would be willing to pay $800 for a promise to receive $80 annually for the indefinite future.

The preceding may be stated in more formal terms. If *PMT* is the annual interest payment and i is the rate of return that is being earned on comparable investments, then the present value is

$$P = \frac{PMT}{(1+i)^1} + \frac{PMT}{(1+i)^2} + \frac{PMT}{(1+i)^3} + \cdots.$$

This is a geometric series, and its sum may be expressed as

$$P = \frac{PMT}{i}. \tag{16.1}$$

Equation 16.1 gives the current value of an infinite stream of equal interest payments. If this equation is applied to the previous example in which the annual interest payment is \$80 and alternative investments can earn 10 percent, then the present value of the bond is

$$P = \frac{\$80}{0.10} = \$800.$$

If market interest rates of alternative investments were to increase, say, to 20 percent, the value of this perpetual stream of interest payments would decline; if market interest rates were to fall to, say, 8 percent, the value of the bond would rise. These changes occur because the bond pays a *fixed flow of income;* that is, the dollar amount of interest paid by the bond is constant. Lower interest rates mean that more money is needed to purchase this fixed stream of interest payments, and with higher interest rates, less money is needed to buy this fixed flow of income.

The inverse relationship between interest rates and bond prices is illustrated in Exhibit 16.1, which presents the value of the preceding perpetual bond at different interest rates. As may be seen from the exhibit, as current market interest rates rise, the present value of the bond declines. Thus, if the present value is \$1,000 when interest rates are 8 percent, the value of this bond declines to \$400 when interest rates rise to 20 percent.

A simple example may show why this inverse relationship between bond prices and interest rates exists. Suppose two investors offered to sell two different bond issues. The first is the perpetual bond that pays \$100 per year in interest. The second is also a perpetual bond, but it pays \$120 per year in interest. If the offer price in each case is \$1,000, which bond would be preferred? Obviously, if they are equal in every way except in the amount of interest, a buyer would prefer the second bond that pays \$120. What could the seller of the first bond do to make the bond more attractive to a buyer? The obvious answer is to lower the asking price so that the yield the buyer receives is identical for both bonds. Thus, if the seller were to ask only \$833 for the bond that pays \$100 annually, the buyer should be indifferent as to which he or she chooses. Both bonds would then offer a yield of 12 percent (i.e., \$100 ÷ \$833 for the first bond and \$10 ÷ \$1,000 for the second bond).

EXHIBIT 16.1

Relationship Between Interest Rates and the Price of a Perpetual Bond

Current Interest Rate (i)	Annual Interest Paid by the Bond (PMT)	Present Price of the Bond $\left(P = \frac{PMT}{i}\right)$
4%	\$80	\$2,000
6	80	1,333
8	80	1,000
10	80	800
15	80	533
20	80	400

Bonds with Maturity Dates

The majority of bonds are not perpetual but have a finite life. They mature, and this fact must affect their valuation. A bond's price is related not only to the interest that it pays but also to its face amount (i.e., the principal). The current price of a bond equals the present value of the interest payments plus the present value of the principal to be received at maturity.

Annual Compounding[1]

The value of a bond with a finite life is the present value of its cash flows (interest and principal repayment). This value is expressed algebraically in Equation 16.2 in terms of the present value formulas discussed in Chapter 5. A bond's value is

$$P_B = \frac{PMT}{(1+i)^1} + \frac{PMT}{(1+i)^2} + \cdots + \frac{PMT}{(1+i)^n} + \frac{FV}{(1+i)^n} \qquad (16.2)$$

in which P_B indicates the current price of the bond; *PMT*, the annual interest payment; *n*, the number of years to maturity; *FV*, the future value, or the principal; and *i*, the current interest rate.

The calculation of a bond's price using Equation 16.2 may be illustrated by a simple example. A firm has a $1,000 bond outstanding that matures in three years with a 10 percent coupon rate ($100 annually). All that is needed to determine the price of the bond is the current interest rate, which is the rate being paid by newly issued, competitive bonds with the same length of time to maturity and the same degree of risk. If the competitive bonds yield 10 percent, the price of this bond will be par, or $1,000, for

Calculator Solution

Function Key	Data Input
PV =	?
FV =	1000
PMT =	100
N =	3
I =	10
Function Key	Answer
PV =	−1000

$$\begin{aligned} P_B &= \frac{\$100}{(1+0.10)^1} + \frac{\$100}{(1+0.10)^2} + \frac{\$100}{(1+0.10)^3} + \frac{\$1{,}000}{(1+0.10)^3} \\ &= \$100(0.909) + 100(0.826) + 100(0.751) + 1{,}000(0.751) \\ &= \$999.60 \approx \$1{,}000. \end{aligned}$$

If competitive bonds are selling to yield 12 percent, this bond will be unattractive to investors. They will not be willing to pay $1,000 for a bond yielding 10 percent when they could buy competing bonds at the same price that yield 12 percent. For this bond to compete with the others, its price must decline sufficiently to yield 12 percent. In terms of Equation 16.2, the price must be

Calculator Solution

Function Key	Data Input
PV =	?
FV =	1000
PMT =	100
N =	3
I =	12
Function Key	Answer
PV =	−951.96

$$\begin{aligned} P_B &= \frac{\$100}{(1+0.12)^1} + \frac{\$100}{(1+0.12)^2} + \frac{\$100}{(1+0.12)^3} + \frac{\$1{,}000}{(1+0.12)^3} \\ &= \$100(0.893) + 100(0.797) + 100(0.712) + 1{,}000(0.712) \\ &= \$952.20. \end{aligned}$$

The price of the bond must decline to approximately $952; that is, it must sell for a **discount** (a price less than the stated principal) in order to be competitive with comparable bonds. At that price investors will earn $100 per year in interest and

discount (of a bond)
The extent to which a bond's price is less than its face amount, or principal.

[1]Although bonds pay interest semiannually, this discussion uses annual compounding to facilitate the explanation. Semiannual compounding is illustrated in the next section.

Calculator Solution

Function Key	Data Input
PV =	?
FV =	1,000
PMT =	100
N =	3
I =	8
Function Key	**Answer**
PV =	−1051.54

approximately \$50 in capital gains over the three years, for a total annual return of 12 percent on their investment. The capital gain occurs because the bond is purchased for \$952.20, but when it matures, the holder will receive \$1,000.

If comparable debt were to yield 8 percent, the price of the bond in the previous example would have to rise. In this case, the price of the bond would be

$$P_B = \frac{\$100}{(1+0.08)^1} + \frac{\$100}{(1+0.08)^2} + \frac{\$100}{(1+0.08)^3} + \frac{\$1,000}{(1+0.08)^3}$$
$$= \$100(0.926) + 100(0.857) + 100(0.794) + 1,000(0.794)$$
$$= \$1,051.70.$$

premium (of a bond) The extent to which a bond's price exceeds the face amount of the debt.

The bond, therefore, must sell at a **premium** (a price greater than the stated principal). Although it may seem implausible for the bond to sell at a premium, this must occur if the market interest rate falls below the coupon rate of interest stated on the bond.

These price calculations are lengthy, but the number of computations can be reduced when one realizes that the valuation of a bond has two components: a flow of interest payments and a final repayment of principal. Since interest payments are fixed and are paid every year, they may be treated as an annuity. The principal repayment may be treated as a simple lump-sum payment. If a \$1,000 bond pays \$100 per year in interest and matures after three years, its current value is the present value of the \$100 annuity for three years and the present value of the \$1,000 that will be received after three years. If the interest rate is 12 percent, the current value of the bond is

$$P_B = \$100(2.402) + \$1,000(0.712) = \$952.20,$$

in which 2.402 is the interest factor for the present value of a \$1 annuity at 12 percent for three years and 0.712 is the interest factor for the present value of \$1 at 12 percent after three years. This is the same answer that was derived earlier (except for the rounding error), but the amount of arithmetic has been reduced.

These examples illustrate the same general conclusion that was reached earlier concerning bond prices and changes in market interest rates: They are inversely related. *When market interest rates rise, bond prices decline. When market interest rates fall, bond prices rise.* This relationship is illustrated in Figure 16.1, which plots the

FIGURE 16.1

Relationship Between Interest Rates and a Bond's Price

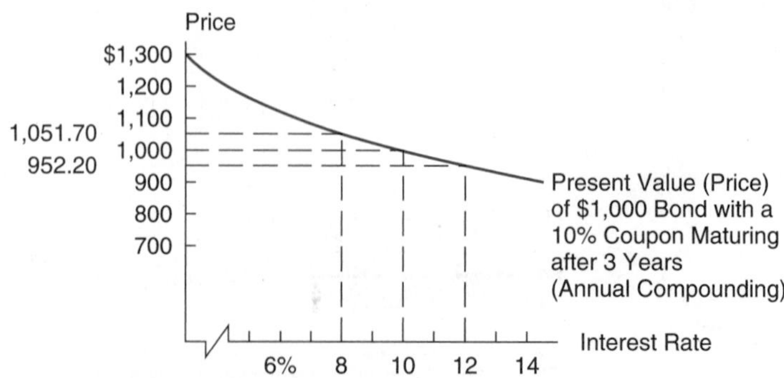

price of the $1,000 bond at various interest rates. As may be seen from the figure, higher interest rates depress the bond's current value. Thus, the bond's price declines from $1,000 to $952.20 when interest rates rise from 10 to 12 percent, but the price rises to $1,051.70 when interest rates decline to 8 percent. (Factors that affect the amount of price change are covered later in this chapter.)

The inverse relationship between the price of a bond and the interest rate suggests a means to make profits in the bond market. All that investors need to know is the direction of *future* changes in the interest rate. If investors anticipate that interest rates will decline, then they are expecting the price of previously issued bonds with a given number of years to maturity and of a certain risk to rise. This price increase must occur in order for previously issued bonds to have the same yield as currently issued bonds. The reverse is also true, for if investors anticipate that interest rates will rise, they are also anticipating that the price of currently available bonds will decline. This decline must occur for previously issued bonds to offer the same yield as currently issued bonds. Therefore, if investors can anticipate the direction of change in interest rates, they can also anticipate the direction of change in the price of bonds.

Investors, however, may anticipate incorrectly and thus suffer losses in the bond market. If they buy bonds and interest rates rise, then the market value of their bonds must decline, and the investors suffer capital losses. These individuals, however, have something in their favor: The bonds must ultimately be retired. Since the principal must be redeemed, an investment error in the bond market may be corrected when the bond's price rises as the bond approaches maturity. The capital losses will eventually be erased. The correction of the error, however, may take years, during which time the investors have lost the higher yields that were available on bonds issued after their initial investments.

Semiannual Compounding

The valuation of a bond with a finite life presented in Equation 16.2 is a bit misleading, because bonds pay interest twice a year (i.e., semiannually), and the equation assumes that the interest payments are made only annually. However, Equation 16.2 may be readily modified to take into consideration semiannual (or even quarterly or weekly) compounding. This is done by adjusting the amount of each payment and the total number of these payments. To adjust the previous example, each interest payment will be $50 if payments are semiannual, and instead of three annual payments, the bond will make a total of six $50 semiannual payments. Hence, the flow of payments that will be made by this bond is

Year 1		Year 2		Year 3		
$50	$50	$50	$50	$50	$50	$1,000

This flow of payments would then be discounted back to the present to determine the bond's current value. The question then becomes, what is the appropriate discount factor?

If comparable debt yields 12 percent, the appropriate discount factor is not 12 percent; it is 6 percent. Six percent interest paid twice a year yields 12 percent interest compounded semiannually. Thus, to determine the present value of this bond, the comparable interest rate is divided in half (just as the annual interest payment is divided in half). However, the number of interest payments to which this 6 percent is applied is doubled (just as the number of payments is doubled).

Hence, the current value of this bond, which pays interest twice a year (is compounded semiannually), is

Calculator Solution

Function Key	Data Input
PV =	?
FV =	1000
PMT =	50
N =	6
I =	6
Function Key	**Answer**
PV =	−950.83

$$\begin{aligned} P_B &= \frac{\$50}{(1+0.06)^1} + \frac{\$50}{(1+0.06)^2} + \frac{\$50}{(1+0.06)^3} + \frac{\$50}{(1+0.06)^4} \\ &\quad + \frac{\$50}{(1+0.06)^5} + \frac{\$50}{(1+0.06)^6} + \frac{\$1{,}000}{(1+0.06)^6} \\ &= \$50(0.943) + 50(0.890) + 50(0.840) \\ &\quad + 50(0.792) + 50(0.747) + 50(0.705) + 1{,}000(0.705) \\ &= \$47.15 + 44.50 + 42.00 + 39.60 + 37.35 + 35.25 + 705 \\ &= \$950.85. \end{aligned}$$

With semiannual compounding, the current value of the bond is slightly lower (i.e., \$950.85 versus \$952.20). This is because the bond's price must decline more to compensate for the more frequent compounding. An investor would prefer a bond that pays \$50 twice per year to one that pays \$100 once per year, because the investor would have use of some of the funds more quickly. Thus, if interest rates rise, causing bond prices to fall, the decline will be greater if the interest on bonds is paid semiannually than if it is paid annually.

Equation 16.2 may be altered to include semiannual compounding. This is done in Equation 16.3. Only one new variable, c, is added, which represents the frequency of compounding (i.e., the number of times each year that interest payments are made).

$$P_B = \frac{\frac{PMT}{c}}{\left(1+\frac{i}{c}\right)^1} + \frac{\frac{PMT}{c}}{\left(1+\frac{i}{c}\right)^2} + \cdots + \frac{\frac{PMT}{c}}{\left(1+\frac{i}{c}\right)^{n\times c}} + \frac{FV}{\left(1+\frac{i}{c}\right)^{n\times c}}. \tag{16.3}$$

When Equation 16.3 is applied to the earlier example, the price of the bond is

$$\begin{aligned} P_B &= \frac{\frac{\$100}{2}}{\left(1+\frac{0.12}{2}\right)^1} + \frac{\frac{\$100}{2}}{\left(1+\frac{0.12}{2}\right)^2} + \cdots + \frac{\frac{\$100}{2}}{\left(1+\frac{0.12}{2}\right)^{3\times 2}} + \frac{\$1{,}000}{\left(1+\frac{0.12}{2}\right)^{3\times 2}} \\ &= \$50(0.943) + 50(0.890) + \cdots + 50(0.705) + 1{,}000(0.705) \\ &= \$950.85, \end{aligned}$$

which, of course, is the same answer derived in the immediately preceding example.

Fluctuations in Bond Prices

As the preceding examples illustrate, a bond's price depends on the interest paid, the maturity date of the bond, and the yield currently earned on comparable securities. The illustrations also demonstrated that when interest rates rise, bond prices fall, and when interest rates fall, bond prices rise.

The amount of price fluctuation depends on (1) the amount of interest paid by the bond, (2) the length of time to maturity, and (3) risk. The smaller the amount of interest, the larger the relative price fluctuations will tend to be. The longer the term, or time to maturity, the greater the price fluctuation will be. Riskier bonds will also experience greater fluctuations in their prices.

This section is concerned with the first two factors that affect price fluctuations, the amount of interest and the term to maturity. The impact of risk is covered in a subsequent section. The effect of the amount of interest and the length of time to maturity may be seen by the following illustrations. In the first case, consider two bonds with equal lives (e.g., ten years to maturity) but unequal coupons. Bond A pays $40 a year (a 4 percent coupon), and bond B pays $140 annually (a 14 percent coupon). If interest rates are 10 percent, the bonds' prices are

$$P_A = \$40(6.145) + \$1{,}000(0.386) \approx \$632$$
$$P_B = \$140(6.145) + \$1{,}000(0.386) \approx \$1{,}246.$$

If interest rates rise to 14 percent, the bonds' prices become

$$P_A = \$40(5.216) + \$1{,}000(0.270) = \$478.64$$
$$P_B = \$140(5.216) + \$1{,}000(0.270) = \$1{,}000.$$

Bond B falls by 20 percent from $1,246 to $1,000. As may be seen in Figure 16.2 (p. 500), if interest rates continue to rise, the bonds' prices decline further. At 20 percent, the values of the bonds are $330 and $749, respectively. These prices represent declines of approximately 48 and 40 percent from the bonds' initial values and suggest a general pattern in which the prices of bonds with smaller coupons tend to be more volatile. Their prices decline more when interest rates rise, but their prices also rise more when interest rates fall.

The length of time to maturity also affects the fluctuation in a bond's price. Consider the following two bonds. Each pays $100 interest annually (a 10 percent coupon). Bond A matures after ten years, and bond B matures after one year. If interest rates are 10 percent, the price of each bond is

$$P_A = \$100(6.145) + \$1{,}000(0.386) = \$1{,}000$$
$$P_B = \$100(0.909) + \$1{,}000(0.909) = \$1{,}000.$$

If interest rates rise to 12 percent, the price of each bond declines to

$$P_A = \$100(5.650) + \$1{,}000(0.322) = \$887.00$$
$$P_B = \$100(0.893) + \$1{,}000(0.893) = \$982.30.$$

The price of bond A falls approximately 12 percent from $1,000 to $887, but bond B suffers only a modest price decline to $982.30.

If interest rates fall, the prices of both bonds will rise, but the price of the bond with the longer term to maturity will rise more. This price increase (and the price decline caused by higher interest rates) is illustrated in Figure 16.3 (p. 501), which shows the larger price fluctuation in the ten-year bond. Figure 16.3 clearly illustrates that investors in long-term debt bear more risk from changes in bond prices caused by fluctuations in interest rates. For this reason, individuals who are speculating on a decline in interest rates will favor bonds with a longer term to maturity, but investors who are concerned with both interest income and safety of principal will prefer shorter-term debt. These investors are willing to accept less interest income for safety and liquidity. Of course, the extreme form of such investments is the money market mutual fund, which invests solely in short-term investments (e.g., commercial paper and Treasury bills), for such investments offer liquidity that cannot be obtained through investments in longer-term debt.

FIGURE 16.2

Relationship Between Prices of Bonds with Different Coupons and Various Interest Rates

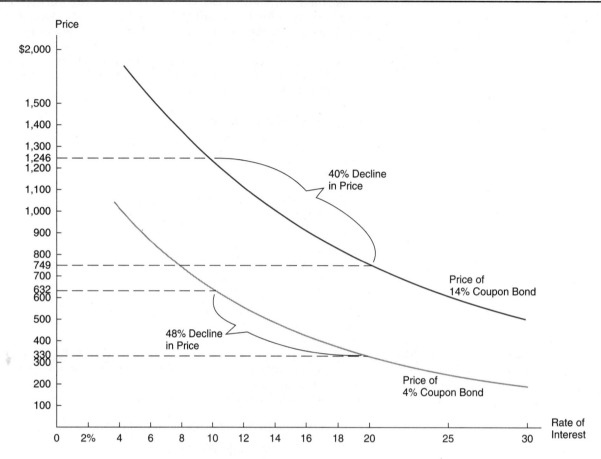

Bond Valuation Applications to Nontraditional Bonds

In the previous examples of valuation, all the bonds paid interest annually and were retired at maturity. In the previous chapter, bond features were not limited to a fixed payment and maturity date. For example, zero coupon bonds pay no interest, and several high-yield securities (e.g., the split coupon bond, the reset bond, or the extendable bond) have features that differ from the traditional bond.

Although bonds can have these varying features, their valuations remain the same: the present value of future cash flows. For example, what would an investor pay for a $1,000 zero coupon bond that matures after ten years? The answer has to be the present value of the $1,000—that is, the present value of the future cash flow. If the investor requires a return of 7 percent, then the value is

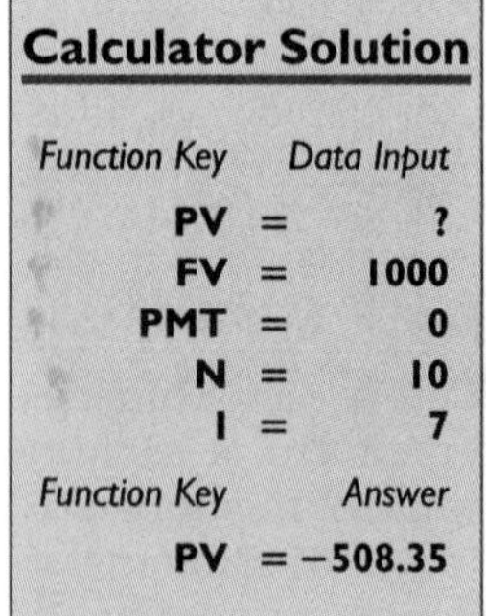

Calculator Solution

Function Key	Data Input
PV =	?
FV =	1000
PMT =	0
N =	10
I =	7
Function Key	**Answer**
PV =	−508.35

$$P_B = \frac{\$1,000}{(1 + 0.07)^{10}}.$$

That is, $1,000(0.508) = $508. If the required return had been 10 percent, the value of the bond would be $1,000(0.386) = $386.

FIGURE 16.3

Relationship Between Bond Prices and Time to Maturity (for a Given Coupon)

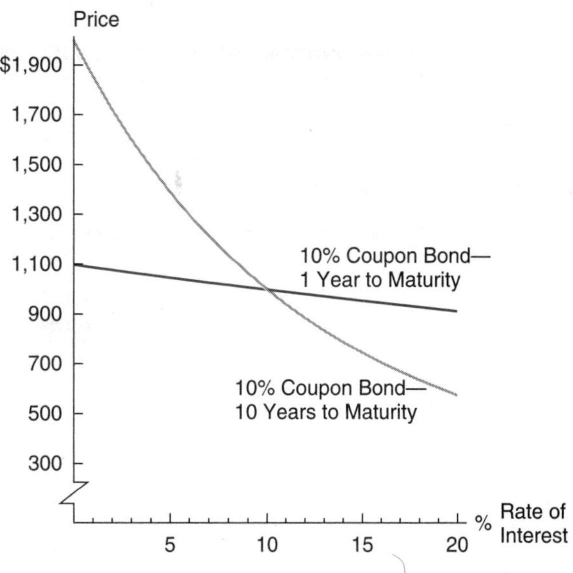

Calculator Solution

Function Key	Data Input
PV =	?
FV =	1000
PMT_1 =	0
PMT_2 =	0
PMT_3 =	0
PMT_4 =	0
PMT_5 =	115
PMT_6 =	115
PMT_7 =	115
PMT_8 =	115
PMT_9 =	115
PMT_{10} =	115
N =	10
I =	15

Function Key	Answer
PV =	−496

(This solution requires a financial calculator that accepts uneven cash payments.)

The valuation of split coupon and reset bonds is essentially the same. Consider the Dr Pepper bond in the previous chapter that illustrated a split coupon bond. That bond paid $0 in interest during the first four years, $115 annually for the next six years, and matured after ten years. How much would an investor pay if the required return were 15 percent? The answer is

$115 × the present value of an annuity for six years at 15 percent

× the present value of one dollar for four years at 15 percent

+ 1000 × the present value of one dollar at 15 percent for ten years

= $115(3.785)(0.572) + $1,000(0.247)

= $496.

If interest rates declined (or the firm's financial condition improved) so the comparable rate is 12 percent, the bond's price would rise to

$115(4.111)(0.636) + $1,000(0.322) = $623

for a 20.4 percent increase. Of course, the converse is also true; higher yields would cause the price of the split coupon bond to decline.

The valuations of zero coupon and split coupon bonds are essentially no different from the valuation of a regular coupon bond since the payments (their amounts and timing) are known. With a reset bond or an extendable bond, the payments and their timing are not known. The interest payments or the maturity date or both are permitted to vary. While the valuation process remains the present value of future cash inflows, the investor must make assumptions concerning these inflows. For example, in the case of an extendable bond, the investor must assume a particular repayment date. If the investor expects the bond's maturity date to be extended, then the longer term is used to value the bond. Using a shorter term may result in the bond receiving a higher valuation, in which case the investor would pay too much and realize a smaller return if the maturity is extended.

Yields

The word *yield* is frequently used with regard to investing in bonds. There are three important types of yields with which the investor must be familiar: the current yield, the yield to maturity, and the yield to call. This section will differentiate among these three yields.

The Current Yield

The current yield is the percentage that the investor earns annually. It is simply

$$\frac{\textbf{Annual interest payment}}{\textbf{Price of the bond}}. \tag{16.4}$$

The discounted bond discussed previously has a coupon rate of 10 percent. Thus, when the price of the bond is $952, the current yield is

$$\frac{\$100}{\$952} = 10.5\%.$$

The current yield is important because it gives the investor an indication of the current return that will be earned on the investment. Investors who seek high current income prefer bonds that offer a high current yield.

However, the current yield can be misleading, for it fails to consider any change in the price of the bond that may occur if the bond is held to maturity. Obviously, if a bond is bought at a discount, its value must rise as it approaches maturity. The opposite occurs if the bond is purchased for a premium, because its price will decline as maturity approaches. For this reason it is desirable to know the bond's yield to maturity.

The Yield to Maturity

The yield to maturity considers the current income generated by the bond as well as any change in its value when it is held to maturity. If the bond referred to earlier is purchased for $952 and is held to maturity, after three years the investor will receive a return of 12 percent. This is the yield to maturity, because this return considers not only the current interest return of 10.5 percent but also the price appreciation of the bond from $952 at the time of purchase to $1,000 at maturity. Since the yield to maturity considers both the flow of interest income and the price change, it is a more accurate measure of the return offered to investors by a particular bond issue.

The yield to maturity may be determined by using Equation 16.2.[2] That equation reads

$$P_B = \frac{PMT}{(1+i)^1} + \frac{PMT}{(1+i)^2} + \cdots + \frac{PMT}{(1+i)^n} + \frac{FV}{(1+i)^n}.$$

[2]The yield to maturity is a specific application of the internal rate of return discussed in Chapter 10. Equation 16.2 is simply a restatement of Equation 10.2 for the determination of an investment's internal rate of return.

The i is the current rate of interest paid by newly issued bonds with the same term to maturity and the same degree of risk. If the investor buys a bond and holds it to maturity, the yield that is being paid by newly issued bonds (i) will also be the yield to maturity.

Determining the yield to maturity when the coupon rate of interest, the bond's price, and the maturity date are known is not easy, except with the use of a financial calculator. For example, if the bond were selling for $952 and the investor wanted to know the yield to maturity, the calculation would be

$$\$952 = \frac{\$100}{(1+i)^1} + \frac{\$100}{(1+i)^2} + \frac{\$100}{(1+i)^3} + \frac{\$1{,}000}{(1+i)^3}.$$

Solving this equation can be a formidable task because there is no simple arithmetical computation to determine the value of i. Instead, the investor selects a value for i and plugs it into the equation. If this value equates the left-hand and right-hand sides of the equation, then that value of i is the yield to maturity.

If the value does not equate the two sides of the equation, another value must be selected. This process is repeated until a value for i is found that equates both sides of the equation. Obviously, that can be a long process. For example, suppose the investor selects 14 percent and substitutes it into the right-hand side of the equation. The result is

$$\begin{aligned} P_B &= \frac{\$100}{(1+0.14)^1} + \frac{\$100}{(1+0.14)^2} + \frac{\$100}{(1+0.14)^3} + \frac{\$1{,}000}{(1+0.14)^3} \\ &= \$100(2.321) + 1{,}000(0.675) \\ &= \$232.10 + 675 \\ &= \$907.10. \end{aligned}$$

POINTS OF INTEREST

The Accuracy of the Approximation Formula

If the student does not have access to a financial function calculator, the approximation formula is a convenient means to estimate the yield to maturity. How accurate is the approximation? To help answer that question, consider two bonds that each have a 10 percent coupon paid semiannually. Bond A matures in 5 years, while bond B matures in 20 years. The following table is constructed to show the correct and the approximate yield to maturity at various prices.

As may be seen in this illustration, the approximate yield to maturity is a reasonable estimate of the actual yield to maturity. Only when the bond sells for a large discount does the approximation significantly understate the true yield the bond offers over its lifetime.

Bond A			Bond B		
Price	Correct Yield to Maturity	Approximate Yield to Maturity	Price	Correct Yield to Maturity	Approximate Yield to Maturity
$1,100	7.56%	7.62%	$1,100	8.92%	9.05%
1,000	10.00	10.00	1,000	10.00	10.00
900	12.77	12.63	900	11.27	11.05
800	15.95	15.55	800	12.79	12.22
500	29.88	26.67	500	20.43	16.67

Unfortunately, $907.10 does not equal $952. That means the selected yield to maturity was too high, so the investor selects another, lower rate. If the investor had selected 12 percent, then

$$\begin{aligned} P_B &= \$100(2.402) + \$1{,}000(0.712) \\ &= \$240.20 + 712 \\ &= \$952.20, \end{aligned}$$

and thus 12 percent is the yield to maturity (compounded annually).[3]

This process for determining the yield to maturity is not accurate if the yield is not a number available in the interest table. For example, if the price of the bond had been $963.66, the yield to maturity is 11.50 percent. This yield cannot be determined using interest tables, since the percent 11.50 is not given. The yield to maturity may be approximated by Equation 16.5.

$$i = \frac{I + \dfrac{1{,}000 - P_B}{n}}{\dfrac{\$1{,}000 + P_B}{2}} \qquad (16.5)$$

The symbols are the same that were used in Equation 16.2. If the current price of a $1,000 bond with a 10 percent coupon (PMT = $100) is $952 ($P_B$ = $952) and the bond matures in three years ($n = 3$), then the approximate yield to maturity is

$$\begin{aligned} i &= \frac{\$100 + \dfrac{\$1{,}000 - 963.66}{3}}{\dfrac{\$1{,}000 + 963.66}{2}} \\ &= \frac{100 + 36.34/3}{981.83} \\ &= 11.42\%. \end{aligned}$$

This answer, 11.42 percent, approximates the 11.5 percent. (For a discussion of the accuracy of the approximation formula, see the accompanying Points of Interest.)

The yield to maturity may be readily computed using a financial calculator. To determine the yield to maturity, enter the amount of each interest payment (PMT = 100), the principal repayment in the future (FV = 1,000), the term to maturity (N = 3), and the current price of the bond (PV = −963.66), and instruct the calculator to determine the interest (I). (Enter the present value as a negative number, since the calculator is programmed to view the price as a cash outflow and the interest and principal repayment as cash inflows.) When these figures are entered, the calculator determines the interest rate—or the yield to maturity—to be 11.50 percent. This procedure is considerably easier than the process described using interest tables and more accurate than Equation 16.5 for the approximation of the yield to maturity.[4]

---

[3]If the investor obtains a price greater than the correct price, the yield to maturity is too low, and the investor should select a higher rate.

[4]If the bond pays interest semiannually, enter each six-month interest payment (PMT = 50), the principal repayment (FV = 1,000), the term on the bond (N = 6), and the current price of the bond (PV = −963.66). Instruct the calculator to determine the interest (I). The calculator determines the yield to maturity to be 5.73 percent per period or 11.46 percent compounded semiannually. Notice that the yield to maturity is marginally lower because the timing of the interest payments is slightly faster ($50 after six months followed by the next $50 after twelve months instead of the entire $100 after twelve months.). To equalize the yields, the bond with the semiannual interest payments would sell for a slightly lower price ($963 instead of $963.66). Since the interest is paid semiannually, you do not have to invest as much to earn a specified return (i.e., 11.5 percent), so the price would be lower. If the prices of the two bonds were the same ($963.66), you would have overpaid for the bond with the semiannual interest payments and your return would have been lower (11.46 percent versus 11.5 percent).

A Comparison of the Current Yield and the Yield to Maturity

The current yield and the yield to maturity are equal only if the bond sells for its principal amount, or par. If the bond sells at a discount, the yield to maturity exceeds the current yield. This may be illustrated by the bond in the previous example. When it sells at a discount (e.g., $952), the current yield is only 10.5 percent. However, the yield to maturity is 12 percent. Thus, the yield to maturity exceeds the current yield.

If the bond sells at a premium, the current yield exceeds the yield to maturity. For example, if the bond sells for $1,052, the current yield is 9.5 percent ($100 ÷ $1,052) and the yield to maturity is 8 percent. The yield to maturity is less in this case because the loss that the investor must suffer when the price of the bond declines from $1,052 to $1,000 at maturity has been included in the calculation.

Exhibit 16.2 presents the current yield and the yield to maturity at different prices for a bond with an 8 percent annual coupon that matures in ten years. As may be seen in the table, the larger the discount (or the smaller the premium), the greater are both the current yield and the yield to maturity. For example, when the bond sells for $850, the yield to maturity is 10.49 percent, but it rises to 12.52 percent when the price declines to $750.

Discounted bonds offer conservative investors attractive opportunities for financial planning. For example, a person who is currently 60 years old may purchase discounted bonds that mature after ten years to help finance retirement. This investor may purchase several bonds that mature five, six, seven years, and so on, into the future. This portfolio will generate a continuous flow of funds during retirement as the bonds mature. Of course, such a portfolio can be constructed only if yields have risen and bonds sell for a discount. In the late 1990s, interest rates were relatively low and few coupon bonds sold for a discount, so the strategy could not be executed. However, in the early 1990s, some bonds were selling at a discount. For example, in January 1993, an individual could have bought the discounted bonds illustrated in Exhibit 16.3 (p. 506). The first column gives the coupon rate, the second column gives the year of maturity, the third column presents the discounted price for $1,000 in face value of debt, and the last column gives the yield to maturity. By purchasing this portfolio for a total cost of $4,633.00, the investor will own $5,000 worth of bonds that mature between 1996 and 2001. Of course, by purchasing more discounted bonds, the investor will have an even greater flow of income during the particular time period to meet his or her financial goals (e.g., financing retirement or paying for children's college education).

EXHIBIT 16.2

Current Yields and Yields to Maturity for a Ten-Year Bond with an 8 Percent Annual Coupon

Price of Bond	Current Yield	Yield to Maturity
$1,100	7.27%	6.60%
1,050	7.62	7.28
1,000	8.00	8.00
950	8.42	8.77
900	8.89	9.60
850	9.41	10.49
800	10.00	11.46
750	10.67	12.52

EXHIBIT 16.3

Selected AT&T Bonds Selling at a Discount (as of January 1, 1993)

Coupon Rate	Maturity Year	Price (per $1,000 Face Value)	Yield to Maturity
4⅜	1996	$957.50	5.65%
5½	1997	977.50	6.14
4¾	1998	935.00	6.18
4⅜	1999	888.75	6.55
5⅛	2001	881.25	7.04

Source: *Moody's Bond Record,* January 1993.

EXHIBIT 16.4

Selected U.S. Treasury Zero Coupon Bonds (as of June 4, 2001)

Coupon Rate	Maturity Year	Price (per $1,000 Face Value)	Yield to Maturity
0%	2010	$611.10	5.54%
0	2011	571.60	5.64
0	2012	532.90	5.73
0	2013	502.00	5.78
0	2014	471.20	5.86

Source: *The Wall Street Journal,* June 4, 2001, C10.

Discounted bonds generally result from an increase in interest rates. If interest rates fall, bonds would sell for a premium, so the previous strategy cannot be executed. An alternative but similar strategy uses zero coupon bonds, which always sell for a discount. This strategy is illustrated in Exhibit 16.4, in which the individual needs funds for the years 2010 through 2014 and buys a series of U.S. Treasury zero coupon bonds. For a total outlay of $2,688.80, the investor will receive $1,000 for each of the five years.

While the two strategies illustrated in Exhibits 16.3 and 16.4 are similar, there are differences. First, as was previously explained, bonds with higher coupons experience less price fluctuation with changes in interest rates, so the zero coupon bond strategy subjects the investor to more price volatility. Such price fluctuations are relevant only if interest rates rise and the investor seeks to sell the bonds before their maturity dates. Second, the discounted bonds do pay some interest each year, while the zero coupon bonds pay nothing. If the investor wants cash flow each year prior to the bonds' maturity dates, the discounted bonds may be the better choice.

The Yield to Call

Some bonds will never reach maturity but are retired before they become due. In some cases the issuer may call the bonds before maturity and redeem them. In

yield to call
The yield earned on a bond from the time it is acquired until the time it is called and retired by the firm.

other cases, the sinking fund will randomly call selected bonds from the issue and retire them. For these reasons the **yield to call** may be a more accurate estimate of the return actually earned on an investment in a bond that is held until redemption.

The yield to call is calculated in the same way as the yield to maturity except that (1) the expected call date is substituted for the maturity date and (2) the principal plus the call penalty (if any) is substituted for the principal. Note that the anticipated call date is used. Unlike the maturity date, which is known, the date of a call can only be anticipated.

The following example illustrates how the yield to call is calculated. A bond that matures after ten years and pays 8 percent interest annually is currently selling for $935.00. The yield to maturity is 9 percent. However, if the investor believes that the company or government will call the bond after five years and will pay a penalty of $50 per $1,000 bond to retire the debt permanently, the yield to call (i_c) is

Calculator Solution

Function Key	Data Input
PV =	−935
FV =	1050
PMT =	80
N =	5
I =	?
Function Key	Answer
I =	10.55

$$\$935 = \frac{\$80}{(1+i_c)^1} + \cdots + \frac{\$80}{(1+i_c)^5} + \frac{\$1{,}050}{(1+i_c)^5}$$

$$i_c = 10.55\%.$$

In this example, the yield to call is higher than the yield to maturity because (1) the investor receives the call penalty and (2) the principal is redeemed early and hence the discount is erased sooner. Thus, in the case of a discounted bond, the actual return the investor earns exceeds the yield to maturity if the bond is called and retired before maturity.

However, if this bond were selling for a premium such as $1,147 with a yield to maturity of 6 percent and the firm were to call the bond after five years, the yield to call would become

Calculator Solution

Function Key	Data Input
PV =	−1147
FV =	1050
PMT =	80
N =	5
I =	?
Function Key	Answer
I =	5.46

$$\$1{,}147 = \frac{\$80}{(1+i_c)^1} + \cdots + \frac{\$80}{(1+i_c)^5} + \frac{\$1{,}050}{(1+i_c)^5}$$

$$i_c = 5.46\%.$$

This return is less than the anticipated yield to maturity of 6 percent. The early redemption produces a lower return for the investor because the premium is spread out over fewer years, reducing the yield on the investment.[5]

Which case is more likely to occur? If a firm wanted to retire debt that was selling at a discount before maturity, it would probably be to its advantage to purchase the bonds instead of calling them. (See the section on repurchasing debt in the previous chapter.) By doing so, the firm would avoid the call penalty and might even be able to buy the bonds for less than par. If the firm wanted to retire debt that was selling at a premium, it would probably be advantageous to call the bonds and pay the penalty. If the bonds were selling for more than face value plus the call penalty, this would obviously be the chosen course of action.

Calculator Solution

Function Key	Data Input
FV =	1050
PMT =	80
N =	5
I =	6
PV =	?
Function Key	Answer
PV =	−1122

An investor should not expect a firm to call prematurely a bond issue that is selling at a discount. However, if interest rates fall and bond prices rise, the firm may refinance the debt. It will then issue new debt at the lower (current) interest rate and use the proceeds to retire the old and more costly debt. In this case the yield to the anticipated call is probably a better indication of the potential return offered by the bonds than is the yield to maturity.

[5]If an investor expected the bond to be called for $1,050 after five years and wanted to earn 6 percent, the price would have to be $1,122.

The preceding example also illustrates the importance of the call penalty. If an investor bought the bond in anticipation that it would yield 6 percent at maturity (i.e., the investor paid $1,147) and the bond is redeemed after five years for the principal amount ($1,000), the return on the investment is only 4.6 percent. Although the $50 call penalty does not restore the return to 6 percent, the investor does receive a yield of 5.46 percent, which is considerably better than 4.6 percent.

Risk and Fluctuations in Yields

Stock investors will bear risk only if they anticipate a sufficient return to compensate for the risk, and a higher anticipated return is necessary to induce them to bear additional risk. This principle also applies to investors who purchase bonds. Bonds involving greater risk must offer higher yields to attract investors. Therefore, the lowest yields are paid by bonds with the highest credit ratings, and low credit ratings are associated with high yields.

This relationship is illustrated by Exhibit 16.5, which presents Moody's ratings and the anticipated yields to maturity for three bonds that will mature in the year 2013. As may be seen in the exhibit, the bonds with the highest credit ratings have the lowest anticipated yield to maturity. A Wal-Mart bond with a Aa2 rating was selling to yield less than the Baa-rated bond of USX (6.79 percent to 7.57 percent). The difference, or *spread,* in the yields is partially due to the difference in risk between the two bonds. While the Wal-Mart bond is considered to be relatively safe (as judged by its rating), the USX bond is viewed as involving more risk.

Because interest rates change over time, the anticipated yields on all debts vary. However, the yields on debt involving greater risk tend to fluctuate more. This is illustrated in Figure 16.4, which plots the yields on Moody's Baa-rated bonds in the top line and the yields on its Aaa-rated bonds in the bottom line. In this particular period there was considerable change in the yields to maturity. During periods of higher interest rates, the poorer-quality debt offered a higher yield and the spread between the yields was also greater. For example, during 1982 the yields rose to 14.8 and 16.9 percent, and the spread between the bonds also rose to 2.1 percent. When interest rates subsequently declined, the spread also declined.

In the late 1990s, the spread tended to be smaller than it had been during the late 1980s and early 1990s. From 1986 through 1989, triple-A-rated bonds had yields that ranged from 8.6 to 9.6 percent, while yields on triple-B-rated bonds ranged from 10.3 to 11.0 percent. The average spread was 1.4 percent. This spread was necessary to induce investors to absorb the large amount of debt issued to finance takeovers and leveraged buyouts by firms with less than investment-grade

EXHIBIT 16.5

Credit Ratings and Yields to Maturity for Selected Bonds Maturing in the Year 2013

Bond Issue	Moody's Bond Rating	Yield to Maturity
Wal-Mart 7¼ 13	Aa2	6.79%
IBM 7½ 13	A1	7.16
USX 9⅛ 13	Baa1	7.57

Source: *Mergent's Bond Record,* January 2001.

FIGURE 16.4

Fluctuations in Yield to Maturity for Moodys Aaa- and Baa-Rated Industrial Bonds (1980 to December 2000)

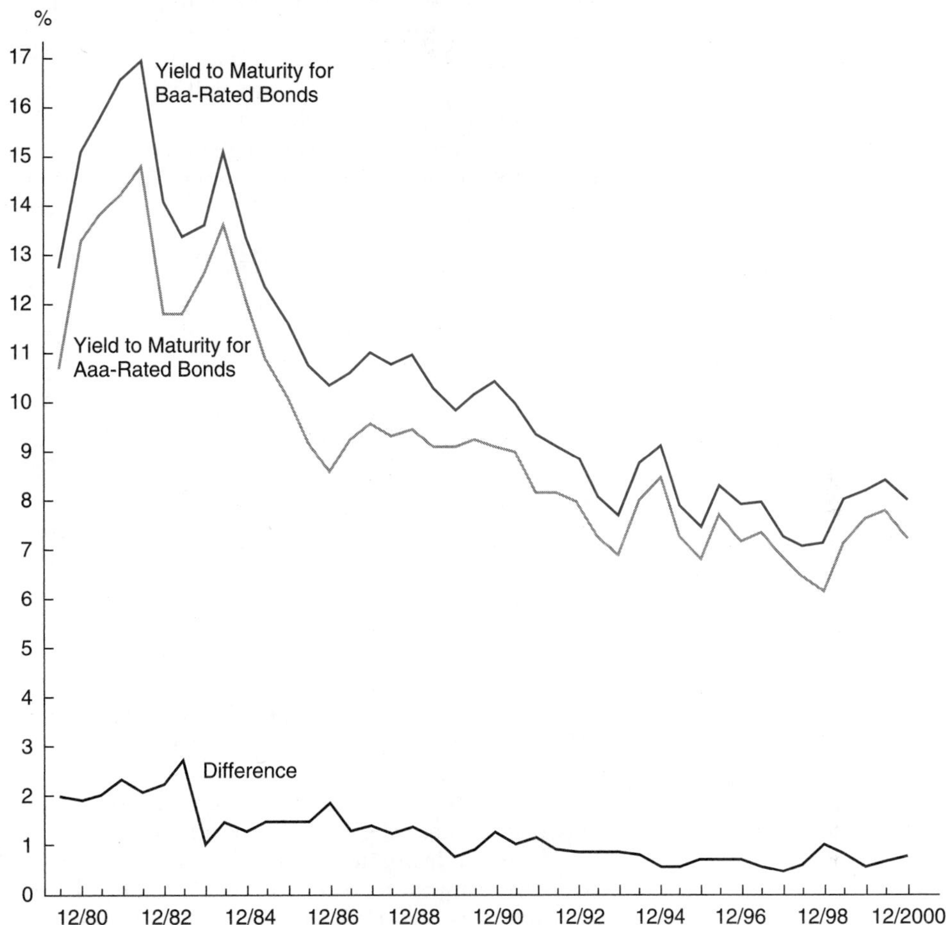

Source: *Moody's Bond Record*, various issues, 1980–2000, *Mergent's Bond Record*, various issues, 2000.

ratings. With the return to financial conservatism in the 1990s, the amount of poor-quality debt issued declined, and the spread narrowed so the difference between the yields consistently averaged below 1.0 percent.

Changes in Risk

Previous sections demonstrated that when interest rates change, bond prices fluctuate in the opposite direction. If interest rates rise after a bond is issued, it will sell for a discount as the price adjusts so that the yield to maturity will be comparable with bonds being currently issued. If interest rates fall after the bond is issued, it will sell for a premium so that once again the yield to maturity is comparable to current interest rates.

The amount of price change depends on the coupon, the term of the bond, and the risk. The smaller the coupon, the greater the price fluctuation for a given maturity and level of risk. The longer the term of the bond, the greater the price fluctuation for a given coupon and level of risk. For given coupons and maturity dates, the prices of riskier bonds tend to fluctuate more.

The coupons and maturity dates of a bond are set when the bond is issued. However, the risk of default on a bond may vary over time as the financial condition of the issuer varies. Firms that were financially sound when their bonds were issued may fall on hard times. Their credit ratings deteriorate. Other firms' financial positions may improve. These changes in risk will, of course, affect the value of outstanding bonds.That risk and bond ratings change is illustrated by the following table giving the Moody's ratings for AT&T and Jersey Central Power and Light bonds.

Year End	AT&T	Jersey Central Power and Light
1977	Aaa	Baa
1978–1979	Aaa	Ba
1980–1981	Aaa	Ba3
1982–1983	Aa1	Ba3
1984	Aa1	Baa2
1985	Aa1	Baa2r
1986	Aa3	Baa1r
1987	A1	Baa1
1988–1990	A1	A2

The threat of and subsequent divestiture of AT&T's phone operation increased the risk associated with the firm. Its sources of revenue were no longer related to regulated phone service, and the ratings of the AT&T bond, therefore, decreased from triple A to A1 to acknowledge the increased risk. Jersey Central Power and Light is part owner of the Three Mile Island nuclear power plant. Obviously, the 1979 accident at that power plant changed the risk exposure of JCP&L's bonds. The ratings dropped from Baa, the lowest investment-grade rating, to Ba. The price of the bonds declined dramatically, and they sold at a substantial discount. However, the subsequent improvement in the firm's financial condition resulted in improved credit ratings, so that by 1990, the rating was only one step below the rating given the AT&T bond.

The Reinvestment Assumption

The yield to maturity makes an important assumption that answers the following questions: What happens to the interest received in year one, year two, and so on (i.e., does the recipient pocket the money or reinvest the funds)? If the funds are reinvested, what rate do they earn? The yield to maturity calculation assumes that *all interest payments are reinvested at the yield to maturity.* This is an exceedingly important assumption because if the payments are not reinvested at that rate, the yield to maturity will not be realized. This also means that when an investor purchases a bond, the yield to maturity is an expected yield that will not necessarily be the realized yield.[6] The debtor could make all the interest payments and redeem

[6]The reinvestment assumption also applies to the yield to call, which assumes that cash inflows are reinvested at the yield to call. All time-value calculations assume that inflows are reinvested at the discount rate, or interest rate. If this reinvestment rate is not achieved, then the present value, or future value, or rate of return, or number of years being determined by the calculation to solve a specific problem are inaccurate.

the bond at maturity, but the yield over the lifetime of the bond could be different from the yield to maturity the investor anticipated when the bond was purchased.

The reinvestment rate assumption is the essential difference between compounding and not compounding. If an investor buys a $1,000 bond with an 8 percent coupon at par and spends the interest as received, the investor is earning a simple, noncompounded rate of 8 percent. The yield to maturity, however, assumes that the interest received will be reinvested at 8 percent (i.e., compounded at 8 percent). If the funds are not being reinvested, the compounded yield will be less than the simple 8 percent rate.

The reinvestment rate that the investor does achieve could be greater or less than the anticipated yield to maturity. If interest rates rise (and the price of this bond declines), the individual can reinvest the interest payments at the now higher rate. The yield earned over the lifetime of the bond will exceed the anticipated yield to maturity. If interest rates fall (and the price of this bond rises), the individual can only reinvest the interest payments at the lower rate. The yield earned over the lifetime of the bond will be less than the anticipated yield to maturity.

Perhaps the best way to see the importance of the reinvestment rate assumption is through several illustrations. In each of the following cases, the investor purchases an 8 percent, $1,000 coupon bond that matures after ten years. The investor wants the funds to accumulate and is curious as to how much will be available at the end of the tenth year. Essentially, this question may be restated in the following way: If I invest $80 each year at some rate for ten years and receive $1,000 at the end of the tenth year, how much will I have accumulated? The final amount will depend on the rate earned each year. This is the reinvestment rate.

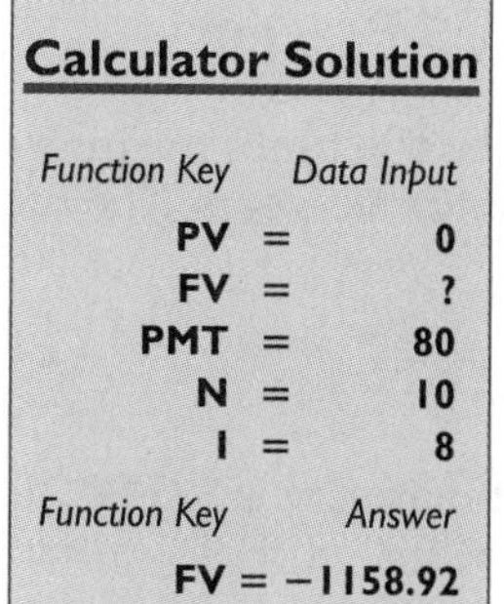

Calculator Solution

Function Key	Data Input
PV =	0
FV =	?
PMT =	80
N =	10
I =	8
Function Key	*Answer*
FV =	−1158.92

Case 1: All Interest Payments Are Reinvested at 8 Percent

In this case, the terminal value will be $80 times the interest factor for the future sum of an annuity of $1 at 8 percent for ten years. The future value of this annuity is

$80(14.487) = $1,158.96.

This amount is added to the $1,000 principal received at maturity so the investor has a total of $2,158.96 at the end of ten years.

What is the return on this investment that initially cost $1,000 and has grown into $2,158.96? This is a future value of $1 problem:

$1,000(interest factor for 10 years at *i* percent) = $2,158.96

$1,000*IF* = $2,158.96

***IF* = 2.159.**

Calculator Solution

Function Key	Data Input
PV =	−1000
FV =	2158.96
PMT =	0
N =	10
I =	?
Function Key	*Answer*
I =	8

An interest factor (*IF*) for the future value of $1 of 2.159 indicates that $1,000 grows to $2,159 in ten years at 8 percent. The yield on this investment over its lifetime (i.e., the yield to maturity) is the anticipated 8 percent.

Case 2: All Interest Payments Are Reinvested at 12 Percent

Suppose immediately after buying the bond, interest rates rise to 12 percent. Of course, the bond would now sell for a discount and the investor has sustained a loss. But the bond was purchased to receive a flow of interest payments that the individual intended to reinvest at the current rate. So the loss of value is only a paper loss. The bond is not sold, and the loss is not realized. Instead, the bond is held and the interest payments are now reinvested at the higher rate. What will be the return on this investment? Will this return be equal to the 8 percent yield to maturity that was anticipated when the bond was purchased?

Calculator Solution

Function Key	Data Input
PV =	0
FV =	?
PMT =	80
N =	10
I =	12
Function Key	Answer
FV =	−1403.92

In this case, the terminal value of the interest payments will be \$80 times the interest factor for the future sum of an annuity of \$1 at 12 percent for ten years. The future value of this annuity is

$$\$80(17.549) = \$1,403.92.$$

This amount is added to the \$1,000 principal received at maturity so the investor has a total of \$2,403.92 at the end of ten years.

What is the return on this investment that initially cost \$1,000 and has grown into \$2,403.92? Once again this is a future value of \$1 problem:

$$\$1,000(\text{interest factor for 10 years at } i \text{ percent}) = \$2,403.92$$
$$\$1,000IF = \$2,403.92$$
$$IF = 2.404.$$

Calculator Solution

Function Key	Data Input
PV =	−1000
FV =	2403.92
PMT =	0
N =	10
I =	?
Function Key	Answer
I =	9.17

The interest table reveals that an interest factor of 2.404 means that in ten years \$1,000 grows to \$2,404 at between 9 and 10 percent (9.17 percent to be more precise). The actual yield on this investment over its lifetime (i.e., the realized yield to maturity) exceeds the anticipated 8 percent. Thus, the investor who purchased the bond anticipating a yield to maturity of 8 percent actually earns more. Even though interest rates rose, which caused the market value of the bond to fall, the return over the lifetime of the bond exceeds the expected yield to maturity.

Case 3: All Interest Payments Are Reinvested at 5 Percent

Calculator Solution

Function Key	Data Input
PV =	0
FV =	?
PMT =	80
N =	10
I =	5
Function Key	Answer
FV =	−1006.23

In this case, the terminal value of the interest payments will be \$80 times the interest factor for the future value of an annuity of \$1 at 5 percent for ten years. The future value of this annuity is

$$\$80(12.578) = \$1,006.24.$$

The sum of this amount and the \$1,000 principal received at maturity is \$2,006.24.

What is the return on this investment that initially cost \$1,000 and has grown into \$2,006.24? The answer is

$$\$1,000(\text{interest factor for 10 years at } i \text{ percent}) = \$2,006.24$$
$$\$1,000IF = \$2,006.24$$
$$IF = 2.006.$$

Calculator Solution

Function Key	Data Input
PV =	−1000
FV =	2006.24
PMT =	0
N =	10
I =	?
Function Key	Answer
I =	7.21

An interest factor of 2.006 indicates that \$1,000 grows to \$2,006 in ten years at less than 8 percent (7.21 to be more precise). Even though interest rates fell and the price of the bond initially rose, the yield on the investment in this bond is only 7.21 percent. The actual return is less than the expected yield to maturity (i.e., the anticipated 8 percent).

These three illustrations are compared in Figure 16.5, which shows the initial \$1,000 and the terminal values achieved through the investment of the interest at the different reinvestment rates. Lines *OA, OB,* and *OC* represent the growth in each investment at 12 percent, 8 percent, and 5 percent, respectively. The terminal values, \$2,403.92, \$2,158.96, and \$2,006.24, generated through the reinvestment of interest income, are shown on the right-hand side of the figure. Of course, the highest terminal value and consequently the highest realized return occur at the highest reinvestment rate.

FIGURE 16.5

Terminal Values at Different Reinvestment Rates

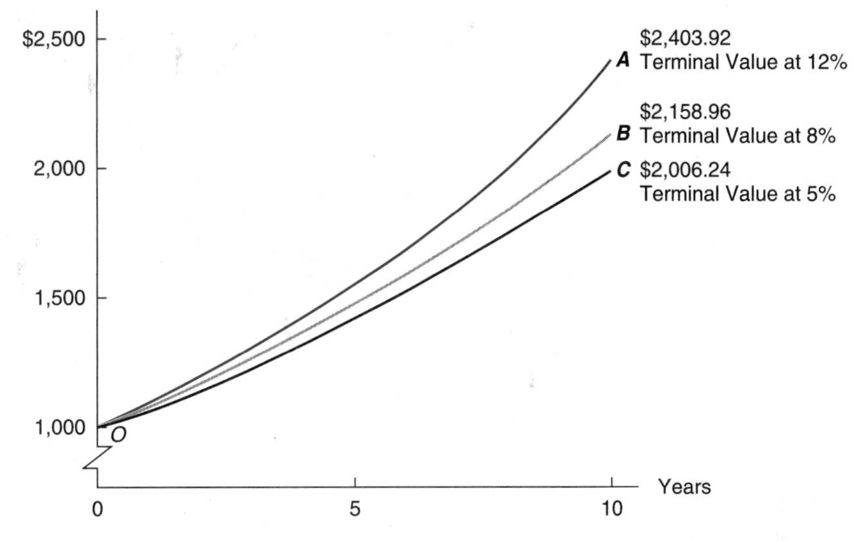

Actually, there is little reason to expect the investor will earn the anticipated yield to maturity. To obtain that yield, interest rates must remain unchanged and the bond must be held to maturity. The probability of these conditions being met is very small. Interest rates change virtually every day, and few bonds remain outstanding to maturity. Most bonds are retired through sinking funds or are called. In either case, only a few bonds of the initial issue may remain outstanding at maturity.

Since many bonds are retired prior to maturity, the investor may want to purchase only those bonds that are noncallable. Some bonds have this feature written into their indentures. They cannot be retired prior to maturity, in which case there is no uncertainty concerning when these bonds will be redeemed. Since this uncertainty has been erased, such bonds tend to sell for lower yields. Thus, the investor purchases the certainty of when the bond will be retired by forgoing some interest income.

Even if the investor acquires noncallable bonds, there is still the uncertainty associated with changes in interest rates. Thus, the realized yield over the lifetime of these noncallable bonds may not equal the yield to maturity that was anticipated when the bonds were purchased. A noncallable feature may reduce one source of risk but cannot erase all the possible sources of risk associated with investing in bonds.

There is only one type of bond that erases both the uncertainty of when the bond will be retired and the reinvestment rate. That bond is the noncallable, zero coupon bond. The entire yield occurs at maturity, and the discounted price considers the compounding of the implicit interest. These bonds offer actual yields to maturity that are equal to the expected yields. As long as the issuer does not default (i.e., repays the principal on the maturity date), the yield to maturity will be the realized return.

Duration

The price volatility of bonds with equal coupons and different terms may be compared on the basis of time. For a given risk class, the price of the bond with the longer term to maturity should be more volatile. Bonds with equal maturities but different coupons may be compared on the basis of the interest payments. For a given risk class, the price of the bond with the smaller coupon will tend to be more volatile. Bonds, however, may have different coupons and different maturity dates. Computing the yield to maturity is one method for comparing bonds.[7] However, the yields to maturity on bonds with different maturities and different coupons may not be comparable, and the yield to maturity does not indicate which bonds' prices tend to be more volatile.

The previous discussion also indicated that the actual return the investor earns over a bond's lifetime will not equal the yield to maturity if the reinvestment rate differs from the yield to maturity. An alternative calculation that may be used to compare bonds with different coupons and different terms to maturity has been developed. This technique is called the bond's **duration** and seeks to compare bonds with different coupons and different maturity dates by determining each bond's price sensitivity to changes in interest rates.

duration
The average time it takes to collect a bond's interest and principal repayment.

Duration is defined as the average time it takes the bondholder to receive the interest and the principal. It is a weighted average that encompasses the total amount of the bond's payments and their timing, then standardizes for the bond's price. To illustrate how duration is determined, consider a $1,000 bond with three years to maturity and a 9 percent coupon. The annual payments are as follows:

Year	Payment
1	$ 90
2	90
3	1,090

Currently, the rate of interest on comparable bonds is 12 percent, so this bond's price is $927.95. The bond's duration is the sum of the present value of each payment weighted by the time period in which the payment is received, with the resulting quantity divided by the price of the bond.[8] Thus, for this bond, the duration is determined as follows:

[7]As is explained in the second appendix to this chapter, bonds in the same risk class and the same maturity but with different coupons may have different yields to maturity. Thus, it cannot be assumed that all bonds with the same maturity date offer the same returns.

[8]Duration may be computed when payments are semiannual, in which case the annual payment and interest rate on comparable debt are divided by 2 and the number of payments is multiplied by 2. If this example had used semiannual compounding, the bond's price would be $926.24, and the computation of duration is

Number of Each Payment		Amount of Payment		Present Value Interest Factor at 6 Percent		
1	×	$ 45	×	0.943	=	$ 42.44
2	×	45	×	0.890	=	80.04
3	×	45	×	0.840	=	113.40
4	×	45	×	0.792	=	142.56
5	×	45	×	0.747	=	168.08
6	×	1,045	×	0.705	=	4,420.35
						$4,966.87

$$\text{Duration} = \frac{\$4{,}966.87/2}{\$926.24} = 5.3624/2 = 2.68 \text{ years.}$$

The duration is marginally smaller because the cash inflows are received slightly faster as the result of semiannual compounding.

Number of Each Payment		Amount of Payment		Present Value Interest Factor at 12 Percent		
1	×	$ 90	×	0.893	=	$ 80.37
2	×	90	×	0.797	=	143.46
3	×	1,090	×	0.712	=	2,328.24
						$2,552.07

$$\text{Duration} = \frac{\$2{,}552.07}{\$927.95} = 2.75 \text{ years.}$$

A duration of 2.75 years means that the bondholder collects, on the average, all the payments in 2.75 years. Obviously, all the payments are not made exactly at 2.75 years into the future. Ninety dollars is received at the end of year one; $90 is received at the end of year two; and $1,090 is received at the end of year three. The weighted average of all these payments is 2.75 years.

The calculation of duration (D) may be formally expressed as:

(16.6)
$$D = \frac{\sum_{t=1}^{m} PVCF_t \times t}{P_B}.$$

The numerator states that the cash flow in each year (CF_t) is stated in present value terms (PV) and weighted by the number of the period (t) in which the payment is received. The individual present values are summed from $t = 1$ to $t = m$ (maturity), and the resulting amount is divided by the current price of the bond (P_B).

Notice that duration is not the sum of the present value of each payment. (That sum is the price of the bond.) Duration takes the present value of each payment and weights it according to when the payment is received. Payments that are to be received farther into the future have more weight in the calculation. If two bonds pay the same coupon but the term of one bond is 10 years while the term of the other is 20 years, the weights given to the payments in years 11 through 20 result in a larger weighted average. The duration, or the weighted average of when all the payments will be received, is longer for the second bond.

The preceding calculation of duration can be tedious. An alternative method simplifies the problem.[9]

(16.7)
$$D = \frac{1 + y}{y} - \frac{(1 + y) + n(c - y)}{c[(1 + y)^n - 1] + y}.$$

Although this equation looks formidable, its application is relatively easy. The variables represent the following:

c = the annual coupon (as a percentage)

n = the number of years to maturity

y = the yield to maturity (reinvestment rate)

[9] See Zvi Bodie, Alex Kane, and Alan J. Marcus, *Investments* (Homewood, IL: Irwin, 1989), 441–447.

Applying the numbers from the preceding illustration yields

$$\textbf{Duration} = \frac{1 + 0.12}{0.12} - \frac{(1 + 0.12) + 3(0.09 - 0.12)}{0.09[(1 + 0.12)^3 - 1] + 0.12}$$

$$= 2.75,$$

which is the same answer (2.75) derived earlier.

By making this calculation for bonds with different coupons and different maturities, the investor standardizes for price fluctuations. Bonds with the same duration will experience similar price fluctuations, while the prices of bonds with a longer duration will fluctuate more. For example, consider the following two bonds. Bond A has a 10 percent coupon, matures in 20 years, and currently sells for $1,000. Bond B has a 7 percent coupon and matures after 10 years with a current price of $815.66.[10] If interest rates rise, the price of both bonds will fall, but which bond's price will fall more? Since the bonds differ with regard to maturity date and coupon, the investor does not know which bond's price will be more volatile.

In general, the longer the term to maturity, the more volatile the bond's price. By that reasoning, bond A will be more volatile. However, lower coupons are also associated with greater price volatility, and by that reasoning bond B's price should be more volatile. Thus, the investor cannot tell on the basis of term and coupon which of these two bonds' prices will be more volatile. However, once their durations have been determined (9.36 and 7.22, respectively), the investor knows that the price of bond A will decline more in response to an increase in interest rates. For example, if interest rates rise to 12 percent, the prices of the two bonds become $850.61 and $717.49, respectively. Bond A's price declined by 15 percent while bond B's price fell by 12 percent, so bond A's price was more volatile.

Duration may also be used to determine the amount by which a bond's price will fluctuate for small changes in interest rates. The percentage change in a bond's price for a change in the yield to maturity is

$$\frac{\Delta P_B}{P_B} = -D \times \frac{\textbf{Change in the yield to maturity}}{1 + y}$$

$$\frac{\Delta P_B}{P_B} = -D \times \frac{\Delta y}{1 + y},$$

in which P_B is the current price of the bond, D is the bond's duration, and y is the yield to maturity. By rearranging terms, the change in the price of a bond is

$$\Delta P_B = -D \times \frac{\Delta y}{1 + y} \times P_B. \quad \textbf{(16.8)}$$

The equation may be illustrated by using bond A above, which sold for $1,000 when the yield to maturity was 10 percent, and whose duration was 9.36. If interest rates rise to 10.2 percent, the change in the price of bond A is

$$\Delta P_B = \frac{(-9.36)(0.002)}{1.1} \times \$1{,}000 = -\$17.$$

[10] In this illustration it is assumed that the bonds sell for the same yield to maturity. While generally the long-term bond should offer a higher yield, this assumption facilitates comparisons for a given change in interest rates.

The increase in interest rates from 10.0 to 10.2 percent causes the price of the bond to decline from $1,000 to $983. If interest rates were to fall from 10.0 to 9.8 percent, the price of the bond would rise to $1,017.[11]

Since bonds with larger durations are more volatile, investors reduce the risk associated with changes in interest rates by acquiring bonds with shorter durations. This, however, is not synonymous with buying bonds with shorter maturities.[12] If two bonds have the same term to maturity, the bond with the smaller coupon will have the longer duration, since a larger proportion of the bond's total payment is repayment of principal. If two bonds have the same coupon, the one with the longer maturity will have the longer duration, as the payments are spread over a longer period of time. However, if one bond has a smaller coupon and a shorter term, its duration could be either greater or smaller than the duration of a bond with a higher coupon and longer term to maturity. Thus, it is possible to buy a bond with a longer term to maturity that has a shorter duration. In such a case, the longer-term bond will experience smaller price fluctuations than the bond with the shorter maturity but longer duration.

Duration is used by professional portfolio managers, such as managers of pension plans, who know when and what amount of funds will be needed. These professional investors seek to match the duration of their portfolios with the timing of the need for funds. Such matching reduces the interest-rate risk associated with the portfolios. Consider an investor who needs $2,210 at the end of seven years and purchases at par a high-yield 12 percent coupon bond that matures at the end of seven years. If interest rates remain at 12 percent, the investor will have $2,211 because the coupons are reinvested at 12 percent. The terminal value is

$$\$1{,}000 + \$120(10.089) = \$2{,}211.$$

(The $1,000 is the repayment of the principal and the $120[10.089] is the future value of all the interest payments compounded annually at 12 percent.)

If interest rates rise and the investor reinvests at 14 percent, the terminal value is

$$\$1{,}000 + \$120(10.730) = \$2{,}288,$$

and the investor is even better off. A problem arises only when interest rates fall and the coupons are reinvested at a lower rate. For example, if interest rates decline to 8 percent, the terminal value is

$$\$1{,}000 + \$120(8.923) = \$2{,}071,$$

and the investor does not have the required $2,210. The lower reinvestment of the interest payments resulted in an insufficient terminal value.

The investor could have avoided the shortage by acquiring a bond whose duration (and not its term) is equal to seven years. For example, if the investor purchases a bond with a 12 percent coupon that matures in 12 instead of 7 years, that bond has a duration of 6.9 years that almost matches when the investor needs the $2,210. (The 12 percent 7-year bond has a duration of 5.1 years.) As will be subsequently illustrated, the purchase of the 12-year bond instead of the 7-year bond eliminates the reinvestment risk.

[11]The usefulness of duration to forecast a bond's price change due to a given change in interest rates diminishes as the change in interest rates increases. For example, if interest rates had increased from 10 to 12 percent, Equation 16.8 indicates that bond A's price would have declined by $170, whereas the bond valuation equation indicates that the price should be $851, a decline of $149. (See the next section on bond convexity.)

[12]The only time duration equals the term to maturity occurs when the bond makes no interest payments (i.e., it is a zero coupon bond). All the payments then occur at maturity.

Since the 12-year bond will have to be sold at the end of seven years, the obvious question is: At what price? The price could rise (if interest rates fall) or decline (if interest rates rise). Must the investor be concerned with interest rate risk (i.e., the fluctuation in the bond's price), which would not apply if the bond matured at the end of seven years? The answer is no. The bond's price of course will change, but the impact of the price fluctuation is offset by the change in the reinvestment of the interest payments. The effect, then, of both reinvestment rate risk and interest rate risk is eliminated.

Suppose interest rates immediately rise to 14 percent after the investor buys the bond. The investor holds the bond for seven years and reinvests the interest payments at 14 percent. How much will the investor have at the end of seven years? The answer is the sum of the interest payments reinvested at 14 percent for seven years [$120(10.730) = $1,288] plus the sale price of the bond. Since the bond has five years to maturity, its price is

$$\$120(3.433) + \$1,000(0.519) = \$931.$$

Thus, the investor has $1,288 + $931 = $2,219, which meets the desired amount ($2,210). The loss on the sale of the bond is offset by the increased interest earned when the annual interest payments are reinvested at the higher rate.

Suppose interest rates immediately decline to 8 percent after the investor buys the bond. The investor holds the bond for seven years and reinvests the interest payments at 8 percent. How much will the investor have at the end of seven years? The answer in this case is the sum of the interest payments reinvested at 8 percent for seven years [$120(8.923) = $1,071] plus the sale price of the bond. Since the bond has five years to maturity, its price is

$$\$120(3.993) + \$1,000(0.681) = \$1,160.$$

Thus, the investor has $1,071 + $1,160 = $2,231, which once again meets the desired amount ($2,210). The gain on the sale of the bond offsets the reduction in interest earned when the interest payments are reinvested at the lower rate.

Notice that in both cases the individual achieves the investment goal of $2,210 at the end of seven years. Lower reinvestment income from a decline in interest rates is offset by the increase in the price of the bond, while higher reinvestment income from an increase in interest rates is offset by the decline in the price of the bond. Thus, the impact of reinvestment rate risk and interest rate risk is eliminated. Of course, the investor has lost the opportunity to earn a higher return, but the purpose of the strategy is to ensure a particular amount in the future.

As this discussion indicates, the concept of duration is exceedingly important for any investor who knows when funds will be needed and at what amount. For example, pension managers know both when payments must be made and their amount. Mortality tables help establish the same information for life insurance companies. Portfolio managers can use duration to reduce risk exposure and ensure that the desired funds are available when needed. (These portfolio managers, of course, still have the risk of default or incorrect forecasts, such as changes in a mortality table.)

Individual investors will probably find duration less useful. For example, even if parents know when their children will attend college, they do not necessarily know the cost—hence the future value is unknown. In addition, the duration of each bond is not readily available and, as is explained in the next section, the value changes with each change in the bond's price. Thus, individual investors who want to apply this concept will have to perform the calculation themselves and frequently adjust their portfolios as the duration of each bond in the portfolio fluctuates.

Bond Price Convexity and Duration

Duration may be used to rank bonds with regard to their price volatility and to determine their price change for a given change in interest rates. The accuracy of the price change, however, varies with the amount of the fluctuation in interest rates. Consider an 8 percent, 10-year bond that is currently selling for par ($1,000). The first three columns in Exhibit 16.6 list various interest rates, the price of the bond based on the rates, and resulting change in price from the initial par value. As expected, the price of the bond rises in response to lower rates, and the price of the bond declines in response to higher rates.

The fourth column gives the bond's duration at the various prices. This value may be used in Equation 16.8 to forecast the price change in the bond for a given

EXHIBIT 16.6

Forecasted Bond Prices Using Duration and Actual Prices

Interest Rate	Price of the Bond	Change in Bond's Price	Duration	Forecasted Change in Price	Difference
20.0%	$497	−$503	6.000	−$805	$302
15.0	649	−397	6.524	−470	119
14.0	687	−313	6.628	−403	90
13.0	729	−271	6.733	−336	65
12.0	774	−226	6.837	−268	42
11.0	823	−176	6.941	−201	25
10.0	877	−123	7.044	−134	11
9.6	900	−100	7.085	−107	7
9.2	924	−76	7.126	−81	5
9.0	936	−64	7.146	−67	3
8.8	948	−52	7.166	−53	1
8.6	961	−39	7.186	−40	1
8.4	974	−26	7.207	−27	1
8.2	987	−13	7.227	−13	—
8.1	993	−7	7.237	−7	—
8.0	1,000	—	7.247	—	—
7.9	1,007	7	7.257	7	—
7.8	1,014	14	7.267	13	1
7.6	1,027	26	7.287	27	1
7.4	1,041	41	7.307	40	1
7.2	1,056	56	7.327	53	3
7.0	1,070	70	7.347	67	3
6.8	1,085	85	7.366	81	4
6.4	1,116	116	7.406	107	9
6.0	1,147	147	7.445	134	13
5.0	1,232	232	7.542	201	31
4.0	1,324	324	7.637	268	56
3.0	1,427	427	7.731	334	93
2.0	1,539	539	7.823	403	136
1.0	1,663	663	7.912	470	193

change in interest rates. The fifth column presents the forecasted price change using Equation 16.8 and starting with the bond selling for par with a duration of 7.247. The last column presents the absolute difference in the forecasted price change and the actual change in column 3. As may be seen in the sixth column, the forecasted error is small for a small change in interest rates. For example, a change in interest rates from 8 percent to 9 percent or from 8 percent to 7 percent produces an error of $3. However, the difference between the actual change and the forecasted change increases with larger changes in interest rates. If interest rates were to rise or fall by 4 percentage points to 12 percent or 4 percent, the error is $42. These differences between the actual and forecasted price changes reduce the usefulness of the duration.

The source of the error may be seen in Figure 16.6. Line *BB* plots the various prices of the bond against the different interest rates. (In effect, line *BB* replicates the second column in Exhibit 16.5.) Line *AA* gives the bond prices forecasted using duration, with the difference between *AA* and *BB* being the error. Notice that as interest rates move further above or below the initial 8 percent, the error increases.

The source of the error is that duration predicts the same price change for each one percent point movement in the interest rate, but the actual price change varies. As may be seen in the figure, *AA* is a straight line while *BB* is a curve and is convex to the origin. The price of the bond moves along the curve. For a given change in interest rates (e.g., 8 percent to 9 percent or 9 percent to 10 percent), the amount of price change varies. The forecasted price moves along the straight line. For a given change in interest rates (e.g., 8 percent to 9 percent or 9 percent to 10 percent), the amount of price change is the same, so the forecasted error increases.

This "convexity" of line *BB* decreases the practicality of using a unique value of duration (e.g., the 7.247 used to construct Exhibit 16.5 and Figure 16.6) to forecast

FIGURE 16.6

Bond Prices Forecasted by Duration and Actual Prices

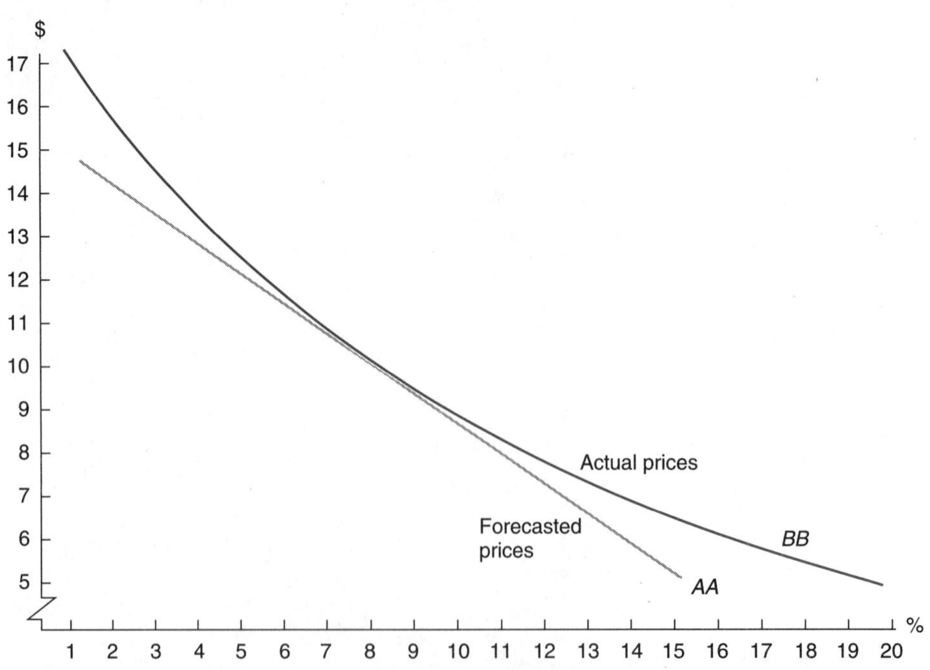

price changes. Equation 16.6, which determines the numerical value of duration, uses the price of the bond in the denominator. As the price of the bond changes, so must its duration. This change in the bond's duration is also illustrated in Exhibit 16.5 in the fourth column. While the initial duration is 7.247 when the bond sells for $1,000, the value rises to 7.445 when interest rates decline to 6 percent and falls to 6.524 when interest rates rise to 15 percent.

To use duration as a tool for managing a bond portfolio, the investor must adjust for changes in the value of a bond's duration. An immediate implication of the change in duration is the need to alter the composition of a bond portfolio when a specific numerical value for duration is desired. Such changes in the portfolio suggest that an actively managed bond portfolio requires constant supervision and that such a portfolio cannot be a passive investment in which the portfolio manager accumulates a collection of bonds and then idly sits and collects the interest. Although a bond portfolio may be passively managed, a bond portfolio designed to generate a specified amount of funds at a specified date cannot be passively managed if the portfolio duration is to be matched with the specified time when the funds are needed.

Management of Bond Portfolios

Since bonds pay a fixed income and mature at a specified date, they are conducive to passive management. The investor may acquire a portfolio of bonds and simply hold them to maturity (i.e., a buy-and-hold strategy). Each year the interest is received and at maturity the principal is repaid. During the interim, the value of the portfolio could rise (i.e., interest rates fall), or the value of the portfolio could fall (i.e., interest rates rise). Such fluctuations in the value of the portfolio may have little meaning to the investor who is passively holding the portfolio and collecting the interest until the bonds mature. Of course, if the individual had to sell the bonds for any reason, their prices would become crucial since the investor would only receive what the bonds are currently worth.

Not all bondholders, however, are passive investors. As was explained in the previous section, using duration for the management of reinvestment rate risk requires frequent trading of bonds. A strategy designed to take advantage of an expected change in rates paid by one type of bond relative to a different type requires the swapping of one bond for another. A strategy designed to reduce interest rate risk may require the construction of a portfolio with many bonds with different maturity dates. A strategy designed to match the timing of a bond portfolio's cash flows with when the funds are needed may require frequent trading of bonds. None of these constitutes passive management of a bond portfolio.

Bond Swapping

bond swap
The selling of one bond and using the proceeds to acquire a different bond.

Bond swapping is the selling of one type of bond and the purchasing of another.[13] Such bond swaps may be used to alter bond holdings to save on taxes, increase yields, change the quality of the portfolio (reduce risk), or take advantage of mispricings.

If an investor has bonds whose prices have declined for some reason (i.e., interest rates rose), the investor may sell the bonds for a loss in order to reduce capital gains taxes. The proceeds are then invested in bonds of similar quality and maturity. For example, the investor may sell bonds issued by one utility and acquire

[13] For the development of bond swaps, see Sidney Homer and Martin Liebowitz, *Inside the Yield Book: New Tools for Bond Market Strategy* (Englewood Cliffs, NJ: Prentice-Hall, 1972).

bonds issued by a comparable utility. Such a transaction is a *tax swap,* and its benefit is the potential tax savings generated by the realized loss.

In a *substitution swap* the investor trades one bond for a different bond with virtually the same characteristics (i.e., same maturity, coupon, credit rating, and call and sinking funds) when their yields differ. If, for example, two virtually identical bonds had different yields, the investor would move out of the bond with the lower yield into the bond with the higher yield. A variation on this strategy is referred to as the *intermarket spread swap* in which the difference in yields between two markets seems excessive. If, for example, the spread between the yields on triple-A-rated bonds rises relative to the yield on federal government bonds, the investor may swap the government bonds for the corporate bonds. In both the substitution swap and the intermarket spread swap, the investor is seeking to take advantage of perceived mispricings of the two bonds.

Figure 15.3 illustrated that generally yields on longer-term bonds exceed yields on short-term debt obligations. The investor may seek to increase interest income by selling short-term bonds and purchasing long-term bonds. Such a strategy is referred to as a *pure yield pickup swap* and is designed to take advantage of the higher yields associated with longer maturities.

All of these strategies or swaps are illustrations of actively managed bond portfolios, but they are not concerned with the interest rate risk. *Rate anticipation swaps* seek to take advantage or avoid the impact of expected changes in interest rates. If the investor anticipates higher rates, bonds with longer terms to maturity are swapped for short-term bonds. Anticipation of lower rates leads to swapping short-term debt obligations for long-term bonds.

Management of Interest Rate Risk

Since interest rates change daily, the value of a bond portfolio fluctuates daily. Of course, the investor could avoid these fluctuations by acquiring only short-term debt obligations. This strategy generates less income since shorter maturities generally have lower yields than bonds with longer maturities. The opposite strategy of purchasing only very long-term bonds will increase income but also increases the risk associated with changes in interest rates.

The investor could construct a portfolio of bonds with maturities distributed over a period of time. Such a strategy is sometimes referred to as a *laddered* approach. For example, a $100,000 portfolio could acquire $10,000 worth of bonds that mature for each of the next ten years. If interest rates change, the prices of the bonds with the shorter terms (i.e., the bonds with one to five years to maturity) will fluctuate less than the prices of the bonds with the longer terms (i.e., years six through ten). Hence, such a portfolio reduces the impact of changes in interest rates.

In addition to reducing the impact on the value of the portfolio from fluctuating interest rates, a laddered portfolio offers two important advantages. First, since the structure of yields is generally positive, the interest earned on the bonds will tend to be greater than would be earned on a portfolio of short-term debt instruments. (Correspondingly, it would be smaller than the interest earned on a portfolio consisting solely of bonds with long terms to maturity.) Second, some of the bonds mature each year. If the individual needs the funds, they are available; if the individual does not need the funds, they may be reinvested. If the funds are reinvested each year in bonds with a ten-year maturity, the original structure of the portfolio is retained.

The primary disadvantage of such a portfolio is that if the investor anticipates a change in interest rates and wants to alter the portfolio, virtually all the bonds have to be liquidated. If the investor anticipates lower interest rates, then a portfolio consisting of only long maturities is desirable. All the bonds with short to intermediate terms would have to be sold and reinvested in bonds with long maturities. The opposite would occur if the individual anticipates higher rates. In that case, the individual wants only short-term securities, so all the bonds with intermediate to long terms would have to be sold.

This lack of flexibility and the need to change a large proportion of the portfolio if the investor seeks to take advantage of anticipated changes in interest rates has led to an entirely different strategy for management of a bond portfolio. In this strategy, which is sometimes referred to as a *barbell,* the investor acquires a portfolio consisting of very long- and very short-term maturities. If the individual has $100,000 to invest, $50,000 may be used to purchase bonds with short maturities (e.g., six months to a year) and $50,000 to purchase 20-year bonds. If the investor then anticipates a change in interest rates, only half of the portfolio needs to be changed. Expectation of lower rates would imply selling the short-term bonds and investing the proceeds in the long-terms. If the investor anticipates higher interest rates, he or she would do the opposite: sell the long-terms and move into the short-term bonds.

A barbell strategy will reduce the impact of fluctuating interest rates if the investor anticipates correctly. It will magnify the impact if the investor is incorrect. A movement into long-term bonds just prior to an increase in interest rates could inflict a substantial loss on the value of the portfolio. The strategy also has a second major disadvantage: With the passage of time, the short-term bonds will mature, and the maturities of the long-term bonds will diminish. Thus, this bond strategy requires active management, as the proceeds of the maturing bonds will have to be reinvested and some of the longer bonds may have to be sold and the proceeds invested in bonds with even longer maturities. Failure to take these steps means that the investor's cash position will increase and the term of the remaining bonds will decrease.

Matching Strategies

The barbell strategy is designed to facilitate swapping bonds of different terms to benefit from anticipated changes in interest rates. Other bond strategies may be designed to match the portfolio with the investor's need for the funds. Two of these strategies are called *immunization* and *dedication.* An immunized portfolio seeks to match the duration of the portfolio with the duration of the investor's cash needs. As previously explained, the concept of duration facilitates comparisons of the price volatility of bonds with different coupons and maturity dates. The individual determines the time period over which he or she wants to lock in current yields. Then the individual constructs a portfolio of bonds with different maturities such that the duration of the portfolio is matched with the desired time period. This strategy will require the investor to monitor the portfolio and adjust it should the duration differ from the time when the funds will be needed.

A *dedicated* bond portfolio matches the receipt of cash flows with the need for the funds. Thus, interest payments and principal repayments are matched with the investor's anticipated payments. For example, a parent may construct a portfolio of zero coupon bonds, each of which matures when the child's tuition is due. While that is perhaps an exceptionally obvious example, the strategy would also apply to the trustees of a pension plan. In that case, the timing and amount of the payments to the retirees is known. The trustees then acquire bonds such that the interest payments and principal repayments match the required payments.

An individual retiree could construct a similar portfolio with funds in an IRA account or funds received from a distribution from a pension plan or corporation savings plan. While the individual investor will not know exactly when the funds will be needed, he or she can estimate cash requirements. For example, suppose a retiree owns a house with no mortgage, a new car, and supplementary medical insurance. That individual may not know exactly how much each payment will be in the future, but he or she knows when property taxes and insurance payments are due. The retiree may also have an estimate of annual maintenance requirements for the house and the car and when the car would be replaced. Acquiring bonds that pay interest or mature at the same time these payments fall due should facilitate making the payments.

Interest rate risk is irrelevant for both immunized and dedicated bond portfolios. By matching the duration of the portfolio with the duration of the investor's liabilities or by timing the cash received with cash needs, the impact of fluctuations in interest rates is minimized. Such strategies are better than a simple buy-and-hold strategy because they seek to match the portfolio with the need for funds. Since a simple buy-and-hold does not consider when the funds will be needed, the investor will be subject to interest rate risk. The funds may possibly be needed during a period of higher interest rates, in which case the investor will not realize the value of the initial investment.

Interest Rate Swaps

Interest rate swaps have emerged as one of the major recent innovations in finance and are discussed in Chapter 21. Interest rate swaps, however, should not be confused with the swaps just discussed. Few individual investors are concerned with the market for interest rate swaps. Instead, these swaps are a means by which financial institutions, such as commercial banks or savings and loan institutions, manage risk.

Many financial institutions have mismatched assets and liabilities. For example, a savings and loan's primary assets may be long-term mortgages, while its primary liabilities are short to intermediate term (i.e., deposits and certificates of deposit). When interest rates rise, a savings and loan institution loses on two counts: The higher interest rate reduces the value of its assets and increases the interest it must pay to attract depositors. To reduce this risk, the savings and loan needs a flow of payments that will vary with changes in interest, so the savings and loan swaps the flow of fixed-interest payments it will receive on the mortgages for a series of variable payments.

The swap is made with a corporation that has the need to make fixed payments. For example, suppose a utility has a large number of fixed-coupon bonds outstanding. The utility agrees to make variable payments to the savings and loan in exchange for the fixed-interest payments. Now the utility will have the funds coming in to make the interest payments. In effect, the utility is substituting variable-interest payments to the savings and loan for the fixed-interest payments that it would have to make to its bondholders, while the savings and loan substitutes the receipt of variable-interest payments for fixed-interest payments from the mortgages. The swap helps both firms better match their receipts and disbursements and manage their assets and liabilities.

Preferred Stock

preferred stock
A class of stock (i.e., equity) that has a prior claim to common stock on the firm's earnings and assets in case of liquidation.

Preferred stock is an equity instrument that usually pays a fixed dividend that is not guaranteed but receives preference over common stock dividends. While most firms have only one issue of common stock, they may have several issues of preferred stock. (Some corporations have also issued a *preference* stock, which is subordinated to preferred stock but has preference over common stock with regard to the payment of dividends. Such stock is another level of preferred stock, and in this text no distinction is made between the two.) As may be seen in Exhibit 16.7, Virginia Electric and Power has 13 issues of preferred stock. In 7 cases the dividend is fixed. Thus, for the series $5.00 preferred, the annual dividend is $5.00, which is distributed at the rate of $1.25 per quarter. In the six remaining preferred stocks (the money market preferred stocks), the dividend is reset every 49 days with changes in money market rates.

The dividend is expressed either as a dollar amount or as a percentage based on the preferred stock's par value. The par value is the stated value of the shares and is also the price at which the shares were initially sold. In the case of the Virginia Electric $5.00 preferred, the par value is $100, so the dividend rate is 5.0 percent based on the par value.

Preferred stock dividends are paid from the firm's earnings. If the firm does not have the earnings, it may not declare and pay the preferred stock dividends. If the firm should omit the preferred stock's dividend, the dividend is said to be *in arrears*. The firm does not have to remove this **arrearage**. In most cases, however, any omitted dividends have to be paid in the future before dividends may be paid to the holders of the common stock. Such cases in which the preferred stock's dividends accumulate are called **cumulative preferred**. Most preferred stock is cumulative, but there are examples of **noncumulative preferred stocks** whose dividends do not have to be made up if missed (e.g., the Sierra Capital Realty 7 percent preferred stock is noncumulative). For investors holding preferred stock in firms experiencing financial difficulty, the difference between cumulative and noncumulative may be immaterial. Forcing the firm to pay dividends to erase the arrearage may further weaken it and hurt the owners of the preferred stock more than forgoing the dividends. Once the firm has regained its profitability, erasing the arrearage may become important not only to holders of the stock but also to the company, as a demonstration of its improved financial condition.

arrearage
Cumulative preferred dividends that have not been paid.

cumulative preferred stock
A preferred stock whose dividends accumulate if they are not paid.

noncumulative preferred stock
Preferred stock whose dividends do not accumulate if the firm misses a dividend payment.

An example of a firm clearing its arrearage of preferred stock is Unisys, which suspended preferred stock dividend payments in 1991 but resumed them in 1993.

EXHIBIT 16.7

The Preferred Stocks of Virginia Electric and Power

Preferred Stock Not Subject to Mandatory Retirement		
	Annual Dividend per Share	**Outstanding Shares**
	$4.04	12,926
	4.20	14,797
	4.12	32,534
	4.80	73,206
	5.00	106,677
	7.05	73,206
	6.98	600,000
1987-1	Money market preferred	500,000
1987-2	Money market preferred	750,000
1988	Money market preferred	750,000
1989	Money market preferred	750,000
1992-1	Money market preferred	500,000
1992-2	Money market preferred	500,000

Source: 2000 Dominion Resources *Annual Report.*

The 1993 payments totaled \$5.625 per share, which consisted of \$3.75 for the current year and \$1.875 toward the arrearage. The company subsequently followed a similar policy until the arrearage was erased.

Once the preferred stock is issued, the firm may never have to concern itself with its retirement: It is perpetual. This may be both an advantage and a disadvantage. Since the firm may never have to retire the preferred stock, it does not have to generate the money to retire it but may instead use its funds elsewhere (e.g., to purchase plant and equipment). However, should the firm ever want to change its capital structure and substitute debt financing for the preferred stock, it may have difficulty retiring the preferred stock. The firm may have to purchase the stock on the open market, and, to induce the holders to sell the preferred shares, the firm will probably have to bid up the preferred stock's price.

The Valuation of Preferred Stock

The process of valuing preferred stock is essentially the same as that used to price bonds. The future payments are brought back to the present at the appropriate discount rate. If the preferred stock does not have a required sinking fund or call feature, it may be viewed as a perpetual debt instrument. The fixed dividend (D) will continue indefinitely. These dividends must be discounted by the yield being earned on newly issued preferred stock (k). This process for determining the present value of the preferred stock (P) is:

$$P = \frac{D}{(1 + k)^1} + \frac{D}{(1 + k)^2} + \frac{D}{(1 + k)^3} + \cdots.$$

As in the case of the perpetual bond, this equation is reduced to

(16.9)

$$P = \frac{D}{k}.$$

Thus, if a preferred stock pays an annual dividend of \$4 and the appropriate discount rate is 8 percent, the present value of the preferred stock is

$$P = \frac{\$4}{(1 + 0.08)^1} + \frac{\$4}{(1 + 0.08)^2} + \frac{\$4}{(1 + 0.08)^3} + \cdots$$

$$= \frac{\$4}{0.08} = \$50.00.$$

If an investor buys this preferred stock for \$50.00, he or she can expect to earn 8 percent (\$50.00 × 0.08 = \$4) on the investment. Of course, the realized rate of return on the investment will not be known until the investor sells the stock and adjusts this 8 percent return for any capital gain or loss. However, at the current price, the preferred stock is selling for an 8 percent dividend yield.

If the preferred stock has a finite life, this fact must be considered in determining its value. As with the valuation of long-term debt, the amount that is repaid when the preferred stock is retired must be discounted back to the present value. Thus, when preferred stock has a finite life, the valuation equation becomes

(16.10)

$$P = \frac{D}{(1 + k)^1} + \frac{D}{(1 + k)^2} + \cdots + \frac{D}{(1 + k)^n} + \frac{S}{(1 + k)^n}$$

Calculator Solution

Function Key		Data Input
PV	=	?
FV	=	100
PMT	=	4
N	=	20
I	=	8
Function Key		*Answer*
PV	=	−60.73

where S represents the amount that is returned to the stockholder when the preferred stock is retired after n number of years. If the preferred stock in the previous example is retired after 20 years for $100 per share, its current value would be

$$P = \frac{\$4}{(1 + 0.08)^1} + \cdots + \frac{\$4}{(1 + 0.08)^{20}} + \frac{\$100}{(1 + 0.08)^{20}}$$
$$= \$4(9.818) + \$100(0.215)$$
$$= \$60.77,$$

in which 9.818 is the interest factor for the present value of an annuity of $1 for 20 years at 8 percent and 0.215 is the present value of $1 to be received after 20 years when yields are 8 percent. Instead of selling the stock for $50.00, the nonperpetual preferred stock would sell for $60.77. At a price of $60.77, the yield is still 8 percent, but the return in this case consists of a current dividend yield of 6.58 percent ($4 ÷ $60.77) and a capital gain as the price of the stock rises from $60.77 to $100 when it is retired 20 years hence.

Preferred Stock and Bonds Contrasted

Since preferred stock pays a fixed dividend, it is purchased primarily by investors seeking a fixed flow of income, and it is analyzed and valued like any other fixed-income security (i.e., long-term bonds). But preferred stock differs from bonds. Preferred stock is riskier than debt. The terms of a bond are legal obligations of the firm. If the corporation fails to pay the interest or meet any of the terms of the indenture, the bondholders may take the firm to court to force payment of the interest or to seek liquidation of the firm in order to protect their principal. Preferred stockholders do not have that power, for the firm is not legally obligated to pay the preferred stock dividends. In addition, debt must be retired, while preferred stock is often perpetual. If the security is perpetual, the only means to recoup the amount invested is to sell the preferred stock in the secondary market. The investor cannot expect the firm to redeem the security.

Market price fluctuations tend to be greater for preferred stock than for bonds. Possible explanations for the differences in price volatility include the term of the preferred stock (which may be perpetual) and the greater risk (uncertainty) associated with the dividend payments. However, given the greater risk associated with preferred stock from the perspective of the investor, the yields on preferred stock may not exceed and may even be less than is available from bonds.

The small difference in yields between bonds and preferred stock is explained by the federal corporate income tax laws. Dividends paid by one corporation to another receive favorable tax treatment. Seventy percent of the dividend is excluded and only 30 percent of the dividend is taxed as income of the corporation receiving the dividend. Thus, for a corporation such as an insurance company in the 34 percent corporate income tax bracket, this shelter is very important. If the company receives $100 in interest, it nets only $66, as $34 is paid in taxes. However, if the same corporation were to receive $100 in preferred stock dividends, only $30 would be subject to federal income tax. The corporation pays only $10.20 ($30 × 0.34) in taxes and gets to keep the remaining $89.80 of the dividend payment.

For this reason, a corporation may choose to purchase preferred stock instead of long-term bonds. This preference drives up the price of preferred stock, which reduces the yield. Since individual investors do not enjoy the tax break, they may prefer bonds, which offer comparable yields but are less risky. To induce individual investors to purchase preferred stock, the issuing firm may offer other features, such as convertibility of the preferred stock into common stock.

While the tax laws may encourage firms to buy preferred stock, they also discourage firms from issuing it. The interest on bonds is a tax-deductible expense, while the dividend on preferred stock is not. Preferred dividends are paid out of earnings. This difference in the tax treatment of interest expense and preferred stock dividends affects the earnings available to the firm's common stockholders. Using debt instead of preferred stock as a source of funds will result in higher earnings per common share.

Consider a firm with operating income (earnings before interest and taxes) of $1,000,000. The firm has 100,000 common shares outstanding and is in the 40 percent corporate income tax bracket. If the firm issues $2,000,000 of debt with a 10 percent rate of interest, its earnings per common share are

Earnings before interest and taxes	$1,000,000
Interest	200,000
Earnings before taxes	800,000
Taxes	320,000
Net income	$480,000
Earnings per common share: $480,000/100,000 =	$4.80

If the firm had issued $2,000,000 in preferred stock that also paid 10 percent, the earnings per common share would be:

Earnings before interest and taxes	$1,000,000
Interest	0
Earnings before taxes	1,000,000
Taxes	400,000
Earnings before preferred stock dividends	600,000
Preferred stock dividends	200,000
Earnings available to common stock	$400,000
Earnings per common share: $400,000/100,000 =	$4.00

The use of preferred stock has resulted in lower earnings per common share. This reduction in earnings is the result of the different tax treatment of interest, which is a tax-deductible expense, and preferred stock dividends, which are not deductible.

Analysis of Preferred Stock

Since preferred stock is similar to debt, similar tools are used to analyze it. Because preferred stock is an income-producing investment, the analysis is primarily concerned with the capacity of the firm to meet the dividend payments. Although dividends must ultimately be related to current earnings and the firm's future earning capacity, preferred dividends are paid from cash. Even if the firm is temporarily running a deficit (i.e., experiencing an accounting loss), it may still be able to pay dividends to the preferred stockholders if it has sufficient cash. In fact, cash dividends might be paid despite the deficit to indicate that the losses are expected to be temporary and that the firm is financially strong.

An analysis of the firm's financial statements (such as the ratios used to analyze common stock in Chapter 13) may reveal its liquidity position and profitability. The more liquid and profitable the firm, the safer the dividend payment should be. The investor may also analyze how well the firm covers its preferred dividend. This analysis is achieved by computing the **times-dividend-earned ratio**, which is

times-dividend-earned ratio

Earnings divided by preferred dividend requirements.

$$\frac{\textbf{Earnings after taxes}}{\textbf{Dividends on preferred stock}}.$$

The larger this ratio, the safer the preferred stock's dividend should be. Notice that the numerator consists of *total* earnings. Although the preferred stock dividends are subtracted from the total earnings to derive the earnings available to the common stockholders, all the firm's earnings are available to pay the preferred stock dividend.

earnings per preferred share
The total earnings divided by the number of preferred shares outstanding.

A variation on this ratio is **earnings per preferred share**. This ratio is

$$\frac{\textbf{Earnings after taxes}}{\textbf{Number of preferred shares outstanding}}.$$

The larger the earnings per preferred share, the safer the dividend payment. However, neither of these ratios indicates whether the firm has sufficient cash to pay the dividends. They can only indicate the extent to which earnings cover the dividend requirements of the preferred stock.

How each ratio is computed can be illustrated by the following simple example. A firm in the 40 percent tax bracket has earnings of \$6 million before income taxes. It has 100,000 shares of preferred stock outstanding, and each share pays a dividend of \$5. The times-dividend-earned ratio is

$$\frac{\$6{,}000{,}000 - \$2{,}400{,}000}{\$500{,}000} = 7.2,$$

and the earnings per preferred share are

$$\frac{\$6{,}000{,}000 - \$2{,}400{,}000}{100{,}000} = \$36.$$

Both ratios, in effect, show the same thing. In the first, the preferred dividend is covered by a multiple of 7.2:1. The second ratio shows an earnings per preferred share of \$36, which is 7.2 times the \$5 dividend paid for each share.

Disadvantages of Preferred Stock

While most preferred stock offers the investor the advantage of a fixed flow of income, this may be more than offset by several disadvantages. Like any fixed-income security, preferred stock offers no protection from inflation. If the inflation rate were to increase, the real purchasing power of the dividend would be diminished. In addition, increased inflation would probably lead to higher interest rates, which would drive down the market value of the preferred stock. Thus, higher rates of inflation doubly curse preferred stock, as the purchasing power of the dividend and the market value of the stock both will be diminished. This disadvantage, of course, applies to all fixed-income securities.

Preferred stock also tends to be less marketable than other securities. Marketability of a particular preferred stock depends on the size of the issue. However, most preferred stock is bought by insurance companies and pension plans. The market for the remaining shares may be quite thin, so there can be a substantial spread between the bid and ask prices. While this may not be a disadvantage if the investor intends to hold the security, it will reduce the attractiveness of the preferred stock in cases in which marketability is desired.

Several other disadvantages were alluded to earlier. The first of these is the inferior position of preferred stock to debt obligations. The investor must realize that preferred stock is perceptibly riskier than bonds. A second disadvantage is that the yields offered by preferred stock are probably insufficient to justify the additional risk. The yields on preferred stock are not necessarily higher than those available on bonds because of the tax advantage preferred stock offers corporate investors and pension managers. As was explained before, only 30 percent of the preferred dividends are subject to corporate income tax, and none of the dividends paid to pension plans are subject to tax. Unfortunately, individual investors are unable to take advantage of these tax breaks except as part of retirement plans. Thus, individual investors may earn inferior yields after adjusting for the risks associated with investing in a security inferior to the firm's bonds.

Summary

The price of a bond depends on the interest paid, the maturity date, and the return offered by comparable bonds. If interest rates rise, the price of existing bonds falls. The opposite is also true—if interest rates fall, the price of existing bonds rises.

The current yield considers only the flow of interest income relative to the price of the bond. The yield to maturity considers the flow of interest income as well as any price change that may occur if the bond is held to maturity. The yield to call is similar to the yield to maturity, but it substitutes the call date and the call price for the maturity date and the principal.

Discounted bonds may be attractive to investors seeking current income, some capital appreciation, and the return of the principal at a specified date. Since many such bonds are redeemed at maturity, the investor knows when the principal is to be received.

All bond prices fluctuate in response to changes in interest rates and changes in risk, but the prices of bonds with smaller coupons, longer maturities, or poorer credit ratings tend to fluctuate more. These bonds may sell for larger discounts or higher premiums than bonds with shorter maturities or better credit ratings. Such bonds may be attractive investments for individuals who want higher returns and who are willing to bear additional risk.

Investors may determine bonds' duration to ascertain which bonds' prices will fluctuate more. Duration is a weighted average of all of a bond's interest and principal payments standardized by the bond's price. Bonds with smaller durations tend to have smaller price fluctuations in response to changes in interest rates. Duration may also be used to manage reinvestment rate risk by timing a bond's duration with when the funds will be needed.

The individual may passively or actively manage a bond portfolio. Passive strategies range from buy and hold to a laddered portfolio consisting of bonds with different maturity dates. Active strategies include swapping among different bonds to take advantage of mispricings, expected changes in interest rates, and tax losses and to match the need for funds and the receipt of interest payments and principal repayments.

Preferred stock is legally equity, but because it pays a fixed dividend, it is similar to debt. Preferred stock's value fluctuates with changes in interest rates. When interest rates rise, the price of preferred stock falls; when interest rates decline, the price of preferred stock rises. Because its price behavior is the same as the price behavior of bonds, preferred stock is valued and analyzed as an alternative to long-term debt.

The prime advantage to the firm issuing preferred stock is that it is less risky than debt because preferred stock does not represent an unconditional obligation to pay dividends. The major disadvantage to the issuing firm is that the dividends are not a tax-deductible expense.

The primary purpose for purchasing a preferred stock is the flow of dividend income. However, since preferred stock is riskier than debt (from the viewpoint of the individual investor), preferred stock is not a popular investment with individuals. The majority of preferred stock is purchased by corporations, especially insurance companies, which receive favorable tax treatment on the preferred stock dividends they receive.

Summary of Equations

Perpetual Bond

(16.1)
$$P = \frac{PMT}{i}$$

Bond with Finite Maturity—Annual Compounding

(16.2)
$$P_B = \frac{PMT}{(1+i)^1} + \frac{PMT}{(1+i)^2} + \cdots + \frac{PMT}{(1+i)^n} + \frac{FV}{(1+i)^n}$$

Bond with Finite Maturity—Semiannual Compounding

(16.3)
$$P_B = \frac{\frac{PMT}{2}}{\left(1+\frac{i}{2}\right)^1} + \frac{\frac{PMT}{2}}{\left(1+\frac{i}{2}\right)^2} + \cdots + \frac{\frac{PMT}{2}}{\left(1+\frac{i}{2}\right)^{n\times 2}} + \frac{FV}{\left(1+\frac{i}{2}\right)^{n\times 2}}$$

Current Yield

(16.4)
$$\text{Current yield} = \frac{\text{Annual interest payment}}{\text{Price of the bond}}$$

Approximate Yield to Maturity

(16.5)
$$i = \frac{I + \frac{1{,}000 - P_B}{n}}{\frac{\$1{,}000 + P_B}{2}}$$

Duration

(16.6)
$$D = \frac{\sum_{t=1}^{m} PVCF_t \times t}{P_B}$$

(16.7)
$$D = \frac{1+y}{y} - \frac{(1+y) + n(c-y)}{c[(1+y)^n - 1] + y}$$

Change in the Price of a Bond

(16.8)
$$\Delta P = -D \times \frac{\Delta y}{1+y} \times P_B$$

Perpetual Preferred Stock

(16.9)
$$P = \frac{D}{k}$$

Preferred Stock with Finite Maturity

(16.10)
$$P = \frac{D}{(1+k)^1} + \frac{D}{(1+k)^2} + \cdots + \frac{D}{(1+k)^n} + \frac{S}{(1+k)^n}$$

Questions

1) What causes bond prices to fluctuate?
2) Define the current yield and the yield to maturity. How are they different?
3) What advantages do discounted bonds offer to investors? Why may a bond be called if it is selling at a premium?
4) Although all bond prices fluctuate, which bond prices tend to fluctuate more?
5) What is the yield to call? How does it differ from the yield to maturity?
6) What differentiates the term of a bond and its duration? If bond A has a 10 percent coupon while bond B has a 5 percent coupon and they both mature after ten years, which bond has the shorter duration?
7) Why is a barbell strategy more flexible than a laddered strategy if an investor anticipates a decline in interest rates?
8) If interest rates rise, bond prices will fall. Given the following pairs of bonds, indicate which bond's price will experience the greater price decline.
   a) Bond A Coupon: 10%
      Maturity: 5 years
      Bond B Coupon: 6%
      Maturity: 5 years
   b) Bond A Coupon: 10%
      Maturity: 7 years
      Bond B Coupon: 10%
      Maturity: 15 years
   c) Bond A Coupon: 10%
      Maturity: 5 years
      Bond B Coupon: 6%
      Maturity: 8 years
   d) Bond A Coupon: 10%
      Maturity: 1 year
      Bond B Coupon: zero percent
      Maturity: 10 years
9) What are the features common to most preferred stock? What does it mean if a preferred stock is in arrears? What is the advantage associated with cumulative preferred stock? Why is the earnings-per-preferred-share ratio important for the selection of a preferred stock?
10) From the viewpoint of the issuing corporation, preferred stock is less risky than bonds. From the viewpoint of the investor, the reverse is true: Preferred stock is more risky than debt. Why are these statements true?

Problems*

1) A $1,000 bond has the following features: a coupon rate of 8 percent, interest that is paid semiannually (i.e., $40 every six months), and a maturity date of ten years.
   a) What is the bond's price if comparable debt yields 8 percent?
   b) What is the bond's price if comparable debt yields 10 percent?
   c) What is the current yield if the bond sells for the prices determined in questions (a) and (b)?
   d) Why are the prices different for questions (a) and (b)?

*Generally, bonds make interest payments semiannually. Interest tables, however, may preclude semiannual calculations. Except for problem #1, the principles being illustrated are independent of annual or semiannual interest payments. Appendix B provides answers to selected problems using both annual and semiannual calculations.

2) A $1,000 bond has a coupon rate of 10 percent and matures after eight years. Interest rates are currently 7 percent.
   a) What will the price of this bond be if the interest is paid annually?
   b) What will the price be if investors expect that the bond will be called with no call penalty after two years?
   c) What will the price be if investors expect that the bond will be called after two years and there will be a call penalty of one year's interest?
   d) Why are your answers different for questions (a), (b), and (c)?
3) A company has two bonds outstanding. The first matures after five years and has a coupon rate of 8.25 percent. The second matures after ten years and has a coupon rate of 8.25 percent. Interest rates are currently 10 percent. What is the present price of each $1,000 bond? Why are these prices different?
4) If a $1,000 bond with a 9 percent coupon (paid annually) and a maturity date of ten years is selling for $939, what is the current yield and the yield to maturity?
5) A $1,000 zero coupon bond sells for $519 and matures after five years. What is the yield to maturity?
6) Given the following information:

   XY Inc. 5% bond
   AB Inc. 14% bond

   Both bonds are for $1,000, mature in 20 years, and are rated AAA.
   a) What should be the current market price of each bond if the interest rate on triple-A bonds is 10 percent?
   b) Which bond has a current yield that exceeds its yield to maturity?
   c) Which bond would you expect to be called if interest rates are 10 percent?
   d) If CD Inc. had a bond outstanding with a 5 percent coupon and a maturity date of 20 years but it was rated BBB, what would you expect its price to be relative to the XY Inc. bond?
7) a) If a preferred stock pays an annual dividend of $6 and investors can earn 10 percent on alternative and comparable investments, what is the maximum price that should be paid for this stock?
   b) If the preferred stock in part (a) had a call feature and investors expected the stock to be called for $100 after ten years, what is the maximum price that investors should pay for the stock?
   c) If investors can earn 12 percent on comparable investments, what should be the price of the preferred stock in part (a)? What would be the price if comparable yields are 8 percent? What generalization do these answers imply?
8) What should be the prices of the following preferred stocks if comparable securities yield 6 percent, 8 percent, and 10 percent?
   a) MN, Inc., $4 preferred ($100 par).
   b) CH, Inc., $4 preferred ($100 par with the additional requirement that the firm must retire the preferred after 20 years).

   Why should the prices of these securities be different?
9) Company X has the following bonds outstanding:

Bond A		Bond B	
Coupon	8%	Coupon	Variable—changes annually
Maturity	10 years	Maturity	10 years

   Initially, both bonds sold at $1,000 with yields to maturity of 8 percent.
   a) After two years, the interest rate on comparable debt is 10 percent. What should be the price of each bond?
   b) After two additional years (i.e., four years after issue date), the interest rate on comparable debt is 7 percent. What should be the price of each bond?
   c) What generalization may be drawn from the prices in questions (a) and (b)?

10) A bond has the following features:

Principal amount	$1,000
Interest rate (the coupon)	11.5%
Maturity	10 years
Sinking fund	None
Call feature	After two years
Call penalty	One year's interest

a) If comparable yields are 12 percent, what should be the price of this bond?
b) Would you expect the firm to call the bond if yields are 12 percent?
c) If comparable yields are 8 percent, what should be the price of the bond?
d) Would the firm call the bond today if yields are 8 percent?
e) If you expected the bond to be called after three years, what is the maximum price you would pay for the bond if the current interest rate is 8 percent?

11) What is the price of the following split coupon bond if comparable yields are 12 percent?

Principal	$1,000
Maturity	12 years
Annual coupon	0% ($0) for years 1–3
	10% ($100) for years 4–12

If comparable yields decline to 10 percent, what is the appreciation in the price of the bond?

12) A bond has the following terms:

Principal amount	$1,000
Annual interest payment	$140 starting after five years have passed (i.e., in year 6)
Maturity	12 years
Callable at $1.14 (i.e., face value + one year's interest)	

a) Why do you believe that the terms were constructed as specified?
b) What is the bond's price if comparable debt yields 12 percent?
c) What is the bond's current yield?
d) Even though interest rates have fallen, why may you not expect the bond to be called?

13) An extendable bond has the following features:

Principal	$1,000
Coupon	9.5% ($95 annually)
Maturity	8 years but the issuer may extend the maturity for 5 years

a) If comparable yields are 12 percent, what will be the price of the bond if investors anticipate that it will be retired after eight years?
b) What impact will the expectation that the bond will be retired after 13 years have on its current price if comparable yields are 12 percent?
c) If comparable yields remain 12 percent, would you expect the firm to retire the bond after eight years?

14) You purchase a 7 percent $1,000 bond with a term of ten years and reinvest all interest payments. If interest rates rise to 10 percent after you purchase the bond, what is the return on your investment in the bond?

15) The prices of longer-term bonds are more volatile than the prices of shorter-term bonds with the same coupon. The prices of bonds with smaller coupons are more volatile than bonds with larger coupons for the same term to maturity. However, you cannot compare the relative price changes on bonds with different coupons and maturities unless you consider their durations. Consider the following bonds:

Bond	Coupon	Term
A	8%	8 years
B	14%	10 years

The price of which bond will fall more if interest rates rise from the current yield to maturity of 8 percent? To answer the question, calculate the duration of both bonds.

16) Compute the duration for bond C, and rank the bonds on the basis of their price volatility. The current rate of interest is 8 percent, so the prices of bonds A and B are $1,000 and $1,268, respectively.

Bond	Coupon	Term	Duration
A	8%	10 years	7.25
B	12%	10 years	6.74
C	8%	5 years	?

Confirm your ranking by calculating the percentage change in the price of each bond when interest rates rise from 8 to 12 percent. (Bond A's and B's prices become $774 and $1,000, respectively.)

17) a) What is the price of each of the following bonds ($1,000 principal) if the current interest rate is 9 percent?

Firm A	Coupon	6%
	Maturity	5 years
Firm B	Coupon	6%
	Maturity	20 years
Firm C	Coupon	15%
	Maturity	5 years
Firm D	Coupon	15%
	Maturity	20 years
Firm E	Coupon	0% (zero coupon bond)
	Maturity	5 years
Firm F	Coupon	0% (zero coupon bond)
	Maturity	20 years

b) What is the duration of each bond?

c) Rank the bonds in terms of price fluctuations with the least volatile bond first and the most volatile bond last as judged by each bond's duration.

d) Confirm your volatility rankings by determining the percentage change in the price of each bond if interest rates rise to 12 percent.

e) What generalizations can be made from the above exercise concerning (a) low- versus high-coupon bonds, (b) intermediate- versus long-term bonds, and (c) zero coupon bonds?

18) A 10-year bond with a 9 percent coupon will sell for $1,000 when interest rates are 9 percent. What is the duration of this bond? Using duration to forecast the change in the price of the bond, calculate the difference between the forecasted and the actual price change according to the bond valuation model for the following interest rates: 9.2, 9.4, 9.6, 9.8, 10.0, 10.5, 11.0, and 12.0 percent.

19) In the section on the yield to call, a bond pays annual interest of $80 and matures after ten years. The bond is valued at $1,147 if the comparable rate is 6 percent and the bond is held to maturity. If, however, an investor expects the bond to be called for $1,050 after five years, the value of the bond would be $1,122. (See footnote 5.) Investor A expects the bond to be called and investor B expects the bond not to be called. Investor A sells the bond to B for $1,122. What is the annual return earned by B if the bond is not called? Why is this yield greater than the 6 percent earned on comparable securities?

20) Determine the times-dividend-earned ratio given the following information:

30% corporate income tax rate
$10,000 EBIT (earnings before interest and taxes)
$2,000 interest owed
$2,000 preferred stock dividends

21) A firm with earnings before interest and taxes of $500,000 needs $1 million of additional funds. If it issues debt, the bonds will mature after 20 years and have a coupon of 10 percent. The firm could issue a preferred stock with a dividend rate of 10 percent. The firm has 100,000 shares of common stock outstanding and is in the 30 percent corporate income tax bracket. What are the earnings per common share under the two alternative financings?

22) (This problem uses the material in Appendix 16B concerning bond valuation.) Two bonds have the following features:

Bond A		Bond B	
Principal	$1,000	Principal	$1,000
Coupon	6%	Coupon	12%
Maturity	5 years	Maturity	5 years

The structure of yields is

Term	Interest Rate
1 year	6%
2 years	7%
3 years	8%
4 years	9%
5 years	10%

a) What is the valuation of each security based on the yield to maturity for a five-year bond?
b) What is the valuation based on the structure of yields?
c) Given the valuations in (b), what is each bond's yield to maturity?
d) Do the yields to maturity in (c) differ from each other and from the assumed yield to maturity in (a)?
e) Given the price of bond A in (a), what would you do? Why?

THE FINANCIAL ADVISOR'S INVESTMENT CASE

Bonds, Bonds, and More Bonds

Karita Canela is an individual with low risk tolerance who has just inherited $100,000. She has no immediate needs for the funds but would like to supplement her current income. Thus, Canela is considering investing these funds in debt instruments, since the interest and repayment of principal are legal obligations of the issuer. While she realizes that the borrower could default on the payments, she believes this is unlikely, especially if she limits her choices to triple- or double-A-rated bonds. Canela does realize that she could earn more interest by purchasing lower-rated bonds but is not certain that she is capable of bearing the risk.

Besides risk and expected return, Canela decides that tax considerations must also play a role in this investment decision. She is currently in the 28 percent federal income tax bracket and pays state income tax of 5 percent. She believes that her job is relatively secure and that her salary will increase over time but does not expect it to rise sufficiently so that her income tax brackets will be significantly increased.

Canela quickly learned that there are many bonds among which to choose. For example, the PHONE Company has four double-A bonds outstanding. Their annual interest payments (or coupon rate), term to maturity, price, and yield to maturity are

Bond	Interest per $1,000 Bond	Coupon
A	$ 50	5%
B	100	10
C	100	10
D	80	8

Bond	Term	Price	Yield to Maturity
A	1 year	$ 981	7.0%
B	5 years	1,035	9.1
C	10 years	1,000	10.0
D	20 years	742	11.3

Currently the interest rate of long-term debt ranges from 9 to 11.5 percent, but Canela expects that this rate will fall, as inflation is declining. In addition, the level of unemployment is increasing, so Canela anticipates that the Federal Reserve will take actions to stimulate the economy through reductions in the rate of interest. She believes that interest rates could fall to 8 percent within a year. Of course, she also realizes that this decline may not occur—or even if it does, that interest rates could rise again after the initial decline. Canela decided to analyze the four PHONE Company bonds to determine which may be the best investment under various assumptions concerning future interest rate behavior. To do this she sought your help in answering the following questions:

1) a) What would be the expected price of each bond one year from now if interest rates were 8 percent?

b) What would be the expected price two years from now if interest rates initially fall but subsequently rise to 12 percent at the end of the second year?

2) If interest rates were expected to fall and not rise back to 12 percent, which alternative is best?

3) If interest rates were expected to decline initially and then rise, which alternative should be selected?

4) If bond A were selected, what would happen after a year elapses? What decision must then be made?

The answers to these questions emphasize to Canela the importance of expected future interest rates on the selection of a bond. Since she firmly believes that interest rates will fall and remain below current levels for several years, she has decided to select bond D, the longest-term bond that would lock in the current high yields. However, she has also decided to consider other bonds to determine what additional returns she could earn for bearing more risk, along with the tax implications of her selections. She has noticed that the following ten-year bonds are available:

Bond	Interest per $1,000	Price	Yield to Maturity	Rating
U.S. Treasury	$ 0	$ 463	8%	—
U.S. Treasury	80	1,000	8	—
WEAK Inc.	140	1,000	14	B
WEAK Inc.	120	896	14	B

At this point Canela is sufficiently frustrated and asks your advice. As her financial advisor, which bond(s) do you recommend? In your advice, specifically explain the tax implications (both in terms of income and capital gains) of each bond. Also consider her willingness to bear risk and the anticipated flow of income both from the bonds and her job. Then construct a portfolio that you believe meets her needs and willingness to bear risk. Assume that the bonds are sold in units of $1,000 with a minimum purchase of $10,000. Exclude the impact of commissions and accrued interest.

THE FINANCIAL ADVISOR'S INVESTMENT CASE
High-Yield Securities and Relative Risk

Stephanie Waldron is an aggressive individual whose career as a self-employed management consultant has blossomed. Waldron is both willing and able to bear substantial risk in order to earn a higher return. She is also very independent, preferring to make her own investment decisions after considering various alternatives. She has a Keogh account that she manages herself. Although she could select various types of mutual funds as investment vehicles for the account, she prefers to select specific assets. The account's value exceeds $200,000, and Waldron recently liquidated several securities whose prices had risen sufficiently so that she believed further price increases to be unlikely.

As her financial planner, you believe that high-yield debt instruments would be an attractive alternative to stocks, whose prices have risen recently. High-yield securities offer larger returns but may involve substantial risk. The combination of high risk and high return are consistent with Waldron's investment philosophy, so she has asked you to suggest several alternative high-yield bonds. The terms of several B-rated bonds are as follows:

Company	Coupon	Maturity Date (Years)	Price	Yield to Maturity
A	10%	10	$ 900	11.752%
B	15	15	1,200	12.055
C	0	7	487	10.825
D	7	10	772	10.847

Waldron is interested in each of the bonds but has several questions concerning their risk. Since each bond has the same rating, it seems reasonable to conclude that the probability of default is about the same for each bond. However, there may be considerable difference in their price volatility. Waldron has asked you to rank each bond from the least to the most price volatile. She also wants you to compare the bonds' price volatility with the triple-A-rated bonds with the same terms to maturity. To do this, you have found four triple-A-rated bonds with the following terms:

Company	Coupon	Maturity Date (Years)	Price	Yield to Maturity
E	6.5%	10	$ 900	7.990%
F	10.5	15	1,200	8.143
G	0	7	587	7.908
H	4.5	10	772	7.879

If interest rates rise by 3 percent across the board, what will be the new price of each of the eight bonds? What do these new prices suggest about the price volatility of high-yield versus high-quality bonds? To answer this last question, compare bond A to bond E, B to F, C to G, and D to H. Which bonds' prices were more volatile? If two bonds with the same term to maturity sell for the same price, which bond may subject the investor to more interest rate risk? Does acquiring bonds with higher credit ratings and less default risk also imply the investor has less interest rate risk?

APPENDIX 16A

Bond Discounts/Premiums & Duration Compared

The discussion in the body of the chapter explained how increases in interest rates cause the prices of existing bonds to fall. Declining interest rates have the opposite effect; bond prices rise. For bonds with the same coupon, the amount of the price change varies with the term of the bond. The longer the term, the greater is the price fluctuation. The discussion also indicated that longer duration is associated with greater price fluctuations. Since both discussions were concerned with price fluctuations, both were also concerned with risk.

The two concepts, however, are different. Consider the two bonds in Exhibit 16A.1 and illustrated in Figure 16A.1. Both bonds have an 8 percent coupon rate of interest; the difference between the bonds is the term, 10 years and 20 years. The exhibit and figure give the premium or discount and the duration for each bond at different interest rates. At a current rate of 3 percent, both bonds sell for a premium, but the 20-year bond sells for a larger premium. As the current interest rate rises, the prices of both bonds fall. They sell for their face value when the coupon and the current rate of interest are equal at 8 percent. As the market rate of interest continues to rise, both bonds sell for a discount. Both the discount and the premium are larger for the bond with the longer term, but the difference between the discounts diminishes as the interest rate continues to rise. Since the maximum possible discount is the face amount of the bond ($1,000), the discount for the bond with the shorter term approaches the discount for the bond with the longer term.

Duration also declines for both bonds as the market interest rate rises. While the duration for the 10-year bond does decline, the change is small (e.g., from 7.6 to 6.37 years as interest rates rise from 3 to 14 percent). The decline in the duration of the 20-year bond is much larger (e.g., from 12.65 to 7.75 years as interest rates rise from 3 to 14 percent). The duration of the 20-year bond approaches the dura-

EXHIBIT 16A.1

Premiums or (Discounts) and the Durations for 8 Percent Bonds with Terms to Maturity of 10 and 20 Years at Different Rates of Interest

	10-Year Bond		20-Year Bond	
Interest Rate	Premium/(Discount)	Duration	Premium/(Discount)	Duration
3%	$429	7.60	$748	12.65
4	327	7.50	547	12.18
5	234	7.39	377	11.71
6	149	7.29	231	11.23
7	71	7.18	107	10.76
8	0	7.07	0	10.29
9	(65)	6.95	(92)	9.83
10	(125)	6.84	(172)	9.39
11	(179)	6.73	(241)	8.95
12	(229)	6.61	(301)	8.53
13	(275)	6.49	(354)	8.13
14	(318)	6.37	(400)	7.75
⋮	⋮	⋮	⋮	⋮
20	(511)	5.65	(587)	5.85

tion of the bond with the smaller term. At 21.5 percent the durations are equal, and for higher interest rates, the duration of the 20-year bond is actually less than the duration of the 10-year bond.

Exhibit 16A.2 (p. 542) and Figure 16A.2 (p. 543) present the premiums and discounts and the durations for bonds with *different coupons* and 10- and 20-year terms to maturity when the current rate of interest is 8 percent. Exhibit 16A.1 held constant the bond's coupon and varied the rate of interest; Exhibit 16A.2 holds constant the rate of interest and varies the coupon. The bonds with the lower coupons sell for a larger discount, and the longer the term, the greater is the discount. The zero coupon 20-year bond's price is $208 (a discount of $792), while the

FIGURE 16A.1

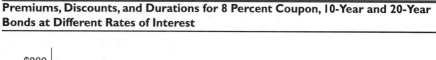

Premiums, Discounts, and Durations for 8 Percent Coupon, 10-Year and 20-Year Bonds at Different Rates of Interest

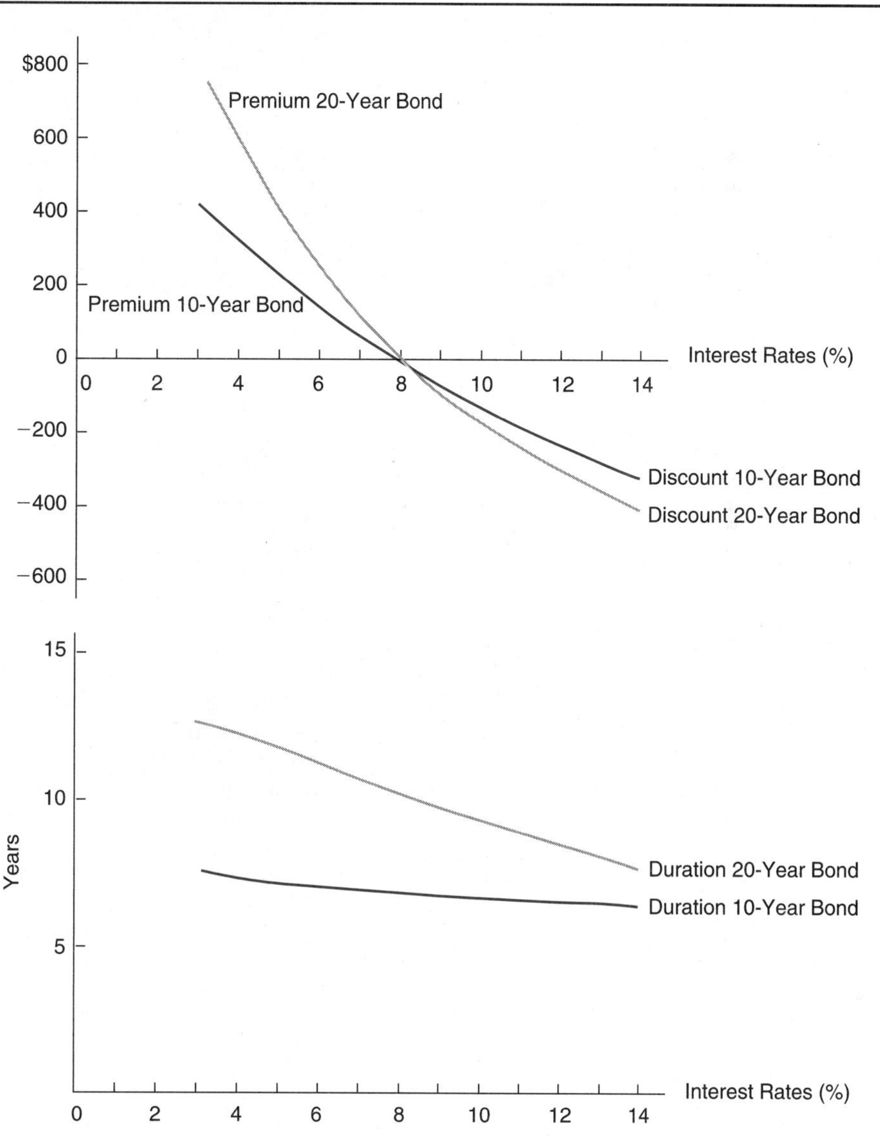

EXHIBIT 16A.2

Premiums or (Discounts) and the Durations When Interest Rates Are 8 Percent for Bonds with Terms to Maturity of 10 and 20 Years at Different Coupons

	10-Year Bond		20-Year Bond	
Coupon Rate	Premium/(Discount)	Duration	Premium/(Discount)	Duration
0%	($554)	10.00	($792)	20.00
2	(407)	8.76	(594)	14.03
3	(340)	8.33	(495)	12.79
4	(272)	7.99	(396)	12.00
5	(204)	7.70	(297)	11.38
6	(136)	7.45	(198)	10.92
7	(68)	7.25	(99)	10.57
8	0	7.07	0	10.29
9	68	6.91	99	10.06
10	136	6.78	198	9.87
11	204	6.65	297	9.71
12	272	6.61	396	9.57
13	340	6.44	495	9.45
14	407	6.35	594	9.34
⋮	⋮	⋮	⋮	⋮
20	815	5.96	1188	8.91

10-year bond would sell for $446 and a $554 discount. As the coupon increases, the discount decreases. When the coupon exceeds the current rate of interest, the bond sells for a premium, and the longer the term of the bond, the larger is the premium. For example, the 10- and 20-year bonds with the 12 percent coupons sell for premiums of $272 and $396, respectively.

The coupon also affects each bond's duration. Higher coupons imply that cash is received faster, so the duration declines as the coupon increases. This relationship is also verified in Exhibit 16A.2. While the durations are equal to the term of the bond for the zero coupon bonds, the durations diminish as the coupons increase. As is also indicated in the exhibit, the numerical value of the 20-year bonds' duration declines more rapidly than the duration of the 10-year bonds.

Notice that in both exhibits as the numerical value of the left-hand column increases, that is, the interest rate or the coupon increases, the duration diminishes. Higher interest rates (i.e., lower bond prices and larger discounts) and higher coupons produce smaller durations. The investor is receiving more cash flow earlier, so the duration is smaller. This relation is different than the relationship between the values in the left-hand column and the premium/discount column. Higher interest rates and *lower* coupons produce larger discounts, while smaller interest rates and *larger* coupons generate larger premiums.

FIGURE 16A.2

Discounts, Premiums, and Durations for 10- and 20-Year Bonds with Different Coupons (Interest Rate = 8 Percent)

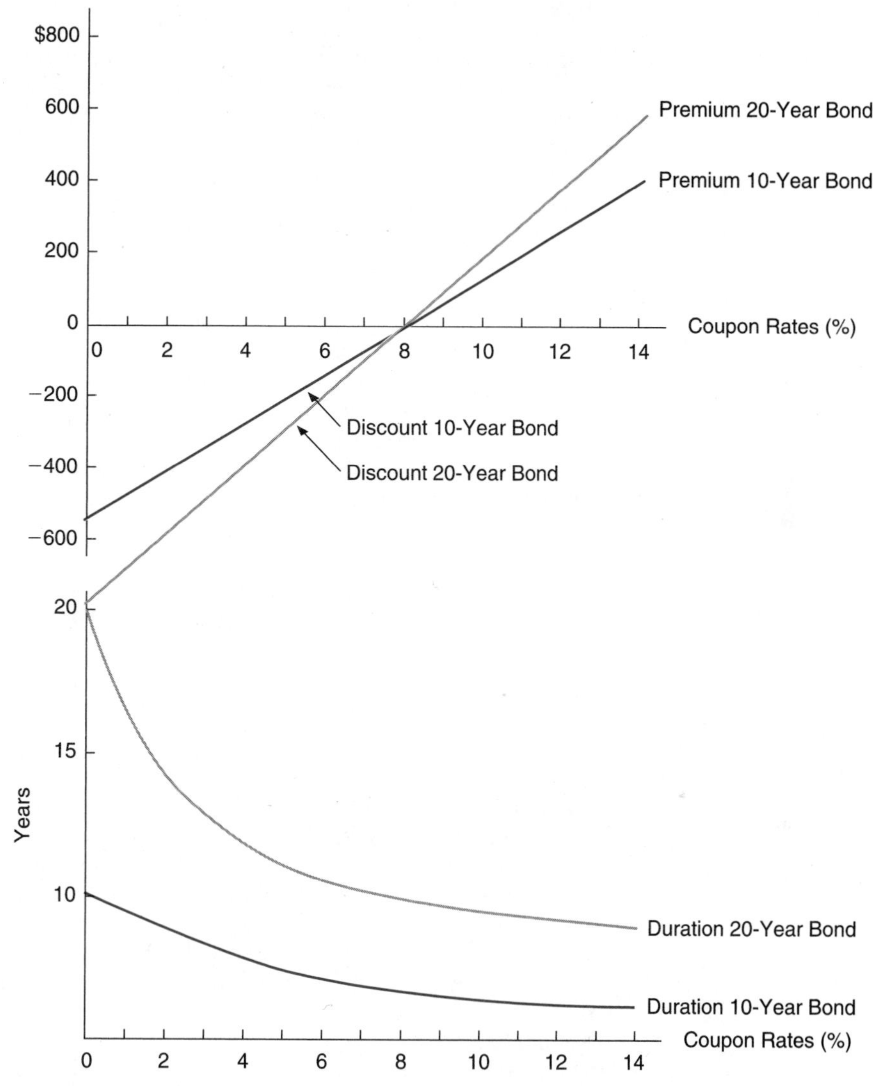

APPENDIX 16B

Using the Yield to Maturity to Price a Bond

In the body of this chapter, once the price of a bond is known, the yield to maturity can be determined. That yield is the discount rate that equates the cash inflows (the interest payments and principal repayment at maturity) from the bond and its price (the initial cash outflow). The discussion also illustrated how the price of a bond may be determined. The price of a bond is the present value of all the cash flows discounted back at the appropriate discount factor (i.e., rate of interest).

The use of the yield to maturity to determine that value, however, may misprice the bond. The source of this mispricing is the assumption that the yield to maturity is the appropriate rate to discount all the future payments. For this assumption to apply, the yield curve (the structure of yields) must be flat so that all payments should be discounted at that unique rate, the yield to maturity. (The same assumption was made in the illustrations of the impact of changes in the reinvestment rate on the terminal value. Since all interest payments were reinvested at the same rate, the assumption has to be that the yield curve is flat. That is, the yield is the same for all terms to maturity.)

If the yield curve is positively sloping, then using the yield to maturity to price a bond undervalues the security. Consider a five-year bond with an 8 percent coupon. The structure of yields is as follows:

Term	Interest Rate
1 year	6%
2 years	7
3 years	8
4 years	9
5 years	10

If 10 percent (the yield on a five-year bond) is used to determine the value, the bond is worth \$924.18. (PMT = \$80; FV = \$1,000; N = 5, and I = 10; PV = −\$924.18.) Is this valuation accurate? Since the value of a bond is the present value of the cash flows, the value of the first \$80 should be discounted at 6 percent. The second, third, and fourth interest payments should be discounted at 7, 8, and 9 percent, respectively. The \$1,080 to be received at the end of the fifth year is discounted at 10 percent. What is the present value of these cash inflows, each of which is discounted at a different rate? The answer is \$936.13 [\$80(0.943) + 80(0.873) + 80(0.794) + 80(0.708) + 1,080(0.621)].

Given the structure of yields, the bond should sell for \$936.12 and not the \$924.18 determined when 10 percent was used to discount all the cash inflows. If the investor does buy the bond for \$936.13, the yield to maturity is 9.67 percent. (PMT = \$80, FV = \$1,000, N = 5, and PV = −\$936.13; I = 9.67.) The actual yield to maturity is less than 10 percent. The use of 10 percent underprices the bond, which overstates its yield.

If the bond did sell for \$924.18, an opportunity for an arbitrage profit would exist.[1] The investor buys the bond and strips the coupons (removes the interest payments from the principal). Each of the coupons and the principal are then sold separately as if they were a zero coupon bond. That is, the \$80 coupon paid after one year is sold as a one-year zero coupon bond priced to yield 6 percent (\$75.47).

[1]Arbitrage is the act of buying in one market and simultaneously selling in another to take advantage of differences in prices between the two markets. It is explained in more detail in the sections on the intrinsic value of an option, put–call parity, and programmed trading and index arbitrage.

The second coupon is sold as a two-year zero coupon bond priced to yield 7 percent ($69.88). The third-, fourth-, and fifth-year coupons are sold as three-, four-, and five-year zero coupon bonds. The principal is also sold as a five year zero coupon bond at 10 percent. What is the value of all these zero coupon bonds? The answer is $936.13, the price of the bond when the structure of yields is used to value the bond. Thus, if an investor could purchase the bond for $924.18 (the value using the yield to maturity based on the bond's term), separate the individual cash payments, and sell each payment as a zero coupon bond, that individual would be assured of a profit. The source of the profit is, of course, the undervaluation of the bond that results from using the yield to maturity to price the bond.

When the yield to maturity is used to determine the value of a bond, all bonds with the same term and risk class (i.e., same credit rating) must have that same yield. This would be true even if the bonds have different coupons. When valuation is based on the structure of yields, bonds with different coupons may have different yields to maturity. Consider two five-year bonds, one of which has a 4 percent coupon and the other a 10 percent coupon. The current structure of yields is as follows:

Term	Interest Rate
1 year	5%
2 years	6
3 years	7
4 years	8
5 years	9

Their valuations based on the structure of yields are $811.72 and $1,054.30, respectively. Given these prices, the yield to maturity for the 4 percent coupon bond is 8.82 percent. (PV = $−811.72, PMT = $40, FV = $1,000, N = 5; I = 8.82.) The yield to maturity for the 10 percent coupon bond is 8.62 percent. (PV = $−1054.3, PMT = $100, FV = $1,000, N = 5; I = 8.62.) The differences in the coupons and the use of the structure of yields to value the bonds result in their having different yields to maturity even though their terms to maturity are the same.

17 Government Securities

In the late 1990s, one of the big political issues in Washington was what to do with the projected federal government surplus. During most of the 1990s, the issue was the opposite: the size of the federal government's deficit. Deficits occur when disbursements (expenditures) exceed receipts (revenues). Whenever a deficit occurs, the general public or the various financial institutions must finance it. In order to raise money to cover its expenditures, the federal government issues a variety of debt instruments. This variety helps the government tap the different sources of funds that are available in the money and capital markets.

Even if the federal government is currently operating at a surplus, prior deficits mean there are many federal government securities already outstanding. This chapter is primarily concerned with these securities. The first section discusses the various types of debt issued by the federal government, which range from short-term Treasury bills to long-term Treasury bonds. The second section briefly considers the debt issued by the various agencies of the federal government, and the last section discusses the debt issued by state and local governments. Special emphasis is placed on the feature that distinguishes state and local government debt from other securities: The interest paid to bondholders is exempt from federal income taxation.

Learning Objectives

After completing this chapter you should be able to:

1. Distinguish among the types of federal government debt.
2. Identify the sources of risk from investing in federal government securities.
3. Distinguish between the federal government's moral obligation and its full faith and credit obligations to its agencies' debt.
4. Isolate the primary advantage of state and local debt.
5. Illustrate how to equalize yields on corporate and state and local debt.
6. Differentiate revenue bonds from general obligation bonds.
7. Compare Treasury bonds, T-bills, inflation-indexed securities, federal agency debt, municipal bonds, and anticipation notes.

The Variety of Federal Government Debt

According to the Economic Report of the President, the federal government made interest payments of $222.8 billion in 2000 on its debt. This sum was substantial and amounted to about 12.5 percent of the total expenditures made by the federal government in that year. The debt was financed by a variety of investors, including individuals, corporations, and financial institutions. To induce this diverse group of investors to purchase its debt, the federal government has issued different types of debt instruments that appeal to the various potential buyers.[1]

---

[1]Information concerning the public debt is available through the Treasury's public debt Web site (http://www.publicdebt.treas.gov) and includes yields on savings bonds and Treasury bills (as of the auction date), and how the investor may buy these Treasury obligations directly from the federal government.

EXHIBIT 17.1

The Variety of Federal Government Debt as of July 31, 2000

	Length of Time to Maturity	Value (in Billions of Dollars)	Percentage of Total Debt
Treasury bills	Less than 1 year	$ 616.2	10.9%
Intermediate-term notes	One to 5 years	1,611.3	28.4
Long-term bonds	Over 5 years	635.3	11.2
Savings bonds	Various maturities	177.7	3.1
Other debt*	Various maturities	2,633.7	46.4

*Debt held by U.S. government agencies and trust funds and state and local governments.
Source: *Federal Reserve Bulletin*, February 2001, p. A27.

For investors, the unique advantage offered by the federal government's debt is its safety. These debt instruments are the safest of all possible investments, for there is no question that the U.S. Treasury is able to pay the interest and repay the principal. The source of this safety is the federal government's constitutional right to tax and to print money. Because there is no specified limitation on the federal government's capacity to create money, only Congress can enact legislation (e.g., the debt ceiling) that restricts the federal government's ability to retire or refinance its debt.

The various types of federal government debt and the amount outstanding of each are illustrated in Exhibit 17.1. As may be seen in the exhibit, there has been an emphasis on the use of short- and intermediate-term (five years or less) financing by the Treasury. This emphasis is partially explained by interest costs. Interest rates on short-term debt are usually lower than those on long-term debt. (See Figure 15.3 for the yields on short-term and long-term federal government debt.) Hence, the use of short-term financing reduces the Treasury's interest expense. Furthermore, Congress restricts the interest rate that the Treasury may pay on long-term debt, but it does not restrict the interest rate on short-term securities. Thus, during periods of high interest rates, the Treasury may not be permitted to sell long-term securities even if it desires to do so.

Nonmarketable Federal Government Debt

series EE (Patriot) bonds
Savings bonds issued in small denominations by the federal government.

Perhaps the most widely held federal government debt is the series E and **series EE bonds**. (On November 16, 2001, the Treasury announced that EE bonds sold through financial institutions would be designated as "Patriot bonds.") The series E bond was designed to encourage saving by people of modest means, as it was sold in small denominations (e.g., $25, $100, $500, and up to $10,000). Although virtually every person should have been able to place modest amounts of savings in these bonds, an individual was allowed to purchase no more than $10,000 worth of series E bonds in a calendar year.

Series E bonds paid no interest but were purchased at a discount (i.e., below their face value). For example, if a saver purchased a $25 series E bond for $18.75 and held it until maturity five years and five months later, he or she received $25 and earned 6 percent annually on the investment. If the bonds were cashed in prior to maturity, the holder received less than $25 and earned a yield of less than

6 percent. (The yield started at 4 percent and rose over the lifetime of the bond until it reached 6 percent at the bond's maturity. This ascending structure of yields is an incentive to hold the bonds until maturity.)

Series E bonds were initially issued in 1941 to help finance World War II expenditures. At that time the bonds had a maturity of ten years and a yield of 2.9 percent. As interest rates have risen, the length of time to maturity has been reduced, which has had the effect of increasing the yield on the bonds.

Although series E bonds did mature, the Treasury initially did not require that the bonds be redeemed. Instead, the maturities were extended and interest continued to accrue. The rate earned on these older bonds has been increased, so the yield is comparable to that earned by the series EE (Patriot) bond that is currently being sold. The Treasury, however, will no longer extend the maturity of E bonds. As they reach final maturity, the bonds will cease to earn interest, and holders will have to redeem or exchange them for other bonds. Failure to redeem or exchange the bonds will result in a loss of interest.

On January 2, 1980, the Treasury started to issue a new bond, series EE, to replace the series E bonds. Like the E bonds, the new bonds were issued at a discount. The smallest denomination was $50, which cost $25. In November 1982, the Treasury changed the method for computing interest on EE bonds from a fixed rate to a variable rate, which is changed every six months. (You may find the current rate by dialing 1-800-US BONDS. Additional information concerning E and EE bonds may be obtained from savingsbonds.com inc. (http://www.savingsbonds.com), which offers a service that provides interest earned, cash-in values, and final maturity dates of all issues of E and EE bonds. The service also tells you which bonds have ceased earning interest.) The variable rate permits the small investor to participate in higher yields when interest rates rise, but the investor will earn less when interest rates fall.

Effective May 1, 1995, the terms of series EE bonds were once again changed, but bonds issued before that date are not affected by the changes. The term of the new EE bonds was set at 17 years. If the bonds are not redeemed at maturity, they will continue to earn interest for an additional 13 years, for a total of 30 years. The interest rate is announced every May 1 and November 1 and applies for the following six months. The new rate is 90 percent of an average of the rate paid by five-year Treasury securities for the preceding three months. Interest is added to the value of the bonds every six months after they are purchased.

There are several major differences between series EE (Patriot) bonds and most other investments, such as savings accounts. The interest earned on Patriot bonds is not subject to federal income taxation until the bonds are redeemed or reach final maturity. (For bonds purchased in 1990 or later, the interest is free of federal income tax if an amount equal to the proceeds is used to pay college tuition and fees. Proceeds used to pay room and board are *not* exempt from federal income taxation.) The interest earned on other investments, including savings accounts, is subject to federal income taxation during the year in which it is earned. Although the federal income tax on the EE series may be deferred until the bonds are redeemed, are disposed of, or mature (whichever comes first), the owner does have the option to have the interest taxed each year. Even though the funds are not received until the bond is redeemed, the owner may report the interest to the Internal Revenue Service on an accrual basis. However, most holders of previously issued series EE bonds have preferred to defer the tax payment.

The deferment of interest income until the bonds are redeemed can be advantageous in that the saver can cash in the bonds in those years when income from other sources is lower. For example, these bonds may be redeemed during retirement or times of temporary unemployment. It is likely that the individual's taxable income will be lower during these periods, and thus the taxes paid on the accrued interest earned by the bonds will be lower. By allowing investors to determine when the interest will be subject to taxation, series EE (Patriot) bonds offer the investor an opportunity to reduce the amount of taxes paid on the interest. Since they are sold in small units, these bonds offer a means that is available to virtually every investor to shelter income from taxes. Such tax sheltering of interest income is not available through other savings instruments, such as accounts in commercial banks or savings and loan associations.

Another important difference between series EE (Patriot) bonds and other bonds is that there is no secondary market in these bonds. If the owner wants immediate cash, the bonds cannot be sold. Instead, the investor redeems them at a commercial bank. Nor can the bonds be transferred as a gift, although they can be transferred through an estate. The Treasury also forbids the use of series EE bonds as collateral. Thus, while corporate debt may be used to secure a personal loan, these bonds cannot.

series HH bonds
Income bonds issued by the federal government.

The investor may exchange series EE (and old series E) for **HH bonds**. The HH series (like the EE bonds) is a new series designed to replace the series H bonds. Series H and HH bonds are different from E and EE bonds in several ways. They are sold at par in larger denominations, with $500 being the minimum investment. The bonds mature in 20 years and pay 4 percent interest if held to maturity. The interest is paid every year and does not accumulate as it does with the series EE bonds. Interest is subject to federal income taxation each year, while taxation on series EE bonds may be deferred until the bonds are redeemed. Series HH bonds are more attractive to investors who need safe sources of current income, while series EE bonds are attractive to conservative investors who wish to build up capital but who do not need current income.

Marketable Securities

Treasury Bills

Treasury bills
Short-term federal government securities.

Short-term federal government debt is issued in the form of **Treasury bills**. These bills are sold in denominations of $10,000 to $1,000,000 and mature in 3 to 12 months. Like series EE (Patriot) bonds, they are sold at a discount; however, unlike series EE bonds, the discounted price is not set. Instead, the Treasury continually auctions off the bills, which go to the highest bidders. For example, if an investor bids $9,700 and obtains the bill, he or she will receive $10,000 when the bill matures, which is a yield of 3.1 percent ($300 ÷ $9,700) for the holding period. If the bid price had been higher, the interest cost to the Treasury (and the yield to the buyer) would have been lower.

Once Treasury bills have been auctioned, they may be bought and sold in the secondary market. They are issued in book-entry form and are easily marketed. There is an active secondary market in these bills, and they are quoted daily in the financial press and many city newspapers. These quotes and the quotes for other federal government securities are illustrated in Exhibit 17.2 (p. 550). For Treasury bills the quotes are given in the following form:

Maturity	Days to Maturity	Bid	Asked	Ask Yield
12/06/01	126	3.49	3.47	3.56

These quotes indicate that for a Treasury bill maturing on December 6, 2001, buyers were willing to bid a discounted price that produced a discount yield of 3.49 percent. Sellers, however, were willing to sell (offer) the bills at a smaller discount (higher price) that returned a discount yield of 3.47 percent. The annualized yield on the bill based on the asked price is 3.56 percent.

EXHIBIT 17.2

Prices and Yields for Selected Treasury Bills, Notes, and Bonds and Selected Government Agency Issues

TREASURY BONDS, NOTES & BILLS

Wednesday, August 1, 2001

Representative Over-the-Counter quotation based on transactions of $1 million or more.

Treasury bond, note and bill quotes are as of mid-afternoon. Colons in bid-and-asked quotes represent 32nds; 101:01 means 101 1/32. Net changes in 32nds. n-Treasury note. i-Inflation-Indexed issue. Treasury bill quotes in hundredths, quoted on terms of a rate of discount. Days to maturity calculated from settlement date. All yields are to maturity and based on the asked quote. Latest 13-week and 26-week bills are boldfaced. For bonds callable prior to maturity, yields are computed to the earliest call date for issues quoted above par and to the maturity date for issues below par. *-When issued.

Source: Telerate/Cantor Fitzgerald

U.S. Treasury strips as of 3 p.m. Eastern time, also based on transactions of $1 million or more. Colons in bid-and-asked quotes represent 32nds; 99:01 means 99 1/32. Net changes in 32nds. Yields calculated on the asked quotation. ci-stripped coupon interest. bp-Treasury bond, stripped principal. np-Treasury note, stripped principal. For bonds callable prior to maturity, yields are computed to the earliest call date for issues quoted above par and to the maturity date for issues below par.

Source: Bear, Stearns & Co. via Street Software Technology Inc.

GOVT. BOND & NOTES

RATE	MATURITY MO/YR	BID	ASKED	CHG.	ASKED YLD.
7⅞	Aug 01n	100:04	100:06	....	2.56
13¾	Aug 01	100:10	100:12	– 1	2.75
5½	Aug 01n	100:03	100:05	....	3.43
6½	Aug 01n	100:05	100:07	– 1	3.62
5⅝	Sep 01n	100:08	100:10	– 1	3.61
6⅜	Sep 01n	100:12	100:14	– 1	3.57
5⅞	Oct 01n	100:16	100:18	– 1	3.50
6¼	Oct 01n	100:18	100:20	– 2	3.61
7½	Nov 01n	101:01	101:03	– 2	3.57
15¾	Nov 01	103:12	103:14	– 2	3.47
5⅞	Nov 01n	100:22	100:24	– 2	3.53
6⅛	Dec 01n	101:00	101:02	– 2	3.48
6¼	Jan 02n	101:09	101:11	– 2	3.48
6⅜	Jan 02n	101:10	101:12	– 2	3.54
14¼	Feb 02	105:20	105:22	– 2	3.44
6¼	Feb 02n	101:17	101:19	– 1	3.44
6½	Feb 02n	101:22	101:24	....	3.41
6½	Mar 02n	101:29	101:31	– 1	3.45
6⅝	Mar 02n	101:31	102:01	– 1	3.48
6⅝	Apr 02n	102:02	102:04	– 1	3.45
6⅝	Apr 02n	102:08	102:10	– 1	3.44
7½	May 02n	103:01	103:03	– 2	3.46
6½	May 02n	102:13	102:15	– 1	3.44
6⅝	May 02n	102:16	102:18	– 1	3.45
6¼	Jun 02n	102:13	102:15	– 1	3.47
6⅜	Jun 02n	102:16	102:18	– 1	3.49
3⅝	Jul 02i	101:29	101:30	– 3	1.56
6	Jul 02n	102:12	102:14	– 1	3.48
6¼	Jul 02n	102:20	102:22	– 1	3.48
6⅜	Aug 02n	102:27	102:29	....	3.49
6⅛	Aug 02n	102:21	102:23	– 1	3.53
6¼	Aug 02n	102:25	102:27	– 1	3.54
5⅞	Sep 02n	102:18	102:20	– 1	3.54
6	Sep 02n	102:22	102:24	– 1	3.56
5¾	Oct 02n	102:18	102:20	– 1	3.57
11⅝	Nov 02	109:29	110:01	....	3.56
5⅝	Nov 02n	102:17	102:19	– 1	3.60
5¾	Nov 02n	102:22	102:24	– 1	3.61
5⅛	Dec 02n	102:00	102:02	....	3.61
5⅝	Dec 02n	102:22	102:24	....	3.60
4¾	Jan 03n	101:16	101:18	....	3.67
5½	Jan 03n	102:19	102:21	+ 1	3.66
6¼	Feb 03n	103:23	103:25	....	3.69
10¾	Feb 03	110:09	110:13	– 1	3.71
4⅝	Feb 03n	101:11	101:13	....	3.70
5½	Feb 03n	102:22	102:24	+ 1	3.69
4¼	Mar 03n	100:26	100:28	....	3.70
5½	Mar 03n	102:25	102:27	....	3.72
4	Apr 03n	100:12	100:14	....	3.74
5¾	Apr 03n	103:09	103:11	....	3.75
10¾	May 03	111:25	111:29	– 1	3.78
4¼	May 03n	100:24	100:26	....	3.78
5½	May 03n	102:30	103:00	– 1	3.78
3⅞	Jun 03n	100:04	100:05	– 1	3.79
5⅜	Jun 03n	102:26	102:28	– 1	3.80
3⅞	**Jul 03n**	**100:03**	**100:04**	**– 1**	**3.81**
5¼	Aug 03n	102:21	102:23	– 1	3.85
5¾	Aug 03n	103:19	103:21	– 2	3.86
11⅛	Aug 03	113:29	114:01	– 2	3.89
4¼	Nov 03n	100:18	100:20	– 2	3.96
8⅛	Aug 19	128:08	128:14	– 12	5.60
8½	Feb 20	132:30	133:04	– 13	5.60
8¾	May 20	136:03	136:09	– 12	5.60
8¾	Aug 20	136:08	136:14	– 14	5.61
7⅞	Feb 21	126:11	126:17	– 12	5.62
8⅛	May 21	129:14	129:20	– 13	5.62
8⅛	Aug 21	129:19	129:25	– 13	5.63
8	Nov 21	128:09	128:15	– 13	5.63
7¼	Aug 22	119:18	119:22	– 12	5.64
7⅝	Nov 22	124:09	124:15	– 13	5.64
7⅛	Feb 23	118:06	118:10	– 12	5.65
6¼	Aug 23	107:13	107:15	– 11	5.65
7½	Nov 24	123:24	123:30	– 11	5.64
7⅝	Feb 25	125:15	125:21	– 11	5.64
6⅞	Aug 25	115:27	115:31	– 10	5.65
6	Feb 26	104:14	104:16	– 9	5.66
6¾	Aug 26	114:16	114:20	– 10	5.65
6½	Nov 26	111:07	111:11	– 9	5.65
6⅝	Feb 27	112:30	113:02	– 10	5.65
6⅜	Aug 27	109:25	109:27	– 9	5.65
6⅛	Nov 27	106:15	106:17	– 9	5.64
3⅝	Apr 28i	104:00	104:01	– 6	3.39
5½	Aug 28	98:00	98:02	– 7	5.64
5¼	Nov 28	94:17	94:19	– 9	5.64
5¼	Feb 29	94:19	94:21	– 7	5.63
3⅞	Apr 29i	108:22	108:23	– 5	3.39
6⅛	Aug 29	106:31	107:01	– 9	5.62
6¼	May 30	109:10	109:11	– 10	5.59
5⅜	**Feb 31**	**97:24**	**97:25**	**– 10**	**5.53**
....	Feb 31wi	5:54	5:53	....	....

U.S. TREASURY STRIPS

MATURITY		TYPE	BID	ASKED	CHG.	ASKED YLD.
Aug	01	ci	99:29	99:29	....	3.16
Aug	01	np	99:28	99:28	....	3.54
Nov	01	ci	99:03	99:03	....	3.21
Nov	01	np	99:01	99:01	....	3.48
Jan	02	ci	98:23	98:23	....	2.90
Feb	02	ci	98:15	98:16	....	2.88
May	02	ci	97:11	97:11	– 1	3.45
May	02	np	97:09	97:10	– 1	3.53
Aug	02	ci	96:13	96:14	– 1	3.54
Aug	02	np	96:10	96:10	– 1	3.66
Nov	02	ci	95:26	95:27	– 1	3.33
Feb	03	ci	94:18	94:20	– 1	3.65
Feb	03	np	94:12	94:13	– 1	3.79
May	03	ci	93:19	93:20	– 1	3.72
Jul	03	ci	92:31	93:00	– 1	3.75
Aug	03	ci	92:19	92:21	– 1	3.79
Aug	03	np	92:14	92:16	– 1	3.87
Nov	03	ci	92:01	92:03	– 1	3.65
Nov	03	np	91:11	91:13	– 1	3.98
Jan	04	ci	90:24	90:26	– 3	3.98
Feb	04	ci	90:12	90:14	– 3	4.01
Feb	04	np	90:08	90:10	– 3	4.06
May	04	ci	89:07	89:09	– 2	4.12
May	04	np	89:01	89:03	– 3	4.19
Jul	04	ci	88:19	88:22	– 3	4.12
Aug	04	ci	88:07	88:09	– 3	4.15

TREASURY BILLS

MATURITY	DAYS TO MAT.	BID	ASKED	CHG.	ASKED YLD.
Aug 09 '01	7	3.66	3.58	+0.21	3.63
Aug 16 '01	14	3.77	3.69	+0.19	3.75
Aug 23 '01	21	3.76	3.68	+0.18	3.74
Aug 30 '01	28	3.80	3.72	+0.18	3.78
Sep 06 '01	35	3.73	3.69	+0.17	3.75
Sep 13 '01	42	3.70	3.66	+0.20	3.73
Sep 20 '01	49	3.67	3.63	+0.17	3.70
Sep 27 '01	56	3.66	3.62	+0.16	3.69
Oct 04 '01	63	3.62	3.60	+0.17	3.67
Oct 11 '01	70	3.62	3.60	+0.18	3.68
Oct 18 '01	77	3.61	3.59	+0.17	3.67
Oct 25 '01	84	3.60	3.58	+0.15	3.66
Nov 01 '01	**91**	**3.59**	**3.58**	**+0.14**	**3.66**
Nov 08 '01	98	3.57	3.55	+0.14	3.63
Nov 15 '01	105	3.56	3.54	+0.14	3.63
Nov 23 '01	113	3.55	3.53	+0.14	3.62
Nov 29 '01	119	3.51	3.49	+0.12	3.58
Dec 06 '01	126	3.49	3.47	+0.13	3.56
Dec 13 '01	133	3.47	3.45	+0.11	3.54
Dec 20 '01	140	3.47	3.45	+0.11	3.55
Dec 27 '01	147	3.45	3.43	+0.12	3.53
Jan 03 '02	154	3.43	3.41	+0.10	3.51
Jan 10 '02	161	3.44	3.42	+0.11	3.52
Jan 17 '02	168	3.45	3.43	+0.11	3.53
Jan 24 '02	175	3.48	3.46	+0.13	3.57
Jan 31 '02	**182**	**3.44**	**3.43**	**+0.09**	**3.54**
Feb 28 '02	210	3.35	3.34	+0.03	3.45

GOVERNMENT AGENCY & SIMILAR ISSUES

Wednesday, August 1, 2001

Over-the-Counter mid-afternoon quotations based on large transactions, usually $1 million or more. Colons in-bid-and asked quotes represent 32nds; 101:01 means 101 1/32. All yields are calculated to maturity, and based on the asked quote. *-callable issue, maturity date shown. For issues callable prior to maturity, yields are computed to the earliest call date for issues quoted above par, or 100, and to the maturity date for issues below par.

Source: Bear, Stearns & Co. via Street Software Technology Inc.

RATE	MAT.	BID	ASKED	YLD.
Fannie Mae Issues				
6.75	8-02	103:04	103:06	3.57
6.38	10-02	103:02	103:04	3.67
6.25	11-02	103:02	103:05	3.69
5.25	1-03	101:29	102:00	3.82
5.00	2-03	101:18	101:21	3.87
5.75	4-03	102:25	102:28	3.98
4.63	5-03	100:31	101:02	4.00
4.75	11-03	101:00	101:03	4.24
5.13	2-04	101:19	101:22	4.42
4.75	3-04	100:21	100:24	4.44
5.63	5-04	102:25	102:28	4.51
6.50	8-04	105:09	105:12	4.58
7.10	10-04*	101:05	101:08	4.28
7.13	2-05	107:14	107:17	4.78
5.75	6-05	102:29	103:00	4.89
7.00	7-05	107:05	107:08	4.96
6.00	12-05	103:19	103:22	5.04
5.50	2-06	101:18	101:21	5.08
5.50	5-06	100:23	100:26	5.30
5.25	6-06	100:11	100:14	5.14
5.50	7-06*	100:09	100:12	5.30
7.13	3-07	108:31	109:02	5.24
6.63	10-07	106:22	106:25	5.32
5.75	2-08	101:22	101:26	5.41
6.00	5-08	103:00	103:04	5.44
5.25	1-09	98:02	98:06	5.55
6.50	4-09*	100:17	100:21	5.57
6.40	5-09*	101:17	101:21	5.74
6.38	6-09	104:23	104:27	5.61
6.63	9-09	106:05	106:09	5.65
7.25	1-10	110:08	110:12	5.69
7.13	6-10	109:19	109:23	5.71
6.63	11-10	106:03	106:07	5.75
6.25	2-11	101:12	101:16	6.04
5.50	3-11	97:29	98:01	5.77
6.00	5-11	101:17	101:21	5.77
6.25	7-11*	100:08	100:12	5.44
6.25	5-29	98:31	99:03	6.32
Freddie Mac				
6.63	8-02	102:31	103:01	3.59
6.25	10-02	102:30	103:00	3.66
4.75	3-03	101:07	101:10	3.91
5.75	7-03	102:31	103:02	4.10
6.38	11-03	104:13	104:16	4.28
5.00	1-04	101:11	101:14	4.38
6.88	1-05	106:18	106:21	4.76
7.00	7-05	107:05	107:08	4.96
5.25	1-06	100:18	100:21	5.08
5.75	4-08	101:20	101:24	5.43
5.13	10-08	97:20	97:24	5.51
5.75	3-09	100:29	101:01	5.58
6.45	4-09*	100:13	100:17	5.70
7.63	9-09	100:16	100:20	7.52
6.63	9-09	106:05	106:09	5.65
7.00	3-10	108:20	108:24	5.70
6.88	9-10	107:27	107:31	5.74
5.63	3-11	98:26	98:30	5.77
5.88	3-11	98:20	98:24	6.05
Federal Farm Credit Bank				
6.75	9-02	103:05	103:07	3.67
6.25	12-02	103:05	103:08	3.72
Federal Home Loan Bank				
6.75	8-02	103:01	103:03	3.66
6.38	11-02	103:03	103:06	3.81
6.38	11-02	103:05	103:08	3.75
5.13	1-03	101:22	101:25	3.84
5.00	2-03	101:17	101:20	3.92
6.88	8-03	105:06	105:09	4.14
5.13	9-03	101:27	101:30	4.15
5.38	1-04	102:06	102:09	4.38
6.88	8-05	106:19	106:22	5.02
5.13	3-06	100:02	100:05	5.08
5.80	9-08	101:11	101:15	5.55
GNMA Mtge. Issues				
5.50	30Yr	95:16	95:18	6.32
6.00	30Yr	98:19	98:21	6.27
6.50	30Yr	100:18	100:20	6.43
7.00	30Yr	102:08	102:10	6.57
7.50	30Yr	103:14	103:16	6.61
8.00	30Yr	104:09	104:11	6.28
8.50	30Yr	104:28	104:30	6.19
9.00	30Yr	105:10	105:12	6.55
9.50	30Yr	105:20	105:22	6.96

Source: *The Wall Street Journal,* Eastern Edition (August 2, 2001, C12, C15). Staff-produced copy.

The reason for the difference between the discount yield and the annualized yield is that Treasury bills are sold at a discount and are quoted in terms of the discount yield. The discount yield is not the same as (nor is it comparable to) the annualized yield on the bill or the yield to maturity on a bond. The discount yield is calculated on the basis of the face amount of the bill and uses a 360-day year. The annualized yield, which is sometimes referred to as the "bond-equivalent yield," depends on the price of the bill and uses a 365-day year.

The difference between the two calculations may be seen in the following example. Suppose a three-month \$10,000 Treasury bill sells for \$9,800. The discount yield (i_d) is

$$i_d = \frac{\text{Par value} - \text{Price}}{\text{Par value}} \times \frac{360}{\text{Number of days to maturity}}$$

$$\frac{\$10{,}000 - \$9{,}800}{\$10{,}000} \times \frac{360}{90} = 8\%.$$

The annualized yield (i_a) is

$$i_a = \frac{\text{Par value} - \text{Price}}{\text{Price}} \times \frac{365}{\text{Number of days to maturity}}$$

$$\frac{\$10{,}000 - \$9{,}800}{\$9{,}800} \times \frac{365}{90} = 8.277\%.$$

Since the discount yield uses the face amount and a 360-day year, it understates the yield the investor is earning. The discount yield may be converted to the annualized yield by the following equation:

$$i_a = \frac{365 \times i_d}{360 - (i_d \times \text{Days to maturity})}$$

Thus, if the discount rate on a three-month Treasury bill is 8 percent, the annualized yield is

$$i_a = \frac{365 \times 0.08}{360 - (0.08 \times 90)} = 8.277\%,$$

which is the same answer derived using the annual yield equation.[2]

Treasury bills may be purchased through brokerage firms, commercial banks, and any Federal Reserve bank. These purchases may be new issues or bills that are being traded in the secondary market. Bills with one year to maturity are auctioned once a month. Shorter-term bills are auctioned weekly. If the buyer purchases the bills directly through the Federal Reserve bank, there are no commission fees. Brokers and commercial banks do charge commissions, but the fees are

Calculator Solution

Function Key	*Data Input*
PV =	−9800
FV =	10000
PMT =	0
N =	.24657
I =	?
Function Key	*Answer*
I =	8.54

[2]The annualized yield is a simple (i.e., noncompounded) rate. The determination of the compound rate (i_c) is

$$\$9{,}800(1 + i_c)^n = \$10{,}000,$$

in which $n = 90/365$. The solution is

$$\$9{,}800(1 + i_c)^{90/365} = \$10{,}000$$

$$(1 + i_c)^{0.2466} = \frac{\$10{,}000}{\$9{,}800} = 1.0204$$

$$i_c = (1.0204)^{4.0556} - 1 = 0.0853 = 8.53\%.$$

modest compared with those charged for other investment transactions, such as the purchase of stock.

Treasury bills are among the best short-term debt instruments available to investors who desire safety and some interest income (i.e., a liquid asset). The bills mature quickly, and there are many issues from which the investor may choose. Thus, the investor may purchase a bill that matures when the principal is needed. For example, an individual who has ready cash today but who must make a payment after three months may purchase a bill that matures at the appropriate time. In doing so, the investor puts the cash to work for three months.

Perhaps the one feature that differentiates Treasury bills from all other investments is risk. These bills are considered the safest of all possible investments. There is no question concerning the safety of principal when investors acquire Treasury bills. The federal government always has the capacity to refund or retire Treasury bills because it has the power to tax and the power to create money.

The primary buyers of Treasury bills are corporations with excess short-term cash, commercial banks with unused lending capacity, money market mutual funds, and foreign investors seeking a safe haven for their funds. Individual investors may also purchase them. However, the minimum denomination of $10,000 excludes many savers. Individual investors who desire such safe short-term investments may purchase shares in money market mutual funds that specialize in buying short-term securities, including Treasury bills.

Treasury Notes and Bonds

Treasury notes
The intermediate-term debt of the federal government.

Treasury bonds
The long-term debt of the federal government.

Intermediate-term federal government debt is in the form of **Treasury notes**. These notes are issued in denominations of $1,000 to more than $100,000 and mature in one to ten years. **Treasury bonds**, the government's debt instrument for long-term debt, are issued in denominations of $1,000 to $1,000,000, and these bonds mature in more than ten years from the date of issue. Notes and bonds are issued in book-entry and registered forms. These issues are the safest intermediate- and long-term investments available and are purchased by pension funds, financial institutions, or savers who are primarily concerned with moderate income and safety. Since these debt instruments are so safe, their yields are generally lower than that which may be obtained with high-quality corporate debt, such as AT&T bonds. For example, in January 2001, Johnson & Johnson bonds that were rated triple A yielded about 7.1 percent, while Treasury bonds with approximately the same time to maturity yielded 5.5 percent.

Like Treasury bills, new issues of Treasury bonds may be purchased through commercial banks and brokerage firms. These firms will charge commissions, but the individual may avoid such fees by purchasing the securities from any of the Federal Reserve banks or their branches. Payment, however, must precede purchase, except when the individual pays cash. Unless the individual investor submits a competitive bid, the purchase price is the average price charged institutions that buy the bonds through competitive bidding. By accepting this noncompetitive bid, the individual ensures matching the average yield earned by financial institutions, which try to buy the securities at the lowest price (highest yield) possible.

Once the bonds are purchased, they may be readily resold, as there is an active secondary market in U.S. Treasury bonds. Like corporate stocks and bonds, Treasury bonds are quoted in the financial press under the general heading *Treasury Issues*. How these bonds are reported was illustrated in Exhibit 17.2, which presented quotes for selected Treasury notes and bonds. These price quotes are different from the bid and ask prices for stocks because Treasury securities are quoted in 32nds. Thus, the $6\frac{1}{4}$ percent note due in 2023, which was quoted 107:13–107:15 had a bid price of $107\frac{13}{32}$ and an asking price of $107\frac{15}{32}$ (i.e., $10,740.63 and $10,746.88 per $10,000 face amount).

Treasury bonds are among the safest investments available to investors. As with Treasury bills, there is no question that the federal government can pay the interest and refund its debt, but there are ways in which the holder of Treasury notes and bonds can suffer losses. These debt instruments pay a fixed amount of interest, which is determined when the notes and bonds are issued. The fixed interest means the bonds are subject to interest rate risk. If interest rates subsequently rise, existing issues will not be as attractive, and their market prices will decline. If an investor must sell the debt instrument before it matures, the price will be lower than the principal amount and the investor will suffer a capital loss.

Interest rates paid by Treasury debt have varied over time. The extent of this variation was illustrated by Figure 15.3, which showed the yields on Treasury bills and Treasury bonds from 1980 to 2001. Yields also can fluctuate rapidly. For example, yields on three-month Treasury bills changed from a high of 15 percent in March 1980 to 8.7 percent only two months later. These fluctuations in yields are due to variations in the supply of and demand for credit in the money and bond markets. As the demand and supply vary, so will the market prices and the yields on all debt instruments, including the debt of the federal government. When demand for bonds becomes strong and exceeds supply at the old prices, bond prices will rise and yields will decline. The reverse occurs when supply exceeds demand: Bond prices decline and yields rise.

An investor may also lose through investments in Treasury debt when the rate of inflation exceeds the interest rate earned on the bonds. For example, during 1974 the yields on government bonds rose to 7.3 percent, but the rate of inflation for consumer goods exceeded 10 percent. The investor then suffered a loss in purchasing power, for interest payments were insufficient to compensate for the inflation.

These two factors, fluctuating yields and inflation, illustrate that investing in federal government debt, like all types of investing, subjects the investor to interest rate risk and purchasing power risk. Therefore, although federal government debt is among the safest of all investments with regard to the certainty of payment of interest and principal, some element of risk still exists.

Foreign investors have the additional risk associated with exchange rates when they purchase U.S. federal government securities. If the value of their currency rises relative to the dollar, then the interest and principal repayment is reduced. However, the value of the dollar could rise, in which case the return on the investment is enhanced. During periods of economic uncertainty in other countries, foreign investors will buy dollars both as a safe haven and for the enhanced return that will occur if their currency declines and the value of the dollar rises.

The Variability of Federal Government Bond Returns

One argument for investing in federal government securities is their safety. Prior to the 1995 budget impasse, no question existed that the federal government would fail to service its debt. The probability of default on interest and principal repayment was believed to be nil. However, as was previously discussed, there always existed the possibility of loss from inflation and higher interest rates driving down the price of federal government bonds. This variability of returns was illustrated in Exhibit 10.2 in which the return on the federal government long-term bonds was 5.6 percent with a standard deviation of 9.2 percent. During the 1980s, returns on federal government bonds became more variable.

This increased variability is illustrated in Figure 17.1, which plots the annualized standard deviations of monthly returns for stocks and for long-term government securities for the period 1950–1999. For 1950–1978, the standard deviations of the bond returns averaged 5.5 percent and, except for 1958, were always less than the standard deviations of the stock returns. With the exception of 1969–1970, the numerical values of the standard deviations were less than 10 percent, whereas the standard deviations of the stocks consistently exceeded 10 percent.

In 1979, the returns on government bonds became more variable. For the period 1979–1988, the standard deviations of the bond returns exceeded 10 percent and in several years exceeded the standard deviations of the stock returns. During this period, risk of loss from an adverse movement in bond prices increased, suggesting that government bonds were not as safe as was generally believed.

During the late 1980s, the variability of bond returns declined. While the standard deviations of the returns has not reverted to the levels experienced during 1950 through the mid-1960s, they are perceptibly below the levels experienced during 1979–1988. Although 1979–1988 was an aberration, the data suggest that government bonds have become riskier as the returns have become more variable.

Zero Coupon Treasury Securities

With the advent of Individual Retirement Accounts (IRAs), corporations started issuing zero coupon bonds. Because the Treasury did not issue such bonds at that time, selected brokerage firms created their own zero coupon Treasury securities. For example, Merrill Lynch created the Treasury Investment Growth Receipt (TIGR, generally referred to as *Tigers*). Merrill Lynch bought a block of Treasury bonds, removed all the coupons, and offered investors either the interest to be received in a specific year or the principal at the bonds' maturity. Since payment was limited to the single payment at the specified time in the future, these tigers were sold at a discount. In effect, they were zero coupon bonds backed by Treasury securities originally purchased by Merrill Lynch and held by a trustee.

Other brokerage firms created similar securities by removing coupons from existing Treasury bonds. Some of these zero coupon Treasury securities were given clever acronyms, such as Salomon Brothers' CATS (Certificates of Accrual on Treasury Securities). In other cases they were just called Treasury Receipts (T.R.s). In each case, however, the brokerage firm owns the underlying Treasury securities. The actual security purchased by the investor is an obligation of the brokerage firm and not of the federal government.

Strips

In 1985, the Treasury introduced its own zero coupon bonds, called STRIPS, for Separate Trading of Registered Interest and Principal Securities. Investors who purchase such STRIPS acquire a direct obligation of the federal government. Since these securities are direct obligations, they tend to have slightly lower yields than Tigers, CATS, and the other zero coupon securities created by brokerage firms.

In any case, the primary appeal of these securities is their use in retirement accounts. The interest earned on a zero coupon bond is taxed as it accrues, even though the holder does not receive annual cash interest payments. Thus, there is little reason to acquire these securities in accounts that are not tax sheltered. They are, however, excellent vehicles for retirement accounts, since all the funds (i.e., principal and accrued interest) are paid in one lump sum at maturity. Because any tax on a retirement account is paid when the funds are withdrawn, the tax disadvantage of zero coupon bonds is circumvented. The investor can purchase issues that mature at a desired date to meet retirement needs. For example, a 40-year-old

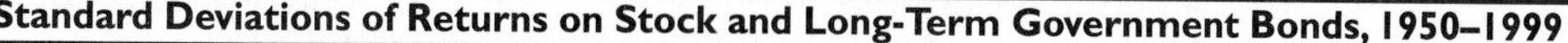

FIGURE 17.1

Standard Deviations of Returns on Stock and Long-Term Government Bonds, 1950–1999

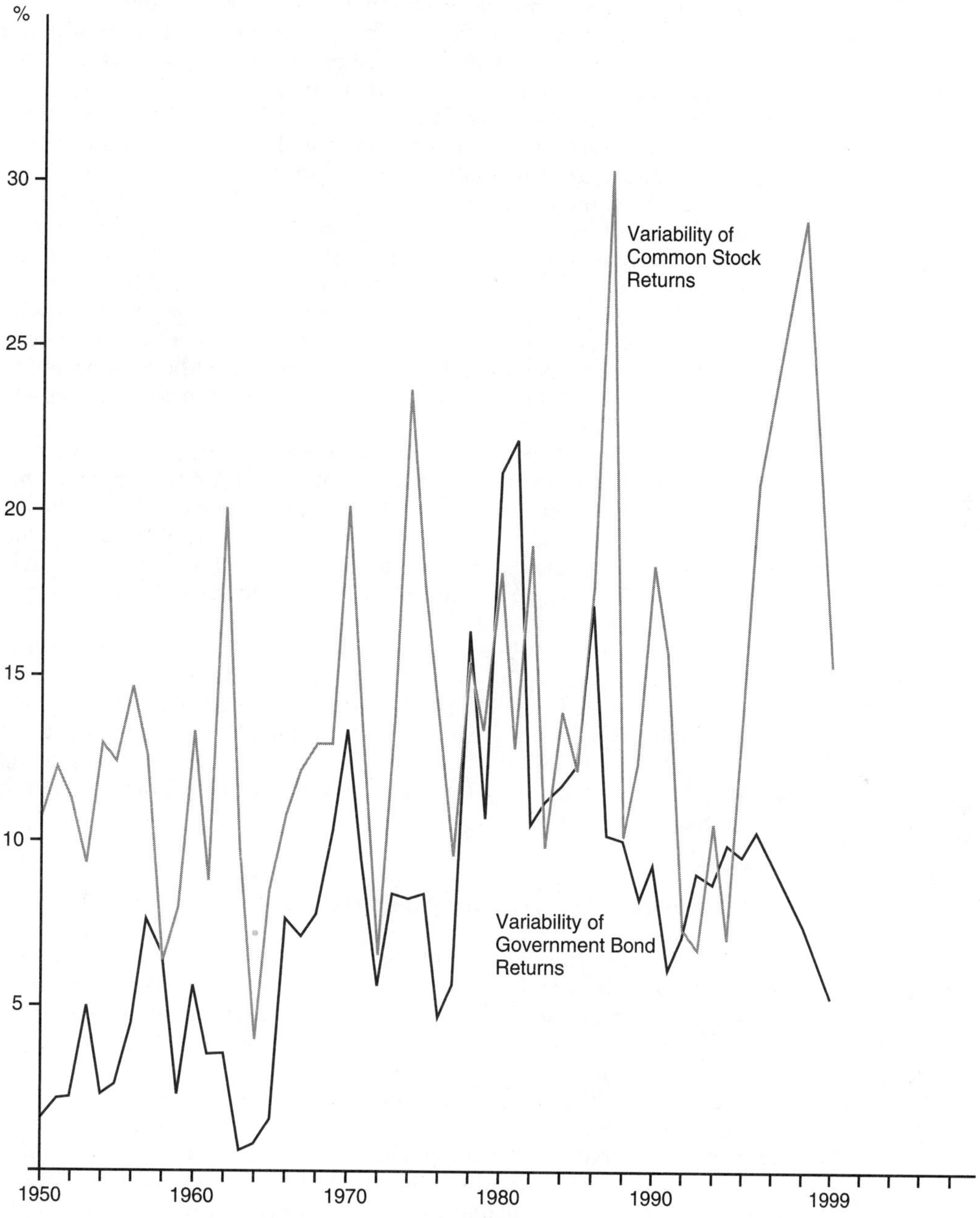

%
30
25
20
15
10
5
Variability of Common Stock Returns
Variability of Government Bond Returns
1950
1960
1970
1980
1990
1999

Source: *Stocks, Bonds, Bills, and Inflation 2000 Yearbook* (Chicago: Ibbotson Associates), 117.

investor could purchase zero coupon government securities that mature when he or she reaches the age of 65, 66, and so on. Such a laddered bond strategy would ensure that the funds were received after retirement, at which time they would replace the individual's earned income that ceases at retirement.

If the investor does acquire zero coupon bonds, that individual should be aware that these securities have the most price volatility of all federal government bonds. As was discussed in Chapter 16, changing interest rates generate fluctuations in bond prices. The longer the term or the smaller the coupon, the greater is the price fluctuation. Zero coupon bonds make no periodic interest payments; thus, for a given term to maturity, their prices are more volatile than coupon bonds with the same maturity. For example, if interest rates were 8 percent compounded annually, a ten-year zero coupon bond would sell for $463.19, while a ten-year 8 percent coupon bond would sell for $1,000. If interest rates rose to 10 percent, the price of the zero coupon bond would fall to $385.50 for a decline of approximately 17 percent. The price of the 8 percent coupon bond would fall to $877.11 for a decline of approximately 13 percent. If the terms of these bonds had been 20 years, the respective prices at 8 percent would be $214.55 and $1,000 and would fall to $148.64 and $829.73 at 10 percent. Such price declines are approximately 30 and 17 percent.

The reason for a zero coupon bond's increased price volatility in response to changes in interest rates is that the entire return falls on the single payment at maturity. Since the current price of any bond is the present value of the interest and principal payments, the price of a zero coupon bond is solely the result of the present value of the single payment received at maturity. No interest payments will be received during the early years of the bond's life that reduce the responsiveness of the bond's price to changes in interest rates.

This price volatility suggests that zero coupon bonds may well serve a laddered bond strategy and may be excellent candidates for purchase in anticipation of lower interest rates. In the laddered strategy, there is no intention to sell the bond prior to maturity. Instead, the investor expects to collect the payment at the bond's maturity, so price volatility is unimportant. Bond purchases made in anticipation of lower interest rates are made to take advantage of the price increase that would accompany lower rates.

Inflation-Indexed Treasury Securities

inflation-indexed securities
Securities whose principal and interest payments are adjusted for changes in the Consumer Price Index.

In addition to traditional marketable debt instruments, the federal government also issues **inflation-indexed securities**, sometimes referred to as TIPS (Treasury Inflation-Protection Securities). There are two basic types of marketable federal government inflation-indexed debt. The first is notes, which are issued annually on January 15 and July 15 and mature after ten years. The second is the inflation-indexed bond, which is a 30-year security issued every October 15.

Inflation-indexed notes and bonds pay a modest rate of interest plus make an adjustment for changes in the Consumer Price Index (i.e., the rate of inflation). The interest rate is the "real yield" earned by the investor. The adjustment occurs by altering the amount of principal owed by the federal government; *no* adjustment is made in the semiannual interest *rate.* The amount of the change in the principal depends on the current CPI relative to the CPI when the securities were issued. For example, the ten-year notes issued in January 1999 have a real interest rate of 3⅞ percent. The base CPI to be used for determining subsequent changes in the principal is 164. Two years later, in January 2001, the CPI was 174, and the principal was increased by a factor of 1.06098 (174/164). A $1,000 note was increased to $1,060.98. The investor would then receive interest of $41.075 ($1,060.98 × .03875) instead of the $38.75, which was the amount initially earned when the note was issued.[3] Since the principal and the amount of interest received are increased with the rate of inflation, the investor's purchasing power is maintained.

Inflation-indexed bonds appeal to individuals who are primarily concerned that the rate of inflation will increase so that an investment in a traditional, fixed-rate bond will result in a loss of purchasing power. If, for example, the rate of inflation is 2 percent and an investor purchases a 5 percent, ten-year bond and the rate of inflation rises to 6 percent, the interest is insufficient to cover the higher rate of inflation. The purchasing power of the investor's principal is also eroded. If that investor had acquired an inflation-indexed security, the principal owed and the interest earned would rise sufficiently to cover the increased inflation and provide a modest return.

While federal government inflation-indexed notes and bonds are a means to manage purchasing power risk, there are risks associated with an inflation-indexed bond. The fixed, real rate paid by the bonds is less than the nominal rate that could be earned by an investment in a traditional bond. For example, the rates of interest on ten-year notes in 1999 were 5.5 to 6.0 percent, which is more than the 3⅞ percent real rate on the inflation-indexed note just illustrated. Of course, if the rate of inflation were to increase, the real return on the traditional note would diminish while the inflation-indexed note would continue to earn its 3⅞ percent real rate. If, however, inflation abates, the inflation-indexed security produces an inferior return.

Inflation-indexed federal government notes and bonds are, of course, illustrative of an important trade-off investors must accept. To obtain protection and reduce the risk from inflation, investors may acquire the indexed bonds. If, however, the rate of inflation does not increase, this strategy earns a lower rate of interest. Investors could earn a higher rate by not acquiring the indexed bonds, but then they bear the risk associated with inflation. Although the traditional bond may generate more current interest income, the investors who acquire them in preference to the indexed bond bear the risk associated with the loss of purchasing power from inflation.

The possibility also exists that the CPI may decline. If deflation were to occur, the inflation-indexed principal would be *reduced,* which decreases the periodic interest payments. If the inflation-adjusted principal were less than the original par value at maturity of the security, the federal government will repay the initial par value. The buyer is assured of receiving the initial amount invested in inflation-indexed securities (when they are issued) if they are held to maturity. Only the periodic interest payments would be reduced.

In addition to these risks, there is a tax disadvantage associated with the federal government's inflation-indexed debt securities. The addition to the principal is considered taxable income even though it is not received until the instrument matures (or is sold). In the preceding example, the principal amount rose from $1,000 to $1,060.89. The $60.89 is taxable income during the two years in which the accretion occurred even though the investor only received interest of 3⅞ percent of the principal value. This tax treatment of the accretion in the principal value may reduce the attractiveness of inflation-indexed notes and bonds except for usage in tax-deferred retirement accounts.

Federal Agencies' Debt

In addition to the debt issued by the federal government, certain agencies of the federal government and federally sponsored corporations issue debt. These debt

[3]This illustration assumes annual interest payments, while the notes (and the bonds) distribute interest semiannually. The index factors for adjusting the principal may be found at http://www.publicdebt.treas.gov under the subhead of inflation-indexed notes and bonds.

instruments encompass the entire spectrum of maturities, ranging from short-term securities to long-term bonds. Like many U.S. Treasury debt issues, there is an active secondary market in some of the debt issues of these agencies, and price quotations for many of the bonds are given daily in the financial press (see, for instance, the Fannie Mae or The Federal Home Loan Bank bonds in Figure 17.2).

Several federal agencies have been created to fulfill specific financial needs. For example, the Banks for Cooperatives were organized under the Farm Credit Act. These banks provide farm business services and make loans to farm cooperatives to help purchase supplies. The Federal Home Loan Mortgage Corporation was established to strengthen the secondary market in residential mortgages insured by the Federal Housing Administration. This federal corporation buys and sells home mortgages to give them marketability and thus increase their attractiveness to private investors. The Student Loan Marketing Association was created to provide liquidity to the insured student loans made under the Guaranteed Student Loan Program by commercial banks, savings and loan associations, and schools that participate in the program. This liquidity should expand the funds available to students from private sources.

federal agency bonds
Debt issued by an agency of the federal government.

moral backing
Nonobligatory support for a debt issue.

Federal agency bonds are not issued by the federal government and are not the debt of the federal government. Hence, they tend to offer higher yields than those available on U.S. Treasury debt. However, the bonds are extremely safe because they have government backing. In some cases, this is only **moral backing**, which means that in case of default the federal government does *not* have to support the debt (i.e., to pay the interest and meet the terms of the indenture). Some of the debt issues, however, are guaranteed by the U.S. Treasury. Should these issues go into default, the federal government is legally bound to assume the obligations of the debt's indenture.

The matter of whether the bonds have the legal or the moral backing of the federal government is probably academic. All these debt issues are excellent credit risks, because it is doubtful that the federal government would let the debt of one of its agencies go into default. Since these bonds offer slightly higher yields than those available on U.S. Treasury debt, the bonds of federal agencies have become very attractive investments for conservative investors seeking higher yields. This applies not only to individual investors who wish to protect their capital but also to financial institutions, such as commercial banks, insurance companies, or credit unions, which must be particularly concerned with the safety of the principal in making investment decisions.

Federal agency debt can be purchased by individuals, but few individual investors do own these bonds, except indirectly through pension plans, mutual funds, and other institutions that own the debt. Many individual investors are probably not even aware of the existence of this debt and the potential advantages it offers. Any investor who wants to construct a portfolio with an emphasis on income and the relative safety of the principal should consider these debt instruments.

Ginnie Mae Securities

Ginnie Mae
Mortgage pass-through bond issued by the Government National Mortgage Association.

One of the most important and popular debt securities issued by a government agency and supported by the federal government is the **Ginnie Mae**, a debt security issued by the Government National Mortgage Association (GNMA or Ginnie Mae), a division of the Department of Housing and Urban Development (HUD). The funds raised through the sale of Ginnie Mae securities are used to acquire a pool of FHA/VA guaranteed mortgages. (FHA and VA are the Federal Housing Administration and Veteran's Administration, respectively.) The mortgages are originated by private lenders, such as savings and loan associations and other savings institutions, and packaged into securities that are sold to the general public and guaranteed by GNMA. The minimum size of each issue is $1 million, and the minimum size of the individual Ginnie Mae securities sold to the public is $25,000.[4]

Ginnie Mae securities serve as a conduit through which interest and principal repayments are made. An investor who buys a Ginnie Mae acquires part of the pool. As interest payments and principal repayments are made to the pool, the funds are channeled to the Ginnie Mae's owners. The investor receives a monthly payment that is his or her share of the principal and interest payment received by the pool. Since such payments may vary from month to month, the amount received by the investor also varies monthly. Thus, the Ginnie Mae is one example of a long-term debt security whose periodic payments are not fixed.

Ginnie Mae securities have become particularly popular with individuals financing retirement or accumulating funds in retirement accounts. The reason for their popularity is safety, since the federal government insures the payment of principal and interest. Thus, if a mortgage payer were to default, the federal government would make the required payments. This guarantee virtually assures the timely payment of interest and principal to the holder of the Ginnie Mae.

In addition to safety, Ginnie Maes offer higher yields than federal government securities. Since the yields are ultimately related to the mortgages acquired by the pool, they depend on mortgage rates rather than on the yields of federal government bills and bonds. This yield differential can be as great as 2 percentage points (sometimes referred to as 200 basis points, with one basis point equaling 0.01 percentage point) over the return offered by long-term federal government bonds.

Ginnie Mae securities are also useful to investors seeking a regular flow of payments, since interest and principal repayments are distributed monthly. The mortgage repayment schedules define the minimum amount of the anticipated payments. However, if the homeowners speed up payments or pay off their loans before the full term of the mortgage, the additional funds are passed on to the holder of the Ginnie Mae securities.

While these securities are supported by the full faith and credit of the federal government, there are risks associated with Ginnie Maes. One is the loss of purchasing power through inflation. Of course, investors will not purchase Ginnie Maes if the anticipated yield is less than the anticipated rate of inflation.

Even if the anticipated return is sufficient to justify the purchase, investors could still lose if interest rates rise. All the mortgages in a particular pool have the same interest rate, and since Ginnie Maes are fixed-income debt securities, their prices fluctuate with interest rates. Higher interest rates will drive down their prices. Thus, if an investor were to seek to sell the security in the secondary market (and there is an active secondary market in Ginnie Maes), he or she could sustain a capital loss resulting from the rise in interest rates. Of course, the investor could experience a capital gain if interest rates were to decline, thus causing the security's value to rise.

The last source of risk concerns the reinvestment rate, which reduces the certainty of the monthly payments. Homeowners can (and do) repay their mortgage loans prematurely. This occurs when individuals move and sell their homes and when interest rates fall. Lower rates encourage homeowners to refinance their mortgages (i.e., obtain new mortgages at the current, lower rate and pay off the old, higher-rate mortgages). Since the old loans are retired, the owners of the Ginnie Mae receive larger principal repayments but can only relend the funds at the

[4]Individuals with less to invest may acquire shares in a mutual fund that invests in mortgage-backed securities. Since Ginnie Maes convert an illiquid asset (a mortgage loan) into a marketable security, they are an illustration of securitization. Few investors are willing to hold a mortgage, because mortgage notes are difficult to sell. A Ginnie Mae, however, may be readily sold. The effect, then, is to convert an illiquid asset into a marketable asset. See the discussion of securitization in Chapter 15.

current, lower rate of interest. (Such repayments also limit the amount of any capital gains from lower rates.) The opposite would occur if interest rates rise. Homeowners will not refinance and prepayments will decline, so the holder of the Ginnie Mae receives lower principal repayments.

This uncertainty of the timing of payments affects the valuation of Ginnie Mae securities. Pricing Ginnie Maes is essentially the same as any other bond: The interest and principal repayments are discounted back to the present at the current rate of interest. Because of reinvestment rate risk, the amount of each principal payment is not certain. If a large number of homeowners rapidly pay off their mortgages, the payments will quickly retire the Ginnie Maes. (This disadvantage associated with Ginnie Maes may be reduced by acquiring collateralized mortgage obligations [CMOs], which are discussed later.)

This uncertainty of future payments can lead to differences in the estimated yields. Consider a Ginnie Mae that has an expected life of 12 years[5] and that is currently selling for a discount (which could result if interest rates rose after this Ginnie Mae pool had been assembled and sold). In such a case, the price of the Ginnie Mae would decline so that the anticipated yield is comparable with securities currently being issued. For the Ginnie Mae selling at a discount, the yield would depend on the flow of interest payments and how rapidly the mortgage loans are paid off.

If the mortgages are paid off more rapidly than expected (i.e., if the life of the pool is less than the expected 12 years), the realized return will be higher because the discount will be erased more rapidly. However, if the mortgages are retired more slowly, the realized return will be less than the expected return. Thus it is possible that the actual yield may differ from the yield assumed when the security was purchased. This makes it possible for two security dealers to assert different yields for the same Ginnie Mae sold at the same discounted price. If one dealer assumes that the mortgage loans will be retired more quickly, a higher yield is anticipated. However, another security dealer may make a more conservative assumption as to the rate at which the mortgages will be retired.[6]

The speed with which the mortgages are paid off depends in part on the interest rates being paid on mortgage loans. If the Ginnie Mae mortgage loans have relatively high rates, homeowners will seek to refinance these loans when rates decline, so the original mortgages are retired rapidly. The opposite holds when the rates on the Ginnie Maes' mortgage loans are lower than current interest rates. In this case, there is less incentive for early retirement, which will tend to extend the life of the mortgage pool. Thus, a Ginnie Mae that sells for a discount because the mortgage loans have lower interest rates will tend to have a longer life than a Ginnie Mae selling at a premium because its mortgage loans have a higher rate of interest.

The investor who purchases a Ginnie Mae security should be aware that the payment received represents both earned interest income and return of invested funds. If the investor spends all the payment, that individual is depleting his or her principal. Thus the investor should be fully aware that the individual payments received are composed of both interest and principal repayment and that the latter should be spent only if there is reason for the investor to consume the principal.

---

[5]While the maturity of a Ginnie Mae may be 25 to 30 years, the average life (according to the Government National Mortgage Association) is 12 years.

[6]The impact of faster or slower principal repayments on the value of a mortgage is considered in Chapter 23 in the section on investing in real estate.

Other Mortgage-Backed Securities

While Ginnie Maes were the first mortgage-backed securities, other issues have been created by the Federal Home Loan Mortgage Corporation (FHLMC or *Freddie Mac*), the Federal National Mortgage Association (FNMA, commonly called *Fannie Mae*), and other lending institutions. The FHLMC Participation Certificate (PC) is similar to the Ginnie Mae; they are both conduits through which interest and principal payments pass from the homeowner to the certificate holder. There is, however, one important difference: Freddie Mac PC payments are not guaranteed by the federal government. The absence of this guarantee means that even though the individual mortgages are insured by private mortgage insurance companies, Freddie Mac PCs offer a higher yield than is available through Ginnie Maes.

Mortgage-backed securities are also issued by Fannie Mae. These funds are used to finance mortgages, and like the Freddie Mac Participation Certificate, the bonds are secured by mortgage loans. Since the company is a private corporation (i.e., is not a government agency) whose stock is traded on the NYSE, its debt obligations are not guaranteed by the federal government. Fannie Mae bonds thus offer higher yields than Ginnie Maes. During 1998, FNMA officially changed its name to Fannie Mae. Financial information concerning the company, its securities, and mortgages it issues is available at its Web site: http://www.fanniemae.com.

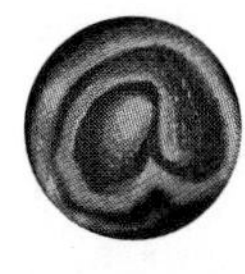

Collateralized Mortgage Obligations (CMOs)

While Ginnie Maes are supported by the federal government so the investor knows that the interest and principal will be paid, the amount of each monthly payment is unknown. Because principal repayments vary as homeowners refinance their homes, the amount of principal repayment received by the investor changes every month. This variation in the monthly cash flow may be a disadvantage to any individual (e.g., a retiree) seeking a reasonably certain flow of monthly cash payments.

collateralized mortgage obligation (CMO)
Debt obligation supported by mortgages and sold in series.

tranche
Subdivision of a bond issue.

A **collateralized mortgage obligation (CMO)** reduces, but does not erase, this uncertainty. Collateralized mortgage obligations are backed by a trust that holds Ginnie Mae and other federal government-supported mortgages. When a CMO is created, it is subdivided into classes (called **tranches**). For example, a $100 million CMO may be divided into four tranches of $25 million each. The principal repayments received by the CMO are initially paid to the first class until that tranche has been entirely retired. Once the first tranche has been paid off, mortgage principal repayments are directed to the holders of the CMOs in the second tranche. This process is repeated until all the tranches have been repaid.

Within a tranche, principal repayments may be made on a pro rata basis or by lottery. Whether a pro rata or a lottery system is used to determine repayment is specified in the CMO's indenture; thus, investors know which system applies to a particular CMO. In either case, no principal repayments are made to the next tranche until all the funds owed the first tranche are paid.

This pattern of payment is illustrated by the following CMO with four tranches. Each tranche consists of a $200,000 loan ($800,000 total outstanding), $100,000 of which is retired each year. Interest is paid annually on the amount of the loan outstanding in each tranche. The rate of interest varies with the expected life of each tranche. The interest rates start at 7 percent for tranche A and rise to 10 percent for tranche D. For accepting later repayment of principal, the investor can expect to earn a higher interest rate. The tranche with the shortest expected life earns the lowest interest rate, while the one with the longest expected life earns the highest rate.

The annual payments to each tranche are as follows if the anticipated payment schedules are made:

Tranche Payment

	A		B		C		D	
Year	**Interest**	**Principal**	**Interest**	**Principal**	**Interest**	**Principal**	**Interest**	**Principal**
1	$14,000	$100,000	$16,000	$ 0	$18,000	$ 0	$20,000	$ 0
2	7,000	100,000	16,000	0	18,000	0	20,000	0
3	0	0	16,000	100,000	18,000	0	20,000	0
4	0	0	8,000	100,000	18,000	0	20,000	0
5	0	0	0	0	18,000	100,000	20,000	0
6	0	0	0	0	9,000	100,000	20,000	0
7	0	0	0	0	0	0	20,000	100,000
8	0	0	0	0	0	0	10,000	100,000

This schedule indicates that tranche D is a loan for $200,000 at 10 percent, so the annual interest payment is $20,000 for the first 7 years and $10,000 in year 8. Repayment of principal does not occur until all the preceding tranches are retired. Under the anticipated schedule, the principal repayments of $100,000 occur in years 7 and 8, which is why the interest payment is $10,000 instead of $20,000 in year 8.

Over the eight years, the borrower pays a total of $326,000 in interest for the use of the funds and retires the $800,000 loan. While the owners of the different tranches receive different interest rates, the borrower pays the same rate on the entire loan. The trustee structures the tranches to coincide with the loan payments. In this illustration, the borrower's repayment schedule is as follows:

Year	Principal Owed at the End of the Year	Interest Payment	Principal Repayment
0	$800,000		
1	700,000	$ 72,448	$100,000
2	600,000	63,392	100,000
3	500,000	54,336	100,000
4	400,000	45,280	100,000
5	300,000	36,224	100,000
6	200,000	27,168	100,000
7	100,000	18,112	100,000
8	0	9,056	100,000
		$326,016	

The rate of interest on the loan is 9.056 percent on the declining balance. (9.056 percent is a forced number. Generally, the terms of the loan are established and the trustee constructs the tranches to match the borrower's payments. Since the purpose of this example is to illustrate the payments to the tranches, the loan is being forced to approximate the payments to the investors.)

The total interest paid by the borrower is $326,016, and the interest payments approximate those received by the tranches. Notice that the borrower's interest rate of 9.056 percent applies to the entire $800,000 loan, while each tranche receives a different rate of interest. In effect, the early tranches subsidize the later tranches. Investors in the early tranches accept a lower rate for a more rapid repayment of principal, while the investors who acquire the longer tranches accept later payments in order to earn a higher rate of interest. The borrower's payments, however, do not make this distinction. The trustee who makes the loan to the borrower establishes the tranches and converts the borrower's debt obligation into a series of securities that different investors with different financial needs find acceptable.

When an investor purchases a CMO, an estimated *principal repayment window* is known. As in the preceding illustration, the schedule gauges when the investor can expect to receive principal repayments and when a particular tranche will be entirely redeemed. As with Ginnie Mae payments, the CMO payment schedule is based on historical repayment data, but the actual timing of the repayments cannot be known with certainty. Lower interest rates will tend to speed up payments as homeowners refinance, while higher interest rates will tend to retard principal repayments.

Since the actual timing of principal repayment is not known, CMOs reduce but do not erase this source of risk. However, less timing risk exists with CMOs than with a Ginnie Mae. When the investor acquires a Ginnie Mae, the repayments are spread over the life of the entire issue. With a CMO, the repayments are spread over each tranche. The investor who acquires a CMO can better match the anticipated need for cash. For example, a 65-year-old retiree may have less immediate need for cash than an 80-year-old. The latter may acquire the first tranche, while the former acquires the third tranche within a CMO. The 65-year-old would receive the current interest component but the principal repayment would be deferred until the first and second tranches were entirely retired.

State and Local Government Debt

State and local governments also issue debt to finance capital expenditures, such as schools or roads. The government then retires the debt as the facilities are used. The funds used to retire the debt may be raised through taxes (e.g., property taxes) or through revenues generated by the facilities themselves.

Unlike the federal government, state and local governments do not have the power to create money. These governments must raise the funds necessary to pay the interest and retire the debt, but the ability to do so varies with the financial status of each government. Municipalities with wealthy residents or valuable property within their boundaries are able to issue debt more readily and at lower interest rates because the debt is safer. The tax base in these communities is larger and can support the debt.

The Tax Exemption

municipal (tax-exempt) bond
A bond issued by a state or one of its political subdivisions whose interest is not taxed by the federal government.

The primary factor that differentiates state and local government debt from other forms of debt is the tax advantage that it offers to investors. The interest earned on state and municipal government debt is exempt from federal income taxation. Hence, these bonds are frequently referred to as **tax-exempt** or **municipal bonds**. Although state and local governments may tax the interest, the federal government may not. The rationale for this tax exemption is legal and not financial. The Supreme Court ruled that the federal government does not have the power to tax the interest paid by the debt of state and municipal governments. Since the interest paid by all other debt, including corporate bonds, is subject to federal income taxation, this exemption is advantageous to state and local governments, for they are able to issue debt with substantially lower interest rates.

Investors are willing to accept a lower return on state and local government debt because the after-tax return is equivalent to higher yields on corporate debt. For example, if an investor is in the 28 percent income tax bracket, the return after taxes is the same for a corporate bond that pays 10 percent as for a state or municipal government bond that pays 7.2 percent: The after-tax return is 7.2 percent in either case.

The willingness of investors to purchase state and local government debt instead of corporate and U.S. Treasury debt is related to their income tax bracket. If an investor's federal income tax rate is 28 percent, a 6.5 percent nontaxable municipal bond gives the investor the same yield after taxes as a 9.03 percent corporate bond, the interest of which is subject to federal income taxation. The individual investor may determine the equivalent yields on tax-exempt bonds and nonexempt bonds by using the following equation:

(17.1) $$i_c(1 - t) = i_m$$

in which i_c is the interest rate paid on corporate debt, i_m is the interest rate paid on municipal debt, and t is the individual's tax bracket (i.e., the marginal tax rate). This equation is used as follows. If an investor's tax bracket is 28 percent and tax-exempt bonds offer 6.5 percent, then the equivalent corporate yield is

$$i_c(1 - 0.28) = 0.065$$

$$i_c = \frac{0.065}{0.72} = 9.03\%.$$

If the investor lives in a state that taxes income, Equation 17.1 may be modified to include the impact of the local tax. Equation 17.2 includes the impact of the federal income tax rate (t_f) and the state and/or local income tax rate (t_s):

(17.2) $$i_c(1 - t_f - t_s) = i_m.$$

If the investor's federal income tax bracket is 36 percent and the state income tax bracket is 6 percent, then a high-yield, low-quality bond offering 10.8 percent has an inferior after-tax yield to a local municipal bond offering more than 6.264 percent (10.8 percent[1 − 0.36 − 0.06] = 6.264 percent).

Exempting the interest on these bonds from federal income taxation has been criticized because it is an apparent means for the "rich" to avoid federal income taxation. Since the minimum denomination for municipal bonds is $5,000 and dealers may require larger purchases (e.g., $15,000 − $20,000), individuals with modest amounts to invest are excluded from this market except through investing in mutual funds that invest in tax-exempt bonds. The exemption does, however, reduce the interest cost for the state and municipal governments that issue debt, which in effect subsidizes those governments. From an economic point of view, the important question is whether the exemption is the best means to aid state and local governments. Other means, such as federal revenue sharing, could be used for this purpose. Thus, the interest exemption is primarily a political question. Changes in the legal structure may alter the tax exemption in the future. Until that time, however, the interest on state and municipal debt remains exempt from federal income taxation, with the effects being that (1) state and local governments can issue debt with interest rates that are lower than those individuals and corporations must pay, and (2) these bonds offer the wealthier members of our society a means to obtain tax-sheltered income.

Although state and local government debt interest is tax-exempt at the federal level, it may be taxed at the state level. States do exempt the interest paid by their own local governments but tax the interest paid by other states and their local governments. While interest earned on New York City obligations is not taxed in

FIGURE 17.2

Average Yields and the Spread between Aaa- and Baa-Rated Municipal Bonds (1980–April 2001)

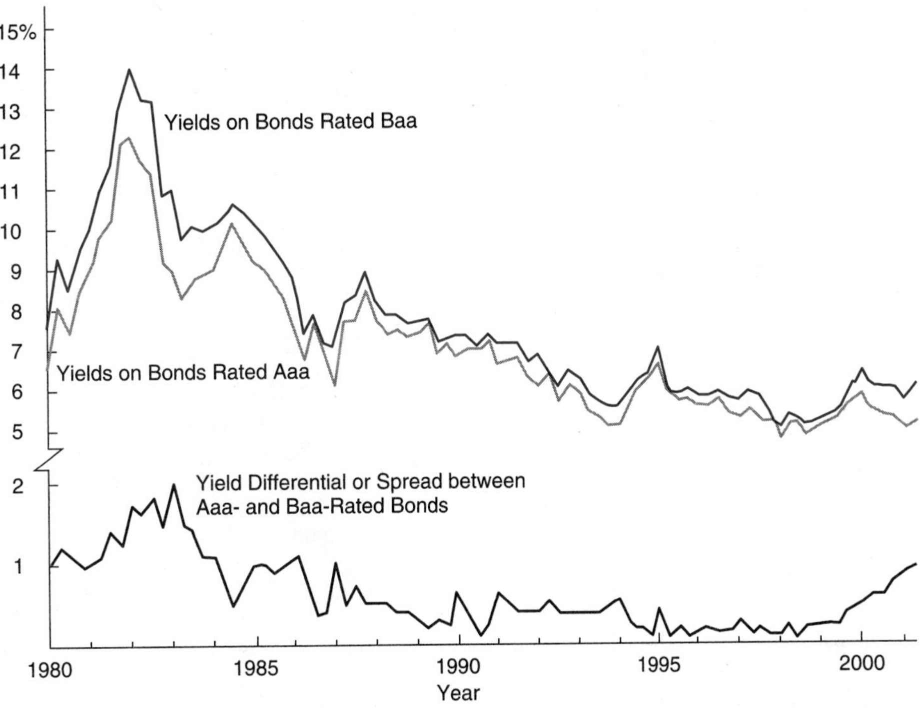

Source: *Mergent's Bond Record*, various issues.

New York, it is taxed in New Jersey. The converse is also true: New Jersey taxes the interest earned on New York City obligations but exempts interest earned on New Jersey municipal bonds.

It should also be noted that state and local governments cannot tax the interest paid by the federal government. While interest earned on series EE and HH bonds and Treasury bills, notes, and bonds is taxed by the federal government, this interest cannot be taxed by state and local governments. In states with modest or no income taxes, this exemption is meaningless. However, in states with high income taxes, such as Massachusetts or New York, this tax exemption may be a major reason for acquiring U.S. Treasury securities. For example, the yield on a Treasury bill on an after-tax basis may exceed the yield on a federally insured certificate of deposit or the yield offered by a money market mutual fund. In such cases, the tax laws will certainly encourage the investor to acquire the federal security, because that investor has both a higher after-tax yield and less risk (i.e., the full faith and credit of the federal government).

Yields and Prices of State and Local Government Bonds

Like yields on other securities, yields on tax-exempt bonds have varied over time. Figure 17.2 shows the average yields on Moody's Aaa- and Baa-rated bonds over

FIGURE 17.3

Yields on Federal Government Bonds and Aaa-Rated Municipal Bonds (1980–April 2001)

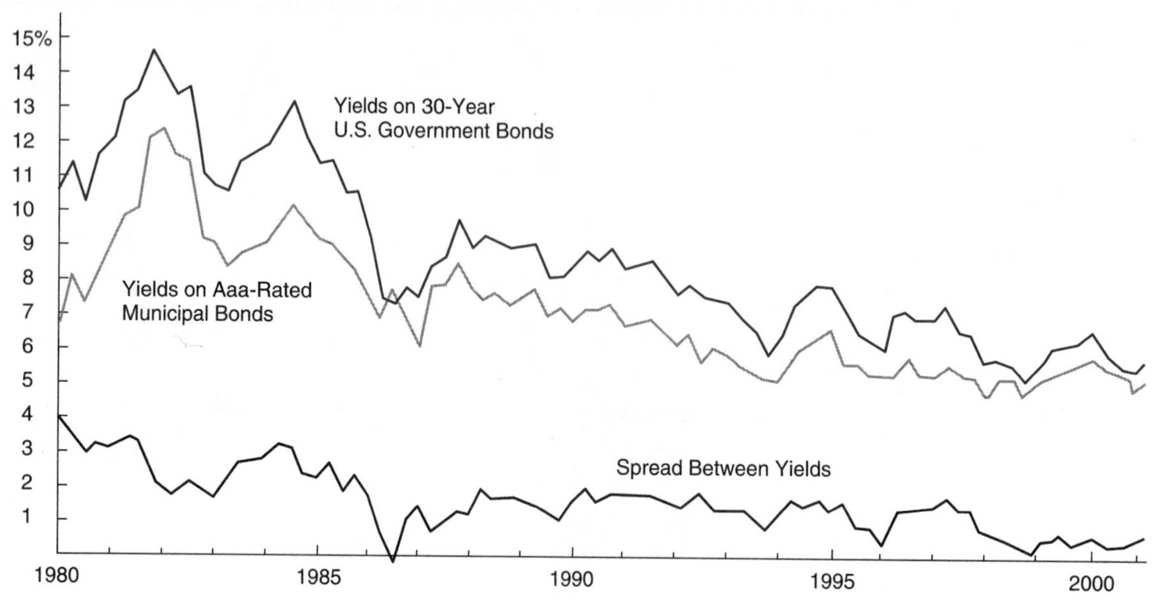

Source: *Mergent's Bond Record,* various issues; *Federal Reserve Bulletin,* various issues.

several years. During this period there was considerable fluctuation in the interest rates paid by tax-exempt bonds. For example, in 1980 the yields to maturity were 6.6 percent for the Aaa-rated bonds, but these yields rose to 12 percent in 1982. There was a comparable fluctuation in the yields of the Baa-rated bonds, which rose from 7.6 percent to 13.3 percent during the same period. A yield of 12 percent is comparable to a yield of 16.7 percent on a corporate bond for an individual in the 28 percent income tax bracket.

In addition to showing the fluctuations in yields, the figure shows the difference in yields. As would be expected, the yields on Baa-rated bonds exceed those on the Aaa-rated bonds, but the spread in the yields between the Aaa- and Baa-rated bonds varies. During the periods of higher interest rates, the spread widens. For example, the spread rose to 2 percentage points during 1983. However, when interest rates declined, the spread between the yields on the Aaa- and Baa-rated bonds declined to less than 30 basis points from 1995 to 1998.

Figure 17.3 presents similar information except it plots the yields on U.S. government bonds and Moody's Aaa-rated municipal bonds. A similar pattern emerges. When interest rates in general rose, the yields on both bonds rose (e.g., 1980 to 1982), and when interest rates fell, the yields on both federal government and municipal bonds fell (e.g., 1987 through 1992). Except briefly during 1986, the yields on the federal government securities exceeded the yields on the municipal bonds throughout the time period. After 1985, the differential between the yields was lower as tax reform and lower federal income tax rates reduced the attractiveness of municipal securities vis-à-vis the bonds of the federal government. Since 1990, the differential has been relatively stable, rarely less than 1 percentage point and never exceeding 2 percentage points.

This change in the relative attractiveness of one bond to another points out that the yields (and prices) of municipal bonds, like the prices and yields on corporate and federal government debt, ultimately depend on the demand for and supply of the various types of bonds. When many state and local governments seek credit and desire to issue bonds, the yields on tax exempts will rise. In addition, the conditions in the financial markets will affect yields. As Figures 17.2 and 17.3 illustrate, when interest rates rise in general, the yields on tax-exempt bonds will also rise.

Of course, an increase in yields means that the prices of existing municipal bonds must fall. The equations used to determine the value of a bond that were presented in Chapter 16 also apply to the valuation of municipal and state bonds. The yields on these bonds are inversely related to their prices. When a state or municipal government bond's price rises, its yield declines. When the bond's price falls, the yield rises. Like corporate debt, these bonds can sell at a discount or for a premium, depending on the direction of change in interest rates. Hence, investors in tax-exempt bonds bear the risk associated with fluctuations in interest rates.

Types of Tax-Exempt Securities

State and local governments issue a variety of debt instruments; these can be classified either according to the means by which the security is supported or according to the length of time to maturity (i.e., short- or long-term). State and municipal debt is supported by either the taxing power of the issuing government or the revenues generated by the facilities that are financed by the debt. If the bonds are secured by the taxing power, the debt is a **general obligation** of the government.

general obligation bond
A bond whose interest does not depend on the revenue of a specific project; government bonds supported by the full faith and credit of the issuer (i.e., authority to tax).

revenue bond
A bond whose interest is paid only if the debtor earns sufficient revenue.

A bond supported by the revenue generated by the project being financed with the debt is called a **revenue bond**. Revenue bonds are issued to finance particular capital improvements, such as a toll road that generates its own funds. As these revenues are collected, they are used to pay the interest and retire the principal.

General obligation bonds are commonly thought to be safer than revenue bonds, since the government is required to use its taxing authority to pay the interest and repay the principal. General obligation bonds may have to be approved by popular referendum. Such referendums can be costly, and public approval of the bonds may be difficult to obtain. These characteristics associated with issuing the debt reduce the risk of investing in general obligation bonds. Revenue bonds are supported only by funds generated by the project financed by the sale of the bonds. If the project does not generate sufficient revenues, the interest cannot be paid and the bonds go into default. For example, the Chesapeake Bay Bridge and Tunnel did not produce sufficient toll revenues, so its publicly held bonds went into default. The default, of course, caused the price of the bonds to fall. Since the bondholders could not foreclose on the bridge, their only course of action was to wait for a resumption of interest payments. After several years elapsed, toll revenues rose sufficiently, such that interest payments to the bondholders were resumed.

Tax-exempt bonds are issued in minimum denominations of $5,000 face value. There is an active secondary market in this debt; however, the bonds are traded only in the over-the-counter market, and only a handful are quoted in the financial press. Small denominations (e.g., $5,000) tend to lack marketability, but that does not mean that an investor trying to sell one $5,000 bond issued by a small municipality cannot sell it. It does imply, however, that the market is extremely thin and that the spread between the bid and ask prices may be substantial.

Although most corporate bonds are issued with a particular term to maturity and a sinking fund requirement, many tax-exempt bonds are issued in a series.

POINTS OF INTEREST
COPs

In addition to general obligation and revenue bonds and notes issued in anticipation of taxes and other revenues, some municipalities have sold *certificates of participation* (COPs). COPs are issued to finance specific projects (e.g., equipment such as police vehicles, correction facilities, or administrative buildings) that are subsequently leased to the municipality. The rental payments cover the debt-service payments to the holders of the certificates. The municipal government is not responsible for payments to the investors who purchase the COPs; the municipality only makes the lease or rental payments.

COPs are often issued by governments seeking to circumvent limits on their ability to issue debt or to avoid having to obtain voter approval to sell debt. Since the government makes lease payments and not interest and principal repayments, the debt is not considered an obligation of the government. This exclusion of the debt from the municipality's balance sheet understates its obligations.*

The removal also increases the investor's risk. Unlike the required interest and principal repayment of general obligation bonds, there is no assurance the government will allocate the funds to make the lease payments. Legislative bodies in Brevard County, Florida, and Florence, South Carolina, have threatened to withhold the lease payments. Without such appropriations, payments to the investors would not be made and the COPs would go into default. While such a default has not occurred, any default on a specific certificate could affect all COPs and lead to their downgrading by the rating services. This increased risk associated with COPs results in their offering higher yields (from 0.1 to 0.5 percentage points) than are available through traditional municipal bonds of the same credit rating.

*An analogous situation applies to firms that lease plant and equipment. However, corporate accounting may require that the firm *capitalize* the lease. That is, the corporation must determine the present value of the lease obligation and put that amount on its balance sheet as a long-term obligation. In effect, the lease obligation is acknowledged as an alternative to a bond. Both require periodic payments, and both increase the financial risk associated with the firm.

Managements that do not want the lease obligation to appear on the firm's balance sheet must be certain that the terms of the lease do not meet the accounting requirements that cause the lease to be capitalized. Even if the lease obligation does not have to be capitalized, it must be disclosed in a footnote to the firm's accounting statements.

With a serial issue, a specific amount of the debt falls due each year. Such an issue is illustrated in Exhibit 17.3, which reproduces a tombstone advertisement for bonds sold by the North Carolina Eastern Municipal Power Agency. (These advertisements are placed by the underwriting syndicate to describe a public offering. They are frequently referred to as *tombstones* because of their resemblance to an epitaph on a tombstone.) About half of the $113 million issue is in serial bonds. A portion of the issue matures each year. For example, $2,895,000 worth of the bonds matures on January 1, 2003, and another $5,185,000 matures on January 1, 2013. Serial bonds offer advantages to both the issuer and the buyer. In contrast to corporate debt, in which a random selection of the bonds is retired each year through the sinking fund, the buyer knows when each bond will mature. The investor can then purchase bonds that mature at the desired time, which helps in portfolio planning. Because a portion of the issue is retired periodically with serial bonds, the issuing government does not have to make a large, lump-sum payment. Since these bonds are scheduled to be retired, there is no call penalty. If the government wants to retire additional debt, it can call some of the remaining bonds. For example, if the agency wanted to retire some of these bonds prematurely, it would call the term A bonds that are due in 2021 or the term B bonds due in 2026. (Most issues like the bonds shown in Exhibit 17.3 require that any debt retired before maturity be called in reverse order. Thus, the term bonds with the longest time to maturity are called and redeemed first.)

anticipation note
A short-term liability that is to be retired by specific expected revenues (e.g., expected tax receipts).

Although most of the debt sold to the general public by state and local governments is long-term, there are two notable exceptions: tax or revenue anticipation notes. A tax or revenue **anticipation note** is issued by a government anticipating certain receipts in the future—it issues a debt instrument against these receipts. When the taxes or other revenues are received, the notes are retired. The maturity

EXHIBIT 17.3

Tombstone for an Issue of Serial and Term Bonds

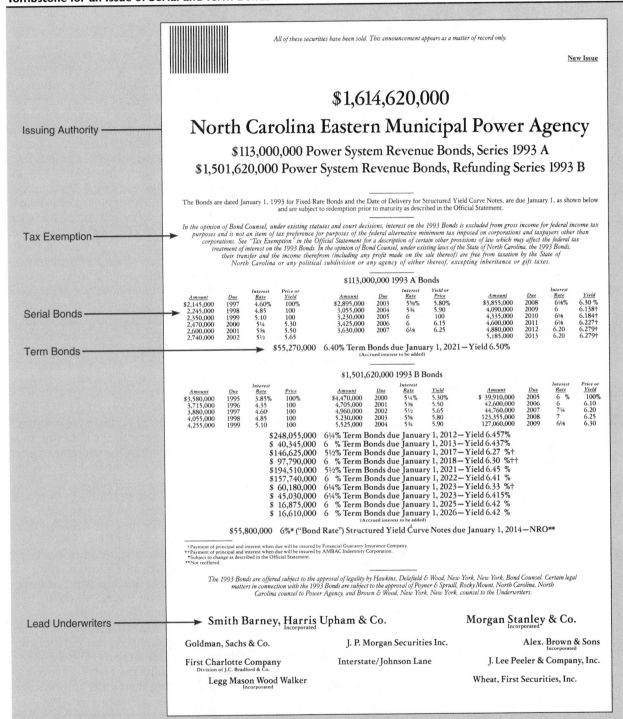

All of these securities have been sold. This announcement appears as a matter of record only.

New Issue

$1,614,620,000

Issuing Authority →

North Carolina Eastern Municipal Power Agency

$113,000,000 Power System Revenue Bonds, Series 1993 A
$1,501,620,000 Power System Revenue Bonds, Refunding Series 1993 B

The Bonds are dated January 1, 1993 for Fixed Rate Bonds and the Date of Delivery for Structured Yield Curve Notes, are due January 1, as shown below and are subject to redemption prior to maturity as described in the Official Statement.

Tax Exemption →

In the opinion of Bond Counsel, under existing statutes and court decisions, interest on the 1993 Bonds is excluded from gross income for federal income tax purposes and is not an item of tax preference for purposes of the federal alternative minimum tax imposed on corporations and taxpayers other than corporations. See "Tax Exemption" in the Official Statement for a description of certain other provisions of law which may affect the federal tax treatment of interest on the 1993 Bonds. In the opinion of Bond Counsel, under existing laws of the State of North Carolina, the 1993 Bonds, their transfer and the income therefrom (including any profit made on the sale thereof) are free from taxation by the State of North Carolina or any political subdivision or any agency of either thereof, excepting inheritance or gift taxes.

$113,000,000 1993 A Bonds

Serial Bonds →

Amount	Due	Interest Rate	Price or Yield	Amount	Due	Interest Rate	Yield or Price	Amount	Due	Interest Rate	Yield
$2,145,000	1997	4.60%	100%	$2,895,000	2003	5⅝%	5.80%	$3,855,000	2008	6⅛%	6.30 %
2,245,000	1998	4.85	100	3,055,000	2004	5¾	5.90	4,090,000	2009	6	6.138†
2,350,000	1999	5.10	100	3,230,000	2005	6	100	4,335,000	2010	6⅛	6.184†
2,470,000	2000	5¼	5.30	3,425,000	2006	6	6.15	4,600,000	2011	6⅛	6.227†
2,600,000	2001	5⅜	5.50	3,630,000	2007	6⅛	6.25	4,880,000	2012	6.20	6.279†
2,740,000	2002	5½	5.65					5,185,000	2013	6.20	6.279†

Term Bonds → $55,270,000 6.40% Term Bonds due January 1, 2021—Yield 6.50%
(Accrued interest to be added)

$1,501,620,000 1993 B Bonds

Amount	Due	Interest Rate	Price	Amount	Due	Interest Rate	Yield	Amount	Due	Interest Rate	Price or Yield
$3,580,000	1995	3.85%	100%	$4,470,000	2000	5¼%	5.30%	$ 39,910,000	2005	6 %	100%
3,715,000	1996	4.35	100	4,705,000	2001	5⅜	5.50	42,600,000	2006	6	6.10
3,880,000	1997	4.60*	100	4,960,000	2002	5½	5.65	44,760,000	2007	7¼	6.20
4,055,000	1998	4.85	100	5.230,000	2003	5⅝	5.80	123,355,000	2008	7	6.25
4,255,000	1999	5.10	100	5,525,000	2004	5¾	5.90	127,060,000	2009	6⅛	6.30

$248,055,000 6¼% Term Bonds due January 1, 2012—Yield 6.457%
$ 40,345,000 6 % Term Bonds due January 1, 2013—Yield 6.437%
$146,625,000 5½% Term Bonds due January 1, 2017—Yield 6.27 %†
$ 97,790,000 6 % Term Bonds due January 1, 2018—Yield 6.30 %††
$194,510,000 5½% Term Bonds due January 1, 2021—Yield 6.45 %
$157,740,000 6 % Term Bonds due January 1, 2022—Yield 6.41 %
$ 60,180,000 6¼% Term Bonds due January 1, 2023—Yield 6.33 %†
$ 45,030,000 6¼% Term Bonds due January 1, 2023—Yield 6.415%
$ 16,875,000 6 % Term Bonds due January 1, 2025—Yield 6.42 %
$ 16,610,000 6 % Term Bonds due January 1, 2026—Yield 6.42 %
(Accrued interest to be added)

$55,800,000 6%* ("Bond Rate") Structured Yield Curve Notes due January 1, 2014—NRO**

†Payment of principal and interest when due will be insured by Financial Guaranty Insurance Company.
††Payment of principal and interest when due will be insured by AMBAC Indemnity Corporation.
*Subject to change as described in the Official Statement.
**Not reoffered.

The 1993 Bonds are offered subject to the approval of legality by Hawkins, Delafield & Wood, New York, New York, Bond Counsel. Certain legal matters in connection with the 1993 Bonds are subject to the approval of Poyner & Spruill, Rocky Mount, North Carolina, North Carolina counsel to Power Agency, and Brown & Wood, New York, New York, counsel to the Underwriters.

Lead Underwriters → **Smith Barney, Harris Upham & Co.** Incorporated **Morgan Stanley & Co.** Incorporated

Goldman, Sachs & Co. J. P. Morgan Securities Inc. Alex. Brown & Sons Incorporated

First Charlotte Company Division of J.C. Bradford & Co. Interstate/Johnson Lane J. Lee Peeler & Company, Inc.

Legg Mason Wood Walker Incorporated Wheat, First Securities, Inc.

Source: Reprinted with permission of North Carolina Eastern Municipal Power Agency.

date is set to coincide with the timing of the anticipated receipts so that the notes may be easily retired.

Tax-Exempt Securities and Risk

While the sources of risk associated with investing in tax-exempt bonds were alluded to in the preceding discussion, it is helpful to summarize them. First, there is the market risk associated with changes in interest rates. Higher interest rates will drive down the prices of existing bonds. This source of risk, of course, applies to all bonds and is not unique to the bonds of state and municipal governments. The investor may reduce this source of risk by purchasing bonds of shorter maturity, because the prices of bonds with longer terms to maturity fluctuate more. If the investor is concerned with price fluctuations and the preservation of capital, then shorter-term tax-exempt bonds should be preferred to long-term bonds. The investor, however, should realize that shorter-term bonds generally pay less interest.

The second source of risk is the possibility that the government might default on the interest and principal repayment. Unfortunately, finding information on particular bond issues can be difficult for the individual investor. Municipal bonds are not registered with the Securities and Exchange Commission (SEC) prior to their sale to the general public, and many state and local governments do not publish annual reports and send them to bondholders. Instead, investors may consult the latest issues of Mergent's *Municipal and Government Manual* or *Standard & Poor's Bond Guide.* Fortunately for investors, several firms rate a considerable number of the tax-exempt bonds that are sold to the general public. These ratings are based on a substantial amount of data, for the rating services require the municipal and state governments to provide them with financial and economic information. Since failure of the bond issue to receive a favorable rating will dissuade many potential buyers, the state and local governments supply the rating services with the required information.

The investor can take several steps to reduce the risk associated with default. The first is to purchase a diversified portfolio of tax-exempt bonds, which spreads the risk associated with any particular government. Second, the investor may limit purchases to debt with high credit ratings.[7] If the investor purchases only bonds with AAA or AA credit ratings, there is little risk (perhaps no real risk) of loss from default.

A third means by which the investor may limit the risk of default is to purchase municipal bonds that are insured. Several insurance companies guarantee the payment of interest and principal of the municipal bonds they insure. For example, Monroe Township, New Jersey, bonds are insured by AMBAC and have a AAA rating by Standard & Poor's. AMBAC stands for American Municipal Bond Assurance Corporation, which is part of AMBAC Financial Group, a company traded on the NYSE (ABK). Other municipal bond insurers include MBIA (Municipal Bond Insurance Association), which is also traded on the NYSE (MBI), and FGIC (Financial Guaranty Insurance Co.), which is part of GE Capital.

The investor who acquires insured bonds should realize that lower yields accompany lower risk.[8] As a result of the insurance guarantees, the yield on the bonds will be lower than the yield available on noninsured bonds. The reduction in risk and yields is also affected by the quality of the company offering the insurance. If the insurance company has a lower credit rating than other insurers, the

[7]Some tax-exempt bonds are secured by lines of credit with commercial banks. If the government defaults, the banks pay the interest and principal.

[8]Insuring municipal bonds decreases the risk to bondholders and reduces required interest payments. However, there may be no net savings to the issuing government if the savings in interest is consumed by the cost of the insurance.

POINTS OF INTEREST
WPPSS/WHOOPS

In recent years, tax-exempt bonds have generally been free from default. Only two municipal governments with investment-grade ratings have defaulted on general obligation bonds: New York City in 1975 and Cleveland in 1978. (New York claims that it did not default but had a "moratorium.") Such safety, however, need not apply to non-general obligation tax-exempt bonds. For example, in 1988, Standard & Poor's downgraded the debt of Verex Assurance, which insured tax-exempt housing authority bond issues. Lowering the credit rating of the insurance company implied an increase in the bonds' risk. The insured bonds' prices tumbled, and bonds that were trading at par ($1,000) quickly declined to $950 (i.e., $0.95 per dollar face amount) for a 5 percent price decrease. The price decline occurred even though the issuers of the bonds had not defaulted.

The most spectacular demonstration of risk through default is the Washington Public Power Supply System (WPPSS and cynically referred to as WHOOPS), which sold $2.25 billion of debt to build two nuclear power plants. The plants, however, were not completed, so the utilities that initially agreed to buy the power refused to make construction payments. In addition, the power authority was not allowed by the courts to raise its rates for electricity generated in the authority's other facilities. Because the plants were not completed and the authority could not recover its costs, the bonds went into default.

quality of the insurance may be lower, raising the possibility of default by the insurance company should the municipality default.

In addition to the risks associated with fluctuations in security prices and the possibility of default, the investor should be aware that tax-exempt bonds may lack marketability.[9] Bonds issued by small governments may be resold, but the secondary markets are thin (i.e., small). Common sense should tell the investor that bonds issued by the School District of Medium-Town, USA, are not liquid. If the investor must sell the bonds before maturity, he or she may suffer a loss as the price of the bonds is marked down to induce someone to purchase them. Many investors may not be aware of this lack of marketability until they try to sell the bonds and receive bids that are below the anticipated price. This is particularly true during periods of high interest rates when the market for existing municipal bonds dries up and prices are significantly marked down.

The existence of these risks does not imply that an investor should avoid tax-exempt bonds.[10] The return offered by these bonds is probably consistent with the amount of risk the investor must bear. If a particular bond were to offer an exceptionally high return, it would be readily purchased and its price driven up so that the return was in line with comparably risky securities. Tax-exempt bonds should be purchased by investors with moderate-to-high incomes who are seeking tax-free income and who do not need liquidity. Like any investment, tax-exempt bonds may fit into an individual investor's portfolio and offer a return (after tax) commensurate with the risk the investor must endure.

Taxable Municipal Securities

The previous discussion indicated that the interest on state and local government securities is exempt from federal income taxation. Although that is generally true, there are exceptions. There is no requirement that localities issue tax-exempt

[9]One municipal bond salesperson referred to the $5,000 municipal bond as a "roach motel." Once you are in, you can't get out. The unit is just too small for bond dealers to buy. If an investor does acquire municipal securities in units of $5,000, he or she had best plan to hold the bond until it is retired.

[10]The investor also bears the risk associated with inflation and reinvestment rate risk, if the purpose of the bond portfolio is to accumulate funds instead of generating current tax-free income.

bonds; they may issue taxable bonds. For example, the Alaska Housing Finance Corporation has issued over $2 billion in taxable bonds. Few other state and local governments have followed the Alaska Housing Finance Corporation's policy. Tax reform, however, has limited the ability of local governments to issue tax-exempt bonds as a means to raise funds for financing some projects, such as housing and industrial development.

Prior to tax reform, a local government could create an industrial authority that would issue bonds, build a facility, and then lease it to a firm. Local governments sold these industrial revenue bonds to stimulate economic growth or obtain a desired facility, such as a hospital. Since the local government authority and not the user issued the debt, the interest is tax-exempt. The interest payments are the responsibility of the industrial authority and not the local or state government that created the authority (i.e., the bonds are revenue bonds of the authority and not general obligations of the state or its municipalities). If the firm using the facilities were to fail to make the required payments, the industrial authority would be unable to make the interest payments to the bondholders. While this suggests industrial revenue bonds can be risky investments, many are among the safest tax-exempt bonds because the interest is supported by major corporations. For example, the Waynesboro, Virginia, Industrial Authority bonds are supported by Du Pont.

Tax reform has limited the ability of state and local governments to issue tax-exempt bonds to finance these "private" (as opposed to "public") projects. While tax reform has imposed limits on tax-exempt financing, it has not precluded state and local governments from issuing taxable bonds to raise funds to finance private enterprise. Such taxable municipal bonds are sometimes referred to as *private activity bonds,* since the funds are used for private purposes.

In addition to taxable municipal bonds, the interest on some nontaxable bonds may be subject to the alternative minimum tax that some individuals must pay. This alternative tax is designed to ensure that individuals who may not be subject to federal income tax under the regular tax laws will be required to make some federal income tax payments. Hence, tax-exempt interest may be subject to the alternative taxation.

POINTS OF INTEREST

Prerefunded Municipal Bonds

Municipal bonds are initially issued with terms of 15, 20, or 25 years. Bonds may even have maturity dates that are farther in the future. Some are noncallable, and the call date for others is often many years after the date of issue. For example, the University of Virginia Hospital Authority issued nontaxable revenue bonds in 1985 with coupons in excess of 8 percent and maturities extending beyond the year 2000. The bonds could not be called until 1995, ten years after being issued. After 1985, interest rates declined, so it would have been advantageous to refinance. Issuing new bonds with lower coupons and retiring the more expensive debt would reduce interest expense, but the inability to call the bonds meant such an action was not feasible.

Although the bonds could not be called, an alternative strategy was used to reduce interest expense. A second series of bonds was issued, and the proceeds were used to acquire U.S. Treasury bonds that matured when the original issue was callable. The interest earned on the Treasury bonds was then used to pay the interest on the original bonds. In effect, the municipal authority only paid interest on the new bonds: When the original bonds became callable, the proceeds from the maturing Treasury securities retired the original debt issue.

Once a municipal government (or authority in the case of the UVA hospital bonds) issues the new bonds, segregates the proceeds, and acquires the Treasury securities, the original issue of bonds is referred to as *prerefunded.* The bonds will be retired on the call date, and the maturity date is no longer relevant. From the investor's perspective, the uncertainty as to when the bonds will be retired is eliminated. In addition, since the proceeds of the Treasury securities are earmarked to pay the interest and retire the debt, default risk is eliminated. While prerefunded municipal bonds still have some interest rate and reinvestment rate risk, these tax-free bonds are as safe as Treasury securities.

An example of tax-exempt debt subject to the alternative minimum tax was the issue of bonds sold by the Richmond, Virginia, Redevelopment and Housing Authority. The funds raised by the issue were used to develop and renovate a section of the city referred to as Tobacco Row by building condominiums, apartments, and retail space. Part of the financing, which included both private and public participation, was a $100 million issue of authority bonds. While the interest was exempt from regular federal income taxation, it was subject to the alternative minimum tax.

Bonds that are subject to the alternative tax are not as attractive as other debt instruments, such as bonds issued by the state of Virginia to finance general improvements or the city of Richmond to finance public schools. Bonds subject to the alternative minimum tax tend to have higher yields than bonds not subject to the tax. Individuals who are subject to the regular federal income taxes but are not subject to the alternative minimum tax may find these debt obligations to be attractive investments. They offer higher yields and do not affect these individuals' tax obligations.

Foreign Government Debt Securities

American investors are not limited to the securities issued by the federal government, its agencies, the states, and their political subdivisions. Investors can also purchase the debt of foreign governments. These foreign securities may offer a higher yield because they have additional risk, such as the risks associated with changes in exchange rates and with default.

Investments in foreign government securities have exchange rate risk—that is, the currency in which the debt is denominated. Unless the debt is denominated in dollars, the American investor bears the risk associated with fluctuations in exchange rates. Since the value of the dollar relative to other currencies changes daily, higher promised yields in the local currency may translate into modest or even negative returns once the local currency is converted into dollars.

The second source of risk is the risk of default. The failure to pay the interest and redeem the bonds is highly unlikely by the governments of world financial powers, such as the United Kingdom. The risk of default, however, is perceptibly greater for the governments of such countries as Russia and China. Such default could be based on political as well as economic events. For example, when Castro came to power, Cuba nationalized assets held by U.S. firms and repudiated debts the government owed. (Cuban bonds continued to trade in the United States even after their maturity dates had passed and interest had not been paid for years.) More recent defaults led to the development of Brady bonds.

Brady Bonds

During the 1980s, the economies of many developing nations experienced a period of rapid growth. These nations, especially those with such natural resources as oil reserves, were able to issue debt that was readily bought by Western commercial banks. The countries were eager to issue this debt to avoid constraints imposed by accepting grants from Western nations or borrowing from Western government-sponsored banks (e.g., the World Bank). The commercial banks readily granted the loans to the developing nations to earn higher rates of interest. Increasing commodity prices suggested that these countries could easily service the debt.

Commodity prices, however, did not indefinitely increase, and many of these governments either defaulted or had to borrow additional funds to pay the interest on their bonds. Such borrowing, of course, only further increased the amount they owed. Many of the bonds sold in the secondary markets for substantial discounts. In effect, these bonds became another illustration of a high-yield, junk security. The defaults led to a period of restructuring, and it was during this period that Brady bonds were developed.

Brady bonds, named for Nicholas Brady, who was responsible for their development, advanced a plan to reduce the amount of foreign debt through an exchange of old bonds for new bonds. For the debt restructuring to occur, the debtor nation had to undergo economic reforms. After economic progress had been made, the old bonds were exchanged for new bonds—the Brady bonds. The face value or principal amount of the new bonds was less than the original amount of the debt (i.e., some of the debt was forgiven). Initial interest payments were less than current interest rates but would rise over time.

Lower interest payments and principal forgiveness are common features in restructuring. What differentiated Brady bonds was that the principal was guaranteed by U.S. federal government securities. U.S. zero coupons with maturity dates that coincided with the maturity dates of the exchanged bonds were used as collateral for the new bonds issued by the emerging nation's government. This guarantee was exceedingly important because it removed default risk (at least for the principal). It also removed exchange rate risk because the principal amount is collateralized in dollars.

It is important to realize that Brady bonds are not obligations of the federal government and that the federal government is not making the loans. Instead, the Brady bonds were created through an exchange of old bonds for new bonds, and are not new loans. Once issued, Brady bonds may be bought and sold in the secondary market like any other debt security. Investing in Brady bonds still involves risk. Interest payments may not be made, and a bond's price will vary with changes in interest rates, so yields are higher than available on investment-grade debt. In effect, Brady bonds are a type of government, high-yield security, whose principal repayment is guaranteed by U.S. federal government obligations. (Information concerning Brady bonds, such as prices and ratings, may be found at BradyNet Incorporated's Web address: http://www.bradynet.com).

Government Securities and Investment Companies

Closed-end investment companies and mutual funds are tailor-made for investing in government securities. Although investment companies are available for equities, some individuals prefer to manage their own portfolios. There is no denying the potential excitement or satisfaction of acquiring a stock and then having its price rise. (The converse would be true if the individuals sold the stock short and its price subsequently declined.) Even if the investor does not outperform the market over a period of time (and efficient markets suggest that the individual will not outperform the market on a risk-adjusted basis), there is satisfaction from the process of security selection and personal management of the portfolio.

Even these individuals, however, may prefer to use mutual funds for the acquisition of government securities. Several reasons have been alluded to throughout this chapter, two of which are the lack of marketability of some government securities and the lack of readily available information on which to base an investment decision. A third reason is the size of the unit of trading, and a fourth is diversification.

While federal government securities have active secondary markets, that is not true for many tax-exempt securities. Even if the investor is able to acquire the bonds, the spread between the bid and ask prices can be substantial, especially for small issues or if the individual acquires small denominations, such as a $5,000 face amount.

The inability of the investor to obtain financial information concerning the issuing government authority is also related to the size of the issue. Municipal bonds are not registered with the SEC. Information on many issues is not readily available through brokerage firms or other sources, such as the Internet. Prices are not quoted, and though bond values may be provided by brokers on monthly statements to customers, the values are at best approximations and are not indicative of actual trades or available bid prices.

The third disadvantage is the size of the unit of trading, and that minimum size has implications for diversification. For example, the size of trading is $1,000 face amount for Treasury bills and $25,000 for Ginnie Maes. Municipal bonds are sold in units of $5,000, but it may be difficult to find bonds available for $5,000 and virtually impossible to find a specific issue available in that small a unit. Of course, if the individual is determined to acquire and manage his or her own bond portfolio, brokers will execute the buy and sell orders. This may be especially true if the investor is concerned with the composition of the portfolio and not specific issues. For example, the investor can construct a laddered municipal bond portfolio in which the emphasis is on the maturity dates and not on acquiring bonds issued by specific municipalities. It may take some patience on the part of the investor while bonds with the various maturity dates are located, but a broker can execute the strategy.

Diversifying a municipal government bond portfolio also requires purchasing a variety of issues. However, diversifying may not be important if the investor limits the bonds to those with investment-grade ratings, since bonds with these ratings should not default. (Of course, the investor still must bear the risk associated with changes in interest rates since all bond prices will change with an increase or a decrease in the rate of interest.) Diversifying a bond portfolio will require a variety of issues, whose features would differ in order for their returns to not be perfectly correlated. Such diversification would obviously be important if the investor constructed a portfolio of less-than-investment-grade municipal bonds or a portfolio of foreign government debt issues. Such a diversified portfolio will probably require a substantial investment, since the minimum unit of trading increases the total cost of diversifying the portfolio.

These disadvantages associated with managing an individual government bond portfolio are avoided by acquiring shares in investment companies. The shares are easily bought and redeemed (in the case of mutual funds) or bought and sold (in the case of closed-end investment companies). Information is, of course, readily available on the investment company, such as its size, past performance, management, and fees. Information on the specific securities held by the investment company may be irrelevant to the individual investor. Instead, the information is relevant to the fund's professional managers.

The size of the unit is also not a problem for the investor. Presumably the fund has the resources to buy and sell the individual debt security using a cost-efficient unit of trading. The investor then buys the shares of the closed-end investment company on the open market or buys the shares directly from the open-end mutual fund. The amount of the purchase can be as small as the investor wishes, subject to minimum size of purchase from the fund (e.g., $1,000) or the minimum amount to be cost-effective to acquire the publicly traded shares of the closed-end investment company.

Last, diversification is one of the advantages offered by investment companies. Unless the individual acquires shares solely in specialized investment companies, the individual has a piece of a diversified portfolio. Even if the investor acquires a position in a specialized fund, that portfolio is diversified within the specialization.

Specialized Government Investment Companies

Many investment companies have portfolios that specialize in particular debt instruments. While many money market mutual funds hold a cross section of short-term debt instruments, some hold only Treasury bills and other short-term securities guaranteed by the U.S. government. These funds pay the lowest rates available from money market funds, but they are also the absolute safest of all the money market funds.

Other mutual funds specialize in intermediate-term federal government bonds, while others hold long-term bonds. The latter funds may move into intermediate-term bonds if the portfolio manager anticipates higher interest rates. Such a movement would protect investors if long-term rates did rise. This portfolio manager would follow an opposite strategy in anticipation of lower rates, since the prices of the longest-term bonds would increase the most in response to lower rates. Other portfolio managers may follow a more passive strategy, which emphasizes the collection of interest and the repayment of principal and not the timing of interest rate changes.

Among the most important government security funds are those specializing in municipal bonds. These include (1) money market mutual funds that acquire short-term municipal debt, (2) general bond funds that hold a cross section of municipal bonds, and (3) state municipal bond funds with portfolios devoted entirely to the government bonds issued in a particular state. While the short-term municipal bond funds are always open-end mutual investment companies, the general bond funds and the specialized state funds can be either open-end or closed-end investment companies whose shares are traded on the secondary markets.

The appeal of the general municipal bond funds is primarily directed to investors seeking income that is exempt from federal income taxation. For example, Dreyfus Muni Bond Fund holds 100 percent of its assets in municipal bonds issued in various states. In 2000, this fund earned (and distributed) $0.59 a share on a net asset value of $11.94 for a yield of 4.94 percent. All the income was exempt from federal income taxation. The distributions, however, were subject to state income taxes, but if the individual lived in a state with no income tax, then the distribution was not taxed at the state level.

Individuals who live in states with high state income taxes may prefer the specialized municipal bond funds. These specialized funds are obviously designed to attract the funds of investors who live in the particular state. For example, Nuveen New Jersey Premium Income Municipal Fund (NNJ) is a closed-end investment company that owns investment-grade municipal bonds issued by the state of New Jersey and its political subdivisions. NNJ's shares are traded on the New York Stock Exchange, and, although any investor may acquire the stock, its primary appeal is to residents of New Jersey, who pay both federal and state income tax. For residents in the top bracket, the total tax rate is 41.37 percent (35.00 percent federal plus 6.37 percent state). If the investor in the top bracket acquires the shares of NNJ and earns 4.94 percent, that is the equivalent of 8.43 percent on a taxable investment.

Summary

In order to tap funds from many sources, the federal government issues a variety of debt instruments. These range from Series EE and HH bonds, which are sold in small denominations, to short-term Treasury bills and long-term bonds, which are sold in large denominations.

Because there is no possibility of default, federal government debt is the safest of all possible investments. However, the investor still bears the risk of loss through fluctuations in interest rates and (except for indexed bonds) inflation. If interest rates rise, the prices of federal government bonds decline. If the rate of inflation exceeds the yield on debt instruments, the investor experiences a loss of purchasing power.

In addition to the debt issued by the federal government itself, bonds are issued by its agencies. These bonds tend to offer slightly higher yields, but they are virtually as safe as the direct debt of the federal government. In some cases, the agency's debt is even secured by the full faith and credit of the U.S. Treasury.

Among the most popular securities issued by a federal government agency are the mortgage pass-through bonds issued by the Government National Mortgage Association, or *Ginnie Mae.* These bonds serve as a conduit through which interest and principal repayments are made from homeowners to the bondholders. Payments are made monthly, so Ginnie Mae bonds are popular with individuals desiring a flow of cash receipts. These bonds expose investors to risk of loss from fluctuating interest rates or from inflation, but the interest payments and principal repayments are guaranteed by an agency of the federal government.

Alternatives to Ginnie Maes are collateralized mortgage obligations (CMOs), which are issued by a trust that holds mortgages guaranteed by the federal government. CMOs are sold in series, or tranches, with the obligations in the shortest tranche being retired before any of the CMOs in the next series are retired.

State and local governments issue long-term debt instruments to finance capital improvements, such as schools and roads. The debt is retired over a period of time by tax receipts or revenues. Some of these bonds are supported by the taxing authority of the issuing government, but many are supported only by the revenues generated by the facilities financed through the bond issues.

State and municipal debt differs from other investments because the interest is exempt from federal income taxation. These bonds pay lower rates of interest than taxable securities (e.g., corporate bonds), but their after-tax yields may be equal to or even greater than the yields on taxable bonds. The nontaxable bonds are particularly attractive to investors in high income tax brackets, because the bonds provide a means to shelter income from taxation.

Tax-exempt bonds can be risky investments, since the capacity of state and local governments to service the debt varies. Moody's and Standard & Poor's rating services analyze this debt based on the government's ability to pay the interest and retire the principal. Such ratings indicate the risk associated with investing in a particular debt issue. In addition, investors must bear the risks associated with fluctuations in security prices and the lack of liquidity associated with tax-exempt bonds.

Questions

1) Why is the debt of the federal government considered to be the safest of all possible investments?
2) What distinguishes series EE (Patriot) bonds from Treasury bills?
3) When interest rates rise, what happens to the price of federal government bonds? What happens to the price of state and local government bonds?
4) What is the difference between the following:
   a) A bond secured by a moral obligation and a bond secured by full faith and credit?
   b) A revenue bond and a general obligation bond?

   Are there any similarities between a bond secured by a moral obligation and a revenue bond?
5) What are the sources of risk investing in
   a) Federal government debt?
   b) Municipal debt?
6) How do Treasury inflation-indexed securities help the investor manage risk?
7) What is the difference between a term bond issue and a serial bond issue? Why are many capital improvements made by state and local governments financed through serial bonds?
8) What is a mortgage pass-through bond? What risks are associated with investing in Ginnie Mae bonds? What is the composition of the payment received from a mortgage pass-through bond?

9) If interest rates increase, what should happen to
   a) The price of a Ginnie Mae bond and the price of a municipal bond?
   b) The payments received from a Ginnie Mae bond and the payments received from a municipal bond?

   Contrast your answers to parts (a) and (b).
10) Identify which government securities may be appropriate for the following investors:
    a) A retired couple seeking income
    b) An individual in the highest tax bracket seeking a liquid investment
    c) An individual seeking a government bond for inclusion in an individual retirement account (IRA)
    d) A child with no income and a modest amount to invest
    e) A corporation with $100,000,000 to invest for less than three months
    f) A church seeking to invest a modest endowment fund

11) Selected interest rates may be found in Federal Reserve Economic Data (FRED), which may be accessed through the Federal Reserve Bank of St. Louis's home page: http://www.stls.frb.org/fred. Based on this information, what is the current difference between the yield on a six-month Treasury bill and the 30-year Treasury bond? What is the difference in the yields on corporate bonds rated Aaa and Baa by Moody's?
12) What is the yield currently being offered by series EE bonds? (Information concerning EE bonds may be found through the Bureau of Public Debt: http://www.publicdebt.treas.gov.)

Problems

1) If a six-month Treasury bill is purchased for $0.9675 on a dollar (i.e., $96,750 for a $100,000 bill), what is the discount yield and the annual rate of interest? What will be these yields if the discount price falls to $0.94 on a dollar (i.e., $94,000 for a $100,000 bill)?
2) An investor is in the 28 percent income tax bracket and can earn 6.3 percent on a nontaxable bond. What is the comparable yield on a taxable bond? If this same investor can earn 8.9 percent on a taxable bond, what must be the yield on a nontaxable bond so that the after-tax yields are equal?
3) An investor in the 35 percent tax bracket may purchase a corporate bond that is rated double A and is traded on the New York Stock Exchange (the bond division). This bond yields 9.0 percent. The investor may also buy a double-A-rated municipal bond with a 5.85 percent yield. Why may the corporate bond be preferred? (Assume that the terms of the bonds are the same.)
4) What is the price of the following zero coupon bonds if interest rates are (a) 4 percent, (b) 7 percent, and (c) 10 percent?
   - Bond A: zero coupon; maturity 5 years
   - Bond B: zero coupon; maturity 10 years
   - Bond C: zero coupon; maturity 20 years

   What generalization can be made concerning the term of a zero coupon bond and its price in relation to changes in the level of interest rates?
5) You are in the 28 percent federal income tax bracket. A corporate bond offers you 9.8 percent while a tax-exempt bond with the same credit rating and term to maturity offers 8.1 percent. On the basis of taxation, which bond should be preferred? Explain.
6) A six-month $10,000 Treasury bill is selling for $9,844. What is the annual yield according to the discount method? Does this yield understate or overstate the true annual yield? Explain.

7) What is the current taxable equivalent yield for an individual in the 35 percent federal income tax bracket for intermediate bonds (10 or fewer years to maturity) and long-term bonds (30 years to maturity)? Estimates of prevailing yields on municipal bonds may be found through Bloomberg's information on U.S. financial markets: http://www.bloomberg.com/markets.

8) The federal government issues two four-year notes. The first is a traditional type of debt instrument that pays 6 percent annually ($60 per $1,000 note). The second pays a real yield of 3 percent with the amount of interest being adjusted with changes in the CPI. The CPI was 100 when the notes were initially issued.

   a) What is the annual amount of interest paid each year on each security if the CPI is as follows?

Year	CPI
1	102
2	96
3	103
4	110

   b) What is the amount of principal repaid at maturity by each note?
   c) Using the dollar-weighted return explained in Chapter 10, what is the nominal, annual rate of return on each security?
   d) Based on the answer to part (c), which alternative produced the higher return and why?

THE FINANCIAL ADVISOR'S INVESTMENT CASE
Building a Bond Portfolio

Kris Kazim, who recently retired, has come to you for financial help. At the initial consultation, you realized that he is a very low risk tolerance investor who wants to increase current income. Kazim has $300,000 invested in certificates of deposit with maturities of one to three years earning rates of 3.0 percent. While you believe that such a large amount invested in one type of asset at one financial institution is a decidedly inferior strategy, you also realize that Kazim would not be willing to alter the portfolio in any way that would largely impact on risk.

Since he is primarily concerned with income and safety of principal, you believe that initially the best strategy would be to alter the portfolio by substituting quality bonds for a substantial proportion of the certificates of deposit. Thus, you suggest that $250,000 be invested in bonds. Of the $250,000, $25,000 would be invested in triple-A- or double-A-rated bonds with one year to maturity, $25,000 with two years to maturity, and so on until the last $25,000 is invested in bonds with ten years to maturity. Thus, none of the bonds would have a maturity exceeding ten years, none of the bonds would have a rating of less than double A, and each year $25,000 of the bonds' face amounts would mature.

Kazim agreed to the basic strategy but required that all the bonds be federal government obligations. Currently the structure of interest rates is as follows:

Term to Maturity	Coupon Rate of Interest
1	4.0%
2	4.0
3	4.0
4	5.0
5	5.0
6	5.0
7	6.0
8	6.0
9	7.0
10	7.0

All the bonds are currently selling at par ($1,000 per $1,000 face amount). Kazim still has doubts concerning the risk of loss of principal, but he likes the fact that additional income can be generated by the bonds with the higher coupons. To help convince him this is an acceptable strategy, answer the following questions:

1) If the interest on the CDs was $9,000, what is the increase in income generated by this laddered strategy?
2) What is the advantage of investing $25,000 in bonds maturing each year instead of investing the entire $250,000 in the ten-year bonds?
3) How much could Kazim lose of the $250,000 if he follows this strategy and, *after one year,* interest rates rise across the board by 1 percent (100 basis points)?
4) Would the earned interest offset the loss from the rise in interest rates?
5) How much additional loss would be incurred compared to the loss in question 3 if Kazim invests the entire $250,000 in the ten-year bonds and one year later the interest rates rise to 10 percent?
6) What should Kazim do with the $25,000 from the bond that matures after one year if he finds that he does not need the principal?

APPENDIX 17

Using Yield Curves

Yield curves relate the term, or time to maturity, and yields to maturity (not coupon or nominal rates) for bonds of a given risk class. These curves were illustrated in Figures 15.1 and 15.2, which plotted yields and time to maturity for U.S. Treasury securities during three different time periods. Figure 15.1 presented a positive yield curve, indicating that longer-term bonds offered higher yields. Figure 15.2 presented (1) a negatively sloped yield curve, which indicated that as the term of the bond increases, the yield to maturity declines; and (2) a flat yield curve, in which yields are essentially the same no matter how long the bond is outstanding.

Yield Curves and Active Bond Strategies

Generally, yield curves are positively sloping, but curves do shift and change their shape. These fluctuations may offer investors an opportunity to increase returns or decrease risk by adjusting their portfolios of debt securities. For example, in Figure 17A.1, the original, negatively sloped yield curve (YC_1) shifts to a positively sloped yield curve (YC_2). While all yields decrease, the shape of the yield curve changes. Short-term rates decline more than the decline in long-term rates, and the yield becomes upward sloping, indicating that long-term yields now exceed short-term yields. (A shift from YC_2 to YC_1 would indicate the opposite: that short-term rates now exceed long-term rates.)

The individual may infer that a negatively sloped yield curve argues for investing in short-term and avoiding long-term bonds in order to earn the higher rates

FIGURE 17A.1

Shifting Yield Curves

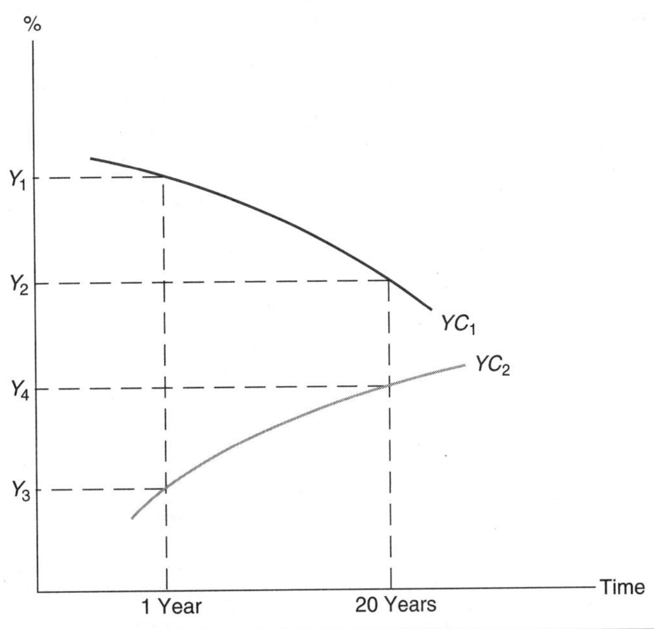

(i.e., shift funds from long-term to short-term). The investor may execute this strategy if he or she expects rates to remain unchanged or to increase.

The shift from long-term to short-term, however, will not benefit from a decline in interest rates. If the yield curve returns to its normal, positive slope (i.e., YC_1 shifts to YC_2), acquiring short-term securities precludes the opportunity to lock in currently high long-term rates. For example, if the investor acquires one-year securities offering yield Y_1, that individual will experience a large decline in yields if the curve shifts from YC_1 to YC_2. If this investor had purchased the 20-year security with a yield of Y_2, that individual would have locked in the higher rate. If the investor had initially acquired higher-yielding short-term securities, that individual will earn only Y_3 if the short-term securities are retained and Y_4 if the funds are invested for 20 years.[1]

Acquiring the long-term debt does run the risk that the bonds will be called after interest rates fall and the yield curve returns to its normal shape. Even if the bonds are called, the investor can roll over the funds, and any call penalty offsets (at least partially) lost interest. (Financial managers of corporations realize that they may save interest expense if they borrow for the short-term at the higher rate on YC_1 and refinance at the subsequent lower rate on YC_2. One reason why the short-term rate is higher on YC_1 than the long-term rate is that financial managers expect rates to fall and are reluctant to borrow for the long-term. Instead, they increase the demand for short-term funds, which increases the short-term rate of interest.)

Another possible shift in yield curves is illustrated in Figure 17A.2, in which the yield curve shifts upward from YC_1 to YC_2. While the positive slope of both curves

FIGURE 17A.2

An Upward Shift in Yield Curves

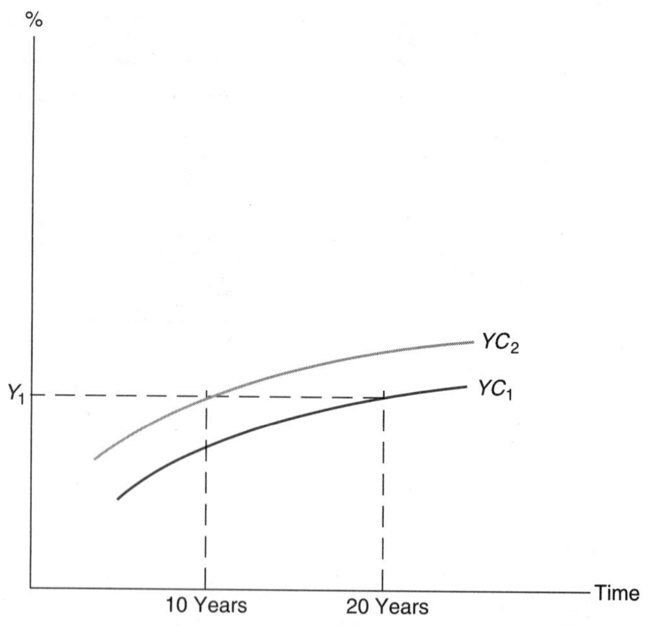

[1]These fluctuations in yield curves also illustrate reinvestment rate risk. If the investor acquires long-term debt (e.g., the 20-year bond yielding Y_2 in Figure 17A.1), the actual return will be less if the yield curve shifts from YC_1 to YC_2 because the interest payments cannot be reinvested at Y_2.

FIGURE 17A.3

Yield Curves for Different Risk Classes

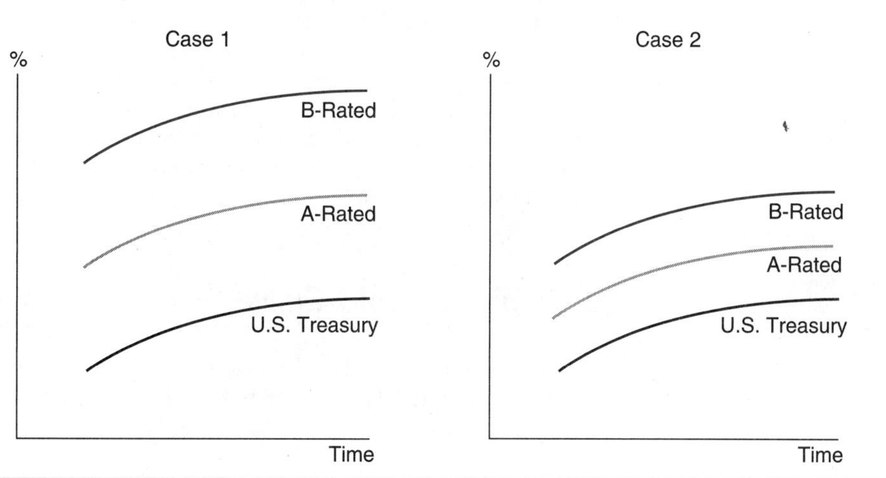

indicates that the longest-term bonds continue to offer the highest yields, higher yields are now available with shorter maturities. The investor can earn Y_1 but will have to commit the funds for only 10 years instead of 20 years. By shortening the maturity of the portfolio, the investor may be able to reduce risk from fluctuations in interest rates, the reinvestment rate, having the bond called prior to maturity, and the loss of purchasing power. The risk reduction may be achieved without having to forgo interest income.

Of course, if the investor had purchased the 20-year bond prior to the shift in the yield curves from YC_1 to YC_2, that individual will experience a capital loss. In this case, the better strategy would be to acquire short-term debt and forgo some interest income. Unfortunately, few investors can predict the direction of change in interest rates and must bear the risk associated with their fluctuations.

The prior discussion was limited to yield curves for bonds with the same default risk (i.e., bonds with comparable ratings such as U.S. Treasury securities). Figure 17A.3 illustrates two cases for yield curves of bonds with different credit ratings. In both cases, the yield curves are positively sloped, and lower ratings are associated with higher yields. The difference between case 1 and case 2 is the distance or spread between the yield curves. Figure 16.4 illustrated fluctuations in the yields of triple-A- and triple-B-rated corporate bonds. The same information for Aaa- and Baa-rated municipal bonds was presented in Figure 17.1. The yields on the lower-quality bonds always exceeded the yields on the higher-quality debt, but the difference between the yields (i.e., the spread between the yield curves) fluctuated over time.

When the spreads increase (i.e., when the yield curves are farther apart as in case 1), the investor may sell the safer bonds and purchase the riskier bonds. This strategy will earn the higher return. If increased default risk is excluded, this bond swap may also decrease the investor's risk exposure. First, if the term remains the same (e.g., ten years), the investor earns the higher return without increasing purchasing power risk. Second, interest rate risk is related to the decline in the price of the bonds when interest rates increase. If rates do increase, there may be less of a decline in the market value of the riskier bonds because they pay higher coupons. The relationship between a bond's coupon and the fluctuation in its price was shown in Figure 16.2. The smaller price fluctuation from the higher coupon bonds suggests that swapping the safer, lower-coupon bond for the higher-coupon bond may reduce rather than increase interest rate risk.[2] Third, reinvestment rate risk is related to the rate earned when the interest payments are reinvested and applies if interest rates decline. After the swap the additional interest offsets (at least partially) any interest lost from reinvesting the coupons at lower rates.

This suggests that the investor can use yield curves to actively manage a bond portfolio. Shifts in the curves may encourage alterations in the composition of a bond portfolio to increase returns or reduce risk. Such a plan opposes the laddered strategy discussed in the section on managing interest rate risk in Chapter 16. By staggering maturities in a laddered strategy, the investor adopts a passive strategy and is not concerned with the shape of or shifts in the yield curve.

Riding the Yield Curve to Enhance Short-Term Yields

In addition to active bond strategies, the investor may use a positive yield curve as a means to magnify the return on a short-term investment. Consider an individual with $10,000 to invest in Treasury bills. Four investment possibilities follow:

Term	Price	Annual Yield
3 months	$9,800	8.42%
6 months	9,500	10.80
9 months	9,100	13.40
12 months	8,800	13.64

Notice that in this example the yield curve in Figure 17A.4 is positively sloped because as the term of the bill increases, the yields become higher (e.g., 8.42 percent for the three-month bill and 13.64 for the 12-month bill).[3]

The investor may purchase any of the four T-bills. For example, if the individual wants to invest the funds for one year, he or she can buy the 12-month bill or buy the 3-month bill and reinvest the funds for an additional 9 months when the 3-month bill matures. Even if the individual wants the investment for only 6 months, any of the T-bills may be purchased, because the 3-month bill can be rolled over into another bill and the 9-month or 12-month bills can be sold after 6 months. Since there are active secondary markets in T-bills, the investor could buy the 12-month bill, hold it for 6 months, and then sell it.

Whether the individual wants to invest for 3 months, 6 months, or a year, it may be possible to increase the yield by purchasing the 12-month bill and selling it after a period of time. This strategy is referred to as *riding the yield curve.* To see how the yield may be increased, consider the investor who buys the 12-month bill

Calculator Solution

Function Key	Data Input
PV =	−9800
FV =	10000
PMT =	0
N =	.25
I =	?
Function Key	*Answer*
I =	8.42

[2]The higher coupon weights the cash flows toward the earlier years of the bond's life. The duration of these bonds is smaller, which indicates that their price volatility is less than those bonds with the smaller coupons.

[3]The exaggerated difference in the yields is designed to illustrate this concept—it is not typical of the actual differences in yields. The determination of the annualized (compound) yield is

$$\$9{,}800(1 + i)^n = \$10{,}000,$$

in which $n = 0.25$. The solution is

$$\$9{,}800(1 + i)^{0.25} = \$10{,}000$$

$$(1 + i)^{0.25} = \frac{\$10{,}000}{9{,}800} = 1.0204$$

$$i = (1.0204)^4 - 1 = 0.0842 = 8.42\%.$$

(This answer may be obtained using a financial calculator or a calculator with a y^x key.)

FIGURE 17A.4

Riding the Yield Curve

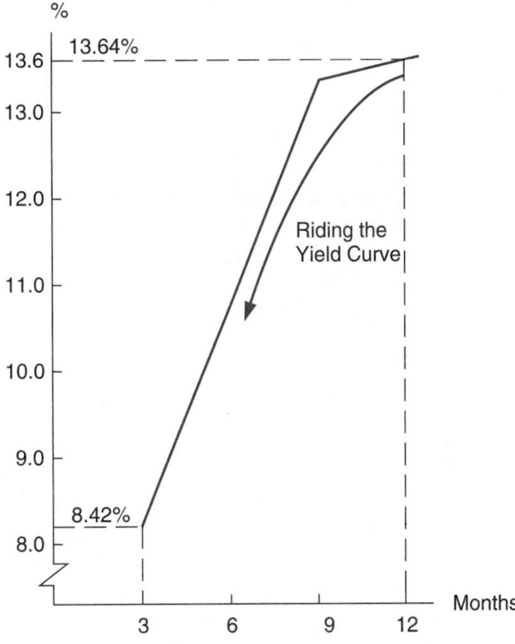

with the intention of selling it after 6 months. What will be the price of the bill when it is sold? There are three general possibilities: (1) the structure of yields will remain the same, (2) yields will rise, and (3) yields will fall.

If after 6 months the structure of yields has not changed, the 12-month bill becomes a 6-month bill with a price of \$9,500 and an annual yield of 10.80 percent. (Remember: T-bills are sold at a discount that declines as the bill approaches maturity.) The bill has moved up two steps in the preceding table of prices and yields and has moved down the yield curve in Figure 17A.4. That means the investor may sell the bill for a profit of \$700 (\$9,500 − \$8,800), for a 6-month holding period return of 7.95 percent (\$700/\$8,800). The annualized yield is 16.54 percent.[4] This gain is greater than the \$500 earned by purchasing the 6-month bill for \$9,500 and redeeming it for \$10,000 at maturity, thus realizing an annualized return of 10.80 percent.

If interest rates have risen, the prices of the bills will not rise as much. For example, suppose after 6 months the structure of yields is

Calculator Solution

Function Key		Data Input
PV	=	−8800
FV	=	9500
PMT	=	0
N	=	.5
I	=	?
Function Key		*Answer*
I	=	16.54

[4]The determination of the annualized (compound) rate (i) is

$$\$8{,}800(1 + i)^n = \$9{,}500,$$

in which $n = 0.5$. The solution is

$$\$8{,}800(1 + i)^n = \$9{,}500$$

$$(1 + i)^{0.5} = \frac{\$9{,}500}{\$8{,}800} = 1.07955$$

$$i = (1.07955)^2 - 1 = 0.1654 = 16.54\%.$$

Term	Price	Annual Yield
3 months	$9,750	10.66%
6 months	9,410	12.93
9 months	9,000	15.08
12 months	8,600	16.28

The original 12-month bill can now be sold for $9,410, which generates an annual return of 14.3 percent. The investor did not fare as well in this case (14.3 percent versus 16.8 percent) because the bill's price did not rise as much. However, unless interest rates rise precipitously and rapidly, as did occur during 1980 (see Figure 15.3), the investor will earn a return that exceeds the yield available through purchasing the 6-month bill and holding it to maturity.

If interest rates have fallen, the strategy of buying the 12-month bill produces an even higher return. Suppose after 6 months the structure of yields is

Term	Price	Annual Yield
3 months	$9,850	6.23%
6 months	9,600	8.51
9 months	9,400	8.60
12 months	9,120	9.65

Since interest rates have fallen, the price of the 12-month bill has risen even more than it would have had there been no change in the yield structure. In this case, the investor may now sell the bill for $9,600, generating a profit of $800 and an annual return of 19.0 percent. This is obviously the best scenario since the investor benefits from both riding the yield curve and the declining interest rates.

The opportunity to increase returns by riding the yield curve suggests that a positively sloped yield curve may be unstable. If many investors try to ride the yield curve, they will sell the shorter-term bills in order to purchase the longer-term bills. The sales will depress the price of the shorter-term bills and increase their yields while simultaneously increasing the price of the longer-term bills and decreasing their yields. These forces will tend to flatten the yield curve. The actual shape of the yield curve at a point in time will depend on the interplay of many factors, including individuals' preference for liquidity and expectations of future interest rates as well as the impact of individuals seeking higher returns by riding the yield curve.

Convertible Bonds and Convertible Preferred Stock

18

The previous chapters discussed the variety of bonds and preferred stock and the valuation of these securities. This chapter considers bonds and preferred stock with a special feature: The owner may convert the security into the issuing firm's common stock. Generally, convertible securities offer more income (higher interest or higher dividends) than may be earned through an investment in the firm's common stock. In addition, convertible securities have some potential for capital gains if the price of the underlying stock rises. Convertibles are issued by a variety of firms, generating a range of securities from high-quality to extremely risky convertibles.

This chapter discusses investing in convertible bonds and convertible preferred stocks. Initially, the features and terms of convertible bonds are described, followed by a discussion of their pricing. This includes the premiums paid for convertible bonds, and the relationship between their price and the price of the stock into which they may be converted. The third section is devoted to convertible preferred stock. These shares are similar to convertible bonds but lack the safety implied by the debt element of convertible bonds. Next follows the brief histories of three convertible bonds that illustrate the potential profits and risk associated with investing in them. The chapter ends with a description of a bond that permits the holder to sell the security back to the issuer prior to maturity for the bond's face value.

Learning Objectives

After completing this chapter you should be able to:

1 Describe the features common to all convertible bonds.
2 Determine the *floor,* or minimum price, of a convertible bond.
3 List the factors that affect the price of a convertible bond.
4 Identify the two premiums paid for a convertible bond.
5 Explain why the two premiums are inversely related.
6 Compare convertible bonds with convertible preferred stock.
7 Explain the advantage offered by a put bond.

Features of Convertible Bonds

Convertible bonds are debentures (i.e., unsecured debt instruments) that may be converted at the holder's option into the stock of the issuing company. Since the firm has granted the holder the right to convert the bonds, these bonds are usually subordinate to the firm's other debt. They also tend to offer a lower interest rate (i.e., coupon rate) than is available on nonconvertible debt. Thus, the conversion feature means that the firm can issue lower-quality debt at a lower interest cost. Investors are willing to accept this reduced quality and interest income because the market value of the bond will appreciate *if* the price of the stock rises. These investors are thus trading quality and interest for possible capital gains.

EXHIBIT 18.1

Selected Convertible Bonds

Corporation	Coupon Rate of Interest	Year of Maturity	Standard & Poor's Rating
Advanced Micro Devices	6%	2005	CCC+
Charming Shoppes	$7\frac{1}{2}$	2006	B−
Loews	$3\frac{1}{8}$	2007	A+
Seagram & Sons	0	2006	A−
Sun Company	$6\frac{3}{4}$	2012	BBB−

Source: *Standard & Poor's Bond Guide*, January 2001.

convertible bond

A bond that may be exchanged for (i.e., converted into) stock.

Convertible bonds have been a popular means for firms to raise funds in the capital markets. A sample of firms and their convertible bonds is presented in Exhibit 18.1. As may be seen in the exhibit, the bonds are not issued just by lower-quality firms with poor credit ratings. Some of the country's most prestigious firms, including IBM and Pfizer, have raised funds by issuing convertible bonds.

Since convertible bonds are long-term debt instruments, they have features that are common to all bonds. They are usually issued in $1,000 denominations, pay interest semiannually, and have a fixed maturity date. However, if the bonds are converted into stock, the maturity date is irrelevant because the bonds are retired when they are converted. Convertible bonds frequently have a sinking fund requirement, which, like the maturity date, is meaningless once the bonds are converted.

Convertible bonds are always callable. The firm uses the call to force the holders to convert the bonds. Once the bond is called, the owner must convert, or any appreciation in price that has resulted from an increase in the stock's value will be lost. Such forced conversion is extremely important to the issuing firm, because it no longer has to pay the interest and retire the debt.

Convertible bonds are attractive to some investors because they offer the safety features of debt. The firm must meet the terms of the indenture, and the bonds must be retired if they are not converted. The flow of interest income usually exceeds the dividend yield that may be earned on the firm's stock. In addition, since the bonds may be converted into stock, the holder will share in the growth of the company. If the price of the stock rises in response to the firm's growth, the value of the convertible bond must also rise. It is this combination of the safety of debt and the potential for capital gain that makes convertible bonds an attractive investment, particularly to investors who desire income and some capital appreciation.

Like all investments, convertible bonds subject the holder to risk. If the company fails, the holder of a bond stands to lose the funds invested in the debt. This is particularly true with regard to convertible bonds, because they are usually subordinate to the firm's other debt. Thus, convertible bonds are riskier than senior debt or debt that is secured by specific collateral. In case of a default or bankruptcy, holders of convertible bonds may at best realize only a fraction of the principal amount invested. However, their position is still superior to that of the stockholders.

Default is not the only potential source of risk to investors. Convertible bonds are actively traded, and their prices can and do fluctuate. As is explained in detail in the next section, their price is partially related to the value of the stock into which they may be converted. Fluctuations in the value of the stock produce fluctuations in the price of the bond. These price changes are *in addition* to price movements caused by variations in interest rates.

EXHIBIT 18.2

The Outcomes of Selected Convertible Bonds

	Prices as of December 31		
Bond	**1981**	**1985**	**1990**
Ampex 5½ 94	74½	Called and converted	N/A
Gulf & Western 5½ 93	Called and converted	N/A	N/A
Pan American World Airlines 4½ 86	46¼	96	Redeemed in 1986
Seatrain 6 95	16	No price quote	N/A

During periods of higher interest rates and lower stock prices, convertible bonds are doubly cursed. Their lower coupon rates of interest cause their prices to decline more than those of nonconvertible debt. This, in addition to the decline in the value of the stock into which they may be converted, results in considerable price declines for convertible bonds. Such declines are illustrated in Exhibit 18.2, which gives year-end prices for four convertible bonds, each of which was originally issued for $1,000.

Exhibit 18.2 also illustrates the three possible outcomes for a convertible bond. The first outcome occurs when the value of the stock rises, causing the value of the bond to rise and ultimately be converted. For example, the Gulf & Western and Ampex convertible bonds were called and converted after the underlying stocks rose in value. The value of the Ampex stock rose more slowly than that of the Gulf & Western stock, since the G&W bond was called earlier. A second outcome occurs when the firm defaults and the bond is reissued as part of a reorganization or the bond becomes worthless. Seatrain defaulted and declared bankruptcy, and the market for its bonds ceased to exist (i.e., there were no price quotes). An investor who purchased this bond when it was issued lost the entire $1,000. The third possible outcome for a convertible bond occurs when the value of the stock does not rise, so that the bond remains outstanding until the issuing corporation retires the debt at maturity or through the bond's sinking fund. The Pan Am convertible bond was outstanding for 20 years and retired at maturity. (Holders of Pan Am convertible bonds that matured in the 1990s were not so lucky because Pan Am, like Seatrain, went bankrupt and ceased to operate.)

The Valuation of Convertible Bonds

This section considers the valuation of convertible bonds. The value of a convertible bond is related to (1) the value of the stock into which it may be converted and (2) the value of the bond as a debt instrument. Although each of these factors affects the market price of the bond, the importance of each element varies with changing conditions in the security markets. In the final analysis, the valuation of a convertible bond is difficult, because it is a hybrid security that combines debt and equity.

This section has three subdivisions. The first considers the value of the bond solely as stock. The second covers the bond's value only as a debt instrument, and the last section combines these values to show the hybrid nature of convertible bonds. To differentiate the value of the bond as stock from its value as debt, subscripts are added to the symbols used. S will represent stock, and D will represent debt. Although this may make the equations appear more complex, it will clearly distinguish the value of the bond as stock from the value as debt.

The Convertible Bond as Stock—The Conversion Value

conversion value as stock
Value of the bond in terms of the stock into which the bond may be converted.

The value of a convertible bond in terms of the stock, its **conversion value** (C_s), depends on (1) the face value or principal amount of the bond (FV), (2) the conversion (or exercise) price of the bond (P_e), and (3) the market price of the common stock (P_s). The face value divided by the conversion price of the bond gives the number of shares into which the bond may be converted. For example, if a $1,000 bond may be converted at $20 per share, then the bond may be converted into 50 shares ($1,000 ÷ $20). The number of shares times the market price of a share gives the value of the bond in terms of stock. If the bond is convertible into 50 shares and the stock sells for $15 per share, then the bond is worth $750 in terms of stock ($15 × 50).

The conversion value of the bond as stock may be expressed in equation form. The number of shares into which the bond may be converted is called the *conversion ratio,* or

$$\textbf{Conversion ratio} = \frac{FV}{P_e}.$$

The conversion value of the bond is the product of the conversion ratio and the price of the stock.[1] The conversion value of the bond as stock is expressed in Equation 18.1:

(18.1)

$$C_s = \frac{FV}{P_e} \times P_s$$

and is also illustrated in Exhibit 18.3. In this example a $1,000 bond is convertible into 50 shares (i.e., a conversion price of $20 per share). The first column gives various prices of the stock. The second column presents the number of shares into which the bond is convertible (i.e., 50 shares). The third column gives the value of the bond in terms of stock (i.e., the product of the values in the first two columns). As may be seen in the exhibit, the value of the bond in terms of stock rises as the price of the stock increases.

This relationship between the price of the stock and the conversion value of the bond is illustrated in Figure 18.1. The price of the stock (P_s) is given on the horizontal axis, and the conversion value of the bond (C_s) is shown on the vertical axis. As the price of the stock rises, the conversion value of the bond increases. This is shown in the graph by line C_s, which represents the intrinsic value of the bond in terms of stock. Line C_s is a straight line running through the origin. If the stock has no value, the value of the bond in terms of stock is also worthless. If the exercise price of the bond and the market price of the stock are equal (i.e., $P_s = P_e$, which in this case is $20), the bond's value as stock is equal to the principal amount (i.e., the

[1]The *conversion price* is the face value divided by the number of shares into which the bond may be converted. That is,

$$\text{Conversion price} = \frac{FV}{\text{Conversion ratio}}.$$

If the bond is convertible into 50 shares, the conversion price is

$$\frac{\$1{,}000}{50} = \$20.$$

EXHIBIT 18.3

The Relationship Between the Price of a Stock and the Value of a Convertible Bond as Stock

Price of the Stock	Shares into Which the Bond is Convertible	Value of the Bond in Terms of Stock
$ 0	50	$ 0
5	50	250
10	50	500
15	50	750
20	50	1,000
25	50	1,250
30	50	1,500

bond's face value). As the price of the stock rises above the exercise price of the bond, the bond's value in terms of stock increases to more than the principal amount of the debt.

The market price of a convertible bond cannot be less than the bond's conversion value. If the price of the bond were less than its value as stock, an opportunity to arbitrage would exist. Arbitrageurs would sell the stock short, purchase the convertible bond, exercise the conversion feature, and use the shares acquired through the conversion to cover the short sale. They would then make a profit equal to the difference between the price of the convertible bond and the conversion value of the bond. For example, if in the preceding example the bond were selling for $800 when the stock sold for $20 per share, arbitrageurs would enter the market. At $20 per share, the bond is worth $1,000 in terms of the stock (i.e., $20 × 50). Arbitrageurs would sell 50 shares short for $1,000. At the same time they would buy the bond for $800 and exercise the option (i.e., convert the bond). After the shares had been acquired through the conversion of the bond, the arbitrageurs would cover the short position and earn $200 (before commissions).

As arbitrageurs purchase the bonds, they will drive up their price. The price increase will continue until there is no opportunity for profit. This occurs when the

FIGURE 18.1

The Relationship Between the Price of the Stock and the Conversion Value of the Bond

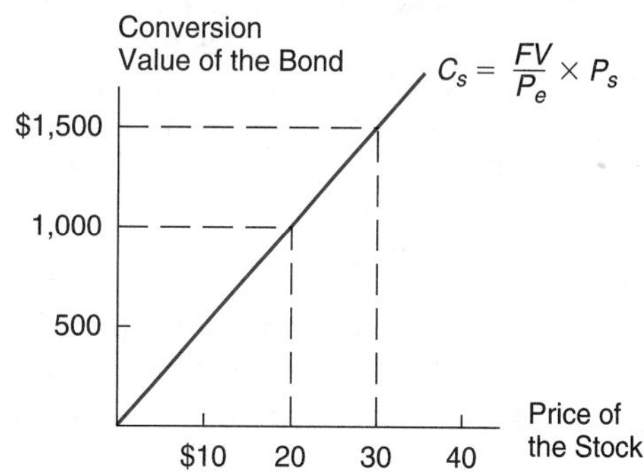

price is equal to or greater than the bond's value as stock. Thus, the conversion value of the bond as stock sets the minimum price of the bond. Because of arbitrage, the market price of a convertible bond will be at least equal to its conversion value.

However, the market price of the convertible bond is rarely equal to the conversion value of the bond. The bond frequently sells for a premium over its conversion value because the convertible bond may also have value as a debt instrument. As a pure (i.e., nonconvertible) bond, it competes with other nonconvertible debt. Like the conversion feature, this element of debt may affect the bond's price. Its impact is important, for it also has the effect of putting a minimum price on the convertible bond. It is this price floor that gives investors in convertible bonds an element of safety that stock lacks.

The Convertible Bond as Debt—The Investment Value

investment value as debt
The value of a convertible as if it were nonconvertible debt.

The **investment value** of a convertible bond (C_D) is related to (1) the annual interest that the bond pays (*PMT*), (2) the current interest rate that is paid on comparable nonconvertible debt (*i*), and (3) the requirement that the principal (*FV*) be retired at maturity (after *n* number of years) if the bond is not converted. In terms of present value calculations, the value of a convertible bond as nonconvertible debt is given in Equation 18.2:

(18.2)
$$C_D = \frac{PMT}{(1+i)^1} + \frac{PMT}{(1+i)^2} + \cdots + \frac{PMT}{(1+i)^n} + \frac{FV}{(1+i)^n}.$$

(Equation 18.2 is simply the current price of any bond and was discussed in Chapter 16.)

Equation 18.2 may be illustrated by the following example. Assume that the convertible bond in Exhibit 18.3 matures in ten years and pays 5 percent annually. Nonconvertible debt of the same risk class currently yields 8 percent. When these values are inserted into Equation 18.2, the investment value of the bond as nonconvertible debt is \$798.50:

Calculator Solution

Function Key	Data Input
PV	= ?
FV	= 1000
PMT	= 50
N	= 10
I	= 8
Function Key	**Answer**
PV	= −798.70

$$C_D = \frac{\$50}{(1+0.08)^1} + \frac{\$50}{(1+0.08)^2} + \cdots + \frac{\$50}{(1+0.08)^9} + \frac{\$50}{(1+0.08)^{10}} + \frac{\$1{,}000}{(1+0.08)^{10}}$$

$$C_D = \$50(6.710) + \$1{,}000(0.463) = \$798.50.$$

This equation may be solved by the use of present value tables or a financial calculator. The 6.710 is the interest factor for the present value of an annuity of \$1 for ten years at 8 percent, and 0.463 is the interest factor for the present value of \$1 to be received ten years in the future when it is discounted at 8 percent. To be competitive with nonconvertible debt, this bond would have to sell for \$798.50.

The relationship between the price of the common stock and the value of this bond as nonconvertible debt is illustrated in Figure 18.2. This figure consists of a horizontal line (C_D) that shows what the price (\$798.50) of the bond would be if it were not convertible into stock, in which case the price is independent of the value of the stock. The principal amount of the bond is also shown in Figure 18.2 by the broken line *FV*, which is above line C_D. The principal amount exceeds the value of the bond as pure debt because this bond must sell at a discount to be competitive with nonconvertible debt.

FIGURE 18.2

The Relationship Between the Price of Common Stock and the Value of the Bond as Nonconvertible Debt

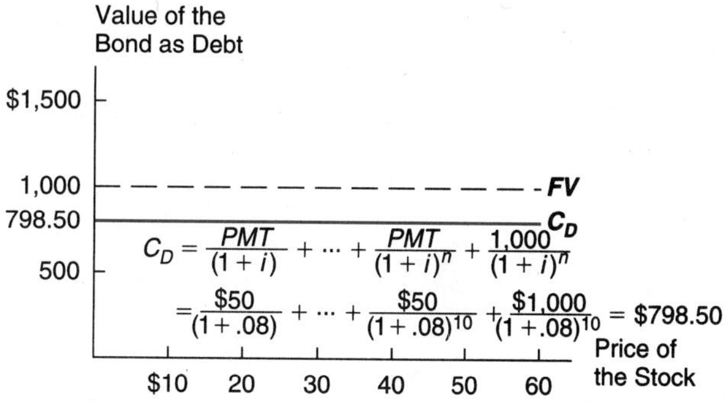

The investment value of the convertible bond as debt varies with market interest rates. Since the interest paid by the bond is fixed, the value of the bond as debt varies inversely with interest rates. An increase in interest rates causes this value to fall; a decline in interest rates causes the value to rise.

The relationship between the value of the preceding convertible bond as debt and various interest rates is presented in Exhibit 18.4. The first column gives various interest rates; the second column gives the nominal (i.e., coupon) rate of interest; and the last column gives the value of the bond as nonconvertible debt. The inverse relationship is readily apparent, for as the interest rate rises from 3 to 12 percent, the value of the bond declines from $1,170.60 to $604.48.

The value of the bond as nonconvertible debt is important because it sets another minimum value that the bond will command in the market. At that price the convertible bond is competitive with nonconvertible debt of the same maturity and degree of risk. If the bond were to sell below this price, it would offer a more attractive (i.e., higher) yield than nonconvertible debt. Investors would seek to buy the bond to attain this higher yield. They would bid up the bond's price until its yield was comparable to that of nonconvertible debt. Thus, the bond's value as

EXHIBIT 18.4

The Relationship Between Interest Rates and the Investment Value of a Bond

Interest Rate	Coupon Rate	Investment Value of a Ten-Year Bond (Interest Paid Annually)
3%	5%	$1,170.60
4	5	1,081.11
5	5	1,000.00
6	5	926.40
7	5	859.53
8	5	798.70
10	5	692.77
12	5	604.48

FIGURE 18.3

The Actual Minimum Price of a Convertible Bond

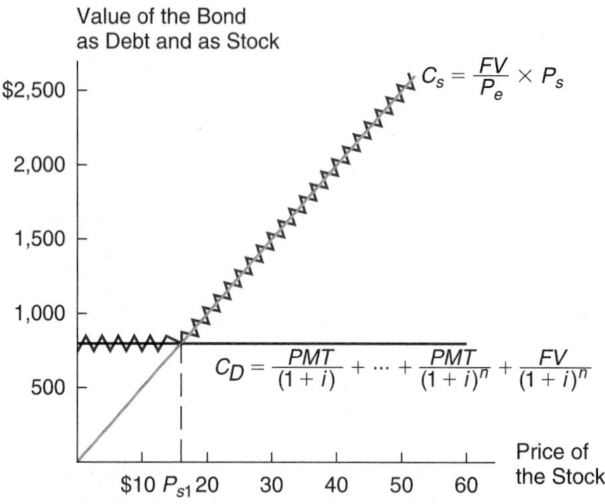

nonconvertible debt becomes a floor on the price of the convertible bond. Even if the value of the stock into which the bond may be converted were to fall, this floor would halt the decline in the price of the convertible bond.

The actual minimum price of a convertible bond combines its value as stock and its value as debt. This is illustrated in Figure 18.3, which combines the preceding figures for the value of the bond both in terms of stock and nonconvertible debt. The bond's price is always greater than or equal to the higher of the two valuations. If the price of the convertible bond were below its value as common stock, arbitrageurs would bid up its price. If the bond sold for a price below its value as debt, investors in debt instruments would bid up the price.

The minimum price of the convertible bond is either its value in terms of stock or its value as nonconvertible debt, but the importance of these determinants varies. For low stock prices (i.e., stock prices less than P_{s1} in Figure 18.3), the minimum price is set by the bond's value as debt. However, for stock prices greater than P_{s1}, it is the bond's value as stock that determines the minimum price.

The Bond's Value as a Hybrid Security

The market price (P_m) of the convertible bond combines both the conversion value of the bond and its investment value as nonconvertible debt. If the price of the stock were to decline significantly below the exercise price of the bond, the market price of the convertible bond would be influenced primarily by the bond's value as nonconvertible debt. In effect, the bond would be priced as if it were a pure debt instrument. As the price of the stock rises, the conversion value of the bond rises and plays an increasingly important role in the determination of the market price of the convertible bond. At sufficiently high stock prices, the market price of the bond is identical with its conversion value.

These relationships are illustrated in Figure 18.4, which reproduces Figure 18.3 and adds the market price of the convertible bond (P_m). For prices of the common stock below P_{s1}, the market price is identical to the bond's value as nonconvertible debt. For prices of the common stock above P_{s2}, the price of the bond is identical to its value as common stock. At these extreme stock prices, the bond may be ana-

FIGURE 18.4

Market Price of a Convertible Bond

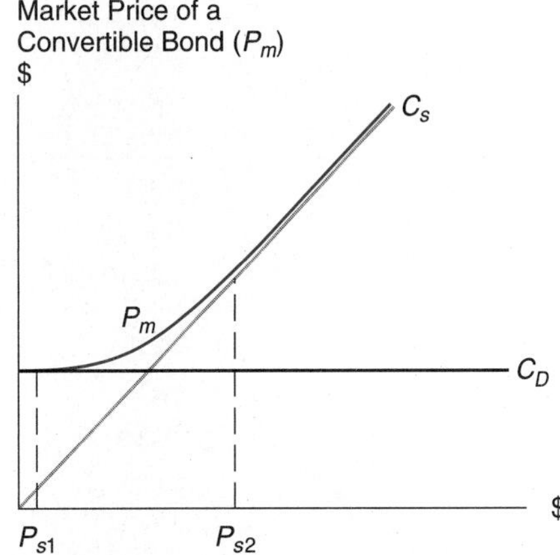

lyzed as if it were either pure debt or stock. For all prices between these two extremes, the market price of the convertible bond is influenced by the bond's value both as nonconvertible debt and as stock. This dual influence makes the analysis of convertible bonds difficult, since the investor pays a premium over the bond's value as stock and as debt.

Premiums Paid for Convertible Debt

One way to analyze a convertible bond is to measure the premium over the bond's value as debt or as stock. For example, if a particular convertible bond is commanding a higher premium than is paid for similar convertible securities, perhaps this bond should be sold. Conversely, if the premium is relatively low, the bond may be a good investment.

The premiums paid for a convertible bond are illustrated in Exhibit 18.5 (p. 596), which reproduces Exhibit 18.3 and adds the value of the bond as nonconvertible debt (column 4) along with hypothetical market prices for the bond (column 5). The premium that an investor pays for a convertible bond may be viewed in either of two ways: the premium over the bond's value as stock or the premium over the bond's value as debt. Column 6 gives the premium in terms of stock. This is the difference between the bond's market price and its conversion value as stock (i.e., the value in column 5 minus the value in column 3). This premium declines as the price of the stock rises and plays a more important role in the determination of the bond's price. Column 7 gives the premium in terms of nonconvertible debt. This is the difference between the bond's market price and its investment value as debt (i.e., the value in column 5 minus the value in column 4). This premium rises as the price of the stock rises, because the debt element of the bond is less important.

The inverse relationship between the two premiums is also illustrated in Figure 18.5 (p. 596). The premiums are shown by the difference between the line representing the market price (P_m) and the lines representing the value of the bond in terms of stock (C_s) and the value of the bond as nonconvertible debt (C_D).

When the price of the stock is low and the bond is selling close to its value as debt, the premium above the bond's intrinsic value as stock is substantial, but the premium above the bond's value as debt is small. For example, at P_{s1} the price of

EXHIBIT 18.5

Premiums Paid for Convertible Debt

Price of the Stock	Shares into Which the Bond May Be Converted	Conversion Value of the Bond in Terms of Stock	Investment Value of the Bond as Non-convertible Debt	Hypothetical Market Price of the Convertible Bond	Premium in Terms of Stock*	Premium in Terms of Non-convertible Debt†
$ 0	50	$ 0	$798.50	$ 798.50	$798.50	$ 0.00
5	50	250	798.50	798.50	548.50	0.00
10	50	500	798.50	798.50	298.50	0.00
15	50	750	798.50	900.00	150.00	101.50
20	50	1,000	798.50	1,100.00	100.00	301.50
25	50	1,250	798.50	1,300.00	50.00	501.50
30	50	1,500	798.50	1,500.00	0.00	701.50

*The premium in terms of stock is equal to the hypothetical price of the convertible bond minus the value of the bond in terms of stock.

†The premium in terms of nonconvertible debt is equal to the hypothetical price of the convertible bond minus the value of the bond as nonconvertible debt.

the stock is $10, the bond's value in terms of stock is $500 (line *AB* in Figure 18.5), and the premium is $298.50 (line *BC*). However, the bond is selling for its value as nonconvertible debt ($798.50), and there is no premium over its value as debt. When the price of the stock is $25 and the bond is selling for $1,300, the premium in terms of stock is only $50 (line *EF*). However, the bond's premium over its value as nonconvertible debt is $501.50 (line *DF*).

As these examples illustrate, the premium paid for the bond over its value as stock declines as the price of the stock rises. This decline in the premium is the result of the increasing impact of the conversion value on the bond's market price and the decreasing impact of the debt element on the bond's price.

FIGURE 18.5

Premium Paid for a Convertible Bond

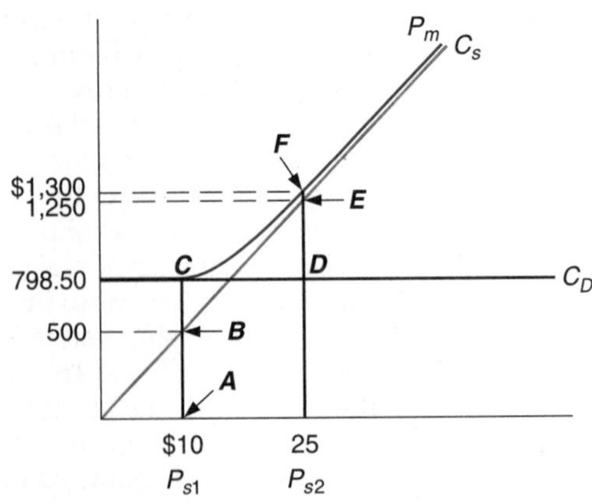

As the price of the stock rises, the safety feature of the debt diminishes. If the price of the common stock ceased to rise and started to fall, the price of the convertible bond could decline considerably before it reached the floor price set by the nonconvertible debt. For example, if the price of the stock declined from $30 to $15 (a 50 percent decline), the price of the convertible bond could fall from $1,500 to $798.50 (a 46.8 percent decline). Such a price decline would indicate that the floor value of $798.50 had little impact on the decline in the price of the bond.

In addition, as the price of the stock (and hence the price of the convertible bond) rises, the probability that the bond will be called rises. When the bond is called, it can be worth only its value as stock. The call forces the holder to convert the bond into stock. For example, when the price of the stock is $30, the bond is worth $1,500 in terms of stock. Should the company call the bond and offer to retire it for its face value ($1,000), no one would accept the offer. Instead, they would convert the bond into $1,500 worth of stock. If the investor paid a premium over this conversion value (such as $1,600) and the bond were called, the investor would then suffer a loss. Thus, as the probability of a call increases, the willingness to pay a premium over the bond's value as stock declines, and the price of the convertible bond ultimately converges with its value as stock.

This decline in the premium also means that the price of the stock will rise more rapidly than the price of the bond. As may be seen in both Exhibit 18.5 and Figure 18.5, the market price of the convertible bond rises and falls with the price of the stock, because the conversion value of the bond rises and falls. However, the market price of the convertible bond does not rise as rapidly as the conversion value of the bond. For example, when the stock's price increased from $20 to $25 (a 25 percent increase), the convertible bond's price rose from $1,100 to $1,300 (an 18.2 percent increase). The reason for this difference in the rate of increase is the declining premium paid for the convertible bond. Since the premium declines as the price of the stock rises, the rate of increase in the price of the stock must exceed the rate of increase in the price of the bond.

Some investors may have the misconception that convertible bonds offer the best of both worlds: high return plus the safety of debt. In many cases, a convertible bond may prove to be an inferior investment. For example, if the price of the stock rises rapidly, the stock is a superior investment because it will produce a larger capital gain. The stock outperforms the bond because the investor paid a premium for the convertible bond. In the opposite case when the price of the stock does not rise, a nonconvertible bond will outperform the convertible bond because it pays more interest. Thus, the very sources of a convertible bond's attractiveness (i.e., the potential capital growth plus the safety of debt) are also the reasons for its lack of appeal (i.e, the inferior growth relative to the stock and the inferior interest income relative to nonconvertible debt).

In addition to inferior growth and income, convertible bonds may inflict substantial losses if stock prices decline simultaneously with rising interest rates. In this scenario, the convertible bond is doubly cursed: The value of the underlying stock declines, which decreases the value of the convertible bond, and the value of the bond as debt declines, reducing the safety associated with the convertible bond as a debt instrument.

There is also potential for loss if the convertible bond is purchased for a substantial premium over its value as debt (i.e., over its investment value). For example, when the price of the stock was $30 in Exhibit 18.5, the bond sold for $1,500 (its conversion value). At that price the investor paid a premium of $701.50 over the bond's value as debt. If the price of the stock were to decline to $10, the value of the bond could fall to $798.50, inflicting a capital loss of $701.50 on the investor. While the decline in the bond's value is less than the decline in the value of the

POINTS OF INTEREST
The Conversion Parity

In the body of the text, the analysis is based upon the value of the bond as stock (the conversion value) and the value of the bond as a debt instrument (the investment value). The analysis may be reversed to express the value of the stock in terms of the price of the bond, which is referred to as the *conversion parity*. This indicates what the stock is worth given the price of the bond. That is,

$$\text{Conversion parity} = \frac{\text{Price of the bond}}{\text{Conversion ratio}}$$

If the price of the bond is $900 and the bond is convertible into 20 shares (i.e., convertible at $50 a share), the conversion parity is

$$\frac{\$900}{\$1{,}000/\$50} = \frac{\$900}{20} = \$45.$$

The conversion parity indicates that a share of stock is worth $45 in terms of the bond. If the price of the stock is $35, the bond is selling for a premium of $10 a share (i.e., a total premium of $200 based on the number of shares into which the bond may be converted).

The conversion parity offers another means to determine the premium paid for a convertible. In Exhibit 18.5, the bond's premium over its value as stock is the price of the bond minus the conversion value of the bond ($900 − $700 = $200 in this illustration). The conversion parity reverses the process. If the price of the bond is $900, the stock is worth $45 a share. Since the stock sells for $35 ($10 less than $45), the bond commands a premium of $200 ($10 × 20 shares) over its value as stock. The premium is $200 in either case.

stock (47 versus 67 percent), the significant decrease certainly suggests that investors in convertible bonds could sustain a substantial loss even when interest rates remain the same and the company does not default.

These risks suggest that investors should approach convertible bonds cautiously. However, convertible bonds do offer some combination of potential capital gains, interest income, and the safety associated with debt. If the price of the stock rises, the price of the bond must also rise, and the investor receives interest income. If the stock's price does not rise, the convertible bond must eventually be retired because it is a debt obligation of the firm. Hence the bond does offer an element of safety that is not available through an investment in stock, as well as some growth potential that is not available through an investment in nonconvertible debt.

Convertible Preferred Stock

convertible preferred stock
Preferred stock that may be exchanged for (i.e., converted into) common stock.

In addition to convertible bonds, many firms have issued **convertible preferred stock**. As its name implies, this stock may be converted into the common stock of the issuing corporation. For example, the Rouse Company 6 percent preferred is convertible into 1.311 shares of the company's common stock.

Several of these issues of convertible preferred stock are the result of mergers. The tax laws permit firms to combine through an exchange of stock, which is not taxable (i.e., it is a tax-free exchange). If one firm purchases another firm for cash, the stockholders who sell their shares have an obvious realized sale. Profits and losses from the sale are then subject to capital gains taxation. However, the Internal Revenue Service has ruled that an exchange of *like securities* is not a realized sale and thus is not subject to capital gains taxation until the investor sells the new shares.

This tax ruling has encouraged mergers through the exchange of stock. In many cases, the firm that is taking over (the surviving firm) offers to the stockholders of the firm that is being taken over an opportunity to trade their shares for a new convertible preferred stock. Since the stock is convertible into the common stock of the surviving firm, it is a "like" security. Thus, the transaction is not subject to capital gains taxation. To encourage the stockholders to tender their shares, the surviving firm may offer a generous dividend yield on the convertible preferred stock. For this reason many convertible preferred stocks have more generous dividend yields than that which is available through investing in the firm's common stock.

Convertible preferred stock is similar to convertible debt, but there are some important differences. The differences are primarily the same as those between nonconvertible preferred stock and nonconvertible debt. Preferred stock is treated as an equity instrument. Thus, the firm is not under any legal obligation to pay dividends. In addition, the preferred stock may be a perpetual security, and unlike debt, may not have to be retired. However, many convertible preferred stocks do have a required sinking fund, and all convertible preferred stocks are callable, so the firm can force stockholders to convert.

The value of convertible preferred stock (like convertible bonds) is related to the price of the stock into which it may be converted and to the value of competitive nonconvertible preferred stock. As with convertible bonds, these values set floors on the price of the convertible preferred stock. It cannot sell for any significant length of time below its value as common stock. If it did, investors would enter the market and buy the preferred stock, which would increase its price. Thus, the minimum value of the convertible preferred stock (like the minimum value of the convertible bond) must be equal to the conversion value of the stock (P_c). In equation form that is

$$P_c = P_s \times N, \tag{18.3}$$

where P_s is the market price of the stock into which the convertible preferred stock may be converted, and N is the number of shares an investor obtains through conversion. Equation 18.3 is similar to Equation 18.1, which gave the intrinsic value of the convertible bond as stock.

The convertible preferred stock's value as nonconvertible preferred stock (P_{pfd}) is related to the dividend it pays (D_{pfd}) and to the appropriate discount factor (k_{pfd}), which is the yield earned on competitive nonconvertible preferred stock. In equation form that is

$$P_{pfd} = \frac{D_{pfd}}{k_{pfd}}, \tag{18.4}$$

which is essentially the same as the convertible bond's value as debt except that the preferred stock has no definite maturity date. (Equation 18.4 was derived in Chapter 16.) However, this value does set a floor on the price of a convertible preferred stock because at that price it is competitive with nonconvertible preferred stock.

As with convertible bonds, the convertible preferred stock is a hybrid security whose value combines its worth both as common stock and as nonconvertible preferred stock. Convertible preferred stock tends to sell for a premium over its value as common stock and its value as straight preferred stock. Figures 18.4 and 18.5, which illustrated the value of the convertible bond at various prices of the stock into which it may be converted, also apply to convertible preferred stock. The only difference is the premium that the preferred stock commands over the value as common stock, which tends to be smaller. The reason for this reduced premium is that the preferred stock does not have the element of debt. Its features are more similar to common stock than are the features of the convertible bond. Thus, its price usually commands less of a premium over its value as common stock.

Convertible-Exchangeable Preferred Stock

Convertible-exchangeable preferred stock is a security that includes two options. The holder may convert the shares into the firm's common stock, or the company may force the holder to exchange the shares for the firm's bonds.[2] For example, the Federal Paper Board $2.3125 convertible-exchangeable preferred stock could be converted at the holder's option into 2.51 shares of common stock. However, the firm had the option to exchange each share for $25 worth of the firm's 9¼ percent convertible debentures.

The exchange option gives the firm more control over the preferred stock, as it is a means to force retirement of the shares without an outlay of cash if the value of the common stock rises *or* falls. If the value of the common stock were to rise, the investor may voluntarily convert the preferred stock. However, the firm may exercise its option to exchange the bonds for the preferred stock, thus forcing the stockholder to convert or lose the appreciation in the preferred stock's value. In this case the exchange option operates as a call feature—it forces conversion.

If the value of the common stock were to decline, no one would exercise the option to convert the stock. Without the exchange option, there is nothing the firm could do to retire the stock and rid itself of the required dividend payments except repurchase the shares. However, the exchange option allows the firm to force the preferred stockholder to exchange the shares for debt. The firm will now have to make interest payments, but these are tax-deductible expenses, while preferred dividends are paid from earnings and are not tax deductible.

Preferred Equity Redemption Cumulative Stock (PERCS)

Preferred equity redemption cumulative stock (PERCS) is a preferred stock that will be exchanged in the future for the issuing firm's common stock. Like convertible preferred stock it combines elements of preferred stock with some potential for growth. The cash dividend paid by a PERCS is established when the security is issued and is generally about twice the amount of the dividend being paid by the common stock. Since the stock pays a fixed dividend, the security is similar to preferred stock.

The potential for growth occurs through the redemption feature. This preferred stock may not be converted at the holder's option and will not be called by the firm. Instead, the preferred stock is redeemed (i.e., exchanged) at a specified future date into the firm's common stock (usually three years after date of issue). For example, the PERCS issued on February 21, 1992, by Sears would be exchanged for Sears common stock on February 21, 1995. The PERCS paid an annual dividend of $3.75 while the common paid a dividend of $2.00. At the end of three

[2]A variation on the convertible-exchangeable preferred stock is the Premium Income Equity Securities or PIES. (Lehman Brothers Inc. has the rights to the terms "Premium Income Equity Securities" and "PIES".) These securities consist of a stock purchase contract that the holder must fulfill and a debt obligation that the issuer must meet. For example, in November 2000, Dominion Resources issued PIES with a 9.5 percent coupon that must be converted into common stock at $61.20 in 2004. If the price of the stock rises above $61.20, the value of the PIES will rise. But the converse is also true. If the price of the stock declines below $61.20, the holder is obligated to exchange the PIES for the stock. If an investor purchases a convertible bond and the price of the underlying stock falls, the investor may hold the bond and receive the principal at maturity. With a Premium Income Equity Security, the investor must exchange the security for the underlying stock.

years, the stock would be exchanged for one share of common as long as the price of the common was $59.00 or less. If the price of the common exceeded $59, the number of common shares exchanged would be adjusted so that the holder of the PERCS received common stock worth $59.00. Thus, if Sears were selling for $75, the holder of the PERCS would receive 0.7867 ($59/$75) shares. On February 21, 1995, Sears stock did not sell for more than $59, so each share of preferred was exchanged for a share of common stock.

What advantages do PERCS offer investors? The primary advantage is the higher dividend yield. Suppose the price of Sears stagnates; at the end of the three years, the investor receives one share of common stock whose value has not changed, but the investor has received more dividends during the three years than would have been paid to holders of the common stock. If the value of the common stock declines, the additional dividends offset some of the price decline. Thus, if the price of the stock remains stable or declines, the investor ends up better off with the PERCS compared to holding the underlying common stock.

If the price of the common stock rises, the value of the preferred equity cumulative redemption stock also rises up to the specified maximum price, which sets a ceiling on the price increase. If the price of the common continues to rise, the price of the PERCS cannot rise since further price increases are offset by the decline in the number of shares into which the PERCS will be exchanged. Thus, PERCS are of interest to investors who seek additional dividend income and who do not believe that the price of the underlying stock will rise dramatically during the time period. Of course, the best outcome for the investor in the PERCS would be for the price of the stock to rise to the maximum exchange price. Then the investor would receive the higher dividend and realize the highest possible capital gain. The only loss would be an opportunity loss from the price of the common stock rising above the exchange price.

Selecting Convertibles

Because convertible bonds are a hybrid security, they are more difficult to analyze than nonconvertible bonds. These securities are debt instruments and pay a fixed flow of interest income, so they appeal to conservative, income-oriented investors. However, since the bonds sell for a premium over their investment value as debt, investors forgo some of the interest income and safety associated with nonconvertible bonds.

A convertible bond also offers the potential for capital gains if the value of the stock into which the bond may be converted were to rise. Possible capital gains increase the bond's attractiveness to investors seeking capital appreciation. Since the investor pays a premium over the bond's value as stock, the potential price appreciation is less than is available through an investment in the firm's common stock. However, the investor who purchases the bond does collect the interest, which usually exceeds the dividends paid on an equivalent number of shares into which the bond may be converted.

The interest advantage may be seen by considering the 8 percent convertible bond issued by Petrie Stores. Each bond may be converted into 45.2 shares of common stock. The stock paid dividends of $0.20 a share (i.e., the equivalent of $9.04 on 45.2 shares), but the bond paid interest of $80. The bondholder collected $70.96 more in interest income than the stockholder collected on an equivalent number of shares.

This additional flow of income offers one way to analyze the premium paid for a convertible bond. If the bond is held for a sufficient amount of time, the additional income will offset the premium. This time period is sometimes referred to as *years to payback* or the *breakeven time*. The following example illustrates how this breakeven time period may be computed. Consider a $1,000 convertible bond with a 7 percent coupon that is convertible into 50 shares of stock. The stock currently sells for $16 a share and pays a dividend of $0.40 a share. In terms of stock the bond is worth $800 (50 × $16), so the premium over the bond's value as stock is $200 ($1,000 − $800). The bondholder receives $70 a year in interest but would receive only $20 ($0.40 × 50) on the stock. Thus purchasing the bond instead of an equivalent number of shares generates $50 in additional income, which offsets the premium over the bond's value as stock in four years ($200/$50 = 4).

This series of calculations may be summarized as follows:

Market value of the bond	$1,000
Minus bond's conversion value	800
Premium over the conversion value	$ 200
Bond's annual income	$ 70
Minus annual income from stock	20
Annual income advantage to bond	$ 50

$$\textbf{Payback period} = \frac{\textbf{Premium over the conversion value}}{\textbf{Annual income advantage}}$$

$$= \frac{\$200}{\$50} = 4 \text{ years.}$$

If the additional income offsets the premium paid over the bond's value as stock in a moderate period of time (e.g., three to four years), the convertible bond may be an attractive alternative to the stock. (This, of course, assumes that the stock is also sufficiently attractive and offers the potential for growth.) If the time period necessary to overcome the premium is many years (e.g., ten years), then the bond should not be purchased as an alternative to the stock but should be viewed solely as a debt instrument and analyzed as such.

The individual should realize that this technique is relatively simple and does not consider (1) differences in commission costs to buy bonds instead of stock, (2) possible growth in the cash dividend, which will increase the time period necessary to recapture the premium, and (3) the time value of money. The premium is paid in the present (i.e., when the bond is purchased), but the flow of interest income occurs in the future. However, the technique does permit comparisons of various convertible bonds. If the individual computes the time period necessary to recapture the premium for several bonds, he or she may identify specific convertible bonds that are more attractive potential investments.

The History of Selected Convertible Bonds

Perhaps the best way to understand investing in convertible bonds is to examine the history of several convertible bonds. The first is a success story, in that the price of the common stock rose and therefore the value of the bond also rose. The second is a not-so-successful story, for the price of the stock declined and so did the value of the bond. However, the story of this bond is not a tragedy, for the bond was still a debt obligation of the company and was retired at maturity even though it was not converted into stock. The third bond illustrates a more typical case in which the bond's price rises but the increase occurs over an extended period of time.

The American Quasar Convertible Bond

American Quasar was a firm devoted to exploring and drilling for oil and gas. The discovery of oil wells (called *wildcats*) can prove to be highly lucrative; however, the majority of drilling leads only to dry holes (i.e., no oil or natural gas is found). Because of the nature of its operations, American Quasar was a speculative firm at best. Speculative firms, however, need funds to operate, so the firm issued \$17,500,000 in face value of convertible bonds. The coupon rate was set at 7¼ percent and the exercise price of the bond was \$21 (i.e., it was convertible into 47.6 shares), which was a premium of 17 percent over the approximate price of the stock (\$18) at the date of issue.

After the bond was issued, American Quasar's stock did particularly well, and the value of the convertible bond rose along with the price of the stock. The prices of the bond and the stock moved closely together, and less than two years after being issued the bond was called, which forced conversion of the bond into the stock.

What was the return earned by investors in these securities? Obviously, an investment in either the stock or the bond was quite profitable, since the price of the stock rose so rapidly. The bond's price rose from \$1,000 to \$1,500 during the time it was outstanding. The bond paid \$72.50 in interest. The holding period return earned over the 15 months on an investment in the bond was

$$\frac{\textbf{Price appreciation + Interest earned}}{\textbf{Cost}} = \frac{\$1{,}500 - \$1{,}000 + \$72.50}{\$1{,}000}$$

$$= \frac{\$572.50}{\$1{,}000} = 57.25\%.$$

For the stock the holding period return was

$$\frac{\textbf{Price appreciation + Dividends}}{\textbf{Cost}} = \frac{\$32 - \$18 + \$0}{\$18} = \frac{\$14}{\$18} = 77.7\%.$$

(The bond paid only one year's interest since it was converted prior to the next interest payment, and the stock did not pay any cash dividends while the bond was outstanding.) As may be seen by these calculations, the returns are both positive. The stock did better because the bond was initially sold for a premium over its value as stock. However, an investor who purchased this convertible bond certainly would have little cause for complaint.

The Pan American World Airways Convertible Bonds

While the previous example illustrated how the price of convertible bonds may rise as the price of the stock rises, the Pan American World Airways convertible bonds demonstrate the opposite. The 4½ percent convertible bond was issued when Pan Am was riding the crest of popularity. For investors purchasing either the stock or the bond, Pam Am's popularity vanished, and through years of continued deficits, the price of the stock declined drastically. Both the stock and the bond fell to "bargain basement" prices, as the market expected the firm to default. At that time the bond reached a low of \$130 for a \$1,000 bond!

Pan Am, however, did not default, and the bond remained an obligation that had to be retired. Thus, when Pan Am did redeem the bond, investors who purchased it initially for \$1,000 received their principal. Holders of the Pan Am convertible bonds due in 2010 and the nonconvertible debt due in 2003 and 2004 were

POINTS OF INTEREST
Convertibles and Information

Only a modest number of convertibles are currently traded and available for purchase by individual investors. Issuers have determined that it is cost-effective to sell a new issue of convertibles to financial institutions such as pension plans and mutual funds. Such private placements may be tailor-made for the needs of the buyer and avoid the costs of registering the securities with the SEC. (The securities must be subsequently registered if the financial institutions desire to sell the securities to the general public.)

Even though most investors may prefer to acquire shares in mutual funds or closed-end investment companies that specialize in convertibles, it is possible to put together a convertible portfolio. (Commissions on bonds tend to be less than on stock, so many full-service brokers may discourage the purchase of convertible bonds.) Descriptive materials concerning convertible bonds are available from financial institutions. For example, Equity Analytics (http://www.e-analytics.com) has information on convertibles as a subsection of its material on bonds. One site devoted exclusively to convertibles is Convert-Bond.com (http://www.convertbond.com), which includes a convertible index, research reports, and a tutorial.

Other possible sources of information include Value Line (http://www.valueline.com), which provides convertible recommendations as part of its subscription services.* Convertible bonds that are traded are generally enumerated in Standard & Poor's monthly *Bond Guide,* which gives basic information such as a bond's coupon, maturity date, recent price, yield to maturity, the value of the bond as stock, and S&P's credit rating. More detailed information concerning a particular company (e.g., its financial statements) may then be found in EDGAR, the SEC database on stocks (http://www.sec.gov or http://www.edgar-online.com). After determining that the firm has a convertible security, this data may be used to analyze the firm and its convertible. If, however, the investor does not know whether a firm has convertible securities, using EDGAR to look through a large number of 10Ks or 10Qs to determine if a particular corporation has a convertible is potentially very time-consuming.

*At least one study suggests that Value Line convertible bond recommendations earn significant returns over time but that using Value Line stock rankings for selecting convertible bonds produces even higher returns. See Craig M. Lewis, Richard J. Rogalski, and James K. Seward, "The Information Content of Value Line Convertible Bond Rankings," Financial Markets Research Center, Vanderbilt University, August 1995. These findings are consistent with the prior discussion that the Value Line rankings generate higher returns. See the material in Chapter 4, especially footnotes 2 and 3 and the Value Line anomaly discussed in Chapter 9.

not so lucky, because the firm eventually failed and ceased operations in 1991. These bonds thus illustrate that investors who acquire both convertible and nonconvertible bonds of financially weak firms can lose their entire investments if the firm fails.

The Seagate Technology Convertible Bond

The American Quasar bond was in existence only briefly because the underlying stock price rose and the bond was converted soon after it was issued. The Pan Am convertible bond lasted the entire term and was retired at par. Between the two extremes is the Seagate Technology convertible bond. Issued in 1993, this 6¾ percent bond continued to trade, with its price moving with the price of the underlying stock. The Seagate convertible illustrates the importance of holding the bond for many years if the bondholder expects to earn a higher return on the bond than on the stock. For example, an investor could have bought the bond in 1993 for $860, while the stock sold for $16. Since the bond was convertible into 23.529 shares, its value as stock was $376 (23.529 × $16). At those prices the bond sold for a premium of $484 ($860 − $376) over the value of the underlying stock. Since the bond paid annual interest of $67.50, it would take over seven years ($484/$67.50) for the interest to offset the premium.

In 1996, the stock had risen to over $60, and Seagate called bonds for $1,013.50 plus accrued interest. At $60, the bonds were worth $1,411.74, so it was obviously advantageous to convert. The call occurred three years after the bonds were issued, so the interest could not cover the premium. The investor who purchased the stock for $16 and sold it for $60 earned an annualized return in excess of 55 percent. The investor who purchased the bond for $860, collected the interest, and sold the bond for $1,412 earned an annualized return of 24.7 percent.

Put Bonds

Most of this chapter has been devoted to convertible bonds, which are debt instruments that investors may, at their option, exchange for stock. If the price of the stock rises, the investor profits because the conversion value of the bond rises.

put bond
A bond that the holder may redeem (i.e., sell back to the issuer) at a specified price and a specified time.

During the 1980s, another type of bond was created with a different type of option. This **put bond** permits the holder to sell the instrument back to the issuer. In effect, the firm must redeem the bond at a specified date for its principal amount. Since the owner of these bonds has the option to sell the bond back to the firm, this option is analogous to a put option—hence the name, *put bond*. (Put options to sell stock are explained in the next chapter.) A typical illustration of a put bond is the Dominion Resource bonds issued in 2000, which the investor may redeem in 2004 for the principal amount.[3]

Fear that interest rates would increase and thereby inflict losses on bondholders led to the development of put bonds. Firms and governments need long-term financing, but some investors do not want to commit their funds for extended periods of time, especially if they fear rising interest rates. Put bonds permit firms and governments to sell long-term debt to investors who are reluctant to buy bonds with maturity dates 20 to 30 years into the future.

If, after these put bonds were issued, interest rates were to rise and thereby drive down the price of the bonds, the investor would exercise the put option at the specified redemption date. He or she would receive the principal and could immediately invest it at the current (and higher) rate of interest. Of course, if interest rates were to fall, the individual would not exercise the option. There would be no reason for the investor to seek the early redemption of the principal if interest rates have fallen. Instead, the investor may sell the bond on the market for more than the principal amount (i.e., for a premium).

Firms and governments are willing to offer investors this put option for much the same reason that they were willing to offer convertibility: lower interest costs. If an investor acquires an option, he or she must pay a price. For regular puts and calls that price (or *premium* as it is called in the jargon of options) is the amount paid to purchase the option. With a convertible bond or a put bond, the option's price is more subtle. Its price is the reduction in interest the investor must accept to acquire the option.[4] Without the option the bond's coupon would have had to be higher to induce investors to purchase the long-term bond.

The put option's potential impact on the value of a bond as interest rates fluctuate may be seen by the following illustration. A firm issues a bond due in 20 years with a 10 percent coupon. It grants the investor the option to redeem the bond at par at the end of 5 years. If the option is not exercised, the bond will remain outstanding for an additional 15 years. (This is a simple illustration with only one future date at which the investor may exercise the put option. Some

[3]These bonds also have a call feature, which gives the company the right to redeem the bonds. Thus, both the issuer and the buyer have options to redeem the bonds at par as of a specified date.

[4]This price may be expressed in present value terms—it is the difference between the value of the bond with and the value of the bond without the option.

Calculator Solution

Function Key	Data Input
PV =	?
FV =	1000
PMT =	100
N =	20
I =	8
Function Key	**Answer**
PV =	−1196.36

bonds may grant the bondholder the option to redeem the bond more frequently, such as every 5 years.)

If the current interest rate is 8 percent, the value of the bond is

\$100(9.818) + \$1,000(0.215) = \$1,196.80.

The interest factors are 9.818 and 0.215 for the present value of an annuity and the present value of \$1 at 8 percent for 20 years. Twenty years is the appropriate number of years because, since interest rates have fallen, the investor will not redeem the bond. The option thus has no impact on the increase in the price of the bond.

If the current interest rate is 12 percent, the value of the bond is

Calculator Solution

Function Key	Data Input
PV =	?
FV =	1000
PMT =	100
N =	5
I =	12
Function Key	**Answer**
PV =	−927.90

\$100(3.605) + \$1,000(0.567) = \$927.50.

The interest factors are 3.605 and 0.567 for the present value of an annuity and the present value of \$1 at 12 percent for *five* years. Five years is the appropriate number of years because if the current rate of interest exceeds 10 percent, the investor will exercise the option and redeem the bond.

The impact of the put option on the value of the bond can be seen by comparing the value above and the bond's value *without* the put option. In that case, if the current interest rate were 12 percent, the value of the bond would be

\$100(7.469) + \$1,000(0.104) = \$850.90.

Calculator Solution

Function Key	Data Input
PV =	?
FV =	1000
PMT =	100
N =	20
I =	12
Function Key	**Answer**
PV =	−850.61

The interest factors are 7.469 and 0.104 for the present value of an annuity and the present value of \$1 at 12 percent for 20 years. Twenty years is the appropriate number of years because the bond lacks the put option. In this illustration, the put option increases the value of the bond by \$76.60 (\$927.50 − \$850.90). Thus the put option affects the value of the bond if interest rates increase. Its impact is to reduce the amount by which the bond's price will decline, because the expected life is the redemption date rather than the maturity date.

Since bonds with put options are relatively new securities, one can only speculate as to their future popularity. However, granting the option does alter the interest paid, so one of the participants (i.e., the issuer or the investor) profits from the option. If interest rates remain below the coupon rate, the issuer profits, because the firm (or government) was able to sell a debt instrument with a lower rate than would have been required to sell the bonds without the put option. However, if interest rates rise, investors profit, because they are no longer locked into a debt instrument with an inferior yield. The issuer then will have to pay the higher rates in order to reborrow the funds. Obviously, if the investor (1) anticipates rising interest rates or (2) is particularly uncertain as to the direction of future interest rates and wants to hedge against rates increasing, bonds with put options may be attractive alternatives to other types of long-term debt instruments.

Investment Companies and Convertible Securities

Although an investor may acquire convertible securities, they are not as actively traded as the underlying stock, and the spreads between the bid and ask prices tend to be larger for the convertible bonds than for the stock. Only a handful of convertible prices are reported daily in the financial press. In addition, the large increases in security prices experienced during the late 1990s resulted in many convertibles being called, so the existing supply of convertible bonds and preferred stocks diminished.

These factors suggest that investors wanting to buy convertible securities may prefer to acquire shares in investment companies that hold convertibles. Both mutual funds and closed-end investment companies exist that specialize in the shares of convertibles. However, just a handful of closed-end investment companies specialize in convertible securities. (As of 2001, *The Wall Street Journal* listed only nine convertible security funds in the Monday edition that reported closed-end fund net asset values and discounts and premiums.)

Fidelity Convertible Securities (symbol: FCVSX) illustrates a no-load mutual fund that specializes in convertibles. In 2001, over 80 percent of its portfolio consisted of convertible bonds and preferred stocks. Castle Convertible Fund (CVF) and Gabelli Convertible Securities (GCV) are illustrations of closed-end investment companies whose stocks are traded on the American Stock Exchange and the New York Stock Exchange. Like Fidelity Convertible Securities, their portfolios emphasize convertible securities. However, unlike a mutual fund, the shares of a closed-end investment company often sell for a discount from the net asset value. As of June 2001, both Castle and Gabelli shares were trading for discounts of 10.2 and 0.4 percent, respectively, from net asset value.

Summary

A convertible bond is a debt instrument that may be converted into stock. The value of this bond depends on the value of the stock into which the bond may be converted and on the value of the bond as a debt instrument.

As the value of the stock rises, so does the conversion value of the convertible bond. If the price of the stock declines, the conversion value of the bond will also fall. However, the stock's price will decline faster, because the convertible bond's investment value as debt will halt the fall in the bond's price.

Since a convertible bond's price rises with the price of the stock, the bond offers the investor an opportunity for appreciation as the value of the firm increases. In addition, the bond's value as a debt sets a floor on the bond's price, which reduces the risk of loss to the investor. Should the stock decline in value, the debt element reduces the risk of loss to the bondholder.

Convertible bonds may sell for a premium. For these bonds, the premium may be viewed relative to the bond's value as stock or its value as debt. These two premiums are inversely related. When the price of the stock rises, the premium that the bond commands over its value as stock diminishes, but the premium over its value as debt rises. When the price of the stock falls, the premium over the bond's value as stock rises, but the premium relative to the bond's value as debt declines.

Convertible preferred stock is similar to convertible debt, except that it lacks the safety implied by a debt instrument. Its price is related to its conversion value, the flow of dividend income, and the rate that investors may earn on nonconvertible preferred stock.

A recent innovation in the debt instrument market is the put bond, which permits the holder to redeem the bond for its principal amount at some specified time in the future. If interest rates increase, the bondholder may exercise the put option. He or she redeems the bond, receives the principal, and thus is able to reinvest the funds at the higher current rate of interest. However, if interest rates fall, the bondholder will not exercise the option, as there is no reason to redeem the bond prior to maturity. Hence, the advantage put bonds offer investors is protection against being locked into an inferior rate of interest if the rates were to increase in the future.

Summary of Convertible Bond Equations

$$\text{Conversion ratio} = \frac{FV}{P_e}$$

$$\text{Conversion price} = \frac{FV}{\text{Conversion ratio}}$$

Conversion value (value of the bond as stock):

(18.1)
$$C_s = \frac{FV}{P_e} \times P_s$$

$$\text{Conversion premium (in dollars)} = \text{Price of the bond} - \text{Conversion value}$$

$$\text{Conversion premium (percentage)} = \frac{(\text{Price of the bond} - \text{Conversion value})}{\text{Conversion value}}$$

$$\text{Conversion parity (value of the stock based on the price of the bond)} = \frac{\text{Price of the bond}}{\text{Conversion ratio}}$$

Investment value (value of the bond as debt):

(18.2)
$$C_D = \frac{PMT}{(1+i)} + \cdots + \frac{PMT}{(1+i)^n} + \frac{FV}{(1+i)^n}$$

$$\text{Investment premium (in dollars)} = \text{Price of the bond} - \text{Investment value}$$

$$\text{Investment premium (percentage)} = \frac{(\text{Price of the bond} - \text{Investment value})}{\text{Investment value}}$$

$$\text{Payback period (breakeven time)} = \frac{\text{Conversion premium}}{(\text{Bond income} - \text{Stock income})}$$

Questions

1) What differentiates convertible bonds from other bonds?
2) How is the value of a convertible bond in terms of stock determined? What effect does this conversion value have on the price of the bond?
3) How is the value of a convertible bond in terms of debt determined? What effect does this investment value have on the price of the bond?
4) Why may convertible bonds be called by the firm? When are these bonds most likely to be called?
5) Why are convertible bonds less risky than stock but usually more risky than nonconvertible bonds?
6) Why does the premium over the bond's conversion value decline as the value of the stock rises?
7) How are convertible preferred stocks different from convertible bonds?
8) What advantages do convertible securities offer investors? What are the risks associated with these investments?

9) Why may an investor prefer a debenture with a put feature in preference to a bond with a call feature?
10) If you expected a common stock's price to appreciate over a period of time, would you prefer to invest in a put bond, a callable convertible bond, or a convertible-exchangeable preferred stock issued by the firm?

Problems

1) Given the following information concerning a convertible bond:

Principal	$1,000
Coupon	5%
Maturity	15 years
Call price	$1,050
Conversion price	$37 (i.e., 27 shares)
Market price of the common stock	$32
Market price of the bond	$1,040

a) What is the current yield of this bond?
b) What is the value of the bond based on the market price of the common stock?
c) What is the value of the common stock based on the market price of the bond?
d) What is the premium in terms of stock that the investor pays when he or she purchases the convertible bond instead of the stock?
e) Nonconvertible bonds are selling with a yield to maturity of 7 percent. If this bond lacked the conversion feature, what would the approximate price of the bond be?
f) What is the premium in terms of debt that the investor pays when he or she purchases the convertible bond instead of a nonconvertible bond?
g) If the price of the common stock should double, would the price of the convertible bond double? Briefly explain your answer.
h) If the price of the common stock should decline by 50 percent, would the price of the convertible bond decline by the same percentage? Briefly explain your answer.
i) What is the probability that the corporation will call this bond?
j) Why are investors willing to pay the premiums mentioned in parts (d) and (f)?

2) The following information concerns a convertible bond:

Coupon	6% ($60 per $1,000 bond)
Exercise price	$25
Maturity	20 years
Call price	$1,040
Price of the common stock	$30

a) If this bond were nonconvertible, what would be its approximate value if comparable interest rates were 12 percent?
b) Into how many shares can the bond be converted?
c) What is the value of the bond in terms of stock?
d) What is the current minimum price that the bond will command?

e) If the current market price of the bond is $976, what should you do?
f) Is there any reason to anticipate that the firm will call the bond?
g) What do investors receive if they do not convert the bond when it is called?
h) If the bond were called, would it be advantageous to convert?
i) If interest rates rise, would that affect the bond's current yield?
j) If the stock price were $10, would your answer to part (i) be different?

3) Given the following information concerning Continental Group $2.00 convertible preferred stock:

One share of preferred is convertible into 0.50 shares of common stock	
Price of common stock:	$34
Price of convertible preferred stock:	$25

a) What is the value of the preferred stock in terms of common stock?
b) What is the premium over the preferred stock's value as common stock?
c) If the preferred stock is perpetual and comparable preferred stock offers a dividend yield of 10 percent, what would be the minimum price of this stock if it were not convertible?
d) If the price of the common stock rose to $60, what would be the minimum increase in the value of the preferred stock that you would expect?

4) Two bonds have the following terms:

Bond A	
Principal	$1,000
Coupon	8%
Maturity	10 years

Bond B	
Principal	$1,000
Coupon	7.6%
Maturity	10 years

Bond B has an additional feature: It may be redeemed at par after five years (i.e., it has a put feature). Both bonds were initially sold for their face amounts (i.e., $1,000).

a) If interest rates fall to 7 percent, what will be the price of each bond?
b) If interest rates rise to 9 percent, what will be the decline in the price of each bond from its initial price?
c) Given your answers to questions (a) and (b), what is the trade-off implied by the put option in bond B?
d) Bond B requires the investor to forgo $4 a year (i.e., $40 if the bond is in existence for ten years). If interest rates are 8 percent, what is the present value of this forgone interest? If the bond had lacked the put feature but had a coupon of 7.6 percent and a term to maturity of ten years, it would sell for $973.16 when interest rates were 8 percent. What, then, is the implied cost of the put option?

5) Two firms have common stock and convertible bonds outstanding. Information concerning these securities is as follows:

	Firm A	Firm B
Common stock		
Price of common stock	$46	$30
Cash dividend	none	$1
Convertible bond		
Principal	$1,000	$1,000
Conversion price	$50	$33⅓
	(20 shares)	(30 shares)
Maturity	10 years	10 years
Coupon	7.5%	7.5%
Market price	$1,100	$1,100

a) What is the value of each bond in terms of stock?
b) What is the premium paid over each bond's value as stock?
c) What is each bond's income advantage over the stock into which the bond may be converted?
d) How long will it take for the income advantage to offset the premium determined in part (b)?
e) If after four years firm A's stock sells for $65 and the firm calls the bond, what is the holding period return and the annual rate of return earned on an investment in the stock or in the bond? (You may wish to review the material on calculating rates of return presented in Chapter 10.)

6) Corporation RTY has the following convertible bond outstanding:

Coupon	7%
Principal	$1,000
Maturity	10 years
Conversion price	$64.516
Call price	$1,000 + one year's interest

The bond's credit rating is A. Other bonds issued by the company have a AA rating. Comparable AA-rated bonds yield 9 percent, and A-rated bonds yield 10 percent. The firm's stock is selling for $60 and pays a dividend of $2 a share. The convertible bond is selling for par ($1,000).

a) What is the value of the bond in terms of stock?
b) What is the premium paid over the bond's value as stock?
c) What is the bond's income advantage?
d) Given the bond's income advantage, how long must the investor hold the bond to overcome the premium over the bond's value as stock?
e) What is the probability that the firm will currently call the bond?
f) If after three years the price of the stock has risen annually by 10 percent to $80, what must have happened to the price of the bond?
g) If the price of the bond rises to $1,240 at the end of three years, what is the *total* percentage return (i.e., the holding period return) the investor earns on the stock and on the bond?
h) Why is the holding period return misleading?

i) If the price of the bond rises to $1,240 at the end of three years, what is the annualized return the investor earns? Does this return exceed the return earned on the stock?
j) If the stock is split 2 for 1, what impact will that have on the price of a convertible bond?
k) If the convertible bond is held to maturity, what does the investor receive? What is the annualized return?
l) If the price of the stock rises to $90 a share while interest rates on A-rated bonds rise to 12 percent, what impact does the increase in interest rates have on this convertible bond?

7) A company issued a $100 preferred equity redemption cumulative stock with an annual dividend of $8. The preferred may be exchanged for two shares of common stock as long as the price of the stock is $60 or less. If the price of the stock exceeds $60, the number of shares is adjusted so the investor receives stock worth $60 a share. The preferred stock currently sells for $95. The common stock sells for $40 and does not pay a dividend.

a) What is the value of the exchangeable preferred stock based on the current value of the common stock?
b) Is the preferred stock selling for a premium over its value as common stock?
c) What may explain the existence of the premium?
d) What is the preferred stock's current yield?
e) What will be the value of the preferred stock as stock if the common stock sells for $30, $40, $50, $60, $70, and $80?
f) If at the end of four years the common stock sells for $75 a share, which alternative generated the higher annualized return?

THE FINANCIAL ADVISOR'S INVESTMENT CASE

The Pros and Cons of Investing in a Convertible Bond

Many of your clients own small to medium-sized private businesses. One of your clients, Alban Schoenberg, is planning to finance the education of his two children, ages 10 and 12. Currently, neither child has any assets, so Schoenberg is considering investing a modest amount in convertible bonds in their names with his wife, Alma, as custodian. Alma Schoenberg has doubts because she does not believe that it is wise to risk their hard-earned money on risky investments. Mr. Schoenberg believes that the money to be transferred is small enough to risk. Besides, he is fascinated with the convertible bonds issued by UT&T, a large company with a good, if not superior, credit rating.

Currently, the UT&T bonds trade for par ($1,000), have a coupon of 8 percent, mature in ten years, and are convertible into the stock at $10 a share (100 shares per $1,000 bond). Other bonds issued by the company pay 10 percent interest; its stock sells for $8.50 and pays no cash dividends. While Mr. Schoenberg believes that the bonds are a fine investment, Mrs. Schoenberg has doubts and raises several questions for you to answer.

1) If the bonds were not convertible, what would they be worth?
2) Since the bonds are convertible, what is their stock value?
3) If the value of the stock rose to $15, what would happen to the value of the bonds?
4) If the price of the stock declined to $5, what would happen to the value of the bonds?
5) If the money were invested in the nonconvertible bonds and the price of the stock changed, what would happen to the value of the bonds?
6) If the price of the stock rose, would the Schoenbergs have to exchange the bonds for the stock?
7) If Mrs. Schoenberg changed her mind, could she get the principal back?
8) If the company were to fail, what would happen to the bonds?
9) Would buying the bonds be preferable to putting the money in the firm's stock?
10) Would buying the bonds be preferable to putting the money in a certificate of deposit in a federally insured commercial bank?
11) What are the federal income tax implications of owning convertible bonds? Would putting the bonds in the children's names result in any tax savings?

Given the nature of Mrs. Schoenberg's questions, do you believe that the money should be invested in convertible bonds?

Derivatives

4

PART

Part IV is devoted to derivative securities. As their name implies, derivatives are based on another asset, and a derivative's value is dependent on the value of that underlying asset. Initially, Part IV is devoted to options. An option is a contract that gives the holder the right to buy or sell a security at a specified price within a specified time period.

Options can be very speculative investments, and only those individuals who are willing and able to bear the risk should consider buying and selling them to take advantage of anticipated price movements. Options, however, may also be used in conjunction with other securities to manage risk. Thus, options are both a means to speculate on price movements in stocks and a means to reduce risk. Chapter 19 covers the basic features and positions using options. Chapter 20 presents the Black-Scholes option valuation model and a variety of strategies using options. Because options offer the possibility of a large return, those investors who are willing to bear the risk may find this material to be the most fascinating in the text.

Chapter 21 considers an alternative speculative investment: the futures contract. This contract is for the delivery of a commodity, such as wheat, or a financial asset, such as U.S. Treasury bills. Like options, the value of a futures contract is derived from the value of the underlying commodity. Futures contracts can produce large and sudden profits or losses, and they require that the individual actively participate in the day-to-day management of the investments. While futures contracts are considered very speculative, they may be combined with other assets to hedge positions and reduce risk. Thus, futures contracts, like options, may be used as a means to speculate or to manage risk.

19 An Introduction to Options*

In January 2001, you could have bought an option to buy Cisco Systems stock at $50 for $625. Eight months later, the option was selling for $80. In January 2001, you could have bought an option to sell Cisco Systems stock at $50. That option would have cost you $1,638, but in August 2001, that option was worth over $3,400. Why did the prices of these options change so dramatically and in opposite directions? This chapter will help you answer that question.

An option is often defined as the right to choose. In the security markets, an option is the right to buy or sell stock at a specified price within a specified time period. The value of an option is derived from (that is, depends on) the underlying security for which the option is a right to buy or sell. Hence, options are often referred to as *derivative* securities. Options take various forms, including calls, puts, and warrants. Some securities, such as the convertible bonds discussed in the previous chapter, have options built into them.

Investors in options do not receive the benefits of owning the underlying stock. These investors purchase the option because they expect the price of the option to rise (and fall) more rapidly than the underlying stock. Since options offer this potential leverage, they are also riskier investments; an individual could easily lose the entire amount invested in an option.

This chapter is a general introduction to investing in options. Initially, the features common to all options (their intrinsic value, the leverage they offer, and the time premiums they command) are covered. Next follows a discussion of particular options: the call and the put. With the formation of the Chicago Board Options Exchange (CBOE), a secondary market was created for the purchase and sale of call and put options. These options permit investors to take long and short positions and to construct hedge positions to reduce risk. The CBOE transformed security markets by creating an opportunity for individuals to readily buy and sell options.

The initial success of the CBOE led to the trading of options on other exchanges and to the creation of new types of options, such as the stock index option, which is not based on a specific company's securities but on an index of the market as a whole. These index options permit investors to take long or short positions on the market without having to trade individual securities. The chapter ends with a discussion of warrants and rights offerings to buy stock issued by firms. While warrants and rights are similar to call options, they are infrequently used by firms as a means to raise funds.

Learning Objectives

After completing this chapter you should be able to:

1 Define the word *option* as it applies to securities and differentiate between an option's market value and its intrinsic value.

*This chapter uses material from Herbert B. Mayo, *Using the Leverage in Warrants and Calls to Build a Successful Investment Program* (New Rochelle, NY: Investors Intelligence, 1974). Permission to use this material has been graciously given by the publisher.

2 Identify the risks associated with purchasing an option and the factors affecting an option's time premium.
3 Differentiate the profit and loss from writing a covered call option versus a naked call option.
4 Explain the relationship between the price of a stock and a put option.
5 Compare buying a put option with selling short.
6 Identify the advantages offered by stock index options.
7 Differentiate warrants and rights offerings from calls.

The Intrinsic Value of an Option

option
The right to buy or sell something at a specified price within a specified time period.

expiration date
The date by which an option must be exercised.

intrinsic value
What an option is worth as stock.

exercise (strike) price
The price at which the investor may buy or sell stock through an option.

premium
The market price of an option.

An **option** is the right to buy or sell stock at a specified price within a specified time period. At the end of the time period, the option expires on its **expiration date.** The minimum price that an option will command is its **intrinsic value** as an option. For an option to buy stock, this intrinsic value is the difference between the price of the stock and the per-share **exercise (strike) price** of the option. The market price of an option is frequently referred to as the **premium.** If an option is the right to buy stock at $30 a share and the stock is selling for $40, then the intrinsic value is $10 ($40 – $30 = $10).

If the stock is selling for a price greater than the per-share exercise price, the option to buy has positive intrinsic value. This may be referred to as the option's being *in the money.* If the common stock is selling for a price that equals the strike price, the option is *at the money.* And if the price of the stock is less than the strike price, the option has no intrinsic value. The option is *out of the money.* No one would purchase and exercise an option to buy stock when the stock could be purchased for a price that is less than the strike price of the option. However, as is explained subsequently, such options may still trade.

The relationships among the price of a stock, the strike price (i.e., the exercise price of an option), and the option's intrinsic value are illustrated in Exhibit 19.1 and Figure 19.1 (p. 618). In this example, the option is the right to buy the stock at

EXHIBIT 19.1

The Price of a Stock and the Intrinsic Value of an Option to Buy the Stock at $50 per Share

Price of the Stock	*minus*	Per-Share Strike Price of the Option	*equals*	Intrinsic Value of the Option
$ 0		$50		$ 0
10		50		0
20		50		0
30		50		0
40		50		0
50		50		0
60		50		10
70		50		20
80		50		30
90		50		40

FIGURE 19.1

The Relationship Between the Price of a Stock and the Intrinsic Value of an Option to Buy the Stock at $50 per Share

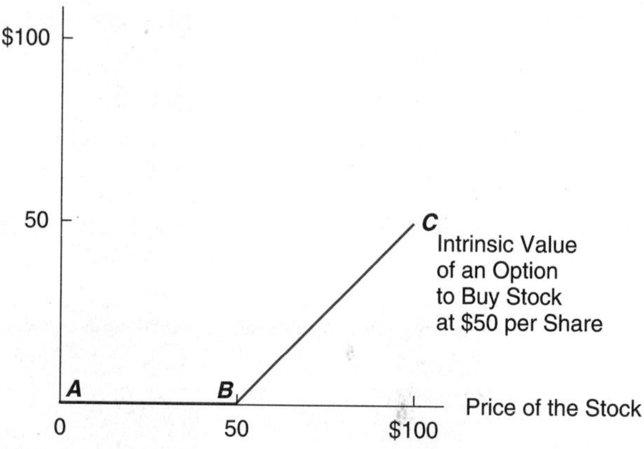

$50 per share. The first column of the exhibit (the horizontal axis on the graph) gives various prices of the stock. The second column presents the strike price of the option ($50), and the last column gives the intrinsic value of the option (i.e., the difference between the values in the first and second columns). The values in this third column are illustrated in the figure by line *ABC*, which shows the relationship between the price of the stock and the option's intrinsic value. It is evident from both the exhibit and the figure that as the price of the stock rises, the intrinsic value of the option also rises. However, for all stock prices below $50, the intrinsic value is zero, since security prices are never negative. Only after the stock's price has risen above $50 does the option's intrinsic value become positive.

The market price of an option must approach its intrinsic value as the option approaches its expiration date. On the day that the option is to expire, the market price can be only what the option is worth as stock. It can be worth only the difference between the market price of the stock and the exercise price of the option. This fact means that the investor may use the intrinsic value of an option as an indication of the option's future price, for the investor knows that the market price of the option must approach its intrinsic value as the option approaches expiration.

Because of arbitrage, the intrinsic value of an option sets the minimum price that the security will command. As was explained in Chapter 7, arbitrage is the act of simultaneously buying and selling a commodity or security in two different markets to make a profit from the different prices offered by the markets. In the case of an option, the two markets are the market for the stock and the market for the option. The essence of the arbitrage position is a short sale in the stock and a long position (i.e., a purchase) in the option. After these transactions are effected, the arbitrageur will exercise the option. Then the shares acquired by exercising the option will be used to cover the short position in the stock.

This act of arbitrage may be clarified by using the simple example presented in Exhibit 19.2. If the price of the stock is $60 and the strike price of the option is $50, the option's intrinsic value is $10. If the current market price of the option is $6, an investor can buy the option and exercise it to acquire the stock. By doing so the investor saves $4, for the total cost of the stock is $56 (i.e., $6 for the option and $50 to exercise the option). The investor then owns stock that has a market value of $60.

EXHIBIT 19.2

The Steps Required for Arbitrage

Givens		
Price of the stock		$60
Per-share strike price of the option		50
Price of the option		6
Step 1		
Buy the option for $6		
Sell the stock short for $60		
Step 2		
Exercise the option, thereby acquiring the stock for $50		
Step 3		
After acquiring the stock, cover the short position		
Determination of Profit or Loss		
Proceeds from the sale of the stock		$60
Cost of the stock		
Cost of the option	$ 6	
Cost to exercise the option	50	
Total cost		56
Net profit		$ 4

If the investor continues to hold the stock, the $4 saving can evaporate if the stock's price falls. However, if the investor simultaneously buys the option and sells the stock short, the $4 profit is guaranteed. In other words, the investor uses arbitrage, the required steps for which are presented in Exhibit 19.2. The investor sells the stock short at $60 and purchases the option for $6 (step 1). The stock is borrowed from the broker and delivered to the buyer. Then the investor exercises the option (step 2) and covers the short position with the stock acquired by exercising the option (step 3). This set of transactions locks in the $4 profit, because the investor sells the stock short at $60 per share and simultaneously purchases and exercises the option for a combined cost of $56 per share. By selling the stock short and purchasing the option at the same time, the investor ensures that he or she will gain the difference between the intrinsic value of the option and its price. Through arbitrage the investor guarantees the profit.

Of course, the act of buying the option and selling the stock short will drive up the option's price and put pressure on the price of the stock to fall. Thus, the opportunity to arbitrage will disappear, because arbitrageurs will bid up the price of the option to at least its intrinsic value. Once the price of the option has risen to its intrinsic value, the opportunity for a profitable arbitrage disappears. However, if the price of the option were to fall again below its intrinsic value, the opportunity for arbitrage would reappear, and the process would be repeated. Thus, the intrinsic value of an option becomes the minimum price that the option must command, for arbitrageurs will enter the market as soon as the price of an option falls below its intrinsic value as an option.

If the price of the option were to exceed its intrinsic value, arbitrage would offer no profit, nor would an investor exercise the option. If the option to buy the stock in the previous examples were to sell for $5 when the price of the common stock was $50, no one would exercise the option. The cost of the stock acquired by exercising the option would be $55 (i.e., $50 + $5). The investor would be better off buying the stock outright than purchasing the option and exercising it.

Actually, the opportunity for the typical investor to execute a profitable arbitrage is exceedingly rare. Market makers are cognizant of the possible gains from arbitrage and are in the best possible position to take advantage of any profitable opportunities that may emerge. Hence, if the opportunity to purchase the option for a price less than its intrinsic value existed, the purchases would be made by the market makers, and the opportunity to arbitrage would not become available to the general public. For the general investor, the importance of arbitrage is not the opportunity for profit that it offers but the fact that it sets a *floor* on the price of an option, and that floor is the minimum or intrinsic value.[1]

Leverage

leverage
Magnification of the potential return on an investment.

Some options offer investors the advantage of **leverage**. The potential return on an investment in an option may exceed the potential return on an investment in the underlying stock (i.e., the stock that the option represents the right to purchase). Like the use of margin, this magnification of the potential gain is an example of leverage.

Exhibit 19.3, which illustrates the relationship between the price of a stock and an option's intrinsic value, also demonstrates the potential leverage that options offer. For example, if the price of the stock rose from $60 to $70, the intrinsic value of the option would rise from $10 to $20. The percentage increase in the price of the stock is 16.67 percent ([$70 − $60] ÷ $60), whereas the percentage increase in the intrinsic value of the option is 100 percent ([$20 − $10] ÷ $10). The percentage increase in the intrinsic value of the option exceeds the percentage increase in the price of the stock. If the investor purchased the option for its intrinsic value and the price of the stock then rose, the return on the investment in the option would exceed the return on an investment in the stock.

EXHIBIT 19.3

The Relationship Between the Price of a Stock, the Value of an Option, and the Hypothetical Market Price of the Option

	Option		
Price of the Common Stock	Per-Share Strike Price	Intrinsic Value	Hypothetical Market Price
$ 10	$50	$ 0	$ 0
20	50	0	0.02
30	50	0	0.25
40	50	0	1
50	50	0	6
60	50	10	15
70	50	20	23
80	50	30	32
90	50	40	41
100	50	50	50

[1]As is explained in the next chapter on the Black-Scholes option valuation model, prior to the expiration date the minimum price *must exceed* the option's intrinsic value.

Leverage, however, works in both directions. Although it may increase the investor's potential return, it may also increase the potential loss if the price of the stock declines. For example, if the price of the stock in Exhibit 19.3 fell from $70 to $60 for a 14.2 percent decline, the intrinsic value of the option would fall from $20 to $10 for a 50 percent decline. As with any investment, the investor must decide if the increase in the potential return offered by leverage is worth the increased risk.

The Time Premium Paid for an Option

time premium
The amount by which an option's price exceeds the option's intrinsic value.

If an option offers a greater potential return than does the stock, investors may prefer to buy the option. In an effort to purchase the option, investors will bid up its price, so the market price will exceed the option's intrinsic value. Since the market price of an option is frequently referred to as the *premium,* the extent to which this price exceeds the option's intrinsic value is referred to as the **time premium** or time value. Investors are willing to pay this time premium for the potential leverage the option offers. This time premium, however, reduces the potential return and increases the potential loss.

The time premium is illustrated in Exhibit 19.3, which adds to Exhibit 19.1 a hypothetical set of option prices in column 4. The hypothetical market prices are greater than the intrinsic values of the option because investors have bid up the prices. To purchase the option, an investor must pay the market price and not the option's intrinsic value. Thus, in this example when the market price of the stock is $60 and the intrinsic value of the option is $10, the market price of the option is $15. The investor must pay $15 to purchase the option, which is $5 more than the option's intrinsic value.

The relationships in Exhibit 19.3 between the price of the stock and the option's intrinsic value and hypothetical price are illustrated in Figure 19.2. The time premium paid for the option over its intrinsic value is easily seen in the graph, for it

FIGURE 19.2

The Relationships Among the Price of the Stock and the Option's Intrinsic Value and Hypothetical Price

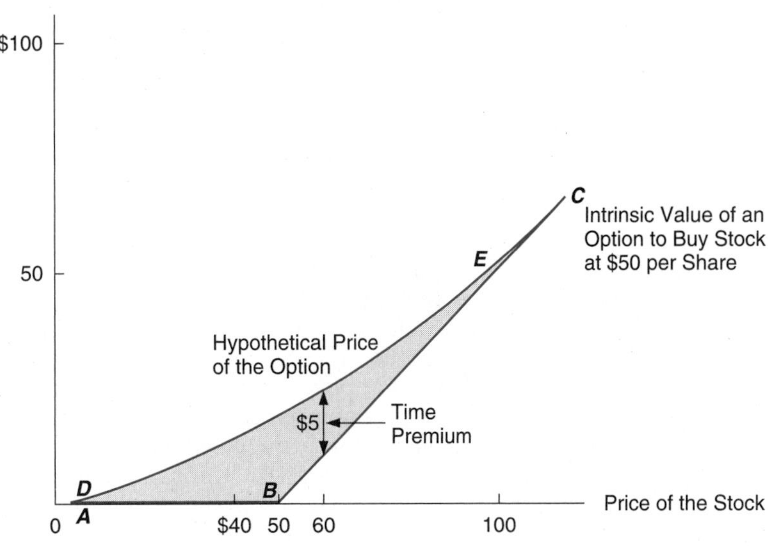

is the shaded area indicating the difference between the line representing the market price of the option (line *DE*) and the line representing its intrinsic value (line *ABC*). Thus, when the price of the stock and option are \$60 and \$15, respectively, the time premium is \$5 (the price of the option, \$15, minus its intrinsic value, \$10).

As may be seen in the figure, the amount of the time value varies at the different price levels of the stock. However, the amount of the time premium declines as the price of the stock rises above the option's strike price. Once the price of the stock has risen considerably, the option may command virtually no time premium over its intrinsic value. At \$100 per share, the option is selling at approximately its intrinsic value of \$50. The primary reason for this decline in the time premium is that as the price of the stock and the intrinsic value of the option rise, the potential leverage is reduced. In addition, at higher prices the potential price decline in the option is greater if the price of the stock falls. For these reasons investors become less willing to bid up the price of the option as the price of the stock rises, and hence the amount of the time premium diminishes.

The time premium decreases the potential leverage and return from investing in options. If, for example, this stock's price rose from \$60 to \$70 for a 16.7 percent gain, the option's price would rise from \$15 to \$23 for a 53.3 percent gain. The percentage increase in the price of the option still exceeds the percentage increase in the price of the stock; however, the difference between the two percentage increases is smaller, since the option sells for more than its intrinsic value. The time premium has substantially reduced the potential leverage that the option offers investors.

Investors who are considering purchasing options should ask themselves what price increase they can expect in the option if the price of the underlying stock should rise. For the option to be attractive, its anticipated percentage increase in price must exceed the anticipated percentage increase in the price of the stock. The option must offer the investor leverage to justify the additional risk. Obviously an investor should not purchase the option if the stock's price is expected to appreciate in value more rapidly than the option's price. The previous example illustrates that the time premium paid for an option may substantially decrease the potential leverage. Thus, recognition of the time premium that an option commands over its intrinsic value is one of the most important considerations in the selection of an option for investment.

The valuation of an option determines the amount of the time premium (i.e., valuation determines where line *DE* in Figure 19.2 lies in the plane relating the price of the stock and the option's value). Several factors affect an option's value; since these factors differ among companies, time premiums commanded by options on their stocks also differ. While a detailed discussion of option valuation (and hence the time premium) is deferred until the next chapter, the following gives an overview of the determinants of an option's time premium.

As an option approaches expiration, its market price must approach the option's intrinsic value. On the expiration date, the option cannot command a price greater than its intrinsic value based on the underlying stock. Thus, as an option nears expiration, it will sell for a lower time premium, and that premium disappears at the option's expiration.

Other determinants of an option's time premium include the payment of cash dividends, the volatility of the underlying stock, and interest rates. Options of companies that pay cash dividends tend to sell for lower time premiums. There may be two possible explanations for this relationship. First, companies that retain (do not distribute) earnings will have more funds available for investments. By retaining and reinvesting earnings, a company may grow more rapidly, and this growth may be reflected in the price of its stock. Hence, the potential gain in the price of the option to buy that stock may be greater if the firm retains its earnings and does not pay a cash dividend. Second, if a company pays a dividend, the owner of the option does not receive the cash payment. The option will be less attractive relative to the common stock, for the owner of the option must forgo the dividend. Therefore, investors will not be willing to pay as much for the option and it will sell for a lower time premium.

Another factor that affects the time premium paid for an option is the price volatility of the common stock. (In the next chapter this volatility will be measured by the variability of the stock's return as measured by the standard deviation of the return.) If the stock's price fluctuates substantially, the option may be more attractive and command a higher time premium. Since the price of the option follows the price of the underlying stock, fluctuations in the price of the stock will be reflected in the option's price. The more volatile the price of the stock, the more opportunity the option offers for a price increase. Thus, options on volatile stocks tend to be more attractive (at least to speculators) and command a higher time premium than options on stocks whose prices are more stable and less volatile.

Interest rates affect options by their impact on the present value of the funds necessary to exercise the option. Since options are exercised in the future, higher interest rates imply that the investor must set aside a lower amount of money to exercise the option. Since an option's intrinsic value is the price of the stock minus the strike price, a lower strike price must increase the value of the option. In effect, higher interest rates reduce the present value of the strike price, which makes the option more valuable.

Calls

call option
An option sold by an individual that entitles the buyer to purchase stock at a specified price within a specified time period.

put option
An option to sell stock at a specified price within a specified time period.

In contrast to the previous discussion of options in general, the remainder of this chapter is devoted to specific types of options. A **call** is an option to buy a specified number of shares of stock (usually 100) at a specified price (which is frequently referred to as the *strike* price) within a specified time period.[2] The owner of a call has the right to *call forth* the shares of stock and to purchase the shares at the specified price. The opposite option, which is called a **put**, grants the right to sell a specified number of shares (usually 100) at a specified price within a specified time period. A put is an option to *place or put* with someone else shares owned by the holder of the option. (Puts are discussed later in this chapter.)

Notice the phrase "within a specified time period" in the preceding definitions. American call (and put) options may be exercised prior to expiration. Comparable European options may be exercised only "at expiration." This difference means an investor could exercise an American call option prior to a dividend payment and receive the dividend. Such is not the case with European call options. Although American options are infrequently exercised prior to expiration, this increased flexibility makes American options more valuable than European options.

Chicago Board Options Exchange (CBOE)
The first organized secondary market in put and call options.

The Chicago Board Options Exchange

Prior to the formation of the **Chicago Board Options Exchange (CBOE)** (http://www.cboe.com), calls were purchased only in the over-the-counter market. If an investor wanted to buy a call option, it was obtained from an options dealer. Each option sold was different, because the exercise price and the expiration date were negotiated with each sale. Once the option was purchased, the investor who desired to sell it had difficulty, because there was no secondary market in options.

[2]Actually, call options are not new. They have existed since the 1630s, when options on tulip bulbs played a role in the speculative tulip bulb craze that swept Holland. For a fascinating portrait of such speculative periods, see Burton G. Malkiel, *A Random Walk Down Wall Street,* 7th ed. (New York: W. W. Norton and Company, 2000).

With the advent of the CBOE, an organized market in call options on selected securities was created. For the first time investors could buy and sell call options through an organized exchange (i.e., an organized secondary market). An investor purchasing a call on the CBOE knew that there would be a market for that option in the future. This ability to sell options that had been previously purchased gave a degree of marketability to call options that had not existed earlier.

There are several features of the CBOE that are conducive to the development of secondary markets for the calls. First, transactions are continuously reported and daily summaries of transactions appear in leading newspapers. Exhibit 19.4 presents a clipping of selected calls and puts traded on various exchanges as reported in *The Wall Street Journal.* As may be seen in the exhibit, there are several options traded on each stock. The company, such as AMD (Advanced Micro Devices), is listed first, followed by the strike price and the expiration month. The last four entries are the volume (number of contracts traded) and the closing price for call options at that strike price, followed by the volume and closing price for put options. If there are no entries, the option did not trade or does not exist. The number of existing options, which is referred to as the **open interest**, is also reported for the day's most actively traded options.

open interest
Number of option contracts with a specified strike price and expiration date on a particular stock.

Second, a clearinghouse was established for the CBOE that maintains a daily record of options issued in the accounts of its members. The members are required to keep a continuous record of their respective customers' positions in options. No actual options certificates are issued; only the bookkeeping is maintained by the clearinghouse. A centralized clearinghouse greatly facilitates trading in the options, for it serves as the intermediary through which purchases and sales of the calls are recorded.

Third, the CBOE is self-regulated. It has the power to impose requirements that must be met before calls may be traded on the exchange, and options on only a selected number of securities have been accepted for trading on the exchange. Investors must be approved before they can purchase and sell through the CBOE, and there is a limit to the number of options on a single stock that an investor may own. Brokers on the floor of the exchange must have a minimum amount of capital. Although such self-regulation does not guarantee the absence of illegal transactions, it is conducive to the development of organized security markets.

The initial success of the CBOE exceeded expectations. Soon after its formation, other exchanges started to list call options. Currently, call options are traded not only on the CBOE but also on the New York, American, Pacific, and Philadelphia exchanges. While all companies do not meet the criteria for having options listed, over a thousand firms are eligible to have call options traded on their stock.[3]

Options and Leverage

Calls may be purchased by investors who want to leverage their position in a stock. Should the price of the stock rise, the price of the call will also rise. Since the cost of the call is less than the cost of the stock, the percentage increase in the call may exceed that of the stock, so the investor earns a greater percentage return on the call option than on the underlying stock. If the price of the stock declines, the value of the call also falls, so the investor sustains a larger percentage loss on the option than on the stock. However, since the cost of the call is less than the stock, the absolute loss on the investment in the call may be less than the absolute loss on the stock.

[3]The criteria for having call options listed on an exchange include the following: The firm must have at least 8,000,000 shares outstanding, 10,000 shareholders, and an annual turnover of 2,000,000 shares for the last two years. During 1998, the CBOE and the Pacific Exchange proposed a merger. This was in addition to the proposed acquisition of the Philadelphia Exchange by the American Stock Exchange.

EXHIBIT 19.4

Listing of Selected Options

LISTED OPTIONS QUOTATIONS

Wednesday, August 1, 2001

Composite volume and close for actively traded equity and LEAPS, or long-term options, with results for the corresponding put or call contract. Volume figures are unofficial. Open interest is total outstanding for all exchanges and reflects previous trading day. Close when possible is shown for the underlying stock or primary market. **CB**-Chicago Board Options Exchange. **AM**-American Stock Exchange. **PB**-Philadelphia Stock Exchange. **PC**-Pacific Stock Exchange. **XC**-Composite. **p**-Put. **o**-Strike price adjusted for split.

MOST ACTIVE CONTRACTS

OPTION/STRIKE				VOL.	EXCH	LAST	NET CHG	a-CLOSE	OPEN INT
Nasd100Tr	Aug	43		82,054	XC	160	+ 050	4310	97,181
Intel	Jan	35		65,265	XC	210	+ 025	3075	53,844
Microsft	Jan	70	p	55,417	XC	870	+ 020	6647	108,899
Intel	Oct	3750		47,559	XC	045	...	3075	59,848
Nasd100Tr	Aug	41	p	43,987	XC	070	– 045	4310	43,755
Microsft	Aug	75	p	43,862	XC	870	– 010	6647	20,534
Cisco	Aug	20		30,973	XC	120	+ 040	2030	134,947
Lucent	Sep	750		26,504	XC	040	– 005	613	28,188
SiebelSys	Aug	25	p	24,548	XC	030	+ 005	3607	30,203
VeritasSf	Aug	25	p	22,225	XC	010	– 005	4323	30,295
SunMicro	Aug	1750		22,216	XC	075	+ 045	1735	23,465
Nasd100Tr	Aug	44		17,628	XC	110	+ 040	4310	51,306
Lucent	Jan 03	5	p	17,420	XC	135	+ 020	613	19,088
A M D	Oct	20		16,939	XC	210	+ 010	1890	17,829
Cisco	Aug	2250		16,774	XC	035	+ 015	2030	52,711
Intel	Aug	3250		16,611	XC	040	+ 020	3075	68,318
Nasd100Tr	Aug	45		15,781	XC	075	+ 030	4310	117,900
ADC Tel	Aug	5		15,542	XC	025	– 005	494	1,653
Intel	Oct	3750	p	15,000	XC	710	– 140	3075	22,733
Intel	Aug	30		14,729	XC	150	+ 040	3075	88,368

OPTION/STRIKE				VOL.	EXCH	LAST	NET CHG	a-CLOSE	OPEN INT
Cisco	Aug	1750	p	14,721	XC	030	– 015	2030	68,468
EMC	Aug	20		14,482	XC	160	+ 075	2090	18,943
SunMicro	Sep	1750		13,278	XC	140	+ 050	1735	7,391
Nasd100Tr	Sep	45		12,368	XC	195	+ 045	4310	41,946
Nasd100Tr	Aug	42		12,057	XC	210	+ 060	4310	118,929
Nasd100Tr	Aug	46		11,190	XC	050	+ 015	4310	42,380
RschMot	Sep	20	p	11,010	XC	210	+ 010	2312	1,023
RschMot	Sep	125		10,524	XC	265	– 065	2312	590
JPMorgCh	Dec	60		10,030	XC	025	...	4350	13,266
Nasd100Tr	Aug	42	p	9,508	XC	1	– 055	4310	36,697
Nasd100Tr	Sep	48		8,694	XC	095	+ 020	4310	55,227
PepsiCo	Aug	45		8,008	XC	050	– 170	4369	5,750
Cisco	Aug	20	p	7,935	XC	095	– 060	2030	18,133
RF MicD	Aug	35		7,640	XC	075	+ 050	3096	3,425
TexasInst	Aug	30		7,482	XC	660	+ 180	3663	14,311
AMCC	Aug	20		7,346	XC	085	+ 040	1869	13,365
QuakrO	Aug	95		7,275	XC	550	+ 360	10030	11,786
CirCty	Aug	1750		7,035	XC	215	+ 040	1918	2,266
PepsiCo	Aug	45	p	7,033	XC	165	+ 115	4369	6,158
CienaCp	Aug	30	p	6,822	XC	105	– 045	3565	12,457

Journal Link: Complete equity option listings and data are available in the online Journal at **WSJ.com/JournalLinks**

Strike Price

Closing Price of the Stock

Expiration Month

OPTION/STRIKE		EXP.	CALL VOL.	CALL LAST	PUT VOL.	PUT LAST
ACT Mfg	10	Aug	100	045	587	195
ADC Tel	5	Aug	15542	025	134	035
AES Cp	35	Nov	800	6	11	195
3888	40	Sep	851	180	40	360
AmOnline	1750	Sep	2502	185	101	3
4608	4250	Aug	23	390	1541	040
4608	45	Aug	559	2	544	1
4608	45	Oct	112	430	1644	285
4608	4750	Aug	1214	070	14	210
4608	50	Aug	2446	020	48	410
4608	50	Sep	556	095	12	5
4608	50	Oct	433	180	15	550
4608	50	Jan	479	360	54	670
4608	55	Oct	1087	065	63	950
4608	60	Oct	559	030	33	1410
ATT Wrls	1750	Aug	805	175	...	...
1901	20	Sep	387	060	14	165
AT&T o	20	Aug	4220	075	350	030
2030	20	Sep	7	120	1000	085
2030	2250	Aug	2161	010	...	...
AberFitch	1250	Sep	864	120	...	...
Acterna	5	Sep	1470	190	...	...
AdobeS	40	Aug	649	150	239	280
Adtran	25	Sep	550	2	...	...
A M D	1750	Aug	975	170	587	050
1890	1750	Oct	58	340	396	190
1890	20	Aug	1506	050	582	185
1890	20	Sep	624	130	285	255
1890	20	Oct	16939	210	81	330
1890	20	Jan	3217	320	1050	4
1890	2250	Aug	448	010	...	...
1890	2750	Jan	1167	105	...	...
AethrSys	10	Feb	...	...	3150	270
Alcoa	40	Sep	432	150	100	275
Alkerm	35	Feb	700	330	...	...
AldWaste	1750	Sep	401	230	10	045
1932	20	Aug	8	030	500	095
Allste	3250	Sep	...	...	4600	070
3525	35	Sep	11	170	4600	150
Alltel	70	Oct	462	130	...	...
Altera	30	Aug	1042	3	5656	080
3223	3250	Aug	1508	150	399	185
3223	35	Aug	6306	085	72	360
A Hess	80	Aug	25	090	1295	430
AEagleO	35	Aug	506	220	790	135
AmExpr	3750	Aug	516	390	171	020
4149	40	Aug	478	2	181	050
4149	40	Jan	89	480	2021	320
4149	4250	Aug	408	055	56	185
4149	4250	Sep	3492	145	...	...
AmIntGp	80	Aug	402	3	...	...
8260	80	Sep	100	490	1075	155

OPTION/STRIKE		EXP.	CALL VOL.	CALL LAST	PUT VOL.	PUT LAST
4830	50	Aug	2207	150	818	330
4830	50	Sep	582	330	66	510
4830	55	Aug	836	030	24	7
4830	55	Sep	951	155	3	810
4830	55	Oct	389	260	21	890
4830	55	Jan	369	510	...	...
4830	60	Aug	465	005	...	...
AMCC	15	Aug	1628	380	576	025
1869	20	Aug	7346	085	454	205
1869	20	Sep	864	2	383	330
1869	2250	Aug	543	025	55	390
1869	4750	Aug	1397	2	623	090
ArrowEl	20	Dec	...	...	500	050
...	25	Dec	3	430	500	185
Atmel	10	Aug	659	085	23	045
AuroraBio	30	Jan	508	360	...	...
Autdsk	40	Aug	412	140	...	...
AutoDt	50	Aug	107	140	404	150
AutoZn	50	Sep	400	120	12	430
Aviron	25	Aug	398	110	93	295
Avon	50	Sep	38	060	500	480
BEA Sys	20	Aug	296	440	2814	070
2366	2250	Aug	1038	275	208	145
2366	2250	Sep	495	380	118	270
2366	25	Aug	1166	130	44	280
2366	25	Sep	399	265	27	410
2366	30	Sep	450	120	11	740
BJ Svc	25	Aug	591	150	93	155
BakrHu	3750	Aug	381	050	10	290
BallardPw	40	Aug	6	340	3039	170
BancOne	40	Sep	396	060	...	...
3835	4250	Nov	570	050	...	...
Bk of Am	60	Aug	1016	360	148	055
63	60	Sep	550	450	23	150
63	65	Aug	574	060	361	265
63	70	Feb	1473	290	...	...
63	75	Feb	1470	160	...	...
BankNY	50	Aug	750	010	10	550
BarickG	15	Sep	447	065	531	080
1476	15	Jan	450	140	...	...
1476	1750	Jan	718	060	...	...
BestBuy	60	Aug	2	920	805	105
6645	65	Sep	11	650	532	490
Biogen	55	Sep	1001	510	65	290
BiotechT	110	Aug	30	1220	663	140
12019	115	Sep	...	...	2779	550
12019	120	Aug	115	450	1305	440
12019	125	Aug	744	230	...	...
BlackBox	55	Aug	1	330	410	320
Block	55	Oct	1160	1750	...	...
7248	65	Oct	1004	850	...	...
Boeing	60	Aug	788	075	104	2

OPTION/STRIKE		EXP.	CALL VOL.	CALL LAST	PUT VOL.	PUT LAST
8665	85	Oct	2	680	519	440
8665	95	Aug	1135	035	553	830
CVS Corp	40	Aug	370	015	...	...
3506	45	Aug	...	...	1000	990
3506	50	Aug	...	...	1000	1490
Cabltrn	1750	Aug	857	255	31	065
Cadence	15	Nov	500	860	...	...
2280	20	Nov	3565	430	...	...
2280	20	Feb	3565	520	...	...
Calpine	40	Aug	2418	050	...	...
CapOne	60	Aug	300	510	520	055
CaremkRx	1750	Mar	380	225	...	...
Caterp	50	Aug	135	460	460	030
5395	55	Aug	714	090	45	210
CellGens	15	Jan	...	...	750	170
Cendant	1750	Sep	5	280	1219	045
1973	20	Aug	5070	045	3023	070
1973	20	Sep	2636	090	1802	110
1973	2250	Nov	1020	075	10	330
ChartCm	2250	Sep	2107	095	...	...
ChartOneF	25	Aug	750	7	...	...
3211	30	Aug	750	2	...	...
ChkPoint	40	Aug	472	610	318	075
4549	45	Aug	1225	275	577	235
4549	50	Aug	405	080	30	560
ChinaTlc	20	Dec	1000	450	...	...
CienaCp	30	Aug	969	610	6822	105
3565	35	Aug	2748	310	1040	250
3565	40	Aug	2002	120	21	590
CirCty	1750	Aug	7035	215	10	045
1918	20	Aug	6534	055	...	...
Cirrus	20	Sep	852	230	15	265
1961	2250	Sep	465	135	3	430
Cisco	15	Jan	252	640	368	110
2030	1750	Aug	4820	3	14721	030
2030	1750	Sep	269	360	512	070
2030	1750	Oct	935	390	1141	110
2030	1750	Jan	4317	480	277	185
2030	20	Aug	30973	120	7935	095
2030	20	Sep	5646	2	1106	160
2030	20	Oct	1851	240	167	205
2030	20	Jan	953	350	415	295
2030	2250	Aug	16774	035	132	255
2030	2250	Sep	2732	085	24	3
2030	2250	Oct	1932	140	48	340
2030	2250	Jan	1892	245	44	430
2030	25	Aug	617	010	40	490
2030	25	Sep	2370	035	304	510
2030	25	Oct	942	070	72	540
2030	25	Jan	1151	160	245	6
2030	2750	Sep	554	010	105	740
2030	30	Jan	1918	065	...	...

FIGURE 19.3

Profits and Losses at Expiration for the Buyer of a Call

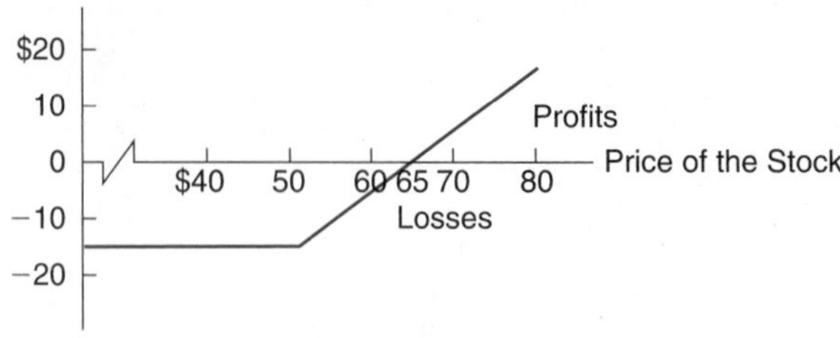

To see the potential for profit and loss, consider a call option to buy stock at $50 when the price of the stock is $60 and the call sells for $15. (These numbers were used in Exhibit 19.3 and Figure 19.2 to illustrate the time premium paid for an option.) The investor buys the call (i.e., establishes a long position in the option) to take advantage of the potential leverage. As was previously explained, a price increase in the stock from $60 to $70 causes the price of the call to rise from $15 to $23—respective price increases of 16.7 and 53.5 percent. If the price of the stock were to decline from $60 to $50, the price of the call would decline from $15 to $6—respective price decreases of 20 and 60 percent. Leverage cuts both ways.

The previous example assumes that the price of the stock changed soon after the call was purchased so that the time premium continues to exist. Such will not be the case if these prices of the stock occur at the call's expiration. At expiration, the call will only sell for its intrinsic value. The call will sell for $20 when the stock sells for $70, and for $0 if the stock sells for $50 or less.

The potential profits and losses at expiration on the purchase of the call for $15 when the stock sells for $60 are illustrated in Figure 19.3. As long as the price of the stock is $50 or less, the entire investment in the call ($15) is lost. As the price of the stock rises above $50, the loss is reduced. The investor breaks even at $65, because the intrinsic value of the call is $15—the cost of the option. The investor earns a profit as the price of the stock continues to rise above $65. (Remember that in this illustration the starting price of the stock was $60. The price has to rise only by more than $5 to assure the investor of a profit on the position in the call.)

Figure 19.4 replicates Figure 19.3 and adds the profits and losses from buying the stock at $60. Both involve purchases and therefore are long positions in the securities. If the price of the stock rises above or declines below $60, the investor earns a profit or sustains a loss. The important difference between the lines indicating the profit and losses on the long positions in the two securities is the possible large dollar loss from buying the stock compared to the limited dollar loss on the call. In the worst-case scenario, the investor could lose $60 on the stock but only $15 on the call.

Writing Calls

The preceding section considered purchasing call options to obtain leverage; this section will cover the opposite: selling call options. In the jargon of options, the act of issuing and selling a call is referred to as *writing* the option. While a long position in a call gives the investor an opportunity to profit from the leverage the option offers, the short position (i.e., writing and selling calls) produces revenues from their sale.

FIGURE 19.4

Profits and Losses of a Long Position in the Stock Compared to a Long Position in the Call

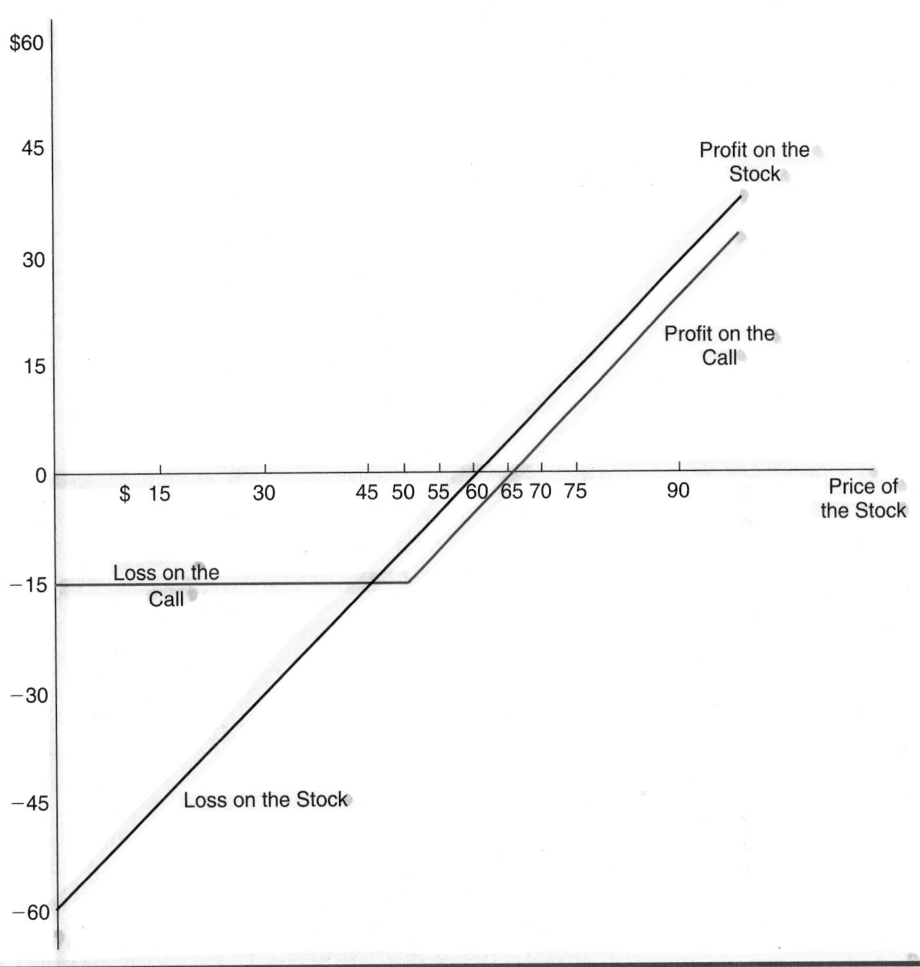

covered option writing
Selling an option for which the seller owns the securities.

naked option writing
The selling (i.e., writing) of an option without owning the underlying security.

There are two ways to write options. The first is the less risky strategy, which is called **covered option writing**. The investor buys (or already owns) the underlying stock and then sells the option to buy that stock. If the option is exercised, the investor supplies the stock that was previously purchased (i.e., *covers* the option with the stock). The second method entails selling the call without owning the stock. This is referred to as **naked option writing**, for the investor is exposed to considerable risk. If the price of the stock rises and the call is exercised, the option writer must buy the stock at the higher market price in order to supply it to the buyer. With naked option writing the potential for loss is considerably greater than with covered option writing.

The reason for writing options is the income to be gained from their sale. The potential profit from writing a covered option may be seen in Exhibit 19.5 (p. 628), which continues the illustration used in the discussion of buying a call. In this example the investor purchases the common stock at the current market price of $60

EXHIBIT 19.5

Profit on a Covered Call (at Expiration) Consisting of the Purchase of Shares of Stock and the Sale of One Call to Buy Shares at $50 a Share

Price of Stock at Expiration of the Call	Net Profit on the Stock	Value of the Call at Expiration	Net Profit on the Sale of the Call	Net Profit on the Position
$35	$−25	$ 0	$15	$−10
40	−20	0	15	−5
45	−15	0	15	0
50	−10	0	15	5
55	−5	5	10	5
60	0	10	5	5
65	5	15	0	5
70	10	20	−5	5

per share and simultaneously sells for $15 a call to buy the shares at the strike price of $50. Possible future prices for the stock at the expiration of the call are given in column 1. Column 2 presents the net profit to the investor from the purchase of the stock. Column 3 gives the value of the call at expiration, and column 4 presents the profit to the investor from the sale of the call. As may be seen in column 4, the sale of the call is profitable to the investor as long as the price of the common stock remains below $65 per share. The last column gives the net profit on the entire position. As long as the price of the common stock stays above $45 per share, the entire position will yield a profit before commission fees. The maximum amount of this profit, however, is limited to $5. Thus, by selling the call the investor forgoes the possibility of large gains. For example, if the price of the stock were to rise to $70 per share, the holder of the call would exercise it and purchase the 100 shares from the seller at $50 per share. The seller would then make only the $5 that was received from the sale of the call.

If the price of the stock were to fall below $45, the entire position would result in a loss to the seller. For example, if the price of the common stock fell to $40, the investor would lose $20 on the purchase of the stock. However, $15 was received from the sale of the call. Thus, the net loss is only $5. The investor still owns the stock and may now write another call on that stock. As long as the investor owns the stock, the same shares may be used over and over to cover the writing of options. Thus, even if the price of the stock does fall, the investor may continue to use it to write more options. The more options that can be written, the more profitable the shares become. For individuals who write options, the best possible situation would be for the stock's price to remain stable. In that case the investors would receive the income from writing the options and never suffer a capital loss from a decline in the price of the stock on which the option is being written.

The relationship between the price of the stock and the profit or loss on writing a covered call is illustrated in Figure 19.5, which plots the first and fifth columns of Exhibit 19.5. As may be seen from the figure, the sale of the covered option produces a profit (before commissions) for all prices of the stock above $45. However, the maximum profit (before commissions) is only $5.

Option writers do not have to own the common stock on which they write calls. Although such naked or uncovered option writing exposes the investor to a large

POINTS OF INTEREST

Big Profits; Big Losses

Profits and losses can be sustained very rapidly in option trading. Combine options with corporate takeovers and the possible price movements are magnified. Consider the attempted takeover of Cities Service by Gulf Oil. On Wednesday, June 16, 1982, the following options on Cities Service were traded when the stock sold for $37¾.

June Option Exercise Price	Option's Closing Price (6/16/82)
$20	$17⅛
25	12
30	7⅜
35	2
40	7/16
45	⅛
50	1/16
55	1/16

On Thursday, June 17, 1982, there was no trading in Cities Service stock pending an announcement. The announcement turned out to be that Gulf Oil would buy Cities Service for $63 a share. When trading resumed on Friday, June 18, 1982, Cities Service stock rose to $53⅛. The options' price increases (and the percentage increases from the previous closing prices) were as follows:

June Option Exercise Price	Option's Closing Price (6/18/82)	Percentage Increase in Price
$20	$33¼	94.2%
25	28½	137.5
30	22⅞	210.2
35	18	800.0
40	13⅛	2,900.0
45	9½	7,500.0
50	3½	5,500.0
55	1/16	—

The irony of this incident is that the options were to expire on June 18, 1982. Thus the individual who bought the 40s at 7/16 ($43.75) with only *two days to expiration* would normally have lost this money. But as a result of the attempted takeover, this speculator earned 2,900 percent in two days!

While few investors earned such a return, *The New York Times* (June 19, 1982, p. 33) reported that several traders who had sold these options without owning the stock (i.e., had sold the options naked) had sustained heavy losses. If a trader had sold 100 contracts at 40 for 7/16 ($43.75) per contract on Wednesday, those options were worth $4,375 (100 contracts times $43.75 per contract = $4,375). On Friday those calls were worth $131,250 (100 × $1,312.50 = $131,250). The loss to the naked call writer would be $126,875($4,375 − $131,250). Thus naked call writers of Cities Service stock suffered large losses as the unexpected happened and gave value to options that normally would have been worthless at expiration.

FIGURE 19.5

Profit or Loss on Selling a Covered Call (at Expiration of the Call)

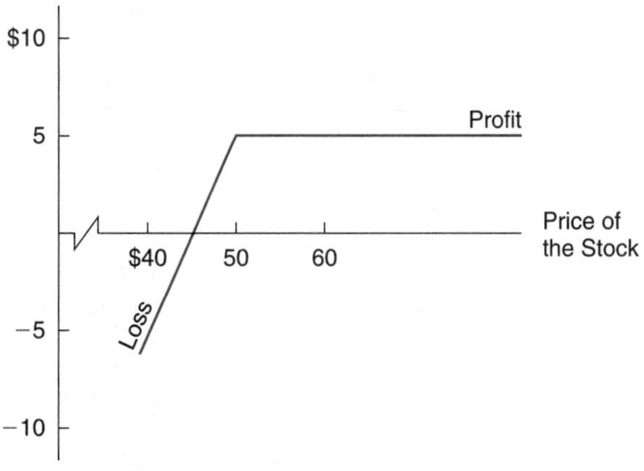

FIGURE 19.6

Profits and Losses at Expiration for a Naked Call Writer

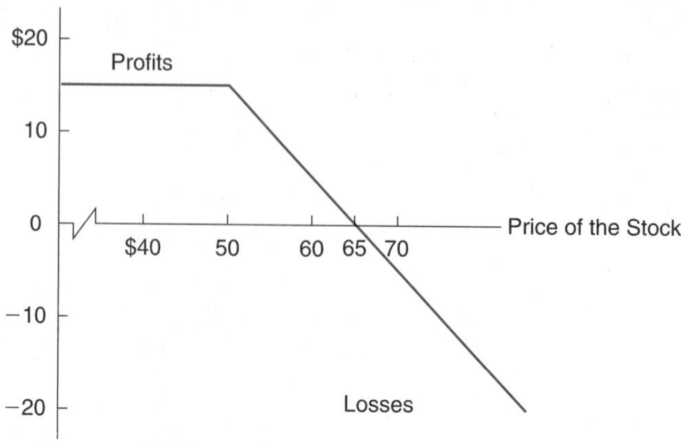

amount of risk, the returns may be considerable. If the writer of the preceding option had not owned the stock and had sold the option for $15, the position would have been profitable as long as the price of the common stock remained below $65 per share at the expiration of the call. The potential loss, however, is theoretically infinite, for the naked option loses $100 for every $1 increase in the price of the stock above the call's exercise price. For example, if the price of the stock were to rise to $90 per share, the call would be worth $4,000 ($40 per share × 100 shares). The owner of the call would exercise it and purchase the 100 shares for $5,000. The writer of the call would then have to purchase the shares on the open market for $9,000. Since the writer received only $1,500 when the call was sold and $5,000 when the call was exercised, the loss would be $2,500. Therefore, uncovered option writing exposes the writer to considerable risk if the price of the stock rises.[4]

The relationship between the price of the stock and the profit or loss on writing a naked call option is illustrated in Figure 19.6. In this case the option writer earns a profit (before commissions) as long as the price of the stock does not exceed $65 at the expiration of the call. Notice that the investor earns the entire $15 if the stock's price falls below $50. However, the potential for loss is considerable if the price of the stock increases.

Investors should write naked call options only if they anticipate a decline (or at least no increase in) the price of the stock. These investors may write covered call options if they believe the price of the stock may rise but are not certain of the price increase. And they may purchase the stock (or the option) and not write calls if they believe there is substantial potential for a price increase.

When Figures 19.3 and 19.6 are combined in Figure 19.7, it becomes apparent that the potential profits and losses from selling a naked call present a mirror image of the losses and profits from purchasing the call. The short position (the sale of the call) exactly mirrors the long position (the purchase). Excluding the impact of commissions, the profits earned by one participant come at the expense of the investor with the opposite position. The buyer is anticipating that the price of the stock will rise and seeks to take advantage of the call's potential leverage. The writer is anticipating that the price of the stock will not rise. Both cannot be right,

[4]This risk may be reduced by an order to purchase the stock at $65. If the price of the stock rises, the stop-loss order is executed so that the option writer buys the stock and the position in the call is no longer naked.

FIGURE 19.7

Profit or Loss on the Purchase of a Call and on the Sale of a Naked Call

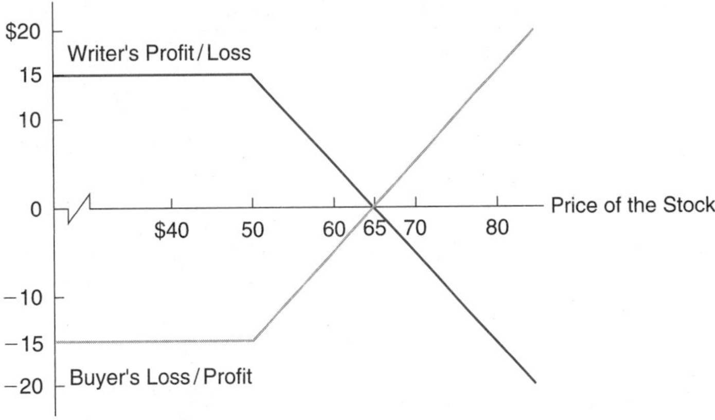

so the source of profits to one of the participants has to be the source of the loss to the other.

If, however, the writer had sold the call covered, the profits and losses are not directly opposite. The covered writer has a type of hedged position that reduces the risk associated with fluctuations in the price of the stock. The covered writer seeks to take advantage of the option's time premium and accepts a smaller profit. In the previous illustration, that maximum profit was $5—the option's time premium. The naked writer, however, could earn $15 if the price of the stock declined and would earn the $5 time premium even if the price of the stock did not rise (i.e., remained stable). The potential profits and risks assumed by the naked and covered writers are obviously different. Theoretically, the naked writer has no limit to the possible loss whereas the covered writer's worst-case scenario occurs in the unlikely event that the price of the stock declines to $0.

Puts

A put is an option to *sell* stock (usually 100 shares) at a specified price within a specified time period. As with a call, the time period is short: three, six, or nine months. Like all options, a put has an intrinsic value, which is the difference between the strike price of the put and the price of the stock.[5] The relationship between the price of a stock and the intrinsic value of a put is illustrated in Exhibit 19.6 (p. 632). This put is an option to sell 100 shares at $30 per share. The first column gives the strike price of the put, the second column presents the hypothetical prices of the stock, and the third column gives the intrinsic value of the put (i.e., the strike price minus the price of the stock).

If the price of the stock is less than the strike price, the put has a positive intrinsic value and is said to be *in the money.* If the price of the stock is greater than the strike price, the put has no intrinsic value and is said to be *out of the money.* If the price of the stock equals the strike price, the put is *at the money.* As with call options, the market price of a put is called *the premium.*

[5]Note that the intrinsic value of a put is the reverse of the intrinsic value of an option to buy (e.g., a call). Compare Exhibits 19.1 and 19.6.

EXHIBIT 19.6

The Relationship Between the Price of a Stock and the Intrinsic Value of a Put

Strike Price	*minus*	Price of the Stock	*equals*	Intrinsic Value of the Put
$30		$15		$15
30		20		10
30		25		5
30		30		0
30		35		0
30		40		0

As may be seen in Exhibit 19.6, when the price of the stock declines, the intrinsic value of the put rises. Since the owner of the put may sell the stock at the price specified in the option agreement, the value of the option rises as the price of the stock falls. Thus, if the price of the stock is $15 and the exercise price of the put is $30, the put's intrinsic value as an option must be $1,500 (for 100 shares). The investor can purchase the 100 shares of stock for $1,500 on the stock market and sell them for $3,000 to the person who issued the put. The put, then, must be worth the $1,500 difference between the purchase and sale prices.

Buying Puts

Why should an investor purchase a put? The reason is the same for puts as it is for other speculative options: The put offers potential leverage to the investor. Such leverage may be seen in the example presented in Exhibit 19.6. When the price of the stock declines from $25 to $20 (a 20 percent decrease), the intrinsic value of the put rises from $5 to $10 (a 100 percent increase). In this example a 20 percent decline in the price of the stock produces a larger percentage increase in the intrinsic value of the put. It is this potential leverage that makes put options attractive to investors.

As with other options, investors are willing to pay a price that is greater than the put's intrinsic value: The put commands a time premium above its intrinsic value as an option. As with warrants and calls, the amount of this time premium depends on such factors as the volatility of the stock's price, the time to the expiration of the put, and the potential for *decline* in the price of the stock.

The relationships among the price of the stock, the strike price of the put, and the hypothetical prices for the put are illustrated in Exhibit 19.7. The first three columns are identical to those in Exhibit 19.6. The first column gives the strike price of the put, the second column gives the price of the stock, and the third column gives the put's intrinsic value as an option. The fourth column presents hypothetical prices for the put. As may be seen in Exhibit 19.7, the hypothetical price of the put exceeds the intrinsic value, for the put commands a time premium over its intrinsic value as an option.

Figure 19.8 illustrates these relationships among the price of the common stock, the intrinsic value of the put, and the hypothetical market value of the put. This figure shows the inverse relationship between the price of the stock and the put's intrinsic value. As the price of the stock declines, the intrinsic value of the put increases (e.g., from $5 to $10 when the stock's price declines from $25 to $20). The

EXHIBIT 19.7

Relationships Among the Price of the Stock, the Strike Price of the Put, and the Hypothetical Price of the Put

Strike Price of the Put	Price of the Stock	Intrinsic Value of the Put	Hypothetical Price of the Put
$30	$15	$15	$15.25
30	20	10	12
30	25	5	8
30	30	0	6
30	35	0	3.50
30	40	0	1
30	50	0	—

figure also readily shows the time premium paid for the option, which is the difference between the price of the put and the option's intrinsic value. If the price of the put is $8 and the intrinsic value is $5, the time premium is $3.

As may be seen in both Exhibit 19.7 and Figure 19.8, the hypothetical market price of the put converges with the put's intrinsic value as the price of the stock declines. If the price of the stock is sufficiently high (e.g., $50 in Exhibit 19.7), the put will not have any market value because the price of the stock must decline substantially for the put to have any intrinsic value. At the other extreme, when the price of the stock is low (e.g., $15), the price of the put is equal to the put's intrinsic value as an option. There are two reasons for this convergence. First, if the price of the stock rises, the investor may lose the funds invested in the put. As the

FIGURE 19.8

The Relationships Among the Price of the Stock, the Intrinsic Value of a Put Option, and the Hypothetical Price of the Option

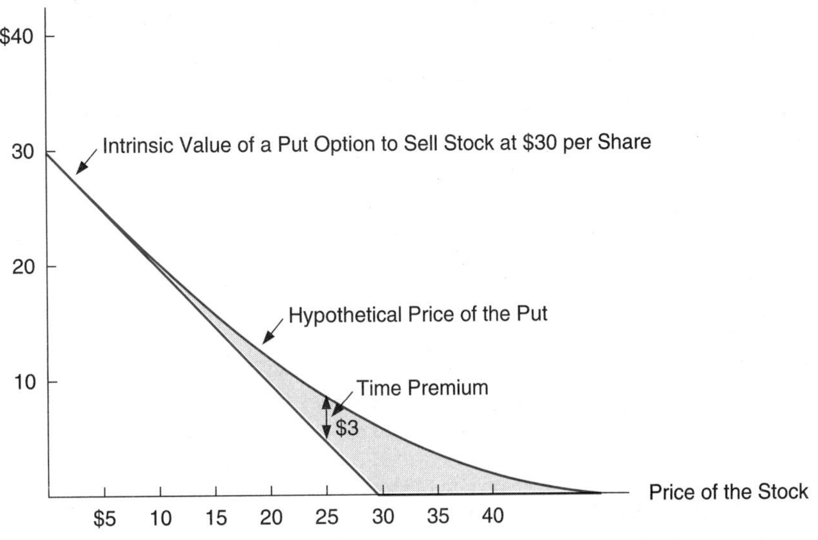

EXHIBIT 19.8

Profits and Losses at Expiration from Purchasing a Put

Price of the Stock	Intrinsic Value of the Put	Net Profit (Loss) on the Purchase
$15	$15	$ 7
20	10	2
25	5	−3
30	0	−8
35	0	−8
40	0	−8

price of the stock declines below the strike price of the put, the potential risk to the investor if the price of the stock should start to rise becomes greater. Thus, put buyers are less willing to pay a time premium above the put's intrinsic value. Second, as the intrinsic value of a put rises when the price of the stock declines, the investor must spend more to buy the put; therefore, the potential return on the investment is less. As the potential return declines, the willingness to pay a time premium diminishes.

The potential profit and loss from purchasing a put is illustrated in Exhibit 19.8 and Figure 19.9. If the price of the stock is $25 and the strike price of the put is $30, the intrinsic value is $5 (i.e., the put is in the money). Suppose the price of the put is $8, so it commands a time premium of $3. As may be seen in both Exhibit 19.8 and Figure 19.9, the purchase of the put is profitable as long as the price of the stock is less than $22, and the profit rises as the price of the stock declines. In the unlikely case that the price of the stock were to fall to $0, the maximum possible profit is $22 (the strike price minus the cost of the put).

If the price of the stock were to rise, the position sustains a loss. As long as the price of the stock is $30 or greater, the put has no intrinsic value (the put is out of the money). No one would exercise an option to sell at $30 if the stock could be

FIGURE 19.9

Profits and Losses at Expiration from Purchasing a Put

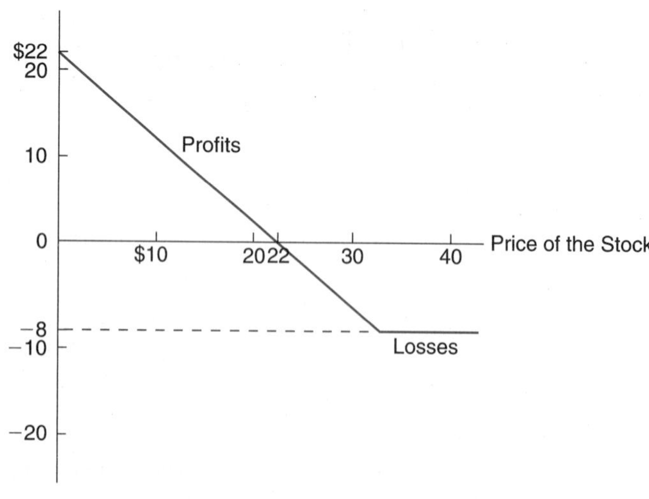

sold for a higher price elsewhere. The option would have no value and expire. In this case the investor loses the entire cost of the option ($8). This is, of course, the worst-case scenario, but it emphasizes that the most the investor can lose is the cost of the option. As is explained when comparing purchasing a put to selling a stock short, the latter strategy can generate greater losses.

Writing Puts

Whereas the previous section discussed buying a put, this section will consider its opposite—selling a put. As with call options, investors may either buy or sell a put (i.e., they may *write* a put). The investor buys a put in anticipation of a fall in the price of the stock. The investor who writes a put, on the other hand, believes that the price of the stock will *not* fall. The price of the stock could rise, which is certainly acceptable from the writer's perspective, but the emphasis is on the stock's price *not falling*.

The writer may be either naked or covered. If the investor only sells the put, the position is naked. If the writer simultaneously shorts the stock, the writer is covered. If the put were exercised and the writer buys the stock, the writer could then use the stock to cover the short position. However, since covered put writing is rare, the following discussion is limited to naked put writing.

The possible profits and losses from writing a put may be seen by continuing the example in Exhibit 19.8 and Figure 19.9. In that illustration, the investor purchased the put for $8 to sell stock at $30 when the stock was selling for $25. In the opposite case, the investor writes the put to sell the stock at $30, and receives the $8 proceeds. The writer's possible profits and losses are shown in Exhibit 19.9 and Figure 19.10 (p. 636). As long as the price of the stock exceeds $22, the position generates a profit. The profit rises along with the price of the stock and reaches a maximum of $8 when the price of the stock is $30. The position sustains a loss if the price of the stock is less than $22, and the loss increases as the price of the stock declines. The maximum possible loss is $22 if the price of the stock were to fall to $0.

Figure 19.11 (p. 636) combines the two previous graphs to illustrate the profits and losses to both the buyer and the writer of the put. Like the purchase and sale of a call in Figure 19.7, it should be immediately apparent that the writer's profits and losses mirror the buyer's losses and profits. If the stock sells for $22 at the expiration of the put, the option's intrinsic value is $8—which is exactly what the buyer paid and the writer received. Neither buyer nor seller earns a profit or sustains a loss (before commissions on the trades). If the price of the stock is less than $22, the buyer earns a profit at the writer's expense. If the price of the stock exceeds $22, the writer earns a profit at the buyer's expense. If the price of the stock is $30 or greater, the maximum possible profit to the writer is $8, which is also the

EXHIBIT 19.9

Profits and Losses at Expiration from Selling (Writing) a Put

Price of the Stock	Intrinsic Value of the Put	Net Profit (Loss) on the Sale
$15	$15	$−7
20	10	−2
25	5	3
30	0	8
35	0	8
40	0	8

FIGURE 19.10

Profits and Losses from Selling (Writing) a Put

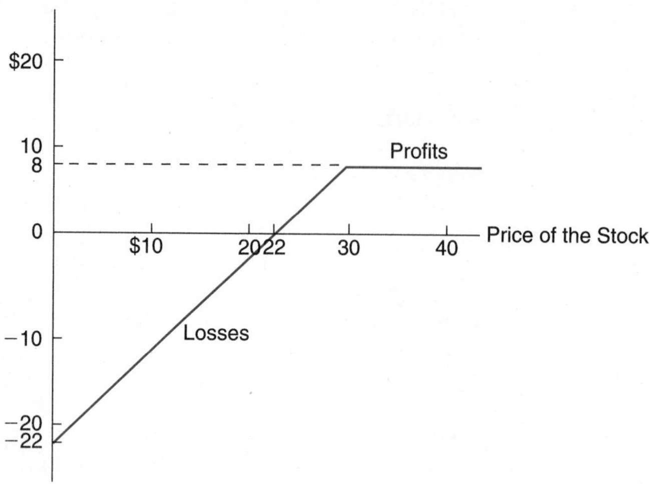

buyer's maximum possible loss. If the price of the stock declines to $0, the maximum possible profit to the buyer is $22, which is also the writer's maximum possible loss. Excluding the impact of brokerage commissions on the transactions, the gains and losses offset each other.

Puts Compared with Short Sales

Investors purchase put options when they believe that the price of the stock is going to decline. Purchasing puts, however, is not the only method investors can use

FIGURE 19.11

Profits and Losses to the Buyer and Seller of a Put

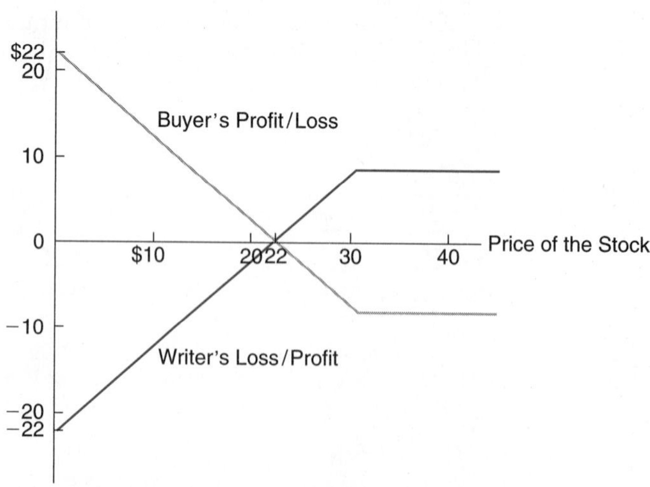

to profit from falling security prices. As was explained in Chapter 3, an investor who believes that the price of a stock is going to fall may profit from the decline by selling short. Buying a put is another form of a short position. However, the put option offers the investor two major advantages over selling short. First, the amount of potential loss is less; second, puts may offer a greater return on the investor's capital because of their leverage.

In order to execute a short position, the investor must sell the stock, deliver the borrowed stock, and later purchase the stock to cover the position. The profit or loss is the difference between the price at which the borrowed stock was sold and the price at which the stock is purchased to repay the loan. If the price of the stock declines, the investor reaps a profit, but if the price of the stock rises, the investor suffers a loss. This loss may be substantial if the stock's price rises significantly. For example, if 100 shares are sold short at $30 and later purchased at $50, the investor loses $2,000 plus commissions on the investment. The higher the price of the stock rises, the greater is the loss that the short position inflicts on the investor.[6]

Purchasing a put option does not subject the investor to a large potential capital loss. If the investor purchases for $300 a put that is the option to sell 100 shares at $30, the maximum amount that the investor can lose is $300. If the price of the common stock rises from $30 to $50, the maximum that can be lost with the put is still only $300. However, the loss on the short position is $2,000 when the price of the stock rises from $30 to $50. Puts reduce the absolute amount that the investor may lose.

Besides subjecting the investor to potentially large losses, the short sale ties up a substantial amount of capital. When the investor sells short, the broker will require that he or she put up funds as collateral. The minimum amount that the investor must remit is the margin requirement set by the Federal Reserve, and individual brokers may require that the investor supply more collateral than this minimum. Selling short thus requires the investor to tie up capital, and the larger the amount that the investor must remit, the smaller the potential return on the short position.

Less capital is required to invest in a put. While the amount of margin varies at different time periods, it certainly will not be as low as the price of the put. Thus, purchasing the put instead of establishing the short position ties up a smaller amount of the investor's funds. The potential return is greater if the price of the stock declines sufficiently to cover the cost of the put, because the amount invested is smaller. Puts thus offer the investor more leverage than does the short position.

Short sales, however, offer one important advantage over puts. Puts expire, but a short position can be maintained indefinitely. If an investor anticipates a price decline, it must occur during the put's short life for the investment to be profitable. With a short sale, the investor does not have this time constraint and may maintain the position indefinitely.

Protective Puts

Purchasing put options may be viewed as a speculative investment strategy. The buyer profits as the value of the underlying stock declines, which causes the value of the put to rise. Since the long-term trend in stock prices is to increase as the economy expands, purchasing a put seems to be betting against the natural trend in a stock's price.

Although purchases of puts by themselves may be speculative, they may, when used in conjunction with the purchase of stock, reduce the individual's risk exposure. Such a strategy—the simultaneous purchase of the stock and a put—is called

[6]Once again the investor may limit this potential loss by establishing an order to purchase the stock should the price rise to some predetermined level.

EXHIBIT 19.10

Profit and Loss Resulting from a Protective Put

Price of the Stock	Profit on the Stock	Intrinsic Value of the Put	Profit on the Put	Total Profit
$20	($20)	$20	$17.50	−$2.50
25	(15)	15	12.50	−2.50
30	(10)	10	7.50	−2.50
35	(5)	5	2.50	−2.50
40	0	0	(2.50)	−2.50
45	5	0	(2.50)	2.50
50	10	0	(2.50)	7.50
55	15	0	(2.50)	12.50
60	20	0	(2.50)	17.50

a *protective put* because it conserves the investor's initial investment while permitting the investor to maintain a long position in a stock so the profit can grow.

Suppose an individual buys a stock for $40 but does not want to bear the risk associated with a decline in the price of the stock. This investor could purchase a put, whose value would rise if the price of the stock were to decline. Suppose there is a six-month put with a strike price of $40 that is currently selling for $2.50.[7] Exhibit 19.10 presents the benefit of buying the put in combination with the stock. The first two columns give the price of the stock and the profit (loss) on the position in the stock. The third and fourth columns give the intrinsic value of the put at its expiration and the profit (loss) on the position in the put. The last column gives the net profit (loss), which is the sum of the profits (losses) on the positions in the stock and the put.

As shown in the last column of the exhibit, the worst-case scenario is a loss of $2.50. No matter how low the price of the stock falls, the maximum loss to the investor is $2.50. If the price of the stock rises, the maximum possible profit is unlimited. The only effect, then, is that the potential profit is reduced by $2.50, the price of the put. (This reduction in potential profit may be seen by comparing columns 2 and 5.) What the investor has achieved by purchasing the put in conjunction with the purchase of the stock is the assurance of a maximum loss of $2.50.

This protective put strategy may be viewed as an alternative to placing a stop-loss order to sell the stock at $37.50. The advantage of the protective put is that the investor is protected from the price of the stock falling, the stock being sold, and the price subsequently rising. Day-to-day fluctuations in the price of the stock have no impact on the protective put strategy. The disadvantage is that the put ultimately expires, whereas the limit order may be maintained indefinitely. Once the put expires, the investor no longer has the protection and would once again be at risk from a decline in the price of the stock. To maintain the protection, the investor could buy another put. In the previous example, the cost of the put was $2.50. If the put were in existence for six months, expired, and the investor bought another put for the same price, the annual cost of the protection is $5.[8] The limit

[7]This strategy requires the existence of a put option on the stock. Obviously, it cannot be executed for stocks for which there are no put options.

[8]The protective put is similar to buying car or home insurance. The individual must renew the policy in order to maintain the coverage. The cost of insuring one's home, however, is perceptibly less (as a percentage of the value of the asset) than the cost of using the protective put to reduce the risk of loss from a decline in security prices.

POINTS OF INTEREST

Love a Stock? Then Sell a Put

If you believe a stock is undervalued, the usual strategy is to buy it. Alternative strategies may be to buy a call option or sell a covered call option. Selling a put is also a possibility, but selling a put on a stock you like may appear perverse.

Suppose a stock is trading for $86; four-month calls and puts with strike prices at $85 are trading for $10.50 and $8.25, respectively. You believe that the stock will rise, so your choices are (1) buy the stock, (2) buy the stock and sell the call (the covered call position), (3) buy the call, or (4) sell the put. The cash outflows are as follows:

Buy the stock:	$86
The covered call:	$86 − $10.50 = $75.50
Buy the call:	$10.50
Sell the put:	($8.25)

While the first three strategies result in cash outflows, the sale of the put generates a cash *inflow.*

The possible profits and losses (before commissions) from each strategy are given in the following profit–loss profile:

Price of the Stock	Bought the Stock	Covered Call	Bought the Call	Sold the Put
$110	$24	$9.50	$14.50	$8.25
100	14	9.50	4.50	8.25
95.50	9.50	9.50	.00	8.25
90	4	9.50	(5.50)	8.25
86	0	9.50	(9.50)	8.25
80	(6)	4.50	(10.50)	3.25
76.75	(9.25)	1.25	(10.50)	.00
75.50	(10.50)	.00	(10.50)	(1.25)
70	(16)	(5.50)	(10.50)	(7.75)
60	(26)	(15.50)	(10.50)	(17.75)

The investor profits in each strategy if the price of the stock rises. Of course, in absolute dollars, buying the stock produces the largest potential profit (and largest potential loss), but that strategy requires the largest cash outlay.

Analyzing the profit–loss profile indicates that selling the put is a viable alternative strategy for taking a position in a stock you like. Consider the following:

1) Selling the put is similar to the covered call, but selling the put generates a cash inflow of $8.25 while the covered call requires a $75.50 cash outflow. If the investor earns more than $1.25 on the difference in cash outflows, the sale of the put is the superior strategy.
2) Buying the call produces the lowest possible loss, but the price of the stock must rise to above $95.50 for the strategy to generate a profit. For the sale of the put, the price does not have to rise at all for the strategy to be profitable. Buying the call beats selling the put only if the price of the stock exceeds $103.75.
3) If the price of the stock were to fall, buying the stock or the call produces losses. The covered call and the sale of the put provide some protection from the price decline, but if the price declines below $75.50, all the strategies generate losses.
4) At $75.50 the put may be exercised, forcing you to buy the stock for $85. But your actual cost is $76.75 ($85 − $8.25). For four months you had the use of the $8.25 from the sale of the put and the $85 you would have spent to buy the stock. Instead of buying the stock you liked for $86 (or buying the call for $10.50 and losing the entire amount), you get the stock for a lower price, $76.75.

As this brief discussion indicates, selling a put on a stock you like is a viable strategy. It may seem backwards to sell an option on a stock you expect to go up, but if you are correct, you make money without a cash outflow. If you are wrong, you may end up buying the stock at a lower price. Although it is not quite "Heads I win, tails you lose," it is a reasonable strategy for a stock you believe is undervalued.

order, however, has no costs—although the investor may periodically have to instruct the broker to reinstate the limit order.

There is not a clear answer as to whether the limit order or the protective put is the better strategy. The limit order involves no cost but does subject the investor to being sold out on a dip in the price of the stock. The protective put avoids the risk of being sold out by a temporary price decline but requires the investor to pay the cost of the option, which reduces the potential profit from the position in the stock.

Price Performance of Puts and Calls

The prices of puts and calls depend on what happens to the price of the underlying stock. This is illustrated in Figures 19.12 and 19.13 for puts and calls on USX (United States Steel) and Teledyne. Figure 19.12 clearly illustrates the impact of the decline in USX's stock price. The stock continuously declined during the time period, causing the price of the call to fall while the price of the put rose. The call, which initially traded for $2.50, was worthless at expiration, but during the same time period the price of the put rose from less than $1 to $5.

Figure 19.13 illustrates what happens when the price of the stock does not change. Initially, Teledyne's stock was $34. During the next three and a half months it fell to below $31, then rose to $36, and at the option's expiration was trading for $35, which was the option's strike price. As may be seen in the figure, the price of the put rose rapidly at first (i.e., its price doubled in January); however, the price fell almost as rapidly in February, and the option was worthless at

FIGURE 19.12

Prices of USX Stock and April Put and Call at $25

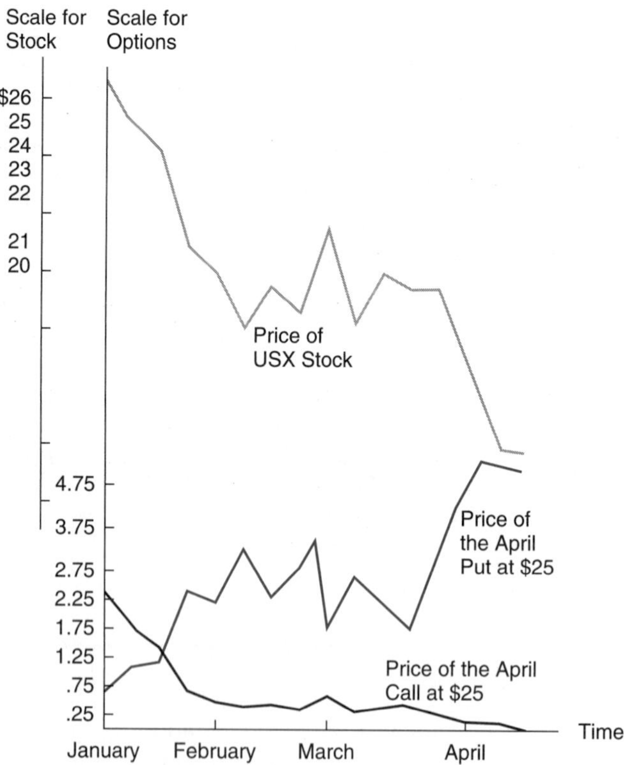

Source: *The Wall Street Journal*, various issues.

FIGURE 19.13

Prices of Teledyne Stock and the April Put and Call at $35

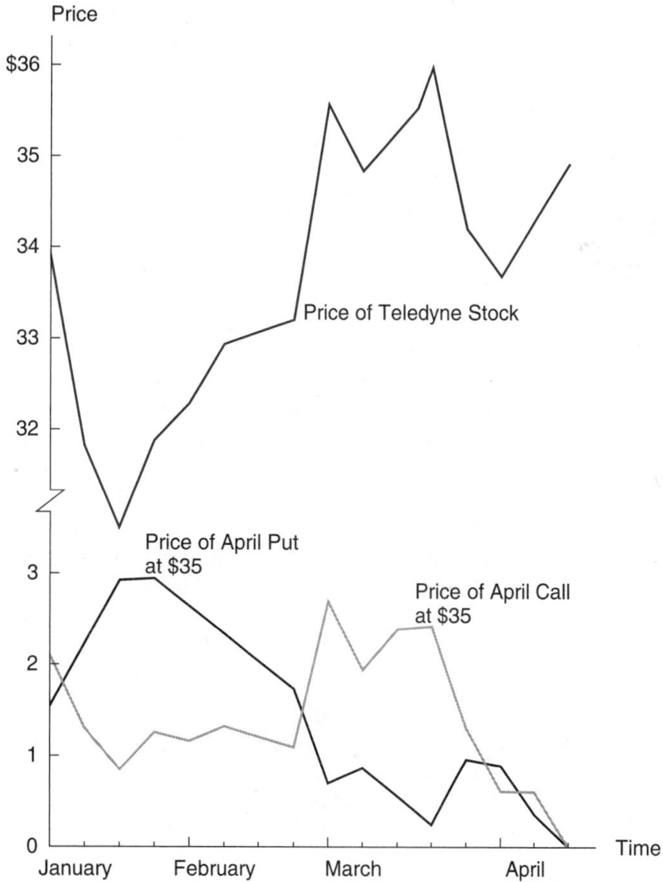

Source: *The Wall Street Journal*, various issues.

expiration. The price of the call initially fell and then rose in late February in response to the increase in the stock's price. However, in late March the price of the call fell and at expiration the call was worthless.

Perhaps what is most striking about Figure 19.13 is the fact that the ending price of Teledyne's stock was only $1 above the starting price. This small percentage increase of less than 3 percent from January to mid-April caused the value of the put to fall from $1.62 to $0, for a 100 percent decline, and caused the value of the call to fall from $2.12 to $0, also for a 100 percent decline. Even though the price of the stock did rise from $34 to $35, the increase was insufficient to offset the time premium the call initially commanded, so the price of the call fell.

It should be obvious from these illustrations that there can be large variations in the returns from investments in options. Since there are many options for a given stock (Exhibit 19.4 gave the prices for 19 call options and 18 put options on Cisco), the investor has a mind-boggling array of possible strategies.[9] No particular strategy can be expected to yield consistently superior results. If such a strategy existed, many investors would seek to use it, which would reduce the strategy's potential for profit. As with investments in other securities (such as stocks and bonds), profits from investments in options should not tend to exceed the return consistent with the risk borne by the investor.

Stock Index Options

stock index options
Rights to buy and sell based on an aggregate measure of stock prices.

While put and call options were initially created for individual stocks, **stock index options** have developed. (As is explained in Chapter 21, there are also stock index futures.) These stock index options are similar to options based on individual stocks, but the index option is based on an aggregate measure of the market, such as the Standard & Poor's 500 stock index. In addition to puts and calls based on the aggregate market, there are options based on subsets of the market, such as computer technology stocks or pharmaceutical stocks. A listing of selected index options is given in Exhibit 19.11. Stock index options have proved to be particularly popular and account for a substantial proportion of the daily transactions in options.

These options are popular because they permit the investor to take a position in the market or in a group of companies without having to select specific securities. For example, suppose an investor anticipates that the stock market will rise. What does this individual do? He or she cannot buy every stock but must select individual stocks.[10] Remember from the discussion of risk in Chapter 7 that there are

EXHIBIT 19.11

Selected Index Options

Traded on the CBOE

- DJ Industrials
- Nasdaq 100
- Russell 2000
- S&P 100 Index
- S&P 500 Index
- Value Line

Traded on the AMEX

- Internet Index
- Major Market Index
- Japan Index
- MS Technology
- Pharmaceutical Index

Traded on the Philadelphia Exchange

- Oil Service Index
- Semiconductor Index
- Utility Index

[9] The next chapter explores several strategies for using options.

[10] The investor could buy an index mutual fund, since such funds construct portfolios that mirror aggregate measures of the stock market.

POINTS OF INTEREST
LEAPS

Initial trading in puts and calls was limited to options of three, six, and nine months. However, in 1990 puts and calls with terms up to two years commenced trading on the CBOE and the AMEX. These options, called LEAPS (Long-Term Equity AnticiPation Securities), work essentially the same as traditional puts and calls, but because the term is longer, LEAPS command a larger time premium. For example, in 2001 a 5-month call to buy Cisco at $25 sold for $3 and the 19-month call sold for $7.10, while the price of the underlying stock was $23.48. The same price relationship holds for puts. The 5-month and 19-month puts sold for $4.10 and $7.10, respectively.

Investors who anticipate that the price of Cisco will rise may prefer to acquire the LEAPS instead of the short-term option because LEAPS offer additional time for the price of the stock to rise. Conversely, the writer may prefer to sell the longer-term call because the premium is larger. Of course, for the LEAPS option to be profitable for the buyer, the price of Cisco must rise sufficiently to cover the cost of the option. And if that price increase does occur, the writer of the option will sustain a loss.

two sources of risk associated with the individual stock: nondiversifiable systematic risk and diversifiable unsystematic risk. One source of systematic risk is the tendency of a stock's price to move with the market. Unsystematic risk results from price movements generated by the security that are independent of the market (e.g., a takeover announcement, dividend cut, or large increase in earnings).

If the investor buys a particular stock on the expectation of a rising market, it does not necessarily follow that the individual stock's price will increase when the market rises. Investors construct diversified portfolios to reduce the unsystematic risk associated with the individual asset. As the portfolio becomes more diversified, unsystematic risk is reduced further and the return on the portfolio mirrors the return on the market. (Whether the return on the portfolio exceeds the market depends on the portfolio's beta. If the individual selects stocks with high betas, the diversified portfolio should tend to earn higher returns than the market as a whole in rising markets but sustain larger losses than the market in declining markets.)

Index options offer the investor an alternative to creating diversified portfolios as a means to earn the return associated with movements in the market. For example, if the investor anticipates that the market will rise in the near future, he or she may purchase a call option based on an index of the market as a whole (such as the Standard & Poor's 500 stock index). If the market does rise, the value of the call option also increases. The investor has avoided the unsystematic risk associated with the individual stock. In addition, the investor has avoided the commission costs necessary to construct a diversified portfolio.

If the investor anticipates the market will decline, he or she will purchase a stock index put. If the investor is correct and the market does fall, the value of the stock index put rises. Of course, if the market does not decline but rises instead, the investor loses the amount invested in the put option, but *the maximum that the investor can lose is the cost of the option*. An investor who sells stocks short instead of purchasing stock index put options may be exposed to a large loss if stock prices rise.

Stock index options also give investors a means to manage existing portfolios. This is particularly important for portfolio managers with large holdings or individuals who want to improve the tax management of these holdings. Consider a substantial stock portfolio that has appreciated in value. If the investor anticipates declining stock prices and sells the shares, this is a taxable transaction. Instead of selling the stocks, the investor may sell stock index calls or purchase stock index puts (i.e., construct a protective put using stock index puts). Then if the market declines, profits in these positions will help offset the losses on the individual stocks.

If the investor were to sell stock index call options, the value of these options would decline as the market decreased. The gain on the sale would then offset the loss in individual stocks. If the investor were to purchase stock index put options, the value of the options would increase if the market declined. The loss on the portfolio would be offset by the gain on the put option. (The amount offset would depend on how many put options the investor purchased. The number of options necessary to hedge a portfolio is discussed in the next chapter in the section addressing the hedge ratio.) As these two cases illustrate, stock index options offer the investor a means to hedge existing portfolios against a decline in the market without having to liquidate the positions and thus incur the capital gains tax liability. By buying or selling the appropriate stock index option, the investor achieves protection of capital without selling the appreciated securities.[11]

There is one major difference between stock index options and put and call options on specific stocks. With a call option to buy shares of IBM, the owner may exercise the option and buy the stock. With a put option to sell shares of IBM, the owner may exercise the option by delivering shares of IBM stock. Such purchases or deliveries are not possible with a stock index option. The owner of the call cannot exercise it and receive the index. Instead, stock index options are settled in cash. For example, suppose the owner of a call based on the Standard & Poor's 500 index does not sell the option prior to expiration (i.e., does not close the position). At expiration the intrinsic value of the option is determined and that amount is paid by the seller of the option to the owner. Of course, if the option has no intrinsic value at expiration, it is worthless and expires. The seller of the option then has no further obligation to the option's owner. In that case the premium paid for the option (i.e., its price) becomes profit for the seller.

In addition to stock index options, there are options on debt instruments (e.g., Treasury bonds) and foreign currencies. Each of these options permits the investor (1) to take long or short positions on the underlying assets without actually acquiring them or (2) to establish hedge positions that reduce the risk of loss from price fluctuations. For example, if an investor anticipates declining interest rates, he or she will buy a call option to purchase bonds. If interest rates do fall, the value of bonds will rise, increasing the value of the call option. However, if interest rates rise, the investor's maximum possible loss would be limited to the cost of the option.

Warrants

warrant
An option issued by a company to buy its stock at a specified price within a specified time period.

The preceding material covered options in general, calls, and puts. The remainder of this chapter is devoted to warrants and rights offerings. A **warrant** is an option issued by a company to buy its stock at a specified price within a specified time period. This definition includes the essential elements of all warrants, but there can be subtle differences. For example, the specified exercise price may rise at predetermined intervals (e.g., every five years) or the firm may have the right to extend the expiration date or to call the warrant.

An example of a warrant is the option traded on the American Stock Exchange issued by SFBC International. The warrant is an option to purchase one share of SFBC common stock for $9.60 through October 11, 2005. If this option is not exercised by the expiration date, it will expire and become worthless.

Most warrants are an option, or right, to buy one share of common stock. Some warrants, however, are the option to buy more or less than one share. Such terms

[11]In addition to stock index options, another possibility for managing risk is to trade put and call options on mutual fund indexes. In 1998, the CBOE started trading in options based on the Lipper Salomon mutual fund index and on the Lipper-Salomon Growth & Income index. Each index is an aggregate measure of the value of the 30 largest mutual funds with common objectives. While these options give investors another means to speculate on the direction of the market, they may also be used to write covered positions against existing mutual fund holdings or to construct protective puts.

may be the result of stock dividends, stock splits, or a merger. For example, a warrant that is the option to buy 0.4 share may have evolved through a merger. The warrant initially represented the option to purchase one share of the company. However, when the company subsequently merged into another firm, the terms of the merger were 0.4 share of the acquiring firm (i.e., the surviving company) for each share of the company being acquired. The warrant then became an option to buy one share that had been converted into 0.4 share of the surviving company.

If a warrant is an option to buy more or less than one share, the strike price and the market price of the warrant can be readily converted to a per-share basis. Such conversion is desirable to facilitate comparisons among warrants. Consider, for example, an option that gives the right to buy 0.4 share at $10 and is currently selling for $4. The warrant's strike price and market price are divided by the number of shares that the warrant is an option to buy. Thus, the per-share strike price is $25 ($10 ÷ 0.4), and the per-share market price is $10 ($4 ÷ 0.4). Stated differently, 2.5 warrants are necessary to buy one share for $25.

Warrants are usually issued by firms in conjunction with other financing. They are attached to other securities, such as debentures or preferred stock, and are a sweetener to induce investors to purchase the securities. For example, AT&T and Chrysler Corporation issued bonds and preferred stock with warrants attached. The warrants were an added inducement to purchase the securities.[12]

When a warrant is exercised, the firm issues new stock and receives the proceeds. For this reason, most warrants usually have a finite life. The expiration date ultimately forces the holder to exercise the option if the strike price is less than the current market price of the stock. However, if the strike price exceeds the stock's price at expiration (i.e., if the warrant has no intrinsic value), the warrant will not be exercised and will expire. After the expiration date, the warrant is worthless. This was the case with the Berkshire Realty warrant, which was the option to buy the stock at $11.79 through September 8, 1998. Although the stock traded above $12 during the first part of 1998, the stock sold for $9.625 on the expiration date. No one would exercise a warrant to buy stock at $11.79 that could be bought for $9.625, so the warrant expired.

Warrants are very similar to calls; their definitions are essentially identical. They offer speculators potential leverage because the price of a warrant moves with the price of the underlying stock. Since the warrant sells for a lower price than the underlying stock, the percentage increase in the price of the warrant tends to exceed the percentage increase in the price of the stock. The converse is also true: The percentage decline in the price of the warrant will exceed the percentage decline in the price of the stock. Again, leverage works both ways.

Warrants, just like calls, ultimately expire and must sell for their intrinsic value at expiration. Prior to expiration, the price of a warrant will exceed its intrinsic value. For example, the SFBC International warrant referred to earlier sold for $9.95 in June 2001 when the stock sold for $16.44. At $16.44, the warrant's intrinsic value was $7.84 ($16.44 − $9.60), so the warrant sold for a time premium of $2.11 ($9.95 − $7.84).

While warrants are similar to calls, they have several distinguishing features. First, warrants are issued by companies, whereas call options are issued by individuals or financial institutions like pension plans. Second, the term of a warrant tends to be longer than the term of a call. The expiration date of a warrant may be several years into the future. Calls are of relatively short duration: three, six, or nine months. (There are some longer-term calls; see the Points of Interest box on LEAPS.) Third, when a warrant is exercised, the firm issues new stock and receives the proceeds. The seller of a call, however, cannot issue new stock when the

[12]Warrants are often used in private placements of new securities. In 2001, RCN Corp. sold $50 million worth of stock with warrants. The sale price of the stock was $6.53, which approximated the current market price of the stock at the time of the sale. The exercise price of the warrant was $12.93 with an expiration date of 4½ years. If the price of RCN rises to above $12.93, the buyer can exercise the warrant and subsequently sell shares for a profit. The effect is to increase the potential return on the initial sale without the investor's making an additional current cash outlay.

POINTS OF INTEREST

Investment Companies' Use of Options

While options are purchased and sold by individuals, the managers of some investment companies also use options as part of their portfolio strategies. Funds that do use derivatives employ them for the same purposes as individual investors: to magnify returns (e.g., the purchase of a call option), to generate cash inflows (e.g., the sale of a covered call), or to reduce risk (e.g., the construction of a protective put). For example, the Alliance All-Market Advantage (AMO) is a closed-end investment company traded on the NYSE. The purpose of the fund is capital appreciation, and to achieve this objective, management acquires growth stocks and uses derivatives. The fund buys calls on stocks that are anticipated to rise in price and puts on stocks whose prices are anticipated to decline. The fund's portfolio managers also sell index calls in anticipation of a market decline.

Such an aggressive strategy resulted in Alliance All-Market Advantage's earning a higher return for 1995–1997 than was achieved by both the average growth fund and the S&P 500 stock index. However, during the July–August 1998 market decline, the fund's net asset value declined more than the S&P 500. Leverage, of course, works both ways, but market declines are often considered buying opportunities by the management of an aggressive fund seeking capital appreciation.

call is exercised but must either purchase the stock on the open market or surrender the stock from personal holdings. When the stock is supplied for the exercised call option, the option writer and not the firm receives the proceeds.

Rights Offerings

As explained in Chapter 9, some stockholders have preemptive rights that enable them to maintain their proportionate ownership in the corporation. If the firm wants to raise additional equity capital by issuing more shares of stock, it must first offer these shares to its current stockholders. The stockholders are not required to buy the new shares, but they do have the privilege of purchasing or refusing them. If the stockholders do purchase the new shares to which they are entitled, they maintain their proportional ownership in the firm.

Firms that have granted preemptive rights present a rights offering when they issue new stock.[13] This offering gives the stockholder the option to purchase the additional shares at a predetermined price. Evidence of this option is called a **right**, and one right is issued for every existing share of stock. This right specifies the exercise price of the right, the expiration date, and the number of shares that the right is an option to buy.

right
An option given to stockholders to buy additional shares at a specified price during a specified time period before the offer is made to the general public.

For example, suppose a company has 1,000,000 shares outstanding and wants to raise $12,500,000. The price of its stock is currently $60, and management believes that it can sell additional shares to its current stockholders at $50. The firm then will have to issue 250,000 new shares at $50 each to raise the $12,500,000. These 250,000 new shares will increase the number of shares outstanding by 25 percent. The firm offers its current stockholders the right to buy additional shares. Each existing share receives a right to buy one quarter of a new share at $50 per share. Thus, it takes four rights to buy an additional share. If the stockholder has 100 shares, he or she may purchase 25 additional shares for $1,250 (25 × $50). If the stockholder does buy the new shares, the individual's proportionate ownership in the firm is unaltered. The stockholder then owns 125 shares of the

[13]The number of rights offerings has diminished; in 2000 only 12 firms listed on the NYSE issued new stock through a rights offering. Most of the issuers were either foreign firms or investment companies (i.e., closed-end investment companies). (See *Mergent Annual Dividend Record,* 2000, 748–750.)

1,250,000 shares outstanding, whereas before the rights offering that stockholder owned 100 of the 1,000,000 shares outstanding.

The issuing of rights, like the declaration and distribution of dividends, occurs over time. The following series of dates illustrates the time frame of a rights offering. On January 1 stockholders have no knowledge of a rights offering. On January 10 the firm announces that a rights offering will be made and that stockholders owning shares at the close of the business day on January 31 will receive the rights to purchase the new shares. From January 10 through January 31 the stock continues to trade on the open market, and anyone who purchases the stock during that period and holds the stock until February will receive the rights to purchase the new shares. During this time the price of the stock includes the value of the right. The stock trades with the *rights on* (i.e., the stock still confers the rights).

Stockholders as of February 1 no longer receive the rights, and the stock trades exclusive of the rights, or *ex-rights*. Purchasing the stock after the ex-rights date means the purchaser may not participate in the rights offering. However, the price paid for the stock will be lower because the existing shares have been diluted. As with the distribution of cash dividends, stock dividends, or stock splits, the price of the stock must decline to account for the dilution of the existing shares.

The stockholders who own the shares on January 31 receive their rights from the company. These stockholders may exercise the rights or *sell them*. The rights now trade independently of the common stock. The only constraint on these stockholders is that they act (i.e., exercise or sell the rights) by the expiration date of the right, which is usually about four weeks after the rights are issued (in this case March 1). The market price of the right may rise or fall. If speculators anticipate that the price of the stock will rise, they will seek to buy the right and may even bid up the price so that it sells for a time premium over its intrinsic value as stock. If the stock's price does subsequently rise, these speculators will realize a profit because the value of the rights must also increase.

How is the intrinsic value of a right determined? The answer depends on whether the individual wants the value of the right when it is still affixed to the stock (i.e., when the stock is trading rights on) or after the right has been issued and is trading independently of the stock. There is a simple formula for determining the intrinsic value of the right as an option in either case. If the stockholder wants the rights-on value of the option (i.e., the value of the rights before they trade independently of the stock), the simple formula is

$$V = \frac{P_s - P_e}{n + 1}, \tag{19.1}$$

in which V indicates the intrinsic value of the right; P_s, the current market price of the stock including the rights; P_e, the exercise price of the right (which is also referred to as the subscription price); and n, the number of rights necessary to purchase one share. If the investor applies this formula to the example presented previously, the intrinsic value of the right is

$$\begin{aligned} V &= \frac{\$60 - \$50}{4 + 1} \\ &= \frac{\$10}{5} \\ &= \$2. \end{aligned}$$

This formula helps to illustrate the dilution that occurs when additional shares are issued. The "$n + 1$" in the denominator adjusts for the dilution that will occur when the stock trades ex-rights. The " + 1" represents the new share that will be created for every n number of the firm's current shares. In this case, the firm issues one new share for every four shares currently outstanding.

After the stock goes ex-rights, its price declines by the value of the right. Thus, in this case, the market price of the stock declines by \$2, from \$60 to \$58. The rights are now traded independently of the stock (i.e., traded *rights off*). The formula for the intrinsic value of a right after the stock trades ex-rights is

$$V = \frac{P_s - P_e}{n}. \qquad (19.2)$$

The difference between the two formulas is the "+ 1." Since the price of the stock has already been adjusted in 19.2 for the new share, the " + 1" is no longer necessary. Now the intrinsic value of the right is

$$V = \frac{\$58 - \$50}{4} = \$2.$$

Notice that the market price of the stock is lower as a result of the dilution but the value of the right is unaltered. The terms of the option have not been changed, but the increase in the total number of shares that will occur when the new shares are issued has caused a dilution of the old shares, and this dilution caused the price of the stock to decline by the value of the right.

These rights are an example of an option and like calls or puts may attract speculative interest. Should the price of the stock rise, the value of the right will tend to rise more rapidly because the rights offer potential leverage. If this occurs, speculators may be rewarded for purchasing the right from those stockholders who did not wish to exercise the option. For example, consider the impact of a 4-point increase in the price of the preceding stock from \$58 to \$62. What effect does that have on the intrinsic value of the right? The answer is

$$V = \frac{\$62 - \$50}{4} = \$3.$$

The small increase in the price of the stock causes the value of the right to rise by 50 percent ([\$3 − \$2] ÷ \$2).

Such potential leverage may attract speculators who anticipate an increase in the price of the stock. Of course, if the price of the stock declines, then the intrinsic value of the right will decline. Leverage works both ways, and speculators who purchase rights for the potential increase in the value of the stock must also bear the risk of loss that will occur if the price of the stock falls.

Summary

In the security markets, an option gives the holder the right to buy or sell a stock (or index of stocks) at a specified price within a specified time period. The value of an option depends in part on the value of the underlying security, so options are often referred to as *derivative* securities. A call is an option written by an individual to buy stock. A put is an option to sell stock. A call writer may either own the underlying stock and write *covered* call options or not own the stock and write *naked* call options. If the call writer does not own the stock, that individual is exposed to a large potential loss should the price of the stock rise dramatically.

Options permit investors to buy and take long positions without acquiring the stock. Options also permit investors to sell and take short positions without selling the stock. Investors purchase options in anticipation of price changes. Options are a means for buyers to leverage the potential profits and limit the potential losses. Writers seek to take advantage of the time premiums that buyers are willing to pay for the options. Options may be used to hedge against a price change. For example, the owner of a stock may acquire a put to protect against a decline in the stock's price.

The intrinsic value of an option to buy is the difference between the price of the stock and the strike (exercise) price of the option. As the price of the stock rises, the value of the call rises. The intrinsic value of a put is the reverse: the difference between the strike price and the price of the stock. As the price of the stock declines, the value of the put rises.

Options tend to sell for more than their intrinsic values—that is, they command a *time premium.* This time premium works against the holder of the option, because it reduces the option's potential leverage. This premium declines with the passage of time, because on the expiration date the option must sell for its intrinsic value. Unless the price of the underlying stock changes sufficiently, the disappearance of the time premium inflicts a loss on the investor who purchased the option.

Since the creation of the Chicago Board Options Exchange (CBOE), put and call options have been traded on organized exchanges. These secondary markets have increased the popularity of options because investors know there are markets in which they may liquidate their positions. The initial success of option trading has led to the creation of varied types of puts and calls, such as stock index options. These index options are puts and calls based on an aggregate measure of the stock market instead of a specific security. Stock index options offer investors a means to manage their exposure to systematic risk by permitting them to take positions in the market as a whole.

In addition to call options, warrants and rights are options issued by a firm to buy a stock at a specified price within a specified time period. While warrants and rights are similar to calls, the firm issues new shares and receives the proceeds when the option is exercised.

The following table summarizes the maximum possible gains and losses for the basic positions using options:

Bullish	
Buy the stock	Maximum possible gain: unlimited
	Maximum possible loss: cost of the stock
Buy the call	Maximum possible gain: unlimited
	Maximum possible loss: cost of the call
Sell the put	Maximum possible gain: price of the put
	Maximum possible loss: strike price of the put minus the cost of the put
Bearish	
Short the stock	Maximum possible gain: price of the stock
	Maximum possible loss: unlimited
Buy the put	Maximum possible gain: strike price of the put minus the cost of the put
	Maximum possible loss: cost of the put
Sell the call	Maximum possible gain: price of the call
	Maximum possible loss: unlimited
Neutral	
Covered call	Maximum possible gain: time premium of the call
	Maximum possible loss: price of the stock minus the price of the call

Questions

1) What is an option? How is an option's minimum (or intrinsic value) determined? How does arbitrage ensure that the price of an option will not be less than the option's intrinsic value?
2) What is the source of leverage in a call option? Why may an option be considered a speculative investment?
3) If you saw that the price of a share of stock was $20, the exercise price of an option to buy the stock was $10, and the price of the option was $5, what would you do?
4) What is the CBOE, and why are secondary markets crucial to the popularity of options?
5) What is the difference between covered and naked call writing? Why do some individuals buy call options while others write calls?
6) If an individual buys a call option and the price of the underlying stock declines, what should happen to the option? What is the maximum amount the investor can lose?
7) In what ways are calls similar to warrants? How do they differ?
8) Why does the intrinsic value of a call rise with the price of the stock, whereas the intrinsic value of a put declines as the stock's price rises?
9) What should happen to an option's time premium as the option approaches expiration? What happens to an out-of-the-money option at expiration?
10) If an individual sells a call option, how may that investor close the position?
11) What advantage does purchasing a stock index option offer over buying options on individual securities?
12) Why does a protective put reduce the potential loss from a long position in a stock?
13) Why do rights offerings maintain stockholders' relative position in a corporation?

Problems

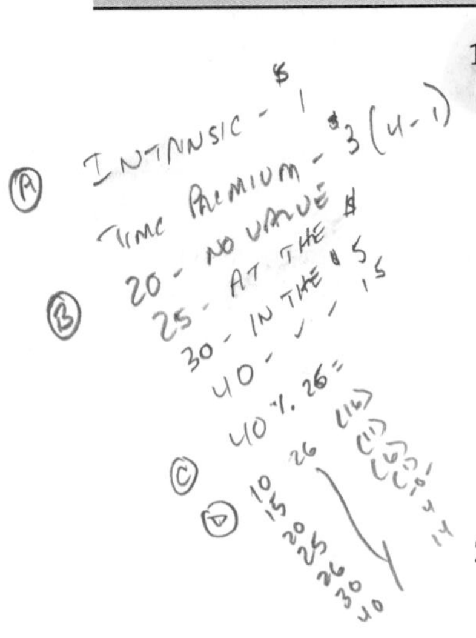

1) A particular call is the option to buy stock at $25. It expires in six months and currently sells for $4 when the price of the stock is $26.
   a) What is the intrinsic value of the call? What is the time premium paid for the call?
   b) What will the value of this call be after six months if the price of the stock is $20? $25? $30? $40?
   c) If the price of the stock rises to $40 at the expiration date of the call, what is the percentage increase in the value of the call? Does this example illustrate favorable leverage?
   d) If an individual buys the stock and sells this call, what is the cash outflow (i.e., net cost) and what will the profit on the position be after six months if the price of the stock is $10? $15? $20? $25? $26? $30? $40?
   e) If an individual sells this call naked, what will the profit or loss be on the position after six months if the price of the stock is $20? $26? $40?
2) What are the intrinsic values and time premiums paid for the following options?

Option	Price of the Option	Price of the Stock
Calls: XYZ, Inc., 30	$7.00	$34
XYZ, Inc., 35	2.50	34
Puts: XYZ, Inc., 30	1.25	34
XYZ, Inc., 35	4.25	34

If the stock sells for $31 at the expiration date of the preceding options, what are the profits or losses for the writers and the buyers of these options?

3) The price of a stock is $51. You can buy a six-month call at $50 for $5 or a six-month put at $50 for $2.
   a) What is the intrinsic value of the call?
   b) What is the intrinsic value of the put?
   c) What is the time premium paid for the call?
   d) What is the time premium paid for the put?
   e) If the price of the stock falls, what happens to the value of the put?
   f) What is the maximum you could lose by selling the call covered?
   g) What is the maximum possible profit if you sell the stock short?

   After six months, the price of the stock is $58.
   h) What is the value of the call?
   i) What is the profit or loss from buying the put?
   j) If you had sold the stock short six months earlier, what would your profit or loss be?
   k) If you sold the call covered, what would your profit or loss be?

4) A particular put is the option to sell stock at $40. It expires after three months and currently sells for $2 when the price of the stock is $42.
   a) If an investor buys this put, what will the profit be after three months if the price of the stock is $45? $40? $35?
   b) What will the profit from selling this put be after three months if the price of the stock is $45? $40? $35?

5) A LEAP with an expiration date of two years is an option to buy stock at $24. The current market price of the stock is $35, and the market price of the LEAP is $15.
   a) What is the option's intrinsic value?
   b) What is the time premium paid for the LEAP?
   c) If after two years the stock is selling for $50, what will be the price of the LEAP? What is the percentage increase in the value of the stock and in the value of the option?
   d) Why does the time premium disappear?
   e) If after two years the stock is selling for $22, what will be the price of the LEAP? What is the percentage decrease in the value of the stock and in the value of the option?

6) A stock that is currently selling for $47 has the following six-month options outstanding:

	Strike Price	Market Price
Call option	$45	$4
Call option	50	1
Put option	45	2

   a) Which option(s) is (are) in the money?
   b) What is the time premium paid for each option?
   c) What is the profit (loss) at expiration given different prices of the stock—$30, $35, $40, $45, $50, $55, and $60—if the investor buys the call with the $45 strike price and the put?
   d) What is the profit (loss) at expiration given different prices of the stock—$30, $35, $40, $45, $50, $55, and $60—if the investor buys the call with the $50 strike price and the put?
   e) What is the range of stock prices that will generate a profit if the investor buys the stock and sells the call with the $50 strike price?
   f) What is the range of stock prices that will generate a profit if the investor buys the stock and sells the call with the $45 strike price? Compare your answers to (e) and (f).

7) An investor buys a stock for $36. At the same time a six-month put option to sell the stock for $35 is selling for $2.
   a) What is the profit or loss from purchasing the stock if the price of the stock is $30, $35, or $40?
   b) If the investor also purchases the put (i.e., constructs a protective put), what is the combined cash outflow?
   c) If the investor constructs the protective put, what is the profit or loss if the price of the stock is $30, $35, or $40 at the put's expiration? At what price of the stock does the investor break even?
   d) What is the maximum potential loss and maximum potential profit from this protective put?
   e) If, after six months, the price of the stock is $37, what is the investor's maximum possible loss?

8) Options may also be used with other securities to devise various investment strategies. For example, an investor has the following alternative investments and their prices:

Common stock	$50
Six-month call to buy 100 shares at $50	$400
Six-month $10,000 U.S. Treasury bill	$9,600

The investor has $10,000 and thus could buy (a) 200 shares of the stock or (b) one call plus the Treasury bill. After six months how much profit or loss will the investor have earned on each alternative (excluding commissions) if the price of the stock is $60, $55, $50, $45, or $40? Which alternative is less risky?

9) A company has 10,000,000 shares outstanding and needs to raise $100,000,000 in equity funds. Stockholders have preemptive rights, so the firm must initially offer new stock to current stockholders. While a share sells for $35, management believes that it can successfully offer new stock to existing stockholders for $32, a discount of approximately 8.5 percent.
   a) How many shares must be issued to raise the desired amount of funds?
   b) A stockholder who owns 100 shares will be offered the right to buy how many shares? How many rights are necessary to purchase a new share?
   c) By how much will the price of the stock decline when it trades "rights off"?
   d) If the price of the stock subsequently rises to $36 after the stock trades "rights off," what is the value of a right?
   e) If investors who receive the rights do not sell them and do not exercise the rights, what happens to their relative position in the firm?

THE FINANCIAL ADVISOR'S INVESTMENT CASE

A Speculator's Choices

Tamika Wynn is an optimist who likes to speculate. She enjoys watching prices change rapidly and believes that she could make large profits by judiciously taking advantage of price swings. Thus it is easy to see why she is attracted to options whose prices may change rapidly from day to day. She especially likes the securities associated with Fasolt Construction Corporation, a large building and engineering firm that also has considerable holdings of coal and oil reserves.

Currently the economy is in a recession. Fasolt is doubly cursed: The recession has resulted in a significant decline in construction, and commodity prices, including oil and gas, are declining. These two factors have reduced Fasolt's profit margins so that per-share earnings have plummeted from $5.50 to $1.00 during the latest fiscal year. The stock, which at one time had been an outstanding performer, has declined from a high of more than $80 to its current price of $15.

Wynn believes that the stock market has overreacted to the decline in earnings. Furthermore, there are signs that the recession is ending. Retail sales have risen and interest rates are falling. A more robust economy should certainly help Fasolt's sales and earnings, which Wynn believes would result in a higher stock price. Fasolt's fundamentals are sound, as its profit margins have historically been among the highest in the industry. However, the firm has a considerable amount of long-term debt outstanding. Even though the company pays no cash dividends, it has had to issue long-term bonds because retained earnings were insufficient to finance expansion and acquisitions.

Wynn firmly believes that Fasolt Construction offers an excellent opportunity for profit, but she is very uncertain as to the correct strategy to follow. In addition to the stock, the firm has outstanding a ten-year, high-yield debenture with a 7.2 percent coupon. The bond is currently selling for $780 per $1,000 face amount for a yield to maturity of 10.92 percent. It is rated double B by one rating service but only single B by another service.

Options on Fasolt stock are also actively traded. Currently the following options and their prices are available:

Exercise Price	Three-Month Call	Three-Month Put	Six-Month Call	Six-Month Put	Nine-Month Call	Nine-Month Put
$15	$2.00	$1.50	$3.50	$2.25	$5	$3
20	0.75	5.50	1.50	6	2	6.25

To help determine the potential returns from the various alternatives, Wynn decided that answers to the following questions may be useful.

1) What is the current yield offered by the stock, the bond, and the calls and puts?
2) What is the value of the bond in terms of the stock?
3) What is the intrinsic value of each option?
4) What are the time premiums paid for each option?
5) What will be the price of each security if after six months the fundamental economic picture is not changed and the price of the stock remains at $15?
6) While Wynn considers a further decline in Fasolt's situation to be unlikely, the possibility does exist that after six months the stock would fall to $10. What impact would that have on the prices of the various securities?
7) Wynn believes that the price of the stock will rise to $25 a share within six months. What impact would such a price increase have on the prices of the various securities?

As an outside financial advisor to Tamika Wynn, what course of action would you suggest with regard to Fasolt's securities? In formulating your answer, consider the pros and cons of each of the alternatives and which conditions favor each security.

INVESTMENT PROJECT

By now your chart should have a substantial amount of data, and you should be able to see changes in the market as indicated by the S&P 500 stock index, and individual stock prices as indicated in rows 2–9. In this part, options on Microsoft's stock are added. Select a call and a put with a strike price that approximates the current market price of the stock and has approximately two months to the option's expiration. If you are in the 11th week of the semester, record these prices in the column for the 11th week. Now work your way back to record the same data for prior weeks. Do not be surprised if the option did not trade on a specific day, in which case there would be no entry. Also do not be surprised if the data indicate large swings in the prices of the options. During one semester a Teledyne call used in the Investment Project initially cost $10 and sold for over $50 by the end of the semester because of a dramatic increase in the stock price. Of course, during the same time period the put became worthless.

Option Valuation and Strategies

20

The previous chapter presented the basics concerning options. It described their features, the reasons why investors may purchase or sell them, and how they are used as speculative investments or as a means to reduce risk. The chapter also explained how an option sells for a time premium that disappears with the passage of time, so that the option sells for its intrinsic value on the day it expires.

This chapter develops the material on options by (1) discussing the Black-Scholes option valuation model, (2) explaining how stock, bond, and option markets are interrelated so that changes in one are transmitted to the other markets, and (3) illustrating several strategies using options. Options are a very involved topic that can be approached from a sophisticated mathematical perspective. The approach used in this chapter seeks to reduce the abstractions while liberally illustrating the concepts, so that the individual investor can understand the fundamentals and importance of option valuation even if he or she never intends to apply them.

Learning Objectives

After completing this chapter you should be able to:

1 Determine the relationship between the value of an option and the variables specified in the Black-Scholes option valuation model.
2 Calculate the value of a call option using the Black-Scholes option valuation model.
3 Illustrate how arbitrage ensures that a change in the market for stock is transferred to the market for options and vice versa.
4 Explain how the hedge ratio is used to reduce the risk associated with a position in a stock.
5 Determine the potential profits and losses from option strategies.
6 Differentiate speculative from risk management strategies using options.
7 Explain how incentive-based stock options may affect a firm's earnings.

Black-Scholes Option Valuation

Valuation is a major theme in finance and investments. The valuation of bonds, preferred stock, and common stock composes a substantial proportion of the chapters devoted to these securities. The valuation of options is also important but is more difficult than most of the material covered in this text. This section will briefly cover the model initially developed by Fischer Black and Myron Scholes for the valuation of warrants and subsequently applied to

FIGURE 20.1

The Relationship Between the Value of an Option to Buy and the Underlying Stock

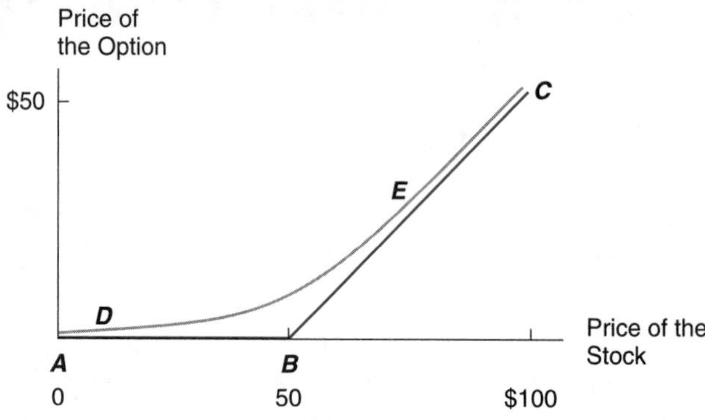

call options.[1] This valuation model, commonly referred to as Black-Scholes, permeates the literature on put and call options. It has also been applied to other areas of finance in which there are options. For example, if a firm has the right to retire a bond issue prior to maturity, the bond has a built-in option. By valuing the option and separating that value from the amount of the debt, the financial analyst determines the cost of the debt.

The following discussion explains and illustrates the Black-Scholes option valuation model. The derivation of the model is not given, so the reader will have to take the model on faith. You may, of course, pursue its development and subsequent option valuation models in further readings cited in footnote 1.

The question of valuation of an option is illustrated in Figure 20.1, which essentially reproduces Figure 19.2. Lines *AB* and *BC* represent the option's intrinsic value, and line *DE* represents all the values of the option to buy for the various prices of the stock. The questions are: "Why is line *DE* located where it is? Why isn't line *DE* higher or lower in the plane? What variables cause the line to shift up or down?" The Black-Scholes model determines the value of the option for each price of the stock and thus locates *DE* in the plane.

In Black-Scholes, the value of a warrant or call option (V_o) depends on

P_s, the current price of the stock;

P_e, the option's strike price;

T, the time in years to the option's expiration date (i.e., if expiration is 3 months, $T = 0.25$);

σ, the standard deviation of the stock's annual rate of return; and

r, the annual risk-free rate of interest on an asset (e.g., Treasury bill) with a term equal to the time to the option's expiration.

[1]The initial model was published in Fischer Black and Myron Scholes, "The Pricing of Options and Corporate Liabilities," *Journal of Political Economy* (May/June 1973): 637–654, and is reproduced in Robert W. Kolb, ed., *The Financial Derivatives Reader* (Miami, FL: Kolb, 1992).

More advanced information on option valuation and option strategies may be found in Don M. Chance, *An Introduction to Derivatives and Risk Management*, 5th ed. (Fort Worth, TX: South-Western, 2001), and Robert W. Kolb, *Futures, Options, and Swaps*, 3rd ed. (Malden, MA: Blackwell Publishers, 2000).

Except for price quotations and educational materials, most information on options available through the Internet is by subscription. Sites that may offer some complimentary information include Schaeffer's Investment Research, Inc. (http://www.schaeffersresearch.com), McMillan Analysis Corp. (http://www.optionstrategist.com), and Option Vue Systems (http://www.optionvue.com).

The relationships between the value of the option (the dependent variable) and each of these independent variables (assuming the remaining variables are held constant) are as follows:

- An increase in the price of the stock (an increase in P_s) increases the value of the option (V_o). This is true since the intrinsic value of the option rises as the price of the stock rises.
- An increase in the strike price (an increase in P_e) decreases the value of an option. Higher strike prices reduce the option's intrinsic value for a given price of the stock.
- An increase in the time to expiration (an increase in T) increases the value of an option. As time diminishes and the option approaches expiration, its value declines.
- An increase in the variability of the stock (an increase in σ) increases the value of the option. A speculator will find an option on a volatile stock more attractive than an option on a stock whose price tends to be stable. Decreased variability decreases the value of an option.
- An increase in interest rates (an increase in r) increases the value of the option. Higher interest rates are associated with higher option valuations.

Most of the relationships between the independent variables and an option's value seem reasonable with the exception of a change in the interest rate. Throughout this text, an increase in interest rates decreases the value of the asset. Higher interest rates reduce the present value of a bond's interest payments and principal repayment, thus reducing the value of the bond. Higher interest rates increase the required return for a common stock, thus decreasing the valuation of the common stock. This negative relationship between changes in interest rates and a security's value does not hold for call options. Higher interest rates increase the value of an option to buy stock.

The positive relationship between interest rates and the value of a call option seems perverse given the previous material in this text, but the relationship makes sense. Remember that the intrinsic value of a call option is the difference between the price of the stock and the strike price. The investor, however, does not have to exercise the call option immediately but may wait until its expiration. The funds necessary to exercise the option may be invested elsewhere. Higher interest rates mean these funds earn more. You need to invest less at the higher rate to have the funds to exercise the option at expiration. Thus the present value of the strike price (i.e., the funds necessary to exercise the call option) declines as interest rates rise. This reduction in the present value of the strike price increases the value of the option.

It should be noted that dividends are excluded from the Black-Scholes model. In its initial formulation, the valuation model was applied to options on stocks that did not pay a dividend. Hence the dividend played no role in the determination of the option's value. The model has been extended to dividend-paying stocks. Since the extension does not significantly change the basic model, this discussion will be limited to the original presentation.

Black-Scholes puts the variables together in the following equation for the value of a call option (V_o):

(20.1)
$$V_o = P_s \times F(d_1) - \frac{P_e}{e^{rT}} \times F(d_2).$$

The value of a call depends on two pieces: the price of the stock times a function, $F(d_1)$; and the strike price, expressed in present value terms, times a function, $F(d_2)$. While the price of the stock (P_s) presents no problem, the strike price (P_e) expressed as a present value (P_e/e^{rT}) needs explanation. The strike price is divided by the number $e = 2.71828$ raised to rT, the product of the risk-free interest rate and the option's time to expiration. The use of $e = 2.71828$ expresses compounding on a continuous basis instead of discrete (e.g., quarterly or monthly) time periods.

The definitions of the functions $F(d_1)$ and $F(d_2)$ are

(20.2)
$$d_1 = \frac{\ln\left(\frac{P_s}{P_e}\right) + \left(r + \frac{\sigma^2}{2}\right)T}{\sigma\sqrt{T}}$$

and

(20.3)
$$d_2 = d_1 - \sigma\sqrt{T}.$$

The ratio of the price of the stock and the strike price (P_s/P_e) is expressed as a natural logarithm (ln). The numerical values of d_1 and d_2 represent the area under the normal probability distribution. Applying Black-Scholes requires a table of the values for the cumulative normal probability distribution. Such a table is readily available in statistics textbooks, and one is provided in Exhibit 20.1 (pps. 660–661) for convenience. Once d_1 and d_2 have been determined and the values from the cumulative probability distribution located, it is these values that are used in the Black-Scholes model (i.e., substituted for $F(d_1)$ and $F(d_2)$ in Equation 20.1).

How the model is applied may be seen by the following example. The values of the variables are

Stock price (P_s)	\$52
Strike price (P_e)	\$50
Time to expiration (T)	0.25 (three months)
Standard deviation (σ)	0.20
Interest rate (r)	0.10 (10% annually)

Thus the values of d_1 and d_2 are

$$d_1 = \frac{\ln\left(\frac{52}{50}\right) + \left(0.1 + \frac{0.2^2}{2}\right) \times 0.25}{0.2\sqrt{0.25}}$$

$$= \frac{0.0392 + (0.1 + 0.02)0.25}{0.1} = 0.692$$

and

$$d_2 = 0.692 - 0.2\sqrt{0.25} = 0.692 - 0.1 = 0.592.$$

The values from the normal distribution are[2]

$$F(0.692) \approx 0.755$$
$$F(0.592) \approx 0.722.$$

These values are represented by d_1 and d_2 in Figure 20.2, which shows the areas under the normal probability distribution for both d_1 and d_2.

The probability distribution seeks to measure the probability of the option being exercised. If there is a large probability that the option will have positive in-

[2] $F(0.69) = 0.7549$ and $F(0.59) = 0.7224$, which approximates the values given in the text.

FIGURE 20.2

A Normal Curve with the Areas for d_1 and d_2

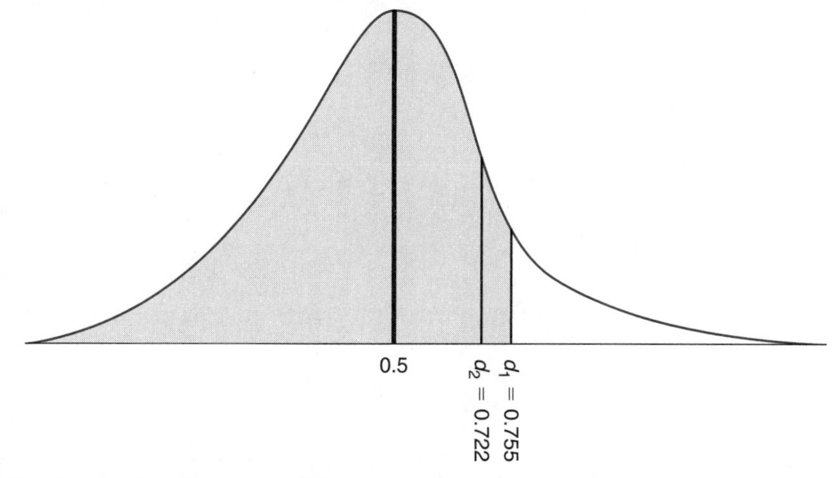

trinsic value at expiration, the numerical values of d_1 and d_2 approach 1, and the option's value will approach the price of the stock minus the present value of the strike price:

$$V_o = (P_s)(1) - \frac{(P_e)}{e^{rT}}(1) = (P_s) - \frac{P_e}{e^{rT}}.$$

If there is little probability that the option will have positive intrinsic value at expiration, the numerical values of d_1 and d_2 will approach 0, and the option will have little value:

$$V_o = (P_s)(0) - \frac{(P_e)}{e^{rT}}(0) = 0.$$

Given the values for $F(d_1)$ and $F(d_2)$ determined from the normal distribution, the value of the call option is

$$V_o = (\$52)(0.755) - \frac{50}{2.71828^{(0.1)(0.25)}}(0.722) = \$4.00.$$

If the call is selling for more than \$4.00, it is overvalued. If it is selling for less, it is undervalued.

If the price of the stock had been \$60, the Black-Scholes model determines the value of the option to be \$11.25. If the price of the stock were \$40, the value of the option is \$0.04. By altering the price of the stock, the various values of the option are determined. As shown in Figure 20.3 (p. 662), the different prices of the stock generate the general pattern of option values illustrated by line *DE* in Figure 20.1.

If one of the other variables (i.e., T, σ, P_e, and r) were to change while holding the price of the stock constant, the curve representing the value of the option would shift. If the life of the option had been nine months instead of three months, the curve would shift up. Increased price volatility, a lower strike price, or higher interest rates would also shift the Black-Scholes option valuation curve upwards.

EXHIBIT 20.1

Cumulative Normal Distribution

d	F(d)	d	F(d)	d	F(d)	d	F(d)	d	F(d)	d	F(d)		d	F(d)	d	F(d)	d	F(d)	d	F(d)	d	F(d)
−3.09	.0010	−2.51	.0060	−1.93	.0268	−1.35	.0885	−0.77	.2207	−0.19	.4247		0.39	.6517	0.94	.8264	1.49	.9319	2.04	.9793	2.59	.9952
−3.08	.0010	−2.50	.0062	−1.92	.0274	−1.34	.0901	−0.76	.2236	−0.18	.4286		0.40	.6554	0.95	.8289	1.50	.9332	2.05	.9798	2.60	.9953
−3.07	.0011	−2.49	.0064	−1.91	.0281	−1.33	.0918	−0.75	.2266	−0.17	.4325		0.41	.6591	0.96	.8315	1.51	.9345	2.06	.9803	2.61	.9955
−3.06	.0011	−2.48	.0066	−1.90	.0287	−1.32	.0934	−0.74	.2297	−0.16	.4364		0.42	.6628	0.97	.8340	1.52	.9357	2.07	.9808	2.62	.9956
−3.05	.0011	−2.47	.0068	−1.89	.0294	−1.31	.0951	−0.73	.2327	−0.15	.4404		0.43	.6664	0.98	.8365	1.53	.9370	2.08	.9812	2.63	.9957
−3.04	.0012	−2.46	.0069	−1.88	.0301	−1.30	.0968	−0.72	.2358	−0.14	.4443		0.44	.6700	0.99	.8389	1.54	.9382	2.09	.9817	2.64	.9959
−3.03	.0012	−2.45	.0071	−1.87	.0307	−1.29	.0985	−0.71	.2389	−0.13	.4483		0.45	.6376	1.00	.8413	1.55	.9394	2.10	.9821	2.65	.9960
−3.02	.0013	−2.44	.0073	−1.86	.0314	−1.28	.1003	−0.70	.2420	−0.12	.4522		0.46	.6772	1.01	.8438	1.56	.9406	2.11	.9826	2.66	.9961
−3.01	.0013	−2.43	.0075	−1.85	.0322	−1.27	.1020	−0.69	.2451	−0.11	.4562		0.47	.6808	1.02	.8461	1.57	.9418	2.12	.9830	2.67	.9962
−3.00	.0013	−2.42	.0078	−1.84	.0329	−1.26	.1038	−0.68	.2483	−0.10	.4602		0.48	.6844	1.03	.8485	1.58	.9429	2.13	.9834	2.68	.9963
−2.99	.0014	−2.41	.0080	−1.83	.0336	−1.25	.1057	−0.67	.2514	−0.09	.4641		0.49	.6879	1.04	.8508	1.59	.9441	2.14	.9838	2.69	.9964
−2.98	.0014	−2.40	.0082	−1.82	.0344	−1.24	.1075	−0.66	.2546	−0.08	.4681		0.50	.6915	1.05	.8531	1.60	.9452	2.15	.9842	2.70	.9965
−2.97	.0015	−2.39	.0084	−1.81	.0351	−1.23	.1093	−0.65	.2578	−0.07	.4721		0.51	.6950	1.06	.8554	1.61	.9463	2.16	.9846	2.71	.9966
−2.96	.0015	−2.38	.0087	−1.80	.0359	−1.22	.1112	−0.64	.2611	−0.06	.4761		0.52	.6985	1.07	.8577	1.62	.9474	2.17	.9850	2.72	.9967
−2.95	.0016	−2.37	.0089	−1.79	.0367	−1.21	.1131	−0.63	.2643	−0.05	.4801		0.53	.7019	1.08	.8599	1.63	.9484	2.18	.9854	2.73	.9968
−2.94	.0016	−2.36	.0091	−1.78	.0375	−1.20	.1151	−0.62	.2676	−0.04	.4840		0.54	.7054	1.09	.8621	1.64	.9495	2.19	.9857	2.74	.9969
−2.93	.0017	−2.35	.0094	−1.77	.0384	−1.19	.1170	−0.61	.2709	−0.03	.4880		0.55	.7088	1.10	.8643	1.65	.9505	2.20	.9861	2.75	.9970
−2.92	.0018	−2.34	.0096	−1.76	.0392	−1.18	.1190	−0.60	.2743	−0.02	.4920		0.56	.7123	1.11	.8665	1.66	.9515	2.21	.9864	2.76	.9971
−2.91	.0018	−2.33	.0099	−1.75	.0401	−1.17	.1210	−0.59	.2776	−0.01	.4960		0.57	.7157	1.12	.8686	1.67	.9525	2.22	.9868	2.77	.9972
−2.90	.0019	−2.32	.0102	−1.74	.0409	−1.16	.1230	−0.58	.2810	−0.00	.5000		0.58	.7190	1.13	.8708	1.68	.9535	2.23	.9871	2.78	.9973
−2.89	.0019	−2.31	.0104	−1.73	.0418	−1.15	.1251	−0.57	.2843	0.01	.5040	$d_2 \rightarrow$	0.59	.7224	1.14	.8729	1.69	.9545	2.24	.9875	2.79	.9974
−2.88	.0020	−2.30	.0107	−1.72	.0427	−1.14	.1271	−0.56	.2877	0.02	.5080		0.60	.7257	1.15	.8749	1.70	.9554	2.25	.9878	2.80	.9974
−2.87	.0021	−2.29	.0110	−1.71	.0436	−1.13	.1292	−0.55	.2912	0.03	.5120		0.61	.7291	1.16	.8770	1.71	.9564	2.26	.9881	2.81	.9975
−2.86	.0021	−2.28	.0113	−1.70	.0446	−1.12	.1314	−0.54	.2946	0.04	.5160		0.62	.7324	1.17	.8790	1.72	.9573	2.27	.9884	2.82	.9976
−2.85	.0022	−2.27	.0116	−1.69	.0455	−1.11	.1335	−0.53	.2981	0.05	.5199		0.63	.7357	1.18	.8810	1.73	.9582	2.28	.9887	2.83	.9977
−2.84	.0023	−2.26	.0119	−1.68	.0465	−1.10	.1357	−0.52	.3015	0.06	.5239		0.64	.7389	1.19	.8830	1.74	.9591	2.29	.9890	2.84	.9977
−2.83	.0023	−2.25	.0122	−1.67	.0475	−1.09	.1379	−0.51	.3050	0.07	.5279		0.65	.7422	1.20	.8849	1.75	.9599	2.30	.9893	2.85	.9978
−2.82	.0024	−2.24	.0125	−1.66	.0485	−1.08	.1401	−0.50	.3085	0.08	.5319		0.66	.7454	1.21	.8869	1.76	.9608	2.31	.9896	2.86	.9979
−2.81	.0025	−2.23	.0129	−1.65	.0495	−1.07	.1423	−0.49	.3121	0.09	.5359		0.67	.7486	1.22	.8888	1.77	.9616	2.32	.9898	2.87	.9979
−2.80	.0026	−2.22	.0132	−1.64	.0505	−1.06	.1446	−0.48	.3156	0.10	.5398		0.68	.7517	1.23	.8907	1.78	.9625	2.33	.9901	2.88	.9980
−2.79	.0026	−2.21	.0136	−1.63	.0516	−1.05	.1469	−0.47	.3192	0.11	.5438	$d_1 \rightarrow$	0.69	.7549	1.24	.8925	1.79	.9633	2.34	.9904	2.89	.9981

−2.78	.0027	−2.20	.0139	−1.62	.0526	−1.04	.1492	−0.46	.3228	0.12	.5478	0.70	.7580	1.25	.8943	1.80	.9641	2.35	.9906	2.90	.9981
−2.77	.0028	−2.19	.0143	−1.61	.0537	−1.03	.1515	−0.45	.3264	0.13	.5517	0.71	.7611	1.26	.8962	1.81	.9649	2.36	.9909	2.91	.9982
−2.76	.0029	−2.18	.0146	−1.60	.0548	−1.02	.1539	−0.44	.3300	0.14	.5557	0.72	.7642	1.27	.8980	1.82	.9656	2.37	.9911	2.92	.9982
−2.75	.0030	−2.17	.0150	−1.59	.0559	−1.01	.1562	−0.43	.3336	0.15	.5596	0.73	.7673	1.28	.8997	1.83	.9664	2.38	.9913	2.93	.9983
−2.74	.0031	−2.16	.0154	−1.58	.0571	−1.00	.1587	−0.42	.3372	0.16	.5636	0.74	.7703	1.29	.9015	1.84	.9671	2.39	.9916	2.94	.9984
−2.73	.0032	−2.15	.0158	−1.57	.0582	−0.99	.1611	−0.41	.3409	0.17	.5675	0.75	.7734	1.30	.9032	1.85	.9678	2.40	.9918	2.95	.9984
−2.72	.0033	−2.14	.0162	−1.56	.0594	−0.98	.1635	−0.40	.3446	0.18	.5714	0.76	.7764	1.31	.9049	1.86	.9686	2.41	.9920	2.96	.9985
−2.71	.0034	−2.13	.0166	−1.55	.0606	−0.97	.1660	−0.39	.3483	0.19	.5753	0.77	.7793	1.32	.9066	1.87	.9693	2.42	.9922	2.97	.9985
−2.70	.0035	−2.12	.0170	−1.54	.0618	−0.96	.1685	−0.38	.3520	0.20	.5793	0.78	.7823	1.33	.9082	1.88	.9699	2.43	.9925	2.98	.9986
−2.69	.0036	−2.11	.0174	−1.53	.0630	−0.95	.1711	−0.37	.3557	0.21	.5832	0.79	.7852	1.34	.9099	1.89	.9706	2.44	.9927	2.99	.9986
−2.68	.0037	−2.10	.0179	−1.52	.0643	−0.94	.1736	−0.36	.3594	0.22	.5871	0.80	.7881	1.35	.9115	1.90	.9713	2.45	.9929	3.00	.9987
−2.67	.0038	−2.09	.0183	−1.51	.0655	−0.93	.1762	−0.35	.3632	0.23	.5910	0.81	.7910	1.36	.9131	1.91	.9719	2.46	.9931	3.01	.9987
−2.66	.0039	−2.08	.0188	−1.50	.0668	−0.92	.1788	−0.34	.3669	0.24.	5948	0.82	.7939	1.37	.9147	1.92	.9726	2.47	.9932	3.02	.9987
−2.65	.0040	−2.07	.0192	−1.49	.0681	−0.91	.1814	−0.33	.3707	0.25	5987	0.83	.7967	1.38	.9162	1.93	.9732	2.48	.9934	3.03	.9988
−2.64	.0041	−2.06	.0197	−1.48	.0694	−0.90	.1841	−0.32	.3745	0.26	.6026	0.84	.7995	1.39	.9177	1.94	.9738	2.49	.9936	3.04	.9988
−2.63	.0043	−2.05	.0202	−1.47	.0708	−0.89	.1867	−0.31	.3783	0.27	.6064	0.85	.8023	1.40	.9192	1.95	.9744	2.50	.9938	3.05	.9989
−2.62	.0044	−2.04	.0207	−1.46	.0721	−0.88	.1894	−0.88	.3821	0.28	.6103	0.86	.8051	1.41	.9207	1.96	.9750	2.51	.9940	3.06	.9989
−2.61	.0045	−2.03	.0212	−1.45	.0735	−0.87	.1922	−0.29	.3859	0.29	.6141	0.87	.8078	1.42	.9222	1.97	.9756	2.52	.9941	3.07	.9989
−2.60	.0047	−2.02	.0217	−1.44	.0749	−0.86	.1949	−0.28	.3897	0.30	.6179	0.88	.8106	1.43	.9236	1.98	.9761	2.53	.9943	3.08	.9990
−2.59	.0048	−2.01	.0222	−1.43	.0764	−0.85	.1977	−0.27	.3936	0.31	.6217	0.89	.8133	1.44	.9251	1.99	.9767	2.54	.9945	3.09	.9990
−2.58	.0049	−2.00	.0228	−1.42	.0778	−0.84	.2005	−0.26	.3974	0.32	.6255	0.90	.8159	1.45	.9265	2.00	.9772	2.55	.9946		
−2.57	.0051	−1.99	.0233	−1.41	.0793	−0.83	.2033	−0.25	.4013	0.33	.6293	0.91	.8186	1.46	.9279	2.01	.9778	2.56	.9948		
−2.56	.0052	−1.98	.0239	−1.40	.0808	−0.82	.2061	−0.24	.4052	0.34	.6331	0.92	.8212	1.47	.9292	2.02	.9783	2.57	.9949		
−2.55	.0054	−1.97	.0244	−1.39	.0823	−0.81	.2090	−0.23	.4090	0.35	.6368	0.93	.8238	1.48	.9306	2.03	.9788	2.58	.9951		
−2.54	.0055	−1.96	.0250	−1.3	.0838	−0.80	.2119	−0.22	.4129	0.36	.6406										
−2.53	.0057	−1.95	.0256	−1.37	.0853	−0.79	.2148	−0.21	.4168	0.37	.6443										
−2.52	.0059	−1.94	.0262	−1.36	.0869	−0.78	.2177	−0.20	.4207	0.38	.6480										

	Critical Values of z for		
Significance Level	**Two Tails**	**Lower Tail**	**Upper Tail**
0.10	±1.65	−1.28	+1.28
0.05	±1.96	−1.65	+1.65
0.01	±2.58	−2.33	+2.33

FIGURE 20.3

Black-Scholes Option Values

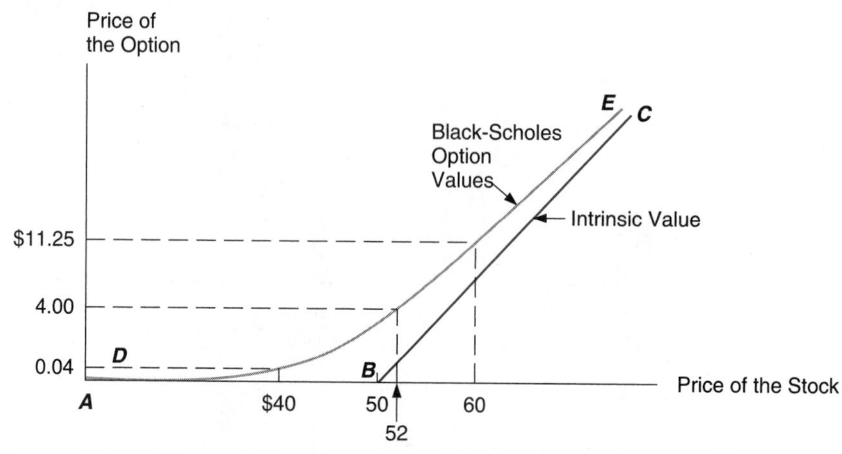

A shorter time to expiration, a lower interest rate, a higher strike price, or smaller volatility would shift the curve downward.

These relationships are illustrated in Exhibit 20.2, which shows the impact of each variable on a call's value using Black-Scholes. This illustration uses the previous example and is divided into five cases. In each case one of the variables is changed while all the others are held constant. The value derived in the initial illustration is underlined in each case. In case 1, the price of the stock varies from \$40 to \$70, and as the price of the stock rises, so does the valuation of the option. When the option is way out of the money (i.e., when the stock is selling for \$40), the valuation is a minimal \$0.04. The value rises to \$11.25 when the stock sells for \$60. At a stock price of \$70, the option is way in the money with an intrinsic value of \$20, and the Black-Scholes valuation is \$21.22.

In case 2, the strike price varies from \$40 to \$70. As would be expected, the value of the option declines with higher strike prices. While the option is worth \$12.98 when the strike price is \$40, the option is virtually worthless at a strike price of \$70.

Case 3 illustrates the decline in the value of the option as it approaches expiration. A year prior to expiration, the option at \$50 is worth \$8.08 when the stock sells for \$52. This value declines to \$4.00 when three months remain. With two weeks to expiration, the option is worth \$2.36, and at expiration, the option is only worth its \$2.00 intrinsic value.

In case 4, the variability of the underlying stock's return is altered. While greater variability usually decreases the attractiveness of a security, the opposite occurs with call options. Increased variability means there is a greater chance the underlying stock's price will rise and increase the intrinsic value of the option. Thus, increased variability is associated with higher option valuations, and lower variability is associated with lower option valuations. This relationship is seen in case 4. As the standard deviation of the stock's return declines, so does the value of the option.

In the last case, the interest rate is changed. As was explained earlier, a higher interest rate decreases the present value of the strike price and increases the value of the call option. This relationship is seen in case 5. At an annual interest rate of 20 percent, the option is worth \$4.91, but this value decreases as the interest rate declines.

EXHIBIT 20.2

Black-Scholes Option Valuations

Initial values:

Price of the stock	$52.00
Strike price	$50.00
Time to expiration	0.25 (three months, or 90 days)
Standard deviation	0.20
Risk-free interest rate	0.10 (10 percent annually)
Black-Scholes valuation	$ 4.00

Case 1: Price of the stock is altered

Stock Price	Black-Scholes Option Value
$40	$0.04
45	0.55
50	2.62
52	4.00
55	6.50
60	11.25
65	16.22
70	21.22

Case 2: Strike price is altered

Strike Price	Black-Scholes Option Value
$40	$12.98
45	8.18
50	4.00
55	1.37
60	0.31
65	0.03
70	0.01

Case 3: Time to expiration is altered

Days	Black-Scholes Option Value
360	$8.08
270	6.86
180	5.53
90	4.00
60	3.41
30	2.74
15	2.36
7	2.14
1	2.01

Case 4: Standard deviation is altered

Standard Deviation	Black-Scholes Option Value
1.0	$11.56
0.6	7.71
0.3	4.87
0.2	4.00
0.15	3.62
0.1	3.34
0.05	3.22
0.001	3.21

Case 5: Interest rate is altered

Interest Rate	Black-Scholes Option Value
0.20	$4.91
0.15	4.45
0.12	4.18
0.10	4.00
0.08	3.83
0.06	3.66
0.04	3.50
0.02	3.33
0.001	3.18

POINTS OF INTEREST
Black-Scholes and Employee Stock Options

As explained in Chapter 6, firms grant stock incentive options to selected employees. The strike price is set equal to or greater than the market price of the stock, so there is no immediate income tax obligation. If the strike were less than the market price of the stock, the option would have immediate positive intrinsic value. That value would be taxable as income, so incentive-based stock options never have a strike price that is less than the current market price of the stock. They are always out of the money.

Many firms offer incentive stock options as a form of compensation, so a question arises: Does this practice have a cost to the firm? The initial answer may seem to be no. The practice has no cost because there is no expense or cash outflow when the options are issued.

The conclusion that the option has no value, however, is incorrect. The Black-Scholes option valuation model indicates that the value of an option depends not only on the price of the stock and the strike price but also on the risk-free rate of interest, the time to expiration, and the volatility of the underlying stock. Out of the money options still have value even though they lack positive intrinsic value. That an out of the money incentive stock option may have value is obvious when you realize that these options often have five to ten years to expiration. The present value of this exercise price, which is so many years into the future, has to be lower than the actual strike price and this lower present value increases the valuation of the option in the Black-Scholes model.

Why is the conclusion that incentive stock options are not free important? The answer depends on the impact on a firm's earnings. Instead of granting the option to employees, the firm could have sold the option. By granting the option, the firm loses the potential proceeds of the sale. This is an implied cost, and failure to consider this cost overstates earnings. The accounting profession has acknowledged the cost of incentive-based compensation, especially incentive stock options. Under current reporting requirements, a firm must estimate the cost of incentive-based compensation and provide that information in the footnotes to its financial statements. Hershey Foods' income statement for 1999 (in Exhibit 13.2) reported earnings of $460.3 million and earnings per share of $3.29. The footnotes, however, estimate that using a Black-Scholes option pricing model would reduce earnings by more than $10 million to $449.9 million and reduce earnings per share by $0.08.[1]

In the case of Hershey Foods, the impact is relatively small. The reduction in earnings is about 2 percent. However, for small or newly created companies the impact can be substantial. Wind River, a software company, reported a net loss of $76.4 million in its 2001 annual report. In the footnotes, the company stated that the loss would have been $125.7 million if the estimated cost of incentive-based compensation were included. The effect of the exclusion was to reduce the loss per share from $1.75 to $1.05.

[1]A financial analyst would have to decide whether to use these lower earnings or the earnings reported on the income statement in the various ratios that measure performance, such as the return on assets and the return on equity.

While Black-Scholes may appear formidable, it is easily applied because computer programs have been developed to perform the calculations. All the variables but one are readily observable. Unfortunately, the standard deviation of the stock's return is not observable, so the individual will have to develop a means to obtain that data to apply the model.

One method to overcome that problem is to reverse the equation and solve for the standard deviation. If the individual knows the price of the stock, the strike price, the price of the option, the term of the option, and the interest rate, Black-Scholes may be used to solve for the standard deviation of the returns. Historical data are then used in Black-Scholes to determine the implied historical variability of the underlying stock's returns. If it can be assumed that the variability has not changed, then that value for the standard deviation is assumed to be the correct measure of the stock's current variability and is used to determine the present value of an option.[3]

[3]For a discussion of the use of implied variability, see Robert W. Kolb, *Futures, Options, and Swaps*, 3rd ed. (Malden, MA: Blackwell Publishers, 2000), 400–402; or William F. Sharpe, Gordon J. Alexander, and Jeffery V. Bailey, *Investments*, 5th ed. (Upper Saddle River, NJ: Prentice-Hall, 1999), 627–628.

Put–Call Parity

Once the value of a call has been determined, so has the value of a put with the same strike price and term to expiration, because the price of the stock, put, and call are interrelated.[4] A change in the value of one must produce a change in the value of the others. If such a change did not occur, an opportunity for a riskless arbitrage would exist. As investors sought to take advantage of the opportunity, prices would change until the arbitrage opportunity ceased to exist.

The relationship between the prices of a put and a call, the price of the underlying stock, and the option's strike price is referred to as put–call parity. In effect, put–call parity says a pie may be cut into pieces of different sizes, but the total pie cannot be affected. According to put–call parity, the price of a stock is equal to the price of the call plus the present value of the strike price minus the price of the put:

(20.4) $$P_s = P_c + \frac{P_e}{(1+i)^n} - P_p.$$

In the previous example, the price of the stock was \$52, the strike price of the call was \$50, and the value of the call was \$4 when the annual rate of interest was 10 percent and the option expired in three months. The values imply that the price of a three-month put to sell the stock at \$50 must be

$$\$52 = \$4.00 + \frac{\$50}{(1+0.1)^{0.25}} - P_p$$

$$P_p = -\$52 + \$4.00 + \$48.82 = \$0.82.$$

Rearranged, the equation says that the price of the stock plus the price of the put minus the price of the call and the present value of the strike price must equal 0. That is,

$$0 = P_s + P_p - P_c - \frac{P_e}{(1+i)^n}.$$

If the equation does not hold, an opportunity for arbitrage exists. Consider the following example. A stock sells for \$105; the strike price of both the put and call is \$100. The price of the put is \$5, the price of the call is \$20, and both options are for one year. The rate of interest is 11.1 percent (11.1 percent is used because the present value of \$100 at 11.1 percent is \$100/1.111 = \$90, which is easier to work with in this illustration). Given these numbers, the equation holds:

$$0 = \$105 + 5 - 20 - 90.$$

If the call sold for \$25, then an opportunity for arbitrage would exist. The investor (or the computer) perceives the disequilibrium and executes the following trades:

1. Buy the stock	Cash outflow	\$105
2. Buy the put	Cash outflow	5
3. Sell the call	Cash inflow	25
4. Borrow \$90 at 11.1%	Cash inflow	90

[4]Put–call parity ensures that if the value of a call is determined, the value of the put must also be determined. Since the Black-Scholes model calculates the value of a call, the value of a put with the same strike price and expiration date is also determined. For this reason, software that applies the Black-Scholes model includes the value of a put with the same strike price and expiration date.

(Notice there is an important assumption that the investor can either lend funds and earn 11.1 percent or *borrow* funds at that rate.) There is a net cash inflow of $5 ($25 + 90 − 105 − 5), so the investor has committed no cash and has actually received funds.

What are the potential profits from this position a year from now when the options expire if the prices of the stock are $110, $105, and $90? The question is answered as follows:

Price of the Stock	Profit on the Stock Purchased	Profit on the Call Sold	Profit on the Put Purchased	Interest Paid	Net Profit
$110	$ 5	$15	$−5	$−10	$5
105	0	20	−5	−10	5
90	−15	25	5	−10	5

At the highest price ($110), the investor makes $5 on the stock. Since the call's intrinsic value is $10, $15 is made on the sale of the call. Since the put's intrinsic value is $0, $5 is lost on the purchase of the put. Interest paid was $10 ($ 90 × 0.111), so the net profit is $5. At the lowest price ($90), the investor loses $15 on the stock. Since the call's intrinsic value is $0, $25 is made on the sale of the call. Since the put's intrinsic value is $10, $5 is made on the put. Ten dollars was paid in interest, so the net profit is $5. By similar reasoning, if the price of the stock remains at $105, the net profit on the position is $5. No matter what happens to the price of the stock, the investor nets $5. There is no cash outlay and no risk; the $5 is assured.

In the previous illustration the call was overpriced, which led to an arbitrage opportunity. Suppose the put were overpriced and sold for $10. Once again an opportunity for arbitrage would exist. The following trades are executed:

1. Sell the stock (short)	Cash inflow	$105
2. Sell the put	Cash inflow	10
3. Buy the call	Cash outflow	20
4. Lend $90 at 11.1%	Cash outflow	90

There is a net cash inflow of $5 ($105 + 10 − 20 − 90), so the investor has once again committed no funds but has actually received cash.

What are the potential profits from this position? The answer may be illustrated as follows:

Price of the Stock	Profit on the Stock (Short)	Profit on the Call Purchased	Profit on the Put Sold	Interest Received	Net Profit
$110	$−5	$−10	$10	$10	$5
105	0	−15	10	10	5
90	15	−20	0	10	5

At the $110 price of the stock, the investor loses $5 on the stock. Since the call's intrinsic value is $10, $10 is lost on the purchase of the call. Since the put's intrinsic value is $0, $10 is made on the sale of the put. Ten dollars was collected in interest, so the net profit is $5. At $90, the investor earns $15 on the stock, but loses $20 on the call. Since the put's intrinsic value is $10, there is no gain or loss on the put, and $10 was collected in interest. Once again the net profit is $5. No matter what happens to the price of the stock, the investor nets an assured $5.

Both examples illustrated an opportunity for a riskless arbitrage. In either case, the act of executing the positions would cause the prices of the securities to change until the opportunity ceased to exist and the condition that

$$0 = P_s + P_p - P_c - \frac{P_e}{(1 + i)^n}$$

is fulfilled. In the first example, the call was overpriced, and in the second example, the put was overpriced. In actuality, if any of the securities was mispriced, there would be an opportunity for arbitrage.

Put–call parity may also be used to show interrelationships among financial markets and why a change in one must be transferred to another. Suppose the Federal Reserve uses open-market operations to lower interest rates. The Fed buys short-term securities, which drives up their prices and reduces interest rates. This means the equilibrium prices in the preceding example will no longer hold. The lower interest reduces the present value of the strike price. At the existing prices, investors would borrow funds at the new lower rate, buy the stock, sell the call, and buy the put. Executing these transactions generates a net cash inflow and ensures the individual of a profitable riskless arbitrage. Of course, the act of simultaneously trying to buy the stock and the put and to sell the call alters their respective prices until the arbitrage opportunity is negated. The effect of the Federal Reserve's action in one market will then have been transferred to the other financial markets.

The Hedge Ratio

In addition to option valuation and the development of put–call parity, the Black-Scholes model provides useful information to investors seeking to hedge positions. Hedged positions occur when the investor takes one position in the stock and the opposite in the option (e.g., a long in the stock and a short in the option). Unfortunately, the price movement in an option and the underlying stock are not equal. This was illustrated in Exhibit 19.3 in which the price of the call option increased from \$15 to \$23 when the price of the stock rose from \$60 to \$70. The percentage increase in the call exceeded the percentage increase in the price of the stock, and the absolute price changes were not equal. Since absolute price changes are not equal, the investor cannot use one call option to exactly offset price changes in the stock. Thus a hedge position of one call option cannot exactly offset the price movement in 100 shares of the stock.

To exactly offset a stock's price change, the investor must know the *hedge ratio* of the option. This is the ratio of the change in the price of the call option to the change in the price of the stock (i.e., the slope of the line *DE* relating the price of an option to the price of the stock in Figures 20.1 and 20.3). The hedge ratio is also referred to as an option's *delta.* For a call option, the delta must be a positive number. (For a put the delta is a negative number.) If the delta is 0.5, this means that the price of the option will rise \$0.50 for every \$1.00 increase in the price of the stock. Thus, if the investor owns 100 shares of the stock and has written two calls, a \$1.00 increase in the stock should generate a \$1.00 loss in the options (i.e., a \$0.50 increase in the value of each option, which produces a total loss of \$1.00 for the individual who has written two options). The gain in one position (e.g., the long position in the stock) is exactly offset by the loss in the other position (e.g., the short position in the option). The entire position is completely hedged.

If an investor or a portfolio manager wants to exactly offset price changes by using options, the hedge ratio is crucial information. The reciprocal of the hedge ratio, which is

(20.5) $$\textbf{Number of call options to hedge 100 shares} = \frac{\textbf{1}}{\textbf{Hedge ratio}},$$

defines the number of call options that should be sold for each 100 shares purchased.[5] Thus, in the previous example, the number of call options sold to construct a complete hedge is

$$\frac{1}{0.5} = 2.$$

The hedger must sell two call options for every 100 shares purchased to have a perfectly hedged position.

The hedge ratio may also be viewed as the number of shares of stock that must be purchased for each option sold. In the preceding example, the hedge ratio of 0.5 implies that 50 shares purchased for every call option sold is a completely hedged position. Either view of the hedge ratio is essentially the same. One view determines the number of shares to buy per call option, while the other determines the number of call options to sell per 100 shares of stock.

Fortunately, the hedge ratio is easy to obtain. The numerical value of $F(d_1)$ in the Black-Scholes option valuation model is the hedge ratio. In the preceding illustration of the valuation model, $F(d_1)$ was determined to equal 0.755. Thus at a price of the stock of $52, the number of call options necessary to hedge completely a position in the stock is $1/0.755 = 1.325$ options. Since the investor cannot buy or sell 1.325 call options, the hedge could be expressed as follows: For every call option, the investor takes the opposite position in shares of the stock. Thus one call option hedges 76 shares of the stock.

While the hedge gives the number of call options that must be bought (or sold) for every 100 shares of stock, the numerical value of the ratio frequently changes. This may be seen by observing the curved line *DE* in Figure 20.1, which represents the value of the option at various prices of the stock. The slope of the line changes from being relatively flat for low prices of the stock to being parallel with the line representing the option's intrinsic value. Since the slope of the line increases with a rise in the stock's price, the numerical value of the hedge ratio also increases. This implies that fewer call options must be sold to construct a perfectly hedged portfolio. To maintain a perfectly hedged position, the individual must frequently adjust the positions in the call options or in the underlying securities.

The prior discussion focused on the use of call options and the hedge ratio to reduce the risk associated with a position in a particular stock. Investors, however, may wish to reduce the risk associated with their entire portfolios and may use stock index options to hedge their portfolios. To hedge a portfolio using stock index options, the investor must consider (1) the value of the portfolio, (2) the volatility of the portfolio, (3) the implied value of the option, and (4) the option's hedge ratio.

The value of the portfolio is the sum of the value of all the securities in the portfolio. The volatility of the portfolio is measured by the portfolio's beta. (Failure to include the beta assumes that the portfolio moves exactly with the market [i.e., that the beta = 1.0].) The implied value of the option is the product of the option's

[5]For short positions in the stock, the ratio indicates the number of calls the individual must buy for every 100 shares sold short.

EXHIBIT 20.3

Using Stock Index Call Options to Hedge a $200,000 Portfolio

Givens

Value of portfolio: $200,000

Beta: 0.75

Value of S&P 500 stock index call: 550

Strike price of S&P 500 stock index call: 560

Implied value of S&P 500 stock index option: $100 × 560 = $56,000

Price of the stock index option: $8 ($800)

Hedge ratio: 0.4

Number of calls necessary to hedge: ($200,000/$56,000)(0.75)(1/0.4) = 6.7

Number of call index options sold: 6

Proceeds from the sale of one option: $800

Total received: 6 × $800 = $4,800

Market declines by 2 percent to 539

Price of one option: $350

Cost of the repurchase of options: $350 × 6 = $2,100

Gain on call options sold: $4,800 − $2,100 = $2,700

Loss on portfolio: ($200,000[1 − 0.02] − $200,000)(0.75) = −$3,000

Net loss: $2,700 − $3,000 = −$300

Market rises by 2 percent to 561

Price of one option: $1,100

Cost of the repurchase of options: $1,100 × 6 = $6,600

Loss on call options sold: $4,800 − $6,600 = −$1,800

Gain on portfolio: ($200,000[1 − 0.02] − $200,0000(0.75) = $3,000

Net gain: $3,000 − $1,800 = $1,200

strike price and $100. (If an S&P 500 index option's strike price is 560, the implied value of the option is 560 × $100 = $56,000.) The hedge ratio is derived from the Black-Scholes option valuation model.

The number of index options necessary to hedge a portfolio is given in Equation 20.6.

$$\textbf{Number of index options} = \frac{\textbf{Value of the portfolio}}{\textbf{Implied value of the option}} \times \textbf{Portfolio's beta} \times \frac{1}{\textbf{Hedge ratio}} \tag{20.6}$$

Exhibit 20.3 illustrates how an investor may hedge a $200,000 portfolio by writing index call options. The S&P 500 stock index stands at 550, and an out of the money index stock call with a strike price of 560 sells for $800. (The price would be reported as $8 in the financial press, but the cost to the buyer and the proceeds to the seller are $8 × 100.) The stock index call option's hedge ratio is 0.4.

Equation 20.6 indicates that the investor should write 6.7 calls. Since fractional sales are not possible, the investor sells six calls for $800 each and receives $4,800 before commissions. In case 1, the market declines by 2 percent (the S&P 500 declines from 550 to 539). The decline in the market causes the price of the index option to fall from $8 to $3.50. The investor repurchases the six options for $2,100 and earns a profit of $2,700, which almost offsets the $3,000 loss on the portfolio. In case 2, the S&P 500 rises by 2 percent from 550 to 561, and the price of the call rises from $8 to $11. The investor loses $1,800 on the sale of the index options and earns a net profit of $1,200.

As these examples illustrate, using stock index options in hedged positions can reduce the risk of loss, but hedging also reduces and may erase the potential gain from the portfolio. Unlike covered call writing, which seeks to take advantage of the time premium disappearing as the option approaches expiration, the purpose of hedging is to reduce the impact of price fluctuations. This example illustrates the reduction in loss if the market were to decline, but the hedge reduces any gain when the market rises because the option is not at expiration and still commands a time premium. (The call's intrinsic value is $561 - 560 = 1$, but the option sells for $11. The profit would be even smaller if the option commanded a larger time premium and the option price had been higher. At a price of $14, the position would have generated a $200 loss even though the market rose.)

Constructing this hedge requires active portfolio supervision. The data necessary to construct a hedge includes the portfolio's beta, which changes with the composition of the portfolio, and the option's hedge ratio. As was discussed earlier, the hedge ratio changes as the price of the option responds to changes in the underlying stock. Maintaining a well-hedged portfolio requires continuous supervision and frequent rebalancing of the number of index options in the hedge. For the individual investor, using stock index options to hedge a portfolio can be both time-consuming and costly (when commissions are considered) and simply may be impractical. However, using stock index options in hedge positions could be a viable means to reduce the risk of loss for short periods of time when the investor is no longer bullish and does not want to liquidate the portfolio.[6]

Additional Option Strategies

Even if arbitrage drives option markets toward an equilibrium so that the investor cannot take advantage of mispricings, fairly priced options may still be used in a variety of strategies. For example, in the previous chapter the protective put was illustrated as a means to reduce potential loss. The investor bought a put when buying a stock, so if the value of the stock were to fall, the value of the put would rise and at least partially offset the loss on the stock.

This section covers several other strategies involving options. These include the covered put and the protective call, which mirror the covered call and protective put presented in the previous chapter. Next follow the *straddle,* which combines buying (or selling) both a put and a call, and the *spreads,* which involve the simultaneous purchase and sale of options with different strike prices on the same stock. The last strategy, the *collar,* which involves the stock and both a put and a call, is a means to limit the impact of a decline in the price of the stock. Although these additional strategies do not exhaust all the possible strategies using options, they do give an indication of the variety of possible alternatives available that employ puts and calls.

The Covered Put

The *covered put* is the opposite of the covered call. To construct a covered put, the investor sells the stock short and sells the put. If the put is exercised (forcing the

[6]Another possibility for hedging a stock or a portfolio is the "collar" strategy considered in the section on additional option strategies. For the individual investor, a collar may be more practical since it avoids rebalancing and is a passive strategy.

investor to buy the stock), that individual may use the shares to cover the short in the stock. This is, of course, the opposite of the covered call, in which the writer supplies the previously purchased stock if the call option is exercised.

As with the covered call, the covered put limits the potential profit, but it also reduces risk. An investor constructs this position in anticipation of a stable stock price. If the investor anticipates a large change in the price of the stock, an alternative strategy is superior to the covered put. For example, if the investor anticipates a large price decline, selling the stock short or buying the put offers more potential gain if the stock's price were to fall. To see the potential profit and loss from the covered put, consider the following example:

Price of the stock (P_s)	$52
Strike price of the put (P_e)	$55
Price of the put	$ 5.50

The put is in the money, since it has a positive intrinsic value ($P_e - P_s$ = $55 − $52 = $3). It is also selling for a time premium ($5.50 − $3 = $2.50). Because the investor expects the price of the stock to remain stable or decline modestly, a covered put is constructed by selling the stock short at $52 and selling the put for $5.50. The potential profit and loss at the expiration of the put from this position at various prices of the stock are as follows:

Price of the Stock	Profit (Loss) on the Short	Intrinsic Value of the Put	Profit (Loss) on the Put	Net Profit (Loss)
$40	$12	$15	$(9.50)	$2.50
45	7	10	(4.50)	2.50
50	2	5	.50	2.50
52	0	3	2.50	2.50
55	(3)	0	5.50	2.50
57.50	(5.50)	0	5.50	0
60	(8)	0	5.50	(2.50)
65	(13)	0	5.50	(7.50)

As long as the price of the stock remains below $57.50, the position generates a profit, but the maximum possible net profit is $2.50 (the time premium of the put).

The profit/loss profile is illustrated in Figure 20.4 (p. 672). The horizontal axis presents the price of the stock, and the vertical axis gives the profit and loss on the position. As may be seen in the figure, the maximum possible profit is $2.50 (whenever the price of the stock is equal to or less than $55, the option's strike price). There is no limit to the possible loss if the price of the stock rises. The break-even price of the stock is $57.50.

The Protective Call

Obviously, if the investor anticipates a large decline in the price of the stock, the previous strategy is inappropriate because it limits the potential profit from a price decline. Instead, the investor would short the stock (or buy a put). However, there is no limit to the possible loss from a short position if the price of the stock were to rise. The investor could limit the loss by entering a limit order to buy the stock and cover the short if the price of the stock were to rise. A limit order, however, could result in the investor's position being closed by a brief run-up in the

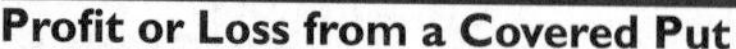

FIGURE 20.4

Profit or Loss from a Covered Put

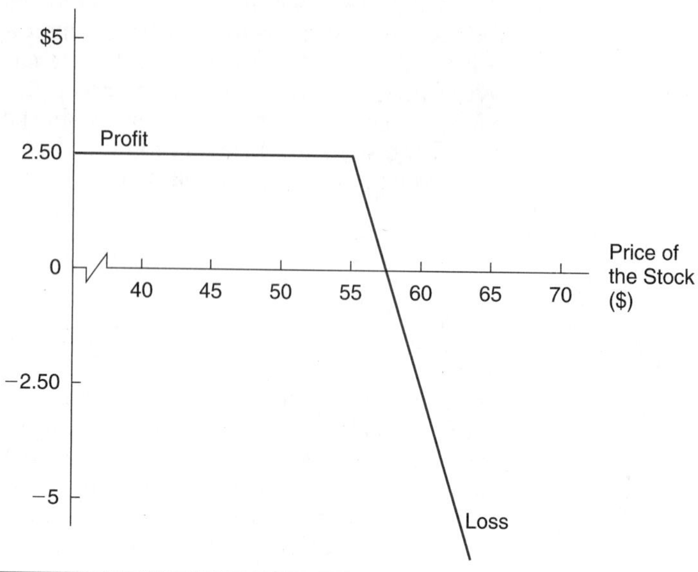

price of the stock. An alternative strategy would be for the investor to buy a call. Combining a short in the stock with a call is the *protective call* strategy. The protective call is the opposite of the protective put strategy in which the investor buys the stock and a put. In that case, losses on the stock are partially offset by profits on the put. To see how the protective call strategy works, consider the following extension of the previous illustration.

Price of the stock	$52
Strike price of the call	$55
Price of the call	$ 1.50

In this illustration, the call is out of the money since the strike price exceeds the price of the stock. The option sells for a time premium of $1.50.

To construct a protective call, the investor shorts the stock at $52 and purchases the call for $1.50. The possible profits and losses from the position are as follows:

Price of the Stock	Profit (Loss) on the Short	Intrinsic Value of the Call	Profit (Loss) on the Call	Net Profit (Loss)
$40	$ 12	$ 0	$(1.50)	$10.50
45	7	0	(1.50)	5.50
50	2	0	(1.50)	.50
52	0	0	(1.50)	(1.50)
55	(3)	0	(1.50)	(4.50)
60	(8)	5	3.50	(4.50)
65	(13)	10	8.50	(4.50)

FIGURE 20.5

Profit or Loss from a Protective Call

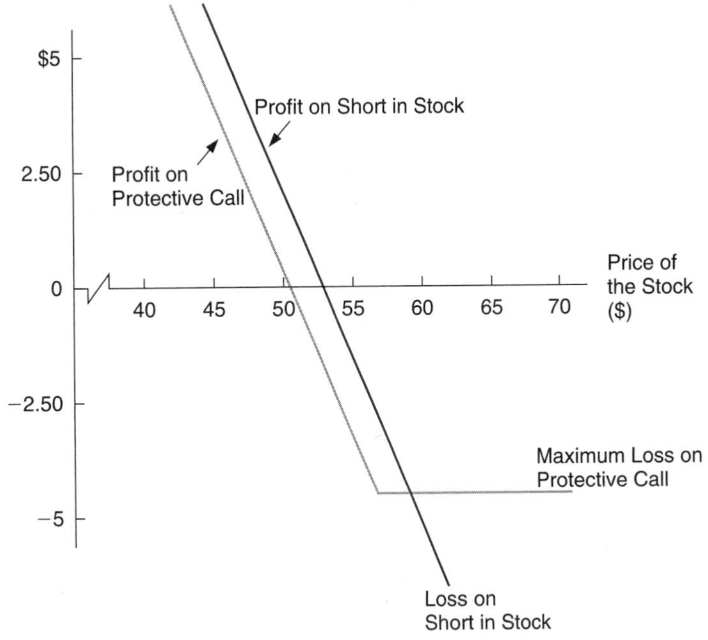

In this illustration, the worst case occurs when the price of the stock rises; however, the maximum possible loss is $4.50. Since theoretically there is no limit to the possible loss from a short position, the protective call limits the possible loss from an increase in the price of the stock. To achieve this increased safety, the investor forgoes some possible profit on the short in the stock.

The possible profits and losses at the various prices of the stock are illustrated in Figure 20.5. If the price of the stock rises, the maximum possible loss is limited to $4.50. As long as the price of the stock is less than $50.50, the position is profitable. This figure also includes the possible profits and losses from a short in the stock. While the potential profit is larger if the price of the stock declines, there is no limit on the possible loss from selling the stock short. There is, however, limited loss from the protective call.

The Straddle

A *straddle* consists of a purchase (or sale) of a put and a call with the same exercise price and the same expiration date. If the investor buys both options, it is possible to earn a profit if the price of the stock rises or falls. The price increase may generate a profit on the call, and the price decline may generate a profit on the put.

Investors construct straddles if they expect the stock's price to move but are uncertain as to the direction. Consider a stock that is trading for $50 as the result of takeover rumors. If the takeover does occur, the price of the stock should rise. That argues for a long position in the stock. If the anticipated takeover does not occur and the rumors abate, the price of the stock will probably decline. That argues for a short position.

A long or a short position by itself may inflict losses if the investor selects the wrong position. To avoid this, the investor purchases both a put and a call. A price movement in either direction generates a profit (if the price movement covers the two premiums), and the maximum possible loss is the cost of the two options.

To see these potential profits and losses, consider the stock and the two options used in the previous illustrations:

Price of the stock	$52
Price of a call at $55	$ 1.50
Price of a put at $55	$ 5.50

Instead of purchasing or shorting the stock, the investor buys both options. The possible profits and losses at the expiration of the options for various prices of the stock are as follows:

Price of the Stock	Intrinsic Value of the Call	Profit (Loss) on the Call	Intrinsic Value of the Put	Profit (Loss) on the Put	Net Profit (Loss)
$40	$ 0	$ (1.50)	$15	$9.50	$8
45	0	(1.50)	10	4.50	3
48	0	(1.50)	7	1.50	0
50	0	(1.50)	5	(.50)	(2)
52	0	(1.50)	3	(2.50)	(4)
55	0	(1.50)	0	(5.50)	(7)
60	5	3.50	0	(5.50)	(2)
62	7	5.50	0	(5.50)	0
65	10	8.50	0	(5.50)	3
70	15	13.50	0	(5.50)	8

FIGURE 20.6

Profit or Loss from Purchasing a Straddle

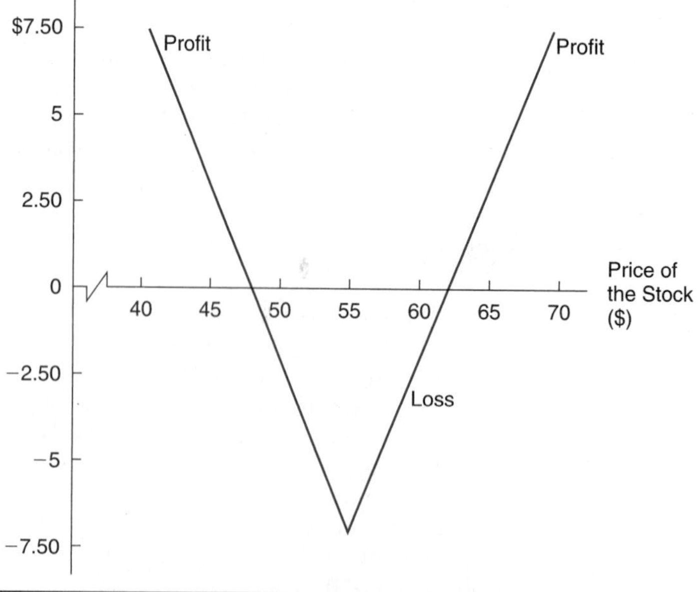

The position generates a profit as long as the stock price exceeds \$62 or is less than \$48 (i.e., the range of stock prices that generates a loss is $\$48 < P_s < \$62$). If the price of the stock moves either above \$62 or below \$48, the investor is assured of a profit. The maximum possible loss is \$7, which occurs when the price of the stock equals the options' strike price at their expiration. At that price, neither option has any intrinsic value and both expire, so the investor loses the entire amount invested in both options.

The profits and losses from purchasing a straddle are illustrated in Figure 20.6. As may be seen in the figure, the position sustains a loss if the price of the stock is greater than \$48 or less than \$62, with a maximum possible loss of \$7. There is no limit to the potential profit if the price of the stock rises, and the position could generate a profit of \$48 in the unlikely case that the price of the stock declines to \$0.

Why would the investor construct a straddle in which it is possible to sustain a loss, even if the price fluctuates but does not fluctuate sufficiently to cover the cost of the two options? The answer is that the investor anticipates a large movement in the price of the stock but is uncertain as to the direction. This position offers potential profit if such a price change occurs and limits the loss if the anticipated change does not materialize.

If the investor expects the price of the stock to be stable, that individual writes a straddle. The investor sells a put and a call. This strategy is, of course, the opposite of buying a straddle and its profit/loss profile is the exact opposite:

Price of the Stock	Intrinsic Value of the Call	Profit (Loss) on the Call	Intrinsic Value of the Put	Profit (Loss) on the Put	Net Profit (Loss)
\$40	\$ 0	\$ 1.50	\$15	\$(9.50)	\$(8)
45	0	1.50	10	(4.50)	(3)
48	0	1.50	7	(1.50)	0
50	0	1.50	5	.50	2
52	0	1.50	3	2.50	4
55	0	1.50	0	5.50	7
60	5	(3.50)	0	5.50	2
62	7	(5.50)	0	5.50	0
65	10	(8.50)	0	5.50	(3)
70	15	(13.50)	0	5.50	(8)

The writer of the straddle profits as long as the price of the stock exceeds \$48 but is less than \$62. The maximum possible profit is \$7, which occurs when the price of the stock is \$55 and both options expire worthless. Of course, the writer could sustain a large loss if the price of the stock makes a large movement in either direction.

The profile of profit and loss to the writer of the straddle is illustrated in Figure 20.7 (p. 676). Notice that this figure is the exact opposite of Figure 20.6. The writer accepts a modest possible profit, but there is no limit to the possible loss if the price of the stock were to rise, and there is also the potential for a large loss if the price of the stock falls below \$48.

The Bull Spread

The covered put, the protective call, and the straddle do not exhaust all the possible strategies using puts and calls. The investor can also construct *spreads,* using options with different strike prices and/or expiration dates. In this case, the investor takes a long position in one option and a short position in the other. Consider the following:

Price of the stock	\$52
Price of a call at \$50	\$5
Price of a call at \$55	\$1.50

FIGURE 20.7

Profit or Loss from Selling a Straddle

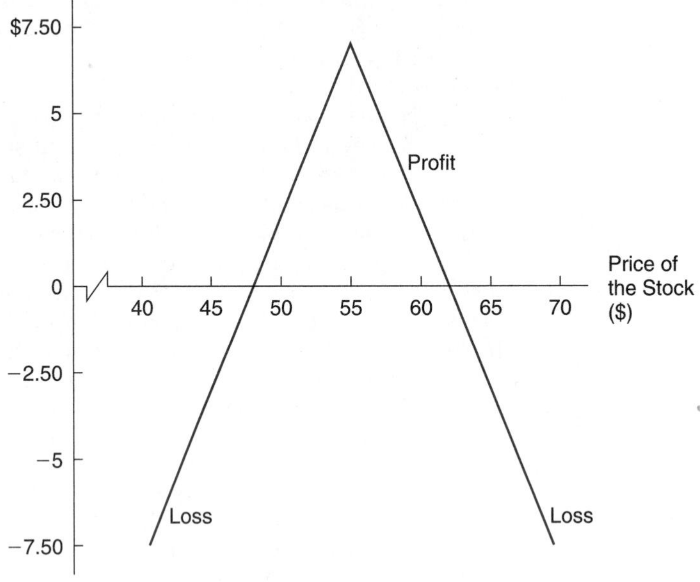

The investor may construct a *bull spread* by purchasing the call with the lower strike price and selling the call with the higher strike price. In this illustration, the investor buys the $50s for $5 and sells (writes) the $55s for $1.50. The net cash outlay is $3.50 (the $5 cost of the call at $50 minus the $1.50 received from the sale of the call at $55). The profile of the possible profit and loss at the options' expiration for various prices of the stock are as follows:

Price of the Stock	Intrinsic Value of the Call at $50	Profit (Loss) on the Call at $50	Intrinsic Value of the Call at $55	Profit (Loss) on the Call at $55	Net Profit (Loss)
$40	$ 0	$ (5)	$ 0	$1.50	$(3.50)
45	0	(5)	0	1.50	(3.50)
50	0	(5)	0	1.50	(3.50)
53.50	3.50	(1.50)	0	1.50	0
55	5	0	0	1.50	1.50
60	10	5	5	(3.50)	1.50
65	15.50	10	10	(8.50)	1.50

The position generates a profit as long as the price of the stock exceeds $53.50, with a maximum possible profit of $1.50. The maximum possible loss is $3.50 (the net cash outlay). The amount of the profit may seem trivial, but since only $3.50 was at risk, the percentage return (before commissions) is 42.8 percent ($1.50/$3.50).

The Bear Spread

The investor could also reverse the preceding position and construct a *bear spread*. The investor buys the option with the higher strike price and sells the option with

FIGURE 20.8

Profit or Loss from Bull and Bear Spreads Using Call Options

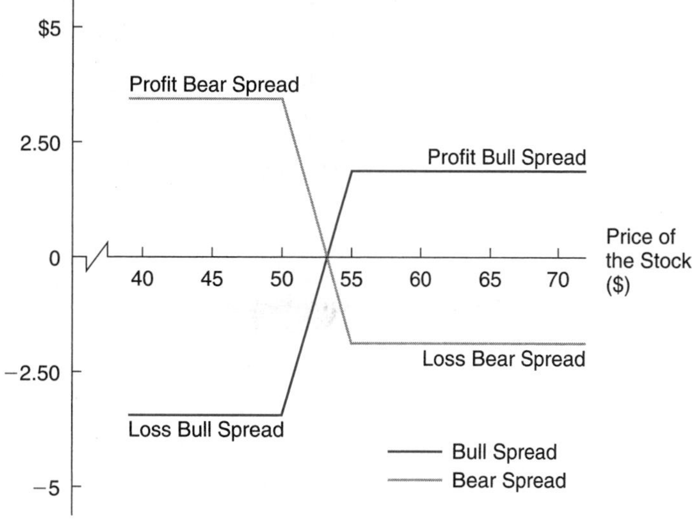

the lower strike price. In this illustration, the investor buys the option at $55 for $1.50 and sells the option at $50 for $5. This produces a net cash inflow; however, margin requirements will not permit the individual to remove the entire net proceeds. The possible profits and losses at the options' expiration for various prices of the stock are as follows:

Price of the Stock	Intrinsic Value of the Call at $50	Profit (Loss) on the Call at $50	Intrinsic Value of the Call at $55	Profit (Loss) on the Call at $55	Net Profit (Loss)
$40	$ 0	$ 5	$ 0	$(1.50)	$3.50
45	0	5	0	(1.50)	3.50
50	0	5	0	(1.50)	3.50
53.50	3.50	1.50	0	(1.50)	0
55	5	0	0	(1.50)	(1.50)
60	10	(5)	5	3.50	(1.50)
65	15	(10)	10	8.50	(1.50)

As long as the price of the stock is below $50, the investor earns the maximum profit of $3.50, while the maximum possible loss is $1.50 if the price of the stock is $55 or higher.

Figure 20.8 presents the potential profits and losses at various prices of the stock for the bull and bear spreads. Since they are opposite, the graphs mirror each other. The maximum possible loss is $3.50 in the bull spread if the price of the stock declines, while $3.50 is the maximum possible gain in the bear spread. Conversely, the maximum possible profit in the bull spread is $1.50, and $1.50 is the maximum possible loss in the bear spread.

Both of these spreads are types of hedge positions because they combine a long position and a short position. The effect in both cases is to limit the possible loss, which has the corresponding effect of limiting the potential profit. Neither may be appropriate if the investor anticipates a large movement in the price of the stock in a particular direction. Instead, these spreads are appropriate when the investor anticipates modest price movements in a particular direction. If this expected price change is downward, the investor should sell the option with the lower strike price and buy the option with the higher strike price (i.e., construct the bear spread). Conversely, if a modest price increase is anticipated, the investor buys the option with the lower strike price and sells the option with the higher strike price (i.e., constructs the bull spread). In either case, if the price of the stock moves in the anticipated direction, the investor earns a modest profit on a small outlay. If the price of the stock moves against the investor, the spread protects the investor from a large loss.

The Butterfly Spread

A *butterfly spread* involves three options at different strike prices. The position is established when the investor buys (or writes) two options with the middle strike price and takes the opposite position in the options with the higher and lower strike prices. To see how a butterfly spread is constructed, consider the following options when the price of the underlying stock is $52:

Price of a call at $50	$8
Price of a call at $55	$5
Price of a call at $60	$3

The investor buys two of the options with the $55 strike price and writes one each of the options with the $50 and $60 strike prices. The profile of the possible profits and losses generated by this butterfly spread at the expiration of the options at various prices of the stock is as follows:

Price of the Stock	Intrinsic Value of the Call at $50	Profit (Loss) on the Call at $50	Intrinsic Value of the Call at $55	Profit (Loss) on the Calls at $55	Intrinsic Value of the Call at 60	Profit (Loss) on the Call at $60	Net Profit (Loss)
$40	$ 0	$8	$ 0	$(10)	$0	$3	$1
45	0	8	0	(10)	0	3	1
50	0	8	0	(10)	0	3	1
51	1	7	0	(10)	0	3	0
55	5	3	0	(10)	0	3	(4)
59	9	(1)	4	(2)	0	3	0
60	10	(2)	5	0	0	3	1
65	15	(7)	10	10	5	(2)	1

As long as the price of the stock is less than $51 or greater than $59, the spread generates a $1 profit with a maximum possible loss of $4 at a stock price of $55. This butterfly spread is constructed if the investor expects the butterfly to flap its wings and not hover around the $55 strike price.

The investor could reverse the butterfly spread and write (sell) two options with the $55 strike price and buy one each of the other two options. In this case, the profit (loss) profile at various prices of the stock is as follows:

Price of the Stock	Intrinsic Value of the Call at $50	Profit (Loss) on the Call at $50	Intrinsic Value of the Call at $55	Profit (Loss) on the Calls at $55	Intrinsic Value of the Call at 60	Profit (Loss) on the Call at $60	Net Profit (Loss)
$40	$ 0	$(8)	$ 0	$10	$0	$(3)	$(1)
45	0	(8)	0	10	0	(3)	(1)
50	0	(8)	0	10	0	(3)	(1)
51	1	(7)	0	10	0	(3)	0
55	5	(3)	0	10	0	(3)	4
59	9	1	4	2	0	(3)	0
60	10	2	5	0	0	(3)	(1)
65	15	7	10	(10)	5	2	(1)

In this butterfly spread the investor earns a modest profit when the price of the stock ranges from above $51 to below $59; however, the maximum possible loss is only $1. Such a butterfly may be attractive if the individual anticipates that the price of the stock will be stable (i.e., the butterfly hovers around the strike price). But if the butterfly does flap its wings (i.e., the price of the stock fluctuates), the maximum possible loss is small.

Figure 20.9 presents the possible profits and losses at various prices of the stock for the butterfly spreads. As in the case of the bull and bear spreads, the two butterflies are in opposite positions. Their profit and loss profiles are exactly opposite. However, in both butterflies, the potential profits and losses are limited because butterfly spreads are types of hedges. The investor has both long and short positions. The purpose of these positions is to take advantage of anticipated price movements in the underlying stock while limiting the investor's potential loss.

As the preceding discussion illustrates, the introduction of options with different strike prices alters the number of possible strategies the individual may follow in anticipation of changes in stock prices. These strategies do not exhaust all the

FIGURE 20.9

Profit or Loss from Butterfly Spreads Using Call Options

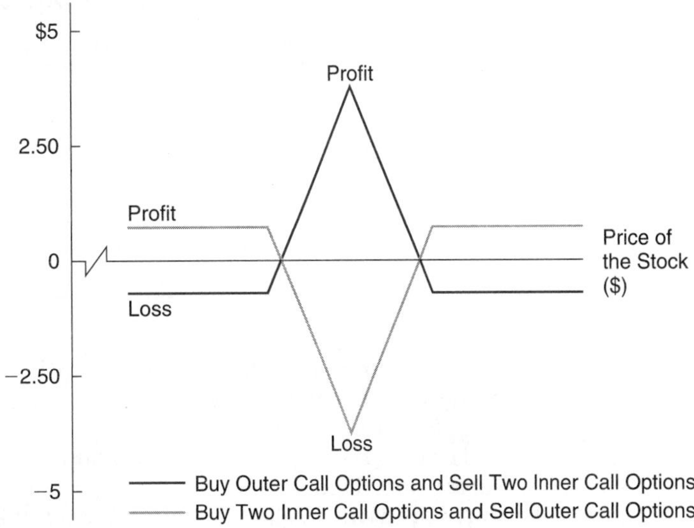

possibilities since the illustrations primarily used call options. The investor could, for instance, construct spreads and butterflies using puts, or the investor could alter the number of options in the positions, such as varying a spread by buying two call options at one strike price and selling only one call option at the other strike price.

Collars

If you look at a shirt, there is an opening for the head and the cloth covers the shoulders. Both shoulders are protected but there is room for the individual's head. A collar in investments is similar. The individual is protected on both sides from price movements.

A collar is constructed when an investor owns a stock and for some reason (possible reasons are considered later) wants to hedge against a movement in the stock's price. The investor constructs a collar by selling a call at one strike price and buying a put at a lower strike price. Since this strategy involves both a purchase and a sale, the cash flows offset each other, resulting in either a small cash inflow or, at worst, a modest cash outflow. Consider the following options and their prices:

Strike Price	Price of a Call	Price of a Put
$45	NA	$2
50	$3	NA

The stock is currently selling for $48, and the investor owns 100 shares. The collar requires the investor to sell the call at $50, a $3 cash inflow, and purchase the put at $45, a $2 cash outflow. The result is a net cash inflow of $1. (This small inflow may cover the commissions, in which case the investor has no net cash outflow.) The investor now has three positions: (1) a long position in the stock, (2) a short position in the call, and (3) a long position in the put.

The profit/loss profile of these positions at the expiration of the options for various prices of the stock is as follows:

	Profit on the			
Price of the Stock	Stock	Call	Put	Net Profit
$60	$12	($7)	($2)	$3
55	7	(2)	(2)	3
50	2	3	(2)	3
48	0	3	(2)	1
45	(3)	3	(2)	(2)
40	(8)	3	3	(2)
35	(13)	3	8	(2)

In this illustration, if the price of the stock rises, there is a modest gain. If the price of the stock declines, there is a modest loss. The investor's aim to avoid a possible large loss has been achieved.

The profit/loss profile for the collar is similar to the profit/loss profile for a bull spread. (See Figure 20.8.) The positions, however, are different and serve different purposes. With a collar, the investor *owns* the stock and is attempting to avoid the impact of a price decline. Movements in the price of the stock in either direction have little or no effect. In a bull spread the investor buys the call with the lower strike price and sells the call with the higher strike price. The investor does *not own the stock.* In a bull spread, the investor anticipates an increase in the price of the stock and wants to make a large percentage return on the modest amount invested. The purpose of the spread is to magnify the price increase while limiting the potential loss if the price of the stock declines.

Why would an investor construct a collar? There are several reasons, which revolve around the timing of sales and limits on the investor's ability to sell. Consider the situation of an investor who bought the preceding stock at $20 and would like to sell at $48. The sale, however, produces a capital gain, which the investor would prefer to defer to the next taxable year. Constructing the collar locks in the price and the profit on the stock because if the price does change, the profits/losses on the various components cancel each other. The original appreciation in the stock from $20 to $48 is retained and the taxes are deferred until the positions are unwound, which could occur in the next taxable year.

Another, and more likely, reason for constructing the collar is to protect a gain when the investor is forbidden to sell the stock. Prior to an initial public offering, a firm may issue employees stock as compensation or grant employees options to buy the stock. For instance, a firm expects to go public and sell stock at $50 and grants current employees shares based on the following formula. Each employee is to receive stock based on 40 percent of that individual's prior year's compensation. That dollar value then will be divided by $50, the initial anticipated price of the IPO, to determine the number of shares that will be granted prior to the initial public offering. If an employee earned $80,000, the number of shares to be received is 640 shares (0.4[$80,000/$50]). The employee, however, cannot immediately sell the shares. Shares are restricted units, one third of which may be sold on the anniversary dates of the initial public offering for the next three years. The employee can only sell 213 shares a year for the next three years.[7]

Suppose six months after the initial public offering the price of the stock is $72. The employee would like to sell and realize the $22 profit, but the stock cannot be sold. Of course, further price increases would be welcome, but a price decline could inflict a loss or at least reduce existing gains. By constructing a collar, these employees are able to freeze the price of the stock until they are able to sell it. While they forgo the possibility of further gains, they lock in existing profits. Since the investment objective is to hedge against a price decline, the collar protects these employees against the possibility of a price decline.

A third reason for constructing a collar is essentially a variation on the previous case. Many top executives receive additional compensation in the form of stock options instead of cash. (See the Points of Interest on stock-based compensation.) These stock options are similar to calls and give the executives the right to buy the stock at specified prices for specified time periods. While the calls traded on the CBOE and other exchanges are of relatively short duration, options granted executives often may be exercised after many years.

Once again, the use of collars protects the investors from a price decline. If an executive exercises a profitable stock option, there may be legal or tax reasons why the stock may not be immediately sold. By constructing the collar, the executive freezes the current price of the stock and protects the gain.

Collars are also used in merger agreements to lock in a specified price or range of stock prices. When Georgia Pacific (GP) offered to buy Fort James, the terms established a maximum price of $40. GP offered $29.60 plus 0.2644 shares of Georgia Pacific for every share of Fort James. If GP sold above $40, the number of shares

[7]The purpose of such restrictions is to avoid the dumping of stock right after an initial public offering, especially if the price of the stock rises. (See the discussion of lock-ups in Chapter 2.)

would be decreased. The effect is to set a maximum cost and a minimum cost to Georgia Pacific. If GP sold for more than $40, the reduction in the number of shares limits the upside cost to $40. Thus, if GP were to sell for $50, the stockholders of Fort James would receive $29.60 plus 0.208 shares. The 0.208 shares would be worth $10.40, which plus the $29.60 is a total of $40. At the other extreme, in the unlikely case that the price of Georgia Pacific stock collapsed, the stockholders of Fort James would receive $29.60. The effect is to guarantee Fort James stockholders $29.60 to $40 and to limit the cost to Georgia Pacific of the acquisition from $29.60 to $40. Such merger agreements, which guarantee a minimum but limit the upside price, are common when the acquiring firm offers to swap its stock for the other firm's stock.

Summary

While the previous chapter presented the basics concerning options, this chapter expanded that material by covering the Black-Scholes option valuation model; by explaining how the stock, bond, and option markets are interrelated so that changes in one are transmitted to the others; and by illustrating several strategies using options.

The Black-Scholes option valuation model specifies that the value of a call option is positively related to the price and to the volatility of the underlying stock. As the price of the stock rises, the value of the option rises. The same relationship holds for variability of returns, as options on volatile stocks command higher valuations. Call option values are also positively related to the life of the option. As the term of the option diminishes and the option approaches expiration, the option's value declines.

While an increase in interest rates generally depresses the value of a financial asset, this negative relationship does not apply to options to buy stock. An increase in interest rates increases the value of the option, because higher rates reduce the present value of a call's strike price. The lower strike price then increases the value of the option to buy the stock.

The Black-Scholes option valuation model also calculates the hedge ratio, which determines the number of options necessary to completely hedge a stock portfolio. A completely hedged portfolio means that any loss generated on one side (e.g., a long position in stocks) is offset by the gain on the opposite side (e.g., a short position in the options). Such a hedging strategy is executed by portfolio managers to reduce risk. Such risk reduction may not be available to individual investors, since the portfolio has to be frequently rebalanced as the hedge ratio changes.

Put–call parity explains the interrelationships among financial markets. In equilibrium, the price of the underlying stock, the price of the puts and calls on the stock, and the present value of the strike price (as affected by the rate of interest) must balance or an opportunity for a risk-free arbitrage would exist. As investors seek to execute the arbitrage, the prices of the various securities are affected. An implication of put–call parity is that any change in one of the markets (e.g., an increased demand for stocks) must be transmitted to the other markets.

Strategies using options include the covered put and the protective call, which are the reverse of the covered call and the protective put. Other possible option strategies are straddles; bull, bear, and butterfly spreads; and collars. Straddles and spreads involve buying or selling more than one option on the same stock. Straddles and spreads permit investors to take long, short, or hedged positions in stocks without actually owning or selling the stocks. Collars permit investors who own stock but cannot sell it to lock in the current price. All these strategies using options alter the individual's potential returns and risk exposure from investing in financial assets. Options, thus, are both a means to speculate on anticipated price movements in the underlying stocks and to manage the risk from actual price movements in the underlying stocks.

Questions

1) What, according to the Black-Scholes option valuation model, is the relationship between the value of a call option and each of the following?
   a) Risk as measured by the variability of the underlying stock's return
   b) Interest rates
   c) The term of the option (i.e., the length of time to expiration)
2) According to Black-Scholes option valuation and put–call parity, what will happen to the value of a put option if interest rates decline?
3) How may the Black-Scholes option valuation model be used to determine the risk associated with the underlying stock?
4) An investor sells a stock short in July and its price declines in November—the position has generated a profit. However, the individual does not want to close the position and realize the profit during this tax year. Instead, the investor wants to maintain the position until January so the gain will be taxed next year. How can the hedge ratio be used to reduce the risk associated with the price of the stock rising while still transferring the gain to the next tax year?
5) An investor expects the price of a stock to remain stable and writes a straddle. What is this individual's risk exposure? How may the investor close the position?
6) You expect the price of a stock to decline but do not want to sell the stock short and run the risk that the price of the stock may rise dramatically. How could you use a bear spread strategy to take advantage of your expectation of a lower stock price?
7) You sell a stock short. How can you use an option to reduce your risk of loss should the price of the stock rise?
8) How do collars, the hedge ratio, the protective call, and the protective put help investors manage risk?
9) If you thought a stock was fairly valued and its price would not change, how could you use a butterfly spread to take advantage of your valuation? If you follow this strategy and the stock's price does not remain stable, have you increased your risk exposure?
10) The Black-Scholes valuation model shows that higher interest rates result in higher call option valuations. Do these higher interest rates and call valuations imply that put values will also rise?

Problems

Apply the Black-Scholes option valuation model to solve the following problems.

1) A stock sells for \$30. What is the value of a one-year call option to buy the stock at \$25, if debt currently yields 10 percent? (Assume $F(d_1)$ and $F(d_2) = 1$.)
2) A call option is the right to buy stock at \$50 a share. Currently the option has six months to expiration, the volatility of the stock (standard deviation) is 0.30, and the rate of interest is 10 percent (0.1 in Exhibit 20.2).
   a) What is the value of the option according to the Black-Scholes model if the price of the stock is \$45, \$50, or \$55?
   b) What is the value of the option when the price of the stock is \$50 and the option expires in six months, three months, or one month?

c) What is the value of the option when the price of the stock is $50 and the interest rate is 5 percent, 10 percent, or 15 percent?
d) What is the value of the option when the price of the stock is $50 and the volatility of the stock is 0.40, 0.30, or 0.10?
e) What generalizations can be derived from the solutions to these problems?

3) In the body of this chapter, disequilibrium of the following equation indicated an opportunity for a riskless arbitrage:

$$0 = P_s + P_p - P_c - \frac{P_e}{(1 + i)^n}.$$

The equation was illustrated as follows. A stock sells for $105; the strike price of both the put and call is $100. The price of the put is $5, the price of the call is $20, and both options are for one year. The rate of interest is 11.1 percent, so the present value of the $100 strike price is equal to $90. Given these values, the equation holds:

$$0 = \$105 + 5 - 20 - 90.$$

The opportunity for the riskless arbitrage was then illustrated by two cases, one in which the call was overpriced ($25) and one in which the put was overpriced ($10). For each of the following sets of values, verify that a riskless arbitrage opportunity exists by determining the profit if the price of the stock rises to $110, falls to $90, or remains unchanged at $105.

	Price of the Stock	Price of the Call	Price of the Put	Interest Rate
a.	$105	$10	$5	11.1%
b.	105	20	3	11.1
c.	105	20	5	5.263
d.	105	20	5	19
e.	112	20	5	11.1
f.	101	20	5	11.1

When will the opportunity for arbitrage cease, and what are the implications for the prices of each security?

4) Put–call parity in effect states that a combination of a put, a call, and a risk-free bond must be the same value as the underlying stock. If not, at least one market is in disequilibrium. The resulting arbitrage alters the securities' prices until the value of the three securities equals the value of the stock. Currently, the price of a stock is $50, while the price of a call option at $50 is $3, the price of the put option is $1.50, and the rate of interest is 10 percent—so that the investor may purchase a $50 discounted note for $45.50.

Given these prices, an arbitrage opportunity exists. Verify this by setting up a riskless arbitrage. Show the possible profit if the price of the stock is $45, $50, or $55 at the expiration of the options. (Since the problem does not specify which market is in disequilibrium, all prices would simultaneously change. To facilitate answering the problem, assume that only the market for the call option is in disequilibrium. Since the problem only asks to verify the arbitrage opportunity, the actual final price of each security is irrelevant to the answer.)

5) One useful piece of information derived from the Black-Scholes model for the valuation of a call option is the hedge ratio, which gives the slope of the

line relating the change in the price of an option to the change in the price of the stock.

a) If the delta is 0.6 and the investor owns 600 shares of stock, how may the investor use call options to hedge the position?

b) If the investor buys a call option on 100 shares, what position in the stock and how many shares will offset movement in the price of the option?

The body of the text explained put–call parity through the use of arbitrage. Arbitrage is not limited to put–call parity. Problems 6 through 8 also illustrate arbitrage.

6) Many warrants were issued attached to bonds. In some cases the warrant holder could use the bond in lieu of cash to exercise the warrant. If a warrant is the option to buy stock at $10 a share and currently sells for $4 when the stock sells for $13 and a $1,000 bond (which may be used in lieu of cash) sells for $700, what would you do and why would you do it?

7) Given the following:

Price of the stock	$26
Price of a six-month call at $25	2
Price of a six-month call at $30	4

An investor buys the $25 call and sells the $30 call. What are the profits if the stock's price at expiration is $20, $25, $30, or $35? Arbitrage implies what about the price of the call with the higher strike price?

8) Currently a stock that sells for $57 has a put option at $55 and another at $60. The prices of the options are $6 and $3, respectively. What would you do? Illustrate and explain your actions.

Various option strategies (e.g., the straddle, the butterfly) were explained in this chapter. The following problems apply these strategies.

9) Given the following:

Price of the stock	$26
Price of a six-month call at $25	4
Price of a six-month call at $30	2

An investor buys the $25 call and sells the $30 call. What is the net cash outflow? What are the profits if the stock's price at expiration is $10, $15, $20, $25, $26, $30, or $40? Compare these answers with your answers to problem 1(d) in Chapter 19. What inference can be drawn from the comparison?

10) Given the following:

Price of the stock	$18
Price of a three-month call at $20	2
Price of a three-month call at $15	5

a) What is the profit (loss) at the expiration date of the options if the price of the stock is $14, $20, or $25 and if the investor buys the option with the $20 strike price and sells the other option?

b) Compare the profit (loss) from this strategy with shorting the stock at $18.

c) What is the profit (loss) at the expiration date of the options if the price of the stock is $14, $20, or $25 and if the investor buys the option with the $15 strike price and sells the other option?

d) Compare the profit (loss) from this strategy with buying the stock at $18.

11) A straddle occurs when an investor purchases both a call option and a put option. Such a strategy makes sense when the individual expects a major price movement but is uncertain as to the direction. For example, a firm may be a rumored takeover candidate. If the rumor is wrong, the stock's price could decline and make the put profitable. If the rumor is correct and a takeover bid does occur, the price of the stock may rise and the call become profitable. There is also the possibility (probably small, at best) that the price of the stock could rise and subsequently fall, so the investor earns a profit on both the call and the put. The following problem works through a straddle.

Given the following:

Price of the stock	$50
Price of a six-month call at $50	$5
Price of a six-month put at $50	3.50

the individual establishes a straddle (i.e., buys one of each option).

a) What is the profit (loss) on the position if, at the expiration date of the options, the price of the stock is $60?

b) What is the profit (loss) on the position if, at the expiration date of the options, the price of the stock is $40?

c) What is the profit (loss) on the position if, at the expiration date of the options, the price of the stock is $50?

12) In 1995, an offer was made to purchase Chrysler. Prior to the offer, the stock was selling for around $35. Suppose the offer was for $55, and the stock immediately rose to $45. Since the price did not rise to $55, that indicates the market doubted whether the takeover would occur. As an investor, you expected the stock to rise if the takeover occurred or decline if the takeover failed. There were call options to buy the stock at $40, $45, and $50, and their prices were $8, $4, and $1, respectively. Set up a butterfly spread designed to take advantage of your expectation.

a) Describe the position you established.

b) Show the potential profits and losses on the position if the price of the stock is $30, $35, $40, $45, $50, $55, or $60.

c) What is the maximum possible loss? What must happen for this loss to occur?

d) What is the maximum possible gain? What must happen for this gain to occur?

e) If you expected the takeover to be protracted and last at least a year, what butterfly spread would you construct and why?

13) As a well-paid executive, you received stock options that you recently exercised. However, you cannot legally sell the stock for the next six months. Currently the stock is selling for $38.25. A call to buy the stock at $40 is selling for $3.38 and a put to sell the stock at $35 is selling for $1.94. How could you use a collar to reduce your risk of loss from a decline in the price of the stock? Verify that the collar does achieve its objective.

THE FINANCIAL ADVISOR'S INVESTMENT CASE

Profits and Losses from Straddles

Sean Alicandri, a sophisticated investor who is both willing and able to take risk, has just noticed that Mid-West Airlines has become the target of a hostile takeover. Prior to the announcement of the offer to purchase the stock for $72 a share, the stock had been selling for $59. Immediately after the offer, the stock rose to $75, a premium over the offer price. Such premiums are often indicative that investors expect a higher price to be forthcoming. Such a higher price could occur if a bidding war erupts for the company or if management leads an employee or management buyout of the firm. Of course, if neither of these scenarios occurs, the price of the stock could fall back to the $72 offer price. In addition, if the offer were to be withdrawn or defeated by management, the price of the stock could fall below the original stock price.

Alicandri has no reason to anticipate that any of these possibilities will be the final outcome, but he realizes that the price of the stock will not remain at $75. If a bidding war erupts, the price could easily exceed $100. Conversely, if the takeover fails, he expects the price to decline below $55 a share, since he previously believed that the price of the stock was overvalued at $59. With such uncertainty, Alicandri does not want to own the stock but is intrigued with the possibility of earning a profit from a price movement that he is certain must occur.

Currently there are several three-month put and call options traded on the stock. Their strike and market prices are as follows:

Strike Price	Market Price of Call	Market Price of Put
$50	$26.00	$0.125
55	21.50	0.50
60	17.00	1.00
65	13.25	1.75
70	8.00	3.50
75	4.25	6.00
80	1.00	9.75

Alicandri decides the best strategy is to purchase both a put and a call option (to establish a straddle). Deciding on a strategy is one thing; determining the best way to execute it is quite another. For example, he could buy the options with the extreme strike prices (i.e., the call at $80 and the put at $50). Or he could buy the options with the strike price closest to the original $72 offer price (i.e., buy the put and the call at $70).

To help determine the potential profits and losses from various positions, Alicandri developed profit profiles at various stock prices by filling in the following chart for each position:

Price of the Stock	Intrinsic Value of the Call	Profit on the Call	Intrinsic Value of the Put	Profit on the Put	Net Profit
$50					
55					
60					
65					
70					
75					
80					
85					

To limit the number of calculations, he decided to make three comparisons: (1) the purchase of two inexpensive options—buy the call with the $80 strike price and the put with the $60 strike price, (2) the purchase of the options with the $70 strike price, and (3) the purchase of the options with the price closest to the original stock price (i.e., the options with the $60 strike price).

Construct Alicandri's profit profiles and answer the following questions.

1) Which strategy works best if a bidding war erupts?
2) Which strategy works best if the hostile takeover is defeated?
3) Which strategy works best if the original offer price becomes the final price?
4) Which of the three positions produces the worst result and under what condition does it occur?
5) If you were Alipcandri's financial advisor, which strategy would you advise he establish? Or would you argue that he not speculate on this takeover?

APPENDIX 20

Binomial Option Pricing

The Black-Scholes model determines the value of an option, and put–call parity demonstrates through arbitrage the linkage among the prices of put and call options, the underlying stock, and the rate of interest earned by lending or paid from borrowing. This appendix adds the binomial option pricing model. The model is referred to as "binomial," because it is initially built on an assumption that there are only two possible outcomes.

Illustrating this process of valuation requires an extended example. Consider an option to buy stock at $50 at the end of a time period such as a year. To ease the analysis, assume that the option can be exercised *only* at expiration (i.e., it is a European option). Currently, the price of the stock is $50, so the option is at the money. The price of the stock could rise to $65 or decline to $40. These prices are the only two possible outcomes, one of which involves a rising stock price and the other of which involves a declining stock price. The investor can purchase or sell the stock or the investor can purchase or sell the call. Since sales produce cash inflows, the funds may be invested at the going rate of interest (i.e., the investor can purchase a bond). Since purchases require cash outflows, the funds may be borrowed at the going rate of interest. Assume the borrowing and lending rates of interest are both 10 percent and that the principal amount is $50, the current price of the stock. Given this information, what should be the value of the call? To answer that question, consider the two possible outcomes:

Current price of the stock	**$50**	
Future price of the stock	$65	$40
Future value of the option	$15	$ 0

If the price of the stock rises to $65, the value of the call must be $15 at expiration. If the price of the stock declines to $40, the call must be worth $0. The binomial option pricing model asks the following question: What combination of the stock and the bond produces the same result?

To answer that question, set up two equations for the possible outcomes:

$$65S + 55B = 15$$

$$40S + 55B = 0$$

The 65 and 40 are the two future prices of the stock, and the 55 is the value of the bond plus the 10 percent interest ($50 + $5). Since there are two equations with two unknowns, they may be solved. First, subtract the second equation from the first and solve for S:

$$\begin{aligned} 65S + 55B &= 15 \\ -\ 40S + 55B &= \ \ 0 \\ \hline 65S - 40S &= 15 \\ (65 - 40)S &= 15 \\ S = 15/25 &= \ 0.60 \end{aligned}$$

Next, substitute this value in equation 2 and solve for B:

$$40(0.6) + 55B = 0$$

$$B = -40(0.6)/55 = -0.436$$

The next question is, what are the interpretations of the values 0.6 and −0.436? This information tells us that 0.6 unit of the stock and −0.436 unit of the bond produce the same outcome as buying the call. That is, if an investor is long 0.6 share of the stock and short 0.436 in the bond (the investor borrows 0.436 unit), this combination generates the same results that would be obtained if the investor bought the call.

To verify this statement, consider the cash inflows and outflows. That is, what would be the cash flows if an investor bought 0.6 share of stock and borrowed 0.436 unit of the bond? The answers are

$$\textbf{Stock: } (0.6)(\$50) = \$30$$

$$\textbf{Bond: } (0.436)(\$50) = \$21.80.$$

The stock purchase is a cash outflow and borrowing is a cash inflow, so there is a net cash outflow of \$8.20 (\$30 − \$21.80). As will be shown, that \$8.20 must be the value of the call to buy a share of stock at \$50. However, before verifying that the price of the call must be \$8.20, it is necessary to confirm that the outcome from buying the stock plus borrowing is the same as buying the call.

Consider the outcome if the price of the stock is \$65. The stock is worth \$65(0.6) = \$39, but the borrowed funds must be repaid plus interest. That cash outflow is (\$50)(0.436) + (0.1)(\$50)(0.436) = \$23.98 ≅ \$24. The cash balance is \$15 (\$39 − 24), which is the same result obtained by purchasing the call. If the price of the stock is \$65, the call is worth \$15 at expiration, so the ending cash is \$15 in either case.

If the price of the stock is \$40, the investor has stock worth \$40(0.6) = \$24. When the borrowed funds plus interest [(\$50)(0.436) + (0.1)(\$50)(0.436) = \$23.98 ≅ \$24] are repaid, the balance is \$0. This is the same result obtained by purchasing the call. If the price of the stock is \$40, the call is worthless at expiration. In either case, the balance is \$0.

The preceding illustration stated that the initial cash outflow was \$8.20 and that the value of the call must also be \$8.20. To see that the value of the call must be \$8.20, consider what would happen if the price of the call were not \$8.20. For instance, if the option were \$10 (i.e., it is overvalued), the investor would sell the call (a cash inflow of \$10), buy 0.6 share of stock (cash outflow of \$30), and borrow \$21.80. The sum of the cash inflows and outflows is an inflow of \$1.80 (\$10 − \$30 + \$21.80 = \$1.80). What is the profit or loss on this position if at the expiration of the call, the price of the stock is \$65 or \$40, the two possible outcomes? The answer is

	Profit (Loss) on			
Price of the Stock	**The Call**	**The Stock**	**Interest on the Bond**	**Net Profit**
\$65	(\$5)	0.6(\$15) = \$9	−\$2.20	\$1.80
40	10	0.6(−\$10) = −6	− 2.20	1.80

Either of the two final outcomes, a higher or a lower stock price, produces the \$1.80 profit.

If the option were \$5 (i.e., it is undervalued), the investor would reverse the process. The investor buys the call (a cash outflow of \$5), sells 0.6 share of stock (cash inflow of \$30), and lends \$21.80. The sum of the cash inflows and outflows is an inflow of \$3.20 (−\$5 + \$30 − \$21.80 = \$3.20). What is the profit or loss on this position if the price of the stock is \$65 or \$40? The answer is

Price of the Stock	Profit (Loss) on The Call	Profit (Loss) on The Stock	Interest on the Bond	Net Profit
$65	$10	0.6(−$15) = −$9	$2.20	$3.20
40	(5)	0.6($10) = 6	2.20	3.20

Either of the two final possible outcomes produces the $3.20 profit.

It is this process of taking both long and short positions that assures the price of the option must be $8.20. Once again, the opportunity for an arbitrage profit drives prices to eradicate the opportunity. Given the assumptions of the example, the option value must be $8.20. In addition, the investor can replicate the call by using the stock and the bond. That is, the investor can construct a position in the stock and the bond (borrowing) that produces the same outcome as the call. The investor can buy the call for $8.20 or achieve the same final outcome by buying 0.6 share of stock and borrowing $21.80.

In the preceding illustration, the number of shares that had to be purchased (0.6) and the number of bonds (0.436) were determined by solving the two equations. The values could have been found by doing the following calculations. The 0.6, which is the hedge ratio discussed in the body of the chapter, indicates the amount by which the call rises for every $1 increase in the stock. This value may be determined by dividing the difference between the call's two possible outcomes by the difference between the ending prices of the stock. That is, the hedge ratio is

$$\frac{\$15 - 0}{\$65 - 40} = 0.6$$

The amount to be borrowed is equal to the present value of the difference between the lower value of the stock ($40) and the profit associated with that outcome ($0 in this illustration). That value is

$$\frac{(0.6)(\$40) - 0}{1 + 0.1} = \$21.82$$

and is 0.436 times the current price of the stock. Thus, if an investor knows the two possible outcomes (e.g., $65 and $40), the rate of the interest (e.g., 10 percent), the price of the stock (e.g., $50), and the strike price (e.g., $50), that individual can determine the value of the call. If the price of the call is not equal to that value, the investor can arbitrage away the price differential. If the individual knows the price of the stock, the interest rate, price of the call, and the strike price, the investor can replicate the call by buying the stock and borrowing the appropriate amount such that either outcome is the same.

The preceding discussion was premised on only two possible outcomes and the time period was a year. What happens if there are more than two outcomes and the time period is not a year? Consider what may happen if the time period is two six-month time periods instead of one twelve-month time period. The following decision tree starts with the same current price of the stock and the original ending prices but adds two possible prices at the end of six months and an additional price at the end of the twelve months.

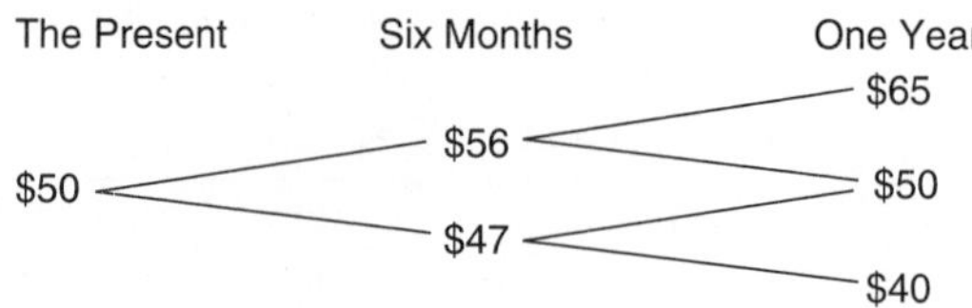

The price of the stock could go from $50 to $56 or $47 after six months and then proceed to $65, $50, or $40 after a year. Given this information, could the value of the call option be determined? The answer is yes, by following the process previously described for each time period. If the logic holds for the option pricing using two possible outcomes, it can be expanded to encompass three possible outcomes. A current value for the option will be determined, and arbitrage assures that the price is the one and only price.

The preceding illustration could be expanded to encompass a large number of possible outcomes and time periods. As the time periods become smaller, the number of outcomes approaches an infinite number. Computer applications can process a large number of possible time periods and outcomes, but that becomes unnecessary. As the number of outcomes increases, the binomial option pricing model approaches the Black-Scholes option valuation model. The Black-Scholes model reduces option valuation to a single equation that is easily applied.

The importance of the binomial option pricing model is not its applicability but its underlying explanation of option valuation. Through the process of arbitrage and the replication of options using long and short positions in the underlying stock and the bond, the value of an option is determined. The model also identifies the factors that are crucial to option valuation. These include the current price of the stock, the option's strike price, the time to expiration, the rate of interest, possible future prices of the stock, and the risk. This risk is measured by the extreme possible outcome prices. If the range in the extreme possible outcomes were smaller, the stock is less volatile and the outcome is less risky. Notice that the bionomial option pricing model (and the Black-Scholes model) does not include investors' expected future stock prices and investors' aversion to risk. This means that option pricing is independent of investors' expectations and willingness to bear risk. Both are based on the simple premise that two identical positions (the call or the stock and the bond) must have the same price.

Commodity and Financial Futures 21

Do you want excitement and rapid action? Would you prefer to speculate in pork bellies (i.e., bacon) instead of investing in the stock of Swift or Armour? Then investing in commodity futures may satisfy this speculative desire. These futures contracts are among the riskiest investments available, as prices can change rapidly and produce sudden losses or profits.

There are two participants in the futures markets: the speculators who establish positions in anticipation of price changes and the hedgers who seek to employ futures contracts to reduce risk. The hedgers are growers, producers, and other users of commodities. They seek to protect themselves from price fluctuations, and by hedging they pass the risk of loss to the speculators. The price of a futures contract ultimately depends on the demand for and supply of these contracts by the hedgers and speculators.

This chapter is an elementary introduction to investing in contracts for the future delivery of commodities. The chapter describes the mechanics of buying and selling the contracts, the role of margin, the speculators' long and short positions, and how the hedgers use the contracts to reduce risk. Next follows a discussion of financial futures, since commodity contracts are not limited just to physical assets. There are also futures contracts for the purchase and sale of financial assets and foreign currencies. There are even futures based on the Standard & Poor's 500 stock index or the New York Stock Exchange Composite Index. The chapter continues with a discussion of programmed trading and stock index futures and how changes in the futures markets are transferred to the stock market and vice versa. The chapter ends with a brief discussion of swaps, in which participants agree to trade (swap) payments.

Learning Objectives

After completing this chapter you should be able to:

1 Define a futures contract and differentiate between the long and short positions in a commodity futures contract.

2 Contrast the role of margin in the stock market with its role in the commodity futures markets.

3 Distinguish speculators from hedgers and describe the role played by each in the futures markets.

4 Identify the forces that determine the price of a commodity futures contract.

5 Demonstrate how speculators may earn profits or suffer losses in financial and currency futures.

6 Explain how programmed trading links the futures and stock markets.

7 Demonstrate how futures and swaps help manage risk.

What Is Investing in Commodity Futures?

A commodity may be purchased for current delivery or for future delivery. Investing in commodity futures refers to a contract to buy or to sell (deliver) a

futures contract
An agreement for the future delivery of a commodity at a specified date.

commodity in the future. For this reason these investments are sometimes referred to as *futures.* A **futures contract** is a formal agreement between a buyer or seller and a commodity exchange. In the case of a purchase contract, the buyer agrees to accept a specific commodity that meets a specified quality in a specified month. In the case of a sale, the seller agrees to deliver the specified commodity during the designated month.

Investing in commodity futures is considered to be very speculative. For that reason investors should participate in this market only after their financial obligations and primary financial goals have been met. There is a large probability that the investor will suffer a loss on any particular purchase or sale of a commodity contract. Individuals who buy and sell commodity contracts without wanting to deal in the actual commodities are generally referred to as *speculators,* which differentiates them from the growers, processors, warehousers, and other dealers who also buy and sell commodity futures but really wish to buy or sell the actual commodity.

The primary appeal of commodity contracts to speculators is the potential for a large return on the investment resulting from the leverage inherent in commodity trading. This leverage exists because (1) a futures contract controls a substantial amount of the commodity and (2) the investor must make only a small payment to buy or sell a contract (i.e., there is a small margin requirement). These two points are discussed in detail later in this chapter.

The Mechanics of Investing in Commodity Futures

Like stocks and bonds, commodity futures may be purchased in several markets. One of the most important is the Chicago Board of Trade (CBT) (http://www.cbt.com or http://www.cbot.com), which executes contracts in agricultural commodities, such as corn, soybeans, and wheat. Other commodities are traded in various cities throughout the country. Over 50 commodities are traded on ten exchanges in the United States and Canada. As may be expected, the markets for some commodity futures developed close to the area where the commodity is produced. Thus, the markets for wheat are located not only in Chicago but also in Kansas City and Minneapolis. The market for several commodity futures is in New York City, where cocoa, coffee, sugar, potatoes, and orange juice are bought and sold. This geographical diversity does not hamper commodity traders, who may buy and sell commodity contracts in any market through their brokers.

Like stocks and bonds, commodity contracts are purchased through brokers. The broker (or a member of a brokerage firm) owns a seat on the commodity exchange. Membership on each exchange is limited, and only members are allowed to buy and sell the commodity contracts. If the investor's broker lacks a seat, then that broker must have a correspondent relationship with another broker who does own a seat.

The broker acts on behalf of the investor by purchasing and selling contracts through the exchange. The investor opens an account by signing an agreement that requires the contracts to be guaranteed. Since trading commodity contracts is considered to be speculative, some brokers will open accounts only after the investor has proved the capacity both to finance the account and to withstand the losses.

Once the account has been opened, the individual may trade commodity contracts. These are bought and sold in much the same way as stocks and bonds; however, the use of the words *buy* and *sell* is misleading. The individual does not buy or sell a contract, but enters a contract to buy or sell. A buy contract specifies that the individual will *accept* delivery and hence "buy" the commodity. A sell contract specifies that the individual will *make* delivery and hence "sell" the commodity.

A commodity order specifies whether the contract is a buy or a sell, the type of commodity and the number of units, and the delivery date (i.e., the month in which the contract is to be executed and the commodity is bought or sold). The investor can request a market order and have the contract executed at the current market price, or he or she may place orders at specified prices. Such orders may be for a day or until the investor cancels them (i.e., the order is good till canceled). Once the order is executed, the broker provides a confirmation statement for the sale or purchase and charges a commission for executing the order. This fee covers both the purchase and the sale of the contract.

Although a futures contract appears to involve a buyer and a seller, the actual contract is made between the individual and the exchange. If an individual buys a contract, the exchange guarantees the delivery (the sale). If an individual sells a contract, the exchange guarantees to take delivery (the purchase). When a contract is created, the exchange simultaneously makes an opposite contract with another investor. While the exchange has offsetting buy and sell contracts, the effect is to guarantee the integrity of the contracts. If one of the parties were to default (for example, the buyer), the seller's contract is upheld by the exchange.

Commodity Positions

The investor may purchase a contract for future delivery. This is the long position, in which the investor will profit if the price of the commodity and hence the value of the contract rises. The investor may also sell a contract for future delivery. This is the short position, in which the seller agrees to make good the contract (i.e., to deliver the goods) sometime in the future. This investor will profit if the price of the commodity and hence the value of the contract decline. These long and short positions are analogous to the long and short positions that the investor takes in the security market. Long positions generate profits when the value of the security rises, whereas short positions result in profits when the value of the security declines.

futures price
The price in a contract for the future delivery of a commodity.

The way in which each position generates a profit can be seen in a simple example. Assume that the **futures price** of wheat is $3.50 per bushel. If a contract is purchased for delivery in six months at $3.50 per bushel, the buyer will profit from this long position if the price of wheat *rises*. If the price increases to $4.00 per bushel, the buyer can exercise the contract by taking delivery and paying $3.50 per bushel. The speculator then sells the wheat for $4 per bushel, which produces a profit of $0.50 per bushel.

spot price
The current price of a commodity.

The opposite occurs when the price of wheat declines. If the price of wheat falls to $3.00 per bushel, the individual who bought the contract for delivery at $3.50 suffers a loss. But the speculator who sold the contract for the delivery of wheat (i.e., who took the short position) earns a profit from the price decline. The speculator can then buy wheat at the market price (which is referred to as the **spot price**) of $3.00, deliver it for the contract price of $3.50, and earn a $0.50 profit per bushel.

If the price rises, the short position will produce a loss. If the price increases from $3.50 to $4.00 per bushel, the speculator who sold a contract for delivery suffers a loss of $0.50 per bushel, because he or she must pay $4.00 to obtain the wheat that will be delivered for $3.50 per bushel.

Actually, the preceding losses and profits are generated without the goods being delivered. Of course, when a speculator buys a contract for future delivery, there is always the possibility that this individual will receive the goods. Conversely, if the speculator sells a contract for future delivery, there is the possibility that the goods will have to be supplied. However, such deliveries occur infrequently, because the speculator can offset the contract before the delivery date. This is achieved by buying back a contract that was previously sold or selling a contract that is owned.

This process of *offsetting existing contracts* is illustrated in the following example. Suppose a speculator has a contract to buy wheat in January. If the individual wants to close the position, he or she can sell a contract for the delivery of wheat in January. The two contracts cancel (i.e., offset) each other, as one is a purchase and the other is a sale.[1] If the speculator actually received the wheat by executing the purchase agreement, he or she could pass on the wheat by executing the sell agreement. However, since the two contracts offset each other, the actual delivery and subsequent sale are not necessary. Instead, the speculator's position in wheat is closed, and the actual physical transfers do not occur.

Correspondingly, if the speculator has a contract for the sale of wheat in January, it can be canceled by buying a contract for the purchase of wheat in January. If the speculator were called upon to deliver wheat as the result of the contract to sell, the individual would exercise the contract to purchase wheat. The buy and sell contracts would then cancel each other, and no physical transfers of wheat would occur. Once again the speculator has closed the initial position by taking the opposite position (i.e., the sales contract is offset by a purchase contract).

Because these contracts are canceled and actual deliveries do not take place, it should not be assumed that profits or losses do not occur. The two contracts need not be executed at the same price. For example, the speculator may enter a contract for the future purchase of wheat at $3.50 per bushel. Any contract for the future delivery of comparable wheat can cancel the contract for the purchase. But the cost of the wheat for future delivery could be $3.60 or $3.40 (or any conceivable price). If the price of wheat rises (e.g., from $3.50 to $3.60 per bushel), the speculator with a long position earns a profit. However, if the speculator has a short position (i.e., a contract to sell wheat), this individual sustains a loss. If the price declines (e.g., from $3.50 to $3.40 per bushel), the short seller earns a profit, but the long position sustains a loss.

The Units of Commodity Contracts

To facilitate trading, contracts must be uniform. For a particular commodity the contracts must be identical. Besides specifying the delivery month, the contract must specify the grade and type of the commodity (e.g., a particular type of wheat) and the units of the commodity (e.g., 5,000 bushels). Thus, when an individual buys or sells a contract, there can be no doubt as to the nature of the obligation. For example, if the investor buys wheat for January delivery, there can be no confusion with a contract for the purchase of wheat for February delivery. These are two different commodities in the same way that AT&T common stock, AT&T preferred stock, and AT&T bonds are all different securities. Without such standardization of contracts there would be chaos in the commodity (or any) markets.

The units of trading vary with each commodity. For example, if the investor buys a contract for corn, the unit of trading is 5,000 bushels. If the investor buys a contract for eggs, the unit of trading is 22,500 dozen. A list of selected commodities, the markets in which they are traded, and the units of each contract are given in Exhibit 21.1. While the novice investor may not remember the units for a contract, the experienced investor is certainly aware of them. As will be explained later, because of the large units of many commodity contracts, a small change in the price of the commodity produces a considerable change in the value of the contract and in the investor's profits or losses.

[1]This process is analogous to the writer of an option buying back the option. In both cases the investor's position is closed.

EXHIBIT 21.1

Selected Commodities, Their Markets, and Their Units of Trading

Commodity	Market	Unit of One Contract
Corn	Chicago Board of Trade	5,000 bushels
Soybeans	Chicago Board of Trade	5,000 bushels
Barley	Winnipeg Commodity Exchange	20 metric tons
Cattle	Chicago Mercantile Exchange	30,000 pounds
Coffee	Coffee, Sugar & Cocoa Exchange, New York	37,500 pounds
Copper	COMEX (Div. of New York Mercantile Exchange)	25,000 pounds
Platinum	New York Mercantile Exchange	50 troy ounces
Silver	COMEX (Div. of New York Mercantile Exchange)	5,000 troy ounces
Lumber	Chicago Mercantile Exchange	100,000 board feet
Cotton	New York Cotton Exchange	50,000 pounds

Reporting of Futures Trading

Commodity futures prices and contracts are reported in the financial press in much the same way as stock and bond transactions. This is illustrated in Exhibit 21.2 (p. 698), which was taken from *The Wall Street Journal.* As may be seen in the exhibit, corn is traded on the Chicago Board of Trade (CBT). The unit for trading is 5,000 bushels, and prices are quoted in cents per bushel. The opening price for December delivery was 230¼¢ ($2.3025) per bushel, while the high, low, and closing (i.e., the *settle*) prices were 231½¢, 226¢, and 226¾¢, respectively. This closing price was 3½¢ below the closing price on the previous day. The high and low prices (prior to the reported day of trading) for the lifetime of the contract were 275¢, and 202¼¢, respectively. The **open interest**, which is the number of contracts in existence, was 190,943.

open interest
The number of futures contracts in existence for a particular commodity.

This open interest varies over the life of the contract. Initially, the open interest rises as buyers and sellers establish positions. It then declines as the delivery date approaches and the positions are closed. This changing number of contracts is illustrated in Figure 21.1 (p. 699), which plots the spot and futures prices and the open interest for a September contract to buy Kansas City wheat. When the contracts were initially traded in November, there were only a few contracts in existence. By June the open interest had risen to over 10,000 contracts. Then, as the remaining life of the contracts declined, the number of contracts fell as the various participants closed their positions. By late September only a few contracts were still outstanding.

As is explained in the section on pricing, futures prices tend to exceed spot prices. If speculators anticipate higher prices, they will buy contracts for future delivery. This anticipation of inflation and the cost of storing commodities usually drives up futures prices relative to the spot price, so the futures price exceeds the current price.

Figure 21.1, however, illustrates that this relationship does not always hold. The figure gives the futures price and the spot price of Kansas City wheat, and, except for a brief period, the spot price exceeds the futures price. This inversion of the relationship occurs if speculators believe the price of the commodity will decline. These speculators sell contracts now to lock in the higher prices so they may buy back the contracts at a lower price. This selling of the futures contracts drives their price down below the spot price.

The futures price must converge with the spot price as the expiration date of the contract approaches. As with options such as puts and calls, the value of the

EXHIBIT 21.2

Selected Futures Prices

FUTURES PRICES

Wednesday, August 1, 2001

Open Interest Reflects Previous Trading Day.

GRAINS AND OILSEEDS

Corn (CBT) 5,000 bu.; cents per bu.

	OPEN	HIGH	LOW	SETTLE	CHANGE	LIFETIME HIGH	LIFETIME LOW	OPEN INT.
Sept	218½	220	214¾	215¼	– 3½	276½	192	119,913
Nov	....	....	....	223	– 3¼	242½	199	230
Dec	230¼	231½	226	226¾	– 3½	275	202¼	190,943
Ja02	233½	233½	230¼	230½	– 3	243	213½	370
Mar	240	241½	236½	237¼	– 2¾	270	205	36,794
May	244¾	245	241¼	241¾	– 2	266½	221	10,606
July	247½	249¼	245¼	246¼	– 2	279½	227¼	15,168
Sept	246½	248	244	244¾	– 2½	262	233	1,264
Dec	250½	252½	248¾	249	– 2¼	272	239¾	11,616
Jl03	....	....	....	264	– 1	272	260	39
Dec	259	262	258	262	– ¾	269	253½	1,081

Est vol 46,000; vol Tue 75,833; open int 388,024, –2,474.

Oats (CBT) 5,000 bu.; cents per bu.

	OPEN	HIGH	LOW	SETTLE	CHANGE	LIFETIME HIGH	LIFETIME LOW	OPEN INT.
Sept	140½	140½	135½	136¼	– 4¼	154½	103¾	4,766
Dec	139	139	133½	134	– 3	146¼	108½	5,496
Mr02	137½	137½	134½	134½	– 3½	144½	114½	1,936

Est vol 900; vol Tue 933; open int 12,359, –12.

Soybeans (CBT) 5,000 bu.; cents per bu.

	OPEN	HIGH	LOW	SETTLE	CHANGE	LIFETIME HIGH	LIFETIME LOW	OPEN INT.
Aug	513	517¾	507	509	– 3¾	549	421	9,006
Sept	513	517½	506½	507½	– 4¾	549	414½	21,342
Nov	513¼	516	504¼	506¼	– 6¼	605	417½	93,264
Ja02	517	518½	509½	510	– 4½	540	427¾	11,971
Mar	514	518	511	511½	– 3	546	436½	13,801
May	517½	518½	509	509	– 7	531	444	16,488
July	515	516	509	509½	– 6	533	450½	6,910
Nov	494	499	493	493	– 2	561	460	1,342

Est vol 54,000; vol Tue 69,490; open int 174,179, –620.

Soybean Meal (CBT) 100 tons; $ per ton.

	OPEN	HIGH	LOW	SETTLE	CHANGE	LIFETIME HIGH	LIFETIME LOW	OPEN INT.
Aug	179.00	180.00	175.50	176.20	– 2.40	190.40	142.50	15,858
Sept	176.00	176.00	170.30	170.60	– 1.60	182.80	140.20	25,436
Oct	167.00	168.70	166.00	166.10	– 1.30	181.00	138.80	13,405
Dec	167.80	168.00	165.20	165.50	– .90	180.00	139.00	51,514
Ja02	166.00	167.20	165.00	165.10	– 1.20	175.50	139.50	10,188
Mar	164.20	164.50	162.40	162.90	– 1.80	174.00	141.00	8,413
May	160.80	161.50	159.50	160.00	– 1.50	171.50	142.00	6,845
July	160.80	161.10	159.50	159.50	– 1.70	170.50	143.00	2,977
Aug	158.50	159.00	158.00	158.00	– 1.00	168.50	150.00	859
Sept	156.50	157.00	155.70	155.70	– .30	168.00	150.50	406

Est vol 25,000; vol Tue 29,800; open int 136,063, +828.

Soybean Oil (CBT) 60,000 lbs.; cents per lb.

	OPEN	HIGH	LOW	SETTLE	CHANGE	LIFETIME HIGH	LIFETIME LOW	OPEN INT.
Aug	19.12	19.12	18.68	18.78	– .14	20.98	14.65	7,662
Sept	19.21	19.21	18.77	18.80	– .21	21.15	14.79	34,526
Oct	19.16	19.24	18.93	18.94	– .23	20.35	14.94	17,034
Dec	19.67	19.70	19.28	19.29	– .23	21.25	15.22	65,146
Ja02	19.53	19.75	19.42	19.45	– .25	19.75	15.43	12,589
Mar	19.81	19.90	19.60	19.63	– .23	19.90	15.72	8,057
May	19.90	20.10	19.70	19.70	– .30	20.10	16.00	8,754
July	20.05	20.05	19.95	19.97	– .23	20.12	16.30	4,126
Aug	....	....	....	19.70	– .20	19.65	17.30	694
Sept	....	....	....	19.70	– .20	17.50	16.90	555
Oct	....	....	....	19.70	– .20	18.35	17.60	257
Dec	....	....	....	20.50	....	20.50	17.10	896

Est vol 39,000; vol Tue 40,989; open int 160,296, +1,135.

Wheat (CBT) 5,000 bu.; cents per bu.

	OPEN	HIGH	LOW	SETTLE	CHANGE	LIFETIME HIGH	LIFETIME LOW	OPEN INT.
Sept	277½	279½	274	274½	– 4	325	254	58,812

INTEREST RATE

Treasury Bonds (CBT)-$100,000; pts 32nds of 100%

	OPEN	HIGH	LOW	SETTLE	CHANGE	LIFETIME HIGH	LIFETIME LOW	OPEN INT.
Sept	103-27	104-04	103-14	103-25	– 8	106-25	96-22	477,459
Dec	102-28	103-10	102-24	103-01	– 8	104-24	97-25	30,502

Est vol 144,000; vol Tue 194,963; open int 508,230, –2,211.

Treasury Notes (CBT)-$100,000; pts 32nds of 100%

	OPEN	HIGH	LOW	SETTLE	CHANGE	LIFETIME HIGH	LIFETIME LOW	OPEN INT.
Sept	106-01	106-04	05-195	05-275	– 8.0	106-28	101-26	549,306
Dec	05-005	105-10	04-285	05-035	– 8.5	105-15	100-26	33,575

Est vol 176,000; vol Tue 236,898; open int 582,881, +13,090.

10 Yr Agency Notes (CBT)-$100,000; pts 32nds of 100%

	OPEN	HIGH	LOW	SETTLE	CHANGE	LIFETIME HIGH	LIFETIME LOW	OPEN INT.
Sept	101-05	101-11	100-27	01-015	– 10.5	02-035	97-145	51,967

Est vol 2,200; vol Tue 4,304; open int 51,967, –1,504.

5 Yr Treasury Notes (CBT)-$100,000; pts 32nds of 100%

	OPEN	HIGH	LOW	SETTLE	CHANGE	LIFETIME HIGH	LIFETIME LOW	OPEN INT.
Sept	105-12	105-16	05-035	105-09	– 4.5	105-16	101-03	469,451
Dec	105-02	05-035	104-27	104-31	– 5.5	05-055	103-17	9,607

Est vol 73,000; vol Tue 90,426; open int 479,058, –1,083.

2 Yr Treasury Notes (CBT)-$200,000; pts 32nds of 100%

	OPEN	HIGH	LOW	SETTLE	CHANGE	LIFETIME HIGH	LIFETIME LOW	OPEN INT.
Sept	103-17	103-21	03-155	03-172	– 1.5	103-21	02-085	56,934

Est vol 4,600; vol Tue 3,809; open int 56,934, –815.

30 Day Federal Funds (CBT)-$5 million; pts of 100%

	OPEN	HIGH	LOW	SETTLE	CHANGE	LIFETIME HIGH	LIFETIME LOW	OPEN INT.
July	96.230	96.235	96.230	96.235	....	96.280	96.230	25,648
Aug	96.37	96.37	96.35	96.36	....	96.46	94.18	25,620
Sept	96.52	96.52	96.51	96.52	– .01	96.53	95.50	44,948
Oct	96.61	96.63	96.59	96.61	– .01	96.63	95.62	25,238
Nov	96.65	96.66	96.63	96.64	– .02	96.66	96.08	30,858
Dec	96.65	96.66	96.62	96.64	– .02	96.66	96.35	10,476
Ja02	....	....	....	96.59	....	96.31	96.22	615
Feb	96.55	96.55	96.53	96.54	– .02	96.55	96.05	1,705
Mar	96.51	96.51	96.47	96.47	– .04	96.51	96.05	1,832
Apr	96.40	96.40	96.39	96.39	– .04	96.43	96.27	600

Est vol 16,500; vol Tue 13,439; open int 167,540, +1,239.

Muni Bond Index (CBT)-$1,000; times Bond Buyer MBI

	OPEN	HIGH	LOW	SETTLE	CHANGE	LIFETIME HIGH	LIFETIME LOW	OPEN INT.
Sept	106-17	106-17	105-30	106-05	– 8	106-17	100-12	11,972

Est vol 600; vol Tue 457; open int 11,974, –8.

Index: Close 105-31; Yield 5.33.

Treasury Bills (CME)-$1 mil.; pts of 100%

	OPEN	HIGH	LOW	SETTLE	CHANGE	YIELD	CHANGE	OPEN INT.
Sept	96.66	96.68	96.66	96.67	+ .02	3.33	–.02	2,265

Est vol 65; vol Tue 178; open int 2,265, +105.

Libor-1 Mo. (CME)-$3,000,000; pts of 100%

	OPEN	HIGH	LOW	SETTLE	CHANGE	YIELD	CHANGE	OPEN INT.
Aug	96.38	96.38	96.37	96.37	....	3.63	....	16,737
Sept	96.46	96.46	96.46	96.46	....	3.54	....	7,768
Oct	96.52	96.53	96.52	96.53	....	3.47	....	2,029
Nov	96.53	96.53	96.52	96.52	....	3.48	....	539
Dec	....	....	....	96.28	....	3.72	....	610
Fb02	96.39	96.39	96.38	96.39	....	3.61	....	235

Est vol 2,700; vol Tue 3,989; open int 27,983, +1,046.

Eurodollar (CME)-$1 Million; pts of 100%

	OPEN	HIGH	LOW	SETTLE	CHANGE	YIELD	CHANGE	OPEN INT.
Aug	96.41	96.42	96.40	96.41	....	3.59	....	27,301
Sept	96.46	96.47	96.42	96.46	....	3.54	....	703,360
Oct	96.40	96.40	96.37	96.39	....	3.61	....	2,851
Nov	....	....	....	96.35	....	3.65	....	200
Dec	96.32	96.33	96.29	96.32	....	3.68	....	667,358
Ja02	96.32	96.33	96.31	96.33	– .01	3.67	+.01	450
Mar	96.19	96.22	96.14	96.18	– .01	3.82	+.01	493,772
June	95.88	95.91	95.83	95.87	– .02	4.13	+.02	537,271
Sept	95.53	95.56	95.48	95.53	– .03	4.47	+.03	414,479
Dec	95.15	95.18	95.11	95.15	– .02	4.85	+.02	334,185
Mr03	94.93	94.95	94.88	94.92	– .03	5.08	+.03	249,569
June	94.65	94.70	94.63	94.67	– .03	5.33	+.03	155,296
Sept	94.48	94.50	94.43	94.47	– .03	5.53	+.03	145,484
Dec	94.26	94.28	94.21	94.25	– .03	5.75	+.03	113,352

EXCHANGE ABBREVIATIONS

(for commodity futures and futures options)

CANTOR-Cantor Exchange; **CBT-Chicago Board of Trade; CME**-Chicago Mercantile Exchange; **CSCE**-Coffee, Sugar & Cocoa Exchange, New York; **CMX**-COMEX (Div. of New York Mercantile Exchange); **CTN**-New York Cotton Exchange; EUREX-European Exchange; **FINEX**-Financial Exchange (Div. of New York Cotton Exchange; **IPE**-International Petroleum Exchange; **KC**-Kansas City Board of Trade; **LIFFE**-London International Financial Futures Exchange; **MATIF**-Marche a Terme International de France; **ME**-Montreal Exchange; **MCE**-MidAmerica Commodity Exchange; **MPLS**-Minneapolis Grain Exchange; **NYFE**-New York Futures Exchange (Sub. of New York Cotton Exchange); **NYM**-New York Mercantile Exchange; **SFE**-Sydney Futures Exchange; **SGX**-Singapore Exchange Ltd.; **WPG**-Winnipeg Commodity Exchange.

METALS AND PETROLEUM

Copper-High (Cmx.Div.NYM)-25,000 lbs.; cents per lb.

	OPEN	HIGH	LOW	SETTLE	CHANGE	LIFETIME HIGH	LIFETIME LOW	OPEN INT.
Aug	66.90	68.30	66.85	68.30	+ 0.50	92.50	66.85	1,116
Sept	68.25	68.80	67.10	68.75	+ 0.50	93.00	67.10	45,361
Oct	68.10	68.10	68.10	69.10	+ 0.50	92.40	68.10	2,096
Nov	68.50	69.60	68.50	69.45	+ 0.50	91.75	68.50	1,673
Dec	69.20	69.85	68.20	69.80	+ 0.55	92.00	68.20	14,828
Ja02	69.15	70.15	69.15	70.20	+ 0.55	90.80	69.15	1,531
Feb	69.55	70.15	69.55	70.55	+ 0.55	90.00	69.55	1,006
Mar	69.60	70.90	69.35	70.85	+ 0.50	91.00	69.35	5,475
Apr	70.00	70.30	69.75	71.15	+ 0.50	89.70	69.75	761
May	70.25	70.60	70.10	71.40	+ 0.45	89.60	70.10	1,994
June	70.95	71.30	70.95	71.65	+ 0.45	89.50	70.95	812
July	70.85	70.85	70.80	71.90	+ 0.40	88.90	70.80	1,222
Aug	....	....	....	72.15	+ 0.40	82.90	73.75	547
Sept	71.50	71.70	71.50	72.40	+ 0.35	88.00	71.50	1,115
Oct	....	....	....	72.65	+ 0.35	85.50	74.00	736
Nov	....	....	....	72.90	+ 0.35	85.50	74.00	452
Dec	72.30	72.30	72.20	73.20	+ 0.30	83.00	72.20	1,678

Est vol 12,000; vol Tue 10,375; open int 82,429, –1,876.

Source: *The Wall Street Journal,* Eastern Edition (August 2, 2001, C14). Staff-produced copy.

FIGURE 21.1

Spot and Futures Prices and Open Interest for a September Contract for Kansas City Wheat

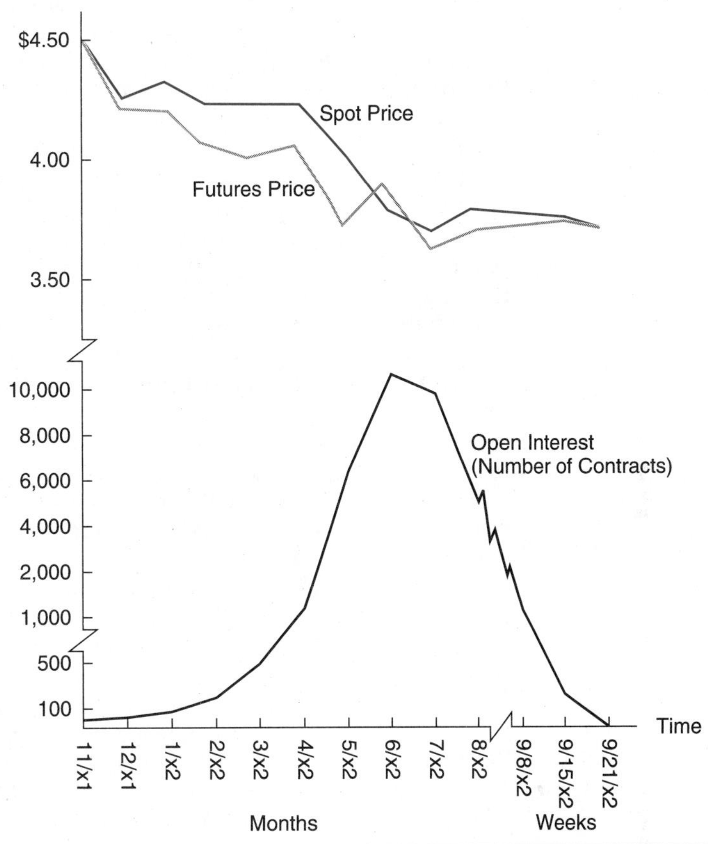

futures contract can be worth only the value of the underlying commodity at the expiration date. This pattern of price behavior is also illustrated in Figure 21.1. In March, April, and May there was a considerable differential between the two prices. However, in late September the futures and spot prices converged and erased the differential.

The Regulation of Commodity Markets

The commodity exchanges, like stock exchanges, are subject to regulation. Until 1974, federal laws pertaining to commodity exchanges and commodity transaction laws were enforced by the Commodity Exchange Authority, a division of the Department of Agriculture. In 1974, Congress created the Commodity Futures Trading Commission (http://www.cftc.gov) to control entry into and operation of the futures markets. As with the regulation of security transactions, the regulations do not protect investors or speculators from their own folly. Instead, the regulations establish uniform standards for each commodity. The regulatory authority also has control over trading procedures, the hours of trading, and the maximum allowable daily price movements.

Leverage

margin
Good faith deposit made when purchasing or selling a commodity contract.

Commodities are paid for on delivery. Thus, a contract for future delivery means that the goods do not have to be paid for when the individual enters the contract. Instead, the investor (either a buyer or a seller) provides an amount of money, which is called **margin**, to protect the exchange and the broker and to guarantee the contract. This margin should not be confused with the margin that is used in the purchase of stocks and bonds. In the trading of stocks and bonds, margin represents the investor's equity in the position, whereas margin for a commodity contract is a deposit to show the investor's good faith and to protect the broker against an adverse change in the price of the commodity.

In the stock market, the amount of margin required varies with the price of the security, but in the commodity markets, the amount of margin does not vary with the dollar value of the transaction. Instead, each contract has a fixed minimum margin requirement. These margin requirements for selected commodities and financial futures are given in Exhibit 21.3. Thus, an investor who purchases a futures contract for cocoa must put up $1,000. These margin requirements are established by the commodity exchanges but cannot be below the minimums established by the Commodity Futures Trading Commission. Individual brokers may require more, especially for small accounts.

The margin requirements are only a small percentage of the value of the contract. For example, the $1,000 margin requirement for cocoa gives the owner of the contract a claim on 10 metric tons of cocoa. If cocoa is selling for $1,400 a metric ton, the total value of the contract is $14,000. The margin requirement as a percentage of the value of the contract is only 7.14 percent ($1,000/$14,000). This small amount of margin is one reason why a commodity contract offers so much potential leverage.

The potential leverage from speculating in commodity futures may be illustrated in a simple example. Consider a contract to buy wheat at $3.50 per bushel. Such a contract controls 5,000 bushels of wheat worth a total of $17,500 (5,000 × $3.50). If the investor buys this contract and the margin requirement is $1,000, he or she must remit $1,000. An increase of only $0.20 per bushel in the price of the commodity produces an increase of $1,000 in the value of the contract. This $1,000 is simply the product of the price change ($0.20) and the number of units in the contract (5,000). The profit on the contract if sold is $1,000.

EXHIBIT 21.3

Margin Requirements for Selected Commodity Contracts

Commodity	Margin Requirement	Financial Futures	Margin Requirement
Broilers	$ 500	S&P 500	$20,000
Cocoa	1,000	NYSE Composite Index	7,000
Cotton	1,000	Value Line index	20,000
Hogs	800	Treasury bonds	5,000
Lumber	1,200	Treasury bills	1,500
Potatoes	500	Municipal bonds	4,000
Soybeans	1,500		
Wheat	1,000		

What is the percentage return on the investment? With a margin of $1,000 the return is 100 percent, because the investor put up $1,000 and then earned an additional $1,000. An increase of less than 6 percent in the price of wheat produced a return on the speculator's money of 100 percent. Such a return is the result of leverage that comes from the small margin requirement and the large amount of the commodity controlled by the contract.

Leverage, of course, works both ways. In the previous example, if the price of the wheat declines by $0.10, the contract will be worth $17,000. A decline of only 2.9 percent in the price reduces the investor's margin from $1,000 to $500. To maintain the position, the investor must deposit additional margin with the broker. The request for additional funds is referred to as a **margin call**. Failure to meet the margin call will result in the broker's closing the position. Since the contract is supported only by the initial margin, further price declines will mean that there is less collateral to support the contract. Should the investor (i.e., the buyer or the seller) default on the contract, the exchange becomes responsible for its execution. The margin call thus protects the exchange.

margin call
A request by a broker for an investor to place additional funds or securities in an account as collateral against borrowed funds or as a good faith deposit.

Actually, there are two margin requirements. The first is the minimum initial deposit, and the second is the maintenance margin. The **maintenance margin** specifies when the investor must deposit additional funds with the broker to cover a decline in the value of a commodity contract. For example, the margin requirement for wheat is $1,000 and the maintenance margin is $750. If the investor owns a contract for the purchase of wheat and the value of the contract declines by $250 to the level of the maintenance margin ($750), the broker makes a margin call. This requires the investor to deposit an additional $250 into the account, which restores the initial $1,000 margin.

maintenance margin
The minimum level of funds in a margin account that triggers a margin call.

Maintenance margin applies to both buyers and sellers. If, in the previous example, the price of wheat were to rise by $250, the speculators who had sold short would see their margin decline from the initial deposit of $1,000 to $750. The broker would then make a margin call, which would require the short sellers to restore the $1,000 margin. Once again this protects the exchange, since the value of the contract has risen and the short seller has sustained the loss.

These margin adjustments occur daily. After the market closes, the value of each account is totaled. In the jargon of futures trading, each account is *marked to the market.* If a position has gained in value, funds are transferred into the account. If a position has lost value, funds are transferred out of the account. The effect is to transfer the funds from the accounts that have sustained losses to those accounts that have experienced gains. If, as a result of the transfer of funds, the account does not meet the maintenance margin requirement, the broker issues a margin call that the individual must meet or the broker will close the position.

The process of marking to the market and daily cash flows may be seen in the following example for a futures contract for 5,000 bushels of a commodity (e.g., wheat or corn). The futures price is $3.00, the margin requirement is $1,500, and the maintenance margin requirement is $800. There are two speculators, one of whom expects the price to rise and buys the contract (i.e., is long) and the other who is short and sells the contract. Both make the initial $1,500 margin payment, so at the end of the first day their respective positions are

Day 1 Futures price: $3.00
Value of the contract: $15,000
Margin positions:

Speculator Long	Speculator Short
$1,500	$1,500

During the second day, the futures price rises to $3.05 and the margin accounts are as follows:

Day 2 Futures price: $3.05
Value of the contract: $15,250
Margin positions:

	Speculator Long	Speculator Short
Beginning balance	$1,500	$1,500
Change in balance	+250	−250
Required deposits	—	—
Voluntary withdrawals	250	—
Ending balance	$1,500	$1,250

Notice that Speculator Long has gained $250 while Speculator Short has lost $250 and the appropriate adjustments are made at the end of the day as each account is marked to the market. Since both accounts have more than $800, both meet the maintenance margin requirement, so no deposits of additional funds are needed. Speculator Long, however, may remove $250, since the account exceeds the initial margin requirement. These funds may be invested (e.g., in a money market account) to earn interest.

During the third day, the futures price continues to rise to $3.20 a bushel, so the value of the contract is $16,000. The positions for each account are now

Day 3 Futures price: $3.20
Value of the contract: $16,000
Margin positions:

	Speculator Long	Speculator Short
Beginning balance	$1,500	$1,250
Change in balance	+750	−750
Ending balance	$2,250	$ 500

Speculator Long may remove an additional $750 since the account again exceeds the margin requirement. Speculator Short's position is now less than the maintenance margin requirement. He or she will have to restore the account to the initial margin ($1,500), which will require an additional $1,000. After these changes the accounts will be

	Speculator Long	Speculator Short
Beginning balance	$1,500	$1,250
Change in balance	+750	−750
Balance	2,250	500
Required deposits	—	1,000
Voluntary withdrawals	−750	—
Closing balance	$1,500	$1,500

Notice that Speculator Long's $1,000 gain equals Speculator Short's $1,000 loss. If the futures price had declined from $3.00 to $2.80, the cash flows would have been reversed. Speculator Short would have $2,500 in the account and could remove $1,000, while Speculator Long would have only $500. Speculator Long would receive a margin call for $1,000 to restore the account to $1,500.

Whether the speculator chooses to meet the margin call is, of course, that person's decision, but a primary purpose of daily marking all positions to the market is to let the process of transferring funds occur. If a participant fails to meet a margin call, the broker closes the position, so that losses will not continue to increase (and put the brokerage firm at risk). Since speculators are highly aware of their risk exposure and often rapidly close positions, the probability they will receive a margin call is small. Such speculators rapidly close losing positions in order to limit their losses.

daily limit
The maximum daily change permitted in a commodity future's price.

While commodity prices can and do fluctuate, limits are imposed by the markets on the amount of price change permitted each day. The **daily limit** establishes the maximum permissible price increase or decrease from the previous day. The purpose of these limits is to help maintain orderly markets and to reduce the potentially disruptive effects from large daily swings in the price of the futures contract.[2]

Once the price of the futures contract rises by the permissible daily limit, further price increases are not allowed. This does not necessarily mean that trading ceases, because transactions can still occur at the maximum price or below should the price of the commodity weaken. The same applies to declining prices. Once the daily limit has been reached, the price cannot continue to fall, but transactions can still occur at the lowest price or above should the price strengthen. For example, when the 1992 Florida orange crop came in at the higher end of expectations, orange juice futures prices quickly fell. Contracts for January, February, and March delivery declined by the 5¢ daily limit. Although trading could have continued at the lowest price, trading ceased because no one was willing to buy at that level and speculators anticipated further price declines. The same principle applies to price increases. In 1995 Hurricane Erin threatened lumber supplies and September lumber rose by the $10 daily limit and trading ceased.

Hedging

hedging
Taking opposite positions to reduce risk.

One major reason for the development of commodity futures markets was the desire of producers to reduce the risk of loss through price fluctuations. The procedure for this reduction in risk is called **hedging**, which consists of taking opposite positions at the same time.[3] In effect, a hedger simultaneously takes the long and the short position in a particular commodity.

Hedging is best explained by illustrations. In the first example, a wheat farmer expects to harvest a crop at a specified time. Since the costs of production are determined, the farmer knows the price that is necessary to earn a profit. Although the price that will be paid for wheat at harvest time is unknown, the current price of a contract for the future delivery of wheat is known. The farmer can then sell a contract for future delivery. Such a contract is a hedged position, because the farmer takes a long position (the wheat in the ground) and a short position (the contract for future delivery).

Such a position reduces the farmer's risk of loss from a price decline. Suppose the cost to produce the wheat is $2.50 per bushel and September wheat is selling in June for $2.75. If the farmer *sells* wheat for September delivery, a $0.25 per bushel

[2]The daily limit applies to many futures prices but not all, especially financial futures based on federal government debt and stock index futures.

[3]Hedging cannot erase risk and may even increase it. For a discussion of how such an increase may occur, see Richard J. Teweles and Frank J. Jones, *The Futures Game—Who Wins? Who Loses? Why?* 2nd ed. (New York: McGraw-Hill, 1987), 32–53.

POINTS OF INTEREST

Forward Contracts

In addition to futures contracts, there are also "forward contracts." These are essentially the same as futures contracts with different features. A futures contract is a standardized contract between two parties that specifies the amount of the commodity and the delivery date. Since the contract is standardized, futures may be bought and sold through organized futures markets. A forward contract is a contract between two parties but is tailor-made for each transaction. The uniqueness of each forward contract makes it adaptable to the specific needs of the respective parties.

Forward contracts are common in the normal course of business. Any contract for the future delivery of a commodity or service is a forward contract. For example, a magazine subscription or an airline ticket illustrate a forward contract. In each case one party contracts to deliver a commodity (the magazine) or service (the plane ride) at specified future dates and for a specified amount of money. The money may be paid when the contract is executed or upon delivery.

Many businesses could not exist without forward contracts in which one party agrees to provide something in the future for a specified price and the other party agrees to take delivery and pay the specified price. Firms, governments, and households enter such contracts, and each contract creates legal obligations on both parties.

Although a forward contract specifies the amount and delivery date, the uniqueness of its features reduces the marketability of the contract. When the contract is written, the intention is to maintain the contract until delivery, so there are no organized forward markets. In effect, forward contracts are illiquid futures contracts. There is, however, some trading of forward contracts over-the-counter among financial institutions. In addition, if a firm has a forward contract to buy a commodity, it may enter into another contract to deliver the commodity. In effect, the two forward contracts cancel each other.

In addition to the lack of liquidity, the other important difference between forward and futures contracts is daily settlement, which applies to futures contracts but not to forward contracts. Forward contracts are not marked to the market daily, and funds are not transferred between the two parties. Final settlement thus occurs when the commodity is delivered and paid for as specified in the contract.

profit is assured, because the buyer of the contract agrees to pay $2.75 per bushel on delivery in September. If the price of wheat declines to $2.50, the farmer is still assured of $2.75. However, if the price of wheat rises to $3.10 in September, the farmer still gets only $2.75. The additional $0.35 gain goes to the owner of the contract who bought the wheat for $2.75 but can now sell it for $3.10.

Is this transaction unfair? Remember that the farmer wanted protection against a decline in the price of wheat. If the price had declined to $2.40 and the farmer had not hedged, the farmer would have suffered a loss of $0.10 (the $2.40 price minus the $2.50 cost) per bushel. To obtain protection from this risk of loss, the farmer accepted the modest profit of $0.25 per bushel and relinquished the possibility of a larger profit. The speculator who bought the contract bore the risk of loss from a price decline and received the reward from a price increase.

Users of wheat hedge in the opposite direction. A flour producer desires to know the future cost of wheat in order to plan production levels and the prices that will be charged to distributors. However, the spot price of wheat need not hold into the future, so this producer *buys* a contract for future delivery and thereby hedges the position. This is hedging because the producer has a long position (the contract for the future delivery of wheat) and a short position (the future production of flour, which requires the future delivery of wheat).

If the producer buys a contract in June for the delivery of wheat in September at $2.75 per bushel, the future cost of the grain becomes known. The producer cannot be hurt by an increase in the price of wheat from $2.75 to $3.10, because the contract is for delivery at $2.75. However, the producer has forgone the chance of profit from a decline in the price of wheat from $2.75 to $2.40 per bushel.

Instead, the possibility of profit from a decline in the price of wheat rests with the speculator who sold the contract. If the price of wheat were to decline, the speculator could buy the wheat in September at the lower price, deliver it, and collect the $2.75 that is specified in the contract. However, this speculator would suffer a loss if the price of September wheat rose over $2.75. The cost would then exceed the delivery price specified in the contract.

These two examples illustrate why growers and producers hedge. They often take the opposite side of hedge positions. If all growers and producers agree on prices for future delivery, there would be no need for speculators; but this is not the case. Speculators buy or sell contracts when there is an excess or an insufficient supply. If the farmer in the preceding example could not find a producer to buy the contract for the future delivery of wheat, a speculator would buy the contract and accept the risk of a price decline. If the producer could not find a farmer to supply a contract for the future delivery of wheat, the speculator would sell the contract and accept the risk of a price increase.

Of course, farmers, producers, and speculators are simultaneously buying and selling contracts. No one knows who buys and who sells at a specific moment. However, if there is an excess or a shortage of one type of contract, the futures price of the commodity changes, which induces a certain behavior. For example, if September wheat is quoted at $2.75 per bushel, but no one is willing to buy at that price, the price declines. This induces some potential sellers to withdraw from the market and some potential buyers to enter the market. By this process, an imbalance of supply and demand for contracts for a particular delivery date is erased. It is the interaction of the hedgers and the speculators that establishes the price of each contract.

The Selection of Commodity Futures Contracts

As with the selection of securities, there are two basic methods for the selection of commodity futures contracts: the technical approach and the fundamental approach. The technical approach uses the same methods that are applied to the selection of securities. Various averages, point-and-figure charts, and bar graphs and their patterns are constructed for various commodities and are used to identify current price movements and to predict future price movements. Since this material was covered in Chapter 14, it is not repeated here.[4]

The fundamental approach is primarily concerned with those factors that affect the demand for and the supply of the various commodities. Although the approach is similar to the selection of securities in that it uses economic data, the specifics are different. The price of a commodity depends on the supply of that commodity relative to the demand. Since the commodities are produced (e.g., wheat) or mined (e.g., silver), there are identifiable sources of supply. Correspondingly, there are identifiable sources of demand. However, there is also a variety of exogenous factors that may affect the supply of or the demand for a particular commodity, and these factors can have a powerful impact on the price of a specific commodity.

To illustrate these points, consider a basic commodity such as wheat. It takes several months for wheat to be produced. It has to be planted, grown, and harvested. The amount of wheat that is planted is known because statistics are kept by the U.S. Department of Agriculture. Such statistics are necessary for government forecasts of the economy, and this information is certainly available to those firms and individuals concerned with the size of the wheat crop.

[4]The investor who is interested in the application of technical analysis to commodity selection may consult Teweles and Jones, *The Futures Game—Who Wins? Who Loses? Why?* 2nd ed. (New York: McGraw-Hill, 1987), Chapter 7.

The size of the crop that is planted and the size that is harvested, however, may be considerably different. The actual harvest depends on other factors. Particularly important is the weather, which can increase or decrease the yield. Good weather at the appropriate time can result in a bountiful harvest. A larger than anticipated supply of wheat should depress its price. On the other hand, bad weather, be it drought or excess rain, will significantly reduce the anticipated supply. A reduction in supply should increase the price of wheat.

Demand, like supply, depends on both predictable and unpredictable forces. The demand for wheat depends on the needs of the firms that use the grain in their products. The producers of flour and cereals are obvious potential customers for wheat. However, the total demand also includes exports. If a foreign government enters the market and buys a substantial amount of wheat, this may cause a significant increase in its price.

Such government intervention in the market is not limited to foreign governments. The U.S. government also buys and sells commodities. Sometimes it buys to absorb excess supplies of a commodity and thus supports the commodity's price. In other cases the federal government may sell from its surplus stocks of a given commodity. This, of course, has the opposite impact on the price of the commodity. The increased supply tends to decrease the price or at least to reduce a tendency for the price to rise. These exogenous forces in the commodity markets are just another source of risk with which the speculator must contend.

Obviously the speculator needs to identify shifts in demand or supply before they occur in order to take the appropriate position. Anticipation of a price increase indicates the purchase of a futures contract, whereas an anticipated price decline indicates the sale of a futures contract. Unfortunately, the ability to consistently predict changes in demand and supply is very rare. This should be obvious! If an individual could predict the future, he or she would certainly make a fortune not just in the commodity futures markets but in any market. Mortals, however, lack such clairvoyance, which leaves them with fundamental and technical analysis as means to select commodity futures for purchase.

Whether an investor uses technical or fundamental analysis, there is an important strategy for trading futures. The speculator should limit losses and permit profits to run. Successful commodity futures trading requires the speculator's ability to recognize bad positions and to close them before they generate large losses. Many speculators, especially novices, do the exact opposite by taking small profits as they occur but maintaining positions that sustain losses. Then, when price changes produce margin calls, the speculator is forced either to close the position at a loss or to put up additional funds. If the speculator meets the margin

POINTS OF INTEREST

Taxation of Gains and Losses from Trading in Futures

Realized profits from trading in futures are taxed as capital gains. In addition, all positions in futures are considered to have been closed at the end of the tax year. Open positions then must be marked to the market on the last day of the tax year and any paper profits taxed as if they were realized capital gains. Any paper losses are treated as realized capital losses.

The profits are arbitrarily apportioned as 60 percent long-term capital gains and 40 percent short-term capital gains. A $1,000 profit would be separated into a $600 long-term capital gain and a $400 short-term capital gain and taxed according to the applicable rates. Losses are treated as capital losses and are used to offset capital gains from trading in futures, capital gains from other security transactions, and income from other sources, subject to the limitations discussed in Chapter 6.

call by committing additional funds, that individual is violating the strategy. Instead of taking the small loss, this investor is risking additional funds in the hope that the price will recover.

Financial and Currency Futures

financial futures
Contract for the future delivery of a financial asset.

currency futures
Contract for the future delivery of foreign exchange.

In the previous discussion, commodity contracts meant futures contracts for the delivery of physical goods. However, there are also **financial futures**, which are contracts for the future delivery of securities such as Treasury bills, and **currency futures**, which are contracts for the future delivery of currencies (e.g., the British pound or the European euro).[5] The market for financial futures, like the market for commodity futures, has two participants: the speculators and the hedgers. It is the interaction of their demands for and supplies of these contracts that determines the price of a given futures contract.

While any speculator may participate in any of the financial or currency futures markets, the hedgers differ from the speculators because they also deal in the currency itself. The hedgers in currency futures are primarily multinational firms that make and receive payments in foreign moneys. Since the value of these currencies can change, the value of payments that the firms must make or receive can change. Firms thus establish hedge positions to lock in the price of the currency and thereby avoid the risk associated with fluctuations in the value of one currency relative to another.

As interest rates and bond prices change, the yields from lending and the cost of borrowing are altered. To reduce the risk of loss from fluctuations in interest rates, borrowers and lenders may establish hedge positions in financial futures to lock in a particular interest rate.

Speculators, of course, are not seeking to reduce risk but reap large returns for taking risks. The speculators are bearing the risk that the hedgers are seeking to avoid. The speculators try to correctly anticipate changes in the value of currencies and the direction of changes in interest rates and to take positions that will yield profits. The return they earn (if successful) is then magnified because of the leverage offered by the small margin requirements necessary to establish the positions.

How financial futures may produce profits for speculators may be illustrated with an example using an interest rate futures contract for the delivery of U.S. Treasury bonds. Suppose a speculator expects interest rates to fall and bond prices to rise. This individual would *buy* a contract for the delivery of Treasury bonds in the future (i.e., the *long* position). If interest rates do fall and bond prices rise, the value of this contract increases because the speculator has the contract for the delivery of bonds at a lower price (i.e., higher yield). If, however, interest rates rise, bond prices fall and the value of this contract declines. The decline in the value of the contract inflicts a loss on the speculator who bought the contract when yields were lower.

If the speculator expects interest rates to rise, that individual *sells* a contract for the future delivery of Treasury bonds (i.e., establishes a *short* position). If interest rates do rise and the value of the bonds declines, the value of this contract must decline, but the speculator earns a profit. This short seller can buy the bonds at a lower price and deliver them at the price specified in the contract. Or the speculator may simply buy a contract at the lower value, thereby closing out the position at a profit. Of course, if this speculator is wrong and interest rates fall, the value of

[5]Exhibit 21.2 presented prices not only for selected commodities but also for currency and interest rate futures. While the reporting provides prices for currencies, bonds and other interest rate futures are expressed in percentages. For example, a Treasury bond at 103-27 means 103 and 27/32s ($1,038.4375) per $1,000 face amount for an 8 percent coupon bond. Since Treasury bills are sold at a discount, a percentage such as 96.66 means $966.60 per $1,000 bill.

POINTS OF INTEREST

The Variety of Financial Futures

While the text discussion features U.S. Treasury bonds and NYSE Composite Index futures, there are a variety of financial futures available to the investor. These contracts and their respective markets include those in the table below.

In addition to financial futures, there are options available on U.S. Treasury securities. Put and call options on Treasury bonds are traded on the Chicago Board of Trade, and put and call options on Treasury notes and bills are traded on the American Stock Exchange. And in 1983, put and call options on financial futures were created and commenced trading. The investor may now purchase a put or call option based on Standard & Poor's 500 futures contracts.

Contract	Market
U.S. Treasury bonds	Chicago Board of Trade (http://www.cbt.com)
U.S. Treasury notes	Chicago Board of Trade
U.S. Treasury bills	International Monetary Market at the Chicago Mercantile Exchange (http://www.cme.com)
Bank CDs	International Monetary Market at the Chicago Mercantile Exchange
Dow Jones Industrial Average	Chicago Board of Trade
Dow Jones Transportation Average	Chicago Board of Trade
Dow Jones Utility Average	Chicago Board of Trade
Dow Jones Composite Average	Chicago Board of Trade
Standard & Poor's 500 Index	Chicago Mercantile Exchange
KC Value Line Index	Kansas City Board of Trade (http://www.kcbt.com)
Major Market Index	Chicago Board of Trade
Muni Bond Index	Chicago Board of Trade
Eurodollar	International Monetary Market at the Chicago Mercantile Exchange
British pound	International Monetary Market at the Chicago Mercantile Exchange
Canadian dollar	International Monetary Market at the Chicago Mercantile Exchange
Japanese yen	International Monetary Market at the Chicago Mercantile Exchange
Swiss franc	International Monetary Market at the Chicago Mercantile Exchange

the bonds increases, inflicting a loss on the speculator, who must now pay more to buy the bonds to cover the contract.

The same general principles apply to currency futures. Suppose the price of the British pound is \$2. A speculator who anticipates that the price of the pound will rise establishes a long position in the pound. This individual buys a contract for the future delivery of pounds. The futures price may be \$2.02 or \$1.96. It need not necessarily equal the current, or spot, price. (If many speculators expect the price of the pound to rise, they will bid up the futures price so that it exceeds the current price. If speculators expect the price of the pound to fall, they will then drive down the futures price.) If this speculator buys the futures contract for \$2.02 and is correct (i.e., the price of the pound rises), that individual makes a profit. If, for example, the price of the pound were to rise to \$2.20, the value of the contract may rise by \$0.18 per pound (i.e., \$2.20 − \$2.02).[6] Of course, if the speculator is wrong and the price of the pound declines to \$1.80, the value of the contract also declines, and the speculator suffers a loss.

[6]At expiration the futures and spot prices must be equal. Thus, if the pound is \$2.20 on the expiration date, the value of the contract must be \$2.20 per pound.

If the speculator had anticipated a decline in the value of the pound, that individual would establish a short position and sell contracts for the future delivery of pounds. If the speculator is right and the value of the pound declines, the speculator may close the position for a profit. Since pounds are now worth less, the speculator may buy the cheaper pounds and deliver them at the higher price specified in the contract.[7] If the speculator had been wrong and the price of the pound had risen, that individual would have suffered a loss, as it would have cost more to buy the pounds to make the future delivery required by the contract.

Financial and currency futures, like all futures contracts, offer the speculator an opportunity for profit from a change in prices. Although such securities are not suitable for the portfolios of most individuals, they do offer more sophisticated investors an opportunity for large returns. Whether the returns justify the large risks is, of course, a decision that each individual investor must make.

While most individuals think of futures contracts as a means to speculate on price changes, financial futures may be used to reduce the risk of loss from an increase in interest rates. Consider an investor who desires a flow of income and has constructed a large portfolio of bonds. The portfolio's market value would decline if interest rates rose. To offset the potential loss, the investor could hedge using financial futures. Since the individual has a long position in the bonds, the investor must take a short position in the futures. Therefore, the investor sells contracts for the future delivery of bonds. If interest rates rise (and therefore cause the value of the bonds to fall), the value of the futures contracts also falls. Since the investor has a short position in the contracts, the individual profits from the rising interest rates. The profits on the futures contracts then offset the decline in the value of the bonds.[8]

Stock Market Futures

stock index futures
A contract based on an index of security prices.

Futures contracts are also based on an index of the stock market (e.g., the Value Line stock index, the Standard & Poor's 500 stock index, or the New York Stock Exchange Composite Index). These **stock index futures** contracts offer speculators and hedgers opportunities for profit or risk reduction that are not possible through the purchase of individual securities. For example, the NYSE Composite Index futures contracts have a value that is 500 times the value of the NYSE Index. Thus, if the NYSE Index is 140, the contract is worth $70,000. By purchasing this contract (i.e., by establishing a long position), the holder profits if the market rises. If the NYSE Index were to rise to 145, the value of the contract would increase to $72,500. The investor would then earn a profit of $2,500. Of course, if the NYSE Index should decline, the buyer would experience a loss.

The sellers of these contracts also participate in the fluctuations of the market. However, their positions are the opposite of the buyers (i.e., they are short). If the value of the NYSE Index were to fall from 140 to 135, the value of the contract would decline from $70,000 to $67,500, and the short seller would earn a $2,500 profit. Of course, if the market were to rise, the short seller would suffer a loss. Obviously, if the individual anticipates a rising market, that investor should buy the futures contract. Conversely, if the investor expects the market to fall, that individual should sell the contract.

NYSE Index futures contracts are similar to other futures contracts. The buyers and sellers must make good faith deposits (i.e., margin payments). As with other

[7]Actually the speculator would close the short position by buying an opposite contract (a contract for the future delivery of pounds).

[8]To determine the exact number of contracts that should be sold to offset the potential loss, see Nancy H. Rothstein, *The Handbook of Financial Futures* (New York: McGraw-Hill, 1984), 262–264.

futures contracts, the amount of this margin ($7,000) is modest relative to the value of the contract. Thus, these contracts offer considerable leverage. If stock prices move against the investor and his or her equity in the position declines, the individual will have to place additional funds in the account to support the contract. Since there is an active market in the contracts, the investor may close a position at any time by taking the opposite position. Thus, if the investor had purchased a contract, that long position would be closed by selling a contract. If the investor had sold a contract, that short position would be closed by buying a futures contract.

There is one important difference between stock market index futures and commodity futures contracts. Settlement at the expiration or maturity of the contract occurs in cash. There is no physical delivery of securities as could occur with a futures contract to buy or sell wheat or corn. Instead, gains and losses are totaled and are added to or subtracted from the participants' accounts. The long and short positions are then closed.

One reason for the development of futures markets was the need by producers and users of commodities to hedge their positions against price fluctuations. Stock index futures (and other financial and currency futures) developed in part for the same reason. Portfolio managers buy and sell stock index futures in order to hedge against adverse price movements. For example, suppose a portfolio manager has a well-diversified portfolio of stocks. If the market rises, the value of this portfolio rises. However, there is risk of loss if the market were to decline. The portfolio manager can reduce the risk of loss by selling an NYSE Composite Index futures contract. If the market declines, the losses experienced by the portfolio will be at least partially offset by the appreciation in the value of the short position in the futures contract.

To execute such a hedge, the portfolio manager uses a futures contract that matches the composition of the portfolio. The NYSE Composite Index contract is suitable for a well-diversified stock portfolio but would not be appropriate for a specialized portfolio. Instead, the portfolio manager, who is responsible for a portfolio of smaller companies, would more likely use futures on the S&P Midcap index, which gives more weight to smaller companies.

To hedge using stock index futures, the portfolio manager divides the value of the portfolio by the value of the contract to determine the number of contracts to sell. For example, if the value of the portfolio is $1,000,000 and the futures contracts are worth $85,000, the individual would sell 11 to 12 contracts ($1,000,000/$85,000 = 11.76). It may not be possible to exactly hedge the portfolio, since the futures contracts may be unavailable in the desired units. In this example, the portfolio manager would not be able to sell 11.76 futures contracts, but would have to sell either 11 or 12 contracts. This question of units is less of a problem for managers of large portfolios. If the portfolio's value had been $100,000,000, the number of contracts would be 1,176 ($100,000,000/$85,000 = 1,176.47), and the difference between 1,176 and 1,177 is immaterial. The problem facing this portfolio manager will be the market's ability to absorb such a large number of contracts. Is there sufficient demand at current prices to absorb $100,000,000 worth of futures contracts? If the answer is no, then prices will change (which changes the required number of contracts) or the portfolio manager will not be able to hedge completely the long position in the stocks.

In addition to the number of contracts, the portfolio manager must consider the volatility of the portfolio relative to the market. The preceding illustration implicitly assumes that the value of the portfolio exactly follows the index on which the futures contract is based. In effect, the example assumes that the portfolio's beta equals 1.0. If the beta is greater than 1.0, more contracts must be sold to hedge against a price decline, since the value of the contracts sold short will decline less

EXHIBIT 21.4

Using Stock Index Futures to Hedge $2,000,000 Portfolios

	Portfolio A	Portfolio B
Value of portfolio:	$2,000,000	$2,000,000
Beta:	1.25	0.75
Value of S&P 500 stock index:	$500 × 563.65 = $281,825	$500 × 563.65 = $281,825
Number of contracts necessary to hedge:	($2,000,000/$281,825)(1.25) = 8.87	($2,000,000/$281,825)(0.75) = 5.32
Number of contracts sold:	9	5
Gain on futures contracts sold short after market declines by 10 percent to 507:	$281,825 × 9 − 507($500)9 = $254,925	$281,825 × 5 − 507($500)5 = $141,625
Loss on portfolio:	[$2,000,000(1 − 0.1) − $2,000,000] (1.25) = −$250,000	[$2,000,000(1 − 0.1) − $2,000,000] (0.75) = −$150,000
Net gain (loss)	$254,925 − $250,000 = $4,925	$141,625 − $150,000 = ($8,375)

than the value of the portfolio. If the portfolio's beta is less than 1.0, fewer contracts must be sold, since the value of the market will decline more than the value of the portfolio.

The entire process of hedging is illustrated in Exhibit 21.4, in which two individuals seek to hedge $2,000,000 portfolios against a price decline. Portfolio A has a beta of 1.25, while portfolio B has a beta of 0.75. Since the portfolio betas differ, portfolio A requires that 9 contracts be sold, while portfolio B requires the selling of only 5. The market subsequently declines by 10 percent. Each portfolio sustains a loss, but the short positions in the futures contracts generate profits that offset the losses. Except for the problem of units, each investor has successfully hedged against the price decline but has also forgone the opportunity for a gain. If the market had risen, the increase in the value of the contracts would offset the gain in the stocks. Hedging with stock index futures works in both directions but is the most appropriate strategy when the portfolio manager expects a price decline and is unwilling to sell the portfolio. For example, the portfolio manager may wish to hedge during a period of greater uncertainty but does not want to sell the securities and generate taxable capital gains.

Besides selling the index futures contract (establishing a short position in futures), the portfolio manager could have hedged by writing an index call option (establishing a covered call position) or by purchasing an index put option (establishing a protective put position). Each of these strategies is designed to protect against a decline in the market as a whole. Each offers potential advantages and has disadvantages, so there is no clear argument to use one exclusively. Selling a futures contract is an easy position to establish and tends to have low transaction costs. If, however, the market were to rise, the loss on the futures contract will offset the gain on the market. Selling the futures eradicates the upside potential.

Selling the call generates income from the sale but the downside protection is limited. If the market were to decline sufficiently to offset the proceeds of the sale of the call, the portfolio will sustain a loss. In addition, if the market rises, the value of the call will increase, which offsets the gain in the portfolio. The protective put does not limit the upside potential. If the market were to rise, the increase in the value of the portfolio is not offset by an equal decrease in the value of the put. But buying the put requires a cash outlay, and the process must be repeated (and cash outlays increased) if the portfolio manager wants to retain the protection from a market decline.

POINTS OF INTEREST

Single-Stock Futures

There are futures contracts on individual commodities (e.g., wheat); there are contracts on individual stock indices (e.g., the S&P 500) and broad baskets of stocks; contracts exist on individual currencies (e.g., the pound); and there are even contracts on individual federal government securities (Treasury bills). Beginning in 2001, the Chicago Board Options Exchange, the Chicago Mercantile Exchange, and the Chicago Board of Trade formed a joint venture for trading in single-stock futures.

Single-stock futures essentially work the same as any other futures contract. The participant enters into a contract to buy or to sell the specified stock at the current futures price. If the futures price of the stock rises, the long position wins and the short position loses. The appeal of such contracts is the small margin requirement, so the participant is able to obtain substantial amounts of leverage. However, unlike options, which also may be used to obtain leverage, single-stock futures are marked to the market daily, so gains and losses are settled daily. The cost of an option also varies daily, but the margin requirement for single-stock futures is set and does not change with the futures price. This means that if the price of the stock rose so that the futures price of the stock also rose, the cost of buying or selling the single-stock futures remains the set margin requirement.

Programmed Trading and Index Arbitrage

One of the more controversial developments in the security markets has been the consequence of programmed trading and index arbitrage. Programmed trading arose after the creation of stock index futures and has become a major link between the stock market and the futures market. Through programmed trading and index arbitrage, price changes in one market are transferred to the other and vice versa as the participants move funds between the markets to take advantage of price differentials.

programmed trading
Coordinated buying or selling of portfolios triggered by computers.

The term **programmed trading** refers to the coordinated purchases or sales of an entire portfolio of securities. The managers of mutual funds or financial institutions cannot physically place individual orders to buy and sell large quantities of stocks. Instead, large orders are placed through computers that are programmed (hence the name *programmed trading*) to enter the trades if certain specifications are met.

As explained earlier in this text, arbitrage refers to the simultaneous establishment of long and short positions to take advantage of price differentials between two markets. If, for example, the price of the British pound were $2.46 in Paris and $2.50 in Bonn, the arbitrageur would buy pounds in Paris and simultaneously sell them in Bonn. The pounds bought in Paris could be delivered in Bonn; hence, the individual is assured of a $0.04 profit on the transaction. This riskless arbitrage position ensures that the price of the pound will be approximately the same in Paris and Bonn with minute differentials being explained by transactions costs.

Conceptually, index arbitrage is no different, except the arbitrageur is buying or selling index futures and securities instead of pounds. The principle is the same. If prices deviate in different markets, an opportunity for arbitrage is created. Arbitrageurs will seek to take advantage of the price differentials, and through their actions the differentials are erased. This type of arbitrage is frequently done by mutual funds with large holdings of securities that duplicate the various indices of stock prices. These funds shuffle money between stocks and futures to take advantage of price differentials.

Programmed trading index arbitrage combines the two concepts: Computers are programmed to enter orders to sell or buy blocks of securities designed to take advantage of arbitrage opportunities that exist in the securities and futures markets. If stock index futures prices rise, the arbitrageurs will short the futures and buy the stocks in the index. If futures prices decline, the arbitrageurs do the opposite. They go long in the futures contracts and short the stocks in the index.

Three potential problems arise: (1) There are some transactions costs that must be covered, so the difference between the value of the futures contracts and the underlying securities must be sufficient to cover this cost. (2) There is an obvious problem with buying or shorting all the securities in a broad-based index. Since the Standard & Poor's 500 stock index uses 500 different stocks, positions would have to be taken in all 500. To get around this problem, the arbitrageurs have developed smaller portfolios called *baskets* that mirror the larger index. The price performance of these stock baskets then mimics the price movements in the index. (3) For arbitrage to be riskless, both positions must be made simultaneously. If they were not, there would be a period when the investor is either long or short (i.e., has only one position) and thus would be at risk. This need for simultaneous executions led to the use of computers that are programmed to coordinate the purchases or sales of the baskets. It is the use of the computers that permits the arbitrageur to enter simultaneously orders to buy or sell large quantities of many individual stocks.

In Chapter 19 it was explained why an option's intrinsic value sets a floor on the option's price. If the price were to decline below the intrinsic value, an opportunity for arbitrage would exist. The same concept applies to stock index futures, except in this case the option is replaced by the index futures and the individual stock by the stock basket.

The idea may be explained by a simple example. Suppose the S&P 500 stock index stands at 300 and the futures contract is trading for 301.5. Assume that the contract has a value of 500 times the index, so the value of each contract is $150,750. The arbitrageur shorts the futures and buys the $150,000 worth of the stocks in the index (or the shares in the basket). In effect, the arbitrageur has paid $150,000 for $150,750 worth of stock, because the arbitrageur has already entered into a contract for the sale of the stock at $150,750 through the short position in the futures.

If, after executing the position, the futures price declines or the prices of the stocks in the index rise, the arbitrageur will close both positions (referred to as *unwinding*) and make a profit. For example, suppose the prices of the stocks rise sufficiently that the index is 301.50 and the futures contract has only risen to 302. The arbitrageur may now sell the stocks and repurchase the futures contract. The loss on the futures is $250 (301.5 × $500 minus 302 × $500), while the gain on the stocks is $750 (301.5 × $500 − 300 × $500). Since all the transactions can occur in a matter of minutes, the cost of carrying the positions is negligible. The arbitrageur need only cover the transaction cost associated with the trades.

If the differential between the values of the futures and index are not rapidly erased, the arbitrageur can maintain the positions until the expiration date of the futures contracts. As the expiration date approaches, the futures price must converge with the current (i.e., spot) price. Options can only be worth their intrinsic value at expiration, and futures prices must equal the spot prices when the contracts expire. Thus the arbitrageur knows that the differential between the value of the futures contract and the index must disappear and thus assure the profit. The only difference between this and the previous situation is the cost of carrying the stocks, which may be partially offset by income generated by the securities.

If the prices had been reversed (e.g., the futures were trading at 298.5 when the index was 300), so would the procedure. The arbitrageur goes long in the futures and short in the stocks. The simultaneous long and short positions lock in the differential and assure the arbitrageur of the profit. If the price differential rapidly disappears, the positions are unwound and the profit realized. Even if the differential persists, the arbitrageur knows that at expiration the differential must be erased.

FIGURE 21.2

Differential Between the Value of a Stock Index Futures Contract and the Underlying Stocks

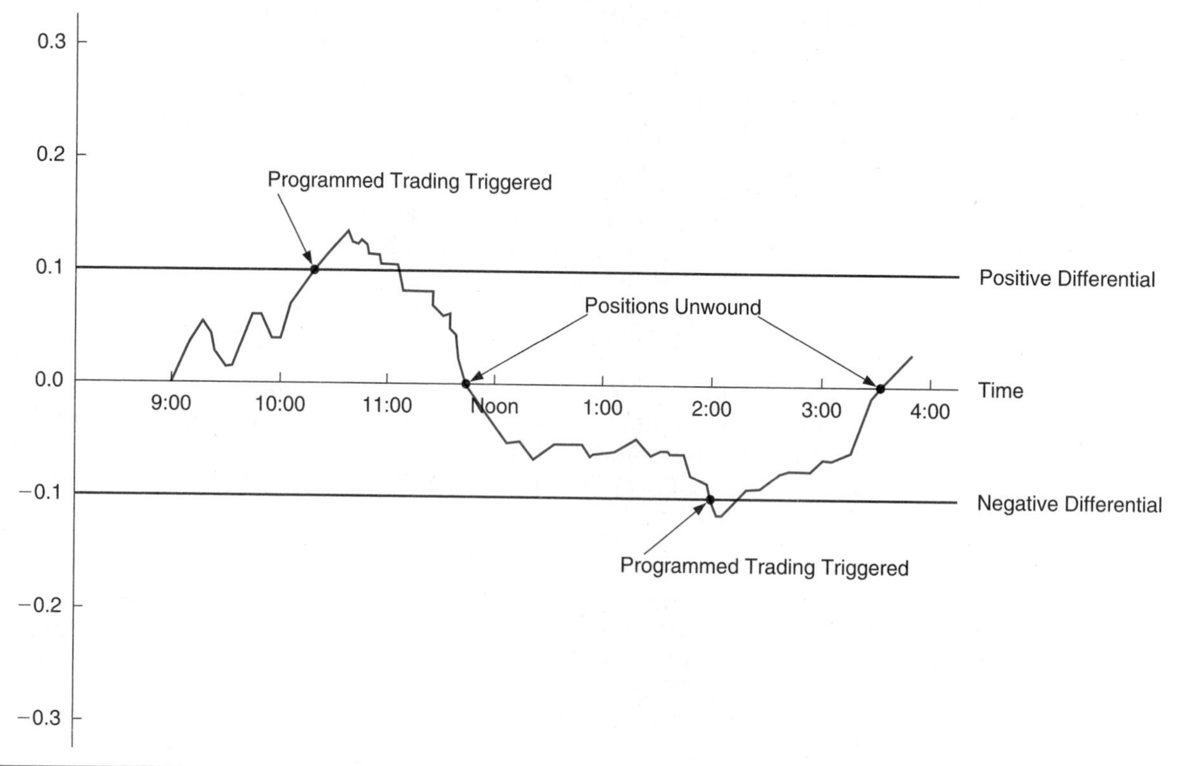

This process of index arbitrage is illustrated in Figure 21.2, which presents the differential between the value of the futures contract and the underlying stocks in the index during a trading day. The line at zero represents no differential, and the lines at +0.1 and −0.1 represent the transaction costs of executing index arbitrage. Once the differential between the futures and the index exceeds +0.1 or −0.1, the opportunity for a profitable arbitrage exists.

The computers are then programmed to enter the appropriate buy and sell orders when the differential is sufficient to cover the costs associated with the transactions. For example, at 10:15 A.M., the differential is sufficient on the plus side that the arbitrageur would short the futures and buy the stocks. By 11:45 the differential has vanished, so the positions are closed and the profits are realized. At 2:00 P.M. the differential has once again sufficiently increased (on the negative side) that the arbitrageur goes long in the futures and shorts the stocks. By 3:30, the differential is again erased, and the arbitrageur unwinds the positions.

Of course, as the differentials are erased, the impact is felt in the various markets. Increased demand for futures contracts relative to the underlying stocks generates demand by the arbitrageurs for the stocks and hence their prices rise. In a similar way, an increase in stock prices would be transferred to the futures markets. The converse would also be true. A decline in stock prices would tend to drive down the futures prices.

It is important to realize that index arbitrage–programmed trading does *not* depend on the level of stock prices or the level of futures prices. Instead, it depends on (1) spot prices relative to futures prices and (2) synchronized trading. Index arbitrage–programmed trading does not depend on technical analysis, fundamental analysis of a firm's financial statements, changes in information such as an increase in earnings or dividends, or forecasts of the economy.

Programmed trading can distort a stock's price. An individual stock can be fairly valued based on fundamental analysis but experience a large swing in its price if it becomes caught up in programmed trading. As arbitrageurs seek to establish long positions in stocks, the prices of individual securities included in the index or basket can rise rapidly and dramatically. Of course, the converse would be true if arbitrageurs seek to unwind long positions in the stocks or establish short positions. Thus it is possible for the prices of individual securities to be whipsawed during a trading day in response to the establishing or unwinding of arbitrageurs' positions. Such price volatility can create buying (or shorting) opportunities in individual stocks if their prices deviate from their values as indicated by fundamental analysis.

This price volatility may be particularly noticeable near the expiration dates and especially on the four days during the year that are referred to as the *triple witching hour.* On these days the Standard & Poor's 500 stock index futures contract, the Standard & Poor's 100 stock index option contract, and individual option contracts expire. This convergence of expirations can lead to large volatility in the prices and the volume of the securities traded.

On the triple witching day, the time period is so short that even small differentials can create arbitrage opportunities. The various participants in the markets (i.e., the owners and writers of option contracts and the speculators and hedgers with futures contracts) seek to close their positions, so price differentials can develop, and computers can spot them. If, for example, the futures price becomes marginally higher than the value of the underlying stocks, the arbitrageurs immediately short the futures and buy the stocks knowing that the differential must disappear in a matter of hours. Conversely, if the values of the stocks rise, the arbitrageurs sell the stocks and buy the futures because any difference between the futures contracts and the underlying stocks must disappear at the expiration of the contracts and the options. The possibility of such arbitrage profits, of course, has the effect of increasing the volume of transactions and driving prices so that any disparity is erased.

The large swings in stock prices may create buying (or shorting) opportunities in individual stocks if they become under- or overvalued. Evidence exists that large price changes in individual stocks on the triple witching day are quickly erased during trading on the day after the expiration date.[9] This is, of course, consistent with efficient markets. If, for some reason, an individual stock were to be mispriced, investors would buy or sell the security so that its price would be indicative of what the market believed the security was worth. The unwinding of stock index arbitrage positions can create, albeit briefly, such opportunities.

The volatility of security prices has raised the question of the desirability of programmed trading. The answer partially revolves around whether programmed trading and index arbitrage are viewed as a cause or as a reaction to other events that are occurring in the security and futures markets. Consider the case in which speculators believe that the Federal Reserve will ease credit and interest rates will fall. These speculators seek to take long positions and purchase stock index call options and futures contracts. The prices of these contracts rise above the value of the underlying stocks, which triggers programmed selling of futures contracts and large purchases of securities. Stock prices rise dramatically.

[9]See, for instance, Hans R. Stoll and Robert E. Whaley, "Program Trading and Expiration-Day Effects," *Financial Analysts Journal* (March/April 1987): 16–28.

The converse applies if speculators expect security prices to fall. They sell futures contracts that will be transferred to the security markets. The decline in the futures price would result in programmed trading taking long positions in the futures and short positions in the stocks (i.e., selling stocks). These illustrations, of course, suggest that it is not programmed trading and index arbitrage that are the cause of the changes in stock prices. Instead, it is the speculators who initiated the changes; the programmed trading was only in response to the initial cause.[10]

The Pricing of Futures

Several factors may affect a futures contract's price. For example, expectations have frequently been discussed as motivating speculators. The expectation of higher prices leads speculators to take long positions, and the expectation of lower prices results in their establishing short positions. Thus, the futures price mirrors what speculators anticipate prices will be in the future. In addition, the futures price and the spot price are not independent of each other. Such factors as the cost of carrying the commodity link the spot and futures prices. The pricing of futures contracts is an involved topic. The following material covers only the basics so an investor can have an understanding of the pricing of a futures contract. More detailed discussions may be found in texts devoted solely to derivatives.[11]

The following discussion is based on a commodity whose spot price is $100; the futures contract is for delivery after one year. Suppose individuals expect the price of the commodity to be $110 after one year. What should be the current price of a one-year futures contract? The answer is $110. Consider how individuals would react if the price were $108. They would buy the futures contract and, after one year, when the price of the commodity was $110, they would exercise the contract to buy the good for $108 and promptly sell it for $110, making a $2 profit. If the futures price exceeded $110 (e.g., $113), they would reverse the procedure and sell the futures contract. After one year, they would buy the commodity for $110, deliver it for the contract price of $113, and clear $3. For any futures price other than $110, speculators would take positions in the futures contracts. Only if the futures price equals the expected price in the future will the market be in equilibrium and speculators will take no action.

For this reason, futures prices are often considered to be measures of what investors, speculators, and other market participants currently expect the price of the commodity to be in the future. That is, the current futures prices are an indication of what the future holds. (This concept previously appeared in the appendix to Chapter 15, in which the expectations theory of interest rates suggested that the current long-term interest rate is an average of the current short-term rate and *expected* future short-term rates.) The process of using futures prices as a forecasting tool is sometimes referred to as "price disclosure." The current futures price discloses what market participants believe the future price will be.

[10]The existence of index arbitrage is one reason why index futures are followed by some investors prior to the opening of the stock market. If index futures are trading higher, that means the stock market will open higher. If the futures are lower, the stock market will open lower. Unfortunately, just because you know that futures are trading higher does not mean that you will be able to take advantage of the information. The market makers will adjust the stocks' prices as trading starts in response to the increased demand resulting from the increase in the futures price. The existence of index arbitrage assures that you will not be able to profit by the price differentials and is another illustration of why financial markets are considered so efficient.

[11]For a more detailed discussion of futures pricing, see Don M. Chance, *An Introduction to Derivatives and Risk Management*, 5th ed. (Fort Worth, TX: The Dryden Press, 2001); or Robert W. Kolb, *Futures, Options, and Swaps*, 3rd ed. (Malden, MA: Blackwell Publishers, Inc., 2000).

If expectations concerning future prices were to change, then the futures price must also change. A major failure of the coffee crop would be expected to increase the future price of coffee, so the expectation of high prices would drive up the current futures price. Of course, if the price of coffee did not rise, those speculators who bought in anticipation of the price increase would lose, while those who sold in anticipation that the price increase would not occur would win.

An additional factor that affects futures prices is the cost of carrying the commodity. In the previous examples, the speculator took only one side, that is, he or she bought or sold the futures in anticipation of a price change and the futures price mirrored the speculator's expected price change. Suppose the individual could buy the commodity now for $100 and sell the futures contract at $110. If the price rises to $110, the investor wins because the commodity that cost $100 can be delivered for $110. If the price exceeds $110, this individual still gets $110 and earns the $10. If the price is less than $110, the profit remains $10 because the price is set in the contract at $110. What is the catch?

The problem is the cost of carrying the commodity. If the individual buys the commodity for $100, those funds will not be earning interest (if the investor uses his or her own money) or will be requiring interest payments if the funds were borrowed. Suppose the interest rate is 8 percent. Now the individual can borrow $100, buy the commodity for $100, enter into a contract to deliver the commodity after a year for $110, and clear a $2 profit. Thus, if the futures price exceeds the spot price plus the cost of carry, then an opportunity for a risk-free arbitrage exists. The arbitrageurs will buy the commodity and sell the futures; they would long the commodity and short the futures. The act of executing these positions will drive up the spot price of the commodity and drive down the futures price. Speculators who anticipate a price of $110 in the future will gladly buy the futures contract for less than $110, since they anticipate earning the difference between $110 and whatever amount they buy the contract for.

If the interest rate were 12 percent, the arbitrageurs would reverse the procedure. They would sell the commodity at the current spot price (receiving the $100) and buy a contract for future delivery at $110. That is, the arbitrageurs would short the commodity and long the futures. Next they would invest (lend) the money received from the sale at 12 percent. At the end of the year, the arbitrageurs would receive the commodity that previously had been sold and make $2 on the transaction. Although the cost of the commodity was $110 and the arbitrageurs received only $100 from the sale, they earned $12 on the sale proceeds and netted $2 on the set of transactions.

Once again the act of executing these positions affects the prices of the commodity. Selling the commodity in the spot market will decrease its price, and buying the futures contract will increase its price. As the futures price increases, the speculators, who anticipate the price will be $110, gladly supply (i.e., sell) the contracts as the futures price rises above $110.

In the previous illustration, the cost of carry was limited to the rate of interest. Although that limitation may apply to a financial contract, it does not apply to a contract for a commodity. For commodities, the cost of carry includes interest expense and warehouse expenses, insurance, and shipping.

Consider the preceding case in which the spot price was $100, the futures price was $110, and the interest rate was 8 percent; the arbitrageurs bought the commodity with borrowed funds and sold the futures contract. Now, however, add a $9 cost of warehousing and shipping the commodity. These additional expenses alter the potential for an arbitrage profit. The futures price must exceed $117 for the arbitrageurs to earn a profit. If they sell the futures contract for $120, they can buy the commodity today for $100 with borrowed funds, pay the $8 interest, cover the $9 in other expenses, and earn a $3 profit without bearing any risk. However, now the futures price must greatly exceed the spot price for the arbitrage opportunity to exist.

Swaps

swap
An agreement to exchange payments.

In addition to options and futures, another derivative is the swap. A **swap** is an agreement between two parties who contract to exchange (i.e., swap) payments. A swap is as if I agree to pay your electric bill if you will agree to pay my phone bill. We agree to trade payments. Individuals rarely, if ever, swap payments, but firms and financial institutions often participate in the swap market. Firms make their profits through operations and not from speculating on anticipated price changes. To reduce the risk of loss from price changes, management may enter into a swap agreement. Since accounting disclosure requires swaps to be discussed in annual reports, the investor needs to understand swaps and how corporations use these derivatives to manage the firm's risk exposure.

Currency and Interest Rate Swaps

There are a variety of swap agreements between firms. For example, two firms may swap payments in different currencies (a currency swap). In another case, one firm swaps a series of fixed payments for a series of variable payments. The opposing firm (called the *counterparty*) swaps the variable payments and receives the fixed payments.

The large increase in foreign investments and foreign operations by global firms has greatly increased the use of swap agreements to manage exchange rate risk. Consider a U.S. firm with operations in the United Kingdom that is required to make payments in British pounds. The dollar value of the payments will rise if the pound increases (dollar declines), but the dollar value declines if the pound decreases (dollar increases). The converse is true for a British firm with American operations that must make payments in dollars. Earnings, however, can be increased or *decreased* by fluctuations in the value of the foreign currencies.

One means to reduce the risk of loss is to hedge using the currency futures discussed earlier in this chapter. Swapping payments is another means to reduce the foreign exchange risk. The British firm agrees to make the American firm's required payments in pounds, and the American firm agrees to make the British firm's dollar payments. Since both firms are now making the payments in their native currency, neither has the risk associated with changes in the exchange rate. If the dollar rises (pound falls), the effect on both firms is immaterial.

Swaps involving funds borrowed abroad may also reduce interest expense. Suppose an American firm can borrow in the United States under favorable terms but needs the funds in England where the cost of the loan will be greater. A British firm can borrow in England at a lower rate but needs the funds in the United States. In both cases the firm saves interest expense if it borrows in the domestic market. However, since the funds are needed abroad, they will have to be converted into the local currency. Once converted, the firm now faces exchange rate risk when the funds are exchanged back to retire the loans.

If the American firm could borrow in the United States and the British firm could borrow in England and then agree to swap the liabilities, each firm would have a loan denominated in its currency. To accomplish this swap, the firms use a swap dealer (usually a large financial institution, such as a major commercial bank) who charges a fee for the service. The American firm issues dollar-denominated debt and passes the funds to the dealer. The dealer, in turn, passes the funds to the British firm. Simultaneously, the British firm issues debt denominated in pounds and passes the funds to the dealer, who passes the funds to the American firm.

The British firm now pays interest in pounds, and the American firm pays interest in dollars. The net effect is that the American firm has a dollar-denominated debt on its balance sheet but is able to use pounds. Since the debt is denominated in dollars by the swap agreement, there is no exchange rate risk. In addition, the interest expense may actually be lower if the firm is able to issue debt domestically at a lower interest rate. The converse is true for the British firm, which has borrowed in pounds but can use dollars.

For this swap to occur, both parties must perceive a benefit and the amounts must be comparable. The potential benefits are (1) potential savings in interest expense, (2) reduction in exchange rate risk, or (3) a combination of both. By acting as an intermediary, the swap dealer facilitates the creation of the swap. For this service, the dealer receives a fee.

The potential benefits may be seen by the following simple example in which an American firm needs £625,000 and a British firm needs $1,000,000. A pound costs $1.60. (Conversely, $1.00 buys £0.625.) Given this exchange rate, $1,000,000 equals £625,000. The American firm can borrow $1,000,000 from a domestic bank at 6 percent but must pay 7 percent if it borrows £625,000 from a British bank. The interest payment will be £43,750, and the loan will be denominated in pounds. The British firm can borrow £625,000 for 6 percent in the United Kingdom but must pay 8 percent for $1,000,000 in the United States. The interest cost will be $80,000, and the loan will be denominated in dollars.

In this case, there is an interest savings if the two firms swap obligations. A swap dealer arranges the swap in which each firm borrows the funds in the domestic market and exchanges the obligations. The American firm has the use of £625,000 with an interest cost of £37,500. The interest savings is £6,250, which is $10,000 at the current exchange rate. The British firm has the use of $1,000,000 with an interest cost of $60,000. The interest savings is $20,000, which is £12,500 at the current exchange rate. There is a net interest savings to both firms from the swap.

The previous example illustrates the potential interest savings if each party can borrow at a lower interest cost in a particular market. The next example illustrates the reduction of exchange rate risk. Assume the amounts borrowed and the exchange rate are the same as in the previous example, and the interest rate is 6 percent for both parties in both markets. (Equal interest rates removes the savings from interest payments, so the impact of changing exchange rates is highlighted.) Under these assumptions the American firm borrows $1,000,000 at 6 percent ($60,000 interest payment) and the British firm borrows £625,000 at 6 percent (£37,500 interest payment). The firms swap the funds so both firms get the use of the money in the foreign currency.

Suppose after a year when the loan is repaid, the exchange rate is $1.00 = £0.50 (£1.00 = $2.00). The American firm pays $1,060,000 to retire the loan. If the firm had borrowed £625,000, it would owe £625,000 + £3,750 = £628,750. The cost in dollars of the pounds would be $1,257,500. The savings from the swap is $197,500. The British firm pays £628,750 to retire the loan. If the firm had borrowed $1,000,000, it would owe $1,060,000, which would have cost £530,000. The British firm has lost an opportunity to gain £98,750 ($197,500) from the increased value of the pound. However, the British firm has also avoided any loss that would have occurred if the dollar had risen in value. (The American firm has also lost the opportunity to gain from an increase in the value of the dollar.)

Since firms are generally in business to generate profits from operations and not from exchange rate fluctuations, many firms with international operations participate in swap agreements. For example, in its *2000 Annual Report,* Coca-Cola stated that it had currency swap agreements at the end of 2000 totaling $580,000,000 and that all derivative activities using interest rate swaps, currency swaps, and commodity futures contracts were to manage risk. Without the existence of these derivatives (options, futures, swaps), a firm's exposure to fluctuations in foreign exchange, interest rates, and commodity prices would be increased.

Equity Swaps

In addition to interest rate swaps and currency swaps, there are also equity swaps in which investors swap payments based on a stock index. Consider Investor A with a substantial portfolio of stocks who expects their prices to decline and who would like to move into debt securities. The sale of the stocks may generate taxable gains and will involve transaction costs (commissions). Investor B has substantial holdings of debt securities and anticipates that stock prices will rise. Investor B would like to sell the bonds and purchase stocks. However, the bonds may be illiquid (especially if they are nontaxable municipal bonds) and the sales will involve transaction costs. These two investors could execute a swap agreement that meets each investor's needs.

To see how this equity swap works, assume an amount such as $1,000,000 (the notational principal). If the interest rate is 10 percent, the $1,000,000 earns $100,000 annually. Investor A, who wants the bonds, agrees to pay Investor B the return on the S&P 500 stock index. If the index rises by 5 percent, A pays $50,000 ($1,000,000 × 0.05). Investor B, who wants the stocks, agrees to pay Investor A $100,000 annually. For each year during which the swap agreement is in effect, Investor A receives $100,000 from Investor B and pays B an amount based on the S&P return. If the S&P 500 rises by 10 percent, A pays B $100,000 and B pays A $100,000, so the amounts cancel. The following table sets out other possible cash flows between the two investors based on the return on the stock index.

Cash Flows Investor A

S&P 500 Return	Payment to B	Payment from B	Net
15%	$150,000	$100,000	($50,000)
4	40,000	100,000	60,000
−3	−30,000	100,000	130,000

Cash Flows Investor B

S&P 500 Return	Payment to A	Payment from A	Net
15%	$100,000	$150,000	$50,000
4	100,000	40,000	(60,000)
−3	100,000	−30,000	(130,000)

If the S&P return is 15 percent, A receives $100,000 but must pay $150,000, so there is a net cash outflow of $50,000 to B. If the S&P return is 4 percent, A receives $100,000 but only has to pay $40,000, so A nets $60,000. In the case when the S&P return is −3 percent, A receives $100,000 from B plus an additional $30,000 because the index return is negative.

Investor B's cash flows are, of course, the mirror image of A's. When the return on the S&P index exceeds 10 percent, Investor A's payments to B exceed the $100,000 B has agreed to make. B then receives a net cash inflow. If the S&P return is less than 10 percent, B's payments to A exceed the cash received, and B experiences a net cash outflow. Actually, only the net cash flow payments are made. If the return on the market is 15 percent, there is no need for A to pay B $150,000 and for B to pay A $100,000. Only the net cash flow payment is made, which in this case would be the $50,000 payment from A to B.

What advantage does this swap offer each investor? The answer is that the swap approximates what would have happened if the parties had made their portfolio changes. Suppose A had sold $1,000,000 worth of stock to buy the 10 percent bonds and the market rose 15 percent. The investor would earn $100,000 in interest but had an opportunity loss of $150,000 in capital appreciation. By entering the swap, the investor experiences a cash outflow of $50,000, so the end result is essentially the same, except the investor avoided all the transaction costs associated with security sales and subsequent purchases and avoided all the tax consequences of the sales.

From B's perspective, selling the bonds would have resulted in forgoing $100,000 in interest but the stock purchases would have generated $150,000 in appreciation. The net difference is the $50,000, which is essentially the same as the $50,000 cash inflow from the swap. By executing the swap, Investor B avoided the transaction costs and any marketability or liquidity problems associated with selling the debt instruments.

In this illustration, the swap occurred when two investors wanted to alter their portfolios from equity to debt (and vice versa). Other possible equity swaps may occur if investors want to move from one sector to another or to alter their exposure to foreign securities. For example, one investor wants to reduce holdings of large cap stocks in favor of small cap stocks, while another investor wants fewer small cap stocks in favor of large cap stocks. In this case, a swap is based on indices of large and small cap stocks. The investor who wants the large cap stocks would receive payments based on the large cap index and make payments based on the performance of the small cap index. The investor wanting greater exposure to small cap stocks would make and receive the opposite payments (i.e., receive payments based on the small cap index and make payments based on the large cap index).

The same basic principle applies to equity swaps involving foreign securities. Consider an American investor who wants to diversify by including foreign securities. Simultaneously, a foreign investor wants to diversify by owning American securities. Instead of each investor acquiring foreign securities, a swap is arranged. The American investor would receive payment based on an index of foreign securities and make payments based on an index of American securities. The foreign investor would make payments based on his or her domestic index and receive payments based on the performance of the index of American securities. The American investor will receive a net cash inflow if the foreign index generates the higher return but will have to make payments if the foreign index has the lower return. That is essentially the same result that would have occurred if American stocks had been sold to buy foreign stocks. Higher returns abroad would have resulted in an increased return to the American investor, while lower returns abroad would have produced lower returns. The swap agreement achieves a similar result without having to buy and sell individual stocks.

Summary

Investing in commodity futures involves the buying or selling of contracts for future delivery. The speculator may take a long position, which is the purchase of a contract for future delivery, or a short position, which is the sale of a contract for future delivery. The long position generates profits if the commodity's price rises, while the short position results in a gain if the price falls.

Commodity contracts are purchased through brokers who own seats on commodity exchanges. The contracts are supported by deposits, which are called *margin,* that signify the investor's good faith. The margin requirement is only a small fraction of the value of the contract, and this produces considerable potential for leverage. A small change in the price of the commodity produces a large profit or loss relative to the small amount of margin. For this reason, commodity contracts are considered very speculative.

Hedging plays an important role in commodity futures markets. Growers, miners, and users of commodities often wish to reduce their risk of loss from price fluctuations and thus hedge their positions. Growers sell contracts for future delivery, and users buy contracts for future delivery. Frequently, it is the speculators who are buying and offering the contracts sought by the hedgers. In this way the risks that the hedgers seek to reduce are passed on to the speculators.

The price of a commodity, and thus the value of a futures contract, is related to the supply of and the demand for the commodity. Speculators may use technical or fundamental analysis to help forecast supply, demand, and price movements. Unfortunately, many exogenous factors, such as the weather or government intervention, make accurate forecasting difficult. These forces also contribute to the price fluctuations experienced in the commodity markets and are a major source of the risk associated with investing in commodity futures.

Besides commodity futures there are financial futures, currency futures, and stock index futures. Financial futures are contracts for the delivery of financial assets, such as U.S. Treasury bills and bonds. Currency futures are contracts for the future delivery of foreign moneys, such as Japanese yen or British pounds. Stock index futures are based on a broad measure of the market (e.g., the New York Stock Exchange Composite Index). Speculators who anticipate movements in interest rates, foreign currencies, or the stock market can speculate on these anticipated price changes by taking appropriate positions in futures contracts. As with all commodity contracts, the potential return may be quite large, but the risk of loss is also large. Speculating in commodity futures is probably best left to those few investors who understand these potential risks and can afford to take them.

The creation of stock index futures and the rise of programmed trading have resulted in stock index arbitrage. When the value of a stock index futures contract deviates from the value of the underlying stocks in the index, an opportunity for arbitrage is created. If the value of the contract exceeds the value of the shares, arbitrageurs will short the contracts and buy the shares. The converse occurs when the value of the contract is less than the value of the shares, in which case the arbitrageurs buy the futures and sell the shares. These transactions are done simultaneously through the use of computers that are preprogrammed to enter the buy and sell orders when a divergence between the stock index futures and the stock index develops.

The combining of stock index futures and programmed trading links the securities and futures markets. Changes in one are quickly transferred to the other. This linkage has resulted in significant swings in the prices of individual stocks when the arbitrageurs enter large numbers of buy or sell orders. This increased price volatility has led to the suggestion that programmed trading be banned.

A swap is an agreement in which two parties agree to exchange payments. Swap agreements are not a method to increase profits but a means to manage risk, especially exchange rate or interest rate risk. A firm with operations in a foreign country may swap payments with a firm in that country to avoid having to convert one currency to another. A firm that is required to make fixed payments but would prefer to make variable payments may swap the fixed payments with a firm that is obligated to make variable payments. As a result of the swap both firms may be better able to match their cash inflows with required payments.

Questions

1) What is a futures contract? What are the spot price and the futures price of a commodity? When must the two prices be equal?
2) Why is investing in commodity futures considered to be speculative?
3) What is the difference between a long and a short position in a commodity future?
4) What is margin and why is it a source of leverage? What is a margin call? How does margin for futures differ from margin for stocks?
5) Why do farmers and other users of commodity futures hedge their positions?
6) If an investor anticipates a decline in a commodity's price, which futures position should he or she take?
7) How may government intervention affect commodity prices? Are commodity futures markets subject to government regulation?
8) What is a financial futures contract? If you expect interest rates to rise, should you buy or sell a financial futures contract?
9) If you anticipated that the price of the British pound would rise and wanted to speculate on that increase, should you sell or buy a contract for the delivery of pounds?
10) What is the difference between the long and the short positions in a contract for the future delivery of the S&P 500 stock index? If you expect stock prices to fall, do you buy or sell stock index futures?
11) How do changes in the futures market for stock indices affect the stock market? Why may stock index futures and programmed trading result in dramatic price changes in individual stocks?
12) How does the swapping of payments reduce a firm's risk exposure? When would an individual find it desirable to enter a swap agreement?

Problems

1) You expect the stock market to decline, but instead of selling a stock short, you decide to sell a stock index futures contract based on the New York Stock Exchange Composite Index. The index is currently 138, and the contract has a value that is 500 times the amount of the index. The margin requirement is $3,500 and the maintenance margin requirement is $1,000.
   a) When you *sell* the contract, how much must you put up?
   b) What is the value of the contract based on the index?
   c) If after one week of trading the index stands at 140, what has happened to your position? How much have you lost or profited?
   d) If the index rose to 144, what would you be required to do?
   e) If the index declined to 136.6 (approximately 1 percent from the starting value), what is your percentage profit or loss on your position?
   f) If you had purchased the contract instead of selling it, how much would you have invested?
   g) If you had purchased the contract and the index subsequently rose from 138 to 144, what would be your required investment?
   h) Contrast your answers to parts (d) and (g).
2) This problem illustrates hedging with currency futures. The questions lead you through the process of hedging. While this material was not explicitly covered in the text material, your instructor may use this problem to show how hedging may reduce the risk of loss from fluctuations in the price of a foreign currency.

You expect to receive a payment of 1,000,000 British pounds after six months. The pound is currently worth $1.60 (i.e., £1 = $1.60), but the six-month futures price is $1.56 (i.e., £1 = $1.56). You expect the price of the pound to decline (i.e., the value of the dollar to rise). If this expectation is fulfilled, you will suffer a loss when the pounds are converted into dollars when you receive them six months in the future.

a) Given the current price, what is the expected payment in dollars?
b) Given the futures price, how much would you receive in dollars?
c) If, after six months, the pound is worth $1.35, what is your loss from the decline in the value of the pound?
d) To avoid this potential loss, you decide to hedge and sell a contract for the future delivery of pounds at the going futures price of $1.56. What is the cost to you of this protection from the possible decline in the value of the pound?
e) If, after hedging, the price of the pound falls to $1.35, what is the maximum amount that you lose? (Why is your answer different from your answer to part (c)?)
f) If, after hedging, the price of the pound rises to $1.80, how much do you gain from your position?
g) How would your answer be different to part (f) if you had not hedged and the price of the pound had risen to $1.80?

3) One use for futures markets is "price discovery," that is, the futures price mirrors the current consensus of the future price of the commodity. The current price of gold is $350 but you expect the price to rise to $400. If the futures price were $390, what would you do? If your expectation is fulfilled, what is your profit? If the futures price were $418, what would you do? What futures price will cause you to take no action? Why?

4) The current price of wheat is $3.70 and the expenses for carrying wheat (combined cost of storage, insurance, shipping) are 20 percent of the price. Based on this information, what should be the price of wheat after a year? What would you do if the futures price were $4.55?

5) Two institutional investors execute a swap agreement for $10,000,000 in which one party agrees to remit to the counterparty the return on the EAFE, an index of European, Australasian, and Far-Eastern stocks. The counterparty agrees to remit payments based on the return on the S&P 500. During the next four time periods, the returns on the two indices are as follows:

Period	S&P 500	EAFE
1	5%	12%
2	−5	8
3	15	0
4	−2	−7

What are the cash flows between the two parties for each time period?

THE FINANCIAL ADVISOR'S INVESTMENT CASE

Futures to Defer Taxes

One of your most sophisticated investors, David Lyman, believes that the stock market will decline and hence reduce the value of his substantial portfolio. However, he does not want to sell the stocks, because the sales would generate a substantial federal capital gains tax liability in the current tax year. He recently read that futures may be used to reduce the risk of loss from price changes as well as vehicles designed to speculate on price changes. You have been his personal financial planner for many years, and he has asked you to develop a strategy using futures to achieve his goal of protecting his gains without selling the securities in the current year.

Since Lyman has a long position in stocks, you realize that he needs a short position in futures to reduce the risk of loss. Since his portfolio is both substantial and well diversified, you decide to limit your choices to index futures. The portfolio is worth several million dollars, but you decide to use $1,000,000 as the basis for all comparisons since any other amount could be expressed as a multiple of $1,000,000. You notice that an index of the market is 100 and there exists a futures contract with a value that is 500 times the index. The margin requirement is $2,000 per contract. You decide that the best means to explain the strategy using futures is to answer a series of questions that illustrate how the futures may be used to meet Lyman's goal of deferring the tax obligation until the next year while protecting his gains. These questions are as follows:

1) What is the value of the contract in terms of the index?

2) How many contracts would Lyman have to sell to hedge $1,000,000? Why should Lyman sell rather than purchase the contracts?

3) How much cash will Lyman have to put up to meet the margin requirement? If the annual interest rate on money market securities is 6 percent, what is the interest lost from the margin requirement if the position must be maintained for two months?

4) If the market declined by 5 percent, what will happen to the value of the contracts? Could Lyman take funds out of the position to reduce the interest lost?

5) If the beta of his portfolio is 1.0 and the market declines by 5 percent, how much would he lose on a $1,000,000 portfolio?

6) If the beta of the portfolio were less than 1.0, could Lyman hedge his portfolio by selling fewer contracts?

7) If the market rose by 10 percent, what would be the impact on Lyman's stocks and his position in the futures? How would the market's increase affect his margin? What is the possible impact on the interest earned or lost by hedging the portfolio?

8) When the contracts expire, will Lyman have to deliver his securities?

Portfolio Management

5

PART

The last three chapters in this textbook are concerned with the individual's portfolio. Chapter 22 adds international investments, and Chapter 23 adds nonfinancial assets, such as collectibles, precious metals, natural resources, and real estate. While each of these investments offers a potential return, they also help diversify the individual's portfolio. Risk reduction is a primary reason for including foreign securities and nonfinancial assets in a portfolio since their returns may not be highly correlated with returns from financial assets.

The text ends with a discussion of portfolio planning and construction. This process is not easy since it requires analytical thought and possibly extensive calculations. There are so many assets from which to choose; the economic environment can be very dynamic; the tax code is complex; and individuals' obligations and resources change throughout their lives. But these difficulties are no reason to avoid planning one's financial future and constructing a well-diversified portfolio that offers as high a return as possible consistent with one's willingness to bear risk.

Of course, investors must also determine how actively they want to manage their portfolios. While some investors do manage their own funds, many individuals delegate this responsibility. They employ the service of a financial planner and acquire shares in investment companies instead of selecting individual securities. The text ends with a discussion of factors to consider when selecting a money manager or an investment company. The factors include historical returns earned on investments, taxation, and the implications of the efficient financial markets for financial planning.

22 Investing in Foreign Securities

For many individuals living in the United States, investment in stocks or bonds means the purchase of securities issued by American firms even though many corporations (e.g., Coca-Cola) have substantial foreign operations. However, confining investments to the securities of U.S. corporations is a narrow approach to security selection. Stocks and bonds are actively traded in many countries. The shares of large, global American firms (e.g., IBM) are traded on several foreign exchanges. Conversely, the shares of large foreign companies (e.g., SONY) trade in the United States. Trading occurs 24 hours a day. While specific markets (e.g., the New York Stock Exchange) have limited trading hours, the shares of many American and foreign firms trade virtually all the time on global markets. The effect is to have a continuous market or "around-the-clock trading" in these securities. Events that occur while a particular exchange is closed still have an immediate impact on the value of stocks and bonds traded on international security markets.

Interest in foreign securities by American investors increased during the late 1980s. Today, stock prices for many foreign companies and foreign stock indexes are reported daily in *The Wall Street Journal*. These include the Tokyo Nikkei Average, the London FT 30-share index, the London FT-SE 100-share index, the Frankfurt DAX, the Paris CAC index, and the EAFE index. The EAFE is a general index of non-U.S. stocks, computed by Morgan Stanley, comprising stocks in Europe, Australasia, and the Far East, hence the EAFE acronym. Salomon Brothers, First Boston, Goldman Sachs, and Dow Jones also publish indexes of world equity markets.

This chapter is concerned with foreign investments from the perspective of a U.S. investor. It stresses the special risks associated with foreign investments, the reduction of risk through derivative securities, the use of foreign securities to diversify the individual's portfolio, and investment companies that offer a means to take a position in foreign securities without having to select specific foreign stocks and bonds.

Learning Objectives

After completing this chapter you should be able to:

1. Enumerate the advantages and risks associated with foreign investments.
2. Define foreign exchange, foreign exchange markets, and exchange rate risk and contrast devaluation and revaluation.
3. Differentiate balance of payments from balance of trade and the current account from the capital account.
4. Explain how hedging is used to reduce exchange rate risk.
5. Explain how and why foreign investments diversify a domestic portfolio.

Global Wealth and World Financial Markets

The value of the world's equity markets is substantial. Exhibit 22.1 presents an estimate of the value of the 12 largest stock markets.[1] The United States is a dominant world economic power; its equity markets accounted for over half the total value of the world's stock markets. The growth of a common economic unit in Europe and the development of Far-Eastern economies such as Korea suggest that the U.S. market may become a declining part of the world's total equity market. However, the decline in many of these stock markets during the late 1990s has produced the opposite effect. In 1994, the U.S. stock market accounted for only 41.0 percent of the total. By 2000, that amount had risen to 54.8 percent.

The existence and size of global assets argues for foreign assets to be included in the portfolios of American investors. Foreign investments generally imply the acquisition of assets in advanced economies (i.e., developed countries, or DCs), but emerging economies (i.e., less-developed countries, or LDCs), such as Chile, Korea, and Thailand, also offer investment opportunities for growth or possible diversification.

In addition to LDCs, the change in the political environment in eastern Europe and the states of the former Soviet Union offer opportunities for the adventuresome investor. Equity markets are developing in former communist countries. Even if the U.S. investor does not purchase securities issued in these countries, the individual may purchase stock in firms expanding operations in eastern Europe and less-developed economies. Of course, for this strategy to generate a positive return, the firm's earnings must increase as a result of the foreign investments. Because most of the firms capable of making these investments will be large, global

EXHIBIT 22.1

Estimated Size of the 12 Largest Equity Markets, 2000

Country	Value of Equity (in Billions of U.S. Dollars)	Percent of Total
United States	$13,112	54.8%
Japan	2,892	12.1
United Kingdom	2,111	8.8
France	1,154	4.8
Germany	896	3.7
Italy	587	2.5
Switzerland	577	2.4
Netherlands	555	2.3
Canada	435	1.8
Sweden	326	1.4
Spain	253	1.1
Australia	222	0.9

Source: Morgan Stanley Capital International Inc.; reported in *Business Week*, July 10, 2000, 114–144.

[1]Descriptions of foreign security markets, the growth in new foreign security issues, the development of dual-tranche offerings (offering of securities in two or more countries), and the regulation of foreign securities issued in the United States and domestic securities issued abroad may be found in Jonathan Clements, ed., *Stock Answers—A Guide to the International Equities Market* (New York: Nichols Publishing, 1988); Roger G. Ibbotson, *Global Investing* (New York: McGraw-Hill, 1993); and Summer Levine, ed., *Global Investing* (New York: Harper Business, 1992).

firms, it may be impossible to isolate the impact that eastern Europe will have on these firms' bottom lines.

The Special Considerations Associated with Foreign Investments

U.S. residents invest in foreign securities to earn a return through the receipt of income (dividends or interest) and price appreciation. These investments involve special considerations that affect the return the investor earns and the risk that must be borne. These factors include political risks, local taxation, and the fluctuation of the U.S. dollar relative to foreign currencies (i.e., exchange rate risk). The latter is particularly important since any return received in foreign funds must be converted into U.S. dollars before the investor can use the money in the United States. Obviously, the investor who receives dividends in British pounds can spend the funds in London, but those pounds must be converted into dollars before they can be spent in the United States.

Political Risks

The political climate of a foreign nation creates risks because governments and political systems do change. The potential for this change must be considered by a U.S. business seeking to expand its market through foreign operations. Firms with foreign investments have experienced nationalization and expropriation of assets. These firms are not guaranteed compensation for any seized assets. For example, Cuba did not offer compensation when Fidel Castro came to power and nationalized the facilities of U.S. firms.

Political risk, which is also referred to as "sovereign" risk, could be considered a type of unsystematic risk in that it applies to a specific country. As with other sources of unsystematic risk, political risk may be reduced and perhaps virtually erased through investing in several countries. Just as diversification across industries reduces firm-specific risk, investing in firms in different countries reduces country-specific political risk.

Foreign Taxation

Foreign taxation further complicates foreign investments and reduces the return earned by the individual. Just as the U.S. government taxes dividend income, foreign governments may also tax dividend and interest payments. To facilitate the collection of the funds, these taxes are usually withheld before the U.S. investor receives the money. For example, if the usual withholding is 10 percent and a British firm distributes a cash dividend of £100, £10 are withheld and £90 remitted to the U.S. holder. For example, BP ADRs (British Petroleum Amoco) paid a per-share dividend of $0.35 in June 2001, but $0.035 was withheld to pay British taxes.

If the American investor owns the actual stock, the payment is made in pounds, which must be converted into dollars to be used in the United States. If the U.S. investor owns the American depositary receipts (ADRs), the bank that is the stock's transfer agent receives the payment, converts the pounds into dollars, and remits the funds to the holder of the ADR. The bank collects a fee for this service. However, since the bank exchanges large amounts of foreign currency, any fee charged will probably be less than the individual investor would have to pay to have the pounds converted into dollars.

The dividends (and interest) received from foreign investments are also subject to income taxation in the United States. If the investor is in the 28 percent federal income tax bracket, then 28 percent of the £100 is subject to tax. To facilitate the illustration, assume a pound is worth $2, so the dividend is $200 ($2.00 × 100). The federal income tax would be $56 ($200 × 0.28). This tax is in addition to the £10 ($20) that the British government has already withheld. The U.S. federal government permits the U.S. investor to take a foreign tax credit for the amount of the foreign tax. Thus, the net amount owed to the U.S. federal government is $36 ($56 − $20).

Fluctuations in Exchange Rates

In addition to income, investors acquire assets for possible capital gains. In the case of foreign investments, capital gains may occur because the value of the asset rises or because the value of the foreign currency in which the asset is denominated rises. Since capital gains are related to the price of the asset as well as the value of the currency, it is possible for the price of the foreign asset to rise but for this price increase to be offset by a decline in the value of that country's currency. It is also possible for the price of the foreign asset to decline but for the price decline to be offset by an increase in the value of that country's currency.

The previous section considered political risks and foreign taxation; this section covers the risk from fluctuations in the value of the U.S. dollar relative to other currencies. Since fluctuations in the value of currencies can enhance or reduce the return earned on foreign investments, these fluctuations affect the risk associated with investing in foreign assets. This risk is in addition to the usual risks the investor must bear: the diversifiable, unsystematic risk associated with the particular asset and the nondiversifiable, systematic risk from fluctuations in market prices, changes in interest rates, and the loss of purchasing power through inflation.

The value of currencies responds to changes in the demand and supply for the currencies. The demand for foreign investments (as well as foreign goods and services) is also a demand for foreign money. To acquire these funds, buyers must exchange their currency for the foreign currency. For example, if U.S. citizens want to purchase stocks and bonds denominated in British pounds, they must exchange dollars for pounds. The opposite is true when British citizens seek to purchase securities denominated in U.S. dollars. These investors must exchange pounds for dollars.

foreign exchange market
Market for the buying and selling of currencies.

exchange rate
The price of a foreign currency in terms of another currency.

The market for foreign currencies is called the **foreign exchange market**. The price of one currency in terms of another is referred to as the **exchange rate**. Currencies are traded daily, and the prices of major currencies are reported in the financial press. Although these prices change daily, such reporting gives the investor a close indication of the currencies' current prices.

Exhibit 22.2 (p. 732), a clipping from *The Wall Street Journal*, gives the exchange rates for various currencies as of August 1, 2001. At that time the price of a British pound was $1.4345. Anyone holding American dollars would have to pay $1.4345 to purchase a British pound. (Conversely, 1 pound would have purchased $1.4345.) The clipping also expresses the value of the foreign currency in terms of $1, which would have purchased 0.6971 pounds. This amount (0.6971) may be derived by dividing $1.00 by the dollar price of the foreign currency. For example, $1/1.4345 = 0.6971 units of the British currency. Exhibit 22.2 also includes a table of cross rates. This is the same information as in the table of exchange rates. Reading down the Dollar column indicates that $1 would have bought 0.6971 pounds. Reading down the Pound column indicates that 1 pound would have bought $1.435. You may obtain the same information by reading across. For the U.K., the 0.6971 indicates the cost of $1; for the United States, 1.4345 indicates the cost of a pound.

An imbalance in the demand for or supply of a currency causes its price to change. Excess demand generates a higher price and excess supply depresses the

EXHIBIT 22.2

Selected Foreign Exchange Rates, August 1, 2001

CURRENCY TRADING

Wednesday, August 1, 2001

EXCHANGE RATES

The New York foreign exchange mid-range rates below apply to trading among banks in amounts of $1 million and more, as quoted at 4 p.m. Eastern time by Reuters and other sources. Retail transactions provide fewer units of foreign currency per dollar. Rates for the 12 Euro currency countries are derived from the latest dollar-euro rate using the exchange ratios set 1/1/99.

Country	U.S. $ EQUIV. Wed	U.S. $ EQUIV. Tue	CURRENCY PER U.S. $ Wed	CURRENCY PER U.S. $ Tue
Argentina (Peso)	1.0006	1.0004	.9994	.9996
Australia (Dollar)	.5186	.5093	1.9281	1.9633
Austria (Schilling)	.06404	.06363	15.616	15.715
Bahrain (Dinar)	2.6525	2.6525	.3770	.3770
Belgium (Franc)	.0218	.0217	45.7810	46.0712
Brazil (Real)	.4023	.4044	2.4855	2.4730
Britain (Pound)	1.4345	1.4259	.6971	.7013
1-month forward	1.4327	1.4241	.6980	.7022
3-months forward	1.4289	1.4205	.6998	.7040
6-months forward	1.4236	1.4152	.7024	.7066
Canada (Dollar)	.6504	.6521	1.5375	1.5335
1-month forward	.6501	.6518	1.5382	1.5342
3-months forward	.6495	.6513	1.5397	1.5355
6-months forward	.6487	.6504	1.5415	1.5374
Chile (Peso)	.001471	.001492	679.65	670.25
China (Renminbi)	.1208	.1208	8.2769	8.2770
Colombia (Peso)	.0004347	.0004366	2300.50	2290.50
Czech. Rep. (Koruna)				
Commercial rate	.02595	.02578	38.532	38.795
Denmark (Krone)	.1183	.1176	8.4536	8.5057
Ecuador (US Dollar)-e	1.0000	1.0000	1.0000	1.0000
Finland (Markka)	.1482	.1473	6.7477	6.7905
France (Franc)	.1343	.1335	7.4443	7.4915
1-month forward	.1342	.1334	7.4491	7.4967
3-months forward	.1341	.1332	7.4593	7.5065
6-months forward	.1339	.1330	7.4695	7.5179
Germany (Mark)	.4505	.4477	2.2196	2.2337
1-month forward	.4502	.4474	2.2211	2.2353
3-months forward	.4496	.4468	2.2241	2.2382
6-months forward	.4490	.4461	2.2271	2.2416
Greece (Drachma)	.002586	.002570	386.71	389.07
Hong Kong (Dollar)	.1282	.1282	7.7997	7.7996
Hungary (Forint)	.003546	.003531	281.99	283.24
India (Rupee)	.02123	.02122	47.110	47.130
Indonesia (Rupiah)	.0001039	.0001053	9625	9500
Ireland (Punt)	1.1188	1.1117	.8938	.8995
Israel (Shekel)	.2374	.2374	4.2130	4.2120
Italy (Lira)	.0004551	.0004522	2197.44	2211.36
Japan (Yen)	.008031	.007997	124.52	125.05
1-month forward	.008057	.008024	124.12	124.63
3-months forward	.008105	.008069	123.38	123.93
6-months forward	.008177	.008143	122.30	122.81
Jordan (Dinar)	1.4069	1.4069	.7108	.7108
Kuwait (Dinar)	3.2595	3.2552	.3068	.3072
Lebanon (Pound)	.0006605	.0006605	1514.00	1514.00
Malaysia (Ringgit)-b	.2632	.2632	3.8001	3.8000
Malta (Lira)	2.2070	2.1968	.4531	.4552
Mexico (Peso)				
Floating rate	.1084	.1090	9.2215	9.1710
Netherlands (Guilder)	.3999	.3973	2.5009	2.5168
New Zealand (Dollar)	.4184	.4135	2.3901	2.4184
Norway (Krone)	.1099	.1096	9.0959	9.1220
Pakistan (Rupee)	.01562	.01565	64.025	63.900
Peru (new Sol)	.2858	.2866	3.4990	3.4895
Philippines (Peso)	.01860	.01867	53.750	53.550
Poland (Zloty)-d	.2350	.2348	4.2550	4.2596
Portugal (Escudo)	.004395	.004367	227.52	228.97
Russia (Ruble)-a	.03408	.03407	29.344	29.354
Saudi Arabia (Riyal)	.2666	.2666	3.7509	3.7505
Singapore (Dollar)	.5541	.5546	1.8047	1.8030
Slovak Rep. (Koruna)	.02038	.02021	49.078	49.469
South Africa (Rand)	.1213	.1210	8.2454	8.2638
South Korea (Won)	.0007740	.0007704	1292.00	1298.00
Spain (Peseta)	.005296	.005262	188.83	190.03
Sweden (Krona)	.0948	.0945	10.5450	10.5870
Switzerland (Franc)	.5836	.5789	1.7135	1.7275
1-month forward	.5838	.5791	1.7128	1.7268
3-months forward	.5843	.5795	1.7115	1.7255
6-months forward	.5851	.5804	1.7090	1.7229
Taiwan (Dollar)	.02880	.02878	34.720	34.750
Thailand (Baht)	.02188	.02188	45.705	45.705
Turkey (Lira)-f	.00000075	.00000075	1329500	1330000
United Arab (Dirham)	.2723	.2723	3.6729	3.6729
Uruguay (New Peso)				
Financial	.07508	.07508	13.320	13.320
Venezuela (Bolivar)	.001377	.001379	726.36	725.37
SDR	1.2614	1.2588	.7928	.7944
Euro	.8812	.8756	1.1348	1.1421

Special Drawing Rights (SDR) are based on exchange rates for the U.S., German, British, French , and Japanese currencies. Source: International Monetary Fund.

a-Russian Central Bank rate. b-Government rate. d-Floating rate; trading band suspended on 4/11/00. e-Adopted U.S. dollar as of 9/11/00. f-Floating rate, eff. Feb. 22.

Price of a British Pound in Dollars

Price of $1.00 in British Pounds

KEY CURRENCY CROSS RATES

Late New York Trading Wednesday, August 1, 2001

	Dollar	Euro	Pound	SFranc	Guilder	Peso	Yen	Lira	D-Mark	FFranc	CdnDlr
Canada	1.5375	1.3548	2.2055	0.8973	.61478	.16673	.01235	.00070	.69269	.20653	....
France	7.4443	6.5599	10.6788	4.3445	2.9766	.80728	.05978	.00339	3.3539	....	4.8418
Germany	2.2196	1.9559	3.1840	1.2954	.88752	.24070	.01783	.00101	....	.29816	1.4436
Italy	2197.4	1936.4	3152.2	1282.4	878.65	238.29	17.647	....	990.01	295.18	1429.2
Japan	124.52	109.73	178.62	72.670	49.790	13.503	....	.05667	56.100	16.727	80.989
Mexico	9.2215	8.1260	13.228	5.3817	3.6873	....	.07406	.00420	4.1546	1.2387	5.9977
Netherlands	2.5009	2.2038	3.5875	1.4595	....	.27120	.02008	.00114	1.1267	.33595	1.6266
Switzerland	1.7135	1.5099	2.4580	....	.68515	.18582	.01376	.00078	.77199	.23018	1.1145
U.K.	.69710	.6143	....	.4068	.27874	.07560	.00560	.00032	.31407	.09364	.45340
Euro	1.13480	....	1.6279	.66228	.45376	.12306	.00911	.00052	.51127	.15244	.73809
U.S.	....	.8812	1.4345	.58360	.39986	.10844	.00803	.00046	.45053	.13433	.65041

Source: Reuters

Source: *The Wall Street Journal,* Eastern Edition (August 1, 2001, C10). Staff-produced copy.

devaluation

A decrease in the value of one currency relative to other currencies.

revaluation

An increase in the value of one currency relative to other currencies.

price. Such price changes are often referred to as devaluation (or depreciation) and revaluation. With a **devaluation**, the price of one currency declines relative to all other currencies. A **revaluation** (or appreciation) is an increase in the price of one nation's currency relative to all other currencies.

Under the current international monetary system, such devaluations and revaluations occur daily, for the prices of currencies are permitted to fluctuate. If the demand for a particular currency rises so that the demand exceeds the supply, the price of that currency rises relative to other currencies. If the supply of the currency exceeds the demand, the price falls. There are continual devaluations of some currencies and revaluations of others as their prices vary daily in accordance with supply and demand.

The demand for and supply of a currency are related to the demand for and supply of the goods and services the country produces and the flow of investments into and out of the country. If British goods and services are cheaper than those in other countries, this will generate an increase in the quantity demanded. If Great Britain offers good investment opportunities, firms and individuals will seek to buy British securities and invest in plant and equipment located in Britain. In both cases, the buying of foreign goods and services and the making of foreign investments create a demand for the British currency and a supply of other currencies. The price of the pound should rise to equate the demand for and supply of each currency. Since demand and supply constantly change, currency prices fluctuate daily in an effort to equate the demand for and supply of each currency.

Demand for and supply of a currency are ultimately related to the demand for and supply of goods, services, and capital—but costs of production, consumer tastes for particular goods, and barriers to trade are some of the root causes of changes in exchange rates.[2] For example, consider the 1994 decline in the dollar vis-à-vis the yen. Although U.S. demand for domestically produced cars certainly improved during the 1990s, considerable demand existed for foreign cars, especially luxury cars manufactured in Germany and Japan. Barriers to trade with Japan artificially altered the demand for and supply of automobiles. Japanese "voluntary" export quotas of cars reduced the U.S. supply. Japanese restrictions on both exports to Japan and firm operations in Japan altered their domestic supply of cars. These imbalances in the supply and demand of cars (and other consumer goods) contributed to the decline in the dollar and the rise in the yen.

During the late 1990s, the dollar reversed its decline against many currencies, especially those of the countries of the Far East. As the economies of Japan and other countries fell into severe recessions, and political turmoil developed in Russia, investors wanted a "safe haven" for all their funds. Such non-American investors bought dollars, so the value of the dollar rose against the yen, the ruble, and other currencies. In mid-1995, $1.00 bought 100.98 yen, but by mid-1998, $1.00 bought 133.24 yen. Subsequently, the dollar has remained strong against the yen and in July 2001, $1.00 bought 124 yen.

Discrepancies in interest rates between countries and differences in the rate (or expected rate) of inflation also affect exchange rates. Declines in interest rates or increased inflation encourage currency to flow to countries with higher rates or more stable prices. Lower U.S. short-term rates during the mid-1990s and the continuing deficit in the federal government's budget encouraged holders of dollars to exchange them for currencies in countries with higher short-term rates and less probability of future inflation. Dollars flowed into some currencies, such as the German mark, rather than others, such as French francs, because of their perceived price stability. Hence, the German mark rose (just as the yen was rising) but the values of other currencies, such as the franc and the peso, declined. (The low rate of inflation and the federal government surplus subsequently helped strengthen the dollar.)

Balance of Payments

All monetary transactions for a period of time between a country and the rest of the world are recorded in the **balance of payments**.[3] While the general time period is a year, many countries compile and report the data quarterly. The balance of payments records transactions by double-entry bookkeeping. Each transaction is recorded as both a debit and a credit, so the total of all debits must equal credits.

balance of payments
An accounting statement that enumerates purchases and sales and currency flow between a country and the rest of the world.

[2]For a general discussion of the factors affecting exchange rates, see David S. Kidwell, Richard L. Peterson, and David W. Blackwell, *Financial Institutions, Markets, and Money*, 7th ed. (Fort Worth, TX: The Dryden Press, 2000), 382–388.

[3]Some transactions do avoid being counted. The value of goods smuggled because they are illegal or because the smugglers wish to avoid tariffs is obviously excluded. In addition, the flight of capital from politically unstable countries may also evade being counted.

However, individual parts or subsets of the balance of payments statement may have a surplus or deficit.

While an elaborate discussion of all the parts of the balance of payments is beyond the scope of this text, the essential parts are (1) the current account, (2) the capital account, and (3) the official reserve account. The **current account** enumerates the value of goods and services imported and exported, government spending abroad, and foreign investment income for the time period. It is the broadest measure of a country's international trade in goods and services.

current account
Part of the balance of payments that enumerates the importing and exporting of goods and services by a nation over a period of time.

The difference between the value of imports and exports is often referred to as a country's *balance of trade.* If a country imports more goods than it exports, it is running a deficit in its "merchandise trade" account. If a country is exporting more goods than it imports, it is running a surplus. A country can run a surplus or a deficit in its balance of trade but not in its balance of payments. For every credit in the balance of payments, there is a corresponding and offsetting debit, so the balance of payments must balance even though the current account may have a surplus or deficit.

The **capital account** consists of investment flows and measures capital investments made between the domestic country and all other countries. Capital investments include direct investments in plant and equipment in a foreign country and the purchases of foreign securities. Security transactions may be long- or short-term. Long-term transactions are purchases and sales of foreign bonds and stocks. Short-term capital transactions primarily take the form of changes in bank balances held abroad and in foreign money market instruments.

capital account
Part of the balance of payments that enumerates the importing and exporting of investments and long-term securities.

The third account, the **official reserve account**, is a balance account and reflects the change in a country's international reserves. If a country imports more than it exports or makes more foreign investments, its foreign reserves will decline. If a country exports more than it imports and experiences foreign investments, its holding of foreign reserves will rise. These changes in its reserves may also affect its drawing rights on its account with the International Monetary Fund (IMF).

official reserve account
Part of the balance of payments that enumerates changes in a country's international reserves.

An illustration of a balance of payments is presented in Exhibit 22.3. The exhibit is divided into the current account, the capital account, and the official reserve account. The vertical columns give the debits (−) and the credits (+). Credits represent currency inflows while debits are currency outflows, and the sum of the debits and credits must be equal.

The current account starts with merchandise exports, a credit of $224.40, and merchandise imports, a debit of $368.70. The difference ($224.40 − $368.70 = −$144.30) is the merchandise balance of trade, and since the amount is a negative number, that indicates a net currency outflow. The next entry is government spending abroad, a debit of $15.30. If a government spends abroad, that has the same impact on currency flows as individuals' spending abroad. It does not matter whether the government buys goods and services abroad or the nation's citizens buy foreign goods and services. Both are currency outflows (i.e., both are debits).

Net income from investments abroad, a credit of $20.80, is a currency inflow. This currency inflow is the result of previous currency outflows. Current foreign investments in plant and equipment or in foreign securities require currency outflows that are reported in the capital account. These investments may generate future income that will produce a currency inflow in the current account. Of course, foreign investors will also be earning income on their investments in the domestic country. For the country to experience a net currency inflow, the income received from the foreign investments must exceed the income paid foreign investors. In this illustration, the net investment income is a currency inflow of $20.80, which is reported in the credit column. A currency outflow would have been reported in the debit column.

The sum of all these transactions (−$138.80) is the balance on the current account. In this illustration, the net income from previous investments helped offset

EXHIBIT 22.3

Simplified Balance of Payments for the Time Period 12/31/X0 through 12/31/X1

	Debit (−)	Credit (+)	Balance
Current Account			
Exports		$224.40	
Imports	$368.70		
Balance of trade			$(144.30)
Government spending abroad	15.30		
Net income from investment abroad		20.80	
Balance on current account			$(138.80)
Capital Account			
Long-term			
Direct investment abroad	130.10		
Foreign investments in the country		117.60	
Purchases of foreign securities	27.40		
Foreign purchase of domestic securities		41.00	
Short-term			
Purchases of short-term foreign investments	9.30		
Foreign purchases of short-term investments		95.70	
Balance on capital account			87.50
Official Reserves			
Statistical adjustment		3.90	
Net change in foreign reserves		47.40	
	$550.80	$550.80	

some of the current outflow from the merchandise trade balance, but the total on the current account indicates a currency outflow.

The capital account represents currency flows resulting from investments in physical assets, such as plant and equipment, and financial assets, such as stocks and bonds. It also includes investments in short-term financial assets. If a country has a net currency outflow in the current account, that outflow may be offset by an inflow in the capital account. If foreigners use the currency to make investments in that country, the money is returned. Correspondingly, if a country is running a surplus in its current account, it is receiving money it may use to invest in the foreign country. Such investments, of course, may be in actual physical assets or in financial assets. If the receiving country just holds the other country's cash, it is investing in a financial asset. However, the currency is usually invested in an income-earning asset, since holding the money itself earns nothing.

In this illustration, direct investments generate an outflow (a debit of $130.10), while direct foreign investments in the country generate an inflow (a credit of $117.60). Purchases of long-term foreign securities were $27.40, and foreign purchases were $41.00. Purchases of short-term foreign securities were $9.30, while foreign purchases were $95.70. The total credits on the capital account exceeded the debits by $87.50, indicating a cash inflow. If there had been a currency outflow (in other words, debits exceeded credits), the balance would be negative.

The sum of the currency inflows and outflows on the current and capital accounts still may not balance. The official reserve account is the final balancing item that equates the currency inflows and the outflows. If there is a net credit balance on the current and capital accounts, there has to be a debit on the official reserve account. A net credit balance on the official reserve account indicates the opposite, a net debit on the current and capital accounts.

Transactions involving the reserve account can result when the country borrows or repays credit granted by the International Monetary Fund and when it uses or adds to its international reserves created by the IMF. Also, there is a statistical discrepancy account for errors and omissions. These errors can occur when transactions are not recorded (such as illegal transactions). For example, if individuals in a politically unstable country smuggle out money to invest in a safe haven, the transaction may not be recorded on the country's current or capital accounts.

Of all the three accounts in the balance of payments, the merchandise trade balance receives the most publicity. A debit on the merchandise trade account indicates that the country is importing more goods than it is exporting. Money is flowing out of the country into other countries. That money does not disappear, so the question becomes: What happens to this money and what are the implications of the cash outflow? These are not easy questions to answer but are obviously important from the perspective of the country, its commercial banks, and financial managers. The merchandise trade balance for goods and services for the United States from 1970 through 2000 is presented in Figure 22.1. In recent years, the United States has imported a large amount of goods relative to its exports, so the balance is negative and dollars have been flowing out of the country.

Until August 15, 1971, foreigners could demand payment for dollars in gold. When they bought the gold, the currency would be returned to the United States. Today the dollar is not convertible into gold, so foreigners must take another course of action. They may simply hold the dollars. However, since dollars do not earn anything, they will be used to acquire something, such as short-term federal government securities (i.e., Treasury bills). Thus, the willingness of foreigners to hold U.S. financial assets absorbs a large amount of the dollars that flow abroad as a result of the merchandise trade deficit. The purchase of these securities, of course, returns the dollars to the United States.

Even if the foreigners do not return the dollars by purchasing financial assets issued in the United States, they do not retain dollars as such. Instead, the holders deposit the dollars in foreign commercial banks. These deposits may be denominated in dollars (i.e., the dollars are not converted into the local currency). Such dollar-denominated deposits placed in banks in Europe are referred to as **Eurodollars**. A Eurodollar, then, is a deposit in any foreign bank that is denominated in dollars. (The bank need not necessarily be located in Europe: A dollar-denominated deposit located in a Hong Kong bank is still called a Eurodollar.)

Eurodollars
Dollar-denominated deposits in a foreign bank.

The creation of Eurodollar deposits led large European banks to accept deposits in other currencies. For example, a bank in London could have deposits denominated in Swiss francs, dollars, and yen, as well as British pounds. Such deposits resulted in the creation of the term *Eurocurrency.* Eurocurrency deposits, like any deposits, are a source of funds that the bank can lend. Thus, foreign banks may create loans that are denominated in many currencies, as well as those denominated in their local currency.

From the U.S. investor's perspective, the importance of the balance of payments and the deficit or surplus on the current account is the potential impact on the value of the dollar. If the current and capital accounts are running a deficit and dollars are flowing abroad, that suggests the value of the dollar will decline as the holders supply dollars and demand other currencies. Such a decline will increase the value of foreign securities and may increase their return when the foreign currency is converted back into dollars. The converse would apply to a surplus in the current account as foreign dollars flow into the United States, which may cause the value of the dollar to rise and the value of foreign currencies to fall.

FIGURE 22.1

U.S. Merchandise Trade Balance, 1970–2000 (in Billions)

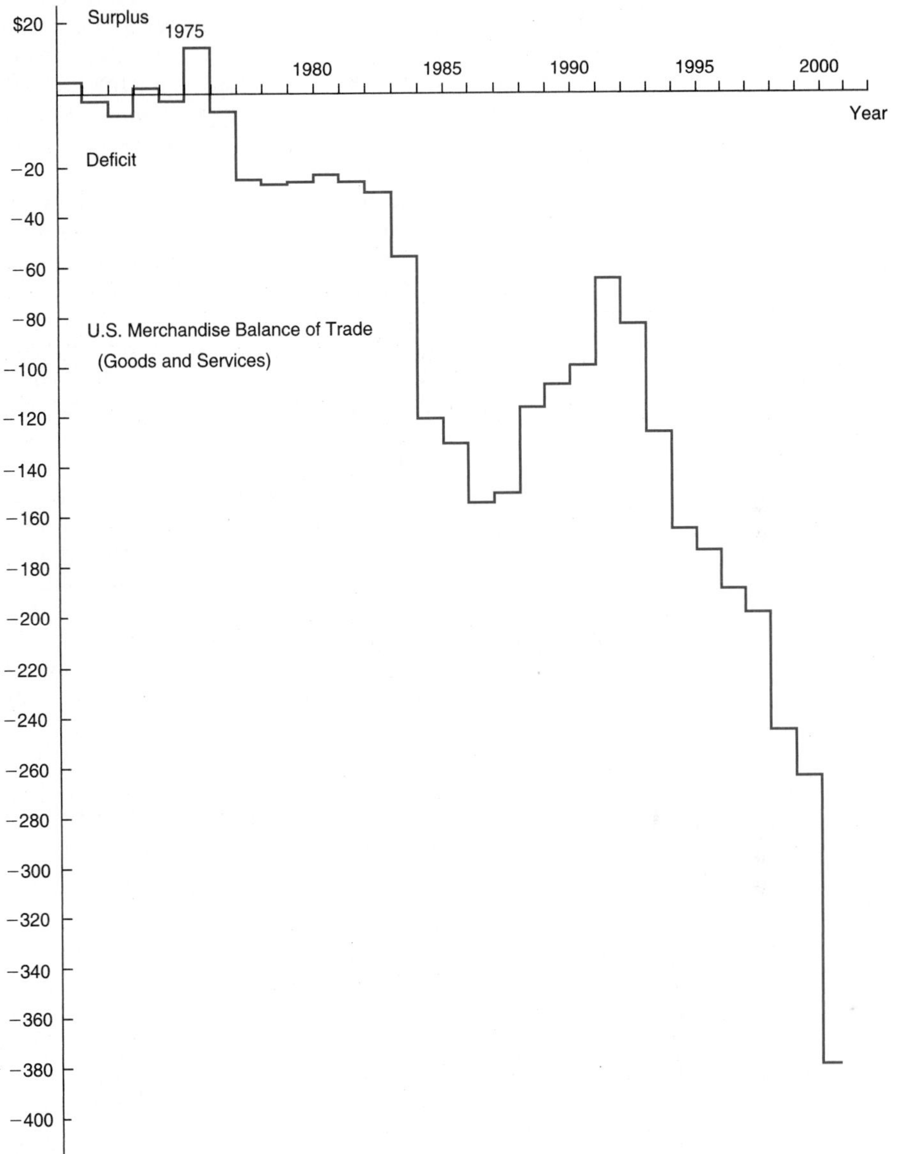

Source: Summary of U.S. International Transactions: U.S. Department of Commerce. Data available through the Federal Reserve Bank of St. Louis (http://www.stls.frb.org/fed/data).

Risk Reduction Through Hedging with Currency Futures

U.S. investors who acquire foreign stocks and bonds and U.S. firms that invest abroad have to bear the risk associated with fluctuations in exchange rates. As was previously explained, such investors can earn a profit on a foreign investment even if its price declines—as long as the decline in the dollar's value more than offsets the decline in the value of the particular asset. The converse is also possible: The value of the particular asset can appreciate, but if the value of the currency falls, the U.S. investor can still sustain a loss. And if the value of the dollar rises sufficiently, it can more than offset the gain in the value of the foreign security.

If the prices of currencies were stable, there would be little risk associated with currency price fluctuations. However, this is not the case, as is illustrated in Figure 22.2, which plots the price of the British pound from 1975 to 2000 (e.g., in 1992 the pound fell from over \$1.80 to about \$1.50, a decline in excess of 15 percent). A decline of that magnitude during a year could easily wipe out all positive returns earned on assets denominated in British pounds. The question then arises: Can the investor reduce the risk associated with the variability in the price of foreign exchange? The answer is yes, as the investor may reduce the risk of loss by hedging with derivatives, such as futures contracts. Of course, for such risk reduction to occur there must be speculators who are willing to accept that risk.

As with all futures contracts, speculators buy and sell foreign exchange futures to take advantage of changes in exchange rates. If a speculator anticipates that the value of the British pound will rise relative to the U.S. dollar, he or she enters into a contract to buy pounds (i.e., supply dollars) in the future. The investor has a long position in pounds (which may also be viewed as a short position in dollars). If the speculator is correct and the price of the pound rises, the value of the contract rises, and the speculator earns a profit. As with other futures trading, the

FIGURE 22.2

Dollar Value of the British Pound, 1975–2000

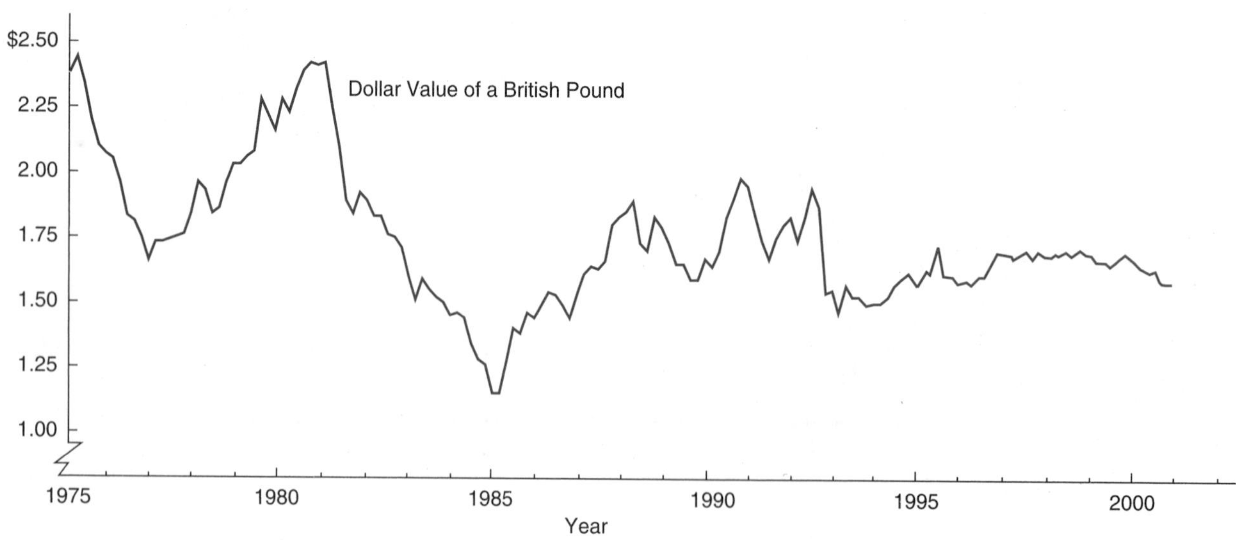

Source: *Federal Reserve Bulletin*, various issues.

margin requirement is so modest relative to the value of the contract that the percentage earned on the margin is substantial.

If the speculator anticipates that the value of the British pound will fall relative to the U.S. dollar, he or she enters into a contract to sell pounds (i.e., buy dollars and deliver pounds) in the future. The investor has a short position in pounds (which may also be viewed as a long position in dollars). If the speculator is correct and the price of the pound falls, the value of the contract declines and the speculator earns a profit. Once again, since the margin requirement is modest relative to the value of the contract, the percentage earned on the margin can be substantial.

Of course, the speculator bears the risk that the currency's value may move in the wrong direction. If a speculator has a long position in the British pound, a decline in the value of the pound inflicts a substantial loss. (Of course, speculators with short positions profit.) If the speculator has a short position in the British pound and the value of the pound rises, then this individual sustains a loss. (Conversely, speculators with long positions profit.) The willingness of speculators to accept the risk associated with fluctuations in exchange rates means that other investors are able to hedge their positions to reduce the risk of loss from exchange rate fluctuations.

Individuals who acquire foreign securities purchase them for the returns offered by the investments, not for the potential return offered by correctly anticipating changes in exchange rates. For example, a U.S. investor purchases $10,000 worth of stocks and/or bonds denominated in Swedish kronor (e.g., the investor buys stock in Electrolux, Ericsson, or Volvo). If the value of the krona is $0.125, the securities are worth 80,000 kronor. Should the value of the krona rise, this investor could experience a profit on the price increase. If the value of the krona were to fall, the investor could sustain a loss on the decline in the krona's value. To reduce this risk, the U.S. investor constructs a hedge position. Since the investor has a long position in the Swedish securities, he or she establishes a short position in kronor by entering into a contract for future delivery. If the value of the krona declines, the resulting loss on the investment in the securities is offset by the profit on the futures contract.

To see how this works, continue the example started earlier. Assume that the current price (i.e., the spot price) of the krona is $0.125 ($1.00 = 8 kronor) and that the futures price of the krona is $0.127 ($1.00 = 7.87 kronor). (In this example, the futures price exceeds the spot price. The converse, in which the spot price exceeds the futures price, is also possible.) The investor enters into a contract for the future sale of kronor—for example, the delivery of 80,000 kronor at $0.127 per krona. The value of this contract (80,000 × $0.127 = $10,160) is almost the same as the value of the securities acquired by the investor ($10,000). Suppose the value of the krona then declines to $0.11. The securities are now worth $8,800 (80,000 kronor × $0.11), and the investor has sustained a loss of $1,200 ($10,000 − $8,800). However, this investor can buy kronor for $0.11 and deliver them for the $0.127 specified in the futures contract. The investor makes $0.017 per krona on the short position in the futures contract. The total profit is $1,360 (80,000 × 0.017), which more than offsets the loss from the decline in the value of the securities denominated in kronor.

The Swedish investor who acquires U.S. securities would follow the opposite strategy. That individual has a long position in the U.S. securities and thus would take a short position in dollars (long position in kronor). If this individual acquires $10,000 worth of U.S. stocks for 80,000 kronor, he or she would sustain a loss if the value of the krona rises. For example, if the krona were to rise to $0.13 from $0.125 (7.69 kronor versus 8 kronor per $1.00), the value of the investment would be 76,900 kronor ($10,000 × 7.69). The investor sustains a loss of 3,100 kronor.

To protect against this loss, the investor enters into a futures contract for the sale of dollars (purchase of kronor). Such a contract would appreciate if the value of the dollar were to decline. If the investor acquires a futures contract to sell $10,000 when the futures price is 1 krona = \$0.127 (\$1.00 = 7.874 kronor), the value of the contract is 78,740 kronor (10,000 × 7.784 kronor). This amount is approximately equal to the value of the securities (80,000 kronor). If the value of the dollar declines to 1 krona = \$0.1333 (\$1 = 7.5 kronor), the securities are worth 75,000 kronor, and the individual loses 5,000 kronor on the investment in the stock. However, the investor can now buy \$10,000 with an outlay of 75,000 kronor and deliver them for the 78,740 kronor specified in the contract and make 3,740 kronor. This profit partially offsets the loss resulting from the decrease in the value of the dollar.

It should be noted that in both these examples, the investor did not completely hedge the position. In the first example, the investor profited by the change in the value of the currency, while in the second case, there was a net loss. This inability to hedge completely results from (1) the difference between the futures price and spot price and (2) differences between the size of the contract and the amounts invested in the foreign securities. The inability to hedge completely and to offset exactly the potential loss does not mean that a substantial amount of the risk associated with exchange rate fluctuations cannot be eliminated through the use of futures contracts in hedge positions.

Advantages Offered by Foreign Securities

Investing in foreign securities offers three possible advantages. The first is the obvious advantage associated with investing in economies and firms experiencing economic growth. The two other advantages, however, may be more important for an individual's portfolio, since economic growth is not unique to foreign firms and foreign economies. (IBM during the 1970s, The Limited during the 1980s, and Microsoft during the 1990s all exhibited superior growth in earnings.) The remaining advantages, then, are (1) excess returns if foreign markets are less efficient than U.S. security markets and (2) reduction in risk through diversification using foreign instead of domestic investments.[4]

Market Efficiency

As explained in Chapter 9, the rapid dissemination of new information and the intense competition among investors produce efficient U.S. financial markets. If new information becomes available that implies a security is undervalued (or overvalued), its price changes rapidly. The opportunity to profit from incorrect valuations disappears before most investors learn the new information. Unless the investor is able to anticipate new information and to adjust his or her position before it becomes generally available, the individual cannot expect to outperform the market consistently. Thus, according to the efficient market hypothesis, higher returns can be achieved only by bearing more risk (i.e., by purchasing assets whose returns tend to be more volatile than the market as a whole).

Foreign markets may not be so efficient. Less analysis may be applied to foreign securities, and the results of the analysis may not be widely disseminated. This suggests that the astute investor may be able to isolate securities that are undervalued or overvalued. If this is true, the opportunity for an excess return would exist. Foreign investments would offer individuals a means to increase returns on their portfolios that is generally not available with domestic investments.

Of course, obtaining information on which to base foreign investment decisions may be difficult. While foreign firms with securities traded on U.S. exchanges

[4]For a survey of international diversification, including an extensive bibliography, consult Jeff Madura and Thomas J. O'Brien, "International Diversification for the Individual," *Financial Services Review* (1991–1992): 159–175.

POINTS OF INTEREST
European Options

Put and call options are not unique to American financial markets but are also available in some foreign security markets. However, these put and call options can differ significantly from American options. Specific differences vary from country to country but revolve around the duration of the option and existence of secondary markets. For example, the duration of the traditional British option is three months. Six-month and nine-month options are not available.

Some secondary markets do exist, but not for all foreign puts and calls. For example, there is no secondary market for the traditional three-month British option. Once purchased, the option cannot be sold. The investor must either exercise the option at a specified time or let it expire. Thus the most important difference between an American option and a so-called European option is the requirement that the investor must exercise the European option to realize any gain achieved through appreciation in the option's value.

must meet SEC disclosure requirements, this reporting does not apply to nonlisted foreign securities. In general, foreign firms do not publish as much information as U.S. firms. For example, many firms do not publish quarterly operating results. Even obtaining an annual report may be difficult, and there is no reason to assume the information is available in English.

Even if foreign security markets are not efficient, the individual U.S. investor may be unable to take advantage of the inefficiencies, especially with regard to the selection of individual securities. For this reason, foreign investments are often made through investment companies. (These investment companies are discussed later in this chapter.) However, even if the individual cannot take advantage of foreign inefficiencies, the possibility of diversification still argues for the inclusion of foreign securities in a domestic portfolio.

Diversification

Historical average returns and their standard deviations for 1970 through 1990 for selected countries are presented in Exhibit 22.4. Of the 10 countries represented, 7 generated higher stock returns than the U.S. equity markets. But none had lower

EXHIBIT 22.4

Annual Rates of Return on Stocks, 1970–1990

	Rate of Return	Standard Deviation of Returns
Australia	7.7%	28.5%
Canada	10.1	17.9
France	12.4	33.3
Germany	12.1	33.8
Japan	19.1	38.7
Netherlands	15.3	20.7
Spain	8.5	35.5
Switzerland	11.6	27.4
United Kingdom	13.5	34.7
United States	10.0	16.6

Source: Adapled from Roger C. Ibbotson and Gary Brinson, *Global Investing* (New York: McGraw-Hill Inc., 1993), p. 140.

FIGURE 22.3

Annual Returns on the EAFE and S&P 500 Stock Indexes (1978–2000)

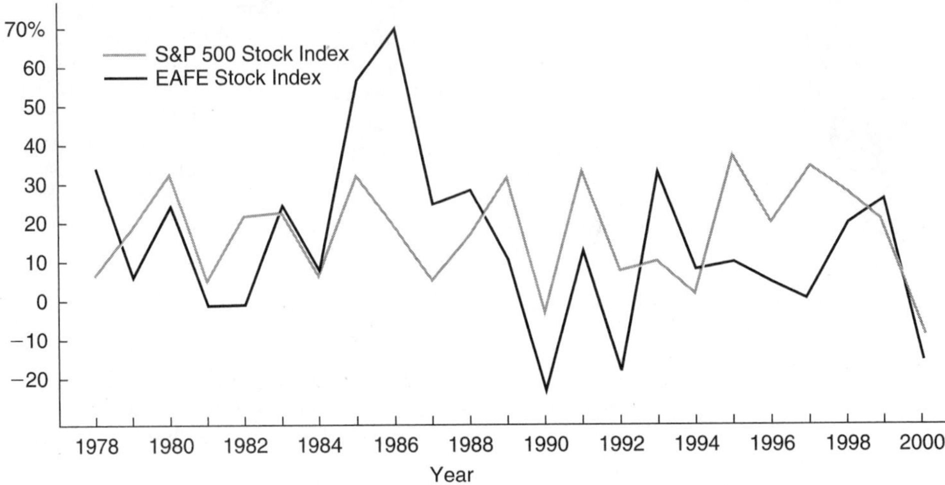

Source: Data derived from the *Individual Investors Guide to Low-Low Mutual Funds*, various issues.

standard deviations, indicating that U.S. returns were less variable. The higher returns generated by a specific country's equities are associated with higher risk and thus cannot be taken as evidence that these markets are less efficient.

More variability by itself is not important from an American investor's perspective if the purpose of including foreign investments is their potential impact on diversification. The inclusion of foreign investments may reduce the risk associated with the portfolio even though the individual assets are riskier. As is explained in Chapter 7, for risk to be reduced, the returns on the assets included in the portfolio should not be positively correlated—that is, the returns should not be related.

The correlation, or lack of it, between the annual returns on the U.S. stock market and the world stock market is illustrated in Figures 22.3 through 22.6. Figure 22.3 presents the annual return on the S&P 500 stock index and the EAFE (the index comprised of stocks in Europe, Australia, and the Far East). While the two returns tended to move together, there were year-to-year differences. In particular, the EAFE generated very large returns in 1985 and 1986. The explanation of these abnormally large security returns, however, is not that foreign security markets generated such high returns during those two years but that the value of the dollar perceptibly declined. (See, for instance, Figure 22.2, which illustrated the rise in the dollar cost of the British pound from mid-1985 through mid-1988.)

Figure 22.4 presents a scatter diagram of the returns from Figure 22.3. The x-axis gives the annual return in the S&P 500 stock index, and the y-axis gives the annual return in the EAFE. If the returns on the S&P 500 and the EAFE were perfectly and positively correlated, all dots would lie on the line *AB;* if the returns were perfectly and negatively correlated, all the dots would lie on line *CD*. The dots appear to lie closer to line *AB* than to *CD*. In this case, the correlation coefficient is 0.369, which indicates that there is a positive correlation. The lack of perfect correlation indicates the potential for risk reduction by including foreign stocks in an American equity portfolio and vice versa (i.e., including American equities in a Japanese or other foreign stock portfolio).

FIGURE 22.4

Scatter Diagram of Annual Returns on the EAFE and S&P 500 Indexes (1978–2000)

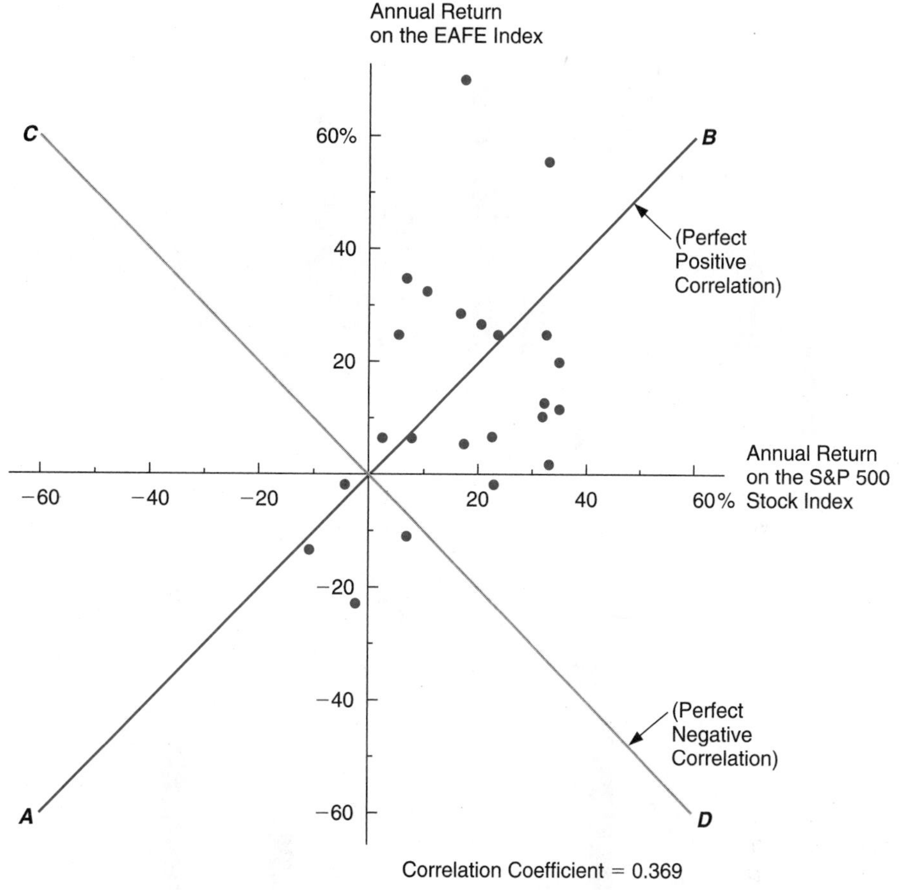

Since the EAFE is a weighted aggregate index in which the values of Japanese and British stocks comprise approximately two-thirds of the index, investors may not be able to purchase securities that are comparable to the composition of this index.[5] These investors may be more concerned with the correlation coefficients relating the returns on U.S. stocks to stocks in individual foreign countries. Figure 22.5 (p. 744) presents the 1991–2000 annual percentage change for the Japanese, German, British, and U.S. stock markets. The top half of the figure presents the percentage changes for each market over time, and the volatility of the German market is readily apparent. The bottom half compares the percentage changes in each index for each year. While the percentage changes tended to move together, especially in 1999 and 2000, the direction of change did differ among the markets for some of the years. For example, the British and U.S. markets rose during 1992 while the Japanese declined. Even when the markets moved together, the annual changes differed, indicating that the markets are, at least partially, independent of one another.

[5]One means to invest in the EAFE is to acquire shares in the Morgan Stanley index fund that tracks the EAFE.

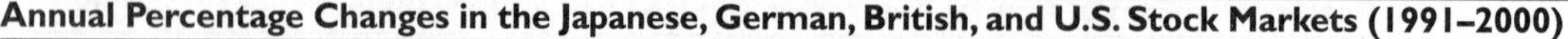

FIGURE 22.5

Annual Percentage Changes in the Japanese, German, British, and U.S. Stock Markets (1991–2000)

Japan: Nikkei 225

Germany: DAX

United Kingdom: FT–SE 100

United States S & P 500

Japan

Germany

United Kingdom

United States

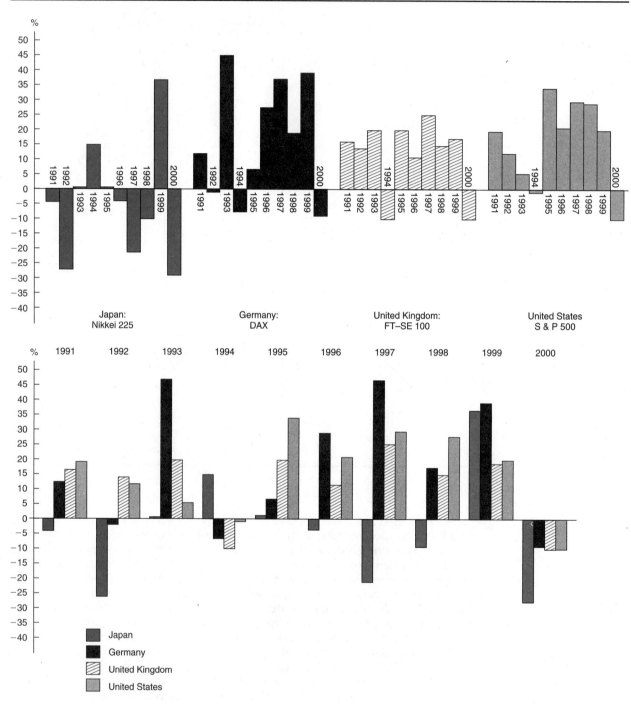

Source: *The Wall Street Journal*, author's calculations.

EXHIBIT 22.5

Correlation Coefficients Between U.S. and Foreign Stock Markets

Country	1970–1990	June 1981 to September 1987	November 1987 to December 1989	January 1980 to January 1994
France	0.47	0.39	0.79	0.44
Germany	0.35	0.21	0.71	0.37
Italy	0.24	0.22	0.56	—
Netherlands	0.57	0.47	0.42	—
Switzerland	0.50	0.50	0.74	—
UK	0.50	0.51	0.95	0.53
Japan	0.28	0.33	0.15	0.26
Canada	0.72	0.72	0.92	0.73

Sources: 1970 to 1990 data adapted from Roger G. Ibbotson and G. P. Brinson, *Global Investing* (New York: McGraw-Hill, 1993), 146; June 1981 to September 1987 data adapted from Richard Roll, "The International Crash of October 1987," *Financial Analysts Journal* (September/October 1988): 20–21; November 1987 to December 1989 data adapted from S.V. Le, "International Investment Diversification Before and After the October 19, 1987, Stock Market Crisis," *Journal of Business Research* (June 1991): 305–310; January 1980 to January 1994 data adapted from Roger G. Clarke and Mark P. Kritzman, *Currency Management: Concepts and Practices* (Charlottesville, VA: Research Foundation of the Institute of Chartered Financial Analysts, 1996). The correlation coefficients for Figure 22.4 are 0.099 for the Japanese market, 0.440 for the German market, and 0.820 for the British market.

Exhibit 22.5 presents estimates of correlation coefficients during several periods for the United States and several industrialized nations. The coefficients of each time period indicate a strong positive relationship between the U.S. and Canadian stock markets. For the remaining countries, the relationship was positive, but the coefficients were generally less than 0.5, which suggests an advantage from international diversification.

A past potential for diversification, however, makes no guarantees for the present. The trend toward globalization of security markets and the creation of futures and options tied to various stock indexes may increase interdependence of global financial markets. Factors affecting prices in one market are rapidly transferred to other markets. Much of the historical record predates these developments, so that the past benefits of global diversification may be reduced, if not erased.

To explore this possibility, Exhibit 22.5 includes the correlation coefficients for the periods before and after the October 1987 stock crash. During 1987, major U.S. and international security markets rose together, and when prices dramatically declined during October 1987, 19 of 23 major stock markets fell by more than 20 percent. This suggests that some factor or variable is common to all markets, so that during a major price decline, international diversification may have only marginal benefits.[6]

Exhibit 22.5 appears to corroborate the diminished benefits of international diversification. Six of the eight countries have higher coefficients for the period after the October crash than for the period preceding it. The major exception is the Japanese stock market, whose correlation coefficient was among the lowest for the entire time period. The exhibit, however, does not include correlation coefficients for emerging markets, such as those of Korea, Singapore, or Brazil. These developing markets may now offer the benefits of diversification that previously existed from investments in the major international financial markets.

[6]See Richard Roll, "The International Crash of October 1987," *Financial Analysts Journal* (September/October 1988): 22–27.

Emerging Markets

Prior to the 1990s, foreign investments were essentially limited to securities in developed countries. During the 1990s, security markets began to develop and prosper in less-developed countries.[7] For American investors, these emerging markets have provided an important alternative to domestic securities. Several reasons have been given for this growth in foreign security markets. In addition to rapid economic growth in emerging economies, ideological shifts led to the privatization of industries (i.e., the sale of state-owned businesses to the general public). More-open economies spawned private firms that needed funding. Both privatization and the creation of new firms led to the issuing of securities to raise funds. These securities necessitated the creation and development of secondary markets.

The development of security markets in emerging nations was aided by improved communications and technological change that were easily transferred from developed nations to the emerging economies. The development of free trade associations (e.g., the Latin American Free Trade Area, or LAFTA), political reform in former communist countries, and improvements in health also facilitated the development of these economies. Domestic confidence improved and contributed to the growth of local stock markets as citizens became more willing to invest at home and repatriated funds from abroad.

The arguments for investing in emerging markets are essentially the same as the arguments for investing abroad in firms located in developed countries: potential growth and potential diversification. Many emerging nations did experience economic growth during the 1990s, but economic recession occurred during the late 1990s, especially in the economies of the Far East. The economic recession caused their stock markets to decline. As is illustrated in Exhibit 22.6, some of the declines in the Dow Jones global stock indexes during 1998 were severe. For example, the stock markets in Brazil and Hong Kong declined by 53.3 and 27.5 percent, respectively. During the same period, the stock market in the United States rose by 4.4 percent, and the European market exceeded 15 percent.

EXHIBIT 22.6

Percentage Change for Ten Emerging Stock Markets

Country	Percent Change in the Dow Jones Country Index (January 1, 1998–September 8, 1998)
Brazil	−53.3%
Chile	−43.6
Hong Kong	−27.5
Malaysia	−39.5
Mexico	−51.4
Philippines	−39.4
South Korea	9.5
Taiwan	−22.3
Thailand	−28.3
Venezuela	−72.8

Source: *The Wall Street Journal*, September 9, 1998, C16.

[7]For descriptions of the emerging security markets and the growth of emerging economies, consult Michael Keppler and Martin Lechner, *Emerging Markets* (Chicago: Irwin Professional Publishing, 1997); and J. Mark Mobius, *Mobius on Emerging Markets* (London: FT Pitman Publishing, 1996).

EXHIBIT 22.7

Correlation Coefficients Between the U.S. Stock Market and Emerging Stock Markets

January 1989–December 1995		January 1991–December 1995	
Argentina	−0.04	Argentina	0.31
Brazil	0.21	Brazil	0.42
Chile	0.08	Chile	0.26
China	0.14	China	0.00
Colombia	0.06	Colombia	−0.02
Hungary	0.44	Hungary	0.29
India	0.00	India	−0.08
Indonesia	0.14	Indonesia	0.28
Korea	0.14	Korea	0.00
Malaysia	0.45	Malaysia	0.20
Mexico	0.25	Mexico	0.19
Peru	0.38	Peru	0.19
Philippines	0.28	Philippines	0.18
Poland	0.43	Poland	0.24
Taiwan	0.27	Taiwan	0.05
Thailand	0.31	Thailand	0.05
Turkey	0.03	Turkey	−0.11
Venezuela	−0.14	Venezuela	0.03

Source: Data for 1989–1995 from Michael Keppler and Martin Lechner, *Emerging Markets* (Chicago: Irwin Professional Publishing, 1997), 96; data for 1991–1995 from J. Mark Mobius, *Mobius on Emerging Markets* (London: FT Pitman Publishing, 1996), 216–217.

The diversification argument revolves around the correlation between the returns earned on the U.S. markets and the returns on the foreign markets. While Exhibit 22.5 provided correlation coefficients between the U.S. and foreign stock markets in advanced economies, Exhibit 22.7 provides the correlation coefficients between the U.S. stock market (as measured by the S&P 500 stock index) and stock markets in 18 emerging nations. The exhibit reports the coefficients for each country from two sources. Although the coefficients differ, the differences are small.

In all cases, the correlation coefficients between the U.S. market and the emerging markets are low. In many cases, the coefficients are close to 0.00, which indicates no relationship between the two markets. During this period, emerging market returns did not move with the returns on U.S. stocks. This evidence, of course, supports the diversification argument. However, it is doubtful that increased diversification offsets the negative returns from these investments in the eyes of most investors who held these securities during the late 1990s.[8]

An individual who is considering an investment in a company in an emerging market needs to be aware if the nation is "investable" or "noninvestable." An

[8] If you were a "contrarian investor," the increased interest in emerging markets that occurred during the middle to late 1990s would suggest the opposite strategy: Avoid these securities! The essence of this argument boils down to this: Once there is widespread interest in a particular investment, such as emerging stock markets, too many individuals are participating and the opportunity has passed. Conversely, after these securities were battered during 1998 and no one appeared to want to own these stocks, the investor should have considered the emerging markets as possible investments.

emerging market is considered investable if the market is open to foreign investors and meets other criteria concerning size and liquidity.[9] Some emerging markets are not considered investable because the national government has placed limits on foreign participation in its equity markets. The need for emerging firms to raise funds, however, puts pressure on governments to allow foreign investments, so the trend is toward permitting foreign participation. But participation may still be limited or foreign investors may be excluded from investing in firms in specific industries. For example, Philippine law requires that nationals own at least 60 percent of domestic firms and media; retail trade and rural bank stocks are closed to foreign investors.

Mutual Funds with Foreign Investments

global funds
Mutual funds whose portfolios includes securities of firms with international operations that are located throughout the world.

international funds
American mutual funds whose portfolios are limited to non-American firms.

regional funds
Mutual funds that specialize in a particular geographical area.

emerging market fund
Investment company that specializes in securities from less-developed countries.

From a U.S. perspective, there are basically four types of mutual funds with international investments. **Global funds** invest in foreign and U.S. securities. Many U.S. mutual funds are global, as they maintain some part of their portfolios in foreign investments. Although these funds do not specialize in foreign securities, they do offer the individual investor the advantages associated with foreign investments: returns through global economic growth, diversification from assets whose returns are not positively correlated, and possible excess returns from inefficient foreign financial markets.

In addition to global funds, there are **international funds**, which invest solely in foreign securities and hold no U.S. securities, and **regional funds**, which specialize in a particular geographical area, such as Asia. (There are also mutual funds that specialize in a particular area within the United States, such as the North Star Fund, which invests in firms located in seven upper Midwest states.) The regional funds obviously specialize, and the international funds may also specialize during particular time periods. Thus it is not unusual for a fund to invest a quarter or more of its assets in the shares of firms in a particular country.

The last type of mutual fund with international investments is the **emerging market fund**, which specializes in securities of firms located in less-developed nations. In many cases, emerging market funds specialize in specific countries, such as the Indonesia Fund or the Turkish Investment Fund. Such funds permit the U.S. investor the opportunity to invest in specific markets without specialized knowledge of local firms or laws concerning security transactions in that country. In addition, the governments of some countries with emerging security markets forbid foreign ownership of securities (perhaps to avoid foreign control or influence). Such governments, however, may grant a specific investment company the right to own securities issued in that country. In such cases, the only means by which the U.S. investor may participate in that specific market is through the ownership of shares in the emerging market fund.

Many of the regional and emerging market funds are closed-end investment companies. A list of these funds traded on the New York Stock Exchange is given in Exhibit 22.8. (Ticker symbols are given to facilitate obtaining information on a particular fund.) The prices of these shares can be very volatile since the price depends on both the fund's net asset value and speculative interest in the shares. This volatility is illustrated in Figure 22.6 (p. 750), which plots the price and the premium over net asset value of the Germany Fund during the fall of 1989 when

[9]This distinction between investable and noninvestable emerging stock markets is used by the International Finance Corporation (IFC), whose mission is to "promote the growth of productive and profitable private enterprise in emerging markets." (See *The IFC Indexes—Methodology, Definitions, and Practices,* Washington, DC: International Finance Corporation, 1998, p. 2.) The IFC has databases on foreign companies that include financial statements, security prices (in the local currency and in dollars), trading volume, and local stock market indexes. IFC may be reached through its Web site: http://www.ifc.org.

EXHIBIT 22.8

Selected Specialized Country Closed-End Investment Companies Traded on the New York Stock Exchange

Fund	Ticker Symbol
Developed Nations	
Austria Fund	OST
France Growth Fund	FRF
Germany Fund	GER
Italy Fund	ITA
Japan Equity Fund	JEQ
Spain Fund	SNF
Swiss Helvetia Fund	SWZ
United Kingdom Fund	UKM
Emerging Markets	
Brazilian Equity Fund	BZF
Chile Fund	CH
China Fund	CHN
First Philippine Fund	FPF
India Growth Fund	IFN
Indonesia Fund	IF
Jakarta Growth Fund	JGF
Korea Fund	KF
Malaysia Fund	MF
Singapore Fund	SGF
Taiwan Fund	TWN
Thai Fund	TTF
Turkish Investment Fund	TKF
iShares (World Equity Benchmark Shares) Traded on the American Stock Exchange	
Australia Index Series	EWA
Austria Index Series	EWO
Belgium Index Series	EWK
Canada Index Series	EWC
France Index Series	EWQ
Germany Index Series	EWG
Hong Kong Index Series	EWH
Italy Index Series	EWI
Japan Index Series	EWJ
Malaysia (Free) Index Series	EWM
Mexico (Free) Index Series	EWW
Netherlands Index Series	EWN
Singapore (Free) Index Series	EWS
Spain Index Series	EWP
Sweden Index Series	EWD
Switzerland Index Series	EW I
U.K. Index Series	EWU

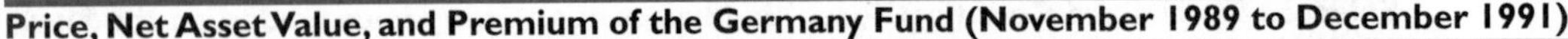

FIGURE 22.6

Price, Net Asset Value, and Premium of the Germany Fund (November 1989 to December 1991)

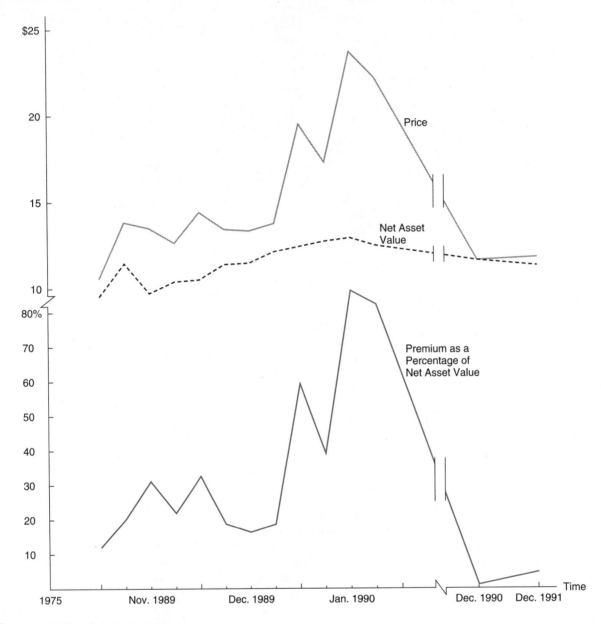

Source: *The Wall Street Journal*, various issues.

the political climate changed very rapidly. The price of these shares rose dramatically and sold for a premium that exceeded 80 percent of the fund's net asset value, but by the end of 1991, the premium had declined to 4 percent.

Such a large premium has not been limited to the Germany Fund. At various times, the shares of many funds that specialize in a particular country sell above their net asset value. Buying these shares for a large premium over their net asset value may seem illogical. However, these funds may be the only means by which the individual investor may participate in a country's stock markets, since local laws may ban or severely limit foreign ownership of the securities.

American investors may also acquire shares in foreign investment companies, such as the British mutual funds called *unit trusts*. Thus, if a U.S. investor cannot find an acceptable domestic fund, the search may be extended to a foreign fund. However, since these securities are not registered with the SEC, some foreign funds will not sell shares directly to U.S. investors, as these funds believe such sales are illegal. In other cases, purchases may be made for a fee through foreign banks with branches in the United States. However, the individual should probably question whether the potential return is worth the additional expense required to acquire the shares.

iShares (WEBS)

An alternative to investing in mutual funds and closed-end investment companies that specialize in foreign securities are iShares, which were initially called World Equity Benchmark Shares (WEBS). iShares were created by Morgan Stanley and track an index of a country's stock market. U.S. investors may readily buy and sell iShares because they trade on the American Stock Exchange. (iShares that are traded and their ticker symbols are provided in Exhibit 22.8.)[10] In effect, these securities are exchange-traded index funds for foreign stock markets, and their prices fluctuate with changes in their underlying markets.

While iShares are index funds, they do not necessarily own every security in a particular index. Instead, the sponsors construct a portfolio that is highly correlated with the index. This strategy reduces commission and management costs for the fund. iShares are virtually 100 percent invested at all times, so there is minimal

POINTS OF INTEREST
Global Investing and the World Wide Web

Finding information on foreign firms is not as easy as on American firms, especially since most foreign firms do not have their shares registered with the SEC for trading in the United States. Global Investor (http://www.global-investor.com) may be used to determine which foreign securities have American Depositary Receipts and where the securities are traded. The Bank of New York (http://www.bankofny.com/adr provides similar service and offers company profiles and Web site links. Global Financial Data, Inc. (http://www.globalfindata.com) furnishes historical databases that cover stock markets, interest rates, and exchange rates for over 50 countries. Although Global Financial Data offers information through subscription, it does provide some complimentary data such as annual data for many stock indexes, including markets in developed countries and the emerging markets.

As you would expect, foreign stock markets have Web sites, usually with information in English. For example, the Mexican stock market (Bolsa Mexicana de Valores) may be found at http://www.bmv.com.mx. If you do not have the Web address for the foreign exchanges, one means to obtain links is the Institute of Finance and Banking at the University of Goettingen (http://www.gwdg.de/~ifbg/stock1.html). Other sites, such as Wall Street Research Net (http://www.wsrn.com) or ADR.com (J.P. Morgan) (http://www.adr.com) also provide links to foreign markets. One especially convenient Web source is the *Financial Times* which reproduces surveys at its Web site (http://surveys.ft.com). Coverage includes financial markets, emerging markets, global industries, and individual countries. If, for example, you wanted information on Singapore, this Web site is a good place to start. Topics include an overview, financial services, the country's foreign policy, and even social issues such as individual freedoms.

[10]Additional information on iShares may be found at http://www.ishares.com.

turnover of their portfolios. This lack of turnover also reduces the cost of managing the portfolio.

iShares offer U.S. investors another means to participate in foreign markets, and their prices on the AMEX are expressed in dollars. That price represents the dollar value of the iShares portfolio. The securities they own, however, are denominated in the local currency, so an American investor's return is affected by (1) changes in the exchange rate, (2) changes in the value of the index, and (3) any dividends distributed by the stocks in the portfolio. Dividends received by iShares are, in turn, distributed to their stockholders. If the value of the dollar were to rise, the value in dollars of an iShares portfolio would decline. Thus, the investor could sustain a loss even though the stock market in that particular country rose.

This exchange rate risk, of course, applies to all foreign investments, but an iShares' management cannot take actions that might offset this risk. Since an iShares portfolio is always fully invested, its management cannot sell the securities and convert to dollars in anticipation that the dollar will rise. The management of a specialized country index fund, however, can liquidate the portfolio and move the funds into dollars to reduce the impact of an increase in the value of the American dollar.

Recent Developments: The Creation of the "Euro"

euro
Common currency of 11 European nations.

Effective January 4, 1999, 11 European nations joined the Economic and Monetary Union (EMU) and adopted a common monetary unit, the **euro**. In July 2002, French francs, Italian lira, German marks, and the currencies of the other member nations ceased to exist. (The other countries are Austria, Belgium, Finland, Ireland, Luxembourg, Netherlands, Portugal, and Spain. Denmark, Sweden, Switzerland, and the United Kingdom chose not to join.) In addition to a common monetary unit, the countries that joined the Economic and Monetary Union agreed on the creation of a new European central bank. Each country had to relinquish control of its domestic supply of money and the level of interest rates. The new central bank establishes monetary policy for the area just as the Federal Reserve sets monetary policy in the United States.

The potential economic impact of this change in the financial structure is substantial and should stimulate economic activity in the countries that join the Economic and Monetary Union. For example, the creation of a European central bank should decrease inflationary pressures and lower interest rates. The existence of the same monetary unit in each of the 11 countries facilitates the comparison of prices by consumers. Businesses no longer have to convert one currency to another. A German company does not have to convert marks to francs when it invests in France and does not have to convert francs back to marks to realize its profits. Thus, the uncertainty concerning exchange rates ceases. Individual firms may achieve economic efficiencies, and increased merger activity may result as European firms combine to better compete in global markets.

All of this suggests that the creation of the euro should create an important opportunity for global investors. Under the new monetary system, the investor can place less emphasis on the country in which a firm is located and more emphasis on the firm's fundamentals. Monetary union, however, should also increase market efficiency, and security prices may become more correlated. Market inefficiencies and the potential to diversify a portfolio were previously given as two important reasons for investing abroad. Thus, the development of the Economic and Monetary Union may reduce their importance for investing in European securities. However, the potential for economic growth remains and may become the primary reason for investing in firms located in the countries of the Economic and Monetary Union.

Summary

Many individuals take a global view of investing and acquire stocks and bonds issued in foreign countries. These investments involve additional sources of risk: an unstable political climate and fluctuations in exchange rates. If the individual buys securities in politically unstable security markets, there is little the investor can do but accept that risk. The values of foreign currencies (foreign exchange rates) fluctuate daily with the demand for and supply of each currency. When foreign securities are sold and converted back into U.S. dollars, the value of the dollars may have risen or declined, depending on what has happened in the foreign exchange markets.

The investor may reduce the risk of loss from fluctuations in exchange rates by constructing a hedge position using currency futures. For example, if the individual acquires a long position in foreign securities, he or she can hedge against loss by selling contracts for the future delivery of the currency. The investor thus has a long position in the securities and a short position in the currency, which reduces the risk resulting from fluctuations in the dollar value of the foreign currency.

Foreign investments offer the individual several advantages. Since the returns on foreign securities are not perfectly correlated with returns on domestic securities, such investments are a means to diversify the individual's portfolio. In addition, foreign security markets may not be as efficient as U.S. security markets. Such inefficiencies suggest that foreign investments may offer astute investors an opportunity to increase the return earned on their portfolios.

Instead of selecting specific foreign securities, U.S. investors may prefer to acquire shares in mutual funds that make foreign investments. Many U.S. funds maintain a portion of their assets in foreign securities. Other mutual funds invest exclusively abroad while others specialize in particular countries or geographic regions. Such investment companies relieve the investor of having to select individual foreign securities but still offer the advantages of global diversification and possible increased returns through investments in less efficient markets.

The recent creation of the Economic and Monetary Union and the creation of one currency, the euro, should have a profound impact on economic development in Europe. For the first time, 11 European countries have combined into a single economic unit whose ability to compete on a global basis should be enhanced. This potential for growth may create opportunities for investors but may also reduce potential diversification if the correlation among security markets is increased.

Questions

1) What are foreign exchange and the foreign exchange market? What causes the prices of currencies to fluctuate?
2) What are the sources of risk associated with foreign investments? How can the individual investor manage those risks?
3) Would a U.S. investor who owned foreign securities prefer a devaluation or revaluation of the U.S. dollar?
4) What does a deficit in a country's balance of trade imply? Can a country have a surplus in its balance of payments?
5) If a British investor who purchased French securities anticipates that the value of the euro may fall but does not wish to sell the securities, what should this investor do?
6) Why may the addition of foreign securities to a U.S. investor's portfolio reduce this individual's risk exposure?

7) Why may investing in mutual funds with foreign investments be preferable to purchasing foreign stocks?
8) Why may the development of the European Economic Monetary Union reduce the potential for diversification but increase the potential for economic growth?

9) Using a source such as Global Investor (http://www.global-investor.com), determine which Chinese companies have ADRs and in which U.S. market the ADRs trade.
10) From Exhibit 22.8 select a country iShares and a closed-end investment company specializing in the same country (e.g., the Germany Fund and the Germany Index Series). Compare their monthly returns for three years and compute the correlation between the two sets of returns. You may be able to obtain historical prices from Yahoo! Finance. From its home page, http://quote.yahoo.com, enter the security's ticker symbol. Then go to "Chart," and from "Chart" click on "Table." Table has a menu for daily, weekly, and monthly prices. The price information also includes any dividends necessary to compute returns. You may be able to reach the same destination from http://chart.yahoo.com/m?s= and enter the ticker symbol.

Problems

1) What is the cost of $1.00 in each of the following currencies?

British pound	$1.62
Canadian dollar	0.65
Russian ruble	0.14
Japanese yen	0.007

2) If you purchase 100,000 pesos for $5,000, what is the price of a peso?
3) You purchase 100 ADRs of British Oil for $12 per ADR. What is the value of the shares in dollars, given the following information?

Time	Price of the Stock in Pounds	Dollar Price of the Pound
1/1/X0	£ 6.00	$2.00
4/1/X0	7.80	2.10
7/1/X0	9.30	1.85
10/1/X0	10.20	1.70
1/1/X1	14.00	1.65

Compare the percentage returns for each quarter earned by a U.S. investor and a British investor.
4) You anticipate buying a Volvo in six months for $30,000. Currently the spot price of the Swedish krona is $0.50 and the six-month futures price is $0.505. You anticipate that the value of the dollar relative to the krona will decline. What course of action should you take and how much will it cost you (excluding brokerage commissions)?
5) A portfolio manager owns a bond worth £2,000,000 that will mature in one year. The pound is currently worth $1.65, and the one-year future price is $1.61. If the value of the pound were to fall, the portfolio manager would sus-

tain a loss. If the value of the pound were to rise, the portfolio manager would experience a profit.

a) What is the expected payment based on the current exchange rate?
b) What is the expected payment based on the futures exchange rate?
c) If, after a year, the pound is worth $1.53, what is the loss from the decline in the value of the pound?
d) If, after a year, the pound is worth $1.72, what is the gain from the increase in the value of the pound?
e) To avoid the potential loss in part (c) the portfolio manager hedges by selling futures contracts for the delivery of pounds at $1.61. What is the cost of the protection from a decline in the value of the pound?
f) If, after hedging, the price of the pound falls to $1.53, what is the maximum amount the portfolio manager can lose? Why is this answer different from the answer to part (c) above?
g) If, after hedging, the price of the pound rises to $1.72, what is the maximum amount the portfolio manager can gain? Why is this answer different from the answer to part (d) above?

THE FINANCIAL ADVISOR'S INVESTMENT CASE
Foreign Country Funds and Diversification

You believe that many of your clients could benefit from using international investments to diversify their portfolios, but many are reluctant to invest abroad—especially since they may be unfamiliar with foreign economies and businesses. Previously, all suggestions to diversify internationally have met resistance. At best, your clients have been willing to invest in U.S. firms with international operations, such as Coca-Cola or IBM.

To overcome this reluctance, you have decided to demonstrate the reduction in portfolio risk from foreign investments. For the demonstration, you have selected two single-country funds to illustrate the variability of returns from combining a country fund with an index fund based on the S&P 500 stock index. The S&P 500 has averaged a return of 10 percent with a standard deviation of 10 percent. The first country fund specializes in Japanese stocks and has a beta of 1.0 when compared to the returns on the Japanese market. The return has averaged 10 percent with a standard deviation of 14 percent. The second country fund specializes in Brazilian stocks and also has a beta of 1.0 when compared to returns on that stock market. Its return has also averaged 10 percent but has a greater standard deviation of 20 percent. Neither fund has any investments in U.S. stocks and historically the correlation coefficients relating the returns on the funds to the S&P 500 stock index have been 0.4 and −0.2, respectively. To isolate the impact of selecting one of these funds for diversification, you assume that the returns on the funds and on the S&P 500 stock index will continue to be 10 percent, so that the investor can anticipate earning 10 percent regardless of which choice is made. The only consideration will be the reduction in the variability of the returns (i.e., the reduction in risk as measured by the standard deviation). To show the reduction, compute the standard deviation of the return when combining the U.S. index fund with the Japanese fund or the Brazilian fund for each of the following investment proportions:

Proportion Invested in the U.S. Fund	Proportion in the Foreign Fund
100%	0%
90	10
80	20
70	30
60	40
50	50
40	60
30	70
20	80
10	90
0	100%

1) What happens to the portfolio standard deviation as the investor substitutes the foreign securities for the U.S. securities? What combination of U.S. and Japanese stocks and U.S. and Brazilian stocks minimizes risk?
2) Even though the risk reduction is greater for the Brazilian fund, why may the U.S. investor prefer the Japanese fund?
3) Should a Japanese investor who owns only Japanese stocks acquire U.S. stocks?
4) How would each of the following affect a U.S. investor's willingness to acquire foreign stocks?
   a) The dollar is expected to strengthen.
   b) Inflation in the foreign country is expected to increase.
   c) Globalization of financial markets should accelerate.

Investing in Nonfinancial Assets: Collectibles, Resources, and Real Estate

CHAPTER 23

Anyone who has watched *Antiques Roadshow* on PBS knows that individuals collect an amazing variety of items. Some of these collectibles fetch prices that many people probably find incomprehensible. Of course, the vast majority of items brought to *Antiques Roadshow* to be appraised have, at best, only sentimental value and are not included in the broadcast. But it is the possibility of locating that valuable item that makes collecting both fun and potentially rewarding.

Many collectors started when they were young. Valuable collections of baseball cards, Barbie dolls, or teddy bears are often the result of an individual continuing a childhood love that grows into a lifetime of satisfaction and possible profit. While the general public's interest in collectibles varies over time, a collection constructed with thoughtfulness and foresight can both be satisfying and serve as a store of value.

Investing in collectibles and other nonfinancial assets is essentially no different from investing in financial assets. In both cases, the investments are made in the present and the return earned in the future. The return comes from possible income and price appreciation. In order to realize capital gains, secondary markets must exist, and realized gains are subject to capital gains taxation. And, as with any investment, there is risk.

Although investing in nonfinancial, real assets is similar to investing in financial assets, there are important differences. In several cases, these investments require specialized knowledge that is different from the knowledge used to select financial assets. An individual could spend an entire lifetime learning the fine points that make one an expert in a particular type of asset, such as art or real estate.

This chapter briefly covers investment in a variety of nonfinancial assets: collectibles, gold and other natural resources, and real estate. The largest section is devoted to real estate and ranges from home ownership to rental properties and real estate investment trusts (REITs), which are investment companies that specialize in real estate. Throughout the chapter, emphasis is placed on the elements most similar to those associated with investing in financial assets: the potential returns, an asset's marketability, and the risks. Implicit throughout the chapter is the assumption that the individual needs specialized information concerning these investments. Such information can best be obtained through a careful and extensive study of the particular nonfinancial assets that are of interest to the individual investor.

Learning Objectives

After completing this chapter you should be able to:

1. Compare the sources of risk and return from investing in nonfinancial assets and financial assets.
2. Explain the role of auctions, dealers, and secondary markets for nonfinancial assets.
3. List the mediums for investing in gold, metals, and other natural resources.
4. Demonstrate the importance of the inelasticity of supply for investing in resources.

5 Differentiate the means for investing in real estate.
6 Compare the sources of funds to finance the purchase of a home.
7 Determine the cash flow from an investment in rental properties and the importance of funds from operations to the valuation of real estate investments.
8 Distinguish among the types of real estate investment trusts (REITs).

Returns, Markets, and Risk

A market brings together buyers and sellers in order to transact the exchange of goods and services. When a mutually acceptable price is determined, the goods are transferred from the seller to the buyer. This is obviously what occurs in the organized security markets, such as the New York Stock Exchange (NYSE). Sellers and buyers of securities are brought together, and they trade securities for money. Many securities, however, are bought and sold in the informal over-the-counter market. There is no centralized place where transactions in the over-the-counter market are consummated. It exists wherever a buyer and a seller can trade cash for securities.

The market for collectibles and many nonfinancial assets is also an informal market, for there is no organized center such as the NYSE for the transfer of these physical assets. While there may be certain centers, such as the diamond district in New York City, the market is geographically dispersed and not formally organized.

Because there is no formal market, there are none of the advantages offered by such formality. For example, price quotations (i.e., bid and ask prices) are not readily available. The volume of transactions is generally not recorded, and when it is, this information is not widely disseminated as are reports of security trades, which are published in the financial press. Specialized publications may report some of this information, but these are frequently not well known to the investor and may not be readily available.[1]

POINTS OF INTEREST
Tangible Assets and Diversification

Perhaps the strongest rationale for acquiring collectibles and other nonfinancial assets is their possible impact on diversification. The returns on most financial assets tend to be positively correlated. When stock prices rise, the prices of most individual stocks rise in sympathy. The factors that cause stock prices to rise often cause bond prices to rise. Lower interest rates tend to be bullish for both stocks and bonds. Inflation tends to cause the prices of both stocks and bonds to fall as earnings are squeezed and tighter monetary policy raises interest rates.

The returns on some physical assets (e.g., gold and other precious metals, real estate, and art objects) may be negatively correlated with returns on financial assets. The inflation that hurts stocks and bonds may be beneficial for precious metals or real estate. This suggests that these assets can play an important role in the construction of a diversified portfolio. The attractiveness of tangible assets then may not be the returns they offer but the possibility of risk reduction, in which case they are not alternatives to financial assets but complementary to them.

[1]For a general reference on collectibles, consult the following encyclopedia: Jack P. Friedman, ed., *The Encyclopedia of Investments*, 2d ed. (Boston: Warren, Gorham & Lamont, 1990). This book contains chapters devoted to art nouveau and art deco, books, coins, folk art, gemstones, motion pictures, paintings, furniture, photographs, porcelain, prints, rugs, sculpture, and stamps. Each chapter covers the basic characteristics of the assets, its attractive features and its potential risks, special factors to consider, and custodial care. Each chapter also has a glossary and suggested readings.

These characteristics mean that the markets for some nonfinancial assets (e.g., collectibles) may not be efficient, while the markets for some tangible assets, such as gold, are efficient. If the price of gold were $400 in one market and $350 in another, arbitrageurs would quickly pounce on the opportunity for a risk-free profit by buying gold for $350 in one market and simultaneously selling it for $400 in the other. Of course, this would equalize the price of gold in both markets.

In addition to inefficiencies, there is little or no regulation of the markets for many nonfinancial assets. The Securities and Exchange Commission reduces fraud and ensures the timely disclosure of pertinent financial information that may affect the value of a firm's securities, but no such government organization exists to protect the buyers of many physical assets. It is a case of "let the buyer beware," and the unsuspecting investor is certainly an easy target for the forger or any other shady dealer who can prey on the individual's desire to find an asset that will offer an exceptional return.

The return offered by an investment in an asset such as gold comes from the potential for price appreciation and is taxed as a capital gain when the gain is realized. The return earned through price appreciation is the difference between the net sale price and the purchase price. The net sale price is the realized price minus any commissions or fees necessary to make the sale. While the commissions for buying and selling stock may be 2 or 3 percent of the price, the commissions for buying and selling nonfinancial assets such as real estate may be considerably more. These fees vary with the different types of assets, but they can consume a substantial portion of any profit earned through price appreciation.

In addition to commissions, other expenses may be incurred with an investment in nonfinancial assets that are not incurred with financial assets. The investor may take out special insurance to cover insurable risks. For example, insurance may be desirable for investments in art, which are subject to theft and fire. Or the investor may rent space (e.g., a safe deposit box) to store the assets. This certainly would apply to valuable stamps, coins, and gold. These additional expenses reduce the return earned by the investment.

Besides the return earned through price appreciation, the investor may receive a flow of services. Oriental rugs may be functional, works of art are decorative, and housing provides shelter and space. The potential flow of services offered by some physical assets should be the prime reason for buying them.

Investing in art and collectibles subjects the investor to the same basic risks associated with investing in financial assets. These are the elements of risk attributable to the market (i.e., the risk associated with price changes of a class of assets) and the risk associated with a particular company or asset. In addition, the investor must face the risk of loss from inflation and the problems associated with theft and fraud.

The markets for nonfinancial, real assets vary over time. Prices do fluctuate and presumably, if prices in general move in a particular direction, the value of specific assets will move accordingly. Hence, if the price of gold rises, then the value of gold coins will rise. Conversely, if the price of gold declines, the value of gold coins will fall. The investor who buys gold and gold coins cannot avoid this market risk, which applies to all physical assets.

The investor must bear the risk associated with the specific investment. Changes in taste alter the public's demand for specific goods. For example, if the demand for Oriental rugs increases, the value of Oriental rugs also will appreciate. However, even within this group some will appreciate more than others. The rugs that are popular today will not necessarily be those that are popular tomorrow. Thus, the investor may experience losses on specific investments even though the market as a whole moves upward in price.

A major reason for purchasing nonfinancial assets as an investment is that they may help the individual beat inflation. The value of financial assets, such as stocks and bonds, often declines when the inflation rate increases. However, the value of physical assets may keep pace with the rate of inflation, as individuals seek to buy them in preference to financial assets, thus driving up their prices.

The investor should realize that for this strategy to work, he or she must anticipate inflation in order to purchase physical assets before the price increases. In addition, even if inflation were to occur, it is not necessarily true that the price of all nonfinancial assets will rise. Their prices can rise, fall, or remain the same. Inflation inflicts a loss of purchasing power on any investor whose particular portfolio does not keep pace with the rate of inflation. While some real assets have appreciated in price (e.g., housing), this is not true for all physical assets. For example, the price of gold has stagnated for over a decade, but the Consumer Price Index continued to rise, at least moderately. The rate of inflation exceeded the return on an investment in gold during that particular period.

The last sources of risk are theft and fraud. Although financial assets such as stocks and bonds can be left with custodians (e.g., stock registered in street name), that is not necessarily the case with nonfinancial assets. One's house is not left with the real estate broker. The investor in paintings will want to display them in order to enjoy them. The coin and stamp collector probably enjoys looking at the collection and does not leave it with coin and stamp dealers. These items are kept at home, where they are subject to theft and fire. Although the individual may protect these investments with insurance, adequate protection requires detailed records to verify the asset's value.

Finally, the investor must bear the risk of fraud. Fakes and misrepresentations may be sold to unsuspecting buyers who lack the knowledge to appraise them properly. This applies not only to novices but also to sophisticated professionals who, on occasion, have been completely deceived. The possibility of fraud, or at least of excessive pricing, truly makes investing in art and collectibles areas in which the novice should move with caution.

These risks suggest several practical steps for investing in these assets. First, investors should buy only after doing their homework. Second, investors should specialize in those particular nonfinancial assets that appeal to them. For example, one should not buy Oriental rugs because they are Oriental rugs but should collect them because they can be enjoyed and are functional. Third, one should invest in collectibles only after sufficient financial assets have been accumulated to meet financial emergencies and contingencies. Such physical assets offer little, if any, liquidity (although some may be used as collateral to secure a loan). Fourth, the investor should be willing to lose the entire investment in the art object or other

POINTS OF INTEREST

Insuring Your Collectibles

If the investor has a sizable collection of collectibles, it may be desirable to insure it against loss from fire, theft, and other perils. Before purchasing this insurance, the investor should consider the costs and benefits of such coverage. Special insurance may not be necessary since the investor's homeowner's policy generally covers the contents of the house up to one-half the value of the home. There may, however, be a limit on the coverage of a particular item or class of items.

The investor may remedy this limitation by adding a floater to the policy to cover specific items. This will require that the investor and the insurance company agree on the value of each specific item. Instead of a floater, the investor may buy a specialized policy (e.g., a fine art policy). This also requires enumeration and valuation of specific items. Such coverage should be updated annually.

Insurance is not free, and for sizable collections (e.g., over $100,000) the insurance company will probably require a security system. The investor should never overinsure, since the companies will pay only the market value of the item. Claim adjusters are not fools and will not accept inflated claims. Overinsurance is a waste of funds that may be used more profitably elsewhere.

collectible. Under these circumstances the investor will not be deluded into thinking that the asset will offer extraordinary gains. Such gains rarely, if ever, accrue to the novice, and investors in art and other collectibles are competing with professionals who have a lifetime of experience on which to base decisions.

Art and Other Collectibles

Art objects may be purchased in a variety of ways. One means is the dealer who makes a market (i.e., buys and sells). The art and security markets are very similar in that they are primarily secondhand markets. Since van Gogh and Rembrandt are no longer producing, sales of their work can only be secondary transactions. The same applies to all collectibles, such as Barbie dolls, baseball cards, and even beer cans. Any exchanges after the initial sale are in the secondary markets. In order for dealers to have these items for sale (i.e., inventory), many either acquire them or hold them on consignment.

When dealers make markets, they, in effect, establish bid and ask prices. While such prices may not be known to the investor, any dealer who is willing to buy used rugs, antiques, or art is offering a bid. Of course, the offer to sell establishes an asking price. Since the volume of transactions is low and the number of dealers in these specialized areas is relatively small, the spread between the bid and the ask will be substantial. The buyer may be paying the retail price but only receiving the wholesale price, which will certainly consume a substantial amount of any price appreciation.

Some dealers sell on consignment. Title remains with the owner, and if a sale occurs, the dealer receives a set percentage of the price. This commission can be as high as 30 or 40 percent of the sale price. If the commission on the sale of a collectible is 30 percent of the sale price, that's like buying a stock at an asking price of $50 and selling it at a bid price of $35. The price of the stock would have to rise above $71 (if the spread remained 30 percent of the sale price) for the investor to start to earn a profit. Obviously, the prices must rise substantially for these investors to recoup the initial cost, pay the commissions, and still net a profit.

An alternative market for valuable art and collectibles is the auction. The word *auction* may imply the Saturday afternoon sale of an estate, but many major works are sold through auctions. The important auction houses of the world, such as Sotheby's (http://www.sothebys.com) and Christie's (http://www.christies.com), hold auctions that handle many valuable art treasures. Such auction houses permit the owners of valuable art, antiques, and other collectibles to offer them for sale to a larger audience, but the sale price that will be realized is unknown in advance. Although the auction house places an estimated value on the item, the realized price can be higher or lower than the estimate. After the sale, the auction house takes its fee or commission from the realized price. Buyers as well as sellers may have to pay a fee for items bought at an auction. Both Christie's and Sotheby's add a premium that the buyer must pay of up to 10 percent of the cost of the purchase. This charge is in addition to their fees charged the seller, which range from 2 to 10 percent of the proceeds of the sale.

The Return on Collectibles

The return on investments in art, antiques, and other collectibles comes from potential price appreciation. It is obvious how price appreciation generates a return, since it is the difference between the net proceeds of the sale (the sale price minus the commissions) and the purchase price. As has already been discussed, the commissions may consume a substantial portion of any gross profits.

An Oriental rug, an antique, or a painting may offer a superior total return when both the flow of services and price appreciation are considered. For example, if the investor compares the cost of wall-to-wall carpeting with the cost of an Oriental rug, the return offered by the Oriental rug will probably be superior. The wall-to-wall carpeting depreciates and cannot be readily moved if the investor changes homes. The Oriental rug performs the same service, may appreciate in value, and is easily moved. No wonder such rugs may be viewed by some individuals as investments, because these rugs generate many years of service and offer the potential for price appreciation.

The same applies to art and antiques. Paintings, lithographs, and sculpture all generate a flow of service. The owner derives pleasure from them, which is part of the reason for buying the works. Of course, quantifying this pleasure is impossible, so the true return on an investment in these items cannot be determined.[2]

The Valuation of Collectibles

What gives art, antiques, or Oriental rugs their value? The answer to this question is both simple and complex. The obvious answer is scarcity relative to demand. There are only so many paintings by a master, and certainly this scarcity enhances their value. Although there is a paucity of works by major artists, there is an abundance of what passes for art. This abundance (or an abundance relative to the demand) has resulted in low prices for the vast majority of paintings, graphics, and poor-quality Oriental rugs.

The valuation of art objects depends on many factors. Value is affected by the reputation of the artist and quality of the work as well as by many other factors, including attributes of the work itself and exogenous factors.

The creator of the work and its quality are the easiest attributes to isolate. The paintings of old and modern masters are readily identified, and the quality of their work is well known. However, the cost of their works frequently exceeds $100,000 and may reach into millions of dollars. Such prices virtually exclude all but a handful of collectors and museums.

Even many lesser-name artists are readily identifiable, and an investor may determine the quality of their work through reading, studying, and viewing the art firsthand. A minor name in art history is usually minor for a reason. Investments in this type of art may appreciate (especially if art prices rise in general), but the probability of a large increase in value is small.

In addition to the artist and the quality of the work, value depends on several factors that are both inherent in and external to the specific price. Factors indigenous to the work itself include the medium and the subject matter. For example, oil paintings tend to cost more than watercolors by the same artist. Landscapes command higher prices than portraits. Dark or somber scenes may be less valuable than brightly colored and cheerful ones.

Factors affecting value that are independent of the piece itself include the condition of the work, the former owners, the museums or shows in which the work was previously exhibited, and the seller.

Condition obviously affects value. As one would expect, a damaged painting or antique or a badly worn Oriental rug commands a lower price. However, the

[2]One means to measure investment performance is to use an index. The performance of the index can then be compared to indices of the stock market. (Of course, using an art index measures only price changes. It is not possible to measure the value of the pleasure received from the art.) One possibility is the Mei/Moses art indices, which were created by Jianping Mei and Michael Moses. These indices cover (1) all paintings, (2) American paintings, (3) impressionist and modern paintings, and (4) old master and nineteenth-century paintings. Information concerning the indices may be found at Professor Mei's home page: http://www.stern.nyu.edu/~jmei/.

POINTS OF INTEREST

What Goes Up Must Come Down

The market for collectibles, like the markets for stocks, options, and commodities, is not immune to speculation fever. As with other speculative binges, the bubble will ultimately burst and prices will decline dramatically. In 1982, rare stamps and coins declined 40 to 50 percent; in 1992, limited edition prints sold for less than half their 1990 prices. For example, Rauschenberg's *Booster* sold for $20,000 after reaching a high of $165,000 in 1990. In some cases the markets entirely dried up, as there were few buyers, and owners were reluctant to sell at distress prices. The causes of this dramatic price decline included the reduction in the rate of inflation, increased interest in equity investments, and the recession. These large price declines in stamps, limited edition prints, and other art objects taught investors in collectibles a lesson that investors in securities already know (but must periodically relearn): Speculative excesses ultimately correct themselves and prices fall. Unfortunately, the lesson can be expensive for those investors who are sucked in when prices reach their peak.

owner may be able to have damaged works restored (for a price). Such restoration should help increase the value of the work. Just the cleaning of an old painting or an Oriental rug will bring out the colors and perhaps make the piece both more attractive and marketable.

Who has previously owned the work, where it has been exhibited, and who is selling it may also affect the value of an art object. If a painting has passed through the collection of an important museum or major collector, its value is enhanced. In a sense, previous owners and exhibitions are like a pedigree. They establish authenticity and credibility that can enhance the value of a particular art object.

As the preceding discussion suggests, the valuation of art is very subjective. Professionals (e.g., art dealers and museum curators) know this and are capable of making reasonably accurate appraisals. When a piece is offered at an auction, these professionals know approximately how much the work should bring. If it appears that such a price will not be obtained, these professionals may enter the bidding and purchase the piece for their own galleries or collections. For this reason the novice investor should not expect to acquire quality art, antiques, or Oriental rugs at bargain prices. Those in the know will outbid such a naive investor.

The Selection of Collectibles

How does the investor tackle the problem of selecting among the works of art or other collectibles? Essentially the choice is either to buy the works of known artists or to try to identify the artists that will gain acceptance in the future. In a sense, this is similar to buying stock issued by IBM or GE, which are known firms in excellent financial condition, versus buying stock in the over-the-counter market that is issued by some small company that offers promise for the future. The works of an unknown artist will tend to be inexpensive, and if the artist subsequently acquires a "name," his or her works will appreciate in value. However, the probability of this occurring is small, in which case the investor will probably be lucky to recoup even the meager cost of the investment.

There are, however, several things that the investor can do to help increase the chance of earning a positive return on an investment in a painting or any collectible. First, the investor should buy from reputable dealers, since their reputation verifies the authenticity of the work. Exhibit 23.1 (p. 764) presents the confirmation statement from a dealer for the purchase of a painting. In addition to the title of the work and the medium (oil), the statement presents the year of the painting's execution (1974) and the work's identifying number (58). Such a statement is

EXHIBIT 23.1

Confirmation for the Purchase of a Painting

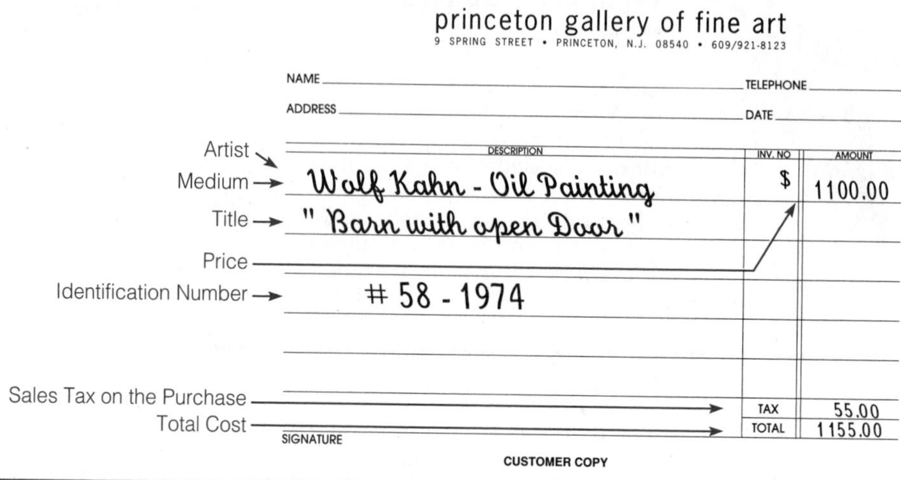
princeton gallery of fine art
9 SPRING STREET • PRINCETON, N.J. 08540 • 609/921-8123

NAME ____ TELEPHONE ____
ADDRESS ____ DATE ____

DESCRIPTION	INV. NO	AMOUNT
Wolf Kahn - Oil Painting	$	1100.00
" Barn with open Door "		
# 58 - 1974		
	TAX	55.00
SIGNATURE	TOTAL	1155.00

CUSTOMER COPY

not only proof of purchase but also serves to authenticate the work. Notice also that the purchase may be subject to sales tax. Such taxes do not apply to the purchase of stocks and bonds.

Second, the investor should avoid buying prints and other objects that masquerade as potential investments. Unsigned prints and reproductions may be an excellent means to decorate a room and to learn about art, but they are not originals, nor are they unique. Generally, unsigned prints and reproductions are not investments, and the individual should realize this fact and not be deluded into believing that such items will appreciate in value.[3]

Third, the investor should develop a specialty. Just as one cannot learn about all possible firms and their securities, the individual cannot know everything concerning all forms of art. The best strategy, then, is to develop an area of expertise that will permit the investor to learn which factors affect the value of particular art objects. In this way the investor can accumulate a collection that may be both decorative and serve as a store of value.

Precious Metals and Natural Resources

The previous section considered collectible tangible assets; this section covers different types of tangible assets. It begins with a discussion of investing in gold. Much of this material would also apply to other precious metals, such as silver, but the coverage is limited to gold. Next follows a brief discussion of investing in natural resources, such as timber and oil.

Gold

Gold has held a specific fascination for centuries. It has been minted into coins and used as a medium of exchange. Its color and durability have made it a

[3]In the past, print makers (e.g., Dürer) did not sign their works, but these unsigned original prints are potential investments. However, prints and reproductions of these originals should not be considered to be investments.

FIGURE 23.1

Year-End Price of Gold and the Annual Percentage Change in the Consumer Price Index (1971–1997)

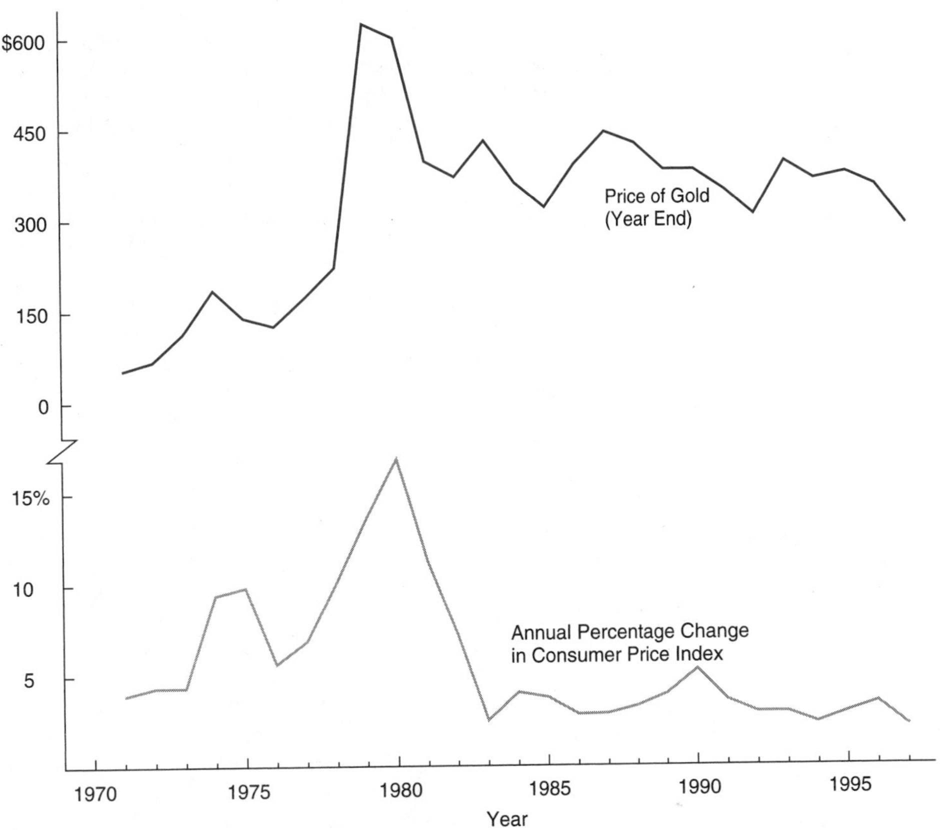

Source: *Federal Reserve Bulletin,* various issues; *The Wall Street Journal,* various issues.

popular metal for jewelry. Gold has also been a popular store of value. Some investors, who are frequently referred to as *gold bugs,* consider it to be a superior investment. A few investment advisory services have even recommended that investors hold a substantial proportion of their portfolios in some form of gold.

The main reason for investing in gold is a belief that it is the best insurance against inflation. The universal acceptability of gold makes it the one commodity to own during a period of rapid inflation. The price of gold tends to mirror fears of inflation. If the rate of inflation rises, purchases of gold will increase along with its price. Conversely, during periods of declining inflation, the price of gold tends to decrease. This is illustrated in Figure 23.1, which plots the price of an ounce of gold and the rate of inflation. As may be seen in the figure, the price of gold does respond to the rate of inflation. Once inflation abated during the early 1990s, the price of gold fell. For the period 1992 through 2000, the Consumer Price Index increased annually at less than 3 percent, and the price of gold languished. As of January 2001, its price was 25 percent less than the price as of January 1991.

Figure 23.1 also points out another fact: Investors can lose money by buying gold. As with any other investment, there is always the risk of loss. Holders of gold not only forgo income, such as dividends and interest, but also have to store the metal and bear the risk of fraud and capital loss from declining prices. Investors who bought gold in the 1970s may have earned a substantial return, as the price of gold rose to over $800 in 1980. Of course, if those investors chose not to realize their paper profits, they watched the profits melt away, as the price of gold has steadily declined since it reached those historic highs. Two decades later the price still languished well below the historic high.

There are several mediums for investing in gold: jewelry, coins, bullion (which is usually in the form of gold bars), stocks of mining companies, and futures contracts. As an investment, gold jewelry is a poor choice, because the cost of the jewelry includes not only the cost of the gold but also the cost of the copper used to strengthen the gold and the wages of the craftspeople who design and construct the jewelry. There may be excellent reasons for buying gold jewelry, but it is not a good choice as an investment. (Jewelry, especially rare gems, may prove to be an acceptable investment. However, the individual is primarily buying the gems instead of the gold, and such investments are very illiquid and produce no monetary income.)

Gold Coins

Gold coins are a better vehicle than jewelry for investing in gold. These coins initially came into existence as currency, but in the United States they no longer serve as a medium of exchange. Many coins still exist from the past and may be purchased through coin dealers and at auctions.

Like jewelry, gold coins have a serious weakness as an investment. Their price is related to two things: the bullion content and the coin's numismatic value. The bullion value of a coin depends on the gold content and the price of gold. This price, in turn, depends on the market's demand for and supply of gold. Gold is used in various products (e.g., jewelry) and is continually being mined. The demand for gold in its various uses (including investments) relative to the supply that is offered determines the market price of gold bullion.

In addition, the value of gold coins depends on the numismatic value of the coin. Some coins are much scarcer than others and hence are more valuable as collector's items. If the investor is concerned only with accumulating gold, then numismatic rarities are of little interest because the investor pays more for the same amount of gold. The premium paid over the bullion value can be substantial; the investor, therefore, is really speculating on the coin as a collector's item and not on its gold content.[4]

One coin of particular interest to gold collectors is the Canadian Maple Leaf, which is issued by the Canadian government. Canada is second to South Africa as the Western world's main producer of gold. It mints the Canadian Maple Leaf to sell to gold collectors.[5] While the coin may be used as money, it is not circulated, for such use would scar the coins and reduce their value.

The primary attractiveness of the Canadian Maple Leaf is that the coin is issued in exactly one troy ounce of fine gold. This uniformity of metal content increases its marketability in the secondary markets. In addition, the coin sells for a modest premium over the value of the gold bullion in the coin. Other gold

[4]Investors who wish to acquire coin collections may prefer such rarities. These will probably increase in value more rapidly than the more common gold coins. In general, it is the rarer items that appreciate the fastest. Collectors of gold coins (and stamps, antiques, and other collectibles) may find that the best strategy is to buy a few expensive, high-quality representations instead of trying to amass large collections of less rare and cheaper specimens.

[5]South Africa also mints a coin to sell to collectors, the Krugerrand.

coins, especially commemorative coins or foreign limited edition coins, are frequently sold (at least initially) at a considerable premium over their value as bullion. The investor runs a substantial risk in that the price of these commemorative coins may decline relative to the value of the gold bullion in the secondary markets. This potential price decline, however, does not apply to Canadian Maple Leafs.

Gold Bullion

Until January 1, 1975, gold coins and jewelry offered Americans the only legal means to own gold. However, Americans can now own gold bullion in the form of gold bars. These may be bought through gold dealers and brokerage firms. Once the investor purchases the gold, he or she may take possession of it or leave it with the dealer or broker. Leaving the gold with the broker involves storage and insurance costs, which increases the price of the investment.

The investor may take delivery and store the gold in a presumably safe place. The gold ingots should be stamped and numbered by the refiner, who also supplies correspondingly numbered certificates. These must be delivered with the gold should the investor ever sell the ingots. If the certificates are lost, the ingots will have to be assayed to prove their gold content. This expense must be paid by the investor to ensure the marketability of the gold bars. Even if the documentation is not lost, the investor may have to have the gold assayed because taking possession results in a loss of the guarantee of the gold's quality, and this guarantee can only be restored by having the gold assayed.

Gold Mining Stocks

The investor may also buy the shares of gold mining companies. This, of course, is not owning gold. Instead, the firm may own gold mines and mining equipment. Presumably, the value of the shares is related to the value of the gold, but it is possible for the price of gold to rise while the price of the mining company's stock declines. Various factors, such as a strike or a fire, can affect the value of the mining firm and its securities, but such events may have no impact on the price of gold.[6]

These exogenous factors (especially political forces) are particularly important in the valuation of gold mining stocks. South Africa alone accounts for about two-thirds of the world's output of newly mined gold. The political climate in South Africa is somewhat unstable, and this instability can have an impact on the value of gold mining shares in South African companies.

The investor may avoid these political problems by limiting purchases to shares in gold mining companies in the United States and Canada whose values tend to follow closely the price of bullion. This is illustrated in Figure 23.2 (p. 768), which shows the price performance of shares of Homestake Mining (a Canadian firm) and the price of gold. As may be seen in the figure, the price of these shares moved in tandem with the price of gold. Since the price of gold languished during the 1990s, it is not at all surprising that the price of Homestake Mining also languished. Gold stocks, however, do offer several advantages over gold bars. Such shares not only avoid the costs of storage, insurance, and assaying but also may pay dividend income, which is not possible from an investment in gold bars.

However, this strategy of buying gold shares instead of gold also has disadvantages. Buying shares in gold firms may be more risky than taking a position in the metal. The prices of gold stocks tend to be more volatile than the price of gold. These

[6]The investor may reduce the impact of such events by purchasing the shares of an investment company that specializes in the securities of gold mining companies. For example, American–South African Investment Company (or ASA) is a closed-end investment company whose shares are traded on the New York Stock Exchange. ASA specializes in the stocks of South African gold mining firms.

FIGURE 23.2

Price of Gold and Yearly Price Range of Homestake Mining Stock (1981–1997)

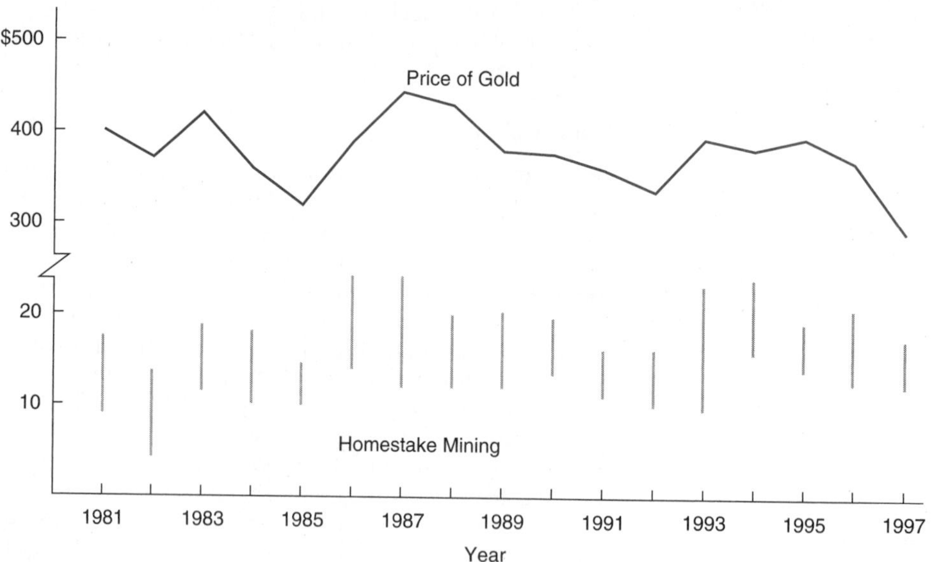

Source: *Standard and Poor's Stock Guide*, various issues; *The Wall Street Journal*, various issues.

companies have costs (e.g., wages, interest, depreciation of equipment) that are independent of the price of gold. Once these expenses have been met, further increases in the price of gold tend to increase earnings. Thus a small change in the price of gold can generate a larger change in the earnings of gold mining companies.

The converse is also true since a small decline in the price of gold can cause a profitable mine to operate at a loss. The difference between a profitable and a losing mine can be a matter of a few dollars. For this reason the analysis of gold mining shares tends to stress two considerations: (1) the estimated life of the mine and (2) the cost of recovering the metal. Low-cost, long-lived mines are obviously the most desirable. They will tend to be the most profitable during periods of higher gold prices but may still generate a profit (or smaller loss) during periods when the price of gold declines.

Gold Mutual Funds

The individual may acquire shares in investment companies that specialize in gold investments. For example, Franklin Gold and Bull & Bear Gold Investors LTD invest primarily in gold (i.e., gold mining stocks and bullion) and other precious metals (i.e., silver and platinum). (The funds may also have temporary holdings of short-term money market securities.) One advantage of these funds is the diversification of their portfolios. If the individual expected the price of gold to rise but was uncertain whether to invest in the bullion, gold mining stocks, or other assets that are complementary to gold, then investing in a gold mutual fund gives the investor a diversified mix of gold investments. The individual avoids having to select a specific gold investment or a particular gold stock.

Gold Futures and Options

In addition to gold coins, gold bullion, and gold mining shares, the investor may speculate in gold futures and gold options.[7] Like many other commodities, there is an active market in contracts for the future delivery of gold. The principal markets for these gold futures are the Chicago International Monetary Market and the New York Commodity Exchange (COMEX).

As with other commodity contracts, the appeal of gold futures is in the great leverage that they offer investors. A contract for the future delivery of gold is for 100 troy ounces. At $350 an ounce, the contract has a face value of $35,000. If the margin requirement were $3,500, the speculator would have a claim on $35,000 worth of gold for an outlay of only $3,500. If the price were to rise by only $10 per ounce, the value of the contract would rise by $1,000 to $36,000. The speculator would then make $1,000 on an investment of only $3,500. Of course, if the price of gold were to fall by only $10 per ounce, the speculator would lose $1,000. Since gold prices do fluctuate, there exists considerable potential for large profits (and losses), which is a primary reason for the attractiveness of gold futures to speculators.

Although all forms of investing in gold involve several sources of risk, gold futures involve a special source of risk. Government and international agencies participate in the market for gold. For example, the U.S. Treasury may sell gold, and this additional supply tends to reduce its price. In addition, the International Monetary Fund of the United Nations sells gold to raise currency for its international transactions. These sales make investing in gold futures more risky, as they alter the supply of and demand for the metal.

The New York Commodity Exchange also offers gold futures options, which are put and call options to sell and buy gold futures contracts. Although they are not options to buy and sell gold, their prices move with the price of gold. As with other put and call options, one reason for purchasing them is the potential leverage they offer. Suppose the investor pays $1,000 for a call option to purchase a gold futures contract for 100 ounces at $320. The value of the call option will rise as the price of gold (and the futures price) rises above $320. For example, if the price of gold rose to $350 by the expiration date of the call, the option would be worth $3,000. This $3,000 is the $30 difference between the current price ($350) and the price specified in the call option ($320) times 100, since the option is the right to buy a contract for 100 ounces. Thus, in this illustration the price of gold rose less than 10 percent (from $320 to $350), but the value of the option tripled from $1,000 to $3,000. If the investor had purchased the option for $1,000, this individual would have earned a $2,000 profit on the transaction.

If the price of gold were to decline, the value of the call option would also decline. If the price of gold fell to $300, then the call option to buy the gold futures contract at $320 would become worthless. No one would exercise the option to buy at $320 what could be purchased elsewhere for $300. In that case, the investor would lose the $1,000 invested in the call option.

While both futures contracts and put and call options are means to leverage one's position when speculating on changes in the price of gold, the gold option offers one major advantage over the futures contract. With a futures contract, the investor could lose a substantial amount if there were a large and sudden change in the price of the commodity. This is because the investor has not purchased anything but has entered into a contract to buy (or sell) gold at a specified price. If the price moved against the investor, that individual could sustain a large loss in order to fulfill the contract. However, with a put or a call option the investor actually

[7]Refer to Chapter 21 for a general discussion of investing in commodity futures and Chapter 19 for a general discussion of options.

owns something (i.e., the option). Thus, the maximum amount that may be lost is the cost of the option. This limit on the possible loss reduces the risk associated with speculating in the movements of the price of gold.

Natural Resources

The previous material considered investing in collectibles (e.g., art) and precious metals (especially gold). This section will focus on investing in natural resources. Although the principles developed here may apply to many natural resources, the analysis is limited to oil and timber.

As with any asset, the reason for investing in natural resources is the potential return, which is the result of the nature of the aggregate supply of the resource. At a given moment in time, the supply of natural resources is fixed. For example, the amount of oil and gas reserves is known and will not readily change. While more oil and gas reserves will be discovered, the process takes time and expense. Environmental concerns may limit drilling, and while older wells may hold additional reserves, current technology may not be sufficient to recover these reserves profitably.

The supply of timber is also fixed. The time period necessary to plant a new crop and bring it to harvest is long. Of course, advancements in technology may alter the usage of the current supply. Recycling of newsprint and cardboard or the development of products such as particle board affect the demand for and the price of timber, but they will not immediately affect the supply. As in the case of the recovery of oil in old wells, technology's impact on the resource and its pricing is usually minimal during a short period of time.

Oil and timber illustrate an important factor to consider when investing in natural resources: the elasticity of supply. Economists use the term *elasticity* to refer to responsiveness in a dependent variable, such as the quantity supplied, to a change in an independent variable, such as price. If the quantity demanded of a good or service or the quantity supplied does not respond to a change in price, the demand or supply is said to be *inelastic.*

Such inelasticity is important for individuals considering an investment in a natural resource. If higher demand and the resulting higher prices induce an increase in the quantity supplied, the price increase is dampened. Consider the supply curves presented in Figure 23.3. Supply curve S_1 is relatively flat, or elastic. An increase in the price of the good generates a large increase in the quantity supplied. Supply curve S_2 is relatively steep, or inelastic. A price increase generates a small increase in the quantity supplied.

Consider what happens when demand rises from D_1 to D_2 and the price starts to increase from P_1. In the case of the more inelastic supply curve S_2, there is a small increase in the quantity supplied to Q_3, so the price rises to P_3. However, in the case of the elastic supply curve S_1, there is a larger increase in the quantity supplied to Q_2, and the price does not rise as much (only from P_1 to P_2). The larger response in the quantity supplied dampens the price increase and obviously reduces the potential return.

An individual who desires to invest in natural resources should seek those resources whose supply cannot readily respond to a higher price. The time lapse necessary to locate and drill for oil or the long growing period for timber suggest that the supply of these resources is inelastic. Increased demand causes their prices to rise, and the inelastic supply means that price will remain at a higher level for a longer period of time. This price pattern would not be possible if supply were elastic and could quickly respond to the change in demand.

Of course, this inelasticity works in both directions. If demand were to fall, the existing supply does not disappear. The quantity supplied does not respond, and

FIGURE 23.3

Price Responses to a Change in Demand

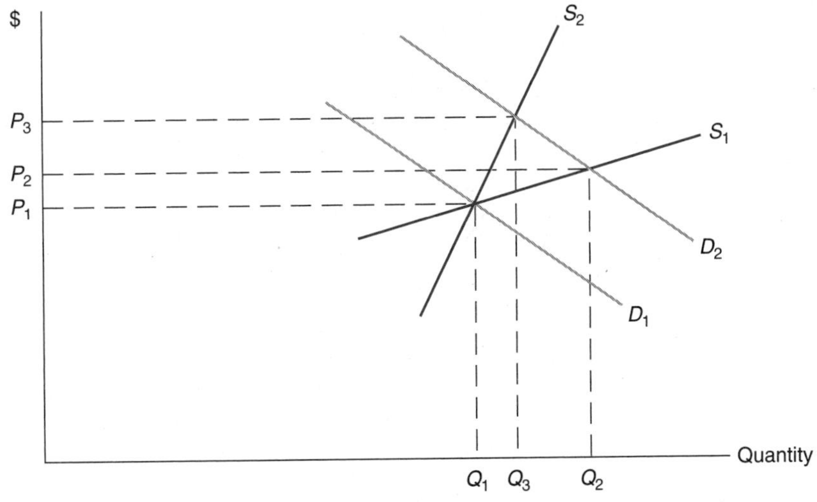

the price decline will be more severe and remain at a depressed level for a longer time until the existing supply is absorbed.[8]

In addition to the potential return, investments in natural resources may offer the additional advantage of diversifying the portfolio. Often, natural resource prices rise when the prices of financial assets decline. This is particularly true during an inflationary period, which is accompanied by higher commodity prices, higher interest rates, and lower security prices. Fixed-income securities (such as bonds) or income stocks (such as the shares of electric utilities) may sustain a major price decline during a period of higher interest rates.

Once the individual decides to invest in natural resources for their potential return or their ability to diversify the portfolio, the individual must decide on the vehicle for making the investments. One possibility is the stock of firms with large oil, gas, coal, and mineral reserves or timber holdings. This strategy of acquiring a financial asset rather than the resource itself requires that the price of the stock rise in response to an increase in the price of the natural resource.

Another alternative is to buy units in a limited partnership specializing in a type of resource. For example, Kinder Morgan Energy Partners (NYSE: KMP) is a limited partnership with investments in natural gas and gas pipelines. Partnership units offer the advantages of limited liability for the unit holders, marketability, and possible tax deferral. The partnership's cash flow and resulting distributions may be sheltered from current taxation by depreciation and depletion allowances. For income tax purposes, distributions of cash flow are treated differently from dividend or interest income. They require additional tax schedules, and more detailed record-keeping is necessary than for investments in stocks and bonds, which only generate dividend or interest income and possible capital gains.

[8]The large fluctuations in the price of oil and oil-based products, especially gasoline and heating oil, are the result of the fact that both supply and demand tend to be inelastic. Small shifts in the supply curve can have a large impact on price because the quantity demanded changes only marginally.

It is, however, easy to confuse cash flow distributions with taxable dividend income. Tax-free distributions are a return of the investor's initial capital that reduce the cost basis of the investment.[9] If the partnership units are subsequently sold, capital gains are determined by subtracting the adjusted and lower cost basis from the proceeds of the sale. Thus, tax-free distributions may lead to future capital gains taxes if the units' value does not decline by the amount of the distributions.

If the individual does not want to invest in units of limited partnerships, there may be opportunities to invest directly in natural resources. For example, the climate and soils of some parts of the country may be acceptable for growing a stand of timber. In the Southeast, timber such as pine may be sold for lumber or pulpwood. Even though the crop takes decades to grow sufficiently to harvest, it should appreciate in value as the trees mature and inflation consistently increases the price of timber. Any current cash received from the timber may not be taxable depending on depreciation or depletion allowances, and if the individual meets specified conditions, the IRS applies capital gain instead of income tax rates. The ability to treat the cash flow generated by harvesting the timber as a capital gain means that current losses from the operation may be used to offset capital gains from other sources.

Such investments in timber, however, require active management by the individual. In reality, this investment involves the business of growing, managing, and harvesting the crop, in contrast to the passive nature of an investment in units in a partnership or stock in a natural resource company. Running an active business is perceptibly different from managing a financial portfolio. The individual may have to hire employees to run the operation; purchase insurance against loss from fire, theft, or liability; pay taxes and fees, such as Social Security taxes or workers' unemployment insurance; and offer employees retirement plans or health insurance.

Real Estate

Collectibles, precious metals, and natural resources are investments that may not appeal to many individuals, but virtually every investor is interested in real estate. Since people must live somewhere, their choices are either to rent and consume space or to own and simultaneously consume space and make an investment in the property. In addition to home ownership, an investor may acquire rental properties or shares in companies whose primary operations are in real estate. These alternatives range from passive investments in companies that own and manage real properties to active investments in which the individual owns properties and rents the space.

The following discussion begins with home ownership and considers the tax advantages associated with owning a home, the returns, and sources of mortgage money. The balance of this section covers investing in rental properties and real estate investment trusts that acquire properties. Owning rental properties is essentially operating a business in which the investor must play an active role. In addition, real estate assets are not readily sold. Like collectibles, real properties can be a very illiquid asset. Owning shares in a real estate investment trust is a

[9]These payments are analogous to receipts from mortgage pass-through securities such as Ginnie Maes (discussed in Chapter 17). Payments are partly taxable interest income and partly return of principal—which, since it is the initial investment, is not taxable as income.

passive investment since the management of the trust makes the decisions concerning the properties. However, shares in these trusts are actively traded, so they offer the most liquidity of all real estate investments.

Home Ownership

Acquiring a home is not the same as purchasing most goods and services. Few individuals can make in one single payment the entire cost of a home. Instead, they make an initial payment (i.e., the down payment) and borrow the balance with a loan secured by the property (i.e., the mortgage). The initial down payment may be substantial. For example, a down payment of 20 to 25 percent on a $200,000 home requires the buyer to have between $40,000 and $50,000 in cash. Obviously, the individual will have had to accumulate the funds in order to make this required initial payment.

The primary sources of mortgage loans are savings and loans and other financial institutions, such as commercial banks. The potential buyer must apply for these loans, and whether the lending institution grants them will depend on the amount of the down payment and the buyer's capacity to service the debt (i.e., pay the interest and retire the principal). Although the loan is secured by the property, the lender is primarily concerned with collecting the mortgage payments and not with seizing the home in case of default. Thus, having sufficient income to service the loan is crucial to obtaining a mortgage.

Besides having the down payment and obtaining the mortgage, the buyer must be able to meet other expenses when the home is acquired. Transferring title from the seller to the buyer requires the services of a lawyer. The potential buyer may want the home professionally inspected for possible defects (especially if the home is several years old). Title insurance, which guarantees the title is free and clear of claims, also increases the initial costs associated with the purchase of the home (or any other real estate).

There are many reasons for owning a home instead of renting. These include the psychic income that comes with the pride of owning a place that can be called one's home. However, owning involves considerable costs and possible headaches that the renter may avoid. Suppose your hot water heater breaks. If you rent, you call the manager. You don't have the headache associated with getting the problem fixed. (Your headache may be getting the landlord to fix the problem.) Responsibility for many repairs rests with the owner, who also pays expenses, such as property taxes, interest on the mortgage, general maintenance, fire insurance, and supervisory personnel. The owner seeks to recover these expenses through the rents, but failure to cover these costs may result in the investment generating a loss instead of a profit.

Homeowners, of course, have to cover these expenses out of their own pockets. Expenditures such as general maintenance (e.g., painting and repairs), necessary equipment (e.g., lawn mowers), insurance, property taxes, and interest on the mortgage may consume a substantial proportion of a family's budget. Many of these costs are not recaptured when the home is sold but must be made in order to maintain the property's value. If the individual does not want to perform required tasks or is reluctant to employ others to maintain the property, then renting and passing the expenses (and headaches) to the landlord is a reasonable strategy, especially if the funds that could have been invested in a home are not frittered away but are used to obtain some other alternative investments.

Home ownership, however, offers a very pragmatic advantage over renting. It is a means to force saving. Every payment on a mortgage loan represents interest and principal. The amount that the individual has invested in the home increases with each mortgage payment. These payments become a convenient means to force oneself to save. In addition, any repairs and improvements made in the property accrue to the owner and not to the landlord.

There are two major financial reasons for home ownership. The first pertains to the tax benefits, and the second is the potential return on the investment. Of course, this return depends partially on the tax shelters generated by home ownership. These tax breaks are tax shelters, because they either reduce taxable income or defer tax payments. The tax shelters or tax advantages of home ownership are (1) the deductions from income that the homeowner who itemizes is able to take and (2) the possible deferment or even avoidance of capital gains taxes when the property is sold.

Income Tax Deductions

The vast majority of homes are purchased through the use of mortgage loans. The interest paid is a tax-deductible expense, which reduces taxable income and thus results in a tax savings. If the homeowner is carrying a $100,000 mortgage at 8 percent, the approximate interest charge is $8,000 in the first year of the mortgage. Itemization of this interest expense reduces taxable income by $8,000.

The effect of this deduction is a reduction in the true or effective cost of a mortgage loan. The individual's true cost of a mortgage is related to (1) the interest rate and (2) the marginal income tax rate. If an investor borrows funds and pays 8 percent, the *before-tax* interest rate is 8 percent, but the true cost of the loan is less.

A simple example illustrates how the deduction reduces the effective cost of the debt. If an investor has a marginal tax rate of 28 percent and borrows funds at 8 percent interest, then the effective cost of the mortgage is 5.76 percent. The **effective interest rate** is

effective interest rate
The interest rate paid adjusted for any tax savings.

Before-tax interest rate (1 − Marginal tax rate).

For this individual the calculation is

$$0.08\ (1 - 0.28) = 5.76\%.$$

This effective interest rate (i_e) is expressed in symbolic form in Equation 23.1:

$$i_e = i(1 - t). \qquad (23.1)$$

The effective interest rate (i_e) is simply the product of the stated interest rate (i) and the tax effect ($1 - t$), in which t represents the investor's marginal income bracket. Obviously, the higher the individual's marginal tax rate, the lower is the true cost of borrowing.

The homeowner is also permitted to deduct from taxable income the property taxes that are paid on the home. The effect of itemizing property taxes is a reduction in the individual's taxable income and therefore a reduction in the federal income tax liability. Since the property tax charged by some local governments amounts to over $2,000 on even moderately valued homes (e.g., $70,000 to $100,000 homes), the property tax deduction can result in substantial savings on income taxes for middle-income homeowners.

Owing to these deductions, several important expenditures or cash outlays associated with home ownership come from *before-tax* dollars. Most expenditures made by individuals come from *after-tax* dollars. Renters, who cannot take advantage of these deductions, pay rent with after-tax dollars. If an individual is in the 28 percent tax bracket, that person must earn $1,042 to make $750 in rental payments. However, that same individual could reduce taxes by $28 for every $100 paid in interest or property taxes on a house.

Capital Gains Taxation of the Sale of a Principal Residence

In addition to the previous deductions, a homeowner will probably receive a tax break when the residence is sold. The profit on the sale of a principal residence is excluded from taxation if the gain is less than $500,000 for a joint return and $250,000 for a single return. The home must have been the principal residence for at least two of the five years prior to the sale, and the exclusion applies only to one sale every two years. Since the vast majority of home sales will be for less than the exclusions, the effect is that few home sales will generate sufficient profits to be subject to capital gains taxation.

Condominiums

condominium
An apartment that is owned instead of rented.

These reasons for home ownership also apply to **condominiums**. A condominium is similar to an apartment, but instead of renting, the individual owns the "apartment." The grounds and general facilities belong to all the owners of the condominiums, who pay a fee for their maintenance.[10] The portion of the building that the individual owns may be subsequently sold, and the seller may earn a capital gain if the property is sold for a profit. In addition, since the individual owns and does not rent the space, the tax advantages of home ownership apply. Thus, in some ways ownership of a condominium is no different from ownership of a home; a condominium may be treated as an investment just as a home is.

The condominium is particularly attractive to people who have little need or desire for lawns and shrubs. The maintenance of a home and the grounds can be expensive in terms of both time and money. Although the condominium owner does not avoid the monetary cost of this maintenance, he or she may not have to expend the effort. If the individual lacks the time or the inclination for home maintenance, the condominium may offer the best of both worlds: the advantage of home ownership and the convenience of renting.

Risks and Returns

Many people believe that homes are among the best investments. The appreciation in the value of the home acts as a hedge against inflation, and at the same time the investor receives the services of the home.

The price appreciation in homes is illustrated in Figure 23.4 (pp. 776–777), which presents the median prices of new and existing homes for 1973 through 2000.[11] The figure also includes the Dow Jones Industrial Average for the same period. Part (a) of the figure presents yearly home prices, while part (b) presents annual percentage changes.

The prices of new and existing homes and the Dow Jones Industrial Average rose during this time period. Over the entire time period, the annual growth rate in the median price of a new home was 6.37 percent, while the prices of existing homes grew by 5.99 percent. The Dow Jones rose 9.87 percent (compounded annually). These numbers, however, cannot be considered rates of return, since the growth in the Dow Jones does not consider dividends and hence understates the return the investor would have earned. Correspondingly, the growth in the home prices may overstate returns, since costs (e.g., repairs) associated with home ownership are excluded.

[10]The investor should read carefully the agreement that specifies what is covered by the maintenance fee. Some managements have defaulted and not fulfilled their part of the contracts, which leaves condominium owners with additional obligations that must be met to comply with local health and fire regulations.

[11]Figure 23.4 uses the median price and not the average price of single-family residential homes since the average is raised by the sales of a few expensive homes. The median price may be more representative of the price of a home to the typical buyer. Data concerning home prices are collected by the U.S. Bureau of the Census. This data may also be found (along with additional information on homes) at the Web site of the National Association of Home Builders (http://.www.nahb.com).

FIGURE 23.4

Dow Jones Industrial Average and Median Prices of New and Existing Homes, 1973–2000

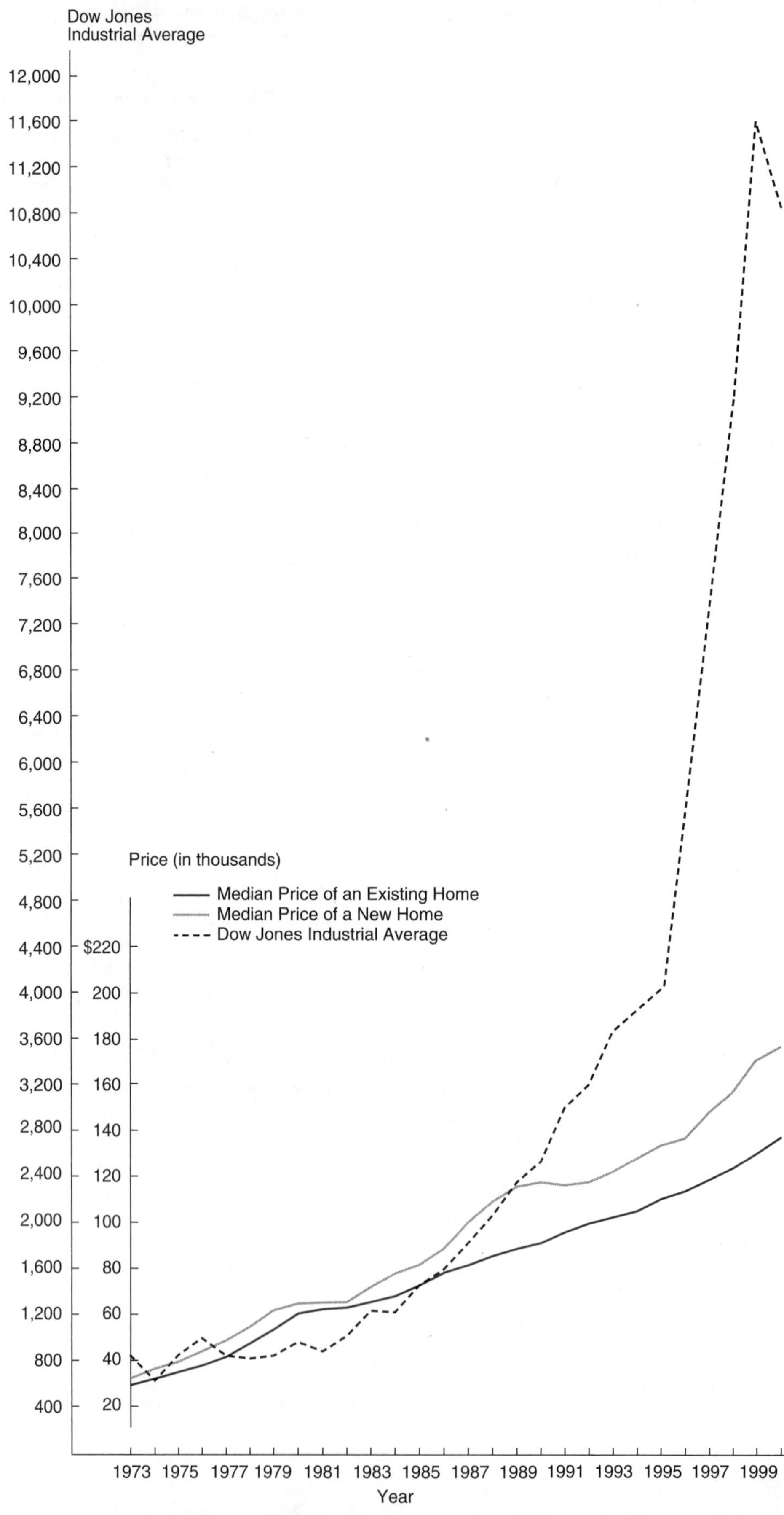

FIGURE 23.4 CONTINUED

Dow Jones Industrial Average and Median Prices of New and Existing Homes, 1973–2000

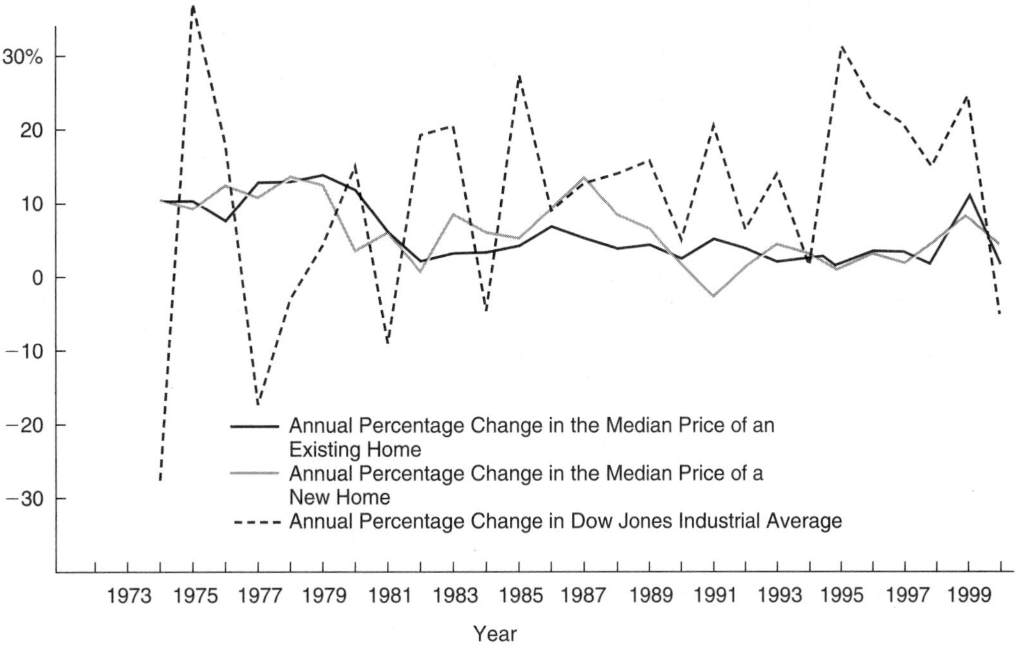

Source: *Federal Reserve Bulletin*, various issues; *The Wall Street Journal Index* (Ann Arbor, MI: UMI Company), various issues.

Figure 23.4 also illustrates considerable differences in the year-to-year price fluctuations. While home prices rose virtually every year, the Dow Jones experienced losses in several years (e.g., 2000). There were also periods when stock prices rose dramatically (e.g., 1995–1999) while home prices rose only modestly. This variability in returns is mirrored by the standard deviations of the annual price changes. For existing homes and new homes, the standard deviations were 4.1 and 3.6, respectively. This indicates only modest year-to-year changes in the median prices of existing homes and new homes. The standard deviation for the Dow Jones Industrial Average, however, was 15.1—indicating considerable year-to-year variation in the percentage change in the average.

Part of the explanation for the increase in home values is the increased cost of construction. The rising building costs of new homes translate into increased values for old homes. Old and new homes are substitutes for each other. If the cost of one rises relative to the cost of the other, buyers will seek to purchase the cheaper home. As the cost of new homes rises, some individuals will seek to purchase existing homes. This, in turn, will drive up the prices of older homes to keep them in line with the prices of newly constructed homes.

Another explanation for the increased value of homes is the continued increase in demand. Conventional wisdom suggests that home ownership serves two purposes—as a place to live and as an investment. This belief encourages individuals to buy homes even though they may have to take on more financial obligation than is prudent for their capacity to service the debt. As is subsequently discussed, the tendency on the part of some homeowners to use excessive amounts of debt financing (i.e., excessive financial leverage) is a major source of risk of investing in homes. However, to the extent that individuals are willing and able to obtain this mortgage money, they increase the demand for homes and hence help to increase their prices.

Is an investment in a home really one of the best hedges against inflation? One study found that *only* private residential real estate offered complete protection against inflation.[12] Other investments, such as debt instruments, were a successful hedge against anticipated inflation, because their yields adjusted for the anticipated rate of inflation. However, these assets did not protect against unanticipated inflation. Only private residential real estate provided a safeguard against both expected and unexpected inflation. This study thus supports the conventional wisdom that home ownership is one of the best investments available, especially during inflationary times.

Although Figure 23.4 shows steady increases in home prices, the recession of 1990 and 1991 took its toll, as home prices in some geographical areas stagnated and even fell and the rate of increase declined in other localities. From 1989 through 1994, the annual rate of growth in the median prices of new and existing homes was only 1.6 and 3.4 percent, respectively. (During the same time period the Dow Jones Industrial Average annual compound rate of growth was 9.0 percent.) Changes in family structure (such as delaying marriages or children returning home after graduating from college) and economic conditions (such as the creation of lower-paying service jobs at the expense of manufacturing jobs) may discourage individuals from taking on the responsibilities of home ownership. In addition to financing costs and day-to-day expenses, owners are responsible for maintenance, whose costs (even if recouped when the home is sold) still require a current cash outlay.

While inflation may help generate a return on an investment in a home, it may also be a major source of risk associated with home ownership. The cost of running a home rises with the rate of inflation. The increased costs of insurance, energy, and various other expenses (which are not deductible from taxable income) may strain the individual's budget if personal income does not rise as rapidly. Even though the resale value of the house may be increasing, it does not supply the current cash necessary to meet the expenses associated with running the home.

Another source of risk is the use of mortgage financing to acquire the home. The mortgage is a fixed monthly expense that must be met, or the holder of the mortgage may seize the home (through a court proceeding) and sell it to recoup the funds lent to the homeowner. Investors thus run risk of loss should they be unable to maintain mortgage payments. Some individuals purchase expensive homes and anticipate that home values and their salaries will rise while mortgage payments remain constant, only to find that the mortgage payment becomes a real burden when adversity strikes (e.g., the loss of a job or extended illness).

The last source of risk is the fact that not all property values increase. Real estate values are dependent on the economies of their local region. Plant closings and corporate relocations affect real estate values in specific regions, because they cause an imbalance of the supply of housing and industrial properties relative to the demand. For this reason, local governments may encourage firms to locate in their areas by offering tax relief, lower-priced loans, or other services.

Individuals' tastes also affect the value of local properties. During the 1970s, suburban homes appreciated in value more rapidly than city properties. However, pockets within some cities have appreciated more rapidly since 1980, as some in-

[12]Eugene F. Fama and G. William Schwert, "Asset Returns and Inflation," *Journal of Financial Economics* 5 (November 1978): 115–146.

POINTS OF INTEREST

The Housing Affordability Index

A measure of the potential demand for housing is the affordability index. This index compares individuals' income to a measure of required debt service. If the index exceeds 1.0, the typical American family has sufficient income to purchase a median-priced house. If the index is less than 1.0, the cost of a median-priced house exceeds the ability of most families to afford it.

Obviously, higher median incomes or lower housing prices increase the index while higher debt service reduces it. Houses are usually purchased through the use of mortgage loans, which require monthly payments by the homeowner. The mortgage payment depends on the amount of the loan, its terms, and the interest rate. Lower interest rates will mean lower debt service, so the value of the index rises. Conversely, higher interest rates reduce the index.

The affordability index changes from month to month with changes in income, house prices, and interest rates. In mid-1989 the index fell below 1.0 for the first time since March 1986. This meant that the typical American family with median income of $32,760 could not afford the median-priced house (i.e., $93,200) using conventional financing (i.e., a 20 percent down payment and a fixed-rate mortgage). Since 1989 was a period of continuing economic prosperity, it seems almost perverse that the affordability index declined.

Actually, the ability to afford a house may rise during periods of economic stagnation since declining interest rates may more than offset declining aggregate incomes. The converse may hold when the economy is expanding and incomes are rising. More economic activity is often accompanied by both higher home prices and higher interest rates because the demand for funds is increased and the Federal Reserve may tighten credit to reduce inflationary pressure. Thus it is possible that during periods of economic expansion, many potential buyers will be unable to afford a single-family home.

dividuals moved back into urban areas. People who had the foresight to buy in an area where home values subsequently appreciated did well. But many individuals were not so lucky. During the early 1990s, some homeowners experienced such large price declines that the resale values of their homes were less than the amount owed on the mortgages. In many cases these individuals were locked into their homes: They could not sell, because they lacked the funds to retire their mortgages once they realized the losses.

Sources of Mortgage Money

One problem facing the individual buying a home is financing. Few individuals have sufficient funds to pay the entire purchase price and hence must borrow to finance the purchase. Funds are obtained through mortgage loans from a financial intermediary, such as a commercial bank or a savings and loan association.[13] There are basically two types of mortgage loans: conventional loans and loans backed by an agency of the federal government.

conventional mortgage loan
A standard loan to finance real estate (and secured by the property) in which the loan is periodically retired, and the interest paid is figured on the declining balance owed.

With a **conventional mortgage loan** the individual buys the house with a down payment and borrows the balance. The loan is retired over a period of years by payments (usually monthly) that pay the interest and retire the principal. The amount of the periodic payment is fixed, and the interest is determined on the balance owed. Exhibit 23.2 (p. 780) presents parts of a mortgage schedule for a loan of $150,000 at 8 percent for 25 years. Each monthly payment is $1,157.72, which consists of an interest payment and a principal repayment. The first column of the table gives the number of payment. These range from 1 to 300 because the loan requires 12 monthly payments for 25 years for a total of 300 payments. The second

[13]On-line information concerning mortgage rates may be found through HSH Associates (http://www.hsh.com), Home Finance of America (http://www.hfamerica.com), or mortgage.com (http://www.mortgage.com).

EXHIBIT 23.2

Selected Payments from a Repayment Schedule for a $150,000 Mortgage Loan at 8% for 25 Years (Monthly Payment: $1,157.72)

Number of Payment	Interest Payment	Principal Repayment	Balance of Loan
1	$1,000.00	$157.72	$149,842.28
2	998.95	158.78	149,683.50
3	997.89	159.83	149,523.67
—	—	—	—
—	—	—	—
—	—	—	—
148	738.84	418.89	110,407.01
149	736.05	421.68	109,985.33
150	733.24	424.49	109,560.84
—	—	—	—
—	—	—	—
—	—	—	—
298	22.85	1,134.88	2,292.50
299	15.28	1,142.44	1,150.06
300	7.67	1,150.06	0.00

column presents the interest payment, and the third column gives the amount of principal repayment. The balance of the loan is given in the last column. Since the amount of interest is determined on the balance owed, the amount of interest remitted with each payment declines, and the amount of the payment used to retire the principal rises. For example, the amount of interest in the third payment is $997.89, but in payment number 148, interest is $738.84. Since the amount of interest declines, the principal repayment increases from $159.83 in payment number 3 to $418.89 in payment number 148. Payments during the early years of the mortgage loan primarily cover the interest owed, but payments near the end of the life of the loan primarily reduce the balance of the loan.

The periodic payment required to cover the interest and retire the loan is determined through the use of present value calculations presented in Chapter 5. The following simple example illustrates this calculation. An individual borrows $10,000 for ten years and agrees to make annual payments that retire the loan and pay 12 percent interest on the declining balance owed. What is the annual payment? The answer is

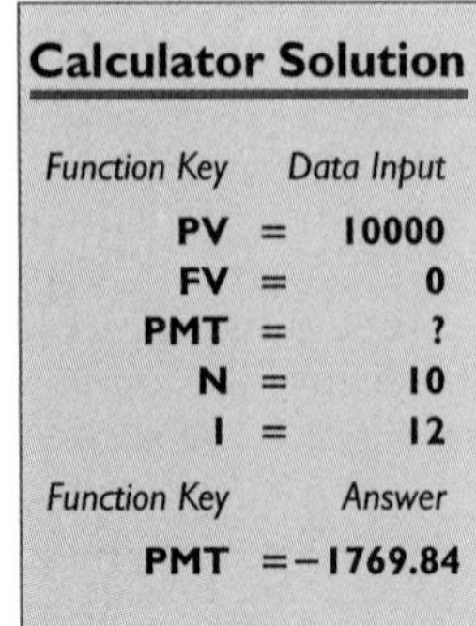

$$\$10,000 = \frac{PMT}{(1 + 0.12)^1} + \cdot \cdot \cdot + \frac{PMT}{(1 + 0.12)^{10}}.$$

Since the periodic payments will be equal, this equation may be solved by the use of the present value of an annuity table. The problem collapses to

$10,000 = *PMT* times the interest factor for the present value of an annuity of $1 at 12% for 10 years

$$\$10,000 = PMT\ (5.650)$$

$$PMT = \frac{\$10,000}{5.650} = \$1,769.91.$$

Annual payments of $1,769.91 for ten years will retire the loan and pay 12 percent on the declining balance owed.[14]

If the borrower defaults and does not make the monthly payment, the lender may seize the property through a legal process called *foreclosure*. The property then may be sold to recoup the principal and interest owed. Banks and other lenders thus consider the amount of the down payment and the borrower's capacity to service the debt as conditions for granting the mortgage loan.

To broaden the market for homes, the federal government has followed a policy of encouraging mortgage loans. Although the government does not originate mortgage loans, it may guarantee them through insurance issued by the **Federal Housing Administration (FHA)**. FHA-insured loans started during the 1930s. This insurance reduces the element of risk to the lender because if the borrower defaults, the FHA will make good the loan. The effect of this guarantee has been to make mortgage money available to low- and middle-income individuals who lack the necessary down payment or who may not be able to meet other requirements necessary to obtain conventional mortgage financing.

Federal Housing Administration (FHA)
An agency of the federal government that will insure mortgages granted to qualified recipients.

A similar program was started in 1944 by the **Veterans Administration (VA)** when the VA began to guarantee mortgage loans made to veterans. As with FHA-insured loans, VA-guaranteed loans reduce the risk of loss to the lender and hence encourage the flow of funds into the mortgage market. The requirements for veterans to obtain the guarantees are less than with conventional, noninsured mortgages, especially the amount of the initial down payment required to obtain mortgage funding.

Veterans Administration (VA)
An agency of the federal government that will guarantee mortgages granted to qualified veterans.

One variation on the conventional mortgage is the substitution of an adjustable interest rate (an **adjustable-rate mortgage** or **ARM**) for a fixed rate. As interest rates vary, the rate of interest on the loan changes. For example, the rate may change ½ percent each year with a limit of 2½ percent over the lifetime of the loan. Thus, if a borrower obtains funds for 8 percent, the rate could rise as high as 10.5 percent. The length of the loan may still be 20 or 25 years. If the lender does not correctly anticipate the amount of change in interest rates in the future, the lender would own a mortgage note that offers an inferior yield if interest rates rose above the upper cap.

adjustable-rate mortgage (ARM)
A mortgage loan in which the interest rate is periodically adjusted to reflect current interest rates.

A **two-step mortgage loan** combines the conventional and the adjustable-rate mortgages. During the initial period, the rate is fixed. After a period of time (for example, five or ten years), the interest rate is changed. The initial rate on a two-step mortgage will exceed the rate of an adjustable mortgage but be less than the conventional rate. If rates are higher at the adjustment period, monthly payments are increased. The converse occurs if interest rates are lower.

two-step mortgage loan
A mortgage loan in which the interest rate is changed once at a predetermined time.

Calculator Solution

Function Key	Data Input
PV =	10000
FV =	0
PMT =	?
N =	120
I =	1
Function Key	**Answer**
PMT =	−143.47

[14]This illustration is an oversimplification because interest payments, (at least on a mortgage) are generally made monthly and not annually. Adjustments may be made to determine monthly payments. Divide the interest rate by 12 months and multiply the number of periods by 12. In this case, that is

$$\$10{,}000 = \frac{PMT}{\left(1+\frac{0.12}{12}\right)} + \cdots + \frac{PMT}{\left(1+\frac{0.12}{12}\right)^{10\times 12}}$$

$10,000 = x times the interest factor for the present value of an annuity of $1 at 1 percent for 120 time periods

$10,000 = x(69.698)

x = $143.48.

The monthly payment is $143.48 and is not $1,769.91 divided by 12 months ($147.49). Since the loan is being retired more rapidly (i.e., every month the principal is reduced), the effect is to reduce the total amount of interest paid and thus decrease the total monthly payment to $143.48 instead of $147.49.

This example also illustrates the limitation of using interest tables, which have a limited number of percents and time periods. Financial calculators permit the use of any interest rate and time period. For example, the payment on a $10,000 loan at 7.35 percent for 11.5 years is $1,318.06 annually, or $107.56 monthly.

POINTS OF INTEREST

Points

"Heads I win; tails you lose." That saying may appropriately describe *points*, which many financing institutions charge to grant a mortgage loan. These points are in addition to other costs associated with buying a home, such as a mortgage application fee, lawyers' fees to transfer title, surveying, and title insurance.

Points are expressed as a percent of the mortgage loan. Two points means that two percent is added to the amount being borrowed. If the home owner requests a loan for $100,000, the cost of the loan is increased by $2,000. This money is paid to the lending institution up front. If the home owner does not have the $2,000, he or she will have to borrow an additional $2,000 to cover the points. This effectively increases the cost of the loan, since the individual does not have the use of the entire $102,000 that has been borrowed.

Points charged by lending institutions vary. One lender may offer the loan for 8 percent plus one point while a competing lender may offer the loan for 7.5 percent plus two points. The differences in the interest rates and the points increase the difficulty in comparing the loans. Points may also be tax deductible (if the individual itemizes), which further complicates the analysis.

If the individual anticipates living in the home for a short period (e.g., less than five years) before selling, accepting the loan with the higher interest rate and lower points is usually preferable. The anticipation of lower interest rates and the possibility of refinancing also argues for accepting the higher interest and lower points alternative. If, however, the individual expects to be paying the mortgage over many years (i.e., not moving or refinancing), then accepting the lower interest rate and paying the higher points is a better option. Over the extended number of years, the lower interest costs will tend to more than offset the higher points.

renegotiable-rate mortgage loan
A mortgage loan in which the parties have the option to renegotiate the interest rate charged on the loan.

graduated-payment mortgage loan
A mortgage loan in which the periodic payments rise over time.

Another variation is the **renegotiable mortgage**. In this type of loan the terms may be renegotiated at specified intervals. For example, while the term of the mortgage may be 25 years, the lender may renegotiate the interest rate every 3 to 5 years. If interest rates rise, the borrower is forced to pay the higher current rate of interest.

A fourth variation on the conventional mortgage is the **graduated-payment mortgage**. Under this type of mortgage loan the amount of the payment is not fixed (although the rate of interest may be fixed) but rises during the lifetime of the loan. Such loans may be beneficial to homeowners who anticipate rising incomes that can service the higher mortgage payments over time. However, such loans could prove to be disastrous if the borrower's income does not rise or if other expenses consume any increase in income. Then the burden of the debt would obviously increase, and since the loan is secured by the home, default could lead to the borrower losing the property.

Besides adjustable-rate, two-step, renegotiable-rate, and graduated-payment mortgage loans, shorter-term mortgage loans have developed. With this type of loan, the borrower has the funds for a short time, such as three years, pays the interest for the term of the loan, but then refinances the loan at the end of the time period. Such an arrangement obviously protects the lender from being locked into a lower rate if interest rates increase. However, these loans place borrowers in a precarious position, because they may not be able to find new financing when the loan becomes due.

As is illustrated in Figure 23.5, interest rates on mortgages do rise and fall with changes in the supply of and demand for mortgage funds. As may be seen in the figure, there was a rapid and large increase in interest rates on conventional mortgages from 1980 through 1981. The figure also depicts the different mortgage environment in the 1990s and early 2000s. Fluctuations in mortgage rates were smaller and rates fell to their lowest levels in 20 years.

FIGURE 23.5

Interest Rates on Conventional Mortgage Loans, 1980–July 2001

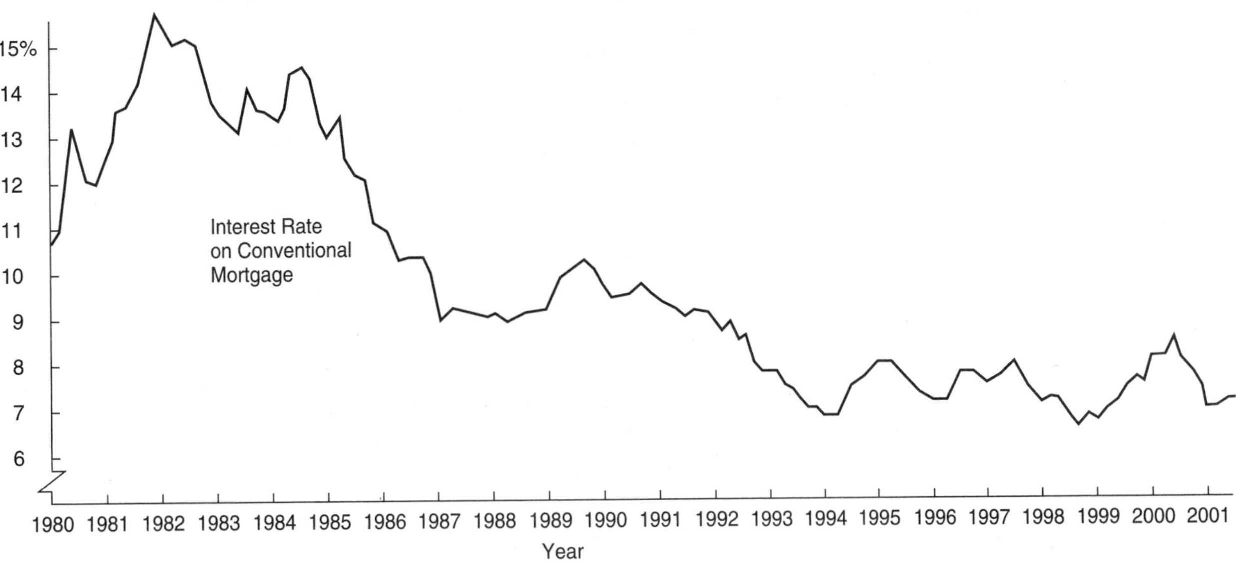

Source: *Federal Reserve Bulletin*, various issues.

These lower mortgage rates resulted in many homeowners refinancing existing mortgages.[15] Just as a firm may refinance its high-interest-rate bonds when rates fall, homeowners may also refinance by borrowing at the current, lower rate and using the funds to pay off the older, more costly mortgage. A firm, however, will not automatically retire existing debt when interest rates fall because there are costs associated with refinancing; the same applies to individuals. These costs will vary among lending institutions and may include application fees, points, and closing costs (e.g., lawyers' fees as the new loan is recorded). A new survey and new title insurance may also be required. Thus, lower interest rates do not automatically lead to refinancing an existing mortgage since the interest savings over the years of the new loan must cover the upfront costs of refinancing.[16]

Land and Rental Properties

unimproved land
Land that has not been cleared and that lacks improvements, such as curbs and gutters.

improved land
Land that has been cleared or that includes improvements, such as curbs, gutters, or buildings.

An alternative means to invest in real estate is to purchase land and/or rental properties. Land is either unimproved or improved. **Unimproved land** is raw land, whereas **improved land** has curbs and sewers, has buildings constructed on it, or has been cleared for farming or other agricultural uses. Unimproved land is generally a passive investment, but improved land may require considerable attention from the investor.

[15]Refinancing is a major source of risk to owners of Ginnie Maes, CMOs, and other mortgage pass-through securities. As was pointed out in Chapter 17 on government securities, increased refinancings return the investor's principal faster. The individual then has to reinvest the proceeds at the current, lower rate.

[16]While not illustrated in the body of this chapter, factors to consider in the refinancing decision are covered in Problem 6 at the end of this chapter.

Unimproved Land

Unimproved land by itself produces nothing and hence cannot generate a flow of income. Any income generated is the result of using the land for some activity, such as farming or mining. Even cutting down trees for sale as firewood requires expenditures of labor and tools. Since unimproved land cannot by itself generate income, the source of the return on such an investment is solely the potential for price appreciation.

The return on an investment in unimproved land is often reduced by several factors. First, many state and local governments tax land as well as other real estate investments. Second, land may be difficult to sell. Although the title can be transferred, finding a buyer may take several months or even years. Third, real estate commissions on the sale of land may be as high as 10 percent of the sale price. Therefore, the price of the land must appreciate sufficiently to recoup these commissions plus any other fees that may be associated with the sale (e.g., lawyers' fees) and still earn a profit.

For most investors, raw, undeveloped land is a poor investment. However, for those knowledgeable individuals who are willing to wait, forgo current income, and even pay out cash to carry the land, the return may be considerable if economic trends alter the unimproved land's potential.

Improved Land

The investor may buy improved land, which includes land on which buildings, such as apartments, are constructed, or land with other improvements, such as curbs and sewers. Such purchases are alternatives to investments in financial assets, but they may also be viewed as business ventures. As with any business venture, the management of improved land requires specialized knowledge that differs markedly from the knowledge employed in the selection of financial assets. Management needs to know such things as zoning and other land-use laws, the laws regulating the relationship between landlord and tenant, and the administration of accounts receivable (i.e., rent owed).

For those investors who are willing to invest in rental property, the potential benefits are illustrated in Exhibit 23.3[17] (pp. 786–787). This exhibit projects the cash flow estimates for an investment in a rental property and illustrates several facets concerning investing in properties: the initial tax savings, the reinvestment of the cash flow generated by the property, and the appreciation of the rental property's value. The benefits of such an investment require time. This particular example has a 20-year time horizon. While the investor may sell the property at any time (assuming that a buyer can be found), rental properties should be viewed as long-term investments whose returns are a combination of initial tax advantages, annual flows of cash, and potential long-term growth in property values.

In the example in Exhibit 23.3, the investor purchases a rental property for \$100,000. The purchase is financed with a \$20,000 down payment and a conventional loan for \$80,000 at 12 percent for 20 years. To simplify the analysis, the loan is amortized (i.e., retired) in 20 equal annual installments of \$10,710.30 (Column 7). The breakdown of this annual payment into interest and principal repayment is given in columns 8 and 9, respectively, in the exhibit.

[17]An additional reason for acquiring real estate is its potential to diversify a portfolio of financial assets. For example, one study found virtually no correlation (a correlation coefficient of 0.052) between the S&P 500 stock index and the National Council of Real Estate Investment Fiduciaries (NCREIF) index. The NCREIF index of real properties is used to measure returns on real estate and is an accepted benchmark for the real estate industry. See Michael Paladino and Herbert Mayo, "Investments in REITs Do Not Help Diversify Stock Portfolios," *Real Estate Review* (summer 1995): 23–26.

The first two columns give the year and the annual rental income. Rents are assumed to increase annually by 5 percent. (The assumptions used in this illustration are discussed in the next section.) Thus rental income is $12,000 in the first year but grows to $30,323.40 during the 20th year. The third and fourth columns give the depreciation expense on the property and the resulting cost basis of the property. To simplify the analysis, the property is depreciated by an equal amount ($5,000) for 20 years. Thus, the cost basis declines annually by $5,000, so that at the end of the 20 years, the cost basis has been reduced to $0. (In reality, the asset could not be completely depreciated because there would be some residual value, such as the value of the land, that cannot be depreciated. The rate at which the asset may be depreciated and the time period over which it is depreciated is established by the tax laws. Under current tax law, residential real estate is depreciated over 27.5 years and other real estate over 31.5 years.) While the asset is being depreciated, its market value may increase. In this example the value is assumed to increase by 5 percent annually, so the property that initially cost $100,000 is worth $265,329.77 at the end of 20 years.

To determine the net income generated by the property, all expenses must be deducted from the rental income. These expenses include depreciation (column 3), interest (column 8), and maintenance expenses (column 6). This last expense includes all the operating expenses (e.g., insurance and property taxes) and repair expenses associated with the building. This expense rises by 5 percent annually to adjust for increases in the running expenses that tend to occur over time. The total expenses are subtracted from the rental income to determine taxable income (column 10).

The tax paid on the income is given in column 11. A tax rate of 30 percent is assumed in this example, but the actual tax that would be paid would depend on the rates set by Congress plus any taxes established by state legislatures. After the taxes have been paid, net earnings are determined (column 12). In this illustration, the operation generates a loss during the first ten years. The investor uses these losses to offset income from other properties and thus to reduce taxes paid on the other income. These initial losses are an important tax shelter that reduce the investors' total taxes. For example, this tax shelter reduces taxes by $1,980 in year 1 and continues to reduce taxes for the next ten years. However, eventually the property earns income and requires the investor to pay taxes.

The individual who invests in rental property is more concerned with cash flow than with net earnings. Cash flow may be used for reinvestment purposes and is the sum of net earnings plus depreciation minus principal repayment (column 12 plus column 3 minus column 9 = column 13). Depreciation is added back to net income because it is a *noncash* expense that allocates the cost of the investment over a period of time. Since it is a noncash expense, it is a source of funds that may be reinvested. Principal repayment is subtracted because it is a cash outlay that has not been previously subtracted. All other cash outlays were tax-deductible expenses (e.g., interest and maintenance) and therefore were deducted from the rental income to determine taxable income. Principal repayment is not a tax-deductible expense; thus, to determine the cash flow generated by the operation, this repayment must be subtracted from the sum of net income plus depreciation.

If the cash being produced exceeds the cash outflow, the property is generating a positive cash flow. If, however, the cash coming in is less than the cash going out, the cash flow is negative. In this illustration, the cash flow is negative for the first three years, so the owner of the property will have to put in more funds to cover this shortage. In year 4 the property starts to generate positive cash flow. The cumulative cash flow (column 14) becomes positive in year 8 and continues to grow as these funds are reinvested.

In this example, the cash flow is reinvested in other assets that earn 12 percent annually. It is presumed that the investor can earn at least 12 percent because if

EXHIBIT 23.3

Cash Flow Projections for a Real Estate Investment

Year (1)	Rents (2)	Depreciation (3)	Cost Basis (4)	Value (5)	Maintenance (6)	Mortgage Payment (7)
1	$12,000.00	$5,000.00	$95,000.00	$105,000.00	$4,000.00	$10,710.30
2	12,600.00	5,000.00	90,000.00	110,250.00	4,200.00	10,710.30
3	13,230.00	5,000.00	85,000.00	115,762.50	4,410.00	10,710.30
4	13,891.50	5,000.00	80,000.00	121,550.63	4,630.50	10,710.30
5	14,568.08	5,000.00	75,000.00	127,628.16	4,862.03	10,710.30
6	15,315.38	5,000.00	70,000.00	134,009.56	5,105.13	10,710.30
7	16,081.15	5,000.00	65,000.00	140,710.04	5,360.38	10,710.30
8	16,885.21	5,000.00	60,000.00	147,745.54	5,628.40	10,710.30
9	17,729.47	5,000.00	55,000.00	155,132.82	5,909.82	10,710.30
10	18,615.94	5,000.00	50,000.00	162,889.46	6,205.31	10,710.30
11	19,546.74	5,000.00	45,000.00	171,033.94	6,515.58	10,710.30
12	20,524.07	5,000.00	40,000.00	179,585.63	6,841.36	10,710.30
13	21,550.28	5,000.00	35,000.00	188,564.91	7,183.43	10,710.30
14	22,627.79	5,000.00	30,000.00	197,993.16	7,542.60	10,710.30
15	23,759.18	5,000.00	25,000.00	207,892.82	7,919.73	10,710.30
16	24,947.14	5,000.00	20,000.00	218,287.46	8,315.71	10,710.30
17	26,194.50	5,000.00	15,000.00	229,201.83	8,731.50	10,710.30
18	27,504.22	5,000.00	10,000.00	240,661.92	9,168.07	10,710.30
19	28,879.43	5,000.00	5,000.00	252,695.02	9,626.48	10,710.30
20	30,323.40	5,000.00	0.00	265,329.77	10,107.80	10,710.30

other alternatives were not available, the mortgage loan could be paid off more rapidly. Since the loan has an interest rate of 12 percent, it is reasonable to assume that the cash flow can be reinvested at that rate. At the end of 20 years, the investor will have accumulated $69,949.11 by reinvesting the cash flow received each year.

The investor should note that in this illustration net earnings start to exceed cash flow in year 15. The principal repayments have risen sufficiently that they exceed depreciation. Thus while the operation now appears profitable, the investor has a large principal repayment that (1) is not tax deductible and (2) consumes cash. Unlike the early years when the cash generated exceeded earnings, earnings now exceed the cash being generated.[18]

If the individual holds the property to the end of the time period, the investor has $69,949.11 through the reinvestment of the cash flow plus property worth $265,329.77. Thus, the original $20,000 investment has grown to $335,278.88. Of course, the individual over time has invested a total of $100,000 in the property as the mortgage is retired. However, while the total investment is $100,000, the final value of the investor's assets (before tax)[19] is $335,278.88—the $100,000 invested in

[18]It is possible that the taxes owed on the income will exceed the cash being generated, which could occur if principal repayment consumes the cash.

[19] The illustration does not assume that any tax has been paid on the earnings generated by the reinvestment of the cash flow. Nor does it consider any capital gains tax on the property if it were sold.

EXHIBIT 23.3

continued

Year (1)	Interest (8)	Principal Repayment (9)	Earnings before Taxes (10)	Taxes (11)	Net Earnings (12)	Cash Flow (13)	Cumulative Cash Flow (14)
1	$9,600.00	$1,110.30	$−6,600.00	$−1,980.00	$−4,620.00	$−730.30	$−730.30
2	9,466.76	1,243.54	−6,066.76	−1,820.03	−4,246.73	−490.27	−1,308.21
3	9,317.54	1,392.76	−5,497.54	−1,649.26	−3,848.28	−241.04	−1,706.23
4	9,150.41	1,559.89	−4,889.41	−1,466.82	−3,422.59	17.52	−1,893.46
5	8,963.22	1,747.08	−4,239.17	−1,271.75	−2,967.42	285.50	−1,835.17
6	8,753.57	1,956.73	−3,543.32	−1,063.00	−2,480.32	562.95	−1,492.44
7	8,518.76	2,191.54	−2,797.99	−839.40	−1,958.60	849.86	−821.67
8	8,255.76	2,454.52	−1,998.98	−599.69	−1,399.28	1,146.20	225.92
9	7,961.23	2,749.07	−1,141.59	−342.48	−799.11	1,451.82	1,704.85
10	7,631.34	3,078.96	−220.71	−66.21	−154.50	1,766.54	3,675.98
11	7,261.87	3,448.43	769.29	230.79	538.50	2,090.07	6,207.17
12	6,848.06	3,862.24	1,834.65	550.40	1,284.26	2,422.02	9,374.04
13	6,384.59	4,325.71	2,982.26	894.68	2,087.58	2,761.87	13,260.80
14	5,865.50	4,844.80	4,219.69	1,265.91	2,953.78	3,108.98	17,961.08
15	5,284.13	5,426.17	5,555.32	1,666.60	3,088.73	3,462.56	23,578.97
16	4,632.99	6,077.31	6,998.44	2,099.53	4,898.90	3,821.59	30,230.04
17	3,903.71	6,806.59	8,559.29	2,567.79	5,991.50	4,184.91	38,042.55
18	3,086.92	7,623.38	10,249.23	3,074.77	7,174.46	4,551.08	47,158.74
19	2,172.11	8,538.19	12,080.84	3,624.25	8,456.59	4,918.40	57,736.18
20	1,147.53	9,562.77	14,068.87	4,220.42	9,847.65	5,284.88	69,949.40

the property, plus the assets acquired through the reinvestment of the cash flow, plus the appreciation in the property's value. Of course, for this result to occur in this example, the value of the property and the rental income must increase annually by 5 percent. Changes in the growth rate of expenses, changes in the tax laws, and the inability to earn 12 percent annually on the accumulated cash flow will also affect the return ultimately earned on the investment in the rental property.

Uncertainties and Investing in Real Estate

Exhibit 23.3 illustrates the determination of a property's income and cash flow, but the example makes several important simplifying assumptions. First, it assumes that rents will increase every year by 5 percent. Such consistent increases are highly unlikely, because rental properties rarely remain 100 percent occupied. Rental income varies with occupancy rates, which are tied to the local economy. Although the long-term trend in rents may be positive, assuming that increase will consistently occur is one means to overestimate the attractiveness of a property.

Second, the illustration assumes expenses grow in tandem with rental income. Maintenance and repairs, property taxes, insurance, and management expenses should tend to rise over time, but the increases may be erratic. Large increases in expenses may occur when the properties are not completely leased, because improvements may have to be made to attract new tenants. Cash flow may become negative when the owners most need the funds to finance the improvements.

Third, the illustration assumes that the value of the property increases annually by 5 percent, from $100,000 to $265,329.77. Figure 23.4, however, suggests that during the last decade such growth was not achieved by many residential homes. Even if real estate values do average a 5 percent increase, that need not apply across the board. Economic conditions in various regions differ and affect the values of real estate. Some geographic areas tend to be more recession-proof than others. For example, during the early 1980s, the oil boom produced strong real estate markets in Texas and Colorado. However, the late 1980s produced the exact opposite, with many properties in Texas and Colorado remaining vacant for extended periods of time, thus generating no rental income for their owners.

Political factors also affect real estate investments. Changes in zoning or rent control and rent stabilization can be imposed. While rent control laws generally are not applied to commercial properties, they may be applied to residential apartment buildings. Even a region such as residential Washington, DC, may prosper during periods of economic growth *and* recession but become stagnant when the political climate develops more cost consciousness.

Real Estate Valuation

Although Exhibit 23.3 has many simplifying assumptions, it does illustrate the fundamentals of determining a real estate investment's cash flow. As the previous discussion suggests, these funds from operations are uncertain because so few elements are fixed in the present and the time dimension is long.[20] Cash flow, however, is important for the valuation of real estate, since the process does not emphasize earnings. Instead, the emphasis is often placed on funds from operations, which is generally defined as income before gains or losses on investments and extraordinary items plus noncash items, primarily depreciation. Since noncash depreciation is such a large proportion of real estate's operating expenses, especially in the early years of the asset's life, the funds from operations are considered by real estate professionals to be a better measure of profitability than net earnings generated by the property.

Once net operating income is determined, the next step is to determine the present value of the real estate. In essence, this is no different from the models used to value common stock in Chapter 9. In that chapter two models were developed: (1) the dividend-growth model, which discounts future dividends back to the present at the appropriate rate (i.e., the capital asset pricing model's required rate), and (2) P/E ratios, which involve estimated future earnings. Valuation techniques for real estate use similar models. The capitalization of funds from operations determines the present value of the property's estimated cash flows and is analogous to the dividend-growth model. The second technique, the gross income multiplier, is analogous to the use of P/E ratios. The application of these techniques, however, is beyond the scope of this text.

Limited Partnerships

Investing in and managing rental property is a business enterprise. It is virtually impossible for the investor to participate passively in such real estate ownership.[21] However, the investor may buy shares, called *units,* in limited **partnerships** that

partnership
An unincorporated business owned by two or more individuals.

[20] Exhibit 23.3 uses a fixed-rate mortgage. Even the payments required by the mortgage would be uncertain if the loan had a variable interest rate or if the owner anticipated being able to refinance at a lower rate. That leaves only the depreciation schedule as fixed. If Congress were to change the schedules for new investments, acquisitions made under previous depreciation rules would not be adversely affected.

[21] The investor may employ a real estate agent to handle the properties, but this, of course, will consume part of the return earned by the properties.

own and manage real estate. Like the rental property discussed in the previous illustration, these partnerships offer investors a possible return from cash flows and from appreciation in real estate values.

In a real estate partnership there are two types of partners: the general partners who manage the real estate, and the limited partners. The limited partners provide the funds to acquire the properties but are passive owners who do not manage the real estate. Unlike the general partners, the limited partners have limited liability. Since the business is a partnership and not a corporation, the limited partners directly reap the benefits of any profits earned.

In the initial years of the partnership (when the properties are being developed), the partnership generally operates at a loss. After the buildings are completed, the partnership may still generate losses from depreciation expense. Once again this depreciation expense is a noncash expense (i.e., it does not require a disbursement of funds) that allocates the cost of investment in the properties over a period of time. While the buildings are being depreciated, these properties may generate cash that, when distributed to the limited partners, is a return of their capital invested in the project. Such return of capital is *not* income and hence is not subject to income taxes. Instead, the partners' cost basis in the investment is reduced.

The initial operating losses and the depreciation expense shelter cash payments to the limited partners from income taxation. The losses may also be used to offset income from limited partnerships that are profitable. After a period of years, the cost of the investment will be recouped through the depreciation expenses. When the properties are sold, any appreciation in value of the properties will be treated as capital gains.

The tax laws pertaining to investing in limited partnerships and the tax shelters associated with them are exceedingly complex. These investments are primarily of interest to sophisticated investors. Individuals with only modest sums to invest or who are in lower tax brackets should probably choose an alternative means to invest in real estate, especially the real estate investment trust.

Real Estate Investment Trusts (REITs)

real estate investment trust (REIT)

Closed-end investment company that specializes in real estate or mortgage investments.

An alternative to owning real estate or acquiring shares in limited partnerships is to buy shares in **real estate investment trusts** (commonly called **REITs**). These real estate trusts are a type of closed-end investment company. They receive the special tax treatment granted other investment companies (e.g., mutual funds). As long as a REIT derives 75 percent of its income from real estate (e.g., interest on mortgage loans and rents) and distributes at least 90 percent of the income as cash dividends, the trust is exempt from federal income tax. Thus, REITs, like mutual funds and other closed-end investment companies, are conduits through which earnings pass to the shareholders.

Shares of REITs are bought and sold like the stocks of other companies.[22] Some of the shares are traded on the New York Stock Exchange (e.g., Commercial Net Lease Realty), while others are traded on the American Stock Exchange and in the over-the-counter markets. The existence of these markets means that the shares of REITs may be readily sold. This ease of marketability certainly differentiates shares of REITs from other types of real estate investments.

[22]Information concerning a REIT may be obtained from the trust. Use its name or ticker symbol to locate the trust's Web address. Information may also be obtained through the SEC EDGAR database (http://www.sec.gov), Edgar Online (http://www.edgaronline.com), or specialized sources such as the National Association of Real Estate Investment Trusts (http://www.nareit.com), REITNet (http://www.reitnet.com), and RealtyStocks and Funds (http://www.realtystocks.com). Clarion CRA Securities, which specializes in managing real estate securities, also has an excellent Web site (http://www.crainvest.com) devoted to REITs.

POINTS OF INTEREST

REIT Distributions and Federal Taxes

Many companies make cash distributions to stockholders. These are often called *dividends*, but the use of that term is not necessarily correct when applied to distributions by REITs. In common usage, a cash dividend implies a distribution of earnings. But a REIT's cash distribution could be from earnings, capital gains, or a return of capital.

Consider the following REIT with per-share earnings from operations of $1.00, a per-share gain from the sale of property of $0.60, and per-share funds from operations of $2.10. Since a REIT's expenses include noncash depreciation charges, the firm can generate more funds than earnings. Noncash expenses explain why operating income can be $1.00 while funds from operations is $2.10. (They also explain why financial analysts may use funds from operations instead of earnings when valuing a REIT.)

The REIT now distributes $1.90 per share to its stockholders. What are the tax implications of this distribution? One dollar of the distribution is income and is taxed as income. That is, the $1.00 in dividends from earnings is taxed no differently than a $1.00 cash dividend received from Ford or IBM. $0.60 of the distribution is classified as a capital gain. Since property is generally held for more than a year, the $0.60 will be a long-term capital gain and taxed at a lower rate than the tax on the dividend from earnings.

One dollar in income plus $0.60 in capital gains account for only $1.60 of the $1.90 distribution. What is the tax on the remaining $0.30? The answer is nothing. Thirty cents is a return of the investor's capital and is not taxed. Instead, the investor's cost basis for the stock is reduced by $0.30. If the investor paid $13.45 per share for the stock, the adjusted cost basis becomes $13.15. This adjustment becomes important when the investor sells the stock and must pay capital gains tax on any profits. As the cost basis is reduced by the return of capital, potential capital gains taxes increase. Of course, as long as the stockholder retains the stock, there is no capital gains tax.

Distributions from REITs are occasionally touted as being partially nontaxable. To some extent this is true, since any return of capital is nontaxable. But, the statement is also misleading because the cost basis is reduced by the amount of distribution, which may result in future capital gains taxes. The informed investor realizes that REIT dividends are not necessarily dividends in the traditional sense of the term and that nontaxable distribution can produce capital gains taxes in the future. (If an investor wants to know if previous distributions made by a REIT were nontaxable, that information is available through the National Association of Real Estate Investment Trusts (NAREIT) Web site, http://www.nareit.com.)

EXHIBIT 23.4

Selected REITs and Their Dividend Yields

Firm	Price of Stock as of 6/1/01	Annual Dividend	Dividend Yield
Commercial Net Lease Realty	13.10	$1.26	9.5%
IRT Properties	10.30	0.94	9.1
United Dominion REIT	13.52	1.08	7.9
Washington REIT	23.67	1.27	6.1

Source: *Standard and Poor's Stock Guide*, June 2001.

Since a REIT distributes virtually all its earned income to maintain its tax status, the result is greater dividend yields than may be available through most stock investments. Selected dividend yields offered by REITs are provided in Exhibit 23.4, and yields in excess of 8 percent are common from investments in REITs.

In addition to higher dividend yields, the tax regulations may produce fluctuations in a trust's dividend payments. While other companies tend to maintain stable dividends and increase them only after there has been an increase in earnings that management anticipates will be maintained, the dividends of REITs will fluctuate with changes in earnings. Higher earnings will lead to higher dividend payments, but lower earnings will decrease dividend payments. While many trusts seek to increase dividend payments periodically, there is the obvious possibility that lower earnings will immediately be translated into lower dividend payments. Shares of REITs, therefore, may not be desirable investments for individuals who need assured and stable sources of dividend income. Investors, however, who can tolerate fluctuations in their dividend income may prefer the shares of REITs since the trusts offer both higher yields and the potential for future dividend growth as rents and property values increase.

Classification of REITs

equity trust
A real estate investment trust that specializes in acquiring real estate for subsequent rental income.

mortgage trust
A real estate investment trust that specializes in loans secured by real estate.

REITs may be grouped according to either the types of assets they acquire or their capital structure. **Equity trusts** own property and rent it to other firms (i.e., they lease their property to others). **Mortgage trusts** make loans to develop property and finance buildings. There is a considerable difference between these two approaches to investing in real estate. Loans to help finance real estate, especially developmental loans, can earn high interest rates, but some of these loans can be very risky. Contractors may be unable to sell or lease the completed buildings, which may consequently cause them to default on their loans. In addition, any inflation in the value of the property cannot be enjoyed by the lender, who owns a fixed obligation.

In an equity trust, the REIT owns the property and rents space. This also is risky because the properties may remain vacant. Unleased property, of course, does not generate revenue, but the owner still has expenses, such as insurance, maintenance, and depreciation. These fixed expenses can generate large fluctuations in earnings of an equity trust. However, should there be an increase in property values, the trust may experience capital appreciation.

The second method for differentiating REITs is according to their capital structures or the extent to which they use debt financing. Some trusts use modest amounts of debt financing, while others use a large amount of leverage. The latter can be very risky investments. If a REIT's loans turn sour and the borrowers default, or if the properties become vacant, the trust may have difficulty meeting its own obligations. Thus, while the use of debt financing magnifies fluctuations in a REIT's cash flow and earnings, low use of financial leverage suggests a REIT is better positioned to survive a period of recession.

These differences among REITs are illustrated in Exhibit 23.5 (p. 792), which presents real estate as a percentage of the trust's assets and its use of debt financing as measured by the debt ratio. The entries are listed in descending order according to their debt ratios. Allied Capital Corporation is a mortgage trust that owns no properties. Its property loans finance commercial real estate, such as offices, retail stores, and hotels. United Dominion REIT is an equity trust (primarily apartments) with over 60 percent of its assets debt financed. Commercial Net Lease Realty is also an equity trust but finances its assets with less debt. While Commercial Net Lease Realty's use of less debt financing suggests that it is the less risky of the two trusts, its commercial properties may be subject to increased vacancy rates. It has more business risk than United Dominion.

In addition to equity and mortgage trusts, there are finite-life REITs (called FREITs). Regular REITs have an indefinite life; FREITs do not. Their assets will be liquidated within a specified time period, and the funds will be distributed to stockholders. For example, EQK Realty Investors was organized in 1985 and liquidated in 1997. Of course, such forced sale of the properties could prove to be deleterious to stockholders if the market for real estate is weak when the sale must be made.

EXHIBIT 23.5

Selected REITs by Type of Assets and Capital Structure

REIT	Real Estate as a Percentage of Total Assets	Debt Ratio (Debt to Total Assets)
United Dominion REIT	96.3%	64.7%
IRT Property Company	97.9	59.1
Washington REIT	94.5	59.1
Commercial Net Lease Realty	83.7	48.3
Allied Capital Corporation	0.0	44.0

Source: 2000 annual reports

REITs and Securitization

REITs are another illustration of securitization, the process of converting illiquid assets into a liquid, marketable asset. Even if they had the resources, few investors would be willing to own an apartment complex or office building. And even fewer would be able to own a mall. Contractors and developers are able to package together these types of properties and spin them off as REITs. By this process they convert an asset that is not easily sold (e.g., apartment buildings) into an asset for which a ready market exists (i.e., the shares of the REIT). For example, Cornerstone Realty Income Trust was formed when real estate operations were converted into a trust. Public ownership of the shares then facilitated the trust's acquiring additional properties through issuing publicly traded stock in exchange for the properties. Public ownership also meant that the trust could raise additional funds by selling additional shares to the general public. As a result of the acquisitions, Cornerstone Realty Income Trust has grown from total assets of $322 million in 1996 to total assets of $799 million at the end of 2000.

A company may use the formation of a REIT as a means to divest an operation without actually selling the assets and thereby avoid paying income taxes on any gains from the sale. Other companies may form a REIT to remove assets (and liabilities) that no longer meet their strategic plans. Getty Petroleum split into two operations. One piece received service stations (and any debt such as mortgages associated with the stations). The operation was renamed Getty Realty, and in 2001, Getty Realty was reorganized as a real estate investment trust. Virtually all of Getty Realty's assets are service stations under long-term leases to Getty. Owners of the trust will receive cash flow from the leases but no gain from any increases in the profitability of petroleum products. Getty divests itself of the service stations and their associated liabilities. In effect, the company has converted an illiquid asset, the service stations, into a marketable asset, shares in the trust.

Valuation of Shares in REITs

The valuation of shares in real estate investment trusts is essentially the same as the valuation of any other asset: the present value of future cash flows. Thus, the valuation techniques discussed in Chapter 9 may be applied to REITs. Consider New Plan Excel (NPX), whose per-share dividends have grown from $1.05 to $1.615 during the ten years ending in 2000. NPX's funds from operations grew from $1.01 to $1.85. The annual growth rates are 4.40 percent and 6.24 percent, respectively.

To apply the capital asset pricing model and the dividend-growth model, the required additional data are NPX's beta, the risk-free rate, and the expected return on the market. According to the Value Line *Investment Survey,* NPX's beta is 0.6. As of the day of this application, six-month Treasury bills and 30-year Treasury bonds were yielding 3.7 and 5.7 percent, respectively. If the Ibbotson historical return on small stocks of 12 percent is used as the anticipated return on the market, the required return for NPX is

$$k = r_f + (r_m - r_f)\text{beta} = 0.035 + (0.12 - 0.035)0.65 = 0.9025$$

using the Treasury bill rate, and

$$k = r_f + (r_m - r_f)\text{beta} = 0.057 + (0.12 - 0.057)0.65 = 0.09795$$

using the Treasury bond rate. The dividend-growth model developed in Chapter 9 was

$$V = \frac{D(1+g)}{k-g}.$$

The current annual NPX dividend payment is \$1.65. The valuation using the growth rate for the dividend and the required return based on the Treasury bill rate is

$$V = \frac{\$1.65(1 + 0.040)}{0.09025 - 0.040} = \$37.25.$$

The valuation using the required return based on the Treasury bond rate is

$$V = \frac{\$1.65(1 + 0.040)}{0.09795 - 0.040} = \$31.93.$$

The valuation using the growth rate for funds from operations and the Treasury bill rate is

$$V = \frac{\$1.65(1 + 0.057)}{0.09025 - 0.057} = \$52.45,$$

while using the Treasury bond rate, the valuation is

$$V = \frac{\$1.65(1 + 0.057)}{0.09795 - 0.057} = \$42.33.$$

These valuations produce amounts ranging from \$31.93 to \$52.45. The range of values suggests that the stock should be purchased as long as the price is less than \$31.93 if the analyst believes the historical rate of growth in dividends and the Treasury bond rate are the appropriate data for the valuation.

As of the day of these valuations, New Plan Excel sold for \$17.31, which suggests the stock is exceedingly undervalued. Of course, the other (and more likely) implication is that the analysis is incorrect. Even if the concept (i.e., the discounting of future flows) is accurate, the application may be flawed. The analysis has crucial assumptions that include: (1) the growth rate will be maintained *indefinitely* into the future and (2) the anticipated return on the market is correct. For example, if the values of the growth rate and the required return were 4 percent and 10 percent, respectively, the value of the stock would be

$$V = \frac{\$1.65(1 + 0.04)}{0.12 - 0.04} = 21.45.$$

This value is considerably closer to the actual market price and suggests that the historical growth rate may not be maintained or that the required return was understated.

There is also the implicit assumption that the basic composition of the firm will not change. For example, management could change the firm's use of debt financing or the composition of the real estate holdings (i.e., change NPX's financial risk and business risk). Changes in the use of financial leverage and in the real estate holdings could affect the estimates of the growth rate, the variability of its funds from operations and of the dividend, or the trust's beta. Any of these changes could alter the valuation.

Additional problems with applying the capital asset pricing model to a real estate investment trust include questions concerning the appropriate beta and the appropriate return on the market. In the preceding illustration, a Value Line beta was used as the measure of market risk and return on the market was assumed to be the Ibbotson historical returns for small stocks. Both, however, may be inappropriate for valuing the shares of a REIT. As was explained in Chapter 7, a beta coefficient encompasses the variability of an asset's return and the correlation of the asset's return and the market return. A low beta, such as NPX's beta of 0.6, may be the result of low correlation with the market or low variability of the trust's return. While the lack of correlation with the market is important from a diversification perspective, it may not be the appropriate measure of risk for the valuation of an asset whose cash flows are the result of real estate investments.

The same basic point also applies to using the returns on the market as the implied alternative or benchmark. Essentially, this is the question of why would the return on a real estate investment be compared to the return on the stock market if the analyst wants to know the performance of the trust's management. Instead, an appropriate return would be the return on an aggregate measure of the return on real estate properties. One possible measure of real returns is the Wilshire Real Estate Securities index, which tracks the performance of over 150 real estate investment trusts, real estate operating companies, and real estate limited partnerships, or the National Association of Real Estate Investment Trusts (NAREIT) index of all publicly traded REITs. Information about each index may be found at their respective home pages, http://www.wilshire.com and http://www.nareit.com.

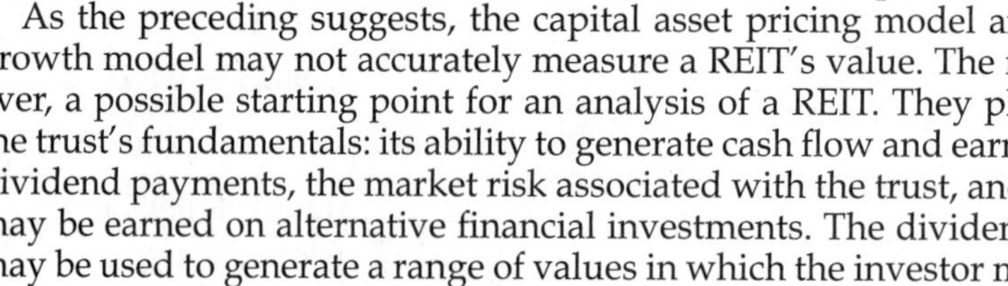

As the preceding suggests, the capital asset pricing model and the dividend-growth model may not accurately measure a REIT's value. The models are, however, a possible starting point for an analysis of a REIT. They place emphasis on the trust's fundamentals: its ability to generate cash flow and earnings that finance dividend payments, the market risk associated with the trust, and the returns that may be earned on alternative financial investments. The dividend-growth model may be used to generate a range of values in which the investor may find the REIT to be fairly priced. If the trust deviates from the range, it may have become a candidate for purchase or sale, at which time further analysis may be warranted before a final investment decision is made.

Summary

Collectibles (e.g., art objects), precious metals (e.g., gold), resources (e.g., timber), and real estate are important alternatives to traditional financial assets. These nonfinancial assets offer potential price appreciation and in some cases potential income.

These assets, however, also subject the investor to risk of loss. This risk is associated with the specific assets themselves as well as the result of fluctuations in prices of assets in general and of inflation, theft, and fraud. To help overcome these risks, the investor needs to be well informed and to specialize in a particular type of physical asset. Instead of diversifying (as is desirable in the case of financial assets), the investor may become exceedingly specialized in a particular type of tangible asset, especially if he or she is investing in art and other types of collectibles.

Precious metals, such as gold, may be acquired in a variety of forms, including jewelry, coins, and bullion. The investor can also buy the stock of mining companies, futures contracts, and options. Jewelry is the poorest means to invest in gold, and a futures contract is probably the riskiest. As with art and other collectibles, investments in jewelry, coins, and bullion may require expenses, such as storage, insurance, or having the metal assayed, that reduce the potential return from the investment.

Individuals may also invest in natural resources, such as timber, that may generate cash flow or possible capital gains. The responsiveness of the supply of the resources to change in demand is an important consideration prior to making the investment, because if the supply is relatively unresponsive to changes in demand, its price will tend to rise more and generate a larger return. The converse, however, is also true. Lower demand will depress the resource's price more if the supply is inelastic and does not respond to the change in demand.

Real estate is another nonfinancial, tangible asset, and this chapter covered several means to invest in properties, including home ownership, land and rental properties, and real estate investment trusts. Home ownership is a particularly attractive investment, since the individual must live somewhere. In addition, the federal income tax laws encourage investing in a home as several expenses (e.g., interest and property taxes) are allowed as deductions in the determination of the individual's taxable income, and the capital gains on the sale of the house may be avoided. Several federal government programs have evolved to encourage home purchases. Mortgage loans are secured by the property, which reduces the risk of loss to the lender, and a variety of mortgage loans are available to provide the funds for the purchase of a home.

Investors may also buy land and rental properties. Unimproved land may appreciate in value if there is potential use for the land. An investment in rental properties is essentially a business venture and may earn a return from the cash flow generated by the properties and the potential for capital appreciation.

Real estate investment trusts (REITs) offer investors an alternative to directly investing in real estate. These trusts are a type of closed-end investment company whose shares are traded on the exchanges or over-the-counter. REITs either make loans to develop properties or own properties that they rent out to various tenants. The federal tax code permits REITs to avoid income taxation as long as they distribute earnings to stockholders as dividends. This distribution of income results in real estate investment trusts being attractive to individuals seeking dividend income. The valuation of the shares of REITs is essentially the same as the valuation of any common stock: Future dividend payments or cash flows are discounted back to the present at the appropriate discount rate.

Questions

1) What are the sources of return from investing in collectibles and other real assets? What are the special expenses associated with investing in collectibles and tangible assets?
2) What are the tax implications of investing in nonfinancial assets?
3) What are the risks associated with investing in nonfinancial assets? What role does specialized knowledge perform in the management of these risks?
4) How do the secondary markets for nonfinancial, tangible assets differ from the secondary markets for financial assets?
5) Why are investments in timber more like operating a business than managing a portfolio of financial assets?
6) What are the different sources of mortgage money for financing the purchase of a home? What are features that differentiate mortgage loans? What advantage does an ARM offer over a fixed-rate mortgage? What advantage does the fixed-rate mortgage offer over an ARM?
7) How is cash flow or funds from operations determined for an investment in rental properties?

8) What impact does each of the following have on a real estate investment's cash flow?
   a) An increase in depreciation expense
   b) A decrease in rental income
   c) An increase in principal repayment
   d) A decrease in interest rates
9) What differentiates a real estate investment trust from a firm involved in building and developing properties? What differentiates a mortgage trust from an equity trust?
10) What are the risks associated with investing in real estate and how are they similar and dissimilar to those of investments in stock and bonds? What advantages do REITs offer over direct investments in real estate properties?
11) Using the information in the Points of Interest on the taxation of REIT distributions, what was the tax status of the 2001 and 2002 distributions made by the following REITs?

    IRT Property Company
    New Plan Excel
    United Dominion REIT
    Washington REIT

12) Find the current mortgage rates for loans and compare the monthly payment for a $150,000 mortgage for 25 years with the payment in Exhibit 23.2. You may find interest rates through MSN Money (http://www.moneycentral.com). Another possible source for rates (including yields on CDs and credit cards) is BanxQuote at http://www.banx.com.

Problems

1) In 1982, Marc Chagall's *Orphee* sold for $120,000. In 2001, approximately 20 years later, it sold for $500,000. If the commission on the sale was 10 percent, what was the annual rate of growth in the value of Chagall's piece? The Mei/Moses American Fine Art Price Index rose from its base of 100 in 1941 to approximately 1100 in 2000 (approximately 60 years). What was the annualized rate of growth in the index?
2) You acquire land for $100,000 and sell it after five years for $150,000.
   a) What was the annual rate of appreciation in the value of the land?
   b) Each year you paid $2,000 in property tax, $300 for liability insurance, and $700 for upkeep (e.g., mowing). What was the true annualized return on the investment?
   c) If there was also a 5 percent commission on the sale, what was the annualized return on the investment?
3) Determine the annual repayment schedule for the first two years (i.e., interest, principal repayment, and balance owed) for each of the following. (Assume that only one payment is made annually.) Compare the payments required by each mortgage.
   a) A $60,000 conventional mortgage for 25 years at 10 percent
   b) A $60,000 conventional mortgage for 20 years at 10 percent
   c) A $60,000 conventional mortgage for 25 years at 8 percent
4) In 1990 the average and median prices of a new single-family home were approximately $95,200 and $118,200, respectively. Ten years later, these prices had risen to $139,000 and $177,000. During the same time period the Dow Jones Industrial Average rose from 2,633 to 10,646 and the S&P 500 stock index rose from 330 to 1,320. Compare the annual rate of increase in home prices to the rate of growth in these two popular aggregate measures of the stock market.

5) What is the expected cash flow and tax liability (or savings) for the first two years for an investment in an apartment building given the following information?

Cost of the building	$800,000
Cost of the land	200,000
Required down payment	25%
Interest on balance owed	10%
Annual principal repayment	20,000
Annual operating expenses	30,000
Rent, year 1	120,000
Rent, year 2	140,000
Annual depreciation expense	40,000
Individual owner's income tax rate	30%

6) As a result of lower interest rates, you are considering refinancing your mortgage. The existing mortgage has a 12 percent interest rate. The balance owed is $50,000, and the remaining term is 18 years, and your annual payment (i.e., interest plus principal) is $6,897. A bank is willing to lend you the money at 10 percent to retire the old loan. The term of the new loan will be 18 years, so you are not increasing the number of years required to pay off the mortgage. (There is no reason why the number of years should be the same. If there is a reduction in your mortgage payment, you could restore the original payment and retire the loan quicker. Or you may increase the amount of the loan and use the additional funds to improve the property.) Unfortunately, the bank will charge you an application fee of $500 and an additional fee (*points*) equal to 2 percent of the amount of the mortgage. There will also be additional costs (e.g., court recording costs of the new mortgage) that are estimated to be $500. To help determine if it is profitable to refinance, answer the following questions.

a) What are the total expenses to obtain the new loan?
b) How much will you have to borrow to retire the loan when the refinancing expenses are included, and what will be the annual payment required by the new loan?
c) What is the difference between the annual payments under the new and the old mortgages? What is the implied course of action?
d) What is the present value (at 10 percent) of the reduction in your annual payment?
e) If you compare your answers to (c) and (d), what is the implied course of action?

7) You acquire a debt security that is a claim on a mortgage pool (e.g., a Ginnie Mae pass-through security). The mortgages pay 9 percent and have an expected life of 20 years. Currently, interest rates are 9 percent, so the cost of the investment is its par value of $100,000.

a) What are the expected annual payments from the investment?
b) If interest rates decline to 7 percent, what is the current value of the mortgage pool based on the assumption that the loans will be retired over 20 years?
c) If interest rates decline to 7 percent and you expect homeowners to refinance after four years by repaying the loan, what is the current value of the mortgages? (To answer this question, you must determine the amount owed at the end of four years.)
d) Why do your valuations differ?
e) You acquire the security for the price determined in part (c) but homeowners do not refinance, so the payments occur over 20 years. What is the annual return on your investment? Did you earn your expected return?

8) (This problem is designed to illustrate the potential savings from paying a mortgage off faster. It may be viewed as an illustration of an assured, risk-free return, except that the return is the interest you save instead of interest you earn.)

You have a 20-year $100,000 mortgage with a 9 percent interest rate. (To reduce the size of this problem, assume that payments are made annually and not monthly as would be the normal case with a mortgage.)

a) Determine the repayment schedule.
b) How much is owed after ten years?
c) How much will be the total payments made over the 20 years?
d) How much interest is paid over the 20 years?
e) If you increase your first-year payment to include the *next year's principal payment*, how much interest will you pay at the end of the second year?
f) If each year our payment includes the current required payment and the subsequent year's principal repayment, what will be the life of the mortgage?
g) If you follow the process in (f), what are the total payments and the interest payments made over the life of the mortgage?
h) What are the advantages and disadvantages associated with this early payment strategy?
i) If interest rates decline to 7 percent, what is the current value of the mortgage based on the assumption that the loan will be outstanding for 20 years? (That is, if you were buying this mortgage as an investment for a mortgage pool, how much would you be willing to pay?)
j) If interest rates decline to 7 percent and the homeowner follows the strategy in (f), what is the current value of the mortgage?
k) If interest rates decline to 7 percent and you expect the homeowner to refinance after four years (i.e., repay the loan with no prepayment penalty), what is the current value of the mortgage?
l) Why do your valuations in (i) through (k) differ?

9) Washington Real Estate Investment Trust's earnings per share (EPS), funds from operations per share (FFO), and dividends per share were as follows:

	EPS	FFO	Dividends
1996	$0.88	$1.13	$1.03
1997	0.90	1.23	1.07
1998	0.96	1.39	1.11
1999	1.00	1.55	1.16
2000	1.16	1.79	1.23

a) Compute the ratio of dividends to earnings and the ratio of dividends to funds from operations.
b) Relate dividends to earnings (EPS) and cash flow (FFO) by computing the R and R^2 relating (1) dividends and earnings and (2) dividends and funds from operations.
c) Determine annual growth rates for dividends, earnings, and funds from operations.
d) Use the dividend-growth model and the capital asset pricing model to value the stock. For illustrative purposes, use the Value Line beta (0.55); a market required return of 12 percent, which approximates the historical return on small company stocks based on the Ibbotson studies of security returns; and a risk-free rate of 4 percent.

THE FINANCIAL ADVISOR'S INVESTMENT CASE

The Apartment

Michael Rossetti is a sophisticated investor with assets in excess of $2.5 million. Rossetti believes he has sufficient funds invested in equities and is considering acquiring a moderate-size apartment complex with ten units. Rents are currently $1,000 per unit per month and each unit is rented. The asking price is $1.1 million; however, Rossetti believes he can acquire the property for less. But, after lawyers' fees, title search and title insurance, inspection fees, and other costs, the total cash outlay will be $1.1 million ($100,000 for the land and $1 million for the building).

Rossetti can obtain 100 percent financing with an 8 percent, 20-year mortgage provided that he pledges his stock portfolio as additional collateral. As an alternative, he could sell stock worth $100,000 for a down payment and borrow the balance at 9 percent for 25 years. Of course, he could liquidate sufficient stock to cover the entire purchase price, but that strategy would generate a large long-term capital gain and would defeat a primary purpose of buying the apartments: to generate cash without significantly increasing his income taxes. Currently, he is in the 35 percent federal income tax bracket and does not want to generate more current income. He plans to personally operate the apartments to reduce expenses, but property taxes, insurance, and maintenance costs will have to be covered by the apartment's cash flows.

To ease his analysis, Rossetti decides that these expenses would average $75,000 annually for the first five years and $100,000 annually for the next five years. He plans to sell the building after ten years, but since real estate values have been increasing slowly he anticipates that rents and the value of the property will, at best, rise by 3 percent annually. Annual depreciation expense is $34,000.

1) What will be the building's annual net profit and cash flow if Rossetti uses the 8 percent mortgage?
2) What will be the building's annual net profit and cash flow if Rossetti uses the 9 percent mortgage?
3) Should the investment be made using either of the mortgages if Rossetti does sell the property after ten years for $1,478,000 (i.e., what is the rate of return on the investment)?
4) How would the answers differ if
   a) The occupancy rate were to fall to 80 percent?
   b) Operating costs are initially 25 percent of the cost of the building and rise to 30 percent after five years?
   c) The anticipated price at which the apartments will be sold after ten years is its book value of $850,000?
5) What are the unsystematic and systematic risks associated with this investment?
6) If the correlation coefficient relating returns on investments in apartments to returns on investments in common stock is −0.1, what impact will the investment have on Rossetti's total risk?

THE FINANCIAL ADVISOR'S INVESTMENT CASE

Collectibles Are Not Commodities

Jason Knapp is a bachelor who has accumulated a substantial sum, primarily through periodic investments in savings accounts at a commercial bank ($80,000), shares in a balanced mutual fund ($125,000), and a pension plan ($68,000). Knapp has also been a lifelong philatelist. Ever since receiving a stamp album for his 12th birthday, he has been fascinated with collecting stamps. As a child he collected any and all stamps, but for the last 20 years he has devoted his efforts to the stamps of Great Britain and its colonies. Knapp has now obtained a reputation for expertise in this area and has accumulated a sufficiently large collection to have received recognition from a regional stamp organization.

The value of Knapp's stamp collection is unknown, and its has never been insured. Knapp believes that over the years he has spent at least $25,000 on the collection. Unfortunately, the exact cost of many of the items is lost in time, as he did not keep records of his early purchases made during the 1970's. Some of these acquisitions have proven to be among the most valuable stamps in the collection.

Knapp has become increasingly concerned with the performance and quality of his financial assets. He realizes the funds in the savings account are insured by the FDIC, but the shares in the mutual fund are not insured. In addition, the fund has not performed well during the preceding year, as it rose less than the Dow Jones Industrial Average. Except for his pension (which he cannot withdraw until retirement), he believes the portfolio needs changing. Knapp knows very little about stocks and bonds and tends to distrust things he cannot touch. He recently read an advertisement that suggested commodities offered large potential returns. Knapp thought he could buy commodities like silver and hold them for subsequent sale in much the way he has acquired and held the stamps.

To finance these purchases, Knapp expects to sell his shares in the mutual fund or some of his stamp collection. His sister Deneen (who is an accountant) was distressed when she learned of Jason's ideas and suggested that they have lunch with you so you could explain some of the features, risks and potential returns associated with Jason's proposed portfolio changes. Jason agreed to the lunch, which Deneen arranged for the next week. Deneen also privately suggested that you should at a minimum discuss the following:

1) The differences between collecting and investing in stamps and investing in commodities.
2) The tax implications (if any) of redeeming the mutual fund shares, closing the bank account, or selling the stamps.
3) The need to insure the stamp collection.
4) Any need to diversify the mutual fund holdings.
5) Alternatives to the savings account with the bank.

How would you respond to each of these considerations? What course(s) of action would you recommend?

Portfolio Planning and Management | 24

Benjamin Britten in his *Young Person's Guide to the Orchestra* describes and illustrates the instruments of the symphony orchestra. Then Britten reconstructs the orchestra one instrument at a time and ends the work with a glorious fugue that combines all the instruments. The preceding chapters of this text have described and illustrated individual investments: bonds, preferred stock, common stock, options, shares in investment companies, commodity futures, physical assets, collectibles, and real estate. In a manner similar to Britten's fugue, the investor combines the individual assets to construct a portfolio. The individual acquires assets one at a time, and they are blended together into a portfolio designed to meet the investor's financial goals.

Portfolio construction, then, is a process in which the individual specifies financial goals, identifies financial resources and obligations, acquires a diversified portfolio designed to meet the goals within the investor's constraints, and evaluates the portfolio's performance. Of course, this process is affected by the economy (e.g., expectation of inflation), changes in the tax laws, the deregulation of financial markets, and the speed of technological change. In addition, changes in the individual's economic or family environment can have an important impact on financial planning and the resulting portfolio.

This chapter is concerned with financial planning. It covers determining the individual's assets, liabilities, and cash flows, and the allocation of the investor's assets to meet the specified financial goals. Some individuals make their own investment decisions, select the specific assets to include in the portfolio, and subsequently manage that portfolio. Other individuals, however, take a more passive approach. They delegate the responsibility for the selection of specific stocks and bonds to the portfolio managers of investment companies. These individuals still must select which mutual funds to own, so a large section of this chapter is devoted to factors to consider when investing in a mutual fund. The chapter and this text end with a reminder that investment decisions are made in efficient financial markets. As the individual selects different assets using different analytical techniques, the portfolio becomes increasingly diversified. Such diversification is among the most important concepts in investing, for it erases the risk associated with a specific investment. But diversification also reduces the impact that a single investment decision has on the portfolio. Over a period of time, the return the individual will earn on this well-diversified portfolio mirrors the return on the markets and the allocation of the assets over the various asset classes.

Learning Objectives

After completing this chapter you should be able to:

1 Identify financial goals and the assets that are appropriate to meet the goals.

2 Enumerate the risk/reward, marketability, and tax status of investment alternatives.

3 Construct an individual's balance sheet and cash budget.

4 Explain the importance of asset allocation to the determination of a portfolio's return.

5 Determine factors to consider when selecting a specific mutual fund as an investment.
6 Contrast the various indexes that may be used for benchmarking.
7 Identify the advantages associated with index and exchange-traded funds.
8 Explain the importance of the individual's perception of efficient financial markets to his or her investment strategy.

The Process of Financial Planning

To construct a portfolio, the investor starts by defining its purpose. There has to be some goal (or goals) to guide the selection of the assets that should be included. After specifying realistic financial objectives, the next step is determining which assets are appropriate to meet the goals. After establishing investment goals and identifying assets that may meet the goals, the investor should analyze his or her environment. Environments vary with individuals and change over an individual's lifetime. The investor needs to be aware of the resources and sources of income with which he or she has to work. The investor then will construct a financial plan designed to fulfill the investment goals within these environmental and financial constraints.

The Specification of Investment Goals

The purpose of investing is to transfer purchasing power from the present to the future. A portfolio is a store of value designed to meet the investor's reasons for postponing the consumption of goods and services from the present to the future. Several reasons for saving and investing were offered in the introductory chapter. Possible goals included

1 The capacity to meet financial emergencies;
2 The financing of specific future purchases, such as the down payment for a home;
3 The provision for income at retirement;
4 The ability to leave a sizable estate to heirs or to charity; and
5 The ability to speculate or receive enjoyment from accumulating and managing wealth.

financial life cycle
The stages of life during which individuals accumulate and subsequently use financial assets.

In addition to these specific investment goals, many individuals have general financial objectives that are related to their age, income, and wealth. Individuals go through phases, often referred to as a **financial life cycle**. The cycle has three stages: (1) a period of accumulation, (2) a period of preservation, and (3) a period of the use or depletion of the investor's assets.

During the period of accumulation, the individual generates income but expenditures on housing, transportation, and education often exceed cash inflows, which increases debt. Yet individuals with debt (e.g., a mortgage, car payments, or student loans) often start the process of accumulating assets, especially by participating in tax-deferred pension plans. Such participation, especially if the employee's contributions are matched by the employer, may be one of the best investment strategies any individual can follow.

Another desirable strategy during the period of asset accumulation is to restructure or retire debt. While stocks and bonds have uncertain returns, retiring debt has an assured return, the interest savings. This return can be substantial if the debt being retired is the balance owed on credit cards. The Ibbotson studies of returns discussed in Chapter 10 found that annual returns on investments in stocks were 11.3 percent for large-company stocks and 12.6 percent for small-company stocks. Corporate and federal government bonds earned less than 6 percent annually. Certainly these returns are less than the high interest rates charged on many credit card balances and argue that credit card debt reduction is a desirable, even superior, alternative to investing in stocks and bonds.

During the period of preservation, income often exceeds expenditures. Individuals reduce debt (e.g., pay off the mortgages on their homes) and continue to accumulate assets. The emphasis, however, may change to preservation of existing assets in addition to the continued accumulation of wealth. Since investors will need a substantial amount of wealth upon reaching retirement, they must continue to take moderate or prudent risk to earn a sufficient return. Without that return they may not have the funds that are needed to finance their retirement.

During the period when assets are consumed, most individuals will no longer have salary or wage income. Even though a pension and Social Security replace lost income, many individuals must draw down their assets to meet expenditures. While the assets that are retained continue to earn a return, both the amount of risk and return are reduced as safety of principal becomes increasingly important. These individuals, however, continue to need some growth. A married couple, both aged sixty-five, have a combined life expectancy of at least 20 years. Such a long time horizon argues for the inclusion of equities in their portfolio.

A large variety of assets (e.g., stocks, bonds, and mutual funds) are available to meet investors' financial goals as they go through their financial life cycles. Within each type of asset there is an almost unlimited number of choices. However, each of the various assets has common characteristics: liquidity/marketability, potential return, risk, and tax implications.

You do not spend your stocks or bonds. The ability to convert the asset into cash is obviously important. The ease of converting an asset to cash with little risk of loss is an asset's liquidity. For many assets this liquidity depends on the asset's marketability, the existence of a secondary market in which the asset may be sold. The potential return from an investment is either the income it generates (e.g., interest), price appreciation, or a combination of both. All investments involve risk that is either specific to the asset or to the type of asset. (The management of risk is so crucial to portfolio management that the methods and strategies for risk management discussed throughout this text are reviewed later in this chapter.) Lastly, federal, state, and local taxation permeates investment decisions since income, capital gains, and wealth are all subject to tax even though the tax rates on income, capital gains, and wealth differ.

An Analysis of the Individual's Environment and Financial Resources

Financial planning requires an analysis of the individual's environment and financial resources. One's environment includes such factors as age, health, employment, and family. A young bachelor in good health who is securely employed does not need the same portfolio as a young man with a family, even if his health is excellent and his employment is secure. The more current obligations an individual has (be they debt or family), the greater the need for a conservative portfolio. The assets should stress safety and liquidity so that short-term obligations may be met as they occur. In contrast, the young bachelor could afford to bear more risk in the selection of a portfolio.

In addition to the individual's environment, the investor should take an accurate account of financial resources. This may be done by constructing two financial statements. The first one enumerates what is owned and owed, and the other enumerates cash receipts and disbursements. The former is, of course, a balance sheet, whereas the latter is a cash budget.

The entries for an individual's balance sheet are given in Exhibit 24.1. It lists all the individual's assets and liabilities. The difference between these assets and liabilities is the individual's net worth (which would be the "estate" if the individual were to die at the time the balance sheet is constructed). For clarity, the individual should list short-term assets and then long-term assets, and the same should be done with liabilities. In effect, an individual's balance sheet is no different from a firm's balance sheet.

pro forma financial statement
A projected or forecasted financial statement.

The entries for the balance sheet given in Exhibit 24.1 consider the individual's financial position as of the present and as of some specified time in the future (e.g., at retirement). For the purpose of financial planning, it is advisable to construct one's current financial position as well as to project what that position will be at some time in the future. Such a projection is often referred to as a **pro forma financial statement**. The construction of a pro forma balance sheet will require that the individual make assumptions concerning (1) his or her ability to accumulate assets and retire liabilities and (2) the rate of return that will be achieved by the assets. While the resulting projections will depend on the assumptions, the projections often bring into sharp focus the individual's future financial needs and can help in establishing current investment strategies.

The balance sheets in Exhibit 24.1 are more detailed than is necessary for most individuals. Few individual investors will have entries for each asset or liability enumerated in the exhibit. For example, many investors may not be eligible for Keogh accounts or have deferred compensation owed them. Also, some of the entries may not apply now but may apply in the future. For example, if the individual has not started an IRA but intends to, this should be included in the projected balance sheet even though it is not currently applicable.

The mechanics of constructing a balance sheet are relatively easy. The difficult part is enumerating the assets and placing values on them. Such valuation is easy for publicly traded securities, such as stocks and bonds. The problem concerns placing values on tangible personal assets, such as collectibles or real estate. Since the purpose of constructing a balance sheet is to determine the individual's financial condition, it is advisable to be conservative in estimating the value of these assets. If, for example, the individual had to sell antiques to finance living expenses, it would be better to underestimate than to overestimate the prices for which these assets may be sold.

cash budget
A financial statement enumerating cash receipts and cash disbursements.

After the individual enumerates what is owned and what is owed and thereby determines his or her net worth, the next step is to analyze the flow of receipts and disbursements. This is done by constructing a **cash budget**. Exhibit 24.2 (pp. 807–808) shows the entries needed for the construction of a cash budget. It lists all the individual's sources of receipts (e.g., salary, interest, and rental income) and all the disbursements (e.g., mortgage payments, living expenses, and taxes). As with the balance sheet, the cash budget may be constructed for the present or projected for a specific time in the future (e.g., at retirement). Exhibit 24.2 thus provides for both a current annual cash budget and a pro forma cash budget. Although the cash budget illustrated in this exhibit is for one year, cash budgets may be constructed to cover other time periods, such as monthly receipts and disbursements.

As with the balance sheet in Exhibit 24.1, the entries in Exhibit 24.2 are probably too detailed for many individuals. Obviously, not everyone receives veterans' benefits or royalty payments. However, such completeness is desirable, for it highlights the variety of possible sources and uses of funds. If the individual's receipts exceed disbursements, the excess receipts become a source of funds that should be invested to meet future financial needs. It is possible that after constructing such a cash budget, the individual will perceive ways to increase receipts and decrease disbursements and thus generate additional funds for investment.

EXHIBIT 24.1

An Individual's Balance Sheet and the Determination of Net Worth

	Present	Future
ASSETS		
1. Bank deposits		
a. Cash, checking accounts	___	___
b. Savings accounts	___	___
c. Certificates of deposit	___	___
d. Money market accounts	___	___
e. Credit union accounts	___	___
f. Other	___	___
Subtotal	===	===
2. Liquid financial assets		
a. Money market mutual funds	___	___
b. Treasury bills	___	___
c. Series EE and HH bonds	___	___
d. Amounts owed and payable on demand	___	___
e. Tax refunds and other payments owed	___	___
f. Cash value of life insurance	___	___
Subtotal	===	===
3. Retirement and savings plans		
a. IRA accounts:	___	___
Tax-deferred IRA	___	___
Roth IRA	___	___
b. Keogh accounts	___	___
c. Lump-sum distributions and/or IRA rollover accounts	___	___
d. Employee savings and investment plan:		
Before tax	___	___
After tax	___	___
e. Employee stock ownership plan	___	___
f. Deferred compensation due	___	___
g. Company options	___	___
Subtotal	===	===
4. Financial assets		
a. Treasury notes and bonds	___	___
b. Corporate bonds	___	___
c. Corporate stock	___	___
d. Municipal bonds	___	___
e. GNMAs and other federal agency debt	___	___
f. Mutual funds:		
Fixed income	___	___
Equities	___	___
Subtotal	===	===
5. Tangible assets		
a. Real estate:	___	___
Home and vacation properties	___	___

(continued on next page)

EXHIBIT 24.1 CONTINUED

An Individual's Balance Sheet and the Determination of Net Worth

		Present	Future
Investment properties		___	___
Other		___	___
b. Collectibles		___	___
c. Cars		___	___
d. Personal tangible property (e.g., furs, silver, furniture, jewelry, boats)		___	___
	Subtotal	___	___
Total Assets		___	___
LIABILITIES			
1. Short-term			
a. Current portion of mortgage owed		___	___
b. Current portion of car payments		___	___
c. Personal debts		___	___
d. Credit card balances		___	___
e. Miscellaneous		___	___
	Subtotal	___	___
2. Long-term			
a. Mortgage balance owed		___	___
b. Balance owed on car or other tangible assets		___	___
c. Bank loans, amount borrowed on life insurance		___	___
d. Other long-term debts		___	___
	Subtotal	___	___
Total Liabilities		___	___
SUMMARY			
Total assets		___	___
Total liabilities		___	___
NET WORTH (value of estate: assets minus liabilities)		___	___

The Establishment of Financial Plans

After specifying goals and analyzing one's financial position, the investor can establish a financial plan or course of action. This plan is the strategy by which the investor will fulfill the financial goals. Although plans will vary among individuals, the importance of such a plan applies to all. It is the means to the end—the means to financial success and security.

Plans require the establishment of priorities. Those financial goals that are most important should be fulfilled first. After investments have been made to satisfy these needs, the next most important goals should be attacked. In this way the investor systematically saves and invests to meet the specified goals. For example, an individual may determine the following goals and their priority:

- Funds to meet financial emergencies
- Funds to finance a child's education
- Funds to finance retirement

The initial goal, then, is sufficient liquid assets to cover emergencies (e.g., unemployment or extended illness). After this goal has been met, the investor proceeds

EXHIBIT 24.2

An Individual's Cash Budget for One Year

	Present	Future
CASH RECEIPTS		
Salary (after deductions)	___	___
Social Security	___	___
Pension	___	___
Interest from savings	___	___
Dividends on stock	___	___
Commissions & bonuses	___	___
Royalties, fees	___	___
Distributions from businesses	___	___
Net rental income	___	___
Veterans' benefits	___	___
Annuity payments	___	___
Distributions from trusts	___	___
Mortgage payments received	___	___
Distributions from IRA, Keogh, and IRA rollover accounts	___	___
Other receipts	___	___
Total Receipts	===	===

	Present	Future
CASH DISBURSEMENTS		
1. Housing	___	___
a. Mortgage payments	___	___
b. Rent	___	___
c. Maintenance	___	___
d. Utilities	___	___
e. Fuel	___	___
f. Property taxes	___	___
2. Food and personal expenditures		
a. Dining at home	___	___
b. Dining out	___	___
c. Personal care	___	___
d. Clothing	___	___
e. Recreation and travel	___	___
f. Furniture, appliances	___	___
g. Hobbies	___	___
3. Transportation		
a. Automobile expense	___	___
b. Car replacement	___	___
c. Public transportation	___	___
4. Medical		
a. Insurance	___	___
b. Deductibles paid	___	___
c. Miscellaneous expense	___	___

(continued on next page)

EXHIBIT 24.2 CONTINUED

An Individual's Cash Budget for One Year

	Present	Future
CASH DISBURSEMENTS		
5. Insurance		
a. Life insurance	___	___
b. Homeowner's insurance	___	___
c. Automobile insurance	___	___
d. Other	___	___
6. Estimated taxes	___	___
7. Other disbursements		
a. Gifts	___	___
b. Contributions	___	___
c. Miscellaneous	___	___
Total Disbursements	═══	═══
SUMMARY		
Total receipts	___	___
Total disbursements	___	___
Difference between receipts and disbursements	___	___

to accumulate assets designed to finance the child's college education. The process is continued until all the goals have been met.

The Capacity to Meet Financial Emergencies

While this financial goal can be well defined, planning to have funds to meet financial emergencies involves uncertainty. The investor does not know when (or even if) the money will be needed. While long-term securities may be used to meet a financial goal that has an identifiable time period, they would probably be inappropriate to meet the goal of having sufficient funds to deal with emergencies. Assets that are very liquid (i.e., that are easily converted into cash without a loss) should be chosen to fulfill this investment goal. These may include savings accounts; high-quality short-term debt, such as certificates of deposit and series EE bonds; and money market mutual funds.

The Financing of Identifiable Future Purchases, Such as a Child's Education

While it is impossible to know when the funds will be needed for an emergency, this uncertainty need not apply to other future purchases of goods and services. The desire to purchase a specified good or service often has a known time dimension. Financing an education and planning for retirement are both examples of expenditures that will occur at a particular time in the future. Individuals know approximately when their children will be in college or when they will retire. Although there may be some deviation in the time of the actual occurrence, the investor knows approximately when these events will happen and can plan to have the funds to finance the purchase.

Consider the financing of a child's college education. If the child is currently eight years old, the funds for a college education will be needed in approximately ten years. Even though the future cost of the education is not known, parents know when the funds will be needed and can systematically accumulate assets to meet this anticipated expense. The assets should be long-term since the funds will not be needed for many years, and they should be relatively safe since the parents would not want to lose the funds. Possible choices may include

growth stocks,
high-yielding stocks, and
intermediate-term bonds.

Each of these alternatives requires that the investor choose an individual asset for purchase.[1] The investor may avoid this decision by purchasing shares in a mutual fund that meets the specific investment goal. Investment companies that specialize in growth or in income-producing securities offer another means to accumulate funds designed to finance a specific expenditure in the future, such as a college education. With this strategy, specific stocks (e.g., IBM or Microsoft) are not purchased. Instead, the individual acquires shares in a variety of mutual funds. One fund might invest in large companies (i.e., *large cap value* stocks) while another fund could specialize in international investments. A third fund might specialize in small companies with exceptional growth potential (i.e., *small cap growth* stocks). When the funds are needed to finance the child's education, the funds are periodically redeemed. By allocating funds among these classes of mutual funds, the individual achieves diversification and potential appreciation without having to determine which individual assets to acquire.

Although the preceding discussion used the financing of a college education as the investor's goal, other, similar goals could have been used. For example, the accumulation of funds to help finance retirement is a similar goal. Once again, the investor knows approximately when the event (i.e., retirement) will occur. The portfolio should then be constructed with assets that can be converted into cash at a specified time in the future. This general principle actually applies to any portfolio whose purpose is to meet a goal whose time dimension is known with some degree of certainty.

Altering the Financial Plan

Financial planning is the backbone of portfolio construction, but the individual must realize that goals and financial conditions do change. Such changes may alter the general financial plan. The birth of a child, the death of a spouse, a promotion, or a new job are just some of the many possible events that shape our lives and can alter our financial goals. The individual must be willing to adjust financial plans accordingly.

Firms also change, so their securities may no longer be appropriate for an individual's portfolio. For example, AT&T is different today than it was prior to the spin-off of Lucent, NCR, and AT&T Wireless. In effect, AT&T is converting itself into a more focused firm and no longer serves the needs of investors who previously acquired AT&T as a low-risk, moderate-growth stock.

One of the most important facets of investing—taxation—is also subject to change. Taxes alter the environment in which investment decisions are made. Some changes encourage investing or favor specific securities that the individual may acquire. Changes in the tax laws can have a profound impact on the individual's portfolio and thus require the investor to reassess the composition of the portfolio and make appropriate adjustments. It is only possible to conjecture as to

[1]There are tax-advantaged accounts that facilitate the accumulation of funds for a child's college education. The 2001 federal tax law increased the amount that may be tax-sheltered in education accounts. However, setting up the account is not the same as deciding what assets to acquire. The investor must still decide which stock or which mutual fund to purchase for the account.

what future changes in the tax code may be enacted, but certainly the investor should be aware of current tax laws and the impact that proposed changes may have on the portfolio.

Finally, the investor must be willing to realize that not all investments will achieve their anticipated return or serve the purpose for which they were acquired. That is the nature of risk; the future is uncertain. If a particular asset is no longer appropriate or the anticipated return has not been realized, the investor should be willing to liquidate that asset and acquire an alternative. This does not mean that the individual should continuously turn over the portfolio. Such a course of action may be counterproductive and perhaps may even reduce the return as the investor pays the fees associated with the sale of one asset and the purchase of another. However, the investor should not become so enamored with particular assets that they are an end unto themselves instead of a means to meet specified financial goals.

Selecting a Money Manager or Financial Planner

Since the management of assets requires specialized knowledge and can be time consuming, some individuals prefer to use the services of a money manager or financial planner. Financial planning is an emerging profession, so the terms *money manager* or *financial planner* can be both broad and vague. Many individuals may offer financial counsel. For example, the accountant who completes the investor's income tax forms may be a natural source for financial advice. The same applies to insurance salespeople, bankers, and stockbrokers. Any of these individuals can (and often do) offer financial advice as part of the usual services they provide. You, however, should question whether their advice is self-serving. For example, an insurance salesperson or stockbroker may recommend purchasing specific investments. While these investments can be valuable as part of the individual's portfolio, their purchase may not necessarily be in the best interests of the investor.

To avoid this problem, the individual may use the services of a fee-only financial planner, who develops financial plans for clients. Unlike bankers, brokers, or insurance salespeople who may be compensated through sales commissions, fee-only financial planners are primarily compensated for constructing the financial plan. The individual may then execute the plan (and pay any related costs associated with the purchase of specific financial assets), or the individual may have the fee-only financial planner execute the plan. Financial planners who administer plans often use low- or no-load mutual funds for the acquisition of financial assets. Even after considering the cost of a financial plan, the use of no-load mutual funds may generate a net savings for the individual investor. That is, the combined cost of the financial plan plus the no-load mutual fund shares may cost less than shares in individual stocks or shares in a mutual fund with a loading fee.

The selection of a money manager/financial planner is a highly individual decision. In some cases the choice may have been forced upon the individual. For example, a spouse may have inherited an estate that is managed by the trust department of a commercial bank. Someone, however, had to initially select that trust department to manage the assets.

The selection of a money manager/financial planner is not made easier when the individual realizes that financial planning requires access to very personal information. As a medical doctor requires confidential, personal information, so too will a money manager/financial planner require information that many individuals do not care to disclose. Sources of income, the value of assets and outstanding debts, or relationships with family are illustrative of the information that a money

POINTS OF INTEREST

Wrap Accounts

In 1990, E. F. Hutton offered individual investors the first account to include financial planning, custodial services, and professional money management. These *wrap accounts* are available to individuals with a specified minimum amount to invest (e.g., $250,000). Brokers initially work with their clients to determine the individual's financial goals and risk tolerance. After this preliminary financial planning, the broker selects a professional money manager who meets the client's needs. The money manager makes all investment decisions, such as purchases and sales of securities designed to meet the investor's goals.

The money manager may work independently of the investor's brokerage firm, but some brokerage firms use only in-house portfolio managers. In either case, the money manager works through the client's brokerage firm. The investor receives periodic account statements, but unless the dollar amount being managed is substantial, the investor does not meet or talk with the money manager. Information on specific assets being included or decisions to buy or sell comes through the broker, thus tieing investors to their brokers and isolating them from the money managers.

The investors pays a fee, such as 3 percent of the value of assets being managed, which is split among the broker, the brokerage firm, and the money manager. (Fees may be less for fixed-income accounts, which involves less active managements.) The fee covers all costs, including commissions on security transactions. However, there may be hidden costs if the money manager does not obtain comparable prices for sales and purchases, a problem that could arise when the money manager works through the client's brokerage firm.*

Wrap accounts' primary advantages to the clients are access to professional management and avoidance of having to make specific investment decisions. Of course, these advantages require relinquishing control over timing of transactions and the composition of the portfolio. For individuals who lack the time or inclination to manage their assets, wrap accounts offer a more complete package than investing in specific mutual funds or other investments vehicles.

Although wrap accounts have professional money managers, the investor should not assume that the account receives individual attention. The wrap account may only give the impression of individualized professional management. Money managers may have certain predetermined portfolios for certain types of investors. For example, a manager may select the same portfolio for each individual seeking conservative investments with accounts of less than $500,000. In effect, each account has a common position in a portfolio constructed by the money manager.

Perhaps the biggest disadvantage to the wrap account is the reliance on the broker. There is the assumption that the broker correctly identifies the investor's financial objectives and risk tolerance and recommends the appropriate money manager. This assumption could easily be violated when in-house money managers are used. In addition, it is assumed that sufficient information is provided to the investor to evaluate the performance of the money manager. Efficient financial markets suggest that few money managers will consistently outperform the market and that the fee will not be covered by superior results. Of course, the individual would pay other costs (e.g., fees for the services of a financial planner or brokerage commissions) if an alternative to a wrap account is used, but these costs may be less than the cost of the wrap account.

While wrap accounts may not generate superior investment results, they have become popular with investors. In less than three years, the amount managed through these accounts grew to over $40 billion. For individuals who seek to avoid investment decisions or who fear brokers may excessively churn their accounts to generate commissions, wrap accounts offer one-stop investment shopping for a fixed price.

*See Albert J. Golly Jr., "The Pros and Cons of Brokerage Wrap Accounts," *AAII Journal* (February 1993), 8–11; and Ellen E. Schultz, "Hidden Costs Can Put the Squeeze on Wrap Accounts," *The Wall Street Journal*, January 28, 1993, C1+.

manager may need. Before an investor seeks the help of a money manager or professional financial planner, it is desirable for the individual to determine his or her willingness to reveal personal financial information.

Several considerations should enter the selection of a knowledgeable money manager. Financial planning is a broad area requiring breadth of knowledge of the various investment alternatives as well as risk management through insurance, tax planning, retirement, and estate planning. Although it is difficult to measure an individual's breadth and depth of knowledge, credentials, such as academic background, previous experience, and professional designations, such as CFP (Certified Financial Planner) or ChFC (Chartered Financial Consultant), help indicate the level of knowledge. In addition, membership in professional associations, such as the National Association of Personal Financial Advisors (NAPFA) for fee-only planners, the International Association for Financial Planning, and the Institute of Certified Financial Planners, is desirable, as these associations establish codes of ethics to which their members must subscribe.

Finally, the money manager/financial planner and the individual must concur on the individual's financial goals and willingness to bear risk. If the individual believes that he or she can bear more risk than the money manager/financial planner believes is prudent, there may be inherent conflicts. There must be a meeting of the minds between the money manager/financial planner and the client for the process to be successful. Also, without rapport and respect, the individual may not be willing to divulge information necessary for the construction of realistic financial plans.

Asset Allocation

The individual establishes financial goals and constructs a portfolio designed to meet the goals. The funds are invested in various assets so that the individual simultaneously achieves both risk reduction through diversification and the financial goals. Often this process is referred to as *asset allocation,* an unfortunately ambiguous term. Does asset allocation simply connote the determination of the proportion of the individual's resources that should be invested in the various types or classes of assets? Does asset allocation mean altering the portfolio in response to changing economic and market conditions? Does asset allocation imply the selection of individual assets to construct a diversified portfolio? Or does asset allocation imply all three? The broadest definition is the first, which suggests that asset allocation is part of the general planning process that determines the optimal allocation prior to the selection of individual assets or classes of assets. That is, asset allocation establishes portfolio policy. The two other definitions imply that asset allocation is an operational concept that helps guide changes in the portfolio.

Asset Allocation as Policy

Asset allocation as part of the financial plan may be illustrated by an individual with only two financial goals: funds for emergencies (such as unemployment) and funds for retirement. The pie charts in Figure 24.1 represent asset allocations designed to meet these two goals at three different points in an individual's life. In the first, the individual is 30 years old and has only a modest amount of assets ($50,000). The allocation policy determines that 60 percent of funds should be used to meet financial emergencies with 40 percent designated for growth. After making this determination, 60 percent of the assets are invested in liquid assets and the remaining funds are allocated to more volatile stocks or growth mutual funds whose potential higher returns are more suited for a long-term financial goal. If the value of these assets were to increase, then some would be sold and the funds transferred into liquid assets to maintain the 60–40 proportion of the portfolio.

In the second pie chart, the individual is now 50 years old and has assets of $300,000. The appropriate allocation is determined to be 15 percent to meet emergencies and 85 percent for growth. Even though the absolute amount of funds necessary to meet the first goal has been increased from $30,000 to $45,000, these funds constitute a smaller percentage of the portfolio. Since retirement is closer, the type of growth security may be less volatile and offer a smaller return than the

FIGURE 24.1

Asset Allocations at Different Stages in an Individual's Life

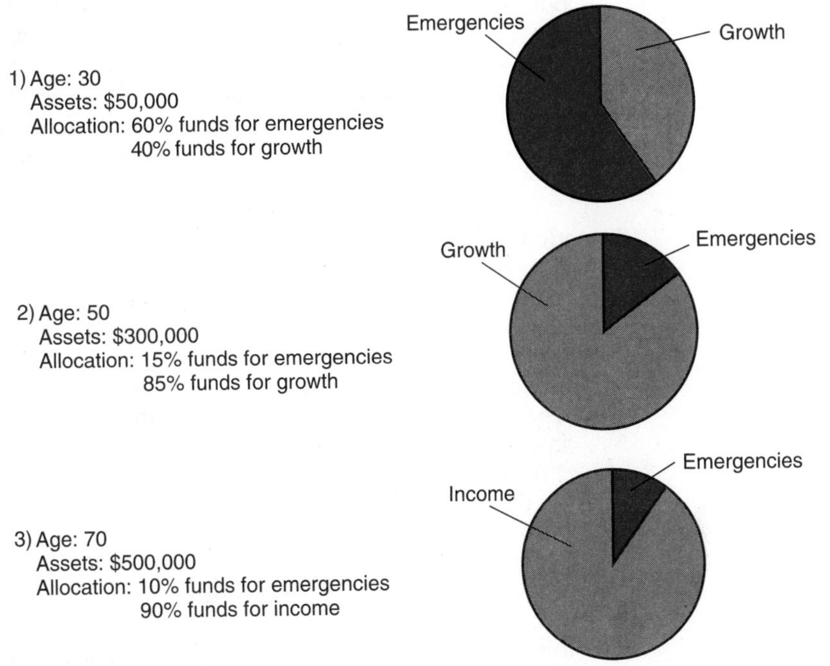

assets selected when the individual was 30 years old. Once again, if the value of assets designed to meet the growth objective were to change, the individual would alter the portfolio to maintain the 15–85 asset allocation.

In the third chart, the individual is now 70 with $500,000 in assets. The need for funds to meet emergencies such as unemployment ceases, but other possible emergencies such as illness may become important. The optimal allocation is determined to be 10 percent for emergencies and 90 percent for income during retirement. The specific assets (e.g., individual stocks and bonds or mutual funds) produce dividend and interest income and expose the individual to less risk than the growth stocks that were appropriate when the individual was younger. Once again, if the value of these income-producing assets were to change, the individual would alter the portfolio to maintain the 10–90 asset allocation.

Changing the portfolio to maintain a percentage allocation implies that the portfolio requires active supervision. Since security prices change daily, this supervision can be taken to an extreme in which the portfolio is rebalanced every day. This extreme may be avoided by defining the percentages as ranges instead of single points. For example, an asset allocation may be 30 to 40 percent liquid assets and 70 to 60 percent growth securities. As long as the components of the portfolio remain within the specified range, no adjustments are required.

Asset Allocation as Market Timing

Asset allocation can also imply the shifting of the portfolio to take advantage of anticipated changes in the economy or in the financial markets—essentially moving among various types of securities, such as selling stocks to acquire bonds. For example, the anticipation of lower interest rates from the Federal Reserve to stimulate economic activity suggests that the investor should alter the allocation of assets to securities that are responsive to changes in interest rates (e.g., long-term bonds) and the stocks of firms that may benefit from economic stimulus. A portfolio allocation of 80 percent growth stocks and 20 percent money market mutual funds may become 20 percent growth stocks, 20 percent money market mutual funds, and 60 percent interest-sensitive stocks and bonds. The anticipation of inflation would suggest an entirely different allocation of assets, away from fixed-income securities to assets whose prices tend to increase in an inflationary environment.

A variant on this interpretation of asset allocation occurs when the investor identifies specific groups of securities within a particular type whose prices are believed to be overvalued and therefore should be sold. The funds could then be used to purchase similar securities whose prices suggest they are undervalued. For example, if the investor believes that stocks of pharmaceutical companies are undervalued while the stocks of oil companies are overvalued, the investor sells the latter in order to buy the former. While the composition of the portfolio with regard to type of security is unchanged (i.e., all investments are in common stocks), the emphasis has changed from one industry to another.

Whether shifting among assets in response to anticipated changes in economic conditions or differing valuations of specific securities can improve portfolio performance is open to dispute. Individuals who believe in the efficacy of market timing or in their ability to identify over- and undervalued individual securities (or classes of securities) would argue this type of asset allocation increases returns. The efficient market hypothesis, however, suggests the opposite: Asset allocation designed to monitor markets and take advantage of different economic conditions should not produce higher risk-adjusted returns. Such strategies may do the opposite and produce lower returns, especially after considering the taxes on realized gains and the transaction costs associated with swapping one security for another.

Asset Allocation as Security Selection to Achieve Diversification

The third definition of asset allocation—the distribution of funds among various types of assets to achieve diversification—is illustrated in Figure 24.2. In the figure, an initial capital market line xy denotes the efficient frontier when only domestic stocks are considered for the portfolio. The inclusion of other types of assets (e.g., international equities, securities of firms in emerging markets, real estate, and collectibles) increases the investor's choices. If the returns on these assets are not highly correlated with the returns on domestic stocks, the investor may achieve a higher return for the same level of risk, and the efficient frontier pivots from xy to xz. Asset allocation then becomes the determination of that combination of various types of assets that achieves the highest return for a given amount of risk.

The Importance of Asset Allocation

Asset allocation took on an entirely new dimension with the publication in 1986 of an article by Brinson, Hood, and Beebower and later confirmed in a subsequent publication. Essentially, the authors wanted to decompose the return earned by a portfolio manager into three components: (1) investment policy, (2) market timing, and (3) security selection.[2] The decomposition would then determine the

[2]Gary P. Brinson, L. Randolph Hood, and Gilbert L. Beebower, "Determinants of Portfolio Performance," *Financial Analysts Journal* (July–August 1986): 39–44; and Gary P. Brinson, B. D. Singer, and Gilbert L. Beebower, "Determinants of Portfolio Performance II: An Update," *Financial Analysts Journal* (May–June 1991): 40–48.

FIGURE 24.2

Impact of Increased Diversification on the Efficient Frontier

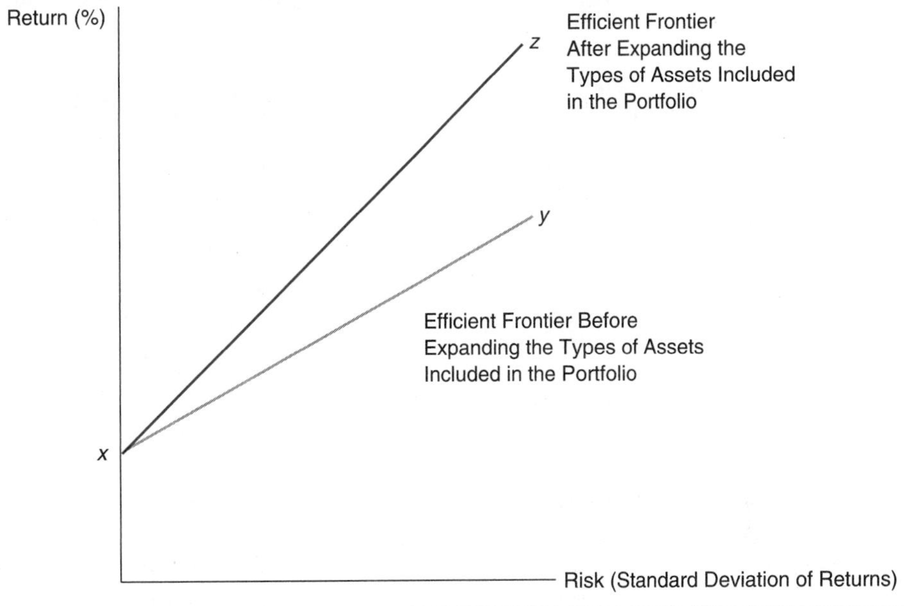

portfolio manager's contribution since the components could be compared to a passive benchmark portfolio, such as the S&P 500 stock index.

While total returns may be compared to a benchmark, part of the return depends on the investment policy, which may be independent of the portfolio manager's decision-making power. For example, suppose a corporation employs a money management firm to oversee its pension plan. The corporation sets the general policy that 30 to 40 percent of the portfolio should be in fixed-income securities and 70 to 60 percent should be in equities. This policy decision is independent of the portfolio manager's decision as to how to execute the policy. The portfolio manager's choices are limited to which fixed-income securities and which stocks will be in the portfolio and when to move from one type of security to the other to maintain the specified allocation.

Brinson, Hood, and Beebower determined a method to isolate each factor's contribution. In effect, their method determined the relative importance of the investment policy, market timing, and security selection. Their results, however, startled the investment management community since 93.6 percent of the observed variation in returns was attributed to the investment policy. The impact of market timing and security selection was minor and (to make matters worse) actually reduced the average return and increased the variability of the return. A passive strategy of buying the stock index generated a higher return than attempting market timing and selecting individual assets.

This seminal work in asset allocation has been expanded. One study identified 11 variables that suggested an active allocation strategy produced higher returns.[3] A more recent study concluded that the portfolio manager's discretion to change the policy also affects the results.[4] Permitting the portfolio manager to alter the

[3]R. C. Klemkosky and R. Bharati, "Time-Varying Expected Returns and Asset Allocation," *Journal of Portfolio Management* (summer 1995): 80–88.

[4]Warren E. Bitters, *The New Science of Asset Allocation* (Chicago, IL.: Glenlake Publishing, 1997).

proportions changes the relative importance of policy, timing, and security selection. Timing and security selection then have a larger impact on total return, but the total amount of variation in returns that was explained by the active management of the portfolio was still small. The policy that determined the asset allocation, however, remained a major determinant of the total return.[5]

Active Versus Passive Management

In addition to determining financial goals and analyzing resources, the individual must determine how actively or passively to manage the portfolio. Some individuals have neither the time nor the inclination to oversee their portfolios and thus employ the services of others (e.g., financial planners, stockbrokers, portfolio managers in trust departments, or the managers of mutual funds). The individual investor, however, must still select who will administer the assets and, of course, suffer any losses that result from poor management of the funds. Ultimately it is the saver who bears the risk and reaps the reward from the portfolio, whether the funds are managed by that individual or by others.

The Self-Administration of a Portfolio and the Belief in Efficient Markets

Individuals who manage their own portfolios have to select the assets that comprise the portfolios. This selection process can range from the active trading of securities to a passive buy-and-hold strategy. Implicit in their decision-making process is the belief in the degree to which financial markets are efficient.

Efficient markets and the efficient market hypothesis are major themes in investments and permeate this text. An important body of information suggests that financial markets are efficient and that few investors consistently outperform the market on a risk-adjusted basis. Returns that exceed market returns are achieved through taking additional risk. On a risk-adjusted basis, higher-than-market returns are not indicative of superior performance but indicate bearing additional risk.

There is also an important body of empirical evidence that suggests financial markets are not completely efficient. This work suggests that anomalies generate returns that exceed market returns even after adjusting for risk. The existence of anomalies offers hope to financial analysts and investors who believe they can outperform the market. For most investors, however, the anomalies can be a diversion. For an anomaly to be useful, the increased return must cover the additional cost associated with executing the strategy. If the additional return is 0.5 percent but increases the cost of investing (e.g., additional transaction costs), the anomaly is of little use for the average investor. The market is effectively efficient even if the anomaly exists.

The belief in the degree of market efficiency affects the individual's selection process, which can range from an active trading to a passive buy-and-hold strategy. Active trading may use many of the techniques and analytical tools discussed in this text. A passive buy-and-hold strategy emphasizes buying securities and holding them until the investor has a need for the funds. A possible passive strategy would be holding index funds, such as the Dreyfus Index Funds: S&P, whose

[5]A study by Roger Ibbotson and Paul Kaplan ("Does Asset Allocation Policy Explain 40, 90, or 100 Percent of Performance?" *Financial Analysts Journal* [January/February 2000]: 26–33) found that policy explained 90 percent of the variability of a fund's return over time but only explained 40 percent of the differences among fund returns. Other factors such as differences in fees, security selection, investment style, and timing account for the differences in returns among funds.

return should mirror the market as measured by the S&P 500 stock index. An alternative index strategy is to invest in funds that invest in different asset classes. The investor could acquire shares in Vanguard Bond Index Long-Term Bond, Vanguard Index Trust 500 Port, Vanguard Index Trust Small Cap Stock, and Vanguard International Equity Index: European. The portfolio would then cover bonds, large U.S. stocks, small U.S. stocks, and European stocks. The investor's return then should mirror the return on each index and each fund's weight in the portfolio.

The more the investor believes that markets are inefficient, the stronger is the argument for an active strategy. Market inefficiency suggests the investor can pursue a particular strategy and earn higher returns. For example, technical approaches such as moving averages may be viable in an inefficient market. However, if the investor believes the weak form of the efficient market hypothesis, this individual will not use any technical approach because this type of analysis will not lead to superior investment results.

If the investor believes the weak form but not the semistrong form of the efficient market hypothesis, fundamental analysis may be employed to select securities. The investor may follow a growth strategy instead of a value strategy or vice versa. With either investment style, the implicit assumption is that the market is sufficiently inefficient to justify the effort to perform the analysis and select the specific assets to include in the portfolio.

If the investor believes both the weak and semistrong forms of the efficient market hypothesis, then technical analysis and fundamental analysis will not lead to superior investment results. That, however, does not preclude using inside information to select securities. Even if the market is very efficient, the efficiency may not be absolute and the strong form of the hypothesis may not hold. Tracking the purchases and sales of insiders assumes this inefficiency.

If the investor is convinced that the financial markets are exceedingly efficient, a buy-and-hold approach to wealth accumulation is a reasonable strategy. The investor constructs a well-diversified portfolio and maintains it for an extended period. The minimal amount of turnover reduces commission costs; plus, with few realized gains the investor has lower capital gains taxes. For the investor who is convinced that financial markets are efficient, this strategy is among the best choices.

The Self-Administration of a Portfolio and Risk-Management Strategies

The uncertain future permeates investment decision making. Although individuals may anticipate and invest based on these expectations, the future cannot be known. That is the essence of the risk associated with investing. Even if the investor believes the financial markets are exceedingly efficient and follows a passive strategy, he or she may continue to use a variety of techniques to manage risk. Many risk-management strategies were covered in various places in this text. This section briefly reiterates them in one convenient summary. These strategies do not create wealth; they help preserve it.

From an investment perspective, risk was divided into two types: unsystematic, diversifiable risk and systematic, nondiversifiable risk. Asset-specific unsystematic risk is, of course, the easiest to manage. The construction of a well-diversified portfolio reduces this source of risk. As long as the returns on the various assets in the portfolio are not positively correlated, asset-specific risk is reduced. This source of risk is virtually eliminated once the portfolio has 15 different assets, but the challenge is finding assets whose returns are not positively correlated.

Diversification, however, has little impact on the other sources of risk because these sources apply to all assets of a given type. All bond prices respond to changes in interest rates. Diversification reduces the impact of a particular bond defaulting, but it does not reduce the impact of higher interest rates decreasing bond prices. (You may also reduce the risk of default by limiting the portfolio to bonds with high credit ratings or bonds that are insured.) To reduce interest rate risk, the investor must execute a different strategy. The same applies to the risk associated with fluctuations in security prices (market risk), inflation (purchasing power risk), the reinvestment of income and proceeds of redemptions and sales (reinvestment rate risk), and fluctuations in exchange rates (exchange rate risk).

The following are several risk-management techniques that the investor may follow. Unfortunately, using one strategy may only affect one source, so the investor may employ several strategies simultaneously. The presentation is in the order in which the strategies were covered in the text.

Insured Bank Deposits (Chapter 2). FDIC-insured bank deposits erase the risk associated with bank failures up to the specified amount of the insurance.

Stop-Loss Orders (Chapter 3). By entering an order to sell a stock after buying it, the long investor reduces the amount of loss from a decline in the price of the stock. By entering a stop-loss order to purchase a stock, the short investor reduces the possible loss from an increase in the price of the stock.

Beta Coefficients (Chapter 7). By providing an index of market risk, beta coefficients can be used by the investor to construct a portfolio consistent with his or her willingness to bear market risk. More risk-averse investors may limit their portfolios to stocks with low betas, while more aggressive investors may construct portfolios consisting of stocks with higher betas.

Index Funds (Chapter 8). By mimicking the movement in an aggregate measure of the market, index funds allow the investor to achieve diversification.

Secured Debt (e.g., equipment trust certificates in Chapter 15 and mortgage loans such as CMOs and Ginnie Maes in Chapter 17). Loans secured by identifiable property reduce the risk of default by permitting the investor through a court proceeding to assume ownership of the asset pledged against the loan.

Duration (Chapter 16). By matching when proceeds are needed and the duration of a bond, the investor avoids both the risk associated with fluctuations in interest rates and reinvestment rate risk.

Laddered Bond Portfolio (Chapter 16). By constructing a bond portfolio in which some of the bonds mature every year, the effects of interest rate risk and reinvestment rate risk are reduced.

Inflation-Indexed Bonds (Chapter 17). Since interest and principal repayments are adjusted with changes in the Consumer Price Index, inflation-indexed bonds erase the risk associated with inflation.

Put Bonds (Chapter 18). These bonds permit the investor to redeem the bond at par at a specified date that is prior to maturity. The put option reduces the impact of an increase in interest rates.

Covered Option Writing (Chapter 19). While primarily a source of income to the writer, covered option writing reduces the possible loss on a stock by the amount of the premium received for the option.

Protective Put (Chapter 19) and Protective Call (Chapter 20). By taking the opposite of long and short positions in a stock or a basket of stocks, protective puts and calls reduce the risk from a price movement in the security while maintaining the possibility of gain.

Hedge Ratio (Chapter 20). The hedge ratio provides the investor with the number of options that may be bought (or sold) to offset movements in a stock's price. When applied to index options, the hedge ratio is a means to manage market risk.

Bull and Bear Spreads (Chapter 20). By buying options with different strike prices, the investor accepts a modest possible gain but reduces the possible loss from an adverse movement in a stock's price.

Collars (Chapter 20). This strategy, which involves the purchase of a put at one strike price and the sale of a call with a higher strike price, is designed to lock in a price for a stock and reduce the risk of loss from a decline in the stock's price.

Interest Rate and Currency Swaps (Chapter 21). Primarily used by portfolio managers and corporate financial managers, swaps alter risk exposure associated with fluctuations in interest rates and in exchange rates.

Hedging Strategies with Futures (Chapter 21). By taking the opposite position than the investor currently has in a security (e.g., an index fund), futures contracts reduce the risk associated with market price fluctuations. A long position in stocks is hedged by a short position in stock index futures and reduces the market risk associated with the long position.

The Decision to Delegate the Administration of the Portfolio

The previous discussion suggested that the investor's belief in efficient markets affects the management of a portfolio. The discussion also suggested that the investor may use a variety of strategies to help manage risk, if not erase it. Many investors, however, delegate their authority over the management of the portfolio. They have substituted choice of portfolio manager for choice of specific assets and active risk management.

Selecting Mutual Funds

Selecting a mutual fund requires matching the goals of the investor with the objectives of the fund. The individual's needs for custodial services, diversification, and professional management also affect the selection. In addition, there are several subtle factors that can have an impact on the decision to acquire the shares of a particular mutual fund, including taxation, the maturity of the fund and its management, and rates of return. These considerations may affect not only the decision to purchase mutual funds instead of other investments but also the decision to purchase a particular fund instead of another competing fund.

There are over 8,000 U.S. mutual funds from which to choose. Obviously the investor cannot buy shares in all of them but must select among the alternatives. Thus, while investment companies may relieve individuals from selecting particular stocks and bonds, they do not relieve investors from having to select among the mutual funds that meet the individual's financial goals (e.g., growth or income).

Fees and Expenses

As was explained in Chapter 8, individuals who acquire mutual funds pay a variety of fees. These may include the loading charge, which is the sales fee paid to the broker or financial advisor for executing the transaction. (Other expenses include management fees, 12b-1 fees, and transaction costs incurred by the fund.) Whether the load charge is worth the cost is, of course, open to considerable debate, but there is little evidence that load funds earn a higher return than no-load funds. The load must be justified on the basis of services received. The investor must find a broker or financial advisor whose advice and help are worth the load fee.[6]

By acquiring no-load funds, the load expense is avoided, but the investor continues to bear the remaining expenses. Management fees, operating expenses, and transaction costs apply to all funds. While these expenses cannot be avoided, they do differ among the various funds. The investor should consider these costs, because they obviously decrease returns. Higher-than-average management and operating expenses and frequent portfolio turnover, which generates higher transaction costs, are possible red flags the investor should take into account when selecting a particular mutual fund for purchase.

The investor may particularly want to analyze 12b-1 fees, which are marketing expenses and are assessed each year by many no-load funds. Over a period of years, 12b-1 fees can exceed load expenses. Excluding the impact of compounding, a \$0.50 annual 12b-1 fee exceeds a \$3.00 load fee after six years. If the investor holds the shares for ten years and pays the 12b-1 fee each year, that investor would have been better off buying a load fund without the 12b-1 fee. (Unfortunately, some load funds also charge 12b-1 fees.)

POINTS OF INTEREST
The Internet and Information Concerning Mutual Funds

As you might expect, the Internet can be a major source of information concerning mutual funds. For example, in Chapter 8, the Web addresses of several mutual fund families (e.g., Fidelity) were given. Presumably, all mutual funds post information on the Internet and have Web addresses. As was explained in Chapter 8, shares of mutual funds are purchased directly from the fund instead of through secondary markets. While such purchases are often made through brokers, shares may also be purchased on-line. (Don't conclude, however, that on-line purchase of a load fund lets you avoid paying the sales charge. You still pay the load fee, but instead of the payment going to a salesperson, it is kept by the fund.

Possible on-line sources of information concerning mutual funds include:

American Association of Individual Investors: http://www.aaii.com
Bloomberg Financial: http://www.bloomberg.com
Brill's Mutual Funds Interactive: http://www.fundsinteractive.com
ICI Mutual Fund Connection: http://www.ici.org
MSN Investing: http://www.investor.msn.com
MSN Money: http://www.moneycentral.com
Morningstar: http://www.morningstar.com
Mutual Funds Investor's Center: http://www.mfea.com
Mutual Funds Magazine Online: http://www.mfmag.com
Quicken: http://www.quicken.com
Value Line Investment Research and Asset Management: http://www.valueline.com
Yahoo! Finance: http://quote.yahoo.com

These sources offer basic information, such as net asset value, performance measures, and comparisons. Several offer links to other sites. For example, *Mutual Funds* magazine's site (http://www.mfmag.com) provides links to a mutual fund's site and to other fund services, such as Morningstar.

[6]For some practical advice, see Marla Brill, "How to Pick a Financial Advisor," *Mutual Funds* (February 1997): 48–59; or Jonathon Burton, "Show Me the Load," *Mutual Funds* (October 1998): 44–49.

POINTS OF INTEREST

Dollar Cost Averaging and Mutual Funds

One of the advantages offered investors by mutual funds is dollar cost averaging. As was explained in Chapter 10, an individual may make equal, periodic investments. With such a strategy, the investor acquires fewer shares when prices rise but more shares when prices fall. The larger purchases reduce the average cost of a share, and, if the value of the stock subsequently rises, the low-cost stock generates more capital gains.

While the individual may follow such a strategy by purchasing stock through brokers, transaction fees reduce the attractiveness of dollar cost averaging, especially if the individual is investing a modest amount (e.g., less than $500). Transaction costs may be eliminated or at least reduced through the use of mutual funds. Avoidance of fees is obvious in the case of no-load funds, but reduction in costs may also apply to load funds. Suppose an individual seeks to invest $300 a month; many brokers may not execute such a small order. If they do buy $300 worth of stock, brokerage firms (including discount brokerage firms) will charge the minimum commission, which is generally at least $50 to $60. Thus even with loading fees, mutual funds can still offer investors with modest sums a cheaper means to achieve the advantage associated with dollar cost averaging.

Tax Considerations

Investment companies receive favorable tax treatment. They pay no federal income taxes and are a conduit through which income and capital gains are passed to stockholders. The investor ultimately has to pay any applicable taxes on the income and capital gains generated by the fund. If the fund's net asset value increases and the investor redeems the shares, he or she pays any applicable capital gains tax. If the mutual fund earns and distributes income, the individual stockholder pays the income tax on the dividends. If the mutual fund realizes capital gains, the investor pays any capital gains taxes.

Taxes can have an important impact on the selection of a particular fund. Tax considerations are numerous, and the following discussion covers hidden capital gains, hidden capital losses, year-end distributions, and tax efficiency. Besides creating problems for financial planning, taxation alters the net return the investor earns and reduces the individual's ability to compare his or her return with the performance claimed by the fund's management. (The fund's return is stated before tax but the investor only gets to keep the after-tax return.) Even if the fund's objectives are consistent with the investor's financial goals, the fund's management may still follow a policy that is not in the best interests of the individual investor's tax strategy.

Hidden Capital Gains

The individual mutual fund can have built into its portfolio the potential for a considerable tax liability that may not be obvious to the investor. In some cases this liability may fall on investors who do not experience the gains. This potential tax liability is the result of the fund experiencing paper profits on its portfolio (i.e., profits that have not been realized). As long as the gains are not realized, there will be no taxation, which only occurs once the investment company sells the appreciated assets and thus realizes the capital gain.

This potential tax liability is perhaps best seen by a simple illustration. If a mutual fund is started by selling shares for $10 (excluding costs), the net asset value of a share is $10. The fund invests the money in various securities, which appreciate in value during the year. At the end of the year the net asset value of a share is now $14. Since the fund has not sold any of its holdings, its stockholders have no tax liability.

This fund is a going concern and like all mutual funds offers to redeem its shares and sell additional shares to investors. Suppose an original investor redeems shares at the net asset value of $14. This individual has a capital gain because the value of the shares rose from the initial offer price of $10 to $14. Such a capital gain is independent of whether or not the fund realizes the capital gain on its portfolio, because the investor realizes the gain.

Suppose, however, this individual had not redeemed the shares but continued to hold them. The fund then realizes the $4 per share profit and distributes the capital gain. Once again this investor must pay the appropriate capital gains tax. These two cases are exactly what the investor should expect. If the investor redeems the shares and realizes the gain or if the fund realizes the gain, the individual stockholder is responsible for the taxes.

It is, however, possible for an investor to be responsible for the taxes without experiencing the capital gain. Suppose the individual purchases shares at the current net asset value of $14 for a cost basis of $14. On the next day the management of the fund realizes the profits on the portfolio (i.e., sells its securities) and distributes the capital gain. The investors who purchased the initial shares at $10 have earned a profit and must pay any appropriate capital gains tax. The individual who has just purchased the shares for $14 also receives a capital gain distribution and thus is also subject to the capital gains tax. Even though this investor paid $14 per share, that individual is the holder of record for the distribution and thus is responsible for the tax.

When the capital gain distribution is made, the value of the stock declines. In this illustration the net asset value of the shares declines by $4 (i.e., the amount of the distribution) to $10. The investor who bought the shares for $14 could offset the $4 distribution by redeeming the shares. Since the shares cost $14 but are now worth only $10, this investor sustains a $4 loss. Such a sale offsets the distribution, and thus the stockholder no longer has any tax obligation. However, the original purchase, the redemption, and any subsequent reinvestment may involve transaction costs that this investor must bear. So the stockholder loses either through having to pay the capital gains tax or having to absorb the fees associated with the redemption designed to offset the tax necessitated by the distribution.

Could the individual have anticipated this potential tax liability? The answer is yes when the investor realizes that the source of the tax is the unrealized capital gains embedded in the mutual fund's net asset value. If a fund's portfolio has risen in value, the fund has unrealized capital gains. When the gains are realized, they accrue to the shareholders to whom they are distributed. These shareholders are not necessarily the stockholders who owned shares when the appreciation occurred. If the individual were to determine the cost basis of the fund's portfolio and the current value of that portfolio, any unrealized capital gains would be apparent. If, for example, the fund has $100,000,000 in assets that cost only $60,000,000, there is $40,000,000 in unrealized gains. If these profits are realized, they will create tax liabilities for current—rather than former—stockholders.[7]

Hidden Capital Losses

Whereas unrealized gains imply the potential for future tax liabilities, unrealized capital losses offer the possibility of tax-free gains. Suppose a mutual fund started with a net asset value of $10 but as the result of a declining market currently has a net asset value of $6. Any individual who originally bought the shares at $10 and now has redeemed them for $6 has sustained a capital loss, and he or she will use

[7]This tax problem could be avoided by purchasing the shares after the distribution and the decline in the net asset value. Ascertaining when the shares may be purchased exclusive of the distribution may save the investor considerable tax expense over a period of years. Many funds report estimated distribution amounts and dates on their Web sites. The investor should check for this information before purchasing the shares.

POINTS OF INTEREST

The Specific Share Method for Identifying Shares Sold or Redeemed

When shares in a mutual fund are sold, the gains are subject to capital gains taxation. When the investor sells only part of the holdings, the general rule is first-in, first-out. That is, the first shares purchased are the first to be sold. Since share values tend to rise, first-in, first-out usually generates more taxes. This potential difference in taxes is illustrated in a simple example in which the investor makes the following three purchases of 100 shares:

	Cost Basis	Holding Period
100 shares	$1,000	4 years
100 shares	$2,000	3 years
100 shares	$3,000	2 years

The cost basis rises with the more recent purchases.

The current price of a share is $40 and the investor redeems 100 shares for $4,000. Under first-in, first-out, the shares bought four years ago were sold; the long-term capital gain is $3,000. Obviously the tax will be larger than if the last shares were sold and the long-term capital gain is only $1,000. Can the investor sell the shares acquired more recently and retain the first shares? If the investor can sell the last shares instead of the first shares, there is an obvious gain in the capital gains tax owed. (If the last shares were held for less than a year and are subject to short-term capital gains tax rates—that is, the investor's marginal income tax rate—it may be more advantageous to use first-in, first-out. Depending on the amount of the gain, the long-term capital gains tax may be lower.)

The answer to the question is yes.* The investor uses the "specific share method," which identifies the particular shares that were sold. The IRS, however, will not accept the investor saying that the last shares were sold. The investor must notify the fund in writing which shares were sold and receive written confirmation of the sale from the fund. The same principle applies to the purchase and subsequent sale of stock. If the purchases were AT&T stock and the investor sold 100 shares, the first-in, first-out rule applies unless the investor informs the broker that the last shares were sold and receives written confirmation that the last shares were sold. Mutual funds and brokers will, of course, provide the written confirmation, but the investor must take the initiative and request it. Without the written confirmation from the fund or the broker, the first-in, first-out rule applies.

*Investors in mutual funds have an additional alternative. They can average the cost of a fund's shares and use that amount for the cost basis. Averaging to determine the cost basis is not available for investors in stock, who must use first-in, first-out or the specific share method. (See the appendix to Chapter 8.)

that loss to offset other capital gains or income (up to the limit allowed by the current tax code).

If, however, an individual purchases shares at the current net asset value of $6, the value of the portfolio could rise without necessarily creating a tax liability for that investor. Suppose the portfolio's net asset value rises back to $10, at which time the mutual fund sells the securities. Since the cost basis to the fund of the sold securities is $10, the fund has no capital gain. The shareholder has seen the net asset value rise from $6 to $10 without any tax liability being created by the mutual fund.

If the net asset value continues to rise to $12 and the fund sells the securities, it realizes a $2 gain ($12 − $10). The investor who bought the shares at $6 will only be subject to capital gains tax on the $2, because the fund's cost basis is $10. The investor has seen his or her investment rise from $6 to $12 but is only subject to tax on the appreciation from $10 to $12. As long as the investor *does not redeem the shares acquired for $6,* the tax on the $4 appreciation from $6 to $10 is deferred even if the mutual fund sells the securities. Thus, if the fund has unrealized losses, this may offer the individual an opportunity for tax savings just as the unrealized capital gains may create future tax liabilities.

The investor should realize that a fund with unrealized losses is not necessarily an attractive investment. The losses may be the result of inept management, and if such performance continues, the fund will generate larger losses. However, if the investor believes that the fund will be acquired or will turn around and perform well so that its net asset value increases, the unrealized tax losses embedded in the fund's portfolio can magnify the investor's after-tax return.

Year-End Distributions and Income Taxation

Distributions from mutual funds are subject to income or capital gains taxation. While many U.S. corporations distribute dividends quarterly during the year, most mutual funds make two distributions. The first is a six-month income distribution. A second and year-end distribution consists of both income and capital gains. As a stock's price is adjusted downward for the dividend (see the discussion of the distribution of dividends in Chapter 11), the net asset value of the fund declines by the amount of the dividend. For example, if the NAV is $34 and the fund distributes $2.00 ($0.50 in income and $1.50 in capital gains), the NAV declines to $32.

The recipient of the distribution is responsible for the tax on the dividend income and the capital gains tax on the capital gain. If the investor buys the shares at the NAV ($34) just prior to the distribution, that individual pays the appropriate tax even though the appreciation occurred prior to the purchase. Thus, it may be desirable to defer the purchase until after the fund goes ex dividend and the NAV declines to $32. (Of course, this tax issue is irrelevant if the shares are held in a tax-deferred retirement account.)

Tax Efficiency

Mutual fund fees obviously affect an investor's return. Load charges, operating expenses, marketing expenses (12b-1 fees), and commissions paid by the fund reduce the return the investor earns. While funds with lower fees may be preferred, there are reasons why some fees are larger and the increased expense is justified. For example, funds that specialize in foreign investments may have larger expenses because foreign operations cost more and obtaining information on which to base security purchases or sales may be more difficult. Obviously, if the investor wants shares in the foreign fund for some purpose (e.g., diversification), the higher fees may be justified.

While fees affect the fund's return, an additional consideration affects the return the investor retains. Mutual fund returns are before tax, but income and capital gains taxes affect the return the investor retains. Consider three funds: The net asset value of each is $20 and each earns a return of 10 percent. The investor buys one share for $20. Fund A consists solely of stocks that are never sold, so at the end of the second year, the fund's net asset value is $22 ($20 × 1.1), and the investor has stock worth $22.

Fund B collects dividends of 10 percent on its investments. Thus, during the first year, the fund earns $2 and distributes $2. The fund's earnings initially increased its NAV to $22, but after the $2 income distribution, the NAV returns to $20. The individual reinvests the $2 into 0.1 shares and has 1.1 shares worth $22.

Fund C invests in stock that appreciates 10 percent, then is sold and the gain distributed. The fund's NAV initially increased to $22, but after the $2 capital gain distribution, the NAV returns to $20. The individual reinvests the $2 into 0.1 shares and has 1.1 shares worth $22.

All three cases end with the investor having stock worth $22. However, there is a tax difference. Fund A had no security sales, and the investor has no tax obligations. Fund B's $2 distribution is subject to income taxes, and Fund C's $2 distribution is subject to capital gains taxation. There is an obvious difference in the investor's tax obligations generated by each fund.

The ability of the fund to generate returns without generating large amounts of tax obligations is the fund's tax efficiency. Obviously, if the fund never realizes any capital gains and does not receive any income, there will be no distributions and the investor has no tax obligations. This, however, is unlikely. (Even a passively managed index fund may receive dividend income from its portfolio. This income is distributed and the investor becomes liable for taxes on the distribution.) At the other extreme are the funds that frequently turn over their portfolios. Each security sale is a taxable event. Such frequent turnover implies the fund will not generate long-term capital gains. The capital gains and the distributions will be short-term and subject to tax at the stockholder's marginal federal income tax rate.

If the fund turns over its portfolio less frequently, the capital gains it realizes and the subsequent distributions may be long-term. Since long-term capital gains are taxed at favorable (lower) rates, the fund's ability to generate long-term instead of short-term capital gains is more favorable to the investor from a tax perspective.

"Tax efficiency" is an index that converts mutual fund returns to an after-tax basis by expressing the after-tax return as a percentage of the before-tax return, which permits comparisons based on a fund's ability to reduce stockholder tax obligations. The computation of tax efficiency requires assumptions concerning tax rates. In the following example, an income tax rate is assumed to be 35 percent, and the long-term capital gains tax rate is assumed to be 20 percent. Fund A's return consisted solely of unrealized capital appreciation. Since there is no tax, the after-tax and before-tax returns are equal so the tax efficiency is 100 percent. Fund B's return is entirely subject to income tax of $0.70 (0.35 × $2 = $0.70). While the before-tax return is 10 percent, the after-tax return is 6.5 percent ($1.30/$2). The tax efficiency index is 65 (6.5%/10%). Fund C's return consisted of realized long-term capital gains, which generated $0.40 in taxes (0.20 × $2.00). The after-tax return is 8 percent ($1.60/$2), so the tax efficiency index is 80. Since the tax efficiency index for each of the three funds is 100, 65, and 80, on an after-tax basis the performance ranking is A, C, and B.

While this index may seem appealing, it has several weaknesses. To construct the tax efficiency index, the investor needs the composition of the returns and the appropriate tax rates in effect when the returns were earned.[8] Tax rates vary with changes in the tax laws, but even without changes in the tax laws, the appropriate income tax rate may differ as the investor moves from one tax bracket to another. The tax efficiency index varies among investors, and published tax efficiency rankings may not be appropriate for an investor whose tax brackets differ from those used to construct the index.

A second weakness is that a high tax efficiency index may be achieved when the fund does not realize capital gains. When these gains are realized, the tax efficiency ratio will decline. In terms of the illustration, Fund A's high rating will fall when the gains are realized. Thus, while a high tax efficiency ratio indicates lower taxes in the past, it may also imply higher taxes in the future. For this reason the index needs to be computed over a period of years so that differences in the timing of security sales from one year to the next are eliminated.

A third weakness is that high efficiency may not alter performance rankings. Funds with similar objectives and styles (e.g., long-term growth through investments in large cap stocks) may generate similar tax obligations. Suppose one fund's return is 20 percent while another fund generates 16 percent. All gains are distributed and are long-term. The tax efficiency for both funds is the same, so the relative ranking is unchanged. Unless the second fund can perceptibly save on

[8] *The Individual Investor's Guide to Low-Load Mutual Funds* provides both actual returns and tax-adjusted returns. In the 2001 edition, the returns for 2000 were adjusted using a 39.6 percent income tax rate and a 20 percent long-term capital gains tax rate. For example, Fidelity Convertible Securities reported a return of 7.2 percent, but the tax-adjusted return was 2.3 percent. While 39.6 percent and 20 percent tax would not apply to all investors, they were a worst-case scenario in 2000.

taxes, its performance is likely to remain inferior on both a before- and after-tax basis.[9]

Actually, the tax efficiency index may only be another measure of a fund's portfolio turnover. Low turnover suggests that the fund will generate more long-term gains and thus reduce taxes relative to a fund with a high turnover. If management turns over the entire portfolio during the year, all gains will be short-term. If the portfolio turns over every two years, many of the gains may be long-term. Thus, if the investor is concerned with the taxes, a portfolio with low turnover should tend to generate lower taxes than a fund with high turnover.

Returns

Investments are made to generate returns. The same obviously applies to investments in mutual funds. But all funds do not earn the same return. Does the age (or size) of the fund affect the return? Do some funds consistently outperform other funds? This section is devoted to these questions. If a type of fund consistently outperforms other funds, the implication for investors is obvious. However, efficient markets suggest that selecting funds is not that easy.

The Mature Versus the New Fund

All funds had to be created. Those that have been successful tend to grow as investors purchase additional shares. Should an investor purchase the shares of new funds or those with the advantage of established track records? *Forbes,* for example, annually publishes performance ratings and separates performances by rising and declining markets. Thus, the investor can learn how well a fund has performed when security prices rose and how well the fund protected capital during a period of declining security prices.

A fund's performance record is also a record of its management. The fund has an indeterminate life; portfolio managers change with the passage of time. The individuals who guided the fund during the period of its initial success and growth may no longer be associated with the fund. A change in a fund's management may reduce continuity and alter investment philosophy. The investor should not assume that new management will be able to match prior management's record.

Over time, mutual funds grow by issuing new shares. As the fund expands, its capacity to perform may decline. It is easier for a small fund to move in and out of the market when it buys or sells in modest-sized blocks. As the fund's portfolio increases, this flexibility decreases. A large fund may be unable to quickly establish a position in an attractive security or to rapidly liquidate a position if the fund is buying or selling large blocks of stock.

Even if the fund is able to establish a position, the market makers may require the fund to pay a higher-than-market price to purchase a large block or to accept a lower-than-market price to sell a large block. The effect is to increase transaction costs. Even if the fund negotiates smaller brokerage commissions on the purchase or sale, the total cost—which includes brokerage commissions, the spread between the bid and ask prices, and any price concessions necessary to execute the transactions—may exceed that which an individual investor pays to buy and sell securities.

Large funds may also have difficulty sustaining growth. It is harder to increase by 20 percent the value of a portfolio worth $2,000,000,000 than a portfolio worth

[9]That the best before-tax performing funds are often the best after-tax performing funds is discussed in Greg Carlson, "Does Tax Efficiency Count?" *Mutual Funds* (February 1999): 76–78.

$200,000,000. The base for the former portfolio is so large that a decent performance in the value of one of the fund's holdings may have little impact on the fund's total value.

A smaller and newer fund may not have these problems. The fund's size permits it to establish a position readily in a given security or to liquidate the position. It is small enough that a major move in the market or selected holdings is readily discernible in the fund's net asset value. And the young management may have an aggressiveness (or incentive) that generates more growth and success.

Unfortunately, a new fund does not have a track record, and investors do not know how well management will perform under varying conditions in the securities markets. The fund may have been created during a bull market and thus management would not have been tested during a period of declining prices. There is also the possibility that only funds that perform well are taken public. For example, a fund may be initially sold privately. If the management is unsuccessful, the shares are never offered to the public, but if it succeeds and the value of the portfolio appreciates, the fund is offered publicly. Management has a record of success that will be detailed in the fund's prospectus. Obviously, such previous success will help market the shares. Whether management will be able to sustain the growth once the fund is public and its total assets are larger is not known when the initial public offering of the shares is made.

Consistency of Returns

One system for selecting mutual funds may be to purchase shares in a fund that has done well. The premise is that the best-performing funds will continue to do well (i.e., going with the "hot hands"). Certainly the large amount of publicity in the popular financial press given to the funds that do well during a particular time period encourages individuals to invest in those funds. Money certainly does flow into funds that have a superior track record, and, since fees increase as the funds under management grow, it should not be surprising to learn that mutual funds tout any evidence of superior performance.

Consistency of mutual fund performance is intuitively appealing. Such consistency seems to apply to many areas of life. For example, several National Football League teams do well and make the playoffs virtually every year. However, the material on efficient markets suggests the opposite may apply to mutual funds. Essentially the question is: If stock market prices have no memory and past stock performance has no predictive power, why should historical mutual fund performance have predictive power? The answer, of course, may be the superior skills of the fund's managers. If fund managers have superior skills, then the portfolios they manage should consistently outperform the portfolios of less-skilled managers.

Studies have been conducted to determine the consistency of fund returns. Nonacademic studies tend to suggest consistency. For example, a study by the Institute for Economic Research indicated that past performance did predict future performance.[10] The results were consistent over different time horizons; for example, 26-week returns forecasted the next 26-week returns and one-year returns predicted the next year returns. Results tended to be best over the longest time horizons. Funds with the highest returns over a period of five years consistently did better during the next two years than the funds with the lowest returns.

---

[10] "Mutual Fund Hot Hands: Go with the Winners," Institute for Economic Research (April 1998). Information concerning this study may be obtained from the Institute at 2200 S.W. 10th St., Deerfield Beach, FL 33442.

The results of academic studies, however, are ambiguous. Although some support consistency, others do not.[11] At least one study explained the observed consistency on the basis of the fund's investment objective or style and not on the basis of the portfolio manager's skill.[12] For example, suppose large cap stocks do well while small cap stocks do poorly. Large cap mutual funds should consistently outperform small cap funds. Once the returns are standardized for the investment style, the consistency of the returns disappears. The superior performance of the large cap mutual funds is the result of market movements and not the result of the skill of the portfolio managers. The consistently better-performing large cap stocks give the impression that the large cap mutual funds are the consistently better-performing mutual funds.[13] These findings, of course, support the concept of efficient markets. One set of portfolio managers is not superior to another. Their better performance in one period does not predict superior returns in the next period. Once again, past performance is not indicative of future performance. Past prices have no memory and do not predict future prices.

One major problem facing all studies of the consistency of returns is "survival bias." Suppose an investment management firm has two mutual funds, A and B, which earn 20 and 5 percent, respectively. For some reason (possibly skill, possibly luck) the management of Fund A did perceptibly better than the management of Fund B. Can the investment management firm erase Fund B's performance? The answer is yes! One possibility is to merge Fund B into Fund A. Since Fund A survives, the performance data of B are buried. That is the essence of survival bias—poorly performing funds cease to exist and their performance data disappear.[14]

Does this happen? The answer is unequivocally yes, and there are stunning illustrations. In 1993, the $334 million Putnam Strategic Income Fund was merged into Putnam Equity Income. Prior to the merger, the Putnam Equity Income Fund had only $1 million in assets, so the merger buried the performance of a much larger fund. During the mid-1990s Dreyfus merged or liquidated 14 funds. In late 1998, a plan existed to merge and combine several Steadman funds, which were among the industry's worst-performing funds.[15]

From the investor's perspective, liquidations and mergers are important when interpreting data concerning the consistency of performance. If funds that did poorly cease to exist while funds that do well continue to operate, the investor may conclude that funds perform better than is the case. Returns from poor funds are ignored. Of course, investors who owned the poorly performing funds will have actual returns that are perceptibly less than the returns reported by the surviving fund.

[11]A sampling of this research includes: Ronald N. Kahn and Andrew Rudd, "Does Historical Performance Predict Future Performance?" *Financial Analysts Journal* (November–December 1995): 43–51. This study found consistency only in fixed-income funds. William N. Goetzmann and Roger G. Ibbotson, "Do Winners Repeat?" *Journal of Portfolio Management* (winter 1994): 9–18. This study found consistency in both raw returns and after adjusting for risk using the Jensen alpha. W. Scott Bauman and Robert E. Miller, "Can Managed Portfolio Performance Be Predicted?" *Journal of Portfolio Management* (summer 1994): 31–39. This study found consistency over long periods of time (i.e., stock cycles).

[12]See, for instance, F. Larry Detzel and Robert A. Weigand, "Explaining Persistence in Mutual Fund Performance," *Financial Services Review* 7, no. 1 (1998): 45–55; and Gary E. Porter and Jack W. Trifts, "Performance of Experienced Mutual Fund Managers," *Financial Services Review* 7, no. 1 (1998): 56–68.

[13]An extreme example would be the gold funds. Since the price of gold has stagnated for years, these funds have consistently been among the worst-performing mutual funds. However, if the portfolio manager's job is to operate a gold fund, such consistent inferior performance would be the result of the sector in which the fund invested and not of the portfolio manager's lack of skill. (See the discussion of appropriate benchmarks later in this chapter.)

[14]For example, Burton Malkiel has suggested that performance consistency is largely explained by survival bias. His study found that mutual funds tend to underperform the market and that consistency, which may have existed in the 1970's, has subsequently disappeared. See Burton G. Malkiel, "Returns from Investing in Equity Mutual Funds, 1971–1991," *Journal of Finance* (June 1995): 549–572.

[15]See "Davis Schedules the Ultimate Fund Killing," *Mutual Funds* (February 1999): 30–32.

The Risk-Adjusted Portfolio and the Importance of Benchmarks

Investments are made in order to generate a return, but these investments require the individual to bear risk. A higher return by itself does not necessarily indicate superior performance. It may simply be the result of more risk. As was previously explained in Chapter 8, several techniques (based on the capital asset pricing model) have been developed to evaluate performance on a risk-adjusted basis. These composite performance measures—the Jensen performance index (alpha), the Treynor index, and the Sharpe index—were illustrated in Chapter 8 and are repeated here to facilitate the subsequent discussion of benchmarks.

(8.4) $$\textbf{Jensen alpha: } a = r_p - [r_f + (r_m - r_f)\textbf{beta}]$$

(8.5) $$\textbf{Treynor Index: } T_i = \frac{r_p - r_f}{\textbf{beta}}$$

(8.6) $$\textbf{Sharpe Index: } S_i = \frac{r_p - r_f}{\sigma_p}$$

Each composite performance measure may be used to compare a portfolio's return to a market return and adjust for risk. The Jensen alpha determines the extent to which the realized return (r_p) exceeds the expected return. The expected return is the risk-free return (r_f) plus the extent to which the return on the market (r_m) exceeds the risk-free rate, with the difference adjusted for the market risk (the beta) associated with the portfolio. The Treynor and Sharpe indexes standardize the realized return in excess of the risk-free return by a measure of risk. While the Treynor index (T_i) uses the portfolio's beta, the Sharpe index (S_i) uses the portfolio's standard deviation of the returns (σ_p).

Each measure may be used to compare the portfolio return to that of the market. The Jensen performance index directly uses the return on the market as part of the calculation of the alpha. If the alpha is positive, the portfolio outperformed the market on a risk-adjusted basis. To use the Treynor and Sharpe indexes for comparisons, the indexes must be computed for the market. If the portfolio's index exceeds the market index, then the individual portfolio outperformed the market on a risk-adjusted basis.

In Chapter 8, the market return was measured by an aggregate stock index, such as the S&P 500. As is discussed throughout this text, alternative investments available to individuals are not limited to the stocks and mutual funds that acquire the securities comprising the S&P 500. Investors may acquire a variety of assets that include corporate and municipal bonds, derivatives, foreign securities, real estate investment trusts, and collectibles. Many mutual funds do not construct broad-based, well-diversified equity portfolios. Instead, these funds have specialized portfolios (e.g., foreign stocks) or invest in specific segments of the financial markets (e.g., municipal bonds) or follow a specific investment style (e.g., small-cap value stocks).

Evaluating the performance of a broad portfolio consisting of many types of assets or the portfolio of a specialized investment company against an aggregate measure of the equity market will not produce meaningful comparisons. It should be obvious that the return on a gold fund or a real estate investment trust should

EXHIBIT 24.3

Asset Classes and Possible Benchmarks

Asset Class	Benchmark
Large cap U.S. stocks	S&P 500 500 largest companies on NYSE, AMEX and Nasdaq
Mid cap U.S. stocks	S&P MidCap 400 medium-sized firms
Small cap U.S. stocks	Russell 2000 Index of 2,000 small stocks
Developed nations international stocks	EAFE Index Morgan Stanley index of European, Australasian, and Far Eastern stocks
Emerging market stocks	IFCI Composite Index Emerging markets open to foreign investors.[1]
Investment-grade long-term bonds	Lehman Brothers Aggregate Bond Index Index of over 5,000 U.S. government and corporate bonds
High-yield bonds	CS First Boston High Yield 600+ publicly traded bonds with BBB or lower ratings
Municipal bonds	Lehman Brothers Municipal Bond Index Index of over 20,000 investment-grade tax-exempt bonds
Equity REITs	NAREIT Index Index to all publicly traded real estate investment trusts
Real estate properties	NCREIF Index National Council for Real Estate Investment Fiduciaries index of properties

[1]International Finance Corporation also has indexes of the individual country stock markets included in the emerging markets composite index.

not be compared to the return on the S&P 500. Even if an investment in a real estate investment trust did outperform the S&P 500 on a risk-adjusted basis, the comparison would indicate nothing about the performance relative to other real estate investment trusts.

If the individual wants to make risk-adjusted comparisons, the data used in the performance models should be an appropriate benchmark. That is, the Jensen alpha or the Treynor or Sharpe indexes should use an appropriate measure for comparisons, and that measure is not necessarily an aggregate of the stock market. This is, of course, the benchmark problem introduced in Chapter 8. That discussion, however, preceded the material on indexes in Chapter 10 and the specific investments in Parts 2, 3, and 4.

Possible appropriate indexes and their coverage are given in Exhibit 24.3. Since there are over 100 indexes from which to choose, the exhibit is at best only a sample of possible indexes that may be used as benchmarks. The exhibit enumerates an asset class, a possible benchmark index, and a brief description of the composition of the index. As may be seen in the exhibit, the S&P 500 is an appropriate benchmark for a large cap portfolio, but the benchmark for an international portfolio may be the EAFE index.

Even if the investor does not use an index in one of the composite performance measures, indexes may still be used to determine a benchmark for a portfolio. Even though the benchmark may not be risk adjusted, it may still be useful for comparison purposes. This is achieved by constructing a weighted average for the investor's portfolio and a weighted average of the comparable indexes. Suppose an investor has a portfolio consisting of the following four classes of assets, their weights in the portfolio, and returns earned:

Asset Class	Weight in Portfolio	Return
Large cap stocks	40%	17%
Federal government bonds	30	6
Foreign stocks	20	−2
Real estate investment trusts	10	12
Portfolio's return		9.4

The return on the portfolio is 9.4 percent [(0.4)(17) + (0.3)(6) + (0.2)(−2) + (0.1)(12)]. How well did the portfolio perform? Without a source for comparison, the question cannot be answered.

While constructing a risk-adjusted composite measure would be best, that will require the investor to calculate (or obtain) standard deviations of returns or beta coefficients. A simple, pragmatic solution is to construct a weighted average of the returns on the comparable benchmarks and compare that return to the portfolio return. For example, suppose the returns on the comparable indexes were

Index	Return
Large cap stocks	19%
Federal government bonds	7
Foreign stocks	−6
Real estate investment trusts	10
Benchmark return	9.5

Using the same portfolio, the weighted average return is 9.5 percent [(0.4)(19) + (0.3)(7) + (0.2)(−6) + (0.1)(10)]. The portfolio return is only 0.1 percent less than the weighted average of the comparable indexes.

This information gives the investor some measure of comparable performance. Financial theory, however, would not conclude that the portfolio performance was inferior to the benchmark because the analysis only considered return. Risk was excluded. If the portfolio were less risky than the benchmark, the portfolio may have actually outperformed the benchmark on a risk-adjusted basis.[16]

Index and Exchange-Traded Funds

Index Funds

As was discussed in Chapter 8, few funds outperform the market over an extended period of time, and many do not match the returns earned on comparable benchmarks. These results make reasonable sense. In efficient financial markets, few investors and portfolio managers should consistently outperform the market on a risk-adjusted basis. In addition, as the portfolio manager adds more securities to the portfolio, the portfolio's composition increasingly mirrors the market as a whole (or the market for the class of securities being acquired).

This result should not be surprising in an efficient financial market, since over time, most returns should mirror the market unless the portfolio is riskier than the market. Since mutual funds have expenses (e.g., operating expenses and management fees), the return after these costs should be lower than the market return,

[16]For a more comprehensive discussion of portfolio evaluation, see Zvi Bodie, Alex Kane, and Alan J. Marcus, *Investments*, 5th ed. (Boston: Irwin McGraw-Hill, 2001).

which is not reduced by any expenses. The individual who manages his or her own account and buys and sells stocks through a broker also has expenses that reduce the return. So the individual is faced with deciding which strategy—self-management or the delegation of security selection—is most appropriate and if the costs are worth the services received.

The inability of many mutual funds to outperform the market or outperform an appropriate benchmark, however, has led to increased interest in index funds, which mirror the market (or a subsection of the market). Their appeal is obvious. It includes (1) portfolio diversification, (2) a passive portfolio whose minimal turnover and minimal supervision result in lower expenses, and (3) lower taxes since the index fund has few realized capital gains.

By 1998, there were about 50 mutual funds that tracked the S&P 500 stock index. Index funds, however, are not limited to funds that mimic the S&P 500. For example, the Dreyfus S&P MidCap Index fund specializes in moderate-sized equities that match the S&P MidCap 400 index. The Vanguard Balanced Index fund mimics a combination of stocks and bonds. The Schwab International Index fund tracks the 350 largest non-U.S. firms.

Since there are so many index funds, the investor may construct a well-diversified portfolio consisting solely of these passive investments. The investor, however, can even move among funds in an effort to market time (e.g., move into stock funds in anticipation of lower inflation and lower interest rates) or to take advantage of anticipated changes in different markets (e.g., sell U.S. index funds and acquire foreign index funds). Thus, the individual can own passive investments but manage them in an active manner. Such a strategy, of course, may seem perverse, but it avoids the expenses associated with the managed funds.

Support for acquiring index funds may be found in both the popular press and the professional literature.[17] It is, of course, not surprising to learn that such a firm believer in efficient markets as Burton Malkiel favors index funds.[18] John C. Bogle, who was chairman and chief executive officer of the Vanguard Group of Investment Companies, also argues persuasively for acquiring index funds.[19] (Bogle's arguments, however, may be self-serving since he introduced the first index fund, the Vanguard 500, in 1976.)

Exchange-Traded Funds and Portfolios

Financial markets are dynamic. New products are developed, and some catch on while others die. One successful new product has been the exchange-traded fund, which is an outgrowth of the index fund. Index funds permit the individual to take a position in the market as a whole without selecting individual securities. Purchases or redemptions of an index fund only occur at the end of the day when the fund's net asset value is determined. Standard & Poor's Depository Receipts or SPDRs (commonly pronounced "spiders"), overcame that limitation, since the shares can be bought and sold on an exchange during operating hours. In effect, SPDRs are index funds that trade like stocks and bonds. That is, they are exchange-traded funds (ETFs). WEBS (World Equity Benchmark Shares) extend the concept to foreign indexes.[20]

[17]See, for instance, James Picerno, "Market Matchers," *Mutual Funds* (April 1995): 57–62.

[18]Burton G. Malkiel, *A Random Walk Down Wall Street* (New York: W.W. Norton, 1996).

[19]John C. Bogle, "Selecting Equity Mutual Funds," *Journal of Portfolio Management* (winter 1992): 94–100.

[20]There are also mutual funds that invest in other funds, so-called funds of funds. While these funds will result in paying two layers of management fees, the investor obtains a diversified fund portfolio without having to select individual funds. Funds of funds that invest in funds with different styles or strategies should also tend to mimic an index.

The first SPDR comprised all the stocks in the S&P 500 stock index. The second SPDR was based on the S&P MidCap stock index and was quickly followed by SPDRs based on subsections of the S&P 500 stock index. The SPDRs covered basic industry, consumer products, cyclical/transportation, energy, financial, industrial, technology, and utility stocks. Because each consists of all the stocks in the S&P 500 stock index that fall into each category, each is a pure play in the particular subsection of the overall index. If you believe that the large energy companies will do well, you do not have to select the specific companies but can buy the energy SPDRs. Since each SPDR is unmanaged, operating expenses should be minimal, and the performance should mirror the return earned on the energy stocks in the S&P 500 stock index.[21]

After the initial success of index funds, SPDRs, and WEBS, the next logical step was to extend the concept to other areas. Today there is a whole spectrum of exchange-traded funds (also referred to as "exchange-traded portfolios"). While the majority are listed on the American Stock Exchange, some are traded on the New York Stock Exchange and Nasdaq market.

In addition to SPDRs and WEBS, which were renamed iShares (and discussed in Chapter 22 on international investments), the investor may acquire streetTRACKS™. These exchange-traded funds track specialized indexes such as the Dow Jones small cap growth index or the Wilshire REIT index.[22] There is even a fund tracking the Fortune 500. Merill Lynch has created HOLDRs™ (Holding Company Depository Receipts), each of which holds a fixed portfolio of approximately 20 stocks in a sector such as biotech, pharmaceuticals, or regional banks.[23] For example, the pharmaceutical portfolio includes Abbott Laboratories, Allergan, Johnson & Johnson, and Merck. Once the portfolio is acquired, it is maintained indefinitely. There is no active management of the portfolio, which reduces annual expenses to a minimum.[24]

Since ETFs are a type of closed-end investment company, the investor might want to know if ETFs can sell for a discount or premium over their net asset value. The answer is no. ETFs permit large institutions to exchange shares in companies for ETF shares and vice versa. Suppose an ETF were to sell for a discount from its net asset value. The financial institution could buy the ETF shares and exchange them for shares in the underlying companies. Simultaneously, the financial institution would sell the exchanged shares in the secondary markets and make the difference between the cost of the ETF shares and proceeds from the sale of the underlying stock. If the ETF shares were selling for a premium, the process is reversed. The financial institution would buy the underlying shares, exchange them for shares in the ETF, and simultaneously sell the ETF shares. Once again, the financial institution makes the difference between the cost of the underlying stock and the proceeds from the sale of the ETF shares. In effect, the financial institution has an opportunity for arbitrage and certainly would take advantage of any price

---

[21]SPDRs collect dividends distributed by the stocks they own. These dividends cover the fund's expenses, and the residual is distributed as cash dividends.

[22]Information concerning streetTRACKS may be found at http://www.streettracks.com. General information on index funds and exchange-traded funds is available through IndexFunds, Inc. at http://www.indexfunds.com.

[23]Information on HOLDRs is available from Merrill Lynch's Web site (http://www.holdrs.com) and the AMEX site at http://www.amex.com. The Bank of New York, which acts as the trustee and transfer agent for the securities, provides a Web site devoted to depository receipts (http://www.adrbny.com) that gives current pricing and a link that provides the composition of each HOLDR's portfolio.

[24]HOLDRs are different than other ETFs. The investors who purchase these shares are considered to own the stocks in the HOLDR's portfolio. An investor may take delivery of the individual securities, in which case the HOLDR ceases to exist. This subtlety means that the HOLDRs must sell for the value of the underlying stocks. If a HOLDR were to sell for a discount, the investor could short the stocks, buy the HOLDR at the discounted price, have the underlying shares delivered, and cover the shorts. This process would guarantee a profit. Of course, the act of shorting the stocks and buying the HOLDR would drive its price back to the value of the underlying stock. Other ETFs offer this opportunity for arbitrage to large financial insitutions but not to individual stockholders. A HOLDR extends the opportunity to all of its stockholders.

differentials between the ETF's share price and its net asset value. Through this act of simultaneously executing both a long and a short position in the ETF and the underlying stocks, any differential between the net asset value of the ETF shares and their underlying stocks is erased.[25]

Exchange-traded funds have become popular vehicles for investors.[26] In 2000, the funds based on the Nasdaq 100, the S&P 500, and the DJIA were the most actively traded securities on the AMEX. The Internet HOLDR was the seventh most active issue, and six of the ten most actively traded issues on the AMEX were exchange-traded funds. However, it cannot be concluded these are riskless investments. From August 2000 to August 2001, the price of the B2B Internet HOLDR reached a high of $60 and within a year traded for less than $5, a decline in excess of 90 percent.

While exchange-traded funds are not riskless, they do offer investors advantages not available through index funds. Investors may easily move from one to another just as they can buy and sell the stock of individual companies. If an investor believes one area or sector is overpriced, the individual may sell the exchange-traded shares short. Such short sales are not possible with index funds and would require substantial commissions if a large number of companies were shorted.

In a sense, exchange-traded funds let passive investors actively manage their positions. Instead of having to select individual securities (as is required by active portfolio management), the investor may move between sectors and rebalance a portfolio's asset allocation. If an investor believes that one sector is overpriced while another is underpriced, exchange-traded funds let the investor move from one sector to the other. Prior to the creation of exchange-traded funds, the investor would have to sell stocks in the overpriced sector to purchase stocks in the underpriced sector. This individual could be correct as to the strategy but incorrect as to which securities to sell and purchase. The exchange-traded fund avoids this problem of security selection since the fund tracks the sector as a whole. If an investor wants to allocate a larger proportion of the portfolio to pharmaceuticals, that individual can more heavily weight the portfolio with an exchange-traded fund based on a pharmaceutical index without having to analyze and buy individual pharmaceutical companies.

Even if the investor wants to acquire individual assets in a specific sector, exchange-traded funds offer increased flexibility. The investor may initially acquire an exchange-traded fund and then research individual stocks. Once the desired stocks have been identified, the investor unwinds (i.e., sells) the position in the fund and substitutes the desired stocks. This process may be spread over a period of time, during which the investor maintains exposure to the sector through the exchange-traded fund. As more individual stocks are added to the portfolio, the position in the fund is liquidated.

Selling (Redeeming) Mutual Fund Shares

An investor may purchase stock because he or she believes that the company is undervalued. If the stock's price rises, the individual may sell the stock and realize the capital gain. Investors may purchase long-term bonds in anticipation of lower interest rates. They want to lock in the higher yields or speculate that the

[25]Other closed-end shares do not permit financial institutions or anyone else to exchange shares in the fund for the underlying stock, so this opportunity for arbitrage does not exist and the shares of the closed-end fund may sell for a discount or for a premium.

[26]Information on index funds and exchange-traded funds may be found at IndexFunds, Inc. (http://www.indexfunds.com).

price of the bonds will rise as rates decline. These investors may subsequently sell the bonds when interest rates fall, anticipating that they will rise again. Positions in stocks and bonds are sold every trading day. If some investors were not selling, markets would cease to exist—there has to be a seller for every buyer.

Shares in mutual funds may also be liquidated, but since there is no secondary market, the shares are sold back to the fund (i.e., redeemed). Most written material on mutual funds is concerned with acquiring the shares and covers such topics as the features and objectives of various funds, the variety of funds, and the returns they have earned. Not much is written concerning the selling or liquidation of positions in mutual funds. There is, however, no reason to assume that shares once acquired will be held forever; indeed, there are several reasons why investors should redeem their shares in mutual funds.

Presumably the individual acquires the shares to meet financial goals, so the most obvious reason for redeeming the shares is that the investor has achieved these goals. For example, funds acquired to finance a college education are redeemed to meet that expense. A growth fund acquired while the investor is working may be redeemed when the individual retires and needs a flow of income provided by a bond or balanced fund.

Meeting one's financial goal(s) is only one of many reasons for liquidating a position in a mutual fund. For example, investors may acquire a particular mutual fund to meet a specific financial goal, but these objectives are not static. The birth of a child, a death in the family, a change in employment, divorce, or a major illness may alter the investor's financial situation and necessitate a change in the portfolio. A mutual fund that met prior financial objectives may no longer be suitable—in which case, the position is liquidated and the funds used for current needs.

Shares may be redeemed for tax purposes. If an investor has a capital loss from another source, the investor may liquidate a position in a mutual fund to offset the tax loss. Conversely, if an investor has a loss in the fund, the shares may be redeemed to offset capital gains from other sources. If the investor has no offsetting capital gains, the loss may be used to reduce ordinary income (subject to the limitations on capital gain losses offsetting ordinary income as discussed in Chapter 6). The proceeds may be used to invest in an alternative fund with the same or similar goals.

The three previous reasons for liquidating a position (financial goals have been met, financial goals have changed, and tax considerations) apply to the individual investor. There are also reasons for liquidating a position that pertain to the individual fund. A fund's specified objective may change, or the fund's portfolio may not appear to meet its objective. For example, an investor may question the appropriateness of a growth fund's purchasing shares in a regulated phone company such as BellSouth. In response, this investor may redeem the shares to place the proceeds in an alternative fund with a more appropriate portfolio.

The fund may change its investment strategies while maintaining its objective. For example, a growth fund may start using derivative securities in an attempt to increase its return. A large proportion of the fund's portfolio may be invested in foreign securities or in securities of firms in emerging economies. While these strategies may be consistent with the fund's objective, they may be inconsistent with the investor's willingness to bear risk, in which case the individual may redeem the shares.

A change in the fund's management may also be cause for liquidating a position. While the management of a corporation may be replaced, it may take years for the firm to be transformed—if it is changed at all. For example, it is doubtful that a new management at Hershey's or Heinz will change the basic products sold by these firms. However, a change in a fund's portfolio manager can have an immediate impact, since the portfolio may be easily altered. A fund with a poor performance record may improve while a fund with an excellent record may deteriorate after a change in its principal portfolio manager. For instance, the investor who supports the theory concerning a fund's consistency of performance would consider a change in a fund's portfolio manager to be exceedingly important and may redeem the shares in response to the change.

Past performance may also induce the investor to redeem shares. If the fund consistently underperforms its peer group, the investor may redeem the shares and invest the proceeds elsewhere. The rationale for such a move again supports the consistency argument: Poor-performing funds will continue to underperform. However, the investor needs to define underperformance and its duration. Does underperformance mean 0.5 percent, 2 percent, or a larger percentage? Is consistency two quarters, two years, or longer?

There are still other possible reasons for redeeming shares: (1) the fund's expenses are high relative to the expenses of comparable funds, (2) the fund becomes too large, or (3) the fund merges with or acquires another fund. Once again, the investor will have to make a judgment as to what constitutes "higher expenses" or "too large" or if the merger is potentially detrimental. If there were obvious answers to these questions, investing would be simple and mechanical. But investing is neither simple nor mechanical, and acquiring shares in mutual funds does not absolve the individual from having to make investment decisions. While the individual does not determine which specific assets to include in the portfolio, investing in mutual funds may require some active management. A portfolio of mutual funds may require less supervision than a portfolio of individual stocks and bonds, but it should not be considered a passive investment strategy.

Common Sense, Efficient Markets, and Investment Strategies

The number of assets available to the investor is so large that no individual could possibly know them all. In addition, the individual may follow a variety of investment styles or strategies. Just as no one could possibly know all the assets, no one could follow all the strategies. Investing requires making choices: the selection of strategies and the selection of specific assets. For example, the individual could choose a small stock ("small cap") strategy. The next decision would be to determine whether to buy the individual small cap stocks or to acquire the shares in a mutual fund with a small cap portfolio. Of course, a small cap style requires the investor to bear the risk associated with the strategy. It is irrelevant if the investor selects the individual stocks or a mutual fund; the risk associated with the small cap strategy continues to exist.

The investor could select stocks on the basis of insider trading on the premise that such purchases forecast higher stock returns. The individual would identify the companies whose shares are being purchased or sold or would invest in a mutual fund that emphasizes insider trading.[27] Of course, the investor who uses insider trading to make investment decisions has to bear the risk associated with that strategy.

A large number of strategies or techniques could be used to construct a portfolio. Each requires the investor to bear risk. As there is the risk associated with a specific asset, so must there be the risk associated with a specific strategy. Asset-specific risk is reduced and perhaps even erased through the construction of a diversified portfolio. The risk that remains is the nondiversifiable, systematic risk associated with movements in the market as a whole, changes in interest rates,

[27] Mutual funds do exist that follow an insider trading strategy. For example, the Bear Stearns Insiders Select Fund bases buy and sell decisions on insider trading and on firm repurchases since both insider trading and share repurchases may suggest the stock is undervalued.

FIGURE 24.3

Frequency of Occurence of Portfolio Returns Over One Year

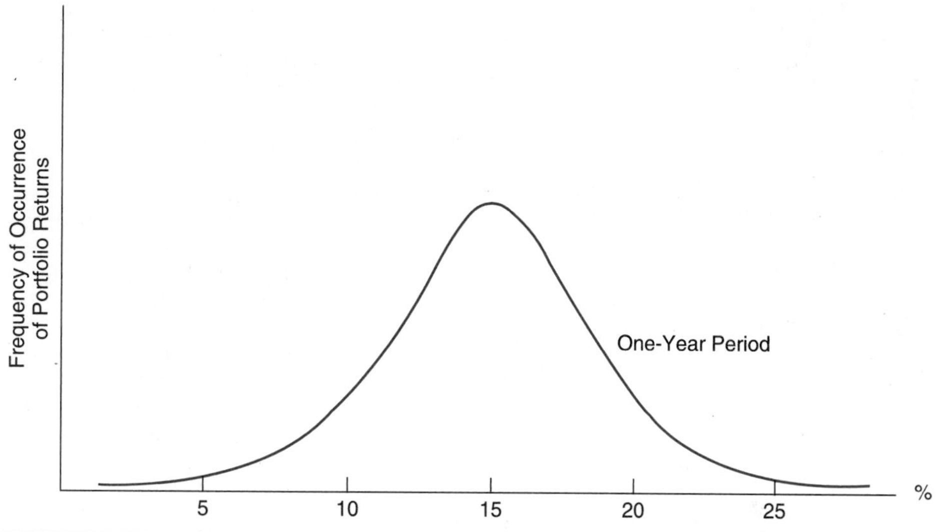

changes in exchange rates, and inflation. These sources of risk cannot be erased through the construction of a diversified portfolio.

This concept of diversification also applies to investment strategies. If the investor buys only large cap stocks, or only follows moving averages to select stocks, or only acquires stocks based on a specific anomaly and *is correct,* that investor should do well. But if the selection process is incorrect, the opposite may occur. The investor suffers the consequences of the one-strategy method of asset selection.

Unless the investor is willing to accept the risk associated with a particular strategy, constructing a portfolio based on various investment styles or methods of security selection reduces the risk associated with a particular style or analytical technique. As the investor adds more investment styles, the contribution of each to the portfolio declines. The individual, in effect, diversifies away the potential the strategy offers, and the portfolio becomes more like an index portfolio whose return should mirror the market.

Such mirroring of the market is what the efficient market hypothesis suggests will happen. Even believers in inefficient markets admit that it is difficult to beat the market.[28] Why, then, is there so much emphasis on those investors who do appear to beat the market?

Part of the answer rests with the distribution of returns. Consider Figure 24.3, the distribution previously used in Figure 7.3 to illustrate the returns on two stocks. In this case, the distribution illustrates portfolio returns for an investment time horizon, such as a year. The mean (15 percent) represents the return on the

[28]See, for instance, Robert A. Haugen, *The Inefficient Stock Market* (Upper Saddle River, NJ: Prentice Hall, 1999). Haugen emphatically believes that a value strategy produces superior results but admits that "it's hard to beat the market because there is a gale of unpredictable price-driven volatility between you and the 'candy'" (p. 145). One recent study even concluded that over an extended period of time (1965–1998) *no* investment style earned positive abnormal returns. See James L. Davis, "Mutual Fund Performance and Manager Style," *Financial Analysts Journal,* (January/February 2001): 19–27.

POINTS OF INTEREST

Investing and the Internet

Throughout this text, a variety of Web addresses have been given that will provide you with additional information and permit you to track individual securities or a portfolio. Some additional addresses that may be helpful include:

BusinessWeek Online Investing:
http://www.businessweek.com/investor
CyberInvest.com:
http://www.cyberinvest.com
The Financial Center:
http://www.tfc.com
Kiplinger.com:
http://www.kiplinger.com
Stock Smart:
http://www.stocksmart.com.

Inclusion of a Web address in this text does not imply that the source is the best, the most complete, or the easiest to use. You may find additional sites that are more helpful and easier to use. In addition, the material covered in a particular site or the cost of assessing the information may change. Many sites offer similar and, in some cases, identical data. You may need flexibility and patience to determine which sites best meet your needs.

Because so much information is available and because you can track your favorite stocks virtually continuously, it is easy to get wrapped up in the Internet. The development of the on-line brokers, whose commissions are trivial relative to the amount invested, may encourage you to frequently trade securities and lose sight of why you are investing. The Internet is an important source of financial information. It can increase your knowledge and help facilitate the management of your portfolio. But the Internet is not the end; it is a means to help you achieve your financial plan and investment objectives.

market. Individual returns are both above and below the mean. The figure indicates that some investors and portfolio managers did beat the market. There were, of course, investors and portfolio managers who underperformed the market.[29]

The figure clearly suggests that some investors *must outperform the market during a specified time period.* If a portfolio manager does outperform the market, that information is disseminated. Money flows into funds that do well, and a portfolio manager's compensation is often tied both to performance and to the amount of assets under management. Obviously, it is beneficial for portfolio managers and money management firms to capitalize on their success.

The answer is also related to the financial press. Portfolio managers who do exceptionally well often receive publicity and are touted in the popular press. Articles appear in *Money* or *Forbes.* The fund managers may be interviewed on talk shows, and the funds they manage receive "five stars." In a few cases, the portfolio managers develop superstar status. Underperforming portfolio managers, of course, do not receive this kind of publicity.

While Figure 24.3 presents a probability for one period, Figure 24.4 adds a probability distribution for a longer time horizon. During a short period, several investors and portfolio managers do exceptionally well as is illustrated by the flatter distribution, but over longer periods of time, their numbers diminish. The distribution becomes narrower and taller and indicates that more investors earn returns that mirror the markets in which they invested and fewer earn exceptional returns. The positive tail, however, remains. A few, exceptional investors earn higher returns. Perhaps their existence gives false hope to the vast investing public, but these investors and portfolio managers may have exceptional skills that are not transferable to the ordinary investor.[30]

[29]The important question, however, should be the return earned over an extended period of time. If an investor's goal is to finance retirement and the portfolio underperformed the market in a given year, that performance may be unimportant when the extended period is considered during which assets are accumulated for retirement.

[30]See Simon M. Keane, "The Efficient Market Hypothesis on Trial," *Financial Analysts Journal* (March–April 1986): 58–63.

FIGURE 24.4

Frequency of Occurrence of Portfolio Returns Over Five Years

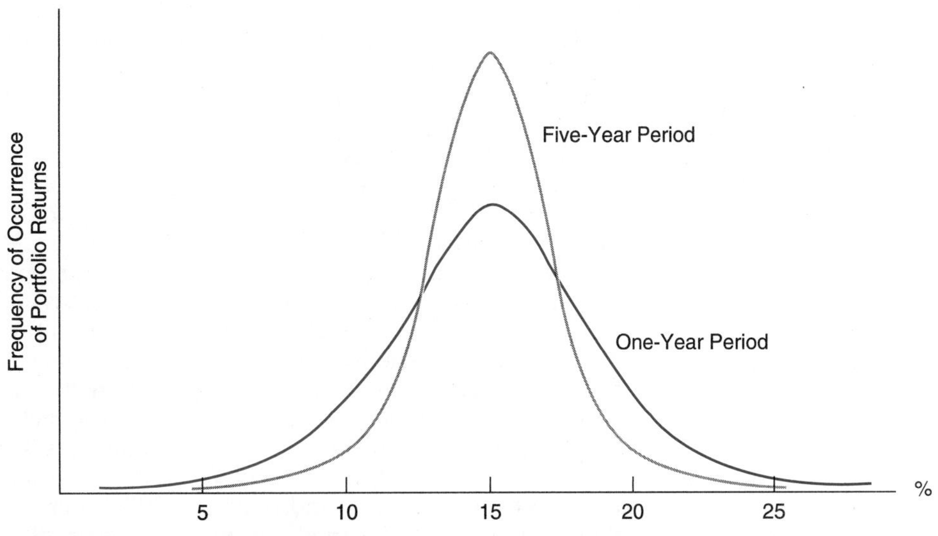

The typical investor, however, should take the concept of efficient financial markets seriously. Instead of trying to emulate the few who have done exceptionally well, most individuals should devote time to developing their financial objectives and constructing well-diversified portfolios that meet those objectives. Correspondingly, they should spend less time trying to beat the financial markets and not follow the day's investment fad or hot mutual fund.

A large proportion of the material covered in this text can aid in this process of financial planning and investment management even if the information cannot produce superior investment results. This text has described the features of alternative investments, explained factors that affect security prices, and illustrated many of the analytical tools used to select securities by portfolio managers. The text has also argued for the construction of diversified portfolios to reduce the unsystematic risk associated with a specific asset. It is through this construction of well-diversified portfolios and the patient waiting for compounding to work its magic that individuals achieve their financial goals.

Summary

Because investments are made in efficient financial markets, it is difficult for an investor to outperform the market consistently. However, this does not imply that securities or other assets should be acquired randomly. Instead, the investor should have a financial plan, in which financial goals are defined and priorities determined. Next, the individual analyzes his or her financial position. This may be achieved through the use of two financial statements: a personal balance sheet that enumerates what the individual owns and owes and his or her net worth, and a cash budget that enumerates the individual's cash receipts and disbursements. These financial statements may be created for the present or may be projected for some time in the future.

After specifying the financial goals and analyzing the financial environment, the investor should construct a diversified portfolio designed to meet the goals.

Diversification reduces (and perhaps eliminates) the unsystematic risk associated with each asset; the remaining systematic risk cannot be reduced through diversification. If the individual is willing to bear more nondiversifiable risk, he or she may achieve a higher return.

Not all assets are appropriate for every goal, so a diversified portfolio will contain various types of assets, each of which plays a role in the portfolio as a whole through its impact on risk and its capacity to meet specific financial needs.

The allocation of the various assets within the portfolio depends on such factors as the investor's age and resources. The asset allocation may also be changed in anticipation of movements in specific sectors of the financial markets. The actual allocation among various assets is also important for it affects the return the individual earns on the portfolio.

Each investor must determine how actively or passively he or she wants to manage the portfolio and whether to delegate or retain that management responsibility. The extent to which the investor believes that financial markets are efficient will affect these decisions. If the investor believes the market is less efficient, the stronger is the tendency to actively manage the funds.

Many investors delegate the decision as to which assets to acquire to professional portfolio managers, especially the managers of mutual funds. The investor, however, has to select the individual funds. Factors to consider include a fund's fees and expenses, taxes, and returns. While it may seem logical to acquire funds that have previously earned the highest returns, efficient financial markets suggest that funds that have done well in the past will not necessarily do well in the future. Historical returns do not predict future returns.

While investors may evaluate the performance of mutual funds by constructing the composite performance measures discussed in Chapter 8, there remains the problem of an appropriate benchmark for comparisons. There are many indexes of the market as a whole or of subsets of the financial markets that may be used for a benchmark. Even if the investor does not construct a risk-adjusted measure of performance, various indexes may be combined in a weighted average that may be used as a benchmark against which to judge the individual's portfolio.

Since many professional portfolio managers have been unable to outperform the market, some investors have turned to index and exchange-traded funds whose returns tend to track the market or a subset of the market. This strategy is reasonable in efficient markets, since index and exchange-traded funds have lower operating expenses and generate lower taxes because there is less portfolio turnover.

Questions

1) What types of assets are appropriate to meet financial emergencies? For income? Do these assets change over an individual's life?
2) What are the steps for constructing a financial plan? What is a pro forma balance sheet or cash budget? How do they differ, and what role do they play in the construction of financial plans?
3) Which of the following should be part of a balance sheet and which should be part of a cash budget?
   a) Mortgage owed
   b) Principal payment to be made
   c) Dividend payments
   d) Social Security payments
   e) IRA account
   f) Gifts to children
   g) Mutual fund shares
   h) Interest owed

i) Antiques
j) Credit card balances
k) 401(k) contribution

4) If the investor follows an active portfolio strategy, what should that individual do if a decrease in interest rates is anticipated?
5) Is the purpose of diversification to eradicate risk? Acquiring shares in an index fund has what impact on which sources of risk?
6) What is the role of compounding if the investor's goal is the accumulation of capital?
7) Which of the following argue for the selection of a particular mutual fund?
   a) Last year's return was the highest among comparable funds.
   b) The fund frequently turns over its portfolio.
   c) The fund specializes in companies located in emerging markets.
   d) The fund has a load charge but no 12b-1 fees.
   e) The fund is newly created.
8) How can an investor determine if a mutual fund has hidden capital gains or losses? If the fund's tax efficiency is high, does that suggest the investor's return is increased?
9) Why may an index fund increase the investor's ability to manage his or her federal income taxes?
10) Which benchmarks are more appropriate for a government bond portfolio, a portfolio of small cap stocks, and a portfolio of real estate investment trusts?
11) If an investor believes that financial markets are not efficient but does not want to take the time to select individual assets, what types of funds should appeal to that investor?
12) Using an Internet source such as those listed in the Points of Interest, "The Internet and Information Concerning Mutual Funds," obtain and compare the following information:
   a) one-, five-, and ten-year returns
   b) 12b-1 fee (if any)
   c) the percentage of the portfolio in stock
   d) the expense ratio
   e) the portfolio turnover

   for the following funds:
   1) Dreyfus New Leaders ((DNLDX)
   2) Heartland Value (HRTVX)
   3) Janus Venture (JAVTX)
   4) Scudder Development (SCDVX)

   (Ticker symbols are in parentheses to facilitate the search.)

Problems

1) You are given the following information concerning a 52-year-old male:

Car and consumer loans	$ 14,000
Cash and savings accounts	3,000
Cash value of life insurance	10,000
Education loans	26,000
Home (estimated value)	175,000
Home mortgage	68,000
Home equity loan	14,000
Pension plan	95,000
Retirement account (IRA)	15,000
Securities (corporate stock)	41,000

a) From this information, construct the individual's current balance sheet.
b) Construct pro forma balance sheets for this individual at ages 62 and 70. To make these projections, assume (1) that the rate of inflation will be 5 percent annually and the value of the house will appreciate at that rate, (2) that no additional contributions will be made to the IRA and the amount of cash and savings will remain $3,000, (3) the IRA and the cash value of the life insurance will grow annually at 6 percent, (4) the annual return on the pension plan and the stock will average 10 percent, (5) $5,000 additional contributions to the pension plan and $3,000 additional stock investments will be made each year, and (6) all liabilities will be retired by age 60. After age 62, contributions to the pension plan will cease.
c) What is the value of the individual's financial assets at ages 62 and 70? Suppose at the age of 70, this individual consolidates all the financial assets into a very safe investment that pays a modest 6 percent annually. How much can the individual spend each year to age 90?

2) The following gives the values of the funds in your portfolio:

S&P 500 Fund	$200,000
Money Fund	35,000
High-Yield Fund	75,000
Small-Cap Fund	120,000
Euro Fund	70,000

During the time period, you earned 12 percent on your investments. During the same time period, the returns of various market indexes were as follows:

S&P 500 index	14%
S&P MidCap index	12
Russell 2000	8
Lehman Bond Index	6
CS First Boston High Yield	12
NAREIT Index	10
EAFE Index	15
IFCI Composite Index	18
Treasury bills	4

How well did your portfolio perform relative to the market? Is your comparison adjusted for risk? How could you bring risk into your analysis?

THE FINANCIAL ADVISOR'S INVESTMENT CASE
Goals and Portfolio Selection

Cathy Lin is a very successful self-employed freelance writer of romantic novels. She has a reputation for writing rapidly and is able to complete at least four books a year, which net after expenses $25,000 to $50,000 per book per year. With this much income, Lin is concerned with both sheltering income from taxes and planning for retirement. Currently she is 40 years old, is divorced, and has a child who is entering high school. Lin anticipates sending the child to a quality college to pursue a degree in computer sciences.

While Lin is intelligent and well informed, she knows very little about finance and investments other than general background material she has used in her novels. Since she does not plan to write prolifically into the indefinite future, she has decided to obtain your help in financial planning.

At your first meeting, you suggested that Lin establish a tax-sheltered retirement plan and consider making a gift to her child, perhaps in the form of future royalties from a book in progress. Both of these ideas intrigued Lin, who thought that funds were saved, invested to accumulate over time, and then transferred to heirs after death. While Lin wanted to pursue both ideas, she thought approaching one at a time made more sense and decided to work on the retirement plan first. She asked you for several alternative courses of action, and you offered the following possibilities.

1) An IRA with a bank with the funds deposited in a variable-rate account.
2) A self-directed Keogh account with a major brokerage firm.
3) A Keogh account with a major mutual fund.
4) An account with a brokerage firm to accumulate common stocks with substantial growth potential but little current income.

Lin could not immediately grasp the implications of these alternatives and asked you to clarify several points:

1) What assets would be owned under each alternative?
2) What are the current and future tax obligations associated with each choice?
3) What amount of control would she have over the assets in the accounts?
4) How much personal supervision would be required?

How would you reply to each question? Which course(s) of action would you suggest that she pursue?

Finally, how would each of the following alter your advice?

1) Lin has a record of poor health.
2) Lin would like to write less and perhaps teach creative writing at a local college.
3) Lin has expensive tastes and finds saving to be difficult.

INVESTMENT PROJECT

By now the conclusion of the semester is approaching. Calculate the holding returns for the S&P 500 and the individual stocks. Dividend payments should be included but since the time period of a semester is short, the exclusion of dividend payments may not affect the results. Obviously, adjustments should be made for any stock splits or stock dividends.

Next, compute the holding period returns assuming that you purchased one share of each stock and assuming that you purchased an equal dollar amount of each stock. If you need help remembering the holding period return, consult the material in Chapter 10. Compare the holding period returns with the holding period return of the S&P 500. If the market rose during the semester, you should have earned a positive return. Conversely, if the market declined, you probably earned a negative return.

Comparing the holding period returns with the S&P 500 return may be misleading because the individual stock returns have not been adjusted for risk. A higher return than the market does not necessarily mean that you outperformed the market if you had a riskier portfolio. To adjust for risk, use the beta coefficients from Chapter 7. In that chapter you were asked to calculate a beta for two portfolios, one assuming the purchase of an equal number of shares of each stock and the other assuming an equal amount invested in each stock.

To give some indication of the risk adjustment, divide your portfolio holding period returns by the appropriate betas. (If the beta is less than 1.0, this will have the effect of raising your risk-adjusted return. The converse is true if the beta is more than 1.0.) Compare this adjusted return with the holding period return for the S&P 500. Did the portfolio outperform the market on a risk-adjusted basis? If you beat the index, congratulations. Achieve similar results for several years, and you will appear in *Business Week, Fortune,* or *Forbes.* If you didn't outperform the market, don't fret. You'll probably do better when you make your next investments because it is difficult to consistently underperform as well as outperform the market on a risk-adjusted basis.

Mathematical Tables

- The Future Value of $1
- The Present Value of $1
- The Future Value of an Annuity of $1
- The Present Value of an Annuity of $1

The Future Value of $1

Period	1%	2%	3%	4%	5%	6%	7%
1	1.010	1.020	1.030	1.040	1.050	1.060	1.070
2	1.020	1.040	1.061	1.082	1.102	1.124	1.145
3	1.030	1.061	1.093	1.125	1.158	1.191	1.225
4	1.041	1.082	1.126	1.170	1.216	1.262	1.311
5	1.051	1.104	1.159	1.217	1.276	1.338	1.403
6	1.062	1.126	1.194	1.265	1.340	1.419	1.501
7	1.072	1.149	1.230	1.316	1.407	1.504	1.606
8	1.083	1.172	1.267	1.369	1.477	1.594	1.718
9	1.094	1.195	1.305	1.423	1.551	1.689	1.838
10	1.105	1.219	1.344	1.480	1.629	1.791	1.967
11	1.116	1.243	1.384	1.539	1.710	1.898	2.105
12	1.127	1.268	1.426	1.601	1.7496	2.012	2.252
13	1.138	1.294	1.469	1.665	1.886	2.133	2.410
14	1.149	1.319	1.513	1.732	1.980	2.261	2.579
15	1.161	1.346	1.558	1.801	2.079	2.397	2.759
16	1.173	1.373	1.605	1.873	2.183	2.540	2.952
17	1.184	1.400	1.653	1.948	2.292	2.693	3.159
18	1.196	1.428	1.702	2.026	2.407	2.854	3.380
19	1.208	1.457	1.754	2.107	2.527	3.026	3.617
20	1.220	1.486	1.806	2.191	2.653	3.207	3.870
25	1.282	1.641	2.094	2.666	3.386	4.292	5.427
30	1.348	1.811	2.427	3.243	4.322	5.743	7.612

Period	8%	9%	10%	12%	14%	15%	16%
1	1.080	1.090	1.100	1.120	1.140	1.150	1.160
2	1.166	1.188	1.210	1.254	1.300	1.322	1.346
3	1.260	1.295	1.331	1.405	1.482	1.521	1.561
4	1.360	1.412	1.464	1.574	1.689	1.749	1.811
5	1.469	1.539	1.611	1.762	1.925	2.011	2.100
6	1.587	1.677	1.772	1.974	2.195	2.313	2.436
7	1.714	1.828	1.949	2.211	2.502	2.660	2.826
8	1.851	1.993	2.144	2.476	2.853	3.059	3.278
9	1.999	2.172	2.358	2.773	3.252	3.518	3.803
10	2.159	2.367	2.594	3.106	3.707	4.046	4.411
11	2.332	2.580	2.853	3.479	4.226	4.652	5.117
12	2.518	2.813	3.138	3.896	4.818	5.350	5.936
13	2.720	3.066	3.452	4.363	5.492	6.153	6.886
14	2.937	3.342	3.797	4.887	6.261	7.076	7.988
15	3.172	3.642	4.177	5.474	7.138	8.137	9.266
16	3.426	3.970	4.595	6.130	8.137	9.358	10.748
17	3.700	4.328	5.054	6.866	9.276	10.761	12.468
18	3.996	4.717	5.560	7.690	10.575	12.375	14.463
19	4.316	5.142	6.116	8.613	12.056	14.232	16.777
20	4.661	5.604	6.728	9.646	13.743	16.367	19.461
25	6.848	8.623	10.835	17.000	26.462	32.919	40.874
30	10.063	13.268	17.449	29.960	50.950	66.212	85.850

$P_0(1 + i)^n = P_n$ Interest factor $= (1 + i)^n$

The Present Value of $1

Period	1%	2%	3%	4%	5%	6%	7%	8%	9%	10%	12%	14%	15%
1	0.990	0.980	0.971	0.962	0.952	0.943	0.935	0.926	0.917	0.909	0.893	0.877	0.870
2	0.980	0.961	0.943	0.925	0.907	0.890	0.873	0.857	0.842	0.826	0.797	0.769	0.756
3	0.971	0.942	0.915	0.889	0.864	0.840	0.816	0.794	0.772	0.751	0.712	0.675	0.658
4	0.961	0.924	0.889	0.855	0.823	0.792	0.763	0.735	0.708	0.683	0.636	0.592	0.572
5	0.951	0.906	0.863	0.822	0.784	0.747	0.713	0.681	0.650	0.621	0.567	0.519	0.497
6	0.942	0.888	0.838	0.790	0.746	0.705	0.666	0.630	0.596	0.564	0.507	0.456	0.432
7	0.933	0.871	0.813	0.760	0.711	0.665	0.623	0.583	0.547	0.513	0.452	0.400	0.376
8	0.923	0.853	0.789	0.731	0.677	0.627	0.582	0.540	0.502	0.467	0.404	0.351	0.327
9	0.914	0.837	0.766	0.703	0.645	0.592	0.544	0.500	0.460	0.424	0.361	0.308	0.284
10	0.905	0.820	0.744	0.676	0.614	0.558	0.508	0.463	0.422	0.386	0.322	0.270	0.247
11	0.896	0.804	0.722	0.650	0.585	0.527	0.475	0.429	0.388	0.350	0.287	0.237	0.215
12	0.887	0.788	0.701	0.625	0.557	0.497	0.444	0.397	0.356	0.319	0.257	0.208	0.187
13	0.879	0.773	0.681	0.601	0.530	0.469	0.415	0.368	0.326	0.290	0.229	0.182	0.163
14	0.870	0.758	0.661	0.577	0.505	0.442	0.388	0.340	0.299	0.263	0.205	0.160	0.141
15	0.861	0.743	0.642	0.555	0.481	0.417	0.362	0.315	0.275	0.239	0.183	0.140	0.123
16	0.853	0.728	0.623	0.534	0.458	0.394	0.339	0.292	0.252	0.218	0.163	0.123	0.107
17	0.844	0.714	0.605	0.513	0.436	0.371	0.317	0.270	0.231	0.198	0.146	0.108	0.093
18	0.836	0.700	0.587	0.494	0.416	0.350	0.296	0.250	0.212	0.180	0.130	0.095	0.081
19	0.828	0.686	0.570	0.475	0.396	0.331	0.276	0.232	0.194	0.164	0.116	0.083	0.070
20	0.820	0.673	0.554	0.456	0.377	0.312	0.258	0.215	0.178	0.149	0.104	0.073	0.061
25	0.780	0.610	0.478	0.375	0.295	0.233	0.184	0.146	0.116	0.092	0.059	0.038	0.030
30	0.742	0.552	0.412	0.308	0.231	0.174	0.131	0.099	0.075	0.057	0.033	0.020	0.015

Period	16%	18%	20%	24%	28%	32%	36%	40%	50%	60%	70%	80%	90%
1	0.862	0.847	0.833	0.806	0.781	0.758	0.735	0.714	0.667	0.625	0.588	0.556	0.526
2	0.743	0.718	0.694	0.650	0.610	0.574	0.541	0.510	0.444	0.391	0.346	0.309	0.277
3	0.641	0.609	0.579	0.524	0.477	0.435	0.398	0.364	0.296	0.244	0.204	0.171	0.146
4	0.552	0.516	0.482	0.423	0.373	0.329	0.292	0.260	0.198	0.153	0.120	0.095	0.077
5	0.476	0.437	0.402	0.341	0.291	0.250	0.215	0.186	0.132	0.095	0.070	0.053	0.040
6	0.410	0.370	0.335	0.275	0.227	0.189	0.158	0.133	0.088	0.060	0.041	0.029	0.021
7	0.354	0.314	0.279	0.222	0.178	0.143	0.116	0.095	0.059	0.037	0.024	0.016	0.011
8	0.305	0.266	0.233	0.179	0.139	0.108	0.085	0.068	0.039	0.023	0.014	0.009	0.006
9	0.263	0.226	0.194	0.144	0.108	0.082	0.063	0.048	0.026	0.015	0.008	0.005	0.003
10	0.227	0.191	0.162	0.116	0.085	0.062	0.046	0.035	0.017	0.009	0.005	0.003	0.002
11	0.195	0.162	0.135	0.094	0.066	0.047	0.034	0.025	0.012	0.006	0.003	0.002	0.001
12	0.168	0.137	0.112	0.076	0.052	0.036	0.025	0.018	0.008	0.004	0.002	0.001	0.001
13	0.145	0.116	0.093	0.061	0.040	0.027	0.018	0.013	0.005	0.002	0.001	0.001	0.000
14	0.125	0.099	0.078	0.049	0.032	0.021	0.014	0.009	0.003	0.001	0.001	0.000	0.000
15	0.108	0.084	0.065	0.040	0.025	0.016	0.010	0.006	0.002	0.001	0.000	0.000	0.000
16	0.093	0.071	0.054	0.032	0.019	0.012	0.007	0.005	0.002	0.001	0.000	0.000	
17	0.080	0.060	0.045	0.026	0.015	0.009	0.005	0.003	0.001	0.000	0.000		
18	0.069	0.051	0.038	0.021	0.012	0.007	0.004	0.002	0.001	0.000	0.000		
19	0.060	0.043	0.031	0.017	0.009	0.005	0.003	0.002	0.000	0.000			
20	0.051	0.037	0.026	0.014	0.007	0.004	0.002	0.001	0.000	0.000			
25	0.024	0.016	0.010	0.005	0.002	0.001	0.000	0.000					
30	0.012	0.007	0.004	0.002	0.001	0.000	0.000						

$P_0 = \frac{P_n}{(1 + i)^n}$ Interest factor $= \frac{1}{(1 + i)^n}$

The Future Value of an Annuity of $1

Period	1%	2%	3%	4%	5%	6%
1	1.000	1.000	1.000	1.000	1.000	1.000
2	2.010	2.020	2.030	2.040	2.050	2.060
3	3.030	3.060	3.091	3.122	3.152	3.184
4	4.060	4.122	4.184	4.246	4.310	4.375
5	5.101	5.204	5.309	5.416	5.526	5.637
6	6.152	6.308	6.468	6.633	6.802	6.975
7	7.214	7.434	7.662	7.898	8.142	8.394
8	8.286	8.583	8.892	9.214	9.549	9.897
9	9.369	9.755	10.159	10.583	11.027	11.491
10	10.462	10.950	11.464	12.006	12.578	13.181
11	11.567	12.169	12.808	13.486	14.207	14.972
12	12.683	13.412	14.192	15.026	15.917	16.870
13	13.809	14.680	15.618	16.627	17.713	18.882
14	14.947	15.974	17.086	18.292	19.599	21.051
15	16.097	17.293	18.599	20.024	21.579	23.276
16	17.258	18.639	20.157	21.825	23.657	25.673
17	18.430	20.012	21.762	23.698	25.840	28.213
18	19.615	21.412	23.414	25.645	28.132	30.906
19	20.811	22.841	25.117	27.671	30.539	33.760
20	22.109	24.297	26.870	29.778	33.066	36.786
25	28.243	32.030	36.459	41.646	47.727	54.865
30	34.785	40.568	47.575	56.085	66.439	79.058

Period	7%	8%	9%	10%	12%	14%
1	1.000	1.000	1.000	1.000	1.000	1.000
2	2.070	2.080	2.090	2.100	2.120	2.140
3	3.215	3.246	3.278	3.310	3.374	3.440
4	4.440	4.508	4.573	4.641	4.770	4.921
5	5.751	5.867	5.985	6.105	6.353	6.610
6	7.153	7.336	7.523	7.716	8.115	8.536
7	8.654	8.923	9.200	9.487	10.089	10.730
8	10.260	10.637	11.028	11.436	12.300	13.233
9	11.978	12.488	13.021	13.579	14.776	16.085
10	13.816	14.487	15.193	15.937	17.549	19.337
11	15.784	16.645	17.560	18.531	20.655	23.044
12	17.888	18.977	20.141	21.384	24.138	27.271
13	20.141	21.495	22.953	24.523	28.029	32.089
14	22.550	24.215	26.019	27.975	32.393	37.581
15	25.129	27.152	29.361	31.772	37.280	43.842
16	27.888	30.324	33.003	35.950	42.753	50.980
17	30.840	33.750	36.974	40.545	48.884	59.118
18	33.999	37.450	41.301	45.599	55.750	68.394
19	37.379	41.446	46.018	51.159	63.440	78.969
20	40.995	45.762	51.160	57.275	72.052	91.025
25	63.249	73.106	84.701	98.347	133.334	181.871
30	94.461	113.283	136.308	164.494	241.333	356.787

$CS = I(1 + i)^0 + I(1 + i)^1 + \cdots + I(1 + i)^{n-1}$ Interest factor $= \dfrac{(1 + i)^n - 1}{i}$

The Present Value of an Annuity of $1

Period	1%	2%	3%	4%	5%	6%	7%	8%	9%	10%
1	0.990	0.980	0.971	0.962	0.952	0.943	0.935	0.926	0.917	0.909
2	1.970	1.942	1.913	1.886	1.859	1.833	1.808	1.783	1.759	1.736
3	2.941	2.884	2.829	2.775	2.723	2.673	2.624	2.577	2.531	2.487
4	3.902	3.808	3.717	3.630	3.546	3.465	3.387	3.312	3.240	3.170
5	4.853	4.713	4.580	4.452	4.329	4.212	4.100	3.993	3.890	3.791
6	5.795	5.601	5.417	5.242	5.076	4.917	4.766	4.623	4.486	4.355
7	6.728	6.472	6.230	6.002	5.786	5.582	5.389	5.206	5.033	4.868
8	7.652	7.325	7.020	6.733	6.463	6.210	5.971	5.747	5.535	5.335
9	8.566	8.162	7.786	7.435	7.108	6.802	6.515	6.247	5.985	5.759
10	9.471	8.983	8.530	8.111	7.722	7.360	7.024	6.710	6.418	6.145
11	10.368	9.787	9.253	8.760	8.306	7.887	7.499	7.139	6.805	6.495
12	11.255	10.575	9.954	9.385	8.863	8.384	7.943	7.536	7.161	6.814
13	12.134	11.348	10.635	9.986	9.394	8.853	8.358	7.904	7.487	7.103
14	13.004	12.106	11.296	10.563	9.899	9.295	8.745	8.244	7.786	7.367
15	13.865	12.849	11.938	11.118	10.380	9.712	9.108	8.559	8.060	7.606
16	14.718	13.578	12.561	11.652	10.838	10.106	9.447	8.851	8.312	7.824
17	15.562	14.292	13.166	12.166	11.274	10.477	9.763	9.122	8.544	8.022
18	16.398	14.992	13.754	12.659	11.690	10.828	10.059	9.372	8.756	8.201
19	17.226	15.678	14.324	13.134	12.085	11.158	10.336	9.604	8.950	8.365
20	18.046	16.351	14.877	13.590	12.462	11.470	10.594	9.818	9.128	8.514
25	22.023	19.523	17.413	15.622	14.094	12.783	11.654	10.675	9.823	9.077
30	25.808	22.397	19.600	17.292	15.373	13.765	12.409	11.258	10.274	9.427

Period	12%	14%	16%	18%	20%	24%	28%	32%	36%
1	0.893	0.877	0.862	0.847	0.833	0.806	0.781	0.758	0.735
2	1.690	1.647	1.605	1.566	1.528	1.457	1.392	1.332	1.276
3	2.402	2.322	2.246	2.174	2.106	1.981	1.868	1.766	1.674
4	3.037	2.914	2.798	2.690	2.589	2.404	2.241	2.096	1.966
5	3.605	3.433	3.274	3.127	2.991	2.745	2.532	2.345	2.181
6	4.111	3.889	3.685	3.498	3.326	3.020	2.759	2.534	2.339
7	4.564	4.288	4.039	3.812	3.605	3.242	2.937	2.678	2.455
8	4.968	4.639	4.344	4.078	3.837	3.421	3.076	2.786	2.540
9	5.328	4.946	4.607	4.303	4.031	3.566	3.184	2.868	2.603
10	5.650	5.216	4.833	4.494	4.193	3.682	3.269	2.930	2.650
11	5.988	5.453	5.029	4.656	4.327	3.776	3.335	2.978	2.683
12	6.194	5.660	5.197	4.793	4.439	3.851	3.387	3.013	2.708
13	6.424	5.842	5.342	4.910	4.533	3.912	3.427	3.040	2.727
14	6.628	6.002	5.468	5.008	4.611	3.962	3.459	3.061	2.740
15	6.811	6.142	5.575	5.092	4.675	4.001	3.483	3.076	2.750
16	6.974	6.265	5.669	5.162	4.730	4.033	3.503	3.088	2.758
17	7.120	6.373	5.749	5.222	4.775	4.059	3.518	3.097	2.763
18	7.250	6.467	5.818	5.273	4.812	4.080	3.529	3.104	2.767
19	7.366	6.550	5.877	5.316	4.844	4.097	3.539	3.109	2.770
20	7.469	6.623	5.929	5.353	4.870	4.110	3.546	3.113	2.772
25	7.843	6.873	6.097	5.467	4.948	4.147	3.564	3.122	2.776
30	8.055	7.003	6.177	5.517	4.979	4.160	3.569	3.124	2.778

$PV = \sum_{t=1}^{n} \frac{1}{(1+i)^t}$ Interest factor $= \frac{1 - \frac{1}{(1+i)^n}}{i}$

Answers to Selected Problems

B

Chapter 3

1) a) 25% margin: 300%
   c) 75% margin: 100%
2) b) 50% margin: −50%
3) At price of stock = $40 and margin requirement of 60%:
   Cash account: −21.2%
   Margin account: −42%
   At price of the stock = $70 and margin requirement of 40%:
   Cash account: 31.2%
   Margin account: 63%
4) At price of the stock = $36: 27.8%

Chapter 5

Your answers may vary from the following depending on rounding off, especially when using interest tables. The use of a financial calculator or the accompanying software may lead to different answers than derived when using the interest tables. If the answer obtained from a calculator is 6.1% but only approximately 6% from the interest table, both are "correct."

1) a) $1,191 total interest
   b) $40 annually; $800 total
2) Approximately 6% (5.8%)
3) a) $85,913
   b) $147,521; $61,608 in additional funds
4) a) Ordinary annuity: $6,391
      Annuity due: $6,903
   b) Ordinary annuity: $7,572
      Annuity due: $7,950
5) Value: $98,181, which is less than $120,000; don't buy.
6) At 4%: $76,685
   At 8%; $150,000 is not sufficient.
7) $19,714
8) a) $87,729
   b) $38,276
   c) $12,619
9) At 6%, select the $900.
   At 14%, select the $150 each year.
   (The higher rate stresses receiving the money faster so it may be invested at the higher rate.)
10) a) Annual compounding: $112
       Semiannual compounding: $112.40
       Monthly compounding: $112.70
    b) Annual compounding: $89.30
       Semiannual compounding: $89.00
       Monthly compounding: $88.70
11) Tom: $102,320
    Joan: $111,529

12) 12 years (12.18)
13) The present value of the annuity payments is $62,868. If the annuity costs $75,000, it is overpriced.
14) At 9%, the present value of the cash flows is $849, which is more than $800. The yield has to be higher than 9% (10.125%) to bring down the present value of the cash flows to $800.
15) $73,212
16) $60,795
17) Budget in year 10: $4,805,550
15: $8,607,060
20: $15,400,665
18) Alternative B's present value: $1,034
19) Monthly payment for the 9% mortgage: $10,181
20) Between 6 and 7 years (6.9 years)
21) He can withdraw $16,021 annually. To withdraw the desired amount, he must earn 11%.
22) Annual payment starting at the end of the year: $5,393
Annual payment starting at the beginning of the year: $5,041
23) a) $30,650
b) $16,250
24) Invest $3,167 annually
25) The loan (payment = $5,678)

Supplemental Problems

1) $1,795
2) Interest ordinary annuity: $1,828
Interest annuity due: $2,503
3) Present value ordinary annuity: $65,848
Present value annuity due: $71,392
4) 18.638%
5) Payment at the end of the year: $8,660
Payment at the beginning of the year: $8,078

Chapter 6

1) a) Capital gains: $4,700
Tax: $1,316
b) Tax savings in current year: $1,188
2) b) Net long-term loss after net short-term capital gain: $1,000
Tax savings: $310
g) Current year tax savings: $930
3) a) $300
d) Loss disallowed
4) a) $500 saved
b) $0
5) b) $8,050
6) a) $10,000 grows to $23,670; the total in all accounts: $172,406 ($172,428 using a financial calculator).
b) over 25 years (28.3 years)
c) $19,690
7) Bob: $60,247
Mary: $77,037
Difference: $16,790

8) Bob contributes $1,500 for ten years and accumulates $23,906. This amount grows for ten years into $62,012. The final sum is drawn over fifteen years at the rate of $8,153 annually. Mike contributes a larger amount ($2,000) for ten years and accumulates $31,874; however, he must start to withdraw the funds after five years, so the final amount grows to $51,349. This final sum is drawn down over twenty years at the rate of $6,031 annually. Even though Mike contributed more than Bob, the fact that he must start withdrawing the funds earlier means that the amount received each year is less. This problem points out the desirability of leaving funds in a tax-deferred account as long as possible in order to take advantage of the growth in tax-deferred interest.
9) The answer depends on the current dividend exclusion. If the exclusion is 70%, the taxes owed are
   $2.35 (10,000)(.3)(.34) = $2,397.

Chapter 7

1) 14% in all three cases
2) a) 10.3%
3) a) 12.4%
   standard deviation = 3.12
4) a) 50% A/50% B: return = 16%; standard deviation = 3.14
   c) 25% A/75% C: return = 18%; standard deviation = 4.56
6) Return = 12% when beta = 1.5
8) a) coefficient of variation stock B: 0.132
9) a) Beta stock x: 0.352
   c) Stock y: $R^2 = 0.82$

Chapter 8

1) $7.68
2) 6.8%
3) percentage (holding period) return: 40.6%
5) a) The risk-adjusted ranking: E, D, C, A, B
   b) The risk-adjusted ranking: C, D, B, E, A

Chapter 9

1) $21
2) $21.40, which is less than $25. (Don't buy!)
3) a) $28.53
4) Required return: 12%
5) b) Stock A: $7.78
   d) $12.94
6) Required return for B: 12.6%
8) Present value of dividend payments: $7.66
   Value of stock: $68.91

Chapter 10

1) Holding period return: 209%
   Annualized return: 11.96%
2) a) Holding period return: 61%
   b) Annualized return: 10%

3) a) 12% (12.38%)
   c) 9% (8.88%)
4) Dollar-weighted return: 19%
   Time-weighted return: 23.1%
5) At 12%, the present value = $35.56, which is less than $40, so the return is less than 12%. (Return = 9.16%.)
6) Between 9 and 10% (9.4%)
7) b) $85.74
   c) −1.7%
8) 10.27%
9) Change in price of Stock A: $50
10) Average price per share: $34.55
11) a) Simple average: $15
    Value-weighted average: $15.60
    Geometric average: $14.50

Chapter 11

1) a) Cash and retained earnings decline by $1,000,000 to $19,000,000 and $97,500,000.
   b) 100,000 shares issued
   Common stock: 1,100,000 shares, $10 par; $11,000,000
   Paid-in capital (new entry): $300,000
   Retained earnings: $97,200,000
2) a) Paid-in capital: $1,800,000
   New price of the stock: $20
   b) Paid-in capital: $2,280,000
   New price of the stock: $54.55
3) 162.9 shares
4) a) Average: 7.2%
   b) Growth rate: 7.18%
   c) Regression: 7.18%

Chapter 13

1) Current ratio: 2:1
   Quick ratio: 0.98:1
   Inventory turnover: 1.5 (using cost of goods sold)
   Average collection period: 108 days
   Operating profit margin: 25%
   Net profit margin: 16.8%
   Return on assets: 9.8%
   Return on equity: 14.5%
   Debt/Net worth: 48.3%
   Debt/Total assets: 32.6%
   Times-interest-earned: 5.0
2) Quick ratio 2000: 0.8
   Times-interest-earned 1998: 4.5
3) Debt ratio: 70%
4) Reduction in inventory: $75,000
5) Issue B: 1.7*x*
6) $4,754,556

Chapter 16

1) a) $1,000
   b) $875
   c) Current yield in b.: 9.1%
2) a) $1,179 (semiannual compounding: $1,181)
   b) $1,054 (semiannual compounding: $1,055)
   c) $1,142 (semiannual compounding: $1,142)
4) Current yield: 9.6%
   Yield to maturity: 10% (semiannual compounding: 10.04%)
5) 14%
6) a) 5% coupon bond: $575 (semiannual compounding: $571)
7) a) $60
   b) $75.48
9) a) Bond A: $894 (semiannual compounding: $892)
   Bond B: $1,000
11) $636
13) a) $876
    b) $839
15) Bond B: 6.6 years
17) b) Bond A: 4.4 years
    Bond E: 5.0 years
    c) C, A, E, D, B
20) Times-dividend-earned: 2.8
21) EPS with debt financing: $2.80
    EPS with preferred stock financing: $2.50

Chapter 17

1) Discount yield: 6.5%; annualized compound yield: 6.83%
2) Taxable yield: 8.75%
4) Bond B: $676, $508, and $386
6) 3.12% discount yield
   3.19% annualized yield

Chapter 18

1) a) 4.8%
   b) $864
   c) $38.52
   d) $176
   e) $817
   f) $223
   g) At least $1,728
   h) At least $817
   i) Virtually nil
2) a) $552
   b) 40 shares
   c) $1,200
   d) $1,200 (value as stock)
   g) $1,040
3) a) $17

4) a) Bond A: $1,070
b) Bond B: $946
d) $4(6.710) = $26.84
5) c) A: $75
d) A: 2.4 years
e) Stock: 9% annual return
Bond: 10.7% annual return
6) c) $39
f) $1,240
i) Bond: 14%
k) $1,000
7) b) $15
d) 8.4%

Chapter 19

1) a) Intrinsic value: $1; time premium: $3
b)

Price of the stock	Value of the call
$20	$0
30	5
40	15

c) 275%
d) Cash outflow: $22

Price of the stock	Profit
$15	($7)
25	3
26	3
40	3

e) $4, $3, and ($11)
2) XYZ calls: $4 and nil
XYZ puts: nil and $1
If the price of the stock is $31, the losses to the buyers of the calls are ($6) and ($2.50).
If the price of the stock is $31, the profits to the writers of the puts are $1.25 and $0.25.
3) a) $1
b) $0
c) $4
d) $2
e) rises
f) $46
g) $51
h) $8
i) ($2)
j) ($7)
k) $4
4) a) ($2), ($2), and $3
b) $2, $2, and ($3)
5) a) $11
b) $4
c) $26 (73.3% increase in the LEAP)
e) $0 (100% decrease in the LEAP)
6) c) Profit at the stock price of $30: $9
Loss at the stock price of $45: ($6)

d) Profit at the stock price of $35: $7
Loss at the stock price of $50: ($3)
e) Loss at the stock price of $35: ($11)
Profit at the stock price of $50: $4

7) b) Net cash outflow: $38
d) ($3)

8) If price of the stock is $60, make $2,000 on the position in the stock versus $1,000 in the call and the Treasury bill. If the price of the stock is $40, lose $2,000 on the position in the stock versus no loss on the position in the call and the Treasury bill.

Chapter 20

1) $30 – $25/(1 + .1) = $7.27
2) a) If the price of the stock is $50, value of the call: $5.45
b) If the expiration is six months, value of the call: $5.45
c) If the interest rate is 5%, value of the call: $4.82
d) If the standard deviation is 40% (.4), value of the call: $6.79
3) a) Profit if
price of the stock is $110: $10
price of the stock is $105: $10
price of the stock is $90: $10
4) $3
6) Arbitrage profit: $200
7) Profit when price of the stock is $20: $2
Profit when price of the stock is $35: $7
9) Cash outflow: $2
Profit when price of the stock is $20: ($2)
Profit when price of the stock is $40: $3
11) a) Make $5 on the call but lose $3.50 on the put; net profit: $1.50
12) b) Profit when price of the stock is $41: 0
Profit (loss) when price of the stock is $45: ($4)

Chapter 21

1) a) $3,500
b) $69,000
c) ($1,000)
e) 20% profit
f) $3,500
2) a) $1,600,000
b) $1,560,000
c) ($250,000)
d) $40,000
e) $40,000
f) $0
g) $200,000
4) $4.44
5) First transaction: counter-party receives $700,000

Chapter 22

1) 0.6173 pounds
   7.1428 rubles
3) At 4/4/X0: $16.38 and 36.5% increase
5) a) $3,300,000
   b) $3,220,000
   c) ($240,000)
   e) $80,000

Chapter 23

1) Orphee's return: about 7% (6.83%)
2) b) About 6% (5.89%)
3) a) Interest payment: $6,000
   Principal repayment: $610.11
   Balance owed: $59,389.89
4) Growth in median price of a new home: 4.11%
   S&P 500: 14.87%
5) Earnings before taxes/year 2: ($3,000)
   Cash flow year 1: $2,500 after tax savings and principal repayment
6) b) $50,000 + $500 + .02($50,000) + $500 = $52,000

Chapter 24

1) a) Total assets: $339,000
   b) Total assets age 62: $813,130
   c) Annual withdrawal: $140,935

GLOSSARY

A

Accelerated depreciation: The allocation of the cost of plant and equipment in unequal annual amounts such that most of the cost is recovered in the early years of an asset's life.

Accrued interest: Interest that has been earned but not received.

Adjustable-rate mortgage (ARM): A mortgage loan in which the interest rate is periodically adjusted to reflect current interest rates.

American Depositary Receipts (ADRs): Receipts issued for foreign securities held by a trustee.

Annuity: A series of equal annual payments.

Annuity due: A series of equal annual payments with the payments made at the beginning of the year.

Anticipation note: A short-term liability that is to be retired by specific expected revenues (e.g., expected tax receipts).

Arbitrage: Simultaneous purchase and sale to take advantage of price differences in different markets.

Arrearage: Cumulative preferred dividends that have not been paid.

Average collection period (days sales outstanding): The number of days required to collect accounts receivable.

B

Balance of payments: An accounting statement that enumerates purchases and sales and currency flow between a country and the rest of the world.

Balloon payment: The large final payment necessary to retire a debt issue.

Banker's acceptance: Short-term promissory note guaranteed by a bank.

Bar graph: A graph indicating the high, low, and closing prices of a security.

Barron's confidence index: An index designed to identify investors' confidence in the level and direction of security prices.

Bearer bond: A bond with coupons attached or a bond whose possession denotes ownership.

Bearish: Expecting that prices will decline.

Best-efforts agreement: Agreement with an investment banker who does not guarantee the sale of a security but who agrees to make the best effort to sell it.

Beta coefficient: An index of risk; a measure of the systematic risk associated with a particular stock.

Bid and ask: Prices at which a security dealer offers to buy and sell stock.

Bond: A long-term liability with a specified amount of interest and specified maturity date.

Bond swap: The selling of one bond and using the proceeds to acquire a different bond.

Book-to-price ratio: The accounting value of a stock divided by the market price of the stock.

Broker: An agent who handles buy and sell orders for an investor.

Bullish: Expecting that prices will rise.

Business cycle: An economic pattern of expansion and contraction.

Business risk: The risk associated with the nature of a business.

Bylaws: A document specifying the relationship between a corporation and its stockholders.

C

Call feature: The right of an issuer to retire a debt issue prior to maturity.

Call option: An option sold by an individual that entitles the buyer to purchase stock at a specified price within a specified time period.

Call penalty: A premium paid for exercising a call feature.

Capital account: Part of the balance of payments that enumerates the importing and exporting of investments and long-term securities.

Capital gain: The increase in the value of an asset such as a stock or a bond.

Capital loss: A decrease in the value of an asset such as a stock or a bond.

Cash budget: A financial statement enumerating cash receipts and cash disbursements.

Cash value: The amount that would be received if a life insurance policy were canceled.

Certificate of deposit (CD): A time deposit with a specified maturity date.

Certificate of incorporation: A document creating a corporation.

Charter: A document specifying the relationship between a firm and the state in which it is incorporated.

Chicago Board Options Exchange (CBOE): The first organized secondary market in put and call options.

Closed-end investment company: An investment company with a fixed number of shares that are bought and sold in the secondary security markets.

Collateralized mortgage obligation (CMO): Debt obligation supported by mortgages and sold in series.

Commercial paper: Unsecured, short-term promissory notes issued by the most creditworthy corporations.

Commissions: Fees charged by brokers for executing orders.

Compounding: The process by which interest is paid on interest that has been previously earned.

Condominium: An apartment that is owned instead of rented.

Confirmation statement: A statement received from a brokerage firm detailing the sale or purchase of a security and specifying a settlement date.

Contrarians: Investors who go against the consensus concerning investment strategy.

Conventional mortgage loan: A standard loan to finance real estate (and secured by the property) in which the loan is periodically retired, and the interest paid is figured on the declining balance owed.

Conversion value as stock: Value of the bond in terms of the stock into which the bond may be converted.

Convertible bond: A bond that may be exchanged for (i.e., converted into) common stock.

Convertible preferred stock: Preferred stock that may be exchanged for (i.e., converted into) common stock.

Coupon bond: A bond with coupons attached that are removed and presented for payment of interest when due.

Coupon rate: The special interest rate or amount of interest paid by a bond.

Covered option writing: Selling an option for which the seller owns the securities.

Covering the short sale: The purchase of securities to close a short position.

Credit rating systems: Classification schemes designed to indicate the risk associated with a particular security.

Cross-sectional analysis: An analysis of several firms in the same industry at a point in time.

Cumulative preferred stock: A preferred stock whose dividends accumulate if they are not paid.

Cumulative voting: A voting scheme that encourages minority representation by permitting each stockholder to cast all of his or her votes for one candidate for the firm's board of directors.

Currency futures: Contract for the future delivery of foreign exchange.

Current account: Part of the balance of payments that enumerates the importing and exporting of goods and services by a nation over a period of time.

Current ratio: Current assets divided by current liabilities; a measure of liquidity.

Current yield: Annual income divided by the current price of the security.

Cyclical industry: An industry whose sales and profits are sensitive to changes in the level of economic activity.

D

Daily limit: The maximum daily change permitted in a commodity future's price.

Date of record: The day on which an investor must own shares in order to receive the dividend payment.

Day order: An order placed with a broker that is canceled at the end of the day if it is not executed.

Dealers: Market makers who buy and sell securities for their own accounts.

Debenture: An unsecured bond.

Debt ratio: The ratio of debt to total assets; a measure of the use of debt financing.

Default: The failure of a debtor to meet any term of a debt's indenture.

Deficit spending: Government expenditures exceeding government revenues.

Devaluation: A decrease in the value of one currency relative to other currencies.

Dilution: A reduction in earnings per share due to the issuing of new securities.

Director: A person who is elected by stockholders to determine the goals and policies of the firm.

Discount: The sale of anything below its stated value.

Discount (of a bond): The extent to which a bond's price is less than its face amount or principal.

Discount (from net asset value): The extent to which the price of a closed-end investment company's stock sells below its net asset value.

Discount broker: A broker who charges lower commissions on security purchases and sales.

Discount rate: The rate of interest that the Federal Reserve charges banks for borrowing reserves.

Discounting: The process of determining present value.

Dispersion: Deviation from the average.

Distribution date: The date on which a dividend is paid to stockholders.

Diversification: The process of accumulating different securities to reduce the risk of loss.

Dividend: A payment to stockholders that is usually in cash but may be in stock or property.

Dividend-growth valuation model: A valuation model that deals with dividends and their growth properly discounted back to the present.

Dividend reinvestment plan (DRIP): A plan that permits stockholders to have cash dividends reinvested in stock instead of received in cash.

Dollar cost averaging: The purchase of securities at different intervals to reduce the impact of price fluctuations.

Dollar-weighted rate of return: The rate that equates the present value of cash inflows and cash outflows; the internal rate of return.

Dow Jones Industrial Average: An average of the stock prices of 30 large firms.

Dow Theory: A technical approach based on the Dow Jones averages.

Duration: The average time it takes to collect a bond's interest and principal repayment.

E

Earnings per preferred share: The total earnings divided by the number of preferred shares outstanding.

Effective interest rate: The interest rate paid adjusted for any tax savings.

Efficient market hypothesis (EMH): A theory that security prices correctly measure the firm's future earnings and dividends and that investors should not consistently outperform the market on a risk-adjusted basis.

Efficient portfolio: The portfolio that offers the highest expected return for a given amount of risk.

8-K report: A document filed with the SEC that describes a change in a firm that may affect the value of its securities.

Emerging market fund: Investment company that specializes in securities from less-developed countries.

Equilibrium price: A price that equates supply and demand.

Equipment trust certificate: A serial bond secured by specific equipment.

Equity trust: A real estate investment trust that specializes in acquiring real estate for subsequent rental income.

Estate tax: A tax on the value of a deceased individual's assets.

Euro: Common currency of 11 European nations.

Eurobond: A bond denominated in U.S. dollars but issued abroad.

Eurodollar CD: Time deposit in a foreign bank and denominated in dollars.

Eurodollars: Dollar-denominated deposits in a foreign bank.

Exchange rate: The price of a foreign currency in terms of another currency.

Exchange rate risk: The uncertainty associated with changes in the value of foreign currencies.

Exchange-traded fund: A mutual fund whose shares are traded in the secondary markets.

Ex-dividend: Stock that trades exclusive of any dividend payment.

Ex-dividend date: The day on which a stock trades exclusive of any dividends.

Exercise (strike) price: The price at which the investor may buy or sell stock through an option.

Expected return: The sum of the anticipated dividend yield and capital gains.

Expiration date: The date by which an option must be exercised.

Extendible security: Bond whose maturity date may be extended into the future.

Extra dividend: A sum paid in addition to the firm's regular dividend.

F

Face value: An insurance policy's death benefit.

Fallen angel: Investment-grade security whose quality has deteriorated.

Federal agency bonds: Debt issued by an agency of the federal government.

Federal Deposit Insurance Corporation (FDIC): Federal government agency that supervises commercial banks and insures commercial bank deposits.

Federal funds rate: The rate of interest a bank charges another for borrowing reserves.

Federal Housing Administration (FHA): An agency of the federal government that will insure mortgages granted to qualified recipients.

Federal Reserve: The central bank of the United States.

Financial futures: Contract for the future delivery of a financial asset.

Financial intermediary: A financial institution, such as a commercial bank, that borrows from one group and lends to another.

Financial leverage: The use of borrowed funds to acquire an asset.

Financial life cycle: The stages of life during which individuals accumulate and subsequently use financial assets.

Financial risk: The risk associated with a firm's sources of financing.

Firm commitment: Agreement with an investment banker who guarantees a sale of securities by agreeing to purchase the entire issue at a specified price.

Fiscal policy: Taxation, expenditures, and debt management of the federal government.

Fixed asset turnover: Ratio of sales to fixed assets; tells how many fixed assets are needed to generate sales.

Flat: A description of a bond that trades without accrued interest.

Foreign exchange market: Market for the buying and selling of currencies.

Full disclosure laws: The federal and state laws requiring publicly held firms to disclose financial and other information that may affect the value of their securities.

Future sum of an annuity: Compound value of a series of equal annual payments.

Futures contract: An agreement for the future delivery of a commodity at a specified date.

Futures price: The price in a contract for the future delivery of a commodity.

G

General obligation bond: A bond whose interest does not depend on the revenue of a specific project; government bonds supported by the full faith and credit of the issuer (i.e., authority to tax).

Ginnie Mae: Mortgage pass-through bond issued by the Government National Mortgage Association.

Global funds: Mutual funds whose portfolios includes securities of firms with international operations that are located throughout the world.

Good-till-canceled order: An order placed with a broker that remains in effect until it is executed by the broker or canceled by the investor.

Graduated-payment mortgage loan: A mortgage loan in which the periodic payments rise over time.

Gross domestic product (GDP): Total value of all final goods and services newly produced within a country by domestic factors of production.

Gross profit margin: Percentage earned on sales after deducting the cost of goods sold.

H

Head-and-shoulder pattern: A tool of technical analysis; a pattern of security prices that resembles a head and shoulders.

Hedging: Taking opposite positions to reduce risk.

High-yield securities: Non-investment-grade securities offering a high return.

Holding period return (HPR): Total return (income plus price appreciation during a specified time period) divided by the cost of the investment.

I

Improved land: Land that has been cleared or that includes improvements, such as curbs, gutters, or buildings.

Income: The flow of money or its equivalent produced by an asset; dividends and interest.

Income bond: A bond whose interest is paid only if it is earned by the firm.

Increasing rate bond: Bond whose coupon rises over time.

Indenture: The document that specifies the terms of a bond issue.

Index fund: A mutual fund whose portfolio seeks to duplicate an index of stock prices.

Inefficient portfolio: A portfolio whose return is not maximized given the level of risk.

Inflation-indexed securities: Securities whose principal and interest payments are adjusted for changes in The Consumer Price Index.

Inheritance tax: A tax on what an individual receives from an estate.

Initial public offering (IPO): The first sale of common stock to the general public.

Inside information: Privileged information concerning a firm.

Interest: Payment for the use of money.

Interest rate risk: The uncertainty associated with changes in interest rates; the possibility of loss resulting from increases in interest rates.

Internal rate of return: Percentage return that equates the present value of an investment's cash inflows with its cost.

International funds: American mutual funds whose portfolios are limited to non-American firms.

Intrinsic value: What an option is worth as stock.

Inventory turnover: The speed with which inventory is sold.

Investment (in economics): The purchase of plant, equipment, or inventory.

Investment (in lay terms): Acquisition of an asset such as a stock or a bond.

Investment banker: An underwriter, a firm that sells new issues of securities to the general public.

Investment tax credit: A direct reduction in taxes owed resulting from investment in plant or equipment.

Investment value as debt: The value of a convertible as if it were nonconvertible debt.

IRA: A retirement plan (individual retirement account) that is available to workers.

Irregular dividends: Dividend payments that either do not occur in regular intervals or vary in amount.

J

Jensen performance index: A measure of performance that compares the realized return with the return that should have been earned for the amount of risk borne by the investor.

K

Keogh account (HR-10 plan): A retirement plan that is available to self-employed individuals.

L

Leverage: Magnification of the potential return on an investment.

Limit order: An order placed with a broker to buy or sell at a specified price.

Liquidation: The process of converting assets into cash; dissolving a corporation.

Liquidity: Moneyness; the ease with which assets can be converted into cash with little risk of loss of principal.

Listed security: A security that is traded on an organized exchange.

Load fund: A mutual fund that charges a commission to purchase or sell its shares.

Long position: Owning assets for their income and possible price appreciation.

M

M-1: Sum of demand deposits, coins, and currency.

M-2: Sum of demand deposits, coins, currency, and savings accounts at banks.

Maintenance margin: (1) The minimum equity required for a margin position in a stock. (2) The minimum level of funds in a futures account that triggers a margin call.

Margin (futures): Good faith deposit made when purchasing or selling a commodity contract.

Margin (stocks or bonds): The amount that an investor must put down to buy securities on credit.

Margin call: A request by a broker for an investor to place additional funds or securities in an account as collateral against borrowed funds or as a good faith deposit.

Margin requirement: The minimum percentage, established by the Federal Reserve, that the investor must put up in cash to buy securities.

Marginal tax rate: The tax rate paid on an additional last dollar of taxable income; an individual's tax bracket.

Market order: An order to buy or sell at the current market price.

Market risk: Systematic risk; the risk associated with the tendency of a stock's price to fluctuate with the market.

Marketability: The ease with which an asset may be bought and sold.

Maturity date: The time at which a debt issue becomes due and the principal must be repaid.

Money market instruments: Short-term securities, such as Treasury bills, negotiable certificates of deposit, or commercial paper.

Money market mutual funds: Mutual funds that specialize in short-term securities.

Moral backing: Nonobligatory support for a debt issue.

Mortgage bond: A bond that is secured by property, especially real estate.

Mortgage trust: A real estate investment trust that specializes in loans secured by real estate.

Moving average: An average in which the most recent observation is added and the most distant observation is deleted before the average is computed.

Municipal (tax-exempt) bond: A bond issued by a state or one of its political subdivisions whose interest is not taxed by the federal government.

Mutual fund: An open-end investment company.

N

Naked option writing: The selling (i.e., writing) of an option without owning the underlying security.

Nasdaq: National Association of Securities Dealers Automatic Quotation system; quotation system for over-the-counter securities.

Negotiable certificate of deposit: A certificate of deposit in which the rate and the term are individually negotiated by the bank and the lender and which may be bought and sold.

Net asset value: The asset value of a share in an investment company; total assets minus total liabilities divided by the number of shares outstanding.

Net profit margin: The ratio of earnings after interest and taxes to sales.

No-load mutual fund: A mutual fund that does not charge a commission for buying or selling its shares.

Noncumulative preferred stock: Preferred stock whose dividends do not accumulate if the firm misses a dividend payment.

NYSE composite index: New York Stock Exchange index; an index of prices of all the stocks listed on the New York Stock Exchange.

O

Odd lot: A unit of trading, such as 22 shares, that is smaller than the general unit of sale.

Odd-lot theory: A technical approach to the stock market that purports to predict security prices on the basis of odd-lot sales and purchases.

Official reserve account: Part of the balance of payments that enumerates changes in a country's international reserves.

Open interest (futures): The number of futures contracts in existence for a particular commodity.

Open interest (options): Number of option contracts with a specified strike price and expiration date on a particular stock.

Open market operations: The buying or selling of Treasury securities by the Federal Reserve.

Open-end investment company: A mutual fund; an investment company from which investors buy shares and to which they resell them.

Operating profit margin: Percentage earned on sales before adjusting for nonrecurring items, interest, and taxes.

Option: The right to buy or sell something at a specified price within a specified time period.

Ordinary annuity: A series of equal annual payments in which the payments are made at the end of each year.

Organized exchange: A formal market for buying and selling securities or commodities.

Originating house: An investment banker that makes an agreement with a firm to sell a new issue of securities and forms the syndicate to market them.

Over-the-counter (OTC) market: The informal secondary market for unlisted securities.

P

Paper profits: Price appreciation that has not been realized.

Partnership: An unincorporated business owned by two or more individuals.

Pay-in-kind (PIK) securities: Bonds or preferred stock whose interest or dividends are paid in additional debt or shares.

Payout ratio: The ratio of dividends to earnings.

PEG ratio: The price/earnings ratio divided by the growth rate of earnings.

Perpetual bond: A debt instrument with no maturity date.

Point-and-figure chart (X-O chart): A chart composed of Xs and Os that is used in technical analysis to summarize price movements.

Portfolio: An accumulation of assets owned by the investor and designed to transfer purchasing power to the future.

Portfolio risk: The total risk associated with owning a portfolio; the sum of systematic and unsystematic risk.

Preemptive rights: The right of current stockholders to maintain their proportionate ownership in the firm.

Preferred stock: A class of stock (i.e., equity) that has a prior claim to common stock on the firm's earnings and assets in case of liquidation.

Preliminary prospectus (red herring): Initial document detailing the financial condition of a firm that must be filed with the SEC to register a new issue of securities.

Premium: The market price of an option.

Premium (of a bond): The extent to which a bond's price exceeds the face amount of the debt.

Premium (over net asset value): The extent to which the price of a closed-end investment company's stock exceeds the share's net asset value.

Present value: The current worth of an amount to be received in the future.

Present value of an annuity: The present worth of a series of equal payments.

Primary market: The initial sale of securities.

Principal: The amount owed; the face value of a debt.

Private placement: The nonpublic sale of securities.

Pro forma financial statement: A projected or forecasted financial statement.

Programmed trading: Coordinated buying or selling of portfolios triggered by computers.

Progressive tax: A tax whose rate increases as the tax base increases.

Property tax: A tax levied against the value of real or financial assets.

Proportionate tax: A tax whose rate remains constant as the tax base changes.

Purchasing power risk: The uncertainty that future inflation will erode the purchasing power of assets and income.

Put bond: A bond that the holder may redeem (i.e., sell back to the issuer) at a specified price and a specified time period.

Put option: An option to sell stock at a specified price within a specified time period.

Q

Quick ratio (acid test): Current assets excluding inventory divided by current liabilities; a measure of liquidity.

R

Rate of return: The annual percentage return realized on an investment.

Rate of return (internal rate of return, or IRR): The discount rate that equates the cost of an investment with the cash flows generated by the investment.

Real estate investment trust (REIT): Closed-end investment company that specializes in real estate or mortgage investments.

Realized return: The sum of income and capital gains earned on an investment.

Recapitalization: An alteration in a firm's sources of finance, such as the substitution of long-term debt for equity.

Receivables turnover: The speed with which a firm collects its accounts receivable.

Recession: A period of rising unemployment and declining national output.

Refunding: The act of issuing new debt and using the proceeds to retire existing debt.

Regional funds: Mutual funds that specialize in a particular geographical area.

Registered bond: A bond whose ownership is registered with the commercial bank that distributes interest payments and principal repayments.

Registered representative: A person who buys and sells securities for customers; a broker.

Registration: Process of filing information with the SEC concerning a proposed sale of securities to the general public.

Regressive tax: A tax whose rate declines as the tax base increases.

Regular dividends: Steady dividend payments that are distributed at regular intervals.

Reinvestment rate risk: The risk associated with reinvesting earnings or principal at a lower rate than was initially earned.

Renegotiable-rate mortgage loan: A mortgage loan in which the parties have the option to renegotiate the interest rate charged on the loan.

Repurchase agreement (repo): Sale of a short-term security in which the seller agrees to buy back the security at a specified price.

Required return: The return necessary to induce the investor to purchase an asset.

Reserve requirement: The percentage of cash that banks must hold against their deposit liabilities.

Reset bond: Bond whose coupon is periodically reset.

Retention ratio: The ratio of earnings not distributed to earnings.

Return: The sum of income plus capital gains earned on an investment in an asset.

Return on assets: The ratio of earnings to total assets.

Return on equity: The ratio of earnings to equity.

Revaluation: An increase in the value of one currency relative to other currencies.

Revenue bond: A bond whose interest is paid only if the debtor earns sufficient revenue.

Right: An option given to stockholders to buy additional shares at a specified price during a specified time period before the offer is made to the general public.

Rights offering: Sale of new securities to stockholders.

Risk: The possibility of loss; the uncertainty of future returns.

Round lot: The general unit of trading in a security, such as 100 shares.

S

Secondary market: A market for buying and selling previously issued securities.

Securities and Exchange Commission (SEC): Government agency that enforces the federal securities laws.

Securities Investor Protection Corporation (SIPC): The agency that insures investors against failures by brokerage firms.

Securitization: The process of converting an illiquid asset into a marketable security.

Semiannual compounding: The payment of interest twice a year.

Serial bond: A bond issue in which specified bonds mature each year.

Series EE (Patriot) bonds: Savings bonds issued in small denominations by the federal government.

Series HH bonds: Income bonds issued by the federal government.

Share averaging: A system for the accumulation of shares in which the investor periodically buys the same number of shares.

Sharpe performance index: A risk-adjusted measure of performance that standardizes the return in excess of the risk-free rate by the standard deviation of the portfolio's return.

Short position: Selling borrowed assets for possible price deterioration; being short in a security or a commodity.

Short sale: The sale of borrowed securities in anticipation of a price decline; a contract for future delivery.

Sinking fund: A series of periodic payments to retire a bond issue.

Specialist: A market maker on the New York Stock Exchange who maintains an orderly market in the security.

Speculation: An investment that offers a potentially large return but is also very risky; a reasonable probability that the investment will produce a loss.

Split coupon bond: Bond with a zero or low initial coupon followed by a period with a high coupon.

Spot price: The current price of a commodity.

Spread: The difference between the bid and the ask prices.

Standard & Poor's 500 stock index: A value-weighted index of 500 stocks.

Statement of cash flows: An accounting statement that enumerates a firm's cash inflows and cash outflows.

Stock: A security representing ownership in a corporation.

Stock dividend: A dividend paid in stock.

Stock index futures: A contract based on an index of security prices.

Stock index options: Rights to buy and sell based on an aggregate measure of stock prices.

Stock repurchase: The buying of stock by the issuing corporation.

Stock split: Recapitalization that affects the number of shares outstanding, their par value, the earnings per share, and the price of the stock.

Stop order: A purchase or sell order designed to limit an investor's loss or to assure a profit on a position in a security.

Straight-line depreciation: The allocation of the cost of plant and equipment by equal annual amounts over a period of time.

Street name: The registration of securities in a brokerage firm's name instead of in the buyer's name.

Surplus: Receipts exceeding disbursements.

Swap: An agreement to exchange payments.

Syndicate: A selling group assembled to market an issue of securities.

Systematic risk: The risk associated with fluctuations in security prices; market risk.

T

Tax anticipation note: Short-term government security secured by expected tax revenues.

Tax shelter: An asset or investment that defers, reduces, or avoids taxation.

Tax-deferred annuity: A contract sold by an insurance company in which the company guarantees a series of payments and whose earnings are not taxed until they are distributed.

Tax-exempt bond: A bond whose interest is excluded from federal income taxation.

Technical analysis: An analysis of past volume and/or price behavior to identify which assets to purchase or sell and the best time to purchase or sell them.

10-K report: A required annual report filed with the SEC by publicly held firms.

10-Q report: A required quarterly report filed with the SEC by publicly held firms.

Term insurance: Life insurance with coverage for a specified time and excluding a savings plan.

Thin issue: An issue of securities with either a small number of securities in the hands of the general public or a small volume of transactions.

Third market: Over-the-counter market for securities listed on an exchange.

13-D report: Document filed with the SEC by an individual who acquires 5 percent of a publicly held firm's stock.

Time premium: The amount an option's price exceeds the option's intrinsic value.

Times-dividend-earned ratio: Earnings divided by preferred dividend requirements.

Time-series analysis: An analysis of a firm over a period of time.

Times-interest-earned: Ratio of earnings before interest and taxes divided by interest expense; a coverage ratio that measures the safety of debt.

Time-weighted rate of return: Average of individual holding period returns.

Total return: The sum of dividend yield and capital gains.

Trader: An investor who frequently buys and sells.

Tranche: Subdivision of a bond issue.

Treasury bills: Short-term federal government securities.

Treasury bonds: The long-term debt of the federal government.

Treasury notes: The intermediate-term debt of the federal government.

Treynor index: A risk-adjusted measure of performance that standardizes the return in excess of the risk-free rate by the portfolio's systematic risk.

Trustee: An appointee, usually a commercial bank, responsible for upholding the terms of a bond's indenture.

12b-1 fees: Fees that a mutual fund may charge to cover marketing and advertising expenses.

Two-step mortgage loan: A mortgage loan in which the interest rate is changed once at a predetermined time.

U

Undercapitalized: Having insufficient equity financing.

Underwriting: The process by which securities are sold to the general public and in which the investment banker buys the securities from the issuing firm.

Unimproved land: Land that has not been cleared and that lacks improvements, such as curbs and gutters.

Unit trust: A passive investment company with a fixed portfolio of assets that are self-liquidating.

Unsystematic risk: The risk associated with individual events that affect a particular security.

U.S. Treasury bill: Short-term debt of the federal government.

V

Valuation: The process of determining the current worth of an asset.

Value: What something is worth; the present value of future benefits.

Variable interest rate bond: A long-term bond with a coupon rate that varies with changes in short-term rates.

Venture capitalist: Firm specializing in investing in the securities, especially stock, of small, emerging companies.

Veterans Administration (VA): An agency of the federal government that will guarantee mortgages granted to qualified veterans.

Voting rights: The rights of stockholders to vote their shares.

W

Warrant: An option issued by a company to buy its stock at a specified price within a specified time period.

Y

Yield to call: The yield earned on a bond from the time it is acquired until the time it is called and retired by the firm.

Yield curve: The relationship between time to maturity and yields for debt in a given risk class.

Yield to maturity: The yield earned on a bond from the time it is acquired until the maturity date.

Z

Zero coupon bond: A bond on which interest accrues and is paid at maturity, and is initially sold at a discount.

INDEX

Bold entries refer to the page on which a term is defined in the margin notes. While the definition usually occurs the first time the word is used, there are instances in which a term is cross-referenced prior to the marginal definition.